Development Economics

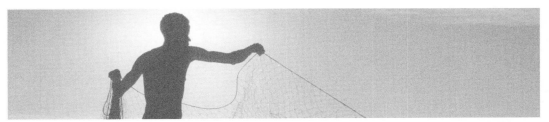

First Edition

First Edition

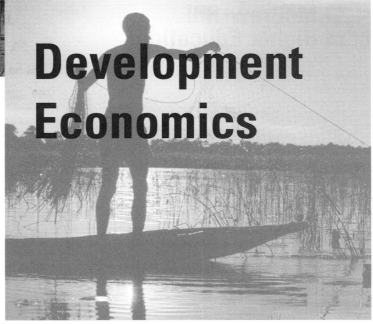

Development Economics

Anthony Clunies-Ross,
David Forsyth
Mozammel Huq
University of Strathclyde, Glasgow

McGraw-Hill
Higher Education

London   Boston   Burr Ridge, IL   Dubuque, IA   Madison, WI   New York   San Francisco
St. Louis   Bangkok   Bogotá   Caracas   Kuala Lumpur   Lisbon   Madrid   Mexico City
Milan   Montreal   New Delhi   Santiago   Seoul   Singapore   Sydney   Taipei   Toronto

Development Economics, 1st Edition
Anthony Clunies-Ross, David Forsyth, Mozammel Huq
ISBN-13 978-0-07-711453-4
ISBN-10 0-07-711453-1

McGraw-Hill
Higher Education

BLACKBURN COLLEGE
LIBRARY
Acc. No. BB51918
Class No. UCL 338.9CLU
Date 23-10-2012

Published by McGraw-Hill Education
Shoppenhangers Road
Maidenhead
Berkshire
SL6 2QL
Telephone: 44 (0) 1628 502 500
Fax: 44 (0) 1628 770 224
Website: *www.mcgraw-hill.co.uk*

British Library Cataloguing in Publication Data
A catalogue record for this book is available from the British Library

Library of Congress Cataloguing in Publication Data
The Library of Congress data for this book has been applied for from the Library of Congress

Acquisitions Editor: Natalie Jacobs
Development Editor: Tom Hill
Marketing Manager: Vanessa Boddington
Head of Production: Beverley Shields

Text Design by Hardlines
Cover design by SCW
Printed and bound in the UK by CPI Antony Rowe, Chippenham and Eastbourne

Published by McGraw-Hill Education (UK) Limited an imprint of The McGraw-Hill
Companies, Inc., 1221 Avenue of the Americas, New York, NY 10020. Copyright © 2009
by McGraw-Hill Education (UK) Limited. All rights reserved. No part of this publication
may be reproduced or distributed in any form or by any means, or stored in a database or
retrieval system, without the prior written consent of The McGraw-Hill Companies, Inc.,
including, but not limited to, in any network or other electronic storage or transmission, or
broadcast for distance learning.

Fictitious names of companies, products, people, characters and/or data that may be used
herein (in case studies or in examples) are not intended to represent any real individual,
company, product or event.

ISBN-13 978-0-07-711453-4
ISBN-10 0-07-711453-1
© 2009. Exclusive rights by The McGraw-Hill Companies, Inc. for manufacture and export.
This book cannot be re-exported from the country to which it is sold by McGraw-Hill.

Dedication

To those many millions of people – now living or yet to be born – whose prospect of even a minimally tolerable, secure and dignified life depends not only on their own effort and ingenuity but also crucially on hard-thinking, imagination, honesty, fairmindedness, and (at least a little) generosity, on the part of the rest of us, whether we live in rich lands or poor.

Brief Table of Contents

Detailed Table of Contents

List of Abbreviations

ACP	African, Caribbean and Pacific (Group)
ADB	Asian Development Bank
AfDB	African Development Bank
AgGDP	Agricultural gross domestic product
ANS	Adjusted net saving
APR	Accounting price ratio
ARI	Accounting rate of interest
AT	Appropriate technology
AWR	Accounting wage rate
BPI	Bribe Payers Index
BRAC	Bangladesh Rural Advancement Committee
CBA	Cost–benefit analysis
CCF	Consumption conversion factor
CCFF	Compensatory and Contingency Financing Facility
CEA	Cost-efficiency analysis
CPI	Corruption Perceptions Index
CRI	Consumption rate of interest
CSOs	Civil society organizations
CTT	Currency-transaction tax
DAC	Development Assistance Committee
DCF	Discounted cash flow
DTT	Double-taxation treaties
EBRD	European Bank for Reconstruction and Development
ECB	European Central Bank
ECLA[C]	Economic Commission for Latin America [and the Caribbean]
ECU	European Currency Unit
EEC	European Economic Community
EF	Ecological footprint
EPZ	Export Processing Zone
FAO	Food and Agriculture Organization
FDI	Foreign direct investment
FTA	Free trade area
GATS	General Agreement on Trade in Services
GATT	General Agreement on Tariffs and Trade
GAVI	Global Alliance for Vaccination and Immunization
GCB	Global Corruption Barometer
GDP	Gross domestic product
GEO-4	Global environmental outlook
GFATM	Global Fund to Fight AIDS, Tuberculosis and Malaria
GM	Genetically modified
GNI	Gross national income
HDI	Human Development Index

HIC	High-income country
HIPCs	Highly indebted poor countries
IADB	Inter-American Development Bank
IBRD	International Bank for Reconstruction and Development
IDA	International Development Association
IFAD	International Fund for Agricultural Development
IFC	International Finance Corporation
ILO	International Labour Office
IMF	International Monetary Fund
IOM	International Organization for Migration
IPCC	Intergovernmental Panel on Climate Change
IRR	Internal rate of return
IT	Information technology
ITDG	Intermediate Technology Development Group
IUCN	International Union for the Conservation of Nature
LDCs	Less developed countries or Least developed countries
LIBOR	London Interbank Offer Rate
LIC	Low-income country
LLDCs	Least developed countries
LMIC	Lower-middle-income country
LM	Little–Mirrlees
LMST	Little-Mirrlees-Squire-van der Tak
M&A	Mergers and acquisitions
MDGs	Millennium Development Goals
MDRI	Multilateral Debt Reduction Initiative
MFN	Most-favoured-nation
MNC/MNE	Multinational corporation/enterprise
MPI	Marginal productivity of investment
NAFTA	North American Free Trade Agreement
NATO	North Atlantic Treaty Organization
NDP	Net domestic product
NEER	Nominal effective exchange rate
NEPAD	New Partnership for Africa's Development
NGO	Non-government organization
NNI	Net national income
NPV	Net present value
NREGS	National Rural Employment Guarantee Scheme
OA	Official aid
ODA	Official development assistance
ODI	Overseas Development Institute
OECD	Organization for Economic Co-operation and Development
OPEC	Organization of Petroleum Exporting Countries
PFI	Portfolio foreign investment
PPP	Purchasing-power-parity
R&D	Research and development
REER	Real effective exchange rate
REI	Regional economic integration
S&T	Science and technology

SCF	Shadow conversion factor
SDRs	Special Drawing Rights
SEEA	System of Environmental and Economic Accounting
SER	Shadow exchange rate
SNA	System of National Accounts
SPS	Sanitary and phytosanitary measures
SWF	Sovereign wealth fund
SWR	Shadow wage rate
TBT	Technical barriers to trade
TI	Transparency International
TRIMS	Agreement on Trade-Related Aspects of Investment Measures
TRIPS	Agreement on Trade-Related Aspects of Intellectual Property
TT	Terms of trade
UMIC	Upper-middle-income country
UNCTAD	United Nations Conference on Trade and Development
UNDP	United Nations Development Programme
UNEP	United Nations Environment Programme
UNESCO	United Nations Educational, Scientific and Cultural Organization
UNFPA	United Nations Population Fund
UNIDO	United Nations Industrial Development Organization
UNIFEM	United Nations Development Fund for Women
UN-HABITAT	United Nations Human Settlements Programme
USAID	US Agency for International Development
VAT	Value-added tax
VITA	Volunteers in Technical Assistance
WB	World Bank
WDI	World Development Indicators
WDR	World Development Report
WHO	World Health Organization
WID	Women in Development
WTO	World Trade Organization
WWF	World Wildlife Fund

Preface

A major attraction for authors writing the first edition of a new textbook is the opportunity of starting with a blank sheet. Their selection of topics, and decisions regarding the emphasis given to each, can take advantage of the latest perceptions as to which themes are likely to be in the forefront of debate over the next two decades, and which – however important in the past – can safely be relegated to footnote status.

Writing a new book on Development Economics late in the first decade of the new Millennium offers particular opportunities. After half a century of frustratingly slow progress in the developing world, massive increases have recently been occurring in the economic output of many (though by no means all) developing countries. At the same time, however, daunting new problems to do with the environment, globalization, governance, and the backwash from accelerating growth itself, must now be confronted. In addition, a significant segment of the world's people was actually going backward materially over the last two decades of the twentieth century. And then from 2007 we began to witness a collapse of financial institutions without precedent over the previous 75 years, and the start of a world recession whose depth and duration are uncertain at the time of going to press.

The authors of this volume on development hope that, through these pages, they can stimulate an interest in, and better understanding of, what they see as the crucial issue of the age.

Unifying theme – what the book is saying

Following Amartya Sen in taking 'development' – the object of the exercise – as consisting fundamentally in enlarging human capacities, we assume as proximate economic objectives for 'developing countries' the differing but linked targets of growth of income and reduction of material poverty, but always on the supposition that gains and losses in income are *fully* taken into account, with the visible benefits that are conventionally registered as income not being allowed to conceal environmental costs. But we recognize too that there are other identifiable objectives with strong claims as components or prerequisites of development in the sense in which we are using the term: objectives such as immunity from armed conflict, equality between women and men, freedom of political expression, and the education and social institutions that allow that freedom to be responsibly exercised.

If there is a unifying theme that emerges, it is in how many instances there are actual or potential virtuous circles – at least synergies – in which pursuing one desirable end contributes to, and is furthered by, the advance of another; and hence there are potential changes in institutions from which all significant parties may hope to gain.

Genuine occasion of conflict between desirable social objectives exists, as does conflict between parties to negotiations, national or sectional; but, as well as revealing intrinsicially beneficent synergies, economic analysis also has certain special capacities for showing how the 'trade-off' in a situation of conflict may be 'improved'. Not all economists' lunches are free of cost, but some are, and those that are not may have their costs reduced through the use of economic observation and analysis.

Moreover the existence of a vicious circle – as between economic stagnation and military conflict, or between economic stagnation and corruption – implies the possibility of a virtuous one if one of the processes in the vicious circle can be decisively blocked.

We hope that this book may advance the habit of looking not only for sources of conflict between objectives – and between human agents – in the business of development, but also for the beneficent synergy, the virtuous circle, the free (or nearly free) lunch, the improved trade-off – and not least where conflict seems to be most challenging, as in the sacrifices that at the moment seem likely to be necessary in order to check the disasters threatened by climate change.

Target readership

The topic coverage and level of treatment in this book make it suitable for undergraduates in third/fourth-year specialist classes on Development Economics, and for graduate students – not necessarily economists – taking courses in Development Economics or Development Studies. Furthermore, individual chapters may be suitable as stand-alone contributions to courses on themes important in *other* important areas of Economics – and of Social Science more generally.

The subject treatment does not incorporate sophisticated mathematical material. Knowledge going beyond basic algebra would be helpful, but is not essential.

Subject coverage – and overall structure of the book

In addition to detailed presentations of the more 'traditional' themes of Development Economics – including population issues, the role of agriculture, industrialization, foreign aid, poverty, rural-urban migration, domestic finance and foreign direct investment – this volume features detailed treatment of important emerging preoccupations – **globalization, governance, corruption, international migration and remittances, gender, sustainability and the environment**, approaches to **building technological capability**, and the role of **civil society**.

Inevitably, coverage of some mainstays of earlier books on development has had to be curtailed – and readers will find, in particular, the treatment of education, land questions and the economic history of the developing world, fairly brief. The authors hope that the resultant balance accurately reflects current priorities in the field.

The volume is divided into five main sections followed by a concluding chapter. Part 1 provides three *scene-setting* chapters which establish the significance of the 'development imperative' and chart the evolution of thinking on development issues, and of development itself, since the mid 20th century. These are followed by two chapters which, respectively, examine key macroeconomic theories of economic growth, and identify 'landmark' theoretical analyses of the development process.

Part 2 focuses on *governance* issues, with chapters on corruption, the public sector in developing countries, and the role and potential of civil society.

This is followed, in Part 3, by detailed examination of four of the areas of most intense, and practically significant, *current debate* on development – globalization, poverty, sustainable development and the environment, and stabilization.

Resource issues are addressed in Part 4 – which looks, in turn, at population, the processes of rural-to-urban labour migration and urbanization, gender issues, agriculture and food-supply problems, industrialization, and possible approaches to building technological capacity in developing countries.

The last of the five main Parts examines, from different angles, a further resource – *finance* for development. Domestic finance, official development assistance ('foreign aid'), loans and debt, foreign direct investment (by multinational companies), and the burgeoning flows of remittances from migrant workers back to their home countries – are all examined in detail. In addition, one chapter is devoted to project appraisal.

The book concludes with a summing up, in Chapter 25, in the form of 'Guidelines, Judgements, and Possibilities'.

On-line material and further features

A major problem in preparing a text-book in development economics is that the sheer volume of relevant material could easily overwhelm a reader new to the field. Accordingly, we have taken the decision to 'streamline' the presentation by focusing on the central themes and issues in the main body of the text – and setting out some larger associated data sets, together with appendices to some of the chapters, in an accompanying 'Online Learning Centre' [OLC] which may be accessed at ***www.mcgraw-hill.co.uk/textbooks/huq***.

This approach has the further advantage of making possible the updating of statistical and other material, and web links, on a rolling basis. The acceleration of structural change in the developing world, and the continual emergence of new issues, make this up-dating capacity a particularly useful one. If a group of readers in an area is unable to access the OLC through lack of local internet connection, they should mention this fact to the publisher at 'the address supplied on page iv. The publisher will then consider some other way of giving access to the material.

At the end of each chapter '*Additional reading*' and '*Questions for discussion*' are provided. Further source material and datasets, on the internet and in other forms such as videos and DVDs, are listed either at the ends of chapters or on the OLC.

The additional reading material cited includes articles and books useful to readers wishing to pursue individual chapter topics further, together with references to material providing easily read supplements to the text – usually topical and often fairly brief. It is hoped that readers will browse this for pleasure rather than as a duty!

The 'Questions' contain both pointers to important issues that should be understood after reading a chapter, and a small number of – frequently controversial – questions which ask the reader to think beyond the confines of the material in the chapter.

Guided tour

Chapter Toolkits
Most chapters have a 'toolkit' that gives explanations of words and abbreviations found in the chapter.

Key Terms
For ease of reference, key terms are often highlighted in the chapters for which they are important.

Figures and Tables
These appear in each chapter either to convey factual information or to represent principles and relationships.

Summary Conclusions
For each chapter a conclusion summarizes the main messages of the chapter.

Questions for Discussion
The questions at the end of each chapter are intended to test understanding of important points and to encourage thought.

Additional Reading
Each chapter has a list of further reading, through which you may extend your knowledge and understanding of the chapter content. In the Online Learning Centre there is a further comprehensive list, chapter by chapter, of Internet and other resources that are freely available.

Appendices
Chapter Appendices contain supplementary information and ideas on themes explored in the chapters.

Technology to enhance learning and teaching

*Visit **www.mcgraw-hill.co.uk/textbooks/huq** today*

Online Learning Centre (OLC)

After completing each chapter, log on to the supporting Online Learning Centre website. Take advantage of the study tools offered to reinforce the material you have read in the text, and to develop your knowledge of development economics in a fun and effective way.

Resources for students include:

- *A glossary of terms*
- *Maps*
- *Background tables of national statistics*
- *Appendices to the chapters*
- *Online datasets*
- *Other learning resources*
- *Index of boxes, figures and tables*

Also available for lecturers:

- *Chapter outlines*
- *PowerPoint presentations*

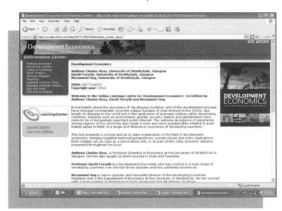

Custom Publishing Solutions: Let us help make our **content** your **solution**

At McGraw-Hill Education our aim is to help lecturers to find the most suitable content for their needs delivered to their students in the most appropriate way. Our **custom publishing solutions** offer the ideal combination of content delivered in the way which best suits lecturer and students.

Our custom publishing programme offers lecturers the opportunity to select just the chapters or sections of material they wish to deliver to their students from a database called Primis at ***www.primisonline.com***

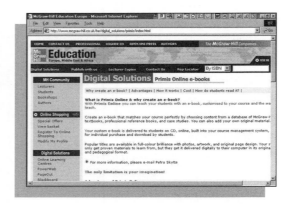

Primis contains over two million pages of content from:

- textbooks
- professional books
- case books – Harvard Articles, Insead, Ivey, Darden, Thunderbird and BusinessWeek
- Taking Sides – debate materials

Across the following imprints:

- McGraw-Hill Education
- Open University Press
- Harvard Business School Press
- US and European material

There is also the option to include additional material authored by lecturers in the custom product – this does not necessarily have to be in English.

We will take care of everything from start to finish in the process of developing and delivering a custom product to ensure that lecturers and students receive exactly the material needed in the most suitable way.

With a Custom Publishing Solution, students enjoy the best selection of material deemed to be the most suitable for learning everything they need for their courses – something of real value to support their learning. Teachers are able to use exactly the material they want, in the way they want, to support their teaching on the course.

Please contact ***your local McGraw-Hill representative*** with any questions or alternatively contact Warren Eels **e:** ***warren_eels@mcgraw-hill.com***.

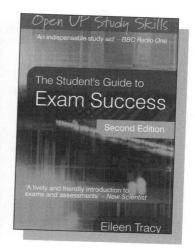

Acknowledgements

Our thanks go to the following reviewers for their comments at various stages in the text's development:

Mauricio Armellini, Durham Business School
Fiona Atkins, Birkbeck University of London
Professor Sue Bowden, University of York
Professor Shanti P. Chakravarty, Bangor University
Gregory Huff, University of Glasgow
Carmen A Li, University of Essex
Dr Julie Litchfield, University of Sussex
Mahmood Messkoub, University of Leeds
Dr Arijit Mukherjee, University of Nottingham
Brian Snowden, Northumbria University
Nicholas Weaver, University of Manchester

Authors' Acknowledgements and Thanks

Various chapters of the book have been used in teaching both undergraduate and post-graduate classes, and we are grateful for the feedback we have received from our students. As the book progressed we have had valued input from a number of our Strathclyde colleagues, principally from Roy Grieve, H.P. Kushari, Eric Rahim and Roger Sandilands, and from Michael Tribe of Bradford University. We also had the privilege of consulting on particular points Mahabub Hossain (Executive Director of BRAC), Mustafa Mujeri (now Chief Economist of the Bangladesh Bank) and Quazi Shahabuddin (Director General of the Bangladesh Institute of Development Studies).

We are grateful for the research assistance we have received, mainly in Glasgow and Dhaka. In Glasgow, we had help from several people including Mikael Adolfsson, Molly Mumtaz Huq and Musa Jega Ibrahim, all of them students at Strathclyde University at the time. We have also received tremendous support from a research team based in Dhaka, consisting of three fresh graduates of Dhaka University: Shamal Kumar Karmaker, Ashiqur Rahman and Syed Al-Helal Uddin. In Bangladesh, we have also been helped by others, in particular Montosh Kumar Roy, Assistant Professor of Economics of Uttar Bangla College, who kindly supplied us with a bunch of good photographs, one of which now features on the cover page. We are also grateful for the logistic support we have received from staff of the Economics Department at Strathclyde, with ever ready and cheerful help from the secretarial team, under the benign tutelage over the period of first Morag Pryce and then Moira Quinn.

When we started writing the book we dealt with Mark Kavanagh at McGraw-Hill, but within a year he handed over the responsibility to Hannah Cooper who, when the book was almost ready for editing and production, passed it to Tom Hill and Natalie Jacobs under the leadership of Alison Holt. All of them have taken such a keen interest in the book that we have felt it a privilege to work with them. We are also grateful to the cover-design team of McGraw-Hill, who had to bear with our idiosyncratic choices.

To all these old and new friends who have contributed to the birth of the book – but emphatically bear no responsibility for its defects – we offer our hearty thanks.

The Authors

Anthony Clunies-Ross

Anthony Clunies-Ross is an Australian long resident in Scotland, graduate of Melbourne and Cambridge. He has taught at Monash University in Melbourne, the University of Papua New Guinea and the University of Strathclyde in Glasgow; briefly also at the University of Melbourne (in history), and part-time at the University of Glasgow, with additional very brief teaching assignments at the Indian Institute of Management Ahmedabad, Government College University Lahore and the University of Peshawar, and a six-month research period at the University of the Philippines. He worked at the University of Papua New Guinea from 1967 to 1974, with subsequent short periods in Papua New Guinea for consultancy and research. His interests have centred round public finance for developing countries. His publications (joint or sole) include *One Per Cent: the case for greater Australian foreign aid* (with R I Downing and others, Melbourne U.P., 1963), *Australia and Nuclear Weapons* (with Peter King, Sydney U.P., 1966), *Alternative Strategies for Papua New Guinea* (ed. with John Langmore, Oxford U.P., 1971), *Taxation of Mineral Rent* (with Ross Garnaut, Oxford U.P., 1983), *Migrants from Fifty Villages* (Papua New Guinea I.E.S.R., 1984), *Economic Stabilization for Developing Countries* (Edward Elgar, 1991), *Albania's Economy in Transition and Turmoil, 1990–1997* (ed. with Petar Sudar, Ashgate, 1998), *Making the World Autonomous: a global role for the European Un ion* (Dunedin Academic Press, 2005), and a report 'Resources for social development' for the ILO's World Commission on the Social Dimension of Globalization (2003).

David J.C. Forsyth

David Forsyth is an Emeritus Professor of Economics at the University of Strathclyde in Glasgow. He studied at Aberdeen University and the University of Virginia before embarking on an academic career which has taken him to lecturing posts at the University of Strathclyde, Aberdeen University, the University of Ghana, Carleton University (Ottawa), and the University of the South Pacific (Fiji), where he was Head of the Department of Economics for twelve years. He has also been a staff member of the International Labour Office (specialising in Technology Policy) and, recently, of the Commonwealth Secretariat (as Multilateral Trade Policy Adviser). His main areas of interest are Development Economics and International Trade. Extensive consultancy work in both fields has involved 'missions' in over twenty African countries, in India, and in all fourteen of the independent island countries of the North and South Pacific. His published work includes books on *Technology Policy for Small Economies* (Macmillan) and on *U.S. Investment in Scotland*, (Praeger), and articles in numerous journals – including *The Economic Journal, Oxford Economic Papers, World Development, The Journal of Developing Areas, The British Journal of Industrial Relations, Sociology of Education, The British Journal of Educational Studies, Regional Studies and The New Scientist*. Professor Forsyth is based, once again, in Scotland – devoting his limited leisure time to discovering, by rail, the many European countries over which, for thirty years, he flew en route to the developing world.

Mozammel Huq

Born in Bangladesh, Mozammel Huq is a graduate of the Universities of Rajshahi (BA Hons and MA) and Glasgow (MLitt and PhD). His career includes extensive teaching (especially in Bangladesh and the UK), and wide-ranging research on Third World development – in which his detailed, first-hand knowledge of the development experience of a large number of countries of Asia and Africa has proved invaluable. He has published in various international journals including *World Development, Pakistan Development Review, Journal of International Development,* and *Bangladesh Development Studies.* He is the author of a number of books including *Machine Tool Production in Developing Countries* (with C.C. Prendergast, Scottish Academic Press, 1983); *The Economy of Ghana: The First 25 Years since Independence* (Macmillan, 1989); and *Machinery Manufacturing in Bangladesh* (with K.M.N. Islam and N. Islam, UPL, 1993). He has also edited several books including *Science, Technology and Development: North-South Co-operation* (with P. Bhatt and others, Frank Cass, 1991), *Strategies for Industrialisation: The Case of Bangladesh,* (with J. Love, UPL, 2000), *Building Technological Capability: Issues and Prospects – Nepal, Bangladesh and India* (UPL, 2003), and *Technology and Development in the New Millennium* (with A. Azhar and others, Karachi University, 2003). He has been a consultant to the ILO, EU, UNDP and the Commonwealth Secretariat. He has worked in and/or collaborated with a number of developing-country institutions including the Bangladesh Institute of Development Studies; the Centre of Development Studies at the University of Cape Coast; the Department of Agricultural Economics, University of Nigeria; the Science & Technology Evaluation and Policy Research Unit of the Royal Nepal Academy of Science and Technology; and the Department of Economics, G.C. University, Lahore. A longtime resident of Scotland, he has taught for over 30 years at the University of Strathclyde and part-time at the University of Glasgow, besides participating in a number of research projects. Currently, he is also a Visiting Professor of Economics at Uttar Bangla College (National University, Bangladesh).

PART 1
History, Ideologies and Methods

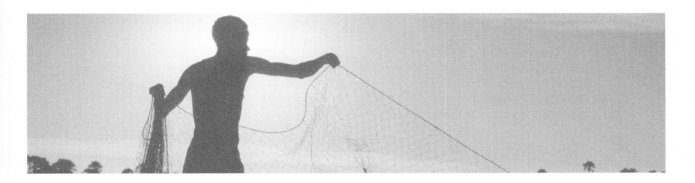

PART 1
History, Ideologies and Methods

CHAPTER 1

Recognizing the Development Imperative

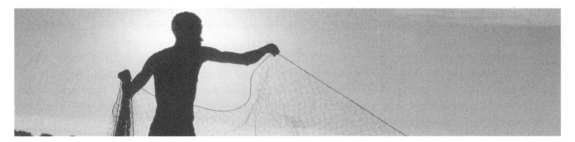

After the Second World War the world woke up to the huge gulf between rich and poor nations. This happened just as hundreds of millions of people were breaking away from the old empires into independent states. The result: a conviction that 'development' was an urgent necessity.

Introduction

This first chapter is designed to explain *why* development economics as a subject of study arose when it did; why from different angles people have widely come to regard the need for development as an *imperative*; *what questions* are covered by development economics; and how we might understand the term *poverty* in a world context and the term *development* itself. It will outline some of the methods by which the *degrees* of development achievement – in average income attained and in equality and aspects of social welfare – in various countries of the world may be compared, together with the limitations of those methods. The final sections will present definitions and explanations of terms used in discourse on development, and also in dealing with national income and related aggregates ('national accounting' or 'social accounting').

The starting-point

The years just after the end of the Second World War in 1945 were an extraordinary period. There was a sense – among the victors, the formerly occupied, even very soon the defeated, and in the overseas colonies of the then world powers – that great changes were possible. As never before – a result in part of the spread of the colonial powers' languages, and of telegraphy, telephones, air mail and broadcasting – there had come to be such a thing as world opinion: divided, fragmented, patchy, with many millions of people by-passed, nevertheless a circuit of communication extending, however tenuously, to most parts of the globe.

At this time an important change in public perceptions and attitudes began to take hold. The world – the segment of it that was within the global conversation – started to think of itself in a new way: as sharply divided into rich and poor – not just into rich and poor within any country, but into rich and poor societies, countries, nations. The fact that there were vast differences between the *average* levels of material subsistence from one country to another began to be understood. Spreading the income equally – if that were possible – across the whole population of Sweden or Britain would provide a level of living hugely different from doing the same in India, say, or the Congo. Moreover, most of the world's people lived in countries at the wrong side of the divide; and the reasons for the great divide *needed to be explained.*

Doubtless this had occurred to people before. They were aware that great changes had been wrought by the original industrial revolution and its spread from its land of origin. Now, however, the rich–poor divide became an explicit assumption, part of the framework within which most educated people came to think about the world. It also became *a matter of general puzzlement and concern.* It was as if our eyes had been opened and we saw a familiar part of the furniture in a new way or with a new intensity. There had been considerable probing of the economic history of some of the richer countries – even of the stories of some among the poorer ones that had diversified into modern industry, such as India and Japan – expounding how those countries had developed. There was also a generalized model, stemming from the classical economists of the late-eighteenth and early-nineteenth centuries, about how growth in productive capacity could occur. There had also been ideas of *stages* through which societies had passed. Yet the general perception that the vast cleavage of the world into rich and poor peoples, nations, countries, was itself a major puzzle, or that closing or narrowing the gap was a crucial challenge for the human family – this was fairly new. Numbers of articulate people began to see the division as a mystery to be solved, or as denoting a set of stages in human development through which all could eventually be expected to pass, or as a problem for enlightened policy, or as a scandal or a crime. One way or another, it began to be taken seriously.

Development economics arose from attempts to unravel the mystery, to catalogue the stages if stages there were, to meet the policy challenges, to reduce the scandal, to atone for the crime. It is one of the new and characteristic cultural phenomena of the second half of the twentieth century. Why development economics – with the view of the world on which it was based – emerged *when* it did and *took the form* that it did will be discussed below.

What is development economics about?

What do we hope to learn from a book about development economics? We may come with 'why' questions, or with 'what is to be done' questions, or both. And they are closely connected.

First, we may want to get some idea of **why the world has become so sharply divided** into rich and poor nations: what is *the process* through which this has happened, given *first* that people all over the world seem pretty much alike when they are separated from their particular cultures and circumstances: at least the variation of inherited characteristics *within* any one nation or ethnic group is immensely greater than *between* nations or ethnic groups – and *second* that the technology on which affluence is based seems readily capable of transfer across national boundaries?

Second, we may want to gain a better idea of **what can be done to improve the living conditions** of the hundreds of millions of people who live in extreme poverty or insecurity: without a clean water supply; with inadequate or unreliable sources of food and prevalent symptoms of under-nutrition; with contagious diseases for which adequate prophylaxis or treatment exists, or forms of blindness or lameness or chronic pain that could be removed or relieved by well-known medicines or simple surgery; and with a lack of elementary schooling and literacy. Our concern may be solely over the severe (and arguably unnecessary) material hardships and insecurity and enforced ignorance and intellectual starvation themselves, or also over the lack of self-confidence, of social influence, and of social respect, that is likely to accompany these deprivations.

Third – partly because we guess this may have some bearing on the answer to the last set of questions – we may want to learn **how the rates of general economic growth in the poorer countries of the world might be increased** – and whether *some* methods of engineering this rather than *others* would lead incomes in those countries to be more equally distributed or the manifestations of extreme poverty to be more extensively reduced.

Fourth, we may wonder whether the ways in which we have been led to analyse economic behaviour in rich countries apply equally to those much poorer countries that seem superficially so different. Do we need *a different style of economics* – with different models, different rules-of-thumb, different policy guidelines – as we move from one to the other?

These questions have had a lot of attention over the sixty years or so since the end of the Second World War: far more than even a short while earlier. The attempt to deal with them has come to be called *development economics.*

Needless to say, it has not come up with complete and universally agreed answers. Indeed, it has touched on highly emotive issues and has been riven with controversy. This is also true of economics in general over some at least of the period, especially when it comes to questions of policy.

Events, dear boy, events . . .

Yet we believe that there is much to be gained by examining the thinking and analysis that have gone into the subject, the interpretations of history, the bright ideas and the deductive reasoning, *against the actual events of the time.* We (the fraternity of those who have gone into the subject) know quite a lot more about development economics – what possibilities there are, what emphatically does not work, how to avoid some of the worst mistakes, maybe also with a clearer understanding of what matters – in 2005 than we did in say 1965, let alone 1950. This is not only because of the careful study and thought that has been deployed in the meantime but also because of what has plainly and strikingly *happened* over those intervening forty years. On being asked what posed the main difficulty in his role as British Prime Minister, Harold Macmillan famously replied: 'Events, dear boy, events'. *Events* have been our main instructor. But events, even spectacular and obvious ones, have to be noted and interpreted. We need to develop a rational framework for *understanding* what has happened.

So, like other textbook writers, the present authors go through the main ideas that have emerged in the study of development economics. Yet, where some among these ideas do not seem to have led to any positive outcome in enlarging understanding or guiding policy, we deal with them fairly briefly.

A proliferation of panaceas

Popular thought about promoting 'development' has been prone to single-issue solutions: that the answer is decolonization, or birth-control, or free trade, or fair trade, or 'South-South' trade, or planning, or market-determined exchange-rates, or fixed exchange-rates, or redistributive land reform, or secure property rights, or nationalization of foreign firms, or privatization of whatever can be privatized, or massive aid, or self-reliance, or revolution, or intermediate technology, or microcredit, or reversing urban-bias, or transparency in governance. Following the main moves that have been made in the debate provides some ground for judging what stands up and what does not; in what sense or in what circumstances some policy may be useful; and how many dimensions there are in which decisions have to be taken and in which taking the right decision can matter.

We shall also try to examine development economics – the study, the governing ideas and tendencies – as a phenomenon in its own right, a major feature of the discourse of its time. We shall suggest explanations of why it took the form it did: to what experiences and needs it had responded.

A game of two halves

British football commentators are fond of the expression 'a game of two halves'. Development economics – until 1990 or shortly after, say – was a game of two halves. The prevailing climate of thought about development policy changed fairly radically over the 1970s. Views that were conventional before that decade tended to be treated as maverick after it, and conversely. To some extent this reversal followed changed thinking about economic policy generally, but there was an even clearer about-turn in development economics. Asking dispassionately why it happened – to what extent any actual observations or greater insight justified the change of direction – may help to sort out how far the new orientation (itself undergoing further modification in the late 1990s and around the turn of the century, so that we can now talk of a third stage) has been valid and useful.

No fortified borders

Like many other disciplines and sub-disciplines, development economics has no clear boundaries. Methods of analysis and investigation that are more readily associated with *sociology* or *political science* than with economics may be used to help answer its questions. Also – because it is much concerned with processes working through long periods – *history*, extending sometimes to prehistory, should have light to throw. The attempt to understand why certain events happen – why they have happened, why they may happen, how they might be made to happen – needs to make use of whatever source of illumination there is. Truth is no respecter of professional fiefdoms.

To acknowledge the broad character of the analysis and evidence that may be useful, the term *development studies* is often used to cover enquiries that include, but extend beyond, what we have normally thought of as 'development economics'; but there is in fact no clear dividing line between development economics and other development studies. Economists' questions may need to rely in part on answers derived from the methods and characteristic interests of other social sciences – and conversely.

Outline of the field

To summarize, we may say that development economics is concerned with:

- **Positive** questions (questions of fact, of generalization of facts, and of cause and effect)
- **Normative** questions (questions of what needs to be done, drawing both on the objectives or values adopted by the investigator and on positive evidence about *what is* and *how the world works*).

The questions may be related to any of the following and their inter-connections:

- Growth in the *economic capacity and average living standards* of nations or societies
- Variation in the degree of *equality* of distribution of income and of other goods
- Reduction of *poverty* in all its aspects
- Correspondingly, enlargement of the *opportunities* open to those most deprived
- Economic *behaviour in* 'developing countries'.

Why did the world in 1945–50 need a new field of study and why just then?

To answer this question, we need to consider the state of the world around 1950 and the few years before.

At the end of the war in 1945, there had been great physical destruction and dislocation in continental Europe extending to the west of the Soviet Union, in Japan, and in China and much of South-East Asia, but the recovery, especially in Japan and Western Europe, was to be surprisingly quick. Immediately after 1945 much of the world was still included in the overseas empires of European powers, which, with the exception of Italy, had retained, or acted to resume, their pre-war 'possessions'.

In mainland East and South Asia and in South-East Asia, the only areas at first acknowledged as independent were the Koreas (recently wrested from Japan and divided), China (then engaged in civil war), the Philippines (newly granted independence by the US in pursuance of a pre-war plan and timetable), Thailand, Outer Mongolia (in fact a Soviet satellite), and a string of landlocked mountain kingdoms (Afghanistan, Nepal, Bhutan, Sikkim). India (including the present Pakistan and Bangladesh) with its vast population was still under British control, together with Ceylon, Burma, Hong Kong, Singapore, and what is now Malaysia. The present Indonesia constituted the then Netherlands East Indies. What are now Vietnam, Laos, and Cambodia made up French Indo-China.

Fully independent in Africa were only Ethiopia (with Eritrea appended), Egypt, Liberia, Libya, and South Africa (with what is now Namibia under its control). Portugal had Mozambique, Angola, Portuguese Guinea (Guinea-Bissau), and São Tomé and Principe; Belgium had what are now the Democratic Republic of Congo, Burundi, and Rwanda; Spain had the Spanish Sahara (Western Sahara), Spanish Morocco (now part of Morocco), Spanish Guinea (Equatorial Guinea), Ceuta and Melilla; Italy continued to hold part of present Somalia as a Trust Territory; Tangier was international; France and Britain under various forms controlled all the rest. Most of the Caribbean and Pacific islands were also dependencies.

By contrast, the whole of mainland South and Central America (apart from what are now Guyana, Surinam, French Guiana, and Belize) was made up of states that had gained independence from Spain or Portugal in the nineteenth century. Like North America, Australasia, and South Africa – and unlike most of the rest of the European empires – they had been in varying degrees settler-colonies in which many Europeans had made their homes. Their colonial heritage varied from the 'Southern Cone' – where, much as in the US, Canada, and Australia, European settlers had greatly outnumbered and more or less marginalized the original inhabitants – through areas where there had been considerable mixing of native and settler genes, though with the settlers' descendants tending to carry social privilege – to the northern Andes and Guatemala, where large and distinct indigenous cultural groups persisted alongside an upper stratum of mainly European or mixed-European descent. In Brazil, much as in the Caribbean and the US, there were also large numbers of people of full or mixed African ancestry whose forebears had been brought in as slaves.

Yet, already by 1950, there had been big changes in South and South-East Asia. India, Pakistan (including what is now Bangladesh), Indonesia, Burma (now Myanmar), and Ceylon (now Sri Lanka) – covering between them perhaps a fifth of the world's population – had joined the ranks of independent nations. By 1965, most of Africa (Portuguese and Spanish possessions apart) was also independent of the European powers, as were Malaysia, Singapore, the Vietnams, Laos, and Cambodia.

Naturally it had been widely supposed in the first batch of countries attaining independence that material benefits would follow. It must have seemed obvious that independence gave at least fresh opportunities for enhanced economic growth, with consequent strengthening of the new states and reduction in poverty; and there would clearly be political advantages for a regime that could recognizably deliver the goods.

So economic development in any ex-colony shifted from being a peripheral concern for the government of the imperial power, pursued conscientiously perhaps but without any great sense of urgency, to become a central preoccupation of an independent government, with its top leaders – often veterans of movements of rebellion against the colonial powers – generally lacking the kind of experience of previous ministerial office or high administrative responsibility that might have shaped their approach into a conventional mould.

If the policies of the colonial power had failed to lift the country out of poverty, if traditional economics had proved unsuitable, then clearly a new approach must be needed. But what new approach precisely? There were new governments looking for answers. In the 1960s their numbers greatly increased. There were also new international institutions that could give attention to this quest. We consider in Chapter 2 the kind of answers that were initially given.

So the first factor demanding a new branch of economics was **the advent of the 'new nations'**.

A second element, helping to signal that something needed to be done and might be possible, was the development in the inter-war period of **systematic national accounting**. Attempts to give accounts of nations' whole income had been made in France and Britain, back to Sir William Petty at the end of the seventeenth century. An attempt to estimate the national income and income per head of India had been made by Dadabhai Naoroji, an opponent of British rule, as far back as 1868, and a series of further Indian estimates followed. But it was not until the 1930s, with the work of pioneers such as Colin Clark in Britain, V.K.R.V. Rao in India, and Simon Kuznets in the US that conventions adopted enabled apparently meaningful international comparisons of total and average incomes to be made. Colin Clark's 1940 book, *The Conditions of Economic Progress*, has been described as 'the first study to make quantitatively evident the gulf between European countries and the rest of the world' (http://cepa.newschool.edu/het/profiles/colin.htm).

Actual numbers for income levels and rates of growth made it possible to think of *growth targets*. Perhaps inputs could be identified that would generate the desired increases in output. Not only did something drastic need to be done but, if we could discover the relevant 'incremental capital–output relationship' – the amount of investment necessary to add an extra unit of output – maybe it *could* be done; and so we could establish objectively how far and on what terms any target could be reached.

Having the figures also gave any contrast a concrete reality, apparently a set of facts beyond argument, potentially a spur to consciences in the affluent part of the world as well as to national aspirations in the newly independent states. The national-income figures did indeed appear to show **a sharp division among nations**, with a great gulf fixed between a comparatively small rich minority and a vast, very poor majority. This was the third element.

Those countries that had been affluent before the War and had not been invaded or significantly bombed – the US, Canada, Sweden, Switzerland, Australia, New Zealand, to a less extent Britain – came out ahead; but most of the rest of Northern and much of Western Europe was quick to reconstruct and for some decades grew consistently faster in average income than the Anglo-Saxon countries and former neutrals. Before long there was a clearly defined group of rich, 'developed', 'industrialized' countries clustered entirely in Northern and Western Europe, North America, and Australasia.

At the other extreme were the poor countries, comprising most of the world's population – with average incomes a tiny fraction of those of the 'developed' nations. These covered virtually all the states of mainland East and South Asia and of South-East Asia, virtually all of Africa, most of West Asia and the Arab world, and at least the poorer parts of Latin America.

In between were admittedly some countries that did not fit clearly into either extreme. These included most of Eastern Europe, the Soviet Union when it too had gone through some reconstruction, much of Latin America, South Africa, and Japan. In some cases (strikingly South Africa and Brazil), the middle-income average concealed an affluent enclave or relatively affluent regions, combined with a very poor majority or poor part of the country.

Like the Soviet Union, Japan at the time had proved an anomaly. Both, with very modest average living standards, had developed industrial sectors that allowed them to be formidable participants in modern warfare.

Yet it was the vast divide between the extremes – the very rich and very poor nations – that provided the challenge. No obvious simple unalterable difference appeared to explain the gap. Technology, skills, investment were all potentially mobile. People from different parts of the world showed at most only slightly different spectra of native aptitudes. Whatever obstacles there were to bridging the gulf could surely be overcome, but at the same time the economics, the policy, applied hitherto had apparently allowed the ravine to emerge. This suggested that new paradigms were needed. Continuation of whatever gradual change poor countries might have experienced in the past would not be enough. Some way had to be found of making a quantum leap.

So these three elements, coming together – the new nations with new governments and new expectations; the national-income figures that appeared to give an anatomy of income and income growth; and the vast rich–poor chasm that those figures revealed – suggested between them that a radical new approach to economic policy in the poor countries was needed and might be possible.

In the years that followed, the combination of television with ever-increasing and ever-wider-ranging business and tourist travel, especially on the part of people from the more affluent countries, enhanced the awareness and immediacy of the rich–poor contrast.

As the 1950s and 1960s proceeded, moreover, the idea that there were models to be emulated could only be enhanced. Both the Soviet bloc – with its ambitious five-year plans – and the Western democracies – with their rapid reconstructions and their new full-employment policies and welfare states – appeared to have solved the problems of unemployment and extreme poverty, and both on the basis of new economic paradigms.

The underdevelopment or poverty problem from three points of view

There were at least three main reasons why the extreme relative poverty of most of the world – as viewed against the affluence of the Northwest Europeans and their overseas descendants – was a cause of concern.

First, many people everywhere were affronted or disturbed by the hunger, the illness, the ignorance, the insecurity, that modern technology and organization *seemed to have made avoidable* and yet still beset hundreds of millions of people. Television, as it took hold and became progressively bolder over the succeeding years, made the poverty and suffering increasingly vivid. A sense of **compassion or justice** or both demanded radical change.

Second, governing groups and elites, and informed people generally, in the new states resented the **external weakness and low international status** – together with the difficulty of meeting the most urgent internal aspirations – that national poverty imposed upon them.

Third, some in the rich countries feared, rightly or wrongly, the **sharp division of the world** into haves and have-nots, believing that it might undermine efforts at international co-operation and provide grounds for attempts to subvert the existing world order. The Cold War between the West and the Soviet Bloc aggravated the fear on the Western side.

For these, and possibly other, reasons, the need for much faster 'development' of the poor countries became virtually uncontroversial. However half-hearted the support might be, however different the prescriptions favoured, there were and still are few voices raised against it. The exceptions have been some sections of the environmentalist movement, mainly from the 1970s on, who argued against economic growth *per se*. Policy may sometimes have yielded to these prejudices, but never or hardly ever on the explicit grounds that income growth in poor countries, such as might lead them eventually to 'catch up', should be discouraged.

In most recent years especially, a fourth source of concern – of a different character– has been added. Much manufacturing, and some services that have become internationally tradable, have moved from the lands of the rich to those of the poor. Some of the 'developing countries', notably China and India, are coming to bulk so large in the world economy that the affluent states in their own interests cannot help taking notice. **Feedback from economic growth in the 'developing' world** has come to be of major direct importance to the high-income countries. So, beside the problem of overcoming the stagnation of many of the developing countries, there is now the (potentially benign) need to adjust constructively to the spectacular growth of others.

Poverty: relative and absolute, primitive and modern

Most of all, it has probably been the sense of compassion and justice that has made world poverty into a recognized world concern. But what do we understand by *poverty*?

The concept of poverty is a difficult one. There is an inevitably subjective element in judgements of others' poverty and of our own. What each of us regards as poor depends greatly on what we ourselves are familiar with and what we expect. **Relative poverty** is distinguished from **absolute poverty**. The same level of material provision that would make a person poor in a rich society might make her rich in a poor society – though the non-material accompaniments of these provisions (status, family ties, social contacts) would surely enter into any assessment that the people concerned made of their own states of poverty or wealth. The *relatively* poor are those who are poor in their own eyes and in the eyes of those among whom they live. They may have reliable and adequate food supplies, tapped water, clothing and shelter, even good health services if they fall sick. Still, if their incomes stand far below the medians or modes for their societies, they may find their social life and contacts limited, feel that their status is low, and be recognized, and count themselves, as poor.

Yet there are people in the world, large numbers of them, whom probably everyone would regard as poor: those who have biologically inadequate and irregular food, or are even affected, as is the case in some parts of Africa, by *frequent* famines; those obliged to work unduly long or hard, or in conditions of extreme discomfort or danger, in order to stay alive and to meet essential family responsibilities; children who have to do physical work for long hours (and their families for whom their work must often be a necessity); those in bondage because of debt; people whose only source of water is polluted or who have to live next to open sewage; older children or grandparents who have families of young children to support; those forced to fossick in rubbish dumps or to beg. Where a large proportion of the children in a country show physical signs of malnutrition in normal times, as in Bangladesh in very recent years, that country is poor; those millions of children and their families are poor, poor in anyone's language. That is **absolute poverty**.

People in **relative poverty** in more or less rich countries may feel miserable on that account. There is plenty of evidence that the satisfaction or unhappiness that people feel about their incomes and material standards of living depends heavily on how these standards compare with the living conditions of those about them. But relative poverty of that sort in rich countries is not generally treated as a *world* concern. Whatever needs to be done about it is seen as a matter for the governments and other institutions of the states in which they live.

The *world's* concern, at least that part of it motivated by compassion and justice, is about absolute poverty. But just where does the absolute poverty that demands our concern start? The many members of the world's population that are rated as very poor when the numbers are now counted stem from various traditional ways of life. While the forebears of some of them were largely isolated from the rest of the world and in conditions that would now be regarded as 'primitive' – living in small autonomous villages or bands – those forebears, provided they had the use of plenty of land, would probably *not* have seen themselves as poor in the sense of miserable or pitiful in normal times – unless and until they came into contact with people or peoples that had much more in the way of material possessions and amenities.

Primitive affluence

The Melanesian peoples of New Guinea and some other islands of the Western Pacific have been described, before they had been much affected by colonial contact, as living in 'subsistence affluence'. There were some gradations of wealth but normally no slavery and probably little variation in access to the essentials of life. Most people in most communities had plenty of food, with little or no risk of crop failure, all the shelter and everyday clothing they desired and expected, fresh water and fuel generally close at hand, plenty of space, and no inordinate burden of work. At least that was how it seemed to outsiders. Yet to most of those outsiders themselves, coming in the twentieth century from the nations that were rich by world standards, that life in its traditional form would still have seemed hard, fitfully uncomfortable, risky perhaps, and monotonous. There would have been no books, no communication beyond the spoken word, no modern surgery or medicine even of the simplest kind, plenty of insect pests, a sameness about the food, and no knowledge of the wider world. In many areas there was malaria, fitfully painful and debilitating where it was endemic, potentially fatal where it was not. Other diseases, to which people might have little immunity, could be occasional visitants. Broken bones and flesh wounds might well be disastrous.

Melanesia, with its subsistence-affluence supported by shifting cultivation in tropical areas mostly of reliable year-round rainfall, may have been an extreme case; but there were other traditional modes of life – hunter-gatherers, nomadic herders, even settled peasant-farmers where land was still reasonably plentiful and landlords and rulers were not unduly rapacious – in which at best most people most of the time may have had what they regarded as the necessities, and yet in which a 'poor' visitant from late-twentieth-century northwestern Europe or North America would have felt seriously deprived.

Was this poverty? Probably the question would have had little meaning to the people in these more 'primitive' societies themselves before contact with Europeans and others with quite different levels of technology and organization. *Then* the traditional systems of values and status and the conditions of life became disturbed. Not only did the outsiders' goods become attractive, creating new wants that could not be satisfied without cash; but also, where there had been no state and no landlords, the newcomers often imposed one and sometimes both, making further demands for cash and hence *either* for devoting part of the people's own land and labour to cash-crops *or* for work on distant mines or plantations under conditions that might be more or less like slavery. Where, as in the Indian Subcontinent, the colonizers took over a peasant society that already had its governments and recruiters and tax-collectors, its own castes and landlords, and its own enclaves of urban civilization, the shock might be less.

Some individuals would have seen themselves as clearly gaining from these alterations; but in the more 'primitive' societies new needs were undoubtedly created; new burdens had to be accepted; there were often new sources of inequality and new opportunities for being relatively poor; and any 'subsistence affluence' that had existed was probably disturbed and would no longer have been seen as enough in any case.

Most serious of all, perhaps, in those societies that were newly colonized or otherwise assailed by European (or Arab) traders or missionaries, it became obvious that the outsiders had the *power*. Traditional dynasties could be overthrown, as with Asante in Ghana, and in Mogul India, Hawaii and Burma. Traditional big-men and chiefs, leading hitherto autonomous village communities and clans, could become of little account. What the outsiders had and valued became increasingly the standard of value. Later *decolonization*, and the accompanying replacement of foreigners by local people – in politics, the civil service and management – would not reverse these changes of outlook, backed as they were by changed material conditions. It was at first simply the personnel, rather than the system, the hierarchy, the values, that were replaced when 'localization' occurred. Yet before long the change in personnel generally came to affect the way the imported institutions worked.

World standards of absolute poverty

What we regard as absolute poverty in the early-twenty-first century has to be defined in relation to what is technically possible and what is necessary for active participation in the wider world now. Much that would not have occurred to people as necessary in most previous centuries, at least in large areas of the globe – such as literacy, and antibiotics, and radio, and aseptic surgery, and a *lingua franca* giving access to world literature and learning, and electricity, and mosquito-nets – have become essentials.

Nonetheless, at the same time the old-fashioned scourges – famine and disease – have been returning with renewed force at certain times and places, especially in sub-Saharan Africa. In spite of the improved technology for the growing of a number of staple crops, frequent and widespread famines have occurred in Africa over the past few decades: probably the result of a combination of increased population pressure, climate change, soil depletion and civil wars, with the migrations that have resulted. What we know now about responding to famines and preventing them has improved matters, but its application has been far from adequate. Added to that, the development of drug-resistance with a number of the diseases that had been more or less controlled over wide areas several decades ago, has allowed them to revive, while the advent of HIV/AIDS has been devastating, especially in southern and eastern Africa.

Famines, other disasters and emergencies (natural or man-made), and common diseases unchecked for which there are medical or surgical treatments or prophylactics either in being or in plausible prospect: these are aspects of absolute poverty that we have widely come to believe the world should not be tolerating and should take available methods to remedy. The same applies to conditions of widespread malnutrition, to the absence of accessible clean water (and, in urban areas, of sewerage), and to the inability of children to obtain the schooling necessary for elementary literacy and numeracy. Other targets accepted include the reduction to a level much closer to rich-country levels of maternal, infant, and young-child mortality. Moreover, for want of a better overall measure, there is general agreement that no household should have to live on a disposable income per person **less than** the purchasing-power-parity (PPP: see below) equivalent of **two US dollars a day**. Anything less than that is regarded conventionally now as 'income-poverty' or simply **poverty**. Household incomes averaging per person **less than one dollar a day** are regarded as constituting **extreme poverty**.

It is of course realized that, with the best will in the world, these objectives – the elimination of these extremes of absolute poverty in all its aspects – cannot be achieved quickly. **The Millennium Development Goals, adopted by the UN General Assembly in the year 2000, comprise interim global targets, mostly expressed in these direct indicators of absolute-poverty reduction, to be attained by the year 2015** (see Chapter 21, Appendix 21.1, p. 616).

'Development' can also be interpreted to include the removal of deprivations of a less material character. A set of quantified world targets may not readily express the need for such objectives as **full political participation, access of all classes to legal and other means of asserting their rights, equality of status and respect in dealings with the agencies of the state and others in positions of power and influence**, and correspondingly the absence of bribery in public and private institutions; but these needs, in many people's view, should be included in 'development' and their absence should be treated as elements of poverty. Similarly, development can be taken to entail **an end to discrimination** against any group of people; and the Millennium Goals themselves specify the objective of gender equality, and, as a vital step, complete equality of access to education for both sexes.

Average income: its limitations as a measure of material welfare

The average level of national income in a country is inevitably used as an indicator of the general level of *potential material welfare* and hence of at least a major component of what development policy aims to increase. But how satisfactory is it for this purpose? It has a number of limitations, even when we limit its claims this way by stressing the *'potential'* and the *'material'* qualification.

First, there is the question of who actually gets the income: its *distribution*. There are good reasons for thinking (other things being equal) that the more equally income is distributed the more it is valued; and the more material deprivation it is likely to relieve. This is the principle (almost self-evidently true) of **diminishing marginal utility of income to any person as that person's income rises**, combined with broad assumptions (much less obviously true but useful as a first stage in analysis) that a given amount of income is **valued equally by all people at a given income level**. But gains from equalizing may go even beyond what this principle implies. *If* we could find some adequate way of measuring the overall losses of those who lose from a change against the gains of those who gain, *and* it is true that people's valuation of their income depends heavily on comparisons with the incomes of others they encounter *and* in any case rising income is subject to diminishing marginal utility, *then* we might find that rises in the incomes of people in the upper part of the income distribution, unaccompanied by similar movements lower down, may be of zero or negative value overall to people's welfare. Hence the importance of the qualification *'potential'* in the use of average income as an indicator of material welfare.

The second limitation is that income, as normally calculated and presented, includes *only those goods and services on which a price can readily be set*. So the beauty of one's surroundings, quiet, opportunities for meeting people without particular effort or expense, a sense of safety or security, freedom from infectious diseases, are not routinely taken into account: in other words, the physical and social environment. Government services provided free of charge are included in national totals and averages, but priced by the cost of their inputs rather than the value of their outputs; so that the *cost of fighting malaria* is treated as a positive item in income or output, whereas *freedom from malaria*, because it does not happen to be endemic in the area concerned, is not counted. Where there is 'subsistence production' – production by people for their own use rather than sale – an allowance is made for it in income, though the means for doing this are necessarily very imperfect.

A third defect is that *value of natural resources depleted in the creation of the income* is not normally deducted from its computed total: non-renewable resources such as oil and metal ores, but also often such resources as forests that are in principle renewable but can be lost without coming under the national accountants' notice. In this category too can be reckoned environmental losses, including those of global character such as ozone-layer depletion and climate change whose costs are often delayed, and felt at times and places quite different from those in which they are generated. Hence the concept of *sustainable development*: change that still counts as gain when we deduct its full resource and environmental costs and that can continue without irreversible damage to renewable resources. (See Chapter 11.)

Fourth, if we are interested in the current living standards of particular households (say, to find out what proportion are in various degrees of poverty), it may be more relevant to compare expenditures than incomes. Poverty statistics are sometimes based on expenditures and sometimes on incomes.

It is in principle possible to devise measures of income that take account of distributional equality, of non-priced benefits and costs, and of the special forms of those costs that count as resource use: so that a rise in the measure would represent 'distribution-weighted, externality-counting, sustainable income growth'. Social appraisal of projects (cost–benefit analysis) does sometimes try to embody all of these elements. But it is important to remember that the national aggregates cited generally do not.

If comparisons of average income are to be made across countries with different currencies, there also has to be some way of translating incomes calculated in one currency into values in another. Official exchange-rates are very imperfect ways of doing this. The fact that 1000 Korean *won* might exchange officially for a US dollar would not imply that a dollar would necessarily buy 1000 times as much in the US as a *won* would in Korea. Instead *purchasing-power-parity* (PPP) equivalents are calculated (see Appendix 1.2).

A recently enhanced critique of the conventional use of income as a measure of what economic policy should be seeking to maximize has come from the more direct study of *happiness*: people's happiness as they themselves report it in response to surveys, evidence now augmented (and arguably fortified) by evidence of related electrical and chemical events in people's brains. This is discussed, on the Online Learning Centre, in Appendix 10.2 of Chapter 10. (See for example Layard (2005); *Economist* (23/12/2006.) There appears in fact to be a very patchy connection between higher income as normally computed and increased happiness as people report it.

All this does not mean that national income as measured is *irrelevant* to well-being, at least in low-income and middle-income countries. Some of the evidence indeed suggests that, at incomes per head below about $10 000 a year in mid-1990s prices, there is a definite, though far from perfect, positive relationship across countries between per capita income and expressed happiness. Even in high-income countries, greater income may well make it easier politically to distribute benefits more equally, partly perhaps by bigger investment in public goods – that is goods that by their nature are available to all if they are available at all. But the limitations should warn us against putting undue weight on this indicator to the exclusion of others.

In spite of other possible ways of presenting the information so as to avoid these biases, it is still normal to present (national) *income* levels (or rates of growth) *side by side* with measures of *inequality* and sometimes (though not often enough) *stability*, and with *more direct measures of the poverty* of those near the bottom of the scale expressed *either* in income terms (poverty rates and poverty gaps, explained in Chapter 10) *or* in specific indicators of, for example, health, education, water access and nutrition.

We may wonder whether this approach is complete *enough* for judging levels of, or progress in, *development* – if development is to be seen as an appropriate comprehensive objective of change in lower-income societies.

A comprehensive view of development and poverty

BOX 1.1 AMARTYA SEN ON DEVELOPMENT AS FREEDOM

'Development can be seen, it is argued here, as a process of expanding the real freedoms that people enjoy. Focusing on human freedoms contrasts with narrower views of development, such as identifying development with the growth of gross national product, or with the rise in personal incomes, or with industrialization, or with technological advance, or with social modernization. Growth of GNP or of individual incomes can, of course, be very important as *means* to expanding the freedoms enjoyed by members of the society. But freedoms depend also on other determinants, such as social and economic arrangements (for example, facilities for education and health care) as well as political and civil rights (for example, the liberty to participate in public discussion and scrutiny). Similarly, industrialization or technical progress or social modernization can substantially contribute to expanding human freedom, but freedom depends on other influences as well.

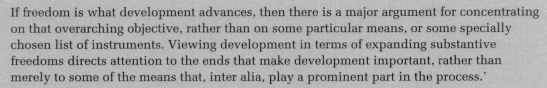

> If freedom is what development advances, then there is a major argument for concentrating on that overarching objective, rather than on some particular means, or some specially chosen list of instruments. Viewing development in terms of expanding substantive freedoms directs attention to the ends that make development important, rather than merely to some of the means that, inter alia, play a prominent part in the process.'
>
> *Source:* Amartya Sen, *Development as Freedom*, Oxford University Press, Oxford, 1999, p. 3.

Sen's *Development as Freedom*

Amartya Sen, in his book *Development as Freedom* (1999), sees *poverty* as *deprivation of various forms of freedom*. This is a view that can embrace poverty's various manifestations: both absolute and relative, material and non-material, in both rich and poor countries. Correspondingly, *development*, covering movement out of any and all the elements of poverty, consists of the enlargememt of freedom.

It follows then that all the constituent elements of development in this understanding of the term involve expanding one form or another of *freedom*. Freedom has 'process aspects' (the absence or removal of constraints) and 'opportunity aspects' (the enhancement of capacities for active choice) (ibid., p. 17). Both are integral to the enlargement of freedom that constitutes development in his use of the term.

> Development requires the removal of major sources of unfreedom: poverty as well as tyranny, poor economic opportunities as well as systematic social deprivation, neglect of public facilities as well as intolerance or overactivity of repressive states. (ibid., p. 3)

Consequently, it would appear to be misleading or meaningless, in Sen's view and use of the words, to ask whether, for example, political freedoms embodied in representative democracy and a free press are favourable to development (by which the questioner commonly understands 'favourable to the growth of average income'). Achieving political freedom of this sort is an integral part of development, valuable in itself. But Sen also appears to believe that, *on the whole*, the various elements of development support each other. (See also Sen, 1995, 1997.) He is famous for the observation that famines do not occur in democracies.[1] In other words, freedom for political participation, even in very poor countries, provides a rough freedom for most people from the *occasional extremes* of want: not from *food poverty*, not from *chronic under-nutrition*; but at least from famines of the kind that have been frequent, and only imperfectly relieved, in much of Africa in recent years; that probably killed 23 to 30 million people in China over 1959–61, more than any other such incident ever recorded; and that had been common in South Asia until the great Bengal famine of 1943–44 but have been avoided since.

The various elements of freedom, whose enhancement constitutes development, Sen characterizes as **capabilities**.

Having a reasonably high disposable income *by world standards*, as is the case with many people in rich countries who are yet relatively *very poor by those countries' standards*,

---

[1] 'Never has a substantial famine occurred in a country that is independent, that has systematic multi-party elections, that permits criticism of the government, and that allows press freedoms' (Sen, 1995, p. 26).

may still leave those people poorer in some respects than individuals elsewhere who have much lower disposable incomes. For one thing, their relative poverty may lead to social exclusion, poor self-esteem, and obstacles to improvement. For another, they may fare worse in some quite specific material ways. Sen (1999, p. 22) refers to the fact that in the early 1990s survival rates among African-American men in the US to various ages over 15 were lower than those of men in the Indian state of Kerala, one of the income-poorer states in a low-income country.

For these and other reasons the average income of a country, though important, is a very imperfect indicator of capability-poverty, and its growth is a very imperfect indicator of development. Sen (ibid., p. 19) sets his view of development as *freedom* – as the enlargement of capabilities – against those that see it essentially as a matter of:

- removing restraints (which leaves out the *opportunities* aspect of freedom);
- increasing mental satisfaction, happiness (which leaves out the *procedural* aspect, the importance of active choice);
- increasing average income (which conceals or ignores many important elements that are not simply or closely related to average income).

The diversity of capabilities embodied in *development* means that there will be *no one natural indicator* of the rate of development or what it has achieved. A number of variables would point up various aspects. A composite indicator might be constructed, but it would have to reflect, in the range of variables that it covered and in the weightings allotted to them, the particular values of those that constructed it.

It will be clear that Sen's view of development is much more than a matter of definition. In classing a number of elements of freedom – a number of capabilities – together under the mantle of 'development', a term that has highly favourable connotations, he is expressing a judgement about the *value* of each of these elements for its own sake, that is for its own direct importance to people's lives.

However, he also, as we understand him, adds to this a broad general (optimistic) presumption on how the world works: that *on the whole* these various elements of freedom tend to be, or can be made, synergistic rather than mutually competitive.

Accordingly, the view of development as freedom can count as one of a fairly fundamental world outlook, applying to high-income, as well as to middle- and low-income, countries. It involves a set of far-ranging values and also a generally optimistic expectation – controversial but based on a volume of experience – that certain diverse types of change, valuable in themselves or instrumentally, can be mutually reinforcing.

In this book we shall do our best to use *development* in this very broad sense: to comprise expansion across the population of any and all of the benign capabilities. So, when we have a chapter on 'gender and development', this is not *only* about the impact that the relative position and status of women and men has on the rate of growth of per capita income, and *vice versa*. Admittedly, we shall inevitably be biased here, in a book on development *economics*, toward those questions susceptible to economic analysis. Yet the opening of capabilities for women comparable to those available for men *will be treated as an element of development in itself*. The topic is in principle about the bearing of gender issues – the comparative positions of women and men – on any of the *other* elements of development, and of *their* bearing in turn on the gender issues. **Development will be used to cover the enlargement of all those immunities and opportunities that societies may offer and secure to the mass of their people for the living of a more abundant life.**

BOX 1.2 AMARTYA SEN

AMARTYA SEN (1933–)
(Harvard University)

Amartya Sen was born in 1933 on the campus of Visva-Bharati College at Santiniketan, in what is now West Bengal. The poet Tagore, founder of the College, was a friend of the family, and was consulted on the naming of the young child. Sen's concern for the sufferings of the local poor during a famine when he was nine years old was to resurface many years later in his influential book *Famine: An Essay on Entitlement and Deprivation*, which shifted perceptions of the root cause of famine from absolute shortage of food to 'entitlement' – or the lack of it. As a student at Cambridge Sen immersed himself in the vigorous debates then raging on macroeconomic policy and on capital theory, benefiting from close contact with a galaxy of eminent economists – one of whom, his research supervisor Joan Robinson, he found 'totally brilliant but vigorously intolerant'. Throughout a subsequent university career centred on the world's top Economics departments, he has maintained an unusually broad range of interests running from philosophy, through social-choice theory and welfare economics, to problems of hunger, poverty, gender and inequality in the developing world. In 1998 Sen commenced a six-year tenure of the position of Master of Trinity College, Cambridge. In the same year he was awarded the Nobel Prize in Economic Sciences 'for his contributions to welfare economics'. The recipient of some ninety honorary degrees, Sen was recently described by the *Guardian* newspaper as 'One of the world's most famous public intellectuals'.

We proceed (Appendices 1.1 and 1.2) to detailed explanations of development terms, and then to outlining national accounting terms (national income and related variables), which leads on to comparison of levels of income and other indicators of material welfare attained in a selection of rich and poor countries.

Summary conclusions

- Development economics is fundamentally about why the world is so sharply divided between rich and poor countries; what can be done to change the situation through economic growth; and how the extremes of world poverty can be eliminated and welfare in poorer countries best promoted.

- Development economics is interested in economic growth; equality; poverty; opportunity for those deprived; and economic behaviour in the lower-income countries.

- The subject arose after the end of the Second World War. It was stimulated by the hopes prevalent at that time of a new beginning, and specifically by the emergence of a number of very poor former colonies as newly independent states; by the systematic estimation of economic aggregates and study of their interrelations; by the huge gap between rich and poor that those aggregates revealed; and by the possible formulas that their interrelations suggested for generating desired rates of economic growth. Then and through the following years those hopes were encouraged by the apparent economic and social achievements of both the Soviet and the post-war Western economies.

■ The concept of poverty raises difficult questions of definition. Some clarification is provided by distinguishing between relative and absolute poverty, with only absolute poverty – for which at least a very crude universal definition can be given – the subject of world, as distinct from national, concern.

■ To measure economic growth, and to compare levels of average material welfare between countries and regions, we inevitably use measures of national income, but these at their best have their limitations, even simply as measures of *potential material* welfare. This is because not all goods have market prices; methods of valuing other goods are highly imperfect and are often not attempted; and depreciation of natural resources and the environment is generally not included as a negative item. Comparisons across countries have further difficulties because of the inadequacy of prevailing exchange rates to represent the relative purchasing powers of currencies. So for this purpose purchasing-power-parity (PPP) exchange-rates are increasingly used.

■ To provide better indicators of *general welfare* than national-income-per-head figures alone, measures of equality of income distribution and objective welfare indicators, such as health, mortality, nutrition and education, need to be cited alongside them.

■ *Development* in its most extended sense, generally used in this book, covers not only growth in income per head; but also other quantifiable elements of *human development* such as increasing equality of distribution, and enhancing health, nutrition and education; and beyond that increasing and strengthening such less-quantifiable conditions as political freedom and participation, the protection of law, and broadly whatever comes into the category of *capabilities* for creative and responsible activity.

From its original concentration on economic growth, the idea of 'development' has shifted to focus on the reduction of poverty in developing countries, with economic growth still vital but more as instrument than as ultimate objective. The concept of development is further extended (in the interpretation followed here) to include the general enlargement of human capabilities and the institutions releasing and encouraging their exercise.

Questions for discussion

1.1 'The development of a society means that its people on average are growing richer.'
'The development of a society means that its people's capabilities are increasing.'
What difference does it make (if any) to choose one of these understandings of development rather than the other?

1.2 What direct-welfare indicators beside those in Table 1.1 on page 24 would you consider particularly important?

1.3 Does the 'relative' poverty of those regarded as poor in rich countries *matter* to the rest of the world? *Should* it matter? If so, why?

1.4 Can you suggest why translating the incomes of various countries into a common currency by purchasing-power-parity (PPP) rather than by currency exchange-rates reduces the apparent proportional gaps between the average incomes of low-income countries and those of high-income countries? Why do you think both sets of income figures are used?

1.5 Why do you think development economics first came to be recognized as a distinct subject of study in the years shortly after the end of the Second World War?

Additional reading

Diamond, Jared (1998) *Guns, Germs and Steel: a Short History of Everybody for the Last 13,000 Years*, Vintage, London.

A highly original (and convincing) and compulsively readable attempt to explain the world distribution of wealth and power as due in part to accidents of biology and geography, including the shapes of the various continents. Jared Diamond is a biologist interested in everything.

Landes, David S. (1998) *The Wealth and Poverty of Nations: why some are so Rich and some are so Poor*, Little, Brown and Company, London.

Takes up the explanation a stage later than Diamond, with tremendous knowledge and imagination, centred on explaining why the industrial revolution came first to Europe, but it's certainly a long work.

Layard, Richard (2005) *Happiness: Lessons from a New Science*, Allen Lane, London.

This is a good read of great general interest, with a wealth of simple, straightforward argument and evidence, and brilliant cartoons, from a distinguished macroeconomist.

Sen, A.K. (1999) *Development as Freedom*, Oxford University Press, Oxford.

Amartya Sen is one of the most original of economists with a commitment to analysing the ethical questions. His interest in the subject, and especially in food deprivation and famines, he traces back to his experience, as a young boy in a middle-class family in Calcutta, during the Great Bengal Famine of 1943–4. In his hands, economics is a hopeful, rather than a dismal, science.

Each of these books is an education in itself, and all can be read for pleasure. Start with Jared Diamond or Richard Layard.

Appendix 1.1 Toolkit on meanings of development terms

There is no doubt that the use of the terms *developing, development,* and *underdevelopment* is inconsistent and confusing. Rather than saying how they *ought to be* used, we set out here (mostly) to sketch their actual uses.

Development. The first thing to be said is that the word can refer to a *process* or to a *state*: either the act of developing or else the state of having developed. The character of the process and the state will be expounded below.

Developing countries. The most common use of '*developing*', in *developing countries*, is a euphemism, but it is one that expresses optimism. It means in practice relatively *poor* – poor of course only in material things, no insult intended – but carries an undertone of hope. *Underdeveloped countries* and later *less-developed countries (LDCs)* have been used with the same meaning, but either is a mouthful; and most people pick up what *developing countries* is intended to mean. (A confusion, however, that may arise from the use of *LDCs* is that some sources use this to mean *least-developed countries – LLDCs* in other sources – by which they understand a very poor subset of the developing countries.) The paradox is that some 'developing countries' have often been developing backwards – growing poorer – while others are more than justifying the expression by surging ahead. The term generally covers both low-income and middle-income countries (see below) and that is how we shall use it, though – for historical reasons, which now seem increasingly irrelevant – *transitional countries* (those Soviet-bloc countries and the successor states to Yugoslavia, but not China or Vietnam or Cuba, that formerly had, but no longer have, highly centrally planned economies) were for some years from 1990 commonly treated as a separate category.

Development and **growth.** This pair embodies two separate distinctions, both of which we need and which, irritatingly, overlap.

In one sense of the difference, *growth* (economic growth) indicates increase in a country's total national income, while *development* means the increase in its national income per head of population.

In the other sense, *growth* can be taken to denote an increase in national income per head of population (considering only the computable material side of economic advance), while *development* is broader and less susceptible to simple measurement, taking into account not only this per capita material growth but also how the additional income per person is distributed; how far the minimum levels of material provision that people can expect – or their probabilities of living above certain floor levels – are raised; or more broadly how far the *capabilities* of people, in Amartya Sen's sense, especially those near the bottom of the heap, are enlarged.

Just how much is covered by this latter use of 'development' is not necessarily agreed. Those aspects of *development* in this sense that are not comprised by *growth* (in average income) are frequently embraced in the term *social development*. But we could reasonably also use the term *political development* for some of the elements in a very broad conception such as Sen's.

We shall try to evade the confusion between 'growth' and 'development' by referring to *growth in total income*, or to *growth in income per head*, when it is one or other of these variables that we mean. Where we use *development* without qualification, it should be taken to mean advance in the broader sense, embodying potentially not only growth in average income but also increased equality of distribution and the other changes implied by 'social development' and 'political development'. *Economic development* will be taken to refer to growth in income per head.

Social development. As outlined in the paragraphs above, this (far from precise) term is used to cover all those aspects counted in as components of 'development' other than what is measured by income per head: namely what is measured or indicated by degree of equality in income distribution, proportions of the population below international poverty lines, educational enrolments, literacy rates, life-expectancy, infant and maternal mortality, nutrition standards, gender equality. Dimensions such as political participation, or access to means for assertion of rights, may be included here – or else separately covered by *political development*.

Underdevelopment. This is the antithesis of development, and is used for a state but generally not for a process. A country or community may be underdeveloped, meaning that it lacks the attributes of a developed society. In Sen's sense, it is poor in a range of capabilities. Its *characteristics*, mostly embodying *what it lacks*, would be along the following lines. It would be:

1   Poor in income terms;
2   Probably more unequal in income than most 'industrialized' high-income countries (though the picture is mixed);
3   Even more probably and markedly *socially* unequal than most 'industrialized' high-income countries;
4   Weak on most of the other items of 'social (and political) development' such as:
    ■   educational institutions and enrolments
    ■   health status and services, life-expectancy, infant and maternal mortality
    ■   nutrition
    ■   accessibility of safe water
    ■   sewerage provision
    ■   housing quality
    ■   extent of literacy
    ■   extent of technical skills of the industrial and post-industrial age
    ■   opportunity for political participation
    ■   effective access among all classes to legal remedies and pursuit of rights
    ■   tendencies to equality in status and respect, including gender-equality.

However, the stereotype should not be taken for a universal. It is possible for a country to have low or lower-middle income but *not* to be particularly deprived of the last three items listed. On the other hand, some of upper-middle income (or even of high income) have had long periods without the impartial rule of law or much opportunity for all but an elite to participate in politics, and with considerable discrimination on various grounds.

There is no convenient term for the antithesis of development as a *process*. Unfortunately the *reality* – low-income and middle-income countries whose incomes per head or important direct-welfare indicators such as life-expectancy are *falling* for significant periods – has become quite prevalent.

Low-income, lower-middle-income, upper-middle-income, and **high-income countries.** There are several categorizations of this type put forward by various organizations. They have the advantage of a kind of precision. Probably the best to follow is that of the World Bank. This division is based solely on GNI (Gross National Income) per head. The dividing lines between the categories are thus expressed in US dollars and their exchange-rate equivalents in other currencies. The dollar values at which the dividing lines are fixed change, of course, as the purchasing power of the dollar falls over time. For 2006 the class ranges in 2006 US dollars per head were (World Bank, 2008, p. 333):

- *low income,* $905 or less;
- *lower-middle income,* $906–$3595;
- *upper-middle income,* $3596–$11 115;
- *high income,* $11 116 or more.

So, in Table 1.1 below, the US, Japan, the UK and Germany would be high income in 2006; Mexico, South Africa and Brazil, upper-middle income; China, lower-middle income; and India, Bangladesh, and Ethiopia, low income. Particular countries move from one category to another as their average real income rises or falls so as to take them across one of the boundaries. China notably changed around the turn of the millennium from the World Bank's low income to its lower-middle-income category, and Brazil in 2006 from lower- to upper-middle, and India from 2007 to lower-middle.

Developed countries. This term is used *either* to mean the same as **high-income countries** *or* to cover only those high-income countries that seem – because of a broad spread of industries, including a range of manufactures and high-level services – to provide a reasonable guarantee that their high-income status is fairly secure. In this latter use, the term might *exclude* economies that were heavily dependent for their high income on the production and export of one or a few primary commodities, or on government transfers as aid from outside, or on being the site of a major power's defence installations, so that the countries' incomes could dive as a result of a large fall in a commodity's price or some interruption in its extraction or export, or on a single decision of some other country's government. This last exclusion might be held to apply to Brunei, Greenland, Guam, Kuwait, New Caledonia, Qatar, and Saudi Arabia, all of them high-income countries by the World Bank's definition in 2006 but probably not generally treated as 'developed'. Yet the criteria for exclusion are not clearly defined or even agreed, and the question, one purely of definition, is hardly worth the argument.

Industrialized countries. The usual meaning here is the same as 'developed countries', except that a one-commodity-based economy, or a transfer-based or foreign-defence-based economy, that happened to stray into high-income territory would be *more unambiguously excluded.* The term again risks being misleading. A number of the 'industrialized' countries – that is, the rich – have in fact for some time been 'de-industrializing' in the sense that the proportions of their workforces in secondary (manufacturing) industry and in the wider category of 'industry' – and also of their output deriving from manufacturing and from 'industry' – have been falling. At the same time some quite poor countries have had higher proportions of the value of their output derived from industry, and from manufacturing, than some of the highly affluent countries that have long been described as 'industrialized'. This is discussed in Chapter 17.

Backward countries. This expression is perhaps best avoided, not just because it sounds derogatory but also because it seems to imply that there is a single natural sequence of stages, or at least a natural path of development, along which every country must move, but at which some have been slow off the mark or have started behind others. That *may* bear *some* relationship to the truth, but it is probably best to keep an open mind.

Third World. This expression was common for a period in the 1970s and 1980s as a way of referring to the *developing countries* (generally the low- and middle-income categories, with the upper income limit not clearly defined), but excluding those in the Communist blocs, which were the *Second World* in this schema, though that expression was hardly ever used. The 'developed' countries formed the *First World*. The disappearance of the *Second World* in the 1990s has helped make the term sound archaic.

North–South. Another bit of shorthand, which became common after the Brandt Report of 1980, was to use *North* for the industrialized countries and *South* for the rest (with the Communist blocs, as they were then, again on the sidelines). This usage has only a very rough fit with the ordinary meanings of the geographical terms that it has adopted (it would make New Zealand 'north' and Mongolia 'south'), and it is dropping out of fashion.

In conclusion: we shall use *developing countries* here to cover low-income and middle-income countries, including, where relevant, transitional countries; and *developed countries* to refer to high-income countries (generally avoiding the term 'industrialized'), with the few minor exceptions mentioned. Otherwise we shall specify *low-income, lower-middle-income, upper-middle-income,* or *high-income countries.*

TABLE 1.1 Comparative measures of aspects of development, selected countries, recent years

Country	(1) GNI per head, at exchange-rate US$, 2006	(2) GNI per head, PPP$, 2006	(3) Human development index, 2003	(4) Gini coefficient (inequality index), (year indicated)	(5) Income or expenditure, ratio richest 10% to poorest 10%, (year indicated)	(6) Adult literacy, %, 2003	(7) Infant mortality, deaths < 1 year old, per 1000 live births, 2003	(8) Per cent of people living on < $1 a day, (year indicated)
US	44 970	44 260	0.944	0.408 (2000)	15.9 (2000)		7	<2
Japan	38 410	33 150	0.943	0.249 (1993)	4.5 (1993)		3	<2
UK	40 180	35 580	0.939	0.360 (1999)	13.8 (1999)		5	<2
Germany	36 620	31 830	0.930	0.283 (2000)	6.9 (2000)		4	<2
Mexico	7 870	11 410	0.814	0.546 (2000)	45.0 (2000)	90.3	23	3.0 (2000)
South Africa	5 390	11 710	0.658	0.578 (2000)	33.1 (2000)	82.4	53	10.7 (2000)
Brazil	4 730	8 800	0.792	0.593 (2001)	68.0 (2001)	88.4	33	7.5 (2004)
China	2 010	7 740	0.755	0.447 (2001)	18.4 (2001)	90.9	30	9.9 (2004)
India	820	3 800	0.602	0.325 (1999)	7.3 (1999)	61.0	63	34.3 (2004–5)
Bangladesh	480	2 340	0.520	0.318 (2000)	6.8 (2000)	41.1	46	41.3 (2000)
Ethiopia	180	1 190	0.367	0.300 (1999)	6.6 (1999)	41.5	112	23.0 (1999/2000)

Notes: (1) The survey variable used for columns (4), (5) and (6) is income in some cases, consumption in others.

(2) As mentioned below in footnotes 2 and 3, there was revision agreed of income figures for 2005 and 2006 in a number of countries; it is not reflected in these figures. The revision was to be downward for China (by 40%), India (36%), Bangladesh, and Ethiopia; and upward for Brazil and Mexico. A number of the figures here would be affected by these changes.

Sources: World Bank, *World Development Report 2006*, pp. 292–5; 2008, pp. 334–7.
UNDP, *Human Development Report 2005*, pp. 219–22; 250–3; 270–3.

Appendix 1.2 Toolkit on measurement and indicators of the level of income attained and the quality of development

National-accounting concepts: GNI or GDP per head

The main aggregates used to indicate the total size of an economy are:

- Gross national income (GNI)
- Gross domestic product (GDP).

GNI, as its name implies, is *a measure of the nation's income, what is earned by its residents.* Until fairly recently it was commonly, and confusingly, called *Gross National Product (GNP).*

GDP is *a measure of the country's output, the value of what is produced within its borders.*

Dividing these aggregates by the country's population number gives its *income per head* and *output per head.*

The difference between the two is seldom important for the purposes of this book, and you will probably not go far wrong if you treat them as interchangeable. The difference is *net property income sent abroad*: remittances abroad of profits, dividends, interest, royalties, and rent derived from production within our country, *minus* the same classes of payment going in the opposite direction. Adding this net sum to GNI gives GDP.

Another aggregate, though one that will not appear much in these pages, is

- Gross domestic expenditure (GDE)

GDE *represents what the residents of the country with which we are concerned buy.* This means that it includes spending on imports (*M*) but not the value of production that goes into exports (*X*). In these two respects it differs from GDP (output). The relationship can be put in an equation:

$$GDE = GDP + M - X$$

Putting values on these aggregates can in principle be done through adding up outputs *or* incomes *or* expenditures. If the process were faultless, all three methods should give the same results for, say, GNI. Of course they do not do so with the imperfect figures that have to be used in practice, and 'national accountants' have to make do with what seem to be the best approximations from the material that they have.

For the sake of readers who may worry about such things, we mention in the next paragraph one of the snags that national accountants must and do avoid. Anyone who is prepared to take it on trust that the experts will not fall into logical traps such as this can ignore the paragraph.

All three methods as a matter of course have to avoid the *double-counting* that could arise if all the incomes, or all the final outputs, or all the purchases, of individual people and firms were simply added together. So GNI includes all incomes (wages, profits, dividends, interest, royalties, rent) earned by people for providing resources (labour, capital, land, risk-taking) *before tax but net of any expenses involved in earning them*, and does not include what people receive *as social-security payments or as gifts or legacies.* It includes in addition that part of company (corporation) income that is not distributed to shareholders. (What goes to shareholders as dividends is already included as part of *the shareholders'* income.)

GDP is the sum of *values-added* of all producing firms including the self-employed and the government: that is in each case their gross outputs *minus* the costs of their material inputs.

GDE includes only purchases of *final* goods and services: those bought directly for consumption or investment, not as materials for further production.

The term *gross* in GNI, GDP, and GDE needs explanation. These totals are all given *without* deduction of the depreciation of capital goods. To get a really satisfactory measure of a country's income (or output or final expenditure) we should actually present it *net* of depreciation. Net versions (NNI, NDP) are sometimes presented. However, estimates of depreciation (such as those presented in company accounts or allowable for tax purposes) follow arbitrary rules; and national totals for depreciation are not deemed very reliable. So it has become normal to use the *gross* totals when we want to present the growth rates of income or to make international comparisons.

Comparison through exchange-rates or through PPP rates

There are two main subjects of interest in the presentation of aggregates of income, output and expenditure: rates of change over time, and international comparisons. For international comparisons, there is a problem. Almost all the 200 or so independent countries have their own currencies. It is in these currencies that their GNI and other aggregates are counted up. How can the various nations' GNIs be compared?

The obvious and easy solution is to use the prevailing exchange-rates to convert each country's GNI into US dollars. So, if there are at the time 100 yen to the dollar, Japan's GNI figure in yen can be simply divided by 100 to give the country a GNI value in dollars. But currencies' purchasing powers do not closely follow their exchange-rates. A hundred yen may exchange for a dollar, but at the same time 100 yen may buy more or less in Japan than a dollar in the US. A currency's exchange value in dollars may also take a sudden big jump (say 20 per cent upward) and so give the impression, when its GNI is turned into dollars, that its income has risen in a year by 20 percentage points more than US income, when in fact – measured in purchasing power – they have been growing at the same rate. The World Bank has devised a method (the Atlas method) to reduce the impact of this kind of change on the comparative figures in its tables. However, this does not wholly remove the possibility of distortion, and it also does not purport to solve the problem of giving purchasing-power figures that are equivalent internationally.

To remedy this, a method now increasingly used is to convert sums expressed in one currency into another by a 'purchasing-power-parity' (PPP) rate. The PPP-dollar rate for the pound sterling would be the number of US dollars that would buy the same bundle of goods in the States as the pound would buy in Britain. That sounds an obvious solution, but as usual it is not all plain sailing. What bundle of goods should you choose? Different bundles will give different rates. The dilemma is greatest when we are dealing with two countries that have very different typical patterns of spending: say the US and Malawi. No representative bundle would really fit well for both. This is what economists call an index-number problem. There is no perfectly satisfactory solution. The best that can be done is to apply a sensible compromise.

However, where international comparisons are to be made, the use of conscientiously calculated PPP rates is likely to be better than that of prevailing exchange-rates, however nuanced. The World Bank, in its *World Development Reports* and *World Development Indicators*, now lists both.

In fact PPP comparisons generally give markedly *smaller gaps* in average incomes between the richest and the poorest countries than exchange-rate comparisons. There are good reasons for this, but we shall not go into them here. The gaps become more credible with PPP, but they are still very big. For examples, see Table 1.1. This shows the compression of the income differences recorded between richest and poorest as we move from exchange-rate comparisons to PPP. On 2006 World Bank figures, the high-income countries, with 16 per cent of the world's population, received 78 per cent of its income on exchange-rate comparisons and 54 per cent on PPP comparisons. For low-income countries, with 37 per cent of the population, the shares of income were 3.2 per cent and 9.7 per cent on the two bases of comparison (World Bank, 2008, p. 335).[2]

Measures of the equality of income distribution

This aspect of 'social development' can be compared between countries (or over time) by two main methods, each of which throws some light on the matter.

One is to look at the proportions of income earned by say the richest decile (10 per cent), or the poorest decile, of people or households. The higher the former and the lower the latter, the more the picture is one of *inequality*. The ratio of one to the other can be used to provide a single measure, as in Table 1.1, column (5). Alternatively, the richest and poorest quintile (20 per cent) might be used, and their ratio, as in Table 10.1 in Chapter 10.

Another is to use the Gini coefficient, an index that can have values between zero and one. The higher the Gini, the more *unequal* the distribution. What the coefficient is and how it is estimated will be explained in Chapter 10.

Examples of both the decile ratio and the Gini appear in Table 1.1. Both show the high degrees of inequality chalked up for Mexico, Brazil and South Africa, by comparison with the other countries, rich and poor, in the table.

Direct welfare (quality-of-life) indicators

Another way of checking elements of 'social-development' ratings between countries or over time is to look at direct welfare indicators such as life-expectancy, infant or young-child death rates, or rates of adult illiteracy. Others commonly cited are the proportions of the population living below the PPP equivalent per person of $2 or $1 a day in 1985 prices[3] (*poverty rate* and *extreme-poverty rate* respectively). The implication of the poverty or extreme-poverty rate in any society is filled out by the corresponding *poverty* or *extreme-poverty gap*, an expression that may be presented in various forms (outlined in Chapter 10) and summarizes the difference between the relevant poverty line and the actual incomes of those who fall below it. Taken with the corresponding poverty rate, 'this measure reflects the depth of poverty as well as its prevalence' (World Bank, 2000, p. 276).

The UN Development Programme's *Human Development Report* cites measures such as these. It also compiles for each country a *Human Development Indicator (HDI)*, which

---

[2] These were the proportions on the PPP-equivalent system used by the World Bank up to and including the 2008 *World Development Report [WDR]*. Thereafter, as reported in the 2008 *World Development Indicators [WDI]* (pp. 1–7), a revision will be used based on more complete price surveys in 2005 and in fact having the effect of rating developing countries' incomes taken together *lower* than the previous system. These give proportions of world GDP in 2005 as changing from 78 to 60 per cent for high-income countries, 19 to 33 for middle-income, and 3 to 7 for low-income, as we move from exchange-rate to PPP comparisons (World Bank, *WDI 2008*, p. 3).

[3] It seems that, with the new prices based on the 2005 survey, the standard for one-dollar-a-day poverty will be lowered by about 14 per cent, from what would have been PPP$1.45 a day in 2005 prices to PPP$1.25 a day in 2005 prices. This would be an arbitrary decision, though reasons are given for taking it.

is a composite of income per head and two direct-welfare indicators (see Box 10.2 in Chapter 10).

Table 1.1 gives examples of HDIs and of some direct-welfare indicators, including extreme-poverty rates. The three direct-welfare indicators there show a rough relationship between each of them and GNI per head, but nothing very neat or close. China and Bangladesh score better on infant mortality, China on literacy, and both China and Ethiopia on the proportion in extreme income-poverty than would be expected from their average incomes; while South Africa seems to rate worse on infant mortality and on the proportion in extreme income-poverty than its average income would predict.

So average GNI (with or without measures of inequality tacked on) and the various direct welfare indicators do not tell exactly the same stories about comparative material welfare between countries. The differences are sometimes important, but all leave us with the same general picture of gaps, often immense, between the materially richest and poorest societies.

What has happened to the picture over the second half of the twentieth century? How has development economics addressed the mystery and the social challenge? Some beginnings of answers to both questions are given in Chapter 2, and sketches of emerging approaches to the second through most of the rest of the book.

Development: the Story over Fifty Years

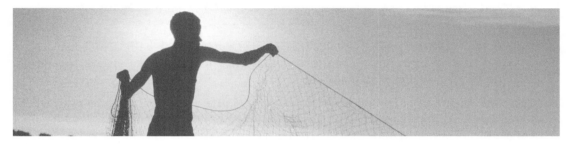

For a number of reasons particular to the time, development economics started with faith in highly activist government. Over the next fifty years much was learned about what worked and what did not. No universal formula for fast economic growth emerged, but some recently poor countries shot to affluence, with others of massive dimensions not far behind, while a further large group stagnated. Yet over the period there were quite big global advances in nutrition, longevity and literacy, and in the closing years of the century a large drop in human fertility and on balance a shift toward democracy and free institutions.

Introduction

This chapter sketches the origin and content of the kernel of ideas with which development economics was launched in the 1940s; the main economic events of the latter half of the century; and quantitative evidence about the extent of economic growth, and improvement in some key welfare indicators, over the period. We shall finish with attempts to summarize this experience and to suggest explanations to which it might point.

BOX 2.1 TOOLKIT FOR CHAPTER 2

Adjustable peg. Exchange-rate system established under the International Monetary Fund [IMF] in which the member countries agreed to keep their exchange-rates against gold (and effectively the US dollar) within a very narrow range of an agreed par value except in conditions of 'fundamental disequilibrium', in which case they could seek the permission of the IMF to alter the par rate. This was the main feature of the 'Bretton Woods system' (see Box 12.1 Toolkit on stabilization). Until the system collapsed when the US abandoned the fixed rate of the dollar against gold in August 1971, such changes of par value were fairly rare – though permission was seldom or never asked in advance.

A few member-countries, notably Canada, did not establish a par value.

▶
> **Autarky** (or **autarchy**). A policy of minimizing inter-dependency with other countries.
>
> **Bretton Woods.** See '**Adjustable peg**' above and Box 12.1 in Chapter 12.
>
> **Convertibility.** A currency is said to be convertible if there is no limitation imposed by its issuing authority on selling it for other currencies. Some currencies have been convertible for non-residents of the country whose currency it is, but not for residents. Moves toward convertibility generally indicate increasing confidence in the issuing country's external position.
>
> **Marshall Plan, Marshall Aid.** Named after General George C. Marshall, US Secretary of State under Harry Truman in the late 1940s, this represented very large-scale economic aid for post-war reconstruction in Europe.
>
> **OPEC.** The Organization of Petroleum Exporting Countries. An inter-government cartel of about eleven countries dominated by Saudi Arabia. OPEC managed the big petroleum price rises of 1973–4 and 1979–80 but had lost control of the price by the mid-1980s.

The initial bias of development economics and why it occurred

In Chapter 1 we gave some reasons why those who began exploring development economics in the 1940s and early 1950s were looking for radical departures in economic thought and policy. However, development economics began with a particular bias, which is largely explained by the recent events and currents of thought that overshadowed its birth.

The first of these was the Great Depression of the 1930s, when world income and international trade had simply collapsed; nominal domestic product in the US had fallen by about 45 per cent from 1929 to 1932; economies that concentrated on the export of primary products had been especially hard hit, and these then included most of the poorer countries; unemployment rates in some industrialized countries had passed 30 per cent; and only the totalitarian states had seemed to have the secret of withstanding the whirlwind or of quick recovery. The helplessness of most governments in the face of this disaster had led to doubts about the value of traditional economics as well as the economic effectiveness of democracies.

Second, though the Depression had been triggered by a fall in asset values and had devastated in greater or lesser degree nearly every state and territory, it had spread from one country to another largely through the depression of inter-country trade. Its effects on countries and regions and individuals were, therefore, worse on the whole the closer their dependence on export trade and especially on primary-commodity exports. Trade, so far from being an engine of growth as it had been for many in the period before the First World War, seemed to have become a source of vulnerability, with reliance on primary-export trade a particular curse. The idea of national self-sufficiency, and especially diversification away from primary products, came to have an obvious appeal.

Third, to this bafflement of traditional economics in the face of disaster had come an apparent saviour in the person of J.M. Keynes with his *General Theory of Employment, Interest and Money* published in 1936. Keynes added an extra dimension to models of how market economies behave, a dimension that took account of the possibility of persistent unemployment. This led to recommendations of state action in the face of falling economic activity, recommendations directly opposite to the measures that governments had commonly taken. Though others had thought along similar lines, Keynes had the merit of not only promoting policies that seemed to many of the lay public like refreshing common sense but also challenging orthodoxy in a way that inspired some of the best minds of the younger generation of economists. This, together with his reputation, eloquence, and contacts, had served to project his argument into the public arena. Paradoxically his position virtually reached the status of orthodoxy in his own country soon after Britain entered the War with Germany in 1939, when it was realized that the terms of his thinking on dealing with *unemployment* could be applied usefully to a situation of labour *shortage*, as set out in his pamphlet *How to Pay for the War*. From the voice crying in the wilderness he had become the indispensable repair man brought in to fix the engine-room.

The impact of Keynes on *economic-development thought* probably arose, first, from the fact that he had advocated not only *different* policies, but also *more active* policies on the part of the state, than had previously been accepted in the main Anglo-Saxon economics tradition; and, second, from his reasoning in economic aggregates, with an interest in the size of totals such as national income, consumption, investment, and the trade balance, and also in their relationships one with another.

It has also been pointed out (Toye, 2006) that as early as the 1930s associates of Keynes such as Joan Robinson had extended the concept of unemployment to 'disguised unemployment' in poorer countries, especially in agriculture. There it seemed to be not primarily demand that was deficient but rather supply: namely the plant and equipment necessary to employ the whole workforce productively. The question addressed by Keynes required, it would seem, a different answer here, but one that again implied the inadequacy of the unaided market to meet the need and required thinking in aggregates. Keynes's work also gave rise to the hope that there might be some fundamental new paradigm to be discovered for dealing with underdevelopment, much as his own new model had transformed the understanding of open unemployment.

Fourth, tremendously important in the newly liberated or about-to-be-liberated colonies, was the reputed success of Stalinist planning in rapidly industrializing the Soviet Union, drawing a large part of the rural workforce into secondary industry, and by so doing restoring the revived Russian empire as a top-rank military power. This seemed to be the *other* answer to the economic despair of the 1930s. Such leaders as Nehru in India and Nkrumah in Ghana saw in the Soviet model the possibility of explosive income growth: perhaps at rates of 10 per cent a year, which could double incomes in seven years. Beside directing hopes toward forceful action by the state, the Soviet example and the thinking that went with it concentrated attention on secondary industry (manufacturing) and on the large scale, with a tendency to think of agriculture – especially small-scale household agriculture – as intrinsically backward. The developmental role of agriculture in this view was to offer its surplus workers and surplus income in order to provide labour and capital for manufacturing, mining and infrastructure. Both Stalinist and Keynesian thinking, in directing attention to aggregates, help to explain the early emphasis among development economists of the 1950s on capital accumulation as a key explanatory element or instrument of growth.

A further set of influences – numbers five, six and seven below – arose from the Second World War and the physical reconstruction and institutional innovation that followed it.

Fifth was the experience of mobilizing for war in the democracies. It had in fact been all too easy to restore full employment when resources had to be found for destruction, and this accentuated the apparent absurdity of accepting mass unemployment in peacetime; but the mobilization involved direction of labour such as the US or Britain or Australia would not have contemplated in peacetime. Britain also practised quite severe rationing of food and other goods – in order to dampen price rises while spreading in some degree the sacrifice entailed by shortage of supplies: making sure that the deprivations should not fall exclusively on the poor and that all should have access to essentials. Miraculously – apparently as a result of the rationing, combined with full employment and measures taken to increase the nutritional value of food – the general nutritional status of children in Britain actually rose during the War, in spite of the reduction in food supplies. Some of the early development thinkers such as Hans Singer (see Chapter 5) lived through these experiences, which strongly suggested that judicious government controls or guidance, even in a democracy, can mobilize extra resources for large national projects, while actually enhancing the position of the poor.

Sixth was the apparent post-war success of America's Marshall Plan in supporting the rapid reconstruction of Europe. Finance from the US government, liberal by any standards and decisively dwarfing, for a few years, the real annual rates of the international economic aid that was to come in later times from all donors taken together, was believed to have played a crucial role in Western European recovery. (It had been offered to Eastern Europe too but was refused.) Certainly support was generous and recovery was swift. So, international aid to countries short of capital seemed to have almost miraculous potential.

Seventh, there should perhaps be mentioned the international public bodies designed or founded in the closing period of the War: the United Nations Organization (with its emerging economic functions and its Specialized Agencies such as the World Health Organization (WHO) and the Food and Agriculture Organization (FAO); and notably too the 'twins' (the International Monetary Fund and World Bank) brought to birth at the Bretton Woods conference of 1944 and intended by the protagonists at that conference, Keynes and the US Treasury economist Harry Dexter White, to make possible a decisive break with the economic disasters of the inter-war period.

Eighth, as we have already mentioned in Chapter 1, was the presence of the elites of those countries that were newly decolonized or about to become so, looking for novel and striking economic solutions that independent governments could introduce.

Result: what optimism, what pessimism

There was a clear result of this constellation of events and influences. The sense of *urgency* felt on both sides of the rich–poor divide over the need to accelerate economic growth for the poor majority of countries was shaped, first, by *optimism* about what was possible with heavy state intervention and abundant capital for investment in non-agricultural industry and infrastructure, capital that might be provided in part by massive international aid; and, second, corresponding *pessimism* about the possibility that large gains could be made by improving resource allocation through freeing markets, about the potential of small-scale and spontaneous entrepreneurship, about the income prospects of poorer countries left to market forces, and particularly about the growth-stimulating opportunities provided by international trade and investment.

So there was a bias not only to state action and large scale but also to what is called *autarky*: self-sufficiency in the sense of minimized interdependence with the rest of the world. The Soviet example, and Soviet planning, had a strongly autarkic bias. So it was considered natural, not only that developing countries should force on the growth of secondary industry, but also that they should turn to import substitution, rather than export promotion – turning inward rather than outward – as a way of doing it.

Import substitution (the production of kinds of goods that have previously been imported) is often easy for governments to engineer (at a cost) by offering sufficient protection by import tariffs or quotas. This contrasts with export development, which, even if subsidized, depends on competing in foreign markets. There was a decided bias toward import substitution at the expense of export promotion.

This mixture of optimism and pessimism – optimism about the state and autarky, pessimism about the market and interdependence – dogged development thought and policy, at least through the 1950s and 1960s.

Fifty years later, at the end of the century, grounds for both the optimism and the pessimism had been seriously undermined. At the same time, there were no correspondingly *simple and universal* alternatives that could be shown to have measured up to the test of events. **There had been both economic growth and economic decline over wide swathes of what had been the world's poorer countries, each as extreme for substantial periods as the most that was probably hoped or feared by early development-economics thinkers.** Success had certainly not gone to the most active interveners, or to those most wary of international trade and investment. Yet there was no guarantee of salvation through taking the opposite road. In fact, the world had not performed neatly according to anyone's script. Dogmas had frequently measured up badly.

However, in order to provide the background to the explanation (to follow in Chapter 3) of the shifts in development ideology, we need to give a brief outline of what happened in the world economy over the second half of the century.

BOX 2.2 GROWTH PERFORMANCE IN THE WORLD ECONOMY, 1950–2000

'The world economy performed better in the last half century than at any time in the past. World GDP increased six-fold from 1950 to 1998 with an average growth of 3.9 per cent a year compared with 1.6 from 1820 to 1950, and 0.3 per cent from 1500 to 1820.

'Part of the acceleration went to sustain faster population growth, but real per capita income rose by 2.1 per cent a year compared with 0.9 per cent from 1820 to 1950, and 0.05 per cent from 1500 to 1820. Thus per capita growth was 42 times as fast as in the protocapitalist epoch and more than twice as fast as in the first 13 decades of our capitalist epoch.

'Interrelations between the different parts of the world economy have greatly intensified. The volume of commodity trade rose faster than GDP. The ratio of exports to world GDP rose from 5.5 per cent in 1950 to 17.2 in 1998 . . . There was a huge increase in international travel, communications and other service transactions. These improved the international division of labour, facilitated the diffusion of ideas and technology, and transmitted high levels of demand from the advanced capitalist group to other areas of the world.

'The flow of foreign investment to poorer parts of the world (Africa, Asia excluding Japan, and Latin America) rose at an impressive pace in the past half century. . . .

'There was a resurgence in international migration . . . From 1950 to 1998, West European countries absorbed more than 20 million immigrants, Western Offshoots 34 million.'

Source: Angus Maddison, *The World Economy*, OECD, Paris, 2006, p. 125.

Development experience, 1950–2000

As we look back over the 50-year period, we can see two clear turning points, the first appearing primarily in the world's economy, the second in its politics, but with economy and politics inevitably interacting. The changes that followed in each case had their impact on development-economics thinking as on much else.

The first of these critical moments can conveniently be dated to the first day of 1974. On that day the 'posted' price of crude oil was fixed by OPEC, the cartel of oil-exporting states, at roughly four times its level of three months earlier. The decision was the culmination of a number of restrictions in supply, and arranged price rises, prompted by the Arab–Israeli War of 6–24 October 1973. This first big oil-price rise seems in retrospect to mark the end of the 'Keynesian golden age' in the rich countries and of the two decades of modest optimism over the prospects of most of the newly independent states. With economic instability, stagflation, unmanageable foreign debt for many developing-country governments, low and volatile primary-commodity prices, and the start of an increasingly visible series of African famines, the next 20 years were to be more gloomy for most, both rich and poor, though with striking exceptions in East, and later also South-East, Asia, and glimpses of light in South Asia.

The second turning point can be dated to 9 November 1989, when crowds began pulling down the Berlin Wall. This signalled the end of the Cold War, of the Soviet external empire, and very soon of the Soviet Union itself. These events terminated not only the life of Marx-Lenin-Stalinism as a crusading world ideology but also the system, risky and for many oppressive, through which the world's system of power had been (after a fashion) organized over the previous 40 years. Together with liberations and shifts toward democracy, and the end of some civil wars where the strings had been pulled from outside, the last decade of the century was unfortunately also one of revived national and cultural fighting, of 'ethnic-cleansing', of currency crises, and coincidentally also of the AIDS scourge.

Modest golden age, 1950–73

The end of the War in 1945 left the US in a more dominant position economically than ever before or since. Most of continental Europe and Japan had been devastated by enemy occupation, fighting and bombing. Britain was less physically damaged but heavily indebted, with its overseas holdings greatly depleted. As a result there was an insatiable demand for American goods for reconstruction, with not enough to sell America in exchange. So (with generally pegged exchange-rates) US dollars were 'scarce': everyone wanted them; everyone hoped to be paid in them. Hence the vital importance of Marshall Aid. The West European countries had at first to impose severe restrictions on foreign exchange, and they formed their own payments union in order to conserve their dollars and facilitate trade among themselves.

However, reconstruction in continental Western Europe (and Japan) was surprisingly swift. Fairly rapid growth in France, West Germany, Italy, the Low Countries and Austria continued through the 1950s and 1960s, so that they came to rank with or surpass Britain in average income and greatly reduced the big pre-war gap with the US. By 1958 most of the restrictions on the use of the West European currencies by non-residents had been abandoned. In 1968 the dollar shortage had decisively passed: foreign official holdings of dollars (that is, short-term claims by other governments on the US) came to exceed US international reserves.

By 1949 the 'cold-war' division of Europe and of much of the world had been established. Over the next 40 years much of Eastern Europe was controlled politically and economically, with a few hiccoughs and qualifications, in a single system from Moscow. Broadly speaking, the Soviet Union and its East European satellites, with a few countries elsewhere in the world – though they were not cut off from trade with the world outside – operated as a kind of economic enclave on their own.

The exchange-rate system established at Bretton Woods and embodied in the IMF was designed to keep exchange-rates fixed within very narrow limits most of the time, with only occasional jumps in cases of 'fundamental disequilibrium'. The rules were also directed at the free flow of transactions without exchange restrictions. In fact restrictions were quite common, but, as we have seen, most of the developed countries had made their currencies 'convertible' to non-residents by 1958. Through the 1960s, in fact, the Bretton Woods system worked – at least for those affluent countries – more or less as intended – until the strains it imposed on the US dollar (as the unofficial linchpin of the arrangement) came to be too great, and the 'adjustable-peg' rule over exchange-rates was effectively ended through President Nixon's move to unfix the dollar price of gold in August 1971.

Altogether the 1950s and 1960s and the first few years of the 1970s seemed a benign time for the developed countries' economies, in sharp contrast to the disasters of the 1930s. The approach to full employment in a number of them was consistently better even than Keynes had hoped. Growth was steady, with the only recessions scarcely worthy of the name. International trade expanded faster than income. 'The ratio of exports to world GDP rose from 5.5 per cent in 1950 to 17.2 [per cent] in 1998' (Maddison, 2006, p. 125). Negotiations under the General Agreement on Tariffs and Trade (GATT) gradually reduced import duties on manufactures.

Of the five periods of capitalist development that Angus Maddison distinguishes from 1820 until the end of the Millennium (see Box 2.3), this 'golden age' from 1950 to 1973, he says, was the one of fastest growth for the world ever, faster than in the period of the 'neo-liberal order', 1974–2000, that followed it.

This meant a climate that should on the face of it have been favourable to growth in the developing countries. Primary-product prices fluctuated, with a sharp rise and then fall for many commodities after the start of the Korean War in 1950; but there were not the prolonged and serious depressions of the prices of many raw materials that accompanied the world recessions of the earlier and later parts of the century.

In fact the growth record of developing countries generally in the 1950s and 1960s was not strikingly disappointing (see Tables 2.1, 2.4). Yet, with the dazzling exception of Japan, there was nothing yet *generally recognized* as prolonged miraculous growth among them. Remember that most of them were not *looking for* growth through exports. Primary exports were inclined to be thought an unfortunate necessity. The emphasis in development of manufactures was on protected import-substitution, which – insofar as it commonly raises not only cash costs, but also real-resource costs, of production – depresses export prospects. Arguably, then, many of the developing countries were probably failing to take full advantage of the opportunities of the 1950s and 1960s by continuing to fight the battles of the 1930s.

Decolonization of East, South, and South-East Asia was complete by the late 1950s (with the exceptions of Hong Kong, Macao and East Timor) and most of it by 1950. African decolonization began in 1958 with the independence of Ghana and was largely complete (except for Portuguese, Spanish, and South African dependencies and Rhodesia/Zimbabwe) by 1965.

Soon after its independence India pioneered the idea of 'democratic planning', with national five-year plans that echoed the Soviet model. It did so, however, under a constitutional and federal democracy and in a mixed economy – where the central government had, even in law and even if there had been perfect implementation of decisions in both, far less power of direction than its Muscovite analogue. More had to depend on consensus (especially between the centre and the various State governments), and more on projections rather than orders, and quite simply on hope. The first Five-Year Plan, of 1951–6, was comparatively modest, depending to some extent on government projects already in the pipeline at the time of independence, but the second, 1956–61, used a developed model of the economy. Its target of 25 per cent growth in *total* (not per capita) income (Bauer, 1961, p. 31) seemed hopeful if not exactly ambitious: implying as it did an annual growth rate in income per head of about 3 per cent, which compared with a realized figure of somewhat less than 2 per cent for the five years of the first Plan (Myrdal, 1968, i, p. 486). Indian economic 'performance' still depended quite significantly on the weather, which was not kind near the end of the second Plan period. The result was that growth of India's income over the five years was less than projected. The third Plan was even more disappointing, with no growth at all in real income per head registered between 1960–61 and 1965–6, though over the first four years of that period, before the war with Pakistan, it had averaged 1.6 per cent (Myrdal, 1968, i, pp. 490–91, n. 8). Cynics, mainly Indians, joked about 'the Hindu rate of growth'.

Nonetheless, Five-Year Plans based on the Indian model became the fashion among developing countries, with even the Washington multilaterals coming to regard them as necessary signs of seriousness.

Mainland China, which had endured various degrees and kinds of internal and foreign warfare for decades, finally came under Communist rule as a single entity in May 1949, with only the island of Taiwan still held by the rival Nationalist Guomindong, and Hong Kong and Macao as small colonial enclaves. A quite promising start economically was interrupted by the collectivization of land, accomplished in a hurry over 1955–7. Then, in what may have been in part a reaction to the apparent depression in farm output that followed the collectivization, came the disastrous moves known as the Great Leap Forward, starting in late 1958 and running through until 1961. This involved amalgamating the newly created agricultural collectives into much bigger units, 'communes', that possibly averaged around 15 000 people apiece (Rawski, 1979, p. 76; see also Eckstein, 1977, ch. 3) and were intended to take over the functions of the main local-government unit, the 'township', as well as determining the allocation of resources and distribution of income.

The idea, only ever incompletely realized, was to collectivize not only agricultural organization and decision-making but also food preparation and the care of children, so that income could be distributed according to need; food consumption could be regulated; and there would be more labour to spare for labour-intensive public works (which the large unit would be able to manage) and for more intensive cultivation. People were also encouraged to increase the production of steel through 'backyard furnaces'. The utopian idea behind this programme – that everything was possible to people with the right 'consciousness', or attitude of mind – was apparently combined with technical ignorance and fantasy on the part of Mao Zedong and some of his associates, a mixture rendered disastrous by the cult implying his infallibility.

The upshot seems to have been that the intensive farming methods were counterproductive, while making huge demands for work on the peasants, and that the backyard furnaces simply wasted resources and destroyed useful assets. The disasters were at first concealed at the top because people reported mainly what their superiors wanted to hear. With the added complication of several bad seasons, however, there was widespread famine, involving, it has been estimated, 23 to 30 million excess deaths: a melancholy record among such frightful occurrences.

Though the full horror of these events was not widely known in the outside world for some time – and China from 1961–2 reorganized rural life under a more rational form of collective ownership in three tiers, with the lowest (the 'team' of 20 to 50 families) the main unit of farm decision-making – the country's possibilities as a showcase for development were further disrupted from 1966 by a new movement devised by Mao and his circle: the Great Proletarian Cultural Revolution. In successive bouts of this campaign, which was to continue off and on until 1976, young people were encouraged to depose, insult, humiliate, and even kill, anyone in authority, even Communist Party officials, on pretexts that could easily be invented, and to destroy relics of past culture. A vivid grass-roots account recounting what the Great Leap Forward and the Cultural Revolution meant for one family and its neighbours can be found in Jung Chang's highly readable *Wild Swans* (1992–3).

What is remarkable is that, in spite of the Cultural Revolution, the periods in which official sanity had the upper hand were apparently enough to effect real improvements in health and longevity after the disasters of the Great Leap Forward.

In the late 1960s came a big boost to the output of the grain-dependent countries in the form of the 'Green Revolution'. This was the introduction of much more productive strains of wheat, maize, and rice developed through conventional plant-breeding at three big research institutions financed by private foundations. The strains of wheat were short-stalked and so less susceptible to damage through heavy rain, and the improved varieties depended upon being able to make more use than pre-existing grains of chemical fertilizers and water. As well as being 'biological and chemical', these improvements represented essentially labour-using technical advance, quite suitable for very small-scale operations, requiring relatively little capital and intensive use of previously underused labour. Seemingly they corresponded well to the needs of the big Asian countries whose general development had proved so constrained by agriculture and hence so susceptible to weather. India, a consistent net grain importer from the time of its independence, became a comfortable net exporter from 1968 onwards.

During the 1950s and 1960s there was one consistent miracle of economic development, namely Japan. Its earlier growth from the time of the Meiji Restoration of 1868, which followed its opening to the world in the 1850s, had been respectable by the standards of earlier industrial revolutions, but it had been still no more than a middle-income country before the War and had been thoroughly devastated in 1945. Yet its per capita income growth through the golden age averaged 8.05 per cent (Maddison, 2006, p. 129). By 1970 it had decisively joined the rich world. (See Tables 2.1, 2.4.)

Though Japan's hectic rate of growth did not continue after it had reached affluent status, it was to continue until 1989 to grow faster than the other big developed countries, and the economic stability and low levels of both inflation and unemployment that it maintained through the global disturbances of the 1970s and 1980s made it an exemplar not only to the developing countries – and especially those of the old civilizations of East and South Asia – but also until 1989 to the affluent economies whose company it had joined. By the late 1960s there were already a few incipient followers of its meteoric rise, but none was yet widely recognized.

The end in August 1971 of the Bretton Woods system of pegged exchange-rates was an omen of the soon-to-change complexion of the world economy. It is notable that no substitute was to follow: no agreed and orderly system of exchange-rates has since emerged, and indeed there has been no stable conventional wisdom about the best way of managing them.

BOX 2.3 GROWTH IN THE 'GOLDEN AGE' AND UNDER THE 'NEOLIBERAL ORDER'

Within the capitalist epoch, one can distinguish five distinct phases of development . . . The 'golden age', 1950–73, was by far the best in terms of growth performance. Our age, from 1973 onwards (henceforth characterised as the 'neoliberal order') has been second best. The old 'liberal order' 1870–1913, was third best, with marginally slower growth than our age. In the fourth best phase (1913–50), growth was obviously below potential because of two world wars and the intervening collapse of world trade, capital markets and migration. The slowest growth was registered in the initial phase of capitalist development (1820–70) when significant growth momentum was largely confined to European countries and Western Offshoots.

Source: Angus Maddison, *The World Economy*, OECD, Paris, 2006, p. 125.

Turbulence and Tigers, 1974–89

The striking turn for the worse was postponed a little longer. The early 1970s were a time of boom and of buoyant primary-commodity prices. Prospects still seemed cheerful until the huge managed rise in the price of crude petroleum at the end of 1973, superimposed on the inflationary tendencies already present, both depressed real income and inflicted tendencies to cost-inflation and external deficit in all countries that were net importers of hydrocarbons. National authorities in these countries generally reacted by demand deflation, and the mid-1970s saw the first OPEC-sparked world recession, with corresponding deep depression before long in the prices of metals and other industrial raw materials.

Yet it was at some time in the 1970s that the extremely fast growth over the previous few years of the four 'East Asian Tigers' (South Korea, Taiwan, Hong Kong and Singapore) – growth little affected by the world slump of the mid-1970s – began to be recognized. At first their growth was mentioned in the same breath as that of Brazil, which had recorded high rates over some years since the war, but, unlike Brazil's, the growth of the Tigers was to continue with little interruption until the end of the century and beyond. What challenged conventional development-economics stereotypes at the time was the means by which these economies had apparently become airborne. With varying degrees of economic liberalism in their foreign trade and investment policies, all seemed to have depended heavily on export expansion. To some observers, this thought was unwelcome, and for years the mantra was repeated that Taiwan and Korea had achieved their fast growth entirely through massive US aid; but this interpretation simply did not fit – in timing, or in other respects. It became ever less tenable as other East and South-East Asian countries came to show similar growth rates in the 1980s and 1990s.

After some recovery of world economic activity in the late 1970s, OPEC showed that it had more shocks to inflict. On the back of an oil-price boost associated with the Iranian revolution of 1979, the cartel imposed a second set of big rises over that year and 1980. This led to a further and deeper recession in the industrial world, which was reflected again, over most of Africa, the Caribbean and the Pacific, in low primary-export prices, and for many countries was to generate actually declining incomes per head over the 1980s.

What seemed at first to be a mitigating factor was the recycling of the surpluses of the richer OPEC countries to a number of mostly non-oil, middle-income countries which were thus enabled to dampen the fall in world expenditure. However, when after 1981 world oil prices themselves began to fall, Mexico, which had become both an oil exporter and a large borrower, began in late 1982 to have difficulty in servicing its debts. This led to a collapse in confidence among lending institutions and a fear that other large debtors would be unable to meet their obligations. The supply of new loans, on which the debtor governments had largely relied for servicing previous debts, began to dry up.

So began the 1980s debt crisis, which threatened a major financial collapse, led to great hardship in the twenty-or-so debtor countries, and continued until around the end of the decade. This is discussed further in Chapter 22. The point here is that there was marked impoverishment as a result for many people in middle-income countries, mainly in Latin America.

Latin America also saw, through the 1980s, a series of stabilization plans, conventional and unconventional, often with new currencies, designed to stabilize prices in the face of chronically high inflation without seriously damaging output. Most of the plans collapsed, with the last state arguably worse than the first. Bolivia alone managed, in the middle of the decade, largely through conventional deflationary measures, to bring down inflation from astronomic to consistently tolerable rates, but this did not avoid considerable human cost that arose through loss of employment. It was not a good decade economically for Latin America, with the part-exception of Colombia, though it saw the end (in Argentina, Brazil, and Chile) of periods of, often brutal, authoritarian military rule.

It was also not a good decade for the low-income and low-middle-income countries heavily dependent on primary exports, which included most of Africa, as well as the Caribbean and Pacific islands. In the late 1970s the apparent success of OPEC in increasing its primary-commodity earnings had prompted hope for a *new international economic order*, under which governments of other primary-commodity producers might exert similar power, or at all events further international schemes for *stabilizing* the prices of individual commodities might be set up. In fact, the few international stabilization schemes for primary-commodity prices that had had any effective life collapsed (tin, 1985) or worked intermittently at best (coffee, whose agreement went into abeyance from 1989) or depended precariously on particular importing-country patrons (several of those for sugar). Commodity prices that were low historically in real terms had their ill-effects augmented in a number of places by various combinations of warfare, drought, weak or corrupt government, and bad policy.

By contrast, the growth of the Tigers continued largely unaffected by the recessions of the 1970s and 1980s. Japan, now numbered among the rich, also showed a capacity to continue stable (though now more modest) growth through those decades in spite of the turbulence of the times.

It was becoming evident in the 1980s that what we can now begin to call the 'East Asian industrial revolution' was being joined in one degree or another by Thailand, Malaysia and Indonesia; and there was an even more momentous addition to their number in mainland China.

After the two great helmsmen – Mao and Zhou Enlai – who had led the Chinese People's Republic through its first 27 years, both died in 1976, there was a surprisingly short period of uncertainty before it became clear, not long after changes in leadership effected around 1978, that a very cautious process of economic liberalization, with an absence of wild experiments, was likely to ensue. Formally, collective ownership was retained in the countryside, but in practice there was a general shift to peasant-household agriculture under what was called the 'household-responsibility system'. Farm prices for food crops were allowed to rise, with (apparently) a considerable positive impact upon both incomes and marginal incentives in the countryside. The real gross value of output in agriculture, like that in 'industry', almost exactly doubled, according to official figures, between 1979 and 1986. Commercial enterprise on the part of townships and villages was often allowed fairly free rein. There were also hesitant moves, gradually extended in a number of dimensions, to admit foreign investment, at first only in limited coastal sites and on condition that it should contribute directly to exports. At the same time indigenous enterprise, much of it financed with the help of overseas Chinese, came to be openly encouraged, though a huge state-run industrial sector remained. While China retained one-party control and was far from a liberal or law-governed society even up to the time of writing, the range of permissible expression of opinion became definitely, if precariously, wider than under Mao; provincial and local governments gained considerable influence over the details of industrial policy; and entrepreneurial dynamism remained such that economic-growth rates of 8 to 10 per cent were normal over much of the last two decades of the century and beyond.

At the same time, India, also moving fitfully toward liberalization, entered on a faster growth path in the 1980s and (more or less) through the 1990s (when it was joined in this movement by Bangladesh) into the early twenty-first century. Soon after 2000 the Hindu rate of growth ceased to be a bad joke (see Table 2.4).

The fall of oil prices in the mid-1980s helped in the recovery of the industrial countries from the second OPEC recession, but it aggravated the difficulties of poorer oil-exporting developing countries, and there were no striking dividends for the exporters of most other primary commodities.

The 1980s had been a dreadful decade economically for most of Latin America and Africa, and gloomy enough for much of Western Europe and North America, but Japan's euphoria had not yet been deflated, and the East Asian industrial revolution was in full swing. The concept of the Third World no longer made much sense: a goodly part of it was soaring, while much of the rest seemed to be bumping along on the level or even sliding downhill.

Transition and turmoil, 1990 onwards

Into this mix of growth and decline came the remarkable events of the last months of 1989, when the Soviet external empire collapsed; the Communist monopoly of power ended then or soon after across Eastern Europe and in the Soviet Union itself; Germany reunited in October 1990; and, at the start of 1992, the Soviet Union broke up into its 15 separate Republics.

Optimists hoped for a new co-operative world order under a UN no longer hobbled by Cold War rivalries, and also for a 'peace dividend' that would arise from disarmament in the NATO and Warsaw Pact countries and release big additional funds for world development. These hopes were at first given some colour by co-operation across the old bloc divisions to end Iraq's occupation of Kuwait in early 1991, and by the fact that there was a big fall in arms spending over the early 1990s.

Yet there seems to have been little immediate direct impact of these changes on most of the developing world. They probably hastened the end of the Ethiopian civil war and the Mengistu regime in 1991, and they deprived Cuba of its highly preferential sugar market. Beyond that, it is hard to think of clear examples. In Southern Africa the Soviet-bloc collapse had less influence in ending civil wars than the radical change of course in South Africa that was signalled by the release of Nelson Mandela in 1990 and consummated in the all-races election of 1994.

Indeed, there were over the last quarter of the century decided shifts in the general direction of democracy and free institutions in a number of countries (after shorter or longer periods of authoritarian rule): in South and Southwest Europe from the mid-1970s; in much of Latin America from the 1980s; in East and South-East Asia from the late-1980s; and in Eastern Europe and parts of Africa from the 1990s.

There was a further world recession in the early 1990s. A part was played in its genesis by the high interest-rates arising from the fiscal deficits incurred by Germany in subsidizing its eastern wing after reunification, but also important (probably) was the exceptional collapse in 1990 of the Japanese stock and property markets and the start of the long Japanese period of slow growth that was to follow. Some contribution was presumably also made by the cataclysmic fall in output of the former satellites and Soviet lands. Authoritative figures put the combined GDP of the twelve members of the Commonwealth of Independent States (CIS) – the former Soviet Republics other than the Baltics – in 1996 at only *51 per cent* of what it had been in 1989 (European Bank for Reconstruction and Development, *Transition Reports*, 1996, 1997) – a larger proportional fall than that of the US in the Great Depression – and in addition almost all the Soviet's former European satellites had lower incomes in 1996 than seven years earlier.

The shift since the early 1980s toward economic liberalism (what the Americans call 'conservatism') in Britain, the US, Australia and New Zealand, seemed to bear fruit in the later 1990s, when they (and even more Ireland) came to lead in growth rates, with the big continental West European countries behind and Japan further back again: the reverse of the order in the 1960s. However, five further developments complicated the impact of the mid- to late-1990s revival on a number of the low- and middle-income countries.

In the first place, and apparently quite unexpected, was a series of currency collapses: first for Mexico over the turn of 1994–5, and then from 1997 for Thailand, Indonesia, South Korea, the Philippines, and Malaysia; shortly after for Brazil and Russia; and then in somewhat different circumstances quite catastrophically for Argentina in 2001. Of the 1997 batch, Indonesia's exchange-rate fall was the most acute: the rupiah at end-June 1998 exchanged for a sixth of the value in dollars at which it had traded exactly a year before. Falls such as this do not leave an economy unscathed, and the disruption in Indonesia has been blamed for riots and disturbances that led eventually (for better or for worse) to a change of regime. Complete freedom for international capital movements was at the time the recommendation of conventional wisdom among the multilaterals. Yet there were grounds for thinking that judicious intervention might have averted the crises. Chile, which against IMF advice had used fiscal methods to check short-term capital inflows, avoided any subsequent corresponding panic outflow. China, with a greater degree of capital control, though admittedly also other differences, was largely unaffected other than through trade relations with its afflicted neighbours.

Since a number of the Asian countries caught in the crises had run quite acceptable macroeconomic policies, it became conventional in hindsight to attribute the currency collapses and the associated domestic financial disturbances to, first, attempts made by the countries involved to stabilize their exchange-rates and, second, their poor banking regulation, so that conveniently they, and not the ultra-liberal advice that they had received from the multilaterals or others, could be blamed. There also was and is serious doubt whether the deflationary measures pressed upon the sufferers during the crisis by the IMF were sensible or might on the contrary have been diametrically wrong. However, all the affected Asian countries, with the exception perhaps of Indonesia, recovered fairly quickly. The currency crises offered only a brief check to the East Asian industrial revolution.

A second complication of the 1990s was the set of international and inter-communal wars that the dissolution of the Soviet system and of Yugoslavia let loose: Armenia against Azerbaijan; Serbs against Croats and Bosniaks and Kosovo Albanians. African development was hampered by new conflicts as the former batch fuelled by the Cold War and the South African apartheid regime became resolved: multiple interventions with millions of deaths in the Democratic Republic of Congo; the Rwanda genocide in 1993; the horror and absurdity of an official international war between the Eritreans and their former revolutionary comrades now running the Ethiopian state; civil wars in Sierra Leone, Liberia, Côte D'Ivoire; a new civil-war-cum-genocide in Sudan.

The third complication was the spread of AIDS, incomparably worse in sub-Saharan Africa, than in any other region, driving down life-expectancies in parts of the south of the continent by *decades*, decimating economically active age-groups, and leaving huge populations of orphaned children.

Fourth, by the second half of the 1990s a new debt crisis was evident, this time among the poorest countries and predominantly of debts not to banks but to other governments and international organizations. Consequently, unlike the crisis of the 1980s, it did not threaten the financial system. The debts were nevertheless a millstone round the neck for a number of very vulnerable societies. In a slow-moving and extremely cautious move to ameliorate the state of the 41 defined as 'heavily indebted poor countries' (HIPCs), the World Bank and IMF began in 1996 to specify conditions under which those countries' debts might be remitted. (See Chapter 22.)

A final feature of this period that was to affect development thinking was the fact that Russia and the rest of the 12 CIS countries remained in varying ways spectacularly unsuccessful societies, their biggest and most 'advanced' members a byword for organized crime and corruption. Rather than following China's example of gradual transition, which seemed to have been very fruitful in output growth, Russia and Ukraine, under the most reputable outside advice, went for quick liberalization and privatization ('shock therapy').

The 1980s picture of quick and slow developers was largely carried on into the 1990s – though with somewhat better times for segments of Latin America, and with instances in Africa of unusual spurts: for example, Mozambique after its emergence from civil war. Yet there was also the addition of the ex-Communist states with their diverse experiences: Vietnam showing signs of joining the East Asian sprinters; the condition of most of the CIS republics still unreservedly gloomy at the end of the decade; but at the same time some of the rest of ex-Communist Europe beginning to recover after the initial shocks of transition and to grow fairly strongly, as indeed a number of the CIS countries also did through the early years of the new century.

China's spectacular growth, and the slower (but by past standards rapid, and increasingly so) growth of India, continued, largely unaffected by the vicissitudes of the 1990s; and generally the East and some South-East Asian economies flourished.

Some developments expressed in figures

Experience of economic growth

Did the developing countries to any extent 'catch up' with the developed over 1950–2000? Did their income per head actually rise at all?

Country group	1950–60	1960–67
World excluding USSR & Europe	2.0	2.9
USSR & E. Europe	3.0	3.3
Developed countries	2.4	3.8
Developing countries	2.4	2.0
Nigeria	8.4	2.2
US	1.2	3.7
Brazil	2.7	0.9
India	1.6	–1.5
Indonesia	n.a.	–0.2
Japan	7.2	8.6
S. Korea	2.5	5.1

TABLE 2.1 Growth rates of real GDP per head, 1950–67, percentage per year
Note: GDP in constant market prices for Japan; at market prices for S. Korea; otherwise at factor cost.
Source: UN *Yearbook of National Accounts Statistics 1968,* volume 2.

Country group	1965–90	1985–95
Low income	2.9	3.8
China and India	3.7	
Excl. China and India	1.7	–1.4
Middle income	2.2	–0.7
Lower middle	1.5	–1.3
Upper middle	2.0	1.2
Low and middle together	2.5	0.4
Sub-Saharan Africa	0.2	–1.1
East Asia and Pacific	5.3	7.2
South Asia	1.9	2.9
Europe & Central Asia		–3.5
M. East & North Africa	1.8	–0.3
L. America & Caribbean	1.8	0.3
High income	2.4	1.9

TABLE 2.2 Growth rates of real GNP per head by region, 1965–95, percentage per year
Source: World Bank, *World Development Report 1992,* p. 218 ; 1997, p. 214. *World Development Indicators,* Table 1.

UN figures, given in Table 2.1, suggest that in the 1950s proportional growth of income per head was roughly the same between developed and developing countries, each taken as a group, with that in the USSR and Eastern Europe somewhat higher than the world average. Over the 1960s to 1967, the developing countries lagged, with lower proportional growth than in the 1950s while that of the developed countries was higher. However, according to Maddison (2002, p. 125) the *poorest* developing countries gained on the richest countries over the whole of the 'golden age', with the ratio of incomes per head falling from 15:1 to 13:1. So: dubious *catching up* for the developing countries overall – though there was significant if modest *growth* in income per head within the developing countries taken as a whole in both 1950s and 1960s. But the few individual countries listed in Table 2.1 already show that there was marked divergence among the members of each of the two groups. The stars are Japan, and in the latter decade South Korea (and, surprisingly, Nigeria in the 1950s). India (with a war) and Indonesia (with multiple political disruptions) both show falling per capita income over 1960–67.

Such divergences mean that after 1970 it makes ever less sense to look at growth rates of the developing countries taken together. Table 2.2 gives some World Bank estimates that separate the developing countries on criteria such as income-level range, and region.

The increased prevalence of negative per capita growth rates in the later period is notable. Over 1965–90 the only developing-country region to show any catching-up with high-income countries is East Asia & Pacific. Over 1985–95 South Asia joins East Asia & Pacific in growing faster than the high-income countries, but all the other regions actually have negative rates for that period, except Latin America & Caribbean, where the rate is (just) positive but low. It is easy to conclude that, except in East and South Asia, developing

Region	1950	2000
World	2519	6086
Africa	224	812
Asia	1396	3676
Europe	547	728
L. America & Caribbean	167	523
North America	172	315
Oceania	13	31
Less developed countries	1707	4892
More developed countries	813	1193

TABLE 2.3 World population by region, 1950 and 2000, millions
Source: Population Division of Department of Economic and Social Affairs, UN Secretariat, *World Population Prospects: the 2004 Revision*, http://esa.un.org/unpp (downloaded 15/1/2006).

countries on the whole over those ten years were going backward.

However, we need to remember that the world supported 6.1 billion people in 2000, as against 2.5 billion in 1950: 2.4 times as many (see Table 2.3). The great majority of these additional 3.6 billion consumers – 3.2 billion – were piled into the developing countries, where most people at the start of the 50-year period were still directly dependent on cultivation and most cultivable land was already occupied. Marked change would be needed just to keep these much larger numbers supported with the same average income as before. Africa increased its population in the ratio of 3.6:1, and Asia of 2.6:1.

Country or group	1960–70	1970–80	1980–90	1990–2000	2000–2004	1960–2004
Low and middle income	2.8	2.9	1.0	2.0	3.3	2.3
High income	4.1	2.6	2.4	1.9	1.4	2.6
Brazil	3.2	5.9	−0.4	1.3	1.0	2.3
Mexico	5.4	3.6	−0.2	1.8	0.1	2.0
Ethiopia				0.7	2.7	1.3[b]
Nigeria	1.7	1.7	−1.9	−0.1	2.2	0.5
S. Africa	3.5	1.1	−0.9	−0.4	2.3	0.9
Bangladesh	1.4	−1.7	1.1	3.0	3.3	1.2
India	1.7	0.7	3.6	3.6	4.6	2.6
Indonesia	1.8	5.4	4.4	2.7	3.2	3.5
China	1.5	4.3	7.7	8.9	7.9	5.8
Japan	9.3	3.3	3.4	1.2	1.2	4.0
S. Korea	5.6	5.4	7.5	5.1	4.0	5.7
Russia				−3.7	6.6	−0.9[b]
Ukraine				−7.6	9.8	−2.9[b]
France	4.5	2.7	1.9	1.5	1.0	2.5
UK	2.2	1.8	2.4	2.2	2.0	2.1
US	2.5	2.2	2.3	2.0	1.5	2.2

TABLE 2.4 Growth rates by decade of real GDP per head in constant 2000 US dollars[a], percentage per year
Notes: [a] The translations across aggregates in different currencies have been made by exchange-rates. Corresponding growth-rate figures derived from PPP aggregates (available in the source from 1980 on) differ from them too little in most cases to be worth noting here.
[b] These rates refer to the period 1990–2004.
Source: Derived from World Bank, *World Development Indicators*, ESDS International, Manchester University, Manchester, England (Internet source, © World Bank).

Measured against the hopes of around 1950, the economic-growth performance of Latin America, Africa, and Western Asia, over the next 50 years was extremely disappointing. Per head there was no *convergence*, no catching up, and there were quite a number of times and places of backward movement. For much of East Asia, however, extending for this purpose first to South-East Asia and then more uncertainly to South Asia, the picture has been promising and increasingly so, with convergence coming from successive waves of fast or even spectacular growth: first, Japan; then the original four Tigers (Hong Kong, Singapore and Taiwan in the high-income class at the end of the century, and South Korea just after); then China, Malaysia, Thailand, Indonesia and Vietnam; then, it seems, India.

Direct welfare experience

Country group	1950–55	2000–05
World	156.9	57.0
Africa	179.3	94.2
Asia	182.1	53.7
Europe	72.4	9.2
Western Europe	45.3	4.5
Latin America	126.2	26.0
Caribbean		
North America	28.6	6.8
Oceania	61.5	28.7
Less-developed countries	179.8	62.4
More-developed countries	59.1	7.7

TABLE 2.5 Infant mortality by region, 1950–55 and 2000–05: deaths under one year old per 1000 live births
Source: As in Table 2.3.

Country group	1950–55	2000–05
World	46.6	65.4
Africa	38.4	49.1[a]
Asia	41.4	57.3
Europe	65.6	73.7
Eastern Europe	64.2	67.9[b]
Latin America	51.4	71.5
Caribbean	52.2	57.5
North America	68.8	77.6
Oceania	60.4	74.0
Less-developed countries	41.5	61.2
More-developed countries	66.1	75.6

TABLE 2.6 Life-expectancy by region, 1950–55 and 2000–05, numbers of years
Notes: [a] Africa's life-expectancy is given as 51.5 in 1985–90, but it *declined* over each of the next three five-year periods, the change presumably reflecting the AIDS epidemic.
[b] Eastern Europe's life-expectancy was 70.3 in 1985–90, but it *fell* by 2.4 over the next 15 years, probably a result, at least in part, of the economic disruption and impoverishment associated with 'transition'.
Source: As in Table 2.3.

A number of variables could be examined. We concentrate here in Tables 2.5 and 2.6 on two that appear likely to be rough indicators of general living standards: infant mortality (the number of children dying in the first year of life per 1000 live births) and life-expectancy. Life-expectancy in year *n* is the average number of years a child born in year *n* would live *if* the proportion of people in each age group dying were to remain at the same rate through that child's life as in year *n*. So it is **not a prediction of the future** but rather a way of summarizing the mortality of people at various ages **in year *n***. Over a shorter period, we also look at changes in the incidence of literacy and of malnutrition

Improvements in life-expectancy and infant survival are not only advantageous in themselves but also point to generally improved health status. So these tables do suggest real advance in certain fundamental elements of living standards over the 50 years. **Out of every twenty children born in the world, two out of the three who would have died within the**

first year of life under the conditions of the early 1950s would have survived 50 years later, as the proportion dying fell between the two periods by nearly two-thirds. To some extent this no doubt reflects general advances in health technology, as against improved and wider application of existing knowledge. But we can also read the figures to suggest some 'catching-up'. In *numbers* of infant deaths avoided per 1000 births, as also in extra years of life-expectancy, the developing countries made greater gains than the developed. Asia reduced its infant deaths per 1000 by nearly 130, and increased its longevity by nearly 36 years; Latin America was close to the world average of about 100 less infant deaths and 20 more years of life; and even Africans avoided 85 infant deaths and (before AIDS) were living 13 years longer. **The infant-mortality rate for less-developed countries in 2000–05 was almost as low as for the more-developed fifty years earlier**. However they happened, these are big changes – even though a child born in the developing world still (2000–2005) apparently has about eight times as great a chance of dying in its first year as one in the developed countries.

The estimates of the extent of undernourishment show improvements over 1980–2001, often quite considerable, for all the large developing countries listed here except Mexico (where the level was low in any case) – and thus over more than half of the world's population. However, a number of countries listed in the source show deterioration. These include at least nine in Africa, as well as Venezuela, Trinidad-Tobago and Panama. The rises in incidence of malnutrition were large in Tanzania, Zambia and Zimbabwe, and immense in the Democratic Republic of Congo (DRC).

Literacy rates given in Table 2.7 rose in all cases, with some striking changes over the 20 years. Given that most of the improvements in proportions of the whole population have presumably come through increased education in school-age groups – a narrow part of the age-range – some of the advances are even more remarkable. Some of those countries in which nutrition over the period seriously deteriorated (DRC, Zimbabwe, Rwanda, for example) still improved their literacy rates substantially over what must have been a highly disturbed time.

Country	1980	2000
Bangladesh	28.9	40.0
Brazil	76.0	86.9
China	67.1	85.2
Egypt	39.3	55.3
Ethiopia	19.9	39.1
India	41.0	57.2
Indonesia	69.0	86.8
Mexico	81.3	91.2
Nigeria	32.9	64.0
South Africa	76.1	85.2

TABLE 2.7 Literacy rates, selected countries, 1980 and 2000, percentage of people aged 15 and over literate
Source: UNESCO estimates (October 2005), from UN Common Database, ESDS International.

Country	1980	2000
Bangladesh	40.0	30.2
Brazil	15.0	9.0
China	30.0	11.0
Egypt	8.0	3.5
Ethiopia	46.5	
India	38.0	21.4
Indonesia	24.0	5.9
Mexico	4.0	5.2
Nigeria	39.0	9.3

TABLE 2.8 Malnutrition, selected countries, 1980 and 2001: those judged undernourished as percentage of total population
Source: FAO estimates, from UN Common Database, ESDS International.

Though static comparisons with rudimentary welfare indicators in the affluent economies are still very unfavourable for much of the rest of the world, there was real quantifiable improvement that went with the decidedly mixed picture of income growth within the developing countries.

Beside all this, we shall mention in Chapter 13 how there was a sharp fall in human fertility in developing countries – in fact by about half – over the last three decades of the twentieth century (see Table 13.10 in that chapter). This in itself meant smaller families, and therefore on the whole a welfare improvement. It also will have made a big contribution to much desired slowing of the rate of population growth in the present century. In addition, though there had been some coercion, notably in China, to bring this result about, much of it probably happened by choice of family size (facilitated by the deliberate spread of family-planning knowledge) or as a result of other decisions made by the parents.

Finally, if we take political freedom to be an important component of development, there is some encouragement from the fact (as we interpret it) that, in spite of setbacks, democracy and free institutions were on balance advancing across the world over the last quarter of the century.

BOX 2.4 ARTHUR LEWIS ON ANALYSING ECONOMIC GROWTH, 1955

'The enquiry into human actions has to be conducted at different levels, because there are proximate causes of growth, as well as causes of these causes. The proximate causes are principally three. First there is the effort to economize, either by reducing the cost of any given product or by increasing the yield of any given input of effort or other resources. This effort to economize shows itself in various ways: in experimentation, or risk-taking; in mobility, occupational or geographical; and in specialization, to mention only its chief manifestations. If the effort is not made, either because the desire to economize does not exist, or else because either custom or institutions discourage its expression, then economic growth will not occur. Secondly, there is the increase of knowledge and its application. This process has occurred throughout human history; but the more rapid growth of output in recent centuries is associated obviously with the more rapid accumulation and application of knowledge in production. And thirdly, growth depends upon increasing the amount of capital or other resources per head. . . .

'The second stage of the analysis takes us behind these proximate causes to ask why it is that they are found strongly operating in some societies but not in others, or at some stages of history but less so in others. What environments are most favourable to the emergence of these forces that promote growth? This stage of the enquiry subdivides itself. First, we must enquire which kinds of institutions are favourable to growth, and which are inimical to effort, to innovation or to investment. Then we must move into the realm of beliefs and ask what causes a nation to create institutions which are favourable, rather than those which are inimical to growth. Is a part of the answer to be found in the different valuations which different societies place upon goods and services relatively to their valuation of such non-material satisfactions as leisure, security, equality, good fellowship or religious salvation? . . . Still further behind this lie questions relating to nature and environment. What causes a people to have one set of beliefs, rather than another set of beliefs, more or less favourable to growth? Are the differences of beliefs and institutions due to differences of race, or of geography, or is it just historical accident?'

Source: W.A. Lewis, *The Theory of Economic Growth*, George Allen and Unwin, London, 1955, pp. 11, 12.

In conclusion: how has the outlook changed?

It seems there are no simple or infallible ways of generating fast economic growth that can be simply introduced as acts of policy – or, if there are, we have not yet discovered them. As will perhaps be clearer when we examine in Chapter 3 the shifts in ideas and ideology relating to development policy, no new paradigm has emerged comparable to that of Keynes on unemployment in rich countries. Neither the hope imposed in the state as mobilizer and in centralized allocation and autarky that was characteristic of the years just after the war, nor the liberal market ideology espoused in the 1980s and 1990s, has proved altogether reliable in delivering the goods.

Yet fast economic growth has occurred, and is occurring, over countries covering a large part of the world's population.

The 1950 division of the world into rich and poor has certainly been disturbed. But a new division has taken over. There are the affluent, now augmented by Japan, South Korea, Taiwan, Hong Kong and Singapore. There is a sub-group of low- and middle-income countries surging ahead, with prospects of 'catching up' within a few decades: China, Vietnam, and Malaysia most clearly on track; then probably India, Thailand, Indonesia – and, in this company, why not soon Bangladesh, Pakistan, the Philippines? Then there are the rest, roughly divided by region: the largest of the twelve CIS successors to the Soviet Union, and also most of ex-Communist Eastern Europe, recovering fast in the early 2000s, after what was certainly a catastrophic fall for all in the early 1990s; most of sub-Saharan Africa, tending to go backward in the last twenty years of the old century, but a number of them then growing relatively fast in the commodity boom at the start of the 2000s; the remainder, including Latin America and the Caribbean, with a more turbulent record, few striking successes, and dismal periods for most.

Yet people in all regions were much more likely to survive in their first year of life and were living longer (in the poorer continents, much longer) than 50 years earlier, and the figures here suggest real 'catching up', not just general technological advance. Over most of the 'developing world' people were also decidedly less likely to be clinically undernourished. Those in the less developed regions were also very much more likely than before to be literate.

It seems that quite striking improvements in conditions of life may still come even where there has not been spectacular growth.

There were still huge gaps between rich and poor and still well over a billion people apparently in the 'extremely poor' category on income grounds; but, on a much more densely populated planet than before, there were some solid objective gains in certain vital conditions of life, and not just among the fast developers.

Why this new division?

The striking feature, which must be telling us something, is that consistent fast growth, at least until the end of the century, has been virtually confined to one region of the world. We have alluded here to the *East Asian industrial revolution*, taking the term to cover also certain parts of South-East Asia. One possibility is that there is a cultural element: some feature of Chinese, Japanese, Korean, and Vietnamese culture that is a precondition. The

South-East Asian countries that have been among the reasonably fast developers (Malaysia, Thailand, and Indonesia) have significant minorities of a Chinese cultural heritage, who have been prominent in business. Could there be something about these cultures that fulfilled a necessary condition (maybe the same as, or possibly an alternative to, the cultural something that was present in the Western European societies that gestated the first industrial revolution)?

An alternative possibility – an explanation more in the realm of conventional economics – is that there is a general pattern of resource endowments that has been conducive to fast growth in the later twentieth century. This might claim support from the fact that India too appears to have joined the consistent fast developers. The fact is that a large part of the world's people were in countries that began the half-century with a high ratio of people to land and natural resources, often quite low education levels on average and for the mass, but a literate traditional culture, centuries of specialized skilled trades, some modern manufacturing, a highly educated elite, and an established administrative tradition. We might postulate a connection in the fact that those economies that were to flourish consistently toward the end of the twentieth century were generally in this class.

Perhaps the characteristics of the global economy at this time somehow made this (natural and human) resource pattern ripe for economic growth through interaction with the wider world, and the necessary switch to 'on' was a change in *policy* that enabled the country to take advantage of this potential.

It could be that these two explanations reduce to one. Certain aspects of the culture, or of the culture of an entrepreneurial minority, may be regarded as part of the resource endowment. Also, the low endowment of land and natural resources, combined with other features of these societies, may have served to generate a culture of enterprising behaviour, as well as offering at first low real wages and low real labour costs to facilitate the growth of export trade with the outside world.

Whichever explanation we choose, there is no insuperable difficulty raised by the fact that in each cultural area – East Asia, South-East Asia, South Asia – fast development has been patchy and, where it has happened, has often begun quite suddenly after a period of relative stagnation. What this may mean is that it is easy enough for governments, or sometimes popular movements, *to prevent growth from occurring* when it otherwise might. The fact that North Korea can hardly feed itself while South Korea has joined the ranks of the affluent does not have to be explained by cultural or resource differences. Nor does it mean, however, that distinctions of culture or resource endowments are *irrelevant* to growth possibilities.

The big difference *there* would appear to be *policy*, the switch that may turn growth off even if it cannot reliably turn growth on.

In fact it is difficult to understand the Asian growth experience without giving some credit to policy as a factor. The change of stance that appeared to flick the switch 'on' was not always unreservedly liberal, but it did appear in all cases to involve encouraging, or at least not discouraging, manufactured exports. This might be done by fairly pure free trade or by various incentives designed to compensate for other handicaps: either indiscriminately or selectively.

Maybe the substratum of culture or resource-endowment *and* the flicking of the policy switch – turning off all the obstacles to enterprise and traffic with the wider world – were both essential.

However, if rapid growth requires a seedbed of a particular cultural or resource endowment, what can be done by or for the rest of the developing countries? Should they continue strenuously to pursue growth in case the preconditions might turn out to be present? Or should they treat rapid growth as something likely to come, if at all, in its own time, and, while rigorously avoiding measures that might strangle it, otherwise concentrate on making the best for their people – especially for their poor – of what they have available?

Or is this a false dichotomy? Does taking reasonable measures for promoting growth include, rather than compete with, making life better for the poor? Or at least *can they be made* mutually consistent? It would seem that, the more important we rate *human capital* as a contributor to growth, the more emphasis growth policy must place on the health, education and nutrition of those who would otherwise be deficient on these scores.

Finally, if filling the gaps to help correct the extremes of poverty in respect of health, education and nutrition must be a large part of the *positive* thrust of both welfare and growth policy, how can the international community best help in this enterprise?

We leave these for the time being as questions.

Summary conclusions

- The character of thought about development economics in its early years was coloured by the experiences of the previous two decades: in particular the Great Depression; the activist element and apparent success of the Keynesian revolution; the achievements of Soviet industrialization; the positive spin-offs of war mobilization in the democracies; the ostensible pay-offs to timely generosity in the Marshall Plan; and the presence of the new international economic institutions created to avoid the mistakes of the recent past.

- The combined effect was a sense of the possibility of radical change and of its urgency, with optimism about what was possible under heavy state intervention, forced development of secondary industry, and abundant capital investment that might be extensively financed by overseas aid; and pessimism about the gains possible through freeing markets, about the potential of small-scale and spontaneous entrepreneurship, about the income prospects of poorer countries left to market forces, and about the opportunities provided by international trade and investment.

- Three periods of development experience can be distinguished within the half-century. First was the 'golden age' to 1973 of generally modest but consistent growth in both rich and poorer countries, with Japan's meteoric rise, the failures of South Asian ambitions, and China's policy catastrophe of 1959–61 striking exceptions. Second was the period of turbulence to 1989, that included two major recessions, the big engineered oil-price rises, the Latin American debt crisis, a fairly disastrous decade in the 1980s for primary exporters and generally for Latin America and Africa, but also the emerging phenomenon of the four East Asian 'Tigers' continuing on a rapid growth path (and, like Japan, little disturbed by the turbulence of the rest of the world), with China and much of South-East Asia already showing signs of fast to explosive growth. Third was the period of 'transition' from 1990, with the initial collapse of the ex-Soviet-bloc economies, the low-income countries' debt crisis and another miserable period for Africa, a further recession in the early 1990s, the currency crises, the phenomenal rise of China, and eventually and more modestly India, and continuing significant growth in much of the rest of East and South-East Asia.

▶

▶
- The upshot in economic growth is a sharp division of the 'developing' world: one segment that covers – on the most optimistic estimate – something like a half of the world's population racing ahead and 'catching up' with the high-income countries or showing prospects of doing so in a foreseeable future; another segment – countries containing perhaps another sixth or eighth of the world's people – stagnating or actually falling in average income much of the time; and still a large number in between.

- In spite of the fact that the world has had to accommodate about 2.5 times as many people in 2000 as in 1950, progress on the objective welfare indicators has not been entirely gloomy. The gaps on these variables between developed and developing countries are still very great. Yet, if life-expectancy and infant mortality are taken as indicators of general living standards, even Africa, the worst-performing of the continents, has shown quite remarkable improvements; and infant mortality across the developing countries in the first five years of the new century was only slightly higher than across the developed world fifty years earlier. Literacy has advanced almost everywhere, even since 1980. Undernourishment also appears to have fallen in almost all of the big developing countries over the last twenty years of the century.

- Two further encouraging changes were the large fall in human fertility in the developing world over the last thirty years of the century, and what we interpreted as on balance a shift in much the same period in the direction of democracy and free institutions.

- We speculated about the circumstances that led to rapid growth, especially about the reasons for thinking that both cultural traditions and attitudes on the one hand – combined with, and possibly related to, particular patterns of resource endowments – and policy on the other, may define necessary conditions.

We have seen that spectacular and transformative growth are possible for 'developing countries' in our time, and so are significant improvements in material welfare and human development. But economic stagnation, and neglect of poverty, have also been an important part of the story.

Questions for discussion

2.1   Would you expect the fact that the low- and middle-income countries of the twentieth century faced a world in which a number of economies were already rich and industrialized would make it *harder* or *easier* for them to make the jump from poverty to affluence themselves?

2.2   Since the late nineteenth century Britain has lost one after another of its export markets to competitors, and jobs have fallen sharply or disappeared in many of its traditional industries. Yet, among the large countries of the world (over 50 million people), Britain in the early twenty-first century remained possibly the third-richest per head; its unemployment rate was in the lowest group among the large rich countries; and its proportion of the active age-groups in work one of the highest. How is this possible?

2.3   Is fighting poverty without economic growth a serious option?

2.4 How if at all can the engineered oil-price rises of 1973–4 be blamed for the bleak economic period through which much of the world went in the 1980s?

2.5 What are possible lessons from the 'debt crisis' of the 1980s?

2.6 What are possible lessons from the currency crises of the 1990s?

Additional reading

Commission on Growth and Development (2008) *The Growth Report: Strategies for Sustained Growth and Inclusive Development*, World Bank, Washington, DC, 'Overview' (9 pages) This was to be published in July 2008, but a preliminary version, the Conference Edition, is or has been available earlier and accessible at www.growthcommission.org. The final report can be ordered through www.worldbank.org/publications. The Overview of nine pages is clear and puts a straightforward position. The members of the Commission were over 20 highly distinguished people from the top levels of government, central banks, business and economic academia.

Maddison, Angus (2002) *The World Economy: a Millennial Perspective*, OECD, Paris. Chapter 3 (pp. 125–67). Angus Maddison has set himself the titanic task of compiling national-income figures for the world and parts thereof going back through the last two millennia. His summaries of more recent, as well as more remote, periods are extremely well-informed and interesting.

CHAPTER 3

Ideologies and Methods in Development Economics

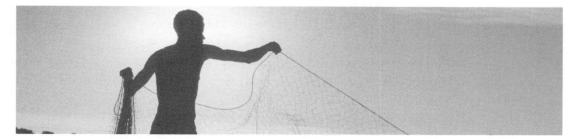

From initial trust in state direction, centralized planning, capital accumulation, and self-sufficiency, the ideology most practically influential in development economics had switched by the 1980s to one of leaving everything possible to the market, opening to the world, and privatizing. Then, over the 1990s, came a shift to a more qualified view of state and market, with an emphasis on the quality of government and on civil society. Throughout, from some rather mechanical views at the start, there was an increasingly realistic awareness of the nature of humanity – with its real needs, failings, and potential – in both ends and means. Because of differences of degree in the characteristics of the societies with which they deal, the methods of development economics differ *in their typical pattern and balance* from those of mainstream economics – over the character of their fields of observation, their theories, and their methods of testing.

Introduction

Economics aspires to be a science but it is always in danger of turning into an ideology or a set of rival ideologies: packages of values and beliefs about the world, each of which may acquire the certainties of a faith. Development economics has not been immune from these tendencies. They may be inevitable in a study concerned with policy of which the subject matter is people. Yet the prevailing views have repeatedly been refreshed and subject to modification and correction by new ideas and experience.

Here we shall follow shifts in the ideology and policy bias of development economics through the three periods of development experience distinguished in Chapter 2.

We shall then outline the methods of development economics, pointing particularly to differences in emphasis from mainstream economics: distinctive ways in which observation, theorizing and testing have been pursued.

BOX 3.1 TOOLKIT ON IDEOLOGIES AND METHODS

Capital-fundamentalism. See 'Investment fetish' below.

Dependency theory. Theory fashionable for some years from the late 1960s to the early 1980s attributing underdevelopment to European and North American colonialism, and the continuation, internationally and internally within developing countries, of the political, property and productive relationships that it had introduced and supported.

Informal sector. That part of countries' economies in which the units consist of individual or one-household firms with few regular employees or none, with minimal records and (except possibly in agriculture) generally without official recognition or registration. Most traditional farming in developing countries can be regarded as within the informal sector.

Intermediate technology. Techniques that represent an advance in efficiency over traditional technology but differ from the most modern methods as used in the rich world in ideally having a smaller efficient scale and being more labour-intensive and generally more accessible to people in developing countries.

Investment fetish (or **Capital-fundamentalism**). The idea that economic growth is closely related to the amount of investment (or capital) and that therefore, because of a further supposition that the amount of saving determines the amount of investment, of which there can never be enough, reducing consumption is necessarily or *prima facie* good. See Box 3.3 below.

Market-fundamentalism. The strong presumption that modes of organizing the economy that rely on market mechanisms are always preferable, where there is a choice, to those that do not.

Marshall Plan/Aid. See Box 2.1 in Chapter 2.

Microfinance. Arrangements for making small production loans to very poor people, usually with the achievement of very low rates of default.

Multiple equilibria. Behaviour in certain markets appears to fit with the view that there is *a range of prices* at any time that may represent an equilibrium consistent with a given set of circumstances that may be regarded as fundamental. Where within that range the price tends to settle will then depend on forces generated *within the market* such as expectations of the future course of prices. Such markets are likely to be those for commodities or assets in which prices fluctuate considerably. Runs on currencies and speculative bubbles of all kinds seem to require a view of multiple equilibria, with the market shifting from one to the other purely as a result of shifts in beliefs about future price levels.

Rent-seeking. See Box 6.1 in Chapter 6.

Structuralism (as opposed in this context to *monetarism* in a particular meaning of the term). View of macroeconomic behaviour (and hence management) that regards inflation in developing countries as due not to excessive expansion of monetary demand but rather to economic growth in the presence of rigidities that follow from the roles allocated to developing countries in the world system.

▶

▶ **Unequal exchange.** Theory briefly advanced in the 1970s by Arghiri Emmanuel to the effect that the relative poverty of countries was *explained by* the prices for which their goods exchanged in international trade, which in turn were determined by the different relative power from one country to another of employees in wage determination. This was taken to imply that real-wage differences between countries were the cause, rather than the effect, of differences in those countries' average incomes.

Urban bias. Superiority (commonly taken to exist in developing countries) of public facilities and infrastructure in towns and cities over those in rural areas. The term is also used for the theory proposed by Michael Lipton in 1977 that urban bias is a, or the, primary reason 'why poor people stay poor'.

Shifts in the ideology of development

1950 to 1973: state direction, planning, capital and autarky

We have tried to explain in Chapter 2 why at the start of the study of development economics, and hence in the first period, roughly 1950–1973, there was considerable trust placed in the transforming power of indigenous governments through national 'planning', much importance being given to capital accumulation independently of the way the capital would be used. This was together with hopes (in the wake of the Marshall Plan) that this could be furthered in developing countries by international aid; expectations pinned on large-scale mechanized manufacturing; and on the other hand pessimism about the value of promoting exports, of agriculture and primary commodities, and of international trade and investment generally (whose structure and institutions were thought to be differentially biased against the interests of poorer countries), and on the whole about the usefulness and importance of market allocation. Export pessimism, influenced by memories of the Great Depression, implied that new ventures in manufacturing must be largely for the domestic market, which meant that each new industry would need to grow at just the right rate to satisfy the demand for its products generated by rising domestic income. Hence the idea of a need for *balanced growth* and for *national planning* to keep the various sectors growing in harmony, and a *big push* so that expansion in all sectors could be financed at once, and could provide markets for each other's products at appropriate scales.

Though the term may not have been much used, great prominence in fact was given to the importance of *market failure* in the explanation of why poor countries had stayed poor. Government must extract the resources and allocate them in order to succeed where market mechanisms had failed.

The strand of thought known as *structuralism*, based in Latin America, added further to the case for active intervention. This started from the view that structures of property and power or of existing specialization, in Latin America or in developing countries generally, acted as a block to the development that might otherwise have taken place through the market, and particularly to favourable influences from transactions with the rich world. These ideas were prompted in part by the experience of unaccustomed industrial growth in South America during the Second World War when imports from Europe and North America had been greatly restricted, and by the lapse of this growth when trade was opened again. They were fuelled by the discovery on the part of Hans Singer and Raúl Prebisch (see Chapters 5 and 17) of an apparent long-term decline in the (net-barter) terms of trade of primary commodities against manufactured goods – that is in the buying-power of one over the other. This was at a time when (far more than was to be the case around the end of the century) the export trade of poorer countries could largely be assumed to be specialized on primary products. Corrective action, it seemed to follow, needed to be taken by the authorities in order to neutralize these drawbacks.

There was often a rather mechanical view of the remedial action needed for lagging industrialization, with the emphasis on the amount of capital investment as the key feature. This bias may have owed something to an implicit interpretation of the Keynesian example as seen through Stalinist spectacles: the idea that there could be a simple quantifiable remedy applied from above.

We suggest that the story of the modifications that the prevailing ideas underwent throughout may be seen as successive corrections of the mechanical simplicities of some of the early theories and models, so as to reach an increasingly realistic appreciation of the nature of the human raw material – with its failings but also its potential – of human institutions including political behaviour, and of human needs.

A few prominent academic dissidents consistently argued against the presumptions of most development economics in this early stage, of whom one of the most persistent and eloquent was P.T. Bauer (e.g., 1961, 1971–6). The World Bank as an institution tended to place more faith in markets and in private enterprise than was common among academic development economists, though it was originally allowed to lend to governments only. The General Agreement on Tariffs and Trade (GATT), to which most countries outside the Communist blocs chose to adhere, ran on the presumption that freeing international trade was advantageous. In Arthur Lewis's 1955 *Theory of Economic Growth* there was an attempt to see the current challenge in the light of the historical experience of development, with many of the themes of subsequent development economics broached. However, it was comprehensive state planning, balanced growth, capital accumulation, inter-governmental aid, and modern large-scale manufacturing, that provided the prevailing furniture in thought about economic growth in the developing countries.

BOX 3.2 DISSENT ON DEVELOPMENT IN THE 1960S AND EARLY 1970S: PETER BAUER

'The ideas examined [in the volume *Dissent on Development*] include the notion (or hypothesis) of the vicious circle of poverty and stagnation in less developed countries; the allegation that rich countries have caused the poverty of the less developed world; the assertions that any substantial progress of poor countries must result in balance-of-payments difficulties, that their terms of trade decline persistently, that economic development depends largely on monetary investment, and that central planning and foreign aid are indispensable for the development of poor countries.

'Since the Second World War these ideas, many of which had their origins in academic writings, have dominated development literature and policy. . . . In the 1960s, when most of these essays were written, the dominance of these ideas was manifest. They are still [1976] dominant, although they are occasionally expressed in a more sophisticated way than they were in the 1950s and 1960s.

▶ 'In these essays I argue that the most prominent and influential of these views are demonstrably invalid. Their inadequacy is obvious on very little reflection. For instance, no elaborate reasoning is required to dispose of the vicious circle of poverty (the notion that societies cannot escape from poverty without external help or prohibitive sacrifices), or the assertion that balance-of-payments difficulties are inevitable concomitants of economic development. Yet . . . these notions are both influential and very widely prevalent.

'The notions in the development literature examined in these essays are endowed with academic respectability which adds to their effectiveness; they are often presented in a variety of different ways which obscure their shortcomings; and they have often come to be protected by a façade of ostensibly technical analysis, which can impress, discourage or deter non-technical readers with no experience of less developed countries. While the presentation and the analysis are often more involved, the ideas are no more substantial now than fifteen or twenty years ago.'

Source: P.T. Bauer, *Dissent on Development*, Student Edition, Weidenfeld and Nicolson, London, 1976, pp. 17–18.

Modifications to these assumptions, however, began to appear. Through this first period, which we are taking as lasting to the mid-1970s, the mechanistic, large-scale, centralized, urban-oriented, aggregated view of development and development policy came to be qualified by increasing recognition of the importance of *the social background* and of the **small-scale, peripheral and rural**.

Over the half-century as a whole – in counterpoint to the other big shifts of the period – there was an awareness of the relevance of *an expanding range of politico-social factors*, and a growing readiness to treat the **distribution** of income and the concrete realities of **poverty** as important considerations in their own right. In this as in other respects, the *human* element came to be taken more seriously, in both means and immediate ends.

Indian experience of planning threw up the constraints placed on national growth by sluggish responsiveness and volatility in crop production and income. India and Pakistan found themselves with big grain deficits that made large demands on their foreign exchange. So agriculture, which in much of the world meant **small-scale peasant agriculture**, had to be taken more seriously.

Then, in 1971, with the ILO Mission to Kenya (Shaw, 2002, pp. 164–7), the development community explicitly recognized the importance of the **informal sector**: individual and family enterprises, generally of very small scale, probably without records and below the effective direct-tax threshold, providing essential or very useful goods and services, supporting operators who might otherwise be destitute, and giving opportunities for accumulation of capital that could be either used for expansion directly or channelled into intermediaries for lending on. Like most Third World food-crop agriculture, the non-agrarian informal sector had to pay its way without protection or subsidy. It had the advantage that it could not afford to misallocate resources. Historically most economic development beyond household self-sufficiency had presumably started with small-scale business rather than massive investments from the state. Moreover, each business opportunity successfully taken directly by a poor household could be presumed to add to material welfare: to 'development' in the broad sense. This strand of thinking linked with the **intermediate-technology** movement, which pre-dated, but came to public attention through, Ernst Schumacher's widely read book, *Small is Beautiful*, published in 1973. The movement promoted a search for techniques that represented improvements on the traditional but were at the same time small scale and on other grounds accessible to the poor. It fitted too with the later emergence of what came to be known as **microfinance**.

The emphasis on *capital* – envisaged primarily as plant, equipment and infrastructure – came to be complicated by the idea of **human capital** – regarded mainly as the result of education and training, often treated as an additional factor of production.

Furthermore, the idea of a need for balanced growth was challenged in the case made by Albert Hirschman (1958) for **unbalanced growth**, which still accepted the idea that the state should make some major decisions on investment in directly productive activities but argued that these should be chosen so as to create *shortages* strategically placed and therefore *opportunities* that would induce private investment in response.

Awareness also emerged of the importance of **entrepreneurship**. David McClelland (1953) attempted to relate the prevalence of certain psychological dispositions in various countries and cultures with those societies' business achievements and economic growth. On the assumption that these dispositions resulted from cultural conditioning, he proposed that it might be possible through early education to generate and nourish them. His views were also applied, with the encouragement of UNIDO (the United Nations Industrial Development Organization), to attempts at working with adults who were believed to start with some entrepreneurial motivation in such a way as to remove psychological blocks to their flowering as entrepreneurs.

Yet through the 1950s and 1960s – though much of the early mechanical simplicity was diluted – the positive role of markets in allocation did not loom large in the discourse of development economics.

1974 to 1989: the shift toward economic liberalism

The big change that began to be evident during the 1970s in the general cast of economic-development discourse can be put down partly to systematic study and analysis relating to developing countries, partly to changes in economic policy thought in the world at large, and partly to new events among the developing countries that eventually could not be ignored.

BOX 3.3 INVESTMENT GOOD, CONSUMPTION BAD? THE INVESTMENT FETISH

'In the Third World the investment fetish is very damaging. The enforced enlargement of investment expenditures and the need to secure particular components of investment projects . . . involve additional taxation and the imposition of controls. These extensions of state economic control damage material progress and often provoke acute political and social conflict in the heterogeneous societies of the Third World. . . .

'Although Third World poverty is often much exaggerated, it is nevertheless true that people at large are much poorer than in the West. They are correspondingly hit harder by economic waste, such as that brought about by the uncritical acceptance of the case for more investment or for the domestic production of capital goods. . . .

▶

'The distinction between investment and consumption is even more tenuous in developing countries than in the West. Much expenditure classified as consumption sustains or increases current productivity by maintaining the health of people and of animals, and by preserving crops or stocks of goods (e.g. spending on insecticides, pesticides and hardware). Moreover, consumption widely serves as inducement for higher economic performance. Especially in the course of emergence from subsistence activity to production for the market, a higher or more varied actual or prospective level of consumption promotes improved economic performance, such as more work (in replacement of leisure), greater readiness to produce for the market rather than for subsistence, more direct investment, and greater saving out of higher cash incomes. . . .

'Thus over a wide range of activity consumption and investment in developing countries are complementary rather than competitive.

'Sir Arthur Lewis is among those who have argued that the extension of human choice is the very essence of economic development. Enforced austerity is proposed and imposed on the ground or pretext that it is necessary for a promised increase in output. The increase is to take place in the unspecified future, and in a form only tenuously related to general living standards. What right have the rulers to coerce their subjects for this purpose?'

Source: P.T. Bauer, *Equality, the Third World and Economic Delusion*, Weidenfeld and Nicolson, London, 1981, pp. 252–4.

First, study and analysis from development economics itself

Careful intellectual challenges to the prevailing consensus came with attempts from the late 1960s to **quantify** the implications of the market distortions and special circumstances that had been supposed to justify widespread intervention, and to set them against the extent of the interventions actually made. Two ventures (with overlapping casts) were probably especially important. *Industry and Trade in Some Developing Countries*, produced in 1970 by Ian Little, Tibor Scitovsky, and Maurice Scott, put some **numbers on the *cost* of protection of manufactures** in the seven countries they examined, and the implied cost per job created. At one extreme (for Pakistan and India) they found (to simplify somewhat) that the average cost of having manufacturing processes performed was *doubled* by the system of protection.

The basis for a similar critique, though from the different angle of individual projects, was laid by two parallel attempts (by Ian Little and James Mirrlees, under OECD auspices in 1968, and by Partha Dasgupta, Paul Marglin and Amartya Sen for UNIDO in 1972) to lay down **a method of social project-appraisal** (cost–benefit analysis) that took into account (with numbers) the grounds for which a developing country was held to require special intervention. (The approach is explained further later in this chapter and the method explored in detail in Chapter 20.) The insights of earlier development thinking did not have to be thrown out, but in each particular case they should be required to face (in quantified form) the insights of traditional economics about the usefulness of market prices in allocation.

The concept of **rent-seeking behaviour** formulated by Anne Krueger (1974) put the matter in a political context: the very clear possibility that ill-considered government intervention that raised the prices of particular goods would create rewards for certain parties that were unrelated to any productive contribution they made; that those interested in these rewards would encourage such intervention; and that it would be politically difficult to reverse the intervention once there were numbers of people who gained from its continuance. The rewards might be lawful (such as the benefit of tariff protection to those with investments in the protected industry), or they might be corrupt (such as the sale by officials of permits and licences), but in either case – unless the prospective measures were specifically justified by some externality – they would have the effect of wasting resources by diverting them from more productive to less productive activities.

Second, reactions in the wider climate of thought: the end of the golden age

In the course of the 1970s, the end of what had seemed, in most developed countries, an era of relatively untroubled economic growth tended to shift fashionable opinion in the main centres of economic thought toward opposite extremes. On one side it moved toward **traditional economic liberalism**, emphasizing the value of openness to international trade and investment, combined with the **monetarist** reaction against Keynesian policies. On the other, the resort was to **dependency theory** which became embedded in briefly fashionable neo-Marxism. Both these lines of thought were taken up (by different groups of course) in the thinking of the time about the developing countries.

There was also, in development economics, an increased emphasis on the actual **distribution** of income, why it was so much less equal in some countries than others, what this had to do (inevitably or not) with economic growth and the level of average income, and how far growth and equity could be enjoyed together. Notable titles from the 1970s that are eloquent of this preoccupation are Hans Singer's *Employment, Incomes and Equality* (1972), a report arising from the same 1971 ILO Mission to Kenya; *Redistribution with Growth* by Hollis Chenery and others (1974); and *Growth with Equity: the Taiwan Case* by John Fei, Gustav Ranis and Shirley Kuo (1979). Distribution became prominent for a while in World Bank thinking during the tenure of Robert Macnamara as its President in the same decade.

Dependency theory represented a strand of the *structuralism* introduced above, associating the handicaps of Latin America and other areas on the 'periphery' of the international system with past colonialism and the economic relationships that it established. Because dependency theory dealt with class-like phenomena of exploitation between and within countries, it provided a way of fitting a view of underdevelopment into the Marxist or quasi-Marxist categories of discourse which in the late 1960s and early 1970s gave an intellectual patina to the movements of radical student and other dissent.

Neo-Marxism of this kind, equipped with dependency theory, saw the world as a vast exploitative system in which all the relatively rich flourished only in zero-sum fashion at the expense of the relatively poor, and any action taken by the governments of rich countries, or by the elites or (with few exceptions) the governments of poor countries, could only be at the expense of the world's poor. Only comprehensive world revolution could remedy these ills and injustices; the international aid and national planning and benevolent state intervention on which much development economics had relied was at least as futile or destructive as unmitigated market capitalism, possibly worse because it concealed the realities of exploitation. Perhaps the most prominent intellectual standard-bearer for this movement was Andre Gunder Frank (1967) (see Chapter 5). The theory of unequal exchange (Emmanuel, 1972) argued further that the differences in wage rates between rich and poor countries were (through trade) the cause, rather than the effect, of those countries' relative wealth and poverty.

The difficulty about much of the neo-Marxism of the late 1960s and 1970s (which bore only a limited relationship to the thought of Marx and Engels) was that by its nature it could make no policy recommendations in the usual sense. Its only remedy was simultaneous world revolution. It also promoted few careers.

Neo-Marxism largely dropped out of sight in the 1980s, but, under international pressure – with ever-increasing bargaining power in the hands of the IMF and World Bank – and the influence of overseas postgraduate education on the technocrats of developing countries (US economics courses becoming increasingly technical and unquestioningly neoclassical in their presumptions), a *liberal* approach[1] to economic policy, emphasizing freedom of markets for goods and capital, both domestically and internationally, and advocating privatization of most state enterprises, became more and more firmly established among the policy-makers of developing countries and in standard development-economic thinking. This tendency was opposed by a few prominent thinkers, some of them surviving from the early post-war period even into the twenty-first century (such as J.K. Galbraith and Hans Singer), and had to battle against vested interests and popular feeling in much of the developing world. Nonetheless, liberalism came to dominate the scene (in simple form verging on the extreme) until challenged by the currency crises of the 1990s and the failings of sudden-shock 'transition'.

Third, the message of events

The shift in the liberal direction and toward export optimism was sealed by striking public events: recognition growing through the 1970s that rapid and sustained growth – drawing on varying degrees of openness to the outside world but with manufactured exports apparently crucial in all cases – had appeared over the previous 10–15 years among the original four East Asian 'Tigers'. The lesson was reinforced in the 1980s when similar events began to be observed in much of South-East Asia and mainland China.

It is perhaps surprising that a major economic disaster of the 1980s – the debt crisis – though it attracted protest, seems to have had little impact on economic-development theory or policy paradigms, and that, even at the end of the century, only very tentative moves to improve the institutions involved were being discussed. No standard ideology could claim that it would have had the recipe for avoiding the crisis or providing a speedy remedy. Hindsight shows us plenty of what ought and ought not to have been done. However, it would have required open-mindedness and foresight rather than any particular dogma.

The 1990s: the liberal lessons modified

The years around 1990 probably represented the high point of faith in markets.

The two big experiences of the world economy in the 1990s were the '**transitions to market**' of the former Communist countries and the **currency crises** that began with Mexico's in 1994–5. Both challenged the extremes of market liberalism as they had generally been championed at the start of the decade by the World Bank and IMF, and, in principle at least, by the US Treasury: what John Williamson called the 'Washington consensus', tending towards what in its most extreme form has been termed **market fundamentalism**.

---

[1] In the British and European sense of 'liberal'.

Whatever other mistakes and weaknesses may have contributed to the currency crises, it appears now that the opening up of a middle-income developing country to **completely free international capital movements** risks a collapse of the currency if at some time a large inflow of short-term capital changes to an outflow. We shall mention in later chapters the advantages claimed for Chile, in the 1997–9 crises, from its defiance of the advice on indiscriminate freedom of capital markets.

More generally, it has probably come to be accepted that the overwhelming presumption in favour of freeing markets, charging for public services other than pure public goods, and privatizing whatever productive enterprises, including public utilities, are capable of being commercialized – without regard to sequence or to other institutions – needs to be modified. *Government failure* is only too common, but governments still have to judge when the risks of various forms of market inadequacy are so great as to demand intervention, and whether their own structures have the capacity for making an intervention successful.

The existence in asset markets of '**multiple equilibria**' – with the players' expectations for the time being *about their fellow-players' expectations* combining to determine which equilibrium if any will be stable – permits rational individual behaviour to lead to socially damaging instability, as happened in the currency crises.

About market fundamentalism a somewhat similar insight to that arising from the currency crises has been drawn from the experience of transition in Eastern Europe and especially the lands of the former Soviet Union. The bias of Western advisers is believed to have been toward the '**sudden shock**': freeing all outputs and prices and privatizing hastily. This, as Stiglitz (2002, pp. 182–7) has argued, was in conflict with the experience of China, which accomplished by very cautious steps what was economically an extremely successful transition, with a growth record probably unsurpassed. By contrast, all the satellite countries of the Soviet Bloc and the successors to the Soviet Union faced big, often catastrophic, initial falls in output, falls that were not fully reversed over a number of years; and rushed privatization often made possible the sheer plunder of state assets by those with political influence or out-and-out gangsters.

BOX 3.4 DISSENT ON DEVELOPMENT IN 2004: HA-JOON CHANG AND ILENE GRABEL

'"There is no alternative." This is the famous pronouncement by former British Prime Minister Margaret Thatcher when she was faced with widespread opposition to her programme of neoliberal reform during the 1980s. Thatcher's dictum captures the triumphalism, hubris and closed-mindedness with which the neoliberal orthodoxy has dominated discussions of economic policy around the world during the past quarter of a century.

'This book [*Reclaiming Development*] begins with the premiss that the "no alternative" dictum is fundamentally and dangerously incorrect. As we demonstrate in great detail throughout the book, feasible alternatives to neoliberal policies exist that can promote rapid economic development that is equitable, stable and sustainable. . . .

'First, there is now abundant and increasing evidence that the economic policies associated with the neoliberal agenda have failed to achieve their chief goals, and have introduced serious problems, especially in the developing world. Second, there is a great deal of historical and current evidence that there are multiple routes to development. We argue

▶ that successful development is the result of diverse types of economic policies, the majority of which run counter to the policies advocated by neoliberal economists today. Third, at the present juncture the unbridled confidence of neoliberal economists seems to be faltering. In fact, a good deal has been published of late by neoliberal economists who tell us that they have grown disenchanted with certain aspects of the neoliberal policies in what is commonly known as the 'Washington Consensus'. . . .

'. . . Part II is the heart of the book. Here we provide activists, policymakers and students of development with an array of concrete policy options that are superior to their neoliberal counterparts. In these chapters we look specifically at policies towards trade and industry . . . , privatization and intellectual property rights . . . , foreign bank borrowing and portfolio and foreign direct investment . . . , domestic financial regulation . . . , and exchange rates and currencies, central banking and monetary policy, and government revenue and expenditure. . . . In each case we explain why the neoliberal policy recommendations have failed, often with disastrous consequences for developing countries. We then counterpoise an array of alternative policies that can promote faster economic development than can neoliberals, while ensuring that it is equitable and sustainable.'

Source: Ha-Joon Chang and Ilene Grabel, *Reclaimimg Development Economics: an alternative economic policy manual*, The University Press Ltd., Dhaka, 2004, pp. 1–3.

There were also more subtle and comprehensive shifts in thinking that probably arose chiefly too from the 'transition' experience. Expressions not heard much before the 1990s that became commonplaces are *civil society* and *governance*. There was also more emphasis than before on the importance of *institutions* generally and on the *capacity* of those institutions and the people working within them.

Governance has come to mean the character, quality, effectiveness, or particular institutions, of government. **Civil society** applies to all non-traditional institutions that are both non-commercial and independent of government and that proceed by peaceful methods. It covers voluntary associations including in some uses those formed to promote the interests of their members as well as those pursuing wider causes. It can be extended to include the public expression of independent opinion, and the arrangements, such as a free press and other media, that make such public expression possible. It can also be taken to include those habits of mind and behaviour that routinely take account of the interests of the wider society.

The **institutions** to which concern was directed were particularly those of law and government but could include those of commercial activity and of civil society.

What appears to have been widely assumed by 'Western' experts brought in as consultants and institutions imposing conditions on loans in the early 1990s was that the swift opening of markets in the ex-Soviet world would fairly quickly boost output and raise general living standards. After all, powerful governments would still be there to curb excesses and to regulate where regulation was necessary. In Russia and Ukraine, the opposite occurred. *Neither the market nor the state 'worked' satisfactorily.* Government officials, the security services, big business and organized crime came to be too closely linked in cohabiting or competing fiefdoms. (On Russia, see, for the witness of a crusading journalist who soon after paid with her life, Anna Politkovskaya, 2004.) Power, arising from governmental or military position or from wealth, was not sufficiently checked by the law as actually administered. Police and judges were widely corrupt, habituated to obeying the strong rather than to interpreting the law, let alone doing justice, impartially. Again, the reliance on removal of central control and reduction in state economic activity as if they could generate a productive and beneficent 'market' had been misplaced.

Hence perhaps the increasingly strong realization that the distribution of responsibility between government and the market was only part of the story. The *quality* of government was also crucial. For this the formal institutions mattered, but even more the habits, the ethos, possessed by those with a role in those governing institutions. *Governance* is about the rules and structures but it is also about the habitual behaviour of the *governors* (politicians, civil servants, judges, the military, the police) and the expectations attaching to them.

From this probably springs the much increased attention to *civil society* (sufficient to require a name for it). For the market to work satisfactorily, government must legislate and support the market institutions and regulate abuses. If, however, the courts, the police, the legislators, and the administrators are corrupt or negligent or without habits of respect for law and the public good, both government and business can easily become systems of plunder. Even when elections are held with universal suffrage, there is no guarantee that the necessary habits can be instilled. What may also be needed is a free press, investigative journalists, disinterested pressure groups and campaigning bodies, to keep the officials within bounds. Totalitarian societies had controlled the press and forbidden any expression of dissenting opinion or any spontaneous voluntary organization. As the state and the market need each other in order to serve the public adequately, they also need the institutions of civil society if they are to perform as they should. The Soviet system had done its best to stamp out civil society. The gap in what otherwise had some of the features of modern economies became painfully obvious when the previous constraints were relaxed.

These insights seemed only too relevant to many developing countries. Development-economic thought came to share then in the wider climate of enhanced awareness of the importance of *institutions* generally, and specifically of *governance* and of *civil society*.

A crack of a different kind in the hardline market approach was the cautious acceptance by the multilaterals of the principle of debt-forgiveness as applied to a number of highly indebted poor countries (HIPCs), many of them in Africa. We shall outline in later chapters how debt-forgiveness under a thin cover had, after long delay, been applied (not only as an extraordinary exception) to the remains of the 1980s debt crisis, with the introduction by the US of 'Brady bonds' in 1989. The later crisis, affecting mainly very poor countries, was less of a challenge to the world financial system, but the human deprivation and reduction in growth prospects caused by intractable debt seems to have been taken more seriously than a decade earlier by the relevant powers when they approved the HIPC Initiative of conditional debt-forgiveness adopted by the World Bank and IMF in 1996 (see Chapter 22).

If anything, 'development' came to be judged increasingly over the 1990s by the extent and intensity of extreme poverty and by objective welfare indicators such as the prevalence of schooling, literacy, immunization, and levels of child and maternal mortality. It is probably significant that the decade ended with the promulgation by the UN General Assembly of the Millennium Development Goals, almost all of which are of this character: **material-welfare *outcomes* rather than *potential***, surviving babies rather than national-income-growth rates. Amartya Sen's innovative work (1981 and later) generated a much more complex outlook on why famines occurred and what responses to them worked. With others (notably in Drèze and Sen, 1989) he brought out means by which in some countries the impact of famines had been averted, a measure of social security provided, and aspects of chronic poverty substantially ameliorated, even in very poor countries.

A further feature of the debate in the late 1990s, running on into the next century, has been the **anti-globalization** movement. So far it represents no single coherent doctrine, but it has provided a vehicle, in both rich and poor countries, for those fearful or resentful of change, for politicians seeking popular causes, for distrust of power and wealth, and for guilt and compassion seeking simple outlets. Removing the artificial barriers between the political units of the world – in movement of goods, capital, and management, if not always of labour – has indeed been the avowed objective of what might be called the 'world economic establishment', especially since the early 1980s. The liberal conventional wisdom has been that this promotes economic growth and is ultimately for the general good. Opposition can be interpreted to include at one end measured criticism such as that of Joseph Stiglitz (2002, 2006) and of Ha-Joon Chang and Ilene Grabel (2004) about certain aspects of the 'consensus' and of how it has been pursued by the Washington multilaterals, and at the other end all the anti-establishment causes that have joined around the turn of the millennium in demonstrations outside intergovernmental summits. Opposing *globalization* has therefore been a response open to all those dissatisfied with the world as it is or as they think it is becoming, and feeling powerless to change it and unable to envisage a coherent programme of desirable reform.

One other increasingly invoked concept, signalling a further need to qualify the freedom of markets, is **sustainability**. Again development thinking has been sharing in the general climate of thought characteristic of the 1990s and the time since. The risks of destruction or depletion of natural resources as population and expenditure increased, and of pollution from industrial and urban-domestic processes, had been a matter of disquiet for decades. In 1972, the 'Club of Rome Report' (Meadows *et al.*, 1972) had caused alarm by projecting from existing trends and coefficients that many raw materials would soon run out and that there would be an environmental crisis with widespread disasters by the mid-1980s. This was certainly far from what happened, with the story of oil in the 1970s and 1980s showing the responsiveness of both demand and supply of that key industrial input to price.

However, there remained increased awareness of the loss of environmental goods and the depletion of certain crucial resources (soils, forests, fresh-water sources) that had arisen from the current patterns of production, consumption and economic and population growth. By the late 1980s this general concern and many specific local concerns had been augmented by two particular environmental dangers of global scope and human generation: ozone-layer destruction and climate change. Amazingly, ozone-layer destruction was fairly satisfactorily addressed by international agreement under the Montreal Protocol of 1987, but the multiple risks of climate change, in spite of an attempt at something similar in the Kyoto Protocol of 1997, have by no means been averted. It has become more and more generally accepted that, even without further economic and population growth, existing techniques of production and patterns of consumption will generate continuing rises in world temperatures on a much faster trend-path than previously recorded – and reversible only after long delay if at all – and that there will be further depletion in limited land-based water supplies, and forest and soil resources. Climate change, already highly visible in the melting of polar and mountain ice-caps, is showing signs of making areas such as much of the Horn of Africa uninhabitable through reduced or more unreliable rainfall, and may well flood the delta areas and coastal cities where hundreds of millions of people live.

Without radical co-ordinated international action to reduce drastically the emissions responsible over the first few decades of the century, *and* to counter the disturbances to living conditions (through flood protection and securing and sharing of water supplies), the survival of huge numbers of people seems likely to require resettlement on a scale that is politically unthinkable. Beyond the great political challenge of reaching an adequate emission-reduction agreement, there is still – because of delays in the effects of emissions already in the atmosphere – the need to agree on, and finance, such flood protection, desalination, water distribution, and resettlement as may soon be necessary – even with very rapid action on climate change starting from now – for tolerable living conditions and harmony to persist.

This seems likely to demand a degree of disciplined co-operation among states across the world that is unprecedented. It will be important – in order to lubricate the politics of this if for no other reason – that proposals to meet these needs should seek the best trade-offs (the most efficient compromises) between emission reduction and economic growth. Rapid industrial growth in China and much of Asia has increased the urgency of finding equitable and acceptable ways of making the necessary changes to modes of production and consumption.[2]

The study of development will probably be increasingly centred on sustainablility.

Methods of development economics

As with all systematic study of the world, development economics rests on three elements:

1 Observations, more or less systematic, more or less matters of common experience.
2 Theories and models, devised in the attempt to make coherent sense of relationships behind the observations or to draw implications from them.
3 Testing of hypotheses based on the theories and models in order to judge how well they fit the world.

Yet every area of study has its own twists and emphases within these categories of activity and its own spectrum of techniques for pursuing them.

Observations

The **observations** that are the raw material of *economics* have been to a large extent those of common experience. Adam Smith, who is generally regarded as the founder of economics as we know it, started with the familiar behaviour of individual people on the one hand and, on the other, such social phenomena as how the productivity of particular industries increased as their markets grew, and how a large variety of components from across the world could be readily available in one place when and where they were needed. The task of the theorizing was then to show how these larger phenomena, the working of the system, followed from the habitual actions of individuals. No special techniques were needed for these observations to be made. Though they were supplemented by experiences of differing policies and outcomes among the various states that Smith had encountered on his travels, and also by historical records, such as the course of food prices in Britain over several

---

[2] The challenge is put forcefully, with analysis of facts and issues and proposals for action, in two independent official reports (UK, 2006; Australia, 2008: the Stern and Garnaut Reports). A highly readable and informative account of the science is given by Tim Flannery (2005).

centuries, much of this raw material was readily available to the amateur or indeed simply comprised what everybody knew.

Modern economists have a far greater stock of systematic information available to them, much of it from official sources, and more techniques for summarizing and analysing it. Though there are elements of laboratory experiment and fieldwork and direct data collection through surveys, their exploring to unearth their raw material is still largely done in the statistics provided by governments and international organizations, or by companies and trade bodies – that is through books, now supplemented by Internet sites.

Development economics shares in this respect much of the character of economics in general. But it is, by the nature of its fundamental questions, more concerned with *comparisons across countries and regions and communities, and also across longer stretches of time: decades and even centuries rather than months and years.* It is concerned with why the same basic raw material (individual human behaviour), faced with more or less the same range of known or knowable productive techniques, works *to such different effects* from place to place and from time to time. What quickly became apparent, insofar as it was not obvious from the beginning, was that a large part of the observational ingredients for an answer would probably lie outside the typical raw material of economics – quantitative information about production, distribution and trade – extending rather to realms such as culture, social relations, law, law enforcement and politics: in the broadest sense of the word, institutions. This was if anything even more consistently the case when the spotlight in the quest for *development* was focused on *poverty* rather than on *average income*: the question of whether and in what circumstances the potential for material well-being could be made to 'trickle down' to the poorest or at least to the 'masses'.

'Unsystematic' observations – what everybody in the society in question knows once their attention is called to it – can still be important here, just as they were to Adam Smith, but the key requirement is that they should be observations made by people who have lived and worked, or otherwise immersed themselves, in *different types of society*, and can therefore recognize when what is taken for granted in one is not necessarily inevitable or universal. What is needed is the capacity to see the institutions of one society (themselves possibly grounded in peculiarities of material circumstances or history) 'in relief': that is in their *contrast* with those of other societies. Theorizing may then be able to link these institutional differences with differences in economic outcomes.

History – how societies have *changed* in the elements regarded as comprising development – is also particularly important to development economics. As Chapter 2 and the earlier part of the present chapter indicate, history as viewed at the start of the present century gives a rather different account of development and its possibilities from the story it was widely supposed to be telling 50 years earlier.

There are also reasons why development economics has been more dependent on *fieldwork* observation than has mainstream economics. Given its concern with poverty – an essential element if any broad view of 'development' is taken – it must focus on the material conditions of the poorest, or at least poorer, part of the population, not simply on the income average. Official statistics in developing countries may often be less complete and reliable than those in more affluent countries, and particularly weak in their cover of the relatively poor, who are typically outside the organized, 'formal' sector. The 'informal sector', comprising mostly very-small-scale family enterprises, often without records, includes traditional agriculture, which supports a large part, still quite often a majority, of the population. In affluent societies, most of the productively engaged people are in employment, earning wages, so that their incomes depend on the activity of the public and private concerns that employ them. In addition, the state takes a more or less comprehensive responsibility for providing or backstopping basic material provision, and it needs precise information about the poor for this purpose. In developing countries by contrast, especially in the rural areas, much more depends upon what individual families can devise *for themselves* – by their own contriving – and what can be done by *local communal activity*. Official statistics may tell little that is relevant to what *works* for these purposes and *why*. Information may have to be collected on the ground.

Theories and models

Theories and models are two categories not clearly distinguishable. Any coherent theory could be described as a model, and any model designed to explain relationships in the world could be described as a theory. The term *theory* tends to be used where the explanation or supposition of a real-world relationship is paramount, and *model* where the emphasis is on the logical consistency of the mechanisms presented; but in practice these are matters of more and less. A model in economics is often designed to *represent* some particular element or elements of the mechanisms operating in the world, so that its terms are *analogues* of real-world variables; and the mechanisms it supposes are analogues of those in the world but with a number of other real-world elements held constant. *Analytical concepts* can play a similar role to that of theories and models in that they may draw attention to underlying processes or distinctions. The meanings given to such development-economics terms as *informal sector, rent-seeking, urban bias, dependency, absorptive capacity, leading sector, intermediate technology,* and arguably *microfinance,* carry implications or suggestions – fruitful or not – about the way things can be expected to work. Defining them and elucidating their meanings can be regarded as implied theorizing. Thirlwall (2006, pp. 8, 9) very interestingly lists 15 concepts, including some of those just mentioned, that development economics has contributed to mainstream economics.

It was in the early stages of development economics, with its search for a new paradigm, that the sub-discipline was most sharply differentiated from what was then regarded as orthodox (that is, neoclassical) economics, either addressing different policy questions (such as how to spark off industrialization) or supposing different circumstances that required modification of conventional models in order to make them relevant (as with the Lewis model or the Prebisch model or the Harris–Todaro model; see Chapter 5.)

Theories and models in economics may be directed primarily either to *explanation* or to *policy*. Several of the grand theories of the early period (mentioned below in Chapter 5) were directly related to *policy*. Such were the Big-push and Balanced-growth theories of Rosenstein-Rodan and Nurkse, and their antithesis, the Unbalanced-growth theory of Hirschman. Such too arguably are Vicious-circle models relating to the interactions of income growth, population growth and saving rates. In the same category we can include the Centre-Periphery theories used by Prebisch and Singer to account for the apparent secular fall in the relative prices of primary commodities in international trade. Where new *analytical concepts* in development economics play a theorizing role, they are usually propounded in arguments leading fairly directly to policy positions.

In others of the notable models of the early period, the element of *explanation* was probably dominant, or at least prior, as a motive. This applies to Lewis's unlimited-supplies-of-labour model and the income-migration-employment model of Harris and Todaro. The authors of these models were undoubtedly interested in policy, but the models could be valued as aids to understanding independent of the policy implications that might be derived from them, and the policy implications drawn might be various, depending on the other circumstances supposed and possibly also the values of those drawing the implications.

A further category is *historical models*. These have often entailed in one form or other the elaboration of *stages* of development, a single track expected to be followed with different timing by societies in different parts of the world. The presumption is usually that the more 'backward' societies will eventually pass through the same stages as those that are ahead, or even that there are stages not yet reached anywhere that all societies can at length be expected to attain. Examples before the twentieth century are the stage models of Adam Smith, Auguste Comte, and most famously Karl Marx, whose model looked forward to future stages not yet exemplified in his own time. In the 1950s Walt Rostow (Chapter 5 again) presented a stages model designed to fit the experience and the preoccupations of the early post-war period.

These may involve implicit or even explicit *explanations* in the account of the forces that drive the process forward, and *policy implications* may be drawn from them if they are seen to indicate that conscious action may speed or hinder it.

A historical model that does not involve stages is presented in John Hicks's *A Theory of Economic History* (1969), which presents material advance as due to the progressive extension of markets and market institutions. Other studies have sought to provide comprehensive or fundamental explanations of why certain areas of the world have developed ahead of others. Jane Jacobs' *Cities and the Wealth of Nations* (1984) puts cities and their trading behaviour at the centre of explanation of the differential development of regions, with a wealth of historical raw material. David Landes in *The Wealth and Poverty of Nations* (1998) sets out to explain the primacy of Europe in industrialization. Jared Diamond in *Guns, Germs and Steel* (1998) explores especially the geographic reasons – related to the likelihood that early innovations could arise in various biological environments and the ease with which they could spread – for the technological primacy of Eurasia, the foundation for the eventual leadership of Northwestern Europe and its colonies of settlement. It is easy enough to derive policy recommendations from Hicks's treatment and to an extent from Jacobs'. But Landes' and Diamond's, fascinating as they are in enhancing our understanding of how the divide has come into being, do not have much obvious bearing on how to close it.

Testing

Empirical **testing** of theories can be taken here to include appraisal of the effects of policies. During the lifetime of development economics as a study, economics has become far more systematic and sophisticated in its empirical testing of hypotheses as well as in simulation and projection.

Econometrics

Econometric methods (a branch of analytical statistics) are, however, not the natural means of empirical testing for *all* the hypotheses that may arise in development economics; other statistical methods may be more appropriate, especially when some of the variables are not naturally quantified. Nevertheless, especially as time series available have become longer and there have been clearly defined policy changes in a number of developing countries, econometric methods have been increasingly used to help answer some of the large questions relating to policy, such as the impact of increased openness of countries to external transactions, or increased freedom in various markets, on the rate of growth and the distribution of income.

Case studies

At the other extreme, there are instances in which the investigation will have of necessity to be a case study, where for example a particular method of catalysing community development is being tested and there is only one case to be examined. This may involve *before and after* measures of some quantitative variables, and also various qualitative judgements of success and failure, and suggestions, some possibly from the participants, on the reasons for these outcomes. The investigator will have to use imagination and the body of experience on this type of venture, to interpret the results.

Non-parametric statistical methods

As the outcomes of a number of similar ventures become available, with a small number of clearly (but qualitatively) defined treatments on which they differ, then non-parametric statistical methods of analysis may be applicable.

Briefly methods of testing range from those now typical of mainstream economics to those more typical of the other social sciences, with probably a greater tendency to the latter than in the economic mainstream because of the nature of the informational material in development economics.

Extended methods of project appraisal

However, an important element in the assessment of policies, and of the premises on which those policies have been based, has been provided by developments, peculiar in the first instance to development economics, in methods of project appraisal. These were the devices (mentioned earlier in this chapter) introduced by Little and Mirrlees (1969, 1974), and by Dasgupta, Marglin and Sen (1971), in order to allow cost–benefit analysis to embody the main considerations that had been held, in developing countries specifically, to justify particularly wide state intervention in the market (see Chapter 20). Such considerations were non-equilibrium exchange-rates, wages above the marginal social product of labour, and valuation of a marginal unit of income available for investment above one available for consumption (on the ground that the existing growth rate was sub-optimal). A later development by Little and Mirrlees of their framework, codified by others and adopted by the World Bank and some of the Regional Development Banks, also allowed income-distribution effects to be taken into account, with greater weight given to the income of the poorer than of the richer.

The authors did not take any position on whether or in what degree market 'distortions' were likely to justify interventions. What they did was to provide a framework that would allow an appraiser to make rational decisions about the extent of the distortions and the figures by which it was reasonable to allow for them in the appraisal. The position of the authors was that it might well be reasonable to compensate by intervention for these conditions, but that the appropriate extent if any of the intervention could and should be rationally judged. The premiss in effect was that of conventional cost–benefit analysis: that market prices should be presumed to offer appropriate signals for efficient allocation – should be taken, in other words, as *social prices – except insofar as there were specific reasons* for reading social prices differently, and that the significance of such reasons should be quantified. The new element was the recognition of additional possible grounds for differences between market and social prices, and the rather fundamental re-casting of the appraisal process that these additional reasons might require. The adoption and encouragement of these methods by the World Bank over projects on which it had influence has probably provided a kind of policy sieve, testing – in the sense of refining – the implied body of loose theory that had to a point been taken unthinkingly as justifying intervention that might take little or no account of efficient allocation.

As suggested above, probably a more immediately persuasive 'test result' of a similar general character had come from Little, Scitovsky and Scott (1970), with their use of a simpler and cruder measure, the *effective rate of protection*, to highlight the extent of the divergence from market prices generated by the protective systems of the countries they considered.

Recognizing pointers provided by events

Yet perhaps some of the most important testing has come from the crude pointers provided by events – often without enough cases to provide a convincing statistical study, yet persuasive nonetheless – especially when the test is a falsification of an asserted universal. The currency crises of the 1990s, discussed above, made it virtually untenable to assert a position that would imply the advantage of a policy of free international capital movements always and everywhere. The experience of 'transition to market' in the Soviet lands and Eastern Europe (seen in contrast with that of China) at least threw great doubt on the view that this process was most efficiently and equitably done by freeing all markets, and privatizing everything privatizable, at once. The East Asian industrial revolution has falsified the generalization that those starting as poor countries in the twentieth-century world could never achieve enough advantageous participation in international trade and investment to proceed through 'open' policies to affluent status. Also, the maxim that a state can never go bankrupt – used to support the case, for both lenders and borrowers, to set no limits to international borrowing by developing-country governments from the private sector – decisively ceased to be conventional wisdom after the debt crisis of the 1980s.

Summary conclusions

- The ideologies and general presumptions attached to development economics changed over the second half of the twentieth century as a result of investigation and analysis of the subject matter itself; of changing fashions in thought about economic policy at large; and of the great public events of the period.

- A bias to state direction and autarky gave way through the 1970s and 1980s to reliance on markets and openness, a position then qualified in various ways in response to events through the last decade of the century.

- Over the course of the whole period, a mechanistic, centralized, and urban-based view of the development process, with emphasis on large units and aggregates, gave way progressively to increasing interest in the diverse socio-political background – often also in the small scale and the rural – and in income distribution and the concrete realities of poverty.

- As with mainstream economics, much of the **observation** that forms the raw material of development economics consists of what is assumed to be common knowledge or is extracted from publicly available quantitative information, much of it from official sources.

▶

- However, development economics depends to a greater extent than mainstream economics on common experience and systematic data *across societies* and on *historical* events and series typically covering longer periods than those with which most ('non-development') economists are concerned.

- It also has to rely more on fieldwork.

- Its **theories** and models and novel analytical concepts may be primarily directed to *policy* or to *explanation*, and some of them, with varying policy or explanatory emphasis, consist of *historical* schemas or interpretations.

- **Testing** of hypotheses in development economics covers the range from econometric studies dealing with large aggregates, through material susceptible to non-parametric testing, to field case studies more characteristic of the other social sciences, but with a greater bias toward the second and third of these than in economics at large.

- Implicit policy-oriented theories relating to developing countries and the promotion of economic growth have been refined in their practical application by novel developments of methods of project appraisal.

- Some generalizations and underlying assumptions about appropriate policy and development possibilities – whether with autarkic, liberal, or what might be called opportunistic, tendencies – have been falsified, at least in the view of many, by events that have served as spectacular public counter-examples.

In counterpoint to the swings of the pendulum in prevailing ideology, we can detect over the fifty or so years progressively advancing recognition of the real needs of the people whom the quest for economic growth is designed to benefit, and of the failings – but also the potential – of the human agents on whom all progress depends.

Questions for discussion

3.1 What factors had shifted economic-development thought and policy in a liberal, market-oriented direction by the 1980s?

3.2 What implications for the 'shock-therapy' prescription might be read from China's experience of 'transition to market'?

3.3 Why do you think the terms *governance* and *civil society* became current and common in the 1990s?

3.4 What do you understand by the *informal sector*?

3.5 Why was *structuralism* so called?

3.6 Why has the idea of *rent-seeking* been considered important?

3.7 In what ways if any would you say that development-economics thinking has come over the first half-century of its existence to take a more realistic view of the needs and capacities of human beings?

Additional reading

Several of the books to which reference is made in the chapter could be worth reading, browsing or skimming, particularly those that have been dissidents in their time (like the first and second below) or have been influential in changing outlooks and opinions (like the fourth and fifth). These are some examples.

Bauer, P.T. (1971–6) *Dissent on Development*, Weidenfeld and Nicolson, London.

Chang, H.-J. and Ilene Grabel (2004) *Reclaiming Development: an Alternative Economic Policy Manual*, Zed Books, London and New York.

Chenery, H.B., M.S. Ahluwalia, C.L.G. Bell, J.H. Duloy and R. Jolly (1974) *Redistribution with Growth*, Oxford University Press, New York.

Krueger, A.O. (1974) 'The political economy of the rent-seeking society', *American Economic Review*, **64**, June, pp. 291–323.

Little, I.M.D., T. Scitovsky and M.F.G. Scott (1970) *Industry and Trade in Some Developing Countries: a Comparative Study*, Oxford University Press, Oxford.

CHAPTER 4

Macroeconomic Theories of Economic Growth

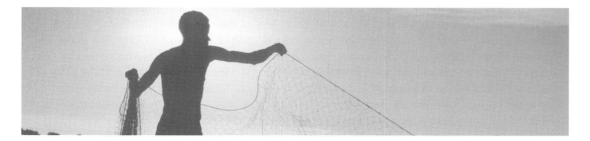

Sustained economic growth is a necessary, though not a sufficient, condition for significant and continuing development in the poor countries of the world – so the search for an understanding of *why* economies grow is fundamental to development economics. Surveying the wide range of macroeconomic growth experience over space and over time, economists have attempted to make sense of the 'seeming chaos' of proliferating potential influences on economic progress by constructing growth models designed to strip the process down to its essentials. However, different economists have constructed very different models; since these, in turn, can generate different – often conflicting – policy recommendations, it is important that students of development are conversant with the diversity of views on the macroeconomics of growth, and of the assumptions and logic that underpin them.

Introduction

Long-term strategies for solving the problem of poverty depend, in part at least, on achieving increases in total output. Some improvement in the living standards of the poor can usually be achieved by redistributing existing output, but this process has limited potential when per capita national income is small – and redistribution is, in any case, much easier to pursue, in terms of political practicality, when output is expanding. Thus **achieving and accelerating economic growth** is of prime importance in development strategy.

Much of this volume is devoted to examining possible means of promoting growth, but, before we look at the detail of development problems and policies, it is instructive to examine the process of economic growth at the macroeconomic level. What are the key **features** of a growing economy? What **changes** may, or must, take place in the overall **structure** of a growing economy, and why?

This is a controversial area which, over the years, has been the battleground for competing schools of economic thought. Much effort has been expended on constructing theories intended to explain how or why economies grow, or fail to grow, and to searching for patterns in the growth paths of today's developing countries and in the earlier evolution of the now-developed countries. An understanding of these issues provides a starting point for the study of development economics.

The key issues – summary preview

This brief summary of key issues in the macroeconomics of growth begins with the ideas put forward by the '**classical**' theorists of the late eighteenth and nineteenth centuries. These early economists 'placed growth at the center of their analyses' (Rostow, 1990, p. 3). Thus Adam Smith (who published his renowned *Wealth of Nations* in 1776) saw economic growth as perfectly feasible, given increases in the stocks of the basic factors of production, in particular capital and labour. However, there was a danger – for some a certainty, for others a possibility – that expansion would come to a halt because of some limiting factor. In its more benign form this might be the arrival at a 'stationary state' resulting from the effects of 'diminishing returns'; or a tendency for population to expand to the point where living standards were depressed to subsistence level; or the drying-up of opportunities for further growth of markets (which had provided opportunities for increasing, rather than diminishing returns); or some combination of these. In its more apocalyptic form the growth process itself might become so disruptive that it destroyed the social and political base on which the economy rested.

The interwar years saw the emergence of Keynesian macroeconomics, later adapted by Harrod and Domar to cast light on the growth process. In the mid-twentieth century these **neo-Keynesian** growth economists struggled with somewhat different problems from those addressed by their predecessors. The key issue was the possible *instability of output and employment* in an economy in which the amount of investment being done might not match the fairly specific investment requirements demanded by the available technology and the growth rate of the labour force. Although this issue was discussed in the context of developed economies, the debate left an important, if unintended, legacy for development economics. This was the conclusion that, given the assumption that technologies had fairly 'rigid' capital requirements per unit of output, the rate of economic growth was bound to be determined by how much could be saved and invested in these technologies.

In the mid-1950s these concerns were to a degree pushed aside by members of the '**neoclassical**' school of economists. They tackled the instability problem by suggesting that the reintroduction of a measure of the classical confidence in market mechanisms would lead to different conclusions regarding the way the growth process worked. In particular, they argued that *market forces would influence the choice of technology* by firms in such a way as to remove any tendency to over-invest or under-invest. Thus, if the capital stock were growing too slowly to employ all available labour, factor-price signals would suggest that more labour-intensive technology should be used. Alternatively, if the capital stock were expanding too rapidly to be fully utilized by the available labour, this would be accommodated by a market-driven increase in the capital intensity of technology.

Furthermore, neoclassical thinking generated the surprising result that, far from being crucial to the determination of the growth rate (as in earlier 'capital-fundamentalist' theories), the rate of saving had no bearing on the long-run equilibrium growth rate of the economy, which was dictated by factors wholly external to the growth process (that is, 'exogenous' factors) such as the rate of growth of population and the rate of technical progress. This view inevitably cast doubt on the effectiveness of neo-Keynesian macroeconomic policies for accelerating growth.

Later still, in the 1980s, reaction against this last view of growth took the form of renewed emphasis on 'endogenous' factors – that is, variables which are part of the growth mechanism itself, rather than external to it. Such a view favoured measures aimed at actively encouraging growth, including – harking back to Adam Smith – promotion of increasing returns in industry.

Last in this sequence is the short-lived flowering around the end of the millennium of the view that, as a result of developments in IT, the world had entered a new age, with a 'new economy', which would grow according to a wholly new set of macroeconomic rules. This optimistic interpretation of the way economies expanded perished, along with the fortunes of many investors, in the collapse of the dot.com share bubble in 2000–1.

In addition to looking at these, and other, attempts to develop theories or models of the growth process, we shall also take into account a second important strand of the analysis of the development process. This is the 'empirical' approach, which seeks to identify regularities in the growth process through the examination of data on GNI and the structure of production in many developing and developed countries.

The analysis of economic growth makes frequent use of algebraic notation and expressions. Key items in this context are set out in Box 4.1.

The value of examining the growth literature

Before we begin our review of the growth literature, it is as well to ask ourselves why we are doing this. Why look at discussions that took place in the past? Why not just master the most up-to-date, 'correct' theory, and leave it at that? Four good reasons are:

1 There is still considerable debate among development economists as to the nature of the growth process and how best to accelerate growth. Many of the ideas currently in vogue were in fact first discussed by earlier generations of economists – more than two hundred years ago. Since we do not yet know which is the 'best' theory, and since the 'best' theory may change with circumstances, it makes sense to look at as wide a range of ideas, and ways of expressing these ideas, as possible.

2 Possession of a working knowledge of the theories of earlier economists may save us from trying to reinvent the wheel and from repeating the mistakes made by others.

3 Looking at theorizing carried out in very different circumstances from the present day can sometimes give a helpfully different perspective on the points being made.

4 Many – indeed most – of the ideas reviewed in this chapter are still alive and kicking in both the highways and the byways of the current literature on development. We will certainly encounter them again as we proceed through this volume. In this chapter we give a quick resumé of where they came from.

BOX 4.1 A BASIC MACROECONOMIC TOOLKIT

Chapter 1 (Appendix 1.2) provided an overview of the key macroeconomic concepts used in national accounting; so there is no need to repeat these here. Instead we focus on the variants of these terms, and associated algebraic notation, used in growth analysis. (Readers familiar with macroeconomic notation may prefer to skip this Box).

- **Output and Income**: In the discussion below we will usually refer to Gross Domestic Product (GDP) or Gross National Income (GNI) as Y, and to per capita output or income as Y/P (where P is total population).

- **Growth of National Income**: The absolute value of the growth in GNI over one year is usually given by ΔY, and the growth *rate* by g, where $g = \Delta Y / Y$. The growth rate of any variable can also be indicated by a subscript g after that variable's symbol.

- **Saving**: The total amount of saving done in a year is given by S. The proportion of GNI going to saving (that is S/GNI or S/Y) is often referred to as s, *the 'savings ratio'* (i.e. $s = S/Y$).

- **Capital**: Savings are invested to form capital. The total accumulated capital stock of the country – machinery, infrastructure, etc. – is given by K.

- **Investment and the Capital–Output Ratio**: The amount invested by a country in one year is indicated by I. This investment will cause output to grow by ΔY in the year it is done. So the amount of additional output per unit of new investment is $\Delta Y / I$, the 'marginal output-to-capital ratio'. The inverse of this ratio, $I/\Delta Y$, is the 'marginal capital–output ratio', often given by v, which indicates the amount of new investment required to generate ΔY new output. This measure is important in growth theory.

- **Allowing for depreciation**: The annual *depreciation* (wearing-out or obsolescence) of the stock of capital is a loss to the nation. If it is subtracted from the total national income (GNI) the corresponding *net* measure NNI results.

- **Profits**: Profits are the returns earned on invested capital. The *rate of profit* on capital invested is given by r, the ratio of annual profits made to capital invested. The size of *total profits*, π, is found by multiplying the total of capital invested by this rate of profit, to give $\pi = r.K$. Thus the share of profits in national income is $r.K/Y$.

- **Wages**: The average wage rate for the economy is indicated by w. Given a total labour force of size L, the total national wage bill will thus be $w.L$, and the share of wages in national income $w.L/Y$.

- **Production Function**: Production functions are mathematical relationships between inputs and output in a production process. They may be pitched at the microeconomic level, where they refer to the production processes of a firm or industry. However, in this chapter, which discusses growth at the macroeconomic level, attention is focused on *aggregate* production functions – which refer to the *total* inputs and outputs for the *entire economy*. The production function is useful in analysis of economic growth. It may be represented algebraically or diagrammatically. As you would expect, the relationship between what goes into a production process (inputs) and what comes out (output) can be complex. However, for the time being we can simply say that output is a function of inputs of labour, capital and improvements in technology. That is:

$$Y = f(L, K, T)$$

Diagrammatic versions of production functions are presented in Figures 4.2, 4.3 and 4.4, and an important application in the section on 'Applying neoclassical growth theory'.

- **Technical Progress**:
Technical progress leads to increased productivity – that is to more output per unit of input. It may stem from new inventions (for example, electronic calculators replacing hand calculation), or from improved design of existing capital goods (for example, more efficient petrol engines which actually cost less than the ones they replace), or, in fact, from any improvement in the *quality* of inputs – including labour (through additional training). In growth economics it may be represented graphically by an outward shift of a production function.

The 'stylized facts' of growth

Before we begin our examination of growth theory it is helpful to consider, in advance of explanations of growth, what it is we are trying to explain. More will be said on this as we proceed. Here we set out what we believe economic growth looks like. Several economists have provided arrays of 'stylized facts' which they believe describe the way economies behave as they grow. The list in Box 4.2 draws on several sources, notably the works of Nicholas Kaldor (1965), Simon Kuznets (1956–67 and 1966) and Hollis Chenery.[1]

BOX 4.2　THE 'STYLIZED FACTS' OF GROWTH: WHAT HAPPENS AS ECONOMIES GROW?

- Continued growth in the aggregate volume of production (Y), in output per capita (Y/P), and in the productivity of labour (Y/L).

- High rates of physical and human capital accumulation, yielding a sustained increase in the amount of capital per worker (K/L).

- A steady rate of profit on capital, r.

- A steady capital–output ratio (K/Y = v) over long periods.

- A strong correlation between the share of profits in national income (r.K/Y) and the share of investment in output (I/Y).

- Steady shares of profits in national income (r.K/Y) and of wages in national income (w.L/Y) – in countries, and/or in periods, in which the share of investment in output (I/Y) is constant.

- Substantial differences in the rates of growth of output and labour productivity *between* countries.

- Structural transformation involving increased industrialization.

- Within manufacturing a shift from light to heavy industry.

- An increase in imports and exports relative to national income, and an increasing emphasis on industrial exports.

- Significant levels of inward transfer of technology, with subsequent appearance of local R&D activity and a shift towards products requiring more sophisticated production and product technology.

Not all growth economists accept the validity of all of these 'facts'. (Nobel Prize winner Robert Solow once observed that 'There is no doubt that they are stylized, though it is possible to question whether they are facts'.) But many accept that they do provide a useful initial guide to what it is that growth theories should be able to explain, or what features growth models should possess. At the very least we may say that theorizing which leads us far away from these 'facts' is probably less useful than theorizing which sticks close to them.

These themes are introduced briefly in this chapter. They will reappear, in various forms and applications, and as the source or underpinning for many specific views on development, throughout this book.

---

[1] For particulars see the discussion of Chenery's work later in this chapter.

Macroeconomic growth theories

Introduction

In this chapter attempts to develop theories of how economies grow at the macroeconomic level are examined. The approach adopted is sequential, because knowledge of the way in which theories evolved, and of the cut and thrust of debate, is often illuminating. As will be seen, key issues argued over by earlier generations of economists reappear in today's controversies.

The origins of modern macroeconomic growth theory: the classical economists

---

BOX 4.3 ADAM SMITH

ADAM SMITH (1723–1790)
Source: National Portrait Gallery, London

Adam Smith, widely regarded as the founding father of modern economics, was born in Kirkcaldy, Scotland, in 1723. He had a difficult early life; his father died before Adam was born – and at one point he was abducted by vagrants. But by the age of 28 he was Professor of Logic at the University of Glasgow. His key work – *An Inquiry into the Nature and Causes of the Wealth of Nations* – is, in the words of Alan Greenspan, 'One of the great achievements of human intellectual history . . . [bringing] conceptual clarity to the seeming chaos of market transactions.' Smith trusted in the impersonal forces of markets, working through prices, together with individual self-interest, to allocate resources efficiently – as if by an 'invisible hand'. Neither much government intervention nor the activities of monopolies were desirable; indeed 'people of the same trade seldom meet together, even for merriment or diversion, but the conversation ends in a conspiracy against the public or in some contrivance to raise prices'. Nor was Smith over-impressed by the politically correct of his times, averring that 'Virtue is more to be feared than vice, because its excesses are not subject to the regulation of conscience'. When he died in 1790 it was discovered that much of his own wealth had been quietly spent on charitable activities.

What actually determines the growth rate – and thus, ultimately, the wealth – of nations?

The expansion process in Smith's growth model depends, as is still the case in most modern growth theorizing, on the level of inputs of three factors of production – land, labour and capital – and on technical progress. Increases in the size of the labour force (L), in the amount of capital (K), and in the available land (H), all lead to increases in total output (Y), suggesting a basic production function of the form:

$$Y = f(L, K, H)$$

Growth in total output (Yg) will be caused by growth in the labour force (Lg), in the capital stock (Kg), and in the supply of land (Hg). In addition, improvements in technology (Tg) lead to expanded output by increasing the productivity of the factor inputs:

$$Yg = f(Lg, Kg, Hg, Tg)$$

If we begin with a 'stationary' economy in which the labour force (and the population), and the stock of capital are constant, then output will also be constant – there will be no economic growth. The real wage earned by labour will be just enough to provide a subsistence living, with no surplus to make possible an increase in population. Similarly, on the capital side, new investment (I), financed by the new saving (S) of capitalists, will be just enough to replace depreciation of existing capital goods, so there is no growth in the stock of productive capital goods. And land, in the absence of new discoveries or improvements in fertility, is also effectively fixed in quantity.

This situation can persist indefinitely, or it may be disturbed by an external 'shock' such as a new invention which improves efficiency of production, or improved opportunities for international trade (perhaps by the opening up of new markets overseas). Increased output makes possible increased saving and investment, which in turn creates conditions favourable for increasing the extent of specialization and further improving productivity. This scenario also permits a rise in wages above subsistence level, which encourages population growth and the expansion of the labour force – a requirement for continued economic growth.

However, in Smith's view, a sustained increase in population and the labour force is likely to exert downward pressure on the wage rate. Increased capital accumulation leads to a corresponding downward pressure on the rate of profit. Eventually, these processes push the real wage rate and the rate of profit back to their original levels. Throughout, the rates of growth of L and of K following the initial 'shock' are determined by 'endogenous' processes, that is processes *internal* to the model itself, and not by some outside process.

Once the original levels of wage and profit rates are re-established the economy is back in a stationary state. The only differences from the starting point for the whole episode are that the population and the capital stock are now larger, and that returns to landlords (the owners of the land input) have risen, since the fixed nature of the stock of land means that no bidding down of its rate of return by expanding the quantity of the factor can happen.

This kind of stop-go growth process, resulting in no permanent growth of per capita incomes, could happen repeatedly. However, in Smith's view, the resultant expansion of the *absolute* size of the economy and total demand for output ('the extent of the market') will eventually create further opportunities for **specialization** ('division of labour') sufficiently great to generate **increasing returns** to inputs of labour and capital. *Now* when an external shock leads to the usual sequence of increased K and L with consequential downward pressures on wage rates and profitability, these pressures are more than counteracted by the expansion of output at a faster rate than factor inputs are expanded. Increasing returns make growth self-reinforcing. The expansion of the market and increased specialization create conditions suitable for further expansion and further specialization.

A period of prolonged economic growth will follow, with living standards improving. So long as technological improvements and the growth of trade permit further market growth, this will continue. However, Smith did recognise the possibility that, eventually, the limits of expansion of the market may be reached. Then the process of downward bidding of wage and profit rates will reappear, resulting in the eventual re-establishment of the subsistence wage and replacement-only investment. No further improvement will now be possible; the long-run 'stationary state' has been reached with population growth and net capital accumulation both at zero. The effect of the entire process will have been to expand the absolute size of the labour force, the capital stock and the economy. However, individual workers and investors will be no better off than at the beginning of the process. Only the owners of land will have benefited from the increased returns from growth.

BOX 4.4 DAVID RICARDO

DAVID RICARDO (1772–1823)
Source: National Portrait Gallery, London

David Ricardo, despite being one of 17 children, having little formal education, and having been disinherited by his father (who was a wealthy banker), carved out a successful career as a stockbroker. By the age of 42 he was sufficiently wealthy to be able to retire, and he devoted the remaining nine years of his life to study, writing and politics. His careful analysis of the early nineteenth-century economy led him to the pessimistic view that the pressure of increasing population on finite land resources must result in diminishing returns, increasing rents, and falling profitability in agriculture. This would encourage investors to divert their capital to other uses where, in turn, profits would be squeezed out. The end result of this process would be a 'stationary state' – a zero-growth trap from which no permanent escape was possible, and which was congenial only to landowners. Ricardo's key work in this field is *The Principles of Political Economy and Taxation*. He died, aged 51, at his home, Gatcombe Park, now the residence of the Princess Royal, daughter of the British Queen. Over a century later his collected writings were brought together by Piero Sraffa in the 10 volumes of the magisterial *The Works and Correspondence of David Ricardo*, which was 43 years in preparation.

Like Smith, David Ricardo expected the macroeconomy to end up in a stationary state after a phase of growth. He saw diminishing returns inevitably limiting agricultural production. As agriculture expands, requiring the bringing into use of progressively less fertile land, the marginal productivity of labour and the marginal productivity of capital are driven down. With wages at minimum subsistence level, increases in output result in a declining rate of profit and redistribute income towards landlords, who are able to charge progressively higher rents while, according to Ricardo, showing little interest in spending this income on productive investment. At the same time, increasing marginal costs in agriculture force the price of food up, which in turn requires an increase in the subsistence (money) wage, and this again cuts into profits. As the profitability of investment in agriculture dwindles, reinvestment in capital goods in agriculture contracts, funds being diverted to non-agricultural investment where they again exert downward pressure on rates of return.

Since, for Ricardo, growth depends on capital investment, a stationary state is eventually reached, with zero net capital investment and thus zero growth. This outcome may be postponed if expanding imports of cheap food head off wage increases, so increasing profitability. Improvements in technology can have a similar effect, though here there is a danger that unemployment will increase because of a net displacement of labour caused by the introduction of labour-saving technology, and because declining profits preclude any increase in capital investment to absorb unemployed labour.[2]

An important element in Ricardo's view of the growth process is his **Iron Law of Wages**. This formalized the 'subsistence theory' of wages which, in one form or another, is a feature of all classical thinking on growth. It suggests that a certain minimum level of consumption is necessary to sustain life, and that the real wage tends to be driven down towards this floor level. As noted above, relief from this dire situation may be found through expansion of the market or technical progress, but this will always be temporary. Long regarded as irrelevant in a world where living standards far above the subsistence floor have either been achieved or are seen as a realistic aspiration, the *Law* is now viewed by some growth economists as regaining relevance because of the trend towards globalization of labour markets in a world where massive pools of unemployed labour still exist.

BOX 4.5 THOMAS MALTHUS

THOMAS MALTHUS (1766–1834)
Source: National Portrait Gallery, London

An ordained minister of the Church of England, Thomas Malthus is best known for his *Essay on Population*. His view that, unless population growth could somehow be contained, famine and its attendant ills would be unavoidable, was unpopular among the social reformers of his day – who believed that social engineering was the answer to man's problems. However, Charles Darwin, who read the *Essay* 'for amusement', was greatly influenced in his thinking on evolution by its focus on the 'struggle for existence' and the consequential importance of what he called 'favourable variations'. Malthus' pessimistic views are responsible for the fact that economics was termed 'the dismal science'.

Probably the most pessimistic of the classical writers, Thomas Malthus subscribed to the view that a stationary state was inevitable. He believed that population tended to expand whenever the food-supply situation permitted this. Any increase in wage rates would be self-correcting, since it would lead to an expansion of population, a consequential increase in the labour force, and the bringing into play of diminishing returns, the supply of agricultural land being fixed. Wages would then be pushed back to the basic subsistence level. Episodes of economic growth could occur as a result of random favourable events such as a run of particularly good harvests, but their effect would soon be swallowed up by increasing population.

Although Malthus acknowledged that a community might deliberately, through 'moral restraint', limit its population growth, and he later came to know of societies in which this had apparently happened, he did not expect any change in the process referred to above, since he doubted the normal willingness of individuals to exercise the necessary restraint

---

[2] David Ricardo (1817/1992) *Principles of Political Economy and Taxation*, Everyman, London. (Ricardo's growing pessimism regarding the impact of technical progress is encapsulated in the chapter 'On Machinery' which first appeared in the third edition of the *Principles*.)

and did not anticipate relief through long-run improvements in technology. So he was pessimistic about the possibility of escape from the low-income trap described by his demographic model.

BOX 4.6 KARL MARX

KARL MARX (1818–1883)
Source: National Portrait Gallery, London

Karl Marx was one of the most influential social scientists of the nineteenth century. Born in Trier in Germany in 1818, he attended school there before enrolling in the Law Faculty at the University of Bonn. At University he was a keen socializer, accumulated large debts, and participated in duels. He also became engaged to Jenny, daughter of Baron von Westfalen. His capacity for prolific and influential publication of his radical views led to his being hounded across Europe, until, in May 1849, he reached London where his 'long, sleepless night of exile' was to last for the rest of his life. Living in acute poverty, he spent much of his time in the Reading Room of the British Museum, studying and writing on capitalist society. The first volume of his key work on *Capital* was not published until 1867. Most of his output appeared posthumously (in particular, volumes II and III of *Capital*, published by his friend Engels). Marx died in 1883. He is buried in Highgate Cemetery in London. Most of his predictions regarding the future of capitalism have not come to pass. Nevertheless, his emphasis on the significance of economic factors in politics, and of class structure for development, have had a major impact on the evolution of social-scientific thought.

Like Smith and Ricardo, Marx believed that the rate of profit would decline as capitalist economies developed, and that this would reduce investment and therefore the rate of economic growth (Marx, 1967). However, where Smith saw the crucial decline in rates of return as stemming from competition among investors, and Ricardo had focused on the pressures of increased rents and wage levels, Marx saw the eventual demise of investment as resulting initially from the pressure of capital accumulation on the labour market, which would tend to push up wages. Capitalists might seek to resist this by direct action to hold wages down, which would give rise to social conflict. Or they might increase the capital-intensity of production by increasing the ratio of spending on capital equipment and industrial raw materials (Marx's *constant capital*) to the wage bill (*variable capital*). But increasing capital-intensity absorbs more capital and reduces the rate of profit, and is thus not a long-term solution either.[3] Furthermore, as machinery replaces men, the labour force can no longer purchase all of the goods being produced, and there is a crisis of deficient effective demand. These problems lead to the collapse of the system and a transition to socialism, a regime under which the dictates of the pursuit of profit (with the attendant problems just mentioned) are no longer paramount.

---

[3] The rate of profit for Marx was defined as the ratio of '*surplus value*' to '*total capital*', where surplus value is the difference between output and the wage bill and total capital is the sum of constant capital and variable capital.

Keynesian Growth – the Harrod–Domar Model

BOX 4.7 ROY HARROD

R oy Harrod was an Oxford economist who made many important advances (often unrecognised or overtaken by others) in economic theory. He is mainly remembered for his pioneering work on 'dynamic' economics, beginning with 'An Essay in Dynamic Theory' published in the *Economic Journal* in 1939. Harrod was personal adviser to Winston Churchill during the War, and later Keynes's official biographer. At the time of his death in 1978 he was being considered for a Nobel Prize.

Evsey Domar, a Russian-born economist researching at MIT on extending Keynes' macroeconomic theories, independently arrived at conclusions similar to those of Harrod – though several years later.

ROY HARROD (1900–1978)
Source: National Portrait Gallery, London

Introduction

In 1939 Roy Harrod published an article in the *Economic Journal* setting out details of a model designed to extend Keynesian analysis into the area of growth. (Harrod, 1939). Similar ideas were put forward some time later, but independently, by Evsey Domar (Domar, 1946) – and the much-used Harrod–Domar growth model was born.

The main interest of the originators of the model was the issue of whether or not a dynamized Keynesian system was capable of stable growth and, if so, under what conditions. The key findings in this context were that there was indeed a problem in that many (indeed, most) possible combinations of values of the savings rate, the level of investment, the capital–output ratio, and the rate of growth of the labour force would result in a tendency for the economy to be unstable – with growing unemployment of either labour or the capital stock – and to possess no self-correcting mechanism. Moreover, even if instability were, by chance, averted, there was no particular reason why the economy should operate at full employment.

Thus the Harrod–Domar model predicted serious inherent instability problems for capitalist economies, and much subsequent discussion of growth focused on this issue. (The neoclassical response is discussed later in this chapter.) Somewhat paradoxically, however, this has **not** been the main interest of those who have used the model in the *development* context. Here the focus has been on the use of the basic *equation* of the Harrod–Domar model to estimate the saving and investment requirements for particular rates of growth. This slant on the model bypasses key problems such as the possibility that savings and investment decisions may not match, but happens to fit well into a 'capital-fundamentalist' view of the growth process – that is, the view that capital accumulation is central to increasing the rate of economic growth. In this chapter the discussion concentrates on the interpretation and presentation of this straightforward (and grossly simplified) perception of the basic Harrod–Domar equation.

The Harrod–Domar equation

The Harrod–Domar equation is explained in this section, first in the form of an illustrative numerical example, then, in Box 4.8, in terms of a simple algebraic derivation. (Readers comfortable with algebra may prefer to go straight to the Box).

Consider the case of an economy in which:

■ There is only one product ('flip-flop' leather sandals)
■ People save 10 per cent of their incomes ($s = 10$ per cent)
■ All savings are automatically invested in sandal-making machinery
■ There is no problem of labour shortage.

Assume that sandal-making machines have a more-or-less fixed output capacity. For instance, a new leather-cutting machine costing £1 000 000 can produce 200 000 pairs of 'flip-flop' leather sandals in a year. These sell for £1.00 per pair, so the total value of annual sales is £200 000. Thus we can say that, for every additional £1 invested each year in capital goods (i.e. machinery), an extra £0.20 of output will be produced each year. Put another way, for this new investment, the capital/output ratio (usually called v) is equal to £1 000 000 divided by £200 000 – or 5.0.

What has this to do with economic growth? The new investment in machinery *adds* to production, since all pre-existing machines are assumed to remain in use.[4] That is, it causes GDP and GNI to grow.

And what is the precise size of the rate of growth (g)? Assume that the leather-cutting machine is the only new investment this year, and that it is financed by savings from last year's GNI. These savings equal 10 per cent of that income (since $s = 10$ per cent). We know that we need to invest £5 for every additional £1 of output produced in a year (since $v = 5$). This is the same as saying that the £ value of annual output will grow by 1/5th of any increase in investment. And, since saving is used to finance investment, it is also the same as saying that output grows by 1/5th of any new saving. So, if saving is equal to 10 per cent of last year's GNI, the resultant growth in output will be 1/5th of that 10 per cent – that is, 2 per cent of last year's GNI. So growth in GNI in this year is 2 per cent, and this is the 'growth rate'.

In symbolic terms: % GNI available for investment $= s$
Investment requirement per £1 of extra output $= v$
So extra output obtainable as % GNI $\mathbf{= s/v = g}$

In our example $s = 0.1$ and $v = 5$;   so $g = s/v = 0.1/5 = 1/50 = \mathbf{2\%}$

*Thus, since v, the capital–output ratio, is assumed fixed, there will also be a fixed relationship between the rate of saving (s, the % of GNI saved) and g, the growth rate of that GNI. In fact, once we know the value of v, the rate of economic growth depends **entirely** upon the amount of saving being done (as a proportion of GNI).*

Graphical presentation of the basic Harrod–Domar relationship

Figure 4.1 illustrates the relationship between the growth rate g and the savings rate s for two different economies. In the economy with the low capital–output ratio (i.e. with $v = 2$), since g must equal s/v, the percentage rate of growth is constrained to be equal to half of the

---

[4] In practice some machines would wear out every year, so part of the new investment would go to replacing these machines. Such 'depreciation' is ignored in this example in the interests of simplicity – and since including it would not change the final outcome in any fundamental way.

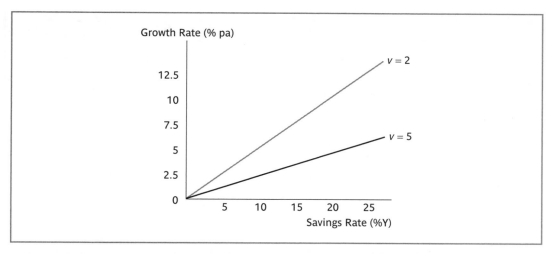

FIGURE 4.1 Growth Rate – Savings Rate Combinations at Two Different Capital–Output Ratios

savings rate. If the savings rate changes, the economy must move along the upper ray through the origin to the new growth rate. Given the rigid nature of the basic Harrod–Domar relationship, no other options are open. Similarly, in the economy characterized by the much higher capital–output ratio ($v = 5$) the available growth rates are always equal to one-fifth of the savings rate – as indicated along the ray. In both cases increasing values for s necessarily go along with increasing values for g.

One implication of the rigidity of the capital–output ratio is that the capital–labour ratio must also be fixed. This important feature of the Harrod–Domar model is illustrated in Figure 4.2 by the fact that the so-called 'Leontief' isoquants permit efficient production of X units of output, and Y units of output at, respectively, the points A and B only.

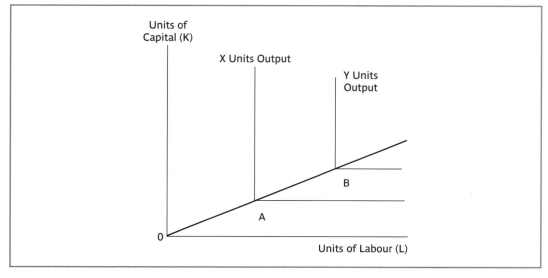

FIGURE 4.2 Fixed Coefficient 'Leontief' Production Function

BOX 4.8 MORE FORMAL DERIVATION OF THE HARROD–DOMAR EQUATION

The Harrod–Domar model makes use of a very simple production function which says that there is a fixed, constant relationship between the amount of capital invested (given by K) and the amount of output produced using that capital (given by Y). That is, the capital–output ratio K/Y is constant. We shall call this ratio v. The constancy of v applies to the *total* capital stock K and the total output it helps to produce, Y. Since constant returns to scale are assumed, it also applies to any *increase* in the capital stock, ΔK, and to the associated increase in output, ΔY, produced by this new capital stock. (That is to say, the *incremental* or *marginal* capital–output ratio is constant and is also equal to v). Thus:

$$v = K/Y$$

and
$$v = \Delta K/\Delta Y \tag{4.1}$$

The rate of growth of total output, which is the same thing as the rate of growth of the economy (given by g), is the increase in output divided by total output:

$$g = \Delta Y/Y \tag{4.2}$$

If we divide both sides of equation (4.1) by Y we get:

$$v/Y = \Delta K/\Delta Y \,.\, 1/Y \tag{4.3}$$

Rearranging:

$$\Delta Y/Y = \Delta K/Y \,.\, 1/v$$

That is:

$$g = \Delta K/Y \,.\, 1/v$$

But, for the economy as a whole, ΔK, the increase in the capital stock, is equal to investment (given by I), which, in turn, is equal to total savings (given by S). Hence ΔK/Y is equal to S/Y, the proportion of total output which is saved – that is, the savings rate, s. Hence:

$$g = s/v \tag{4.4}$$

Equation 4.4 is the fundamental Harrod–Domar relationship: The growth rate of the economy is equal to the savings rate divided by the capital–output ratio.

Thus, if the savings rate were, say, 20 per cent (that is, 20 per cent of output is saved for investment purposes) and the capital–output ratio were 2 (that is, each additional unit of output requires 2 units of capital to produce it), then the growth rate of output would be s/v = 20 per cent / 2, which equals 10 per cent. That is, g = 10 per cent per annum.

Using the Harrod–Domar model as a basis for macroeconomic growth policy

At first sight, the basic Harrod–Domar relationship, $g = s/v$, though a tautology – that is, a statement which is bound to be true because of the way in which g, s, and v are defined – appears to be an insight both simple and powerful. It suggests that, so long as the capital–output ratio can be estimated accurately by policy-makers, it will be possible to work out what the growth rate will be once the current savings rate has been ascertained. More important, it also suggests that policy-makers can readily calculate the *savings rate that would be required in order to achieve a given target rate of growth*. If the savings rate is too low given the desired rate of growth, this will be immediately apparent and, now that both the actual and the required volumes of saving are known, the size of any shortfall – the size of the '*financing gap*' – is also known. The government might then fill this gap, in order to achieve the desired rate of economic growth, by encouraging increased voluntary saving on the part of the population, or by increasing government saving, or by seeking grants or loans from foreign countries, or by some combination of these devices.[5]

However, in practice, application of the Harrod–Domar model in developing countries has usually run into a number of difficulties. Important among these are the following.

- The assumption of a constant capital–output ratio (v) is untenable in the context of long-run economic growth. As is argued by the neoclassical economists (discussed later in this chapter) a 'flexible' technology with a variable v is much more plausible in this context. This means that the economy is not stuck with a permanently fixed capital–output ratio, so there can be no unique 'financing gap' in any given country.

- In any case, calculating the capital–output ratio for an entire economy is difficult as there are often insuperable problems with acquiring the required data. And it is very likely that, in practice, the marginal capital–output ratio (embodied in new investment) differs from the overall v (which is an average measure covering many generations of investment), and the marginal value is unlikely to be known to government statisticians.

- The assumption that funds made available for investment will actually be invested – on schedule – is not necessarily valid. Alternative uses for funds may be preferred, perhaps because of changes in priorities. (For example, in the late 1980s, funds borrowed by the Ethiopian Dergue government from international agencies for investment in factories were largely diverted to purchasing arms.) And delays in project implementation and completion are endemic in many developing countries.

- The expectation that, where funds *are* invested, this will yield the level of output indicated by the computed capital–output ratio, and therefore the predicted growth rate, will be unjustified if the new plant and machinery are not operated at forecast levels of efficiency. This may well be the case as a result of overoptimistic forecasting of machine capacity, or because of 'unforeseen' operating problems of the kind which regularly disrupt production in developing-country conditions (power failures, interruption of raw material supplies, shortages of critical skills, and so on).

- The collateral investment in elements such as education and infrastructure, without which the investment in machinery might fail to pay off, may not be made, or may not be made on time.

For these, and other reasons the predictive power of the Harrod–Domar equation is much less impressive than might have been hoped by development policy-makers.[6]

---

[5] 'Gap' analysis will reappear in Chapter 5 in the discussion of the work of Rostow (on aid for the 'take-off') and of Chenery and Strout (the 'two-gap' model).

[6] Nevertheless, the Harrod–Domar equation is still used to calculate short-run investment requirements for target growth rates. See William Easterly (1997).

The neoclassical response: flexible technology and market forces

Flexible technology

The 'capital-fundamentalist' view of the growth process was challenged very directly by a school of thought on growth led by Robert Solow. He rejected the Harrod–Domar-inspired idea that there is an 'automatic', direct link between the rate of savings out of GNP (and thus the level of investment relative to GNP) and the growth rate of GNP:

> There was [an] . . . implication of the Harrod-Domar model that seemed unsound. If the condition for steady growth is that the savings rate equals the product of the growth rate of employment and a technologically-determined capital-output ratio, then a recipe for doubling the rate of growth in a labor surplus economy was simply to double the savings rate, perhaps through the public budget . . . . In underdeveloped countries, however, where the appetite for new capital is likely to be pretty strong, the recipe looked usable. I believe I remember that writings on economic development often asserted that the key to a transition from slow growth to fast growth was a sustained rise in the savings rate. The recipe sounded implausible to me . . . . It occurred to me very early, as a natural-born macroeconomist, that even if technology itself is not so very flexible for each single good at a given time, aggregate factor-intensity must be much more variable because the economy can choose to focus on capital-intensive or labor-intensive or land-intensive goods.
>
> *(Solow, 1987)*

Solow replaced the 'rigid'-technology assumption central to the Harrod model, where it is embodied in the fixed capital–output ratio (v), by a flexible-technology assumption. The resulting macroeconomic model of the growth process looked very different from the version of the Harrod model popular with development economists.[7]

---

[7] Harrod was, of course, aware of the possibility of factor substitution but thought that, because of the multiplicity of factors affecting factor prices and choices, it was very unlikely that market-driven factor substitution alone would yield the market-clearing solution.

The key assumption underlying the logic of the Solow growth model is that a number of different technologies (that is, alternative sets of plant and machinery with different degrees of capital intensity) are available to choose from when production is planned. For instance, a farmer harvesting sugar cane can choose between using, at one end of the technology spectrum, a very sophisticated, and very expensive, mechanical harvester operated by a small labour force and, at the other end of the spectrum, a large squad of manual workers who cut the cane by hand, using only small cane-knives. Between these two technology options lie others using machinery of different levels of sophistication, each one requiring different numbers of workers to operate it.

In short, firms will often have available to them not just one technology – and hence just one capital–labour ratio (and one capital–output ratio) – but *several* options, and hence several possible capital–labour and capital–output ratios. This reflects the availability, for most jobs, of a range of machinery embodying different levels of labour intensity and capital intensity, as in the case of cane-cutting cited above.

These considerations are still relevant at the aggregate, economy-wide level at which the neoclassical model is pitched. As Solow notes in the passage quoted above, such flexibility of technology is likely to be limited for many individual products, and at any one point in time. However in the aggregate, over time, the range of technology choice is likely to be significant as individual firms take up opportunities to innovate and/or to shift the product composition of their output, and as new firms commence production.

With this kind of production function the capital–labour ratio (K/L), and the capital–output ratio (v), are no longer fixed, but become variables. Put another way, the simple Harrod–Domar production function is replaced by a more complex one in which there is room for substitution of one factor for another – technology becomes 'flexible'. This is the assumption embodied in the familiar isoquant diagram shown in Figure 4.3.

So which of these alternative technologies will be chosen, and why? Since the Solow model assumes that firms are profit-maximizing, the answer is: the technology that maximizes profits. If it is assumed, for simplicity, that there are only two inputs, capital and labour, then firms will consider the price of labour (i.e. the wage rate) and the price of capital (i.e. the rate of interest), and cost out each technological alternative in order to identify the one which maximizes profits. And if the wage rate rises, or the rate of interest falls, there will be an incentive to substitute capital (machinery) for workers – that is, to move to more capital-intensive technology – in order to save money. At the aggregate level,

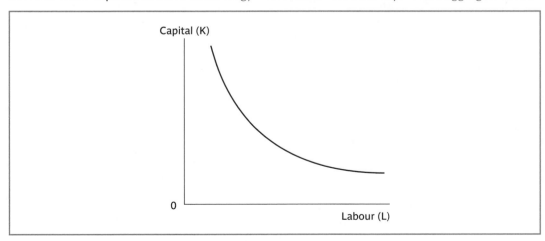

FIGURE 4.3 Variable Factor Proportions Production Function

to this mechanism must be added, as noted above, the possibility of altering the mix of products made by firms in response to changes in relative factor prices.

The assumption of flexible technology has a profound effect on the way in which this growth model works. Increasing the rate of saving out of income (s) is likely to encourage the use of more capital-intensive techniques. These, if investors are to find it worth their while to choose them in preference to the old labour-intensive techniques, will increase output per worker. While the economy is absorbing this change – moving from the original lower output per worker to the new higher level – the growth rate, g, will rise briefly as the economy moves up towards the new growth path characterized by this higher output per worker. But, once the new higher level of output per worker is reached, the growth rate will fall back to its original level. The impact of the rise in the rate of saving has been an important one, since it has raised output per capita (i.e. GNI per capita) so that living standards will have risen. *But the increase in s has not had any permanent effect on g.* (Note that this conflicts directly with the outcome according to the Harrod–Domar process in which increasing s leads to a permanent rise in g.)

So why is it that, according to the neoclassical view, raising s does *not* result in a permanent rise in g? The basic idea is that the workers who now have more sophisticated machines to use, and will certainly *produce more than they formerly did*, will not find, once they get used to their new machines, that their output *grows* any faster than did output with the old machines. Indeed, once they have fully mastered the 'best practice' for using the machines (and their output per day *will* grow while they are 'learning' to use the new machines), there is no reason why output should grow any farther. In other words, with both the old and the new machines, the workers will eventually reach a situation where their output stabilizes – that is, reaches a maximum and stays there. An example of this process is given in Box 4.10.

BOX 4.10 SAVINGS AND GROWTH

While, at first sight, the idea that increasing the rate of saving (s) will raise the rate of growth (g) seems intuitively appealing, a simple example may further clarify the logic of the contrary conclusion arrived at using the neoclassical approach. Consider the case of the 'output' of calculations from hand calculators. Say one student can make 40 calculations per hour with a calculator, provided by the University, costing £5. If the number of students is growing at 5 per cent per annum, the number of calculations being done will also grow by 5 per cent per annum. That is, $g = 5$ per cent. Now, the University decides to save more from its cash flow to permit a higher level of investment in calculators, and replaces the £5 calculators by more powerful units capable of 80 calculations per hour. These cost £12 each, so the capital–labour ratio increases. When the new calculators first come into use there will, of course, be a very rapid increase in the number of calculations being done per hour. That is, the growth rate rises. But soon a new equilibrium will be reached with each student settling down to a regular 80 calculations per hour. There will thereafter be no further growth in the number of calculations being done – other than the 5 per cent per annum increase caused by the increase in student numbers. Thus *the increase in the saving rate, which resulted in higher capital intensity, has increased output per student, so the University community is 'better off', but has **not** increased the long-run equilibrium growth rate of output.* The students are *more productive* because of the move to more capital-intensive technology but, after the rise in g during the disequilibrium (or adjustment) phase following the introduction of the new calculators, their overall output growth rate falls back to the 5 per cent per annum set by the annual expansion of student numbers. In short, increasing s has not increased g.

A more detailed presentation of the neoclassical growth model

In order to confirm and extend the conclusions flowing from the neoclassical model, it is helpful to present its bare bones in a simple algebraic/intuitive form, backed up by a diagrammatic presentation.

Assume that all saving (S) is invested, so that S always equals I (which equals the change in the stock of capital, ΔK, as, for simplicity of exposition, there is no depreciation). Savings have a functional relation to total income, Y, such that $S = s.Y$ (where s is, as usual, the savings ratio, which is constant). The labour force growth rate is constant at n per annum, which (unlike the case in the Smith model) is exogenously determined – that is, is unaffected by the economic variables on which the model is based. The technology available to firms is no longer of the rigid type used in the Harrod–Domar model, but is flexible, permitting the overall capital–output ratio, v, and the capital–labour ratio (K/L, which measures the ratio of capital, K, to labour, L, employed in the production process) to vary. The capital–labour ratio is given by k.

The production function, that is the relationship between inputs and output, is of the form:

$$Y = f(K,L) \tag{4.5}$$

indicating that total output is a function of capital and labour inputs. This production function is also characterised by diminishing returns to both inputs, with the marginal product of capital tending towards zero as k becomes very large.

Constant returns to scale are assumed. That is, output changes at exactly the same rate as inputs when these are changed in step. Hence (4.5) can be divided through by L to yield:[8]

$$Y/L = f(K/L) = f(k)$$

which says that output per capita is a function of the capital-labour ratio (k). The amount of saving (per capita) being done can thus be given as $s.f(k)$. Given that the labour force is growing at n, the capital–labour ratio k will remain constant if, and only if, investment also grows at n, in which case annual investment is $n.k$. But, since annual investment per worker equals annual saving per worker – which is $s.f(k)$ – it follows that the condition under which the capital-intensity of the technology selected remains constant (i.e. has zero rate of change) is:

$$s.f(k) = n.k \tag{4.6}$$

Since the labour force (L) is growing at n while K/L is constant, it follows that K must also be growing at n. And since Y/L must be constant when K/L is constant, it further follows that Y must be growing at n. That is, the capital stock (K), the labour force (L), and – crucially – *output* (Y), are all growing at the same rate of n. So g, the growth rate of output, equals n.

This is the equilibrium, or **steady-state**, configuration for the economy, so-called since there is no tendency to move away from it.

The standard graphical presentation of the **Solow model** is based on Figure 4.4. Here output per capita, (Y/L), is shown on the vertical axis and capital per labourer, (K/L), on the horizontal axis. The production function curve $f(k)$ shows how output per capita increases as capital intensity increases. The impact of diminishing returns is reflected in the 'flattening' of the curve as increasingly capital-intensive technology is used, eventually leading to a zero change in output per capita as more capital is added.

---

[8] With constant returns to scale any change in inputs is precisely mirrored by a change in output. Hence dividing all inputs by L also divides output by L.

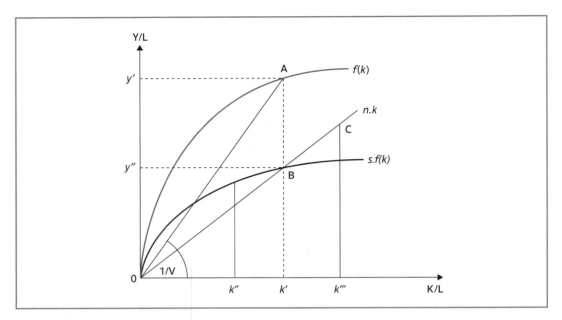

FIGURE 4.4 Neoclassical Growth Model

Saving per capita is shown as the curve $s.f(k)$ which, naturally, mirrors the $f(k)$ curve from which it is derived in becoming flatter as capital-intensity increases and the associated increases in income diminish. The $n.k$ line shows the investment per capita required at each capital–labour ratio, (K/L), to maintain that level of capital intensity given that the labour force is increasing at the rate of n per annum.

Equilibrium is located where the amount of saving being done at a given capital-intensity exactly equals the amount of investment needed to sustain that level of capital-intensity. That is, where:

$$s.f(k) = n.k \tag{4.7}$$

There is, in fact, only one such point – at the intersection B. Thus k' is the equilibrium choice of technology. Given this technology, equilibrium output per capita is y'. And equilibrium saving per capita and investment per capita are y''.

The equilibrium we have identified is a stable one to which the economy will gravitate 'automatically'. It can be seen that, when the technology in use is less capital-intensive than k' (i.e. to the left of k', at, for instance k''), the level of saving will exceed that required to maintain k'', so the capital intensity of production will tend to *rise* towards k'. The converse situation obtains at k''', where saving is insufficient to finance the capital requirements of that technology, so that capital-intensity must fall towards k'. Thus, for any technology other than k', there is a built-in equilibrium mechanism tending to push the economy towards a stable equilibrium at technology k'.

It may also be inferred from Figure 4.4 that, as was shown earlier, changes in the rate of saving will not affect the growth rate. Increasing the savings rate from s to s' would have the effect of shifting the $s.f(k)$ function upward. The new equilibrium will be where this new savings function intersects the $n.k$ function (which is unaffected by the change in savings behaviour) – say at the point C. Here the technology is more capital-intensive, at k''', so output per capita is increased and the economy is better off. But the rate of investment per capita required to maintain any value of k remains unchanged at $n.k$, and the growth rate of income remains at n. That is, increasing the savings rate has *not* affected the growth rate, which remains at g.

It should be noted, however, that, in moving from the first to the second equilibrium, the economy must necessarily have experienced a phase of growth at a higher level than g, while the more capital-intensive technology is being absorbed. (An intuitive example of such necessary temporary acceleration might be that of two cyclists both travelling, in line ahead, at 15 mph. If the second cyclist wishes to move up and ride alongside the leader he must accelerate – to, say, 18 mph – in order to overtake him, at which point he can settle back to 15 mph.) Some commentators have argued that such periods of 'transition', or adjustment, could be lengthy, so that increasing s might raise the growth rate for some time, but this is still a matter of debate.

Thus a key theoretical finding based on this *neoclassical* growth model is that increasing the savings rate in order to increase the rate of accumulation of capital will *not* (contrary to the claims of capital-fundamentalists) result in permanently increased rates of growth. Instead, when the savings rate rises, the rate of growth will rise temporarily (in the 'disequilibrium phase'), only to fall back to the rate determined by population growth.

The steady state, convergence, and technical progress

The growth model developed by the neoclassical economists incorporates the idea of a law of diminishing returns which, as we have seen, preoccupied many of their classical predecessors. As capital is substituted for labour, the operation of the law takes its toll, resulting in progressively smaller gains in productivity from each additional £ spent on new capital equipment – indeed, in a zero marginal return if the process is carried far enough. The actual steady-state configuration, and its determinants, were discussed above. Once the steady state is reached, population growth will continue to raise total GNI. But GNI *per capita* will not change.

This would, then, appear to be the end of the growth process so that, if all countries had access to the same technologies, and had the same savings rates and population growth rates, all would end up, eventually, at the same (zero) growth rate of per capita income and with the same growth rate of GNI, which is then the same as the population growth rate. This process of 'convergence' would be facilitated for the poorer countries by the fact that their marginal productivities of capital, and therefore their rates of return on capital, would be higher than those in the more developed countries (since they are further away from the terminal diminishing-returns state). This would be expected to encourage capital to flow from the more-developed to the less-developed countries, so facilitating the progress of the latter towards the terminal state. Thus, the Solow theory, as explained thus far, would appear to suggest 'convergence' of all economies, subject to the conditions just mentioned. The extent to which this has actually happened is considered briefly in Chapters 2 and 25.

In terms of development policy, the view implied by the previous paragraph, to the effect that 'catching up' is possible and could be facilitated, has provided a further rationale for **aid** flows to the LDCs.

Returning to the steady state: how might growth in per capita incomes be pursued once the steady state has been reached? Why is it that no country, however highly industrialized and with however low a population growth rate, seems to have actually reached this terminal position?

The answer offered by neoclassical theorists is 'improvements in technology'. The argument set out above assumes that the set of available technologies, with their different levels of capital intensity, is fixed, and cannot be varied. But this is clearly not so. *Technical progress* is continually improving existing technologies and introducing new ones. This process does not remove the problem of diminishing returns, but rather continually pushes it back, so that further investment can, indeed, increase total output and per capita output. According to this view, it is *the rate of technical progress* that determines the maximum long-run rate of growth of economies rather than the savings rate or the rate of population growth. In the long run, growth rates in all economies will converge on the rate of technical progress. Should technical progress ever cease, growth of per capita incomes would also cease.

However, there is no internal ('endogenous') mechanism *within* the neoclassical model that leads technical progress to occur – in the way that, for instance, *within* the model, capital intensity of production (K/L) rises because of an increase in the wage rate: that is, technical progress is 'exogenous' to the neoclassical model, having a kind of independent existence, driven by autonomous scientific advances and proceeding at a pace not affected by what is happening within the economic system. Indeed, it was once described by Robert Solow as 'manna from Heaven'. We return to this not entirely plausible scenario in the discussion, later in this chapter, of 'endogenous' growth.

Applying neoclassical growth theory

The neoclassical aggregate production function has been used by Solow and many others in attempts to identify the individual contribution of each of the factors of production to economic growth.

The general approach used is as follows: if the production function is transformed mathematically into a 'growth equation' it splits total growth of GNP into the growth of the individual inputs contributing to that growth and can thus be used to identify the contribution to growth of each input. If capital (K) and labour (L) are the two factor inputs, the estimating equation takes the form:

$$Yg = T + k.Kg + l.Lg + . . . \qquad (4.8)$$

where:

- Yg is the annual growth rate of the economy; Kg is the annual growth rate of the capital stock; and Lg is the annual growth rate of the labour force.
- *k* is the (partial) elasticity of output with respect to inputs of capital; *l* is the (partial) elasticity of output with respect to inputs of labour.

Then T indicates the *shift* in the entire production function resulting from improved efficiency in resource use. That is, T represents the annual rate of growth of total productivity. Once the values of all other terms are known, the value of T is found as a *residual* and is conventionally taken to measure the impact of technical progress on output.

The initial estimates, by Moses Abramovitz (1956) and Robert Solow (1957) were made using data for growth of output and for the inputs of capital and labour. The impact of technical progress on the growth rate was then estimated as a residual – that is, the portion of growth still 'unexplained' after the contributions of capital and labour had been worked out. These investigations yielded the unexpected result that growth of factor inputs (i.e. growth of inputs of labour and capital) appeared to have caused only a small portion of total growth:

> The main result of that 1957 exercise was startling. Gross output per hour of work in the US economy doubled between 1909 and 1949; and some seven-eighths of that increase could be attributed to technical change in the broadest sense and only the remaining eighth could be attributed to conventional increase in capital intensity.
>
> *(Solow, 1957)*

The fact that nearly 90 per cent of growth was ascribed, not to pre-specified variables but rather to a residual somewhat arbitrarily identified with technical progress, was clearly unsatisfactory. It was, in the words of Abramovitz (1956), 'a measure of our ignorance about the causes of economic growth'.

With a view to reducing the extent of this 'ignorance', Solow did suggest that accelerating capital investment might be 'more important than it looked' in that it might lead not only to higher capital intensity, but also to a faster transfer of new technology into actual production, with consequential impacts on the transition rate of growth (though not on the steady-state rate of growth). This was the 'embodiment' effect.

Subsequent investigations using the neoclassical production function – carried out by, notably, Edward Dennison, Zvi Griliches and Dale Jorgenson – sought to expand the proportion of economic growth identified with specific, pre-identified inputs into the production process. This was done by broadening the range of inputs included as sources of growth, by bringing more precision and depth to estimates of the impact of capital and labour, and by correcting, as far as possible, errors in measurement.[9] Thus, for example, Denison decomposed growth in the US economy into a large number of sources, including the following:

(a) *Total factor input:*
Labour:

- employment
- hours worked
- age-sex composition
- education.

Capital:

- inventories
- non-residential structures
- dwellings
- international assets.

Land

(b) *Output per unit of input:*

- Advances in knowledge
- Improved resource allocation
  - Farm
  - Non-farm self-employment
- Economies of scale
- Irregular factors
  - Weather (in farming)
  - Labour disputes.

---

[9] See, for instance, Dennison (1967, 1974); and Griliches and Jorgenson (1972).

In principle, many more inputs could be added to this list, though data availability is a constraint, particularly in developing countries.[10]

The progressive refinement of the growth-accounting process and, in particular, the careful separation of the effects of improvements in factor quality from those of increases in factor stocks, enabled Dale Jorgenson, in a paper published in 1990,[11] to narrow the proportion of US growth, over the period 1947 to 1985, attributed to technical progress to 34 per cent – well below the initial estimate made by Solow.

Empirical macroeconomic analysis – the search for 'patterns'

BOX 4.11 HOLLIS CHENERY

HOLLIS CHENERY (1918–1994)
(World Bank Archive)

Hollis Chenery, for over a decade the World Bank's chief economist, was responsible for the Bank's emergence as a major contributor to research on development issues. His own output included notable work on 'gap models' (an extension of the Harrod model used to determine the levels of domestic savings and foreign exchange required to secure a desired rate of growth); on the need for compatibility of wealth redistribution, poverty alleviation, and growth policies (*Redistribution with Growth* is a key contribution in this context); and on patterns of structural change in developing countries as they grow.

A somewhat different application of macroeconomic analysis to the growth process is the search for regular – 'normal' – patterns of structural change in developing economies. The rationale here is that the identification of systematic changes, tracked over the 'development trajectory' (that is, the key period in the growth history) of those countries for which reliable data are available, could provide a useful guide to understanding their development process and the likely future development patterns of other countries.

Using regression analysis – primarily cross-sectional, but adding time-series data as and where available – such 'morphological' analysis can be adapted to examine a large number of development processes, notably shifts in patterns of *consumption* (for example, between food and non-food products), of *production* (for example, between primary output and manufactures), of *employment* (for example between farm work and non-farm work), of *geographical distribution of population* (rural versus urban), of *international trade* (for example, the product composition of exports and imports), of *savings and investment*, and so on, to include as many 'structural' variables as are of interest to the analyst.[12]

---

[10] A useful summary of the many attempts to improve this kind of growth analysis is presented in David and Wright (1999).

[11] Jorgenson, Dale, 'Productivity and economic growth', in Berndt, E.R. and Jack E. Triplett (eds) (1990) *Fifty Years of Economic Measurement*, University of Chicago Press.

[12] Notable contributions to this line of analysis are: Chenery and Syrquin (1975); Chenery and Taylor (1968); Perkins and Syrquin (1989).

The dominant contributor to this body of analysis was the World Bank economist Hollis Chenery. Mobilizing the massive data resources of, *inter alia*, the World Bank and the United Nations, he and a range of collaborators searched for patterns in the development experience of an ever-increasing number of countries, in the process establishing new 'stylized facts' about the nature, extent and timing of uniformities in development experience.

Endogenous growth theory

BOX 4.12 PAUL ROMER

Paul Romer is one of the founders of the 'New Growth Theory' school which, from the mid-1980s, has sought to integrate Technical Progress into formal growth theory, hence the term 'endogenous growth'. His views imply that increasing returns to investment, especially in knowledge, promise a world of continuing growth, freed from the shackles of diminishing returns. These views have important implications for government policy on technology and education and have earned Romer public recognition, not least in the form of identification by *Time* magazine as 'One of the 25 most influential Americans', and regular nominations for a Nobel Prize. A graduate in Physics as well as Economics, he teaches at Stanford. Much of his published work is mathematically complex; he acknowledges that this can cause problems since, as he has pointed out, 'There are three kinds of Economists – those that can count and those that can't'.

PAUL ROMER (1955–)
(Stanford University)

Interview (text) On 'Growth, Technological Change and an Unlimited Human Future'
http://www.reason.com/0112/fe.rb.post.shtml

Vide Video: On Growth Theory: http://www.leighbureau.com/speaker_documents.asp?view=video&id=148

Endogenous Growth Theory (sometimes called 'New Growth Theory') emerged in the 1980s as a reaction to the limitations of the Solow-style neoclassical view of growth. What were the main problems with the neoclassical model in this context? The summary Box 4.13 identifies these as, briefly:

- The exogenous status of technical progress, the key factor invoked as the source of long-run growth of per capita output;
- The lack of correspondence between predictions of declining (and probably converging) growth rates across countries and the observed actuality;
- The low marginal productivity of investment in most developing countries, where it ought to have been particularly high.

The insistence that the determination of the rate of growth of the economy is a phenomenon *internal* to the workings of the macroeconomy – that is, *endogenous*, proceeding at a rate governed by other variables in the economic system – is a view shared by members of this otherwise quite diverse school of thought, and gives it its name. Different contributors have identified a wide range of relevant issues. In particular, economists such as Paul Romer (1986) argue that, in fact, the orthodox neoclassical insistence on diminishing returns as the central fact of life is misconceived. If the possibility of increasing returns is reintroduced, then there is no need to foresee a ceiling on per capita income. Increased saving and investment can, indeed, increase the long-run rate of growth.

BOX 4.13 THE NEOCLASSICAL MODEL: EXPECTATIONS AND PROBLEMS

Neoclassical expectations

1. Growth rates of per capita income across countries expected to converge towards zero as economies reach ceilings imposed by diminishing returns to capital investment. Appropriate policies on savings rates can also make per capita incomes converge . . . but:

2. Technical progress can save the situation by continually shifting the production function upwards so postponing indefinitely the arrival of the stationary state. Access to improvements in technology enable developing countries to follow the path of developed countries, with growth rates converging on the rate of technical progress.

3. Since developing countries use relatively labour-intensive technologies, their rates of return on capital should be relatively high and/or large flows of capital to them from wealthy countries should be equalizing marginal productivity of capital worldwide.

Problems

1. Growth rates and per capita incomes differ greatly worldwide with little sign of a general slowing of rates or convergence.

2. (i) *Practical*: Accessing and implementing technical progress is often difficult for developing countries;
   (ii) *Theoretical*: Technical progress is simply *assumed* to happen. No explanation is offered of *why* it happens nor of what leads people to spend time and money pursuing it. Opponents argue that it seems likely that factors *integral* to the growth process (*not* outside it) determine the rate of technical progress. What are they?

3. Neither of these phenomena is observed.

This conclusion depends on the hypothesized impact of spending more on research and 'human capital formation' – knowledge and training. Such investment, driven by the profit motive, is seen as having an especially powerful leverage effect on production since it increases productivity directly *and* generates significant 'spillover' effects – positive 'externalities'. When, for instance, an individual invests in training with a view to increasing earnings potential, or a firm invests in R&D with a view to improving profitability, it will often be the case that the gains to the economy as a whole exceed the private gains to these investors because of spillover effects, namely the external benefits conferred on other individuals and firms. Moreover, while it may still be true that an individual firm experiences diminishing returns to its *own* investment in knowledge, yet, when the additional benefits accruing to that firm from the external economies flowing towards it as a result of the *economy-wide totality of such investment* are taken into account, the firm can experience increasing returns overall.

As T.N. Srinivasan (1998) has observed:

> Human capital . . . is not just another input into the production process (albeit complementary to other inputs such as physical capital) with diminishing marginal returns, but one, particularly in the form of knowledge capital, with the characteristics of a non-rival public good whose accumulation can make marginal returns to other inputs, particularly physical capital, increasing rather than diminishing.

Much 'New Growth Theory' has, in fact, been around for some time. Thus, for instance, the idea that the rate of technical progress may be determined directly by the internal workings of the economy (rather than by some external *deus ex machina*) was formalized in the 1960s by Nicholas Kaldor (1961). His 'Technical Progress Function' represented new technological discoveries as causing the rate of growth of output per capita to exceed the rate of growth of capital per capita (i.e., output as an increasing function of investment) so driving up the rate of profit and inducing further investment at this higher rate of growth. And, of course, this line of thinking recalls Adam Smith's idea of increasing returns as a source of growth.[13]

A corollary of these perceptions is the view that growth rates need not decline but can, in fact, be increased by deliberate, appropriate investment in R&D and human capital. Since much training, R&D, and innovation is subsidized by governments, the state does, after all, have an important role to play in accelerating growth and should find ways, particularly ways based on incentives, to reinforce, rather than curtail, such activities. This conclusion is strengthened if we accept Lucas's view that, left to itself, the market tends to under-invest in knowledge, and this spending must be reinforced by government interventions (Lucas, 1988). In this context Romer identifies several possibilities worth considering: 'Tax subsidies for private research, antitrust exemptions for research joint ventures . . . government procurement . . . the scope of protection for intellectual property rights, [and] the links between private firms and universities' (Romer, 1994).

The 'new economy'

In the last decade of the twentieth century, some economists put forward the view that developments in information technology and globalization were creating a 'new economy' characterized by much higher rates of productivity improvement and growth than were known in the 'traditional' economy. Hyperbolic techno-economic phenomena such as **Moore's Law** (the power of a silicon chip doubles every 18 months, resulting in very rapid falls in costs) and **Metcalfe's Law** (the value of a computer network grows roughly in line with the square of the number of users, implying sharply increasing returns to investment) were adduced in support of the 'new economy' growth model.

---

[13] For the original exposition of the associated 'learning-by-doing' hypothesis see Arrow (1962).

In its more extreme forms this view insisted that 'built-in growth' (estimated for the US at well over 4 per cent per annum) ensured that inflation was dead, that the business cycle was finished, and that, more generally, the established theories of economics (from supply and demand to the macroeconomics of growth – and ways of valuing shares) were no longer valid. And these views were frequently put with unusual enthusiasm: 'The dials on our economic dashboard have started spinning wildly, blinking and twittering as we head into new territory. It is possible the gauges are all broken, but it's much more likely that the world is turning upside down' (Kelly, 1999, p. 3).

The fact that, since the bursting of the 'dot.com' stock market bubble in high-tech shares in 2000, very little of importance has been heard from this latest school of growth economists may be seen as support for a sceptical view of these claims.

Specific criticisms include the simple statistical point that to achieve a 4 per cent growth rate (equivalent to over 3 per cent per capita) 'computers and the Internet would need to be a far more important engine of growth than railways or electricity' (*Economist*, 1/9/2000), which underwrote growth of below 1.5 per cent in the nineteenth century and around 2 per cent in the twentieth century – which seems a very tall order. And in terms of economic significance:

> The ultimate test . . . is the impact of a new technology on productivity across the economy as a whole, either by allowing existing products to be made more efficiently or by creating entirely new products. Faster productivity growth is the key to higher living standards.
>
> *(ibid.)*

It is not clear that, in this respect, the IT advances have had the revolutionary effects claimed for them.

There seems little doubt that the view of more orthodox economists such as Carl Shapiro and Hal Varian (2000), to the effect that 'technology changes, economic laws do not', has prevailed. There have, indeed, been many earlier instances when the demise of macroeconomics as we know it has been proclaimed during phases of very rapid technological change or economic distress. In the end, economics has not changed fundamentally; most of the old rules still apply. Nevertheless, it is as well to acknowledge the element of truth in the view that unusually rapid growth can result in the suspension of certain economic phenomena (in this case, *inter alia*, inflation), though these effects are temporary in nature and in a sense akin to the disequilibrium behaviour we have noted in the neoclassical economy as it absorbs increased savings.

Summary conclusions: key differences between growth theories

The main sets of macroeconomic growth theories examined above differ in several crucial respects:

- *Growth and stability*. The neo-Keynesian Harrod–Domar theory emphasizes the likelihood that growth will be associated with instability of output, and thus instability of income and employment. The basic neoclassical model, in contrast, sees the economy as stable and self-equilibrating at full employment.

▶

This disagreement stems from the different assumptions made about the extent to which factor markets will, and can, encourage factor substitution. Harrod's focus on the problem of sustained unemployment of labour, and its causes, predisposed him to be pessimistic about the economy's ability to self-correct to full employment of all resources.

- *Savings and growth.* Harrod, the classical economists, and endogenous-growth enthusiasts, suggest that increased saving rates can increase the rate of growth. The orthodox neoclassical model, however, implies that though increasing s will increase g during the subsequent period of adjustment to the new equilibrium, there will be no long-term impact on g – which depends, instead, on the rate of growth of population. This conclusion in part depends on the assumption of diminishing returns. If this is replaced by the endogenous-growth theorists' assumption of increasing returns to investment, increased savings can indeed increase the growth rate permanently.

- *Technical progress and growth.* Orthodox neoclassical economists are, of course, aware that the basic model, as explained above, tells only part of the story. The outcomes of the model, in particular the stable capital–labour ratio, the stable output-per-capita ratio, and the stable wage rate, do not reflect what has *actually* happened in most economies. As indicated by our 'stylized facts', in most countries there has actually been long-term growth in the values of these variables. It would be possible to argue that such observed changes simply reflect movements towards long-term equilibrium positions. But a more plausible explanation can be had by adding *technical progress* to the model. Technical progress can generate increased g even from unchanged quantities of inputs (measured in £s) by improving their *quality*. It may also be embodied in new capital goods, which suggests a further way in which increased s could increase g.

  More controversial is the matter of the *cause* of technical progress. The neoclassical view that its origins lie, in large part, outside the confines of the growth process is strongly challenged by the 'endogenous' contention that technical progress has its origins within the growth process itself, and can be explained by elements in that process.

- *Returns and growth.* The assumption that diminishing returns to investment will result in a steady, or stationary, state in which per capita incomes are static in the absence of 'exogenous' technical progress is strongly challenged by endogenous-growth theorists, who echo Adam Smith's view (though for somewhat different reasons) that increasing returns are possible and that, with appropriate economic management, advances in knowledge can drive per-capita-income levels up in perpetuity.

The impact and influence of the various macroeconomic theories of economic growth on thinking and policy on development have varied considerably from one to the next. In particular, the emphasis on the importance of capital accumulation found in the Harrod–Domar approach (reappearing in different forms in work by Arthur Lewis, in World Bank research and advice, and in Rostow's 'stages' theory of growth) has been much more influential in practical terms than the neoclassical model – which has been seen by many as portraying a world of smoothly functioning markets, full employment of labour and capital, and equilibrium, remote from the realities of development in many countries.

Questions for discussion

4.1 According to Harrod's view of the process of economic growth the fraction of national income saved is an important determinant of the rate of growth of an economy. According to Solow's view, however, the propensity to save and the rate of growth are, in the long run, unrelated. What explains this contradiction?

4.2 What did Ricardo mean when he said that economic growth must eventually fade away to be replaced by a 'stationary state' – and why? Can you suggest any 'escape routes' from such a stationary state?

4.3 Why does the basic neoclassical growth model developed by Solow suggest that a process of 'convergence' may eventually result in all economies' arriving at the same 'steady state'?

4.4 Explain the economic logic behind the attempts by (i) Dennison and (ii) Chenery to explain the sources of economic growth.

4.5 What role, if any, do you see for technical progress in the process of economic growth?

4.6 Bearing in mind the diverse nature of today's developing countries, consider the problems this poses for economists attempting to construct a single, generally applicable, model of the development process.

4.7 Explain the differing roles played by 'technology' in models of economic growth.

Additional reading

Jones, C.I. (2001) *Introduction to Economic Growth*, Norton, New York.

Sen, A. (ed.) (1970) *Growth Economics*, Penguin Books, London.

Solow, R.M. (1956) 'A contribution to the theory of economic growth', *Quarterly Journal of Economics*, **70**, pp. 65–94.

Temple, J. (1999) 'The new growth evidence', *Journal of Economic Literature*, **37** (1) March, pp. 112–56.

Weil, D.N. (2008) *Economic Growth*, 2nd edn, Addison Wesley, London.

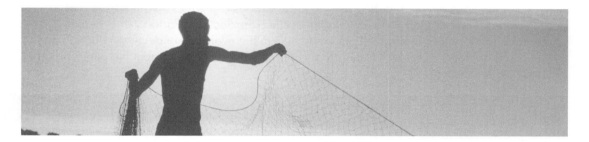

CHAPTER 5

The Development Process: Landmark Theories

Seventy years ago John Maynard Keynes wrote that 'The ideas of economists and political philosophers, both when they are right and when they are wrong, are more powerful than is commonly understood. Indeed the world is ruled by little else.' There is no doubt that, over the last fifty years, the ideas of development economists have had very considerable influence over the policy actions of the major international aid agencies and of many developing countries. An examination of the 'landmarks' along the theoretical journey taken by these economists can explain a great deal about the history of development policy – as well as enabling us to make a more informed judgement as to when it was 'right' and when it was 'wrong'.

Introduction

The previous chapter presented alternative views of how, at the broadest macroeconomic level, economic growth might occur. In the present chapter we show – through summaries of 'landmark' contributions – how development economists have made use of these ideas to formulate in more specific terms their theories of the process of growth in developing countries.

It will be seen that these theories differ widely in their level of sweep and generality, their focus, and in many cases their conclusions as to what is actually important if development is to proceed. Several of the concepts discussed may be viewed as following what is, in a sense, a logically interconnected sequence of ideas. An idea is elaborated until it becomes clear that it does not fit the facts or has failed to yield effective policy measures – this being the fate of most theories of development in a world in which the problem of poverty has clearly not been 'solved' – at which point an alternative view is advanced. In some cases – for instance the advocacy of 'unbalanced-growth' in opposition to a 'balanced-growth' orthodoxy – a 'thesis–antithesis' process has produced sharp reversals of direction. In other cases – notably the 'dependency' challenge to conventional theories of the gains from trade – a wholly new explanation of how the world economy works has been put forward to challenge the orthodox view.

In parallel with this process, but not necessarily integrated into it, specific theories have been advanced to tackle specific policy problems. For instance, the evolution of the 'two-gap' thesis (reviewed later in this chapter) was a response to a need to improve the accuracy of estimates of aid requirements, and made use of Harrod-type concepts which had already been widely rejected by opponents of capital-fundamentalism. Easterly (1997) finds Harrod's legacy still influential in the aid agencies long after the original ideas had come to be regarded as serious over-simplifications.

This chapter is devoted to theories – in these various categories – which have had a major impact on thinking about development since the Second World War. Whether currently in, or out, of fashion, all are landmarks in the evolution of development thinking and all contributed important insights to the debate on how development happens and how it may be accelerated.

BOX 5.1 A LANDMARK THEORY TOOLKIT

Mark-up pricing is a method of pricing such that the producer determines the price of a product by adding a certain percentage (or a certain fixed sum) – the 'mark-up' – to the cost of production. The ability to price in this way, rather than to allow the market to determine price, suggests that the producer has some 'monopoly power'.

Backward linkage refers to the purchasing of inputs (raw materials, components, plant and machinery, know-how, and so on) by a firm from other firms. The size of the backward linkage of a single firm may be measured numerically as the ratio of these purchases to the total selling price of its output. Other things being equal, the higher the extent of the backward linkage of a firm to other local firms, the greater will its 'stimulating' impact be on these firms.

Forward linkage is the corresponding concept relating to the ratio of sales made by a firm to other firms to its total output.

'Commercialization' of agriculture occurs, in the growth model set out by Arthur Lewis, when all of the 'surplus labour' in the subsistence sector has been transferred to the industrial sector. From that point onward the elasticity of supply of labour to the industrial sector is no longer infinite and the agricultural sector and the industrial sector must compete for labour.

Capital-fundamentalism is the view that capital investment, and resultant capital accumulation, are essential requirements of the process of economic growth.

Circles – vicious and virtuous

Modern thinking on development initially focused on the problems of the poorer European countries and (as mentioned in Chapter 3) favoured a seriously interventionist approach. The views of the main contributors to this line of thought are set out in the discussion of 'balanced and unbalanced growth' below. Prior to that, by way of introduction, this section deals briefly with concepts of 'vicious' and 'virtuous' circles.

Underdevelopment and poverty are often seen as being perpetuated by one or more **'vicious circles'** which have the effect of preventing growth and confining the economy to a low-income, or poverty, 'trap'. '**Virtuous circles**' have the opposite effect, promoting growth by setting up self-reinforcing income-raising systems which work through 'circular and cumulative causation'.[1]

A typical vicious circle would see initial low productivity levels leading to low per capita income levels – which place a very low ceiling on attainable levels of saving – which, in turn, rule out the new capital investment needed to improve productivity. The economy is stuck in a low-productivity, low-income trap.

An important characteristic of a vicious circle is that it cannot be breached by small, incremental improvements. Thus poverty is a state of *stable equilibrium* – a condition to which the economy tends to return after a small disturbance, since a disturbance sets up countervailing pressures pushing the system back to the starting point. An example of a favourable 'shock' which produces no lasting effects on poverty was central to the thinking of Malthus (summarized in Chapter 4). Here a minor improvement in, for instance, agricultural productivity raises real per capita incomes above subsistence levels; this results in population growth until the 'surplus' production potential created by the technological improvement is, literally, eaten up and per capita income is pushed back to subsistence level.

Note that the existence of a vicious circle does not necessarily imply that *all* characteristics of the economy return to baseline values after a shock. Permanent change may be possible. In the example above, for instance, population may be permanently increased. Experience of changes in population and income over the last two centuries does, however, suggest an alternative possibility. Population will decline if income falls below subsistence level, and increase temporarily if income rises above subsistence level. Yet, if the favourable shock is large enough and sufficiently prolonged, it may result in an increase in per capita incomes which *permanently* outpaces population growth. Indeed, growing affluence may result in a change in the income-growth/population-growth relationship such that increasing incomes no longer encourage increases in numbers. This indeed fits with the experience of the developed, and a large number of developing, countries.

The critical feature of the 'circle' is that *per capita income* tends to return to its original low-level equilibrium value, thus perpetuating poverty. Escape from the low-level equilibrium poverty trap implies, by definition, that *more than one equilibrium* is, in fact, possible. Nelson (1956) provides a simple example of this based on the population dynamics summarized in the paragraph above (and the assumption that technical progress is absent).

In Figure 5.1 per capita income is measured along the horizontal axis and growth of population and growth of GNI on the vertical axis. The point X indicates the subsistence level of per capita income. Here income is so low that net saving is zero. As a result, the growth rate of GNI is also zero. Should per capita income, shown along curve XG, rise above subsistence level X, net saving will now be possible. From its zero base, the ratio of saving to total GNI will initially rise rapidly. As a result, income growth will take place along curve XG. Population growth will also take place, along curve XP, induced by rising income. Eventually, population growth will reach a maximum, so that XP flattens out. Similarly, savings as a proportion of GNI will reach a maximum value (set by the community's preferences regarding savings versus consumption). As diminishing returns set in as a result of these two effects, the growth rate will fall – shown by the downturn in curve XG.

To see the relevance of multiple equilibria, starting at the subsistence point X, consider the stability of the system along XA and AB, respectively. A favourable 'shock'

---

[1] These processes are discussed in detail in G. Myrdal (1957).

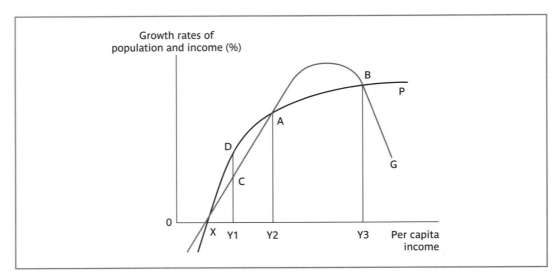

FIGURE 5.1 Escape from the 'Poverty Trap'

(perhaps improved export sales) which increases per capita income from X to a point between X and Y2 – say Y1 – will result in the population growth rate (Y1D) exceeding the growth rate of GNI (at Y1C). This will drive per capita income *down* again until the subsistence level is reached at X. Thus, for improvements which do not raise per capita income as far as Y2, the ultimate equilibrium point to which the economy will gravitate is X. Consider next a shock big enough to push per capita income into the range Y2 to Y3. Now curve XG lies above curve XP, so the growth rate of GNI exceeds the growth rate of population. Hence per capita income will continue to *rise* – to the point B. Beyond this point (i.e. to the right of B) curve XP (population growth) again lies above XG (income growth), so shocks which push up per capita income will be reversed by population growth, and the system will return to B.

In short, the economy depicted in Figure 5.1 has *two possible stable-equilibrium situations* to one of which the economy will tend to return. The first is the low-level income trap at X. The other is B – corresponding to the higher per capita income level Y3. Assuming that the starting point is X, which of these two equilibrium points the economy ultimately settles at depends on the magnitude of the initial 'shock' that drives per capita income above the subsistence level X. A *minor* shock will have no long-term effect on per capita income. But a *major* shock, sufficient to push per capita income above Y2, will lead to the much higher long-run equilibrium per capita income at B.

Recent discussion of this issue suggests that a wide range of overlapping vicious circles can frustrate attempts by the poor to climb out of poverty, and thereby impair national growth performance. In effect, the *consequences* of poverty themselves may prevent people from escaping from it. At the level of the individual, examples of such feedback loops are:

■ The poor cannot afford to build the stocks of physical or knowledge capital needed to improve their productivity and thus their earnings;

■ The poor are much more prone to ill health – which reduces their productivity;

■ The poor are often able to attend only low-quality schools – with the associated diminished earnings potential and reduced labour mobility.

At the macroeconomic level, poverty reinforces poor growth performance, and thus reinforces poverty, since:

■ Poor countries have fewer individuals capable of adopting, managing, and generating the new technologies that would contribute to productivity improvement;

■ Poor countries often lack the infrastructure and/or human capital that would make them attractive to inward foreign investment – and also lack the resources needed to develop such infrastructure;

■ Poor countries often lack the infrastructure and/or resources that would facilitate sectoral and territorial labour mobility in search of higher income opportunities;

■ Poor countries may find ethnic or racial tensions exacerbated by income disparities – leading to interregional tensions that make these regions, and the country as a whole, riskier to invest in.[2]

Virtuous circles may also take several forms. One important example invokes **Verdoorn's Law** – which holds that productivity tends to increase as output rises (as a result, amongst other things, of scale economies and the 'learning by doing' process). Here an external shock – an increase in foreign demand for the home country's exports, say – leads to a rise in output. This triggers the Verdoorn process, increasing the efficiency of the export industries, thus making them even more competitive than at the beginning of the process – so that exports and output increase again.

A second virtuous circle depends on the externalities which form a core part of the endogenous models discussed in Chapter 4. Investment in knowledge by some firms results in knowledge spillovers to other firms, so increasing the latters' rates of return (profitability) above expectations and encouraging increased levels of investment in knowledge by them. This results in further spillovers and investment – in an upward, self-reinforcing spiral process.[3]

Balanced and unbalanced growth – and the big push

Introduction

The possibility that growth may be stalled by the existence of vicious circles has suggested to many economists the need for a special effort to push the economy over a *threshold* into a region where sustained increase in per capita incomes is possible.

The specific nature of this special effort depends, of course, on the nature of the factors inhibiting growth. As we saw in the previous section, in the case of the simplest of Malthusian models the need is to accelerate growth to a rate which is permanently above the maximum possible rate of growth of population – while, in a more realistic neo-Malthusian setting, in which it is expected that population growth rates will decline once some critical per capita income level is reached, the policy aim would be to find a way of pushing income above that critical level.

For many economists in the 1950s and 1960s the answer was a sharp rise in the level of investment out of income – in Solow's words 'a major burst of investment [to] lift the system

---

[2] These points are developed further in Perry *et al.* (2006).

[3] For a brief discussion of vicious and virtuous circles related to investment in knowledge see Easterly (2001).

into a self-generating expansion of income and capital per head.'[4] *Increasing the rate of investment* was seen as the key to growth (a view which contrasted with the neoclassical focus on *efficient allocation* of available investible funds). As we shall see, this conclusion has been embedded, in one form or another, in a variety of competing theories. In this section we focus on an argument for a 'burst of investment' aimed at overcoming not a demographic problem but a technological one – the vicious-circle mechanism that results from the existence of economies of scale in production.

Economies of scale, indivisibilities, and the case for balanced growth

The doctrine of '**balanced growth**' – primarily associated with **Rosenstein-Rodan** (1943) and **Nurkse** (1953), asserts that development requires a broadly based, simultaneous expansion across a wide range of industries. Isolated spurts of growth in just one or two industries are seen as doomed to failure. What is needed is a 'big push' to break the constraints of the 'low-level trap'.

This problem with narrowly based growth is seen as arising because of the existence of *economies of scale* in many modern production processes. These scale economies make small-scale units in the modern sector uneconomic since it is not possible simply to subdivide a production process and maintain its efficiency. In effect, such production processes are 'indivisible'. The nature of many production functions dictates that, to be viable, investment must be made in relatively large-scale units.

This, in turn, leads to *imbalance* on the *demand* side: Specifically, while the total of incomes generated by production in the small number of new, large-scale factories will be sufficient to buy all of their output (since the total selling price of final output will equal the sum of the various incomes spent on producing that output), workers in these factories will not wish to spend all of their incomes on their own output. (For instance, workers in a new shoe factory will not spend all of their incomes on shoes.) They will wish to spend their incomes on a much wider range of products than just those made in their own factories. Meanwhile workers in the non-growing sectors, together with the unemployed (the prime concern of Rosenstein-Rodan's seminal paper), will continue to earn their old levels of income and thus have no additional purchasing power with which to buy the 'surplus' output of the growth sector.[5] The result is a lack of demand for the output of the growing sectors – and their eventual collapse. The process of growth is stalled because of the mismatch between the commodity mix produced by the new factories and the commodity mix demanded by the workers in these factories.

On the *supply* side the indivisibility problem again arises – as a limited investment programme is unlikely to be able to finance the inputs (including infrastructure inputs) which are required by expanding industries, so that their growth will be stalled by bottlenecks and supply failures.

Viewed from a vicious-circle perspective, this situation may be seen as one in which low income levels restrict saving, low saving levels restrict capital formation, and the resulting limitation on the range of investment projects which can be undertaken at any one time condemns investment to failure because of imbalances on both demand and supply sides – so perpetuating low income levels.

---

[4] Solow (1970).

[5] If these workers switched their demand towards the products of the new sector this would simply shift the deficient-demand problem to the products they previously bought.

The answer to this problem was held to be the creation of a *large number* of different, mutually-supporting industries *at the same time*. Careful selection of these industries would ensure that a match (or *balance*) was maintained between what was produced and what was then demanded by the new incomes created in this growing sector. The diversity of goods required by consumers would correspond to the diversity of new output, the result being '*balanced growth*'; and the level of production of these various outputs could be large enough to yield the required economies of scale.

If the requirements for economic expansion are extended to include balance on the *supply* side, new sectors of industry and infrastructure could be expanded in a co-ordinated way to provide the crucial inputs needed by other industries – so preventing bottlenecks from interrupting production and slowing, or stopping, growth.

The role of the *state* would clearly be central to this strategy. As well as assuming the role of co-ordinator and, presumably, securing at least some of the funds required for investment, the state would perform the useful functions of reducing the level of risk faced by private investors (by, in effect, guaranteeing the adequacy of markets for production) and of capturing for the economy as a whole the external economies generated by the balanced-growth process (these being the spillovers which might not be perceived by, or figure in the profitability calculations of, individual private investors).

By definition, the balanced-growth process cannot be undertaken in a limited or piecemeal basis; it is all or nothing – and for this reason the strategy is often referred to as the *Big Push* or *Critical Minimum Effort* approach. Equally, because of the central importance of a major investment programme to the success of the project, 'capital-fundamentalism' is implied; one key prerequisite of growth is the availability of large quantities of investible funds.

Problems with the balanced growth model

- *Resource requirements*: As noted above, large amounts of capital will be required to finance the 'balanced' expansion. Furthermore, sophisticated planning systems must be in place to ensure that the very wide range of consumer goods, and production inputs, needed to keep the whole process going are produced in the required quantities, at the right time, and at the right prices. It is clear that the inputs of investment funds and planning expertise needed to implement a thoroughgoing 'balanced' strategy are likely to be far beyond the reach of poor countries.

- *Impact on prices of inputs*: Even if adequate resources could be mobilized to permit a Big Push to go ahead, the massive new demand for both capital and labour would push up the prices of both – since both capital and skilled labour are likely to be in inelastic supply. This could have damaging consequences for the prospects of successful evolution of the 'balanced' sector, since it would both deter private investors from expanding in certain sectors and erode the beneficial external-spillover benefits, creation of which is held to be one of the key advantages of a balanced approach to growth.

- *The possibility of exporting surpluses*: The proponents of balanced growth tended to be pessimistic about the prospects of a rapid expansion of trade in the post-war period. Had they been willing to admit the possibility of exporting surpluses of particular goods produced by the large-scale factories, then much of the case for balance would have disappeared. (In practice, today many economies have seriously 'unbalanced' trade, and almost all countries import a much wider range of goods than they export.)

- *The possibility of inhibiting imports*: On the demand side, a simpler alternative to the planned construction of 'balanced' industrial complexes might be available through the control of demand for imports. Thus the 'import-substitution' doctrine (reviewed below) proposes setting up barriers to importing in order to stimulate domestic production of a wide range of goods.

■ *Given certain cost structures a 'modern' sector of limited size may be able to establish itself*: It can be shown fairly easily that whether or not a Big Push is required to escape from the low-level trap may depend on the specific cost structures of production by 'traditional' sector producers and 'modern' sector producers, respectively. A simple model illustrating this is set out in Appendix 5.1.

Unbalanced growth

Some critics of the balanced-growth hypothesis have gone further than merely pointing to the problems summarized above, arguing that 'unbalanced' growth may have its own advantages. One of the first, and most influential, of those arguing that actual benefits might accrue from 'unbalancing' an economy was **Albert Hirschman**.[6]

BOX 5.2 ALBERT HIRSCHMAN

ALBERT HIRSCHMAN (1915–)
(Varian Fry Institute)

Albert O. Hirschman was born in Berlin in 1915. He attended the Sorbonne and the London School of Economics, later holding academic posts at Yale and Harvard, and at the Institute for Advanced Study at Princeton. His influential works in the fields of Economics, Politics and Sociology include, most notably, *The Strategy of Economic Development* (discussed briefly in this chapter), *Exit, Voice and Loyalty* (which examines three responses to decline in a corporation or a society), and *The Rhetoric of Reaction* (which sees conservative arguments against change as focusing on its claimed perverse effects, futility, and capacity to jeopardize earlier gains). Although acknowledged to be one of the most brilliant development theorists, he has been criticized for having resisted tight mathematical formulation of development theories – so leading a generation of economists into the wilderness and allowing an oversimplified constant-returns, perfect-competition view of reality to take over development economics and development-policy formulation for two decades.

Hirschman (1958) argued that the key bottleneck in developing countries was not a shortage of capital, but a shortage of entrepreneurial and decision-making capacity. To compensate for this, a mechanism was needed, incorporating incentives and pressures, to facilitate the identification and adoption of appropriate decisions. 'Imbalances', the symptoms of which are private profits and losses, are important guides to decision-making.

---

[6] An interesting perspective on Hirschman's theory (viewed as an important 'wrong turning' from the perspective of the *methodology*, as opposed to the content, of economic analysis) is available on the Web at Krugman (1996). The quotes in the box above are from this source.

Directly productive investment by the state should not be spread across a broad spectrum of activities (which would imply the need for a large input of decision-making) but should be concentrated in those projects which are likely to spark off further investment in other firms through their **backward and forward linkages** – that is, purchases from, and sales to, other local enterprises. The appearance of a new (or significantly increased) demand for a product, or the advent of a new source of much cheaper supply of inputs, would send a clear signal to investors and firms that here were obvious commercial opportunities, and would therefore spark off a further round of investment. This would economize on the need for entrepreneurial capacity (the key bottleneck).

Economies of scale – crucial to 'Big Push' thinking – were also an important element in the Hirschman model. Desirable backward and forward linkages were thought of as those which enabled, respectively, 'upstream' suppliers and 'downstream' customers to expand to the point where advantage could be taken of economies of scale, so making profitable operation possible.

However, the policy implications of Hirschman's view differed radically from those attached to the 'Big Push' approach in that it would now be necessary for government to focus, initially, on promoting investment in *a small number of industries or sectors* selected for their strategic linkage-forming potential. Such investment would create growth-promoting disequilibria – supply/demand imbalances – in the economy. The aim would be that investors would take action to correct these imbalances. This would create further disequilibria in further sectors – and so on.

Structural-change models of growth

Introduction

A more complex view of the development process than that embodied in the 'balanced versus unbalanced' debate sees systematic *structural change*, in one form or another, as the key characteristic of the developing economy. Different theories of growth and development focus on structural change from a variety of different angles and with different emphases.

In this section we look first at one of the most sweeping attempts to capture the dynamics of the entire development process: *Walt Rostow's* 'stages of growth' theory. Beginning with the traditional, 'pre-Newtonian' society and concluding with the modern mass-consumption era, this is one of the most celebrated, criticized and readable, ventures into this field. We than backtrack in time, and in scope, to examine the early, influential, attempt made by *Arthur Lewis* to identify the key process of structural change which he believed propelled the crucial transformation from 'traditional' to 'modern' economy.

Rostow's 'stages of growth'

Much thinking on development views the process as essentially a replication of the industrialization and growth of the now-industrialized countries. One important version of this approach argues that all countries pass through a sequence of clearly defined 'stages' as they develop; poor countries are seen as being on the same development path as wealthy nations – but are at an earlier 'stage' of this *linear* historical process. Probably the

BOX 5.3 WALT WHITMAN ROSTOW

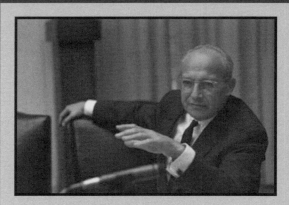

WALT WHITMAN ROSTOW (1916–2003)
Source: LBJ Library Yoichi R. Okamoto

Walt Whitman Rostow, named after the poet Walt Whitman, grew up in New York in a Russian immigrant family. Rostow graduated from Yale at age 19, completed his PhD in 1940, and studied at Oxford as a Rhodes Scholar. His academic career (as a Professor at Columbia University) was interrupted by a secondment, during World War II, to the covert Office of Strategic Services. After the War he held posts at both Oxford and Cambridge Universities. From 1950 to 1961 he was Professor of Economic History at MIT and, from 1969 onward, Professor of Economics and History at the University of Texas. In the intervening years Rostow was Chairman of the Policy Planning Council of the State Department, and later adviser to Secretary for Defence Robert McNamara, and Special Assistant for National Security Affairs in President Lyndon Johnson's administration. In these roles he exerted considerable influence on US foreign policy, being a particularly 'hawkish' proponent of the 'domino theory' with regard to Vietnam. His brother, Eugene Rostow, was also an eminent academic and, like Walt, prominent in government, being head of President Ronald Reagan's Arms Control Agency. Walt Rostow's major contribution to economics was in the field of growth and development – key publications being *The Stages of Economic Growth* and *The Economics of Take-Off into Sustained Growth*.

best-known stages theory is that put forward by Walt Rostow (1960). This divides the growth trajectory for all developing countries into five stages:

1   In the initial stage the **Traditional Society** has over 75 per cent of the population engaged in agriculture. Political power is in the hands of landowners or a central authority backed up by the army and civil servants. There is no general expectation of long-term 'economic progress', though temporary increases in per capita income may occur through random events such as good weather that results in expanded food production for a time.

2   In the **Transitional Stage** 'the preconditions for take-off' are created through:

■   The increasing efficiency of agriculture
■   The broadening of markets through expanded international trade (in particular trade in industrial raw materials)
■   The emergence of a more recognisably 'modern' business class
■   The possibility of long-run economic progress beginning to take hold in the minds of the commercial and governing classes.

3   The **Take-Off** is the critical stage in the development process. As a result of a sharp increase in levels of saving and investment – from around 5 per cent to well over 10 per cent of GNI – the availability of these funds to entrepreneurial groups, and the adoption of 'modern' technologies in a narrow range of 'leading sectors', output per capita

increases swiftly. (It will be noted that the emphasis given by Rostow to the need for a step-change in the level of investment places this scenario in the 'capital-fundamentalist' bracket.) At the same time, the economic and political influence of those elements in society dedicated to economic expansion successfully challenges the influence of the traditional holders of power. The scale of the investment programme, together with the confidence that expansion will continue, cause growth now to become 'built-in' and 'self-sustaining'.

4   In the **Drive to Maturity** the narrowly based growth of a few leading sectors which characterized the 'take-off' spreads to many other industrial sectors, as they too embark on the application of new technologies.

5   The **Stage of High Mass Consumption** is reached once the industrialization process is complete; mass demand for consumer goods is created by the expansion of incomes across the industrial labour force; and the range of consumer goods being made has broadened. This process is reinforced by the recognition by government that maintaining consumer demand is important if unemployment is to be kept at a low level.

Subtitled 'A Non-Communist Manifesto', Rostow's book inevitably attracted much interest – favourable and critical, technical and political. It is now widely accepted that much of the analysis is useful and contains insights into how and why growth actually happened in a number of the now developed countries. However, four decades of 'testing' of the stages hypothesis has produced evidence of many exceptions to the rigid format advanced by Rostow and has seriously eroded its credibility as an adequate 'road-map' of the development process for today's poor countries.

Growth in a two-sector ('dual') economy: the Lewis model

BOX 5.4 ARTHUR LEWIS

Arthur Lewis was born in St. Lucia in the West Indies in 1915. His father died when he was seven years old. On leaving school at age 14, he became a clerk in the civil service. He later won a scholarship to the London School of Economics (despite his desire to be an engineer) where he studied Industrial Economics. Lewis subsequently held professorial posts at Manchester University and Princeton. He helped establish and head the Caribbean Development Bank, was knighted by the Queen in 1963, and won a Nobel Prize in 1979. Lewis spent many of his later years acting as a distinguished economic advisor to the governments of a wide range of African and Asian countries. But the advice he offered to those of his students who aspired to a similar career was non-economic; the keys to success were 'a bottle of champagne and a sleeping tablet – to be taken as soon as you get on the plane'.

W. Arthur Lewis set out, in 1954, what became a very influential model of the growth process which does *not* incorporate virtuous circles and scale economies as essential components – and which owes little to either the Keynesian approach of Harrod or to the neoclassical-production-function approach of Solow. This model (Lewis, 1954) features a 'dual' economy – that is, an economy having *two sectors* – one a 'modern' capitalist sector, the other a 'traditional' subsistence sector. The latter acts as a reservoir containing, in effect,

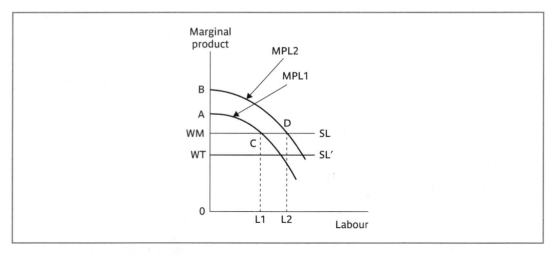

FIGURE 5.2 Growth in the Modern Sector

an 'unlimited supply of labour' – unlimited in the sense that the marginal productivity of labour has been driven down to zero, so labour can drain away from the sector without reducing output. The radical shift in the balance between the two sectors as this labour moves from the traditional to the modern sector is seen as the fundamental structural change driving the development process.

The growth of the modern sector is achieved by the continual ploughing back of the profits made by firms to purchase the new capital goods needed to employ the labour flowing from the traditional sector. (This emphasis on the importance of saving and capital formation again reflects the pervasive influence of 'capital-fundamentalist' thinking in the earlier theorizing on development.) Wage rates in the modern sector are higher than those in the traditional sector – which explains the continuous stream of workers moving into the modern sector – but the differential is nevertheless held down by the availability of large numbers of unemployed and underemployed in the traditional sector. Equally, the availability of surplus labour in the traditional sector ensures that the continual outflow of labour does not reduce output there.

This process is illustrated in Figure 5.2. Assuming a given initial stock of capital equipment in the modern sector, the addition of increasing inputs of labour (flowing from the traditional sector) will increase production, but at a declining rate – because of diminishing returns to the variable factor. Thus the curve showing the marginal product of labour (MPL1) will fall from left to right. Since there is an effectively 'unlimited' supply of labour at a wage rate high enough to induce labour to move from the traditional sector (where the subsistence wage is WT) to the modern sector (where the wage rate is WM), the effective supply curve of labour, SL, is horizontal, indicating infinite elasticity of supply.

How much labour will be employed in the modern sector given these initial conditions? Profit-maximizing firms will continue to hire additional labour until the marginal product of labour falls into equality with the wage rate – that is when the MPL1 curve cuts the SL curve – which occurs at labour force L1. (To hire fewer labourers would mean passing up the profit to be made since their resulting additional output (the marginal product of labour) exceeds the wage rate. To hire more than L1 would mean losing money since the additional output is worth less than the extra wages paid to them.)

When L1 labourers are hired, total output is measured by the area under the MPL1 curve at that point – OACL1. Of this, 0WMCL1 is the total wage bill (equal to the number of labourers, L1, times the wage rate WM), and the remainder, ACWM, is profits.

Assuming that at least some of these profits are reinvested in additional capital goods, productivity of labour will be improved. The marginal-productivity-of-labour curve will be pushed out to MPL2. With L1 labour still hired, the new marginal product of labour exceeds the wage rate WM; so more labour can now be taken on. The new profit-maximizing labour force is L2. Profits have expanded to BDWM – and can be reinvested in order to push the MPL curve still further to the right.

This process can continue as long as the supply of labour remains effectively 'unlimited'. As it proceeds, the modern sector will grow relative to the subsistence economy. Eventually, expansion of the modern sector may create a demand for labour sufficiently large to put pressure on the subsistence-sector labour resources, thus pushing up WT, unifying the labour market and, effectively, 'commercializing' agriculture.[7]

The plausibility of the Lewis model depends on the validity of a number of key assumptions. Thus, its accuracy as a description of how countries actually develop would be diminished if profits were not regularly reinvested in significant volume by capitalists (perhaps being used for consumption or to purchase non-productive assets and/or overseas assets); if profits were reinvested in increasingly capital-intensive technologies (so cutting the rate of growth of demand for labour); or if modern-sector wage rates were pushed up by trade-union pressure, by minimum-wage legislation, or by rising wage rates in the subsistence sector (possibly caused by rising demand for food coupled with inelastic production in agriculture). Even more fundamental is the possibility that the existence of zero-marginal-product labour in the rural areas is a fiction and that, as subsequent research has suggested, marginal products in traditional occupations are, with possible seasonal exceptions, generally positive – if often very small. Again, the assumption that migration flows match job availability in the modern sector has been widely challenged. (An alternative view, provided by Todaro, is outlined later in this chapter.)

However, it is generally accepted that Lewis' path-breaking work continues to provide a helpful insight into the situations of many poor countries in the twenty-first century.

The 'Two-Gap' model

The logic of the model

The requirements for, and effectiveness of, foreign aid were key issues in the development debate in the 1950s and 1960s. **'Two-Gap'** models developed by, amongst others, Ronald McKinnon (1964) and Hollis Chenery and colleagues (1962, 1966) were an important element in the attempt to identify appropriate policies in this context. Their emphasis on the key role of external funding as a means of breaking barriers to growth places these models in the 'capital-fundamentalist' tradition.

The starting point of the Two-Gap analysis is the familiar point that in a developing country growth may be constrained by a shortage of capital for investment – caused by a shortfall of savings below the level required to achieve the target level of growth.

[7] J.C.F. Fei and G. Ranis (1964), in their extension of the Lewis model, differentiate between the 'shortage' point – where the marginal product of labour in the traditional sector first rises above zero – and the 'commercialization' point, where the marginal productivities of labour in the two sectors are finally equalized.

BOX 5.5 BASIC ALGEBRA OF THE TWO-GAP MODEL

Students familiar with national-accounting aggregates may be puzzled as to how imbalances of the kinds basic to the Two-Gap model can arise. Starting with the fundamental macroeconomic national income identities set out in (5.1) and (5.2) below – (where Y is income, C consumption, I investment, X exports, M imports and S saving):

$$Y = C + I + X - M \tag{5.1}$$

and:

$$Y = C + S \tag{5.2}$$

it follows that:

$$C + I + X - M = C + S$$

so that:

$$I - S = M - X \tag{5.3}$$

Equation (5.3) tells us that any gap between imports and exports *must* be counterbalanced by an *identical gap* between investment and saving. If, last year, a country imported more than it exported (that is M > X), the resources used by the country to permit this must have exceeded the volume of resources domestically generated – local savings – by the same amount (that is I > S). Equally, if, last year, investment exceeded domestic saving, this must have been counterbalanced in the national accounts by a current account deficit, with M > X.

These equalities are *ex post* results of national-accounting procedures and follow from the definitions of the macroeconomic variables and relationships themselves. However, there is no particular reason why the difference between the amounts of investment and saving *planned in advance* (that is *ex ante*) should exactly equal the difference between the planned levels of imports and exports. What is important from a policy point of view is the feasibility of *ex ante* plans or expectations. For a clarification of this distinction we return to the basic Harrod–Domar model. Assume that the desired, or target, growth rate (*g*) in a developing country is 5 per cent. Assume also that the savings ratio (*s*) is 10 per cent and the capital–output ratio (*v*) is 4. We know, from Harrod, that *g* = *s*/*v*. Thus, with the given values for *s* and *v*, the rate of growth will be given by:

$$g = s/v \tag{5.4}$$

that is:

$$g = (10/100) / 4 \tag{5.5}$$

so:

$$g = 2.5\%$$

which is well below the target rate. Since the capital–output ratio is largely fixed by technological factors, the problem lies with the savings rate, which is too low. Assuming that there are plentiful investment opportunities, there is a *savings-investment gap*, which can be corrected by increasing the level of saving to the equivalent of 20 per cent of GNI. Since this will almost certainly prove difficult, foreign resources may have to be drawn in to fill the gap.

The possibility of a foreign-exchange gap arising *ex ante* may be shown using a parallel form of the Harrod–Domar equation. In this case the key problem is that a certain quantity of machinery and materials (given by M) must be imported if growth targets are to be

▶ achieved. The growth rate can now be seen as depending on the ratio of these imports to GNI (that is M/GNI – given by m). The counterpart of the capital–output ratio is the import-to-output ratio (that is M/GNI – given by z). The growth rate, g, is now:

$$g = m/z \qquad (5.6)$$

If the target growth rate is, once again, 5 per cent, the ratio of imports to GNI is 16 per cent, and the import-to-output ratio is 8, then:

$$g = (16/100) / 8 \qquad (5.7)$$

so:
$$g = 2.0\%$$

In this case the growth rate feasible given the foreign-exchange requirement implied by equation (5.7) is lower, at 2.0 per cent, than the growth rate feasible given the savings requirement implied by equation (5.5) – so the foreign-exchange gap is the dominant gap.

This 'savings-investment gap' may be filled by bringing in foreign resources in some combination of aid, borrowing from abroad, inward foreign investment, and balance of payments (current-account) surpluses. However, removing the shortage of savings in this way may not clear the path to growth. In order to grow at an acceptable rate most developing countries require to import significant quantities of foreign goods – capital goods and other inputs needed by local producers – and for this foreign exchange is required. If the amount of foreign exchange available is less than the required amount there will be a 'foreign exchange gap' which will have the effect of retarding growth *even if there are adequate funds to finance investment*.

In brief, then, the Two-Gap model sees growth as being, potentially, retarded by one of two 'gaps' – a shortage of investment funds relative to investment opportunities, or a shortage of foreign exchange relative to the amounts needed for essential imports. Since there is no reason why these gaps should be of equal size, filling one will not necessarily fill the other. For example, given a shortfall of investment funds of £200 million and a shortage of foreign exchange of £300 million, filling the savings-investment gap by giving aid to the tune of £200 million would not solve the problem, since a foreign exchange gap of £100 million (i.e. £300 – £200 million) would remain. In this case the foreign-exchange gap is the 'binding' gap (that is the 'dominant') gap. Unless it is filled growth will be retarded – so assistance worth £300 million is required to correct the situation.

It is also possible to imagine, in a different country, a situation in which the shortfall in availability of foreign exchange (of, say, £100 million) is a minor problem relative to the shortage of savings (of, say, £250 million). Here simply filling the foreign-exchange gap by making a donation of £100 million in aid will not solve the 'dominant' problem of the lack of investment funds – and growth will again be retarded. Again, the larger gap must be filled.

An important assumption made at this point is that local savings cannot easily be turned into foreign exchange – that is, that local resources cannot easily be substituted for foreign ones – especially in the short run. If this were not so, the foreign-exchange problem could be solved by mobilizing unused local resources to generate more foreign exchange by increasing exports, or by economizing on unnecessary imports. Neither of these strategies has proved easy to implement in practice; at the time the Two-Gap analysis was developed, widespread pessimism regarding the prospects for expanding exports would have made the problem appear even more intractable than it does today.

It should be noted that the two 'gaps' do not both have to be filled separately. Filling the 'dominant' gap (*with resources in the form of foreign exchange*) will always, at the same time, more than fill the smaller, non-dominant, gap. For instance, in the example given above of a binding savings-investment gap of £250 million and a foreign-exchange gap of £100 million, aid totalling £250 million will provide the resources required to fill the binding gap, while (since that aid is denominated in foreign exchange) more than filling the foreign-exchange gap. A similar argument applies where the foreign-exchange gap is dominant; filling it will more than fill the savings gap.

Thus the Two-Gap analysis identifies the important *dual* role of aid (or other forms of augmentation of local resources from external sources). Not only do these funds add to the quantity of resources available for investment in the developing country, but they also provide these additional resources in the form of foreign exchange. Both may be important.

In practice, for most developing countries – other than oil-producing countries – the foreign-exchange gap is today the dominant gap, with chronic deficits in the current account of the balance of payments being common. Shortages of foreign exchange act as a bottleneck and prevent the purchasing of the producer goods and technical expertise which are needed to bring all domestic resources into use (and to increase exports significantly). The result is widespread unemployment of resources, especially labour.

Broadening development policy and the definition of 'development'

The growth of interest in development economics was accompanied by a progressive broadening of both the scope of development policy and the definition of 'development' itself. The boundaries of capital-fundamentalism were first expanded to make room for the accumulation of both physical capital and 'human capital'. The latter involves the creation of skills through education and training, and its supposed importance has been reflected in greatly increased emphasis on spending on skill creation at all levels in developing countries. This innovation led, in turn, to the view that factors correlated to successful skill creation – health status of the population, physical and financial access to education, and so on – also had, by extension, an important bearing on growth.

A parallel innovation has been the broadening of the definition of what constitutes 'development' itself. A notable contributor to this process was Dudley Seers, who attacked the conventional view that development and economic growth were synonymous. He argued that genuine development necessarily involved extensive social change, and suggested that, in order to assess a country's economic performance it was appropriate to ask the following questions: 'What has been happening to poverty? What has been happening to unemployment? What has been happening to inequality?' Then 'If all three of these have become less severe beyond doubt, there has been a period of development for the country concerned. If one or two of these central problems have been growing worse, and especially if all three have, it would be strange to call the result "development", even if per capita income had soared' (Seers, 1969).

Since Seers expressed these views the boundaries of what is held to constitute development have expanded progressively – to include political evolution, a shift from social relations rooted in custom and tradition to contract-based relationships, and a transformation of both business methods and the legal framework within which business operates.

In a further twist in the evolution of development economics (discussed in a later section of this chapter), recent theorizing now sees many of these desirable *outcomes* of development as important *inputs* into the development process.

Structuralist, centre-periphery and dependency theories

Introduction

In the mid-1950s a major new rival to the neoclassical view of the development process emerged. Instead of emphasizing the importance of trade and, in that context, the need to adhere to the export structures dictated by comparative advantage, 'Structuralist' economists viewed the heavy concentration of developing-country exports on primary products as a symptom of a fundamental problem with the structure of the world economy which retarded growth in these countries.

BOX 5.6 HANS SINGER

HANS SINGER (1910–2006)
(IDS, University of Sussex)

Hans Singer was born in Germany in 1910. He fled to England as a refugee in 1933, where he took up a research post at Cambridge under the aegis of J.M. Keynes. Singer was one of the first economists to join the United Nations and eventually headed the UNIDO. Amongst his other left-liberal recommendations, his advocacy of 'soft' loans for developing countries led Eugene Black (then President of the World Bank) to describe him as 'One of the wild men of the UN'. He is also well known for originating the Singer–Prebisch view that the terms of trade of developing countries are subject to secular decline. Singer returned to academic life, at the University of Sussex, in 1969. His publication record is prodigious – over 100 books and over 200 significant major published articles. He was knighted in 1994.

These economists argued that, far from being simply backward versions of developed countries, which they were destined to follow up the growth escalator (with the assistance of inflows of capital from the wealthier nations) the developing economies had distinctive *structural* characteristics, and faced distinct *structural* problems, with which the prevailing orthodoxy did not deal adequately. In particular, the developing countries of the late twentieth century faced one major problem not confronted by developing countries in earlier eras – in that the former were now attempting to industrialize in a world where many powerful industrialized economies already dominated international trade. The probable outcome of this situation was that developing countries would find it impossible to compete with developed countries' exports of industrial goods and would thus be permanently relegated to the 'peripheral' role of supplying the 'centre' (the developed world) with the raw materials it required for industrial production. Since industrialization was seen as the *sine qua non* for economic growth, the corollary of this view was that the 'centre-periphery structure barred the path to development'.

The Singer–Prebisch thesis

Building on this contention, a specific mechanism restraining development was identified, in 1950, in the so-called **Singer–Prebisch thesis**. Hans Singer and Raul Prebisch[8] had both discovered an apparent long-run tendency for the terms of trade of primary products in relation to manufactures to fall. The observations were based on UK trade statistics reaching back some seventy years. In interpretation they proposed that fundamental differences in character, and conditions of production, between primary products and manufactures were responsible, and that primary-product prices would continue to decline relative to those of manufactures. The deterioration in the terms of trade of countries specializing in producing primary products – mainly developing countries – would lead to a fall in their incomes relative to those of countries producing industrial products (mainly developed countries). It was further argued that manufacturing industries enjoyed a degree of monopoly power (possibly through mark-up pricing and union–employer bargaining) which enabled their workers and capitalists to get the preponderant share of the benefits of technical improvement in either category of product. In contrast, primary-commodity markets, being much more competitive, and faced by income-inelastic demand, would see any productivity gains passed on to consumers in the form of price reductions – *not* to their own workers as wage increases. Furthermore, as the terms of trade continued to shift in favour of the producers of manufactures in the developed world, *their* profitability would be reinforced, inducing further industrialization and growth there – while the opposite happened in the 'periphery'. Thus, contrary to the orthodox view, exports of primary products could not be relied upon as an 'engine of growth' for developing countries.[9]

As an addendum to this contention, Singer suggested that the volatility which he held to be a characteristic of prices of primaries constituted a further disadvantage as it disrupted the growth process.

Import substitution[10]

The response suggested to these perceived structural problems was the expansion of developing-country industry, especially manufacturing, behind a barrier of government-imposed protective tariffs on imports supplemented by an artificially overvalued exchange-rate for the local currency (which cheapened imports of machinery). This policy of 'import substitution' was designed to permit industrialization in poor countries free from the destructive competition offered by established developed-country exporters, so permitting growth to take place after all.

Import-substitution proved, initially, to be a very popular option with developing countries, and was widely practised. No doubt this was partly due to the *prima facie*

---

[8] This and other aspects of structuralist ideology were particularly closely associated with the UN Economic Commission for Latin America (ECLA).

[9] The debate over the evidence for and against the existence of these terms-of-trade effects is summarized in Chapter 17.

[10] Import substitution is discussed more fully in Chapter 17.

plausibility of the Singer–Prebisch case to developing-country administrations faced with poorly performing nascent industrial sectors, and to high-cost local producers struggling to compete with overseas suppliers. At the same time, this highly interventionist policy fitted well with the broader economic philosophies of the left-of-centre regimes in power in many developing countries. At a somewhat less exalted level, the imposition and operation of import-substitution policies, involving the use of a large number of controlling measures (import-licensing, exchange controls, and the like) and giving considerable discretionary powers to administrators of the system, created widespread opportunities for political or financial gain for officials and politicians.

BOX 5.7 ANDRE GUNDER FRANK

ANDRE GUNDER FRANK (1929– 2005)
(Robinson Rojas Foundation)
Source: Photograph, and biographical information (in part) from © Copyright Michel Chossudovsky, GlobalResearch.ca, 2005

Andre Gunder Frank was born in Germany in 1929. He was the son of the prominent German writer Leonard Frank, who was closely associated with Bertoldt Brecht, whom Gunder met when he was a child. His family fled to Switzerland when Hitler was elected Chancellor, and subsequently settled in the US. Frank completed a PhD at the University of Chicago under the supervision of Milton Friedman – whose market-orientated views later attracted his serious disapproval. Frank's 1966 essay on 'The Development of Under-development' – this time an attack on mainstream 'stages of growth' theory – sparked off an intense, long-running debate and had considerable influence on policy thinking in many developing countries for some years.

An eclectic researcher, Frank taught and researched in Departments of Anthropology, Economics, Geography, History, International Relations, Political Science, and Sociology, in 19 different universities in North America, Latin America, and Europe. He lectured in seven languages (English, French, Spanish, Portuguese, Italian, German and Dutch), and wrote 40 books and nearly 1000 other publications. In the 1990s Frank turned his attention to world history and produced (with Barry Gills) *The World System* (1996) on the last five thousand years of world history.

In the end, import-substitution failed to deliver the promised goods. By and large, even after decades of protection, domestic industries typically remained small, inefficient and unable to compete on the world stage because of high costs, poor quality, and the adverse effect of exchange-rate overvaluation on export prices. Growth rates were low, sometimes negative. Bureaucracy and corruption flourished, absorbing scarce resources to no apparent good end, while presiding over systems of distorted prices which failed to reflect true scarcity values and which pushed resource allocation far from the configuration indicated by the market. The result was a progressive disillusionment with import-substitution and a switch, in varying degrees across countries, to a policy based on freer trade, freer markets, and export-led growth.

The advent of the World Trade Organization (replacing GATT) in 1995, and the rapid expansion of its membership thereafter – culminating, in ideological terms, in the accession of China in December 2001 – would appear to confirm the irrevocable and thoroughgoing nature of this switch. WTO members are pledged, with some provision for 'special and differential treatment' for the poorer developing countries, to the freeing up of merchandise trade. There is also strong pressure for the freeing of service trade (in most of its forms), and for the introduction of 'national treatment' (in effect, most-favoured-nation treatment) on investment and even government procurement. In addition, very large numbers of free-trade areas and 'regional–economic-integration' schemes have been set up (the WTO has been notified of nearly 300), and most developing countries are now members of at least one such organization.

Thus the prevailing orthodoxy of trade policy has turned through 180 degrees since the high-water days of import-substitution. Nevertheless, it is interesting to note that the influential notion embodied in the Singer–Prebisch thesis – to the effect that adverse movements in their terms of trade make life more difficult for developing countries – despite having been subjected to much sceptical analysis, is still alive and well, recent research having produced a considerable body of evidence supporting the basic hypothesis.[11] At the same time it has been claimed that no conclusive analysis has yet been conducted on data for a large sample of developing countries over the period to which the original Singer–Prebisch assertions referred.

Dependency

The serious difficulties encountered by the policies flowing from the Singer–Prebisch school of thought spurred the development of the still more radical 'dependency' thinking – which influenced a significant part of an entire generation of development economists. One of the earliest, and most influential, proponents of the dependency thesis was Andre Gunder Frank. He was clear on the point that:

> Historical research demonstrates that contemporary underdevelopment is in large part the historical product of past and continuing economic and other relations between the satellite underdeveloped and the now developed metropolitan countries. Furthermore, these relations are an essential part of the capitalist system on a world scale as a whole.
>
> *(Frank, 1972)*

The 'dependency' view of the world economic system sees capitalism as being responsible for imposing a division of labour on the world economy such that the 'dependent' (that is the poor) countries are condemned to perform the role of suppliers of cheap industrial raw materials and agricultural products to the economically and politically powerful rich countries. Investment and technology do flow to the dependent states, but only in order to enable the latter to fulfil this role. The resources of the poor countries are thus diverted from their own development and used to serve the purposes of the rich 'centre'.

In this scenario there is no place for the 'growth path' vision of many economists – with developing countries following in the steps of the developed countries towards a prosperous

---

[11] A useful review of evidence is set out in Blattman *et al.* (2003). See also Chapter 17 and (on the OLC) Appendix 7.1.

future. The historical record of expansion enjoyed by the now-developed world is regarded as a one-off, made possible by the specific circumstances prevailing at the time – in many cases involving the creation of colonies. Poor countries have been and – unless they adopt radically new policies – will continue to be, *actively* 'underdeveloped' by the wealthy in the sense that their resource use will be aimed at benefiting the wealthy countries rather then themselves. As a result, their poverty will be permanent.

To make matters worse, this unfortunate experience is reinforced by the complicity of the ruling elites in the developing countries. In some cases these groups may actually benefit directly from the relationship but, in many countries, they are simply imposing on their own countries a capitalist-inspired economic doctrine which they have come to accept because of their close ties with corresponding elites in the developed countries.

A further strand in dependency thinking takes issue with the neoclassical view that economic growth will 'trickle down' to the poor and to various disadvantaged minorities in developing countries. It is argued that, given the relatively slow and weak operation of the market there, with attendant gross inefficiencies in resource allocation and reallocation, the poor will be shut out from the benefits of local economic growth, marginalized and ignored by the economic system. For them economic growth brings no benefits. Thus, an alternative to market capitalism must be found in order to distribute the fruits of growth fairly across the community.

Policies advocated by the dependency school reflect the above preoccupations. They include:

- Backing off from further integration into the world economy and moving to a degree of self-sufficiency;
- As a less extreme form of (1), uncoupling dependent economies from the existing world economic system and substituting a new set of non-exploitative trading relationships amongst dependent countries;
- Involving the state to a much greater extent in ensuring 'distributive justice' within developing countries.

Todaro's model of urbanization and unemployment

In Lewis's model, rural-to-urban migration, one of the central demographic characteristics of developing countries, is the main mechanism through which labour transfers physically from agriculture to city-based industrial employment, thus facilitating the expansion of the modern sector and the eventual integration of the two sectors of the dual economy. However, while it is apparent that a clear understanding of the factors influencing the pace of movements from rural to urban areas is required for policy formulation in this area, it is generally accepted that Lewis's model is seriously incomplete. Thinking on this issue was for long dominated by Todaro's[12] model of urbanization and unemployment, presented in summary form below. This short-run model comes to very different conclusions from those of Lewis.

---

[12] Set out in J.R. Harris and M.P. Todaro (1970). An extended version is presented in Todaro (1971).

We again begin by assuming the existence of two sectors – a modern, urban sector in which the wage rate is Wu, and a traditional, rural sector in which the wage rate is Wr. It is to be expected that, for much of the time, Wu will exceed Wr. It is also assumed that Wu is inflexible downwards – because of inevitable resistance by the labour force to wage cuts, coupled with unwillingness on the part of employers to risk increasing rates of labour turnover and associated search costs for replacing employees.

Decisions made by rural workers on whether or not to migrate to town are based not on a simple comparison of the relative wage rates in the two locations (as in the Lewis model) but on a comparison of *expected values* of earnings – that is the observed differential between urban and rural wages adjusted for the probability of actually finding employment in the two areas, respectively. In rural areas there is no significant open unemployment, so this probability takes the value 1 and the expected wage, Wr*, will be:

$$Wr^* = Wr$$

In the urban labour market, where the probability of finding a job is p, the expected wage, Wu*, is:

$$Wu^* = p.Wu$$

The probability of finding a job, p, is defined as:

$$p = Eu/(Eu + Uu)$$

where Eu and Uu measure urban employment and urban unemployment, respectively. If the probability of finding a job is assumed to be the same for all members of the urban labour force, then p reduces to the urban rate of employment, and Wu* is equal to that rate times Wu, that is, p.Wu. (An alternative, perhaps more realistic, assumption is that only a limited proportion of all urban jobs fall vacant in any given period. This would have the effect of reducing the probability of finding a job, so reducing the value of p.)

The actual level of migration from rural to urban areas, given the above, will depend on the responsiveness – indicated by 'a' – of rural labour to the adjusted wage differential (Wu* – Wr). Thus migration in any time period t can be given by:

$$Mt = a (p.Wu - Wr)$$

Inward migration to the urban area will continue so long as the expected value of the urban wage, Wu*, exceeds the rural wage Wr. This flow will cease if urban unemployment rises sufficiently to bring Wu* into equality with Wr.

One striking outcome of the working of this model is that, if the urban–rural wage differential is large and growing, even a fairly low probability of securing a job might be sufficient to encourage an inward flow of labour, with the result that urban *unemployment rates might rise* steadily.

While the introduction of a probabilistic element into the migration model is a useful innovation, several criticisms have been advanced. In particular, it has been suggested that it seriously oversimplifies the migration process by failing to take into account several factors affecting the decision to migrate and migration patterns, notably the influence of family networks and social ties, the distance of the rural area from the urban area, the seasonal nature of much rural work (which may give rise to 'circular migration'), the practice of migrating to town simply to earn a 'target' sum before returning to the rural area, and the presence of the urban informal sector as a provider of jobs when calculating the probability of finding employment. (These, and other features of the current analysis of rural–urban migration, are discussed in detail in Chapter 14.) Despite these criticisms, however, Todaro's model remains a 'landmark' contribution to development theory in this field.

The neoclassical/neoliberal 'counter-revolution'

As we have indicated in Chapter 3, the publication by Little, Scitovsky and Scott (LSS) of *Industry and Trade in Some Developing Countries* in 1970[13] proved to be the turning point in the debate between those favouring the then dominant structuralist view, which endorsed autonomous industrialization based on import substitution and extensive government intervention (including central planning), and their opponents – the 'neoliberals' – who advocated a much more market-orientated approach emphasizing export-based growth and integration into the world economy.

LSS argued that the analysis of the performance of a number of important developing countries (notably India, Mexico, Taiwan and the Philippines) showed clear evidence that import substitution and associated policies were having a counterproductive impact and should be abandoned. In the following decade the intellectual tide turned decisively in favour of the neoliberals as more and more developing countries faced worsening problems in the form of slow (or negative) growth, growing poverty and income disparities, and rapidly worsening problems over servicing international debt.

The debt problem, in particular, played an important role in reversing the tide of development policies. Many developing countries were compelled to seek financial assistance from the International Monetary Fund and the World Bank. Both of these institutions strongly favoured the neoliberal approach and required adoption of a radical reform programme of 'Structural Adjustment', based on neoliberal principles, as a condition for giving assistance.

The specific programmes recommended varied across countries, but important elements were:

- Significant reduction in the extent of government intervention in the economic process – via decontrol and deregulation (especially of trade, financial markets, investment and the foreign exchange market) – aimed at greatly improving the allocation of resources according to market signals (including, very importantly, prices in world markets);
- Adoption of policies favouring export-oriented industrialization (in place of ISI);
- Privatization of state-owned enterprises;
- Reduction in power of trade unions to influence wage levels and manning practices;
- Running down of government-funded social-welfare programmes (notably in education and health).

In the 1980s further impetus was imparted to the neoliberal 'counter-revolution' by the coming to power in the US and the UK of, respectively, the Reagan and Thatcher regimes – both of which were strongly opposed on ideological grounds to large state participation in the economy.

[13] Little, I.M.D., *et al.* (1970).

Summary conclusions

- A number of fairly diverse ideas – theories and models – have contributed to thought about development economics over the sixty or so years of the subject's life.

- Some have appeared to point policy in almost diametrically opposite directions from others. None can be said to have triumphed in quite the same way as the ideas of Keynes, let alone those of Adam Smith – in setting novel terms in which an important part of human experience is almost universally discussed among the educated for a generation, or in Smith's case for centuries.

- Some have been influential, for better or worse, such as contributions to the train of thought that seemed to justify highly protected import-substitution in manufactures and centralized planning.

- Some, such as the Two-Gap model, appeared useful in their day but have gradually ceased to be invoked as times have changed.

- Some, such as the Lewis model of unlimited supplies of labour, in spite of reservations and qualifications, have remained important to current thought – and Lewis's insights will probably continue so until the phenomenon of overcrowded household agriculture has ceased to be pervasive.

- What can hardly be doubted is that ideas in development economics have been of great practical importance.

Thinking on development strategy is, as we have seen, characterized by intermittent, but sizeable, changes in direction. It is difficult to discern any clearcut evolutionary path except perhaps – as we suggested earlier – that thinking has become progressively more realistic about the possibilities and limitations of human beings and about their wants and needs. However, this has, if anything, led the factors believed to influence development to multiply and the focus to soften – so that the probability of finding a 'silver bullet' answer to the problem of poverty continually dwindles. Yet, while the peoples of many developing countries struggle in vain to improve living standards, in others growth has, in a very short space of time, accelerated to breakneck speed – promising to lift hundreds of millions out of poverty in one generation. What 'landmark' lessons may be learned from their experience?

Questions for discussion

5.1 What is meant by a 'vicious circle'? And by a 'virtuous circle'?

5.2 Why did Rosenstein–Rodan believe that, without a 'big push' growth in developing countries would be stifled?

5.3 What does William Easterly mean when he says that 'The ghost of the Financing Gap lives on.'?

5.4 What criticisms have been made of 'Big Push' models?

5.5 What do you understand by a growth model which focuses on 'structural change'?

5.6 How did Arthur Lewis visualize the basic growth process in a 'dual' economy?

5.7 What is meant by a 'binding constraint' in a Two-Gap model?

5.8 What is import substituting industrialization (ISI), and why has it fallen out of favour as a policy for promoting development?

5.9 What did the dependency theorists mean when they said that a world economy run on free market lines would 'underdevelop' poor countries?

Additional reading and web references

Clark, C. (1939) *The Conditions of Economic Progress*, Macmillan, London.

Little, I.M.D., T. Scitovsky and M. Scott (1970) *Industry and Trade in Some Developing Countries*, Oxford University Press, London.

Meier, G. (2004) *Biography of a Subject: an Evolution of Development Economics*, Oxford University Press, New York.

Paul Krugman *The Fall and Rise of Development Economics* in http://www.wws.princeton.edu/pkrugman/dishpan.html, 1996.

Rostow, W.W. (1960) *The Stages of Economic Growth*, Cambridge University Press, Cambridge, Mass.

Rostow, W.W. (1990) *Theorists of Economic Growth from David Hume to the Present*, Oxford University Press, Oxford, pp. 313–14.

Video presentation on growth by Solow, Samuelson and Modigliani at http://mitworld.mit.edu/stream/76/

PART 2
Governance

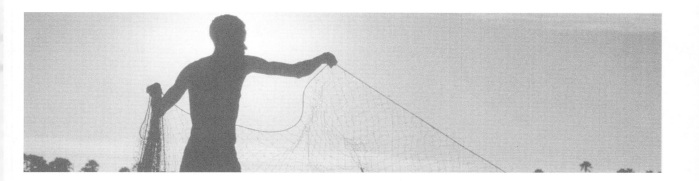

CHAPTER 6

Governance Questions 1: Corruption

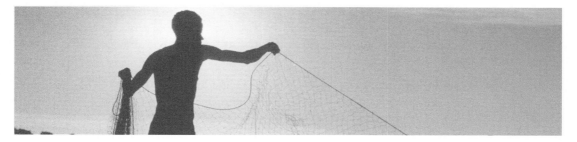

Corruption converts government from a potential servant of the public into a system of plunder – and one that hits the poor hardest. It is much more common on the whole in poorer countries and worst in failed states. Though its connection with low income might, on *a priori* reasoning, be either as cause or as effect, there are strong grounds for thinking that *the contribution of corruption to poverty* is at least an important part of the story.

Introduction

Since the 1990s, **governance** – the quality of government – has become explicitly and generally recognized as a highly important element in economic growth and in the enhancement of all the aspects of welfare that are covered by 'development'.

In this chapter we first try to distinguish between good government and good policy, and we represent government, the market and civil society as three resources on which countries can draw to enhance their people's welfare. We review briefly the closely interconnected elements that go to determine the quality of government; and explain the reason for concentrating on questions of **corruption**, by implication embracing within that topic what is in large measure its antithesis, **the rule of law**.

Next we consider the basic meaning of corruption and its definitions (broad and narrow) and varieties. We outline the concepts of regulatory rent and of rent-seeking in the business of explaining corruption. We follow one explanation of why patterns in various countries of either extensive bribery or of prevailing honesty in government tend to persist. We outline attempts at regularly measuring corruption in the sense of comparing its incidence across countries; and from one of these regular assessments we observe the marked, though far from perfect, negative relationship across countries between the incidence of corruption and income per head.

We consider briefly arguments sometimes heard for justifying corruption; and we review the question of the various factors that are empirically related to corruption, and which way the causal relationships if any are likely to run.

Finally we consider the fields of national life in which corruption is likely to be especially damaging, the directions to which we might look for combating corruption, and the measures that might be taken.

BOX 6.1 TOOLKIT ON GOVERNANCE AND CORRUPTION

Active humanity. Term used by the present authors to refer to the human propensities for trust/trustworthiness, responsibility, and creation that are asserted here to underlie *civil society* (see below) and to be vital to the healthy functioning of any human society – including large, complex societies for which the institutions of government and the market are also necessary.

BPI. Bribe Payers Index. One of the annual indexes used by TI (see below) to compare the extent of corruption between countries and periods. It measures 'the propensity of firms from leading export countries to bribe abroad' and is based on surveys of people working in those firms.

Civil society. Used in a narrow sense to refer to non-governmental, non-commercial *organizations*, especially those with public-interest objectives; and in a broader sense to refer also to *habits, attitudes and conventions* of mutual responsibility and trustworthiness and creativity that underlie the organizations and, partly through them – along with government and market institutions – enable large, complex societies to function fruitfully.

Corruption. Used in a narrow sense to refer to the giving and taking of bribes by officials (sometimes exclusively government officials) and in a broader sense for any misuse of public office (or sometimes of any position of trust) for private gain.

CPI. Corruption Perception Index. Another of the annual indexes used by TI to measure the extent of corruption, this time as it is perceived by expert and business observers. It is based on a number of opinion surveys.

Failed state. A state in which the government has minimal capacity to pursue policies, or lacks effective authority over a significant part of its internationally recognized territory.

GCB. Global Corruption Barometer. The third of the annual indexes used by TI to measure corruption, this time from the viewpoint of the general public. It is 'concerned with attitudes toward and experience of corruption among the general public': such questions as how much people pay in bribes, to whom and for what.

Governance. The quality of government.

NGOs. Non-government organizations (also called *civil-society organizations, CSOs*). Organizations that are both non-governmental and non-commercial. The term is usually confined to public-interest bodies, such as charities and groups that campaign for causes other than the special financial interests of their members.

Regulatory rent. Rent (in the economists' sense, see below) created by government regulation that renders some good artificially scarce.

Rent. In the sense used by economists, rent refers to the income that a person receives solely as a result of being in possession of some scarce and valued asset – such as land or a mineral deposit or native ability, or, as extensions of the original idea, an acquired skill,

▶ or an exclusive right conferred by government to undertake certain activities or engage in certain transactions. Rents from the two last-mentioned sources are referred to as *quasi-rents* and *regulatory rents* respectively.

Rent-seeking behaviour. This term generally refers to attempts to lobby for the granting or retention of regulatory rents, for example through the protection of a particular industry against imports or through the issue of a restricted number of taxi licences.

TI. Transparency International. An international NGO based in Berlin that aims, through research and the dissemination of information, to reduce corruption across the world.

Good governance and good policy

Good governance can be distinguished conceptually from *good policy*, though the dividing line can sometimes be hard to draw. Unless a line is drawn, consideration of governance becomes simply consideration of any and all elements of policy, and the question of 'governance for development' becomes the same as government policy for development.

So, we attempt a distinction as follows. *Policy* is what a government decides explicitly to do: its executive and legislative decisions, such as whether it taxes foreign trade, how much it is prepared to borrow, whether it caps interest-rates. *Governance* concerns the workings of the mechanisms by which government operates: through which policy decisions are implemented, laws enforced, and recognized rights upheld. However, the term is also extended to cover the nature of those recognized rights. It is in such areas as this last – over *the nature of the laws, explicit or implicit, that define people's rights* – that distinguishing between good governance and good policy becomes especially difficult. Some laws are products of current policy, and some are elements in the way government works, and the categories overlap.

Governance in a particular instance may be considered good *instrumentally*, that is for what it achieves – for example, economic growth and reduction in material poverty – or good *in itself*: because it treats people impartially, predictably, tolerantly, responsively, as on the whole people desire to be treated, and as – to state a (surely) widely held judgement of value – they ought to be treated. Whether or not governance is to be rated only instrumentally, and if so with what ends in view, has a bearing on the criteria on which it should be judged. Recent studies distinguishing between 'thin' and 'thick' concepts of the *rule of law* (*Economist*, 15/3/2008, pp. 95–7) reflect this distinction. If the test is the extent to which government promotes growth in income per head, then it may be enough that law should effectively defend *property rights*, so reducing the uncertainty and other transaction costs of productive investment and supporting economic growth. If, however, the test is the contribution that government makes to development in the broadest sense of enhancing human freedom and capabilities, this inevitably involves the *distribution* as well as the *growth* of income; the public provision, or shoring up, of certain essentials of *social welfare*; and the enforcement of what are agreed under international conventions to be *human rights*.

The separation for the present purpose of questions of *governance* from those of *policy* and the concentration in this chapter on the *avoidance of corruption* leaves out of account some vital issues about the role and character of the state. So in Chapter 7 we move to necessary functions and desirable limits of the public sector, the scope for government intervention and leadership in non-state-sector activities, and measures for improving the quality of government decision-making and implementation.

Civil society as means alongside market and government for harmonious and productive living

Civil society covers the organizations, institutions, and practices that are not coercive and at the same time not motivated by the pursuit of the private individual or corporate profit of those engaged in them.

The importance of **civil society** in social and economic development, like that of the quality of government, has also been recognized explicitly from the 1990s. Its role may be seen as analogous to that of **the market** and of **government**. Each of the three represents a mode of organization that depends on harnessing, potentially for the common good, certain fundamental human propensities. These are respectively: the exercise of *rational and flexible activity for one's own and one's family's benefit*, which is the foundation for **the market**; the readiness *to accept certain kinds of rule*, and, on the part of certain people, a readiness or desire *to exercise authority*, which between them form the base for **government**; and what may be called *active humanity*, namely a propensity for accepting responsibility in the interest of others, for trust and trustworthiness, and for creation: which three elements constitute the seedbed of what we call **civil society**. It is the mobilization of these three sets of propensities that gives the three vital organizational ingredients for living together harmoniously and efficiently in large integrated societies.

The meaning and roles of civil society, the potential of the propensities underlying it, and its relationship to market and government are expounded in Chapter 8. This chapter will make some reference to the dependence of good government on civil society.

Essence, dimensions and tests of good governance

The World Bank, in its Worldwide Governance Indicators, judges governance on six characteristics:

1 Voice and accountability
2 Political stability and absence of violence
3 Government effectiveness
4 Regulatory quality
5 Rule of law
6 Control of corruption.

In other words, to be judged good in the way it works, government should:

- be based on institutions that keep it responsive and responsible to the populace;
- be able to maintain the peace and to implement its decisions;
- attempt to regulate only what it can effectively and usefully regulate and do so in ways that are advantageous to the population;
- be subject consistently to rules of justice and public interest rather than being available at discretion for the benefit of any of those in power and authority.

The Bank has rated over 200 countries on each of these six criteria (World Bank, 2007, http://info.worldbank.org/governance/wgi2007/).

The six are causally linked. Much of the discussion of good governance revolves around control of corruption. This is closely connected with the rule of law in that each is in some degree a condition of the other. If corruption is extensive enough, the effective rule of law is impossible. Conversely, arbitrary government, unchecked by law, makes corruption (in the broad sense employed below) extremely likely and not easy to identify as a prelude to eradicating it. 'Voice and accountability' requires not only popular elections for those in power (and a degree of activity from civil society) but also transparency and openness in decision-making, and elections that are subject to law and substantially free from corruption. Unenforceable regulations, or those that are not respected by the public for their manifest usefulness, greatly increase the likelihood of corruption, and, like any attempt of government to undertake more than it can perform, undermine its effectiveness for doing what it needs to do. It is also virtually a precondition of all the other desirable characteristics that a government should be able to keep the peace throughout its jurisdiction, and that each layer of government should be able to have its lawful decisions on specific tangible action implemented.

The term **failed state** is applied to one in which the government cannot keep the peace, nor exercise its legal powers, over the whole, or at least the great bulk, of the area and population within its jurisdiction. As we shall see, failed states – such as Somalia and arguably Myanmar – are among those in which corruption is identified as most extreme.

Perhaps a seventh item should be added to the list. If 'development' is taken to include expanded individual freedoms and immunities, then the governance conducive to development should also be biased by its institutions to **upholding human rights**, which, as the term is normally understood, involves, first, strictly limiting state violence, and, second, defending the weak from the strong, the poor from the rich, and the minorities from the majority. This entails the rule of law, but law which, although of course impartial *in its administration*, tends to be biased *in its content* in favour of the poor and socially weak. Because – as with the avoidance of corruption – law, political rhetoric, and the preponderance of world ethical judgements, *largely* favour this human-rights objective, the circumstances that foster it will overlap considerably with those discouraging corruption.

Because the issue of **corruption** in its broadest sense – its causes and effects and the means for controlling it – is so closely tied to the other criteria of good governance, and because of its apparent importance in the economic systems of many developing countries and its ostensible bearing on economic growth and the reduction of poverty, we focus on corruption in this first chapter upon governance.

Corruption: nature, definitions, explanation, measurement, incidence, causes, effects, and reduction

Nature of corruption

One salient feature that distinguishes a state of good governance from bad is **impartiality**. One general view of governmental corruption is that it is a **departure from impartiality** in government. The structures and culture and practices of government should be such that it is not exercised in the interest of the officials or the politicians or the judges or the police or military officers in power, or of those whom they favour or to whom they owe favours.

That is a demanding ideal. Probably it is never completely attained. Politicians and high officials acting quite legally may well play a part in determining their own remuneration, for example, and they are likely to be more interested in their own pay than in that of say office messengers or farm workers. It will be no surprise if this influences their judgement. Nevertheless, the *closer* those with any authority can be brought by the system to use that authority *completely regardless* of whatever connection – personal or political or commercial – they themselves have to the particular people that their decisions affect, the better governance can be judged to be. There will inevitably be an element of chance – of a lottery – in how any particular citizen or alien is affected by official decisions, such as which firm will be engaged to undertake some public project, or who will be offered some position in government service, but it should be an *unbiased* lottery. Then it will be *possible at least* – not of course guaranteed but possible – for social priorities to be observed over public spending, for the most competent person to be chosen for each public role, and for incentives to be related to performance and social efficiency. Less-than-ideal decisions will still be made, since it is humans, no matter how well motivated, who must do the deciding. However, honest mistakes, we suggest, are far less damaging over the long haul than a regular habit of siphoning off – say for the Minister's wife's overseas shopping trips – 10 per cent of the funds appropriated to build a road or equip a set of clinics; or than giving the management of a public project to a charming nephew who happens to be no use in the family business; or than deciding the winner of a works contract by the generosity of the gifts that the lucky firm has been prepared to offer. (Some opinions contesting, or seeking to qualify, such judgements as these will be considered later.)

Governmental *corruption*, in the broadest sense in which we shall define it below, can be taken to cover all departures from impartiality.

Definitions and classifications of corruption

There are narrow and wide definitions of corruption. The narrow definition would confine it to *bribery*, which is the form of malpractice with which ordinary people have most contact in their day-to-day lives. Senior (2006, p. 27) defines corruption in this **narrow** sense, saying that it requires 'five conditions that *must all be satisfied simultaneously*' [his italics here and below]:

> Corruption occurs when a corruptor (1) *covertly* gives (2) *a favour* to a corruptee or to a nominee to influence (3) *action(s)* that (4) *benefit* the corruptor or a nominee, and for which the corruptee has (5) *authority*.

He notes that the favour must be a positive good or service, so as to exclude from his definition extortion and blackmail.

Much of what people mean when they complain of government corruption is indeed bribery, corruption in this narrow sense. Senior's definition deliberately *includes* comparable dishonesty perpetrated by officials of private bodies such as corporations, which no doubt breeds on similar social attitudes.

The term 'corruption' is also used **more widely** to cover virtually any misuse, or unlawful use, of *government* power in the interest of particular individuals or groups.

Transparency International (TI) defines corruption for the purposes of its Corruption Perceptions Index simply as '**the abuse of public office for private gain**' (TI, 2008). The World Bank definition, '**the abuse of public power for private benefit**' (Tanzi, 1998, p. 564) is virtually identical. These, unlike Senior's definition, include not only forms of financial malpractice that go well beyond bribery, but also the improper use or threat, by the state and its officials, of violence or other harm. However if we are to consider corruption only in the abuse of *public office*, we shall ignore practices that entail cheating, theft, or misdirection in which the parties *on both sides* are non-government entities, and also misdemeanours in which no politician or official is culpable; and in these respects the definition would be *narrower* than Senior's.

Forms of broad-definition official corruption

Items in the following list are adapted from those in Caiden (1988) and in Johnson and Sharma (2004) with the exclusions mentioned above and some amalgamations. Official corruption may be taken to cover:

- Bribery (accepting or demanding gifts for official services, favours, or influence)
- Kleptocracy (stealing by politicians or officials of public funds or property)
- Misappropriation (any other illegal use of public funds or property)
- Illegal use of coercive power (intimidation, torture, unlawful detention)
- Perversion of justice by police, judges, or other officials
- Nepotism and cronyism (favouring relatives and friends in official appointments and contracts)
- Clientelism and patronage (biased political decisions made to keep a segment of popular or influential support)
- Concealment to protect maladministration and malpractice
- Links of officials or politicians with organised crime
- Electoral manipulation (falsification of results, gerrymandering, voter-intimidation)
- Misuse of inside information obtained through official channels
- Tax-evasion, and facilitation of tax-evasion, through the use of official position
- Illegal use of surveillance for private purposes.

There is clearly some overlap among these categories; not all are equally bad; and some are quite legal. There may be considerable favouritism ('cronyism') in the award of government contracts and franchises that is not against any law, even though it may be costly for the country. Also most elected politicians will be expected to seek some favours for the districts or cultural groups that elected them, and that will often be completely legal and not subject to wide disapproval, especially as it will probably be fairly open. Other practices on the list, however, can seriously undermine the function of the state as a benevolent institution, and risk reducing it to the level of an association for plunder.

It will be seen that corruption in this broad sense covers a great variety of activities. One distinction is between micro and macro corruption. On the one hand there is the more or less petty corruption that ordinary people meet in their daily lives and that constitutes a highly tangible burden. This accounts probably for all or most of the corruption recorded on TI's Global Corruption Barometer (see below). On the other hand there is the monstrous plunder of public assets, on the part of heads of government and similarly exalted people of the Mobutu, Suharto, Sukarno, Saddam, and Marcos variety, which may greatly affect people's lives but is often largely invisible to the general public until either the big man is toppled or a disaffected intimate or determined journalist or investigator brings it to light. In between the micro and macro in scale, and also hidden from the general public, is the fairly large-scale bribery of officials, including some below the very highest, that often goes with the award of contracts for big public projects.

Tanzi (1998, p. 565) lists *seven distinctions* among forms of corruption:

1 . . . 'petty'. . . or 'grand' . . . [micro or macro]
2 cost-reducing (to the briber) or benefit-enhancing
3 briber-initiated or bribee-initiated

4 coercive or collusive

5 centralized or decentralized

6 predictable or arbitrary

7 involving cash payments or not.

Explaining corruption

Basis for bribery of officials: the idea of regulatory rents

The term **rent** in economics refers to the returns to the holders of property simply because it is their property, independently of any rewards to effort, saving, or risk-taking on their part. Regulation that restricts, whether for good or bad reasons, any form of gainful activity raises its market price and therefore its value to whoever engages in it. This potential gain in value to the person who is able to engage in the restricted activity is described as a *regulatory rent*. Area planning – deciding who can build or operate what where – and allocation of quotas on foreign trade or capital movement are examples. Officials who determine the result of planning applications or who allocate import quotas, and those whose job is to enforce planning decisions or trade restrictions, have a source of rents at their disposal for which members of the public may be prepared to pay. Police who *de facto* have the discretion to enforce, or not to enforce, legal penalties, or to recover, or not, stolen property for its owners, or (with impunity) to fabricate offences, have similar assets of value that they can sell. Corrupt judges in civil cases in which large amounts are at stake may have some big rents at their disposal. The currency of the concept of *regulatory rents* in this sense is attributed to Anne Krueger (1974).

It is an entirely reasonable principle of policy that the value of any regulatory rents should accrue not to the officials who administer them but to the community through central or local governments. (One important school of economic-policy thought, the followers of Henry George (1839–97), holds that the same principle ought to be applied to the rents due to possession of all the 'gifts of nature' – land and other natural resources – on grounds implying that this is both fair and efficient.) This rule is implemented if such payments as fines and taxes on trade are treated as government revenue. There are analogous ways of dealing with other regulatory rents through devices such as auctioning – for state revenue – trade and capital-export quotas and building permits, and increasing local site taxes on defined areas when, and to the extent that, regulatory changes have increased their value. (This last device is discussed in Appendix 19.2, available on the Online Learning Centre.)

Figure 6.1 shows, with a simple demand-supply diagram how regulatory rents might be created by the imposition of a quota on the sale of some good. The quota would have to be allocated to one or more sellers, who would be able to take all the regulatory rent for themselves. Auctioning the quotas, on the other hand, with the revenue going to the state, would mean that the state reaped all the regulatory rent.

Persistence of corruption (and honesty)

Some writers have tried to explain why, as they see it, a routine practice of bribery in some societies and of honesty in others each seems to be self-sustaining (Mishra, 2006). To simplify: Mishra's explanation depends on people's response to net rewards (material and also psychic) in view of two effects. First, the more corrupt people there are, the greater are the net expected material rewards to any official or member of the public from corrupt behaviour (because the less is the risk of prosecution or losing reputation, and the greater

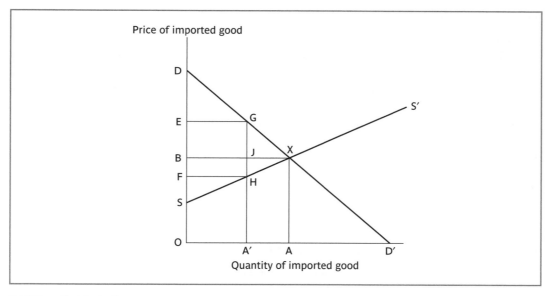

FIGURE 6.1 Regulatory Rent

In Figure 6.1 vertical and horizontal axes represent price and quantity of an imported good.

DD′ and SS′ are demand and supply functions for the good in the domestic market in the absence of restriction.

Then, OA and OB are the free-market equilibrium quantity and price.

Suppose import purchases of the good are limited by regulation to OA′.

The quota raises the buyer price to OE and lowers the seller price to OF.

The area EGHF represents the regulatory rent.

A trader who is allocated the quota free of charge, as the only one allowed to import the good, can buy the good at a price of OF and sell it on domestically at a price of OE. Simply by virtue of being allocated the quota, he is able to make a gain of EGHF, the regulatory rent.

If instead the state auctions the quota, the regulatory rent accrues to the public finances.

is the prospect or ease of finding a corrupt counterpart). Second, the more corrupt people there are, the more being corrupt tends to become the social norm, and the less the psychic (and perhaps reputational) penalties. On both grounds there will be a tendency for any initial movement towards, or away from, corruption, once it passes a certain point, to generate a positive feedback and hence to sustain itself. So there may be *two* potential stable-equilibrium positions for any society: one relatively corrupt, one relatively uncorrupt. Policy measures increasing the size of penalties, or the likelihood of being detected and if detected penalized, will not necessarily be irrelevant, but, with established practices of corruption and ethical norms permitting it, measures such as this will face considerable obstacles to a decisive shift out of the vicious circle that maintains the corrupt equilibrium.

Surveys reported by Miller (2006) in four 'transitional' European countries suggested a gap between people's normative views about corruption (which were predominantly unfavourable) and their readiness nonetheless to offer, demand, pay, or receive, bribes. But the normative views were probably not irrelevant. The countries of the four with the most and least unfavourable views were also those with the least and most reported readiness respectively to engage in bribery. However, one of Miller's inferences from these results was that attempts at moral argument or indoctrination against bribery were unlikely to be effective in seriously reducing it in these countries – since it was already widely disapproved, even by people who felt obliged, or were sufficiently tempted, to practise it.

Measurement of corruption

Given the many forms and the often secret nature of corruption, there are difficulties in measuring it meaningfully, and particularly in giving a single rating for the degree of corruption for each country. Transparency International (TI), however, a non-profit organization centred in Berlin with national branches across the world, attempts to give for each year some critical indicators of corruption on global and national scenes through three sets of summary information, derived from questionnaire-based surveys. The three reflect respectively the judgements of (foreign and national) business people and analysts; the experience of ordinary citizens; and the behaviour of potential bribe-payers in transnational transactions. TI also publishes information on corruption measurement and on research relating to factors affecting corruption and the effectiveness of attempts to combat it. Other surveys (Tanzi, 1998, p. 577) are provided by Global Competitiveness Report (Geneva); Political and Economic Risk Consultancy (Hong Kong); Political Risk Services (Syracuse, NY); and the World Bank.

Transparency International's three sets of ratings

The Corruption Perception Index (CPI) is described by TI (2008) as

> a composite index, a poll of polls, drawing on corruption-related data from expert and business surveys carried out by a variety of independent and reputable institutions. The CPI reflects views from around the world, including those of experts who are living in the countries evaluated.

For the 2007 index, the various countries were assessed from the responses to varying numbers of surveys, between 3 and 9 each. The index drew on altogether 14 different polls and surveys from 12 independent institutions. Each country is given a composite *score* between zero and 10, with 10 representing the *lowest* level of perceived corruption. From their scores, the countries are then given *rankings*, starting from 1 (highest score, least corrupt). The 2007 rankings and scores are shown in Table 6.1. TI recommends judging a country's improvement or worsening by changes in its score rather than in its ranking order, which may have more to do with changes in *other* countries' performance.

The Global Corruption Barometer (GCB) 'is concerned with attitudes toward and experience of corruption among the general public'. It seeks to answer questions such as how often, how much per year, to what groups of officials, and for what, the average person in any particular country pays in bribes. The survey for 2007 took responses from 63 199 people in 60 countries across the world. There was a reasonably close relationship – a correlation coefficient of 0.66 – between countries' scores on the GCB and their scores on the CPI. The 2006 results are summarized with exposition in TI (2007, pp. 314–7) and those of 2007 briefly in TI (2008).

The Bribe Payers Index (BPI) 'focuses on the propensity of firms from leading export countries to bribe abroad – providing an indication of the "supply side" of corruption' (TI, 2008). The 2006 scores for the 30 countries covered are given with discussion and exposition in TI (2007), pp. 331–4. The list of scores and rankings is reproduced in Table 6.2. Further information and discussion in the source shows that there is a greater tendency for the outward investors from quite a number of countries to pay bribes in non-OECD countries, and especially in low-income countries, than in the general sample of recipient countries. This difference is especially marked with investors from the UAE, Singapore, Mexico, and Hong Kong (Mak, 2007). The inference drawn is that the controls exercised by the home countries of those outward investors may be of limited effectiveness in combating bribery, since the outcome seems to vary with the character of the recipient country.

Country	Ranking (least corrupt at 1)	Score (10 least, 0 most, corrupt)
Denmark	1=	9.4
Finland	1=	9.4
New Zealand	1=	9.4
Singapore	4=	9.3
Sweden	4=	9.3
Iceland	6	9.2
Netherlands	7=	9.0
Switzerland	7=	9.0
Norway	9=	8.7
Canada	9=	8.7
Australia	11	8.6
Luxembourg	12=	8.4
UK	12=	8.4
Hong Kong	14	8.3
Austria	14	8.1
Germany	16	7.8
Ireland	17=	7.5
Japan	17=	7.5
France	19	7.3
US	20	7.2
Belgium	21	7.1
Chile	22	7.0
Barbados	23	6.9
St Lucia	24	6.8
Spain	25=	6.7
Uruguay	25=	6.7
Slovenia	27	6.6
Estonia	28=	6.5
Portugal	28=	6.5
St Vincent and Grenadines	30=	6.1
Israel	30=	6.1
Qatar	30	6.0
Malta	33	5.8
United Arab Emirates	34=	5.7
Macao	34=	5.7

TABLE 6.1 Perceived corruption: transparency international's corruption perception index, rankings and scores of 180 countries, 2007
Source: Transparency International website: http://www.transparency.org/layout/set/print/policy_research/surveys_indices/cpi/ , consulted 11/1/2008.

Country	Ranking (least corrupt at 1)	Score (10 least, 0 most, corrupt)
Taiwan	34=	5.7
Dominica	37	5.6
Botswana	38	5.4
Hungary	39=	5.3
Cyprus	39=	5.3
Czech Republic	41=	5.2
Italy	41=	5.2
Malaysia	43=	5.1
South Korea	43=	5.1
South Africa	43=	5.1
Costa Rica	46=	5.0
Bahrein	46=	5.0
Bhutan	46=	5.0
Slovakia	49=	4.9
Cape Verde	49=	4.9
Latvia	51=	4.8
Lithuania	51=	4.8
Oman	53=	4.7
Jordan	53=	4.7
Mauritius	53=	4.7
Greece	56	4.6
Samoa	57=	4.5
Namibia	57=	4.5
Seychelles	57=	4.5
Kuwait	60	4.3
Poland	61=	4.2
Cuba	61=	4.2
Tunisia	61=	4.2
Bulgaria	64=	4.1
Croatia	64=	4.1
Turkey	64=	4.1
El Salvador	67	4.0
Colombia	68	3.8
Romania	69=	3.7
Ghana	69=	3.7
Senegal	71	3.6
Suriname	72=	3.5

TABLE 6.1 (*continued*)

Country	Ranking (least corrupt at 1)	Score (10 least, 0 most, corrupt)
Mexico	72=	3.5
Peru	72=	3.5
Brazil	72=	3.5
China	72=	3.5
India	72=	3.5
Morocco	72=	3.5
Georgia	79=	3.4
Serbia	79=	3.4
Grenada	79=	3.4
Trinidad and Tobago	79=	3.4
Saudi Arabia	79=	3.4
Bosnia and Herzogovina	84=	3.3
Montenegro	84=	3.3
FYR Macedonia	84=	3.3
Jamaica	84=	3.3
Maldives	84=	3.3
Kiribati	84=	3.3
Thailand	84=	3.3
Gabon	84=	3.3
Swaziland	84=	3.3
Lesotho	84=	3.3
Panama	94=	3.2
Madagascar	94=	3.2
Sri Lanka	94=	3.2
Tanzania	94=	3.2
Vanuatu	98	3.1
Armenia	99=	3.0
Mongolia	99=	3.0
Dominican Republic	99=	3.0
Belize	99=	3.0
Lebanon	99=	3.0
Algeria	99=	3.0
Albania	105=	2.9
Argentina	105=	2.9
Djibouti	105=	2.9
Burkina Faso	105=	2.9
Egypt	105=	2.9

TABLE 6.1 (*continued*)

Country	Ranking (least corrupt at 1)	Score (10 least, 0 most, corrupt)
Bolivia	105=	2.9
Moldova	111	2.8
Guatemala	111=	2.8
Solomon Islands	111=	2.8
Eritrea	111=	2.8
Rwanda	111=	2.8
Mozambique	111=	2.8
Uganda	111=	2.8
Ukraine	118=	2.7
Mali	118=	2.7
Malawi	118=	2.7
Sao Tome and Principe	118=	2.7
Benin	118=	2.7
Guyana	123=	2.6
Nicaragua	123=	2.6
Vietnam	123=	2.6
Timor Leste	123=	2.6
Zambia	123=	2.6
Mauritania	123=	2.6
Comoros	123=	2.6
Niger	123=	2.6
Honduras	131=	2.5
Yemen	131=	2.5
Libya	131=	2.5
Iran	131=	2.5
Nepal	131=	2.5
Philippines	131=	2.5
Burundi	131=	2.5
Paraguay	138=	2.4
Syria	138=	2.4
Pakistan	138=	2.4
Ethiopia	138=	2.4
Cameroon	138=	2.4
Russia	143=	2.3
Indonesia	143=	2.3
Gambia	143=	2.3
Togo	143=	2.3

TABLE 6.1 (*continued*)

Country	Ranking (least corrupt at 1)	Score (10 least, 0 most, corrupt)
Angola	147=	2.2
Nigeria	147=	2.2
Guinea-Bissau	147=	2.2
Kazakhstan	150=	2.1
Belarus	150=	2.1
Tadjikistan	150=	2.1
Azerbaijan	150=	2.1
Kyrgyzstan	150=	2.1
Ecuador	150=	2.1
Sierra Leone	150=	2.1
Zimbabwe	150=	2.1
Côte d'Ivoire	150=	2.1
Congo, Republic	150=	2.1
Kenya	150=	2.1
Liberia	150=	2.1
Turkmenistan	162=	2.0
Venezuela	162=	2.0
Bangladesh	162=	2.0
Papua New Guinea	162=	2.0
Cambodia	162=	2.0
Central African Republic	162=	2.0
Laos	168=	1.9
Guinea	168=	1.9
Congo, Democratic Republic	168=	1.9
Equatorial Guinea	168=	1.9
Afghanistan	172=	1.8
Sudan	172=	1.8
Chad	172=	1.8
Uzbekistan	175=	1.7
Tonga	175=	1.7
Haiti	177	1.6
Iraq	178	1.5
Myanmar	179=	1.4
Somalia	179=	1.4

TABLE 6.1 (*continued*)

Source country	Rank (1 = least corrupt)	Score (10 = least corrupt)
Switzerland	1	7.81
Sweden	2	7.62
Australia	3	7.59
Austria	4	7.50
Canada	5	7.46
UK	6	7.39
Germany	7	7.34
Netherlands	8	7.28
Belgium	9	7.22
US	10	7.22
Japan	11	7.10
Singapore	12	6.78
Spain	13	6.63
UAE	14	6.62
France	15	6.50
Portugal	16	6.47
Mexico	17	6.45
Hong Kong	18	6.01
Israel	19	6.01
Italy	20	5.94
South Korea	21	5.83
Saudi Arabia	22	5.75
Brazil	23	5.65
South Africa	24	5.61
Malaysia	25	5.59
Taiwan	26	5.41
Turkey	27	5.23
Russia	28	5.16
China	29	4.94
India	30	4.62

TABLE 6.2 Corruption in international investment: Bribe Payers Index, rankings and scores for 30 outward-investing countries, 2006

Source: D. Mak, 'Bribe Payers Index (BPI) 2006', in TI, *Global Corruption Report 2007*, pp. 331–4.

The empty rows show the divisions made by the author through an agglomerative cluster procedure to split the countries into four clusters.

Rating of corruption across the world: the question of its relationship to the level and growth-rate of average income

Evidence from the GCB on petty bribery

The GCB surveys of 2006 and 2007 show the pervasiveness in ordinary people's lives of the demands for bribes as conditions of receiving basic services or avoiding (just or unjust) penalties or adverse judicial decisions. The poor, as expected, were hit hardest. Worst of the 'services' across the world in both years was the police. In 2006 17 per cent, and in 2007 25 per cent, of respondents who had had dealings with the police had been asked for a bribe: in 2006 the figure was about 55 per cent in Africa; 33 per cent in Latin America; 15–20 per cent in each of South and East Europe, Asia-Pacific, and the region comprising Russia, Ukraine and Moldova; and small percentages in North America and in the EU and Western Europe. Second-worst service overall in 2007 was the judicial system. Other sectors that were large bribe-demanders were registry and permits; health; education; utilities; and taxation. Across the regions there were differences in the *sectors* where bribe demands were apparently *specially* prominent. In the EU and Western Europe, it was medical services; in Africa and Russia-Ukraine-Moldova, both medical services and education; in Latin America, Asia-Pacific, and North America, bribery was especially prevalent in the courts (it is not clear from the source whether these sectors were the *next* most prevalent in all the regions concerned *after the police*) (TI, 2007, pp. 314–17; 2008).

Evidence from the CPI on prevalence of corruption across countries

Table 6.1 shows countries' scores and rankings on the 2007 CPI. The three that came out best that year were Denmark, Finland, and New Zealand, with Singapore and Sweden next. The two worst were Myanmar and Somalia. It is clear that there is a strong tendency for the high-income OECD countries to come out relatively well. Also there is a tendency for those near the very bottom of the list to be more or less *failed states*, where any central government has limited control and there may be, or have recently been, large parts of the country outside its control altogether. Among the high-income OECD countries, Greece is the lowest-ranking, at number 56 out of 180. Of middle-income countries Chile is the highest at 22nd. Botswana is the highest in Africa at 38th. In Asia-Pacific, Japan, Malaysia and the 'Four Tigers' are all in the top 43, with Singapore 4th equal (in company with the Nordics), Hong Kong 14th, and the two lowest of those six, Malaysia and South Korea, roughly on a par with Italy. However, *rapid growth* is no guarantee that a country scores reasonably well on corruption. China, with for long apparently the fastest growing economy in the world, was only 72nd equal on the CPI (together with India, Brazil and Mexico), scoring 3.5 while the least corrupt registered 9.4. Yet, though the positive relationship of CPI score with income *level* is very imperfect, it is inescapable, and, as a rough generalization, it seems to dominate over any independent relationship of the score with region of the world.

Connection of corruption with level and growth-rate of GDP per head

In fact, there is an abundance of cross-sectional econometric evidence that corruption tends *to be associated with lower GDP per head* (e.g., Tanzi and Davoodi, 1997; Senior, 2006, p. 165) and *lower growth-rates* of GDP (e.g., Mauro, 1995; Tanzi and Davoodi, 1997; and, with reservations, Rock and Bonnett, 2004). This in itself, however, leaves open the question *which way the causation works*: from corruption to low level and/or low growth-rate of income, or from the level and/or growth-rate of income to corruption; or perhaps there is a two-way relationship; or perhaps, for each statistical relationship, each variable is associated causally with some 'third factor'. Plenty of reasons and some empirical evidence (see below) can be given for supposing that the first-mentioned direction (from corruption to the level or growth of GDP per head) is important. But what about the second?

Possible reasons why poorer or slower growing countries may generate more corruption

If we presumed, purely for the sake of argument, that it was *the character of the society* – the income level and the other features that tend to go with it, the typical nature of 'developing' as against 'developed' countries – *that at least partly determined the prevalence of corruption*, we could postulate the following reasons why this might be so. There are at least three possible reasons why low level of income per head – or some characteristic closely connected – might favour the possibility of corruption.

First, it might be a greater residue of traditional views of power, which do not distinguish between the personal and the public rights and property of a 'big man', and look to him, *because of* his personal wealth and the influence that goes with it, as a protector and object of loyalty.

Second, maybe some part may be played by the greater gap in poorer countries today between material aspiration and reality for most people.

A third plausible factor, not so obviously related either to poverty or to relics of traditional attitudes, is the fact that in poorer countries there is often a high degree of unnecessary regulation with inadequate capacity for enforcement, so that its main impact is often as an obstacle to necessary or harmless activity and as fertile ground for arbitrary exactions.

It is a partly separate question whether *a low growth-rate* of GDP can be expected to encourage corruption. Mishra (2006, p. 355) speculates that the *process* of economic growth may act against 'collusive behaviour' because it can raise the *opportunity-cost* of resources devoted to collusion. To put it another way, the changes likely to be associated with economic growth may make *production* more rewarding to time and effort for talented people in relation to regulatory rent-seeking.

Ill-effects of corruption

There are various ways of looking at the ill-effects of corruption. Some of them are largely alternative ways of seeing others. They do not all denote mutually independent effects. The following list is informed in large part by Cartier-Bresson (2000, pp. 17–18), and by Tanzi (1998, p. 383) (the items seem in most cases inevitable consequences *a priori*, with the connection in some cases supported by statistical evidence):

1 *Loss of revenue and hence reduction of the state's capacity for high-priority activity.*
2 *Inefficiency in official decisions including appointments and award of public contracts.*
3 *Inefficient and unnecessary levies on useful productive activity.*
4 *Distortion of public spending toward the kinds of projects and techniques in which bribery and overcharging are easy and profitable.* There are likely to be too many capital projects at the expense of recurrent provision and maintenance; a preference for 'custom-built, high-tech equipment' regardless of the optimum choice of techniques; and distortion of sectoral priorities, for example, away from education and toward defence (Cartier-Bresson, 2000, citing evidence from Winston, 1979 (no further reference given) and Mauro, 1997). Mauro (1998) finds that corruption tends to reduce spending on education. There is incidentally evidence that developing countries tend to

spend too much – as judged on grounds of efficiency – on public investment in relation to public consumption (Devarajan *et al.*, 1996).

5 *Increased inequality, especially between 'ins' and 'outs', resentment, civil conflict.* With petty bribery it is disproportionately the poor who pay and those higher up the social ladder who benefit. Where there is any law that can be invoked *against* bribery, wealthier people are the ones most likely to be able to invoke it. With macro-corruption, it is only those near the top who make the large killings. In legal processes, whenever there is competition over who can pay the highest bribe, as in civil cases before corrupt judges, the richer parties are always likely to win. Where there are ethnic or other distinctive subsets of the population that are in any case relatively disadvantaged, corruption is likely to aggravate their grievances, increasing the risk of civil conflict which is always latent in divided societies.

6 *Reduction in the ability of the government to implement necessary regulation in order to correct for market failure, as over environmental externalities* (Tanzi, 1998, p. 383).

7 *Reduction in quality or increase in cost or both of public services and infrastructure.* There are plenty of incidents of buildings that have fallen down because dishonest or incompetent contractors have improperly been awarded contracts or have been allowed by corrupt officials to ignore building regulations. The alternative outcome is that the cost rises, sometimes to an extreme degree. It was estimated that, when the excess costs of corruption in Milan were rooted out by activist magistrates in what was known as the 'clean hands' operation, the cost per kilometre of the underground railway's construction fell by 57 per cent and the cost of building the airport by 59 per cent, and that the additional cost resulting from bribes in construction of telecom and power installations had been around 14 to 20 per cent (Senior, 2006, p. 169).

8 *Profitability of rent-seeking diverting talent from useful activity.*

9 *Increased taxes because of corruption-based loss of revenue discouraging production, driving producers into the informal sector, and (through a likely switch to broad-based indirect taxes) raising the relative burden on the poor.*

10 *Reduction or distortion in 'the fundamental role of the government in such areas as enforcement of contracts and protection of property rights'* (Tanzi, 1998, p. 383).

11 *Reduction in 'the legitimacy of the market economy and perhaps also of democracy'.* (Tanzi, ibid., where he asserts that the criticisms expressed in many countries against democracy and the market economy, especially in 'transitional' countries, are often motivated by the existence of corruption.)

12 *Cynicism and consequent slackness in performance of official and unofficial duties.* Corruption engenders cynicism, which makes it contagious and is likely to stifle public spirit. It is discouraging to those officials who might be disposed to act with integrity, and to those members of the public who might be inclined to take their civic duties – official and unofficial – seriously. Public spirit is a precious resource that no country can afford to squander.

A note: relevance of predictability

Cartier-Bresson (2000, pp. 20–1) cites evidence – from Kaufmann (1997), Kaufmann and Wei (1998), and Brunetti (1997) – suggesting that the ill-effects of corruption on economic activity are less where it is *organized* – as formerly by the KGB in the Soviet Union – and therefore the charges imposed are predictable. He cites World Bank findings from cross-country regressions (*World Development Report, 1997*, p. 103), suggesting that low predictability combined with high corruption goes with a gross-investment-GDP ratio on average of 12.3 per cent; high predictability combined with high corruption, 19.5 per cent; low predictability combined with low corruption, 21.3 per cent; and high predictability combined with low corruption, 28.5 per cent. So the extent of corruption still appears to matter a lot to the propensity to invest, but less when it is predictable.

Arguments used to justify corruption

Nevertheless, a case is sometimes made for *certain forms* of official corruption, notably bribery and official connivance in tax evasion. Here are some examples.

Bribery serves to speed official action, 'oiling the wheels of government'

It is important here not to confuse an assertion that bribing *may in certain circumstances be to the private advantage of the briber* from an assertion that bribery *is of social value as an institution*. The former of these assertions must surely be true; otherwise bribery would not be habitual. In view of the manifest inefficiency and unfairness of the effects of bribery in an economy otherwise working with reasonable efficiency, the latter can only be true if there is no other and socially better way of sparking or speeding official action, which is very much the same as saying that bribery may be of social value if (but only if) the relevant areas of government are irretrievably corrupt. That again may be true, but it does not by any means imply that bribery – and the official corruption (the susceptibility and quest for bribes) that makes it possible and drives members of the public to it – constitute a socially desirable institution, or that rigorous measures should not be taken to eliminate it. The case for the use of bribery to speed up official processes depends on supposing that they would otherwise be unreasonably and unnecessarily slow or that the queuing systems are so faulty that individual cases could easily be postponed indefinitely or regardless of any reasonable priority. There is also the suspicion that, where bribery is possible, processing will be deliberately slowed down in order to attract 'gifts' for speeding it up. In other words, a bribe may speed it up in an individual case *because the prevalence of bribery* has slowed it down across the board.

Market competition for regulatory rents will select the most productive uses and users

The reasoning here is that if, for example, the import of some industrial material is to be quantitatively restricted, (1) the most effective way of discovering which potential use and user will employ the limited supply most productively is to find who is prepared to bid the most for it; (2) the only effective way of finding who is prepared to bid most is to see who is prepared to pay the largest bribe. Though the first step of this reasoning may well be true, the second is not. What the bribery test discovers, at best, is which *dishonest* person is prepared to pay most; and, because of its covert nature, it may not even achieve that. Instead of, more or less secretly, selling the permits to the highest bidder with the proceeds going to the officials who happen to be dishonest enough and in the right place at the time, the administering agency could auction them openly for public revenue. This procedure could be authorized by law; it would indeed be more socially efficient than allocating the permits arbitrarily at some official's discretion; and, because of its obligatory openness, it would at least make bribery *more difficult* than under any set of rules that left the disposition of the scarce supply to be determined by administrative decision. On this ground bribery – even aside from all the arguments against it on grounds of injustice and the cynicism that it generates – is at most second-best to a perfectly simple, legal, and readily applied, device.

Reducing the burden of taxation will benefit the economy, and, if this happens because tax officials bend the rules, those officials are public benefactors

Following the logic of this argument, which is made by some quite respectable commentators, we should easily conclude that it would be better if there were no government revenue at all. However, if taxes on some people are reduced, *either* others pay more *or* the government is further restricted in what it can spend. Proponents of the argument are likely to claim that governments spend too much anyway, and that greater difficulties in raising revenue will lead them to cut waste. Yet, whatever waste there is in government spending, there is no guarantee at all that this is what will be cut. Governments of developing countries so often seem to have not enough resources at their disposal for meeting some of the most urgent humanitarian needs and filling the most glaring gaps in infrastructure. Many of these expenditures that would seem to have a high social priority nevertheless come into the 'discretionary' category: they are the ones that can legally and politically be cut if cuts have to be made. Reducing what the governments have to spend seems very likely to reduce *these critical 'developmental' expenditures.* It is a nice idea that only waste and misappropriation will be hit by diversion of public money to crooked officials, but not one borne out by experience. If the *other* response to the fall in revenue is followed, and reduction in the takings from one tax as a result of corruption in its administration is met by raising the rates applied to that tax or by increasing other taxes, not only will the supposed benefit of a lower tax burden not be realized, but the upshot is also likely to be more inefficient and more unfair. If the rate on the tax concerned is increased to make up, it will discriminate against some of those legally obliged to pay that tax (the ones who happen to be the more honest) in favour of others. If, as is likely, the taxes evaded in this way are mainly direct taxes, the burden may instead be shifted to indirect taxes, which are likely to bear differentially against the poor.

However, the paradox that some very fast-growing 'emerging' countries, such as China and India, have reasonably high levels of corruption has at least raised doubts over the supposition of a wholly adverse influence of corruption on growth. Rock and Bonnett (2004) investigate quantitatively the possibility that corruption may be more damaging to growth in certain kinds of economy than in others. They find that it tends at least to be less harmful in large countries than in small and believe they have found evidence that in Northeast Asia it may actually have been favourable to growth. Their explanation seems to depend on the supposition that China today, and Japan at an earlier stage of development, have been able to establish more predictability for investors through extra-legal arrangements than would have been available in the legal economy. If correct, this would appear to go further in 'justifying' corruption in certain circumstances, even if only as a second-best, than the World Bank (*WDR* 1997, p. 103) evidence mentioned at the end of the earlier sub-sub-section (headed '*A note: relevance of predictability*') would allow. However, 'Northeast Asian countries' constitute a very small sample (presumably China, Japan and the Koreas, maybe Mongolia), and, whatever the estimated statistical significance of the findings, it is difficult to put much weight on econometric results in such a case.

Factors shown econometrically to be related to corruption in government: probably as causes

Senior (2006) tested across countries their perceived levels of corruption – as measured by the countries' rankings on TI's Corruption Perception Index (CPI) – against various economic and non-economic characteristics of the countries concerned. He found that *low* levels of perceived corruption were significantly associated (in several bivariate or multivariate regressions) with high prevalence of ethical standards (personal honesty) in the community, high degree of press freedom, high respect for property rights, low level of regulation, little informal-sector activity, and high GDP per head – all as he expected – but also, unexpectedly, with *low* levels of what he calls religiosity (measured by prevalence of regular attendance at public worship) and *high* levels of government intervention (this last in apparent conflict with findings made by others). Seven other characteristics tested did not give significant results. The precise meaning of the variables used is given in the source (Chapter 3).

Brunetti and Weder (2003) also find a negative relationship between corruption and press freedom, with use of instrumental variables to support the view that at least part of the connection runs *from* press freedom *to* lower corruption.

World Bank evidence (*WDR* 1997, p. 104) shows the extent of corruption positively related to the extent of market distortion (essentially state intervention in the price system), and negatively to the predictability of the judiciary, to the ratio of civil-service wages to manufacturing wages, and to the extent to which recruitment and promotion in the civil service is merit-based. Given the presumption and evidence that the incomes of tax administrators (on grounds both of differential competence and pecuniary advantage) will have a negative relationship to their propensity to corrupt collusion with taxpayers, Ul Haque and Sahay (1996), faced with evidence of declining trends in real public-sector wages in a number of developing countries, use *a priori* reasoning to argue that there will be an optimum combination of tax and wage rate for a country to maximize, other things equal, its fiscal balance, and that departures from this optimum by cutting wages in the revenue service will *reduce* the balance.

It does not necessarily follow of course that any causation is entirely *from* the other characteristic tested *to* corruption. We consider below the question of the direction of the relationship with income. For most of the *other* characteristics among those mentioned in the three sources just cited as showing significant relationships, however, it seems quite reasonable to suppose that corruption is the 'explained' variable. Of these, the degree of press freedom and the extent of regulation, as well as the four identified by the World Bank, seem capable of favourable manipulation by state decision. It is certainly plausible that corruption might be reduced by changes in these variables.

BOX 6.2 POLITICAL RISK FOR INVESTORS WHERE GOVERNMENT IS ARBITRARY

'Political risk is arguably more pervasive and fundamental to who makes or loses money than at any time since the second world war. And not just in Russia. Indeed, although political risk is most prevalent in emerging markets, it is not confined to them. . . .

'In 2006, when Lakshmi Mittal bid for Arcelor, a European steel firm, he met fierce and seemingly racist opposition from the governments of France, Luxembourg and Spain . . . The deal went ahead only when India's government threatened a trade war.

'. . . . Yet most business leaders around the world reckon that political risk is a far greater problem in emerging markets. . . . Western oil and mining companies, having started to improve their behaviour in Africa under pressure from NGOs, now face competition from Chinese, Indian and Russian rivals that seem willing to cut deals with even the most unsavoury African politicians. And how do Western firms compete in countries where bribes are seen as an ordinary cost of doing business?

'Then there are the more humdrum uncertainties about emerging-market governments' attitude to the rule of law. Will theft of intellectual property be punished?. . . . Might the government issue a decree that alters the fundamentals of your business, without consultation or recourse, as often happens in China? Will it decide suddenly to break up local monopolies, or alternatively encourage their formation?'

Source: Economist, 20/9/2008, A special report on globalization by Matthew Bishop, p. 14.

Factors shown to be related to corruption in government: probably as effects

Tanzi (1998, pp. 585–6) lists the following seven relationships supported by econometric studies. In each case he presents the relationship as indicating an *effect* of corruption, with an explanation that makes that interpretation plausible. Leaving out the interpretation and the explanation and giving at first only the relationship and the source of evidence for it, we can say that corruption appears to be related:

1 negatively to investment and hence growth (Mauro, 1995);
2 negatively to expenditure on education and health (Mauro, 1997);
3 positively to public investment (Tanzi and Davoodi, 1997);
4 negatively to public expenditure for operation and maintenance (Tanzi and Davoodi, 1997);
5 negatively to the productivity of public investment and of infrastructure (Tanzi and Davoodi, 1997);
6 negatively to tax revenue (Tanzi and Davoodi, 1997);
7 negatively to inward foreign direct investment (Wei, 1997a; 1997b).

The mechanism supposed as operating in **1** and **7**, is increased cost or uncertainty for investors, and in the case of **5** presumably misallocation of public spending. In **2**, **3**, and **4**, it is the fact that certain kinds of expenditure are easier or more profitable sources of earnings for corrupt officials than others. In **6** it is the readiness of people to bribe in order to reduce their tax bills.

Corruption: cause or effect of low and stagnant income?

From what has been said, it is clear that there are plausible reasons why low or stagnant income may be either a predisposing factor to corruption or a result of it. And there may be a two-way relationship. The important policy question is whether or not corruption is important as a cause, regardless of whether it is also an effect. The seven empirically established relationships just listed do very plausibly suggest that corruption plays an important role in limiting the growth of real income (seen as potential material welfare); we can see good reasons in each case why the causation should run in that direction. And a number of presumed effects enumerated earlier in the chapter tend strongly to the same conclusion. By contrast the case, as we have presented it above, for making poverty, or cultural attitudes that are associated with it, or stagnant income, the *explanatory* variable is fairly speculative. It has been pointed out that migrants from relatively poor and relatively corrupt countries migrating to places in which the institutions of the state are largely effective against corruption do tend to conform in this respect to the behaviour of their adopted areas. This *might* be taken to imply that poverty in itself does not play an overriding part in disposing to corrupt behaviour.

One relevant econometric study is that by Mauro (1995). Here he uses an instrumental variable in two-stage least squares to *eliminate* the possibility that the positive relationship observed between 'bureaucratic efficiency' (a somewhat wider variable including a low level of corruption as one of its components) on the one hand and investment as a proportion of GDP on the other is *entirely* one in which bureaucratic efficiency is the explained element. The 'purged' coefficients meet the usual standard of significance. The implication drawn is that corruption, or something close to it, is at least in some degree the *explaining* variable.

Fields in which it is especially important to guard against corruption

We may speculate that probably the most critical area for maintaining integrity is the **judiciary**, together with the court administration over which the judges preside. So long as the administration of justice is law-driven and impartial, there is a backstop for redressing complaints of corruption in other departments. If the courts are directed to justice (and adequately financed and staffed and free of partisan political pressures), there is hope even for reforming a corrupt police force, provided at least that there is some other strong power in government working to the same end; whereas the converse may not apply: reforming the police can probably not do much to correct unjust judges.

TI devotes its *Global Corruption Report 2007* to 'corruption in judicial systems'. Among other items the publication gives in-country reports on the judicial systems of some thirty individual countries, showing a variety of deficiencies, some of which might appear fairly easily capable of correction, but also a number of attempts at reform more or less comprehensive, revealing some of the obstacles. Especially when it comes to reform of the judiciary, there is the dilemma expressed in the Latin saying: *Quis custodiet ipsos custodes?* Who will control the guardians? If it is vital to their function that the judges should be independent of the executive, how can a reform-minded executive restrain those that are corrupt – and, if not a reform-minded executive, who is or can be empowered and authorized to do it?

Second, in importance probably is the **police**, which TI's recent consumer surveys (the GCB, as mentioned above) identify across the world as the most corrupt service in the sense that it is the one that demands bribes in the highest proportion of its contacts with the public. Honest **courts and police**, if adequately resourced, with support for integrity from the highest levels of the executive, could surely do much to clean up the corruption in other institutions.

A further important candidate is **electoral administration**. It is vital for maintaining civil peace after a close election, and even a modicum of trust in the government elected, that the integrity of the body managing or overseeing elections is, and is believed to be, unimpeachable. This was blatantly lacking after the Kenyan election of 2007, which led to weeks of intercommunal fighting and destruction that was ended only after international mediation.

Vital, for obvious reasons implied above, to pursuing social priorities with fairness and efficiency is the incorruptibility of **tax (and personal-benefit) offices**.

Another characteristic and sometimes huge source of leakage of public resources is **works-contract administration**, which needs to be strictly bound by open-bidding procedures and to be administered in ways that are transparent and as far as possible exclude the possibility of 'conflict of interest'. The huge losses avoided by removing public-works corruption in Milan have already been mentioned.

Permit and regulatory offices are also often foci of graft and need to have similarly strict rules and conventions, to operate transparently, and as far as possible – through auctioning or otherwise – *to reduce or eliminate administrative discretion.*

In addition, to protect, promote, reward honest and capable public servants, and sift out the dishonest and incapable, in all departments, it is important that **public-service appointments bodies and disciplinary tribunals** should follow explicit rules or guidelines, act transparently, and again exclude possible conflicts of interest.

Upholding human rights

As we have suggested, the institutions and practices that are favourable to suppressing corruption tend also to be those favourable to the defence of human rights. This is because, in today's world, law, public rhetoric, and world public opinion, are most commonly both *against* corruption in most of the forms listed and *for* the human rights affirmed by international conventions. So administrative transparency, free comment, limitation of executive power by judicial or quasi-judicial tribunals or investigatory bodies to which there is genuinely free access – whatever makes state official decisions and behaviour public or subject to open review, and much of what checks the discretion of those in power – will be likely to further both objectives.

General approaches to containing corruption and infringements of human rights

We can divide the measures that might be taken to reduce corruption and infringements of human rights within a country into three classes: those that can be promoted respectively by that country's own government; by international action; and by civil society within the country.

Individual forms of institutional change or action under these headings will mostly be simply listed below. However, none of this should be taken to imply that there are plenty of levers easily pulled that will produce the desired effect. A sufficiently repressive or mercenary individual or coterie at the head of government may succeed in blocking all the opportunities of reform or redress, as we have seen in the early twenty-first century in Myanmar and Zimbabwe. Even a reform-minded head of government may have too little control to be able to effect much of the change needed. Where the head of government, possibly with genuinely good intent, has appointed a person of integrity and zeal to prosecute corruption, and the action that person takes is widely popular, the appointee may be rendered ineffective by those whose predatory activities are threatened. So John Githongo, appointed by the Kibaki government to attack corruption in Kenya, was forced in February 2005 to leave the country, apparently because of threats to his life, after he had claimed 'to have discovered ministers looting millions of dollars' (*Economist*, 28/1/2006, p. 14; also 12/2/2005, p. 56). In Nigeria Nuhu Ribadu, who had chaired the Economic and Financial Crimes Commission since 2003, making it 'the second most trusted institution in the country, according to a 2007 poll' and attaining 'almost mythic status among his countrymen by charging and prosecuting the politicians . . . who are responsible for most of the fraud and looting of public funds' (*Economist*, 5/1/2008, p. 46), was forced at the end of 2007 to resign on a technicality, ostensibly for legally obligatory re-education, after he had arrested an extremely rich and powerful state governor. These examples do not prove that the cause is always hopeless. They could indeed be taken to show that a determined and honest official may achieve a lot, but he or she is unlikely to be able to carry a purge through without complete support at the top of government.

BOX 6.3 INTEREST OF FOREIGN BUSINESS IN BEHAVING ETHICALLY

'As developed-country multinationals enter emerging economies, it is crucial that they do not lower their standards on corruption', says Ben Heineman, a former GE [a US multinational] counsel who recently published a book, *High Performance with High Integrity*. . . . Besides everything else, he argues, behaving ethically is in their self-interest. Successful global companies need uniform global cultures, in which everyone adheres robustly to the same rules, even in places where local companies do not. If people in one part of a company start adopting a lower ethical standard, it can have a corrosive effect on the entire corporate culture.

GE's Mr Rice reckons that the firm's hard line on corruption is actually helping it win business in many developing countries. . . . 'Country leaders feel under growing pressure to deliver better infrastructure and to be doing the best they can', says Mr Rice. Increasingly, 'they understand that corruption is a barrier to improving the standard of living of the poorest people, and they want to do business more and more with an ethical firm.'

Source: Economist, 20/9/2008, A special report on globalization by Matthew Bishop, p. 16.

Where corruption has become endemic, reform is likely to require attack from all available directions: action by and through the national government; supportive international action; and civil-society pressure. The list in Appendix 6.1 (available in the Online Learning Centre) gives some idea of the possibilities.

With a highly committed head of government, chief of police, and chief justice; a fully empowered investigatory tribunal; a well-resourced ombudsman office with full investigatory powers; co-operation from the home governments of inward investors; free media; and some organized civil-society activity in support; there could be progress.

Summary conclusions

- **Governance**, here distinguished from the wider question of *policy*, refers to the quality of the mechanisms and processes of government.
- The World Bank lists six dimensions of good governance: voice and accountability; political stability and absence of violence; governmental effectiveness; regulatory quality; rule of law; and control of corruption. To these we added, as a seventh, the upholding of human rights, capable of pursuit by many of the same means as the control of corruption. Recognizing that these seven criteria are interconnected, we approached the subject here through the question of corruption, intimately connected with the rule of law, as among other characteristics the aspect most susceptible to economic analysis, and one that has been regarded as especially important for 'development', with particular implications – because of its prevalence – for low- and middle-income countries.
- **Corruption** may be defined narrowly as *bribery*, the form in which it is most commonly encountered by the general public, or broadly as *the abuse of public office for personal ends*, which covers a wide range of activities, all departing from the rule of *impartiality* in government.

▶

- Officials' opportunity for receiving bribes depends on the existence, lawfully or otherwise, of *regulatory rents*: valuable rights of access or property or particular forms of action of which they are able to dispose.

- Plausible reasons may be adduced why a *stable* corrupt or relatively uncorrupt equilibrium may become established in a particular country and be resistant to change.

- The *comparative extent* of corruption of various types from one country to another can be roughly assessed through surveys such as those conducted and assembled from various sources by Transparency International to compile its annual Corruption Perceptions Index (CPI), Global Corruption Barometer (GCB), and Bribe Payers Index (BPI). A number of other organizations publish comparable assessments, and the World Bank assesses six aspects of governance, of which corruption is one.

- Across countries, the prevalence of corruption seems to have **a strong negative relationship, confirmed in a number of studies, to income per head, and also some negative relationship, though more ambiguous, with the rate of economic growth**. The cross-country relationship of corruption to average income appears to be stronger than any independent relationship of the distribution of corruption to particular regions of the world.

- Though such a correlation does not in itself indicate what leads to what, it is highly plausible that at least part of the story is that corruption *hinders* economic growth. And statistical testing suggests that that is at least a part of the connection.

- However, plausible reasons – though perhaps less compelling – may also be adduced why low income and the institutions that tend to go with it – or stagnant income – might have a role in *generating* corruption.

- There are a number of compelling reasons, generally supported by quantitative analysis, why corruption is likely to **hinder economic growth and the reduction of poverty** and indeed to increase inequality and bear hardest on the poor. However, it seems that any given level of corruption is *less* harmful to economic activity if it is organized and therefore relatively *predictable* in its exactions.

- Arguments purporting to show that corruption (meaning usually bribery) is **harmless or even beneficial** in certain circumstances are still sometimes put forward.

- Various factors that have been shown to have a statistical relationship across countries with corruption – such as the extent of regulation and distortion by government of the price system (positively); and a free press, the predictability of the judiciary, the ratio of civil-service wages to other wages, and the degree to which civil-service recruitment is merit-based (negatively) – are plausible candidates as **part-determinants** of the extent of corruption.

- Other features associated statistically with corruption, and mostly deleterious to growth and poverty reduction, are readily understood as **effects** of corruption, in which capacity they tend to fit with *a priori* expectations.

- Econometric evidence confirms the now prevailing view that at least part of the connection of corruption across countries with low or stagnant income per head reflects **a causal connection *from* corruption *to* low growth**. Coefficients have been estimated for the expected impact on this presumption, such as that a one-standard-deviation

▶

increase in corruption can be expected to reduce investment rates by three percentage points and average annual growth by about one percentage point.

- *Fields* in which it is particularly important to eliminate corruption are the *courts* (whose iniquities are particularly tricky to remedy from outside since their independence is so important to their function), the *police* (whose demands for bribes appear to have been those most frequently experienced recently by the general public across the world), the *electoral system, tax administration, permit-issuing and regulatory bodies*, and *public-service appointments, promotions, and discipline.*

- *Resisting* corruption (and, by many similar measures, upholding human rights) *can be pursued* or assisted by the national government (through its constitution, executive action, processes, and policies); by overseas governments and multilateral agencies (for example, by monitoring elections, and by making illegal and prosecuting, as mandated by the OECD Convention, bribe-paying overseas by persons within the governments' jurisdictions); and by civil society (individuals, organisations, and communication media) both local and foreign.

- *Eliminating* corruption when it has become pervasive across a society *is notoriously difficult* and, without the determined support and leadership by the chief executive, is unlikely to succeed. It probably needs to be attacked from a number of directions at once. We suggested that, with a commitment to reform on the part not only of the head of government but also of the heads of the police and the judiciary, with a fully empowered investigatory body and tribunal, an ombudsman service, a free press and support from the outside world and from local civil society, there may be hope.

The elimination of corruption is in most circumstances an unqualified social good, but a thoroughly corrupt state has strong mechanisms within it tending to perpetuate the corruption, so that removing it presents an enormous challenge. All available forces need to be mobilized – within government, from overseas governments and multilaterals, and from civil society. With wholehearted support from the head of government, the head of the police and the head of the judiciary, a powerful investigatory agency and tribunal, free press, active civil society, and support from the home governments of inward investors, there may be some prospect of success.

Questions for discussion

6.1 What particular difficulties do you see as facing any executive government that aims to reform a corrupt judiciary?

6.2 Why do you think the police rate so highly among the 'services' involved in bribery?

6.3 If lowish-income countries have a particular tendency to overregulate, is there an obvious reason for this? Is it simply that, if they did not overregulate, they would not be lowish-income countries? Or is that interpretation too simple?

6.4 What ground is there for saying that corruption bears especially hardly on the poor?

6.5 Should the home-country governments of international investors take any responsibility for preventing them from bribing host-country governments, even if this may mean that they lose contracts that they might otherwise win? Is such preventative action against bribery unwarranted interference in the host-country's affairs?

Additional reading

We suggest here one short and quite readable book on corruption; Anne Krueger's pioneering article on rent-seeking; a report of a study on the impact of corruption on international investment; and an *Economist* three-page 'Briefing' on the rule of law.

Economist, 20/3/2008, 'Briefing: Economics and the rule of law', pp. 95–7.

Krueger, A.O. (1974) 'The political economy of rent seeking society', *American Economic Review*, **64**, pp. 271–303.

Senior, I. (2006) *Corruption – The World's Big C: Cases, Causes, Consequences, Cures*, Institute of Economic Affairs in association with Profile Books Ltd, London.

Online *Learning* Center

To help you grasp the key concepts of this chapter check out the extra resources posted on the Online Leaning Centre at *www.mcgraw-hill.co.uk/textbooks/huq*

Among other resources, the following appendix is available:

- Appendix 6.1   Channels for suppressing corruption

CHAPTER 7

Governance Questions 2: Public-Sector Scope, Enhancement and Reform

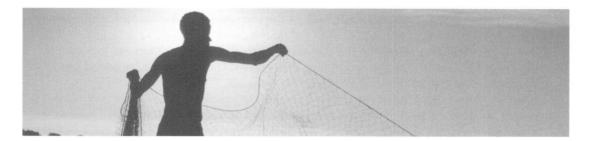

Though there is a wide range of functions in which state activity might in principle be required for the sake of efficiency or equity, it is important to trim any government's scope to its capacity. If the state is short on administrative competence or integrity, the best course may be to stick to the simplest methods and the most essential tasks.

Introduction

The development economics of the mid-twentieth century was inclined to seek salvation through government action. The implicit underlying idea was that **market failure** was responsible for the backwardness of the lower-income countries. By the 1980s the presumption was largely upended: the influential 'Washington consensus' tended rather to see the heavy involvement of the state as a major obstacle to growth and even equity: it was **government failure** that had been principally at fault, and the prevailing message to governments was that they should withdraw from much of their role in economic life. The World Bank's *World Development Report 1997*, 'The State in a Changing World', seems to have been framed with the intention of helping to resolve the conflict by examining the important economic role of government and the reasonable criteria for fixing the boundaries between the state and the private sector in particular circumstances. It then explored how the public sector's performance of its vital task might be improved, and how reforms to re-shape government for fulfilling its proper role might be engineered politically. This chapter draws considerably on that analysis.

The World Bank study says relatively little about macroeconomic management and specifically exchange-rate policy: major subjects of controversy over the role of government through much of the twentieth century. This was the subject matter of one of the two sets of events in the 1990s that in retrospect argued for *reducing the sphere of the market* somewhat further than had been favoured by the prevailing wisdom in the early 1990s.

Shortly after the study's publication, as it happened, the spate of currency crises of 1997 to 2001 in South-East and East Asia and Latin America and in Russia threw doubt on an element of then-prevailing market orthodoxy, in this case the one that would have rejected any control by governments on international capital movements and at the same time sought to put a country's exchange-rate – either by fixing it irrevocably or by allowing it to float freely – outside the range of its government's discretion.

Also, the unfolding story of 'transition' in the countries of the former Soviet Union and ex-Communist Central and Eastern Europe, again during the 1990s, showed the risks of mass privatization in the absence of an already functioning market economy ethically underpinned to a degree by civil society. This could mean handing over highly valuable assets to favoured individuals or limited groups of people who had no particular claim of right to them and might lack the credentials or the incentives conducive to managing them efficiently with the necessary modicum of public responsibility.

Later, in 2008, there was to be the collapse of major financial institutions, especially in the United States, shaking the world financial system. These experiences added further reservations to what had been the Washington consensus.

Here we list the basic justifications for government intervention, and then, following from that, explore the three main questions addressed in the World Bank study: how to fit a government's scope to its capacity; how to improve the performance of the public sector; and how to overcome obstacles to necessary reform. In the course of examining the first of these questions we consider the cases for privatization of state enterprises and functions, and the ways in which it may be practised, while avoiding both the drawbacks of private monopoly and the unfairness and inefficiency of crony and bandit capitalism.

BOX 7.1 TOOLKIT ON ROLE OF THE PUBLIC SECTOR

Asymmetric information. Situation in which one party or class of parties involved in a transaction or transactions knows less of the relevant facts than the other. For example, an investor asking a bank for a loan to support his business is likely to know more about the current state of the business than does the bank. This is not only unfortunate for the less knowledgeable party, but is also unlikely to lead to a contract on the optimum-efficiency locus.

Club good. This is a form of **public-good** (see below) whose enjoyment is **non-rival** (my enjoyment of it does not restrict or reduce yours) but **excludable** (those who don't pay *can* be excluded from enjoying it). A rough approximation to an example is a public highway so long as it is not crowded enough to slow traffic and the charging of tolls is possible.

Common-property good. This form of **public good** gives enjoyment that is subject to **rivalry** but is **not excludable**. An example is a river or canal used for irrigation and nearing its capacity. The more water one user takes the less there is for others, Also, it is difficult to know how much water each user has taken so as to exclude those who take too much.

Externality. An externality is a benefit (**positive** externality or **external benefit**) or cost (**negative** externality or **external** cost) arising from some transaction that is not directly rewarded through the market (if it is a benefit) or charged through the market (if it is a cost). It is thus a source of departure from an efficiency-optimum, unless it is corrected by some intervention, such as by a government subsidy or tax,

▶

Global public good. A good that bears the same relationship to nations in the world as a public good does to inhabitants in a national market. It is **non-rivalrous** or **non-excludable** or both in relation to nations. An example of a pure global public good is action taken under the Montréal Protocol to preserve the ozone layer, or the elimination of an infectious disease such as smallpox or tuberculosis that potentially hits every country. If the action is taken, everyone benefits. No country's enjoyment of the benefits is reduced by the fact than any other country benefits; and it would be impossible to exclude from the benefits a country that did not pay its share of the cost of the corrective action needed. So the market alone – even a market among national governments on behalf of their peoples – cannot provide a satisfactory outcome.

Liberalization. Abolition or reduction of government-imposed taxes or subsidies on particular activities, or of restrictive rules on commercial activities.

Market power. Power that a particular participant in a market possesses because of its size in relation to the size of the market. Extreme cases of market power are **monopoly** (where there is only one seller in the market) and **monopsony** (where there is only one buyer).

Merit good. A good that is not by its nature a public good, but that the government concerned believes should be *available* to everyone in its jurisdiction, or even should be *consumed* by everyone. The most common examples are education and health services. (These may have public-good elements as well, but are merit goods insofar as the public-good elements alone – namely the fact that everyone tends to benefit from an educated and healthy population – are not a sufficient reason for the goods to be provided free of charge or subsidized.)

Public good. A good that is desired and needed but has one or both of the characteristics: **non-rivalry** and **non-excludability**. For that reason it can not be provided to an appropriate degree by the market alone.

Pure public good. A public good, such as street-lighting, that possesses **both non-rivalry and non-excludability**.

Rationales of public-sector activity

Government may need to act in economic affairs (spending, regulating, enterprising, intervening in markets) for three classes of reason: (i) to uphold the **framework** of the market economy; (ii) to correct for **market failure**, that is, for the sake of allocative efficiency or, in other words to provide more abundantly the goods and services that people want or need; and (iii) on grounds of **equity**: that is, for the sake of fairness or the reduction of excessive poverty. In the headings that follow, *market framework* and *macroeconomic stabilization* come under framework questions; *public goods, externalities, monopolies, risk and imperfect credit markets*, and *imperfect or asymmetric information* come under market failure; *redistribution* under equity; and *merit goods* awkwardly under a combination of equity and market failure.

All the cases listed are categories of circumstance in which government intervention of some sort *may* in certain circumstances be necessary or at least be of some value. However, the mere fact that some form of intervention can be fitted under one of these headings **by no means implies that it is necessarily beneficial**, even if it is honestly and effectively pursued.

Also, forms of intervention that might, with a supremely efficient government machine, be useful, **may on balance do harm** if what they aim to do cannot be coherently implemented with the administrative system and the prevailing ethical attitudes that are actually in place.

On the other hand, where there are functions for which no such potential justification – on grounds of upholding the framework, or of economic efficiency or fairness – exists, there are good reasons for the government to leave the field to 'the market' and civil society.

Market framework

Government has an important role in setting or reinforcing the rules under which efficient markets are possible: civil order, and the enunciation and enforcement of commercial law. In this the state generally works best by co-operating with civil society in the broad sense: reinforcing the useful elements among informal rules, habits and attitudes.

Macroeconomic stabilization

The role of maintaining the value of the currency has long been recognized as a critical contribution on the part of government to the efficient working of an economy. In the twentieth century the function was extended to include that of keeping a stable level or growth path of economic activity and income or expenditure for the economy at large. The state has a particular role in circumstances where what is or appears to be privately beneficial to large numbers of people individually may in aggregate be harmful, as in the conditions in which runs on currencies occur, or where there are 'bubbles' in the prices of assets or waves of pessimism among investors. These matters are examined in Chapter 12.

Public goods

'Public-goods' by definition are those that are desired and needed but have one or both of the following two characteristics:

1 *Non-excludability:* they are necessarily enjoyed or consumed in such a way that what is called *exclusion* can not be applied: in other words, if the good is supplied at all, those unwilling to pay cannot be excluded from its benefits. So the goods cannot be financed by charging for their use.

2 *Non-rivalry:* their consumption or enjoyment by one person does not exclude or reduce the possibility of their enjoyment by others – so that, even if those unwilling to pay *can* be excluded, it will, at least in the short term, be socially wasteful to do so (because the extra consumer entails no extra cost).

Examples often cited to which *both characteristics* apply – **pure public goods** – are the provision of law and order through the police and the system of justice; protection from outside attack; and – a more homely example – street-lighting. (The theory derives from Samuelson, 1954, 1958.) The 'framework' benefits mentioned above, including macroeconomic stabilization, may also be classified as pure public goods. In all these cases the market unassisted will not do the job. It will have to be accomplished either by civil society (through consensus, which on the scale required will often be difficult to achieve in modern economies) or by the state (with the backing of coercion). Keeping the peace and protection against external attack may indeed be regarded as the original (beneficent) functions of the state: the main reasons why people by and large have been prepared to tolerate government, in spite of its frequent failings.

There are quite important cases in which enjoyment is *non-rivalrous but exclusion is possible*: so-called **club goods**. An instance is the provision of roads and bridges Potential users who refuse to pay *can* be excluded. On the other hand, unless the road or bridge is congested, the extra social cost of an additional user is often negligible – and enforcing the payment of tolls has costs, including often delay to road users. Some major roads could be, and have been, provided through the charging of tolls by private enterprise, but much of the road networks that countries today enjoy and consider essential could not be so provided without manifest inefficiencies; and without state participation they might not be provided at all. Generally it is taken for granted that the state provides most of the roads.

There may also be *rivalry without excludability*, with so-called **common-property goods**. Examples are grazing rights on common land, and irrigation water. Failing local civil-society rules, of which in fact there are many examples, some of them persisting for centuries (Ostrom, 1990), the state must regulate use of the land to prevent its degradation, and of the water to prevent both the inefficiency and the unfairness of its excessive use by those farmers who happen to be well-placed to draw off as much as they like. (See Case 2 in Chapter 8, pp. 189–91.)

BOX 7.2 GLOBAL PUBLIC GOODS

Mainly since 1990 it has become common to talk of *global public goods*, which stand in much the same relationship to individual states as public goods in the usual sense stand to individual households. They are goods that every state after a fashion desires but which unco-ordinated action by individual states will not deliver. Examples are keeping the peace internationally, or eliminating various contagious diseases such as smallpox or tuberculosis, or meeting some of the global environmental challenges such as ozone-layer destruction or global warming.

For obvious reasons consensual co-ordination among states is necessary for delivering these goods. It has sometimes worked spectacularly well, as over checking ozone-layer destruction under the Montréal Protocol of 1987, and (almost) eliminating smallpox. A number of *consensual* arrangements – agencies, treaties, clubs, and voluntary tribunals – have been set up, throughout the twentieth century and even earlier, that have produced the necessary international co-ordination in important fields, as over civil-aviation rules and collection of meteorological data. Since the late 1940s the UN has run a number of peace-keeping operations – 18 current at the end of 2006 (*Economist*, 6/1/2007, p. 21) – often with very small forces on shoestring budgets, that, despite some failures, have managed to prevent fighting or preserve truces in incendiary situations across the world, often with benefits that extend well beyond the areas concerned.

Yet it is clearly quite possible that relying on co-ordination *through consent* will not be enough in important cases. There will be costs that have to be borne, sacrifices that have to be made, by individual states (including sacrifices of insubstantial but very potent entities such as national myths). There is no overriding global government that might operate courts to settle disputes, or impose tax systems to raise revenue – impartially and with powers of enforcement. Until there is, we must rely on institutions that operate – however imperfectly – through inter-governmental consent to deliver a number of the most crucial global public goods. This must often involve voluntary acceptance by the various governments of rules and procedures under which they agree to be bound very much *as if* they were under an enforced law: what one writer has called *quasi-voluntary compliance* (Ostrom, 1990).

Merit goods

'Merit goods' are more difficult to define than public goods. Public goods can be so designated by virtue of the intrinsic character of the way the service concerned is provided, whereas the classing of a benefit as a merit good has to involve a value judgment by the authority providing it. My list of merit goods is not necessarily yours.

The term *merit good* is applied to any good that is not by its nature a public good (pure, club, or common property) but that the government concerned believes should *be available to* everyone in its jurisdiction or even should actually *be consumed by* everyone. The most important examples in many countries are health and education services. Health services and schooling as goods provided *to individuals* are not intrinsically public goods: they possess 'excludability', and they are also 'rivalrous': those unable or unwilling to pay *can* be excluded; and they use scarce resources so that one person's use of the services *may* reduce what is available for other people or for other purposes.

The main motive behind free health services and free (or even compulsory) schooling is probably a sense of fairness. This implies that the provision has in large part a *distributional* objective. (*Compulsion* over education makes for a further degree of fairness, in that, if effective, it ensures that children have the benefit of schooling even if their parents would not otherwise arrange that they attended.)

Free health services and free or compulsory schooling may also have an *allocative* objective: to secure as far as possible a healthy and suitably competent population. This may be regarded as a public good: there are common benefits arising for the whole society over and above the benefits to the individuals who are taught or treated, and individuals cannot be excluded *from these common benefits* if they refuse to pay for them.

It is probably best to regard the provision of free or subsidized medical treatment and education as having both distributional motives (in which capacity they are merit goods) and allocative motives (based on the public-good elements they deliver).

Checking monopoly and excessive market power

A number of the 'utilities' are *natural monopolies*: they depend on networks such as powerlines which it would be highly inefficient to duplicate. However, this does give the firms operating the utilities monopoly power, under which it may be to their advantage to charge more, and hence to produce and sell less, than would be socially efficient. There may be at least a case for checking monopolistic behaviour. Avoiding private control of natural monopolies has been one of the main pretexts for state enterprise; but controlling or checking monopoly and excessive market power (as manifested, for example, in restrictive trade practices) covers a potentially wider field than the public utilities.

Externalities

Externalities – cases in which market prices differ from 'social prices' – provide a further (allocative) case for intervention by the state. Common examples of *'negative' externalities* are instances of industrial pollution, which represent costs to people at large, but for which neither the producers of the goods in whose production the pollution is generated nor the buyers of those goods are required to pay. An example of a comparable *'positive' externality* is the widely spread social benefit that someone planting trees for timber on a hillside may have through limiting the run-off of water and so moderating fluctuations in the flow of rivers and reducing erosion. Here the defect is that the planter of the trees is not *rewarded* through the working of the market for generating these benefits for others and may therefore have an inadequate incentive for doing so.

Generally the most efficient way – where it is practicable – of correcting the incentives to sellers and buyers of the goods concerned is subsidizing where there are positive, and taxing where there are negative, externalities. Less satisfactory generally are 'command-and-control' methods where permits to operate are given at an official's discretion; but the inefficiency and arbitrariness of such an arrangement may be removed if the permits are auctioned. As an alternative to simply subsidizing, the government may start or acquire itself the producing unit that generates the positive externality and be prepared to run it at a loss.

Risk and imperfect credit markets

The risk of a project entails a cost to the operator. It may render unattractive to private investors an investment *with a (mean) expectation* of being profitable. The risk may be regarded as generating a positive externality: it makes the (mean expected) social benefit of the project greater than the benefit as it appears to the (risk-averse) private investor. This is especially likely to be relevant with infrastructure projects (transport, fuel, power, or communications) in a very poor, or small and isolated, or thinly peopled, territory; and it is probably one of the reasons – more important than a perceived need to control monopoly power – why governments have frequently undertaken such investments. If risk is the only source of the externality, however, and there is no public-good or merit-good element in what is produced, it should not be necessary for the state to subsidize the enterprise (or to run it at a loss) *indefinitely*, or indeed over the lifetime of the project. However, private suppliers of credit may not take a long enough view to consider such investments worth financing, and in that case governments will have to take the risks if the investments are to be made at all.

Imperfect or asymmetric information

Suppliers of services may well know more than their customers about the costs of supplying them and about their own capacity to do so and their prospects of remaining in business. In such cases, government *may* enable markets to work better (more at least in the interests of customers and of reliable suppliers) if it has a system of regulation and certification that will guarantee the general soundness of the suppliers. Such regulation can very easily be overdone and obstruct rather than further transactions, but it is widely agreed that customers need some guarantees or strong presumptions of the soundness of banks, for example, ideally through capital-adequacy and audit requirements and rules against insider-lending (World Bank, 2007b, pp. 66–7).

Straight redistribution: the direct relief of severe poverty

Some government spending – over and above spending on merit goods – can be aimed directly at improving the distribution of income or wealth. First, there are measures to be taken when famine threatens an area or there has been a major disaster: payments to affected individuals (preferably – on several grounds – in exchange for some work of social value). Developing countries, however, have not usually run general systems of 'safety-net' cash payments to the poorest people in normal times. Yet in very recent years there have been some important moves in this direction, such as India's National Rural Employment Guarantee Scheme, *Oportunidades* in Mexico and *Bolsa Familia* in Brazil, to all of which further reference is made in Chapter 10 (*Economist*, 26/4/2008, pp. 71–2; 4/3/2006, p. 58; 18/11/2006, Survey, p. 7; 14/4/2007, Special report on Brazil, p. 11). The two schemes from Latin America have made payments dependent on compliance with schooling and basic health measures for children, so combining straight redistribution with the take-up of merit goods that bring with them some public-good elements. The issues and possibilities are considered further in the material on 'Social safety-nets' in Chapter 10.

Matching public-sector scope to capacity

The World Bank study mentioned in the Introduction to this chapter (World Bank, 1997) puts forward the view that an effective state should be seen as 'central to economic and social development, **not as a direct provider of growth but as a partner, catalyst, and facilitator**' [emphasis ours]. It recognizes that solutions will differ widely from one country to another in response to a large number of variables.

The study enumerates the potential grounds for state intervention much as we have listed them above, but where it goes beyond this standard analysis is to propose *priorities* among the economic tasks of government, and to suggest what might be called *degrees of intensity* of government involvement in the economy, with the appropriate degree depending on the *capacity* of the state's institutions.

It lists what it presents as the five fundamental tasks of the state as:

1   'Establishing a foundation of law
2   Maintaining a non-distortionary policy environment, including macroeconomic stability
3   Investing in basic social services and infrastructure
4   Protecting the vulnerable
5   Protecting the environment' (World Bank, ibid., p. 4).

But it emphasizes that the best mix for fulfilling those tasks may well involve both state and market.

The study's proposal of priorities among forms of government engagement is shown in its Table 1 on p. 27. That table divides the functions of the state into minimal, intermediate, and activist, with decreasing priority. The implication is that some states will be able to fulfil effectively only the first of the classes, which involves the provision of pure public goods and protection of the livelihoods of those in greatest need. Some other states will be able to manage properly only the first two, which deal also with externalities, monopoly, imperfect information, and social insurance. Attempting what cannot be effectively performed is likely to be counterproductive, it is supposed, sowing disillusionment with government and endangering what is essential. It is implied that only those with very high bureaucratic performance should attempt tasks in the third level – the 'activist' functions – such as co-ordinating private-sector activity (such presumably as the 'economic planning' to which so many developing countries aspired in the 1950s and 1960s) that inevitably meant fostering certain industries at the expense of others, and seems to have been successfully practised by Japan and South Korea) or redistribution of assets (such as the post-war land reforms of Japan and Taiwan).

The study (ibid., p. 67) distinguishes *institution-intensive* from *institution-light* approaches to the necessary regulation, relating the choices to three main fields of regulation: financial institutions, utilities, and the environment. 'Institution-light' arrangements, as exemplified there, go for simple rules that are readily enforceable legally, local regulation, public information, and adjustment of incentives, with differing variants for the three main areas of interest. In general they avoid administrative discretion, command-and-control, and reliance on supervisory authorities, which make bigger demands on administrators' competence and integrity and come into the 'institution-intensive' category. A decade later, we might perforce be looking for some much stronger measures on the environment than are foreshadowed here; the world may be simply obliged to apply as best it can cap-and-trade systems on greenhouse emissions, which in their administrative characteristics arguably come into the command-and-control category. Furthermore, some of the proposed 'light' provisions, such as establishing *incentives* for bank owners and managers to maintain bank solvency, may require considerable ingenuity to devise in the first place. However, a system that *thereafter* maintains itself, with little need for bureaucrats' discretion, has obvious advantages.

Attempting functions that are unnecessary, such as much of the regulation of business that often goes on in developing countries, can be positively inhibiting to investment and destructive of economic activity. (Examples of the great difficulty and delay that can be put in the way of starting a business by over-regulation are given in Chapter 19.) Public enterprises also often make consistent losses and provide poor service.

On these grounds there is often an important job for **reforms** that entail *liberalization* and *privatization*.

Liberalization

Liberalization can entail selective removal of regulations, registration requirements, taxes and subsidies. This may need to be extensive but must be discriminating. Some regulation, registration, and monitoring – of financial-service institutions, for example – may be extremely important in order to inform the public about which of them are reliable; and rules on health and safety and on environmental protection may be needed in manufacturing, mining, and construction. Nonetheless, all such regulations and requirements need to be scrutinized to determine whether they are in fact necessary – probably with a presumption against – and whether it will be possible to enforce them with reasonable consistency. Where they are necessary and enforceable, the scope for administrative discretion should be minimized (for example, if capital exports or imports have to be rationed, this should be done by statutory levies or by auctioning of quotas, rather than by some official's judgement or favour).

Privatization

Government enterprises that sell goods and services to the public commonly register consistent financial losses. There are various reasons. Perhaps the overriding one is that those who manage them often *do not have strong incentives to keep them profitable*; but, even if the incentives – imposed or self-generated – were there, other circumstances would often make the achievement of profitability difficult. These come under the general heading of *political interference*. Politicians may regard public enterprises as useful ways of relieving unemployment. They may think it politically imperative to keep the prices charged at levels that happen to be below cost, and particularly to be very reluctant ever to *raise* prices. They may be unwilling to prevent forms of theft from public utilities, such as the illegal tapping-off of power. They may insist that certain individuals be employed regardless of their competence or the need for their services. The interference in other words may shade off into various forms of corruption.

If the enterprises concerned can be transferred into private hands under conditions that make them likely to be managed with rudimentary competence as commercial entities, *and* the transfer process itself can be managed in the public interest, free of favouritism or other forms of corruption, *and* the private firms formed can be prevented from abusing monopoly power, then **privatization** is likely to have clear benefits.

Privatization, even of public utilities, became a fashion, pioneered by the UK under the Thatcher government, and supported by the World Bank and IMF, from the 1980s, before which most *public utilities* in most countries were publicly owned. In a number of the developing countries state enterprises extended well beyond the public-utility range. Where the state enterprises concerned are not natural monopolies, much of the benefit that might be sought by privatization may be derived instead – with less initial difficulties and hazards – by simply allowing private enterprises *to compete on a level playing-field* with those owned and operated by public-sector entities.

Privatization may plausibly bring the following gains through introducing competition and removing political interference:

- It may increase government net revenue (or allow the reduction of taxes) through making loss-making enterprises profitable.

- It may end monopoly in the supply of certain services, providing the spur of competition to reduce prices charged or increase quality or both.

- It may increase the competence of managers in the enterprises concerned and improve their performance incentives.

- In summary, it may make use of the energies and motivations of the private sector in the service of the public.

If the losses of public enterprises, or the net costs of providing services such as those of health and education and roads, can be reduced, that is a *prima facie* social gain. But a number of government-owned enterprises have been public utilities (fuel, power, post, transport, telecoms, water), and some of these industries are *natural monopolies* in at least some of their activities. This is often because they depend on *networks* of infrastructure (pipelines, power lines, railways, roads, telephone lines) which it would be costly, and socially highly wasteful, to duplicate. So fully competitive conditions must often be lacking. A monopoly destined by the nature of its business (or by the regulatory environment in which it works) to remain a monopoly will lack the spur of competition to improve its performance; and in any case, as elementary theory is held to demonstrate, a monopolistic firm pricing so as to maximize its profit will tend to price too highly, and consequently produce too little, for economic efficiency.

There are two plausible ways out of this dilemma, not mutually exclusive. One is to set up an **industry regulator** for each privatized industry that is prone to monopoly. The regulator, working on principles laid down, would set maximum prices and minimum standards of service. To be useful, a regulator would need integrity and well-qualified staff. The World Bank study (ibid., pp. 65–6) stresses that the value of this approach depends heavily on the competence and integrity of the regulator, and that any impression of arbitrariness may deter investors. Where the capacity of the government to staff and brief the regulatory body adequately is dubious, it seems to follow that *the less reliance placed on the use of an industry regulator* the better.

The other expedient for checking monopolistic behaviour on the part of utilities after privatization is **to separate the operation of the *network* part of the business** (such as the electric-power grid), which is by nature monopolistic, **from elements that are potentially competitive** (such as the generation and retail sale of electric power). The network would *either* remain government-owned *or* become the province of a private operator. In the latter case, or possibly both, it might have to be *under regulation* designed to minimize abuses of monopoly power, but the more any regulation could be framed so as to be independent of administrative discretion the better. The other elements of the business might be privatized, especially if there were some possibility of useful competition among firms within them, and, if so – in the measure of their intrinsic propensity to be competitive – they could be subject to *lighter* regulation than the natural monopoly embodied in the network.

A combination of regulation and competition after privatization has been successfully demonstrated by the UK in telecoms, with the previous state monopoly privatized but continuing to provide the network, and the retail (non-network) part of the business subject to open competition but with the prices charged by the network and other terms of access to it subject to regulation in order to keep the field level for the retailing firms.

A similar unbundling of services might be done in the provision of health or education facilities or roads, where their provision by the state is *not* designed to be commercially profitable or even self-supporting. Just as the actual building of roads for the government is commonly done by putting it out to competitive private tender, so the provision of particular ancillary services in hospitals may be *outsourced* to the firm that credibly offers to provide the service – at the standard required – for the lowest charge. Provided the quality of performance and of conditions for workers is upheld by clear specification of requirements and monitoring, any resulting reduction in costs is likely to represent a social gain.

There is frequently **opposition to privatization** on the ground that it is giving away public assets to be used for the sake of private profit. However, shares in the assets are normally sold, not given away, and this may be done by some process equivalent to auctioning in order to maximize the price received by the state. The expectation in such cases – provided there is reason to expect competition among bidders – is that the highest bid would be no lower than the risk-adjusted expected lifetime value of the assets. Also, the profits generated by the privatized firms would be subject to taxation. The buyers would admittedly face risks – of changes in state policy – that the government itself would not have to take into account in valuing the assets, and they would discount their offers accordingly. But against this can be set the likelihood that the assets in private hands would be more commercially profitable and consequently provide more tax revenue. In addition, the more the government can make its policies appear consistent and credible, the less the risk discount that the private bidders would be likely to apply. To see it another way: if a state-owned enterprise would have made zero or negative profit, while its privatized successor managed at least some positive and taxable profit, the state would gain more net recurrent revenue after than before privatization, and this would be a gain over and above the price received from the sale of the assets. If this better financial performance came about through improved technical efficiency and management – under the spur of competition with only the necessary regulation – then it is quite likely too that the customers could be enabled to gain through lower prices or better service.

An alternative approach would be for the state to retain ownership of the whole enterprise, monopolistic or not, but to make it **financially and managerially independent**, with an industry regulator to provide against monopolistic abuse, and perhaps with permission – or even some degree of obligation – for rewards to top management, or to staff generally, to be related to the enterprise's performance, through shareholdings or otherwise. The desirable trick here would be to combine the elements of incentives, public control, accountability, and freedom from 'political interference'. A further variant would be **to sell part of the shares in the enterprise to the private sector**, still with a regulator in operation insofar as industries with monopolistic tendencies were involved. The directors put in place by the private shareholders would be motivated to increase the value of the firm, which would benefit *all the shareholders including the state*, and for this reason they might also help the business to withstand political pressure.

The desirability of privatization, its form and degree, and the importance of a regulator, will no doubt depend considerably on the nature of the industry or service involved. It is clear that successful privatization may require regulatory reform: new regulations as well as the discarding of old ones.

Apart from the need to provide against the formation of private monopolies when certain government enterprises are privatized, experience with the 'transition countries' since 1990 has highlighted a further social hazard of privatization. Unless precautions are taken, even an ostensibly fair and efficient method of selling or giving state shares to the public may result in enterprises' capture by organized groups (with no particular claim of managerial competence, and sometimes of a semi-criminal character) at very little cost to the captors. To take one instance, mass issue to all adult members of the public of tradable vouchers through which they might bid for shares in enterprises to be privatized (as pioneered by the Czech Republic and copied to a point by Albania, for example), with the hope that the shareholders in each enterprise would then engage competent directors and management, can have its good intentions frustrated by the large-scale buying up of vouchers ahead of the bidding process by particular well-informed individuals or groups at knockdown prices, and their consequent control of the enterprises promising the most profit or plunder. If, on the other hand, the shareholders in an enterprise do turn out to be large numbers of ordinary people, there is no guarantee that they will be in a good position to choose appropriate directors and managers. Handing over ownership in an enterprise at an arbitrary or nominal price to its 'workers' – to take another variant – can allow a small group of managers of a capital-intensive concern, if they know the ropes, to capture a vast source of wealth. No doubt there would have been ways to avoid these outcomes. One desirable precaution in privatization is to make the process completely *transparent* to the public. There may never be a repeat sale across a large part of the world on the same scale as in the 1990s, but the hazards are there.

Credibility

The World Bank study stresses that 'the government's credibility – the predictability of its rules and policies and the consistency with which they are applied – can be as important in attracting private investment as the content of those rules and policies' (ibid., p. 4). The study's **credibility index** for countries reflects five variables: unpredictable changes in laws and policies, unstable government, insecurity of property, unreliable judiciary, and corruption (all as judged by survey respondents). The study finds that the index, *negatively* based on those five characteristics, has a strong *positive* relationship with growth of GDP per head, and with gross investment as a proportion of GDP, and also with the average rate of return on World-Bank-financed projects (ibid., pp. 5, 34–7).

One implication of these observations about credibility for the question of fitting scope to capacity is surely that for a government to attempt more than it can carry out consistently and effectively can be damaging to its credibility and hence discourage investment, for that reason alone if for no other, more harm than good may be done to its country's prospects for growth and poverty reduction. Another obvious implication is that it is highly important to introduce reforms in governance that *enhance* credibility: that make for stability in laws and policies, stable government, secure property, an honest and competent judiciary, and generally a reduction of corruption. It is to the question of improving the competence of government that we now turn.

Enhancing public-sector performance

Under the heading 'Reinvigorating state institutions', the World Bank study (ibid., pp. 7 ff.) lists three directions in which action can be taken: toward *effective rules and restraints*, *greater competitive pressure*, and *increased citizen voice and partnership*, drawing respectively on the architecture of the state itself, the possibilities of market-type competition in what are currently government functions both within and without the boundaries of the state, and civil society. The particular classes of measure mentioned often fit under more than one of these categories. Generally they will cover much the same kinds of action as those listed in Chapter 6 as likely to reduce corruption. What helps to remove the incubus of corruption will largely also provide opportunities and incentives for positive improvement. Particular examples (loosely based on the items in the study) are:

- avoiding 'policy-distortion' such as levies, subsidies, and restrictions, other than those justified by externalities; these will misdirect government, as well as private, action;
- protecting the independence of the judiciary;
- watchdogs against corruption and official oppression;
- merit-based recruitment and promotion in the public service;
- public-service pay adequate to attract able people;
- accountability for delivery in the public service; the suggestion is made of reorganizing departments into performance-based public agencies with specific objectives, as in New Zealand and Singapore (ibid., p. 10);
- ending state monopolies by contracting-out, privatization, or allowing private competitors to operate alongside state enterprises;
- increased public information and transparency in state activities;
- citizen-opinion surveys;
- free elections;
- participation of users of public services in their planning and monitoring;
- devolving power to local institutions – 'carefully', the study emphasises, in order to avoid contributing to inequality or to macroeconomic instability, or capture of public operations by 'vocal interest groups'.

The study argues (ibid., p. 92) that – as well as competence – *loyalty* and (if we can interpret) a measure of *inner or social, rather than material, motivation* among public servants will be necessary. This enhances the importance of the last few items on the list above: those that involve active engagement with the public. Such involvement is perhaps becoming increasingly easy (p. 111), it is suggested, since citizen participation through NGOs has been growing in the developing world. In India the proportion of respondents who said that they participated in a social organization or political party doubled between 1971 and 1996. Mention is made of a number of cases of joint community and official action, especially in irrigation (Taiwan and the Philippines cases are mentioned) that are apparently analogous to the irrigation-settlement case described in Chapter 8 (pp. 189–91), at least in the great improvements achieved in water management: co-operation that also seemed in that Sri Lanka case to transform for the better both the target community and the associated bureaucracy. Something similar is reported (ibid.) of 'community monitoring of an innovative community health program' in the State of Ceará in north-eastern Brazil which 'provided the basis not only for a highly successful program but also for more effective co-operation among community members on other mutually beneficial courses of action'. The account of this project is reproduced here as Box 7.3.

BOX 7.3 BUILDING WORKER DEDICATION: GOOD GOVERNMENT IN BRAZIL'S CEARÁ STATE

In 1987 the state government of Ceará in northeastern Brazil confronted a crippling fiscal crisis, superimposed on a legacy of mediocre administrative performance. Yet within four years the fiscal crisis had been overcome, and the quality of services had improved dramatically. Vaccination coverage for measles and polio almost tripled, from 25 percent to 90 percent of the child population. The state's public works program employed more than 1 million unemployed farmers during droughts. And its business extension and public procurement program for small firms was saving more than 30 percent over its previous overall expenditure.

Much of the credit for this success is owed to the civil service itself. The state government contributed in an unusual and sometimes inadvertent way to public workers' newfound dedication. Using rewards for good performance, public screening methods for new recruits, orientation programs, and sheer boasting through the media about its successes, the state created a strong sense of mission around key programs and their workers. Highly motivated workers carried out a larger variety of tasks than usual, often voluntarily. Granted greater autonomy and discretion, workers were able to provide more customized service. This greater discretion did not result, as it often does elsewhere, in greater opportunities for rent seeking, because of pressures to become accountable. Workers wanted to perform better in order to live up to the new trust placed in them by their clients. This in turn was the result of more customized arrangements of their work and the public messages of support from the state. At the same time, the communities where these public servants worked monitored them more closely. The state's publicity campaigns and similar messages had armed citizens with new information about their rights to better government and about how public services were supposed to work. Thus government played a powerful role in monitoring, but it did so discreetly.

These mechanisms created a virtuous cycle in which workers reported feeling more appreciated and recognized, not necessarily by superiors, but by their clients and the communities where they worked. This, in turn, reinforced their dedication to the job.

Source: Reproduced by permission from World Bank, *World Development Report* 1997, p. 97.

The World Bank study also introduces the concept of *social capital*: patterns of habits, conventions, and long-term relationships – in short, under the broad definition that we introduce in Chapter 8, *civil society* – which (to interpret) reinforce trust and responsibility and hence facilitate co-operation. Evidence is cited that ratings of social capital, for example across a set of Tanzanian villages, are positively related to two measures of material well-being: household expenditure per head, and school quality (ibid., p. 115).

Overcoming obstacles to reform

The World Bank study (ibid., p. 145 ff.) uses as examples six specific types of reform: trade liberalization, pension privatization, functional, political, and fiscal decentralization, and public-sector reform (by implication toward greater meritocracy and efficiency). It considers likely opponents and supporters of each, factors affecting the political cost, how the reform might be tactically sequenced, and other relevant issues.

Three general pieces of practical advice for would-be reformers are given or implied, on roughly the following lines.

- Windows of opportunity for reform may open, especially when there are external threats, crises, or changes of government.

- Reformers need to form some idea of the gains and losses, and of the gainers and losers, from the reforms at which they aim, and hence to understand the likely obstacles to the reform and the potential alliances and arguments against the reform and in its favour. They should seek to mitigate the obstacles: for example, by tactical sequencing (probably one item at a time, the items preferably chosen with the objective of demonstrating success), trying to build a consensus for the reform (for example, by packaging together reforms that appeal to different groups), and, where possible, planning to compensate the losers.

- Leadership with clear vision and determination is needed.

Summary conclusions

- There are a number of standard cases in which government intervention in the economy may be justified:
  a In order to establish and maintain a *framework of rules* that allows a market economy to work, and to do so with reasonable short-term stability;
  b For the sake of economic efficiency, to compensate for *market failure*; and
  c For the sake of *equity*.
- Nevertheless not all intervention that might be fitted under these heads is on balance beneficial.
- State actions that might be useful if properly conducted but are not carried out with competence and integrity may on balance do harm – for one thing, because they threaten the *credibility* of government at home and abroad, which plays an important part in encouraging investment.

▶

- For this reason the *scope* of government needs to be matched to its *capacity*. Measures that might otherwise seem ideal for addressing externalities, regulating monopoly, overcoming the effects of imperfect information, or providing social insurance, may have to be forgone in favour of simpler or less fragile devices if administrative competence is inadequate to undertake them consistently and effectively.

- In the extreme case in which capacity is rudimentary, government may need to confine itself to the provision of a small range of essential pure public goods and some protection for the very poorest and those hit by disasters. The presumption must be against devices that require *administrative discretion* or *extensive supervision*. These are devices that generally demand a high level of both integrity and competence on the part of administrators.

- Highly activist interventions, such as attempts to co-ordinate the development of industries in the private sector or to redistribute assets, will make very big demands on the core of most able administrators, and can easily be emptied of any value they might have if the required humanpower and administrative systems are lacking.

- Over-regulation and market-distorting restrictions, duties and subsidies – common, sometimes to an extreme degree, in developing countries – may call for extensive liberalization.

- Public enterprises – often making losses for the state and providing poor service – may often with advantage be opened to private-sector competition or privatized.

- Devices exist for preventing the privatized forms of natural monopolies formerly operated by governments from misusing monopolistic power.

- Enhancing the competence of the public sector can draw on three kinds of approach: (i) '*rules and restraints*' (guaranteed immunities, laws and their repeal, separation of powers, checks and balances, watchdog agencies); (ii) '*competitive pressure*', drawing on competition both within and outside of government (meritocracy in public-service appointments and promotions, 'competitive' public-service pay, liberalization, privatization, contracting-out, exposure to external trade and investment); and (iii) '*voice and accountability*', implying openness to public scrutiny and cooperation with civil society (public information, transparency, free elections, citizen-surveys, consultation with users of services).

- Motivation-to-service of public employees needs to be internalized as far as possible, and for this purpose exposure to public scrutiny and judgement is likely to be specially relevant.

- For the politics of achieving reforms in government, three lessons are enunciated: (i) that opportunities for reform are likely to arise in times of crisis or change; (ii) that reformers need to assess likely supporters and opponents and to think tactically, sequencing reforms in such a way as to start with demonstrable successes, and building alliances by packaging measures appropriately and compensating losers; and (iii) that leadership is needed with determination and clear vision.

Public-sector reform needs to draw on the three staples of policy: rules and restraints (the methods of government itself); competitive pressure (the methods of the market); and 'voice and accountability', namely involving the public through transparency, openness and consultation (the methods of civil society).

Questions for discussion

7.1 In the pursuit of equity, why do you think the World Bank 1997 study gives the *sequence* it does – from more to less essential and from less to more difficult – as starting with antipoverty programmes and disaster relief; proceeding to redistributive pensions, family allowances, and unemployment insurance; and going from there to asset redistribution? What would you interpret the 'antipoverty programmes' in the first stage as likely to include that distinguishes them from the pensions, allowances and social-insurance items in the second?

7.2 What elements in enhancing the competence of the public sector *are not necessarily covered* by simply removing corruption in its broadest sense?

7.3 How do you explain the apparent association between government 'credibility' and economic growth?

7.4 Privatized systems of mass supply of water are rare in both developing and developed countries. Is there likely to be any good reason for this? Are there relevant differences for this purpose between the supply of water and say the supply of electricity?

7.5 Co-ordination by the government of private-sector investment activity is classified in the World Bank study as an 'activist function', that is in the least-essential-most-difficult class of government interventions. Do you regard such intervention as likely to be of value in *any* circumstances?

Additional reading

Samuelson, P.A. (1954) 'The pure theory of public expenditure', *Review of Economics and Statistics*, **36**, November, pp. 387–9.

Samuelson, P.A. (1958) 'Aspects of public expenditure theories', *Review of Economics and Statistics*, **40**, November, pp. 332–8.

World Bank (1997) *World Development Report 1997*, 'The state in a changing world', World Bank, Washington, DC.

CHAPTER 8

The Role and Potential of Civil Society

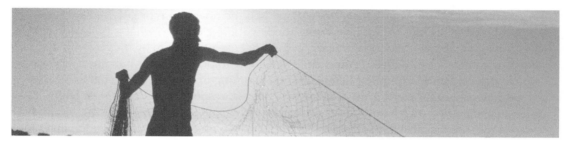

'The output of people and institutions is only roughly related to the inputs they receive.'

(Norman Uphoff, 1996, p. 293)

Civil society, in the sense both of public-interest organizations and of conventions and values of responsibility and trust and creation, is important for the efficient and beneficent performance of both market and state. Releasing and mobilizing propensities for voluntary co-operation and creation may lead to remarkable achievements in solving intractable problems and enhancing welfare.

Introduction

We consider here the meanings attached to the term 'civil society'; its importance for the operation of state and market; its propensity for positive feedback (virtuous circles); its role in resistance to corruption, upholding the law, safeguarding human rights, and shaping law and policy to meet human needs; and means for giving scope for positive achievements to the propensities that we have called 'active humanity'. We then give, in Cases 1 to 4, four quite diverse instances in which active humanity has been mobilized to striking and highly benign effect, and draw out generalizations about the mechanisms, underlying preconditions, and triggers that are involved in generating the remarkable outcomes.

BOX 8.1 TOOLKIT ON CIVIL SOCIETY

For **Active humanity, Civil society, Failed state, NGOs**, see Box 6.1 in Chapter 6.

ARTI. The Sri Lanka Agrarian Research and Training Institute.

OPP. The Orangi Pilot Project, a large sewerage project in Karachi, created and maintained by its users independently of government or any commercial organization.

USAID. Name applied for a number of years to the foreign-aid arm of the US government.

Meanings of the term 'civil society'

'Civil society' has two meanings, narrow and broad. The **narrow** usage, probably the more common, refers to *organizations* **outside both the state and the profit-driven sector**. It is an open question whether the term should include organized interest groups, such as trade unions and bodies representing particular industries or localities, or whether it should be confined to 'public-interest' bodies such as charities and charitable foundations and campaigning groups for causes wider than their members' own or group interests.

The **broader** definition, probably corresponding more closely to what is believed to have been the original (though not particularly approving) use of the term by the Italian Marxist Gramsci in the early twentieth century, refers not only to organizations but also to *values, ethics, and conventions* **tending to maintain the working of society**, which today we may interpret as those **that entail trust and trustworthiness; responsibility for others; and tolerance and encouragement of ideas, creative activity, and innovations**.

Here we use the term *active humanity* for the human propensities that form the basis for civil society.

Importance of civil society for the operation of state and market

Of the three modes of co-ordination – market, state and civil society – on which modern communities depend, civil society is the oldest. Before there was anything that could count as a market or as government, human societies depended – probably for their members' survival – on practices and customs drawing on trust and mutual responsibility and individual and small-group creativity. However, without markets or government, functioning societies had to be small in scale, with only limited material exchange – and with the possibility of destructive conflict – between them.

In the large integrated communities of the modern world, all three of these elements are necessary, and *each of them depends to a degree for its beneficent and efficient practice on the effective operation of the other two*. **The market** depends on government to protect property, to define and enforce the commercial rules, and to settle disputes consistently, so greatly increasing the predictability of the business environment; and it depends on civil society to maintain a culture of trustworthiness and qualified trust. In the absence of either of these elements transaction costs are considerably increased, with the effect of making many desirable economic arrangements impossible. **Governments**, on the other hand, that have tried to dispense altogether with markets have been found to be almost universally oppressive; and governments are also immensely helped in their enforcement of laws and in the equitable raising of revenue if civil society has directed a sense of responsibility into respect for law. Active civil society, with a free and lively press and open public discussion, also contributes to the recognition of people's needs and the formulation of efficient ways of dealing with them. **Civil society** in turn may rely, when matters are well arranged, on being sheltered by government through the independence and accessibility of the courts, the openness of official records and processes, and the liberties and immunities given to campaigning for parties and issues, to dissent, and to 'whistle-blowing'.

We regard civil-society habits and organizations as based upon three human propensities: for trust and trustworthiness, for responsibility, and for creation. The institutionalization of each of these attributes is of routine importance in the operation of large-scale modern, as it is of small-scale primitive, societies.

First, conventional and accepted signals of *trustworthiness* and the resulting *trust* greatly reduce what would otherwise be the transaction costs of commercial buying and selling, lending and borrowing, employing and investing. As a result one party in a transaction often needs to know *not the actual record* of trustworthiness on the part of the other party, but only the general conditions under which trustworthiness can be presumed. The existence of commercial law and its enforcement strengthen these presumptions, but the law would provide rather feeble assurance unless it could be assumed that, in more or less recognizable circumstances, habits of honesty prevailed notably among the police and judges.

Second, it is widely recognized that raising government revenue, especially through direct taxation, would be, and is, difficult except where there is some habitual sense of *responsibility*, on the part of many of those eligible, to pay the amounts prescribed by law. Similarly policing to maintain civil order and to prevent oppression and predation of one person by another is very difficult in any area unless there is among the public a widespread willingness, based upon ideas of what is right, to co-operate in the process or at least not to obstruct it. Effective policing cannot rely on fear alone – unless it lapses into an undesirable degree of violence. Moreover, keeping government honest depends on a measure of responsible self-motivated activity of scrutiny and criticism.

Third, enterprise development and enhancement of public services are unlikely to proceed far unless they draw on the propensity of workers in both sectors for *creation*. Without a habit of innovation and improvement routinely drawn upon and given its head, these activities would presumably have to be coaxed out by material rewards or else forgone.

The saving property of these habits of mind and behaviour so usefully institutionalized by civil society is that their status *as propensities* implies a capacity of our species to *enjoy* their exercise. Once we have experienced a culture of trustworthiness and trust, of responsibility for other people, or of creation, we easily come to enjoy it, a fact that probably has something to do with the need of our hunting-gathering ancestors for these qualities in order for their societies, and consequently for their own genes, to survive. So the institutionalized habits are to a degree self-reinforcing.

The increasing emphasis in the democracies since the 1990s on the need for public *consultation* over government measures seems to be a recognition of these possibilities. As an example of this even in an international context, the Cotonou Treaty between the European Union and its African, Caribbean and Pacific Associates specifically requires consultation with the people affected over measures to be taken under it.

Positive feedback mechanisms

The positive feedback mechanisms in these civil-society institutions appear sometimes to go beyond common expectations if we can judge by the four striking cases presented in this chapter. *Not only* does the prevalence of trustworthiness in certain circles and situations promote the habit of trust, *and* the manifest collective advantages of law-observance once experienced tend (provided the laws are not perversely counterproductive) to make it a socially expected habit. It *also* seems from the examples that voluntary co-operation and mutual responsibility *developed for one immediate purpose* may lead to their mobilization for *other* desirable causes with which the *original goal* has no very obvious connection, such as (in some of the examples that follow) support for gender equality and active opposition to official corruption and to inter-ethnic violence. Perhaps more obviously to be expected, the social improvement achieved through voluntary co-operation on one project arouses hope that voluntary co-operation will be possible on other projects, and these hopes may be realized.

Role of civil society in resistance to corruption, upholding the rule of law, safeguarding human rights, expressing needs, and formulating the means of meeting them

We have argued above that civil society has an important role in maintaining some key elements of good governance. This involves a readiness to *use* whatever freedoms and opportunities are provided by the governmental system to identify and combat abuses. Freedom of the media and of expression and electoral democracy are of course extremely important here, but it is civil society in both its senses that largely determines how far the opportunities provided by the political system will be used. Even where these freedoms do not exist, people of courage, sometimes with international support, may find ways to oppose abuses effectively.

There are two main functions required here: **exposure** and **correction**. **Exposure** involves investigation and publicity either of *abuses* or *of citizens' legal rights, or of opportunities in practice for vindicating those rights.* The publicity may take place through the press or other regular communication media or through *ad hoc* publications, street drama, public meetings, as occasion permits. Academic institutions or charitable foundations or campaigning bodies may finance or otherwise further the investigation, and it may sometimes be necessary also for civil-society organizations to take action – through lobbying and campaigning directed at the executive, through the law, through financial support, or through further exposure – to *protect* those who investigate and publicize.

Correction, within the law and the requirements of public order, may involve *demonstrations, personal lobbying, letters or petiti*ons to those in power, action through the *courts*, or the use of *electoral politics*.

Because of the varied temptations for those in power to misuse their power for private purposes, or to override the law, or to infringe human rights (sometimes with apparently plausible justification), it seems likely that even the 'cleanest' political system will need a readiness from outside government for active exposure and correction.

Amartya Sen (1995, pp. 28–30) stresses the importance of political freedoms for *informing* governments about what is really going on and about the *needs* that people feel and for generating the open discussion that can lead to the *formulation of remedies*. Again the readiness to use these channels and the organization to do so effectively is a function of civil society.

Beyond the support for honest government and the rule of law and defence of civil rights, and the expression to those in power of needs, and the thrashing out of ideas on how they may be met, we suggest through the cases that follow that the *mobilization* of what we have called above 'active humanity', on which civil society rests, has further large potential for improving and supplementing the working of governments and markets in their enhancement of human welfare.

Giving scope to 'active humanity' in social and commercial ventures: four cases

The four 'cases' presented in this chapter reproduce accounts of how innovative mechanisms drawing on active humanity have produced remarkable results in commercial and social projects of significant scale. Of the four examples, three come from developing countries, though in one case from a *relatively* rich area of a country later just making it into upper-middle income. The fourth comes from what was initially a highly disadvantaged area (characterized by having a high proportion of recent immigrants from the 'Third World') in an affluent country. One of the establishments concerned is a major infrastructure project in a squatter settlement within one of the world's mega-cities; one is a government-established irrigation settlement; one is a commercial manufacturing enterprise; and one is a network of community facilities in a highly deprived part of a rich-world conurbation.

In commercial enterprises a device exemplified here, Case 3, is to devolve an extraordinary degree of responsibility to small, face-to-face groups of workers, ensuring that they are provided at the same time with the incentives to pursue the objectives of the larger organization. The somewhat analogous device of 'solidarity groups' of very poor borrowers plays a key part in the Grameen model of micro-credit outlined in Chapter 19 under 'Lending to the very poor: microcredit'.

For public utilities, existing or projected, an approach adopted is to motivate those benefiting from, or subsisting on, a project to play a direct, voluntary part in constructing, maintaining, and managing it. This may, as in Case 2 below, replicate practices followed often in the past by purely non-state local activity for environmental conservation through regulation of access to some natural resource; in such cases the informal systems of management have sometimes persisted for centuries (see Ostrom 1990). Or it may, as in Case 1, work through undertaking a large infrastructure project – technically innovative perhaps but entirely modern – of a kind normally now constructed and managed by government, either directly or through contract with one or more commercial entities.

Alternatively, a big local non-government network of social projects may be built from scratch by starting with work by a small group of volunteers to provide a facility generally recognized as urgently needed, Case 4.

All those described have drawn on propensities for responsibility, mutual trust, and creativity, and all depended at first on one person or a very small group of people to generate the idea and to begin the process of motivation.

BOX 8.2 THE NEGLECTED ELEMENT

'The methods and assumptions of positivist social science do not do justice to values, ideas, and motive forces like human solidarity.'

Norman Uphoff 1996, p. 303.

There are no doubt many case studies that would serve to illustrate these points. We have chosen four, one recounted briefly by the World Bank in its *World Development Report* 1992, and the other three recorded at length in arresting and absorbing books: Norman Uphoff's *Learning from Gal Oya* (1996), Ricardo Semler's *Maverick!* (1993), and Dick

▶

Atkinson's *Radical Urban Solutions* (1994a) and *The Common Sense of Community* (1994b). The stories they recount come from Karachi, from south-eastern Sri Lanka, from São Paulo, and from Birmingham, England. The first is about a sewerage system serving a huge squatter settlement, the second an irrigated-farming project, the third concerns a manufacturing firm in engineering, and the fourth describes a connected set of educational and community ventures in an inner-city neighbourhood. The engineering firm, the irrigation scheme, and the neighbourhood were all there before the stories began, but were in a real sense reborn. Two of them at least had seemed very unpromising material. The interest in the accounts is of how they changed. The other, the sewerage system, was born out of the despair and ingenuity that are part of the story. All could be said to have turned vicious circles into virtuous ones.

We shall present the four cases in turn, and then discuss what generalizations and lessons may be drawn from them.

Case 1: User-provision and -management of sewerage in a metropolitan squatter settlement: the Orangi Pilot Project in Karachi

'In the early 1980s Akhter Hameed Khan, a world-renowned community organizer, began working in the slums of Karachi. He asked what problem he could help resolve and was told that 'the streets were filled with excreta and waste water, making movement difficult and creating enormous health hazards'. What did the people want, and how did they intend to get it? he asked. What they wanted was clear – 'people aspired to a traditional sewerage system . . . it would be difficult to get them to finance anything else.' And how they would get it, too, was clear – they would have Dr. Khan persuade the Karachi Development Authority (KDA) to provide it free, as it did (or so the poor believed) to the richer areas of the city.

'Dr. Khan spent months going with representatives of the community to petition the KDA to provide the service. When it was clear that this would never happen, Dr. Khan was ready to work with the community to provide alternatives. (He would later describe this first step as the most important thing he did in Orangi – liberating, as he put it, the people from the immobilizing myths of government promises.)

'With a small amount of core external funding, the Orangi Pilot Project (OPP) was started. It was clear what services the people wanted; the task was to reduce the cost to affordable levels and to develop organizations that could provide and operate the systems. On the technical side, the achievements of the OPP architects and engineers were remarkable and innovative. Thanks partly to the elimination of corruption and the provision of labour by community members, the costs (for an in-house sanitary latrine and house sewer on the plot and underground sewers in the lanes and streets) were less than $50 per household.

'The related organizational achievements are equally impressive. OPP staff members have played a catalytic role: they explain the benefits of sanitation and the technical possibilities to residents, conduct research, and provide technical assistance. The OPP staff never handle the community's money. (The total cost of the OPP's operations amounted, even in the project's early years, to less than 15 per cent of the amount invested by the community.) The households' responsibilities include financing their share of the costs, participating in construction, and electing a 'lane manager' who typically represents about fifteen households. Lane committees, in turn, elect members of neighborhood committees (typically representing about 600 houses), which manage the secondary sewers.

'The early successes achieved by the project created a 'snowball' effect, in part because of the increased value of properties with sewerage systems. As the power of the OPP-related organizations increased, they were able to put pressure on the municipality to provide funds for the construction of trunk sewers.

'The Orangi Pilot Project has led to the provision of sewerage services to more than 600 000 poor people in Karachi and to recent initiatives by several municipalities in Pakistan to follow the OPP method and, according to OPP leader Arif Hassan, 'have government behave like an NGO.' Even in Karachi the mayor now formally accepts the principle of 'internal' development by the residents and 'external' development (including trunk sewers and treatment) by the municipality.

Source: Reproduced with permission from World Bank, *World Development Report* 1992, p. 109.

Case 2: Civil society is mobilized to transform a dysfunctional irrigation settlement – Gal Oya

Gal Oya was the site of a huge and spectacularly troubled irrigation settlement in a relatively remote and even despised part of Sri Lanka. On the Left Bank, with which the story is concerned, there were over 20 000 farmers. It had been settled by people from a variety of areas and both major language communities, many of them apparently regarded as troublemakers in their places of origin – some even criminals. Irrigation settlements require careful management of water if its use is to be fair and efficient, and conflicts between users readily arise. Management may be provided by the state or by the users as a body. Management through sale of the resource to a single private firm raises too many problems of social control to be a popular expedient. Whatever the mode adopted, management is immensely helped if the farmers are co-operative and are prepared to follow the rules. Gal Oya farmers, in a system controlled from above by officials, were notoriously unco-operative, and there had been much destruction of irrigation facilities and neglect of necessary maintenance. Irrigation officials supposed to be managing the scheme were commonly remote and arrogant toward farmers, and also negligent, and a number were believed to be corrupt. They did not perform the necessary maintenance, and possibly, even with the best of intentions, *could not* through customary official means have done so. Water was used very wastefully and about a third of farmers situated downstream got no irrigation water at all. Tamils, who were a minority in the area, were represented disproportionately among these unfortunate 'tailenders'. There was considerable mutual hostility among farmers over water disputes.

The Gal Oya Water Management Project, starting in March 1981, took place under the auspices of the Sri Lanka Agrarian Research and Training Institute (ARTI) and a unit of Cornell University, with finance from the US government through USAID. The aim was to improve water management through bringing farmers to participate in it. The hope was to elicit more co-operative behaviour among farmers, and thereby also improved performance on the part of local Irrigation Department officials. Social scientists and others from ARTI and Cornell directed the project with more or less frequent presence on the spot, and a key element was the appointment of (initially 32) 'Institutional Organizers' (IOs), young graduates from farming backgrounds, who would be allocated in small groups to particular parts of the scheme, would get to know the farmers, and gradually, it was hoped, would inspire the creation of farmers' organizations.

These organizations were in fact built up from below, eventually into a structure with four layers, representing the hierarchy of connections within the irrigation network. The lowest level (the Field Channel Organization), and the first to be established, was small enough for personal acquaintance and meeting among the farmers it covered. Ostrom (1990, p. 189), in considering this and similar ventures for managing a common natural resource through voluntary cooperation, stresses the importance of such a 'nested' (what might be called federal) form of organization when the number of people altogether involved is large. As we have seen in Case 1, it was also adopted in the Orangi project.

'If we can make progress in Gal Oya, we can make progress anywhere in Sri Lanka', said a senior official before the project began (Uphoff, 1996, p. 4). The idea of farmer participation at first met with varying degrees of hostility from local officials of the Irrigation Department, who were supposed to be co-operating with the venture, and also with scepticism at higher levels. The prime movers in the project believed that they faced a difficult task and were by no means confident of success. They started in a specially bad year, when water supply ran unusually low. They realized that they had no blueprint and needed to learn as they went along. It was not clear whether reform in the Irrigation Department would be necessary *first* before farmers would effectively organize. Circumstances, however, obliged them to gamble on the converse sequence: that, if farmers were effectively organized, the Irrigation Department would respond (ibid., p. 38).

> Yet, within six weeks, 90 per cent of farmers in a pilot area over 2000 hectares were voluntarily undertaking a program which they devised themselves, with organizers' encouragement and facilitation. They cleaned channels, some of which had not been cleaned for 15 or 20 years; rotated water deliveries, so that tail-enders would get a fair share of the available water; and saved water wherever possible to donate to farmers downstream who would otherwise receive little or no supply. Such demonstrations of altruism and co-operation are generally considered unlikely. They were quite remarkable because Gal Oya farmers, resettled into the area two or three decades earlier, had previously been known for their conflictual and individualistic behavior, 'even murders over water', as one farmer told us.
>
> (ibid., p. viii)

The process continued and spread over the project area, with concrete and measurable results. 'Within five years, water use efficiency had almost doubled in the Left Bank system' (ibid., p. 9). Whatever precisely that statement means, other expressions give a striking idea of the achievement. In the same passage Uphoff quotes the Government Agent, the chief generalist official in the District, as saying that previously he had had about 200 complaints a week about water problems but that by late 1984 'not a single farmer comes to complain to me about water problems'. The District Minister is quoted to similar effect as saying that earlier eight out of ten farmers that he spoke to had had problems with water but that later there had been 'practically no complaints about irrigation distribution'. It appears that the same release of water or less, properly husbanded and distributed, had *proved enough to satisfy* virtually all farmers, the majority of whom had regarded themselves as short of water before.

Yet these material achievements (continuing in essentials at least until March 1996, shortly before the second edition of the book went to press) are perhaps no more remarkable than the changes in attitudes that lay behind them, and for these one needs to go to the many anecdotes and farmers' utterances that Uphoff records. It came to be not uncommon for upstream farmers to go out of their way, getting up at night for example, to make sure that the system of conservation worked, so that downstream farmers would get their share of water. Local irrigation officials came as a matter of routine to treat farmers with respect, and became far more diligent and helpful. Most moving of all are the reports of the efforts made on several occasions by Sinhalese farmers to protect the persons and property of Tamil officials, farmers and fishermen in the face of ethnic violence (ibid., pp. 76, 101, 102). 'There are no Sinhalese farmers and Tamil farmers – only farmers', as one old farmer says (ibid., p. 101).

Case 3: Active humanity enlisted in an engineering firm

In 1980 Ricardo Semler took over from his father a successful but threatened marine-engineering producer – in São Paulo, the largest city in Brazil – with about a hundred employees. This occurred just as Brazil's economy was moving into a severely troubled dozen or so years of shocks and lurches. On his first day he sacked 60 per cent of the firm's senior managers. For about four years he led a business run on conventional lines, apparently quite successfully, if unspectacularly. Then, step by step, following his own ideas, though often in response to particular challenges, he presided over a management revolution: surely one of the most radical ever carried out in a firm that continued to thrive.

   Most of the conventional wisdom about management seemed to be thrown to the winds: the status distinctions, the hierarchy of authority, the timekeeping, the stratified pay structure, the appointments and promotion procedures, the records, much of the division of labour, and many of the apparent advantages of large scale. The parts of the business devoted to different types of product came to work largely autonomously, and workers in each determined, or at least had the power of veto over, the appointments of their own leaders. Of pre-tax profits, 23 per cent came to be distributed among the units within the business in proportion to the extent to which they had generated it, and the workers in any unit concerned were free to distribute it among themselves as they saw fit, and generally did so equally to all members. By the end of the 1980s there were only four named 'grades' in the firm, and they were not grades in the usual sense: they were in themselves unrelated to salary. To a point, staff (25 per cent of them at the time the book was written) even came to set their own pay, subject to discussion with their colleagues. The discipline that kept them in check was the opinion of those with whom they worked, backed of course by the market in which they had to sell and cover their costs.

   To interpret: most workers seem clearly to have taken the view that, in working for the firm, they were at least in an important degree working for themselves; and they had adopted this belief because the arrangements under which Semco operated had made it manifestly true. The market in which they sold had required of them frequent and major adaptations through the dozen years before the book was written. A number of workers, including some very able managers, had inevitably to be dropped over the period, but there were rules to protect the jobs of those for whom the loss of employment would be hardest, and efforts were often made to enable those dropped to set up for themselves, sometimes even in potential competition to Semco. By 1991 the firm had begun to make a virtue of this necessity and had encouraged business units to leave the corporation and become independent 'satellites', initially receiving training and support from it, and supplying Semco or any other customer as they saw fit.

Many of these features were not unique. Some even followed fashions – at least minority fashions – of the 1980s in America and Britain and elsewhere, prompted in part by the attention paid to Japanese successes and to books such as Peters' and Waterman's *In Search of Excellence* (1982). But Semco seems to have outdone most of the others in the range of its radicalism, and each step was apparently worked out afresh. Semler had read the books, but appears to have noticed only afterwards the parallels in them to what he was doing.

Yet the firm survived and expanded, its workforce increasing eight-fold and its sales similarly in the seven or so years after Ricardo took over (Semler 1993, pp. 165, 207) – before a decision was made to turn it into something different and smaller with a number of its former functions performed by satellites. Not only that, but it fulfilled other, more broadly social, objectives. Women were given a degree of equality and a range of senior positions unusual in Brazil at the time. All workers were obliged to take 30 days' annual leave. Semco, and Semler personally, also mounted several challenges to official corruption, when it would have been much easier, less risky, and sometimes cheaper, to have played along.

What were the motives behind these changes? At first, Semler had run the firm with a hierarchy, division of task and status, rigorous discipline, masses of 'management information', top executives competing with one another in overwork. Radical changes began to be made on ostensibly pragmatic grounds: to prevent a rebellion among managers, to make deliveries quicker and more reliable, to eliminate wasted effort, to save Semler's own health in the face of excessive stress, above all perhaps to motivate the workforce. Yet behind all this – it must surely seem to the reader – and increasingly making the running, was a respect for people, a satisfaction in seeing them behaving with confidence and enthusiasm, as agents rather than instruments, and an enjoyment of the atmosphere of mutual trust and spontaneous co-operation. Beyond that, as we have seen, there was an impulse to behave responsibly toward the wider society – in an active commitment to equal opportunity for women contrary to prevailing norms; in the setting-up of a foundation to pay for the education of poor children of ability; and in the resistance to corruption, a resistance pursued in apparent conflict with the firm's own interests. It is as if the habit of behaving responsibly within the firm to the many people engaged in it served to generate responsibility in the arena outside.

Something remarkable had happened. Of course the need for the firm to survive had necessarily conditioned every change. That is a fact of life. Nonetheless, where there was a choice, where bets could be laid on one side or the other, Semco seems to have taken the gamble in favour of humanity – the one that respected people, that encouraged them to have their heads, that broke down the barriers between them, that gave them as much security as circumstances allowed; and making this choice seems to have done the firm's commercial performance no harm whatever. After all, especially in a business in which imagination, and adaptation, and ingenuity, are continually needed, workers who are enthusiastic, who enjoy what they are doing, whose opinions are respected and therefore readily offered, who trust each other including their leaders, are decided assets. One volunteer, so they say, is worth however many pressed men.

►
Case 4: Autochthonous generation of a local network of social projects: Balsall Heath in the English West Midlands conurbation

The fourth story is of St Paul's Community Education Project Ltd in Balsall Heath, a district of Birmingham in England's West Midlands. Balsall Heath had been a thriving industrial area until the collapse of much of the industry on which it had depended. By the 1970s much of the population from its active period had moved out, with the exception of those who were old or infirm or otherwise handicapped or incapable, and there was a large proportion of new settlers, mostly poor, including many from the Caribbean and Africa and from South Asia. 'By 1981, the national census revealed that the area fell within the most deprived 2 per cent of neighbourhoods in the whole country' (Atkinson, 1994a, p. 25). It had all the usual inner-city problems in acute form. The parish church, which had once been a centre of community life, was almost deserted, and the church hall was little used and in disrepair. Effectively there was no community centre or community life.

The story starts when, on the initiative of five people, the church hall began to be used for a community purpose.

> In 1970 a teacher, the local curate, two parents and a trade unionist started St Paul's nursery centre in the empty St Paul's church hall. Local parents were desperate for a nursery place for their young children so that they could go to work or have a little respite to ease family difficulties. The nursery centre combines the . . . educational content of a nursery school with the extended day . . . and the social and health care content of a social services daycentre.

The nursery 'brought stability and purpose into the lives of many families'. Its building, previously a church hall, became a place where a variety of community activities could and did take place (ibid., p. 26).

Atkinson mentions altogether ten institutions that constituted the project at the time he wrote. The second of these is the community education and resource centre, which 'started, like the nursery, on the initiative of just a few local people' as an adventure playground and developed in response to local demand and through voluntary effort. It came eventually to be open 72 hours a week for 48 weeks in the year and comprised 'a hall, kitchen, craft and technology room, stables, allotments and a nature area as well as a floodlit sports pitch'.

> Pupils [from a dozen nearby primary schools, the two secondary schools and a sixth-form college which are all located in Balsall Heath] come in school hours to study at the centre. For them, education has become an exciting way of working on and in the real world in out-of-school hours. The centre acts as the playground for the children of the area.
>
> (ibid., pp. 26–7)

A third element in the St Paul's mix is *Language Alive!*, which is among other things a way of stimulating the learning of English by both first-language and second-language speakers. 'It entails a group of teacher/actors working closely with the class teacher and parents both in the classroom and in the community in ways which bring language to life through the use of participatory drama' (ibid., p. 27).

Then there is St Paul's School, a small independent secondary school started by three teachers and five families in 1973 as a means of providing for children whose school

►

behaviour was so bad that they were excluded from school or else who were scarcely attending school at all. The school depends on its small size, which means that everyone knows everyone else, and on making very clear demands of the pupils and their parents and insisting that they are observed. In spite of the fact that the pupils have been selected for being difficult, their rate of meeting the English benchmark achievement for 15–16-year-olds of three good GCSE passes (which at the time was 31 per cent in England and Wales overall and 23 per cent in Birmingham, the city of which Balsall Heath was a deprived segment) was 50 per cent (ibid., p. 30). In 1993 they 'outperformed all but 6 out of the city's 70 secondary schools in the GCSE league tables' (Atkinson 1994b, p. 13).

The other features of the project were a community newspaper, a printing business, a community enterprise centre 'with the potential to generate enough income to cover its own costs and make a contribution to other parts of St Paul's' (Atkinson 1994a, p. 31), twice-yearly neighbourhood celebrations, a management under a completely independent board of directors drawn from local residents, and an attempt to co-ordinate activities with all the agencies and professionals serving the area (ibid., pp. 31–4). Though St Paul's had started in 1971 with £50, its operating costs in 1992 were £500 000, of which £100 000 was raised locally (ibid., p. 24).

But the activity unleashed spread further. Residents started patrolling the streets to eliminate street prostitution. And this had wider effects.

The figures for drug abuse, car theft, burglary and truancy also came down. Residents began to talk of being able to leave their car and front door unlocked.

Today they claim with some justification to have one of the most developed neighbourhood watch schemes in the country. Moving from the need to eliminate the negative, these residents have begun to accentuate the positive . . . [with a variety of other aspirations for enhancing their environment] . . . Lifted by the experience of success, large sections of the population have become engaged in an extensive 'community service' programme.

(Atkinson, 1994b, p. 33)

Generalizations from the four cases

All four of these stories have to do with changes in behaviour.

Ideas, ideals, and friendship

Uphoff suggests that three elements were crucial in the Gal Oya experience: ideas, ideals, and friendship (1996, pp. 108, 377–81). Ideas and ideals may be potently expressed in pithy sayings. *Ideas*, if we understand him correctly, may be more-or-less value-free: about what leads to what or how some end may be attained. *Ideals* are a particular type of idea that expresses a commitment to values. Yet, in practice, the ideals and the value-free ideas are frequently bound up together. The Gal Oya farmers' slogan 'Water has no colour' (where 'colour' refers to political party allegiance) can be read to mean either that *it is possible or most efficient* to deal with water without bringing in politics, or that water is a gift to all and *should not* be appropriated for factional ends – or of course both. Pragmatic ideas shade into ideals. 'We find moral and practical considerations reinforcing each other' (ibid., p. 79).

The weight given to friendship explains itself given that so much depended on the tapping of people's capacity for altruism. 'Once farmers started valuing others' well-being in addition to their own, many new possibilities opened up. . . . People's subjective willingness to contribute to each other's improvement produced measurable, objective consequences in terms of higher water use efficiency and larger harvests' (ibid., pp. 288–9).

In Semco and Balsall Heath, too, we can see a tendency for change to start with ideas of a fairly pragmatic kind but then to move on to ideals, and maybe also for friendships to be formed as events proceed and to help sustain what progress has been made. It is possible to see the reforms that Ricardo Semler began to introduce from about 1984 as pragmatic – unusual only in that he was specially sensitive to what was wrong and exceptionally imaginative and daring in the search for remedies. Eventually, however, the reforms do seem to have come to express a fairly clear set of human values. Similarly, the St Paul's project at Balsall Heath started with a nursery centre where children of working parents and others could be left, if necessary right through the working day, and have among other things the benefit of pre-school: an urgently needed service. The community education and resource centre, the school, the newspaper, the enterprises, the drama, resistance to crime, and all the rest followed, eventually expressing a strong community ideal, and, in Atkinson's words, 'achievement, quality, standards, hard work, neighbourliness and faith'.

Impetus from within set off by a fuse often lit by an outsider

All four experiences depended on the emergence of a strong impetus from *within*: among the workforce, the farmers, the resident community, but it was often outsiders or incomers who set the fuse or pulled the trigger. Sometimes it is easier for outsiders than for insiders to *believe* that change is possible and to convince others. The starting move may be very simple. Neighbours who have similar interests but would not normally meet are led to come together. People geared to regarding each other as opponents or indifferent are brought into conversation. Someone behaves in a generous or accepting or respectful manner contrary to stereotype. A positive achievement breaks the cycle of despair. Some unexpected act or event opens up a new set of possibilities.

Character of the raw material

These stories, to which many analogues could no doubt be given from the experience of some of the 'development' NGOs, remind us of the remarkable character of the human raw material. Remember that these had to be regarded as specially *unpromising* cases for the kind of experiment that was mounted: certainly Gal Oya and Balsall Heath, and, given the labour-relations scene in Brazil and the economic turbulence of the period, probably also Semco. The results suggest that we carry within ourselves, as Uphoff argues, the *capacity* for generosity and co-operation; the capacity, we might add, for creation. It may need only a set of initial stimuli, the right personal move that will start the process, to bring these characteristics into play. The neighbourhood, the school, the farming settlement, the firm, that can tap into these capacities is on to a good thing.

The key to be turned in each case

In each of the stories we may see some ingredient as a kind of key that has to be turned to set the process going.

At Orangi, perhaps, it was the leap of *practical imagination* that generated the idea that a much less costly way of providing sewerage was possible if the residents would contribute labour and management responsibility.

In Gal Oya, the key was perhaps *generosity*. Whatever exactly set the process going in the first place, change became rapid as soon as this element was released. Once there was a framework in which it was clear that generosity need not be wasted, that contributions to the well-being of others formed part of a wider venture with large potential effects, farmers became co-operative, and indeed generous, often beyond the apparent call of duty. From what is recorded we can speculate that the respect for farmers shown by the Institutional Organizers, and indeed their generosity with time and attention, boosted these tendencies, and possibly formed the original stimulus. Uphoff also believes that the action of six (Sinhalese) farmer-representatives in protecting the houses of two minor (Tamil) irrigation officials, when some of the houses of Tamils in the district town had been burned by a mob, may have helped to generate a more respectful attitude to farmers on the part of irrigation officials generally, most of whom were Tamils. Also the constructive activity and effort of farmers made it hard for the demeaning stereotypes of them previously held by officials to persist.

In Semco the key was *autonomy*: autonomy for business units, and manufacturing cells within them, and individuals at large – autonomy of course always limited by the need to keep people and units working together, but this need fulfilled through personal ties of responsibility, and through common sense in response to knowledge and to personal appropriation of the purpose of the exercise, rather than through rules and commands. Autonomy for the very small units meant that it was easy for individuals to command respect and to play a creative role within them.

In Balsall Heath, perhaps, the key was *confidence*. The project, by bringing people together in visible achievements, showed that there were responses other than helplessness, apathy and destruction. Creation was a possibility. All it required was for people to act together with some sense of purpose, and the achievement that generated further confidence would follow. The purpose in turn depended on a certain measure of faith and hope, a vision. Though the mechanics are not spelled out, it seems that the act of providing the nursery both showed the possibility of community action and brought people together. From this combination a positive creative purpose could be born.

In all four cases, active humanity came to the fore: mutual trust, responsibility, creation. Life became so much less nasty and brutish, not because a superior coercive power was introduced – in fact, in one way or another, that was precisely what was abandoned – but because the propensities of people to work together, to take care for each other, and to exercise their ingenuity and imagination – all potentially enjoyable experiences – were brought into play.

BOX 8.3 THE ESSENTIAL COMPONENT

'Attempts to help neighbourhoods, whether in the Third World or in the urban neighbourhoods of the industrialised world, will fail, however well funded, if they do not directly involve those they are designed to assist.'

(Dick Atkinson, 1994b, p. 4)

Common factors or preconditions

Among the common factors (which may have been preconditions) in all four experiences were: *communication* – it was necessary for people to talk to each other when they might not normally have done so; *respect* – the essential actors had to be treated as responsible human beings if they were to behave as such; and *vision*, involving a form of risk-taking – some leaps of faith had to be made, relying on 'the evidence of things not seen'.

Summary conclusions

- 'Civil society' narrowly interpreted refers to **organizations** that are both independent of government and not directed to their members' personal profit. It is an open question whether trade unions and bodies existing to represent the interests of their members in particular industries or other groups should be included.

- A broader definition refers not only to *organizations* external to the government and the market but also to **values, ethics, and conventions** that tend to maintain the beneficial working of society. We interpreted these functions as being built on what we called **active humanity**, namely human propensities for *trust and trustworthiness, a sense of responsibility for others, and creation.*

- We argued for the perennial importance of civil society (in this broad sense) *for the efficient and beneficent working of both market and state.*

- We also submitted that the institutionalized exercise of trust, responsibility, and creation, being based on prevailing human propensities, can easily be enjoyable once experienced, and that this triggers positive feedback mechanisms and a *self-reinforcing character* to the institutions built upon them.

- The role of civil society in resisting corruption, upholding the rule of law, and safeguarding human rights is exercised and stimulated through two activities: **exposure** and **correction**, the two of course overlapping. Exposure involves investigation and factual publication of abuses and of legal and other remedies available. Correction involves lobbying, mobilizing, demonstrating, making what use is possible of the courts and the media. Civil society also has the potential for using free institutions where they exist to make government aware of people's needs and to generate public discourse on how the needs may be met.

- In a series of cases recording some notable ventures, we explore some of the **possibilities of enlisting the ingredients of civil society** – propensities for trust, responsibility, and creation – in the cause of 'development' in its fullest sense.

Beside the *objects* of voluntary or self-motivated co-operative and creative action, the *means* themselves are typically enjoyable and answer human social needs. So the institutions – the organizations and the conventions and understandings – through which those objects are pursued tend to be reinforced and increased in scope by the pursuit.

Questions for discussion

8.1 If the devices and mechanisms manifested in the four main cases described in the chapter were so spectacularly successful on a number of fronts, why are they not more widely applied?

8.2 Are some or all of the distinctive and unconventional practices in Semco likely to be transferable to other firms and in other countries? If not, why not? If so, what kind of firms in what kind of countries?

8.3 In Gal Oya how do you explain the transformation of those farmers who were close enough to the source of the water to be able to take as much as they liked *from* an attitude of neglecting maintenance of channels and ignoring the interests of farmers 'lower down' *to* one of consistent maintenance and exerting themselves to ensure that the 'tail-enders' got their fair share of water?

8.4 Can you see why a 'federal' or 'nested' structure may have been necessary for effective management in Orangi and Gal Oya?

8.5 Can you explain why the Gal Oya experience apparently led some Sinhalese farmers to defend Tamil irrigation officials from racist attacks?

Additional reading

We recommend the absorbing books that are the sources of three of the four main cases that we have used to illustrate the roles of civil society and 'active humanity'. We also suggest at least a glance at Elinor Ostrom's fascinating work that catalogues and analyses a number of cases, some of them lasting for centuries, in which, as at Gal Oya, informal local institutions have acted to conserve a natural resource.

Atkinson, D. (1994) *Radical Urban Solutions: Urban Renaissance for City Schools and Communities*, Cassell, London.

Ostrom, E. (1990) *Managing the Commons*, Cambridge University Press, Cambridge.

Semler, R. (1993) *Maverick!*, Century, London.

Uphoff, N. (1996) *Learning from Gal Oya: Possibilities for Participatory Development and Post-Newtonian Social Science*, IT Publications, New York.

PART 3
Central Global Questions

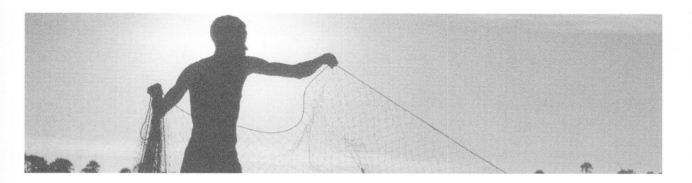

PART 3
Central Global
Questions

CHAPTER 9

Globalization: Trade, Trade Policy, International Economic Relations

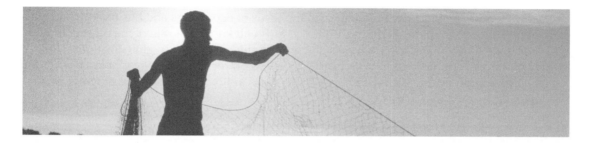

'The evidence strongly supports the conclusion that growth requires a policy framework that prominently includes an orientation towards integration into the global economy.'

Stanley Fischer, 2003

'With appropriate national and global policies, globalization can be an important catalyst for alleviating world poverty. In the absence of these policies, however, this catalyst role is diminished. In a few particular instances, globalization without corrective policies can actually exacerbate certain dimensions of poverty.'

Goldin and Reinert, 2007

'If you're totally illiterate and living on $1 a day, the benefits of globalization never come to you.'

Former US President Jimmy Carter

Introduction

Few, if any, changes in the structure of the international economy have generated as much controversy as **globalization**. The energetic advocacy of globalization by its supporters in government, in international bureaucracies and in segments of academe has been met with equally vigorous opposition from an array of NGOs, trade unions, conservationists, politicians from both far left and far right, segments of academe and other elements of civil society. The opponents of the process include an active element willing to engage in vigorous street protests, sometimes riots, wherever the banner of globalization has been raised with a sufficiently loud fanfare to attract their attention. (Ironically, such opposition would be more muted were it not for the use of the World Wide Web, one of the icons of globalization, both to publicize forthcoming meetings of supposedly pro-globalization personnel, and to rally opposition to such meetings). This polarization of views reflects genuine concern on both sides over the perceived benefits and costs of globalization.

What is globalization?

Readers whose familiarity with literature in the fields of economics and business is confined to material published from 1995 onwards will know that one of the most common words to be found in the titles of books and articles since that year is 'globalization'. They may be surprised to learn that, prior to 1970, there is no record whatsoever of the use of 'globalization' in a title. Stanley Fischer's 'title count' in Box 9.1 follows the progress of the term in America's 'newspaper of record', the *New York Times,* and on the Internet.

BOX 9.1 'GLOBALIZATION' IN THE *NEW YORK TIMES*

'During the 1970s the word "globalization" was never mentioned in the pages of the *New York Times.* In the 1980s the word cropped up less than once a week, in the first half of the 1990s less than twice a week – and in the latter half of the decade no more than three times a week. In 2000 there were 514 stories in the paper that made reference to "globalization"; there were 364 stories in 2001, and 393 references in 2002. Based on stories in the *New York Times,* the idea of being "anti-globalization" was not one that existed before about 1999. Turning from the newspaper to the internet, globalization brings up 1.6 m links through the use of the Google search engine, and typing in "anti-globalization" brings up 80 000 links. Type in globalization and inequality and there are almost 500 000 references, 700 000 references to globalization and environment, almost 200 000 links to globalization and labor standards, 50 000 references to globalization and multinationals, and 70 000 references to globalization and cultural diversity. A search of globalization and the IMF yields 180 000 suggestions.'

Source: Stanley Fischer (2003), *Globalization and its Challenges*, Ely Lecture, American Economic Association, Washington, DC.

Given the wide range of issues debated under the 'globalization' heading, it is necessary to define, and so delimit, the 'economic globalization' discussed in this chapter in such a way as to ensure that our primary focus on economic development is maintained. A much-quoted definition is provided by Joseph Stiglitz, former Chief Economist at the World Bank, for whom globalization is

> the closer integration of the countries and peoples of the world . . . brought about by the enormous reduction of costs of transport and communication, and the breaking down of artificial barriers to the flow of goods, services, capital, knowledge and (to a lesser extent) people across borders.

(Stiglitz, 2002)

To round out this view we may add that this integration process, which is heading in the direction of the creation of single, unified global markets in inputs and outputs, has required not just the technological advances noted by Stiglitz but also extensive political support, active encouragement by a number of international agencies and institutions, and enthusiastic participation by many private-sector firms.

We now take a preliminary glance at the different *forms* of economic globalization studied in this chapter, focusing on *international trade in goods and services, international financial flows* (with special reference to financial markets and foreign direct investment (FDI)), *the international labour market* and *global flows of information and ideas.*

International trade in goods and services

The most salient form of globalization is the continued expansion of international trade in goods and non-financial services. (Trade in *financial* services is discussed later in this section.) There have always been countries whose levels of economic activity were heavily dependent on trading performance – though, for most nations, this has not been the case, and the level of 'trade dependence' has been relatively low. There is, however, a fundamental difference between the trading structures being created today and those of earlier eras. 'Outward-orientation' of economies, including developing economies, is now seen as crucial to sustained growth.

Thus, for instance, the important 'partnership agreement' between the EU and the African, Caribbean and Pacific (ACP) states embodied in the 'Cotonou Agreement' sees 'integration of the ACP countries into the world economy' as the key element in the development package provided by the Agreement for its 77 developing-country signatories – over half of the world's developing nations (*The ACP-EU Courier*, 2000). The vision of world trade implied by this ambition is one in which trading is no longer a peripheral aspect of a nation's economic activity, but central to it – the 'engine of growth'. This greatly increased emphasis on international specialization and interdependence of nations is a key feature of the true globalization of trade, and is regarded as the main reason for the accelerated economic growth that it is expected to bring with it.

International financial flows

Economic globalization processes are also important in relation to international financial flows. 'Modern' financial integration began in the early 1970s following the collapse of the Bretton Woods system which had, in effect, tied other currencies to the US dollar. With the move to flexible, in some cases floating, exchange-rates, the importance attached to controls on foreign-exchange transactions was greatly diminished. In particular, the regulation of international movements of capital was progressively wound down so permitting moves towards a unified, global market in capital.

Deregulation of financial markets in the US, Europe and Japan in the 1980s and 1990s, coupled with broadly favourable global business conditions in the shape of low interest-rates and rapidly rising share prices, encouraged massive increases in demand for international banking services by corporations and governments and opened up many opportunities for banks and other financial institutions wishing to develop and market new financial 'products' across national boundaries. Governments made increasing use of international financial institutions for, amongst other things, issuing government debt in the form of internationally marketed *bonds*, investing reserves, and managing privatizations. Multinational corporations (MNCs – discussed in detail in Chapter 23) became major purchasers of the international expertise and services of international financial institutions – to assist in raising investment capital, to facilitate *foreign direct investment (FDI)* abroad, to oversee mergers and acquisitions, and to provide *regular banking services*. Banks, corporations and financial institutions raised capital across the globe by borrowing, and by selling equity.

BOX 9.2 A GLOBALIZATION TOOLBOX

- **Rules of Origin.** Members of a trading agreement (for instance, a free trade area) giving preferential market access to goods imported from other members need to be sure that these goods are produced entirely, or mainly, by the other members. 'Rules of Origin' comprise a set of criteria used in defining where a product actually 'originates' for purposes of trading.

- **The 'Doha Round'.** Doha is the capital of Qatar. The WTO 'Ministerial' meeting held there in 2001 set the agenda for future negotiations on further dismantling barriers to trade. This 'round' of negotiations collapsed in July 2008.

- **'Leverage'.** In relation to a bank leverage refers to the ratio of liabilities (deposits plus external liabilities) to assets (capital plus reserves). A high level of leverage – a situation in which financial dealings are heavily financed by borrowed funds – increases the risk of insolvency.

- **'Collateral benefits' resulting from financial integration.** These are *indirect* benefits, distinct from the purposes for which the integration was undertaken. Typically, the profit-driven activities of agents engaged in the integration process will have the 'spillover' effect of strengthening the financial system of the 'integrating' country; this has been found to be associated with more rapid economic growth.

- **Portfolio foreign investment (PFI).** This is investment in financial assets (such as bonds or equities) in a foreign country. Portfolio investment is carried out by individuals, banks, and other investing institutions. It does not entail the active involvement in management of enterprises that characterizes **foreign direct investment (FDI)**.

The greatly increased opportunities thus created for banks and other financial institutions to supply an ever-broadening array of financial services has led to intensified competition amongst providers. The shortage of genuine expertise in this booming market, and the difficulty many firms experienced in providing, on their own, adequate, broadly based services, have encouraged mergers and take-overs in the financial-services sector itself (as firms search for, and find, suitably qualified partners).

This process of international expansion of banking operations, of portfolio-investment markets, and of other financial markets, has been enormously encouraged by the rapid improvement in both international communications and data processing (changes discussed in greater detail in the next section) which make possible the tight integration of widely dispersed transactions previously conducted on a more limited and spacially fragmented way in individual national or regional markets.

At the level of the firm, the continued increase in the importance of FDI flows to developing (and developed) countries as a source of investment finance has been parallelled by the building by multinational corporations (MNCs) of worldwide networks of interconnected affiliates and subsidiaries – across which output and earnings (representing, in total, a significant proportion of the world's production and exports) are distributed according to globally optimized plans.

Globalization of the international labour market

A further manifestation of globalization is the gradual emergence of an integrated international labour market. The global market for labour is still fragmented and highly regulated but, as is explained in Chapter 24, the international movement of workers is becoming increasingly important both to host countries, which require the services provided by incoming labour, and to source countries, which in many cases derive considerable benefit from the flow of remittances from their citizens working abroad.

Globalization of information and ideas

Running in parallel with the changes mentioned above has been a very rapid broadening of the range of information, ideas and comment available quickly and cheaply, to economic agents and the general public alike, on all manner of topics. The use of the Internet, in particular, has tied together a worldwide network of information providers and seekers, greatly facilitating the free flow of knowledge and ideas from the highly technical, through news of current happenings in all parts of the world, to the polemical.

Structure of this chapter

In this chapter we discuss, in the following section, the drivers and history of *economic globalization*. We note that the combination of technological advance and political support that sustains the present wave of globalization has precedents, that in many ways the world economy was more extensively globalized in 1914 than it is now, and that waves of globalization can recede if political support is withdrawn. We then look in detail at the main international institutions promoting global integration – their history and current aims. A synoptic account of the evolution of trade policy since the 1950s follows, closing with a summary of the difficulties encountered by the WTO in attempting to pilot the 'Doha Round' negotiations to a successful conclusion in 2008. We then turn to examine the anticipated impact on developing countries – the theoretically predicted costs and benefits – of liberalizing international trade. This is followed by an account of recent trends in the international trade of the developing world and a review of the key results of the massive research effort devoted to ascertaining the impact of liberalization of trade on growth and poverty there. Attention then turns to financial globalization, which is examined in the same way as trade liberalization, special attention being paid to the so-called 'collateral benefits' that may result from the integration process. The impact – actual and potential – of liberalizing the global labour market is then assessed. This is followed by a brief look at key issues raised by globalization of ideas and knowledge. We conclude by assembling a roster of key issues that appear to require urgent action if the globalization process is to continue successfully, and advance policy proposals suggested by our earlier discussion.

Globalization old and new

Pre-First World War globalization

In some respects globalization is not a new phenomenon. Many writers have pointed out that the integration of hitherto 'unconnected' areas into world markets for goods and labour has been going on for centuries, very often with official encouragement. Thus the opening up of the New World following the fifteenth-century discoveries led eventually to the linking of factor markets in Europe and North America as international flows of capital and labour moved across the Atlantic. Indeed, in the case of labour, the pre-First World War flows of migrants from Europe, taking advantage of the introduction of rapid, and relatively safe and cheap, mass ocean travel, dwarfed those we currently observe. Thus:

> It is generally believed that with respect to migration and labor flows the modern system is less globalized than it was a century ago. In 1911, nearly 15 percent of the United States population was foreign born; today that number is probably a bit above 10 percent. Emigration rates from Europe, especially Ireland and Italy, were amazing: 14 percent of the Irish population emigrated in the 1880s, and over 10 percent of the Italian population emigrated in the first decade of the twentieth century.
>
> *(Fischer, 2003, pp. 4–5)*

Migration was not confined to Europe–New World flows. Large-scale movements of population out of China and India were taking place at roughly the same time as the European migrations. All in all, it is estimated that around 10 per cent of the world's population was on the move at some time in the nineteenth century – as part of the 'first wave' of globalization.

Similarly, the transformation of financial-market opportunities by radical new cost-reducing technologies is no new thing. The invention of the telegraph, and the laying of the first successful transatlantic cable in 1866, meant that information could be communicated across the Atlantic in minutes rather than the 10–30 days then taken by ocean-going vessels. This facilitated the closer integration of the financial markets in Europe and North America, making virtually instantaneous financial dealing possible and cutting typical 'settlement times' on deals to only three days.

Certainly, for citizens of the more developed countries, by the late nineteenth century the globalization process was already well advanced in several important dimensions. Thus J.M. Keynes, later to be involved in the founding of the IMF and the IBRD, could reflect (see Box 9.3) on the favoured position of a Londoner (probably a fairly wealthy Londoner) for whom the advent of the telephone, rapid transit by steamship and railroad, and the integration of far-flung colonies into the metropolitan milieu meant that worldwide commercial transactions and travel, and access to a wide array of foreign products, were already commonplace and easy.

Although, when writing in 1920, Keynes was aware of the damage already done to the world economy by the First World War, its causes, and its consequences, he could not be expected to foresee the full extent of the sequence of economic setbacks which was about to ensue. The retreat from global integration associated with economic nationalism and protectionism in the 1920s and 1930s, and the many-faceted loss of productive potential caused by the Great Depression and the Second World War, resulted in a post-war world economy less globalized than that of the late nineteenth century.

BOX 9.3 GLOBALIZATION BEFORE THE GREAT WAR

'The late-19th-century inhabitant of London could order by telephone, sipping his morning tea in bed, the various products of the whole earth, in such quantity as he might see fit, and reasonably expect their early delivery upon his doorstep; he could at the same moment and by the same means adventure his wealth in the natural resources and new enterprises of any quarter of the world, and share, without exertion or even trouble, in their prospective fruits and advantages; or he could decide to couple the security of his fortunes with the good faith of the townspeople of any substantial municipality in any continent that fancy or information might recommend. He could secure forthwith, if he wished it, cheap and comfortable means of transit to any country or climate without passport or other formality, could despatch his servant to the neighbouring office of a bank for such supply of the precious metals as might seem convenient, and could then proceed abroad to foreign quarters, without knowledge of their religion, language or customs, bearing coined wealth upon his person, and would consider himself greatly aggrieved and much surprised at the least interference. But, most important of all, he regarded this state of affairs as normal, certain, and permanent, except in the direction of further improvement, and any deviation from it as aberrant, scandalous, and avoidable. The projects and politics of militarism and imperialism, of racial and cultural rivalries, of monopolies, restrictions, and exclusion, which were to play the serpent to this paradise, were little more than the amusements of his daily newspaper, and appeared to exercise almost no influence at all on the ordinary course of social and economic life, the internationalisation of which was nearly complete in practice.'

Source: J.M. Keynes (1920), *The Economic Consequences of the Peace*, Harcourt, Brace and Howe, New York; quoted in Goldin and Reinert (2007).

The 'second wave' of globalization

Faced with widespread destruction of economic infrastructure, dislocation of national economies, and declining standards of living, post-Second World War governments were eager to rebuild – and to avoid the mistakes made after the Great War. They made energetic efforts to dismantle barriers to trade on a multilateral basis, largely under the auspices of the General Agreement on Tariffs and Trade (the GATT – of which more is said later). The considerable success enjoyed by efforts to rebuild the world economy from the 1950s onwards owed much to *political support* for this liberalizing process – seen by many economic historians as constituting a 'second wave' of globalization.

The new globalization

What differentiates the wave of globalization which has engulfed the world since the early 1990s from earlier, more patchy and incomplete, bursts of international integration is the confluence of a particularly potent combination of factors:

- Technological innovations;
- Political willingness on the part of many influential countries to promote the international integration of markets by removing barriers to trade and other international economic transactions;
- The pro-globalization activities of a growing number of international agencies and institutions;
- An ever-expanding array of private-sector agents engaged in international trade and foreign investment – firms, banks, and other financial and commercial organizations focused on pursuing enhanced profits by participating in the globalization process;

- Feedback from the success of globalization itself: expansion of the global economy, and global income, which provide ever-increasing opportunities for profitable participation in the process – through involvement in trade, international finance, foreign investment, and other activities tending to reinforce globalization.

These are examined in detail below.

Technology

Information technology

Central to the feasibility of the 'new' globalization is the advent of a number of major *technological innovations* applicable to information technology. Particularly important is the use of ever more efficient microprocessors to make possible much faster and much cheaper digital computing. This, together with associated advances in fibre optics and electronic switching devices, has simultaneously greatly speeded up telecommunications and simplified and vastly expanded information-exchange possibilities over long distances while radically reducing communication and data-processing costs. Also, the use of satellite communication technology has ensured that no part of the globe with significant population is outside the range of mobile telephone services or the World Wide Web.

Specific examples of the globalizing effects of these technological innovations are:

- The use by manufacturers, especially the larger multinational corporations, of large amounts of information to adjust product characteristics to better suit market demand, to streamline the paperwork associated with transactions, and to co-ordinate, and optimize, the joint activities of branches and affiliates, however widely dispersed across a country or across the globe.

- The application of computer-based automation to production processes, typically in design and process control, to speed them up, make them more accurate, and cut costs.

- The use by consumers of web-based information sources to improve their access to information on the range of product choice and prices. Given the radical reduction, or elimination, of barriers to international merchandise trade, this can effectively integrate domestic and foreign consumer-goods markets, and significantly affect buying habits.

- In the labour market the much-improved flows of up-to-date information on job vacancies and job-seekers, covering much larger populations than heretofore, and crossing national boundaries to include overseas populations.

Transportation

Improved, cost-reducing technologies interacting with privatization and deregulation, and increasing consumer affluence, have made air travel a cheap, mass-market phenomenon and air-freighting a genuinely competitive means of opening up distant markets for high-value products. At the same time, the steady advance of sea-freight technology has led to continuing and significant reductions in the real cost of transporting goods by sea.

Globalization policy

It is important to recognize that a 'technological revolution' is not a sufficient condition for globalization to take place. The technological developments referred to above, and the political will to embrace them or to encourage their use, are *both* necessary for the pace of globalization to be stepped up radically. While the availability of the Internet and of satellite-communication technology have made possible for the first time easy and cheap communication over long distances, *actually making use of the opportunities* so created could have been, and still can be, made difficult by governments, including governments of developing countries. Thus, with regard to information flows themselves, it is still possible to block, up to a point, private access to long-range Internet and telephone facilities – and where there are technical problems with so doing, some reduction in usage can be achieved by making the use of such facilities illegal.

Second, even if access to international information technology is *not* deliberately restricted, systematic large-scale exploitation of the opportunities for economic globalization created by the availability of cheap information can be severely hampered simply by *imposing traditional barriers (tariffs and non-tariff) on merchandise trade*, by *erecting obstacles to the international movement of persons* (via tougher immigration laws and restrictions on working), by *deterring the inflow of foreign funds* (through denying legal protection to foreign owners of capital engaged in financial or direct investment), by *restricting trade in services* (through denying market access to foreign suppliers), and by *obstructing the commercial trade in information-related services* (through refusing to recognize intellectual-property rights).

Put another way, the massive strides made in globalizing over recent years could not have been taken had all governments been wedded to illiberal, anti-globalization philosophies; the potential of the technological revolution alone was not enough to guarantee the advent of globalization. A crucially important factor in securing the co-operation with globalization of most governments, including those of developing countries, has been the active encouragement (through pursuing policies of deregulation) of the process provided by some of the larger Western countries, together with prompting, even arm-twisting, by powerful international agencies, notably the WTO, the IMF and the World Bank – that owe their origins to the same countries. The role of these institutions in promoting globalization both directly, and indirectly – by creating the conditions in which it has flourished – is discussed in the next section.

International organizations and globalization

The process of globalization has been supported and promoted by a range of international economic institutions which have, in many cases, gained additional global influence as a result of the process. Particularly significant amongst these are the World Bank, the International Monetary Fund (IMF), and the World Trade Organization (WTO). Other supra-national institutions, both 'official' and emanating from civil society and NGOs have been – and may be in the future – influential in accelerating, or retarding, globalization. We look at the nature and evolution of the most important of these in an Appendix to this chapter, which is available on the Online Learning Centre.

The World Bank, the International Monetary Fund, and the World Trade Organization

The origins of all three of these organizations lie in the Bretton Woods Conference (officially styled The United Nations Monetary and Financial Conference) held in the Mount

Washington Hotel in Bretton Woods, New Hampshire, US, in July 1944, just one year before the end of the Second World War.

There a working group, headed by J.M. Keynes, drafted proposals for a body designed primarily to channel funds to repair the devastation done by the Second World War. This became the International Bank for Reconstruction and Development. The activities of this institution were soon to broaden to include providing financial assistance to developing countries, in which role it is better known as the 'World Bank'.

A second working group, headed by Harry Dexter White of the United States, developed the terms of reference and format for an international monetary organization the purpose of which was to assist countries in reaching, and maintaining, balance-of-payments equilibrium, and stability in the foreign-exchange markets. This became the International Monetary Fund (IMF).

The Conference also proposed the creation of an International Trade Organization (ITO) to establish rules and regulations for international trade. Although the ITO's charter was later agreed at the UN Conference on Trade and Employment held in Havana, Cuba, in March 1948, it was not ratified by the US Senate. As a result, the ITO never came into existence. In its place a much more modest undertaking, the General Agreement on Tariffs and Trade (the GATT) – an international *treaty* rather than an institution, aimed at removing or reducing tariff and non-tariff barriers to trade – was agreed. Many years later, in 1994–5, the Uruguay Round of GATT negotiations established the World Trade Organization (WTO), a body charged with extending and developing the GATT principles into a comprehensive, rules-based system for governing world trade, and with administering the new, extended system.

The IBRD/World Bank

The World Bank began operations in 1945. Its main aim, initially, was to provide loans for the speedy rehabilitation of countries devastated by the Second World War. The first loan was made to France to finance a US$250 million purchase of machinery. From the outset, developing countries comprised a substantial proportion of the membership of the Bank, and it was always intended that 'development' projects in these countries would become eligible for financing when the Bank's financial position permitted this. In the event, the advent of the Cold War brought the Marshall Plan, through which American funds were made available for European reconstruction on a scale far larger than could be contemplated by the Bank, so rendering its 'reconstruction' efforts largely redundant. This opened the way for a shift in the focus of its lending, and the first 'development' loan was made in 1947 – to Chile, to pay for electricity-generation equipment and agricultural machinery.

For some years thereafter the Bank acted very much as an orthodox commercial lender to developing-country governments, its main attraction to the latter being its willingness to lend for development projects at unusually low interest-rates made possible by its own 'non-profit' status, coupled with its ability to borrow cheaply from the international capital market because of its 'triple A' credit rating. The latter was achieved because of the perceived 'official' character of the Bank, which meant that lending to it was very low risk. A further reason for the low interest rates charged by the Bank was that the risk of default on loans that it made was also assumed to be very low, so that the Bank itself charged a minimal risk-premium on these loans.

However, from around 1960, when its affiliate, the International Development Association (IDA), was founded to provide low- (or zero-) interest-rate loans, and grants, to low-income countries, the Bank shifted progressively towards its present position as a development institution willing to fund projects and technical assistance in a very wide range of areas, including the social and humanitarian, and now heavily committed to pursuing the Millennium Development Goals of poverty reduction and sustainable development. By 2008 the Bank had increased its membership to 185 countries, had around 1800 ongoing projects (covering virtually every developing country) and an annual disbursement of development funds of the order of US$24 billion. To this figure must be added the project aid provided by the International Finance Corporation (IFC) – another affiliate, formed in 1956 to promote private enterprise (at a time when state finance tended to dominate investment in the developing world).

The World Bank now has two further associates. The Multilateral Investment Guarantee Agency (MIGA) supports direct foreign investment by offering insurance against the adverse financial effects of political turmoil. And the International Center for Settlement of Investment Disputes mediates in cases of dispute between foreign investors and host countries.

The IMF

The Articles of Agreement of the IMF defined its objectives as being 'To facilitate the expansion and balanced growth of international trade, and to contribute thereby to the promotion and maintenance of high levels of employment and real income and to the development of the productive resources of all members'. This was to be done by 'promoting international monetary cooperation through a permanent institution providing the machinery for consultation and collaboration on international monetary problems'. Promoting exchange stability and orderly exchange arrangements, while seeking the elimination of restrictions on any foreign-exchange transactions hindering the growth of world trade, were important elements in its programme, as was the setting up of a multilateral system of payments in respect of current transactions between members. The Fund would also help members to achieve relatively speedy removal of balance-of-payments disequilibria – 'without resorting to measures destructive of national or international prosperity' – by making 'the resources of the Fund temporarily available to them under adequate safeguards' (IMF, 1945).

In return for financial assistance, countries making use of the services of the IMF are usually required to agree in advance to certain conditions regarding policy changes (the 'conditionality' terms). These may be extensive, possibly including the adoption of thoroughgoing 'structural adjustment programmes' (SAPs) aimed at removing the underlying fiscal, monetary or political causes of the troublesome imbalances – typically large and persistent budget deficits, severe inflation, and counterproductive official intervention in the foreign-exchange market.

Decision-making by the World Bank and the IMF

Voting power on the Boards of the World Bank and the IMF is determined, not on the UN system of 'one country one vote', but in proportion to the respective financial contributions ('quotas') of each country. The IMF's Articles of Agreement do not, in fact, indicate precisely how these quotas are to be determined. However, in practice, they are set, for both institutions, relative to the approximate 'economic sizes' of the different member countries. In 2008 the US (which traditionally provides the President of the Bank) had approximately 17 per cent of the total voting power and, as a consequence was, as it had been since 1945, the dominant decision-maker. Japan, Germany, the UK, France, Italy and Canada together had 28 per cent of total voting power and were also influential in deciding policy. European influence has been further increased as a result of the convention of appointing a continental

European as Managing Director of the Fund. A further 14 countries accounted for 27.1 per cent of the votes. The remaining 164 countries – 89 per cent of the total membership, and predominantly developing countries – had only 27.9 per cent of the votes.

Thus, despite being the focus of the activities of the World Bank and the IMF and, in many cases, having been significantly influenced by these activities, developing countries have, over the years since the founding of the Bank and Fund, had little say in determining their policies. These have tended to be set by (primarily) the US, and the wealthier European economies plus Japan. However, a package of reforms to be implemented by 2008 provides for both significant *ad hoc* increases in the quotas of 'the most underrepresented' members (China, Korea, Mexico, and Turkey), and the introduction of a new formula for determining quotas based on four variables – GDP, 'openness', reserves, and variability of current-account aggregates. The overhauling of the formula is seen as providing an important step towards reform of governance of the IMF and the World Bank, as the 'rebalancing' of quota shares will better reflect the current relative weight of member countries in the world economy and strengthen the 'voice and participation' of low-income members.

The role of the World Bank and the IMF in promoting globalization

The relevance of the World Bank and the IMF to globalization is two-fold. First, since they have emerged as the *dominant source of policy advice* (backed up with funding) as to how developing economies should be run, they have, to a greater or lesser degree, induced a large number of developing countries to pursue parallel development strategies, thus in a sense 'globalizing' their development philosophies. Their second, and more directly 'globalizing', influence stems from their *favouring deregulation and 'openness'* and integrating member economies, as far as is practicable, into the global economy.

The World Trade Organization

The World Trade Organization (WTO) is the globalizer *par excellence*. Its creation, as the successor to the GATT, was announced in the *Marrakesh Declaration* of 15 April 1994, which marked the successful conclusion of the long-drawn-out Uruguay Round of multilateral negotiations on removing barriers to international trade. The conclusion of the Round, and the setting up of the WTO, were seen by the Ministers of the countries involved as a 'historic achievement . . . which they believe will strengthen the world economy and lead to more trade, investment, employment and income growth throughout the world'. Key features of the new WTO were 'the stronger and clearer legal framework . . . adopted for the conduct of international trade [in goods] . . . and the establishment of a multilateral framework of disciplines for trade in services and for the protection of trade-related intellectual property rights'. The truly worldwide coverage, and influence, of the new organization were emphasised in the *Declaration* which foresaw 'a new era of global economic cooperation . . . [and] greater global coherence of policies in the fields of trade, money and finance, including cooperation between the WTO, the IMF and the World Bank for that purpose'.

At the end of 1995 the WTO had 112 members. By July 2008 membership had reached 153 (of which 32 were 'least-developed'). A further 30 countries were engaged in the accession process. Thus total membership was heading for at least 183 – very close to the total membership of the United Nations (at 192 in 2008). Like the UN General Assembly – and unlike the World Bank and the IMF – the WTO operates a one-country-one-vote system.

BOX 9.4 CHINA AND THE WTO

'Recognizing the enormous benefits of open international markets, we, the undersigned economists, strongly support China's entry into the World Trade Organization. China's entry will raise living standards in both China and its trading partners. By acceding to the WTO, China will open its borders to international competition, lock in and deepen its commitment to economic reform, and promote economic development and freedom.'

'Open letter to the American people' signed by 149 eminent US economists, including 13 Nobel Laureates, 26 April 2000.

Basic principles

The basic principles upon which much WTO regulation of trade and associated activities are based are the *most favoured nation* (MFN) principle – which requires that any concession offered by one member country to a second member country (the 'most favoured nation') must also be offered to all other member countries (irrespective of whether or not they have been parties to the negotiations between the first two parties) – and the *national treatment* principle which bans discrimination in favour of local nationals and against foreigners in trade-related activities.

Modus operandi

The WTO is not a rule-making body. Rather it provides a forum, framework, guidelines and advice for negotiations between member countries – which themselves make the legally binding agreements which thereafter govern their trade relations. Members negotiate tariff reductions and other forms of deregulation of trade[1] on a bilateral basis or in groups. Such 'concessions' must conform to the fundamental MFN principle which requires that any 'concession' made to one member country – typically a reduction in tariffs on its goods – must be made to all members. (This fundamental 'no discrimination' principle may, in fact, be waived for least-developed countries – and, significantly, in cases where a free-trade area or a customs union is being formed, when discrimination in favour of members of the new body is permitted.) Agreements on cutting tariffs and other barriers to trade are 'binding' in the sense that they cannot be arbitrarily abandoned without potentially serious consequences for the perpetrator. (The WTO provides a dispute-settlement mechanism to which members may resort in the event of disagreement over trade-related issues.) Moreover, since members may *not* agree to permanent *increases* in the bound levels of tariffs, or otherwise to intensify regulation of trade, the agreed changes in the barriers to trade are always in the direction of deregulation. Thus, the entire structure of trade restrictions is always 'ratcheting downward', though it should be noted that this process can give a deceptively optimistic picture of progress if countries agree to 'bind' their tariff rates at levels well in excess of their current actual levels, which leaves them with some room for costless – and often meaningless – 'tariff cuts' in the future.

---

[1] The other forms include the simplification of trade-barrier structures by replacing quotas and other restrictions on imports by 'equivalent tariffs' which are intended to have approximately the same effect on the prices of imported goods as the barriers they replace.

The fundamental, long-term aim of the WTO is to create a world of smoothly functioning, trade-barrier-free, rules-based, non-discriminatory trade and trade-related economic relations. The scope of WTO-inspired intervention would be very broad, covering:

- *Merchandise trade:* Here the main aim is to cut, and eventually remove, tariffs, quotas, and other barriers to trade.

- *Trade in services:* Covered by the principles embodied in the General Agreement on Trade in Services – GATS – the aim is that treatment of services should parallel the treatment of merchandise trade.

- *Trade-related aspects of the activities of inward foreign investors:* Covered by the non-discriminatory rules embodied in the Trade-Related Investment Measures agreement – TRIMs – the aim is to secure equal treatment of foreign and local investors in trade-related matters.

- *Trade-related aspects of intellectual property rights (TRIPS):* This set of interventions seeks to reinforce the effectiveness of devices protecting intellectual property rights – such as patents, royalties, trademarks, copyright, 'geographical indications' (confirming the geographical location of production, where this is important, as with, for example, 'Scotch' whisky); and industrial designs.

- *Technical barriers to trade:* The Technical Barriers to Trade agreement (TBT) seeks to ensure that use of regulations regarding product quality, product certification, technical features of products, and so on – which could, in principle, be used as a form of disguised protection – is fair, and not excessive.

- A similar agreement in the field of *food safety and animal and plant health standards*, the Sanitary and Phytosanitary Measures agreement (SPS) permits countries to set standards appropriate to them. These which must be scientifically based and applied only to the extent necessary to protect human, animal or plant life or health. Such measures must not unfairly discriminate between countries or be used as protective devices.

- Last, a number of *ad hoc* agreements deal with various 'red tape' or legal issues that could constitute hindrances to trade. Examples here include the possible misuse of 'rules of origin' definitions to deny access at WTO-agreed tariff rates to goods from member countries, or the use of inflated valuation of imports in order to offset the effects of tariff cuts.

Other global institutions

In addition to the World Bank, the IMF and the WTO, several other supra-national institutions have emerged in recent years as significant influences on the way in which the global polity, and the global economy, is evolving. Important among these (and discussed in an Appendix to this chapter which is available on the Online Learning Centre) are the International Labour Organization (ILO), the World Health Organization (WHO), the Food and Agricultural Organization (FAO), the United Nations Development Programme (UNDP), the United Nations Environmental Programme (UNEP), and the International Court of Justice (ICJ).

Traders, banks and individuals

While technological innovations, and the encouragement provided by international agencies, have provided the framework within which globalization can take place, the process of actually furthering the integration of the world economy largely falls to firms engaged in international trade, banks and other financial institutions involved in developing integrated international financial systems, and individuals who elect to enter into the international labour market. For the most part these players operate within the private sector, and their responses to the opportunities presented by the evolving global economy are crucial to the globalization process itself.

Feedback from the globalization process

Successful broadening and deepening of globalization processes provide opportunities for continually expanding participation in those areas – international trade, international finance, foreign investment, and employment abroad – which are central to globalization.

A synoptic view of trade policy since the 1950s

In this section we review, very briefly, the main features of international trade policy from the 1950s to the present day.

Import-substituting industrialization

As explained in Chapter 17 the debate on trade policy for developing countries from the 1950s through to the 1970s hinged on the view that the key requirement for successful long-run growth was *industrialization*. One question arising from this perception was whether countries attempting to maintain an 'outward-looking', export-led approach to development could, in fact, achieve industrial expansion and growth through export promotion/substitution, or would find the path to industrialization and growth blocked by, amongst other things, the competitive power of the already industrialized nations. It was argued that developing countries should adopt an inward-looking approach to industrialization – by implication an 'import-substitution' strategy. Such a strategy aimed to foster the growth of domestic industries behind an array of import tariffs and other barriers to trade. The latter might be removed at some later date when, and if, the protected industries were capable of withstanding international competition.

Outward-looking development

The generally favourable (in some cases spectacularly favourable) experience of countries seen as favouring the outward-looking, export-led approach, and the widespread failure of import-substitution to deliver rapid growth, eventually persuaded most policy-makers in the developing world that export-led growth was the more attractive route to follow. In this, as we have noted above, they had the active encouragement, both ideological and financial, of the World Bank. The 'liberal' case gained further credence with the demise of Soviet Union and the end of the Soviet 'Bloc' of satellite countries, and the invigorating effect on many of its former constituent parts (albeit, after a period of reconstruction) of deregulating trade and engaging with the international economy.

Advent and achievements of the WTO

This process of reorientating developing-country economies towards interaction with the global economy was already gaining momentum in 1995, and conditions were thus propitious for the formalizing of national commitments to freer trade, in a more rigorous way than previously, under the auspices of the WTO. As we have seen, this new institution sought to develop a deregulated, global, rules-based system embracing not just international merchandise trade, but also many other dimensions of international economic activity. For some years thereafter it proved possible to press ahead with the liberalizing agenda of the WTO. Considerable progress was made with improving market access by cutting import tariffs and non-tariff barriers across an ever-expanding membership, and with pushing the scope of deregulation well beyond trade in goods and services.

The slowing of WTO-inspired liberalization

Progress with trade liberalization slowed after the 'Ministerial' meeting in Doha in 2001, and finally ground to a halt in mid-2008. This breakdown reflected both the inability to reach agreement on several unresolved issues, and the tardiness of some developed countries in implementing earlier agreements fully. Believed particularly damaging in this respect were:

- The inadequacy of the response by the EU and the US to sustained calls for a reduction in their *subsidies to domestic agriculture* – seen as severely restricting access to their markets by developing-country suppliers and leading to unfair competition in export markets.

- Concern, especially amongst many of the smallest and/or poorest developing countries, that *existing safeguards were inadequate to prevent their domestic industries from being crushed by competition* from large, powerful firms from developed countries.

- The growing unwillingness of developing countries to permit *further access by outside providers to their service sectors* – especially banking, public utilities, health and education – lest incoming firms out-compete local providers, leading to the demise of the latter, and, possibly, to increased charges for poor people currently benefiting from relatively cheap access.

- The insistence of developed countries that *intellectual property rights* – for instance patents, trade marks and copyright – *should be enforced.* The key issue in this context was the desire of developing countries for waivers to be available for the production, or importing, of cheap generic versions of drugs currently used in the treatment of a range of diseases. Strong objections to this proposal had been expressed by the US and Switzerland – both homes to major pharmaceutical-producing firms – who argued that setting aside intellectual property rights in this instance would compromise the capacity of these firms to continue crucial research and new product development.

- The objection of developing countries to what they saw as the illegitimate invoking by the US *of 'anti-dumping' provisions* (which permit increases in import tariff rates if imported goods are being sold at below cost of production) to protect its domestic industries against legitimate competition from abroad.

- Uneasiness on the part of many developing countries regarding the possible reintroduction into the liberalization programme of proposals for the *further deregulation of inward foreign investment, together with enforcement of pro-competition policies*, both of which were widely seen as reinforcing the advantages already possessed by powerful incoming firms – almost certainly to the detriment of domestic firms.

At the time of writing it is not yet clear whether the collapse of the 'Doha round' negotiations represents merely a hiatus on the long march to globalization – or a much more critical turning away from the goal of deregulated global economy. Certainly, it is seen by many as a serious blow to the globalization cause. The reaction of Peter Sutherland (a former

Director General of the GATT) was not unusual: 'A disaster . . . Years of negotiation which were and are important for globalization have been sacrificed by this failure. And there would appear to be no short-term fix.'

Regional economic integration

Either way, one indirect outcome of the activities of the WTO is unlikely to go away – regional economic integration (REI) schemes. The WTO acquiesced in, though it did not encourage, the introduction of large numbers of such schemes for the creation of free trade areas (FTAs) and other forms of economic integration, so much so that it is expected that, by 2010, over 400 schemes will be in place and that more than half of all international trade will take place under their auspices. In some cases REI has been a local response to the slow progress of negotiations for full multilateral improvements in market access – a means of *accelerating* that process across a relatively small group of like-minded countries. In others it has been seen as a means of *delaying* the introduction of full MFN reciprocity of 'concession'-granting. There is considerable debate over the issue of whether such schemes are likely to prove to be 'building blocks' helping in the ultimate creation of full free trade, or 'stumbling blocks' preventing full liberalization. Be that as it may, REI schemes are now a central feature of the international trading landscape, and their impact on the international economy is clearly of crucial importance to the future of the globalization process.

How may globalization affect development?

What development benefits and costs may be generated by the globalization process? In the following sections we discuss six key areas or activities which may be expected to be heavily influenced by globalization – looking first at the potential benefits and costs associated with globalization, and then examining the relevant evidence on each. The discussion focuses on:

- International trade in goods and services
- International financial flows:
  - a Portfolio investment: equity and bonds
  - b Commercial bank lending
  - c Foreign direct investment (FDI)
- International flows of labour
- International flows of information, ideas and knowledge.

Several of these topics are discussed in detail elsewhere in this volume (chapter cross-references are provided as appropriate) and are referred to here in relation to their relevance to globalization only.

International trade

Potential benefits resulting from trade liberalization

The most straightforward manifestation of globalization is increased international trade (henceforth simply 'trade'). The dismantling of tariff, and other, barriers to commerce between nations, and the moves (however halting) towards a single, integrated world market

	Units of labour input/ton output	Units of labour input/ton output
	Fiji	Italy
Maize	6	1
Cement	24	2
Relative price (tons maize per ton cement)	4	2

TABLE 9.1 Hypothetical costs of production of maize and cement in Fiji and Italy

for goods and services,[2] may be expected to lead to a significant increase in the magnitude of world trade. The potential gains to developing countries from deregulating trade are conventionally divided into two components – 'static' efficiency gains, and 'dynamic' gains.[3] These are discussed below.

'Static' efficiency gains from trade: Ricardo's Comparative Advantage theory

The possibility that welfare gains may be had by adopting a free-trade regime is the central conclusion flowing from David Ricardo's celebrated comparative-advantage model.

Consider two countries – one a high-income country, the other a lower-middle-income country. For convenience, we will call them Italy and Fiji. Now make the grossly simplifying assumptions that both countries produce only two goods – maize and cement – and that, in both cases, the sole input is labour. The hypothetical production costs for the two goods in the two countries are expressed, in Table 9.1, in terms of labour inputs per ton of output.

Assuming that *product prices are set with reference to the respective labour inputs*, in Fiji 1 ton of cement (24 units labour) would exchange for 4 tons of maize (24 units labour); that is, the price of 1 ton of cement is 4 tons of maize. In Italy, 1 ton of cement would exchange for 2 tons of maize.

Using a simple example of this sort Ricardo demonstrated that, despite the – at first sight – unattractive nature of Fiji's products to Italian consumers because of their higher unit cost in terms of labour input (bearing in mind that in this simple model labour is the only factor of production), it will, in fact, be to both countries' advantage to trade.

Note that, in *both* industries, production in Italy is more efficient than in Fiji, the labour input per ton output being lower in Italy than in Fiji. Note also that, despite being at an *absolute disadvantage* in maize production, Fiji has a *relative*, or *comparative*, *advantage* in maize production, because it is 'less bad' at producing it. So, if the two economies were now opened to international free trade, Italians would see Fijian maize as a bargain. (By exporting 1 ton of cement they get 4 tons of Fijian maize – whereas at home they get only 2 tons of maize). At the same time, Fijians see Italian cement as a bargain. (By exporting 4 tons of their maize they get 2 tons of cement – instead of only 1 ton). Put another way, by importing both trading partners reduce the opportunity cost of obtaining the imported good.

---

[2] We refer here to non-financial services; financial services are discussed separately later in this chapter.

[3] 'Vent for surplus' gains, which may arise in a situation in which the opening up of trade permits a country to export domestic goods currently available in quantities in excess of possible local use – for instance, fish or fruit – in return for imports, are thought unlikely to have much relevance to today's developing countries, and are not discussed here.

Given this new Italian demand for its maize, in Fiji producers of cement would shift resources into maize production. In Italy the reverse would happen as Italian cement production expands to satisfy the new demand from Fiji. This move in the direction of *specialization* would affect global supply and demand and would thus very probably affect product prices, raising the price of Fijian maize and the price of Italian cement. The final, equilibrium price ratio, in effect now the world price ratio, or the *world terms of trade*, would lie somewhere between the two pre-trade price ratios, for instance at 3 tons of maize per ton cement.

What is the outcome of this process? The key conclusion is *that both countries are better off* with international free trade than without it because of the so-called *static gains from trade* flowing from specialization. Fijians can now import from Italy the same number of tons of cement as they bought before trade began, but at a smaller sacrifice in terms of maize given up. The Italians are in a similar position, with less cement sacrificed to get any particular amount of maize. This also means that specialization and trade have resulted in an *increase in total (world) production*. However, this simple model cannot tell us how the gains from trade will be divided between the two countries – a potentially important issue.

Neoclassical development of the law of comparative advantage: the basic classical law of comparative advantage discussed above hinges on the assumption that labour productivities, though fixed in any one country for the production of a given commodity, differ across countries for production of that commodity. (In fact, if these fixed productivities happen to be the same across countries, or in the same ratio – in our example, if Italy required 4 units of labour to produce one unit of cement – *relative* productivities, and therefore price ratios, would be the same so there would be no incentive to trade.)

A more flexible, neoclassical development of the Ricardian model – the Heckscher–Ohlin model (Ohlin, 1933) – allows for differences in relative factor endowments across countries. These result in different relative prices of factors internationally. Relatively capital-abundant countries will have relatively cheap capital, and relatively labour-abundant countries will have relatively cheap labour. As a result, the former group of countries, which will tend to be high-income countries, will have a cost advantage in production of relatively capital-intensive goods, and will tend to specialize in, and export, them. Countries which are relatively labour-rich – mainly developing countries – will tend to specialize in, and export, relatively labour-intensive goods. Thus, differences in factor endowments, rather than differences in labour productivity or differences in technologies available to countries, become the source of differences in relative product prices, and hence of trading opportunities.

Important conclusions derived from the Heckscher–Ohlin theorem are:

- Specialization by countries in making and exporting those goods which use their relatively abundant factor relatively intensively in production results in 'static' welfare gains.

- Since 'relatively capital-intensive goods' tend to be the more sophisticated manufactures, and since 'relatively labour-intensive goods' tend to be agricultural goods and basic manufactures, production and exporting of the former kinds of goods will tend to be concentrated in developed countries, and production and exporting of the latter kinds of goods will tend to be concentrated in developing countries.

- The process of specialization referred to in the previous paragraph will tend, in each country, to increase demand for the relatively abundant factor. So the price of capital will tend to rise relative to that of labour in the capital-rich (developed) countries, and the price of labour will tend to rise relative to that of capital in the labour-rich (developing) countries. Put another way – relative factor prices will tend to converge in developed and developing countries (this is the *'factor-price-equalization theorem'*). This also means that the relatively scarce factor in each country will tend to *lose* as a result of the opening of trade; that is, labour will lose in capital-rich/labour-poor developed countries, and capital-owners will lose in developing countries. (However, the *dynamic gains* from trade – discussed below – may well outweigh these specific losses.)

The 'dynamic' gains from trade

In addition to reaping the 'static' gains accruing from engaging in international trade, participating countries may benefit from additional *'dynamic' gains* – which could well be much more significant than the static gains. Such gains may take the form of:

- The opportunity for firms to benefit from *economies of scale* through access to markets larger than the domestic ones, especially if production is subject to increasing returns. Even in developing countries with fairly large populations, low per capita incomes can make the local markets effectively 'small'.

- *Improvements in efficiency* of firms' performance. These may arise for several reasons, in particular: the need to cut costs in order to survive in the more competitive international economy; the improvement in products, production processes and managerial systems resulting from contact (competitive or collaborative) with outside firms; and acquisition of 'knowledge'.

- Exchange of exports for imported resources to be used in producing other goods. Where these *imported resources are more productive* than the domestic alternative, they can improve overall efficiency, thus permitting a pushing out of the production-possibility curve (PPC).

- Use by export industries of imported technologies that permit *'learning' by the labour force*, which may be transferred to other occupations, and again help to push the PPC outwards.

- Increases in exports that may make possible increased imports of food and medicinal products. Aside from their humanitarian benefits, these new imports are likely to *improve the health of the population*, and thus improve the productivity of the labour force.

Many analysts believe that the favourable effects resulting from expanding trade under a regime of globalization will have important *pro-development consequences*. It seems likely that improvements in productivity made possible by the combination of the 'static' efficiency gains resulting from specialization along lines indicated by comparative advantage, together with the multi-faceted 'dynamic' gains from trade liberalization, will result in *accelerated growth* which, in turn, will make possible, in addition to generally *higher standards of living, reductions in the incidence of poverty*, and *improvements in income distribution*.

Potential costs resulting from trade liberalization

Although the overall impact is expected to be favourable, liberalizing trade can inflict costs on some individuals and on some sectors of economic activity. Indeed, it is almost inevitable that, in the short term at any rate, there will be losers, as well as gainers, as a result of the economic restructuring which usually follows liberalization. Specific problems may include:

- Increased *unemployment* and *failure of domestic firms* because of intensified competition from imports. In small economies with few alternative employment opportunities, some of the older displaced workers may have to resign themselves to being unemployed for the rest of their lives.

- Localized *increases in poverty* in communities, or regions, particularly badly hit by competition from imports.

- *Deterioration in income distribution* in the period of adjustment following liberalization as some industries expand rapidly while others decline, and so long as increased levels of unemployment and poverty persist.

- *Diminished enthusiasm* on the part of governments for the introduction, or continuation, of measures such as *statutory minimum wages* which may erode competitive advantage in export markets.

- *Relegation to a 'low-growth trajectory'.* The comparative advantage of some developing countries lies in 'non-dynamic' goods, production of which offers few opportunities for improving efficiency by upgrading technology, or by 'learning by doing' on the part of the labour force – and demand for which is slow-growing or declining. In such cases, liberalizing trade may bring to bear market forces, trapping countries in production of these goods. Growth is likely to be weak or non-existent in such situations. A variant of this argument was advanced to justify protective, import-substituting interventions to *change the comparative advantage* of developing countries; behind tariff barriers, it has been argued, local industries might become more efficient by taking advantage of dynamic scale benefits and opportunities for 'learning by doing'.

- *Erosion of local political sovereignty.* The encroachment by the WTO on local legislative autonomy in areas such as trade barriers, business taxation, 'technical', and 'sanitary and phytosanitary' regulations relating to traded goods, and support confined to local firms producing traded goods, seems to many citizens of developing countries to infringe local sovereignty. The impression may be created that national governments in the developing world shape their economic policies along lines set by international agencies on behalf of the US or European countries – and that there is no reciprocity. Such elected national governments are seen as impotent, having influence neither in their own countries nor in the developed world which moulds their policies. This implies what Stiglitz calls a 'democratic deficit'.

- *Adverse environmental impacts.* It is frequently claimed that globalization of trade and environmental deterioration are linked. This allegation can refer simply to the possibility that increases in trade resulting from globalization give rise to increased production and hence more pollution. Or it may be argued that removing restrictions on the freedom of manoeuvre of multinational corporations enables some to relocate pollution-intensive processes in countries where pollution controls are weak – probably developing countries.

Trading performance in the era of globalization

In this section we examine trading performance in the era of globalization before moving on to look at the impact of liberalization on growth and poverty.

Merchandise trade

The rapid expansion of international trade was one of the key features of the world economy in the second half of the twentieth century and into the first decade of the new millennium

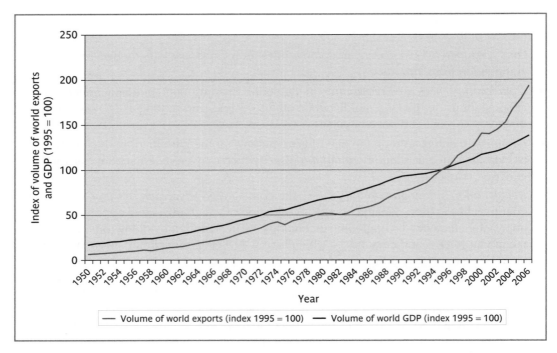

FIGURE 9.1 Volume of world merchandise exports and world GDP 1950–2006 (indexes: year 1995 = 100)
Source: Calculated from data drawn from WTO (2007, Table A1).

	OVERALL PERCENTAGE GROWTH (%)						
	1950–59	**1960–69**	**1970–79**	**1980–89**	**1990–1999**	**2000–2006**	**1996–2006**
World Exports	85.7	109.1	63.0	40.8	68.2	37.4	83.3
World GDP	47.4	62.7	45.4	33.3	20.8	17.9	33.3

TABLE 9.2 Growth of world merchandise exports and GDP, by volume, 1950–1959 to 2000–2006
Source: Calculated from data drawn from WTO (2007, Table A1).

(see Figure 9.1 and Table 9.2). Between 1950 and 2006 the total volume of merchandise exports expanded by a factor of nearly 30 – considerably faster than the volume of world GDP, which rose by around 8 times. (Note that Figure 9.1 shows *index* values of volume measures of exports and GDP. These illustrate relative, not absolute, changes in volumes over time.) The current-price US dollar value of these exports expanded by approximately 192 times over the same period.

Over the 'globalization years' for international trade, following the setting up of the WTO in 1995 – the nominal value of merchandise exports from all major regions of the developing world grew, though at widely differing speeds. As Table 9.3 shows, the overall increase in nominal value over the years 1995–2006 was 273.0 per cent (that is, the total value of exports at current prices more than trebled). The fastest export growth was experienced by the largest exporter, the East Asia and Pacific region. Its exports increased by 313.6 per cent in nominal value over the ten years, expanding its share of world exports

Region	1995		2006		% increase 2006 over 1996
	US$ billion	% World	US$ billion	% World	
East Asia & Pacific	355.2	6.9	1469.0	12.2	313.6
China	*148.8*	*2.9*	*969.9*	*8.0*	*551.8*
Indonesia	*45.4*	*0.9*	*103.5*	*0.9*	*128.0*
Malaysia	*73.9*	*1.4*	*160.7*	*1.3*	*117.5*
Thailand	*56.4*	*1.1*	*130.8*	*1.1*	*131.9*
Europe & Central Asia	205.0	4.0	834.8	6.9	307.2
Russia	*81.1*	*1.6*	*304.5*	*2.5*	*275.5*
Latin America and Caribbean	223.4	4.3	663.6	5.5	197.0
Brazil	*45.6*	*0.9*	*137.5*	*1.1*	*201.5*
Mexico	*79.5*	*1.5*	*250.4*	*2.1*	*215.0*
Middle East & North Africa	68.1	1.3	281.0	2.3	312.6
South Asia	46.7	0.9	157.6	1.3	237.5
India	*30.6*	*0.6*	*120.3*	*1.0*	*293.9*
Sub-Saharan Africa	76.6	1.5	231.3	1.9	202.0
TOTAL DEVELOPING COUNTRIES	974.7	18.8	3635.2	30.1	273.0
TOTAL WORLD	5172.1	100.0	12084.6	100.0	133.6

TABLE 9.3 Nominal value of merchandise exports from developing countries, by region, 1995 and 2006
Source: Based on data drawn from World Bank (2008a).

from 6.9 per cent to 12.2 per cent. All other regions achieved a near trebling, or better, of their merchandise exports over the same period, though the small island developing countries comprising the 'Pacific' component of the East Asia and Pacific region fared much less well as a group, achieving an increase of only around 50 per cent.

Overall, developing countries' merchandise exports grew considerably faster than those of developed countries over the years 1995 to 2006, so substantially increasing their share of total world merchandise exports – from 18.8 per cent to 30.1 per cent. China, the leading developing country exporter, made a major contribution to this increase while extending its own share of world exports over the decade from 2.9 per cent to 8.0 per cent. Other developing countries with a share of world merchandise exports of around, or over, the 1 per cent mark were Russia, Mexico, Malaysia, Brazil, Thailand, India and Indonesia. In 2006 those eight countries were responsible for nearly 60 per cent of all merchandise exports from developing countries and 18 per cent of the global total. If the nine next largest developing country exporters – Kazakhstan, Libya, Nigeria, Philippines, Poland, South Africa, Turkey, Venezuela and Vietnam – are added to this group, in 1995 these countries collectively supplied merchandise exports equivalent to 70 per cent of the developing country total and, in 2006, nearly 75 per cent – indicating clearly how concentrated developing country exports are in terms of the number of suppliers.

At the other end of the scale five countries experienced an actual decline in the dollar value of their merchandise exports between 1995 and 2006 – Burundi, Central African Republic, Eritrea, Gambia and Liberia – all 'least developed' countries. As a group the least developed countries, which had been losing export share in earlier years, did achieve some success in export markets over 1995–2006, increasing the aggregate dollar value of their merchandise exports from $23.1 billions to $96.5 billions – which enabled them to double their collective share of the world market from 0.4 per cent to 0.8 per cent.

These figures, though not providing conclusive evidence of a major favourable impact of trade liberalization on exports of developing countries in the decade following the founding of the WTO, are certainly consistent with the existence of such an impact.

Trade in commercial services

As the figures in Table 9.4 show, exports of commercial services by developing countries grew significantly over the years 1995 to 2006. Although world trade in services is still dominated by developed-country suppliers, the share of developing-country providers is increasing, and reached nearly 20 per cent in 2006 (of which almost half was 'South–South', largely intra-regional, trade). As with merchandise trade, so with commercial services, exports from the developing world are highly concentrated in terms of the number of suppliers. Thus, in 2006, over 43 per cent of the total was provided by only five countries, and around 70 per cent by 15 countries.

The largest component of the commercial-services export sector in developing countries in 2005 was *transport, travel and tourism services*. This trade was dominated by China (with exports of over US$30 billions); other significant exporters were Egypt, India, Mexico, Turkey, Malaysia, Thailand and South Africa. Exports of *computer and information services* by developing countries were dominated by India with sales worth over US$27 billion in 2005 – more than all other developing-country suppliers put together. Exports of *communication services* were important for some developing countries, notably India, Indonesia, Malaysia, and Mexico. Last, exports of *construction services* were dominated by China in 2005 with exports valued at nearly US$2.6 billion.

Region	1995		2006		% increase 2006 over 1995
	US$ billion	% World	US$ billion	% World	
East Asia & Pacific	62.7	5.2	163.5	5.9	160.8
Europe & Central Asia	56.4	4.7	149.8	5.4	165.6
Latin America and Caribbean	37.7	3.1	79.3	2.9	110.3
Middle East & North Africa	n.a.	n.a.	n.a.	n.a.	n.a.
South Asia	10.3	0.9	80.6	2.9	682.5
Sub-Saharan Africa	11.9	1.0	35.7	1.3	200.0
TOTAL	201.5	16.6	566.7	20.5	181.2

TABLE 9.4 Nominal-dollar value of exports of commercial services from developing countries, by region, 1996 and 2006
Source: As for Table 9.3.

Once again, these figures are consistent with the existence of a favourable impact of trade liberalization on the exports of developing countries.

The impact of trade liberalization on growth, and poverty

Does liberalizing trade increase growth rates?

The impact on growth of liberalizing trade has been one of the most worked-over topics in the debate on globalization. In fact, the same topic was regularly analysed long before the advent of current globalization but, as the context is now markedly different, it is instructive to consult the more recent contributions to the literature. Here we look at the results of the major studies by, respectively, Dollar and Kraay (2004), and Frankel and Romer (1999).

Given the breadth and vigour of the attacks on globalization over this issue, it may seem a little unfair of Dollar and Kraay to open their influential analysis with what amounts to a pre-emptive strike on the credentials of critics – 'Openness to international trade accelerates development: this is one of the most widely held beliefs in the economics profession, one of the few things on which Nobel prize winners of both the left and the right agree'. However, it *is* the case that the balance of academic opinion on the matter favours the views that *trade liberalization usually leads to increased trade* (this proposition is not the subject of serious dispute) and that *increases in trade resulting from liberalization make a significant contribution to economic growth and hence to development.*

The Dollar and Kraay study analysed a group of 'globalizers' – developing countries which, post-1980, markedly increased their ratio of trade to GDP and/or significantly reduced their average import tariff rates – and compared their economic performance with that of 'non-globalizing' developing countries. The key findings were that the rate of economic growth in the globalizers (which included China and India) increased from the 1970s through to the 1990s, while the developed countries, and the non-globalizing developing countries, experienced falling growth rates over the same period.

> In the 1990s the globalizing developing countries grew at 5.0% per capita; rich countries at 2.2% per capita; and non-globalizing developing countries at only 1.4% per capita. Thus the globalizers are catching up with the rich countries while the non-globalizers fall further and further behind.

These Dollar and Kraay findings are supported by the results of many other studies, including those of the second major analysis quoted here: Frankel and Romer, using a gravity model and a sample of 63 countries, found a 'substantial' positive relationship between trade and income growth such that 'increasing the ratio of trade to GDP by one percentage point raises income by between one-half and two per cent'.

Further support for this general conclusion is to be found in, *inter alia*, Sachs *et al.* (1995), Dollar (1992), Winters (2004) – and Ades and Glaeser (1999), who use evidence based on the experience of laggard areas in the nineteenth-century American economy to show that backwardness and openness can be (or, rather, have been) an effective combination of characteristics favouring growth.

This area of analysis poses particularly tricky analytical problems because of the difficulty experienced in separating statistically the effects on growth of measures affecting trade from the effects on growth of other measures or characteristics – an 'identification problem'. Thus 'countries with bad macroeconomic policies and weak institutions also have severe trade restrictions. And when countries liberalize their trade regimes, it typically takes place along with a macroeconomic stabilization programme' (Hsieh, 2000, p. 325). In other words, measures of the extent of 'openness', or 'outward-orientation', or 'integration into the world economy', or 'trade liberalization' used in analysis often capture the effects of other policies or country characteristics as well. (Notable examples of criticism of statistical methodology in this context are to be found in the attack on the Dollar and Kraay study by Nye and Reddy (2002), and in the more general broadside by Rodriguez and Rodrik (2000)).

However, it does seem that 'the weight of the evidence supports the by-now conventional view that trade is good for growth.' (Kose *et al.*, 2006 p. 2 note). Lindert and Williamson (2001) certainly believe so. They offer a useful (if not wholly scientific) corrective to excessive preoccupation with fine points of statistical technique in the face of what seems, at the intuitive level, to be overwhelming evidence in favour of the existence of a positive link between trade and growth. They point to the almost complete lack of evidence to the contrary:

> The doubts that one can retain about each individual study threaten to block our view of the overall forest of evidence. Even though no one study can establish that openness to trade has unambiguously helped the representative Third World economy, the preponderance of evidence supports this conclusion. One way to see the whole forest more clearly is to consider two sets, one almost empty and one empty. The almost empty set consists of all statistical studies showing that protection has helped Third World economic growth, and liberalization has harmed it. The second, and this time empty, set contains those countries that chose to be less open to trade and factor flows in the 1990s than in the 1960s and rose in the global living-standard ranks at the same time. As far as we can tell, there are no anti-global victories to report for the postwar Third World.
>
> *(Quoted in Collier and Dollar, 2002)*

Thus it seems safe to assume that, in many countries, globalization has increased trade – which has, in turn, increased growth rates.

BOX 9.5 GROWTH OR DISTRIBUTION?

'I have a choice. I can distribute wealth or I can distribute poverty.'

Deng Xiao Ping [Chinese leader who initiated major economic reforms]

Does liberalizing trade reduce the incidence of poverty?

Turning to the impact of liberalizing trade on poverty, the picture is less clear. Although it might seem likely, at the intuitive level, that the increased growth resulting from trade liberalization will lead to reductions in poverty levels in developing countries, it is necessary to bear in mind that the changes associated with liberalization create losers as well as winners. It is, then, disappointing that no robust evidence has thus far been found linking trade liberalization directly to overall reductions in poverty. Until such time as harder evidence – either way – is available, we must content ourselves with the *indirect* finding that, since trade-driven growth does not seem to affect *income distribution* in developing countries, it is probable that the poor are better off in *absolute* terms as a result of liberalization – since they retain a constant share of an expanding cake. Or, as Dollar and Kraay (2004, p. 27) put it: 'There is no systematic relationship between changes in trade volumes and changes in household income inequality. The increase in growth rates that accompanies expanded trade therefore on average translates into proportionate increases in income of the poor.'

International financial flows[4]

Introduction

In this section the benefits and costs arising in developing countries as a result of financial globalization are examined. The main focus is on 'financial' activities involving capital flows in the forms of cross-border 'portfolio' foreign investment (PFI) in equity and bonds, commercial bank lending, and foreign direct investment (FDI), but mention is also made of the financial flows associated with trade in goods and commercial services (appearing in the current account of the balance as export revenues and payments for imports), foreign aid, and migrant workers' remittances. (Aid, loans, FDI and remittances are examined in greater detail in, respectively, Chapters 21, 22, 23 and 24.)

Types of international financial flows to developing countries

Portfolio investment – equity and bonds

Equity portfolio foreign investment (PFI) refers to the purchasing of shares in a company as an 'indirect' investment – that is, a purely financial investment not related to control of the company. It is thus unlike the foreign 'direct' investment carried out by MNCs, which brings with it participation in management and control of the company. Bonds sold by developing-country governments and corporations to foreign buyers are also classed as portfolio investments.

Commercial-bank lending

Commercial banks involved in international finance lend to foreign governments, firms and individuals. They may do so at arm's length from bank offices in their home countries (technically 'international banking') or, increasingly, from branches set up abroad, often in the countries in which their borrowers reside or operate ('multinational banking').

Foreign direct investment

Foreign direct investment (FDI) is investment, usually by a multinational corporation (MNC), which involves the investor in active participation in the productive activity being financed – generally by *operating* the production facility.

FDI flows to developing countries qualify as an aspect of globalization in two ways. First, and most obviously, an act of direct foreign investment represents the extension of the activities of a firm into the international arena. Moreover, for the larger MNCs, which provide the vast bulk of FDI (and over one-third of total global exports), acts of overseas investment are very often integral parts of global corporate strategies. Thus, many firms scour the globe looking for the optimal locations in which to site subsidiaries, as part of a strategy of global maximization of profits (or market share, or whatever variable the firm seeks to maximize). Indeed, so widespread are the activities of the larger MNCs that it is sometimes difficult to tell what their true nationality (if any) actually is. (See Box 23.5 in Chapter 23 on 'What is an Argentinean company?')

Second, the expansion of FDI may be seen, in part at least, as a response to promotion of globalization by the WTO. The latter clearly seeks to create, as nearly as possible, a global

---

[4] This section draws, in part, on Kose *et al.* (2006).

'level playing field' for all investors – local or foreign – by removing discrimination against incoming MNCs on the part of host governments. The present **Agreement on Trade Related Aspects of Investment Measures (TRIMs)**, goes some way towards this goal by barring member governments from discriminating between local and incoming foreign firms in tax treatment of trade-related activities. It also bans certain devices aimed at restricting the operations of MNCs, for instance requiring that incoming MNCs purchase a certain proportion of their inputs locally (a 'local-content requirement') or restricting an MNC's purchase of imports to an amount equivalent to the level of its exports (a 'trade-balancing' requirement). These TRIMS measures date back to the conclusion, in 1994, of the Uruguay Round, though their implementation by many developing countries has been phased over a lengthy period.

It is worth noting that, although discussion of the foreign-investment issue was dropped from the Doha Round agenda in 2004 in order to make room for discussion of less contentious issues, it seems likely that, in time, it will reappear – as the WTO continues to push towards a truly non-discriminatory 'globalized' framework for trade and investment.

Migrants' remittances

The growth of migration, and the counter-flow of remittances, have been greatly facilitated by the interaction of several aspects of globalization. The sharp falls in the cost of *international air transportation*, together with the improvement in *international information flows* about employment opportunities in other countries, now accessible to residents of developing countries through the Internet, have encouraged migration. In addition, improvements in the geographical coverage, and reliability, *of international money transfer arrangements* facilitate the process of regularly remitting funds between countries.

Foreign aid

Official development assistance (foreign aid), a significant component of financial flows to developing countries, is discussed in detail in Chapter 21.

Exports and imports of goods and commercial services

Trade in goods and commercial services gives rise to flows of current-account expenditures (on imports) and receipts (from exports). The balance of these items – the 'balance of trade' – may be an important element in the overall net cash flow position of a developing country.

Financial globalization: what is being 'deregulated'?

The 'deregulation' which forms the basis of 'integration' or 'globalization' of financial markets is the removal of controls which affect international flows of capital *directly* through explicit administrative measures, or *indirectly* through market-based measures.

The most commonly encountered 'direct' measures are specific limits on the value of capital transactions (including, in some cases, total prohibition), requirements that permission be granted by the authorities for capital transactions (usually above a certain amount), limits on the importing or exporting of currency and gold, rules governing the operation of cross-border bank accounts, regulations affecting the use or surrender of foreign exchange earned by exporters, controls on cross-border transactions in bonds, equities and other securities, restrictions on the granting of credit to non-residents, controls on the financial activities of incoming MNCs – including importing, exporting, funding and liquidation of investments, controls on expatriate transactions in real estate, and prudential regulation of financial institutions. Market-based measures include the use of multiple exchange-rates – with different rates for different uses of foreign exchange – and taxes on foreign-exchange transactions. (A comprehensive account of regulatory measures, and of the current status of legislation in all member countries, is given in IMF (2007).)

A large part of 'deregulation' of international financial markets involves the winding down of these regulatory measures.

Globalizing financial flows: potential costs and benefits

Potential benefits

Increased investment in developing countries   Standard neoclassical theory suggests that deregulation/globalization of capital markets should lead to *more, and cheaper, capital* becoming available to finance increased levels of investment in developing countries. Removing capital controls should lead to a major reorientation of capital flows towards capital-poor countries (that is, towards developing countries) where rates of return on capital should be relatively high. This improvement in the efficiency of resource allocation internationally would, of course, benefit investors, but would also be of major potential benefit to developing countries in which local savings were inadequate and/or local interest-rates high, as the incoming funds could be used to widen the capital base, increase the level of investment, and thus *accelerate economic growth*.

Additionally, increased *overall* investment (worldwide) should result from the broadening and deepening of the international capital base over which risks are spread. This effect, which is logically distinct from the reorientation of funds mentioned above, should further augment capital stocks, and growth potential, in developing countries.

Upgrading financial systems   Increasing inflows of funds of different kinds into developing countries may generate '**collateral benefits**' – in particular by helping to develop the financial systems. This is expected by most commentators to be favourable to *further improvement of growth prospects*. It is discussed in detail later in this section.

Reduction in instability of production and associated macroeconomic aggregrates   The impact of globalization, working through increased inward flows of portfolio investment, commercial bank lending, and FDI, can improve stability of output, employment and incomes in some developing countries – especially countries at a relatively early stage of development – by broadening the production base.

However, for more advanced developing countries, increased investment resulting from globalization, by encouraging greater openness of trade and increased specialization along lines dictated by comparative advantage, can *narrow* the output base. This in turn can increase the risk of output instability, especially in small developing countries – and would, of course, be seen as a cost rather than a benefit.

Potential costs

Capital flight   Abandoning controls on outward movement of capital may encourage capital flight, as nervous owners of capital make use of the opportunity to move their funds abroad in order to earn higher returns, or simply to shift these funds to what they perceive to be more secure locations. Such manoeuvres narrow the resource base of the countries in which they occur.

Volatile inflows of capital   If flows of capital funds into a developing economy fluctuate widely from year to year, so giving rise to unpredictable variations in levels of investment, employment, incomes and budget revenues, problems may be created for both individual firms and workers, and for macroeconomic stabilization. Given the heterogeneous nature of these flows, their sources and their motivation, it would be surprising if there were no year-on-year variation. In view of this, the important considerations are just how volatile these deregulated flows are, and whether or not there are systematic differences in volatility across the different kinds of flow.

Financial crises/panics   Financial deregulation has also been identified as a contributory cause of financial crises in developing countries, these being triggered by the volatile behaviour of certain financial flows. The core element of many financial crises is likely to be the sudden, large-scale withdrawal or liquidation of foreign-owned funds and financial assets – made easier by deregulation.

Such crises often follow a characteristic pattern – with heavy inflows of capital into a developing country being followed by massive expansion of domestic credit and the creation of financial 'bubbles', which trigger a liquidation panic when they burst. The root cause of these crises is believed by some analysts to be a 'market distortion'. This takes the form of asymmetry in the extent and accuracy of information available to lenders and borrowers, respectively, such that borrowers are better informed than lenders of the true nature of the risks associated with any given transaction. Reaction by lenders (who feel themselves to be relatively ill-informed), to a shift in market sentiment may be excessive, going well beyond anything justified by the actual facts of the situation, and may be sufficient to spark off a chain reaction of 'herd instinct' behaviour. Lack of, or inadequacy of, information is common throughout the financial world, but is particularly prevalent in long-range deals between institutions in developed and developing countries. Cultural differences may exacerbate the problem, as may the greater difficulty experienced in enforcing contracts at a distance. Lacking information, investors are likely to over-react to both good and bad news. In the former case they display over-enthusiasm in investing; in the latter they withdraw their funds more quickly, and more completely, than market 'fundamentals' would justify.

Both portfolio and commercial-bank lending have been blamed for triggering financial crises. Debt flows are believed to be particularly sensitive to 'bad news' in this context. They are easily reversible in a crisis, so, in principle, making those developing countries that rely on them rather than on FDI for long-term-investment finance much more vulnerable to negative shocks (Wei, 2006). Also, some analysts argue that commercial bank lending may be particularly prone to setting off panics since the lenders (banks) are highly leveraged and therefore particularly vulnerable, and sensitive to threats of non-repayment (Dobson and Hufbauer, 2001).

It should also be noted that governments are alleged to have, in some cases, intensified 'financial panics'. By assisting financial institutions under threat they may actually have exacerbated the situation by encouraging even more risky behaviour by these institutions – which now perceive themselves to be in a less vulnerable (perhaps totally invulnerable) position.

Experience with globalization and financial flows

The magnitude of financial flows to developing countries

As the figures in Table 9.5 show clearly, *financial flows to developing countries increased sharply* over the years 1998 to 2007 – rising from $275.5 billion to $1150.1 billion. This is in line with the theoretical prediction referred to in the previous section that deregulation

FINANCIAL FLOW	1998	1999	2000	2001	2002	2003	2004	2005	2006	2007
Foreign Direct Investment (net) ($b)	170	178	167	171	157	160	218	281	325	471
% total	*61.7*	*59.9*	*48.8*	*59.4*	*66.5*	*40.1*	*40.2*	*34.8*	*30.9*	*41.0*
Portfolio Equity (net) ($b)	5.8	11.4	13.5	5.7	5.3	24.0	40.4	68.9	104.8	145.1
% total	*2.1*	*3.8*	*3.9*	*2.0*	*2.2*	*6.0*	*7.5*	*8.5*	*10.0*	*12.6*
Bonds (net) ($b)	38.8	25.7	19.5	10.2	8.8	19.6	41.1	52.6	25.3	79.3
% total	*14.1*	*8.7*	*5.7*	*3.5*	*3.7*	*4.9*	*7.6*	*6.5*	*2.4*	*6.9*
Commercial Bank Lending (net) ($b)	49.4	−5.5	−3.9	−2.0	−1.7	15.2	50.4	85.3	172.4	214.7
% total	*17.9*	*−1.9*	*−1.1*	*−0.7*	*−0.7*	*3.8*	*9.3*	*10.6*	*16.4*	*18.7*
Official Development Assistance (net) ($b)	52	53	54	52	58	69	79	107	104	na
% total	*18.9*	*17.8*	*15.8*	*18.0*	*24.6*	*17.3*	*14.6*	*13.3*	*9.9*	na
Workers' Remittances (net) ($b)	73	77	84	95	116	144	164	190	199	240
% total	*26.5*	*25.9*	*24.5*	*33.0*	*49.2*	*36.1*	*30.3*	*23.5*	*18.9*	*20.9*
Exports and Imports of Goods and Commercial Services (net) ($b)	−113.5	−42.6	8.4	−43.8	−107.4	−32.9	−51.2	22.2	122.2	na
% total	*−41.2*	*−14.3*	*2.4*	*−15.2*	*−45.5*	*−8.2*	*−9.5*	*2.8*	*11.6*	na
TOTAL NET FLOWS ($b)**	**275.5**	**297.0**	**342.5**	**288.1**	**236.0**	**398.9**	**541.7**	**807.0**	**1052.7**	**1150.1***

TABLE 9.5   Selected net financial flows to developing countries, 1998–2007 ($ billion and %)
* Excludes Official Development Assistance and Imports and Exports of Goods and Commercial Services.
** Errors due to rounding. na Not available.
Sources: World Bank, *Global Development Finance* (various); WTO (2007); Chapter 23 (Figure 23.5).

would lead to a big increase in capital flows to the developing world. (This said, it should be noted that financial flows to developed countries expanded even more rapidly – as is noted in the Appendix to this chapter, which is available on the Online Learning Centre.)

In all years 1998 to 2007 *FDI* was the largest single resource flow to developing countries, growing rapidly after 2003 to an all-time high of $471 billion in 2007. Over the same period *PFI* (portfolio equity plus bonds) accounted for a proportion of the total flows ranging from just below 6 per cent in 2001 and 2002 to nearly 20 per cent in 2007. The figures for *net lending* to developing countries by *commercial banks* fluctuated sharply over the decade to 2007. In four of the ten years the net flow was, in fact, negative – the only cases of negative net flows (other than those for the balance of trade) recorded for any of the seven categories of financial flow covered by the table.

The rapid expansion of *migrants' remittances* to their homes in developing countries is an important element in the increase in financial flows to developing countries. Over the period covered by Table 9.5 remittances grew from $73 billion to $240 billion – and were always the largest flow after FDI. The dimensions of these remittances, and the costs and benefits associated with them in both source and host countries are discussed in detail in Chapter 24.

Between 1998 and 2006 the nominal value of *official development assistance* (foreign aid) doubled, though it became progressively less important in the totality of annual net financial flows to developing countries, and relative to all other individual forms of finance except bonds.

The net contribution of *exports and imports* to flows of funds into, and out of, developing countries was, for many years, a negative one. However, in the new millennium a number of major developing-country traders began to record surpluses and, in three of the years covered by Table 9.5, developing countries as a group were in surplus, recording a net inflow of funds on this account.

Evidence on financial globalization and economic growth in developing countries

The evidence on the key matter of the impact of financial globalization on growth rates in the developing world is mixed. Some authors find evidence supporting the hypothesis that financial globalization accelerates growth in developing countries. Thus, for instance, Bekaert *et al.* (2005), examining a sample of countries including a large majority of developing countries, 'demonstrates that financial liberalization did increase economic growth' so that 'We find that a financial liberalization leads to a one percent increase in annual real per capita GDP growth over a five year period, and find this increase to be statistically significant.' This result is 'robust', surviving 'a wide variety of experiments including: an alternative set of liberalization dates, different groupings of countries . . . and four different time-horizons for measuring economic growth.'

The rationale offered for these findings includes the possibility, noted earlier, that the improvement in risk-sharing which accompanies financial liberalization may reduce the cost of capital, so encouraging increases in total investment – including investment in riskier-than-usual projects with higher expected rates of return.

Support for the Bekaert finding comes from the results of a large number of studies, including that by Reisen and Soto (2001), who further refine the analysis by differentiating between the positive growth effects of *different kinds of capital flows* resulting from financial integration, They find that the strongest positive impact comes from increased inflows of portfolio equity investment, followed by FDI. Bond sales were found to have no effect on growth, and commercial bank lending had a negative effect.

Despite these, and many other, favourable reports regarding the impact of financial deregulation on growth in developing countries, doubts remain as to the true strength of the pro-growth effects. A wide-ranging study (Kose *et al.*, 2006) draws attention to two analytical difficulties encountered in research in this field. The 'identification problem' again leads to difficulty in separating cleanly the impact on growth of globalization of finance from that of contemporaneous macroeconomic changes and policy shifts. A further major problem arises in measuring the *actual degree of deregulation* of financial markets, as there is frequently a significant difference between *de jure* measures of openness (the legal position) and the *de facto* situation (what happens in practice). Some developing countries have what appears to be a prohibitive battery of controls on capital movements, but do not enforce them effectively. Others have apparently liberal legislation, but maintain effective informal controls over financial flows. Failure to take such discrepancies fully into account – which may be impossible without detailed case-study analysis – can mislead researchers seeking to assess the strength of the impact of financial deregulation on growth.

Kose's agnostic overall finding on this central issue is that, on the basis of a wide-ranging review, there is 'little robust evidence of a 'causal relationship between financial integration and growth' (Kose *et al.*, 2006, p. 3). But, clearly, on this issue the last word has not yet been spoken.

Evidence on financial globalization and financial volatility / instability in developing countries

Relative volatility of different financial flows to developing countries   Looked at from the perspective of their *relative* volatility, portfolio investment (both equity and bonds) and commercial-bank lending, showed much more variability over the decade 1998–2007 than did FDI, foreign aid, or migrants' remittances. (see Table 9.5). Commercial-bank lending, in particular, displayed marked volatility, with an initial swing from positive to negative, then a very rapid recovery over the last five years of the period. This instability is clearly a disadvantage of this form of finance vis-à-vis FDI as a means of funding long-term investment projects.

Volatility and financial crises   As noted earlier, the increased exposure of developing countries to the volatility of portfolio investment and commercial-bank lending following capital-account liberalization has been widely identified as an important precursor of many *financial crises* in developing countries. Indeed, as Kose *et al.* (2006) observe, 'If there is anything close to a consensus in the literature on financial globalization, it is that debt flows, which include portfolio bond flows and commercial bank loans, generate the greatest risks from financial openness.'

This view has special resonance when taken together with the fact that the incidence of financial crises in developing countries has increased dramatically over the period we associate with financial globalization. The Asian crisis of 1997–98 was triggered by a sudden reversal of short-term capital flows – from a net inflow into the affected economies (Indonesia, Thailand, Korea, Malaysia and Philippines) of $92.8 billion in 1996 to a net outflow of $12.1 billion in 1997. This turnaround – in effect, a net shift in the balance of funding of $104.9 billion – made possible by the liberalizing of controls on international capital movements, was equivalent to approximately 11 per cent of the combined GDP of the five countries and, inevitably, had *very costly* consequences for the affected economies.

The initial loss of 'hot money' (much of it flowing to the US in response to favourable interest-rate differentials), triggered a cumulative depreciation of local currencies, the impact of the initial loss of funds being reinforced by increasing debt servicing and repayment costs on outstanding loans (where these were denominated in US$), coupled with the drying-up of further short-term inflows of capital in the face of increasing default by local borrowers. Sharp falls in stock-market prices (by a massive 75 per cent in the case of Thailand), and widespread declines in asset values followed, with an associated rash of bankruptcies, and significantly increased rates of unemployment.

The impact on the real economies of the five Asian countries, in terms of lost output, was severe, especially in Indonesia where the nominal GDP per capita (expressed in US$) fell by around 40 per cent (and was, in 2005, still below its 1996–7 level). Millions in Indonesia were pushed below the poverty line, the proportion of the population 'in poverty' rising from around 11 per cent prior to the crisis to somewhere between 40 per cent and 60 per cent. Thailand also suffered a major economic setback, with a fall in its per capita GDP (again expressed in US$) of somewhere around 21 per cent. And in Korea the corresponding fall was in the region of 18 per cent and unemployment increased from 3 per cent to 10 per cent.

Despite the clear tendency for the number of such crises to grow in recent years, many commentators are optimistic regarding the long-term implications for the developing world, asserting either that the instability arising from financial globalization is a relatively short-run phenomenon which will disappear or, at least, be greatly diminished, in the long run, or else that its ill-effects can be significantly reduced by appropriate policies. Three separate arguments have been advanced in support of this case. First, it can be contended that liberalization permits long-run, cross-country diversification of investment portfolios, so reducing risk levels. Second, there is evidence to suggest that experience with financial crashes leads to a tightening of prudential legislation and the undertaking of institutional reform designed to head off future financial crises. Third, there is room for improvement in the macroeconomic policy-making of many developing countries. Specifically, it is argued that the response to a large new inflow of capital has too often been adoption of an expansionary macroeconomic stance rather than the required contractionary one. The result of such *pro-cyclical* policy action is an intensifying of the 'trigger' problem of the excessive expansion of domestic credit – leading to a financial 'bubble' and a financial crisis. The adoption of c*ounter-cyclical* policies, it is believed, could go a long way to neutralizing this problem.

This having been said, it is important to differentiate between the implications of different kinds of financial liberalization by developing countries in the global context.

Thus, the freeing-up of cross-border financial transactions relating to FDI and other forms of *inherently long-term* investment is unlikely to lead to financial instability or crises. These financial inflows are used to purchase *relatively illiquid* assets in developing countries and cannot easily be reversed in the short-to-medium term. As such they seem very unlikely to cause substantial, unforeseen withdrawal of funds of the kind responsible for many of the financial crises experienced by developing countries in the past.

The situation with regard to *short-term capital flows* into developing countries, PFI and *bank lending in particular*, is quite different. Where comprehensive financial deregulation has been undertaken – involving, typically, the removal of all restrictions on inward and outward movement of capital, on local interest-rates, on currency convertibility, on the kinds of financial transactions that may be undertaken and on the kinds of financial instruments that may be bought and sold – then the probability that large, violent and unpredictable movements of funds into or out of the country will occur is greatly increased. Such volatility may affect both the banking system – where it has pyramided medium/long-term local, or overseas, lending on short-term borrowing – and other enterprises dependent on the stability and reliability of resource flows from abroad.

It is also important to draw attention to the point that, where local banking expertise is not yet fully developed, the risks arising through dealing in complex financial 'products' – such as the mortgage-backed securities problems with which triggered the great global financial crisis of 2007–09 – are even greater than is the case in mature financial systems, and carry with them the potential for precipitating local banking crises.

BOX 9.6 THE GLOBAL FINANCIAL CRISIS OF 2007/09

Unlike the Asian financial crisis of 1997/98, the global financial crisis of 2007/09 had its origins in the wealthier nations of the developed world – the US, the UK, and certain other EU countries. Moreover, the nature of the causes of the worldwide crisis, together with recent structural changes in the financial sectors of many leading developing countries, meant that its impact on developing countries would differ significantly from that of many earlier 'financial panics' in these countries.

The immediate cause of the global crisis was widespread default by mortgage holders in the US. This quickly undermined the financial stability of the lenders – mortgage companies and banks. Defaults on mortgages eroded the short-term *liquidity base* (see online Glossary) of these lenders, a potentially fatal development for institutions which typically borrow short term in order to lend long term, and which can thus stray into insolvency even though their total assets exceed their liabilities. But the problem did not end in the US. The growing integration of the operations of banks and financial institutions around the world resulted in similar problems affecting the many financial institutions that had unwittingly (because of a failure to apply proper checks) invested in 'bundles' of US financial assets that contained 'toxic' mortgages – the so-called 'securitized mortgages'.

Underlying causes of the crisis. A number of factors prepared the ground for the crisis: (i) Extensive deregulation of financial operations of banks and other institutions in the US and elsewhere – permitting more risky behaviour. (ii) The creation of many new, complex, and little understood, financial instruments (such as 'collateralized debt obligations', and 'credit default swaps' (see online Glossary)). (iii) The availability of massive flows of cheap funds into developed countries – especially the US – resulting from the recycling of the huge balance of payments (current account) surpluses run by several countries, notably China and Middle Eastern oil producers. This permitted a major expansion of lending at low interest rates. (iv) The encouragement given by the US government (especially President Clinton's strengthening of the Community Reinvestment Act) to lenders to provide finance, including mortgage finance, for 'the whole community' – including the poorer members of American society. These factors combined to underwrite a decade-long spending spree, especially in the US and other developed countries – mainly on housing, but extending to a wide range of consumer goods – leading on the one hand to a house-price 'bubble' and on the other to the accumulation by many people of unsustainable levels of debt. Once the inevitable defaults on loans reached a critical level, financial 'meltdown' – the progressive collapse of the whole highly-leveraged (see Box 9.2) financial structure – became a serious possibility.

Implications for the developing world? Because a number of the larger Asian countries had reinforced their systems of bank regulation after the events of 1997/98 – and because, in most countries in Africa, the banking sectors were relatively underdeveloped and not closely 'coupled' to developed-country financial systems – the risk that a *banking crisis* might arise in these countries through exposure to the factors causing the problems in developed countries was small. This did, however, still leave a number of developing countries seriously threatened by 'contagion' and consequent damage to their financial sectors (through collapse of institutions resulting from either the need to write off now-worthless assets or from large-scale withdrawal of foreign funds), and thence damage to their 'real' economies. Yet, for those countries, notably China, Russia and Korea, that had been able to reinforce their foreign-exchange reserves significantly since 1997/98, especially if they had also maintained an overvalued currency, the danger that a 'traditional' *foreign-exchange (or 'currency') crisis* might arise through capital flight as foreign banks withdrew deposits in an attempt to bolster their own liquidity, was small. (The Chiang Mai Initiative (see online Glossary) was designed to further reduce this risk). However, for the eighty or more developing countries still running current-account deficits the risk of such a crisis remained.

And purely 'financial' fall-out from the crisis was by no means the only potential problem facing developing countries. One very probable result of the severe decline in the willingness, and ability, of financial institutions in the developed world to lend to both commercial concerns and house buyers was an economic downturn – possibly a recession. The prospect of this, coupled with the weakness or collapse of several important financial institutions, led to major falls in share prices – which, by destroying wealth, and by undermining confidence, intensified the risk of *global recession*. While many developing countries might avoid an all-out financial crisis, all but the least 'globalized' were certain to be affected by any steep decline in activity levels in developed countries. Specific consequences were likely to be: *falling exports* (including exports of services) to developed countries and consequential *declines in employment, economic growth rates, and possibly per capita income* at home (with the possibility of a revival of trade protectionism compounding this fear); *declines in commodity prices* (especially energy, grain, rice, metals, and agricultural raw materials) paid to developing-country exporters as demand by both developing and developed countries weakened; *reductions in inflows of both FDI and PFI* (see Box 9.2) due to retrenchment by developed world multinational corporations – leading to declining investment in developing countries (a process compounded by increased rates of business failure at home and abroad, and by rising costs of borrowing); *rising rates of inflation* in countries unable to sustain their pre-crisis exchange rates; and *cut-backs in foreign aid* because of pressure put on aid budgets by the weak fiscal position of many developed countries following the expensive 'baling-out' of financial institutions. (This, together with falling growth rates worldwide, would increase the difficulty of achieving the Millennium Development Goals.) There was also likely to be *prolonged weakness in emerging-country stock markets* – reflecting the adverse commercial climate – with further associated local declines in economic activity arising from negative wealth effects. And there would very probably be *falling remittances to developing countries* resulting from diminished demand for labour – and hence for migrant labour – in high-income countries.

Policy responses to the crisis available to developing countries were limited and tended to be medium-to-long-term rather than relevant to the immediate crisis. *In the financial sector* these would include: strengthening of prudential controls – including much enhanced surveillance of complex 'financial products' available in international asset markets, and selective intervention to reduce the volatility of international capital flows; and increased international financial co-operation aimed at heading-off future financial crises. *With regard to macroeconomic policy*: improvements in the effectiveness, in many developing countries, of both monetary and fiscal policies made their deployment as an expansionary agent potentially important. (In countries without effective policy instruments of these kinds such intervention would, of course, be impossible.) In addition, active, and internationally co-ordinated, encouragement of continued deregulation of trade was likely to become critical as a means of heading-off a return to protectionism.

The lessons here would appear to be that the risks associated with full liberalization of short-term portfolio and debt flows are so great that financial authorities in developing countries **should proceed with great caution in removing restrictions on these flows** – and that the introduction of *tight prudential regulation* of local banks should be introduced, and validated, *well in advance of such deregulation*.

'Collateral' benefits from capital inflows

Always assuming that adequate measures, along the lines suggested above, are taken to minimize the risk of financial crises arising in developing countries, integration into the global financial system can bring benefits not just from increased capital inflows but also from 'collateral' changes which may be triggered by these flows. Some commentators believe that such effects can, in the long run, have more important *direct* consequences for growth rates in developing countries than the effects of the financial inflows themselves. Moreover, the collateral changes may have favourable, *indirect*, feedback effects on growth by encouraging further increases in capital inflows. The 'changes' we are talking about here fall into one of three categories – *development of the domestic financial sector*, *improvements in institutions* (defined very broadly to include governance, the rule of law, and so on), and *improved macroeconomic policies*. We now look at these 'direct' and 'indirect' effects in turn.

Why and how does financial globalization bring 'collateral benefits'?

Financial globalization encourages improved performance by the domestic financial sector in developing countries

Financial globalization seems likely to improve the quality and performance of the financial sectors in developing countries in the following ways:

Foreign banks now find it easier to set up operations in developing countries This can be expected to yield the following benefits:

- There is now *easier access* to overseas international financial markets and hence enhanced inflows of funds – at interest-rates below those formerly prevailing domestically;

- The *regulatory and supervisory frameworks* used by the incoming banks are very likely to be superior to those used by domestic banks, and will probably be emulated by the latter (in order to appear equally sound commercially to prospective customers);

- The introduction of new financial instruments and technologies, and increased competition, will *improve the quality and range of financial services* offered to customers, probably at reduced cost;

- Foreign banks can provide *an in-country home for funds* when and if there are concerns about the solvency of domestic banks, so these funds do not have to be withdrawn from the local banking system altogether.

At the same time it should be noted that, if the domestic banking sector is very small and weak, it could be wiped out by incoming foreign banks, which might then lose interest in local small depositors and small businesses, with damaging effects on the local economy. Moreover, embarking on financial integration *prior* to strengthening domestic financial institutions could have serious adverse consequences, with deregulation of capital flows leading to net *outward* flows of funds ('capital flight') and negative effects on growth prospects.

Globalization can also promote *deregulation of developing-country equity markets*. This may be expected to lead to increased efficiency as these stock markets become larger and more liquid.

Financial globalization encourages improvement in institutions and governance – including both corporate governance and broader public governance

Corporate governance can be expected to improve with financial globalization because:

- Foreign investors often have the skills and information technologies that enable them to monitor management of firms operating in developing countries better than can local investors.

- Domestic governments may be spurred to tighten up corporate governance systems in response to pressure exerted by international investors.

   Public governance can be expected to improve because:

- Developing countries may find difficulty in attracting FDI and portfolio equity inflows, which are in principle more readily available after globalization, unless and until they improve governance by taking effective action to curb corruption, cut red tape, improve the transparency of policies, and ensure the effective rule of law.

- Incoming banks and multinational companies are often large enough, have the resources and expertise, and are sufficiently 'footloose', to be able to challenge deviations by host governments from good governance practices. Smaller local firms, often wholly dependent on the domestic market, may feel too vulnerable to mount such a challenge.

Financial globalization encourages improvement in macroeconomic policies

Because 'capital account liberalization makes a country more vulnerable to sudden shifts in global investor sentiment, it can serve as a signal of commitment to better macroeconomic policies' (Kose *et al.*, 2006, pp. 37–8). Thus, the opportunities offered by financial globalization may encourage governments of developing countries to make their economies more 'investor-friendly' by, for instance, strengthening their policies on *inflation*, moving towards a freer foreign-exchange market, and avoiding capricious changes in fiscal policy.

Why and how do these 'collateral benefits' feed back to enhance the impact of financial globalization?

If it is the case that financial integration can prompt favourable 'collateral' structural changes in a developing-country economy, this could have advantages for that economy – quite independently of the growth-promoting effects of the financial inflows themselves. As Kose *et al.* (2006 p. 34) observe, 'The fact that well-developed and efficient financial sectors, good institutions, and sound macroeconomic policies contribute to higher growth are, in our view, relatively non-controversial.' The reasons why these collateral improvements would attract further (potentially growth-promoting) inflows of funds are equally obvious.

   However, it is worth noting some additional points in the present context:

- *Financial-sector development* in developing countries, resulting in deeper and better supervised financial markets with a broader range of financial–diversification possibilities, not only enhances the growth benefits of financial globalization but also improves macroeconomic stability by *reducing vulnerability to financial crises* occurring as a result of globalization.

- *The favourable impact of FDI on growth is enhanced by the existence of deep domestic financial markets* willing and able to provide credit to local firms seeking to take advantage of the spillover opportunities offered by incoming MNCs (for instance, the possibility of acting as suppliers of inputs to these firms, or of using their products as inputs, or of copying their production technologies).

■ The *sequence in which globalization policies are introduced* can have crucial implications for their impact. In particular, *earlier trade liberalization* reduces the impact any of financial crises that follow *subsequent financial deregulation*. This is because a major disruptive effect of a financial crisis is to force depreciation of the foreign exchange-rate – and, if trade is already deregulated, the extent of this depreciation will be reduced as exports (increasing) and imports (decreasing) help to restore balance in the foreign-exchange market. If exports and imports were less price-sensitive the currency depreciation would have to go much farther before equilibrium was restored, with correspondingly increased damage to the economy. Research results support this expectation – '. . . among countries that have experienced sudden stops [crises] . . . those that are more open to trade suffer smaller adverse growth effects' (Kose *et al.*, 2006, p. 47).

Globalizing the labour market

In most developed countries, barriers to the free entry of developing-country labour are in place. These take many forms, including quotas, time-limits on period of stay, minimum formal qualification requirements (and unwillingness to recognize qualifications), language-skill requirements, complex procedures for acquiring visas, and restrictions on immigration by family members.

However, strong incentives exist for expanding labour flows from developing to developed countries:

■ The economic gains are potentially enormous. One study has suggested that worldwide efficiency gains from eliminating all controls on labour movement (admittedly, an extreme situation) would lie somewhere between 15 per cent and 67 per cent of world GDP (Iregui, 1999). A much more modest estimate from a more recent analysis puts the potential gain in global welfare from relaxing entry restrictions on the *temporary* movement of workers at all skill levels at between US$150 billion and US$200 billion (Winters *et al.*, 2002) – gains which are, in fact, 'greater than the total gains expected from all other areas of negotiation under the WTO Doha Round' (UNCTAD, 2008b, p. 46). Finally, the study by Walmsley *et al.* (2005) concludes that an increase in the number (stock) of incoming migrant workers in high-income OECD countries equivalent to 3 per cent of the total labour force of the OECD would generate a global welfare gain, shared by all parties, larger than that attainable by removing *all* barriers to trade.

■ The demographic situations in many developed countries are complementary to those in many developing countries. The ageing populations in the former mean that the number of people of working age is declining while the number of non-workers is growing, with inevitable tightening of the labour market. The reverse is true in much the developing world, where youthful populations often have difficulty in finding work. Thus many developed countries are experiencing skill shortages while many developing countries have a surplus of skilled trainees. Indeed, with regard to the latter, it is argued that 'cost-quality competitive labour is one of the strongest endowments of most developing countries' (UNCTAD, 2008b, p. 46).

■ The shift towards service occupations in developed countries has created many posts that are proving difficult to fill because of a growing disinclination of developed-country labour to take on what are often seen as unattractive jobs – in, for instance, nursing and other areas of healthcare and social work – so creating a further set of gaps in the labour market which labour from developing countries may be willing to fill.

■ Many long-term migrants find superior job opportunities and a more fulfilling life in their new home.

Problems with deregulating the international labour market

Flows of migrant labour from developing to developed countries are likely to give rise to costs, as well as benefits, in both source and host countries. The main problems which may arise in source countries are the adverse effects of loss of skilled and professional workers (the 'brain drain') – in particular the negative long-term consequences for output and growth performance. However, although these losses are recognized in most developing countries as a drain on scarce resources and a loss of earlier investment in human capital, few source countries have made serious efforts to block the flow, in part because of the positive effects of remittance flows, where these arise, in part because of the practical difficulties experienced by relatively open societies in preventing departures by people intent on leaving the country.

A very much more important restraint on international labour flows arises from the negative attitudes of significant sections of the population in potential host countries, especially developed countries. These concerns will certainly prevent anything like the free-for-all which Iregui envisages. They take several forms:

■ Fears that large-scale inflows of foreign workers will depress wage levels and add to domestic unemployment;

■ Concern that incoming migrant labour may cause unacceptable additional pressures on public services – especially housing, education, and health-care facilities;

■ Disquiet over the impact of large numbers of immigrants on the existing social fabric, and unease over the prospect of cultural change that is likely to accompany significant levels of immigration.

Last, difficulties experienced by migrants once established in host countries may act as a deterrent to increased migration under the existing regulatory regime. These difficulties may include exploitation by local employers (who may, despite legislation to the contrary, pay wage rates below the legal minimum level and ignore statutory workplace health and safety requirements), ineligibility for social-security benefits, difficulty in finding legal redress or protection, social exclusion, and the like. Life in host countries is also frequently made less attractive to incomers by restrictions on immigration of family members, which often force migrants to live apart from their families for lengthy periods with the associated risk of the break-up of family units.

Globalization of ideas and knowledge

Introduction

In this section we look briefly at two aspects of globalization of ideas and knowledge – the applications of information technology, and issues arising over 'intellectual property'.

Information technology

The capacity, brought by the Internet, to exchange large volumes of information instantaneously across the globe, and to store almost infinite numbers of quickly retrievable pieces of information, all processed through relatively inexpensive, widely available computer equipment, has revolutionized the technology of international telecommunications and data storage, access and processing. As well as greatly reducing the time and cost involved in communicating and handling information, use of the new technology is making possible the emergence of new spatial patterns of location of economic activity for many firms by removing, or greatly reducing, the costs traditionally associated with spatial separation of certain sub-processes – in particular, data-processing and 'back-office' functions. In increasing numbers of cases, these newly 'footloose' activities are being relocated from developed countries to developing countries able to provide the requisite skills at lower cost.

However, the much lower take-up rate of the Internet in Africa and Asia than in Europe and North America, a symptom of the so-called 'digital divide', suggests the possibility that the immense cost-cutting potential of IT applications may be capitalized on in wealthier countries well ahead of poorer countries, so giving the competitive power of the wealthier countries specializing in those industries that are 'Internet-intensive' a major boost and disadvantaging the poorer countries.

In addition to this important economic dimension, the advent of the Internet also has profound political and cultural implications. Free access to the World Wide Web brings with it exposure to the entire range of ideas and information being propagated around the world, and makes the kind of isolation of populations from the international community sought by certain governing regimes in the past much more difficult to achieve. The popularity of this new resource is evident from the data in Table 9.6, which show clearly the dramatic nature of the increase in use of the Internet in the short period 2000–2007 – over which usage in Asia increased five-fold and in Africa by a factor of eleven. At the same time, it is the case in some countries that there are official limitations placed on access to the Internet. It remains to be seen how effective the efforts of governments determined to reverse this particular aspect of globalization will prove to be.

	NUMBER OF INTERNET USERS					
	Users in 2000 (million)	Users in 2007 (million)	Users Per 100 Population 2000 Total	Users Per 100 Population 2007		
				Total	Low	High
Africa	4.5	52.0	0.6	5.4	0.03 (Liberia)	37.0 (Seychelles)
Americas	157.2	376.2	18.9	41.4	1.1 (Bolivia)	85.2 (Canada)
Asia	110.4	569.0	3.1	14.3	0.1 (Timor Leste)	70.0 (Singapore)
Europe	109.3	331.8	13.9	41.2	15.0 (Albania)	91.4 (Netherlands)
Oceania	8.1	15.1	26.5	44.9	1.6 (Solomon Is.)	80.4 (New Zealand)
TOTAL	389.5	1344.1	6.5	20.1		

TABLE 9.6 Internet use in five regions in 2000 and 2007
Source: International Telecommunication Union, ICT Statistics Database. (Available on: http://www.itu.int/ITU-D/icteye/Indicators/Indicators.aspx#)

NUMBER OF MOBILE CELLULAR TELEPHONE SUBSCRIBERS						
	In 1995 (million)	In 2007 (million)	Per 100 Population 2000	Subscribers Per 100 Population 2007		Percentage of all Telephone Subscribers 2007
				Total	Low	High	
Africa	0.6	270.6	2.0	28.1	1.4 (Eritrea)	89.3 (Seychelles)	89.3
Americas	40.3	653.1	21.8	71.8	1.8 (Cuba)	133.6 (Antigua)	69.4
Asia	23.1	1475.1	6.7	37.1	0.4 (Myanmar)	173.4 (UAE)	70.0
Europe	24.1	888.8	36.9	110.3	49.6 (Moldova)	148.4 (Estonia)	72.6
Oceania	2.6	26.9	33.4	78.9	0.8 (Kiribati)	102.5 (Australia)	69.2
TOTAL*	90.8	3314.6	12.2	49.6			71.8

TABLE 9.7 Mobile telephone subscribers in five regions in 1995, 2000 and 2007
*Errors due to rounding.
Source: International Telecommunication Union, ICT Statistics Database. (Available on: http://www.itu.int/ITU-D/icteye/Indicators/Indicators.aspx#)

A second innovation associated with globalization is the mobile telephone. This use of communication via satellites makes possible technological 'leap-frogging' by developing countries, as there is now no need, for those which have not yet done so, to invest in the expensive business of providing, and maintaining, national networks of landlines. The mobile phone is a much cheaper, and less fallible, modern alternative. The new technology has also made it much easier for widely scattered operatives, and branches, of multinational firms to maintain instant contact with one another – an important facilitating factor in, for instance, establishing 'offshoring' in India where, as Stiglitz (2006, p. 43) points out, the telephone system is 'unreliable'.

The figures in Table 9.7 make clear the speed with which this technology has been taken up. In Africa, in particular, the process of bypassing the landline technology is clearly well under way. The 28 per cent of the population subscribing to mobile telephones correspond to 89 per cent of all telephone subscribers.

Intellectual property

An important element in the programme of the WTO is strengthening the protection given to owners of 'intellectual property' by broadening the scope of, and providing more effective enforcement of, copyright, patents, trademarks and other restrictive devices through TRIPS – the Agreement on Trade-Related Aspects of Intellectual Property Rights. Given that compliance with these protective measures tended, traditionally, to be less well observed, and policed, in developing countries than in developed countries, the impact of tightening worldwide compliance under TRIPS has been more burdensome on the former, and constitutes a significant cost of globalization to the developing world.

The most serious issue to emerge in this context has been the aggressive assertion of property rights by drug manufacturers in developed countries over a number of their pharmaceutical products which could be very important for healthcare in developing countries. In most cases the marginal cost of production of these products (or generic versions of them) is low – within the range of users in the developing world – but prices protected by TRIPS are far higher, taking such products beyond their financial reach. While the humanitarian case for waiving price protection is clear, the insistence of the producers on asserting their global intellectual property rights – on the grounds that the prices charged provide funds needed to finance R&D on new, perhaps even more effective, drugs – continues to materially restrict access to many pharmaceutical products by developing country populations.

Benefits and 'discontents' – the globalization 'balance sheet'

'A broad range of critics is arrayed on the other side [against globalization]. Among them are academics, opinion leaders, individuals and groups who see their interests being affected by globalization, politicians, NGOs, and demonstrators – and these categories are not mutually exclusive. To listen to the debate in the terms each side paints the other, one might think that it is a discussion between Dr. Pangloss, who believes that all is for the best in the best of all possible worlds, and those who believe that the world is going to hell in a handbasket. That is doubly misleading. In the first place, many of those who regard themselves as pro-globalization, myself among them, know that there is far too much misery in the world, that there are many wrongs to be righted in the global economy, and that it could be made to operate much better. And on the other side, many – but not all – of the critics are not against globalization. Rather, from NGOs demonstrating for further debt relief and campaigning for greater access of developing country exports to industrialized country markets, to academic critics questioning current policy views, many are seeking a better and fairer globalization.'

(Fischer, 2003, p. 6)

In the above quotation Stanley Fischer implies that much of the wide-ranging public debate on globalization is actually about *how* globalization should be handled rather than whether it should be stopped, or even thrown into reverse. It is clear that many of the points advanced by anti-globalizationists are not properly thought through, embody well-known fallacies, blame globalization for wrongs for which it is blameless, or are hopelessly utopian.

BOX 9.7 ALL CHANGE IS BAD?

'What the protestors are against is not growth or globalization, but change and fear of the impact of change. There once used to be warnings that train travel in excess of fifteen miles per hour would be hazardous to health. Many of the alleged hazards of growth and of joining the international community are similar to such warnings.'

(Krueger, 2002)

Nevertheless, as we have concluded in this chapter, globalization brings with it genuine costs as well as benefits. So what are the critical points at which the present direction of globalization might be changed? What 'discontents' created by or, at least, associated with, globalization need to be tackled? We suggest the following:

- Trade liberalization gives rise to many difficulties but two may be singled out as particularly troublesome. At the local level, liberalization of international trade inevitably gives rise to 'adjustment' costs because of the dislocation involved in transforming economic structures – the most important of these being temporarily increased unemployment and poverty. 'Safety nets' in the forms of retraining of, and welfare payments to, those affected would both reduce local suffering and defuse much of the opposition to this aspect of globalization.

■ At a more general level, the fact that the trade-liberalization process is widely perceived as unbalanced – requiring much more 'give than take' on the part of developing countries – needs to be addressed. Ideally this would involve a rapid reduction in agricultural subsidies by the US and the EU, coupled with greater awareness on the part of the developed nations that many developing countries genuinely require a protracted period of economic restructuring and strengthening before they can safely face the cold, if invigorating, blast of international competition.

■ The vigorous use, by some of the strongest powers, of punitive measures apparently sanctioned by the WTO might be moderated. Worth singling out here are the use of *'anti-dumping'* provisions by some developed countries – notably the US – to beat down competition, and the application of *intellectual property rights* to prevent developing countries from benefiting from access to much-needed medicinal products.

■ The failure of many developed countries to make effective attempts to *tackle environmental problems* – especially global warming – casts doubt on their resolve. Given that most of the accumulated atmospheric carbon dioxide is attributable to the currently developed countries, their obligation to participate actively in this 'most global' of issues is clear, and their involvement essential if developing countries are to be induced to participate.

■ As we have seen, financial globalization can be hazardous for developing countries because of the risk of attracting destabilizing inflows of *hot money*. The co-operation of the developed world in formulating and enforcing, or at least tolerating, policies aimed at reducing the volatility of such capital flows would facilitate this important aspect of globalization in the developing world.

■ A more even-handed, conciliatory, and less doctrinaire, approach in developed-country dealings (and IMF, WTO and World Bank dealings) with developing countries on trade and other globalization issues is required – if the perception that the *national sovereignty* – and the national sentiments of the developing world – do not count for much is to be dispelled.

■ Temporary migration for employment is a major source of income, in the form of remittances, for many developing countries, and also provides major benefits for recipient countries by curbing pressures of excess demand in their labour markets. It is likely that the numbers of migrants could be considerably increased if existing provisions regulating international migration for employment were overhauled. In particular, the concerns expressed by many host countries that migrant workers will 'overstay' might be addressed by revamping the relevant provisions in the WTO's General Agreement in Trade in Services (GATS) aimed at reinforcing the temporary nature of such migration. As a *quid pro quo*, migrant workers might be assisted by the setting up of a global system for validation of credentials and qualifications, together with a provision for accrediting any on-job training they receive in the host countries.

Regarding the benefits accruing from the globalization process, policy should be aimed at increasing their magnitude and broadening their country coverage (bearing in mind that, thus far, the benefits accruing to the developing world have been concentrated on a fairly narrow range of countries). The following measures might be advocated:

- The process of trade liberalization might be slowed down for the smaller and poorer developing countries in order to provide them with a 'breathing space' in which to phase in the structural adjustments needed to avoid serious problems arising when protection is removed. In many countries most of the benefits of trade liberalization could be lost through premature deregulation. A much more flexible, broadly based application of 'special and differential treatment' to developing countries is required to enable this to happen in an orderly manner.

- More thought should be given to the sequence in which different aspects of globalization are introduced – as we know that the impact of financial globalization on growth and volatility is dependent on the initial conditions in the liberalizing economy. In particular, it is important that: trade liberalization is undertaken *before* financial integration; that, also before financial integration, the local financial sector has in place solid, well-managed institutions, using internationally approved accounting and auditing procedures and adequate systems of oversight – and employing competent personnel; that the need for good governance and the elimination of corruption at sectoral and national levels are taken seriously; and that sound macroeconomic policies are adopted.

Summary conclusions

- In this chapter we have seen how a combination of technological advances and widespread political support has created the 'new wave' of economic globalization that has swept across the world in recent years.

- We have noted that in four key dimensions – international trade, international finance, migration of labour, and knowledge – the globalization process holds out the hope of accelerated growth and improved (possibly dramatically improved) living standards for the developing world.

- We have also noted that, inevitably, the upheaval created by economic globalization entrains costs – some short-term, some potentially long-term (and some, perhaps, imaginary!) – and that, unless these are addressed effectively by national governments and international institutions such as the World Bank, the IMF and the WTO, resistance to further change could become a formidable force.

- Thus it is prudent to close by recalling that, as we saw at the beginning of this chapter, there is no certainty that a powerful trend towards globalization cannot be reversed. Were political support to be withdrawn in the face of widespread opposition – however wrongheaded – to globalization, the opportunities created by pro-globalization technological developments might not be strong enough to maintain the momentum of the process. Then the cumulative economic expansion of recent years could be transformed into a cumulative contraction of the kind experienced in the Great Depression – a 'lose-lose' situation that could have serious adverse consequences for the developing world.

'We cannot take it for granted that the world will continue down the road of globalization, greater prosperity and greater democracy. . . . We have special obligations as economists participating in the debate over economic globalization. . . . not to be afraid to take on big untidy issues, but to do so objectively, element by element' (Fischer, 2003).

Questions for discussion

9.1 What case is there for halting – or even reversing – the process of economic globalization? What steps might be taken with a view to achieving this?

9.2 The eminent economist Jagdish Bhagwati has suggested that a World Migration Organization should be set up to co-ordinate policies on migration. What do you think the terms of reference for such a WMO should be? And what problems might it have to face?

9.3 What is the connection, if any, between financial globalization and the recent substantial increase in the incidence of 'financial crises' in developing countries?

9.4 Review the arguments for and against the view that financial globalization will increase the growth rates of developing-country economies.

9.5 Explain how, and why, governments may seek to regulate international trade.

9.6 'The economic theory of resource allocation tells us that the gains from liberalising the world labour market would be maximised by scrapping all controls on international migration'. Comment.

Additional reading

Andres, L., D. Cuberes, M. Diouf and T. Serebrisky (2007) *Diffusion of the Internet*, Policy Research Working Paper No. 4420, World Bank, December.

Cable, Vincent (1999) *Globalization and Global Government*, Chatham House Papers, Royal Institute of International Affairs, London.

Cook, C. (2001) 'Globalization and its critics', *Economist*, 29/9/2001.

Economist, 20/9/2007 'Globalisation and emerging markets'.

Woodhall, P. (2006) 'The new titans' *Economist*, 14/9/2006.

WTO, *The Doha Agenda*, www.wto.org/english/thewto_e/whatis_e/tif_e/doha1_e.htm

Online *Learning* Center

To help you grasp the key concepts of this chapter check out the extra resources posted on the Online Leaning Centre at ***www.mcgraw-hill.co.uk/textbooks/huq***

Among other resources, there are two appendices available:

- Appendix 9.1 'Other' global institutions
- Appendix 9.2 Stocks of foreign assets in developed and developing countries

CHAPTER 10

Poverty, Equity and Well-being

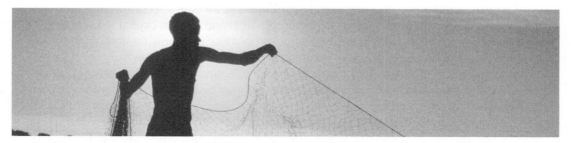

Much effective action of a human-development type against extreme deprivation is possible even in countries of low income. In the face of the more foreseeable emergencies such as crop failures the suffering may be effectively mitigated, and rises in death rates prevented, by appropriate measures adequately prepared that draw on state, market, and civil society. But progressive improvement in living standards for the bulk of a population from a low base requires continuing economic growth generally beyond the point at which labour has become 'scarce' and proceeding substantially faster than population growth. Where there is a capacity for fast growth, combining it with progressive equalization has been shown to be possible, and ideally it can be accompanied and boosted by continuing human-development action, with safety-nets for those who would otherwise lack minimal acceptable means of support.

Introduction

What do we mean by poverty? What are its signs? How do we measure it? How extensive and serious is it? Where is it concentrated? What can be done about it?

Before we get to the big question – what can be done about it – we go through some of the concepts and devices that enable us to make coherent factual statements about poverty across the world and in particular countries, statements not about the averages but about the lower reaches of what life in the society concerned has to offer.

We consider various concepts of poverty: first, the important distinction between **relative** and **absolute** poverty; then poverty seen in its various aspects – as inability to satisfy **basic needs** or as lack of **capacities** and capabilities, poverty as tied to **vulnerability**, poverty as **unjust deprivation**.

We next consider how to measure the **inequality** of income distribution in particular countries, and then how to measure their **poverty in its extent and depth**. For the latter purpose, we compare two ways of gauging the seriousness of poverty in any country or population: first with reference to *income-poverty lines* (or as a substitute food-calorie-poverty lines), and second through the extent to which particular *basic needs* – such as nutritional and health status, literacy, access to water and sanitation, or access to education and health services – are met. There is no single measure, even a composite, that is satisfactory for all purposes.

How may we expect **income-distribution to change with economic growth**? We discuss what observed relationship there is between average-income level on the one hand and income-poverty and inequality on the other and what effect economic growth can be expected to have on income-poverty and inequality. Then we ask the converse question: does poverty have any bearing on the capacity for growth? In other words may poverty itself generate a **vicious circle** for whatever reason, so that an economy may be trapped at a low level, as early development-economists argued?

We next consider how the **functional distribution of income** – its distribution through the market process between labour, land, and physical and human capital – might be used, or altered, or overridden, to reduce inequality and poverty, and how far and on what conditions reliance can be placed on economic growth to reduce poverty.

We also note that poverty and deprivation are not entirely covered by considering income distribution between households: that there may be **discrimination *within* households** by gender and age.

This leads on to the big questions: the various possible **strategies of poverty-reduction**; and the possibilities of combining equalizing redistribution with rapid growth. In order to combat poverty most effectively does it make more sense to target poverty directly or to go primarily for growth? Or is there – or can matters be arranged so that there is – no conflict?

Then we consider two particular topics. The first is the character of **famines** and the means of preventing or ameliorating them, involving not only government but also market mechanisms and civil society. The second is **social safety-nets**: last-resort payments to individuals who would otherwise be destitute or exceptionally deprived.

Appendix 10.1 considers the question of **equity**: whether the world system that permits the existing levels and extent of poverty can be regarded as *unjust*. As a first step toward an answer, this is considered with reference to how much hypothetically it would cost the richer segments of the countries concerned, or the richer outside world, to end each of the two commonly used degrees of income-poverty in each of several large developing countries, and what disruption if any this might entail.

Appendix 10.2 faces the paradox that, though most people would like more income, there seems to be a very weak relationship between **income and happiness**. What bearing does this have on the case for economic growth and for reducing poverty, absolute or relative?

Appendix 10.3 deals with some of the **technicalities of poverty headcounts and gaps**.

Appendix 10.4 presents a recent ILO model of **social safety-nets**.

All four appendices are available on the Online Learning Centre.

BOX 10.1 TOOLKIT ON POVERTY

Absolute and relative poverty. Absolute poverty is poverty judged by a common world standard. Relative poverty is poverty judged by the standard of the country or community within which the person concerned lives.

Basic needs. An approach to judging poverty by the lack of any of a list of specific needs such as a certain level of nutrition, literacy, sanitation, or access to a certain minimum of health care.

Capabilities. An approach (advocated by Amartya Sen) to judging poverty by the lack of any of a list of capabilities to perform certain functions considered necessary for an acceptable human life, such as reading, writing, seeking legal redress, having a voice on

▶ selection of political leaders. Criteria for the capabilities approach are clearly likely to overlap with those for the basic-needs approach.

Disposable income. Income after taxes have been deducted and any payments received from the state have been added; or sometimes only those parts of disposable income in that sense that are at the disposal of the recipients to spend as they wish (rather than being received in the form of general social provisions).

Functional distribution of income. How income is divided by market mechanisms (before any state intervention) among owners of the factors of production: labour, capital, human capital, land (including all natural resources).

Gini coefficient. A measure of the equality of distribution of one variable across another, mostly used to measure the inequality of distribution of income or wealth or of some asset across a population. It has values between zero and one, with higher values indicating greater *inequality*. It is based on a *Lorenz curve* (see below) and is the ratio between (i) the area between the Lorenz curve and the diagonal of the diagram and (ii) the whole area below the diagonal.

Human development. Normally used for (i) increasing the equality of distribution of income or wealth; (ii) increasing the stability over time of the incomes or expenditures of people, especially those at the lower levels of income; (iii) raising the minimum levels – or reducing the proportions of people below certain low levels – of disposable income, or, for example, of education, nutrition, health-service provision, sanitation.

Human development index. Index compiled for individual countries by the UN Development Programme [UNDP] as a weighted average of indexes of income per head, an education index (literacy and school enrolment), and a health index (life-expectancy).

Kuznets curve. Function indicating how countries' degree of inequality typically changes as we move from the poorest countries to the richest *cross-sectionally* (i.e., not necessarily as we move with the same countries over time). Simon Kuznets found that this function, with inequality on the vertical axis and income per head on the horizontal, had roughly *an inverted-U shape*, with inequality first generally rising and then falling as we move from the poorest to the rich.

Lorenz curve. Named after Konrad Lorenz, the Austrian student of animal behaviour, this function, drawn with proportions of people on the horizontal axis and proportions of a variable such as income on the vertical, is used to show the equality of distribution of the latter variable over the population, with complete equality represented by a Lorenz curve that is a diagonal straight line (see Figures 10.1, 10.2).

Poverty headcount and poverty gap. These terms are defined with respect to any particular poverty line, such as the one-dollar-a-day line. The **poverty headcount**, which may be presented as an absolute number of people or as a percentage of the whole population, is the number below the poverty line and represents the *extent* of that degree of poverty. The **poverty gap** represents the *depth* of poverty as defined by the line, and summarizes how far people fall below the line. (See for details Appendix 10.3, available on the Online Learning Centre.)

Rawlsian concept of social justice. This is briefly that inequality in a society can be regarded as just only so far as it is necessary to improve the position of the poorest. (See Appendix 10.1, available on the Online Learning Centre.)

Social safety-nets. Payments or other provisions designed as a last resort to ensure that no one in a society falls below a certain minimally acceptable level of real disposable income.

Conquering poverty is *what it's all about*: certainly *one* central reason behind the interest in development economics for people in the developing countries, and the *overriding* reason for the rest of the world. That very statement risks trivializing poverty as if it were one problem among others – rather than covering the whole range of material deprivations, or at least those that modern technology has made avoidable. Absolute poverty, on the most conservative and restrictive definition, is a matter of desperate importance for over a billion people: at least the billion to a billion and a half generally reckoned to be living in the early twenty-first century on less than the rough equivalent of one US dollar a day and with all the other deprivations likely to go along with that condition. The big question is how poverty can be relieved.

Concepts and definitions of poverty

By poverty we understand inability, through the circumstances of a person's life, to satisfy **essential material needs** for what can be called **well-being or happiness**. Satisfying material needs can never be a *sufficient* condition for happiness, but *some* degree of material satisfaction must be virtually a *necessary* condition for most of us. Most people would judge that there are forms and degrees of material deprivation for themselves, or forms and degrees of material deprivation for anyone, that would make well-being impossible.

However, that definition – failure through circumstances to satisfy the necessary material conditions for well-being – immediately leads us to the important distinction between **absolute and relative poverty**.

Absolute and relative poverty lines

People's sense of well-being is inevitably conditioned by the conditions that they see around them, and what they have come to expect. This is a matter of common experience and is confirmed by more systematic evidence from questionnaires. One family might regard as almost luxury a diet confined to a few vegetables and as much of a staple cereal as its members can eat, and having plenty of clean water available, though only from a nearby public standpipe; while another, in a much richer society, would see this as sheer and utter misery. **Absolute** expressions for poverty set lower limits – absolute levels of disposable income, and minimal provision of social goods such as disease prevention and physical security – below which, it is implied, no one anywhere should be allowed to fall. On the other hand, the authorities in a particular country, concerned with relevantly identifying poverty for their own people, may specify requirements, **relative** to the country's prevailing standards of living, whose absence, they believe, would preclude a sense of minimal well-being *for their citizens*: for example, an income per person in each household not less than half the median for the country.

Poverty lines are set up as signposts of what ought to be. The bearing of various experiences on happiness or well-being may be a matter for empirical investigation, but where exactly a poverty line – absolute or relative – is drawn involves also a value-judgement.

Much of what is said below about measurement of the extent and intensity of poverty with reference to defining limits may be applied to either absolute or relative lines, but it is useful to bear in mind which of the two is being discussed in any instance. In this chapter it will be absolute lines. *International* concern about poverty centres inevitably on absolute limits, but how people stand in relation to their own country's or community's material standards may also still be an important indicator of material limits to their well-being.

Yet even absolute poverty, on these understandings, is in an important sense relative: it is a matter of degree. The interpretation of absolute poverty depends on what needs *are regarded* as essential to every human being and to what extent – food quantity and nutritional quality; access to clean water, to means for sanitary disposal of waste, to clinical health services and to public protection against disease; access to literacy, numeracy, specialized skills, and knowledge about the world; and, in part summary or general indicator, in part supplement, some measure of overall spending-power – all matters of more or less.

So lines defining what is essential are inevitably arbitrary; and, as we shall see, the standard international ones have almost inevitably been subject to change in order to increase their usefulness and relevance. Yet they have a necessary role in setting policy targets. To be useful the lines drawn must bear some relationship to **possibilities** – what social arrangements could in principle achieve – as well as to **ideals**.

Views of poverty: basic needs, basic capabilities, vulnerability, unjust deprivation

The **basic-needs** and **capabilities** approaches to development (Stewart, 2006; Clark, 2006b) can be taken to imply corresponding emphases in the understanding of poverty. The basic-needs discussion arose in the 1970s as a human-centred reaction against the preoccupation with aggregate economic growth. The capabilities approach, stemming from Amartya Sen in a number of publications since the early 1980s (e.g., 2005), attempts a further degree of humanization by emphasising needs that go beyond physical and emotional comfort to include capacities for purposive activity.

A **basic-needs** approach to poverty, then, is one under which policy at any time or place sets minimum absolute standards of (mainly material) need in a number of measurable dimensions. Listing them implies that it is a vital responsibility for each political community, and for the world, to aim to meet them. Yet the operational target does not have to be static. Making the goals realistic often requires them to be reached gradually. This is the view behind the Millennium Development Goals (see Chapter 21), which have set the world intermediate targets to be met by certain dates.

We can also see **poverty as a lack of basic capacities or capabilities**. This is Sen's view of the deficiency to which *development* is the answer (see Chapter 1). The poor are those deprived not only in what they receive but also in what they can achieve, with the one lack closely related to the other. Because of the close connection between material deprivation and the lack of capabilities, it has been argued that the basic-needs and capability approaches can be defined so as to be mutually consistent.

Human development, as the term is used by the United Nations Development Program (UNDP), covers progress or attainment in any and all aspects of human material welfare – but in a very broad sense of 'material' – to include education, for example. The agency's Human Development Index (HDI) for individual countries is a composite of average spending power with ratings on some concrete basic-welfare indicators. The HDI can be no more than a rough pointer which, by including a few health and education statistics, at least gives a more human-centred and poor-oriented assessment of a country's achievement in material well-being than average income alone. Its use of country indicators in constructing the index has to be limited in practice to those that are almost universally available. Insofar as it includes literacy rates and school-enrolment ratios, as well as life-expectancy, it can be regarded as not entirely neglecting capabilities in its assessment of basic needs (see Box 10.2). The UNDP has a corresponding Human Poverty Index (HPI).

BOX 10.2 THE HUMAN DEVELOPMENT INDEX

'The human development index (HDI) is a composite index that measures the average achievements of a country in three basic dimensions of human development: a long and healthy life, as measured by life expectancy at birth; knowledge, as measured by the adult literacy rate and the combined gross enrolment ratio for primary, secondary and tertiary schools; and a decent standard of living, as measured by GDP per capita in purchasing power parity (PPP) US dollars. The index is constructed from indicators that are currently available globally using a methodology that is simple and transparent. . . .

While the concept of human development is broader than any single composite index can measure, the HDI offers a powerful alternative to income as a summary measure of human well-being. . . .'

From: UNDP, *Human Development Report* 2005, p. 214.

Bringing **vulnerability** into the idea of poverty introduces considerations beyond current material deprivation, though to a large degree following from it. Very poor people are not only deprived. What they have is also **precarious**. With no spending-power or time to spare from providing rudimentary food, shelter, and clothing, they would have the greatest difficulty in taking the measures that might protect them from the effects of accidents, such as illness and injury, crop failures, and rises in prices of essentials. If they are city-dwellers, they are quite likely to live in areas that are poorly or predatorily policed and to be subject to coercion or extortion from those with more social power. Because of official corruption and laxity, they may have to pay more for state services than the less poor. They will commonly have minimal opportunity to protest against abuses or to invoke law or public opinion against injustice. They will have the least capacity for protecting themselves against the effects of natural disasters or disorder and conflicts. Writers (such as Ellis, 2006) have identified the need of people for risk-management in advance of setbacks or disasters or for coping strategies after the adverse events occur. The lower people's current income, the less capacity they are likely to have for any form of risk-management.

Vulnerability in these senses is set against **human security**, a comprehensive ideal promoted in the 1990s by the UN Development Programme (UNDP), to indicate that it is not enough to assess how far immediate material needs are being met. With low living standards in normal times, the need is particularly great for some reasonable prospect of stability, of material safety-nets, of aid in emergency, of recourse to help against oppression and injustice. This implies that the attack on poverty requires not only a higher overall level, among the poorest people, of nutrition, water access, sewerage, formal access to schools and clinics, and the like, but also political and social institutions that reduce their *vulnerability*: arguably democracy and free elections (despite their frequent failings and abuses), uncorrupt police and courts, free advocacy where it is needed, and communication media uninhibited politically – as well as some basic material safety-net or social insurance, progress to elimination of the main endemic and epidemic contagious diseases, and public provisions of various kinds to protect people, the poor particularly, against the impact of natural disasters. The need for aid in emergency, or equivalent provision of free services, responds to the fact that a given level of cash spending-power that is minimally adequate in normal times may simply disappear if there is a significant medical expense that the family has to meet or if it feels obliged to pay for advanced education for one of its members.

To see the question another way, the genuine, consistent elimination, through whatever measures, of extreme income-poverty must imply or include a guarantee of a measure of security for everyone. Material deprivation and vulnerability are not fully distinguishable, but the concept of vulnerability shines the light into different places.

A further view is of poverty as **unjust deprivation**. This raises the question of **equity**: how far is the deprivation that exists, all things considered, fair? The classic treatment of this question, challenging at least, and attempting – in its quest for the desirable – not to neglect consideration of what is possible, is that of John Rawls (1971). Rawls asks how we might identify a just social order. Equity (justice) in Rawls's view does not imply *equality*, but it means that there must be pretty good reasons for the inequalities that are allowed to exist. He applies the question to particular countries – political entities – but, *mutatis mutandis*, similar reasoning could be applied to world social justice insofar as there are world institutions, even rather feeble ones, that can affect the world distribution of income and the extent of deprivation and vulnerability. Rawls's reasoning, and its possible application to the injustice of present world poverty, is outlined in Appendix 10.1 (available on the Online Learning Centre). One implication of the argument there is that, insofar as, for example, the *foreign-aid targets* set by the UN Millennium Project or by the rich countries' own paper commitments could be used to better materially and consistently the situation of the world's poorest (which implies, among other things, that they would in so doing *not go beyond a certain point* in blunting economic incentives generally, or risking violent conflict), the poor are unjustly deprived so long as aid at that level is not given. It is a further question how unjust their deprivation is in relation to the resources available *from their own countries*, for which there are also targets for poverty-reducing spending propounded by the Millennium Project, targets for additional spending larger in many cases than those proposed for foreign aid.

Measurement of equality of distribution

There are two main methods used of expressing the degree of inequality of income across a society, with some other more complex variants.

Lorenz curve and Gini coefficient

One method is the **Lorenz curve** and its derivative, the **Gini coefficient**. The Lorenz curve is a curve showing visually the distribution of one variable (here income) across a population. It is plotted from an origin, O in Figure 10.1, at the intersection of two axes, the horizontal one measuring proportions of total population, and the vertical representing proportions of total income. Successive points on the curve, starting from O, are found by plotting the poorest say 1 per cent of the population, x_1, against the proportion, y_1, of total income that that poorest 1 per cent receives; then say the population share, x_2, of the poorest 2 per cent, against the share of income it receives, y_2; and so on until the point is reached at 100 per cent on the x axis and 100 per cent on the y axis, point Z in Figure 10.1.

The farther the Lorenz curve deviates from the diagonal of the diagram, the more unequal the distribution is. The Gini coefficient is a numerical measure of inequality. It is given by

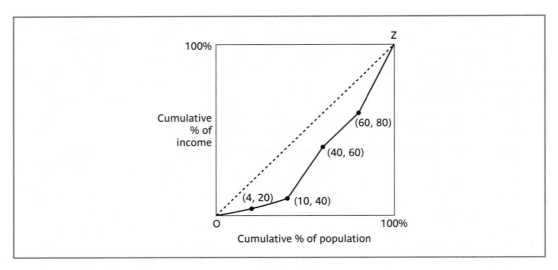

FIGURE 10.1 Lorenz Curve

the ratio of (i) the area between the Lorenz curve and the diagonal to (ii) the total triangular area below and to the right of the diagonal. Gini coefficients for a number of countries are given in Table 10.1, column (4).

However, there are different ways of being unequal. Degrees of inequality cannot be ranked entirely satisfactorily on a single scale. If two countries, A and B, have the same average income and their Lorenz curves imply the same Gini coefficient for both, A's curve may be closer to the diagonal than B's in the lower left of the diagram but further away in the middle and upper right. The poor in A will then be better off than those in B, but a segment of the middle earners, above a certain lowish level of income but below the very richest, will be poorer than the corresponding people in B (see Figure 10.2). There is no compelling answer to the question which of the two countries is the more unequal.

All of this can be taken to illustrate the point that there is no ideal way of measuring inequality.

Richest-to-poorest-quintile ratio

The second common way of expressing the degree of inequality of income in a country is to compare the share of its total income earned by say the top fifth ('quintile') or tenth ('decile') of income earners' income with the share going to the bottom fifth or tenth, for example by showing the ratio between the shares of the top fifth to the bottom fifth. The order of inequality rates on one of these measures will not necessarily be the same as the order of Gini coefficients. In Table 10.1, Colombia, for example, has a slightly lower Gini than South Africa but a higher top-to-bottom-quintile ratio. Still, the ordinal rankings of the countries in that table on the two measures are very similar.

Other measures of inequality

There are other indicators of inequality, some of which are directed at making assessments of material-welfare improvement or achievement that take into account in a single figure both the increase or attainment of income and how it is distributed. The Atkinson (1970)

(1) Country	(2) GNI p.c. PPP$, 2005	(3) HDI* rank	(4) Gini coefficient, %	(5) Inc. or exp. ratio: top to bottom quintile	(6) Poverty line, PPP $1 per day, people below (headcount), %	(7) Poverty line, PPP $1 per day, gap, %	(8) Poverty line, PPP $2 per day, people below (headcount), %	(9) Poverty line, PPP $2 per day, gap, %	(10) Survey years to which cols. (6)–(9) refer; in brackets, for cols. (4), (5) if different
Norway	59 590	1	25.8	3.9	<2	<0.5	<2	<0.5	2000
Korea, Rep.	21 850	28	31.6	4.7					1998
Argentina	13 920	34	52.2****	15.1****	7.0	2.0	23.0	8.4	2003 (2001)
South Africa	12 120	120	57.8	17.9	10.7	1.7	54.1	12.6	2000
Russian Fed.	10 640	62	31.0	4.8	<2	<0.5	12.1	3.1	2002
Malaysia	10 320	61	49.2	12.4	<2	<0.5	9.3	2.0	1997
Mexico	10 030	53	54.6	19.3	4.5	1.2	20.4	6.5	2002 (2000)
Costa Rica	9 650	47	46.5	12.3	2.2	0.8	7.5	2.8	2001 (2000)
Turkey	8 420	94	40.0	7.7	3.4	0.8	18.7	5.7	2003 (2000)
Brazil	8 230	63	59.3	26.4	7.5	3.4	21.2	8.5	2003 (2001)
Iran	8 050	99	43.0	9.7	<2	<0.5	7.3	1.5	1998
Columbia	7 420	69	57.6	22.9	7.0	3.1	17.8	7.7	2003 (1999)
Ukraine	6 720	78	29.0	4.3	<2	<0.5	4.9	0.9	2000 (1999)
China**	6 600	85	44.7	10.7	16.6	3.9	46.7	18.4	2001
Philippines	5 300	84	46.1	9.7	15.5	3.0	47.5	17.8	1994 (2000)
Sri Lanka	4 520	93	33.2	5.1	5.6	0.8	41.6	11.9	1990–1 (1999)
Egypt	4 440	119	34.4	5.1	3.1	<0.5	43.9	11.3	1999–2000
Indonesia	3 720	110	34.3	5.2	7.5	0.9	52.4	15.7	2002
India	3 460	127	32.5	4.9	34.7	8.2	79.9	35.3	1993–4 (1999)
Pakistan	2 350	135	33.0	4.8	17.0	3.1	73.6	26.1	2002 (1998)
Bangladesh	2 090	139	31.8	4.6	36.0	8.1	82.8	36.3	2000
Mozambique	1 270	168	39.6	7.2	37.9	12.0	78.4	36.8	1996
Kenya	1 170	154	42.5	8.2	22.8	5.9	58.3	23.9	1997
Ethiopia	1 000	170	30.0	4.3	23.0	4.8	77.8	29.6	1999–2000
Malawi	650	165	50.3	11.6	41.7	14.8	76.1	38.3	1997–8

TABLE 10.1 Poverty and inequality: summary indicators, based on income or expenditure, selected countries in descending order of PPP GNI per head

Notes: * Human Development Index.

** China excluding Hong Kong, Macao, and Taiwan.

*** Normalized poverty gap (NPG).

**** Data referring to urban areas only.

Sources: World Bank, *World Development Report 2007*, pp. 290–1.
UNDP, *Human Development Report 2005*, pp. 270–1.

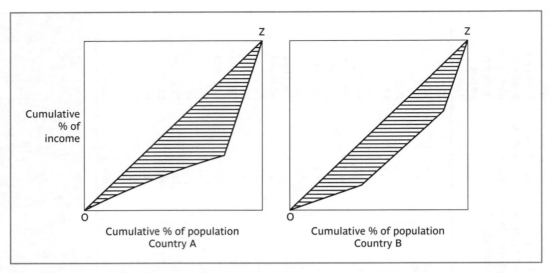

FIGURE 10.2 The same Gini Coefficient in both but A more equal at the lower and of the distribution (lowest 40% of people)

index, directed only at comparisons of inequality, depends for its value in any case on an explicit judgement (arguably one of value): in effect on how the marginal utility of income (the value that is put on a marginal unit of income) should be taken as diminishing as income increases (Fields, 1980, pp. 106–7).

The approach of Ahluwalia and Chenery (Chenery *et al.*, 1974, pp. 38–42) to taking account of distribution in evaluating income *growth* is to apply weighting factors to the aggregate incomes of the various quintiles of income-earners. The point of doing this rather than simply citing an aggregate rate of growth is seen as follows. If the top quintile earns ten times as much as the bottom quintile, giving a rate of *aggregate* growth of income of the whole population in the usual way weights any given proportional rise in income ten times as highly if it occurs in the top quintile as if it occurs to the same number of people who form the bottom quintile. One way of distribution-weighting of growth would be to give the same weight to the income of each quintile. This could be called an equalizing weighting. A 'poverty-weighting' could give even *higher* relative importance to the incomes of the poorer ranks. Again fixing the weighting would be a matter of explicit value-judgement.

Measurement and assessment of poverty

Measurement by income or by objective indicators of well-being

There are two basic approaches to measurement of the poverty of a community or region: by the prevalence and extent of failure on the part of individuals or households to reach certain **income or expenditure levels**; and by the extent of the collective achievement in satisfying certain concrete **basic needs** or attaining other **desirable welfare goals**.

Income-poverty as indicated by poverty headcounts and gaps

The usual summary way of measuring the extent and depth of **income-poverty**, for purposes of comparisons between countries or over time, is by the use of poverty lines. Cross-country comparisons have to be made by some standard that is absolute in the sense of being the same for all the countries compared. The World Bank uses two lines for what can be called *poverty* and *extreme poverty*: respectively where household income per person is below US$2 a day and US$1 a day in PPP ('purchasing-power-parity') equivalents – all in 1985 prices, so that the $1 a day was actually PPP $1.08 a day in 1993 and would have been $1.45 a day in 2005. (The PPP-$1-a-day standard denotes not what a US dollar can actually buy in the country concerned, which for many goods would be appreciably more than in the US, but as near as possible to what a US dollar would buy *in the US in 1985*, which for daily sustenance is not a lot: not much more, at most, than a euro a day would buy in Germany or 60 pence a day in Britain in the early 2000s.)[1] An alternative, which avoids the problem of comparable cash-valuation but has other limitations would be to express the bounding lines as food-calories, instead of US dollars, per day.

The compilers of the World Bank's poverty statistics (*WDR*, 2007, p. 301) recognize the horrendous difficulties of making the poverty figures accurate and comparable across countries. Beside income or output measures in local currencies (which have the usual difficulties such as valuation of non-marketed goods) they depend upon surveys of prices in each country to work out equivalents in PPP dollars. A number of price surveys for this purpose have been conducted since 1970. The eighth of these, for 2005, had the biggest range to date, of 146 economies (101 of them low- or middle-income countries) covering over 95 per cent of the world's people (World Bank, *WDI*, 2008, pp. 1–3). In spite of the great effort clearly put into making the published figures internationally comparable, they have to be taken as approximate at best.

As a result of the 2005 price survey, there was near the end of 2007 news of the need for a massive correction to the factors for converting a numbers of currencies, notably those of India and China, into PPP dollars. This would mean that China's total PPP income was some 40 per cent smaller than previously estimated, and India's some 36 per cent smaller. The change is explained in World Bank *WDI* 2008 (pp. 1–3).

This would clearly raise the headcount of those in extreme poverty in China and India. The figure in Table 10.1 based on a 2001 survey implies a value for China of about 217 million in that year. The 2008 *WDI* does not give revised estimates of poverty headcounts, but a recent set of estimates (apparently using the slightly *lower* line for judging extreme poverty mentioned in footnote 1) raises the number of China's extreme poor in 2005 *as a result of the price re-assessment* by about 130 million to 204 or 208 million (*Economist*, 24/5/2008, p. 110; 30/8/2008, p. 78[2]), about 16 per cent of the population – as it happens roughly the same percentage as implied by the survey *for 2001* reported in Table 10.1 on the old price figures – but on the other hand interprets the change as meaning that *more* people in China than previously thought (407 million as against 240 million) *had come out* of extreme poverty between 1990 and 2004. India's extreme-poverty headcount would also have needed uprating significantly at the same time, apparently to 456 million in 2005 (41.6 per cent of the population). The changes in assessment, it seems, would in any case push the world's extreme-poverty headcount for 2005 from 960–990 million to about 1.4 billion.

---

[1] The standard appears likely to change in the figures to be issued after 2008 to one about 14 per cent lower: $1.25 rather than $1.45 in 2005 US prices. Statements made here about the corrected figures suppose this slightly lower standard.

[2] Reporting work by Martin Ravallion, Shaohua Chen and Prem Sangraula (2008), World Bank Working papers 4620, 4621.

The **extent** of extreme poverty in a country is in this way very roughly indicated by the number of its population meeting the arbitrary test of living in households with less than one PPP dollar a day per member, a 'headcount index'.

What might be called the **weight** or **depth** of extreme poverty can correspondingly be measured by the amount (in, say, PPP dollars) by which the *aggregate incomes* of people in this category *fall short* of a PPP dollar a day per person. This can be expressed as (1) simply an aggregate amount of annual income (the *total poverty gap, TPG*); or as (2) the average gap per person across the total population (the *average poverty gap, APG*); or as (3) the proportion that the TPG bears to total possible income below the poverty line (that is to the poverty-line income per person multiplied by the total number of the population), that proportion being the *normalized poverty gap, NPG*.

The TPG is the amount of extra income that would have to be distributed to those below the poverty line concerned in order to bring all their incomes up to that line. The percentage 'gap', as presented by the World Bank (e.g., 2006, pp. 290–1), is the NPG. If all the extremely poor are just below the extreme-poverty line, the NPG percentage will be low. If they are all living on next to nothing, it will be close to the percentage of people living in extreme poverty.

These (at first glance confusing) indicators (and others!) are summarized, for those interested, in Appendix 10.3, available on the Online Learning Centre. Refer to Figure 10.3 in that appendix.

One-dollar and two-dollar poverty headcounts and gaps for a number of countries are given in Table 10.1 – all inevitably based on figures issued *before* the price revisions that followed from the 2005 price survey.

Table 10.1 shows an income measure, column (2); two inequality measures, columns (4) and (5); and four poverty measures, columns (6) to (9). In the World Bank's classification, all those countries in the table from Argentina to Turkey at the time are upper-middle-income, from Brazil to Indonesia lower-middle-income, and from India downward low-income.[3] South Korea and Norway, inserted for comparison, are high-income countries.

We should expect the incidence and depth of poverty to be determined by a combination of per capita income and inequality of distribution. In principle, if we had enough measures of distribution capturing inequality from various angles, an appropriate selection of them, together with average income, might predict reasonably closely a country's rating on each of the various poverty measures, but that is definitely hypothetical. With the limited inequality indexes we actually have, let alone the much more limited selection given here, that is a long way from being the case. There seem in fact to be loose relationships of the form expected, but some puzzles.

Broadly, as we would expect, the poverty measures become higher as we go down the list, but not consistently. South Africa is higher on three of the poverty measures than any country on the list above the income of China. Beside South Africa, Argentina and Mexico also have higher $2-poverty measures than any other country above Brazil in the table. The relatively high poverty ratings of all three of these countries among those of comparable incomes do, however, fit with the fact that all three have exceptionally high inequality measures in columns (4) and (5). Russia and Ukraine, on the other hand, have low (favourable) poverty ratings for their income range, partly explained by low inequality counts, though in Russia's case the $2-poverty ratings are higher than those of Malaysia and Iran, which have very much higher inequality measures.

---

[3] These classifications apply in 2005. The next year Brazil moved into the upper-middle-income range.

Lower down the list there is similarity among Sri Lanka, Egypt, and Indonesia (with similar incomes) in their inequality measures and also in their poverty indicators (Indonesia, with the lowest of the three incomes, rather higher on $2 poverty than the other two). There is roughly similar consistency among the next three on the list: India, Pakistan, and Bangladesh; though Pakistan, with an average income a third lower than that of India and similar inequality measures, surprisingly shows much lower incidence of $1-poverty. (Difference in timing of the poverty-distribution surveys between countries, and within each country from the timing of the average-income figures, may be part of the explanation.) However, differences in poverty incidence and depth between these South Asian three on the one hand and Sri Lanka, Egypt, and Indonesia on the other – all with very similar inequality measures – are more puzzling, especially the contrast between Indonesia and India, which in 2005 also had very similar average incomes. (Again timing of the surveys – Indonesia's like Pakistan's dates from 2002, India's from two or three years earlier – combined with India's very rapid spurt of growth in the early years of the century, may help in the explanation.) Timing of surveys may also explain the puzzle over the much larger poverty indicators for Mozambique than for Kenya, in spite of the fact that in the tables they have very similar average incomes and Gini coefficients. Surveys relating to income distribution and poverty were conducted eight and nine years respectively before the income year cited here, and Mozambique after the end of its civil war was recording much higher growth rates than Kenya.

One lesson from these figures remains. Poverty, even straight income-poverty, let alone the direct welfare and capability measures, does have some relationship, but a very loose one, with average income taken alone. A *complete* account of distribution must, logically *must*, explain the rest. But favourable figures on *particular measures* of inequality, such as a low Gini-coefficient, do not consistently imply relatively low absolute-poverty indicators at any given average-income level.

What we have seen from Table 10.1, in the comparison between Indonesia and India, is that two countries with very similar average-income levels and similar scores on both indicators of inequality, can have very different headcounts and intensities of poverty. Gary Fields (1980, ch. 3, e.g., p. 58), who looks at a number of such inequality indicators that might be expected to predict the extent of poverty at a particular income level, concludes that it is a mistake to treat one as a surrogate for the other; indeed that summary income-inequality measures and absolute-income measures of poverty are answering different questions motivated by or reflecting different implied value-judgements. So a low Gini or quintile ratio should not console us if absolute-poverty incidence and depth are still high.

Objective welfare indicators

Objective indicators, particularly if they refer to basic needs, may well be thought to provide better poverty comparisons than income-based poverty lines. They could be held to relate to outcomes rather than inputs, as well as being more easily interpreted and for the most part probably more reliable. This is also the case if we are making comparison on grounds of equity. Yet Sen (1998) shows the complexity of *summary* country-to-country comparisons by objective indicators on either absolute-poverty or equity grounds: for example that, though India at the time had a Gini of 33.8 against China's 41.5, 62 per cent of adult women in India were illiterate compared with only 27 per cent in China, and 63 per cent of children in India under 5 were undernourished by the World Bank's definition, while in China the figure was 17 per cent. To take another comparison, India had higher life-expectancy than

(1) Country	(2) Improved water access %, 2002	(3) Life-expectancy at birth, years, 2003	(4) Under-5 deaths per 1000, 2003	(5) HIV, % in 15—49 age group infected 2003	(6) Malaria, cases per 100 000 people 2000	(7) TB, cases per 100 000 people 2003	(8) Under-5s below weight for age, %, 1995—2003 average	(9) Literacy, 15—24 age group, % 2003 or 2002	(10) Primary net enrolment rate, % 2002/2003	(11) Completing primary grade 5, % of grade 1 entry 2001/2002
Norway	100	79.4	4	0.1	..	5	..	..	100	100
Korea, Rep.	92	77.0	5	<0.1	9	118	..	..	100	100
Argentina	..	74.5	20	0.7	1	55	5	98.9	..	92
South Africa	87	48.4	66	21.5	143	341	12	93.8 ***	91	98
Russian Federation	96	65.3	21	1.1	1	157	3	99.7	90	..
Malaysia	95	73.2	7	0.4	57	135	12	97.2	93	87
Mexico	91	75.1	28	0.3	8	45	8	97.6	99	93
Costa Rica	97	78.2	10	0.6	42	18	5	98.4**	90	92
Turkey	93	74.0	39	<0.1	17	40	8	96.6	86	..
Brazil	89	70.5	35	0.7	344	91	6	96.6	97	..
Iran	93	70.8	39	0.1	27	36	11	..	86	95
Colombia	92	72.4	21	0.7	250	80	7	97.6	87	69
Ukraine	98	66.1	20	1.4	..	133	3	99.8	84	..
China *	77	71.6	37	0.1	1	245	10	98.9	..	99
Philippines	85	70.4	36	<0.1	15	458	31	95.1	94	96
Sri Lanka	78	67.8	15	<0.1	1 110	69	29	95.6***	..	98
Egypt	98	69.8	39	<0.1	..	36	9	73.2***	91	98
Indonesia	78	66.8	41	0.1	920	674	26	98.0**	92	89
India	86	63.3	87	[0.4–1.3]	7	287	47	76.4****	87	84
Pakistan	90	63.0	103	0.1	58	358	38	64.5	59***	..
Bangladesh	75	62.8	69	<0.2	40	490	48	49.7	84	54
Mozambique	42	41.9	158	12.2	18 115	567	24	62.8	55	49
Kenya	62	47.2	123	6.7	545	821	20	80.3	67	59
Nigeria	60	43.4	198	5.4	30	518	29	88.6	67	..
Ethiopia	22	47.6	169	4.4	..	507	47	57.4	51**	62
Malawi	67	39.7	178	14.2	25 948	469	22	76.3**	..	44

Table 10.2 Meeting basic needs: some indicators, selected countries in descending order of PPP GNI per head

Notes: * China excluding Hong Kong, Macao, and Taiwan.

** Small difference in year from the one specified, 2003 or 2002, or provisional figures.

*** Greater difference in year from 2003, or other source of incomparability.

Source: UNDP, *Human Development Report 2005*, Oxford U.P., 2005, Human development indicators, Tables 1, 7, 9, and 12.

sub-Saharan Africa, but on the other hand a greater proportion of undernourished children. Also the rating of any one country *as a whole* even on one indicator alone may be a very crude basis of judgement. India has shown a huge variety by state and district in literacy and infant mortality (pp. 34–5). (Comparisons between Kerala and UP states are given below.)

Some comparative figures by country are shown in Table 10.2. International comparisons of various key basic-needs indicators are also given in Tables 2.5 to 2.8 in Chapter 2, with indications of change (mostly improvement, sometimes striking) over various periods.

Information in Table 10.2, especially on life-expectancy and child mortality, generally matches the picture of world concentration of poverty in South Asia and sub-Saharan Africa – with AIDS, especially in southern Africa, an aggravating factor, so that South Africa stands out as strikingly weak on both these measures in relation to its income level. For their incomes, Russia and Ukraine are also prominent as weak on life-expectancy: a finding fairly general in the former Soviet republics. Climate has a bearing on the incidence of diseases, notably malaria, which is likely to be a contributor to early-childhood deaths in heavily infested countries such as Mozambique and Malawi. Figures in Table 9 of the source used show extensive, but fairly patchy and far from complete, use of drug treatment for early-childhood malaria, and for the most part comparatively little use of insecticide-treated bednets for young children, even in some heavily infested countries. South Asia and sub-Saharan Africa are again the regions of the main laggards in meeting the Millennium Development Goals of universal primary-enrolment rates and youth literacy, but there are some other, surprising, defaulters on one or the other, including Turkey, Iran, Egypt, Colombia, and Ukraine.

Poverty, inequality, national-income level and growth: relationships

Bearing of growth and per capita income level on equality and poverty

Whether there is any relationship consistent enough to be meaningful between income level and degree of inequality – and, if there is, what it means for policy – are contentious questions. **Simon Kuznets** (1955, 1963) concluded, from cross-sectional comparison, that inequality, as measured by the proportional shares of various income-quintiles, tended first to increase as one moved from lower to higher per capita incomes, and then beyond a certain income level to fall. A number of subsequent studies (almost all cross-country, not for individual countries over time) found similarly, using various measures of inequality. This pattern could be represented by **an inverted U-shaped curve**, the **Kuznets curve**, with inequality on the vertical axis and per capita income on the horizontal

Gary Fields in 1980 (ch. 3) reviewed a number of these studies to that date, generally accepting the empirical findings but then interpreting what they did and did not mean. This he did with reference to **a threefold division of types of economic growth** in an economy supposed to be 'dualistic' – that is, with a traditional and a modern sector. These types were *traditional-sector-enrichment growth*, *modern-sector-enrichment growth*, and *modern-sector-enlargement growth*. The third of these involved the movement of people and activity into the modern sector (often but not necessarily urban) from the traditional. It was assumed that the modern sector would have higher labour-productivity and higher labour-incomes than the traditional and that the poor would be concentrated disproportionately in the traditional sector. All three types of growth would by definition raise overall income, but in Fields' analysis they would have different impacts on relative inequality and absolute poverty. The first, raising income differentially in the poorer sector, would tend to reduce absolute poverty and relative inequality. The second would increase relative inequality and have little effect on absolute poverty. The third would reduce absolute poverty but might either raise or lower relative inequality, depending on the balance between different effects (pp. 52–6). On the supposition that growth was predominantly of modern-sector-enlargement type, Fields provided a demonstration that, according to his model, relative inequality, as judged in various ways, would indeed first rise and then decline as this growth proceeded, so that the inverted U-curve could in those terms be explained.

However, what did the inverted U-curve, if it existed, mean for policy? One interpretation was that rising inequality had to be accepted in the 'early' stages of growth, and that interfering with distribution in the direction of equalization would tend to inhibit growth. This view could be attacked on various grounds, several of them used by Fields. One was that the observed relationship between income level and distribution was not a close one (as can be seen, for example, by casual inspection of the table in Chenery *et al.*, 1974, pp. 8, 9). A number of other factors showed relationships with income distribution. A second was that the association was not necessarily causal in the direction the argument would imply.

Fields also argued that looking at relative inequality was concentrating on the wrong indicator from a welfare viewpoint. What ought to be of interest was absolute poverty. On that score *growth*, unless confined to modern-sector enrichment (in which case poverty was unaffected), would move in the right direction, so that between absolute-poverty reduction and overall growth there was no conflict. On the other hand (p. 57) *falling relative inequality* might, as possibly for India in the 1960s, be consistent with an increasing headcount of extreme absolute poverty.

A further argument more specifically against the view that growth and equalization *policies* were mutually inconsistent at certain levels of income, was given by Fei, Ranis, and Kuo (1979). They argued that one contrary case was enough to falsify the generalization, and that Taiwan from some time in the late 1950s provided a striking example of continued rapid growth with simultaneously falling inequality indicators. Tables (Fei *et al.*, 1979, p. 66; Fields, 1980, p. 231) show mean household income in Taiwan growing at 3.3 per cent a year between 1953 and 1964 but thereafter at 8.2 per cent a year until 1972; while the income ratio of the top to the bottom tenth fell from 30.4 in 1953 to 8.6 in 1964 and 6.8 in 1972; and the Gini fell from 0.558 in 1953 to 0.328 in 1964 and 0.301 in 1972. Similarly the scatter-diagram in Figure 10.3 on p. 263 shows Taiwan's total GNP over eight years growing at around 7 per cent a year between 1953 and 1961, while the income of its poorest 40 per cent grew at around 12 per cent a year.

So, though there is quite a lot of *cross-sectional* evidence of *some tendency* for inequality to rise and then fall as mean income rises, there is no reason whatever to think that equalizing policies at any stage of growth *ipso facto* limit growth, or (a different question) that growth and the reduction of absolute poverty must be, or are likely to be, competing objectives.

The practical bearing of Fields' supposition that per capita growth *will* always tend to reduce poverty *unless* it is of the *modern-sector-enrichment* type may perhaps be seen in the following way. An increase in income that is registered simply because of a natural-resource bonanza with little direct (first-round) positive employment effect will do little to draw workers into the modern sector and to that extent will constitute *modern-sector enrichment* rather than *modern-sector enlargement* and may have little or no positive effect in poverty reduction. Any increase in employment in the resource industry itself will tend to be

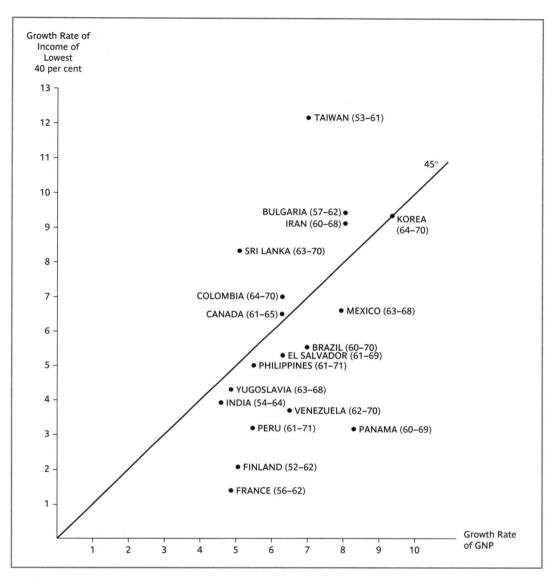

FIGURE 10.3 Growth rate of GNP and of income of lowest 40 per cent: countries and periods indicated
Source: Chenery *et al.* 1974, p. 14. Reproduced by permission.

counterbalanced by a 'Dutch-disease' effect, which in itself will *reduce* modern-sector employment (see Appendix 12.1, available on the Online Learning Centre). However, if the process can be turned into modern-sector *enlargement* through the spending by the recipient (the state itself, at least in part) of the resource rents, especially on projects (such as transport and energy infrastructure) that will be geared to producing growth of other kinds – rather than dispersing the resource rents abroad as personal plunder or hoarding them as reserves – the effect on poverty-reduction may well be positive.

Another possible example of the bearing on poverty of whether growth is concentrated on enrichment or enlargement of the modern sector is provided by the comparison of recent fast growth between India and China. India's spurt in exports has depended heavily on services of back-office type, requiring language, mathematical, and programming skills, but not, in its first-round effects, demanding much unskilled labour. Manufactured exports of comparable value-added, more important relatively in China, have a large appetite for low-skilled workers, drawing surplus labour from the traditional sector, and on the whole increasing the incomes both of those who move and of those who remain. By the late 1990s China had begun to show significantly rising wages in both town and village, suggesting that it had moved out of the 'Lewis' stage (see Chapter 5 and the next section below).

Bearing of poverty on capacity for growth: are there vicious circles?

A further question is whether there are **low-level 'traps'** entailed by low, or at least falling, per capita income nationally or locally, or by absolute poverty beyond a certain extent or intensity, that themselves inhibit economic growth. A 'vicious circle of poverty' model was common in early development-economics thinking, as outlined in Chapter 5. This generally explained the trap by a low or zero rate of net saving (and hence of investment and economic growth) that could be expected with incomes below a certain level. It was one argument for the injection of substantial funds from abroad in order to produce a sufficient once-for-all spurt of growth to turn the vicious circle into a virtuous one.

Subsequent experience has thrown doubt on whether saving rates at the relevant low levels of income are *necessarily* low enough to cause this effect. Microfinance has been held to demonstrate that, with appropriate institutions, even very poor people may consistently save to invest.

However, new forms of vicious-circle argument have recently been put by **Jeffrey Sachs** (2005) and **Paul Collier** (2007), with diagnoses that at least overlap with one another, though the policy implications they draw are not precisely the same.

Sachs's argument (2005, chs 4–7, 10, 12) is applied at both national level (Bolivia in its hyperinflation at the time of the 1980s debt crisis and the collapse of tin prices, and contrasting stories of the treatments of Poland and Russia after the Communist collapse) and local level (the Sauri case outlined below in Chapter 21, Box 21.2). Briefly it is that, when a country or local community has fallen into a sufficiently serious crisis, once-for-all massive help from outside may be necessary to restore it or to stop further deterioration, and failure to provide the help can lead to bad political repercussions locally and even on occasion for the rest of the world. There will often be critical blockages to growth that need to be identified. Removing them within a locality may involve directly humanitarian action such as measures to increase food production and to protect against disease. In those circumstances such assistance with basic needs will itself be a path to economic growth.

Concentrating attention on those poor countries, mainly in Africa, that have stagnant or falling mean income, Collier also explains their plight by expounding various 'traps' that interact negatively with unchanging or increasing poverty and with each other. Those traps most obviously aggravated by poverty and also contributing to it are what he calls the 'conflict trap' and bad government. The implication is that, without some route to significant growth, conditions are likely to become cumulatively worse. Financial or technical aid from abroad may sometimes help but is not always the only or most relevant escape hatch. Natural-resource bonanzas may be more problem than solution because of Dutch-disease effects and because of their propensity to encourage bad government and civil conflict. Sometimes military intervention, possibly in the shape of UN peacekeeping forces, may represent an effective, and the most efficient, way out (Collier, Chauvet and Hegre, 2008; as reported in the *Economist*, 17/5/2008, p. 77).

Implications for poverty of the functional distribution of income

The *functional distribution of income* refers to income's distribution among factors of production (generally before taxes and transfers). The factors of production are commonly simplified for analytical purposes into three or four: *land, labour,* and *capital*, with *human capital* commonly a fourth. In a market economy – such as those of most developing countries now broadly are, at least as concerns their poorer citizens, who are mostly outside *public-sector* employment – returns per unit to the various factors will be determined (other things being equal) by their relative scarcity. The larger the unskilled labour force is in relation to endowments of the other factors, the lower the unskilled wage will tend to be. The 'unskilled wage' in this sense covers not only the rates of pay of those whose only source of income is unskilled wage-work. It includes the part of the income of anyone – self-employed farm family, small-business operator, independent service worker – that is attributable to unskilled work. Income from unskilled or low-skilled labour is liable to play a large part in the incomes of the very poor.

In the logic of the functional distribution of income, policy to increase the gross (i.e., before-tax-and-transfer) income of the very poor can be expected to be largely dependent on *either* transferring to the poor possession of larger shares of the other factors (land, capital and skills) *or* increasing the economy's stocks of the other factors in relation to that of unskilled labour.

In economies that fit the general description of the Lewis model (see Chapter 5), the story is complicated by the existence of 'unlimited supplies of labour' in the traditional sector, that is of labour surplus to the needs of existing production. Increasing the stocks of other factors will then not render unskilled labour 'scarce' (and so raise its return per unit) *until the surplus labour has been drawn into the modern sector*.

As a result of taxes and transfers, the final distribution of *disposable* income in the non-state sector may differ from that determined by relative factor scarcity. The *pattern* of taxation – how it bears differentially on rich and poor – can make a difference. Indirect taxes are likely to bear more severely on the poor than income taxes, which can be tempered to ability to pay and are likely, even if only for administrative reasons, to exempt the very poor. However, deliberate redistribution of cash income through transfers has been thought difficult to manage fairly and efficiently in these countries, and until recently has rarely been tried to any serious extent. (How it can be attempted to a limited degree is discussed below under 'Social safety-nets'.)

Regulating wage levels with a view to increasing them is at best questionable. If it succeeded in raising the level of the wages paid, this would be quite likely to reduce wage-employment in the 'formal' (regulated) sector unless (a) wages had previously been kept low through monopsony power or some form of bondage or (b) the country happened to be in the fortunate situation in which it could safely at the same time expand total demand by macroeconomic means. In the absence of either (a) or (b), it might still be the case that the regulation increased the *share of total income* going to wages. But, even if that were so, it could still be expected to move some workers out of the formal economy, either to no work at all or into the informal sector. Any informal-sector work into which they transferred would presumably be less desirable than the work from which they had been moved; otherwise they would already have chosen it in preference. Also, the movement itself would tend to reduce the returns to work in the informal sector, a change likely to be adverse for the poor.

Except in the special circumstances mentioned, it is likely that at least *some* workers would be impoverished by attempts to raise wages by regulation. This presents a dilemma for policy. How far *should* working conditions be regulated, even in the interests of workers' health and safety, when the regulation, by raising costs, is quite likely to reduce modern-sector employment? There will be gainers and losers from any rules imposed. Whatever compromise is chosen, there will probably be narrow limits at best within which poverty can be reduced by regulating wages upward. It is quite possible that the one-dollar or two-dollar absolute-poverty headcount might be increased.

So the functional distribution itself may appear resistant, except in the rather long term over which extensive investment is possible, to moves that might be made by government policy.

However, beside undertaking and encouraging investment that will increase the endowments of 'physical' and human capital in relation to that of unskilled labour, policy may also encourage (or at least not discourage) the pattern of demand to shift toward more intrinsically labour-intensive goods. For low-wage countries this shift can often be promoted by opening the economy to more uninhibited overseas trade, which will often favour more-labour-intensive exports and less-labour-intensive imports, moving the low-wage economy's *production* in a labour-intensive direction, which in that case would also be the general direction of its comparative advantage. Government may also in some degree tilt public-sector expenditure in a labour-using direction, and it may for the same purpose remove any internal subsidy or privilege (as on the import of capital goods or the use of fuel) that would increase the incentives for substituting other factors for labour. Opening to inward direct investment will also tend to bring technical and managerial skills and know-how. These, even if they are not transferred to the local population (as some surely will be), still contribute to current national income and to raising the unit returns to unskilled labour.

A further possibility of acting in an equalizing direction on the distribution of pre-tax incomes is to redistribute the ownership or usage-rights of productive assets, notably land (as in the radical land reforms of Japan and Taiwan after the Second World War), and also to redistribute the shares of skills among households by reducing the preferential access that richer families may otherwise have to acquiring them.

So, even if it is the case that there are no realistic opportunities for extensive cash transfers to the very poor, other routes are potentially open to government policy, even in the relatively short term, for reducing the extent and depth of absolute income-poverty.

Incidentally, *if there are no realistic opportunities* for cash transfers relevant in size to the extreme-poverty gaps, this, for all but the lowest-income countries, would appear to be primarily *for administrative and political reasons* rather than because it would make unreasonable demands on the richer sections of the countries' populations, let alone on the richer part of the world. The figures given in Tables 10.3 and 10.4 in Appendix 10.1 (available on the Online Learning Centre) put the scale of sacrifice that might be required from the rest of the community in context.[4] In some middle-income countries, they imply,

---

[4] These estimates are based on official World Bank publications available up to the 2008 *WDR* available in early 2008. The lack, at the time of going to press, of new poverty headcounts across the board based on the 2005 price survey precluded a consistently revised version. However, it can be inferred from the bigger numbers in extreme poverty *and* the ratios of market to PPP exchange-rates listed or inferrable from *WDR* 2008, pp. 334–5, and *WDI* 2008, pp. 8–9, that there would clearly be much bigger foreign-exchange transfers required than supposed in the table for India, Bangladesh and Ethiopia, and somewhat bigger at least for Pakistan, so that the conclusions drawn in the text for those countries, from Table 10.4 at least, are almost certainly too optimistic; while this may not be true for Nigeria, Kenya, Brazil and Mexico, where the change in the relationship between the exchange-rates (PPP as compared with official) would in itself be favourable.

the cost for say the richest fifth of the countries' populations for clearing their one-dollar-poverty entirely would be utterly trivial. Even for some of the low-income countries the cost would not be inordinate, and for the rich world eliminating one-dollar poverty from all the low-income countries might require only say tripling Official Development Assistance from its current level.[5] We stress that these calculations are hypothetical – but in many cases only because of the administrative and political difficulties, not because they would make extravagant demands on the rich in low- and middle-income countries or on the rich world.

However, the political and administrative difficulty of attacking poverty by this route turns our attention to direct action on *public* facilities and programmes for health, education, water, sewerage, and the rest. Some of these have a *public-good* character and are necessarily enjoyed by all if they are provided at all. Others, though not intrinsically public-goods, *may be* treated as merit goods and laid open to all without charge or means test. In either of these cases, such provisions avoid the administrative problems of benefits designed to be confined to the poor. Some of them, by increasing human capital and spreading it more widely, may not only contribute to economic growth, as suggested in the next section, but also increase differentially the productive assets in the hands of the poor.

Nevertheless, consideration of the realities determining the functional distribution calls attention to an ultimate limitation. Despite the various ways mentioned here by which poverty might be reduced by redistributing assets or giving production a more labour-intensive cast, we probably have to recognise that general affluence of the degree achieved by Taiwan and South Korea will be impossible without prolonged public and private investment in direct production, physical infrastructure and skills, so that income and output grow at a rate sufficient eventually to render unskilled labour increasingly scarce. Some patterns of production rather than others will help the process along and reduce the time or the volume of investment needed to reach any degree of affluence. Expanded basic-needs provision of public and merit goods can make the intervening period more tolerable for the poor, but, without the investment in capital assets and skills that is fast enough first to mop up surplus labour and then to keep progressively 'farther ahead' of the growth of the workforce, the elusive affluence cannot be attained.

Factors related to poverty not caught in household figures

Absolute-poverty figures used here and in many of the sources count by household. This may leave out of account inequalities that affect the poverty *within households* related to age and gender. The disadvantageous position of women and girls in a number of cultures, and the objections to it not only for its own sake but also because it may well go with a waste of productive resources, are discussed in Chapter 15.

Another element that may escape attention is the differential poverty experienced by certain ethnic or caste groups because of prejudice against them, which may well, as with traditional limitations on women, be productively wasteful as well as bad in itself. There may be vicious circles that will tend to keep the disadvantaged down by denying them channels by which they might otherwise advance their skills and experience.

---

[5] Possibly multiplying by five might be more realistic given the revised PPPs.

The big policy question: priority for growth-targeted *versus* poverty-targeted intervention

'Growth with equity'; 'redistribution with growth'

What is clearly desirable, if a way can be found to do it, is to pursue growth by means that also entail equitable redistribution and poverty-reduction. The concept of **redistribution with growth** is attributed to **Hans Singer** in the course of work on the ILO mission to Kenya in 1971. The term is the title of a book by **Hollis Chenery, Montek Ahluwalia** and others (1974), setting out to re-orient the framework of planning for growth so that the benefits should be differentially distributed toward the poorer. By the late 1970s Taiwan and South Korea seemed to be star examples of how rapid growth could be combined with low Gini coefficients and persisting or even increasingly large shares of total income for the lowest 40 per cent of earners. *Growth with Equity: the Taiwan Case* by **John Fei, Gustav Ranis, and ShirleyW.Y.Kuo** (1979) gave this process a name and set out to explore it.

BOX 10.3 IMPORTANCE OF LAND REFORM TO INCOME DISTRIBUTION IN TAIWAN

'The land reform that government instituted between 1949 and 1953 probably was the most important factor in improving the distribution of income before the beginning of the subphase of export substitution in the early 1960s. Although much of the reform took place before 1952, the year for which sample data on the distribution of income first exist, it continued to have its impact well into the 1950s . . . .

'The first step taken to promote agricultural incentives and output was to reduce farm rents and thereby to increase the share of tenant farmers in farm yields. Promulgated in 1949, this program had five basic provisions: first, farm rents could be fixed at no more than 37.5 per cent of the anticipated annual yield of the main crops; second, if crops failed because of natural forces, tenant farmers could apply to farm-tenancy committees for a further reduction; third, tenant farmers no longer had to pay their rent in advance; fourthly, written contracts and fixed leases of three to six years had to be registered; fifth, tenants had the first option to purchase land from its owners. The reform affected about 43 per cent of the 660 000 farm families, 75 per cent of the 410 000 part-owners and tenants, and 40 per cent of the 650 000 hectares of private farmland. Prices of farmland immediately dropped . . . . Equally important, the requirement for written contracts and the fixing of standard reduced rents enabled tenants to benefit from their own increased efforts for the first time. . . . With higher yields and lower rents, the average income of tenant farmers rose by 81 per cent between 1949 and 1952 . . . .

'Given the success of the program to reduce farm rents, government decided to accelerate the program . . . to sell public land to tenant holders . . . In all 35 per cent of Taiwan's public land was sold during 1948–53; 43 per cent during 1953–58.

'. . . The stage was set for the most dramatic component of the three-pronged package: the compulsory sale of land by landlords . . . . Privately owned land in excess of specified amounts per landowner had to be sold to government, which would resell that land to tenants. The purchase price was set at 2.5 times the annual yield of the main crops.'

Source: J.C.B. Fei, G. Ranis and Shirley W.Y. Kuo, *Growth with Equity: the Taiwan case*, Oxford University Press for the World Bank, New York, 1979, pp. 38, 40.

▶ The authors indicate that the point of selling landowners' land was both to stimulate greater effort of the part of the former-tenant owners, and also to encourage landlords to participate in industrial development. They record that tenant households acquired 16.4 per cent of the total area cultivated in Taiwan during 1951–55 (p. 41). They show how the tenure pattern and size distribution of holdings shifted, and also how the functional distribution of agricultural income changed from 1941 when the island was under Japanese control and the income shares of land, capital and labour were 52.20, 11.48 and 36.32 percent, to 1956 when the shares were 36.28, 7.98 and 55.74 per cent (p. 44).

The Chenery team proposed that planning for growth should separate the effects of particular measures according to their impacts on people at various income levels in the population and on groups otherwise defined as particularly poor such as landless rural labourers. We have mentioned their distribution-weighted growth estimates. Their own cross-sectional analysis of the impact of a number of variables separated national income into three parts: earned by respectively the lowest 40 per cent, the next lowest, and the top 20 per cent. They found for example that the extent of primary schooling was *positively* related to the income share of the lowest 40 per cent; the population growth rate, *negatively*; and the overall per capita growth rate, *positively*. Each of these three findings suggested at least that there need be *no conflict* between growth and poverty reduction (relative as well as absolute).

However, a well-known scatter diagram of overall growth rates against growth rates of income of the lowest 40 per cent (Chenery *et al.*, 1974, p. 14, reproduced here by permission as Figure 10.3, p. 263) for 18 developed and developing countries over various periods suggests to casual inspection little if any relationship between the two, with overall growth rates ranging from about 4 to 9 per cent but growth rates of the income of the poor ranging from 1 to 12 per cent. South Korea (1964–70) has the same rate (about 8.5 per cent) for both variables, and Taiwan (1953–61) 7 per cent for overall growth and 12 per cent for that of the poor. The Taiwan pattern suggests that some important influence other than overall growth had affected the incomes of the poor in that period, even, as Fei *et al.* point out, before the 'turning-point' out of the 'Lewis stage', and (see Box 10.3) they find this influence in the radical land reform. In any case the experiences of both countries certainly confirm the interpretation that there is no *necessary* conflict of priorities between growth and poverty reduction.

Strategies of 'growth-led' and 'support-led security' and 'unaimed opulence'

Drèze and Sen (1995, pp. 34–6), distinguish three policy approaches bearing on what they call 'endemic undernourishment and deprivation': namely *'growth-led security'*, *'support-led security'*, and *'unaimed opulence'*. At the time they wrote (actually in the *early* 1990s), these were typified respectively in their view by South Korea; by Sri Lanka and China (with Chile, Costa Rica, Jamaica, Cuba also mentioned); and by Brazil. (They did of course recognize the extraordinary aberrations in China at times during the Mao period; and on the other hand it is possible that they might have put China into the growth-led category if they had been writing ten years later. A few years later again, and they might also have reclassified Brazil into that category.)

They distinguish the first two types by the *priority in time* assigned to growth promotion as against direct welfare and redistribution measures, rather than by any suggestion of fundamental conflict between growth on the one hand and contemporary poverty-reduction on the other. Growth-led policy does require in addition deliberate attention to poverty if it is to serve the purpose of enhancing human security, but by definition it also gives high priority to growth from the first, whereas support-led security leads with directly poverty-reducing interventions. The 'unaimed-opulence' strategy, attributed at the time to Brazil, relies wholly on economic growth, giving no particular attention to poverty in its selection of policies.

The **growth-with-equity** approach, as described by Fei, Ranis, and Kuo (1979) in their account of Taiwan, however, is not simply growth policy tempered by poverty-reducing interventions. As they see it, what Taiwan had chosen was a growth policy with an equalizing cast written into it throughout. Their most important policy conclusion, as they present it (p. 310) is that:

> It is possible for economic growth to be compatible with an improved distribution of income during every phase of the transition from colonialism to modern growth.

The success of Taiwan in this respect they attribute in part to features of its post-1945 endowment, such as a good rural transport network, but also to the right policies. If we interpret the authors aright, these allowed Taiwan to reallocate resources so as to make use of its endowments while at the same time, and often through the same policies, changing the distribution of income in an equalizing direction. Rural industrialization, promoted by avoiding policies that would positively have encouraged urban concentration, served both purposes; so did the country's abandonment of the promotion of first-stage import-substitution. In place of this Taiwan moved to the export-orientation which, from around 1960, allowed a rapid expansion of labour-intensive manufactured exports.

Fields, drawing on Ranis, identifies four strategies as responsible for Taiwan's success: strategies for *decentralized development*; for *balanced rural development* (expansion of non-agricultural rural industries); to do with *industry and trade* (open economy and export-promotion); and for *human-resource development* (1980, pp. 234–7). (Reference is made in Chapters 14 and 16 of this book to the conflict of opinion over the relative priorities to be given to rural against urban development.)

Fei and colleagues not only recognize the importance in income equalization of the *radical redistributive land reform* that the island underwent in the early 1950s (pp. 314–15). They also highlight the fact that the economy reached a *'turning-point'* around 1968, when urban wage levels began to rise consistently, imparting an equalizing tendency to the urban sector as land redistribution and rural industrialization had earlier done for the rural (p. 312). Taiwan's 'growth with equity', which has considerable analogies with South Korea's experience, seems to be a star example of 'growth-supported security' in the classification of Drèze and Sen. The turning-point, at which labour becomes 'scarce', marks an economy's exit from the Lewis world of 'unlimited supplies of labour', giving those with least economic power, provided that they are not brought down by illness or other personal disaster, the prospect of rising absolutely and perhaps also relatively. If a country starts with some degree of fit with the Lewis model and then grows fast enough and in a sufficiently equalizing way to reach the turning-point, there are reasons for thinking that it is on the path to affluence. If it is possible, growth with equity on this pattern has considerable advantages for an initially Lewis-type economy.

However, the argument that can be made for 'support-led security', even when average income is comparatively low and its growth slow, is supported by cases in which poor countries have attained surprisingly high scores on certain welfare indicators. Sri Lanka was particularly notable here, at least until about 1990. Writing around then Sudhir Anand and Ravi Kanbur (1995) presented the case:

The life expectancy at birth of a Sri Lankan is almost 70 years, which is a figure approaching that found in industrial market economies, and much higher than that typical of developing countries at similar or even higher levels of per capita income. Infant mortality rates in Sri Lanka are below 40 per 1,000 live births . . . Literacy rates are at 80 per cent or more, compared with the developing countries' average of around 50 per cent.

(p. 298)

Sri Lanka's pre-eminence in these respects has not been quite so clear in the early 2000s, as shown in Tables 10.1 and 10.2, though child mortality is still strikingly low and literacy now close to 100 per cent. Poverty headcounts and gaps are also low compared with other South Asian countries of similar income. From the perspective of the earlier date, Anand and Kanbur conclude that 'purposive and directed intervention has had considerable effects on health and education standards both in the early part of the century and in the period after independence'; and moreover, from econometric analysis, that 'income growth alone would not have achieved for Sri Lanka its enviable basic needs record' (p. 329). The comparatively slow growth that might be associated with a support-led-security strategy need not inhibit interventions that considerably improve living conditions for the relatively poor. (If, as Sachs suggests, the welfare-enhancing interventions can be chosen so as themselves to form a path to growth, so much the better.) For other examples of striking 'human-development' achievements, even in a low-income state or under potentially disastrous crop failure, see Box 10.4.

BOX 10.4 FAMINE? WHAT FAMINE?

From the experience of four African countries in the crop failures of 1983–84, Drèze (1995) gives striking evidence showing how human welfare can be safeguarded when the will and the understanding are there. These were the crop failures that affected much of the continent and presented the rest of the world with the horrifying famine pictures from Ethiopia. Yet the four countries – Kenya, Cape Verde, Botswana, and Zimbabwe, one with low income, the other three low-middle – were able to prevent famine deaths or even *reduce* mortality, and to maintain, or in one case (Cape Verde) actually improve, nutrition, even though the four concerned suffered *greater proportional foodcrop reductions* (at least *three times* as great in two of the cases) than Ethiopia and Sudan, where famine deaths were numerous (p. 563).

A further well-known example of important aspects of human welfare preserved in conditions of poverty is Kerala, one of the poorer Indian States, where some social indicators approach First World levels. Kerala's under-five mortality rate in 2000 was 19 per 1000 (contrasting with India, 95; and Uttar Pradesh [UP], the largest State, 123). Its percentage of children receiving all vaccinations was 80 (India, 42; UP, 21); percentage of births attended by a health professional, 94 (India, 42; UP, 22). No doubt as a result in large part of such differences, giving much higher probability of any child's surviving, Kerala's total fertility rate ('expected' births per woman over her lifetime at current age-specific rates[6]) was as low as 2.0 (India, 2.9; UP, 4.0), a figure comparable with that of the US or New Zealand and consistent in the long term with a stable and even slightly falling population (UNDP, 2005, p. 30).

---

[6] Concepts explained in Chapter 13.

It seems that nationally or regionally low income does not preclude important aspects of social provision.

Conversely, it is also the case that reliance cannot be placed on fast economic growth or a relatively high level of income *per se* for quick elimination of income-poverty and adequate social provision. South Africa, an upper-middle-income country, admittedly at the time extremely affected by AIDS, had in 2003 a life-expectancy at birth of 48.4 years, comparable to those of low-income Kenya, Nigeria, and Ethiopia. Its under-five death rate of 66 per 1000 live births was comparable to that of Bangladesh (see Table 10.2).

Above we have not disputed Fields' view that growth – other than of a kind that is solely 'modern-sector-enriching' such as that based on natural-resource proceeds that are purloined or squandered – can be expected to reduce poverty; but to what extent and how fast?

Growth of income might, as we have seen, act to increase or reduce *inequality* or leave the shape of income-distribution unchanged; but *prevailing rates of growth* in a number of countries *on their own* (without a change in distribution at the same time) would take an awfully long time to eliminate extreme poverty. Projecting the impact of growth in itself on absolute poverty on the simplifying assumption that the existing *distribution* would remain, Ravi Kanbur (1991, p. 144) estimated how many years of income-per-capita growth at the rate achieved over the years 1965–84 it would take to raise the *average* less-than-one-dollar-poor person in each of nine Latin American countries over that one-dollar-poverty line. Apart from Chile and Peru, which had shown *negative* per capita growth over 1965–84, and where the answer was therefore infinity, the number of years ranged from 14 in Brazil and 17 in Mexico to 98 in Argentina and 143 in Honduras. Even doubling the rate of growth would only halve the time. Remember this would be enough to raise only the *average* extremely poor person above the line, not by any means everyone currently below it.

'Unaimed opulence' as a policy and objective, it would seem to follow, cannot be relied on to bring a timely solution to poverty.

Unless there was reason to believe that growth in the particular case would of itself have a redistributive cast, *faster* reduction of income-poverty than could be expected to follow from maintaining a constant distribution of income as income grew would demand either that such a cast should be *introduced by policy to the growth process* or that there should be *direct welfare-oriented intervention*. As one possibility for such recasting, redistribution of assets across households, which could include not only land reform but also policies on human capital – training and education – that opened opportunities widely so as to help neutralize the advantages flowing from privileged family income, might be designed to promote both growth and equalization – to that extent speeding poverty reduction beyond the rate that would be set by aggregate growth in the absence of redistribution.

Furthermore it is clear that raising minimal welfare standards in water, sanitation, health, and education, and promoting improved food production, will to a large extent require government action and public spending. Higher income all round will certainly make this easier but will not guarantee it. At the same time – provided the economy is given its head – much of this welfare improvement will itself *contribute to* economic growth, even if only in the longer term. It will not be generally competitive with growth-promotion. However, *at any one time*, it may of course be competitive with *particular valid means* of growth-promotion, such as improvement of transport, power, and communication infrastructure.

To summarize a much-qualified position:

- Effective poverty-reduction with equalizing policies and moderately high human-development standards, even in low-income countries and regions, are not necessarily impossible or indeed unknown, and suitable actions to this end are not inconsistent with economic growth.

- Relatively high income or rapid growth does not necessarily produce high levels of basic-needs provision and human development, though, given the will, it makes their achievement through appropriate policies easier.

- Growth of any significant magnitude with built-in equalization requires policy combinations designed to make full use of endowments of unskilled labour and opportunities of human-capital development.

- Resting content with negative or even zero per capita growth is risky because of its propensity to lead subsequently, through civil conflict or corrupt government or both, to *progressively* worsening conditions, including very probably increasing poverty.

- Public action to improve basic-needs provision and human development is not in general competitive with economic-growth promotion but at any one time may be competitive with particular forms of it, so that priorities may have to be set implying judgements of, among other things, time-preference.

- Though policies shifting allocation in an efficient and labour-using direction may facilitate both economic growth and equalization, and attention to basic-needs provision through public facilities may at the same time greatly ameliorate the welfare of the poor, the attainment of secure affluence by modern standards from low or low-middle income will require a sufficient rate of public and private investment over a sufficiently long period first to use up 'surplus' labour and then to make labour increasingly 'scarce'.

The policy message is then *both* to move progressively into poverty reduction (basic needs and a bias to equalization, safety-nets if possible) *and* to remove impediments to growth, but to seek out ways that reduce any conflict between these objectives and measures and that have the effect of serving both.

Famines and their prevention and alleviation

A **famine** can be said to exist if large numbers of people simultaneously have so little access to food that their lives are threatened. Deaths from famine, however, commonly arise from diseases brought on by severe malnutrition, not necessarily from sheer starvation. A famine in this sense needs to be distinguished from a **crop failure**, however serious, which may or may not lead to famine. It also needs to be distinguished from **chronic hunger and malnutrition**, a much more difficult problem for a reasonably organized and well-motivated government to eliminate.

Much of what applies to famines applies to the **aftermaths of natural disasters** such as floods, cyclones, and earthquakes. In the latter cases the causal events will probably be more difficult to foresee and hence onset of the human damage will be more sudden; the kinds of urgent and extraordinary need will be more varied (shelter and water perhaps as well as food); but on the other hand those in serious need may be easier to identify.

Economic analysis of famines, extending to food deficiency generally, largely began with **Amartya Sen** in the mid-1970s. He is famous for the judgement that famines do not happen in democracies with a free press. This typified his starting-point: **famines are not natural events; they are social phenomena that have to be explained and combated by social arrangements**.

Famines recurred in pre-independence India, culminating in the Great Bengal Famine of 1943–4, in which *millions* died. There have been none in post-independence India: plenty of hunger and malnutrition, plenty of crop failures, but no famines. This is not because the climate has changed for the better. The main reason, in Sen's view, is changed political and social institutions.

China had its last serious famine in the 'Great Leap Forward' time of 1959–61, in which *tens of millions* died. Another remotely similar event is not expected because the extraordinary political conditions of the time are not likely to return. But famines have been still regrettably common in sub-Saharan Africa.

The key concept in Sen's account of famines is **entitlement**.

Famines occur when large numbers of people lose their entitlements to food. A loss of entitlements means in the extreme that people have *neither* food produced by themselves *nor* money or other assets with which they can buy it. There may or may not be less food around than normally, though a famine *is usually* precipitated by a crop failure. But, *if people had enough money and enough warning*, they could buy food from other localities or from abroad. On the other hand – even though there may be as much food grown as normal and importing it may be no more costly than before – if, because of economic disruption or civil conflict, large numbers of people lose their jobs and consequently their incomes, or much trading activity becomes impossible, there may, in the absence of radical government intervention, be no peaceful way in which the people who need it can get their hands on the food.

Why do famines, as Sen repeatedly reminds the world, *not* generally occur in democracies with a free and independent press? On the assumption that the generalization is true, the reason is surely something like this: that the onset or threat of famine becomes widely known and discussed; those likely to be affected complain; the press takes it up; and elected politicians take action to see that essential entitlements are maintained or restored.

How can famines be prevented?

First there is preparation against the possibility of crop failure. **Early-warning systems** of abnormal weather can be and have been set up, though they are by no means infallible. What is essential is that there should be **stocks of basic foods**: stocks continually 'turned over' and sufficient to cover the period from the time when shortages begin to be observed to when extra supplies ordered then can be brought in from other areas in the country or from abroad. The supply of food needs to be adequate to meet basic needs. The necessary stocks and emergency supplies have to be procured, or at least backstopped, by government action. Where collapse of food supply or distribution is possible, it is also important that **administrative arrangements are in place** for dealing with it promptly when it arises.

What *then* needs to be done is to see that people have the resources, the **entitlements**, to buy the food. Those in need may be farmers producing wholly or largely for their own needs, whom a crop failure will deprive of their income. Then there will be agricultural labourers who have lost their employment if there is no harvest work to be done, and the farmers who would normally pay them have no income or motive for doing so. There may be others in industries that depend on agriculture who are similarly deprived; and, with a general fall of purchasing power, the range of affected industries may extend widely.

As far as possible, the state should aspire to **keep up the general level of purchasing-power** through its macro-policy, as well as that of the groups whose well-being and survival is most affected. A standing system of **stabilization planning** as discussed later in Chapter 12 may be needed in advance to make this possible. The more nearly the general level of spending is maintained, the more the ranks of those severely affected or at risk and in need of extraordinary help will be reduced.

What is definitely *counterproductive* is to *subsidize the staple food generally* in response to the tendency of its market price to rise. Subsidy's first-round effect will be to increase *demand* from those that have purchasing power. It will do nothing for those who have none, and if anything it will discourage any tendency to economize on the part of those who still have enough food. *If there is not a corresponding increase in supply*, the consumer price after subsidy will move back towards its pre-subsidy level. Insofar as the consumer price *is* reduced *without* an increase of supply, the subsidizing authority will be supplementing the incomes of those that have the entitlements to buy food, quite possibly increasing the share of the supply taken by those who have more to spend at the expense of those who have less, and leaving out entirely those who have nothing. If, on the other hand, the supply to the market can be increased to its normal level, with confidence established that the supply can be maintained, this will bring the price down to normal without the need for subsidy. Any subsidy to help deal with the inadequacy of certain people's *entitlements* to food will need to be closely *targeted* on the most needy if it is to be serve its purpose, just as any increase in market supply will need to be *supplemented* by other measures to provide entitlements for those who otherwise would have no purchasing power at all or next to none.

In short, both food supply and entitlements must be adequate if the symptoms of famine are to be avoided.

Also counterproductive in most circumstances (and certainly without other measures) will be *controls on food prices*. They will increase the opportunities for persecution and extortion to be practised on traders and will risk destroying the public markets and hence any efficient and reliable access for consumers to the food that there is. During whatever period supplies to the market cannot be restored – while at the same time the authorities themselves may well need to make claims on the limited supply, or else distribute claims on it, for the sake of feeding those who are really destitute – **the market-price must be allowed to rise**. This will encourage economy on the part of those that are above the level of subsistence and will give incentives for supplies to move in from less badly hit areas or from abroad.

On similar grounds *restrictions* imposed by states or districts *on movements of food* will aggravate problems in the worst affected areas. There will of course be gainers as well as losers from such restrictions, but on the reasonable value-judgement that the poorest have the most urgent claims – the highest welfare weightings at the margin – free flow will generate net gain. Ethiopia in 1984 was one of the instances in which food movement had been arbitrarily blocked.

This does not for a moment imply that everything must be left to the market. When significant numbers of people – beyond the likely capacity of charity and informal arrangements to cover – are threatened, the state must step in, not only ensuring that, as far as possible, supplies are minimally adequate but also with feeding programmes, food supplements, coupons, or cash, for those in most need. Similar problems arise to those discussed in the next section on 'Social safety-nets'. Ways have to be found of identifying those in serious need and excluding others.

One way of doing this is **category-targeting**: directing food staples or nutritional supplements to an easily identified category who collectively have a particular claim, such as young children and pregnant and nursing mothers, for whom the shortage of food is likely to have the most serious long-term consequences. Such programmes seem to explain why sometimes nutritional status in the most vulnerable groups *improves* in famines or threats thereof, as mentioned above for Cape Verde in 1983–4.

Another is to require work to be done on **labour-intensive public projects at subsistence wages** for those people who appear able-bodied. Because it commits the workers' time to the programme, this sifts out from support those who might expect to be able to provide for themselves through the informal sector (Chu and Gupta, 1998, p. 17). It is also held to have the advantage of preventing the emergence of a habit of dependency and preserving self-respect, which is often valued by the beneficiaries themselves; and, of course, if proper preparation is made in advance to provide against the need for work programmes, they can do things of local or wider use, such as maintaining local roads, irrigation, soil conservation, and tree planting. Always invoked as a successful example is the Maharashtra Employment Guarantee Scheme in India in 1972–3 and again in the early 1980s. Chu and Gupta (1998, p. 31) mention a similar scheme as preventing famine in Bangladesh in 1988, and relate that the African successes mentioned above in the crop failures of 1983–4, as in Cape Verde and Botswana, also used targeted public works. An example from the US (Friedman, 2007) is of the Civilian Conservation Corps and the Works Progress Administration, set up in 1933, which directly provided work for 8 million people rendered unemployed in the Great Depression, and created a number of public buildings and other great public projects still in use seventy years later.

Drèze and Sen (1989, p. 137) give three elements of the successful responses mentioned in Box 10.4 to food shortage in Cape Verde, a country that is physically especially vulnerable to collapses of supply. These are 'a competent and **planned use of food aid**', with the food supply sold in open market and the proceeds going into a National Development Fund which helps finance the other elements; '**labour-intensive public works programmes** with a "development" orientation'; and '**unconditional relief . . . to particularly vulnerable groups** such as pregnant women, undernourished children, the elderly, and the invalid' *[emphasis ours]*. The same authors cite testimony to the genuine value of the public works performed, and they give evidence (p. 138) of striking *improvements* in the nutritional status of children as measured from 1977, soon after Cape Verde's independence, to the 'famine' year of 1984. (There were similar improvements in the nutritional status of children in Britain during the Second World War, when limitations in the general food supply were met with both rationing – to make sure everyone got a share – and regulations aimed at increasing the nutritional status of some basic foods.)

A further lesson from bitter experience, such as that of Ethiopia in the 1980s, is that as far as possible food should be moved to people rather than people to food. For already weakened people to walk over long distances and assemble with huge numbers of others, also weak and many already sick, is a lethal recipe. Only the worst policy failures and delays are likely to make this concentration of feeding centres necessary.

In general what seems to be needed is a combination of prompt and well-prepared *government* action; no arbitrary blockage to adjustments made by *the market*; and reliance for certain purposes, especially for help with fair distribution, on *civil society*.

International help, bilateral and multilateral, provides a further backstop in the case of famines and natural disasters. The UN World Food Program has access to stocks of staple foods. The UN has a Central Emergency Response Fund, a renamed provision greatly enlarged after the year of disasters in 2005, though still only big enough to make a *contribution* financially in the case of major calamities; but the UN can also play a vital role as a *co-ordinator* of relief activities.

Social safety-nets

The idea of a social safety-net has two related connotations. One is a protection against adverse change, a device to reduce risk, the purpose to which private insurance is directed. The other is a system of supports to bring everyone up to some minimum standard of material well-being. In practice the two cannot be readily distinguished. Either one provided by the state conveys elements of the other. We are concerned here with people in developing countries for whom any form of *private* insurance is likely to be out of the question. They consider themselves too poor to buy insurance and probably they would not in any case be considered insurable by those who purvey insurance policies. So we are concerned with *social* safety-nets: those provided by 'the community', namely the state, possibly with some input from civil society.

A number of developing countries have 'social-insurance' schemes, but usually for relatively privileged workers in the public sector, to provide retirement income and benefits in the case of illness or premature incapacity. These are framed like private insurance, at least to the extent of having contributions from the insured people and their employers, though there is often a degree of state subsidization as well. Access to these schemes can be important benefits attached to certain forms of employment. They allow risks to be spread and also help in the spreading of disposable income over time. Here we consider safety-nets only for those who fall outside the range of these privileges.

One component of the security aspect of safety-nets can be provided by stabilization of the macro-economy. Benefits may also be given to workers who lose their means of livelihood as a result of policy changes such as the removal of trade protection. These latter have been advocated in IMF publications as facilitators of efficiency-directed economic reform in that they are expected to reduce political opposition to it. They have been provided in the US, for example, where other safety-net provisions provide less of a cushion against personal disaster than in most other rich countries. They have the awkward feature for policy that they have to be framed to some extent *ad hoc*.

We concentrate here on the forms of safety-net that are in some places, or might be, provided routinely in developing countries. 'Developing countries' here includes middle-income, even upper-middle-income countries, among which are a number of 'transition countries': former members or satellites of the Soviet Union, and a few others that have moved from systems of planning and centralized economic control toward greater market-orientation. These have often kept a form of the social-security provisions inherited from their ostensibly Marxist pasts. They may provide models that other middle-income countries can follow.

However, setting these models from 'transitional' countries aside, we are faced with the possibilities of three ways in which state support to individual poor households may be given: in cash; as goods in kind or coupons that allow goods of particular kinds (food, for example) to be bought; and in the form of free or highly subsidized access to public services such as schools or clinics.

The potential dilemma of safety-net provisions directed at the poor is the same one we have mentioned in connection with famine relief: to include all those regarded as needy for this purpose and to exclude others.

If the intention with certain health and education facilities is in any case to make them free for all (as is the case with Uganda and Kenya, for example, over primary schooling), their provision without charge avoids this dilemma.

On the other hand, where there must be a means test to fulfil the purpose of the support without excessive expense, there are real difficulties in reliably determining eligibility in any society, rich or poor, but especially where much income may be in non-cash form, where it is irregular, where record-keeping is not a common habit, and where the bureaucracy may be mediocre. The devices used must often be compromises, excluding some of the targeted poor or including some of the non-poor, or both. To this end, some performance conditions may be imposed on the benefits, or their use may be restricted in various ways.

'Category-targeting', mentioned above with reference to famine relief, is one compromise. Food supplements or standard food may be provided for children, or for children who on objective signs are malnourished, and for pregnant and nursing mothers, and perhaps also for old people living alone or serving as principal earners for their households.

Where improving nutrition is an important objective, an ostensibly poor family may either be given nutritious foods directly or be given coupons that can be exchanged for food, or for certain kinds of food, alone. The coupon method (and cash even more so) can be regarded as more efficient in the traditional economic sense than food provided in kind in that it gives the recipient greater choice, but by the same token coupons may be less reliable (and cash less so again) in directing the benefits to nutrition. However, food given directly may also be traded unless it is provided in prepared form through schools or feeding centres, and the alternative of giving the benefits in the form of food coupons – or, even more so, cash – allows the same result to be realized but much more conveniently. Even if it is the nutrition of children that is in question, it can be questioned whether attempts should be made to constrain the choices of parents in these ways rather than trusting them to decide in their children's interests.

In neither of the last two cases mentioned is there any ready guarantee that the non-poor will be excluded, and judgements of fact may also have to be made over category-targeted benefits; but often the size of any land a family possesses, household composition, the character of their dwellings, and their occupations, may give enough indication. These are situations in which use might well be made of 'civil society' in the form of neighbours, local leadership, or any body representative of the village or commune, to help establish the relevant facts. Such use is made now in Bangladesh for determining who is eligible for rudimentary safety-net payments for the destitute old.

The same use of local institutions might be invoked in the absence of adequate government funding to have *local responsibility accepted for minimal support* of the destitute. Models in which something of the sort happened come from modern China, at least in the intervals and areas of comparative normality between 1962 and the reforms of the 1980s, and from England under the 1601 Poor Law, which remained in force for over 200 years, before giving way to the much less humane 1834 Poor Law associated with the workhouses and fixed in public memory by *Oliver Twist*.

Recent examples

Conditional family allowances

One device, recently applied in Brazil, Mexico, Bolivia and Ecuador, is to make cash payments to apparently poor families with children if they meet certain conditions: in Brazil's case that they can give evidence that the eligible children are attending school and that they are receiving the prescribed immunizations. This means at least that the cash is not given automatically, and it serves two social purposes in addition to that of supplementing the cash income of poor families. In Brazil in 2008 the benefits were reported to being received by 11 million families with children (*Economist*, 19/4/2008, p. 81), probably benefiting around a third of the population. Presumably there is some rough objective test applied over whether a family is poor enough to be eligible, maybe with some advice from neighbours or community leaders.

Cash-for-work schemes

India's National Rural Employment Guarantee Scheme (NREGS), which applied across the country from 2008, allows any rural household to demand up to 100 days' paid employment from the government, or unemployment pay in default. The principle seems to be the same as that used in Indian famine employment: that the work provided with its wage is less attractive than full-time normal work, so that it will not attract workers who can otherwise get full-time employment (*Economist*, 26/4/2008, pp. 71–2). If the workers find it worthwhile to apply on those terms, they are regarded as eligible. However, the report points out that the daily rate in Rajasthan state is above that actually received by regular women farm workers. What degree of safety-net is this? If we can take the minimum daily wage set for the scheme by the central government – 60 rupees, $1.50 at the exchange-rate – as 3.0 times as much in PPP dollars,[7] the daily wage works out at $PPP4.5, which, if the 100 days' pay for one person had to be spread over the whole year, would be just about enough to support one person on the extreme-poverty borderline, assuming that it is currently at $PPP1.25 a day. It is clearly not a family wage on the most meagre estimate, but can probably, as the report says, be a useful supplement capable of carrying farm workers over the slack period between sowing and reaping (ibid.), and better than complete destitution. The cost was originally projected at $11 billion a year, but is thought likely to be more like $6 billion, given failings in implementation. A World Bank simulation purports to show that more workers would be removed from poverty if the government simply handed them the cash (ibid.). However, that supposes some practicable rule could be devised for allocating the funds. Providing an income floor that *just allows every household to clear* the extreme-poverty line may be judged administratively impossible, and alternatively giving a *'social dividend'* in which *everyone is paid* at that level would surely be judged far too costly. So a cash-for-work scheme, even if some of the work is of doubtful use, may be the least bad practical option.

There are other safety-net-type schemes.[8] It seems likely that the unusual rises across the world in staple-food prices in 2007–8, which may not be a passing phenomenon, or at least may not be *quickly* reversed, and have generated much hardship and unrest, may compel more and more governments to institute safety-net-type schemes or to increase the rationality of the assistance they give, while at the same time of course the fiscal difficulty of making adequate provision is increased.

---

[7] This is the rate of equivalence that can be inferred from figures in the 2008 *World Development Indicators*, which use the revised PPP estimates arising from the 2005 price survey. They give an implied ratio of 3.0 (for 2005).

[8] For example, in 1997 the Government of Bangladesh introduced various support programmes for helping the aged poor and destitute women.

Summary conclusions

- Poverty can be seen as *lack of basic needs*, as *lack of basic capacities or capabilities*, as *vulnerability*, or as *unjust deprivation*. The question of *poverty* is inevitably bound up with that of *equity*. To be operational and acceptable, approaches to equity (social justice) in a law-governed society need to represent a compromise between, on the one hand, *equality* and on the other recognition of *pre-existing property rights* to income or assets, at least to the extent of retaining some measure of efficient production incentives.

- Poverty may be assessed either *absolutely* – on criteria that apply across the world – or *relatively* to what is normal or expected in a person's own community. In international comparisons, we are mainly concerned with absolute assessments.

- Comparative measures of the extent and depth of poverty across countries or regions, and ideas of its seriousness, can be derived *either* from the use of poverty lines, each representing a certain amount of income per person per day in a common currency converted at purchasing-power parity (PPP) *or* from objective indicators of various aspects of material welfare. A compromise between the two might be provided by an x-food-calorie-per-day line.

- To compare poverty levels across countries by the **first method**, absolute-poverty lines are conventionally fixed at household incomes per person of US$1 and US$2 per day, with those under US$1 regarded as being in *extreme poverty*. As the assessment is applied by the World Bank, the dollars are reckoned at purchasing-power-parity (PPP), with each 'dollar' representing (until the system was amended around 2008) the amount of local-currency that can buy in the country concerned what a US dollar could buy in the US in 1985, this reckoned to be what US$1.08 could buy in 1993, which would be the equivalent of US$1.45 in 2005. The new system of poverty identification would apparently use as standard the slightly lower figure of US$1.25 a day in 2005 prices. Figures provided routinely for each country are the proportions of the population whose incomes or expenditures fall below each of these lines (the **headcount** representing the *extent* of the degree of poverty concerned); and an estimate (for each line) of the percentage **gap**, summarizing how far those below it fall short of it (the *depth* of the poverty). Extreme poverty in the world on these criteria is heavily concentrated now in South Asia and sub-Saharan Africa, with a large (though fast falling) residue persisting also in China. Across countries headcounts and gaps representing extreme poverty generally increase as we move to countries with lower national income per head, but the relationship is far from consistent.

- Various summary measures can be used to express the degree of income-inequality in a community. For countries at a given per capita income level, the higher the inequality on these measures the greater the poverty tends to be, but again the relationship is not an exact one. No *one* of the *inequality* measures that we use gives a reliable indicator of the extent or depth of poverty (as measured by poverty lines) to be expected from a given level of per capita income.

- The **second way** of assessing poverty and comparing it across populations is to present a number of objective indicators of such characteristics as nutrition, health, longevity, literacy, educational level and opportunities, access to water and sewerage. Again these measures bear a relationship to per capita national income, but again not a consistent one, and countries will rank differently on the different indicators. At any level of income there is clearly great scope for performing much better than the income-norm on any one or a number of them.

- On the impact of growth on equality, one finding, confirmed in a number of studies, though most if not all of cross-sectional kind, is taken to imply an inverted U-curve relationship: that, as per capita income rises, the level of inequality first rises and then falls. Another, arguably consistent with the previous one and based on *a priori* theorizing and some evidence, rests on Fields' differentiation of three types of growth: traditional-sector enriching, modern-sector-enlarging, and modern-sector-enriching. The first and the second reduce poverty. The first reduces inequality and the second may or may not do so, with a greater tendency to reduce inequality beyond a certain point of development, which seems to correspond roughly with the 'turning-point' at which surplus labour has been used up. The third, which is most likely to occur when natural-resource developments are the leading element in the growth, increases inequality and leaves poverty unchanged. Fast economic growth and equalization may proceed together as in Taiwan and South Korea if policy is such as to give the growth an equalizing cast.

- Consideration of the functional distribution of income provides the challenge for poverty reduction of transferring more non-labour assets (such as land, education and skills) into the possession of the poor; or increasing the ratio of non-labour factors to labour in the economy through (physical- or human-capital) investment; or increasing the labour-intensity of production. The last of these might be possible for a low-wage economy through removing obstacles to international trade; removing internal disincentives to the use of labour; or switching the pattern of public-sector procurement in a labour-using direction.

- Though advances in the provision of basic needs may be possible in conditions of zero or very slow growth, allowing income per capita to stagnate or fall risks generating vicious circles in which, for example, poverty leads to civil conflict and bad government, which in turn depress income further.

- Though *economic growth* and *poverty-reduction* are mutually consistent, and in fact the former is likely to lead to the latter or at least facilitate it, there are risks to the timely reduction of poverty in deliberate direction to one of the two without concentrating as well on the other. An emphasis on growth may be susceptible to combining the growth with an equalizing cast, such as may be possible to a low-wage economy through greater openness to foreign trade, and additional and widely dispersed education and training. An emphasis on human development, which in important ways may reduce poverty directly, may emphasize those elements in human development, such as education, public health and nutrition, that particularly favour growth.

- Though policies shifting allocation in an efficient and labour-using direction may facilitate both economic growth and equalization, and attention to basic-needs provision through public facilities may at the same time greatly ameliorate the welfare of the poor, the attainment of affluence will require a rate of public and private investment over a sufficiently long period first to use up 'surplus' labour and then to keep the economy growing fast enough to make labour increasingly 'scarce'.

- Famines, though commonly precipitated by crop failure, should be seen as political-social phenomena, avoidable if the institutions are right, and particularly likely to be avoided with electoral democracy and a free press. Though, in cases of crop failure or other disruption in the food markets, public measures may have to be taken to increase food *supply*, it is also crucial to see that all those at risk have *entitlements* to food, whether provided in cash or kind or in some intermediate form. Each country at risk of crop failure needs to have access to a weather-early-warning system, adequate food stocks, and appropriate administrative preparations. Well-prepared administrations, with clear policies, have been able (in parts of Africa in the 1980s, for example) to bring their populations through, in the face of severe crop failures, not only without famine deaths but even with some improvement in the nutrition of vulnerable groups. To be avoided are any *general (non-targeted)* food subsidies, food-price controls, restrictions on movement of food, and, except *in extremis* when all else has failed, moving people or necessitating their movement in order that they may be fed. Work programmes at subsistence wages for able-bodied people who need entitlements to food have several advantages over straight hand-outs, one being a test of need.

- Social safety-nets for guaranteeing the whole population against complete destitution have commonly been absent in developing countries apart from some with Communist ancestry. This is probably, at least in part, because of administrative difficulties. The challenge, where means tests of the kind common in the rich countries face intrinsic obstacles, is to include all those in serious need and to exclude others. However, there are possible compromises, such as category-targeting or using 'civil society' (local informal institutions) to monitor claims. Recently, Mexico, Brazil, Bolivia and Ecuador have begun making regular payments to poor families on condition that they meet certain welfare requirements for their children, such as for immunization or school attendance. Low-wage work programmes, such as those used in famines, open to all prepared to work on the terms offered, are also a possibility; and India has recently provided (in principle across the country) such a scheme from which anyone may demand 100 days' paid work in a year.

Important elements of poverty-reduction through provision of public and merit goods may be achieved even at low levels of income, but there is a risk of various forms of low-level trap if low average incomes remain stagnant. It is vital to exploit the synergies between growth and rising levels of health, nutrition and education, with governments and civil society backing *both* direct investment in human development *and* the business environment that favours economic growth.

Questions for discussion

10.1 What case could be made for confining attention in the analysis of poverty to 'relative' poverty lines fixed in relation to the norm in a particular country rather than giving much weight to uniform worldwide absolute poverty lines?

10.2 What important information, if any, is provided by inequality measures such as Gini coefficients and quintile ratios *that is not given* by absolute-poverty headcounts and gaps?

10.3 In what circumstances would you expect some degree or increase of poverty to lead to a poverty 'trap' or vicious circle?

10.4 What do you consider the most significant indicators of 'human development'?

10.5 How might a government generate a more equal distribution across households of 'human capital'?

Additional reading

Ahluwalia, M.S. (1974) 'Income inequality: some dimensions of the problem', in H.B. Chenery *et al., Redistribution with Growth*, Oxford University Press, Oxford, pp. 3–26.

Drèze, J. and A.K. Sen (1989) *Hunger and Public Action*, Oxford University Press, Oxford.

This (for which other works referred to in the chapter written or edited by Drèze and Sen or either of them might be substituted) is well worth even just browsing. It is moderate, balanced, drawing on a wealth of experience, concerned to face the unpleasant realities of world hunger and under-nutrition, but ultimately optimistic (on the basis of the achievements of some countries that are by no means lucky in their endowments) about what can be done. Or instead you might look at some shorter pieces, such as the two following:

Drèze, J. (1995) 'Famine prevention in Africa: some experiences and lessons', in J. Drèze, A. Sen and A. Hussein (eds) *The Political Economy of Hunger, Selected Essays*, Clarendon Press, Oxford, pp. 554–604.

Sen, A.K. (1998) 'Economic policy and equity: an overview', in V. Tanzi, K.-Y. Chu and S. Gupta (eds) *Economic Policy and Equity*, IMF, Washington DC.

Online
Learning Center

To help you grasp the key concepts of this chapter check out the extra resources posted on the Online Leaning Centre at ***www.mcgraw-hill.co.uk/textbooks/huq***

Among other resources, there are four appendices available:

- Appendix 10.1   John Rawls's undertanding of social justice, and its application to world poverty
- Appendix 10.2   The paradox of income and well-being
- Appendix 10.3   Some technicalities of poverty headcount and gap measurements
- Appendix 10.4   Social safety-nets for low-income countries: the ILO model

CHAPTER 11

Sustainable Development, Environmental Evaluation, Natural Resources

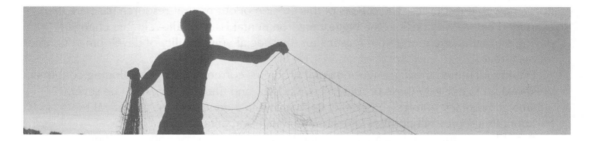

The sustainability of the earth as a home for the human family with rising population and purchasing power is threatened by degradation of soil, air and water, with the consequent exhaustion of pollution sinks and reduction of biodiversity, and at the same time depletion of deposits of a number of metals and hydrocarbons – the threats interacting with one another and with the most urgent, that of climate change. Misleading application of methods of social accounting, ignoring environmental costs and losses and taking too short-sighted a view of future effects of present actions, have obscured the urgency of the challenges by creating an overoptimistic picture of economic growth. For solving the dilemmas, co-operative action across the world is unavoidable.

'Climate change . . . environmental degradation, the loss of biodiversity and the potential for conflict growing out of competition over dwindling natural resources . . . Dealing with these issues is the great moral, economic and social imperative of our time.'

Ban Ki-moon, Secretary-General of the United Nations

Introduction

Because of environmental problems and depletion of the world's natural resources, the possibility that economic growth may not be 'sustainable' in the long run is now widely discussed. The corollary that economic growth in low-income countries must come to a halt – possibly long before the many problems besetting the poor countries of the world have even been significantly ameliorated – is a spectre now haunting the international community.

The structure of this chapter

In this chapter we consider what is meant by **sustainable development**, discuss its relation to the **environment** and the **availability of natural resources**, and examine the relevance of **climate change** – all as they bear on the long-run growth prospects of the developing world.

We begin by looking at possible sources of threat to sustained growth and development. First we reprise briefly our earlier discussion of the concern of some economists that growth is doomed to grind to a halt in some form of *stationary state*. We then assess the extent of the resource-mobilization effort required to enable the peoples of developing countries to reach the much larger per capita income levels to which they aspire – and set beside this the worrying record of depletion and degradation of much of the earth's stock of renewable and non-renewable resources. The drivers of this erosion of our natural-resource base are then examined before we consider the biggest environmental issue of all – climate change – paying particular attention to the reasons for the special vulnerability of developing countries to this threat.

Having identified the key environmental problems currently facing developing countries, we move on to ask *why* these problems have arisen, and find the reasons to be several – an amalgam of lack of foresight, market failure, and inadequacy of the analytical tools traditionally used by economists for examining environmental issues.

Possible definitions of 'sustainability' and their implications for policy are then considered, before we ask the key question: whether or not the global economy, and the developing world in particular, are following a sustainable growth path, or are 'living beyond their means'. An array of possible policies, aimed at fostering sustainable, environmentally sound growth in the developing world, is then set out – before we end the chapter with a brief summary of its content and the conclusions to be drawn from it.

The concept of 'sustainable development' – a provisional definition

What is meant by 'sustainable development'? The discussion in this chapter identifies a number of factors relevant to the operational definition needed as the basis for policy action on sustainability. Pending this, we use, as a working definition, the simple, intuitive formulation proposed by the Bruntland Commission (1987) – and adopted as its masthead slogan by the UN Division for Sustainable Development: Sustainable development is *'Development that meets the needs of the present without compromising the ability of future generations to meet their own needs'*. An important rider to this formula is that it is now generally taken to imply, not just continuation of past growth trends, but also *significant sustainable improvements in the circumstances of the peoples of the developing world*.

Why are prospects for sustainable development believed to be under threat?

Introduction

The prospects for establishing a sustainable development path for the global economy – and, in particular, for developing countries – are widely believed to be under threat. Four key concerns that have been expressed relate to:

1   The possibility that economies naturally gravitate towards a *'stationary state'* in which per capita incomes cannot increase further, and from which there is no escape.

2   The *massive, and growing, resource input needed to raise incomes and living standards in the developing world* to acceptable levels, and the prospect of chronic international political instability if it is not achieved. The discussion, below, of resource depletion reinforces the significance of worries over the feasibility of reaching this goal.

3   *Depletion of the world's natural-resource base* on which growth depends. This threat may be subdivided into the running down of resource stocks as a result of the demands of the production process, and depletion of resources by resource-destroying feedback effects from the economic, and non-economic, activities of humans. This concern is 'environmental' in the sense that natural resources are key elements in the 'endowment' provided by the natural environment.

4   *Climate change* – in particular, *global warming*, which seems likely to inflict a particularly damaging form of resource depletion.

We look at each of these in turn.

The inevitability of a 'stationary state'

The conclusion that economies eventually gravitate to a 'stationary state', in which it is not possible to achieve further lasting increases in per capita income, was reached, from different directions, by various classical and neoclassical economists, whose views were summarized in Chapter 4.

Insofar as the 'stationary state' was reached by 'diminishing returns' which would reduce rates of profit to the point where further net investment would become pointless, it would seem that the modern economy has little to worry about. Even without the reassurance from 'endogenous growth' thinking (that new knowledge brings with it *increasing* returns), it appears that the pipeline of promising opportunities for technological advance and improvements in productivity – from genetic manipulation to nanotechnology – is very far from running dry. Therefore, the possibility that a cessation of economic growth might result entirely from the working of the law of diminishing returns in the industrial sector seems a remote one.

However, this is not the whole story. As we have seen, Thomas Malthus believed that population had a built-in tendency to expand, when and if food supplies increased, to take up all of the new surplus, so pushing living standards back down to subsistence level. Taken seriously at the time of writing of his *Essay* (1798), 'Malthus' Devil' later came to be seen as outdated and irrelevant, an alarming prospect rendered harmless by the unforeseen advent of abundant food supplies from the 'New World' and major improvements in agricultural technology. But this is *not* now a universally accepted conclusion regarding Malthus' 'dismal' prediction of a world stalked by hunger. While the technical capacity currently exists to grow sufficient food for the entire human race, environmental problems now appear to threaten the adequacy of future world food supplies. Food security for the poor in many developing countries is especially at risk. We return to this worrying prospect later in this chapter and in the section of Chapter 16 on 'A challenge to food security'.

BOX 11.1 SUSTAINABILITY TOOLBOX

■ **Sustainable yield.** A sustainable yield is one that can be maintained at a constant size over time. The 'maximum sustainable yield' (MSY) is the largest possible sustainable yield. Harvesting a resource at a rate in excess of the MSY reduces the size of the stock of the resource and will eventually exhaust the resource. It is believed that stocks of several commercially important species of fish are currently being harvested at rates well in excess of their MSY.

■ **'Grandfathering'.** This refers to a situation in which regulations or laws regarding a given activity are changed. Existing participants in the activity are allowed to continue under the 'old' rules, while new participants are required to operate under new rules.

■ **Biosphere.** The biosphere is the outermost layer of the earth's surface – land, water, and air – extending from about five miles below sea level to around five miles above it – within which all life processes occur.

■ **Thermal equivalence of oil, natural gas and coal.** 1 barrel oil = 1.075 tonnes natural gas = 859.8 cubic metres natural gas = 1.429 tonnes coal

■ **Energy reserves.** The extent of energy reserves may be expressed in terms of:

  – **'Proved' (or 'measured') energy reserves.** Quantities of energy sources – oil, natural gas, and coal – the presence of which is *well-established* and which are believed to be recoverable given current economic and operating conditions;

  – **'Probable' (or 'indicated') energy reserves.** Quantities of energy sources that, on the basis of geologic evidence, can *reasonably be* expected to exist and be recoverable under existing economic and operating conditions. This term is equivalent to 'Indicated Reserves'. Measured and indicated reserves, when combined, constitute 'demonstrated' reserves.

Is the resource-mobilization effort needed for development feasible?

The second potential barrier to attaining, and remaining on, the desired sustainable long-run development path is the possible non-feasibility of the immense resource-mobilization effort needed to remove, or even significantly reduce, the massive inequalities in income and consumption levels currently characterizing the international economy.

   The order-of-magnitude figures make striking reading, especially when viewed in the light of the concerns over resource depletion expressed below. If we take as our starting point the 2006 average per capita income levels of US$1997 a year for the developing world as a whole, and $36 608 for developed countries, and accept a global population projection of around nine billion in 2042 (the anticipated 'peak' figure for world population) – of whom 7.8 billion will live in today's developing countries – the expansion of total global GNI required by that year to achieve a worldwide per capita figure of $36 608 (the level required to equalize *if there is no change* in developed-country incomes over the next three decades) would be *6.6-fold*. That is, output and consumption, and, in the absence of technical progress, resource use, would all require to run at over six and one-half times the current annual levels in order to achieve the income target. Even if we lower our sights and assume a long-run per capita income level in developing countries only one-half that of the present developed countries' average, the increase in income and resource use required is still substantial, at 3.8 times present levels. (And an income figure of only one-quarter of the developed-country total would raise the aggregate figures 2.3 times.) Given the picture of intensifying resource constraints painted in this chapter, achieving even the most modest of these targets may prove difficult. Failure to do so may well not be acceptable to the peoples of the developing world, who are increasingly well-informed of global income differentials, and for whom permanent relegation to relative poverty is unlikely to be an acceptable option.

Resource depletion

Resource depletion refers to the running down, and possible eventual exhaustion, of the stock of a natural resource. Natural resources in aggregate comprise the 'natural capital' that is required to produce the flow of goods and services upon which economic development, and indeed life itself, depend.

The distinction between **non-renewable resources** and **renewable resources** is an important one. Resources which by their nature fall into the non-renewable category are the fossil fuels (in particular coal, oil and natural gas), and deposits of minerals and other non-organic materials. Stocks of these are finite and cannot be replaced; once the existing supply is exhausted no more will be available.

BOX 11.2 RESOURCE DEPLETION

'It would be reckless of us to successfully reach the Millennium Development Goals in 2015, only to be confronted by dysfunctional cities, dwindling water supplies, more inequality and conflict, and even less cropland to sustain us than we have now.'

(Johnson, 2003)

Renewable resources, in contrast, are capable of being replenished by natural processes and may have a '**sustainable yield**' – that is, a level of utilization that is capable of being offset, indefinitely, by natural regeneration, and may be capable of expansion given appropriate management. Renewables include plants and animals, together with inanimate resources such as air, water, soil and the biosphere as a whole – as well as energy derived from solar radiation, and geothermal, wind, and wave power. However, while a resource such as solar radiation cannot be exhausted irrespective of how much of it is used – it is a **perpetual resource** – this is not the case for all resources capable, in principle, of regeneration. Excessive use of a resource, for instance serious over-fishing of a particular species – such as currently occurs with yellow-fin tuna in the Pacific Ocean – may reduce the population below the critical minimum level required for regeneration of the stock, and the species may die out. Similarly, excessive removal of vegetation cover from low-quality soils of the kind common in many sub-Saharan African countries, through the use of 'slash-and-burn' cultivation methods or over-grazing by animals, can lead, if no restorative measures are taken, to the eventual loss of *all* vegetation from the area, and to *desertification*. Thus, renewable resources such as fisheries, forests, biomass and water may require active management if they are to avoid overuse, degradation and ultimate exhaustion.

Despite the fairly clear distinction at the intuitive level between renewable and non-renewable resources, in some cases it is possible to process renewable resources to yield fairly close approximations in use to non-renewables. For instance, in the important area of energy, the finite supplies of petroleum (gasoline) and natural gas derived from fossil-fuel sources can be substituted in many uses by biofuels derived from vegetable material – notably ethanol made from corn or sugar cane, and methane. As we shall see, the 'substitutability' of one resource for another is an important consideration in relation to the sustainability of economic growth.

Growing awareness of resource depletion

A recognition that resources might be depleted has been around for a very long time, but only in the last 50 years has what was earlier little more than a subject for philosophical musing been elevated to a matter arousing genuine concern. The understanding that there really was a problem appears to have developed in three stages. First came the appreciation that many resources were in finite supply, that this might indeed affect prospects for indefinitely sustainable economic growth, and that something had to be done about it.

Following this troubling insight came the observation that some of the undesirable side-effects of productive, and domestic, resource-using activities were feeding back into the system and making further growth more difficult. Of course, there had been complaints for a long time about unpleasant by-products of production, such as air pollution – the bringer of 'smogs'. But such phenomena were thought of as localized nuisances rather than serious threats to growth. Only recently has the systematic depletion of, and damage to, renewable resources come to be seen as potentially *irreversible* and a major threat to future growth and development.

Last, by the late 1980s it began to seem likely that human activities were affecting the global *climate* in a number of potentially threatening and destructive ways – notably by causing *global warming* and the damaging changes in climate and acceleration of resource depletion that it might entrain. This possibility, with its potentially calamitous implications for human progress – especially for continued development in the poor countries of the world – has come to dominate the debate on the intertwined issues of natural-resource availability, the environment and sustainable development.

BOX 11.3 EXTINCTION OF SPECIES

The many species currently living on Earth are estimated to amount to no more than 0.5 per cent of all the species that have ever lived. The extinction of species is a natural process – but current rates of loss are far higher than in earlier times. It is estimated that, before the human race appeared, one species per million went extinct each year. The present rate is somewhere between one thousand and ten thousand species per million – with the result that up to half of all existing species could have disappeared by 2100. The main causes of today's relatively very high rates of extinction are: *Destruction of natural habitats* – by climate change or by human encroachment (often the result of *increasing population*); Air and water *pollution*; Destruction by *invasive species* (such as the chestnut fungus, accidentally introduced on imported logs of Asian chestnut, and responsible for virtually wiping out the American chestnut tree); *Over-harvesting* (as with many fish species); and *extinction of other species* in the food chain.

Source: Wilson, E.O. (2002).

From open system to closed system

In 1963, in what then seemed a landmark publication, *Scarcity and Growth*, Howard Barnett and Chandler Morse pronounced that resource scarcity was not, and might never be, the cause of the cessation of economic growth. Yet, within only three years, Kenneth Boulding, in *The Economics of the Coming Spaceship Earth* (Boulding, 1966) was pondering, in what is widely regarded as a watershed publication, the possibility that serious problems might arise from resource shortages in a global economy that was rapidly 'closing'.

Boulding saw the lack of serious concern with resource exhaustion in earlier times as consistent with the characteristics of an economy where there was always a 'new frontier'.

> That is, there was always some place else to go when things got too difficult, either by reason of the deterioration of the natural environment or a deterioration of the social structure in places where people happened to live. The image of the frontier is probably one of the oldest images of mankind, and it is not surprising that we find it hard to get rid of . . . For the sake of picturesqueness, I am tempted to call the open economy the 'cowboy economy', the cowboy being symbolic of the illimitable plains and also associated with reckless, exploitative, romantic, and violent behaviour, which is characteristic of open societies.

In the 'cowboy economy' individuals, and even entire societies, saw their use of natural resources as trivial relative to the apparently infinite reservoirs available, and their pollution of the environment as insignificant relative to its apparently unlimited capacity to absorb their effluent. Given these perceptions, welfare was appropriately measured, as it is in many countries today, by levels of output and consumption. No regard needed to be taken of any 'cost' of resource use or destruction, or of environmental pollution – since these were seen as infinitely small relative to the totality.

However, as human economic activity broadens to become truly 'global', this view loses credibility. The earth is no longer seen as the *open system* of earlier years, but as a *closed system*, akin to

> a spaceship, without unlimited reservoirs of anything, either for extraction or for pollution . . . in which, therefore, man must find his place in a cyclical ecological system which is capable of continuous reproduction of material form even though it cannot escape having inputs of energy.

In such an economy, the old economic logic is stood on its head. Now

> The essential measure of the success of the economy is not production and consumption at all, but the nature, extent, quality, and complexity of the total capital stock, including in this the state of the human bodies and minds included in the system. In the spaceman economy, what we are primarily concerned with is stock maintenance, and any technological change which results in the maintenance of a given total stock with a lessened throughput (that is, less production and consumption) is clearly a gain.

And Boulding observes that

> This idea that both production and consumption are bad things rather than good things is very strange to economists, who have been obsessed with income-flow concepts to the exclusion, almost, of capital-stock concepts . . . Economists in particular, for the most part, have failed to come to grips with the ultimate consequences of the transition from the open to the closed earth.

The key implication of the move to a 'spaceship economy' view is that, sooner or later, the temporary economic bonanza made possible by the use, in a short period of time, of energy stocks which took millions of years to assemble must come to an end, at which point some currently non-existent (or unexploited) alternative will be required if living standards are to be maintained in the developed countries and improved in the developing countries. 'The shadow of the future spaceship . . . is already falling over our spendthrift merriment.'

Resource depletion, the environment and sustainable growth

Boulding's dramatic identification of the exhaustion of energy resources as the key environmental problem threatening the sustainability of world output was followed, over the next decade, by a torrent of studies focused on various aspects of resource availability – or non-availability – and long-run growth prospects.[1] Probably the most influential of all the early contributions to a burgeoning debate was *The Limits to Growth* (Meadows *et al.*, 1972), which painted a particularly dramatic, and gloomy, picture of the future of the global economy. This study, which examined the impact of continued exponential growth of industrial production, population, production of food, and pollution on resource depletion and availability, forecast that, in the absence of any further discoveries, stocks of energy and mineral resources would be exhausted in the near future – notably oil in 1992, only 20 years from the time the book was produced.

Such an outcome was, of course, seen as very worrying in relation to the prospects for continued prosperity in developed countries, and was given additional credibility by the traumatic effects of the 'oil price shocks' of 1974 and 1979–80. From a developing-country perspective, however, it was an apocalyptic view as it meant that the development process might already be over – before it had properly begun. The policy conclusion that, if the nightmare of resource exhaustion were to be avoided, both consumption and population growth would have to be curbed, was heavily criticized at the time as being unduly alarmist. However, many years later, in *Limits to Growth: The 30-Year Update* (Meadows *et al.*, 2004), the same authors were to return to their original theme with renewed conviction and, if anything, more pessimistic warnings for readers in the new century. Resource depletion, in part attributable to environmental degradation, was closing the door on sustainable economic growth and development as these concepts were currently understood.

A 'resource audit': the extent of, and trends in, depletion of non-renewable resources

Introduction

What is the current situation regarding depletion of supplies of *fossil fuels* and other non-renewable *minerals*? Are supplies of any important materials in danger of running out? In this section we summarize the findings of several investigations into the consumption, production and reserves situation of a number of key finite resources.

---

[1] Thus Paul Ehrlich's *The Population Bomb* (1968) revived discussion of the implications of high rates of population growth for resource availability – especially food security. Edward Goldsmith, in *Blueprint for Survival* (Goldsmith and Allen, 1972) focused on non-sustainable levels of resource use. And Robert Heilbroner, in *An Inquiry into the Human Prospect* (1974), argued that, in the face of acute resource scarcity, human survival might be possible only at the expense of considerable loss of freedoms relating to environmental matters. Two further major studies which attracted much attention at the time were *Global 2000: Report to the President* (1981), a report to President Carter by the Council on Environmental Quality, which predicted serious imminent environmental, resource and population problems – and impoverishment – and the much more upbeat response by Simon and Kahn who emphasized, in *The Resourceful Earth* (1984), the capacity of technology to find substitutes for resources in danger of being exhausted.

Region	Oil* (% total)	Natural Gas (% total)	Coal (% total)
Africa	9.5	8.2	5.9
Middle East	20.9	17.9	0.2
Asia and Oceania	2.9	8.2	21.2
China	*1.3*	*1.1*	*13.5*
India	*0.4*	*0.6*	*6.7*
Americas	9.9	4.3	2.0
Developing Europe and CIS	10.5	30.7	29.9
TOTAL	53.7	69.3	59.2

TABLE 11.1 Developing countries' share (per cent) of 'proved recoverable reserves' of oil, natural gas and coal, by region – as at end-2005
* Includes natural gas liquids
Source: British Petroleum (2008).

Fossil fuels

The three main fossil fuels, which provide the bulk of the world's energy supplies, are oil, natural gas and coal. Estimates of the lifetime of known stocks are subject to change (generally increases) as more deposits are found, as extraction technologies improve and as resource prices rise. Between 1971 and 2004 global demand for all forms of primary energy increased by, on average, 2.1 per cent per annum, rising from an annual level equivalent to 38.3 billion barrels of oil to 76.6 billion barrels. The extent of the likely life-span of all in-ground reserves of the main fossil fuels as of 2007 has been estimated a the following levels:

- *Oil:* Reserves of 1.23 trillion (i.e., million million) barrels – sufficient to last until 2050 at current rates of use. As indicated in Table 11.1, the developing-country share of recoverable in-ground reserves as at end-2005 was 53.7 per cent. Four developing countries each have more than 5 per cent of the global total – Iran, Iraq, Venezuela and Russia. The Asian giants China and India have less than 2 per cent of world oil reserves between them.

- *Natural gas:* Reserves of 177.4 trillion cubic metres – sufficient to last until 2077 at current rates of use. It is estimated that around 69 per cent of recoverable reserves of natural gas are located in developing countries. Russia has the largest share with 25 per cent of the total, and Iran has nearly 16 per cent. Again, reserves of gas in China and India comprise less than 2 per cent of the total.

- *Coal:* Reserves of 5 billion tonnes – sufficient to last until 2257 at current rates of use. Some 59 per cent of coal reserves are located in developing countries, notably in Russia (18.5 per cent), China (13.5 per cent), India (6.7 per cent) and South Africa (5.7 per cent). The largest reserves of coal overall are in the US (with 28.6 per cent). Australia (9.0 per cent) is the only other country with more than 5 per cent of total global reserves of coal.

As things stand, supplies of oil are expected to be exhausted well within the lifetime of most people now alive. Supplies of gas are expected to last longer, but are still expected to run out within the lifetime of some of the children born in the twentieth century. Exhaustion of coal will take considerably longer.

Non-fossil minerals

Supplies of minerals come from two sources – metal extracted from the lithosphere (the upper layers of the earth's surface) and metal recycled from old to new products. Calculations regarding the sustainability of supplies are affected as the balance between potential remaining supply and current demand is influenced by technological improvements in extraction and in the use of metals. These tend to extend the apparent life-span of supplies. Nevertheless, the results of recent studies (notably Bringezu *et al.* (2004), Gordon *et al.*, (2006) and Cohen (2007)) suggest that supplies of *certain important minerals will soon be insufficient to meet demand, and in some cases are likely to be exhausted in the near future.* Particularly significant results relate to:

- *Copper* – Widely used in computer chips and circuit boards; annual demand expected to exceed extraction by 2100;
- *Zinc* – Required for galvanizing processes; demand expected to outrun new supplies by 2100;
- *Platinum* – Essential in 'clean-combustion' technologies and 'green' fuel cells; reserves could be exhausted by 2025;
- *Tin* – No problems with availability foreseen;
- *Nickel* – No problems with availability foreseen;
- *Hafnium* – Required for ultra-high-speed computer chips; reserves could be exhausted before 2020;
- *Indium and Gallium* – Required for a new generation of super-efficient solar-power technologies expected to have important applications in developing countries (especially in small-scale power generation and in telecommunications); reserves likely to be exhausted by 2020;
- *Uranium* – Required for nuclear-power production which is once again on the agenda in many countries as fossil-fuel supplies dwindle and become more expensive, and as concern over atmospheric pollution grows; at current rates of use, reserves will be exhausted within 60 years;
- *Phosphorus* – Not a metal, but an essential ingredient in fertilizers used in agriculture; supplies limited and prices rising sharply.

Ownership of remaining supplies of non-fossil minerals

In addition to anticipated problems with the *level* of supplies of many minerals, difficulties may also arise over the *location* of these supplies. A relatively small number of countries often form the sole source of supply of a mineral.

As the figures in Table 11.2 indicate, a substantial proportion of the world's reserves of important non-fossil minerals such as copper, platinum, tin, aluminium (in bauxite), chromium and phosphorus are located in developing countries. However, deposits tend to be geographically concentrated rather than evenly spread. Thus, most of the remaining oil and natural gas is held by a small number of countries in the Middle East; and a sizeable part of the reserves of other minerals are to be found in a handful of developing countries – notably South Africa, China, Brazil and Kazakhstan. Depletion of these stocks may bring with it not just problems to do with adequacy of supplies, but also new, or reinforced, supply difficulties associated with the increasing bargaining power of the controllers of what stocks remain. (The use by Russia, in the mid-2001–10 decade, of its dominant position as a supplier of oil and gas to Eastern Europe as a means of exerting political leverage may be a sign of things to come.)

Mineral	Developing Country Share of Reserves (%)	Mineral	Developing Country Share of Reserves (%)
Chromium	100	Gold	50
Tin	89	Uranium	41
Platinum	88	Silver	35
Antimony	75	Hafnium	34
Aluminium (bauxite)	74	Zinc	33
Phosphorus	73	Lead	30
Nickel	52	Indium	22
Copper	51	Tantalum	Negligible

TABLE 11.2 Developing countries' share (per cent) of reserves of non-renewable, non-fossil mineral resources – as at end-2005
Sources: Cohen (2007) and US Geological Survey (various).

Conclusion on non-renewable resource stocks

The conclusions to be drawn from the above discussion have direct implications for developing countries. It is clear that both the supplies of key fossil fuels, and the reserves of a number of minerals, important either as raw materials in developing country industries or as inputs into new 'green' products of particular interest to developing- country users, have limited life-spans – and, in some cases, may well be exhausted before today's developing countries attain acceptably high living standards. This raises the issue addressed by Gordon in his concluding remarks (which refer to the exhaustion of metal ores but apply equally to fossil fuels):

> 'Concern about the extent of mineral resources arises when the stock of metal needed to provide the services enjoyed by the highly developed nations is compared with that needed to provide comparable services with existing technology to a large part of the world's population . . . [W]orldwide demand continues to increase, and the virgin stocks of several metals appear inadequate to sustain the modern "developed world" quality of life for all Earth's peoples under contemporary technology. These facts compel us to ask two key questions: Do we really envision a developed world quality of life for all of the people of the planet? and if so, are we willing to encourage the transformational technologies that will be required to make that vision a reality?'.
>
> *(Gordon et al., 2006, p. 1214)*

Possible responses to exhaustion of non-renewable resources, with particular reference to the situation of developing countries, are discussed later in this chapter.

The extent of, and trends in, depletion of renewable resources in developing countries[2]

Sustainability of growth requires, in terms of our 'provisional' definition, the passing on by the present generation of a renewable resource base *at least as large* as the one inherited. (More realistically – given that population in developing countries is growing, and that additional renewable resources will be required to substitute for depletion of non-renewable

---

[2] This section draws on UNEP (2007).

resources – the renewable-resource base passed on to the next generation will have to *increase* in size, once allowance is made for any resource-saving effects of technical progress.) So the status of the renewable-resource base in the developing world is a matter of critical importance. Lack of detailed data, and space, preclude presentation of a comprehensive audit of renewable resources here, but indicative information is in plentiful, if patchy, supply. The observable trends it enables us to identify are not reassuring for the future of productive activity in developing countries.

The negative impact of economic growth on the renewable-resource base of developing countries – through direct resource consumption for industrial, agricultural and domestic purposes, and through destructive, depleting feedback loops from these uses, has become increasingly obvious, and costly in recent years. The most important examples of depletion of renewable resources relevant to sustainability of growth in developing countries fall into five categories – land, air, water, biodiversity and environmental 'sinks'. These are discussed below, together with what information is available on their main consequences.

Land

Degradation of land resources and soil quality in developing countries results in a long-term loss of fertility and a decline in productive capacity from which the system may not be able to recover unaided. The principal forms, and causes, of this problem are as follows:

- *Soil erosion* occurs when topsoil (together with its organic matter and nutrients) is removed by the action of wind or water. It is typically caused by poor land management involving clearing forests or grassland for cultivation or grazing (often over-grazing) without ensuring that sufficient ground cover remains to bind soil together, or extending cultivation onto unsuitably hilly terrain exposed to rain and wind with consequential loss of soil. (Subsidiary causes include mining activity and urban and infrastructure development.) The ultimate effect is declining agricultural production, destruction of wildlife habitats, and the introduction of new pests and diseases.

  Evidence from satellite surveys of land quality suggests that between 1981 and 2003 the 'net primary productivity' of land (effectively, the volume of biomass production) declined on over 12 per cent of the earth's surface, with serious adverse implications for both food production and livelihoods. The areas covered were mainly in developing countries and had, at that time, a total population estimated at over one billion people, many of them amongst the poorest in the developing world.

  Particularly badly affected were Africa south of the Equator (particularly South-East Africa), South-East Asia, South China, Central America and the Caribbean, and parts of Brazil and Argentina. Wind erosion is a particular problem in West Asia where up to 1.45 million square kilometres (one-third of the surface area of the entire region) are affected. One study (Biggelaar *et al.*, 2004) estimates a global loss of cultivable surface area of between 20 000 and 50 000 square kilometres every year, losses in Africa, Latin America and Asia running at twice to six times those in Europe and North America. Soil erosion by water is also important, especially in South America.

- *Salinity* of both soils and groundwater is on the increase in many developing countries, and is an important cause of declining fertility. Irrigation is frequently responsible for increasing salinity, and around 20 per cent of irrigated land is now affected. Overall, 16 000 square kilometres of farmland, mainly in developing countries, become unusable each year because of increasing salinity (FAO, 2006).

■ *Nutrient depletion* Continued removal of plant nutrients (nitrogen, phosphorus, potassium) from the soil by crop harvesting and removal of crop residues without replacement through inputs of fertilizers ('nutrient mining'), results in a decline in the nutrient level of soils, and (often) increased soil acidification. These reduce soil fertility and productivity. A similar effect is produced by leaching soluble nutrients from the soil in areas with high rainfall.

   Nutrient deficiency is one of the most important factors inhibiting crop production in the tropics (especially sub-Saharan Africa) where soils are often, in any case, of inherently low quality.

■ *Toxic or damaging chemicals*, in the form of fertilizers and pesticides, are still frequently used in sub-Saharan Africa (notably in Nigeria, South Africa and Zimbabwe). Their use carries with it the risk of long-term contamination, or destruction, of farm land.

■ *Desertification* refers to the degradation of arid land, often through excess pressure of cultivation, removal of ground cover through 'slash and burn' farming, or overgrazing of land (though sometimes as a result of climatic factors such as drought), to the point where severe erosion is set in train, and the land ultimately assumes the characteristics of a desert and can no longer be used for agriculture or support its former level of biodiversity.

   Desertification in developing countries is proceeding at a historically high pace. It is estimated that 10–20 per cent of drylands are already degraded, affecting 200 million people, and further areas currently supporting some 1.8 billion people are at risk. Dramatic examples of desertification are currently on the move in the Sahelian states where the Sahara is encroaching on viable land at a rate of around 30 miles every year, and in northern Ghana and Nigeria, where some 1355 square miles of farmland are lost to desertification each year. The phenomenon is also causing difficulties in the former Soviet republics of Central Asia – in particular in Kazakhstan, where almost half of the area formerly laid to crops has had to be abandoned since 1980, and in China where growing desertification has depleted between 18 and 27 per cent of the country's surface area.

In a wake-up call speech, Karl Harmsen, Director of the UN Institute for Natural Resources in Africa, claimed that, should soil conditions continue to decline in Africa, nearly 75 per cent of the continent might have to rely on some sort of food (and water) aid by 2025. Such a situation would very probably create a tidal wave of 'environmental refugees' which would pose further problems of both social and environmental kinds.

Soil degradation and hunger

The figures in Table 11.3 indicate that, although the proportion of the population undernourished fell in four of the five regions over the decade 1990–92 to 2000–03 (the Near East/North Africa region being the exception), the total number of undernourished people worldwide was virtually unchanged. This was, in part, the result of land degradation. FAO's projections suggest that the incidence of hunger worldwide will decline sharply in both absolute and proportionate terms between 2000–03 and 2015. However, in both sub-Saharan Africa and Near East/North Africa the number of hungry people projected for 2015 will still be larger than it was in 1990–92. By then, sub-Saharan Africa will be home to around 30 per cent of the undernourished people in the developing world, compared with 20 per cent in 1990–92 (FAO, 2006). Given the multidimensional land problems affecting many countries in sub-Saharan Africa and the Near East/North Africa, in particular, it is not

Region	Number of People Undernourished (millions)			Percentage of People Undernourished		
	1990–92	2000–03	2015	1990–92	2000–03	2015
South Asia	290	299	203	26	22	12
East Asia*	279	225	123	17	12	6
Latin Am. & the Caribbean	60	52	41	13	10	7
Near East and North Africa	25	38	36	8	9	7
Sub-Saharan Africa	169	206	179	36	32	21
Total Developing Countries	823	820	582	20	17	10

TABLE 11.3 Prevalence of undernourishment in developing countries in 1990–92 and 2000–03, and projected to 2015
* Includes South-East Asia.
Source: Based on FAO (2006, Table 1 and p. 12).

surprising that undernourishment there has been especially resistant to amelioration, though it is also the case that lack of political will to solve the problem has been an important contributory factor.

Changes in land use – deforestation

A striking change in land use in developing countries in recent decades has been the continued shrinking of forest land. Between 1990 and 2005 the world's forest acreage declined by around 0.2 per cent per annum, the fall in forest cover in developing countries being even faster than this, especially in sub-Saharan Africa, Brazil and Indonesia. Much of this has been for conversion to agricultural uses, often yielding low-grade farmland capable of supporting only small numbers of farmers, at the cost of the loss of the forests' functions of helping to moderate climate, control floods, contain land degradation, and provide a habitat for many animal and vegetable species – thus promoting biodiversity.

A further problem arising from the reduction in forest area is the adverse impact on poorer rural people, some of them traditional forest-dwellers. Research results suggest that, in many developing countries, a significant proportion of the income of poorer rural families (over 20 per cent in the multi-country review quoted here) comes from the forest in the forms of food, firewood, forage for domesticated animals, and medicinal plants. Conversion of forests to cultivated land removes this slender support. (Vedeld and others, 2004, quoted in UNEP, 2007, p. 90).

Air pollution

Air pollution is caused mainly by emissions from road vehicles, factories, power stations, aircraft, and the like, and by the large-scale burning of vegetation. It is the major source of the greenhouse gases responsible for *climate change* – discussed in detail later in this chapter. Aside from this, air pollution imposes costs on individuals through adverse impacts on health, on firms which require clean air for their processes, and on society in general in the form of health problems, increased cleaning expenditures, accelerated decay of buildings, and damage to crops, forests and ecosystems in general by soot deposition and acid rain.

With reference to the health hazard posed by air pollution, Figure 11.1 summarizes the regional distribution of the 800 000 premature deaths in 2000 attributed to outdoor air

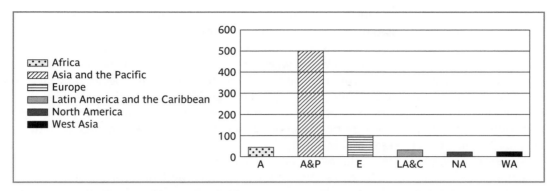

FIGURE 11.1 Premature deaths attributed to outdoor urban PM10* exposure by region in 2000 (measured in 000s)
* Inhalable material classified as 'fine particulates'.
Source: Cohen *et al.*, 2005.

pollution, mainly through respiratory problems. Deaths in Asia and the Pacific account for well over half of the total, a reflection of the acute air-pollution problems in many Asian cities. An even more deadly, though less immediately obvious, form of air pollution in the developing world is *indoor* pollution caused by domestic cooking and heating; within this category, premature deaths in the developing world in 2000 were estimated at around 1.2 million, many of these being women and children.

Trends in emissions are mixed. In Africa and Latin America and the Caribbean small increases have been recorded. However, in many industrializing countries, especially in Asia, emissions of the most damaging gases have increased rapidly since 1990. For example, in China, between 1996 and 2003, emissions of NO_x (mono-nitrogen oxides) rose by 50 per cent, and over the five years 2000 to 2005 emissions of SO_2 (sulphur dioxide) rose by nearly 30 per cent; both of these gases are major threats to health, and cause serious damage to buildings and to man-made materials. Overall, global emissions of NO_x and SO_2 have increased since 1990 (UNEP, 2007) – though there are signs that, in some countries at least, emissions of SO_2 are beginning to fall.

The speed with which air pollution has gone from being seen as something of a 'virility symbol' associated with vigorous industrial expansion to a serious threat to public health and economic growth itself is striking. Certainly it was not always perceived as costly, even to those involved in polluting. In an interview with one of the authors in the late 1960s, Mr. I. Ackom-Mensah, then Managing Director of Ghana Industrial Holding Corporation, declared that he looked forward to the day when local industries had expanded to the point where 'Accra was covered by a pall of smoke'.

Water pollution and scarcity

Water pollution has several causes – and effects. Industrial effluent (including heavy metals) from manufacturing and mining activity accumulates as deposits in lagoons, rivers and coastal areas, and is often toxic to fish and shellfish, and sometimes to humans who eat them. Microbial pollutants in sewage and wastewater, especially in urban slums, transfer to drinking water infectious diseases such as cholera and typhoid, both major killers (especially of infants) in the developing world. Discharges into rivers, lakes and coastal waters of agricultural run-off containing agrochemicals, organic matter and nutrients, result in 'eutrophication' – nutrient overload which promotes the growth of aerobic algae and depletes oxygen, killing fish and other marine organisms and leading in some cases to hypoxia – dead zones created by lack of oxygen in water.

Deteriorating water quality also has significant negative economic consequences, especially for developing countries. Coastal water pollution, notably of mangroves and coral-reef areas, damages or destroys the habitats of a number of marine species on which many coastal dwellers, especially the poor, depend for subsistence, as well as removing the fisheries and reef ecology which attract many tourists. Even more worrying is the possibility that widespread eutrophication coupled with ocean acidification (caused, in large part, by acid rain) could affect food security by fatally damaging fisheries.

Water scarcity, caused by declining rainfall, increased evaporation, and diversion into irrigation schemes, is leading to falling agricultural production and increasing problems with food supplies in a number of countries – including Yemen, a case discussed in Appendix 11.2, which is available on the Online Learning Centre.

Biodiversity

The term 'biodiversity' refers to the diversity of the global stock of renewable natural capital in the forms of diversity of species, genetic diversity, and diversity of overall ecosystems. The broader the biodiversity base available to humans, the greater the number and density of 'ecosystem services' available, and hence the greater the number of options for economic exploitation, the better the prospects for achieving a sustainable form of development, and the smaller the risk of sudden collapse of the life-support system that the planet provides. Conversely, the narrower the biodiversity base, the narrower is the range of economic options open as development paths, and the more precarious, and potentially non-sustainable, these options become.

The destruction of ecosystems supporting biodiversity can lead to the extinction of plant and animal species. This process may result from climate change, destruction of habitats, and air and water pollution. In addition to being ethically unacceptable to those for whom biodiversity has an inherent, or 'intrinsic', value independent of its economic value, its loss carries with it the probable loss for ever of certain commercially exploited species, especially fish – the world's most widely traded foodstuff and a major key source of export earnings for many developing countries, especially smaller island states – as well as materials of potential use as medical ingredients. And *genetic diversity* permits adaptation of plants and animals in response to changes in their environment. It is thus important for the general sustainability and resilience of any development trajectory that animals and plants embody a high level of genetic diversity which may be crucial in the face of major environmental shifts such as those brought about by climate change, and also in the narrower contexts of providing genetic material for developing crop variants with improved yields and greater disease resistance, as well as for developing medicines and other products.

There is little doubt that the reduction of biodiversity is well under way, especially in the developing world. One important destroyer of biodiversity common in the developing world is the transformation of 'biodiversity habitats' by the mobilizing of uncultivated land for crop production. In recent decades forests and virgin savannah have undergone massive conversion to agricultural land in all parts of the developing world. At the same time, the needs of agriculture and urbanization have encouraged the transformation of river systems (and water habitats) to provide reservoirs, dams, hydroelectric schemes, and river diversions, as well as greatly reducing water flows in many river systems to provide water for drinking and irrigation.

Given the diversity of ecosystems themselves, it is inevitable that there are difficulties in actually measuring changes in their status. However a brief summary of the outcomes of recent attempts provides order-of-magnitude indications of important trends in biodiversity. Thus:

- 'Of those *ecosystem services* that have been assessed, about 60 per cent are degraded or used unsustainably.' These include natural systems which relate to 'fisheries, waste treatment and detoxification, water purification, natural hazard protection, regulation of air quality, regulation of regional and local climate, and erosion control' (UNEP, 2007, p. 161).

- The current rate of *extinction of species* is estimated to be many times higher than typical rates in the past as established from fossil records (see Box 11.3). Of the major groups studied, over 23 per cent of vertebrate species (of which 39 per cent of fish), 51 per cent of invertebrates (of which 83 per cent of crustaceans), and 70 per cent of plant species, are 'threatened' (IUCN, 2008, Table 1). Tropical areas contain by far the bulk of these threatened species.

- *Fish stocks* have been seriously depleted, with some 75 per cent of all fisheries overexploited or fully exploited (UNEP, 2007, p. 164).

- In recent years genetic diversity is believed to have been diminished, in both the developing and the developed world, in many of the most important crops because of changes in agricultural practices (Heal *et al.*, 2002).

Sinks

The capacity of the oceans, land, atmosphere and some plants and trees to act as 'sinks' that absorb pollutants and waste products created by industrial and domestic activities is a very important offset to pollution, especially with respect to sequestering or detoxifying dangerous substances (notably nuclear waste and certain toxic chemicals) and absorbing carbon dioxide, the main 'greenhouse gas'. However, the capacity of 'sinks' to absorb pollutants is being weakened through overexposure to these pollutants. This raises the unwelcome prospect that future pollution episodes may become ever more damaging as the natural offsetting capacity of the environment diminishes.

The drivers of resource depletion

In this section we look at the 'drivers' – the proximate causes – of resource depletion (further, *underlying* causes are examined in detail in a later section) as a prelude to identifying appropriate counter-measures.

Since 1950 *economic growth* has hugely increased world (real) GDP – in the order of 9.8 times (Maddison, 2002, and World Bank). This expansion, much of it in the form of manufactures, is now well established in developing countries, and has been greatly reinforced by the globalization of production systems through the expansion of multinational enterprises (see Chapter 23) and the deregulation of world trade (see Chapter 9), which have increased the ratio of international trade to total economic activity.

Further impetus has been given to the growth of output by continuing *population growth*. From some 2.5 billion in 1950 world population increased to around 5 billion by 1987 (the year of the Bruntland Report) and by 2008 had climbed to an estimated 6.7 billion. Current trends suggest that the figure of 9 billion will be reached around the year 2042. Even where incomes have not been rising, as in much of sub-Saharan Africa, expanding population has put additional pressure on the natural endowment, again requiring that more land be brought into production and, in rural areas, depleting water and fuelwood resources.

Huge *increases in the volume of industrial output* have entrained very large increases in inputs of raw materials, both renewable and non-renewable, putting pressure on stocks of finite resources as well as on air, freshwater and energy resources. These trends have strengthened throughout the period since 1950 despite a major shift in the balance of production in developed countries towards services and away from industrial goods (offset by increased output of manufactures by developing countries), and despite significant progress in reducing inputs per unit of output ('material-saving' innovations) in production technology.

The *specific forms taken by economic growth and the development process* impose their own pressures on the global resource base. Thus, while growing population has increased total demand for food, increasing per capita incomes have encouraged significant improvements in diet through consumption, by many individuals, of more and better-quality food. These processes have encouraged *growth in per capita agricultural output*, a sizeable part of which has been achieved by extending the margin of cultivation into hitherto fallow land, by destruction of forests, and by extension of irrigation. Such expedients can, as we have seen, lead to degradation of soil and water resources, in some cases past the point of no return, as well as to loss of species and general degrading of biosystems. In addition, for many crops grown in the developing world, the globalization of agriculture is leading to changes in the location of production, and increases in the scale of production, with inevitable interference in long-established local biosystems, loss of biodiversity, and increased vulnerability of production to external environmental shocks in the areas affected. Good examples of these effects are the expansion of production of such high-value crops as soybeans, coffee, cotton, palm oil and biofuels, which are leading to widespread changes in cropping patterns, often favouring large-scale monoculture (an inherently vulnerable practice) over the original small-farm structure, and encouraging degradation of ecosystems.

Furthermore, the *pattern of demand for consumer goods* in the expanding markets of developing countries – far from reflecting the growing concerns expressed in developed countries over the sustainability of current consumption patterns – is following very closely the lead actually provided by the developed countries, with no shift towards a radical, resource-saving configuration in prospect. Very naturally, the increasingly affluent citizens of many developing countries, being fully apprised through the global reach of television and the Internet of the material comforts taken for granted in high-income countries, do not want to be 'short-changed' at the very point at which they can at last secure some of these prizes for themselves, by being ushered down a more austere – if more sustainable – self-denying path designed to economize on resource use. This reluctance is all the more understandable given that resource-saving pressures are by no means all-pervasive in the wealthy countries. Indeed, while reflecting on the prospect of the exhaustion of certain key metals, Gordon identifies the continuing, and contagious, built-in consumerism of the wealthy countries as a fundamental barrier to achieving a shift to the truly resource-saving patterns of consumption worldwide needed to head off resource depletion: '[W]estern popular and political culture. . . . sees growth and development as absolutes, quickly converting services originating as luxuries or entertainments for the wealthy into necessities for everyone' (Gordon *et al.*, 2006, p. 1214). 'Unsustainable consumption' is clearly a problem not just in developed countries but also, through emulation, in many of the expanding economies of the developing world.

Again, as noted earlier, a large part of year-on-year increases in global production has resulted from, and is channelled through, *international trade* which is, because of the nature of long-haul freight technology (by ship or, in particular, by air), significantly more energy-intensive than domestic commerce. A further form of international trade, the provision of mass *tourism* facilities and services, is a major growth industry in the developing world. It is also a frequent source of environmental disruption, placing excessive pressure on fragile resources such as coral reefs, and is again energy-intensive insofar as it involves international, often intercontinental, travel.

Last, growth has been accompanied by (and almost certainly reinforced by) rapid *urbanization* which brings with it a further set of pressures on the environment of developing countries through slum development, highly concentrated air pollution (rather than dispersed air pollution which might be absorbed by the biosphere), increased outlays on transportation of food, and enormously expanded, but geographically concentrated, demand for water (for both industrial and domestic use) necessitating the diversion of rivers and increased investment in dams and reservoirs – which frequently involves destruction of natural habitats (see Chapter 14). In addition, since much of the recent expansion of cities in developing countries has been in coastal areas – coastal populations are forecast to reach 6 billion by 2025 (Kennish, 2002) – and, since treatment of industrial and domestic waste effluent is patchy at best, offshore water pollution has been significantly intensified with concomitant destruction of marine ecosystems.

Just as new-found affluence in developing countries may drive resource depletion, so may its opposite – desperate *poverty*. Side-by-side with increasing real incomes for large numbers of people is the phenomenon of rising absolute numbers of rural poor. Rural poverty is itself causing further resource depletion, typically in the form of a vicious circle in which poverty both encourages maximum extraction of output from often marginal land, and discourages prudent land husbandry – such as the use of fertilizers and crop rotation. The result of such '*nutrient mining*' is declining land fertility, and, in the extreme, desertification. Again, *lack of land tenure* often leads to failure to maintain the quality of land, there being little incentive to do so when the benefits may well pass to someone other than the improver. Poverty, being frequently associated with lack of collateral assets, itself diminishes the ability to obtain the financial assistance needed to enable tenant farmers to increase their incomes, thus perpetuating the problem by creating a poverty trap that may be very difficult to escape. In any case, ignorance of the requirements of good husbandry and land-improvement techniques is found to be particularly prevalent amongst the rural poor. (The use of slash-and-burn by many poor rural dwellers is a good example of such resource-depleting agricultural practice.)

Accompanying all of the above is the fundamental common denominator – the need for ever-increasing energy inputs for industrial, agricultural, commercial and domestic use. The production, distribution and use of energy affect the environment in a variety of ways, including the often damaging impact of prospecting, mining, and energy-transmission activities. And, of course, the use of many energy sources has important deleterious effects on air, water, land and biodiversity resources.

Climate change

Nature of global warming and evidence of its existence

Air pollution, as we have seen, has long been recognized as an environmental problem, and as a source of costs to both industry and entire communities. Only relatively recently, however, has the full significance of the impact of such pollution become apparent, and the **global warming** that it has promoted been recognized as the dominant, potentially disastrous, environmental problem facing humanity.

Since the mid-eighteenth century the burning of fossil fuels, deforestation and other changes in land use have resulted in substantial increases in the concentrations of carbon dioxide, methane and nitrogen oxides in the atmosphere. By blocking the radiation back into space of much of the heat reaching the earth from the sun, these gases reduce significantly the natural cooling effect of such radiation, thus creating a 'greenhouse effect' and causing a steady increase in temperatures on earth – global warming.

Although the claim that the earth's atmosphere is heating up has been disputed by some climatologists, the balance of scientific opinion is now firmly behind the hypothesis. The supporting evidence includes such salient facts as that:

- Eleven of the years 1995 to 2006 were among the twelve warmest years since 1850, when systematic record-keeping began (IPCC, 2007).

- Mountain glaciers are almost everywhere shrinking.

- Permafrost in northern latitudes is thawing.

- The Arctic ice-cap is becoming smaller each year – to the extent that the Arctic Ocean (and, in particular, the 'North West Passage') is expected to become navigable by 2010.

- River and lake ice is breaking up earlier each year in many parts of the world.

- Growing seasons for plants are lengthening in middle and high latitudes.

- Heat-loving insects, birds, animals and even plants are being found in progressively higher latitudes (formerly colder areas).

- Timing of plant flowering, insect emergence and egg-laying in birds are occurring earlier (all the above, bar the first, from Menzel *et al.*, 2006).

- Systematic changes are observed in rainfall patterns and in ocean currents (Bryden *et al.*, 2005).

No other explanation (for instance, increased solar or volcanic activity) can account for these symptoms of global warming.

The contention that warming can be blamed on 'greenhouse gases' released as result of anthropogenic (human) activity has been disputed, but here, too, the accumulating evidence seems conclusive. Global emissions of 'greenhouse gases' – resulting mainly from industrial and domestic human activities – atmospheric concentrations of CO_2 (carbon dioxide), and global temperatures show a strong degree of association, so that causation seems very likely. Indeed, according to a recent wide-ranging examination of the global-warming issue, there is now 'An overwhelming body of scientific evidence. . . . [showing] that the Earth's climate is rapidly changing as a result of greenhouse gases caused by human activities' (Stern, 2007, p. 2).

Were the rate of greenhouse-gas emissions to *stabilize* at the levels prevailing in 2006, by 2100 gas concentrations in the atmosphere would be more than three times the levels prevailing in the mid-eighteenth century, and would result in an increase in average temperatures of between 3°C and 10°C. To this should be added important feedback effects resulting from warming, reducing the capacity of plants and soils to absorb carbon dioxide, and causing large quantities of methane (a greenhouse gas) to be released from melting permafrost, especially in Russia and Canada, leading to a further rise in temperature of 1°C–2°C.

Threats to developing countries from global warming

It may still be possible to head off the worst consequences of global warming by implementing appropriate pollution-abatement measures of the kind discussed later in this chapter. But, if emissions are unabated, rising temperature seems likely to have important long-term consequences – many of them negative, and many bearing particularly heavily on developing countries. The main expected resource-depletion effects are:

- Accelerating soil degradation and desertification resulting from changing, and only partly predictable, weather patterns, these including episodes of very high temperatures in the tropics and increased variance in precipitation everywhere with some wet areas becoming wetter, and dry and arid areas becoming drier;
- Dwindling water resources;
- Dieback of rainforests, especially in Brazil, radically altering the local biosystem and releasing large quantities of carbon dioxide so intensifying the greenhouse effect;
- Accelerated loss of species;
- Rising sea levels leading to loss of low-lying islands and coastal areas and increased salination of coastal farmland.

Unless effective countervailing action can be taken, these effects will inevitably lead to major economic and social costs including those of falling crop yields,[3] and negative effects on health due to rising temperatures and climate-induced flooding, with significant increases in the incidence of malnutrition, diarrhoea and malaria. Unfortunately, in addition developing countries appear to be especially open to the adverse impacts of climate change. The reasons for this are examined below.

The special vulnerability of developing countries to climate change

Compared with developed countries *many developing countries are particularly vulnerable to the harmful economic backwash from continuing deterioration of the environment caused by climate change*. The reasons for this fall into three broad categories[4] (which, in part, overlap):

- The greater *exposure* of developing countries to these adverse effects. Specific characteristics of developing countries largely, or entirely, unrelated to their developing status – for instance, geographical location and topography – mean that climate change affects them to a greater extent than developed countries.
- Their greater *sensitivity* to the adverse effects of climate change. Any given effect has a bigger adverse impact on a poor developing country, *just because it is poor*, than on a wealthy developed country.
- Their weaker *adaptive capacity*. Developing countries find it more difficult than do developed countries *to prepare for, and deal with*, the impact of global warming.

Exposure

- *Tropical location:* Many developing countries are *located in the tropics* where adverse climatic factors have typically had a much greater impact on economic activity than is the case in the temperate zones, where most developed countries are located. Relevant features of 'harsh climates' which seem likely to worsen as a result of climate change are

[3] It is possible that, while global warming is in its early stages, the initial slight warming effect, together with the fertilizing effect on crops of an increase in atmospheric carbon dioxide, may increase crop yields in some areas. However, this effect will disappear as temperatures continue to rise.

[4] This three-fold classification is based on that used by Stern (2007, pp. 92–9).

excessive heat (with associated heat stress); *erratic rainfall patterns,* leading to problems with water supply for agriculture; *extreme and damaging climatic events* such as hurricanes, tsunamis and local flooding; *heavy rainfall* causing leaching of nutrients and degradation of soils; and *high incidences of pest and parasite problems* and of *vector-borne diseases.* In locations having these characteristics, especially in the many parts of the developing world where agricultural activity is already carried out close to environmental (climate and biosystem) tolerance limits and crop yields are problematic, even marginal climatic deterioration could have serious immediate effects by creating local food shortages and malnutrition, as well as having damaging long-term effects on output and growth.

■ *Rising sea level:* The melting of polar ice is expected to lead to a significant rise in sea levels. *Small islands (especially tropical atolls)* are particularly vulnerable to sea-level rise. The large majority of small-island states are developing countries, and some face extinction as nations if water levels rise by only a few inches. In these countries, and in larger nations such as Bangladesh where most of the population inhabit areas only marginally above sea level, large-scale relocation of population seems inevitable if sea levels do continue to rise, as seems likely.

■ *Water shortage:* Global warming seems likely to be associated with increases in rainfall in the high latitudes and *decreases in precipitation – and droughts – in the tropics and subtropics.* In the cases of many developing countries this would put great pressure on an already difficult situation. In recent years the Sahel, southern Africa and parts of southern Asia have been badly affected by persistent drought – and the UN has forecast that, by 2025, around 1.8 billion people will be living in countries subject to 'absolute water scarcity' and two-thirds of the world's population will be 'water stressed' (UN Water, 2007). This will affect domestic life (with water shortages affecting cooking and sanitation); agriculture, which already depends on irrigation for some 30 to 40 per cent of total world farm output (and accounts for some 70 per cent of water withdrawals in the process); hydro-electric, energy-generating potential; and the environment generally.

Furthermore, where there is a high level of interdependence of neighbouring countries with regard to water supplies, the potential for conflict sparked by climate-induced water shortages is considerable. West Africa and the Nile Basin are both exposed to particularly high risks in this respect.

■ *Forest die-back:* Climate change is predicted by some climate models to create conditions favourable to the dying-back of much rainforest, rendering many inhabitants of those developing countries well-endowed with forests highly vulnerable. Die-back would jeopardize the way of life, even the survival, of many local communities across the developing world, as well as destabilizing many habitats and the ecology of a large tract of the earth's surface. In addition, the demise of the rainforest on any appreciable scale could release large quantities of carbon dioxide which would reinforce the greenhouse effect.

■ The combination of two or more of the above factors – for instance erratic rainfall and poverty – can further extend 'exposure'. For example, in several areas in Ethiopia, where variation in rainfall is marked, water-storage facilities are very limited (on a per capita basis less than 1 per cent of the capacity of storage facilities in the US where the hydrological variability is actually smaller than in Ethiopia) with attendant adverse effects on health and rural productivity. Climate change that results in a decline in rainfall will exacerbate this situation in Ethiopia and in many other developing countries exposed to the same climatic problem.

Sensitivity

■ Negative feedback effects of economic activity on the environment are most direct and most damaging in precisely those sectors – agriculture, fishing and forestry – in which economic activity in developing countries is much more heavily concentrated than in developed countries.

■ Poverty increases sensitivity to climate patterns, and the poor – with minimal reserves of any sort – may find it much more difficult to react adequately (than would the rich) to events such as failure of rains/monsoons, droughts, and to extreme weather events such as floods and hurricanes.

As we have seen, *population growth* is more rapid in the developing world than elsewhere, and tends to be positively associated with environmental damage in a number of ways. Adverse climatic change will intensify the problems already created by population growth.

■ The *structure of developing country production tends to be particularly inflexible* – characterized by limited responsiveness to shifts in resource availability and prices, and to climatic changes. The move from subsistence cropping, which usually involves a wide range of crops, to cash-cropping, which is more specialized, increases vulnerability in this respect. Failure to adjust the product mix (and associated employment mix) to more profitable, or less climate-sensitive, products, in the face of changes in resource availability, resource prices, and the climate, could result in sharp declines in production, employment and incomes.

■ Urban areas in many developing countries (see Chapter 14) are characterized by *large slum areas* where the poor live. These are often built on the least desirable land – on flood plains or on steep slopes – where they are particularly at risk from flooding and landslides.

■ The already *low health status* of many residents of developing countries, their poor diets and rudimentary sanitation facilities, make such populations especially sensitive to the adverse dietary consequences of declining subsistence output – and negative health impacts of global warming are expected to outweigh favourable ones by far. Many additional deaths are anticipated – mainly in Asia and Africa – from flooding, malnutrition, malaria, and diarrhoea. The countries most affected are likely to be those least able to react positively. Escalating health problems, which will further detract from capacity for efficient productive activity, are likely to comprise another negative feedback loop set up by environmental and climatic factors.

Adaptive capacity

The ability to change course promptly in response to changed circumstances is not a characteristic of most developing countries – at either micro or macro level. Thus:

■ Individual enterprises, mainly farms, will often display very little flexibility in crop selection and cultivation techniques used in the face of changes in their resource (including climate) base. Lack of the technical knowledge needed to effect change is often partly responsible for this rigidity. There is also the failure to perceive what is happening in time, or a misjudging of the imminence of collapse of yields (so that the desire to squeeze one more crop from the soil before returns become unacceptably low persists into the period when returns *are* unacceptably low).[5]

---

[5] This form of 'voluntary myopia' has a counterpart in a stock market heading for a crash. Even if all shareholders confidently expect a downturn, many will be caught holding devalued shares when it happens – because of a desire to hold on until the last minute in order to squeeze all possible profit out of shareholdings.

- The combination of low rural incomes and inadequate financial institutions leaves many rural dwellers unable to gain access to the financial resources that might make possible a constructive reaction to resource degradation. Where existing incomes and meagre savings, if any, are needed for survival, there is no realistic prospect of constructive adaptation in the absence of access to the external resources required to effect change.

- Many developing-country governments lack the administrative capacity, or the will, or the funds, needed if they are to react adequately and appropriately to the economic crises and social pressures likely to be brought about by resource depletion and climate change – as itemized above. Failure to tackle these problems could clearly have serious implications for development prospects.

Why have these problems been allowed to become a threat to further growth and development?

Given the magnitude of the problems already created by resource depletion, negative environmental feedback effects from growth, and climate change – and their potentially catastrophic implications for the future growth prospects of developing countries – it is natural to ask: 'Why have problems of such immense importance been allowed to build up unchecked – indeed, largely unremarked – for so long?' Four reasons are suggested here. The first and second (which are related) refer to the failure to *perceive* the problem at an early stage: (1) The extent and/or imminence of the threats were not apparent until relatively recently – so nothing, or very little, was done. And (2) this ignorance was reflected in the logic underlying the system of National Accounting used by virtually all countries until recently – which did not include explicit measures of the costs of resource depletion and negative feedback from growth, and therefore could not alert users to the emerging problem. A third, and more fundamental, reason for the lack of countervailing action until very recently, is that (3) the nature of the 'markets' for natural resources, pollution, and the effects of climate change are such that self-correcting mechanisms are very unlikely to come into play. Last, (4) the time-discounting procedure used in project appraisal has a built-in bias against adequate consideration of the welfare of future generations.

Lack of foresight

It is clear that the serious nature of the onrushing environmental problems that now confront both the developing and the developed worlds was not appreciated until relatively late in the twentieth century. This was very much the case with climate change which, as recently as the mid-1970s, was the subject of much worried speculation – but largely with regard to the dangers of global *cooling*. (It is not mentioned in Boulding's (1966) celebrated publication on *Spaceship Earth*). The long lag between the build-up of carbon emissions and the onset of adverse effects clearly played an important part in masking the nature of the process, making it difficult for many years to match cause and effect. It *was* recognized that, at some time in the distant future, certain finite resources would run out, but that time was seen as a long way off, and there were plausible arguments to the effect that, in any case, synthetic substitutes might be developed long before that.

National-accounting methods

A second, and related reason for the relatively relaxed attitude adopted by most countries to environmental costs until relatively recently is that *they are not reflected explicitly in the traditional barometer of a nation's economic progress – the System of National Accounts (SNA)*. Indeed, the omission of the value of the services of ecosystems from the SNA used in developing countries (and in most developed countries) has been described as 'a major contributing cause' of the problem that 'ecosystems are still deteriorating worldwide, and with them, the capacity to support human wellbeing' (Sachs *et al.*, 2005) – a problem which, as we have seen, is of great concern in developing countries.

Certainly, it has long been recognized that air and water pollution impose costs of diverse kinds on firms and individuals, but these are not recorded as negative values in the SNA, which measures economic activity not social well-being. Thus the value-added resulting from the polluting activity itself is recorded as a 'good', and the clean-up activities required to offset the effects of pollution – from water purification to additional laundering of clothing – appear as a positive item in the production account of the SNA. The reality that these activities amount, in fact, to a *loss* of resources, and have a *negative* impact on living standards, is nowhere recognized in the SNA. Equally, any additional production of air-conditioning plant (and the electricity for its operation) induced by global warming appear as positive items, part of the output comprising GDP, not negative items.

As for the running-down of the resource base, especially the stock of non-renewable resources, this is classified in the SNA, not as a form of real depreciation, but as a positive contribution to GNP equivalent to the sum of the factor incomes it generates. Thus, the extraction of $1 million worth of irreplaceable uranium ore is recorded as a gain (equal to the total of factor incomes generated by the mining operation minus non-factor costs incurred). The loss of the uranium is not recorded in the SNA, which thus overlook this burden on future generations. Similarly with renewable resources such as forests, consumption at a rate exceeding the rate at which regeneration takes place is not recorded as a cost as it is not seen as essentially similar to the depreciation of manufactured capital assets.

Robert Repetto (1989, p. 40), Director of the Economic Research Program of the World Resources Institute, reinforces this point, observing that a nation 'could exhaust its mineral reserves, cut down its forests, erode its soils, pollute its aquifers, and hunt its wildlife to extinction' without affecting its measured income'. He sees GNP as a measure that confuses the using-up of valuable natural assets with the earning of income. This is a particularly important problem for countries – such as many developing countries – dependent on natural resources for employment and revenues, 'because they are using a system of accounting that ignores their principal assets'.

In developing countries, as elsewhere, national-income accounts 'are crucial because they constitute the primary source of information about the economy and are widely used for assessment of economic performance and policy' (Sachs *et al.*, 2005). This being so, the omission of vital information on environmental factors sends misleading signals to governments about the health and performance of their economies. For example, the apparent success of an economic strategy – evidenced by a rapid growth of GDP as measured in the SNA – which is being achieved by speedy liquidation of its natural capital, masks the fact that the asset base is being run down and that no basis for sustained growth is being created.

If policy-makers in developing countries are, in fact, to take adequate note of environmental factors, it is essential that the national-accounting system takes full account of the services of the ecosystem, in particular those provided by *water and soil* resources (which are often particularly vulnerable to depletion in poor countries, precisely the countries worst equipped, through lack of resources, to prevent their loss, or to deal with the consequences of their loss) and those provided by biodiversity (most of the world's biodiversity being located in the developing world, from where it provides crucial services to both host countries and the world as a whole).

A national-accounting system that takes the environment seriously must, therefore, include both market and non-market flows. The approach currently being developed as a System of Environmental and Economic Accounting (SEEA) makes use of 'satellite accounts' (see below).

However, in contrast to what has happened in a number of developed countries,

> . . . there has been little long-term support for implementation of green accounting in developing countries, arguably where green accounts are most needed – resource-dependent economies where faulty economic treatment of environmental changes is likely to be associated with large-scale misallocation of national resources.
>
> *(Sachs* et al.*, 2005)*

The general approach adopted in extending national accounts to include environmental factors – 'green accounting' – is that of developing **satellite accounts** which bring together economic and environmental information attached to, and integrated into, the conventional national accounts used for decision making. They provide information in a common framework on:

- *Physical flows of resources* – which may be used to ascertain the extent to which an economy is dependent on particular environmental inputs, as well as the sensitivity of the environment to specific economic activities;

- *Flows from the environment into the economy* – and from the economy into the environment – in the form of spending, by government, firms, and individuals on reinforcing the environment;

- *Asset accounts* – which measure the physical and monetary value and changes in that value, of assets in the form of natural resources, land and ecosystems;

- *Extension of existing SNA accounts* to include measures of environmental depletion and defensive expenditure (that is, expenditure which makes good depletion).

They thus make it possible to assess the extent to which present patterns of production and consumption are affecting the environment, and the effectiveness of environmental policies. More broadly the SEEA measures

> the contribution of the environment to the economy and the impact of the economy on the environment. It provides policy-makers with indicators and descriptive statistics to monitor these interactions as well as a database for strategic planning and policy analysis to identify more sustainable paths of development.
>
> *(UN, 2003)*[6]

---

[6] It is not possible to go into further detail on satellite accounting in this chapter. Detailed particulars of the aims and techniques of the SEEA system promoted by the United Nations are available at: *Handbook of National Accounting: Integrated Environmental and Economic Accounting 2003* (usually referred to as *UN 2003*).

Market failure – externalities

Stern observed that 'Climate change presents a unique challenge for economics: it is the greatest example of market failure we have ever seen' (Stern, 2007, p. 1). Here he was referring to the third, and by far the most fundamental, of the reasons for the lack of action to mitigate escalating environmental costs associated with economic growth – in particular those caused by pollution and climate change – the *nature of the market framework* within which these problems arise. Most forms of pollution are, in fact, the result of 'market failure'. They are negative externalities, spillovers from damaging activities, which the normal market processes are powerless to correct since they do not pass through any market.

As long as the users of a natural resource – be they polluters of air, water or any other medium, or extractors of, say minerals or fish – are not required to pay compensation to anyone for their use of, or for the damage they do to, open-access or communally-owned environmental resources, and in particular are not obliged to reimburse the individuals and firms who eventually must pay the bills resulting from environmental deterioration, they have no incentive to curb their polluting activities and will *utilize these resources to a greater extent* than if there were a market in them. If a mechanism existed for charging polluters for the damage they do, so 'internalizing' the external diseconomy they create, they would clearly have an incentive to pollute only so long as the benefits accruing to them from the activity which generates the pollution (say, operating a leather-tanning factory which discharges effluent into a river, damaging the stock of a downstream fish farm) exceeded the charge levied. Such a provision would cause polluting activities to be cut back. This applies to both renewable and non-renewable open-access resources.

A number of policy options have been suggested for dealing with this externality problem – from straightforward bans on polluting to taxes. The options are discussed in the 'policy' section later in this chapter.

Time-discounting

When the economic viability of a proposed new project is appraised, either for its likely private profitability or in a broader consideration of the balance of its expected overall costs and benefits (as discussed in Chapter 20), it is standard practice to take into account the *timing* of expected costs and benefits across the entire lifetime of the project. This is done in order to reflect the fact that people have a positive 'time preference' – giving greater weight to cash flows expected to occur in the near future than to those due only in the distant future. Time-preference reflects both the basic human desire to prefer to have benefits now rather than later ('impatience'), and the increasing risk, as we extend our predictions further and further into the future, that, because of unforeseen factors waiting round the bend, our cash-flow projections may turn out to be inaccurate and that the expected benefits may not actually materialize. For these reasons, it is standard practice in conventional project-appraisal to apply progressively higher discount factors to cash flows the later they are expected to occur. As a result, since discounting has geometric effects, the 'present value' of future flows rapidly dwindles as we push farther into the future or increase the discount rate. Thus, if we adopt a discount rate of, say, 5 per cent per annum, the present value of a £1 000 000 cost or benefit expected to occur (all in one year) 20 years from now, would be £377 000, and 50 years from now it would be £87 000. If the discount rate were increased to 10 per cent, the corresponding values would be £149 000 and a near-negligible £9000.

An important effect of the use of time-discounting is that it leads project appraisers to prefer (other things being equal) projects in which the benefits arise early in the project life and the costs arise late in the project life – over projects in which the costs arise early and the benefits arrive late. Unfortunately, since most natural processes cannot be rushed, it is in the nature of many environmental-improvement projects that they are long term, and involve an initial investment followed by a fairly lengthy gestation period, followed by the desired pay-off. This kind of time-profile of project cash flows is liable to be severely penalized by the discounting process. In contrast, a project that promises early benefits at the expense of heavy costs arising many years later (for instance a project with major terminal 'clean-up' costs, such as an off-shore oil rig) will appear relatively attractive as judged by its overall present value. Thus, the use of discounting in project appraisal could lead decision-makers to approve a project which will involve major environmental damage or costs – a nuclear power station, perhaps – simply because the problems will occur a long way into the future. Equally, the major benefits expected to flow in the long term from banning fishing for an endangered species may take so long to materialize – say 25 years – that the present value of the benefits appears negligible and may be ignored. The result may therefore be that banning fishing may be seen as 'not worth doing' (especially given the political trouble regularly associated with imposing such bans), so that fishing continues to be permitted, and that, in 25 years' time, the species becomes extinct, and the sum total of the value of all future catches thereafter is zero.

In even more extreme cases a project leading to catastrophic cost levels in many years' time may still be accepted because the early-year cash flows are good. Thus, some Norwegian project appraiser back in AD 980, when assessing the plan to set up a colony on Greenland (Diamond, 2006), would almost certainly have approved the project in view of the strong cash-flow forecasts for the first 200 years. The fact that, shortly after project year 400, the colony would collapse (because of climate change, as it happens) leaving no survivors and no realizable assets, would not affect the calculation because of the remoteness in time of the disaster. Only if a near-infinite value had been put on the lives lost could the project have been rejected – and, indeed, it is argued by some that, where the risks inherent in a given situation are very serious, applying any positive discount rate is not appropriate. Ignoring the possibly disastrous consequences of climate change when formulating policy is not an option.

It should be noted that embodying time-preference in discounting in this way is not part of an anti-environmentalist plot by project appraisers. Discounting *does make sense for the present generation*, if its members consider themselves in isolation, seeking to maximize their own welfare and taking no responsibility for generations to come. In effect, discounting works **against intergenerational equity in the environmental context** – biasing current decisions towards the interests of the present generation to the exclusion of the interests of generations unborn. This is a complex issue. (It could be argued, for instance, that applying high discount rates rules out many projects as 'unprofitable', hence cutting present levels of investment and resource use – though this point is vulnerable to the counter-argument that this results in the passing on of fewer capital assets to the future). It is also clearly one which cannot be discussed adequately in terms of economic logic alone. Ultimately the decision as to whether the present generation should maximize the gains it extracts from the environment and leave later generations to pay the price, or instead should attempt to pass on the environment in as good shape as possible, is an ethical one. What is at issue is whether or not the present generation owes anything to posterity, a posterity which cannot, of course, speak for itself. The decision made on this core issue will, certainly, have major implications for the kind of 'sustainability' that is built into an environment strategy.

It is sometimes argued that this point is of little practical importance since the next generation is likely to be better off than the present one, and so able to afford to be discriminated against to some extent (through the use of positive discount rates in project selection). However, this is not a plausible argument in the development context when we consider that for many millions in the developing world economic progress from one generation to the next *cannot* be taken for grated. Moreover, if, by using high discount rates we damage the environment through our project selection, this may well bring about a *reduction* in future incomes – so disqualifying this particular argument for discounting.

Valuing the environment

Measuring environmental costs and benefits

Encouraging more environmentally friendly behaviour by both firms and individuals increasingly involves the use of economic instruments – for example, taxes. (A discussion of such instruments is provided in the penultimate section of this chapter.) Successful, and accurate, application of these instruments requires the ability to measure the extent of the *costs* of the environmental damage at which they are aimed, and the extent of the *benefits* resulting from their use. However, as there is no market in many environmental costs and benefits, they do not have market prices. Accordingly, indirect techniques of ascribing money values to environmental costs and benefits have had to be devised.

Important among these are:

- *Hedonic[7] Valuation* (through which money values are derived for the environmental cost of, for instance, noise pollution, by examining the impact of the environmental problem on measurable variables affected by it – in this case, house prices);

- *Contingent Valuation* (through which the value put on an environmental good, perhaps a park, is estimated by simply asking people – often via a survey questionnaire – how much they would be willing to pay to preserve it);

- *Travel-cost Valuation* (which involves valuing an environmental facility, usually a recreational facility, by estimating the total travel cost – the sum of journeys' *cash-costs* and *time opportunity-costs of travelling* – incurred by the users of the facility).

More detail on these valuation techniques is given in Appendix 11.3, which is available on the Online Learning Centre.

'Sustainable development': definitions and broad implications for policy

Having looked at various aspects of 'non-sustainability' and its possible causes we move on to consider whether we can provide a sharper definition of 'sustainable development' than the rather vague one adopted earlier in this chapter. However, as is explained below, the quest for a unique, agreed concept of 'sustainability' is doomed to failure because of the differing standpoints – either technological or ideological – adopted by various analysts.

---

[7] 'Pleasure-oriented'.

Alternative views of sustainability

Ambiguity as to the meaning of 'sustainability' stems in part from the fact that different individuals differ as to how they choose to see the future. Some may feel that they owe nothing to the future and might therefore favour maximizing resource exploitation in their lifetime. Others may prefer to avoid penalizing future generations by (as they would see it) 'overconsuming' environmental resources, and to pass on to the next generation an economy in the same condition as they found it (or as close to this as possible). Still others may feel bound, by ethical convictions, to pass on a world in the best possible condition (perhaps better than they found it) – even going so far as to put an embargo on all avoidable environmental depletion. Again, the emphasis of some commentators may be on *economic* sustainability, while others may focus on social, or political, or even biophysical sustainability as the core of the concept.

Different kinds of capital

If the activities of the present generation are not to compromise the prospects for improving the welfare of future generations, the present generation must, at the very least, leave the globe as productive (on a per capita basis) as it found it. One 'sustainability rule' that might be derived for the world economy as a whole (the closed economy of 'spaceship earth') from this view is that, at a minimum, and in the absence of technological progress, output in any year must be sufficient to provide the same level of consumption as in the previous year and to replace the depreciation of the stocks of manufactured and human capital over the previous year – that is, to pass on to next year what is, in effect, an intact capital stock. Further, if there is to be sustainable *growth* in consumption from one year to the next, output in any year must *exceed* the sum of the previous year's consumption plus depreciation of the capital stock over that year in order to permit the *net increase* in the capital stock needed for an increase in total output in subsequent periods. (To allow for an increasing population, all of the above values would be converted to *per capita*.)

Thus, if GDP represents a particular $ value of the gross (i.e. total) global annual output, all of which is either consumed (C), or used to make good the $ value of the annual depreciation of the stock of capital (d – comprising manufactured capital, human capital and natural capital[8]) required to produce that output, sustainability (without growth) requires that:

$$GDP = C + d \qquad (11.1)$$

that is:
$$C = GDP - d \qquad (11.2)$$

And *sustainable growth* requires that, if the $ value of consumption is once again C, gross output will have to be larger (to permit expansion of the capital stock), at GDP*, and:

$$GDP^* > C + d \qquad (11.3)$$

If a distinction is made between manufactured capital (d_M), human capital (d_H) and natural capital (d_N) sustainability (with growth) would require that, in any year:

$$GDP^* > C + (d_M + d_H + d_N) \qquad (11.4)$$

so:
$$C < GDP^* - (d_M + d_H + d_N) \qquad (11.5)$$

---

[8] Some economists include 'social capital' and 'institutional capital' here.

(Again, all of the above values would be converted to a *per capita* basis by dividing by population).

The discussion in this chapter has emphasized the importance to production of environmental resources in the form of '**environmental capital**' (or 'natural capital'). However, as they stand, equations (11.1), (11.2) and (11.3) make no specific mention of any contribution to production by environmental resources. This conceals a fundamental, highly contentious, assumption – to the effect that there is no practical need to separate out environmental capital from other forms of capital – the rationale being that environmental capital is perfectly substitutable by manufactured or human capital (that is, by d_M plus d_H). *This implies that the running down of the stock of environmental capital can be fully compensated for by increasing the stock of non-environmental capital – so that there is no need to differentiate between the two.* From this perspective, what matters for sustainable long-run development is simply the provision of adequate capital resources for investment, irrespective of whether this capital is man-made or 'natural'.

This extreme view of the nature of capital is known as **very weak sustainability**. It might be interpreted as consistent with a 'business as usual' approach to development which would depend heavily on the market, and would go for maximum growth. It implies the assumption that, in the event of a shortage of a particular kind of natural resource, the operation of free markets will ensure that 'technical fixes' are devised which make possible the substitution of man-made resources for natural ones.

A slightly more demanding requirement for sustainability is embodied in (11.4) and (11.5). This is similar to the condition proposed by Pearce and Atkinson which provides for **weak sustainability**:

$$Z = S/GDP - [d_M + d_H + d_N] / GDP \qquad (11.6)$$

where Z is an index of sustainability, S is aggregate national saving, and GDP and d_M, d_H and d_N are as defined in (11.4). 'Weak sustainability' of economic development is possible if $Z > 0$, requiring no more than that the development pattern ensures that the per capita income of future generations is no less than the per capita income of the present generation (Pearce *et al.*, 1989). This condition asserts that sustained growth is possible on the basis of substitution (with perfect substitutability) of man-made capital for natural capital, and that the implied development path will be satisfactory from an anthropocentric standpoint.

Many analysts would, however, reject these 'weak/very weak sustainability' positions. It is generally agreed that, in certain production processes, natural resources *can* be replaced entirely by man-made resources (manufactured capital) – that is, the two are *perfect substitutes*. For many other products, however, this is not the case – that is, those where natural resources and man-made resources are *complements*. In the future increasing human ingenuity will, in many cases, make it possible not only to economize on resource inputs per unit output (through improvements in the overall technical efficiency of production processes) but also, if desired, to shift the boundary between the contribution of natural capital and manufactured capital, so further reducing the required input of natural resources per unit of output. Nevertheless, so the more cautious 'strong-sustainability' position insists, there is a limit to this. Ultimately, the production process cannot continue to produce total output with a zero input of natural resources. A certain basic minimum input of the natural resource (either renewable or non-renewable) must be available or the process will no longer be feasible – will no longer be 'sustainable'. Moreover, it may well be that certain *non-renewable* natural resources cannot be substituted by either renewable or man-made capital.

Commentators who are less convinced of the feasibility of significant substitution possibilities, and who are very concerned about the dangers inherent in leaving future generations with a natural capital stock which is inadequate, will opt for a more cautious, '**stronger-sustainability**' policy route.

Indeed, it is possible to imagine scenarios more extreme than those just outlined. Equally, it is possible to contemplate a '**very-strong-sustainability**' stance which aims at achieving a zero-growth steady state (probably with no growth of population) with minimum impact on the environment ('decoupling'). Even more extreme 'environmentalist' positions might be adopted – such that use of natural resources was *minimized*, this requiring a reduction in total output.

Sustainability in practice: are we living beyond our means?

How may we work out whether the development path of a particular developing country, or region, is 'sustainable'? Several approaches have been suggested, ranging from simple 'indicators' to complex, comprehensive analyses of resource use by a country relative to resource availability.

We do not have sufficient information on resource availability, resource use, and the true extent of substitutability of man-made for natural capital, to generate hard-and-fast estimates of exactly where developing countries are on the 'sustainability spectrum'. However, we do have information which can be used as 'indicators' of sustainability status. In this section we present the results of two very different approaches to using 'indicators' – an 'adjusted net saving' approach developed by the World Bank (Hamilton, 2000), and the 'biological-footprint' approach pioneered by Wackernagle and colleagues (Wackernagle *et al.*, 2002).

An adjusted-net-savings approach to assessing sustainability status

The World Bank study makes use of the concept of *adjusted net saving (ANS)*, which modifies the traditional national-accounting measure of savings by allowing for environmental factors. Specifically, the level of *genuine saving* in any country is given by the value of 'investment in produced assets and human capital, less the value of depletion of natural resources and the value of accumulation of pollutants' (Hamilton, 2000). This definition of saving differs from the traditional one in that it allows for the cost of depreciation of the stock of natural assets (energy, minerals and forests), includes the cost of damage done by carbon dioxide, and treats expenditure on education as saving rather than as consumption.

The trajectories of ANS for the world, and for developed and developing countries, for the years 1990 to 2005, are shown in Figure 11.2, and the corresponding figures for major regions in Figure 11.3.[9] It will be seen that, according to this indicator of sustainability, all of the main groupings of developing countries included, with the exception of sub-Saharan Africa, are – *on average* – in the 'sustainable' zone, with positive ANS for *all* years 1991 to 2005. By contrast, the sub-Saharan region recorded positive average values in only six of the fifteen years, and was trending down from 1999 onwards.

[9] Data for the Middle East and North Africa were not available for most years.

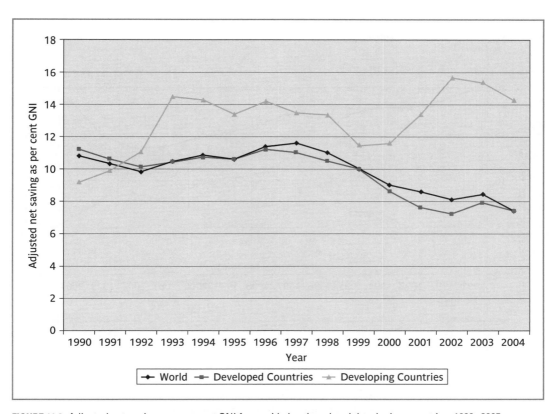

FIGURE 11.2 Adjusted net savings as per cent GNI for world, developed and developing countries, 1990–2005
Source: Based on World Bank data quoted in World Resources Institute 'Earth Trends' site at
http://earthtrends.wri.org/searchable_db/index.php?theme=5&variable_ID=590&action=select_countries

However, looking individually at the 83 developing countries for which data were available for all years in the period 1991–2005, we find that only 28 were unambiguously following a sustainable growth path in the sense that they recorded positive values for ANS in *every* year. Of these only 4 were in sub-Saharan Africa; 11 were Asian countries (notably India – and China, with 25.1 per cent ANS, the highest value recorded by any country); and 8 were in the Central American and Caribbean region. A further 12 developing countries were unambiguously pursuing a *non-sustainable* growth path, displaying negative values for ANS in all years 1991 to 2005. Of these 8 were from sub-Saharan Africa and 3 from the Middle East. The remaining 43 countries had a mixture of positive and negative ANS values over the period examined – suggesting non-sustainability of growth paths in many cases.

Overall, as might be expected *a priori*, non-sustainable growth paths are often recorded by resource-dependent countries such as the oil producers. (For example, Saudi Arabia recorded the very high average depletion rate of −22.4 per cent of GNI, and Nigeria the even higher negative figure of −26.8 per cent, implying a very high rate of net depletion of natural assets.) At the other extreme, the booming non-resource-dependent exporters of Asia generally performed well in terms of the apparent sustainability of their growth paths – as indicated by the Adjusted Net Savings measure.

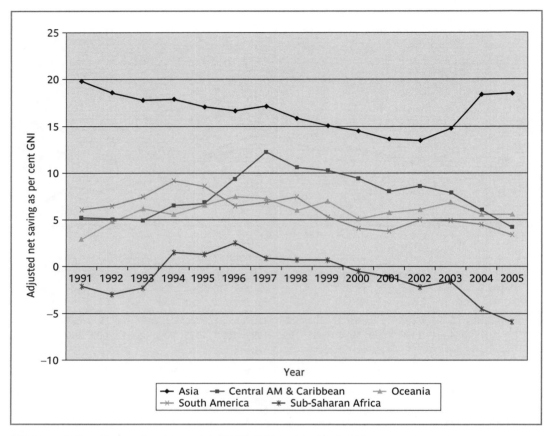

FIGURE 11.3 Adjusted net savings as per cent GNI for major regions: 1991–2005
Source: Based on World Bank data quoted in World Resources Institute 'Earth Trends' site at
http://earthtrends.wri.org/searchable_db/index.php?theme=5&variable_ID=590&action=select_countries

The 'biological-footprint' approach

A second, very different, approach to working out whether, and to what extent, growth
of the global economy is sustainable is to ask whether we are still within the regenerative
capacity of the biosphere. Wackernagel *et al.* (2002) seek to answer this question by making
use of the concept of the 'ecological footprint' (EF) – a measure, expressed in terms of land
area, of the 'ecological demand' placed on the carrying capacity of the natural environment
by a given population. A 'footprint' represents the land area required to maintain the
consumption and waste-disposal activities of that population. At the global level, this
translates into the estimation, using data on aggregate human demands on the environment,
of the minimum 'biologically productive area' (in effect, the land-equivalent area) required
for all productive and waste-absorption activities – the 'ecological footprint' of humanity.
By working out how much area is needed for agriculture (crops and animal grazing),
forests, plantations, fisheries, industry, power generation, housing, transportation and other
infrastructure, and how much area is needed to sequester just enough CO_2 to prevent the
overall level of that gas from increasing because of the burning of fossil fuels – 'nature's
supply of ecological services can . . . be expressed in global hectares of biologically
productive space'.

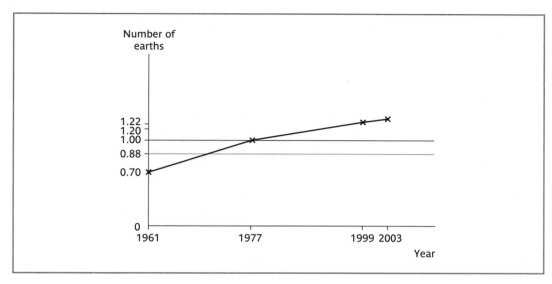

FIGURE 11.4 Ratio of Required to Actual Global Ecological Capacity, 1960–2003

Note: The horizontal line at 0.88 represents 88 per cent of earth's biologically productive area surface area, reflecting the Bruntland proposal that 12 per cent of that area should be reserved for conservation.

Sources: Figures for 1961–1999 from Wakernagel *et al.* (2002); 2003 value from WWF (2006, Table 1).

Comparing demand for land for productive activity with that required for regeneration resulted in the conclusion that, whereas in 1961 total demand for the services of the global biosphere was equivalent to only 70 per cent of the earth's biological productivity, somewhere *around 1977 demand for natural capital had begun to overshoot biological productivity (that is, to deplete the planet's natural capital stock)*, and by 1999 it had reached 120 per cent of the regenerative potential – in effect requiring '1.20 earths' to restore the ecological balance in that year. By 2003, according to Hails (2006), around '1.22 earths' were needed – meaning that the ecological resources consumed in that year took nearly one year and three months to produce. If the Bruntland Report's recommendation that 12 per cent of the earth's biologically productive area surface area should be reserved for conservation is followed, then the annual land requirement increases *pro rata*, and the overshooting process would have begun in the early 1970s, reaching an overshoot of nearly 40 per cent by 2003. These results are summarized in Figure 11.4.

Several other 'environmental-footprint' studies have been conducted, notably that by Chen *et al.* (2007) which finds that China's EF increased between 1981 and 2001, throughout which period the 'EF per capita always exceeded the biocapacity', and that by van Vuuren and Bouwman (2005), which projects EF values forward, by region, from 1995 (when, according to Wakernagel, the global EF was 'already unsustainable') to 2050, and finds that EF rises in all regions, and nearly doubles for the world as a whole (the smallest increase being for the OECD countries).

At the level of individual countries, the most recent figures available (Hails, 2006) indicate a mixed picture for the (per capita) ecological footprint of developing countries. Specifically, in 2003 middle-income developing countries were, overall, in ecological 'credit', while low-income developing countries as a group were – just – in deficit. (Developed countries were heavily in debt.) With regard to individual regions: Africa was, overall, marginally positive. Of the 47 countries for which information was available,

20 were in deficit – and Congo, Gabon, Mauritania and Namibia had the largest 'surpluses'. The footprint bias of the Middle East and Central Asian countries was heavily negative; 15 countries were in ecological deficit (UAE, Kuwait, Israel and Saudi Arabia being the heaviest debtors) and the remaining 5 were only marginally positive. Of 18 developing countries in Asia and the Pacific, 12 (including both China and India) had an ecological deficit in 2003 – and the region as a whole was in deficit. In contrast, Latin America and the Caribbean recorded, overall, a strong 'surplus'. However, this disguised divergent behaviour. All of the reporting Caribbean states had negative values – while all of the South American countries were positive. As for North American and European countries, of the 24 recorded, only 4 were in 'ecological surplus' in 2003 – Canada, Finland, Latvia, and Sweden.

The question may be asked – 'How can the world economy continue to "overshoot"'? The answer lies in the simple logic of a bank account. For much of humanity's span on earth the rate of accumulation of natural assets such as forests and fisheries vastly exceeded the rate of use – resulting in a large and growing positive balance in the ecological account. Since roughly the mid-eighteenth century, however, draw-downs have risen sharply until, at a point in the 1970s (according to the studies quoted here), they exceeded deposits. Thereafter 'Humanity is no longer living off nature's interest, but drawing down its capital' (WWF, 2006), a process that can continue for a time as accumulated stocks of ecological assets are turned into waste. Sooner or later, however, this process of net depletion of resources may compromise the earth's capacity to renew itself. When might this happen?

> A moderate business-as-usual scenario, based on United Nations projections of slow, steady growth of economies and populations, suggests that by 2050 humanity's demand on nature will be twice the biosphere's productive capacity . . . . At this level of ecological deficit, exhaustion of ecological assets and large-scale ecosystem collapse become increasingly likely.
> *(WWF, 2006)*

One final observation: the forecasts generated by 'ecological footprint' analysis seem much more alarming than those of the World Bank's 'adjusted net saving' conclusions on sustainability. Why is this? The answer lies largely in the view taken by the World Bank (and many analysts) that using resources to create various kinds of capital, including human capital, is a positive addition to the resource bank, not a negative drawing-down of resources. Of course, it remains to be seen how productive these investments will be but, should it turn out that today's heavy expenditure on R&D makes possible through biotechnology the virtual disappearance, foreseen by Freeman Dyson (2008) as explained later in the chapter, of the problem of climate change, the arithmetic of ecological-footprint analysis will alter dramatically.

Environmental policies for developing countries

Introduction

It is clear from the foregoing discussion that an effective response to the environmental problems confronting developing countries must be twin-track – pursued simultaneously at two levels – global and national. No amount of enlightened, environmentally friendly policy enactment at the national level can enable a country to avoid depredations wrought by climate change, a phenomenon which, by its nature, must be tackled by concerted, co-operative global action and cannot be solved piecemeal at national level. Equally, successful mitigation, or accommodation, of the negative effects of global warming by the international community will be rendered irrelevant in any individual developing country which fails to tackle local environmental problems; holding the effects of climate change at bay is a necessary, but not a sufficient, condition for avoiding, or mitigating, damaging environmental problems at home. Active domestic policies will also be required; 'business as usual' is not an option in most countries.

In this section we summarize environmental-policy options available at national, and at global, levels, always bearing in mind the overriding assumption on which the whole of the discussion of this chapter is based – that, despite the gravity of environmental problems, the aim of development policy remains that *it must still be possible for developing countries realistically to aspire to achieve, at some future date, standards of living similar to those of developed countries.* It may well be that, in time to come, the life-styles of developed-country populations will change. Reduced emphasis on the role of economic growth as a means of maximizing the quantity of material possessions, in favour of other forms of consumption, may be a necessary adjustment of behaviour reflecting the fact that recovering from centuries of profligate depletion of the earth's limited environmental endowment does involve real costs. But, however 'first-world' life-styles evolve and move away from today's configuration because of environmental imperatives, considerations not only of equity, but also of international political and economic stability, require that these life-styles must still be attainable, in principle at least – and perhaps at some relatively distant date – by all who aspire to them. 'It is neither desirable, nor remotely feasible to seek the removal of the risk of dangerous climate change through reduction in global ambitions for higher . . . living standards' (Garnaut, 2007).

Extension of the market

It has been argued that, if private property (ownership) rights, and associated markets in which these rights could be bought and sold, could be extended to cover *all* of the resources required for, and affected by, production – and this would include water, air, the biosphere, and so on – then resource owners would have an interest in ensuring that their resources were not used without appropriate payment, and were thus never used in the uncompensated and uncontrolled way in which many environmental resources are currently used and depleted (Coase, 1960). Unfortunately, while the idea of bringing environmental resources into the market has attractions as a means of ensuring that their true scarcity value is recognized, and users are charged accordingly, in practice the massive tasks of extending the market in this way, and of enforcing owners' rights, renders this approach impractical as a general solution to the problem of how best to go about 'internalizing externalities'. Other means must be used.

Taxation

Taxing polluters

One answer to the problem of excessive pollution resulting from the ability of a polluter to inflict a negative externality on the community is a pollution tax. The 'Pigovian' tax (named after **A.C. Pigou**, who first suggested it), designed to bring about an 'optimum level of pollution', is illustrated in Figure 11.5. In the figure the line (P1.Q3) represents, for a polluting firm, its marginal operating revenue minus its marginal (private) operating cost – that is, its 'marginal private net revenue' (MPNR). Given that we expect unit private costs of

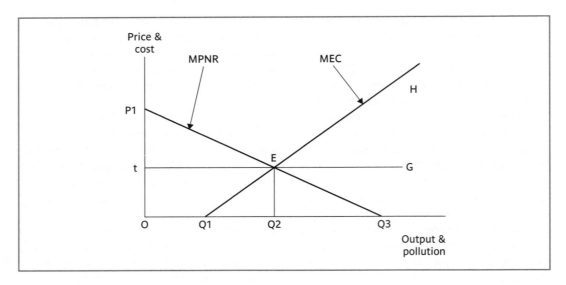

FIGURE 11.5 'Pigovian' optimal pollution tax

production to rise as output increases, and unit revenues to be constant or to fall, the line (P1.Q3) can be expected to be downward-sloping from left to right as rising cost depresses marginal profit. Private profit will be maximized at output Q3 where MPNR is depressed to zero. The line (Q1.H) represents the marginal *external* cost (MEC) of pollution inflicted by the firm on the outside world at different levels of output. This may be expected to increase as output rises.

From the point of view of the community as a whole, so long as MPNR exceeds MEC it makes sense to *increase output* – even though this does entrain increased pollution – since the induced marginal rise in benefits accruing to the firm with each unit increase in output (measured by the height of {P1.Q3}) exceeds the increase in the external cost inflicted on the community by that increase in output (measured by the height of Q1.H). This is the case for all levels of output up to Q2. However, if output is at a level such that MEC exceeds MPNR (which is the case at all points to the right of Q2) then it will be in the community's interest to *reduce output* – until Q2 is reached. It follows that the optimal level of output from the point of view of the community as a whole – and hence the *'optimum level of pollution'* – is not Q3, where the private profitability of the firm is maximized, or Q1, where pollution is minimized, but Q2.

How might the firm be induced to produce output Q2? Pigou suggested the application of a tax on each unit of output at a rate exactly equal to MEC (and MPNR) at the optimal output Q2 – that is, a tax equal to Ot (or E.Q2). With this tax in place, at levels of output below Q2 the firm still makes a profit since MPNR is greater than the tax, and hence will have an incentive to increase output. But, at outputs greater than Q2, MPNR is less than the cost of the tax, so the firm will cut output. Only at output OQ2 will the firm be in profit-maximizing equilibrium. Thus, by setting a tax equal to EQ2, the government induces the firm to produce at the socially optimal level of output.

While the Pigovian tax offers an attractive means of simultaneously making polluters pay for their polluting activities and 'optimizing' pollution, several practical problems make it difficult to use in practice. These fall into two broad categories – valuation problems and information problems. Valuation issues arise most commonly when a polluter damages an asset which lies outside the market – for example, the ambience of a park affected by air or noise pollution. Considerable progress has been made in devising measures of such damage which make it possible to attach money values to non-marketed costs and benefits; some examples of these techniques were given above in the section on 'valuing the environment'. Information problems arise in relation to the Pigovian tax since, before it can be implemented, the positions of the MPNR and MEC curves must be known. Most firms could probably construct their MPNR (or a section of it, at any rate) though they might hesitate to divulge the information to tax authorities if they felt that an increased tax bill might result. The MEC curve, which could summarize damage done to very large numbers of firms and individuals (some possibly not aware of the damage, or of the value of the damage, or of the source of the damage) could, in many cases, be very hard to identify. For these reasons, Pigou's tax on polluters has not been widely used, and alternative financial charges, such as the requirement that polluters' permits up to a 'capped' level be purchased by auction, are applied, or at least discussed, instead.

'Domestic' environmental policies for developing countries

As noted above, while successful international action on climate change is a precondition for ameliorating many of the environmental problems facing developing countries, it will not solve these problems in the absence of appropriate policies at the national level. Nor, of course, will it do anything to improve the situation with regard to environmental difficulties unrelated to global warming. So, what policy initiatives might developing-country governments consider implementing? We divide our proposals into 'direct' and 'indirect' policy options, as follows:

Possible direct domestic environment policies for developing countries

- *Provide direct financial assistance* to farmers in affected areas to fund:
  a *Reforestation* in areas affected by excessive logging in order – (1) to prevent further destruction of local grasslands by promoting soil stabilization and providing windbreaks; (2) to re-establish former forest ecosystems and habitats; (3) to restore forage potential; and (4) to enhance carbon-sequestration capacity;
  b *Soil-stabilization* programmes in marginal areas threatened with desertification. Tree-planting programmes have proved effective in some areas as has the introduction of perennial cropping plants;
  c *Anti-salination* measures – including improved irrigation techniques;
  d Protection, or restoration, of coastal *mangroves*.
- *Strengthen, or ensure more effective enforcement of, legislation* banning excessive levels of logging of forests, especially native forests, and over-fishing of coastal and river fish resources.
- *Introduce land reform* to provide more secure tenure for small farmers and individual-household property rights in land. Having no guaranteed long-term stake in their holdings, tenant farmers with insecure tenure have little incentive to improve their land, and may be tempted to go for maximum short-term exploitation, to the detriment of the quality of the land. Similar problems sometimes affect traditional communal ownership of land. Since individual members of the landowning community in this case derive only a small part of the benefit from any land improvement they carry out, and since 'free riders' who do nothing stand to benefit from others' efforts, land degradation is a constant danger.

■ *Introduce rational pricing regimes* reflecting market conditions for regular agricultural inputs such as fertilizers, water, fuel and electricity – in order to discourage wasteful use (which is common where blanket subsidies are offered in an attempt to encourage agricultural activity).

■ *In urban areas increase spending on sanitation and clean-water provision* especially in slum areas.

■ *Adopt the System of Environmental and Economic Accounting* (SEEA) – an invaluable guide to true changes in GNI (especially in resource-dependent countries of the kind common in the developing world).

Possible indirect domestic environment policies for developing countries

■ *Increase spending on education, primary healthcare, and birth-control* programmes in both urban and rural areas. Environmental pay-offs include improved educational and health status of the labour force – which feed into productivity improvement, increased incomes, and hence enhanced capacity to self-help over environmental problems.

■ *Encourage granting of legal title to property, including slum property*, in order to stimulate enterprise activity by providing collateral against which loans may be raised – hence, in due course, creating a capacity for self-help with environmental problems. Fostering of microcredit schemes can have similar results.

■ In all of the above 'indirect' approaches to environmental improvement, biasing *assistance in favour of women recipients* can appreciably increase the effectiveness of the policy measures.

'Global' environmental policies

The developed countries currently are, and historically have been, the main sources of resource depletion and of emissions causing climate change. The legacy of their earlier, and current, use of natural resources, and their impact on the broader environment, today affect them, and also developing-world countries, profoundly. There is thus a clear moral argument to the effect that developed countries should blaze the trail (that is, foot the bill), in the initial phases at least, on the way to achieving a sustainable growth path for the global economy – including the developing countries. At the same time, if pollution-abatement schemes are to have any hope of success, it will not be possible to ignore for very long the massive, and growing, contributions of China and other developing countries to the pollution problem.

Five different classes of policy measure seem appropriate in this context – those designed:

1 to reduce emissions of greenhouse gases by current emitters using existing technologies
2 to reduce emissions by improving emitting technologies
3 to reduce the volume of already emitted greenhouse gases
4 to economize on depletion of resources
5 to improve substitutability between natural and man-made resources.

These are looked at, briefly, below. All bar the last two concern specifically climate-change mechanisms.

'Optimizing' emissions using existing technology

With regard to climate change, reducing, or at least containing, greenhouse-gas emissions to 'safe' levels is the central priority. As it is generally recognized that market forces alone will not suffice to bring this about, some form of control over current emissions, together with a programmed reduction of emissions to a level well below these currently prevailing, are needed.

Several approaches to emission control have been considered. These include:

- *Fixed upper limits*, set by government, on emissions – backed up by fines for non-compliance;

- *Permits to pollute* which could be sold to firms (some would prefer permits to be given out free[10]) and which could thereafter be traded at prices determined by the commercial valuation placed on the right to pollute by polluters;

- *Pollution or 'carbon' taxes* paid by polluters to compensate others for the external diseconomies being inflicted on them through pollution (including the effects of climate change).

The only significant international agreement, thus far, aimed at reducing greenhouse-gas emissions is the Kyoto agreement. Under the terms of this agreement, which was made in 1997 and formally entered into force in 2005, industrialized countries would be required, by 2008–12, to cut their greenhouse-gas emissions overall to 5.2 per cent below their 1990 levels. (This would equate to a cut by around 29 per cent of the level emissions were expected to reach, if unchecked, by 2010.)

Countries having difficulty in meeting their target reductions may purchase additional emission authorizations by financing emission-saving projects in developing countries – and a secondary market has emerged on which pollution entitlements are bought and sold; in 2007 the turnover on this market was estimated at over US$60 billion.

In addition to controls affecting primarily industrial actors (and consumers and employees only indirectly through the prices they pay and the wages they earn), many governments have introduced, or are considering, legislation affecting the individual citizen directly – such as levying emission taxes on cars, charging for garbage removal, and taxing air travel.

Developing new low-emission technologies

The advent or expectation of financial penalties for failure to meet carbon-emission targets has boosted the drive to develop new, 'greener' production technologies. The aims here are to create a new generation of technologies for industry which yield lower levels of greenhouse gas, and to find more efficient ways of dealing with such gases as are released (for instance, sequestration of emitted gases in artificial underground or marine 'sinks'). These technologies seem likely to be the result of R&D activities primarily in developed countries, but should prove of value to developing countries wishing to abate their own emissions.

Removing greenhouse gases from the atmosphere

A useful contribution to countering global warming using existing know-how could be made by significantly expanding investment in plants and trees that absorb greenhouse gases. This is a proposal with worldwide applicability, but financial support from the wealthy nations would be needed to make it feasible in most developing countries. Much more speculative

---

[10] But this (so-called 'grandfathering') would incur a cost in both efficiency and fairness.

is the prospect, floated by William Nordhaus (2008) that, in due course, increasingly sophisticated bio-engineering techniques will yield a 'low-cost backstop technology' which will save the day – his suggestion here being 'genetically-engineered carbon-eating trees'. Lest this idea appear entirely fanciful, Freeman Dyson (2008) provides some pointers to a possible underlying logic. Starting with the observation that, each year, around 8 per cent of all carbon dioxide in the atmosphere is absorbed by vegetation before being returned to the atmosphere, Dyson suggests that genetic modification of plants, in particular trees, could result in extended, possibly permanent, sequestration periods. Converting this annual capture of carbon dioxide by trees into 'liquid fuels and other useful chemicals' could cut the quantity of this greenhouse gas in the atmosphere by half, so radically changing 'the rules of the climate game'. Such is the momentum behind the advance of biotechnology that Dyson believes this could happen within the next twenty years – and 'almost certainly within fifty years'.[11]

Policies for mitigating resource exhaustion

Many metals cannot be substituted by renewable materials. Aside from developing new terrestrial supplies by redoubling prospecting efforts, or recovering sea-bed 'nodules' of manganese, nickel, copper and cobalt, (or, at the level of science fiction, mining asteroids known to be vastly rich in valuable minerals), the main options available for extending the availability of many minerals are:

- More efficient and parsimonious metal use in production;
- Improved product design aimed at economizing in metal input;
- More, and more efficient, recycling of used metal;
- Redesigning products specifically in order to make them easier to recycle;
- Redeveloping old metal sources – mainly tailings from worked-out mines.

Developing substitute resources

As we have seen, the sustainability of growth paths in the future will depend, not just on how we deal with climate change, but also on just how 'substitutable' man-made resources are for natural resources, and how substitutable natural resources are for one another. The hope of those persuaded by 'weak-substitutability' arguments is that, under pressure of rising resource prices associated with depletion of specific natural resources, 'technical fixes' will emerge which make possible the use of alternative materials not in short supply. While it seems very unlikely that, in the end, a technology will emerge which can transform any resource into any other, past experience does suggest that intensive R&D efforts can yield many new substitution possibilities, as well as suggesting new ways to reduce inputs of particularly scarce material per unit of output. Success in these endeavours will be of great long-term value to both developed and developing countries in spinning out the lifetime of already depleted resources.

---

[11] In response to this exchange, Leigh Sullivan (2008), of the Southern Cross University in Lismore, New South Wales, referring to Parr and Sullivan (2005), writes that the carbon-eating plants (fixing carbon in highly stable form within silicon nodules) are already in existence without the need for genetic modification, in the form of certain cultivars within single species of common plants such as wheat and sugar-cane. These cultivars absorb particularly large amounts of carbon, so that plantings confined to these particular genetic strains could greatly increase the amount of carbon sequestered. Reference is also given to www.goldschmidt2007.org/abstracts/A985.pdf

Similarly, the emergence of successful – in the sense of cost-effective – 'alternative' sources of energy to fossil fuels will be of immense value to all nations, developed and developing. Obvious examples of possible contenders here are low-cost solar, wind, wave, and geothermal power – together with improved energy-storage devices such as fuel cells.

Summary conclusions

- We began this chapter by adopting a 'working definition' of 'sustainable development' requiring that the growth achieved by the present generation should not compromise the capacity of future generations to 'meet their own needs' – which, in the case of developing countries, we took to include the possibility of significant improvement in their living standards.

- Potential 'threats' to sustainability so defined were seen to reside in the revival of the Malthusian concern over the possible inadequacy of food resources in the face of population growth (especially for the very poor), in the sheer size of the resource-mobilization effort needed to make a real difference to living standards across the developing world, in the rapid depletion of the global resource base through the using-up of non-renewable resources and the degradation of many crucial renewable resources, and in the special form of resource degradation which is, perhaps, the most troubling of all – climate change.

- A detailed analysis of the resource-availability situation suggested that clear upper limits were already apparent for availability of supplies of both the major fossil fuels and a number of key non-renewable minerals. In addition, stocks of (in principle 'renewable') environmental resources crucial to achieving sustainable development were seen to be under pressure through over-use and because of destructive, depleting feedback loops from industrial and domestic use. Particularly important in this respect were the widespread degradation of *land* (through erosion, degradation of soil quality, and desertification), *air* (through pollution by emissions from power stations, vehicles, factories and the like), *water* (through pollution by industrial, agricultural and domestic effluents), and *biodiversity* (through destruction of diversity of species and genetic diversity), and also the weakening of *the cleansing effect of pollution 'sinks'* through pressure of use.

- The 'drivers' of this resource depletion were identified as industrial expansion; population growth; a shift in developing-country demand towards better-quality, more resource-intensive food; rapid urbanization; and the continued growth of the 'consumer culture – in both developed and developing countries. A further important cause of resource decay, especially in the countryside, was found to be *poverty* – which was associated with both physical debility (and hence low productivity of labour) and a desperate and immediate need to extract the maximum from the soil, irrespective of the negative implications for its future fertility.

- All of the threats to the natural-resource base were seen to be greatly intensified by the phenomenon of global warming caused by emissions of greenhouse gases. Many developing countries are likely to be particularly hard hit by climate change because they find themselves (for geographic or topographic reasons) relatively exposed to its adverse

▶

effects; because their delicate economies are especially sensitive to its resource-damaging impacts; and because – at several different levels – they lack the adaptive capacity required to change course in order to avoid them.

- That such serious environmental problems should have failed to capture the attention of economists and others until relatively recently was attributed to lack of foresight, market failure, and weaknesses in the analytical techniques (and the assumptions on which these depended) traditionally used by economists. Shortcomings in standard national-accounting methods – in particular, the failure to see resource depletion as a 'cost' – and the excessive discounting of future events by the usual project-appraisal methods, were considered to have played an important part here.

- Attention then turned to the nature of 'sustainable development'. The key requirement for sustainability was found to be the fairly obvious one (derived directly from our 'working definition') that the present generation should pass on to the next a capital stock at least as large as the one it had inherited, and thus capable of maintaining the present level of per capita production. If the aspirations of the developing world for significant growth are to be accommodated, then an augmented capital stock will be required. However, the *precise composition of this required capital stock* remains a matter of considerable debate. The key point at issue is the degree of substitutability that exists between different forms of capital – man-made, human, social, institutional and natural. The optimistic view of the 'weakly sustainable' position is that, given time and investment, human ingenuity can turn most forms of capital into substitute forms of capital – a modern version of the 'philosophers' stone' story. More sceptical analysts, favouring a 'stronger-sustainability' position, fear that certain natural resources will remain unique in the sense that they can never be replaced by a man-made substitute. Insofar as such resources are important for economic development, they must be carefully husbanded and, in the case of renewable resources, not allowed to be depleted to the point beyond which they cannot regenerate naturally. Clearly, the resolution of these uncertainties is a matter of considerable urgency for the framing of long-run development policy in the new world of multilateral resource constraints and depletion.

- The 'strong' versus 'weak' sustainability debate carried over into the two tests we reported of the extent to which the global economy is, or is not, pursuing a sustainable growth path. Here an audit of resource use against the capacity of the globe to regenerate (the 'ecological-footprint' approach) found serious 'overshooting' by over-use of that capacity, leading to the obvious conclusion that use of resources must somehow be cut back. However, no allowance was made in this analysis for the possibility that some of the resources 'wasted' – on, say, R&D – might have powerful long-term pay-offs through enhanced resource substitutability or resource productivity. Starting from a 'weaker-substitutability' standpoint, a second study, which viewed expenditure of resources on education as 'negative resource use' (equivalent to the creation of new resources), came to a much less pessimistic conclusion regarding global sustainability.

- The chapter concluded by suggesting a number of 'environmental policies for development' – ranging from pollution taxes to highly specific financial interventions in productive sectors in the developing world.

It now seems clear that some of the potential economic growth as we have counted it must be sacrificed to maintain a tolerable future. Choices will be hard and contentious. It is vital that ways should be devised for sharing the necessary sacrifices fairly and for using means that offer the most efficient trade-offs.

Questions for discussion

11.1   What is the relationship between the sustainability of development and globalization? What policies might be adopted in order to ensure that globalization processes reinforce sustainable development rather than undermine it?

11.2   Under what circumstances might a project appraiser set the discount rate at zero?

11.3   What are the implications of taking a 'very strong sustainability' view of resource substitutability for growth strategy in developing countries?

11.4   What deficiencies in the 'traditional' approach to National Income Accounting make it unsuitable for 'measuring' the environmental impact of the activities of a nation's industrial sector?

11.5   'Why should we not maximize the welfare of this generation at the cost of posterity?' (Kenneth Boulding). What is the relevance of this question to environmental policy? And how would you answer it?

11.6   A substantial proportion of global reserves of fossil fuels and other important minerals are located in developing countries. Is this likely to prove to be an advantage – or a disadvantage – to these countries in the long run?

11.7   Why are developing countries particularly vulnerable to many of the problems likely to be caused by global warming?

Additional reading

Diamond, J. (2006) *Collapse: How Societies Choose to Fail or Survive*, Penguin, London.

An analysis of the disastrous consequences – actual or potential – for whole societies, of their failure to anticipate, understand, and deal in time with, threatening environmental problems. It ranges from the collapse of such earlier societies as those of the Maya and the islands of the eastern Pacific, to modern China and Australia.

Gore, A. (2006) *An Inconvenient Truth: The Planetary Emergency of Global Warming and What We Can Do About It*, Rodale Books, New York.

A print version of the DVD documentary by the same name produced by Paramount Home Entertainment, summarizing the former US Vice-President's views regarding global warming.

Heal, G., Dasgupta, P., Walker, B., Ehrlich, P., Levin, S., Daily, G., Maler, K.G., Arrow, K., Kautsky, N., Lubchenco, J., Schneider, S., and Starrett, D. (2002) *Genetic Diversity and Interdependent Crop Choices in Agriculture*. Beijer Discussion Paper 170. The Beijer Institute, The Royal Swedish Academy of Sciences, Stockholm.

Lomborg, B. (2007) *Cool It!: The Skeptikal Environmentalist's Guide to Global Warming*, Cyan and Marshall Cavendish, London.

A dissenting view on global warming. Lomborg does not dispute that global warming is a reality, but suggests that investment priorities should be determined using orthodox appraisal techniques – and that this would result in reduced expenditure on climate-related activities.

UN, Department of Economic and Social Affairs, Division for Sustainable Development (2008) *Trends In Sustainable Development: Agriculture, Rural Development, Land, Desertification And Drought*, New York.

On various environmental issues – including environmental indicators – the International Institute for Environment and Development website at:
http://www.iied.org/NR/index.html and http://www.iied.org/
and the International Institute for Sustainable Development website at:
http://www.iisd.org/default.asp

Online *Learning* Center

To help you grasp the key concepts of this chapter check out the extra resources posted on the Online Learning Centre at **www.mcgraw-hill.co.uk/textbooks/huq**

Among other resources, there are three appendices available:

- Appendix 11.1   Supplies of non-fossil minerals
- Appendix 11.2   Water scarcity and hunger in Yemen
- Appendix 11.3   Valuing the environment

CHAPTER 12

Stabilization in Developing Countries

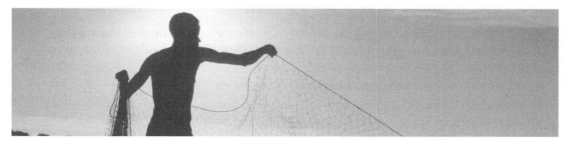

Stabilization is a star example of a win-win game. Other things equal, everyone suffers if there is instability in income or prices. And the poorer the country the more vital stabilization is. Because of heavy dependence on crops and primary-commodity prices, people in many of the poorest countries suffer big fluctuations in income and formal-sector employment, which add greatly to personal insecurity. Much can be done to reduce these shocks, but the measures needed vary with the characteristics of the economy concerned.

Introduction

Economic stabilization is fundamental to human welfare everywhere, and especially in the poorer countries, in many of which instability is pervasive and its human effects overwhelming. People are often on the very edge of subsistence, and any disturbance can easily leave them completely destitute.

So the first set of questions considered here is whether and **why economic stability in developing countries matters**; and, if it does, **stability of what exactly**.

The rest of the chapter is devoted to exploring whether there are accessible and low-cost ways of achieving and maintaining economic stability: through policy measures taken by the developing countries' governments or through international action or a combination of both.

This raises the question whether the framework for making stabilization policy work is broadly the same across all economies. If it is different, is the same recipe appropriate for all developing countries? Does the controversy started in Latin America between **'monetarist' and 'structuralist' views of inflation** have anything to contribute to our present understanding, and, if so, does it put its finger on relevant differences for stabilizing purposes between developed countries on the one hand and some or all developing countries on the other?

From this we proceed to ask what are the main relevant **differences** between various kinds of economy that dictate **different models for stabilization** – with the use of three main classes of instrument: compensatory finance; anti-inflation institutions; and exchange-rate and capital-movement policy.

We look at the framework of stabilization policy now conventional in **developed countries**, with monetary as well as fiscal controls and disciplines; at the **primary-export-dominated developing countries** that must rely on compensatory fiscal finance; and at those **developing countries, including some of low income, that have significant industrial sectors and financial institutions**, and combine some of the characteristics of both the other two classes, with the further complication of a need to guard against currency flight.

In the course of this exploration, answers are given in passing to certain further questions.

- Should countries keep the option of exercising **controls over international capital movements**? If so, to which types of country are controls most likely to be important or useful?
- Is there an ideal **system of exchange-rate management**?
- Under conditions of relatively high inflation, is **indexation** of contracts to the general price level conducive to efficiency and equity, and does it in any of its forms help or hinder the reduction of rates of inflation?

We consider finally systems of **international support for stabilization in primary-export-dominated economies** – by expanded international reserves; by commodity-price-stabilization agreements; by earnings-insurance schemes; and by enabling individual producers to stabilize their earnings through the use of market derivatives.

An Appendix will explain the reasons for speaking of a '**resource curse**'. Another will propound a **formal rule for stabilization in a low-income economy heavily dependent on primary-commodity exports**. These can be found on the Online Learning Centre.

BOX 12.1 TOOLKIT ON STABILIZATION

Bretton Woods. Site in New Hampshire, USA, of the United Nations Monetary and Financial Conference in 1944 that agreed to plans for the International Monetary Fund (IMF) and International Bank for Reconstruction and Development ('World Bank'), the two being known as the Bretton Woods institutions or twins. The 'Bretton Woods system' refers to the 'adjustable-peg' system of relatively stable exchange-rates supervised by the IMF that lasted until August 1971.

CCFF (Compensatory and Contingency Financing Facility). A fund or lending 'window' of the IMF designed to give short-term help to countries whose external accounts are hit by world events. Originally set up (as the Compensatory Financing Facility) in 1963, it was then directed to helping primary-exporting countries, both rich and poor, but since the 1980s or earlier its business has been confined to developing countries, and, especially since 1983, its functions have not been very clearly distinguishable from those of other IMF lending 'facilities'.

Compensatory finance. Government fiscal or monetary action to increase or reduce overall spending in the economy for the sake of stabilizing its level.

Counter-cyclical action. Action to stabilize national (or world) expenditure, usually by fiscal or monetary contraction or expansion.

▶ **Derivative.** A form of contract in which (in the cases relevant here) the parties, instead of making an exchange now at a price agreed now (a **spot** contract), agree to an exchange at some time in the future at a price agreed now (either a **forward** or a **futures** contract), or agree to allow one or other of the parties the option of making a purchase or sale at some point in the future at no more or no less than a certain price agreed now (an **option** contract).

Exchange-rates, NEER, REER. The (nominal) exchange-rate of one currency with another is simply the number of units of one exchanging for a single unit of the other, such as the number of won to the dollar or dollars to the won. The nominal effective exchange-rate (**NEER**) of a currency A is an index that is a weighted average of its exchange-rates (in index form) with all other currencies or all of interest to it. It has to be expressed as an index, that is a ratio of its current value to its value at some base date. The weighting of the various currencies will normally reflect their relative importance as partners for currency A. So the components of the NEER of the Korean won will be weighted according to the importance of each of the other currencies for transactions with Korea. The won's exchange-rates with other individual currencies may be expressed as either won to the dollar, e.g., or dollars to the won. But the NEER index of the won will normally be based on indices of numbers of *other currency units to the won*, so that a *rise* in the index represents an *appreciation* of the won, that is a *rise* in its exchange value. (But it's always as well to check that this is the way the terms are used in a particular case.)

The real effective exchange rate (**REER**) of the won is its NEER (expressed so that a rise in its value represents an appreciation of the won) multiplied by the ratio of a Korean price index to a world price index.

$$REER_K = NEER_K \cdot P_K/P_W$$

So a rise in the Korean REER will occur if *either* Korean prices rise in relation to world prices *or* the won appreciates. Either of these changes on its own will make Korean goods less competitive internationally and to that extent tend both to depress Korean real income and to check any domestic price inflation that has helped to bring about the rise in the REER.

To say that a country's REER is *mean-reverting* means that it tends to return to its previous (equilibrium) level after being disturbed.

Fiscal (policy). 'Fiscal' means concerned with government finance: revenue and expenditure. 'Fiscal policy' now generally denotes using, for macroeconomic-stabilization purposes, the balance between government revenue and spending.

Mackinnon–Shaw hypothesis. This is the assertion that capping interest-rates will depress investment.

Monetary policy. Action to increase or reduce money supply, or to lower or raise interest-rates, for macroeconomic-stabilization purposes, including effects on the overseas balance or the exchange-rate.

Sovereign debt. This refers to the debt of governments.

Special Drawing Rights (SDRs). These are a form of international money that the IMF has been authorized to issue since 1969, though none has in fact been issued since 1981.

Objectives of stabilization policy

What we mean by stabilization here – the **objective** of stabilization policy – has three components: **(1) a steady growth path of real national expenditure; (2) a tolerably low rate of inflation; and (3) the highest growth path that can be maintained steadily over the medium term** (say over any five-year period) – the last being the analogue of the 'full-employment income' objective. All three objectives expressed in this way would appear to depend for their practical definition on judgement: including political or value judgements on what exactly counts as *steady* and as *tolerably low*. But they give enough indication of the *direction* required.

There is a fourth condition that may be regarded as an objective, but perhaps better as a *constraint*; this is **(4) a sustainable external-payments position.** This is essential because it is likely to be a necessary condition of the consistent enjoyment of the others.

Importance of the objectives

Stable total expenditure as an objective

What is required is that *fluctuations around the trend growth path* of expenditure should be as small as possible, whether trend growth is positive, zero or negative. *Expenditure* is used rather than *income* as the aggregate to be stabilized, because it is the point of some of the arrangements discussed here that expenditure can and should be stabilized even while income inevitably fluctuates, just as a prudent household stabilizes its expenditure in the face of fluctuating income through insurance or borrowing or the accumulation of savings in good times.

Keeping the path of total expenditure stable is at least a *necessary* condition for *keeping the expenditure possibilities of most individual households stable*. In general, all instability involves personal costs, which can be extreme in those developing countries that have frequent big fluctuations in national income and no safety-nets. As employment prospects in the formal sector fall, large numbers of people may lose their means of subsistence altogether or at best have either to find ways of entry to the crowded and poorly rewarded urban informal sector, or to return to rural households. Instability of household income reduces the benefit to be derived from any given average level, an effect that hardly needs demonstration to anyone who has had to budget for a household, even a household of one.

Stability – and the expectation of further stability that it generates – also improves the climate for private investment. *Instability*, moreover, reduces the possibility of rational planning for public-sector investment, and may cause public projects already started to be abandoned or delayed, with the extra wasted costs entailed.

Low inflation as an objective

Judgements commonly made for and against inflation (mainly against), on the ground of its impact on economic efficiency, growth, equity, and politics, are based on the following nine observations. But note that some may be questioned, and (at the end of the list) that empirical evidence of the relationship between inflation and *growth* does on balance suggest a *positive* relationship across sufficiently *low* rates of inflation.

1   Inflation is *unpopular* for altering the distribution of income. Though there are gainers and losers, the losers are generally more aware of their losses than the gainers of their gains. Conquering inflation without undesirable side-effects will be popular, and governments that preside over increasing inflation rates will be to that extent unpopular.

2   High inflation (generally, when it is high, also highly *variable* in its rate) introduces serious uncertainty about individual consumers' 'permanent' real incomes, making rational household budgeting difficult, which itself reduces welfare all round.

3   As inflation rates mount, *money* increasingly loses two of its three *vital functions* – as a unit of account and as a store of value – and in extreme cases its function as a medium of exchange too is seriously reduced.

4   As explained later in Chapter 19, inflation is held to enhance the harmful effect generally presumed (under the Mackinnon–Shaw hypothesis) to follow any 'monetary repression' arising through capping of interest-rates. This is because it reduces the *real* interest-rate entailed by any nominal rate, so (under the hypothesis) *further* reducing *investment*, and increasing *further the arbitrariness and hence inefficiency* in the selection of investment projects.

5   Even when there is *no* upper limit on nominal interest-rates, inflation (absolute variability of which tends to increase with its level) *increases uncertainty* over the real value of lending and cost of borrowing, which reduces the attractiveness of both, and on that ground depresses investment and possibly also saving, and in any case, it is argued by some, decreases efficient intermediation through formal-sector institutions.

6   Specifically in the consumer market for ownership of domestic housing, where frequently purchasers rely on long-term loans to finance their purchases, and their readiness to buy therefore depends on their capacity to service the loans from month to month, inflation imparts a *'front-end load'* to the servicing of loans contracted at fixed nominal rates, with the implication that – if servicing in the early part of the life of a housing loan is to be manageable – any borrower household will need a *lower real interest-rate over the life of the loan* than the maximum she or he would accept in the absence of inflation. So, unless servicing of loans is indexed to the price level, the effective demand for housing will be lower than it would have been in the absence of inflation; there will consequently be less private-sector house-building; and consumer choice over consuming housing services will be to that extent (inefficiently) frustrated.

7   Once inflation reaches high rates, reducing it near to zero will usually have serious costs in output and employment, as South American experience since the 1970s appears to demonstrate. Largely avoiding these costs can take considerable discipline and guile on the part of the authorities and tolerance on the part of large sections of the public. *Hyper-inflation*, as in Germany in the early 1920s, Indonesia in 1965–6, Bolivia around 1985, and Zimbabwe in 2007–8 (see Boxes 12.2 and 12.3) typically accompanies (as cause or effect or both) drastic impoverishment and social dislocation.

8   Indexation of prices, possibly including interest- and exchange-rates, to past or projected future price-level changes, may mitigate some of the harmful effects of inflation on the current welfare of the groups of people protected by the indexation, and on investment. However, indexation (especially to past inflation when attempts are being made to reduce the rate) will tend to perpetuate the effect of any initial inflationary impulse, quite possibly increasing the rate as time goes on. Moreover it is quite likely that the people whose real incomes will *not* be shielded by indexation and will consequently undergo falling real

incomes – such as wage-workers in agriculture and in the informal sector, suffering because they have little political clout or because controlling their wages by government or collective bargaining is administratively difficult – will be among the poorest.

9 It has been argued that inflation will tend to increase economic growth by transferring real income from wage-earners to classes with higher propensities to save, or from lenders to investors, or (through 'fiscal drag') from the private sector to the public. But the second effect, and maybe the first too, seems likely to happen only if the inflation or its increase is *unexpected*, or, in the case of the first, if expected inflation *cannot* be countered on the part of wage-earners by raising their wages accordingly (Kirkpatrick and Nixson, 1987, p. 189). Any positive effect that the first of these effects might be expected to have on investment may well be cancelled by the effects on both lending and borrowing of increased uncertainty. The third supposed effect relies on the view that the state will invest more of its resources, or invest them better, than the general public.

Kirkpatrick and Nixson (1987, pp. 189–91) report the results of several empirical studies, some pointing to a positive bearing of inflation on growth, though generally only at low inflation rates, and some to negative effects or none. Thirlwall (2006, pp. 448–50), reviewing a number of empirical studies from the 1990s, shows that they have a fairly consistent tendency to show a positive relationship between inflation and growth for rates of inflation up to about 5–8 per cent (with the critical rate possibly higher in developing than in developed economies), but a negative relationship at higher rates. The implication of the positive relationship over the lower range is not *necessarily* that inflation *causes* faster growth but possibly that the policies or circumstances conducive to growth have moderate inflation as an inevitable or hard-to-avoid by-product. It may be that the structural change inseparable from significant growth, especially in the poorer countries, is likely to entail some inflation, and that it will be counterproductive to check growth-promoting policies by restrictive measures geared say to keeping inflation at 2 per cent or less. To that extent, there may be some basis for the structuralist argument (see below) that growth in developing countries has inflation as an inevitable concomitant.

BOX 12.2 GERMANY 1923: HYPERINFLATION PARTLY RESULTING FROM ACTIONS BY THE WESTERN ALLIES AND ACTING AS SEEDBED FOR NAZISM

'The economic consequences of the Allies' occupation of the Ruhr in 1923 were catastrophic. The German government used deficit spending to subsidise workers summarily dismissed from their posts while [it was] purchasing coal from Britain. The cessation of deliveries of raw materials from the Ruhr resulted in waves of cutbacks in production and layoffs elsewhere. Unemployment rose from 2 to 23 per cent. Tax revenue declined to the point where by October 1923 it covered a mere 1 per cent of total government expenditure. The volume of money circulating in Germany grew astronomically, by the autumn flowing in improbable denominations from nearly two thousand presses operating around the clock. A banknote printers' bill appeared as 32776899763734490417 Marks and 5 pfennige in Reichsbank accounts. Banks had to hire more clerical workers to calculate these lengthening digits. Production slowed as workers trundled carts laden with a day's pay to the banks, and shops shut as owners ceased to be able to purchase new stock with yesterday's takings. . . . A barter economy developed and

Stabilization in Developing Countries **337**

the prudent middle classes began selling their most cherished possessions, although there were only so many Steinway pianos a peasant house could accommodate. Books were devoted to the moral inversions inflation caused . . .

'Differentials between earnings were erased, leading to an acute sense of social declassification, which was soon epitomized by a middle-class Militant League of Beggars. People suffering from clinical malnutrition, and unable to afford adequate food or medicine, were susceptible to tuberculosis or rickets. Although the 'Mark is a Mark' policy. . . . enabled farmers and mortgagees to pay off their creditors, pensioners, savers and elderly people living off modest rental incomes were plunged into poverty and insecurity. Sometimes their only escape from indignity was through suicide.'

Source: Michael Burleigh, *The Third Reich: a new history*, Pan Books, London, 2000, pp. 55–7.

Full-capacity income as an objective

The point here is simply that it is naturally desirable that the level of income at any time should be as high as possible, subject to the two constraints: that its growth path should be steady and that the external balance entailed should be sustainable.

Sustainable external 'balance' as a constraint

'Sustainable external balance' in itself may seem a vague term, because there are various definitions of external balance (as 'on goods and services', 'on current account'), but the reality is important. What needs to be 'balanced' and in what sense? Most countries, and certainly all developing countries, will have certain limits beyond which external deficits cannot go without the need for serious, and quite possibly disturbing, adjustment.

Here the aggregate of importance will be taken to be the *balance on current-and-long-term capital account*, sometimes called the *basic balance*. The necessary objective will be that (once adequate foreign reserves have been accumulated and allowance has been made for any necessary addition over time to these reserves) the *average* of this balance, over some period that might be called *medium-term*, should *approximate to zero*. Of necessity, the period over which this must be so will be determined by the *accommodation* the country can obtain for deficits in the meantime. The possible means of accommodation include pre-existing reserves and opportunities for obtaining accommodating loans from foreign official entities or international institutions.

BOX 12.3 ZIMBABWE 2008: HYPERINFLATION, AGAIN ACCOMPANIED BY EXTREME IMPOVERISHMENT AND SOCIAL DISLOCATION, AND HOW TO END IT

'Inflation [in Zimbabwe] is running officially at more than 11 m.%, and probably, in reality, at more than 40 m.%, with the central bank printing an avalanche of money to cover a massive budget deficit. Last month it slashed ten zeros from the currency but the rate has already slumped from 30 new Zimbabwean dollars to an American one, to 300 today. The bank says it will let some shops trade in foreign cash; petrol in some stations may also be bought in dollars or rand.

▶

'. . . A currency board may be set up to oversee what would in effect be a new currency, most likely pegged, at least at first, to the South African rand. The new government's first priority is to stabilize the currency. During that painful period, which could last several months, more shops will have to be allowed to sell in foreign currency. A massive cash injection from abroad is unlikely while hyperinflation is still at world-record rates.

'The economy has shrunk by more than half in a decade; farming and manufacturing have collapsed; shortages of almost all essential goods, including cooking and heating fuel, sugar and bread, are causing grim hardship. The UN's World Food Programme reckons that 2 m. or so of the 10 m.-odd people still in Zimbabwe (some 3 m. have emigrated) urgently need food handouts. That number could swell to 5 m. early next year, after the failure of this year's harvest.'

Source: Economist, 20/8/2008, p. 64.

Frameworks of stabilization policy relevant in different types of economy

Here there are two main topics: *compensatory finance* and *exchange-rate policy*, with exchange-rate policy inevitably raising the question of the *external-capital-movement controls* that are sometimes necessary to implement exchange-rate policy. Important in the background are the political deals and arrangements that may be needed to make the stabilizing policies possible and to mitigate their undesirable side-effects. However, because of the large part that it has played in thinking about stabilization in the context of economic growth and other aspects of development, we begin with some discussion of the *structuralist–monetarist debate*.

The structuralist–monetarist debate: theory and some Latin American experience on the causes and remedies for high inflation

Inflation has been consistently higher (and more variable) in developing countries taken together than in developed, but much higher in some regions of the world than others, and notably highest most of the time in Latin America (Kirkpatrick and Nixson, 1987, and see Table 12.1).

Rates of inflation in the world, however, have generally been lower since 1990, and in the developing countries especially since 1995, than over the previous period starting around 1975, and, after a number of ambitious but failed attempts at price stabilization in Latin America since the late 1970s, it is precisely there that the change has been especially marked.

In propounding, since the 1950s, so-called *structuralist*, as against more conventional *monetarist*, views of inflation, Latin American thinkers generated the main theoretical controversy, during the early period of development-economics study, about inflation's causes and its bearing on growth in developing countries. The *structuralist* view, with many variants, is that inflation in developing countries should be seen as the outcome of certain 'rigidities': namely forms of property and structures of wealth and power, or the established

	1967–76 av.	1981–90 av.	1991–2000 av.	1998–2007 av. est.	1993	1996	1999	2002	2005
Dev'd c'tries	6.7	5.6	2.6	2.0	3.1	2.4	1.4	1.5	2.3
Dev'g c'tries** *of which*:	13.8	39.0	23.3	6.7	47.3	14.6	10.0	5.7	5.3
Africa	8.5	15.1	21.5	10.5	30.6	25.9	11.9	9.9	8.5
Asia**	9.4	7.1	8.2	3.4	10.7	8.2	2.5	2.0	3.5
M. East & Europe	8.7 (M.E.)	19.2	24.6	6.3 (M.E.)	25.3	24.2	6.7 (M.E.)	5.4 (M.E.)	7.7 (M.E.)
	9.0 (Eur.)			19.5 (CIS)			69.6 (CIS)	13.8 (CIS)	12.3 (CIS)
				13.9 (C.& E. Eur.)			23.0 (C.& E. Eur.)	14.7 (C.& E. Eur.)	4.8 (C.& E. Eur.)
West'n Hemisphere	24.5	145.4	63.5	7.4	209.0	22.4	35.9	13.2	6.3

TABLE 12.1 Average* inflation rates, consumer prices, % per year
* Weighted. **Excluding China before 1978.
Source: IMF, *World Economic Outlook*: 1985, p. 212 (cited Kirkpatrick and Nixson, 1987, p. 174); October 1999, p. 180; September 2006.

product-specialization of countries in the world economy.[1] It cannot therefore be explained by, or entirely controlled by, monetary- and fiscal-policy decisions. In Latin America, or in developing countries generally, on this view, inflation is an inevitable accompaniment of growth. (It will be seen from evidence cited above that there may be some basis for this, at least for very modest rates of inflation.) Accordingly, attempts to suppress inflation by 'monetarist' means will be ineffective, or at least will reduce current income and economic growth.

The *monetarist* view, as the term is used in this context – broader than the expression's customary use in the developed countries from the 1970s, though not inconsistent with it – is that inflation is due to excess money or liquidity or more generally spending power, and that restriction of liquidity or spending power through monetary or fiscal measures is a *necessary* condition for controlling or suppressing it, and also a *sufficient* condition if pressed far enough.

A number of attempts have been made to test structuralist and monetarist claims empirically. (These are reviewed by Kirkpatrick and Nixson, 1987.) The most revealing judgement seems to be some form of synthesis: factors outside the policy range, such as rises in the prices of basic foodstuffs or in world prices generally, or some domestic political decision to overspend, may give the initial impulse to inflation. Then, how far and how fast it proceeds may depend on transmission mechanisms that have much to do with the distribution of social power (such as the strength of trade unions) and institutional arrangements (such as the character of indexation for inflation). At the same time a degree

---

[1] The rigidities supposed by the structuralists may be seen as an example of what has come to be called *hysteresis*, namely the fact that reversing the forces that have brought about a change will not necessarily cause the change to be reversed along the same track through which it has taken place. If doubling the money supply has caused prices to rise, halving it from its new level will not necessarily return everything to what it had been before the money supply was doubled.

of fiscal-monetary restraint will be necessary to halt or slow inflation once the initial impulse has been given; but how far such restraint is pursued, or (alternatively or simultaneously) other – arguably more fundamental – reforms are tried, will itself be a reflection of the power structure. Clearly policies are not independent of politics.

However, structuralism, in the generalized form commonly used for expounding it, does not foreshadow clear policy agenda for keeping inflation within acceptable limits. Nor can it easily explain why South American inflation rates have been typically so much higher than those in most of the rest of the developing world, so much higher at some times than others, and, consistently for long periods, so much higher in some countries within the region than in others.

A series of Latin American plans launched during the late 1970s and the 1980s for suppressing high inflation (plans generally rather short-lived and attempted with weak fiscal control and largely free external capital movement) suggest three lessons.

One lesson – accepted by all sides – is that reducing *expectations* of inflation is an important element, though not easy to sustain.

A second – on the monetarist side – is that, *without fiscal control*, inflation cannot be decisively brought or kept down. With the help of that discipline, however, Bolivia in the mid-1980s, and Israel at about the same time, brought down their very high inflation rates conclusively. Without it, a bevy of other attempts at the time failed. In a further instalment, Argentina's attempt from 1991 to declare the dollar exchange-rate of its peso immutably fixed through a currency board, that is, through limiting the pesos created to the value of the foreign-reserve holdings at the agreed rate, appeared to work well for several years – to international acclaim – but the magic lasted only so long before the much increased *real* exchange-rate (arising largely, it seems, from fiscal indiscipline) led confidence in the one-dollar peso to ebb away, with the self-fulfilling result that the fixed exchange-rate had to be abandoned, as the country went through a massive economic collapse, in 2001.

The third lesson – loosely structuralist – is that, without other elements of a more *political* character, such as bargains with trade unions, safety-nets, and possibly external-capital controls, drastic inflation reduction, if it is politically achievable at all, is likely to come at great social cost. (Bolivia in the mid-1980s is an arguable example of the social cost, though much of this cost may have been due to other contemporaneous events.)

Israel, however, met both requirements – fiscal control and a sustained 'social contract' with the trade unions – as well as, like Brazil and Argentina around the same time, launching a new currency to influence expectations. It succeeded in stabilizing prices at relatively low cost in suffering and disruption. (See for evidence on, and analysis of, these experiments, Corbo, 1985; Dornbusch, 1982; Fernandez, 1985; Bruno, 1985; Blejer and Cheasty, 1988; Blejer and Liviatan, 1987; Bresser Pereira, 1987; Baer, 1987; Kreis, 1989.)

What is *not* true is that there is a monetarist framework appropriate for the developed countries and a structuralist one appropriate for the developing. It would be truer to say that both sets of insights apply to both. (In the turbulent 1970s and 1980s, those rich countries – Japan, Austria, Sweden, and Norway – that maintained, explicitly or implicitly, social contracts over wages achieved considerably better combinations of price stability and high employment than almost all of the rest.)

Compensatory finance: fiscal and monetary measures

Since the Keynesian revolution of the 1930s, the world has been aware that fiscal-cum-monetary control may by expansion increase nominal aggregate demand so as in certain circumstances to increase output and employment, or alternatively by contraction it may reduce aggregate demand so as to reduce inflation.

It seemed at first difficult to apply these insights in developing countries. However, after a period of considerable success in controlling unemployment and inflation, the developed countries too found that the expedients based on simplified Keynesian theory were not working as intended. Decades of theoretical dispute and practical failure led eventually to an uneasy consensus over rules for action, with no clear theoretical justification. This practical outcome is outlined below under 'Stabilization framework in developed countries'

Factors relevant to the choice of methods of stabilization in different types of economy: sources of instability, instruments of control, labour-market behaviour

In spite of the shakiness of this semi-consensus on what are the appropriate stabilization methods in richer countries, we venture to say that there are fairly clear differences among different types of economy in the relative importance of various disciplines and instruments, though these do not fit neatly into a dichotomy between developing and developed countries.

The factors particular to any country that determine the workable and appropriate framework for managing stabilization can probably be reduced to the following three.

1 Relative importance of the main sources of instability – whether internal *'animal spirits' and expectations about investment prospects* (including inflationary expectations and asset-price bubbles in general); or *external market conditions* (especially world prices of key commodity exports); or *international capital movements*.

2 Instruments of control available – whether *monetary as well as fiscal*, or (mainly or only) *fiscal*, this depending largely on the importance of bank credit in the money supply and on the existence or otherwise of 'deep' financial markets. In either case there is also the possibility (within limits) of *manipulating the exchange-rate*, whether through market participation or administrative controls or both.

3 Flexibility of the labour market – *the extent and speed with which real wages will fall or rise* in response to a fall or rise in the domestic demand for labour or *will be restored* after a change in the external value of the currency. A sluggish response can make it possible, given an adequate stock of co-operating non-labour resources, to increase domestic output and employment by increasing monetary demand directly or by allowing the currency to depreciate internationally.

Sources of instability   If instability arises mainly from autonomous fluctuations in *domestic private investment* (related to expectations about the real economy or to speculative booms and slumps in real-property or financial-asset prices), then potentially the authorities have the alternatives of (i) manipulating private investment directly ('at source') through monetary measures, or (ii) compensating for the private-investment fluctuations by fiscal policy. If, however, instability arises primarily from variations in *overseas commodity earnings*, there is no convenient way in the short term for directly checking the instability at source; but with adequate pre-planning fiscal measures may potentially still be used to *compensate* by neutralizing the impact of the instability on the rest of the economy. If the main risk of serious instability lies in *external capital movements*, then, as well perhaps as monetary or fiscal management or both, controls of capital movements will probably be needed. These controls as backstops, together with the authorities' trading of currencies in the markets, may be necessary for allowing the exchange-rate to be stabilized or manipulated.

Instruments available   At the extremes (the rich, developed economies on the one hand, and the poor, primary-export-dominated on the other), the instruments available dovetail well with the sources of instability – and for reasons that appear obvious when we consider them. The developed economies have deep financial systems and depend heavily on bank credit for their liquidity. Their authorities can influence monetary conditions directly through the money markets as well as using fiscal compensation. The poor, primary-export-dominated do not on the whole have highly developed financial and credit systems, and have to rely on fiscal measures. However, as we have suggested and will argue in more detail below, these can be used quite effectively to help meet their stabilization needs. The generally large and often fast-growing middle-income (and some still low-income) countries, which are the main ones that have speculative currency movements to fear, will probably to an extent be able to use monetary as well as fiscal measures, but their other important weapon is *ad hoc* application of external-capital controls, which will generally be accessible if the authorities in these countries choose to use them.

Flexibility (competitiveness) of labour markets   In certain countries, we can regard labour markets as highly competitive (real wages determined by supply and demand, with individual workers *trading their labour independently in a largely free market*). This is likely to mean that, as the nominal exchange-rate falls, prices including nominal wages fairly promptly rise (and conversely), and generally that increased monetary demand will translate quickly into higher money-wages and prices. This in turn implies that downward manipulation of the (nominal effective) exchange-rate will not significantly increase the competitiveness of the country's tradable goods, so that it will have at most a small and transient effect in stimulating output and employment or in reducing real demand for imports. (Also, fiscal or monetary expansion of nominal demand in the economy is unlikely in these circumstances, except very temporarily, to reduce real wages. So, though a resulting expansion of the economy will not be impossible, the expansionary measures will have more tendency than under a more controlled or sticky wage system to be diverted into additional imports or domestic inflation, and the tendency in these directions will be all the stronger if the economy has little industrial capacity for producing manufactured goods for export or for competing with imports.)

By contrast, *where wages are fixed 'politically'*, which usually means that they are above a free-market-equilibrium level, it may be more readily possible to increase employment by currency depreciation or by expanding nominal demand, or on the other hand to suppress inflation by currency appreciation or reducing nominal demand. And currency depreciation, effected by policy or by outside events, *may* have a positive impact on the external balance.

Stabilization framework in developed countries: the eventual uneasy consensus early in the twenty-first century

Early Keynesian ideas of what came to be called 'compensatory' finance depended on manipulating the fiscal balance (surplus or deficit) – supplemented perhaps by monetary measures – in order to keep aggregate demand for the country's output as close as possible, without inflation, to a 'full-employment' level. (Dominance of thinking at the time by the experience of extreme depression in the 1930s, when expansion was the prevailing objective and interest rates had been typically already very low, tended to direct hopes to fiscal, rather than monetary, methods.) The objective of full employment without inflation, however, came to seem increasingly elusive from the 1970s when higher and higher inflation seemed to be consistent with given levels of unemployment.

From the 1970s, then, new models, coming under the broad heading of Monetarism – we give it a capital letter to distinguish it from 'monetarism' in the broader sense, as the term is used in the controversy with structuralism – came into fashion, with a coherent theory behind them, for which there seemed to be empirical support from historical evidence. However, attempts to build systems of macroeconomic management on this body of theory – for example, in both Britain and the US briefly from 1979 (Krugman, 2007) – were not successful. The hope was to adopt a rule that could be applied automatically over considerable periods and might therefore be put beyond the reach of short-term administrative and political decisions. 'Fine-tuning', that is varying actions according to day-to-day circumstances, was to be abjured.

These attempts had soon to be abandoned. '*International monetarism*' as an alternative 'automatic' stabilization policy – involving the gearing of monetary measures to keep a constant *nominal* effective exchange-rate, or a constant nominal rate against some stable currency, such as was practised by Britain in the late 1980s – also failed as a panacea.

The nearest thing to a consensus among developed countries in the early twenty-first century on macroeconomic management, however, is probably represented by versions, often less explicit, of the regime that the UK followed from the mid-1990s and most formally and explicitly after 1997. After that year, a committee independent of government set the guiding interest-rate every month, under a brief that required it to aim at a certain rate of inflation and to keep the rate within a certain range of that target. Its members have based their decisions about the future course of inflation on any indicators they think appropriate, and have made their reasoning public. This *is* a form of *fine-tuning*, with a *monetary* instrument represented by the interest-rate.

Remaining *persistent* unemployment considered to be excessive was by implication to be dealt with by increasing *flexibility* in labour and product markets. As hinted above, it may be that social-contract-type agreements over wages can substitute for high flexibility in labour markets as a means of reducing persistent unemployment. This last has not been part of recent orthodoxy, but it largely retained its hold, and (with the important exception of Japan *after 1990*) to an extent its success, in those developed countries that had relied on it in the 1970s and 1980s.

Under the consensus, active compensatory ('counter-cyclical') *fiscal* policy would be confined to cases of severe negative financial shock, such as a collapse in asset prices of the kinds that occurred in the US in the stock-exchange crashes of 1987 and 2001 and again in most developed countries in the crisis of 2007–09, when there might in response be an emergency reduction in tax rates or a rise in government outlays.

As a huge and very crude generalization we can say that this general approach to policy has lain behind the fiscal and monetary management not only of developed countries but also of those middle- and low-income countries that have substantial industrial sectors and elements of modern financial institutions and markets.

Insofar as there has been a consensus, it has been an uneasy one without clear theory behind it and often without declared rules. Where it has had no answers is to the complications of speculative 'bubbles' in prices of assets, such as stock-exchange and house prices, which are little or not at all reflected in consumer prices but can disrupt the macroeconomy when they are reversed. Should the price indices to which management of the macroeconomy responds take these asset prices into account – or is there any better way out? The dilemma was acute for Japan in the property and stock-exchange boom of the late 1980s, whose collapse began the country's long period of relative stagnation. It has also been acute for the US, Britain and others in the credit crash of 2007–8, which was accompanied by strong upward pressure on food and fuel prices across the world.

There is also a dilemma – more serious when similar stabilization frameworks are applied in those poorer countries that have substantial modern industrial and financial sectors – over how far the monetary response should be confined to 'core' inflation, that is inflation indicators that ignore changes in prices thought to be transient, typically food and fuel prices. This dilemma has loomed large for a number of the big developing countries in 2008. (See *Economist*, 24/5/2008, pp. 101–3.) Food and fuel prices there may amount to an overwhelming part of the cost of living of much of the population.

Compensatory finance in countries highly dependent on primary exports

The rough and uneasy compromise established among the developed countries by the end of the century over the use of monetary and fiscal policy has, for want of anything better, to be part of the framework in a number of middle-income countries – and some low-income countries such as India and Bangladesh – that already have developed industrial sectors and financial markets. In such economies appropriately changing interest rates – as a means of stabilizing inflationary expectations – can have a generally stabilizing effect on the economy at large. Presumably at least some of the main destabilizing influences in these economies are generated *within the domestic financial and investment system.*

However there is a large class of developing countries for which this is far from the case: those heavily dependent on exports of primary commodities. It is fluctuations in the world prices of these products, and also – which is quite important where the commodities are agricultural and subject to weather and diseases – in their outputs, that can, in the absence of compensating policy, impart huge instability to spending in both public and private sectors. Primary-commodity prices fluctuate especially widely because of low world price-elasticity of demand for food-grains, beverages and raw materials; low short-term elasticity of supply for virtually all crops; low medium-term elasticity of supply for treecrops and extractive products; and weather and plant-disease disasters.

To take one extreme example of dependence on a primary commodity, the share in Zambia's GDP of copper production fell irregularly from 48 per cent in 1969 to 11 per cent in 1977 and 1978, and copper's contribution to government revenue varied from 59 per cent in 1969 to 19 per cent in 1972, and then from 53 per cent in 1974 to 3 per cent in 1976 (*Zambia Mining Yearbook*, 1978, p. 24).

Typically in the years just after Zambia's independence in 1964, copper comprised over 90 per cent of the value of its exports (Martin, 1972, p. 146). Copper earnings thus very largely set a limit to its imports, and, since any country's capacity to spend on imports has a considerable bearing on its capacity to spend in general – and pre-eminently so in a country as highly specialized in its non-traditional production as Zambia – we can see that Zambia's spending on consumption and investment must be heavily limited by its copper earnings. If government and private people spent each year to the limit set by current copper earnings, their spending would fluctuate enormously from year to year. Over 2000–4, copper still provided 41 per cent of the export earnings of Zambia, as it did 31 per cent of those of Chile. Other countries whose export earnings were heavily concentrated on one commodity at that time included Suriname (47 per cent) Tajikistan (46 per cent) and Guinea (36 per cent) for bauxite; Cote D'Ivoire (34 per cent) for cocoa; Burundi (43 per cent) for coffee; Burkina Faso (42 per cent) for cotton (IMF, *World Economic Outlook*, September 2006, p. 141). It was reported moreover that between 1983 and 2003 prices of many commodities varied from below 50 per cent to above 150 per cent of their average prices.

In a situation like this, the best that can be done toward keeping national expenditure reasonably stable (rising gradually, or if necessary falling gradually) is a rigorous form of good housekeeping on the part of the authorities, together with the establishment of institutions inducing the equivalent of good housekeeping on the part of some private citizens.

First, what might *government* do with its own revenue? If export earnings come extensively from mining or hydrocarbons, the government is likely to be taking a large amount of the value in revenue, especially in high-price years (while much of the remainder is repatriated abroad). Instead of simply putting all this revenue received in each year into a common fund for public spending, it could create a reserve fund in which a large part of the state receipts from the export products *in high-earning years* could be accumulated. There could then be payments made out of the fund into general government revenue *in years of low earnings*. Ideally *actual* government spending could be kept at the *trend* value of revenue. To check the impulses of governments to draw excessively from the fund or contribute too little towards it, a formula could be devised first for projecting the rules that would have to be observed for government spending to have a good chance of following a stable trend, and then for regularly updating the projections – and the rules could be embodied in law. A rule for determining the 'trend values', and hence which should be the years of paying-in and which of paying-out cannot expect to be perfect, even if subject to regular independent correction of its parameters. That is one reason why international support, discussed later, may be needed.

In the mid-1970s, however, both Botswana and Papua New Guinea set up stabilization funds into which their governments' mineral receipts were to be paid. Papua New Guinea's rules about its Mineral Resources Stabilization Fund seem to have been more prescriptive than Botswana's. In the upshot, neither country was obliged to go to the IMF for help through the late 1970s and 1980s (an extremely difficult period for most primary-exporting countries), until Papua New Guinea did so (possibly unnecessarily) in 1990 when its two largest mines were both closed down and earnings for its main treecrops happened to be specially low.

Second, there is the question of stabilizing *the spending of private citizens* who produce export commodities. In lowish-income countries the profits from *mining and drilling operations* are normally divided between the government and foreign shareholders. This will also often be largely true with *plantation crops*. It is the government's own response to its earnings from these products that has to be curbed in the interest of economic stability. However, where the volatile export earners are *smallholder crops*, the income, and consequently the spending, of the smallholders can also be a source of instability. It is in the smallholders' own interests, moreover, that their individual *disposable incomes* should be stabilized. Schemes directed to producer-price stabilization for cash crops have been devised in various countries, under which levies are collected when export prices are high in order to supplement producer prices when the world prices for the goods are low.

A number of these schemes have come into disrepute because state marketing organizations that do the trading have been highly inefficient or corrupt or because governments have plundered the stabilization funds for other purposes. But the principle is surely valid. If the *disposable* income of the smallholders is stabilized, their spending will be stabilized, and with their spending its multiplier effects on the rest of the economy. In a variant of the same device, the Fiji government managed fairly successfully to stabilize sugar-cane growers' receipts by virtue of owning virtually all the shares in the sugar-mills and absorbing the bulk of sugar-price fluctuations in the mills' profits.

Papua New Guinea has been unusual in giving the responsibility for stabilizing the producer prices of its three main cash-crops to producer organizations in the industries concerned, which served to shield the stabilization funds against misuse; and these arrangements proved fairly durable.

A more formal presentation of the fiscal stabilization rules proposed here, and how they might be derived – with one important complication to take account of fluctuating foreign direct investment – is given in Appendix 12.2, available on the Online Learning Centre.

Somewhat similar considerations may apply in those areas, such as 'Monsoon Asia': – notably much of mainland South and East Asia – where national income fluctuates substantially from year to year because of the weather and its effects primarily on the staple foodcrops. There, however, any attempt to stabilize the incomes of the agrarian population would be complicated by the fact that the balance of gain and loss from a 'bad' year or a 'good' year would differ from one section of that population to another. However, individual crop insurance, as used extensively in Taiwan, where most agricultural households are proprietors, is presumed to have a stabilizing influence on the economy, as well as encouraging investment in productivity improvements through reduced uncertainty of the value that farm activities will generate. Other countries that have practised crop insurance for individual households, with varying degrees of cover, are Mexico, Mauritius, India, Bangladesh, Nigeria, Costa Rica, Jamaica, and Brazil (Ingham, 1995, pp. 316–19; drawing on Mosley, 1989).

Even if other elements of certain economies mean that they require devices and rules for influencing interest- rates or monetary aggregates and short-term capital inflows and outflows, it would seem that any that have high components in the form of primary exports may still gain by employing in addition fiscal or quasi-fiscal stabilization regimes such as those just elaborated. (*Quasi-fiscal* covers the producer-price-stabilization schemes for smallholder cash crops.) Where the financial system is undeveloped, with no large role for bank credit, fiscal balances in fact form the main *domestic* element through which the authorities can influence the money supply.

Anti-inflationary institutions

Inflation at more than a low level (say more than say, 5 to 8 per cent) is unpopular and of itself decreases consumer welfare, independently of its specific impacts on particular classes of people and on investment. It has self-perpetuating tendencies, and attempts to reduce its rate radically are typically painful, wasteful in the sense of reducing output, and politically costly.

Indexation to the general price level has been used to mitigate the pain and inefficiency entailed by inflation. The indexation may be applied, for example, to wages, debts, the exchange-rate, utility prices. Indexing the exchange-rate to domestic prices so as to keep the real effective exchange-rate (REER; see Box 12.1, and explanation below) roughly constant, in effect lowering the exchange-value of the currency as domestic prices rise – as was done by Brazil, Colombia, and Portugal in the 1970s and early 1980s, and as in 1990 was practised by Chile and Madagascar and also later by Colombia and Portugal, (and by Chile still in 1996) – was designed to maintain the competitiveness of the country's exports (IMF, *International Financial Statistics*, 9/1979, 10/1980, 8/1984, 8/1990, 10/1996, pages on 'Exchange rate arrangements'). Indexing of debts, as for housing finance in Colombia for several years from 1972 (see Box 19.3 in Chapter 19), could reduce the uncertainty of the real value of loans to both lenders and borrowers and avoid the destructive 'front-end loading' of servicing payments on long-term loans mentioned above.

Indexing might be 'retrospective', that is based on the inflation of the period just past, as it most commonly has been, or 'prospective', that is based on projections of inflation for the next period.

The trouble is that indexation to the past general price level, widely applied, has a tendency to perpetuate inflation, or at least to increase the social and growth costs of reducing it. This is because it increases nominal costs of production each time the indexation formula is applied.

If an attempt is being made to reduce inflation, retrospective indexation causes particular difficulties, since, if the rate of rise of the price index is actually falling, indexation of wages to the previous period's rise will in fact raise real wage-costs over each successive period after it has been applied. Prospective indexation has a chance of avoiding this effect.

While excessively high inflation lasts, there are dilemmas for any government that aims to reduce it and at the same time to mitigate its harmful effects.

To summarize: indexation may reduce some of the inefficiency introduced by inflation and mitigate its pain for certain classes of the population, but applied widely indexation will tend to perpetuate and even accelerate whatever inflation exists (increasing the pain for those not protected by the indexation and unable to protect themselves), unless it is linked to a 'social contract' or other measures for reducing inflation and preferably if it is in those circumstances applied prospectively.

Exchange-rate and capital-movement policy

The real effective exchange-rate (REER): implications of its behaviour for policy

A country's real effective exchange-rate (REER) is an index of its nominal effective exchange-rate (expressed so that a rise means appreciation) multiplied by the ratio of its domestic price index to the world price index. So a rise in the REER tends to produce (i) a decline in the country's international competitiveness and (ii) a rise domestically in the prices of non-traded goods in relation to traded goods.

A country's REER is described as mean-reverting if it tends to restore itself fairly quickly to its earlier level after any displacement – as by a change in the world price level or in the country's nominal effective exchange-rate. (The mechanism by which this happens is a responsive change in the domestic price level.)

A mean-reverting REER means that measures to depreciate the country's (nominal) exchange-rate will have only transitory effects on the ratio between the prices of tradable and those of non-tradable goods and hence on the country's international competitiveness. (A mean-reverting REER is likely to spring from a high level of competitive behaviour in the labour market.) The weakness or transitoriness of the effects of the depreciation in that case will be the more marked the less the substitutability in production between exports and goods produced for the domestic market, and the less the substitutability in consumption between imports and goods produced domestically.

That form of REER behaviour describes how things are likely to be **with economies heavily dependent on primary exports, and all the more so if their import-competing industries are poorly developed**. The effect of the nominal depreciation in those circumstances will appear mainly as a rise in domestic prices rather than any gain in international competitiveness or (hence) any stimulus to output or favourable impact on the external balance. Correspondingly, however, a nominal appreciation in such economies may be useful for curbing inflation, without much detrimental effect on competitiveness or hence on output or the external balance. All this is likely to be more or less the case with many African, Caribbean, and Pacific Island countries.

It will by contrast be **in the economies that are more industrially developed and less highly specialized internationally** that *depreciation*, though it is always likely to raise domestic prices, may well have some useful function in raising output and 'improving' the external balance; while *appreciation*, introduced perhaps to check domestic price rises, will be prone to depress output and 'worsen' the external balance. Though the balance between these effects of exchange-rate manipulation is a matter of degree, it can be said, as a broad generalization, that the large Latin American and large South and East Asian economies will come much closer to the second of these models than most of those in Africa, the Caribbean, and the Pacific.

Stabilizing the exchange-rate

'Multiple equilibria' and currency collapse   Where there are significant 'autonomous' short-term capital movements, the *expectations* of operators in the exchange markets will have a bearing on their willingness to hold the currency of any particular country. So, for any set of conditions among 'real' factors (here trade in goods and services, and long-term investment), there will be *no unique equilibrium price in a free market for the country's currency*. Hence the expression *multiple-equilibria*. The level at which the exchange-rate settles will depend on the expectations of the traders in currencies, and the relevant expectations will be largely those *about future exchange-rates*. If the authorities can somehow establish the belief that the existing exchange-rate will remain, they may be able to maintain that exchange-rate for considerable periods, without exchange controls and with little intervention in the markets.

So, provided there are stable expectations about the value of the currency, this potential can be a great help to governments hoping to stabilize their currencies in a free market. The trouble arises when 'the markets' suddenly come to take the view that some currency will fall markedly in value; or that the country concerned will impose restrictions on the export of capital; or both. There may be no firmer ground for believing this than that other people say it will happen. To get out before it does, a number of traders sell the currency at once. This of course makes the prediction self-fulfilling: the currency does depreciate drastically, and also the country *may* impose exchange controls in order to stem the collapse. This radical fall in exchange-rates is what happened with Thailand, Indonesia, South Korea, Malaysia, Brazil, and Russia over 1997–9. In the extreme case the Indonesian rupiah fell over the year from end-June 1997 to end-June 1998 to a sixth of its previous dollar value.

Capital-movement controls

This experience led to serious doubts about the wisdom, among middle-income developing countries, of following the then advice of the IMF to free their currency markets completely. Particularly cited in support of these doubts were the experiences of Chile and Colombia on the one hand and Malaysia on the other. Against IMF advice, Chile from 1991 and Colombia from 1993 had imposed controls of a fiscal character *on short-term capital inflows*, and they then escaped the 'contagion' of the collapses elsewhere. Malaysia, in 1998, *after* the initial collapse, had set up *capital-export controls*. Rightly or wrongly it has been alleged that by so doing it avoided the worst effects of the collapse. (Details of these and other recent schemes for 'capital management' – with generally favourable judgments on the extent to which they fulfilled their purposes – are given in Epstein, Grabel and Jomo, 2003.)

Beside longer-running capital-import and capital-export controls as means of avoiding or mitigating currency crises, Paul-Bernd Spahn (1996, 2002) has proposed an emergency device that has come to be called the *circuit-breaker*. This is a means for stopping a rush out of a currency as soon as signs of it appear. Its rules are these. *Set and announce* measures that will come into effect *automatically*. As soon as the *rate of fall* in the effective market value of the currency exceeds a certain figure, a tax at a punitive level (say 50 per cent) will be applied on all sales of the currency other than for certain defined purposes such as imports of goods and services. (On these exempted exchanges the punitive tax, though initially charged, could subsequently be remitted.) Setting the tax rate high enough will make it simply out of the question that sales will occur. Once a rush out of the currency begins, it will in these conditions be quickly halted. All dealers and potential dealers will know this, and will therefore know, before any flight from the currency begins, that it and the fall in value of the currency that it would entail can not proceed beyond a certain point. So, further back in the process, any reason for the fears that might lead to a flight of capital in the first place would be largely removed.

This has not been tried, but, at least in most middle-income countries that are likely to be vulnerable, the institutions for effectively taxing the exchanges appear to exist. (See Schmidt, 2001, where it is argued also that the other controls mentioned here on import and export of capital would be *most efficiently* implemented *through taxing the relevant currency exchanges*, and then remitting the charges on trade transactions.)

Choice of exchange-rate and currency regimes

There are two main dimensions: how *free or fixed* the exchange-rate is; and whether the currency is *convertible*. Both have a bearing on the *controls* that must exist.

Various classifications have been given of exchange-rate regimes over the free-*versus*-fixed question. They are generally presented as a spectrum between fixed and freely-floating.

To define the meanings of the terms we can probably say that *floating rates* may be consistent with a government's participating as a trader in currency markets or in domestic money markets for the purpose of influencing the exchange-rate, but by definition will preclude its use of administrative control of currency movements. (Yet presumably it is possible for a country described as being on a floating rate to hold arrangements for controls *in reserve*.) *Pegged rates*, however, normally do require administrative controls, though fixing the rate permanently through a currency board (see below) is supposed to be achieved by regulating the money-creation process instead.

At the fixed end of the spectrum, a country may simply enter a *monetary union* with others, as the (sixteen at the time of writing) that have joined the euro have done. Or a country may submit to what is called *dollarization* or *currency-substitution*, in which the US currency, or some other, is allowed to replace the domestic currency within the country (full substitution) or circulate alongside it (partial substitution). Ecuador, El Salvador, and Panama are among the countries that have practised full substitution (Chang and Grabel, 2004, p. 168).

If neither of these choices is made, a 'permanently fixed' (or purportedly so) rate generally implies a *currency board*, which must issue domestic currency ('base-money') only so far as it is backed, at the fixed rate laid down, by international-reserve holdings (gold or foreign convertible currency). The theory is that the holder of the domestic currency will be assured that it can always be exchanged at the fixed rate for the currency to which it is tied. However, there is no guarantee that the board and its rules will not some day be abandoned, as happened with Argentina's 1991 currency board a decade after it was established; and what a currency board *does not* preclude is unwise foreign borrowing. It also does not *in itself* (that is, without other rules and conventions) control the bank-credit element in the money supply. Hong Kong and some Eastern European countries, together with a few very small territories, have recently worked with currency boards (Chang and Grabel, 2004, p. 168).

At the opposite extreme – though perhaps more of an ideal to be approached than an actual phenomenon – is a completely *free-market or 'clean' float*, in which by definition the government does not intervene at all in the currency markets directly in order to influence the currency's price. (The IMF uses the term 'independently floating', which seems to imply an approach at least to a clean float.) Yet it seems inevitable, in a country with a developed financial and banking system, that the government will follow *some* domestic monetary policy. Measures taken to influence the interest-rate will have an impact on a 'floating' exchange-rate, and it seems unlikely that the authorities will completely ignore these effects when they manoeuvre interest-rates.

One step away from the 'clean float' is the *managed or 'dirty' float*, under which the authorities may well be intervening directly in the currency markets and may at any time have a definite rate in mind at which they are aiming. The rate against some foreign currency or a basket of them may be kept quite stable for long periods, even if no targeted rate is announced.

In between the fixed rates and the floats are various forms of *peg*, the term generally implying that there is, for the time being, either an *announced rate* against some currency (or a basket of them), or an *announced rule* according to which the rate will be determined. In either case exchange controls would normally be needed.

The former type would cover the *adjustable pegs*, to which (until 1971) all members of the IMF (under its original rules agreed at Bretton Woods in 1944) were in principle (and almost all in practice) committed. Fluctuations were kept within a very narrow band on either side of announced par rates that remained fixed for long periods.

The latter type includes the *'crawling pegs'*, mentioned above as followed for some years by Brazil, Colombia, Chile, and a few others. Those countries carried out a series of predictable depreciations in order (more or less) *to keep the REER constant*, and so maintain international competitiveness in the face of high domestic inflation. The drawback, as we have mentioned, was that these crawling pegs virtually ensured that any existing high inflation would continue. It would be not out of the question, by contrast, for a country that – unlike Brazil, Chile and the rest – had a *mean-reverting* REER to run instead a crawling peg on a different rule, with successive effective nominal *appreciations* designed *to keep the domestic price level constant*. Since the competitiveness effects in such an economy would be minor, the costs of the policy might not be serious. (Papua New Guinea went close to following such a rule in its 'strong-currency policy', during the early years – characterized by world inflation – after its independence.)

An assessment made in 2001 was that about 60 per cent of all developing countries maintained some form of float (Chang and Grabel, 2004, p. 165; citing Bird and Ramkishen, 2001), a considerable change since 1990, when a clear majority of developing countries' currencies (around 80 out of 120 among IMF members) were pegged (IMF, *International Financial Statistics*, 8/1990).

The other important dimension on which a decision must be made is whether the currency is to be convertible, that is whether holders of it are to be allowed to sell it freely for other currencies. This implies giving up much, but not all, of the possibility of capital-flow and exchange-rate management. (For example, it does not stop a country's restricting the *purchase by foreigners of its currency* as a way of limiting the possibility of speculation in its currency through controlling capital inflows.) By the early twenty-first century most developing countries' currencies seem to have been convertible (Chang and Grabel, ibid.), again a big change over the previous decade or so.

There is no agreed view over which of these regimes is best for any particular type of developing economy. Liberal (in the European sense) predilections were for regimes that eliminated administrative discretion, and therefore for either a free float or at the other extreme a currency board. The 'Washington consensus' in the early 1990s tended to favour a market float. (The world's four major currencies in the early twenty-first century float against each other.) The Asian crisis, which had affected mainly currencies with managed floats, or in the case of Thailand an adjustable peg, revived interest in the fixity and supposedly automatic discipline provided by a currency board (e.g., Walters, 1998). However, the very damaging collapse of the Argentine currency in 2001, in spite of its control by a currency board, threw doubt on the currency board as a panacea.

Four cases

Case 1: Significantly industrializing middle-income (and some large low-income) countries with reasonable fiscal discipline   These countries, covering much of South, East and South-East Asia, which are potentially attractive to foreign money and portfolio capital, will reasonably want to keep the option of some control over capital movements in order to avoid speculative crises, and this would appear to rule out completely free market floats. (However, in fact Mexico and the Philippines were both classed by the IMF as 'independently floating' in 1996, and Indonesia and South Korea as well in 1998. If these 'independent float' classifications really preclude the use of administrative controls, it seems probable that for Mexico, Korea and Indonesia, free floating may have seemed inevitable in the early years after their respective currency collapses.) At the same time these countries will probably want the freedom to manipulate the exchange-rate, or to allow it to move, in order to adjust to changes in 'real' conditions. All this would point to either adjustable pegs or else managed floats but with administrative-control powers at least held in reserve. In the wake of 1997 they would appear to have good grounds for allowing themselves access to some form of outflow and inflow controls directed at short-term capital movement, perhaps with a Spahn-type circuit-breaker also in reserve.

Case 2: Industrializing middle-income countries with a history of high inflation and with dubious fiscal discipline   In the absence of fiscal discipline, there would be a dilemma, familiar in Latin America. A fixed exchange-rate, if it could be held, might *eventually* stop, or greatly reduce, the inflation, but at the cost of depressing output and employment in the meantime as the REER rose. Alternatively, a downward-crawling peg designed to keep the country's REER (and hence in the short term its international competitiveness) roughly constant would perpetuate inflation. The dilemma might be mitigated by a 'social contract' over wages, but experience in Latin America has not been favourable to the view that such pacts can be made and held. *Fiscal discipline*, in other words, seems to be a necessary condition for a satisfactory solution. With fiscal discipline for a long enough period, these countries could perhaps escape the dilemma and be able to run a flexible-exchange-rate policy without the risk of igniting or perpetuating inflation. It is arguable that, in its response to the 'Asian crisis' of the 1990s, the IMF (damagingly) treated countries that were really in case 1 as if they were in case 2 and pressed deflationary fiscal policies upon them when what they needed was expansion. (See Krugman, 1999, ch. 6.)

Case 3: Low-income countries heavily dependent on primary exports   Here, because of the likely behaviour of the REER, it is generally reasonable to fix the exchange-rate against the currency of a major trading partner that itself maintains low inflation. (If, as around 1980, there was substantial *world* inflation, there might even be a case for a crawling *appreciation* for the sake of stabilizing the domestic price level.) Because there will be little tendency for traders to hold the currency of the country for speculative purposes, there will generally be no great difficulty over *sustaining* a fixed rate. Economic instability will come about not from domestic waxing and waning of confidence, or from short-term external capital movements, but through fluctuations in export earnings, complicated by the irregular phasing of foreign direct investment. The main methods needed for stability are the medium- or long-term fiscal and quasi-fiscal rules mooted above for this situation and expounded formally in Appendix 12.2, available on the Online Learning Centre. The choice of exchange-rate regime may not matter much except for controlling domestic inflation. (In fact, countries in this class are found in both the 'independently floating' and the 'pegged' ends of the scale.)

Case 4: High-income industrialized countries   Here, it seems, at least until 2008–09, that, on the assumption of reasonable fiscal and monetary discipline, freely floating rates, without the backing of controls, will serve. Krugman (1999, ch. 6) seeks to explain why the rich countries are generally able to allow their currencies to float freely without needing to fear devastating falls, while a number of middle-income countries, however prudent, can have no such assurance. Unfairly perhaps, it seems that, without administrative controls, the institutions of the latter do not inspire enough confidence among traders in the currency markets to keep exchange-rate movements within limits justified by objective conditions.

International support for stabilization in primary-export-dominated economies

The best and most prudent control of public finance for the purpose of stability (in the face of drastic fluctuations in export earnings) may still fail if a run of bad years is longer or more severe than could reasonably have been expected from past experience. We therefore consider whether there are measures that the international community has taken or might take to mitigate the difficulties a country in this position, especially one in Case 3 above, could face. (Consideration of the important question of international management and mitigation of difficulties with sovereign debt will be dealt with in Chapter 22.)

Expanding reserves: use of SDRs

One way of contributing to the possibilities of stabilization in a country is to increase the level of the international reserves on which it can call to accommodate external deficits. However prudently a country plans to keep its cumulative basic external balance within a given range, the unforeseen may always happen to frustrate its intentions. The larger the reserves it possesses, the greater the freedom of action it has to pursue a domestic policy for growth with stability within any given set of other conditions defining the external-balance constraint.

After the currency crises of the 1990s there were large 'investments' in additional reserves. Developing countries' ratio of reserves to their annual imports of goods and services rose by 24 percentage points between 1998 and 2005 (IMF, *World Economic Outlook*, September 2006, p. 248).

The IMF was designed originally to expand the reserves on which all member-countries could effectively draw. In 1969 its members went further and gave it power to create additional credits called Special Drawing Right (SDRs). The original creators of SDRs thought they were protecting the world economic system against a threatened *overall* shortage of international liquidity, and they provided that each issue of SDRs should be divided among member countries in proportion to their IMF quotas, which were effectively their contributions to the organization and reflected in relative size the countries' importance, or past importance, in world output and trade. There was thus no provision for giving SDRs differentially to poor countries or to those with intrinsically unstable economies.

However, it is the poor and unstable countries to which SDRs are most valuable. This is because rich and stable countries are able to borrow, on the markets, reserve assets, such as short-term bonds or bills issued by other rich countries' authorities, and to do so at low interest rates comparable to those that they can earn while they hold the assets. Poorer and more unstable countries, on the other hand, are likely to have to pay *higher* interest-rates in order to borrow the reserve assets *than they receive for holding them*, so that acquiring additional reserves is normally a costly process for them. If they add to their reserves by running an external-payments surplus, there are corresponding (perhaps even higher) opportunity-costs in the form of say forgone public investment that might otherwise be done. The advantage for them of SDR allocations is that they can draw (borrow) the SDRs allocated to them by paying (to the IMF) the same (low) rate of interest that they receive (from the IMF) while they continue to hold the SDRs. (This is explained in Clark and Polak, 2003; and in Boughton, 2001, pp. 924–7.) Adding to their reserves by the SDRs allocated to them is thus virtually costless to themselves and also involves no cost to others. Boughton (2001, p. 926) describes the creation of SDRs as a positive-sum game.

Yet there have been no 'allocations' of SDRs made since 1981. This is partly because the original fear of a general world shortage of liquidity dissipated. It seemed that there was an unlimited supply of reserve assets for all who wanted to hold them, the supply being provided by the readiness of the US and other major industrialized countries to borrow short-term from the rest of the world. Accordingly, after 1981 and until the mid-1990s, the US, Japan, Germany, and the UK opposed any further SDR allocations, and between them they had far more than enough votes in the IMF to prevail. However, in 1997 the Clinton Administration supported a further allocation designed to provide new members of the organization with the stocks of SDRs that they would have had if they had been members from the time SDRs were instituted. Accordingly, the governments represented in the IMF authorized the SDRs and also a change of IMF constitution to make this special allocation legitimate. However, the US Senate was able to effectively veto the change in the IMF constitution when it came for ratification, and as a result the 1997 allocation of SDRs has not at the time of writing been implemented.

Nevertheless, the possibility of further SDR allocations exists, and some, such as the exchange-dealer and philanthropist **George Soros** (2002), have argued not only that they should be made but also that the rich countries, for whom their SDR allocations are of no particular value, should transfer their own shares in the allocations to developing countries – without, or more realistically with, the interest obligations that the original recipients of the SDRs would have taken on. Even with these (low) interest obligations to balance the interest that they would receive while they held the SDRs, the developing countries would still gain through being able either to add to their reserves at next-to-no net cost or else possibly to buy out some of their existing debts on relatively favourable terms. Proposals along these lines, canvassed vigorously by Soros at the time of the Monterrey summit on Financing for Development in February 2002, were opposed by the then US administration and so did not receive enough support.

Possible world counter-cyclical use of SDRs

Logical extension of familiar devices might suggest that the power to issue and withdraw SDRs might be used by the IMF as a world counter-cyclical device. World booms and slumps, which lead to particularly large fluctuations in the prices of industrial raw-materials such as metals, are very damaging to the countries that export these goods. They are also disturbing to the world at large. In a world slump, individual governments and banks may be inhibited over taking the expansionary action which, if taken generally, would restore demand and activity. The IMF, if given the power to do so, might fill the gap by putting out SDRs to governments that could be expected to spend them promptly. These might be governments of poor countries – in which case the action would constitute not only a stimulus to world activity but also aid to lowish-income countries. The IMF, given powers to do this and to make the decisions concerned as executive acts – without needing political sanction from the Executive Directors, who are the politically selected representatives of the member countries – would be acting like a world central bank.

Commodity-price-stabilization schemes

Two types of expedients have had obvious appeal for countries heavily dependent on primary exports. One is for the producing countries to form a cartel, in which they keep the price within the range they desire by jointly controlling output, as was done by OPEC over petroleum from the early 1970s; for bauxite in some degree; very briefly over 1977–80 for coffee; and after 1985 for tin. The problems are those of keeping discipline among the members of the cartel, and not overdoing the price rises in case supply and demand responses in the rest of the world break the cartel's control. (Ten years after their first big engineered price rises of the start of 1974, the OPEC members found themselves selling about half as much oil as before, and by 1986 the oil price had decisively collapsed.)

The other possibility is an agreement *between exporting and importing countries* to stabilize the price – though *in principle* not necessarily to raise its trend value. This has been attempted by the use of one or both of two methods: export quotas and buffer-stocks. Of the two series of commodity agreements that were regarded as reasonably successful over fairly long periods, that for coffee (like the one for sugar) relied on export quotas, and that for tin (like those for cocoa and natural rubber) on both principles simultaneously. Broadly the rest of those started since 1945 have never amounted to much. The International Tin Agreement's buffer collapsed in 1985 with immense debts, though admittedly after 29 years of continuous operation. The International Coffee Council failed to get agreement on quotas in 1989 and has continued to fail since. Though active from 1963, it had had another period of about eight years in the 1970s when there had been no quotas in operation.

The problems of such schemes in general are indiscipline among the members (especially when the producing countries are very numerous, as with coffee); important producer or importer countries that do not join;[2] administrative costs (especially for the exporting countries when – coffee again– there are huge numbers of smallholders each of whom has to be given – or refused – a share of the national quota); technical difficulties over judging appropriate price ranges; and political difficulties over agreeing to them.

There is an even broader objection, though not unconnected with these practical difficulties: that the schemes inevitably have a tendency to favour *existing* producing countries and producing individuals and enterprises – which may be regarded as both inefficient and unfair – and that they depend to an extent on their success in doing this. One factor in the collapse of the tin agreement was held to be the emergence of Brazil as an exporter outside the agreement.

---

[2] As with cocoa, where the biggest producer (Côte D'Ivoire) and the biggest importer (the US) both remained outside the agreement.

In any case, the impulse for producer-importer commodity-price-stabilization agreements is widely regarded as dead. Gilbert (1996), in writing what he called 'an obituary', noted that at the time only the natural-rubber scheme from among the five that had been active was continuing with any market intervention, and that at a very modest level. The tin stabilization scheme had been replaced by a producers' cartel. He did not appear to believe that this kind of venture was necessarily doomed, given enough flexibility in the rules and enough resources; but he recognized that the climate of opinion at the time he wrote was against official market intervention of this type, and that there might be less inefficient, and equally or more effective, ways of stabilizing prices, either through private or national stocks or through the use of futures and options, with the latter of these sets of devices available particularly for increasing the *predictability* of prices.

Insurance to governments of commodity earnings

What about *insurance* over countries' commodity *earnings*, however, or indeed over foreign-exchange earnings in general – or at least over those elements within them that vary independently of those countries' own actions? Is it possible – as with the familiar insurance with which households, by sharing risks, cover themselves against individually unpredictable falls in income or losses in property – to smooth the real income flows of countries?

Two international schemes exist that attempt in some degree to do this, though both depart quite widely from the (tried and sensible) principles of household insurance.

STABEX

This is the scheme established in 1975 by the then EEC for the benefit of its African, Caribbean and Pacific (APC) partners, almost all of whom were and are primary-commodity-dependent. It has, however, dealt only with *biological* exports of those countries – with sugar also excepted, moreover, because it has been dealt with otherwise – and only their exports of these goods to what is now the European Union. (A parallel arrangement, SYSMIN, covers a number of hard minerals.)

The idea is that, when a country's earnings from exports to the EU of any one of the commodities covered falls by more than a certain percentage below 'trend', payments are made to the country's government, which of course might if it chose pass them on to the producers. These payments are not formally grants, but no interest is charged on them and repayment obligations have been applied only in certain rather rare cases. So no revolving fund is built up. Allowances for the purpose are made periodically by the EU to the European Development Fund. In principle, when the amount allocated to a particular year has run out, no more can be paid, though this obstacle has sometimes been overridden. The scheme disbursed over a billion ECUs in its first decade (Hewitt, 1987, p. 621).

From a study made, it is doubtful whether on balance the scheme has increased or decreased stability in the overall export earnings of the countries included (Herrmannn, 1983; citing Hewitt, 1987). The possibility of decrease in stability probably arises first because of delays in payment after the years of shortfall, second because of the commodity-by-commodity treatment, and third because of the confinement of the earnings considered to those from exports *to the EU*. (It is hard to see rational justification for any of these features.)

The STABEX scheme differs from ordinary insurance as we might expect it to apply in a case like this: there is no 'premium' (pay-in) and correspondingly no ironclad obligation for the fund to pay; and, though it is the country, through its government, that is insured, it is not its overall earnings whose shortfalls are compensated, or even its shortfalls from biological exports. On the other hand, provided funds are available, payment of compensation is automatic if the deficiency conditions are met.

The IMF's Compensatory and Contingency Financing Facility (CCFF)

Until 1988 this was the Compensatory Financing Facility (CFF), dating under that name from 1963. Quantitatively it has been many times as important as STABEX. As a 'facility', it represents one set of conditions under which loans may be drawn on the IMF. It was originally intended to cover years of lower-than normal export income, not necessarily only for developing countries. For this purpose exports of all sorts are aggregated, and the range of the 'compensatory' element was progressively extended – until 1983 – to cover by then also deficiencies in tourism earnings and worker remittances and rises above trend in import prices for basic foods. Limitations on the amounts that could be drawn were also progressively relaxed through the 1960s and 1970s. The year ending April 1983, covering the outbreak of the Debt Crisis, was the bumper one for CFF disbursements, which then totalled 3.7 billion SDRs. From 1983, however, the conditions for borrowing under the facility were in practice tightened considerably.

The 'contingency' element, added in 1988, was designed to cover unfavourable departures in levels of tourism earnings, worker remittances, food-import prices, or international interest-rates, as well as merchandise-export conditions, from the levels supposed in any stand-by arrangement agreed with the IMF.

In contrast to STABEX, payments out have been medium-term interest-bearing loans, and they have not been made automatically in response to objective indicators. Judgements have had to be made over whether the balance-of payments position would have been satisfactory were it not for the exogenous changes concerned and on whether the country had been or would be co-operative enough with the IMF. In short, especially since 1983, there has been a high degree of what the IMF calls 'conditionality', a requirement that certain policy conditions should be fulfilled. However, pay-outs, by contrast with those under STABEX, are made quite briskly.

Two studies (Kumar, 1989, and Langlands, 1991; cited Clunies-Ross, 1991, p. 148), on slightly different criteria, both found that the CCFF had *on average* reduced instability in foreign-exchange receipts, but only in small proportions (less than 6 per cent), and less again if repayment obligations were included.

Judged by conventional insurance, the CCFF could be argued perhaps to conform by having a premium of a sort (in the IMF quotas), but to differ in that its pay-outs are not automatic on objective criteria and are fully repayable.

So, neither of these two schemes much resembles conventional commercial insurance, whereas there are reasons for thinking that conventional insurance, which after all grew up commercially in response to customer demand, has broadly the right characteristics to deal with the needs of the insured. The extent to which either STABEX or the CCFF smoothes the path of external receipts (and therefore of potential expenditure) is small at best, and STABEX especially may in particular cases have the reverse effect.

More conventional earnings-insurance

It is quite possible to *conceive* of a system in which governments, on behalf of their populations, hand over to an international fund a share of their primary-export earnings when those earnings are high (in relation to some trend), and receive corresponding payments out of the fund when their earnings are low. There are potentially various ways in which such a procedure can go wrong. Forms of insurance under consideration have to be explored for their susceptibility to *moral hazard* (failure to take due care, or claiming pay-outs for non-existent or self-induced misfortune) and to *adverse selection* (a tendency of those whose circumstances make them especially likely to trigger a pay-out in the near future to enrol in disproportionate numbers and to withdraw once they have been paid). One of the present authors has given reasons for thinking that a simple scheme might be designed in such a way that it was fortified against these hazards; simulations of the scheme over a recent turbulent 20-year period implied that an insurance fund so conceived could, with various sets of detailed provisions, remain solvent, while significantly smoothing net primary-export receipts (Clunies-Ross, 2001).

Stabilizing individual producers' incomes through market derivatives

An idea with a particular appeal for those who distrust governments is that primary-exporting countries or their producers might use the instruments already available in the markets – forward contracts, futures, and especially options – to enable them to keep within defined ranges the future prices they will receive. In principle this is possible, say, through the simultaneous buying and selling of options. (*Importers* of the goods may also be interested in stabilizing the prices they receive in the future.) The question of interest must be whether the concern for stability on both sides is sufficient to make the 'price of stability or predictability' attractive enough to both.

A team under the auspices of the World Bank (International Task Force, 1999, 2001) began in 1999 to explore the possibility of making the purchase of these stabilizing instruments available to individual producers, with the international institutions acting as intermediaries.

Work on this has continued. In 2005 work was beginning on a Global Index Insurance Fund to help ACP countries to access insurance markets against various kinds of disaster. (See the International Task Force's website: www.itf-commrisk.org.)

Summary conclusions

- Stability in the growth path of real income and of the price level is of great importance to current welfare and political stability in developing countries, and can generally be expected to favour economic growth.

- The cause of stability is not hopeless, even in countries highly dependent on primary exports, but it requires internal disciplines and potentially may be greatly helped by appropriate international support in the form of additional reserves or of appropriate forms of insurance.

- In the structuralist-monetarist debate over controlling inflation, there are relevant insights on both sides. These are the importance of positive-sum political bargains and of fiscal-monetary control respectively. But they do not define relevant differences, for stabilization-policy purposes, between developing and developed countries.

- The different policy frameworks appropriate for stabilization in various types of economy depend on three features: their main sources of instability; the policy instruments available; and the behaviour of their labour markets. But fiscal discipline in various guises is important for all; and 'social contracts', involving particularly wages, may facilitate politically the essential fiscal, or fiscal-monetary, control, and ameliorate its effects.

- The crucial disciplines and devices required for stabilization in poor, financially undeveloped countries, heavily dependent on primary exports (which are their main sources of instability), and with relatively competitive labour markets, are *fiscal and quasi-fiscal* with a large *compensatory* ('counter-cyclical') element. Those countries have little need or scope for monetary fine-tuning and little occasion for varying their exchange-rates or allowing them to vary.

- This contrasts with the case of the major rich, industrialized countries, where the main disturbances in normal times come from within the domestic financial, investment, and asset-trading system. There *inflation targeting by monetary fine-tuning* has come to be regarded as an essential element; active compensatory fiscal policy tends to be reserved for *times of occasional large negative financial shocks*; and it is generally believed that exchange-rates can safely be allowed *to float with little deliberate intervention*.

- A further case is that of, often fast-industrializing, middle-income (and some large low-income) countries with important elements of modern financial institutions and markets. Here monetary management will probably require similar rules to those used in developed countries, but currency-flight has turned out to be a major hazard. Provision, at least in reserve, for *control of international capital flows* will probably be necessary. Hence the exchange-rate regime of choice will probably not be a completely free float, and the appropriate option among pegged and intermediate systems will depend on features such as the country's inflationary history and the competitiveness of its labour market, with the choice less constrained the more effective is the fiscal control.

- There is no single best exchange-rate regime. All have potential drawbacks as well as advantages, and the balance of advantage depends mainly on the type of economy, with some bearing also of the character and effectiveness of other aspects of policy.

- Indexation of various forms of contract to the general price level may in certain circumstances avoid inefficiencies and inequities, but there are risks – especially with *retrospective* indexation – of increasing the impulses to inflation and hence the costs of eventually suppressing it, and of protecting certain sections of the population at the expense of others, including many of the poorest.

- Stabilization, especially in low-income countries, may be fortified by various forms of international support. One is potentially costless expansion of their reserves by the issue of SDRs – with the additional possibility that SDR allocations to the richer countries, who, because of their capacity to raise funds at low interest-rates, do not need them, may be passed to developing countries as a form of aid (in effect as very-low-interest-rate loans).

- As what is at the moment a visionary possibility, the IMF might be empowered to use its powers of creation and withdrawal of SDRs counter-cyclically to help iron out world booms and slumps, and to do this through administrative decisions, acting much as if it were a world central bank. While commodity-price-stabilization agreements between producer and consumer countries seem, after the experiences of the last few decades, to

▶

> have little future, there are possibilities of earnings-insurance schemes, though the two at present operating have manifest deficiencies. There is scope for another fund providing earnings-insurance to primary-exporter states, constructed to act more according to the model of commercial insurance, which after all has been able to operate because it meets its customers' needs.
>
> - There is also the possibility, explored and piloted by the World Bank, of giving individual primary-export-producers access to the use of market derivatives for income-stabilizing purposes.

Much of the pain of ordinary people in developing countries that relates to their involvement in the world economy – and can readily be blamed on 'globalization' – is in fact due to instability of incomes and prices. There is much that can be done – by individual countries' governments with international support – to mitigate that pain. Stabilization is in (almost) everyone's interest.

Questions for discussion

12.1 In what way might economic stabilization be important to current welfare?

12.2 In what way might economic instability be (a) conducive, (b) obstructive, to economic growth? Which tendency would you expect to predominate?

12.3 What explanation might be given to explain the inferences drawn from some empirical research that low but positive rates of inflation are more conducive to economic growth than either higher rates (over say 10 per cent) on the one hand or zero inflation on the other?

12.4 Express the definition of the real effective exchange-rate (REER) in an algebraic formula.

12.5 What is meant by a mean-reverting REER, and what features of an economy are likely to lead to it?

12.6 What are the implications of a mean-reverting REER for the effects of various stabilizing policy instruments, such as interventions (a) to appreciate or (b) to depreciate the (nominal) exchange-rate, or fiscal and/or monetary measures for (c) expanding or (d) contracting (nominal) domestic expenditure?

12.7 How would you justify (or question) James Boughton's judgement that creating IMF Special Drawing Rights (SDRs) is a positive-sum game?

12.8 What are the supposed virtues among exchange-rate regimes of (a) a fixed exchange-rate maintained by a currency board, and (b) a freely-floating rate? Why or in what circumstances could these virtues be questioned?

Additional reading

Boughton, J.M. (2001) *Silent Revolution: the International Monetary Fund 1979–1989*, IMF, Washington, DC, pp. 20–21, 925–56 (on SDRs, 'international money').

Kirkpatrick, C. and F. Nixson (1987) 'Inflation and stabilization policy in LDCs', in N. Gemmell (ed.), *Surveys in Development Economics*, Basil Blackwell, Oxford.

Krugman, P. (1999) *The Return of Depression Economics*, Allen Lane, The Penguin Press, London.

Online
Learning Center

To help you grasp the key concepts of this chapter check out the extra resources posted on the Online Learning Centre at ***www.mcgraw-hill.co.uk/textbooks/huq***

Among other resources, there are two appendices available:

- Appendix 12.1   The resource curse
- Appendix 12.2   A stabilization rule for a low-income economy heavily dependent on primary-commodity exports

PART 4
Real Resources and Sectoral Considerations

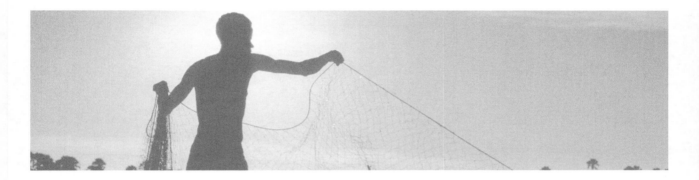

CHAPTER 13

Population and Labour Supply

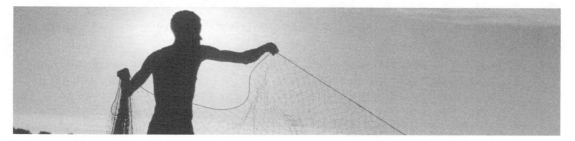

Though the rate of world population growth has declined in recent years, there is still concern over whether the world is able to support sustainably a population that is projected to grow from over 6 billion in 2000 to about 9.2 billion in 2050. Other worries have been augmented by concern over the *effect on the world environment*. Hence, despite some persisting academic dissent, the prevailing view since around 1960 has been that, for developing countries and for the world in general, the lower the growth in population the better. However, coercive and target-driven policies of birth control – as distinct from providing family-planning advice and facilities – had come widely into disrepute by the end of the century, as oppressive, sometimes personally damaging, and unnecessary. Over the last three decades of the twentieth century human fertility in developing countries as a whole fell by about half, and it became clear that fertility decline and falling population growth rate were associated with some other highly desirable social changes relating to the status of women and the health of young children.

Introduction

The growth of population remains an important concern for the world, even though its *rate* has been declining in most countries and overall has been on the way down. This chapter aims to present some issues raised by population growth in Third World countries.

The next two sections deal first with the current population position: **how world population has been changing and is expected to change** over the current half-century. We introduce on the way some **demographic terms** for describing what is happening to the population. We outline the idea of a '**demographic transition**' – a speeding and then slowing of population growth – through which many countries appear to have passed or to be passing. The next section discusses **the bearing of population change on per capita economic growth**, examining the concept of an 'optimum population' to see if it can be of any practical use. This leads to the question of **what factors determine human fertility**. From this we move to **population policy**, the variety of methods that have been used to slow population growth and their relative advantages. Finally we consider the development of that most vital resource, **human capital**. Appendix 13.1 (p. 400) raises the question whether and how it might be possible to enhance the economic growth of the present underdeveloped countries by **using their surplus labour**.

BOX 13.1 TOOLKIT ON POPULATION

Birth control. Various methods – devices, disciplines or medications – to reduce the likelihood of pregnancy.

Crude birth rate. Number of live births per 1000 people each year; so a crude birth rate of 25 per 1000 is the same as a birth rate of 2.5 per cent. The crude birth rate **depends on** age-specific fertility rates and age-gender distribution of the population.

Crude death rate. Number of deaths per year per 1000 people. The crude death rate **depends on** age-gender-specific mortality rates and age-gender distribution of the population.

Demographic transition. A prevalent pattern of changes in population growth in individual countries over time. Initially, there is a virtually stagnant period characterized by high birth and high death rates. This is followed by a period of rapid population growth because of high birth but low death rates, then a period of falling rates of growth, and finally a phase of low population growth with both low birth and low death rates.

Dependency ratio. The proportion of those not working (mostly the young and the old) to working-age people. (It is the ratio of the total number of people, taken to be those in the 0–15 and 65+ age groups, who are dependants to the total number of people who are active in the labour force.)

Determinants of fertility. Various factors that influence fertility, e.g., income of the individuals concerned, availability of family planning services, female education, employment opportunities for women, and the healthcare that affects infant and young-child mortality.

Family planning. A conscious attempt by individuals to plan the births of children – in particular to regulate the size of families – using various contraception methods.

Fertility. Number of live births on average per woman (or per 1000 women). **Total fertility rate** (TFR) is the total 'expected' number of live births to a woman in the child-bearing age group, normally taken as 15 to 49 years, (as distinguished from the **age-specific fertility rate**, which refers for example to the rate in a particular age group, say 20 to 25 years). The 'expected' number at a particular time in this context refers not to the *best prediction* of the number of births a woman will have through that period but to the number she would have if, at every age range, her number of births was the *current* average for that age range, so that the TFR is the sum of the current age-specific fertility rates, a summary account of fertility *now*. (For certain purposes it is desirable to take into account also the current expected rate of dying for a woman in each age range until the end of the child-bearing period.)

Human capital. A key factor in productivity, a composite of acquired knowledge and skills and improvements in nutrition and health.

Infant mortality rate. Number of infants dying before reaching one year of age, per 1000 live births.

Life-expectancy at birth. This is the number of years that a person newly born in year N would be expected (on average) to live if over each year of life she or he were to be subject to the age-specific mortality rate for the relevant gender *that is current for that age range in year N.* So it is *not a best-prediction* of the newly born's length of life but a summary of the mortality conditions *prevailing in year N.* (In this it is analogous to the total fertility rate.) Life-expectancy can be similarly expressed for a man or a woman at any age.

Malnutrition. A state of poor health due to an improper diet or an inadequate quantity of food over an extended period of time.

Malthusian population trap. As postulated by Thomas Malthus (1766–1834), there is a maximum level of population that can be supported by the available agricultural resources; any tendency to increase beyond this level will be capped by starvation, disease, or warfare. Malthus postulated that the trap arises because population increases in a geometric progression, while the increase of food supply is in an arithmetic progression.

Optimum population. A theoretical concept implying a situation in which a country's or a region's population is at the size that enables it to obtain the maximum output per head.

Population density. The average number of people living in a particular area, usually shown as the average number of persons per square kilometre.

Population policy. A conscious attempt to guide and control the growth of a nation's population.

Rate of natural increase. Crude birth rate minus crude death rate per year.

Rate of net immigration. Number of immigrants per year *minus* the number of emigrants per year, per 1000 people.

Rate of population growth. Rate of natural increase plus the rate of net immigration per year.

Current demographic position

Population size: present, recent and projected

As may be seen from Table 13.1, the population of the world has continued to increase, from about 2.5 billion in 1950 to over 6 billion in 2000, and is projected to increase to about 9.2 billion in 2050.

In 1950, 32 per cent of the total population of the world lived in 'developed countries' and the rest (68 per cent) in the 'developing countries'. The percentage of people living in what are now developing countries increased to 80 per cent in 2000, and it is projected to increase further to 87 per cent in 2050. The percentage of world population made up by those living in the 'least-developed' part (LLDCs) of the developing countries increased from 8 per cent in 1950 to 11 per cent in 2000, and is estimated to increase further to 19 per cent in 2050. These figures imply that the population of least-developed countries has increased,

Year	Developing Region*	Least Developed Part (of the Developing Region) *	Developed Region*	TOTAL POPULATION*
1950	1721.5 (68%)	200.3 (8%)	813.6 (32%)	2535.1 (100%)
1955	1906.7 (69%)	221.4 (8%)	864.0 (31%)	2770.8 (100%)
1960	2115.8 (70%)	247.3 (8%)	916.1 (30%)	3031.9 (100%)
1965	2375.8 (71%)	278.4 (8%)	967.0 (29%)	3342.8 (100%)
1970	2690.2 (73%)	315.9 (9%)	1008.5 (27%)	3698.7 (100%)
1975	3028.0 (74%)	358.3 (9%)	1048.1 (26%)	4076.1 (100%)
1980	3368.2 (76%)	405.8 (9%)	1083.3 (24%)	4451.5 (100%)
1985	3739.9 (77%)	461.0 (9%)	1115.4 (23%)	4855.3 (100%)
1990	4145.8 (78%)	525.5 (10%)	1149.1 (22%)	5294.9 (100%)
1995	4543.6 (79%)	601.1 (11%)	1175.4 (21%)	5719.0 (100%)
2000	4929.9 (80%)	679.4 (11%)	1194.2 (20%)	6124.1 (100%)
2005	5299.1 (81%)	766.9 (12%)	1215.6 (19%)	6514.8 (100%)
2010	5674.1 (82%)	863.4 (13%)	1232.5 (18%)	6906.6 (100%)
2015	6050.1 (83%)	966.7 (13%)	1245.0 (17%)	7295.1 (100%)
2020	6413.2 (84%)	1075.1 (14%)	1253.9 (16%)	7667.1 (100%)
2025	6751.5 (84%)	1186.9 (15%)	1259.0 (16%)	8010.5 (100%)
2030	7056.9 (85%)	1300.6 (16%)	1260.8 (15%)	8317.7 (100%)
2035	7327.1 (85%)	1414.7 (16%)	1260.0 (15%)	8587.1 (100%)
2040	7566.7 (86%)	1527.4 (17%)	1256.9 (14%)	8823.5 (100%)
2045	7774.2 (86%)	1637.1 (18%)	1251.8 (14%)	9026.0 (100%)
2050	7964.0 (87%)	1742.0 (19%)	1245.2 (14%)	9191.3 (100%)

TABLE 13.1 Population in developed and developing regions, 1950–2050

* (In Millions). Figures in brackets are in percentages of the respective population total. The least developed part is, however, a sub-set of the developing region.

Source: Population Division of the Department of Economic and Social Affairs of the United Nations Secretariat, *World Population Prospects: the 2006 Revision* and *World Urbanization Prospects: the 2005 revision (http://esa.un.org/unpp).*

and is projected to go on increasing, faster than the rest of the developing countries, with the difference expected to be greater in the present half-century than in the one that preceded it. The LLDCs, containing 11.6 per cent of the total of developing-country people in 1950, had 13.8 per cent in 2000, and on the projections will have 21.9 per cent of them in 2050.

Table 13.2 shows for 152 individual countries the actual population in 1980, 1990 and 2000; the growth rate of population between 1980 and 2000; and also the population projected for 2020.

In 2000, both China and India had over one billion people each, with 1263 million and 1016 million respectively. If we consider a band of countries with 100 million to 300 million people each, in 2000 there were eight members of this group (Bangladesh 131 million, Brazil 170 million, Indonesia 210 million, Japan 127 million, Nigeria 127 million, Pakistan 138 million, Russia 146 million, and the US 282 million), and by 2020 there are projected to

	Actual (Mil.)			Average annual growth rate (%)	Projected (Mil.)	Crude death rate per 1000 people	Crude birth rate per 1000 people
	1980	1990	2000	1980–2000	2020	2000	2000
Afghanistan	16	14.6	26.6	2.5	42.7*	22	48
Albania	2.7	3.3	3.4	1.2	3.4	6	17
Algeria	18.7	25.3	30.4	2.4	40.6	5	25
Angola	7.1	10.5	13.1	3.1	23.8	19	48
Argentina	28.1	32.6	37	1.4	44.5	8	19
Armenia	3.1	3.5	3.8	1	3	6	11
Australia	14.7	17.1	19.2	1.3	23.3	7	13
Austria	7.6	7.7	8.1	0.4	8.3	10	10
Azerbaijan	6.2	7.2	8	1.3	9.4	6	15
Bangladesh	86.7	104	131.1	2.1	181.2	9	28
Belarus	9.6	10.2	10	0.2	8.9	14	9
Belgium	9.8	10	10.3	0.2	10.6	10	11
Benin	3.5	5.2	6.3	3	12.7	13	39
Bolivia	5.4	6.7	8.3	2	11.6	9	31
Bosnia and Herzegovina	4.1	4.3	4	−0.1	3.8	8	12
Botswana	0.9	1.4	1.6	2.8	1.7	20	32
Brazil	121.7	149.4	170.4	1.7	219.2	7	20
Bulgaria	8.9	8.7	8.2	−0.4	6.9	14	9
Burkina Faso	7	8.5	11.3	2.4	20.3	19	44
Burundi	4.1	5.7	6.8	2.5	12.3	20	40
Cambodia	6.5	9.7	12	2.8	18.6	12	30
Cameroon	8.7	11.7	14.9	2.7	20.4	14	37
Canada	24.6	27.8	30.8	1.1	36.4	8	11
Central African Republic	2.3	3	3.7	2.4	5	20	36
Chad	4.5	6.1	7.7	2.7	14.9	16	45
Chile	11.1	13.2	15.2	1.6	18.6	6	17
China	981.2	1135.20	1263	1.3	1424	7	15
Hong Kong, China	5	5.70	7	1.5	8	5	8
Colombia	28.4	35	42.3	2	55	6	23
Congo, Dem. Rep.	27	37.8	50.9	3.2	90	17	46
Congo, Rep.	1.7	2.5	3	3	6.4	14	23
Costa Rica	2.3	3.1	3.8	2.6	5.3	4	20

TABLE 13.2 Population changes: by countries, 1980–2000

Notes: The figures shown with * for Afghanistan, Iraq, and West Bank and Gaza are estimates. In the last row, the total population, shown by s, is the sum of the population of the 152 countries in the table, and the figures, shown by w, for the crude birth and death rates are weighted averages.

Source: World Development Indicators, 1999 (pages 46–48); *2002* (pages 48–50); *2003* (pages 38–40); and *2006* (pages 46–48).

	Actual (Mil.)			Average annual growth rate (%)	Projected (Mil.)	Crude death rate per 1000 people	Crude birth rate per 1000 people
	1980	1990	2000	1980–2000	2020	2000	2000
Côte d'Ivoire	8.2	12.7	16	3.3	23.3	17	37
Croatia	4.6	4.8	4.4	−0.2	4.4	12	10
Cuba	9.7	10.5	11.2	0.7	11.4	7	13
Czech Republic	10.2	10.4	10.3	0	9.9	11	9
Denmark	5.1	5.1	5.3	0.2	5.6	11	12
Dominican Republic	5.7	7.1	8.4	1.9	10.7	6	23
Ecuador	8	10.3	12.6	2.3	16	6	24
Egypt, Arab Rep.	40.9	55.7	64	2.2	94.8	6	25
El Salvador	4.6	5.1	6.3	1.6	8.5	6	26
Eritrea	2.4	3	4.1	2.7	6.6	13	39
Estonia	1.5	1.6	1.4	−0.4	1.3	13	9
Ethiopia	37.7	51.2	64.3	2.7	107.7	20	44
Finland	4.8	5	5.2	0.4	5.4	10	11
France	53.9	56.7	58.9	0.4	63	9	13
Gabon	0.7	1	1.2	2.9	1.7	16	36
Gambia	0.6	0.9	1.3	3.5	2.1	13	39
Georgia	5.1	5.5	5	0	4.1	9	9
Germany	78.3	79.4	82.2	0.2	82.3	11	9
Ghana	10.7	15.5	19.3	2.9	28.8	11	30
Greece	9.6	10.2	10.6	0.5	11.2	11	12
Guatemala	6.8	8.9	11.4	2.6	17.5	7	33
Guinea	4.5	6.2	7.4	2.5	13.4	17	39
Guinea-Bissau	0.8	1	1.2	2.3	2.5	20	42
Haiti	5.4	6.9	8	2	10.3	13	32
Honduras	3.6	4.9	6.4	2.9	9.5	6	31
Hungary	10.7	10.4	10	−0.3	9.6	14	10
India	687.3	849.5	1016	2	1332	9	25
Indonesia	148.3	178.2	210.4	1.7	255.9	7	22
Iran, Islamic Rep.	39.1	54.4	63.7	2.4	85	6	22
Iraq	13	18.5	23.3	2.9	39.7*	9	31
Ireland	3.4	3.5	3.8	0.5	4.9	8	14
Israel	3.9	4.7	6.2	2.4	8.3	6	21
Italy	56.4	56.7	57.7	0.1	57.1	10	9
Jamaica	2.1	2.4	2.6	1.1	2.8	6	21
Japan	116.8	123.5	126.9	0.4	126.7	8	9

TABLE 13.2 (*continued*)

	Actual (Mil.)			Average annual growth rate (%)	Projected (Mil.)	Crude death rate per 1000 people	Crude birth rate per 1000 people
	1980	1990	2000	1980–2000	2020	2000	2000
Jordan	2.2	3.2	4.9	4	7.6	4	29
Kazakhstan	14.9	16.3	14.9	0	14.9	10	15
Kenya	16.6	23.4	30.1	3	49.6	14	35
Korea, Dem. Rep.	17.7	19.7	22.3	1.3	23.7	11	18
Korea, Rep	38.1	42.9	47.3	1.1	49.4	6	13
Kuwait	1.4	2.1	2	1.8	3.7	2	20
Kyrgyz Republic	3.6	4.4	4.9	1.5	6.1	7	21
Lao PDR	3.2	4.1	5.3	2.5	8	13	37
Latvia	2.5	2.7	2.4	−0.4	2.1	14	9
Lebanon	3	2.7	4.3	1.8	4.1	6	20
Lesotho	1.3	1.6	2	2	1.7	17	33
Liberia	1.9	2.1	3.1	2.6	5	17	44
Libya	3	4.3	5.3	2.8	7.5	5	27
Lithuania	3.4	3.7	3.7	0.4	3.2	11	9
Macedonia, FYR	1.9	1.9	2	0.4	2.1	8	13
Madagascar	8.9	12	15.5	2.8	26.6	12	40
Malawi	6.2	9.5	10.3	2.6	17.8	24	46
Malaysia	13.8	17.8	23.3	2.6	31.5	4	25
Mali	6.6	8.9	10.8	2.5	20.9	20	46
Mauritania	1.6	2	2.7	2.7	4.5	15	42
Mauritius	1	1.1	1.2	1	1.4	7	17
Mexico	67.6	83.2	98	1.9	124.7	5	25
Moldova	4	4.4	4.3	0.3	4.1	11	10
Mongolia	1.7	2.1	2.4	1.8	3.1	6	22
Morocco	19.4	23.9	28.7	2	38.3	6	24
Mozambique	12.1	13.4	17.7	1.9	25.5	20	40
Myanmar	33.8	40.8	47.7	1.7	57.1	12	25
Namibia	1	1.4	1.8	2.9	2.4	17	36
Nepal	14.5	19.1	23	2.3	35.7	10	33
Netherlands	14.2	15	15.9	0.6	17	9	13
New Zealand	3.1	3.4	3.8	1	4.4	7	15
Nicaragua	2.9	4	5.1	2.8	7.2	5	30
Niger	5.6	8.5	10.8	3.3	22.6	19	51
Nigeria	71.1	90.6	126.9	2.9	175.8	16	40
Norway	4.1	4.2	4.5	0.5	5	10	13

TABLE 13.2 (*continued*)

	Actual (Mil.)			Average annual growth rate (%)	Projected (Mil.)	Crude death rate per 1000 people	Crude birth rate per 1000 people
	1980	1990	2000	1980–2000	2020	2000	2000
Oman	1.1	1.8	2.4	3.9	3.5	3	28
Pakistan	82.7	108	138.1	2.6	211.7	8	34
Panama	2	2.4	2.9	1.9	4	5	21
Papua New Guinea	3.1	4.1	5.1	2.5	7.6	9	32
Paraguay	3.1	4.2	5.5	2.8	8.3	5	30
Peru	17.3	21.8	25.7	2	34.2	7	23
Philippines	48.3	61.1	75.6	2.3	103.3	5	27
Poland	35.6	38.1	38.7	0.4	37.7	10	10
Portugal	9.8	9.9	10	0.1	10.9	11	12
Puerto Rico	3.2	3.5	3.9	1	4.2	8	15
Romania	22.2	23.2	22.4	0.1	20.4	11	10
Russian Federation	139	148.3	145.6	0.2	133.1	15	9
Rwanda	5.2	7.1	8.5	2.5	12.4	22	44
Saudi Arabia	9.4	16.4	20.7	4	34	4	33
Senegal	5.5	8	9.7	2.7	16	13	37
Serbia and Montenegro	9.8	10.5	10.6	0.4	10.3	11	12
Sierra Leone	3.2	4.1	5	2.2	7.7	23	44
Singapore	2.3	3	4	2.5	5	4	12
Slovak Republic	5	5.3	5.4	0.4	5.4	10	10
Slovenia	1.9	2	2	0.2	1.9	10	9
Somalia		6.7	8.8	1.5	12.3	17	51
South Africa	27.6	35.2	42.8	2.2	48.1	16	26
Spain	37.4	38.8	39.5	0.3	44.4	9	10
Sri Lanka	14.7	17	19.4	1.4	22.9	6	18
Sudan	18.7	26.1	31.1	2.4	47.5	11	34
Swaziland		0.8	1	3.1	1	15	36
Sweden	8.3	8.6	8.9	0.3	9.5	11	10
Switzerland	6.3	6.7	7.2	0.6	7.4	9	10
Syrian Arab Republic	8.7	12.8	16.2	3.1	26	5	29
Tajikistan	4	5.3	6.2	2.2	8.2	5	19
Tanzania	18.6	26.2	33.7	3	49.3	17	39
Thailand	46.7	54.6	60.7	1.3	71	7	17
Togo	2.6	4	4.5	2.9	8.7	15	37
Trinidad and Tobago	1.1	1.2	1.3	0.9	1.3	7	15
Tunisia	6.4	8.2	9.6	2	11.6	6	17

TABLE 13.2 (*continued*)

	Actual (Mil.)			Average annual growth rate (%)	Projected (Mil.)	Crude death rate per 1000 people	Crude birth rate per 1000 people
	1980	**1990**	**2000**	**1980–2000**	**2020**	**2000**	**2000**
Turkey	44.5	56.2	65.3	1.9	86.8	6	20
Turkmenistan	2.9	3.7	5.2	3	5.8	7	21
Uganda	12.8	17.8	22.2	2.8	50.6	19	45
Ukraine	50	51.9	49.5	−0.1	39.6	15	9
United Arab Emirates	1	1.8	2.9	5.1	6.1	3	17
United Kingdom	56.3	57.6	59.7	0.3	62.5	11	11
United States	227.2	249.6	281.6	1.1	338.4	9	15
Uruguay	2.9	3.1	3.3	0.7	3.8	10	16
Uzbekistan	16	20.5	24.8	2.2	32.5	6	22
Venezuela, RB	15.1	19.8	24.2	2.4	33.5	4	22
Vietnam	53.7	66.2	78.5	1.9	99.9	6	19
West Bank and Gaza	1.7*	2	3	1.5*	5.7	4	40
Yemen, Rep.	8.5	12.1	17.5	3.6	32.7	11	40
Zambia	5.7	8.4	10.1	2.8	15.1	21	40
Zimbabwe	7	10.6	12.6	2.9	14.1	18	30
TOTAL	**4429.9s**	**5256.3s**	**6057.3s**	**1.6w**	**7573.5s**	**9w**	**22w**

TABLE 13.2 (*continued*)

be four new members (Ethiopia 108 million, Mexico 125 million, the Philippines 103 million, and Vietnam 100 million).

An extension of the size classification based on bands may be seen in Table 13.3 below. It shows that there were 14 countries with 1 to 2 million people each, 29 from over 2 million to 5 million, 35 from over 5 million to 10 million, 51 from over 10 million to 50 million, 14 from over 50 million to 100 million, and the 10 countries we have mentioned with a population of over 100 million.

Population growth

Table 13.2 shows that between 1980 and 2000 world population grew by 1.6 per cent a year, but in as many as 12 countries – all in Africa or West Asia – it grew by over 3 per cent a year. (The countries were Angola, Congo Dem. Rep., Côte d'Ivoire, Gambia, Jordan, Niger, Oman, Saudi Arabia, Swaziland, Syria, United Arab Emirates and Yemen). There were 40 countries – all of them, except Japan and Cuba, in Europe or the former USSR – with growth rates of less than 1 per cent, of which seven had negative rates. There has been a strong tendency for the rich to be the ones with low population growth rates. Among the affluent countries themselves, those from Europe – and Japan – had distinctly lower growth rates of population than some other developed countries such as Australia (1.3 per cent) or

Total population (millions)	Number of countries N = 152	Countries
1 to 2	14	Botswana, Estonia, Gabon, Gambia, Guinea-Bissau, Jordan, Kuwait, Lesotho, Macedonia, Mauritius, Namibia, Slovenia, Swaziland, Trinidad and Tobago.
>2 to 5	29	Albania, Armenia, Bosnia and Herzegovina, Central African Republic, Congo Rep., Costa Rica, Croatia, Eritrea, Georgia, Ireland, Jamaica, Kyrgyz Republic, Latvia, Lebanon, Lithuania, Mauritania, Moldova, Mongolia, New Zealand, Norway, Oman, Panama, Puerto Rico, Sierra Leone, Singapore, Togo, United Arab Emirates, Uruguay, West Bank and Gaza,
>5 to 10	34	Austria, Azerbaijan, Belarus, Benin, Bolivia, Bulgaria, Burundi, Chad, Hong Kong (China), Denmark, Dominican Republic, El Salvador, Finland, Guinea, Haiti, Honduras, Hungary, Israel, Lao PDR, Liberia, Libya, Nicaragua, Papua New Guinea, Paraguay, Portugal, Rwanda, Senegal, Slovak Republic, Somalia, Sweden, Switzerland, Tajikistan, Tunisia, Turkmenistan.
>10 to 50	51	Afghanistan, Algeria, Angola, Argentina, Australia, Belgium, Burkina Faso, Cambodia, Cameroon, Canada, Chile, Côte d'Ivoire, Cuba, Czech Republic, Ecuador, Ghana, Greece, Guatemala, Iraq, Kazakhstan, Kenya, Korea, Dem. Rep., Korea Rep, Madagascar, Malawi, Malaysia, Mali, Morocco, Mozambique, Myanmar, Nepal, Netherlands, Niger, Peru, Poland, Romania, Saudi Arabia, Serbia and Montenegro, South Africa, Spain, Sri Lanka, Sudan, Syrian Arab Republic, Tanzania, Uganda, Ukraine, Uzbekistan, Venezuela, Yemen, Zambia, Zimbabwe.
>50 to 100	14	Colombia, Congo Dem. Rep., Egypt, Ethiopia, France, Germany, Iran, Italy, Mexico, the Philippines, Thailand, Turkey, United Kingdom, Vietnam,
100+	10	Bangladesh, Brazil, China, India, Indonesia, Japan, Nigeria, Pakistan, Russia, US.

TABLE 13.3 The largest 152 countries in population-size bands, year 2000
Source: Compiled by the authors from information in World Bank, *World Development Indicators.*

Canada and the US (1.1 per cent). The table also shows that, *from 1990 to 2000* – that is during the first decade of 'transition' – a number of the ex-Soviet countries – Russia, Ukraine, Belarus, Kazakhstan, Latvia, Estonia, Georgia, Moldova – as well as the Czech Republic, Hungary, Croatia, Romania and Bulgaria, all *declined* in population.

Births and fertility

Crude birth rates, numbers of births per year per 1000 people, are shown for the year 2000 in Table 13.2, and classified into size bands in Table 13.4. There were 13 countries with a figure of below 10 per 1000; 48 with 10 to below 20; 35 with 20 to below 30; 32 with 30 to below 40; 21 with 40 to below 50; and only two countries with more than 50 births per 1000 people. The developed countries invariably belonged to lower bands, almost all below 20 births per 1000 people, while the sub-Saharan African countries featured strongly in the higher bands.

    Crude birth rates must be distinguished from **fertility**, the frequency with which women of child-bearing age bear children. The **total fertility rate** is defined as the 'total expected [live] births to a woman passing through the age group 15–49' (Benjamin, 1968, p. 60). The '*total*' distinguishes it from *age-specific* **fertility rates**, as, for example, that of women aged from 15 to 19. The 'expected' indicates an average based on what is currently

Crude birth rate (per 1000)	Number of countries N = 152	Countries
Below 10	14	Belarus, Bulgaria, Hong Kong China, Czech Republic, Estonia, Georgia, Germany, Italy, Japan, Latvia, Lithuania, Russian Federation, Slovenia, Ukraine.
10 to <20	48	Albania, Armenia, Australia, Austria, Azerbaijan, Belgium, Bosnia and Herzegovina, Canada, Chile, China, Croatia, Cuba, Denmark, Finland, France, Greece, Hungry, Ireland, Kazakhstan, Korea Dem Rep., Korea Rep., Macedonia, Mauritius, Moldova, Netherlands, New Zealand, Norway, Poland, Portugal, Puerto Rico, Romania, Serbia and Montenegro, Singapore, Slovak Republic, Spain, Sri Lanka, Sweden, Switzerland, Tajikistan, Thailand, Trinidad and Tobago, Tunisia, United Arab Emirates, United Kingdom, United States, Uruguay, Vietnam.
20 to <30	35	Algeria, Bangladesh, Brazil, Colombia, Congo Rep., Costa Rica, Dominican Republic, Ecuador, Egypt Arab Rep., El Salvador, India, Indonesia, Iran Islamic Rep., Israel, Jamaica, Jordan, Kuwait, Kyrgyz Republic, Lebanon, Libya, Malaysia, Mexico, Mongolia, Morocco, Myanmar, Oman, Panama, Peru, Philippines, South Africa, Syrian Arab Republic, Turkey, Turkmenistan, Uzbekistan, Venezuela.
30 to <40	32	Argentina, Benin, Bolivia, Botswana, Cambodia, Cameroon, Central African Republic, Côte d'Ivoire, Eritrea, Gabon, Gambia, Ghana, Guatemala, Guinea, Haiti, Honduras, Iraq, Kenya, Lao PDR, Lesotho, Namibia, Nepal, Nicaragua, Pakistan, Papua New Guinea, Paraguay, Saudi Arabia, Senegal, Sudan, Swaziland, Tanzania, Togo, Zimbabwe.
40 to <50	21	Afghanistan, Angola, Argentina, Burkina Faso, Burundi, Chad, Congo Dem Rep., Ethiopia, Guinea-Bissau, Liberia, Madagascar, Malawi, Mali, Mauritania, Mozambique, Nigeria, Rwanda, Sierra Leone, Uganda, West Bank and Gaza, Yemen Rep., Zambia.
50+	2	Niger, Somalia.

TABLE 13.4 Crude birth rates per thousand; countries by size bands, year 2000

Note: Hong Kong had the lowest birth rate with 8 per 1000, and Niger and Somalia had the highest at 51 per 1000.

Source: Compiled by the authors from information in World Bank, *World Development Indicators.*

happening. The total fertility rate is the number of children a woman entering on child-bearing age could 'expect' (on average) to bear if current age-specific fertility and age-gender-specific mortality rates were to hold through her child-bearing years. It is thus not a *prediction* of the probable number of births to a woman starting the reproductive period *now* over the rest of her life, but a way of summarizing the *current* fertility position: how many children on average a woman *would expect to bear if* the current age-specific rates remained in being for the whole of her reproductive life. The crude birth rate at any time depends on (i) the current age-specific fertility rates of the various child-bearing age-groups and (ii) the proportions of the population who are women within each of those childbearing age-groups.

Deaths, mortality and life-expectancy

Country-by-country enumeration of deaths per 1000 people per year, termed **crude death rates**, shows that (as summarized below in Table 13.5) there were only 10 countries with a figure of less than 5 deaths per 1000; 66 countries in the band of 5 to below 10; 43 with 10 to below 15; 21 with 15 to below 20; and only 11 countries in the highest band of

Crude death rate (per 1000)	Number of countries N = 151	Countries
Below 5	10	Costa Rica, Jordan, Kuwait, Malaysia, Oman, Saudi Arabia, Singapore, United Arab Emirates, Venezuela RB, West Bank and Gaza.
5 to <10	66	Albania, Algeria, Argentina, Australia, Azerbaijan, Bangladesh, Bolivia, Bosnia and Herzegovina, Brazil, Canada, Chile, China, Hong Kong China, Colombia, Cuba, Dominican Republic, Ecuador, Egypt Arab Rep., El Salvador, France, Georgia, Guatemala, Honduras, India, Indonesia, Iran Islamic Rep., Iraq, Ireland, Jamaica, Korea Rep, Kyrgyz Republic, Lebanon, Libya, Macedonia FYR, Mauritius, Mexico, Mongolia, Morocco, Netherlands, New Zealand, Nicaragua, Pakistan, Panama, Papua New Guinea, Paraguay, Peru, Philippines, Puerto Rico, Spain, Sri Lanka, Switzerland, Syrian Arab Republic, Tajikistan, Thailand, Trinidad and Tobago, Tunisia, Turkey, Turkmenistan, United Kingdom, United States, Uzbekistan, Vietnam.
10 to <15	43	Austria, Belarus, Belgium, Benin, Bulgaria, Cambodia, Cameroon, Congo Rep., Croatia, Czech Republic, Denmark, Eritrea, Estonia, Finland, Gambia, Germany, Ghana, Greece, Haiti, Hungry, Italy, Kazakhstan, Kenya, Korea Dem Rep., Lao PDR, Latvia, Lithuania, Madagascar, Moldova, Myanmar, Nepal, Norway, Poland, Portugal, Romania, Senegal, Serbia and Montenegro, Slovak Republic, Slovenia, Sudan, Sweden, Uruguay, Yemen Rep.
15 to <20	21	Angola, Burkina Faso, Chad, Côte d'Ivoire, Gabon, Guinea, Lesotho, Liberia, Mauritania, Namibia, Niger, Nigeria, Russian Federation, Somalia, South Africa, Swaziland, Tanzania, Togo, Uganda, Ukraine, Zimbabwe
20 to <24	11	Afghanistan, Botswana, Burundi, Central African Republic, Ethiopia, Guinea-Bissau, Malawi, Mali, Mozambique, Sierra Leone, Zambia

TABLE 13.5 Crude death rates per thousand; countries by size bands, year 2000
Note: Kuwait had the lowest death rate with 2 per 1000, and Malawi had the highest at 24 per 1000.
Source: Compiled by the authors from information in World Bank, *World Development Indicators*.

20 to 24. As in the case of crude birth rates, the sub-Saharan African countries featured prominently in the two highest bands. Judged by crude rates, they led the field in both being born and dying. For dying they were joined in the late twentieth century by Russia and Ukraine, with most of the rest of Eastern Europe, and indeed of continental Europe in general, not far behind.

Just as crude birth rate has to be distinguished from **fertility**, so crude death rate must be distinguished from **mortality**. Crude death rate depends on (i) the pattern of age-sex-specific mortality rates *and* (ii) the age-sex composition of the population. Age-sex-specific mortality – the number of people per 1000 within any age-sex group (such as women aged 55 to 64) that die in any year – is the **mortality rate** of that age-sex group. Of two communities that have the same age-sex-specific mortality rates as each other, the one with the higher concentration of old people (or of very young children) is likely to have a higher crude death rate than the other. So the country with the highest crude death rate is not necessarily the one with the poorest health or the lowest life-expectancy (as defined below). Given any mortality pattern, the death rate will be boosted by having an unduly high proportion of the very young or very old or both.

The **life-expectancy** of a community is a characteristic that summarizes its overall *mortality* at the time for which it is reported, *abstracting from* the age-sex composition of the population. (The higher the life-expectancy, the lower the mortality.) The life-expectancy of Bangladesh, for example, in the year 2005 was a description of *how things were in 2005, not a prediction* – such as might be made by drawing on all the available evidence – of how long anyone living in 2005 or born in 2005 was likely to live. In this way it is analogous with the total fertility rate. By definition it represents the average number of years anyone born in 2005 *would be expected to live if* the age-sex-specific mortality rates that applied in Bangladesh *in 2005* were to continue through the person's lifetime. (No prediction is made or implied as to whether those mortality rates *will* continue or not.)

Natural increase

Crude birth rate minus *crude death rate* – that is, (births in a year) *minus* (deaths in a year) per 1000 people – equals the **rate of natural increase**.

The **rate of natural increase** has to be distinguished from the **rate of population growth**. Population growth equals natural increase *plus* **net inward migration**.

Gender distribution

Table 13.6 gives the distribution of population by **gender**. In the world as a whole the distribution of males and females has remained almost half and half; in 1980 and 2000 the ratios of males to females were 50.2:49.8 and 50.4:49.6, respectively. However, a comparison of the male–female ratio between less developed and more developed countries shows different ratios, 50.9 to 49.1 in the former and 48.3 to 51.7 in the latter. This is perhaps a consequence of unequal treatment in nutrition, medical care and other benefits generally received by the female population in less developed countries. In rich countries it is common for males to have higher mortality than females in every age-group.

Age distribution

In **age distribution**, the youngest group (0–14) forms a significantly higher proportion of the population in the low- and middle-income countries than in the high-income countries (see Table 13.7); in 2000 the respective figures were 36.9 per cent, 27.4 per cent and 18.5 per cent. The high proportion of the population formed by the youngest group in low-income countries has contributed to the high level there of the **dependency ratio**, defined as the proportion of those not working (mostly the young and the old) to the working-age people in these countries. This is the number reached when the last two columns in Table 13.7 are added, 0.7 for the low-income countries and 0.5 for both middle- and high-income countries in 2000.

Analysis of population changes with a view to *prediction* has to be based on assumptions about future fertility and mortality, and these may turn out to be wrong. For example, in the *World Development Report* (*WDR*) 1984, the population of Bangladesh was projected to grow from 92 million in 1982 to 157 million in 2000, while that of Pakistan was expected to grow from 87 million in 1982 to 140 million in 2000 (see *World Development Report* 1984, p. 254, Table 19). In fact, Bangladesh's population in 2000 was only 131.1 million, thanks to the success of family-planning programmes which had helped to bring down the population growth rate to 2.1 per cent (compared to the projected rate of 2.9 per cent) over the period 1980–2000, while Pakistan (which, as shown above, was projected to have a lower population than Bangladesh in 2000) actually had higher numbers then – though slightly lower than the projected 140 million – because the average annual growth rate in population from 1980 to 2000 there remained almost the same as before, 2.6 per cent, only slightly lower than the projected 2.7 per cent.

	1980				2000			
	Male	Female	Total	Male:Female Ratio	Male	Female	Total	Male:Female Ratio
Less Developed	1 678 598	1 618 709	3 297 306	50.9:49.1	2 474 601	2 407 387	4 881 988	50.6:49.4
More Developed	549 557	587 908	1 137 465	48.3:51.7	619 828	642 793	1 262 621	49.1:50.9
Africa Total	237 707	240 397	478 104	49.7:50.3	447 119	450 498	897 617	49.8:50.2
West Africa	86 007	88 020	174 028	49.4:50.7	165 794	168 190	333 984	49.6:50.4
East Africa	96 967	98 485	195 452	49.6:50.4	188 936	190 971	379 907	49.7:50.3
North Africa	54 733	53 891	108 624	50.4:49.6	92 388	91 337	183 725	50.3:49.7
Asia Total	1 317 830	1 257 155	2 574 985	51.2:48.8	1 819 651	1 750 931	3 570 582	50.9:49.1
East and South-East Asia	980 108	752 543	1 532 651	63.9:36.1	996 499	972 431	1 968 930	50.6:49.4
South Asia	487 072	456 218	943 290	51.6:48.4	737 502	696 172	1 433 674	51.4:49.6
Southwest Asia	50 650	48 394	99 044	51.1:48.9	85 650	82 328	167 978	50.9:49.1
Europe and USSR Total	359 671	389 423	749 094	48.1:51.9	401 790	419 113	820 903	48.9:51.1
Latin and North America	301 520	308 393	609 913	49.4:50.6	411 249	415 357	826 606	49.8:50.2
North America	123 567	130 250	253 817	48.7:51.3	143 838	148 217	292 055	49.3:50.7
Latin America	177 953	178 143	356 096	49.9:50.1	267 411	267 140	534 551	50.0:50.0
Oceania Total	11 426	11 249	22 676	50.4:49.6	14 620	14 281	28 901	50.6:49.4
World Total	**2 228 155**	**2 206 617**	**4 434 771**	**50.2:49.8**	**3 094 476**	**3 050 180**	**6 144 656**	**50.4:49.6**

TABLE 13.6 Gender distribution of population, by regions, 1980 and 2000

Source: Basic Population data were obtained from Vu, M.T. (1984); World Bank (2002) and United Nations (2006a) from which the ratios were derived by the authors.

	Population Age Distribution			Dependency ratios*	
	Ages 0–14 (%)	Ages 15–64 (%)	Ages 65+ (%)	Young	Old
Low Income Countries	36.9	58.7	4.40	0.6	0.1
Middle Income Countries	27.4	66	6.60	0.4	0.1
Lower Middle Income	26.9	66.4	6.80	0.4	0.1
Upper Middle Income	29.1	64.6	6.20	0.5	0.1
Low & Middle Income	31.9	62.5	5.60	0.5	0.1
East Asia & Pacific	26.9	66.8	6.20	0.4	0.1
Europe & Central Asia	22	67.1	10.80	0.3	0.2
Latin America & Caribbean	31.5	63	5.40	0.5	0.1
Middle East & North Africa	37.8	58.6	3.60	0.6	0.1
South Asia	35.1	60.3	4.60	0.6	0.1
Sub-Saharan Africa	44.4	52.6	3.00	0.8	0.1
High Income	18.5	66.9	14.70	0.3	0.2
Europe EMU	16.2	67.3	16.40	0.2	0.2
WORLD TOTAL	30.0w	63.1w	6.9w	0.47w	0.11w

TABLE 13.7 Population by age distribution and dependency ratios: by regions, 2000
Notes: * The dependency ratio is defined as the proportion of the total of young and old people (i.e. those who are dependants) to the working-age people. 'w' indicates weighted average.
Source: World Bank, *World Development Indicators*, Washington, 2002, p. 50.

Demographic transition

From the historical analysis of population, demographers have described a general pattern of changes in birth and death rates, as shown in Figure 13.1. The changes have been schematized to reveal four clear periods differing from one another in their patterns of crude birth and crude death rates. These are known as phases of demographic transition.

Stage 1: High birth rates combined with high death rates

This is the initial stage in population dynamics, experienced all over the world until some 400 years ago or later. High birth rates combined with almost-as-high death rates ensured that the net rate of population growth was extremely low.

Stage 2: High birth rate at a time of declining death rate

At this stage, some countries started experiencing declining death rates, while birth rates remained high, so that there was a more rapid rate of population growth than over most of the countries' previous history (probably the fastest ever in most cases). This was typical of today's developing countries, especially during a large part of the twentieth century.

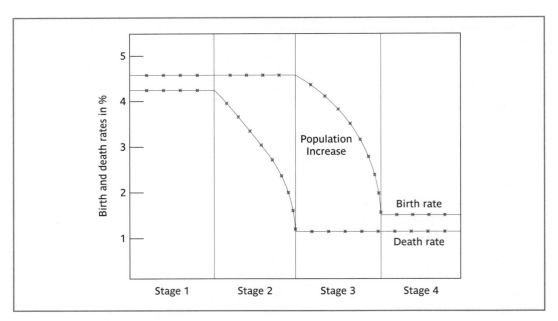

FIGURE 13.1 Stages of demographic transition
Source: Devised by the authors.

Stage 3: Declining birth rates while death rates remained low

At this stage, birth rates started falling while death rates had already fallen and remained at low levels, so that the net population growth rate started to fall. This has been experienced by a number of developing countries, including Bangladesh, China and India, over the last few decades of the twentieth century.

Stage 4: Low birth rates along with low death rates

This is the opposite of Stage 1, with both birth and death rates very low, so that there was once again low net population growth or even declining population. This is the typical case in the developed countries of Western Europe and Japan today, and, as we've seen, also in Eastern Europe including the more westerly of the former Soviet republics. The phenomenon attracted notice first in France. Others, covering virtually the whole continent, are now following the same pattern.

These four stages, reflecting varying birth and death rates and describing changes in population over time, are an integral part of the model of '**demographic transition**'. The model follows from an interpretation by demographer **Warren Thompson** (1929). The model, based on observed transitions or changes in the rates of births and deaths in industrialized countries during the past 200 years or so, implies that there has taken place at some time over that period – or will eventually turn out to have taken place – first a rise and then a fall in the population growth rate. Certainly, some fall in death rates over time has been observed in almost all countries, and – starting some time later – an eventual fall also in birth rates in many or most. (See Tables 13.8, 13.9, 13.10 on p. 392.) From our viewpoint in the early twenty-first century, some approximation to the demographic-transition model seems likely to prove before long to have been a universal phenomenon.

Why does it happen? Where a country is in an early stage of industrialization, income increases, and it is usually supposed that there is some improvement in general living conditions including nutrition and health, though in the case of Britain's trail-blazing industrial revolution there has been controversy among economic historians over how early this improvement started and how long it was before it became significant for the mass of the working population. Sooner or later it seems to have played a part in the fall of mortality. However the causal picture is confused – increasingly as time goes on – by improvements in medical knowledge and techniques, such as the start of inoculation against smallpox at the beginning of the nineteenth century, the later understanding of bacterial infection and of the importance of aseptic methods in surgery and nursing, and – from the mid-twentieth century – the discovery of antibiotics. Mortality in any country may fall, *whether it has rising income or not*, as strongly suggested by the figures in Tables 2.5 and 2.6 in Chapter 2. It seems clear that a fall may be due not only to better nutrition but also to progress in known health technology and in its dissemination and application.

Determinants of fertility

With economic growth beyond a certain point, a country generally experiences an eventual decline in the rate of fertility. The fact that the fall in fertility usually lags behind the fall in mortality explains the initial rise in population growth. However, at any given level of per capita income differing rates of fertility are observed; so there must also be **determinants of fertility other than income**. Again the general progress of technology – this time of **birth control** – continuing at least into the third quarter of the twentieth century, has almost certainly played a part. So a country may experience a fall in fertility because of the increasing range of means of birth control *in existence* as well as because of increasing availability of family-planning services *in that country*. Other factors may be a local **expansion of female education**, or **enhanced employment opportunities for women**, or the **improved healthcare** that reduces death rates in young children. These factors favourable to reducing fertility are likely on the whole to be more prevalent in richer than in poorer countries, but, as with the fall in mortality, there are secular global changes occurring, principally in science and known technology, possibly also in the general climate of thought, that are independent of conditions in any particular country.

Yet what happened during the last 30 years of the twentieth century was astonishing, and probably went well beyond what had been expected only a short while before. There was a big fall in fertility rates, as may be seen from Table 13.10. This surely rates as one of the momentous events of the age. The rate roughly *halved* for low-income countries and for middle-income countries over all, and also for Latin America and the Caribbean; it fell *by nearly half* in the Arab states and in South Asia; and *by two-thirds* in the developing countries of East Asia and the Pacific, where the weight of China, with its one-child policy, was of course very high. This was a period when the seriousness of the prevailing high population growth had become widely recognized with the ready availability of population data. The period also brought better access to family-planning services in many developing countries. During this time, too, female education became increasingly widespread, and there were growing employment opportunities for women.

There is a fairly close negative relationship between female literacy and total fertility rates, as can be seen from Figure 13.2.

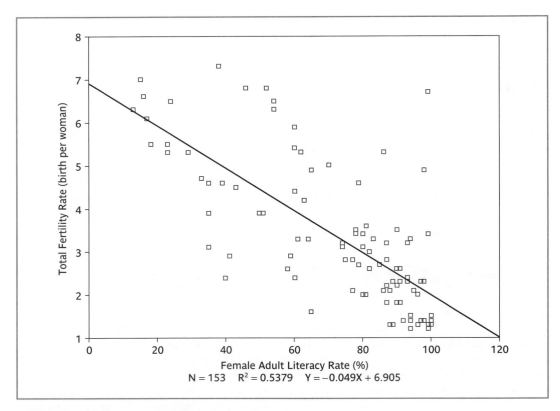

FIGURE 13.2 Rates of fertility and adult female literacy, 2006

The slope is −0.049; the standard error of the slope is 0.0045; the value of the t-statistic is −10.764; and the p-value is 0.000.

Source: Scatter-diagram prepared by the authors from data in World Bank, *World Development Indicators*, 2007, pp. 86–8; and 2008, pp. 102–4.

The diagonal line is the linear regression line of best fit. The relationship is clearly highly significant, as the t-statistic shows.

On the relationship between women's literacy and the fertility rate, Sen also cites a study across Indian districts by Drèze, Guio and Murthi (1995), which again shows 'a very pronounced impact of female literacy on lowering the fertility rate' (1995, p. 33).

On the supposition that lower fertility is beneficial for most developing countries, Figure 13.2 illustrates the basis for one of the *virtuous circles* connected with fertility. Another example is the *positive* relationships between the fertility and population-growth rates on the one hand and infant mortality on the other, illustrated graphically in Sachs (2005, pp. 324–5). Figures 13.3 and 13.4 show similar scatter-diagrams to those of Sachs, with highly significant relationships in both cases. Whichever way the causation works in both these cases (and it is quite plausible that it works in both directions), the possibilities revealed by the relationship are benign. The second regression is done, following Sachs, in addition to the first, to *eliminate the possibility* that, despite any effect of low infant-death rate in reducing fertility, the fact that less babies died might still on balance increase the population-growth rate.

Statistically, the relationships in Figures 13.3 and 13.4 are both highly significant.

It seems very likely from these relationships that increasing the number of women who are educated, and reducing the infant-death rate – both goods of a high order in themselves

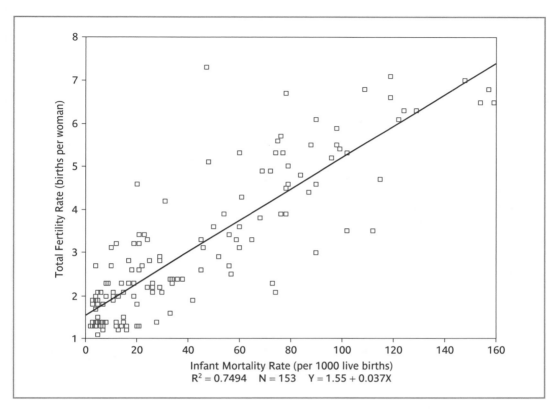

FIGURE 13.3 Total fertility rate (births per woman) and infant mortality rate (per 1000 live births) in 2005
The slope is 0.037; the standard error of the slope is 0.00177; the t-statistic is 20.968; and the p-value is 0.000.
Source: Scatter-diagram prepared by the authors from data in World Bank, *World Development Indicators*, 2008.

– also act to reduce fertility and the average size of families, which of course makes it easier in turn for families or communities to devote resources to educating their daughters and to providing for the health of their babies.

Impact of population change on economic growth

The question whether population growth hinders or promotes economic growth has often been raised by economists and policy-makers. We have supposed in what we have just said about fertility that, for most developing countries, at least as they are at present, greater fertility *hinders* economic growth and human development. For some decades this view has prevailed among policy-makers and scholars in developing countries at large and especially in the big Asian countries, where population control has in notable instances (India, China, Bangladesh, South Korea, Taiwan, for example) been a major government policy. But is that the only possible position?

Optimum population

Discussion of the relationship between population growth and economic development led to the concept of an *optimum population*. *Optimum* in the context is taken to mean consistent

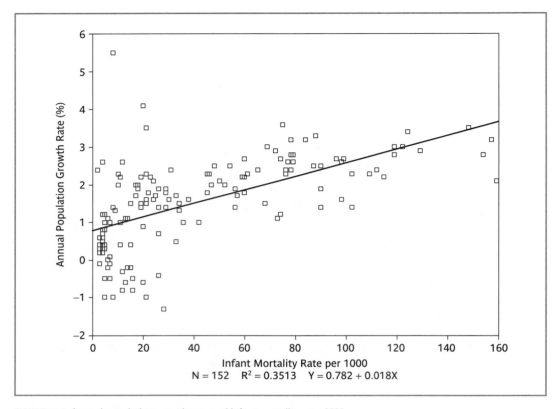

FIGURE 13.4 Annual population growth rate and infant mortality rate, 2006
The slope is 0.018; the standard error of the slope is 0.002; the t-statistic is 8.98; and the p-value is 0.000.
Source: Scatter-diagram prepared by the authors from data in World Bank, *World Development Indicators*, 2008.

with, or leading to, the highest average income. The question is at what level the population of any given state or territory should be to achieve that.

The conventional approach for modelling the determination of the optimum population is illustrated by Figure 13.5.

The line OQ represents the level of total product for various levels of population. The maximum output per person is at the point of tangency (B), i.e., at the point where a ray from the origin touches the total product curve (OQ). At this point, the output per head, i.e., total output (Q) divided by the total population (A), is maximized. Optimum population is shown by the distance OA. An increase or decrease in population from OA will cause the output per head to fall. By definition of terms, at B the marginal product and the average product will be the same.

However, this concept of optimum population can be criticized as being based on a static approach. Changes in other variables, in particular improvements in technology or technical efficiency (which might in principle *result from* increased population, or simply happen exogenously), can cause the total product curve to shift upwards, so that to take any particular level, OA, as the optimum population can be misleading as a guide to policy.[1]

---

[1] What should be the optimum population has been a concern of economists for a long time. See, e.g., Meade (1968) for an in-depth discussion on population growth and standard of living.

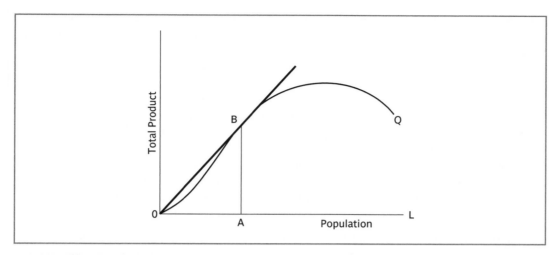

FIGURE 13.5 Maximum output per person

This difficulty or irrelevance is aggravated by the fact that respectable governments can only very slowly influence aggregate population by policy measures. If one of them decides that the optimum population is half the size of the present one, it is hard to see what that government can do about it. By the time any policy it institutes has had time to work itself out, it is quite likely that the parameters of the situation – the position and shape of the OQ curve, for example – will have changed completely.

What then can we learn of a practical character from the optimum-population model? Only that *a priori* we may either be in a position in which extra people would increase output per person or in one in which the reverse is true. There are several possible effects of increasing the workforce. If the endowments of other factors, and also (e.g., as a result of static technology adopted) total factor productivity (TFP), remain constant, then we can expect diminishing marginal returns to labour as more is applied, and consequently diminishing real wages and a diminishing average product of labour. Other effects of increasing population may in principle also, by decreasing net saving propensity, decrease the total capital *stock*, as capital goods are replaced less fast than they depreciate.

On the other hand, it is possible in principle that economies of scale and scope and incentives for the adoption or even invention of improved technology as a result of workforce or population growth may outweigh these adverse factors. *A priori* we cannot tell which set of effects will prevail. But this does not stop us making a judgement. In fact, most low- and low-middle-income countries of any weight, with national authorities of any sophistication, probably do now suppose themselves to be in a situation in which having more people in itself *reduces* average product per person, and consequently, insofar as they can do anything about it, they favour restraint in population growth.

Evidence and presumptions on either side

So the common view of population growth in the latter part of the twentieth century has been a negative one. This pessimistic position was initially championed by **Thomas Malthus** (1766–1834), as we have mentioned in Chapter 4. He was concerned with the diminishing marginal returns from land. In his book, *Essay on the Principle of Population* (1798), he postulated that there was a tendency for the population of a country to grow at a geometric rate, while the food supply would increase at an arithmetic rate. These tendencies would give rise to what has now been termed the **Malthusian population trap**, a supposed level at which the increase in population was bound to come to a halt, with the incomes generally prevailing at that point just adequate to allow survival and enough reproduction to keep the population constant. In development theory, **Harvey Leibenstein** (1957) and **Richard Nelson** (1956) popularized the idea of the Malthusian population trap.

A modern version of that pessimistic viewpoint was advanced, among others, by **Hla Myint** (1964), who argued that developing countries have fallen behind the developed countries *because of* their high population growth. The *World Development Report* 1984, in analysing population changes and demographic issues, argues that the growth rate of population in today's developing countries has become a greater burden than was the case with the comparable level of development of the now-developed countries of Europe, North America and Japan. A number of reasons are listed (World Bank, *WDR* 1984, p. 79):

- 'Population growth is now much more rapid. In industrializing Europe, it seldom exceeded 1.5 per cent a year, compared with the 2 to 4 per cent that many developing countries have averaged since World War II.

- 'Unlike 19th century Europe, large-scale emigration from today's developing countries is not possible.

- 'Compared with Europe, Japan and North America in their periods of fastest population growth, income in developing countries is still low, human and physical capital are less built up, and in some countries political and social institutions are less well established.

- 'Many developing countries whose economies are still largely dependent on agriculture can no longer draw on large tracts of unused land.'

Population growth can affect economic development in various ways. Possible impacts on savings, capital invested, economic efficiency, and the environment have been considered.

The supporters of the pessimistic school of population theory would argue that the high population growth in developing countries has given rise to a high dependency ratio. As a result there are many young mouths to feed, and these children themselves do not produce. Consequently, consumption is high and saving is low when population is fast-growing. The argument, however, fails to consider that in developing countries it is normal for many young children to work. Furthermore, the dependency ratio in countries with *slowly* growing numbers of people will also be boosted by older people who do not produce but do consume. On both these grounds savings rates are not necessarily lower in fast-growing than in slow-growing populations. We are, therefore, required to take into account the impact of *the different components* of the dependency ratio on aggregate savings, which is determined by (i) the relative importance of various age-groups of dependants, and (ii) the savings (or dissavings) propensities of those various groups of dependants. It is possible that, if the *negative* propensity to save of the older people is greater at the margin than that of the inactive young children, a fall in the birth rate and a resulting increase in the proportion of older people will lead to a *fall* in the aggregate savings rate. Regarding the impact on savings of having more children, one also needs to consider that the family may work harder to feed the children, so that there need not be any adverse effect on savings.

However, the subsequent *effect* of a faster-growing population is a *larger* population at any date, so that the ratio of people (potential workers) to a fixed resource such as land is higher than it would otherwise have been. Each person has less land with which to work, and, other things being equal, is likely to produce less. Probably the widespread public concern to slow population growth is not interested *ultimately* in having a *slower-growing* population but in *the effect that follows* from that: namely a *smaller* population. It is *size* of population, rather than or in addition to the *rate of change* of population, whose impact on savings, investment, efficiency and the environment has to be considered.

A priori arguments, and also some empirical evidence, have been adduced to argue that either a faster-growing or a higher population (with rather similar reasoning for the two cases) will tend to depress the rate of net *investment* and hence *productivity*; that it will also (because of its supposed propensity to increase unemployment) depress the general *efficiency* of the society by exerting political pressures for the creation of useless or even obstructive public-sector jobs; and that a larger population has an adverse impact on the *environment*.

Criticisms have been made of these conclusions and of the research findings with which some of them are supported, but they have constituted the standard position of most affected governments, and of international organizations, for several decades.

Among the quantitative studies, an attempt was made by **Ansley Coale and Edgar Hoover** (1958), in a dynamic-modelling simulation, to draw inferences about the effect of population change on material welfare. The study used a macroeconomic model of India's population growth and economic development. The Coale and Hoover study found that a decrease in India's population growth rate would be helpful in raising its per capita income. Such a beneficial effect would take place because of two factors. First, following the reduction in the birth rate, there would be a reduction in the dependency ratio, followed by a fall in consumption and increase in saving at any particular income level. Secondly, the effect of the slower growth of the labour force would be felt some 15 years later as the rate of gross investment required to maintain a fixed sum of capital per labourer for the increasing number of labourers (what is termed 'capital widening') would fall, thus allowing more scope for 'capital deepening', that is it would help to increase capital per labourer. The results thus favoured the case for *reducing* population growth rates in India.

It is clear that the issue of the impact of population growth on income growth is a complex one. Although it has remained a dominant belief that high population growth has been a contributor to underdevelopment or lack of development in developing countries, there have also been voices questioning that viewpoint.

Following Malthus, the pessimistic school of population studies has emphasized the principle of diminishing returns to variable factors (notably labour) when other factors (notably land) are fixed in supply. One criticism of this position is that it fails to recognize that, as resources are depleted, their relative prices will rise and there will be pressures to search for substitutes, thus stimulating technological change. Also, it may be that the benefits of the resulting technological improvements more than compensate for the pressures on resources that have stimulated them. Finally, there are also arguments about the improvements achievable through economies of scale and scope as people are brought increasingly close together.

In fact, a robust challenge to the pessimistic viewpoint was put forward by **Julian Simon** (1981), in what is often referred to as **Simon's challenge**. To quote from his book, *The Ultimate Resource*: 'The ultimate resource is people – skilled, spirited, and hopeful people – who will exert their wills and imagination for the benefit of us all.'

Simon advances both theoretical arguments and empirical evidence to substantiate his hypothesis that, though the initial effects of population growth on living standards are negative, there are positive long-run effects resulting from the stimulus of population growth to technological change, and from the impact of other factors on productivity growth, and that these will outweigh the initial negative impacts. In the case of developing countries, Simon inferred from simulations that *moderate* population growth would be more helpful to the growth of living standards than either a stable population or a very high rate of population growth.

The view of the optimistic school of population study is summarized in the following observation:[2] 'More people implies more ideas, more creative talent, more skills, and thus better technology; in the long run population growth is not a problem but an opportunity' (World Bank, 1984, p. 80).

There are also others, including the Australian economist **Colin Clark** and the Danish agricultural economic historian **Ester Boserup** (see biographical note in Chapter 15), who have doubted the conventional pessimistic view of population. According to Colin Clark (1969, 1970), there is a positive relationship between the rate of growth of population and that of per capita income. A similar observation was made by Ester Boserup (1965) who, from her historical studies of agricultural development, concluded that population growth in fact worked as a motivating factor, thus stimulating agricultural intensification and technological advancement.

A verdict: to multiply or not to multiply?

First, the answer need not be the same across all developing countries, when some are highly crowded and some almost empty. Nearly all the territory of Africa and South America is occupied by countries with less than 20 people per square kilometre, while other countries – India, Bangladesh, Sri Lanka, Vietnam, the Philippines, Burundi, Rwanda – have densities of more than 200. What is right for Burundi is not necessarily right for Botswana.

Yet, in spite of the doubts that may be raised by scholars over the supposed disadvantages of high population growth, there is surely little doubt in the minds of those who have to plan for human development – providing schools and teachers and clinics and health-workers – and public and merit goods generally, that the task is very much easier, and so more effectively performed, if the population is nearly static rather than growing fast. This has come as a revelation to some of those acceding to power for the first time in newly independent countries. Faced with the numbers, they may find that an extra 10 per cent added to the school-age population makes the difference between the possible and the impossible in providing complete primary-school coverage.

Governments in most of East, South and South-East Asia have encouraged population restraint – and, from what we have seen, with some success – and been glad when fertility rates fall. Have they all got it wrong? When marginal labour product for the economy as a whole is extremely low (for example, in a 'Lewis' phase) and consequently prevailing real-income levels for large sections of the population are very low; when cities are already huge, with woeful services for the many; when people are already living uncomfortably close to each other: *in these conditions* increasing the supply of raw labour and accompanying mouths to be fed and bodies to be accommodated seems on the face of it quite the wrong route to a happier and healthier population. 'Unlimited supplies' of (unskilled) labour implies that most people will be extremely poor. We are right to point out that these conditions may not obtain everywhere: maybe not in Zambia, maybe not in Papua New Guinea, maybe not in Kazakhstan, maybe not in Patagonia or Lapland. However, even in

---

[2] In a World Bank publication, but representing a particular view probably not shared by the authors of the publication or the Bank.

those situations, where there may be a rising, rather than horizontal, supply curve of unskilled labour to the modern sector, extra people impose a considerable extra public cost of maintaining or generating suitable health and education facilities, water supplies, sewerage, policing, for even minimally acceptable human development and security.

Some of the arguments for *increasing* population densities and *increasing* the size of cities might have made sense for most of the world in say 5000 BC/BCE when any towns were tiny and widely spaced, or for Western Europe in AD/CE 500, but a world that has its Mumbai, São Paolo and Teheran . . . has surely all it needs in economies of agglomeration that can be realized by sheer numbers of people crowded in together. About Dhaka or Shanghai or Cairo today we could adapt what Dr Johnson said about *Paradise Lost*: 'No one ever wished it longer than it is.' No one could possibly wish them larger than they are. (Would Mumbai be more creative – and a better place to live – if only it could squeeze a few more millions of people into its slums?) We (most of us) believe now that, in the absence of highly expensive adjustments to protect the millions most exposed, the world risks, through climate change, starving or flooding out large segments of its population or depriving them of water where they need it. Since more people mean more greenhouse-gas emissions, more people – whether in the US or Vietnam or China or Mexico, or almost anywhere, even Botswana – can only aggravate the difficulties *for the world* of averting these dangers or palliating their effects.

Reinforcing the observed *negative* correlation or association between population growth and average-income growth (but in fact offering a way of escape from the pessimistic outlook that this has sometimes engendered) is the fact that *rising* per capita income in low-income countries often seems to be associated with *falling* growth rates of population. As a correlation between average-income growth and population growth, this has the same (negative) sign as the relationship described by Malthus, but the direction of causation and the mechanism by which we would explain it are different and the message it gives is hopeful. There is potentially a two-way causal relationship between per capita income and population changes, making possible both vicious and virtuous circles. If the countries trapped in low income and relatively high population growth can break through to higher per capita income and the changes that have frequently gone with it, such as lower child-mortality and more education and job opportunities for women, fertility is likely to decline, so that a virtuous circle ensues.

In concluding discussion of the impacts of population growth, we are inclined to go along with the following statement from the *World Development Report* 1984 (p. 80), which in effect changes the question:

> the costs of rapid population growth differ greatly from country to country. Those differences are not confined to differences in natural resources. In countries heavily reliant on agriculture, a scarcity of natural resources does matter. But the underlying problem is low income and low levels of education, which are sources of rapid population growth and simultaneously make the required adjustments to it more difficult. Much of the world's population lives without the benefit of clear signals to encourage smaller families; yet these are the families and the nations in the worst position to make the adaptive responses that rapid population growth requires. That is why rapid population growth is, above all, a development problem.
> *(World Bank, WDR 1984, p. 80)*

In other words, the most useful question is not whether we want bigger or smaller populations – it is no use just hoping for one or the other (though the clear implication is that we want *lower* fertility) – but what we should do about it. The answer given here seems to be: by some means, break out of the vicious circle of low income and low education. (On the evidence mentioned below, we could add medical and gender-equality requirements as well.) Try by all means to crack one – preferably all – of these constraints decisively. Then we could come into the realm of positive feedback: virtuous circles.

BOX 13.2 CHINA: ONE-CHILD POLICY

With the aim of alleviating the social and environmental problems of the country, the Government of China introduced the One-Child Policy in 1979. This policy can, however, be considered as a continuation of earlier policies. In the 1970s the following slogan was heavily promoted: 'One is good, two is okay and three is too many'. In fact, the country recorded the steepest drop in fertility during the 1970s, i.e., before the adoption of the one-child policy.

The main justification for the one-child policy is economic, as such a policy will reduce demand on natural resources and will help in reducing unemployment. The Communist Party of China, in adopting the policy, took Mao Zedong's ideology in this regard that was based on the Marxist theory of population which had its roots in the Malthusian theory of population.

Though the one-child policy of China, as introduced in 1979, has been somewhat rigidly implemented in urban areas, it is not so rigid in rural areas where a family is allowed to have two children if the first child is disabled or female. Also there are variations depending on the locations and racial groups. While Henan province which has about 100 million people follows the policy strictly, some relaxation is allowed in Beijing. Similarly, in Zhejiang province, a couple living in cities is allowed to have a second child under some special circumstances. Some relaxations were also announced in Sichuan province for parents who lost their children in the severe earthquake which took place on 12 May 2008. Some exceptions are also allowed for [non-Han] ethnic groups who are generally allowed to have more children – two if they live in urban areas and three or four in rural areas. Moreover, by paying a fine or 'social maintenance fee', some couples are allowed to have more children. The returning Chinese from abroad are also permitted to have a second child.

The implementing agency of the policy is the State Family Planning Bureau of the Government of China, which sets overall targets and provides specific directions. The strategy for implementing the once-child policy, in particular the fines to be imposed on those who violate the policy and the rewards to be awarded to those who adopt the One-Child Pledge, is devised by the family planning committees formed at the country and the provincial levels. The minimum marriage age (23 for women and 25 for men) helps to promote late marriage, while couples are also encouraged to plan their families by various slogans heavily publicized, e.g., 'With two children you can afford a 14"-TV, with one child you can afford a 21"-TV'.

There are rewards for those who adopt the One-Child Pledge. In urban areas, the couples with one child are provided with a stipend of around 5 per cent of their wage bill until the child is 14 years old. They also receive preferential treatment in the allocation of housing, and priority in education and healthcare. They will also receive a supplementary pension in their old age. In rural areas, the couples with one child will be allocated a larger farming plot. On the other hand, there are fines and penalties for those who violate the

▶

▶ one-child policy. Not only are there additional fines for violating the policy, but also the workers might lose their bonuses.

In early 2006, Zhang Weiqing, Minister of the State Commission of Population and Family Planning, pledged full support for the continuation of the one-child policy, confirming that it is consistent with China's plan for population growth.

It is true that there are criticisms from within and outside China over the continuation of the policy, but a survey conducted by the Pew Research Centre as late as in August 2008 found strong support for the policy, with over 75 per cent of the people of China supporting it.

Compiled from passages on official websites that can be presumed to express official views of historical events and current practice.

Sources: http://www.bmj.com/cgi/content/full/314/7095/1685
http://content.nejm.org/cgi/content/full/353/11/1171
http://www.bmj.com/cgi/content/full/314/7095/1685

Population policy

Though France between the Wars had a policy designed to *increase* fertility rates, in response to concern – not unique at the time – that the population might be gradually disappearing, population policy in developing countries from the 1960s has implied an attempt to *restrict* population growth.

There are several possible ways of doing this.

1 *Compulsion:* practised, at the time of writing, by China with its 'one-child' policy (see Box 13.2). There was a brief period overlapping with the 'emergency' of extra-parliamentary rule in the 1970s when India also had some *de facto* compulsion. In its most blatant form this was fairly quickly ended because of its unpopularity, but strong pressures continued in other forms. Certain exceptions are allowed under China's policy, but, besides financial penalties for having too many children, women may be forced to have abortions, and both men and women may be compulsorily sterilized. How rigorously and coercively the policy is applied seems to depend, like so much in China, on the arbitrary decisions of local officials.

2 *Financial incentives:* these have been at times a part of the Indian practice. In the Indian 'State of Emergency' period in the 1970s, there were extremely strong incentives both positive and negative. Sterilization 'was made a condition for receiving land allocations and water for irrigation, as well as electricity, rickshaw licences, and medical care . . . Indian officials recruited many men and women for sterilization programs by paying them nearly three times the annual wage of the average Indian at the time' (Epstein, 2008, p. 58).

3 *Family planning:* as it is usually understood; providing advice and facilities, including contraceptive devices for both women and men, oral contraceptives for women and vasectomy operations for men. The ethos of family planning is to enable women (and men) to make their own choices, in a more effective and informed way, about family size. It is contrasted by some writers with 'population policy', which has often worked

with contraceptive or sterilization targets. Though they may not involve compulsion, these have led to abuses, when the priority given to fulfilling targets has gone with a lack of due attention to risks and to the general health and welfare of the clients.

4 *Propaganda for smaller families:* with or without free public discussion. As shown in Box 13.2, there has been heavy propaganda in China aimed at encouraging couples to have small families in accord with the one-child policy introduced in 1979. There is similar propaganda and publicity in Bangladesh and India and elsewhere.

5 *Factors affecting choice of size of family:* and making *use of* what is known about them, such as survival rates of infants and young children, women's education, and their participation in the paid workforce. Increasing girls' education (which also tends to enhance female workforce participation) and better medical care for the very young are good in themselves as well as reducing target family sizes.

An apparent success of the third, fourth, and especially the fifth, method is Kerala state in India. With a quite exceptionally *good* health, education and medical-services record for a low-income country, and specifically with very low infant and young-child mortality, its total fertility rate was recently around 2.0 per woman, quite exceptionally *low*. Sen (1995, pp. 30–2) points out that in Kerala, where there was free public discussion of family size and no attempt at coercion, population policy appears to have been at least as successful as in China, where the opposite was true: authoritarian regulation (with penalties) to enforce the one-child family, and no free discussion.

In 1979 when the one-child policy was introduced in China, its fertility rate was 2.8, compared with 3.0 in Kerala. By 1991, China's fertility rate had fallen, with all its coercive measures, from 2.8 to 2.0. In the same period Kerala's rate fell from 3.0 to 1.8, without any compulsion whatever. The politicization of women's rights and the reformulation of needs drew on high – and rapidly expanding – education (particularly women's education) and on open public discussion of the rights and wrongs of family planning in the contemporary world.

(ibid.)

Official concern to reduce population growth began to be significant around 1950. Not all governments came to take an interest at once. The original governments of newly independent states might come into office with the idea that numbers meant strength and that ex-colonialists were backing population control in order to keep the ex-colonies down. A period in office tended to dispel these views.

BOX 13.3 FAMILY PLANNING *VERSUS* POPULATION CONTROL

'Today, family planning services are available throughout the US and even in remote parts of many developing countries. This is largely the result of an extensive, US-led effort during the 1960s, 1970s, and 1980s. Researchers invented cheap, easy-to-use contraceptives, and a global network of governmental and nongovernmental agencies, research centers, and think tanks developed the means to deliver them through specialized clinics, mobile vans, and door-to-door community distribution programs.

'The family planning movement is one of the great success stories of public health. Birth control enables women to be more economically and socially independent, which may be crucial for sustainable development in general. It also enables them to lengthen the intervals between pregnancies, which improves child health and reduces the risk of fatal birth complications and abortion. However, . . . at one time, these benefits were seen by many US family planning officials as secondary to the goal of reducing the absolute numbers of people in developing countries. The urgency of what came to be known as the "population control movement" contributed to a climate of coercion and led to a number of human rights abuses, especially in Asian countries.'

Source: Helen Epstein, 'The strange history of birth control', *New York Review of Books* LV, 13, 14/8/2008, p. 57.

Helen Epstein, in a review article (2008), traces the trajectory of population policy from the 1940s, when the demographers were generally relaxed about the course of population change, expecting rising incomes and other social changes to reduce fertility. Then, through the next four decades, there was a panic, with rising world population seen as 'threatening economic chaos, ecological disaster, and wars over food. Suddenly population control was the leading edge of development, not the other way around, and the fate of the planet seemed to hinge upon the rapid expansion of family planning programs, especially in Asia' (p. 57). The US used its aid policy actively to promote birth control. And some Asian countries went overboard in the cause. 'By the early 1970s, Bangladesh was spending one third of its entire health budget on family planning and India was spending 60 per cent' (pp. 57–8). In spite of the fact that huge numbers of people undoubtedly benefited from having family-planning advice and facilities available, there were also abuses following from coercion (or inducements that went very close to it) and the pressure imposed by 'targets' to ignore people's general welfare and rights.

A retreat from this phase was signalled by the UN International Conference on Population and Development held in Cairo in 1994, which

committed itself to ending all population programs that were 'target-based', i.e., with specific numerical goals. From then on, programs were to support the right of all women to make their own family planning decisions, and services were to be provided that supported women's health and human rights in general. . . . During the previous two decades, birthrates had declined across the developing world. . . . This occurred just about as rapidly in places with limited population programs as in those with very aggressive programs.

(ibid., p. 59)

However, by that time the political climate in the US had changed, and the 'very first act' of the 1994 Congress was 'to slash USAID's family planning budget by 35 percent' (ibid.) As a result of this and other limitations imposed by that Congress, 'millions of poor women throughout the world still lack access to safe, voluntary family planning services' (p. 59).

If population-restriction policies had been effective, we could expect population growth in the final quarter of the century to be slower than in the third quarter.

It will be clear from Tables 13.8 and 13.9 that world population did grow more slowly in the final quarter-century than in the one before. This was also true of all the regional groups of developing countries given in the tables except Africa and Western Asia. However, the falls are not striking for any of the regions bar Latin America or for any of the individual Asian countries represented there except for China, South Korea and Taiwan. China had its more-or-less compulsory one-child policy. Both South Korea and Taiwan relied on voluntary responses through family planning, but both took the matter seriously from an early stage.

Period	29 West European States	4 Western Off-shoots	44 L. America & Caribbean States	16 E., S. & S.E. Asian States	57 African states	E. European & ex-USSR	15 W. Asian States	World
1950–75	0.68	1.51	2.71	2.09	2.35	1.27	2.82	1.92
1975–98	0.32	1.02	1.98	1.70	2.74	0.50	2.87	1.64

TABLE 13.8 Rates of population growth by region, % p.a., 1950–75, 1975–98
Source: Estimated from A. Maddison, *The World Economy*, OECD, 2002–06, Appendix C

Period	China	India	S. Korea	Taiwan	Bangladesh	Pakistan	Indonesia
1950–75	2.09	2.12	2.13	2.87	2.07	2.59	2.03
1975–98	1.33	2.08	1.20	1.35	2.18	2.61	1.97

TABLE 13.9 Rates of population growth, selected Asian countries, % p.a., 1950–75, 1975–98
Source: Estimated from A. Maddison, *The World Economy*, OECD, 2002–06, Appendix C

	1970–75	2000–05
Developing Countries	5.5	2.9
Least Developed Countries	6.6	5
Arab States	6.7	3.7
East Asia and the Pacific	5.7	1.9
Latin America and the Caribbean	5.1	2.6
South Asia	5.6	3.2
Sub-Saharan Africa	6.8	5.5
Central and Eastern Europe	2.5	1.5
OECD	2.6	1.8
High Income OECD	2.2	1.6
High Income	2.3	1.7
Middle Income	4.6	2.1
Low Income	6	3
WORLD TOTAL	4.5	2.7

TABLE 13.10 Fertility rates in various parts of the world, 1970–75 and 2000–05
Source: UNDP, *Human Development Report 2006*, p. 300.

Given the apparent seriousness of the Indian and Bangladeshi commitments, it is surprising how little the growth rate fell there between the periods; in fact that of Bangladesh rose. But the fertility changes over the last two decades of the century, as shown in Table 13.10, give a much more encouraging picture, as we have seen. They portend larger future falls in the population growth rate as these fertility changes work their way through the age ranges.

The projected figure given in Table 13.1 implies an annual world population growth rate of 0.8 per cent from 2000 to 2050, which compares with 1.9 per cent for the years from 1950 to 1975.

Labour-force participation and human-capital development

Table 13.11 gives an idea of the labour force and its male-female distribution, by regions of the world, for 1980 and 2000. Low- and middle-income countries had an 82 per cent share of the total labour force in the world in 1980. Their share increased to 85 per cent in 2000. However, given that these low- and middle-income countries together had little more than a one-fifth share of the world GNI at exchange-rate valuation (not shown in the table), it is apparent that the average productivity of labour was significantly lower in these countries, *low-income* countries performing particularly badly and having only 3 per cent of the total GNI of the world on this system of valuation, in spite of having a 45 per cent share of the world labour force.

Although there are not significant differences in rates of female participation in the labour force between the developed and developing groups of countries taken as wholes, there are quite large regional differences within the developing countries. The Middle East and North Africa showed the lowest rate among the major world regions in 1980 at 23.8 per cent, which increased to 27.7 per cent in 2000. South Asia also had a relatively low female participation rate, and the figure remained almost the same from 1980 to 2000, at around

	1980 Total (Mil)	1980 % Distribution Male	Female	2000 Total (Mil)	2000 % Distribution Male	Female
Low Income Countries	708.7	62.2	37.8	1115.10	62.2	37.8
Middle Income Countries	969.3	59.8	40.2	1388.80	57.9	42.1
Lower Middle Income	785.4	58.1	41.9	1100.40	56.6	43.4
Upper Middle Income	183.9	67	33	288.40	63.3	36.7
Low & Middle Income	1678.0	60.8	39.2	2503.90	59.8	40.2
East Asia and the Pacific	719.3	57.5	42.5	1051.70	55.6	44.4
Europe and Central Asia	214.1	53.3	46.7	238.10	53.7	46.3
Latin America and the Caribbean	129.8	72.2	27.8	222.10	65.2	34.8
Middle East & North Africa	54.1	76.2	23.8	99.00	72.3	27.7
South Asia	388.7	66.2	33.8	602.60	66.6	33.4
Sub-Saharan Africa	172	58	42	290.50	58	42
High Income	358.1	61.6	38.4	439.40	56.8	43.2
Europe EMU	123.4	63.6	36.4	141.00	58.7	41.3
WORLD TOTAL	**2036.1s**	**60.9n**	**39.1w**	**2943.2s**	**59.4w**	**40.6w**

TABLE 13.11 Total labour force and its distribution by gender, by regions, 1980 and 2000
Note: Aggregates with s are sums of available data, while those with w are weighted averages.
Source: World Bank, *World Development Indicators 2002*, pp. 54 and 62.

33 per cent. Europe and Central Asia had the highest rate among the low- and middle-income countries, around 46–47 per cent in both 1980 and 2000. It was followed by East Asia and the Pacific, with 42.5 per cent and 44.4 per cent in 1980 and 2000 respectively.

Human-capital development

While the size of the population, or for that matter of the labour force, refers to quantity, human-capital development is a matter of quality.

The Nobel Laureate **Theodore Schultz** is emphatic on the importance of human-capital development which he calls *human-capital formation*. The decisive factors in improving the welfare of the people, as Schultz puts it, are 'the improvement in population quality and advances in knowledge' (1981, p. 4). Thus, human-capital development is often viewed as a key factor for improved productivity. The main components for this purpose are gains achieved through knowledge and skills and improvements in nutrition and health. Both these aspects are discussed further below.

Knowledge and skills

The importance of human-capital development will become apparent when (in Chapter 18) we discuss technological-capability-building in developing countries, which is viewed as a learning process. There is now an almost unanimous view that a low level of knowledge and skills is largely responsible for low productivity of labour in developing countries. The developing countries seriously lag behind developed countries in almost all areas that can be considered under the heading of development of knowledge and skills. For example, as may be seen from Table 13.12, in many developing countries a significant portion of the adult population is still illiterate. Also, at the primary-school age, in spite of recent developments, 100 per cent enrolment has not yet been achieved in most developing countries, and, worse, a significant number of students drop out after initial enrolment in primary schools (not shown in the table, but see for some examples Table 10.2 in Chapter 10).

As a percentage of GDP, developing-country governments are generally found to spend significantly less on education than those of developed countries. Indeed, it is clear that most developed countries have taken educational development as a priority sector. This is reflected in compulsory primary schooling. The compulsion is rigorously enforced in most developed countries, and, in order to raise the skill of the people in general, higher education is in many cases not only highly subsidized but also actively pushed. Although, by contrast with primary and secondary, higher education is not regarded as a merit good – a good that should be provided individually for everyone – its subsidization and promotion suggests that participation of a large part of the workforce in higher education is considered to have a public-good element.

Nutrition and health

As with knowledge and skills, the state of nutrition and health in developing countries is far behind that in developed countries, as may be seen from Table 13.13. For example, food-poverty is still common in the least-developed counties, as is reflected in the high level of malnutrition suffered by their people. Another indicator of poor nutrition and health in developing countries is the very high levels of infant and under-five mortality found in these countries, compared to those in developed countries.

	Adult Literacy Rate (1998)	Primary Sch. Enrolment (% of relevant age, 1997)	Public Expenditure on Education (% of GNP, 1995–97)
Developing Countries			
Bangladesh	40	75	2.2
Brazil	85	97	5.1
China	83	97	2.3
Ethiopia	36	35	4.0
Ghana	69	43	4.2
India	56	77	3.2
Indonesia	86	99	1.4
Kenya	81	65	6.5
Nigeria	61	...	0.7
Pakistan	44	...	2.7
Tanzania	74	47	...
Least Developed Countries	50	60	...
Developed Countries			
Canada	...	100	6.9
France	...	100	6.0
Germany	...	100	9.6
Japan	...	100	3.6
United Kingdom	...	100	5.3
United States	...	100	5.4
High Income Countries	...	100	5.0

TABLE 13.12 Indicators of knowledge and skills in selected developing and developed countries, late 1990s
Note: Adult literacy refers to percentage of people 15 years old and above.
Source: UNDP, *Human Development Report* 2000, pp. 194–7.

As is the case with education, developing countries are also generally found to spend a much lower percentage of GDP on health than developed countries. This, combined with very much lower per capita GDP, explains the very much lower figures of per capita health expenditure that prevail in these countries (not shown in the table).

It is, therefore, not hard to believe that, in labour quality, developing countries are at a disadvantage because of their poor state of education and skills and also low levels of health and nutrition. This provides a *prima facie* case for investment in these sectors over and above what is provided by private individuals and firms. There are of course opportunity costs of investment in human capital, and the case for public outlays for this purpose needs to be balanced against other unmet needs for public expenditure. But there seems to be strong ground for supposing that there are positive externalities that would justify a public contribution.

	Prevalence of Malnutrition Rate (under 5, per '000, 1990)	Under-5 Mortality Rate (per '000 2002)	Doctors per hundred '000 Population (1988–92)	Total Health Expenditure as % of GDP (1990)
Developing Countries				
Bangladesh	60	73	15	3.2
Brazil	13	16	146	4.2
China	. . .	38	137	3.5
Ethiopia	. . .	171	3	3.8
Ghana	55	97	40	3.5
India	. . .	61	41	6.0
Indonesia	14	43	14	2.0
Kenya	. . .	84	14	4.3
Nigeria	98	201	15	2.7
Pakistan	61	101	. . .	. . .
Tanzania	20	165	3	4.7
Low Income Countries	. . .	126	. . .	. . .
Developed Countries				
Canada	. . .	7	222	9.1
France	. . .	5	289	8.9
Germany	. . .	5	273	8.0
Japan	. . .	5	164	6.5
United Kingdom	. . .	7	140	6.1
United States	. . .	8	238	12.7
High Income Countries	. . .	7	. . .	. . .

TABLE 13.13 Indicators of nutrition and health in selected developing and developed countries
Source: World Bank, *World Development Report 1993* (pp. 292–3 for malnutrition) WDR 2005 (pp. 256–7, for under-5 Mortality), and for the rest *World Development Report 1993* (pp. 208–11).

Summary conclusions

- World population continued to grow rapidly through the second half of the twentieth century, increasing to 2.4 times its previous size, an average rate of growth of 1.8 per cent a year, from 2.5 billion to 6.1 billion.

- The proportion of that population in the low- and middle-income countries increased in that period from 68 per cent to 80 per cent.

- World population has been projected to increase over the first half of the twenty-first century to 9.2 billion. This implies a much smaller rate of growth, averaging 0.8 per cent, than in the previous 50 years.

- Countries with negative population growth rates, over the 1990s and since, are mostly those of Eastern Europe and the former Soviet Union. Otherwise those with very low rates of growth are typically high-income countries, especially Japan and those of Western Europe. Sub-Saharan African countries, commonly in the low-income category, are prominent among those with highest birth rates and also those with highest death rates, and typically have high rates of natural increase.

- The *demographic transition* is a stylized model, based on historical observations, of the sequence a country is expected to pass through as it moves from a pre-modern demographic pattern through stages that accompany economic growth and transformation. From a typical traditional state of high birth and death rates and near-zero natural increase of population, it enters on a period of much faster population growth when mortality is falling while fertility remains high, and then goes through a phase during which fertility too falls, until finally birth and death rates are once again roughly equal but now low, and the natural increase of population once more is close to zero.

- Reasons responsible for the fall in mortality, followed later by a fall in fertility, that between them generate the demographic transition seem to reflect some combination in each case of *rises in income* in the country concerned; *other social changes and acts of government policy*; and global *progress in science and known technology* bearing on medicine and birth control.

- It has continued to be a matter of controversy in academic circles whether growth in income per head is favoured most by higher or lower populations and by higher or lower rates of population growth, and some arguments may be put for saying that the answer depends on the particular circumstances of the country concerned. Nevertheless, the prevailing view among those at all close to policy-making in developing countries has for some time been – and not only because of its immediate bearing on the growth of income per head – that a smaller, or at least a slower-growing, population is better.

- Concerns about population growth centred on individual countries have been augmented by concern over its *effect on the world environment*, including its bearing on climate change and increasing pressure on resources such as water, soil and forests.

- *Population policy* thus came to be concerned with restricting population growth. It might be implemented through compulsion, as in China; or by financial incentives; or by provision of family-planning services; or by propaganda; or by making use of observed influences of other social changes on fertility. Examples in this last category – and sources of potential virtuous circles – are the facts that fertility is negatively related across countries to the prevalence of female education and female engagement in the workforce, and positively related to infant and young-child death rates. One possible conclusion is that, once we get education, gender relations and health broadly right, the necessary falls in fertility will happen. The prevailing view now over population and family-planning policy (though with official China a major exception) is that family-planning programmes should be based on user choice rather than on pressure to fulfil official targets.

- In the 1950s reducing population growth came to be a fairly general objective among policy-makers and economists, especially with regard to developing countries and particularly in South, East and South-East Asia. *Population growth* was somewhat lower in the fourth quarter of the century than in the third across developing countries taken together, but to a striking extent only in Latin America and in a few East Asian countries. However over 30 years at the end of the century there was *a remarkable fall in fertility rates*: by roughly a half in developing countries as a whole and in Latin America and Caribbean; by nearly a half in the Arab States and South Asia; and by fully two-thirds in East Asia and the Pacific, where fertility rates were brought down close to the levels of the high-income OECD countries. This fall in fertility will increasingly come to be reflected in markedly lower rates of growth of population.

- Growth through modern secondary and tertiary industry depends crucially on the availability of adequate human capital in the form of scientific, technical and business training and experience. This represents a public good, the provision of which makes justified calls on public investment, with the complication that some vital elements of the training are purveyed informally.

- Lewis's unlimited-labour model (Appendix 13.1) led in the 1950s and 1960s to hopes that the surplus labour might be mobilized to generate a rapid and progressive expansion of industrial investment. The failure of these hopes – until the four East Asian Tigers came on the scene – seems to have been due mainly to misguided attempts to effect the desired result without attending to the lessons of experience on the conditions in which it was likely to occur.

The rate of world-population growth has fallen and is falling. Family-planning advice and facilities, and even some coercive policies, probably contributed. But it seems that there is also an important virtuous-circle at work. Human fertility goes down as the extent of women's education and workforce-participation rises and as infant and young-child mortality falls. Smaller families in turn make for more education and opportunities for girls, and healthier children.

Questions for discussion

13.1 Explain the concept of 'demographic transition', showing the various stages of population change.

13.2 In the context of 'disguised unemployment', explain how the Lewis model (refer also to Chapter 5) envisages the process of capital formation in certain developing countries.

13.3 Explain under what conditions rapid population growth might in principle help or hinder per capita economic growth in developing countries.

13.4 How by definition are the following variables for a community related: life-expectancy, age-sex-specific mortality, net inward migration rate, crude death rate, total fertility rate, age-specific fertility, rate of natural increase, crude birth rate, population growth rate?

13.5 With regard to labour supply, list some main components or indicators of realized human-capital development in developing countries and explain how their level compares with that in developed countries.

Additional reading

Clark, Colin (1969) 'The "population explosion" myth', *Bulletin of the Institute of Development Studies*, Sussex, May.

Enke, S. (1971) 'Economic consequences of rapid population growth', *Economic Journal*, **81** (324).

Epstein, Helen (2008) 'The strange history of birth control', *New York Review of Books*, LV, 13, 14/8/2008, pp. 57–9.

Ingham, Barbara (1995) *Economics and Development*, McGraw-Hill, London.

Keynes, J.M. (1933/1972) 'Robert Malthus: the first of the Cambridge economists', in *Essays in Biography*, Macmillan, London.

Schultz, T.W. (1988) 'Education investment and returns', in H. Chenery and T.N. Srinivasan (eds), *Handbook in Development Economics*, Vol. 1, North-Holland, Amsterdam.

World Bank (1984) *World Development Report* 1984, Oxford University Press for the World Bank, New York.

Appendix 13.1 Using surplus labour for economic growth

Developing economies commonly suffer from both open unemployment and underemployment, the latter also being known as **disguised unemployment**. The distinguishing feature of disguised unemployment by definition is that the same output could effectively be produced by a smaller number of people working normal hours. In the process, a large part of the labour force, estimated as over 50 per cent in many developing countries, remains unused. One is thus faced with a double deficiency: a high proportion of the total labour force remaining unemployed and those in employment suffering from low productivity.

In the poorer developing countries an informal labour market typically exists in a large part of the economy, extending to almost every sector, and dominant in agriculture and the more traditional services including trading. Characteristic of labour in the informal sector are its irregular hours and seasonal fluctuations of work. In the case of farming, for example, the work is shared out among the family members, some of them often working for very few hours a day in much of the year, although during the peak season the daily hours of work may be significantly higher than the year-round average.

The situation gives rise to a form of elastic labour supply. The supply of labour can be adjusted in response to the demand, thus providing an opportunity to tap the otherwise untapped reservoir of labour. The untapped reservoir of labour may include young and married women and late school leavers who traditionally would not be seeking employment, but given adequate demand will be willing to enter the labour market, as has been found in the hugely expanding female employment in garment manufacturing in Bangladesh. Part of the expanding industrial employment comes probably from labourers who were previously working elsewhere, for example, as housemaids and cooks, but there is also a significant part who, responding to the new demand, have decided to enter the formal labour market (the non-household sector) for the first time.

It is a perennially attractive idea that the surplus labour could be employed to make the extra capital investment, and staff the additional industries that would be required for rapid economic growth. Arthur Lewis's 'unlimited supply of labour' model, expounded in Chapter 5, seemed to imply that in the countries – covering a large part of the population of the Third World – in which the conditions he described obtained there was a large potential workforce that could be engaged in industrial investment or production without reducing output in other sectors. They could also be employed at wages that would not rise with rising labour demand until the surplus supply of labour had been exhausted, and the industries that employed them would therefore generate substantial reinvestible profits, adding to both savings and investment. In addition, because of the low wages, the techniques adopted in the resulting investments would tend to have low capital-labour ratios, with good potential for the reduction of unemployment.

There is nothing wrong with this reasoning. There are, however, three main suggested reasons to explain why any hopes that rapid growth would easily result from the 'unlimited-labour' syndrome must have appeared – for much of the period since Lewis first propounded his model – to have been exaggerated: (1) that the facts may not have conformed closely enough to Lewis's model or what it was taken to imply; (2) that attempts mistakenly made *to force on* the desired result have been counterproductive, more or less wasting resources and depressing certain industries; or (3) that the conditions represented by the model did not give any reason to believe that the investment contemplated would be automatically forthcoming and that, on the contrary, that investment would have required certain conditions – a certain policy environment – that are normal prerequisites for market-oriented investment but were not in fact present.

1   On the conformity of the world to the model, it has been pointed out that by no means all the profits generated in a developing country have been re-invested in that country (Haq, 1966; Griffith, 1965; Khan and Hossein, 1989, p. 92); that low capital–labour ratios such as had been hoped would make full productive use of the labour have not been universal in agriculture in the economies that are in a 'Lewis' phase or in the industries emerging beside that agriculture (Mabro, 1967); and that in the agricultural systems that Lewis was discussing labour surplus often applied at only certain times of the year (Mehra, 1966)

2   The most extreme and disastrous exercise in channelling surplus labour into investment was Mao's 'Great Leap Forward' of 1959–61, which is blamed for the deaths through food deprivation of an estimated 23 to 30 million people in China. In the centrally planned economies of the Soviet bloc the agricultural surplus was also directed into industry. Indian and Pakistani planning had the idea of altering the terms of trade in favour of secondary industry and against agriculture. This was done through such policies as

> licensing of scarce foreign exchange earned primarily by agriculture to the industrial sector, compulsory procurement of food grains at low prices to subsidize the cost of living of the urban, industrial workers, generous tax concessions to industry and lack of similar incentives for commercial agricultural investment.
> *(Government of Pakistan, Planning Commission*, The Third Five Year Plan 1965–70, *p. 7)*

So there was a deliberate attempt to turn the terms of trade against agriculture. However, in many instances, there was clear evidence that such a policy of deliberate price distortions that artificially handicapped agriculture harmed rather than stimulated the industrial economy. In many countries that pursued such a policy, the output of agriculture failed to increase, and in some cases it even decreased, so that these developing countries were forced to import foodstuffs; and cash-crops for export could also be hit, as was evidenced, for example, in Ghana during the late 1970s and early 1980s. There the effective producer price of cocoa fell so low that farmers lost interest in its production, and export earnings, which depended heavily on cocoa, virtually collapsed partly because of a sharp fall in cocoa output (Huq, 1989). Indeed, the various controls, including protection against industrial imports, which were vigorously pursued, failed to generate a viable industrial sector. Instead, rent-seeking was encouraged, and the industrialists spent their time and attention seeking monopoly power through protection. In the process, there emerged an inefficient industrial structure in many developing countries. (Krueger, 1987. See also Little, Scitovsky and Scott, 1970, for some early evidence.)

These, it is clear now, were policy mistakes for which neither Lewis nor the model can reasonably be blamed.

3   However, probably the most important reason that sanguine hopes from 'unlimited labour' were not fulfilled in the way that was probably envisaged is that investment does not on the whole happen just because funds or labour are available. Except by direct government decision, it happens because of expectations of returns, to which an important contributor is a favourable political climate, a climate in which the investors

have a certain amount of freedom and confidence in the security of property and the support of the law. So, the hope that 'unlimited labour' in a country will lead to an investment boom within it has something of the 'closed-economy illusion' about it. In addition, the fact that funds are generated within a certain country does not mean that they are particularly likely to be invested there and, conversely, investment may boom in a country independently of whether there have been abundant profits realized there shortly before or not. In reality, some countries with initially very low real wages combined with a reasonably efficient workforce – notably the East Asian 'Tigers' – *have* on that account been able to realize considerable economic growth. But it is because they have been able to enter world markets in manufactures, not simply because the low wages have automatically conjured up large amounts of finance for reinvestment.

CHAPTER 14

Migration and Urbanization

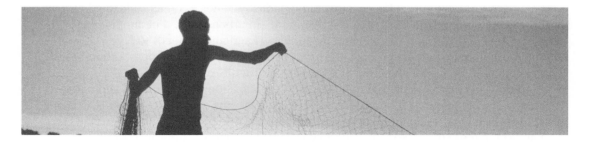

Urban areas in developing countries are expanding at a very rapid rate – the result of a combination of rural-urban migration and natural increase. 'This vast urban expansion in developing countries has global implications. Cities are already the locus of nearly all major economic, social, demographic and environmental transformations. What happens in the cities of the less-developed world in coming years will shape prospects for global economic growth, poverty alleviation, population stabilization, environmental sustainability and, ultimately, the exercise of human rights' (UNFPA, 2007a).

Introduction

Migration and urbanization have been central features of the evolution of human society – often responses to climate change, population growth, the exigencies of a nomadic way of life, or tribal conflict. Much scholarly detective work has gone into tracing the movements of peoples over millennia and dating the gradual establishment and expansion of permanent settlements. For today's development economists interest in the movement of populations and the growth of towns and cities in the developing world goes well beyond the purely 'academic'. These phenomena, and policies which affect them, have come to be seen as important influences on the development process itself. The present chapter is devoted to examining **internal migration**[1] – specifically, migration *within* countries from rural to urban areas – its relationship to **urbanization**, and the significance of the migration-urbanization interaction for economic development and development policy.

Why are rural–urban migration and urbanization, and associated policies, seen as important issues? First, because, as will be seen in later sections, these processes are very important influences on the way in which most developing countries are evolving in the spatial structure, and the fundamental character, of their societies. Second, because a majority of developing-country governments are currently pursuing *anti*-rural-urban-

---

[1] International migration is discussed in Chapter 24.

migration policies, largely in an attempt to head off what are perceived to be the excessive costs of large-scale urbanization. Unfortunately, little attempt has been to think through the long-run implications of these actions, or to integrate them into clear-cut strategies for future growth and development. Indeed, most analysts believe that anti-migration policies are often inappropriate and are likely, in many cases, to damage the prospects for development. Such commentators subscribe to the view that a substantial part of the growth of output and income required for development will stem from increases in industrial production, and, because industry (in particular, manufacturing industry) tends to prefer to locate in towns and cities, future growth must take place primarily in urban areas.[2] Put another way: 'The overarching dualistic approach, whereby traditional agriculture needs to give way to the supposedly more efficient agri-business production system and to modern, urban-based industrial and services sectors, remains pervasive' (Tacoli, 2008).

Thus far our study of internal migration and urbanization has been brief and narrowly focused. Nevertheless, it contains the germ of the concerns referred to above. In Chapter 5 we examined two 'landmark' theories concerning the role played by rural-to-urban migration in the growth process. Arthur Lewis's 'surplus labour' approach saw such migration as a fundamentally benign phenomenon, with rural–urban wage differentials attracting to urban areas the labour supply required for industrialization. Clearly, rural–urban migration and urbanization were an important part of the solution to the development problem. Accordingly, it seemed sensible to warn policy makers to avoid measures that might hinder the inflow of labour to the towns and cities.

Todaro's model linked migration flows into urban areas to both rural–urban wage differentials and urban-unemployment rates. It suggested that it was likely that migration would, in fact, create a serious problem of persistent, probably growing, urban unemployment; and it led to the policy conclusion that priority should be given to discouraging rural–urban migration in order to head off any tendency for towns to become centres of heavy, chronic unemployment and associated social malaise. The fact that unemployment is common in today's developing world's towns and cities has tended to lend plausibility to the 'Todarian' view or, at any rate, to the associated policy conclusion that rural–urban migration causes problems and is to be discouraged, and many developing countries have in place measures designed to do just this.

This conventional wisdom, however, firmly entrenched as it is in the minds of many policy-makers (and aid agencies) over several decades, has come under attack in the early years of the new millennium by economists who believe that, properly handled, internal migration has considerable potential as a spur to development, and who favour policies designed to encourage, or at least accommodate, rural–urban migration.

The structure of this chapter

In this chapter we look first at the dimensions of urban growth and internal migration in the developing world – contrasting the history of slow evolution of urban areas in the now-developed countries with the current headlong pace, and massive extent, of urbanization in developing countries. The contribution that rural-to-urban migration makes to urbanization is then assessed, though figures remain tentative because of the incomplete nature of the data on this matter. This is followed by an examination of the 'pull' and 'push' factors

---

[2] Unless otherwise indicated, in this chapter the terms 'towns', 'cities' and 'urban areas' are used interchangeably.

driving the migration process – who migrates and why? – making use of insights drawn from the 'New Economics of Labour Migration'. The focus then shifts to the *impact* of the migration-urbanization sequence on economic growth. Special attention is paid to the debate over whether rapid urbanization in the developing world is 'pro-growth' or 'anti-growth'. Is the rapid expansion of urban areas (and, within them, slum areas) – sometimes to enormous dimensions – primarily a serious threat to social and economic stability, as many governments appear to believe (given the widespread drift towards policies discouraging rural–urban migration)? Or, on the contrary, is urbanization a prerequisite of economic development for most developing countries – the 'answer' rather than the 'problem'? In the penultimate section we look at the costs and benefits for the populations of the rural areas migrants leave behind. The chapter concludes with an assessment of policy options available to developing-country governments.

The dimensions of urban growth and internal migration

Introduction

Reliable data on internal migration within developing countries are hard to come by. Unlike international migration, movement within countries does not usually require documentation, and thus often goes unrecorded. However, it is apparent that a major segment of internal migration is rural-to-urban, and such migration contributes significantly to growth of urban populations. In this section we examine first the extent of urban growth, then consider the evidence on the contribution of migration to that growth.

Urbanization

The record to 2007

In almost all countries, developed and developing, the extent of urbanization, as measured by the *percentage of a nation's population living in towns and cities*, has increased over time. As the figures in Table 14.1 show, this fundamental demographic change has progressed at a rapid pace since 1900, though the increases in the developing world as a whole easily outstrip those experienced in developed countries. In the former the percentage of the population living in towns and cities doubled between 1900 and 1950, then more than doubled again between 1950 and 2007, implying a rate of increase of urban population over twice that recorded in the developed countries over the same period. The post-1950 increase in urban numbers was even more rapid in the *least developed* countries, where a near four-fold rise was experienced between 1950 and 2005, probably indicating that a 'catch-up' process was at work.

This expansionary surge is often referred to by demographers as the 'second wave' of urbanization in relatively modern times. The 'first wave', beginning in the mid-eighteenth century, spanned some 200 years and transformed, at a fairly gradual pace, the now-developed countries in Europe and North America from a largely rural state into predominantly urban industrial societies. Clearly, the speed with which the 'second wave' of urbanization is advancing in most of today's developing countries far exceeds that achieved by the 'first wave'.

Data on levels of urbanization in the main geographical regions in 2007 are presented in Table 14.1 (corresponding figures for individual countries are given in Appendix 14.1,

	1900	1950	1980	1990	2000	2005	2007	2020	2030	2050
WORLD	14	29	39	43	47	49	50	55	60	70
DEVELOPED COUNTRIES	30	53	69	71	73	74	75	78	81	86
DEVELOPING COUNTRIES	9	18	30	35	40	43	44	51	56	67
Least Developed	na	*7*	*17*	*21*	*25*	*27*	*28*	*35*	*42*	*56*
Africa		15	28	32	36	38	39	45	50	62
Ethiopia		*5*	*10*	*13*	*15*	*16*	*16*	*22*	*27*	*42*
Ghana		*15*	*31*	*36*	*44*	*48*	*49*	*58*	*65*	*76*
Kenya		*6*	*16*	*18*	*20*	*21*	*21*	*27*	*33*	*48*
Nigeria		*10*	*29*	*35*	*43*	*46*	*42*	*57*	*64*	*75*
South Africa		*42*	*48*	*52*	*57*	*59*	*60*	*67*	*71*	*80*
Tanzania		*4*	*15*	*19*	*22*	*24*	*25*	*32*	*39*	*54*
Latin Am & Caribbean		41	65	71	76	78	78	82	85	89
Brazil		*36*	*67*	*75*	*81*	*84*	*85*	*90*	*91*	*94*
Colombia		*33*	*62*	*68*	*72*	*74*	*73*	*78*	*81*	*86*
Mexico		*43*	*66*	*71*	*75*	*76*	*77*	*81*	*83*	*88*
Venezuela		*47*	*79*	*84*	*90*	*96*	*94*	*96*	*97*	*98*
West Asia		29	52	61	64	65	65	69	73	79
Jordan		*37*	*60*	*72*	*78*	*78*	*83*	*80*	*82*	*86*
Saudi Arabia		*21*	*66*	*77*	*80*	*81*	*81*	*84*	*86*	*90*
South-Central Asia		16	2.3	27	30	31	31	37	43	57
Afghanistan		*6*	*16*	*18*	*21*	*23*	*24*	*30*	*36*	*52*
Bangladesh		*4*	*15*	*20*	*24*	*26*	*26*	*34*	*41*	*56*
India		*17*	*23*	*26*	*28*	*29*	*29*	*34*	*41*	*55*
Pakistan		*18*	*28*	*31*	*33*	*35*	*36*	*43*	*50*	*64*
Sri Lanka		*15*	*19*	*17*	*16*	*15*	*15*	*17*	*21*	*34*
East Asia		17	26	33	40	45	46	56	62	79
China		*13*	*20*	*27*	*36*	*40*	*42*	*53*	*60*	*73*
Korea		*21*	*57*	*74*	*80*	*81*	*81*	*84*	*86*	*90*
South-East Asia		15	26	32	40	44	45	56	62	73
Indonesia		*12*	*22*	*31*	*42*	*48*	*50*	*63*	*69*	*79*
Malaysia		*20*	*42*	*50*	*62*	*68*	*69*	*79*	*82*	*88*
Philippines		*27*	*38*	*49*	*59*	*63*	*64*	*72*	*77*	*84*
Thailand		*17*	*27*	*29*	*31*	*32*	*33*	*39*	*46*	*60*
Vietnam		*12*	*20*	*20*	*24*	*26*	*27*	*35*	*42*	*57*

TABLE 14.1 Urbanization: per cent population resident in urban areas: selected years 1900–2050
na Data not available.
Sources: Data for 1900 from Bairoch (1989); Data for 1950–2050 from UNFPA (2008) (www.esa.un.org/unup) and World Bank (2002) (p. 36 and p. 172).

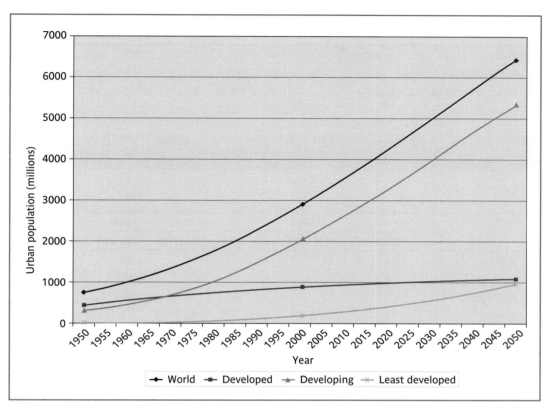

FIGURE 14.1 Urban population, actual and projected: world, developed, developing and least developed countries: 1950–2050 (millions)
Source: Based on data from UNFPA (2008).

which is available on the Online Learning Centre) and, in graphic form, in Figure 14.1. These make clear the diversity of experience of the developing world in this context. Thus, many South American countries – notably Argentina, Brazil, Chile, Colombia, Peru, Uruguay and Venezuela – had by 2007 reached levels of urbanization similar to those in the wealthier developed countries of North America and Northern and Western Europe. Indeed, at 94 per cent of the total population, the figure for Venezuela exceeds those of all developed countries bar Belgium. The regional average level of urbanization in Latin America and the Caribbean was 78 per cent in 2007, some way ahead of the second-ranking developing-country region, West Asia, at 65 per cent. However, within the latter group there was again marked diversity, Kuwait and Israel having 98 per cent and 92 per cent respectively of their populations in urban areas, while Yemen remained predominantly rural with 28 per cent urbanization. In 2007 East Asia and South-East Asia were markedly less urban than West Asia, with 46 per cent and 45 per cent respectively of their populations living in towns. The average for the 47 African countries reported on in Appendix 14.1, (available on the Online Learning Centre), was 39 per cent, though this group contained eight countries with below 20 per cent of their populations resident in towns, and one, Burundi, with 11 per cent, the lowest value reported by the UNFPA for 2007. The figure for South-Central Asia, in the same year, was 31 per cent, a level recorded for the developed world over a century earlier, in 1900, and the lowest of any of the major regions.

	1950	1980	1990	2000	2005	2020	2030	2050
WORLD	736.8	1740.6	2274.6	2853.9	3164.6	4209.7	4965.1	6398.3
DEVELOPED COUNTRIES	427.3	745.0	818.1	872.9	899.8	972.3	1015.6	1017.4
DEVELOPING COUNTRIES	309.5	995.6	1456.4	1981.0	2264.8	3237.3	3949.5	5326.9
Least developed countries	14.6	70.3	110.3	168.6	207.0	376.0	539.4	966.9

TABLE 14.2 Urbanization: total population resident in urban areas, selected years: 1950–2050 (millions)
Source: UNFPA (2008).

REGION	URBAN			RURAL		
	1950–1975	1975–2000	2000–2030	1950–1975	1975–2000	2000–2030
WORLD	2.9	2.4	1.8	1.4	0.9	0.1
DEVELOPED	1.8	0.9	0.6	−0.6	−0.07	−0.9
DEVELOPING	3.7	3.2	2.2	1.6	1.0	0.2
Europe	1.8	0.6	0.04	−0.7	−0.5	−1.3
North America	2.0	1.2	1.0	0.1	0.4	−0.5
Africa	4.6	4.2	3.3	1.9	2.0	1.1
Asia	3.5	3.4	2.2	1.8	1.0	−0.04
Latin Am. & Caribbean	4.2	2.7	1.5	1.0	0.1	−0.3
Oceania	2.5	1.7	1.1	0.7	1.2	0.7

TABLE 14.3 Urbanization: percentage growth rates of population in urban and rural areas, 1950–75, 1975–2000, and 2000–2030 (average annual per cent)
Source: Based on Montgomerie, M.R. *et al.* (2003) (Table 3-1).

The figures in Table 14.1 and Table 14.7 provide clear evidence of the existence of a massive, widespread, and very rapid, transformation of the spatial structure of societies in all parts of the developing world – a transformation both caused by, and inevitably entraining, profound economic and social changes.

Just as the shift in the rural–urban balance of population in today's developing countries is proceeding at a much faster pace than was the case in the corresponding phase in the demographic transition of the now-developed countries so, as is indicated by the data in Tables 14.2 and 14.3, the absolute numbers involved today dwarf those of the 200-year-long 'first wave'. The latter is estimated to have involved a few hundred million people while, over the comparatively short period 1950 to 2005, the population of towns and cities in the developing world increased by nearly two billion, or almost seven-fold – what must be the most dramatic demographic change ever recorded.

The figures in Table 14.3 confirm the fact that while all regions experienced a slow-down in rates of urban growth across the years 1950–2000, major differences were observed across regions. Expansion in the developed world has slowed from an average of 1.8 per cent per annum over the period 1950–75 to 0.9 per cent per annum over 1975–2000, whereas rates of growth in developing countries averaged 3.7 per cent and 3.2 per cent respectively in the same periods, with annual growth in numbers in Africa remaining particularly high across 1975–2000 at 4.2 per cent per annum.

Over the same years rural populations declined in developed countries but continued to expand in the developing world, though at a much slower rate than urban populations. In Asia and Latin America/Caribbean this slow-down was particularly pronounced, with rural numbers in the latter barely increasing across 1975–2000.

The future of urbanization

The UNFPA (2007a) has estimated that in 2008, for the first time, the majority of the world's population (around 3.3 billion) would be living in towns and cities. The 'Urban Millennium' has arrived and the '*urban transition*' – 'the passage from a predominantly rural to a predominantly urban society' – is well under way. The process of urbanization is confidently expected to continue throughout the developing world – barring the introduction of further effective policies to deter migration or severe long-run decline in the economies of urban areas. Such declines seem, in general, unlikely, but should not be ruled out entirely. Thus, 20 years of many-faceted economic failure in Zambia have led to a slow erosion of urban areas there – 'counter-urbanization' – as people drift back to the rural areas (Potts, 2005).

BOX 14.1 CITY GROWTH

'The growth of cities will be the single largest influence on development in the 21st century.'

(UNFPA, 1996)

However, the process of urbanization in developing countries still has a long way to go. UN population projections for urban areas in 2050 compared with 2005 (see Table 14.2 and Figure 14.1) suggest a 13 per cent rise for developed countries as against 135 per cent for developing countries, implying a modest rise of 118 millions in the developed-country cities, and an increase of just *over three billions* in urban areas in the developing world.

> The next few decades will see an unprecedented scale of urban growth in the developing world. This will be particularly notable in Africa and Asia where the urban population will double between 2000 and 2030: that is, the accumulated urban growth of these two regions during the whole span of history will be duplicated in a single generation.
>
> *(UNFPA, 2007a)*

This in turn implies that, in 2050, towns and cities *in the developing world* will be home to over 83 per cent of *the world's* population. The lowest projected degree of urbanization for any of the 'developing' regions is 48 per cent for sub-Saharan Africa, the highest 72 per cent for Western Asia. Overall, it is anticipated that, post-2007, some 93 per cent of all urban growth will be in Asia and Africa.[3]

---

[3] A caveat – population projections should be 'treated with caution'. They are best interpreted as order-of-magnitude guides rather than as precise estimates. A detailed analysis of the accuracy of forecasts made in the past discloses a remarkable degree of imprecision. Notably, the 'mean percentage error' in projections made by the UN for the period 1980–2000 was 14.1 per cent for the world as a whole, and ranged up to 21.8 per cent for sub-Saharan Africa, and a massive 27.2 per cent for South Asia (see Montgomery, M.R. *et al.* 2003, Table 4-9). This should not be interpreted as a criticism of the UN's efforts but rather as an indication of how difficult demographic forecasting is.

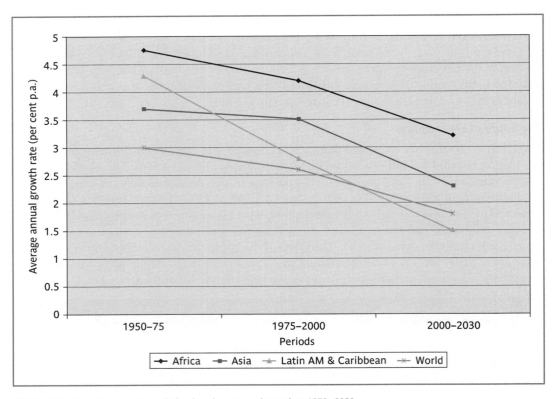

FIGURE 14.2 Growth rates of population in urban areas by region: 1950–2030
Source: Based on data from UNFPA (2007).

However, it should be noted that this further demographic upheaval, while huge in terms of absolute numbers, does *not* depend on the maintaining of very high year-on-year rates of growth of urban populations, but rather stems from the (projected) relatively slow growth of a massive base. Figure 14.2 confirms this, at first sight surprising, conclusion.

Prospects for rural populations

In contrast, rural areas in many developing countries face depopulation. Early signs of this shift are evident in World Bank (2008b, Table A1) data for the period 1990–2005, during which rural populations in a number of countries fell. Particularly noteworthy here were the following *negative* average annual 'growth' rates: China −0.4% Malaysia −0.5%; Indonesia −0.5%; Argentina −0.7%; Korean Republic −1.3%; Uruguay −1.5%; Brazil −1.6%; and, largest of all, Venezuela −3.9%.

Forecasts of future change in the size of the total rural population in developing countries vary slightly – from an (annual) increase of 0.2 per cent between 2000 and 2030 (World Bank) to an annual fall of around 0.5 per cent over the same years (UNFPA). The determining factor will be the balance between continued increases in Africa and Oceania, and declines elsewhere. It is clear, however, that **all, or nearly all**, future net population growth in the developing world is expected to take place in towns and cities.

The nature and extent of rural–urban migration

Forms of internal migration

Internal migration in developing countries takes several forms. Migrants move from poor villages to more affluent agricultural areas (*rural–rural migration*); from rural areas to towns and cities (*rural–urban migration*); from one town to another (*urban–urban migration*); and from urban areas to rural areas (*urban–rural migration*). Rural–urban migration is sometimes carried out in several moves to progressively larger towns (*step migration*) and is sometimes *permanent*, sometimes temporary or *circular*.[4] Urban–rural migration is sometimes in the form of what has been called *counter-urbanization*, indicating movement away from a declining urban area.

In both Africa and Asia circular and temporary migration are growing in magnitude but are often overlooked because they are difficult to capture in national statistics. In this chapter our primary interest is in **rural–urban migration** on the grounds that this is believed to be the most extensive of the various forms of migration, and because the transfer of population from rural areas to urban areas is thought to have the greatest potential for generating development-related benefits – and costs. It is also the form of migration which is, and remains, the focus of much anti-internal-migration policy in developing countries.

BOX 14.2 TOOLKIT ON MIGRATION AND URBANIZATION

The arithmetic of rural–urban migration can cause problems. Here we draw attention to two potential pitfalls in interpreting the ratio '*the percentage of urban population growth attributable to rural–urban migration*' – which can be a slippery concept:

1 If locations of below 'urban' size continue to expand they eventually reach the point where they cross the threshold of 'urban' status and their entire population is at that point reclassified as 'urban'. At the same time, the inflows of rural–rural migrants into these locations are reclassified as 'rural–urban' migrants. Thus, in any one year, marginal changes in migrant flows can have a leveraged effect on the figure calculated for the proportion of urbanization caused by rural–urban inflows. Changes in the classification thresholds themselves also create comparability problems. (Note that the figures in Table 14.4 include 'reclassification effects'.)

2 Significant continued movements from rural to urban areas come to have the effect of apparently *reducing* the impact of rural–urban migration on urbanization of populations because of the purely arithmetical 'feedback effect' whereby in-migration increases the size of towns, and hence increases the denominator of the ratio (in-migrants/urban population).

[4] Circular migration, which typically involves the maintaining by the migrant of close links with relatives in the village, is particularly common in Africa, where the seasonal nature of farm labour inputs is often pronounced, in some cases being reinforced by customary division of labour between men (planting and harvesting) and women (cultivating and tending during the growing season) (White and Lindstrom, 2005).

▶ The **'urban transition'** is analogous to the 'demographic transition' (see Chapter 13) in that it describes a decisive, almost certainly irreversible, change in a country – in this case the spatial population shift transforming what was a predominantly rural country into a predominantly urban one. In 2008 the urban population of the world first exceeded 50 per cent of global population. (According to the UNFPA, in 2007 just under half of the 115 developing countries for which data were available were more than 50 per cent urbanized. In the same year all but one – Trinidad and Tobago – of the 34 high-income countries were more than 50 per cent urbanized.)

Why do slums exist? The Director of the UN-HABITAT agency has argued that, contrary to the general impression, sums are not a planning mistake or the result of market failure. Rather, slums are 'economically useful', a 'market success' – offering low-cost housing options to the poor and making possible the supply of cheap labour needed for competitive production by poor countries (Biau, D. 2007).

The extent of rural–urban migration

It is not possible to deduce from figures on urbanization the precise extent of rural-to-urban migration. Clearly, natural increase of population within towns also augments urban populations. Again, many initially non-urban areas have been reclassified as 'urban' when their growing population passed beyond a threshold level, or when government definitions of what constitutes 'urban' are changed. Nevertheless, it is clear that, given any plausible assumptions about relative fertility in rural and urban areas, taken together with such census data as are available, the increases in urban numbers must be, to a significant extent, attributable to migration from the countryside to towns and cities – that is, to 'internal' rural-to-urban migration.

The limited hard evidence available certainly seems to confirm this. Thus it has been estimated that, during the 1970s, around half of the growth of population in Africa's urban areas was due to in-migration, this figure falling to one quarter in the 1980s (Brockerhoff, 1995). In India, the national Census indicates that, over the 1990s, internal migrants accounted for 30 per cent of urban growth (Lall *et al.*, 2006). In China, where controls on the location of permanent residence are in force,[5] the rapid growth of industry in urban areas has been accompanied by migration on a massive scale. The bulk of this internal migration is rural–urban and temporary, though permanent migration would almost certainly expand sharply were controls relaxed. Numbers of temporary migrants in China rose sharply from around 26 million in 1988 to 150–200 million in 2007. Some projections suggest that the total will reach 300 million by 2015 (Deshingkar, 2006, and Jiang, 2007).

BOX 14.3 MIGRATION, URBANIZATION AND GROWTH

'Internal migration is a prerequisite for urbanization, a phenomenon whose role has long been recognized as the key correlate accompanying economic growth'

(Lall *et al.*, 2006)

---

[5] Under China's *Hukou* system over 100 million rural–urban migrants are still seen as 'rural residents' and do not benefit from the rights accorded to urban residents.

	UN (1980)**	Chen, Valente and Zlotnik (1998)**
1950s	39	
1960s		40.7
1970s		43.2
1980s		40.1

TABLE 14.4 Percentages of urban population growth attributed to rural–urban migration and 'reclassification'* (%)
* i.e. The reclassification of 'rural areas' as 'urban areas'.
** The remaining (approximately) 60 per cent of population growth was attributed to natural increase.
Sources: Publications cited. Values are for median country in country groups covered by surveys.

The figures for all developing countries taken together are somewhat speculative but there is general agreement that, for most of the second half of the twentieth century, rural–urban migration, plus 'reclassification', explained around 40 per cent of the growth of urban populations. (Table 14.4 provides details of two sets of estimates.) It is anticipated that between 250 million and 310 million people in developing countries will become urban dwellers between 2005 and 2015 because of internal migration or reclassification of rural areas as urban areas. (United Nations, 2006).

These figures point to a major change in the speed and magnitude of today's rural–urban migration compared with the corresponding process in the evolution of the now-developed countries. For example, the increase in the urbanized proportion of the population forecast to take place between 2000 and 2030 took around 100 years in the UK (between 1700 and 1800) and, of course, involved far fewer people in absolute terms. The causes and the impact of this massive and very rapid demographic shift (which is much larger than the much discussed international migration from developing countries examined in Chapter 24) are clearly of great potential significance for the development process, and will continue to be so for some decades if the levels of urbanization achieved by developed countries are replicated in all parts of the developing world.

The causes of rural–urban migration

The causes of rural–urban migration are traditionally divided into 'pull' and 'push' factors felt directly by the migrants themselves. In this section we examine these two sets of influences sequentially, adding detail on the personal characteristics and circumstances of migrants and non-migrants which have been found to be associated with the decision to migrate or not to migrate. We also look at the impact of a further factor of considerable importance in many developing countries – government policies designed to curb rural–urban migration.

Pull factors

Economic considerations are usually held to dominate the motivation of rural migrants 'pulled' into urban areas. J.K. Galbraith (1979) saw migration as 'the oldest action against poverty', a view consistent with both Lewis's and Todaro's assessments of the reasons for migration (discussed in Chapter 5) which placed particular emphasis on one 'pull' factor – the *higher wage rates available in the towns than in the countryside*.

More recent analysis, while recognizing the crucial role of earnings differentials as a spur to rural–urban migration, argues that the traditional neoclassical-type approach, which explains migration simply in terms of a desire on the part of the migrant to maximize lifetime earnings, is much too narrowly focused, and does not allow for a number of important considerations that may influence migrants and may affect the character of migration.

In particular, migration is now seen as being a way of 'managing risk' by diversifying the sources of household income; or as a means of securing a given 'target income' with which to finance the purchasing of a residence or productive assets for enterprise purposes (which may be seen as a prudent broadening of the asset base); or as a method of generating the funds needed to make possible 'smoothing' of personal or family consumption over time.

It is also argued that, to explain and understand many examples of migration adequately, attention must be paid to the financial implications of certain *social variables*, especially the role of social networks and interactions involving friends and relatives already living in towns. Specifically, by providing information, contacts, and possibly accommodation, relatives (in many cases themselves established in-migrants now facilitating *chain migration*), effectively provide a labour-market externality – a form of 'social capital' which, when 'spent' by the migrant, reduces job-search costs, including the waiting time before a job is found.

A further striking finding of research on mobility in both Africa and Asia is that *temporary circular* migration appears to be a significant feature of the migration scene. Data here are still inadequate and their coverage very patchy, but figures have been recorded for ratios of urban–rural migration to rural–urban migration as high as 61 per cent (for Malawi) and 76 per cent (for Botswana) (Potts, 2006). It seems likely that circular migration, often overlooked by national statisticians, may be an important component in the strategy of diversifying income sources and asset bases referred to above, 'a key element of the livelihoods of households in both rural and urban settlements . . . an important part of the links between urban and rural development . . . essential to maintain an asset base, and a safety net, spread across different locations' (Tacoli, 2008, p. 7). In some cases, however, the motivation for *temporary* migration may be the intention to emigrate internationally, the move overseas being delayed until the migrant accumulates the required funds and information in the urban area, something that would be much more difficult in the village context (Skeldon, 1997).

The influence of personal characteristics of migrants

These various influences on the migration process will not affect all rural dwellers equally. The personal characteristics and circumstances of individuals affect their desire, and ability, to respond to 'pull' factors. Although circumstances do vary from one country to the next, it is possible to 'profile' migrants to identify a small number of key characteristics that tend to be associated with an increased probability of migrating, other things being equal. Specifically, in most countries rural–urban migrants are more likely than not to be:

- *Male* (though migration by females is on the increase, especially in Asia);
- *Younger* rather than older. (For instance, in China around 70 per cent of migrants heading for the towns are between 16 and 35 years of age);
- *Better educated* or more highly skilled than non-migrants. However, critically, this applies to permanent migrants. Temporary/seasonal migration to towns is often dominated by the less well-educated and unskilled. It is also the case that those currently enrolled in educational institutions are less likely to move than those not enrolled (however, urban–rural migration is dominated by the less well-educated);
- Members of *larger*, rather than smaller, *families*;
- *Unmarried* rather than married – and, if married, having fewer rather than more children;

- Having a *history of past migratory moves* – rather than no such history;
- Having significant *social capital resources* in the shape of contacts in, and information about, the urban areas and the process of finding employment there.

However, the traditional, 'atomistic' approach to analysis of rural–urban migration, which sees migration decisions as being taken in a consistent way over time by autonomous, utility-maximizing individuals, unconnected with others (aside from the use of family contacts to smooth their path), and having clearly defined personal characteristics of the kind identified above, is challenged by research findings highlighting the changing, dynamic, and community-based nature of rural–urban migration and the importance of 'feed-back' to the process. There is evidence that

> The migration history of a community shapes the context of migration for individuals . . . Migration generates common patterns of social, demographic and economic changes in *sending* communities; these changes make future migration more likely; and, due to this dynamic and cumulative mechanism, the effect of individual, household or village level characteristics on migration may depend on the migration history of the individual's community. . . . Migration becomes a *less selective*[6] process as migration experience accumulates, and migrants become increasingly diverse in terms of sex, education and wealth.
>
> *(Garip, 2006)*

Non-pecuniary attractions in urban areas

While 'pull' factors, based in one way or another on calculations relating to financial advantage, are probably crucial in many decisions to migrate to urban areas, they are very unlikely to be the only considerations, and in some cases may not be the decisive ones. To them must be added a number of potentially significant *non-pecuniary attractions*. In particular, migration provides improved access to the range of *public services* available in towns, notably education and health facilities. Furthermore it offers the attractions of the many *social amenities – the 'bright lights'* – of city life, an influence very hard to quantify but potentially very important nonetheless.

Location-specific factors

All of the above considerations may influence the character and magnitude of the flows of people moving from the countryside to the towns in developing countries. The specific geographical pattern of such migration will, of course, depend to a large extent on the nature of the urban areas themselves – some being more attractive than others. Large, rapidly expanding urban areas (often ports in export-led economies) will tend to attract large numbers of migrants, other things being equal. Less prosperous, less dynamic urban areas will attract fewer migrants.

Further, migration from a given village to a given urban area is more likely the closer the latter is to the 'source' village. That is, the probability that the 'pull' of a town will give rise to migration from a village is inversely related to the distance between the two. Proximity encourages migration both because short-distance moves are less expensive than long-range ones, and because information flows regarding conditions in the town are likely to become increasingly attenuated with distance. By the same token, improvements in the national transportation network and/or declining transportation costs are likely to encourage

---

[6] Emphasis added.

migration to towns. One implication of this process is that by no means all moves are to the largest urban areas. In fact, in most developing countries a sizeable proportion of all migrants move to the relatively smaller towns so 'levelling-up' rates of urban growth across the urban sector.

Push factors

Financial pressures may *push* migrants out of the rural areas and towards the urban areas. Thus rural *poverty* caused by rural *unemployment* and *disguised unemployment*, common where rural populations are growing rapidly, employment opportunities are expanding slowly or dwindling, and non-agricultural enterprise activity is inhibited by the lack of access to credit, often drives rural populations into the towns. Again, depletion and degradation of the rural environment, because of poor farming practice and climate change, may lead to a reduction in its carrying capacity and, in extreme cases, crop failures and famine. This again contributes to the growing rural poverty, as do misguided government policies which exhibit 'urban bias' in neglecting agriculture in order to concentrate support on industry.

In view of these threats, rural families may encourage members to migrate to the town in order to diversify collectively the risk they face of loss of income and poverty. Once again, adding urban workers to their 'portfolio' of economic activities acts as 'insurance' for rural families against hard times. It may also facilitate the setting up of a 'migration chain' to assist the migration of further family members.

At the same time it is the case that many other 'push' factors are not directly financial. These include:

- Increasing *landlessness*, due perhaps to consolidation of farms designed to facilitate mechanization of cultivation and harvesting of crops, or to inheritance practices which rule out subdivision of farm acreage amongst farmers' children;
- *Lack of non-farm employment opportunities* because of the slow pace of diversification from agriculture;
- The establishing of *secure property rights* to land. This may encourage rural–urban migration in two distinct ways. It may make possible the 'clearance' by landowners of unwanted tenant farmers from their land, or it may enable landowners to migrate to towns without the fear of losing their property in their absence – sometimes using the land as collateral to help finance the move;
- *Improving educational* levels in the countryside. This may create skills ('human capital') specific to the individual which cannot be fully exploited, and will not be adequately rewarded, in rural employment;
- *Escape from the exploitation and social immobility* which often affect members of the 'underclass' in the countryside;
- Escape from the stultifying *lack of variety*, and lack of opportunity for self-advancement, typical of village life;
- *Warfare* and various forms of *civil unrest*. These can play an important part in prompting internal migration, some of which will certainly be towards towns. (Migrations in Angola, Mozambique, Liberia and Darfur are cases in point.) It is estimated that, in late 2006, there were over 24 million 'internally displaced persons' in the developing world (IDMC, 2007).

Government controls on rural–urban migration

Attempts by governments of developing countries to reduce the level of rural–urban migration by regulation are widespread and growing. Measures may involve actively discouraging migration, especially permanent migration, by limiting the range of jobs open to migrants and restricting access to free welfare benefits (as with China's *Hukou* system), or by denying migrants rights to purchase residential land and to access free education and medical facilities (as with Vietnam's 'KT' registration scheme). Or the focus may be on increasing the relative attractiveness of rural areas by, for instance, improving the welfare benefits available there (as with India's National Rural Employment Guarantee Scheme, which offers guaranteed work or unemployment benefit to some 60 million mainly rural families).

In addition to these explicitly counter-migration policies, slum clearance activities, often involving demolition of dwellings across broad swathes of city-centre land, have forced large numbers of city dwellers into the suburbs, or out of urban areas altogether. In some cases these activities have been financed by international agencies (as with the World Bank's contribution to the costs of clearing areas in Ho Chi Minh City).

In 1976 only 44 per cent of all developing countries reporting on their rural–urban migration policies to the United Nations indicated that their aim was to reduce rural–urban migration. By 1986 this figure had climbed to 56 per cent. And in 2007 some 74 per cent of the 125 developing countries for which information was available had in place measures designed to reduce the flows from the villages to the towns and cities (UNFPA, 2008).

Insofar as these measures have an impact (and it has to be admitted that, in some cases, they are held to be ineffective) this would be to reduce the level of inflows into the towns.

However, the existence of these policies brings us back to issues central to the theme of this chapter: What is the development significance of such restrictions? Are the migrants a brake on economic progress (and thus 'part of the problem') or could they contribute, as urban dwellers, to increasing rates of economic growth (as 'part of the answer')? We pursue these issues in the next section.

The impact of rural–urban migration: urbanization and economic growth

Introduction

Given the massive scale of rural–urban migration in developing countries, and the major stimulus it has given to urbanization, it should be no surprise that the process can have significant impacts at economic, social and political levels. A key issue in the debate over the desirability, or otherwise, of the migration-urbanization process in developing countries concerns *the impact it has on economic growth*. This is an issue of immense practical significance with strong policy implications. It is also one on which, as we have noted, many governments in the developing world appear to have already made up their minds, as is evident from the widespread adoption of anti-migration policies.

However, as we shall see, there is an emerging consensus view amongst analysts that urbanization is, in fact, a necessary condition for long-run growth though not a sufficient one. The case for facilitating migration and urbanization is seen as a strong one provided appropriate measures are put in place to handle the deleterious – indeed, potentially disastrous – effects of urbanization.

The pro-growth potential of urbanization

Largely ignored in earlier years, the pro-growth potential of urbanization (and hence of rural-urban migration) has, since the advent of the new millennium, been widely emphasized in the literature on demography and development. Recognizing that urbanization is closely tied up with the long-run evolution and development of economies and societies, and that all countries have experienced significant shifts over time in the balance of population towards towns and cities, many commentators have hypothesized the existence of a link between migration/urbanization and long-run improvements in living standards.

Some simply note the existence of a strong *association* between urbanization and growth. Thus: 'No country in the industrial age has ever achieved significant economic growth without urbanization' (UNFPA, 2007a), and 'Cities . . . are where the vast majority of modern productive activities are concentrated in the developing world and where the vast majority of paid employment opportunities are located'. Others argue for the existence of an important *causal* connection running from urbanization to growth – 'urbanization is increasingly recognized as a process concomitant with economic development that can play a positive role in promoting development' (UN HABITAT, 2006) – and hence reject anti-urbanization policies: 'There is no economic development without urbanization. Attempts to curb urbanization may have an adverse effect on economic development' (Tannerfeldt *et al.*, 2006).

In the next sub-section we look at the reasoning behind these statements.

Why might we expect urbanization to be 'pro-growth'?

Why might urbanization, and hence the rural-urban migration which is responsible for a sizeable part of it, have favourable effects on economic growth? Several possible reasons can be suggested.

Impact on urban unit labour costs

In-migration to urban areas provides industry with a plentiful supply of relatively cheap, often non-union, labour. In addition, although in-migrants can expect to earn appreciably more than they did in the countryside, their presence has the effect, by increasing the supply of labour in towns, of moderating the rate of increase of urban wage rates. Both of these effects can act as a stimulus to investment and production.

More efficient allocation of labour:

The movement of labour to towns permits a more efficient allocation of a nation's labour, and hence increased output and growth rates, for several reasons:

■ *Switching labour from farm to non-farm employment (in the manufacturing or service sector) can accelerate growth because of the greater productivity of labour* in the latter. As was argued in Chapter 4 – using a production-function approach to the analysis of growth – such switching increases the 'effective size' of the labour force, hence increasing total output (GDP) and growth rates.

■ *Employment opportunities are very much more diverse* in towns than in the countryside, permitting a better match of workers' skills and credentials to job requirements (as well as generating psychic gains from greater employee satisfaction).

■ *The level of activity of the labour force is usually higher in urban areas.* Since enforced idleness is less prevalent in towns than in the countryside, and since the participation rate of female labour in formal employment tends to be higher in towns than in the countryside (in part because of the smaller size of urban families), spatial reallocation of labour via migration permits a fuller use of the labour force.

More efficient production systems

Agglomeration economies   Agglomeration economies (the cost advantages that accrue, because of factors associated with proximity and concentration, to firms clustering together) are much more likely to arise in urban areas, where production is concentrated spatially, than in the countryside where production units tend to be widely scattered and isolated. Lower transport costs (stemming from proximity to markets and suppliers), more efficient and cheaper communications (since shorter range), reduced transaction costs because of the easier recruitment of labour and the more accurate matching of workers to jobs, and the more rapid diffusion of ideas and know-how, all constitute potential agglomeration benefits available in town but not in rural areas. Their creation is encouraged by rural–urban migration. In addition, 'economies of scope' may arise because of the enhanced opportunities offered to firms in urban areas to engage in activities complementary to those of other firms. These considerations give cities a major advantage in the production of goods and services by reducing costs, supporting innovation and fostering synergies among different economic sectors.

Economies of scale   A further source of enhanced efficiency arising from locating production facilities in urban areas, with their large product and labour markets, are the economies of scale which characterize the production functions of many technologies. Interacting with, and combined with, agglomeration economies, scale economies can have a major impact on the dynamism of an urban area.

Improved earnings improve the 'quality' of the migrant labour force

Wage rates, and earnings, tend to be higher in urban areas than in rural areas for several reasons – the higher productivity of labour in formal-sector urban occupations than in many rural occupations, the greater impact of trade-union pressure for higher wage rates in towns than in the rural areas and, in countries in which minimum wage legislation is in place, the greater impact of such legislation in towns than in villages (since it often does not apply to rural occupations and, where it does, because of the much greater practicability of policing employers' compliance in towns). These advantages of higher earnings, both for the present welfare of the employed workers and – because of the effect on labour quality – for future growth have to be set against the impact of migrant workers in keeping labour costs *down* and so making life harder for existing employed workers but probably facilitating future growth in employment and income. From the viewpoint of economic growth, it may be a matter of weighing higher quality against lower price.

For many incoming workers, despite the higher cost of living in urban areas, and the fact that they may be forced, at least initially, to take up less-well-paid urban jobs, migration permits a net improvement in their standard of living compared with their rural, pre-migration situation. As a result, 'urban poverty rates are, overall, lower than those in rural areas; the transfer of population from rural to urban areas actually helps to reduce national poverty rates' (UNFPA, 2007a, ch. 3).

Increased real incomes may be used to improve diet (which will have a beneficial effect on the overall physical 'quality' of the labour force), and to benefit from the proximity of superior, and usually cheaper, urban education/training and healthcare facilities, which will again improve the quality of the migrant labour force.

Region	Infant Mortality*		Child Mortality**	
	Rural	**Urban**	**Rural**	**Urban**
North Africa	73.8	45.8	88.5	50.3
Sub-Saharan Africa	101.7	81.0	153.6	122.0
South-East Asia	49.7	30.4	60.6	36.8
South, Central, West Asia	69.7	54.2	84.6	62.2
Latin America	63.3	46.9	80.7	57.0
TOTAL	**82.8**	**63.7**	**115.9**	**87.8**

TABLE 14.5 Infant and child mortality, rural and urban areas, by region
* deaths under 1 year per 1000 live births; ** deaths under 5 years per 1000 live births.
Source: Montgomerie, M.R. (2003) (Table 4–6). (Based on USAID Demographic and Health Studies – DHS – conducted over 1980s and 1990s).

Future workers, now children, will also benefit from these advantages. The improved income-earning capacity of migrants (including women – see below) in towns compared with the situation in the countryside, provides additional household income some of which will often be earmarked for spending on childrens' health and education with beneficial consequences for the future 'quality' of the labour force, and hence of future productivity and output. Evidence of this favourable effect is to be found in the dramatic comparative figures for town and country on child health. While it might be expected that the squalid, often insanitary, 'close proximity' conditions experienced by the many in-migrants forced to live in slum areas (discussed below) would lead to greater risks to children from communicable diseases in towns than in villages, experience suggests that the opposite is the case. As the figures in Table 14.5 show, in the 1980s and 1990s infant and child mortality were typically *significantly lower* in urban areas than in rural areas in all five regional groupings of developing countries used in the table. This is presumably attributable to the superior healthcare available for children in urban areas.

Beneficial gender effects

The advantages of a move to the town are likely to be particularly important for *women* migrants, who tend to be particularly disadvantaged in the rural context by traditional restrictions on their activities. In addition to the points made above, certain consequences of the much greater degree of 'inclusion' of women in the towns than in the rural areas have macro-level significance. In towns, the greater freedom from cultural norms, together with the expanded opportunities for, and emphasis on, participation in economic activity, mean that women find a wider range of jobs available to them and achieve higher labour-market-participation levels than in rural areas. Participation in regular waged employment also enhances women's status within the family unit; even involvement in informal enterprise activities, or participation in micro-credit schemes, can make a difference in this context. Enhanced access, for some, to education facilities – women's education in the rural areas often being seen as a matter of very low priority and therefore neglected – reinforces this opening-up of employment opportunities. At the same time, superior healthcare (including reproductive healthcare) improves the health status of those women who are able to obtain it and, as mentioned above, the families for which they are responsible.

Last, but by no means least, the generally *lower fertility* of migrants than of non-migrants will be regarded by many female migrants as a 'personal' benefit. Research results indicate that, in all developing-country regions, the fertility of women is significantly lower in urban areas than in rural areas, and that rural–urban migrants have *lower fertility rates* than rural non-migrants. Moreover, this reduction in fertility has important favourable effects on average-income growth at the macro level through its restraining effect on population growth. In this respect the biggest differences are those observed in Latin America (with rural women having, on average, 2.1 more children than urban women) and sub-Saharan Africa (where the figure is 1.4 more children).

It is possible, indeed probable, that this important difference arises, in part, because of a *self-selection* process whereby migrants come from groups which, in terms of age, level of education, marital status and family-size preferences, are already (that is, before migration) predisposed towards lower than average fertility. They will carry this over into their urban life. It is also probable that a *disruption* process is at work – such that plans for rearing children are disrupted by the family dislocation caused by the move to town. It may be that, in time, some families will 'catch up', but, since not all will, the overall effect is likely to be a fall in *de facto* fertility. However, there is ample evidence to support the view that at least as important as these two effects is an *adaptation* process which leads migrants to adopt the social norms, in particular the lower fertility characteristic, of other urban dwellers (White *et al.*, 1995; Hervitz, 1985).

One further advantage stemming from the reduction in fertility mentioned above is that migrant families will have, on average, fewer children competing for funding for education and healthcare and should hence be able to spend more per child. This should reinforce the improvement in the 'quality' of the labour force referred to above. Taking all developing countries together, it is estimated that children aged 0–14 years comprise 39 per cent of the urban population against 45 per cent in rural areas. (Montgomerie *et al.*, 2003).

Increased savings and investment

Over and above what might be termed investment in human capital – in personal health and education – in-migrants to towns are likely to be able to afford, in time, to allocate some of their incomes to small-scale saving and investment activities, so raising the levels of these aggregates and promoting further income growth.

Improvement in the attitudes and motivation of the labour force

By fostering 'modernizing' attitudes towards the possibilities of economic advance at the personal and the national level, and by modifying the restrictive traditional attitudes towards the role and status of women and the work they may undertake, 'the urban transition is having an enormous impact on ideas, values and beliefs' (UNFPA, 2007a).

Intangible benefits

Despite the apparent horrors of many – some would say most – of the features of slum life, there is ample evidence that, on balance, migrant slum-dwellers do not regard their move to town as a mistake. Nowhere, other than in a few declining 'failed towns' that have lost their reason for existence (such as several on the Zambian copper belt), is there a notable move to desert the cities for the countryside (*counter-urbanization*). It is true that some migrants 'burn their boats' when coming to the city and would find it difficult to make their way back into the rural society, but this is not relevant for the many who show no desire to leave the cities, or to the large numbers of *circular* migrants who do return to village life for months at a time, but always with the intention of reverting to the city in due course. Surveys of slum dwellers have in fact typically found that 'migrants generally express a preference for the city over the rural life they left behind' (White and Lindstrom, 2005). It is also likely that, for many migrants, the move to the town will permit a much enhanced and more varied social life, free from the often stultifying boredom of rural life. These improvements in their situation are valuable in themselves – representing increased 'psychic' income. They may even go along with improved performance of the migrants in the labour force.

Some evidence on the direction of causation

The connection between urbanization and economic growth seems intuitively obvious. There is no evidence available to show that any country has achieved sustained improvement in its living standards, and certainly not full 'developed' status, without also achieving fairly high levels of urbanization. But what is the direction of causation? Is urbanization a key, independent catalyst of growth, or do cities grow because countries are prospering and their increasingly affluent populations prefer to spend their rising incomes on urban living, property, and investment? It is certainly true that even rich countries that depend heavily on 'non-urban' products, such as minerals or agricultural output, for example Australia and New Zealand, are, as the figures in Appendix 14.1 (available on the Online Learning Centre) show, heavily urbanized. Similarly, high-income, oil-rich countries, much of whose exports come from rural parts of their surface, are all highly urbanized – even Norway whose oil comes from the ultimate non-urban location – under the North Sea.

A strong case can be made for the view that, in most countries, not only do cities have special qualities which enable them to *generate* growth but, without urbanization, growth might not take place at all. For this large majority of developing countries, it seems likely that urbanization is a *necessary* condition for long-run economic growth.

Cross-sectional statistical evidence points to the existence of a positive association between the level of urbanization and per capita income. The distribution of observations in the scatter diagram in Figure 14.3 (which covers 135 countries, developed, developing and 'transition') suggests that these variables (with income here measured as GNI per head) are, indeed, positively related, though in a non-linear way, such that, as the proportion of the population living in towns and cities increases, per capita income increases at an increasing rate.[7]

At the level of the individual firm, too, studies confirm the existence of a strong relationship between urban location and growth – such that 'productivity rises with city size, so much so that a typical firm will see its productivity climb 5 to 10 per cent if city size and the scale of local industry double.' . . . and 'Evidence from Brazil and the Republic of Korea shows [that] if a plant moves from a location shared by 1000 workers employed in the same industry to one with 10 000 such workers, output will increase an average of 15 per cent, largely because the pool of specialized workers and inputs deepens' (World Bank, 2000, *WDR*, 1999/2000, ch. 6, pp. 126–7).

---

[7] Let us suppose that the cross-sectional picture set out in Figure 14.3, which is, in effect, a snapshot of the situation taken *at a given moment in time*, can be taken to represent a *process occurring over time*, and might thus be used to predict future changes in urbanization levels. If this is, in the event, not so – because the underlying relationship between income and urbanization changes over time (for instance, because, for some reason, the urbanization process is speeding up), the assumption will *not* be valid, and the future path of urbanization may deviate from that suggested by the figure.

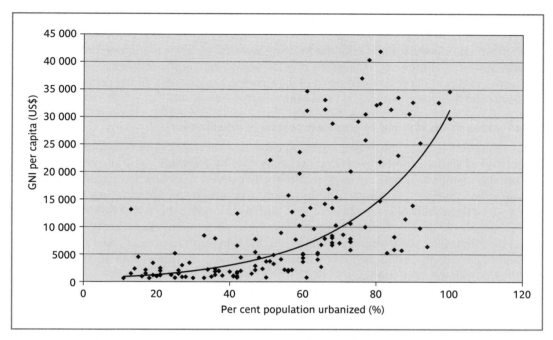

FIGURE 14.3 Urban population as a percentage of total population (in 2007) and per capita GNI (US$*: in 2005) for 135 countries

* A purchasing-power-parity (PPP) measure is used.

Source: Based on data in UNFPA (2008).

Urbanization without growth

Urbanization may be a necessary condition for growth but this does not make it a sufficient condition. Under certain circumstances it is perfectly possible to have rural–urban migration *without* additional growth – especially where the incentives to migrate are provided by the government and do not correspond to genuine economic opportunities. (This point is developed farther, with respect to urbanization without growth in Africa, in Appendix 14.1, which is available on the Online Learning Centre.)

The anti-growth potential of rural–urban migration and urban growth

Thus far in our discussion of the impact of urbanization we have focused on the potentially favourable effects. However there is considerable disquiet regarding the impact of urbanization, to the point at which a majority of developing-country governments have taken action to curb it. In most cases the anti-migration measures have not been set in the context of a coherent growth model or strategy. However, the key concern appears to be that urban populations may rise so rapidly that they give rise to widespread, intractable unemployment which may interact with serious degradation of the urban environment to produce unmanageable social problems.

Unemployment

The message of the Todaro model was that the lure of relatively well-paying jobs would lead to 'excessive' flows of labour to the urban areas, and increasing urban unemployment rates.

In fact, urban numbers are now rising so rapidly that the rate of new job creation in the urban areas lags well behind the rate required to employ all job seekers, or even to hold unemployment rates steady. In addition to being wasteful in terms of forgone production, unemployment is distressing, and after a time demoralizing, for the individual job-seeker. It is also undesirable from a social point of view, being associated with the decay of social cohesion and the rise of anti-social behaviour.

Deterioration in the physical environment caused by urbanization

For many commentators the growth of urban areas in most developing countries means the growth of *slums* – sometimes known as 'shanty towns', '*favelas*', or, more decorously, 'informal settlements'. These are to be found in city centres, in peri-urban locations, and in inter-urban corridors. In some cases they assume enormous proportions, hosting several hundreds of thousands of residents. Mumbai, with a total population of between 14 and 18 million people, is estimated to have some seven to nine million slum dwellers of whom upwards of 600 000 live in one area – Dharavi, 'the biggest slum in Asia'. And 60 per cent of Nairobi's residents live in the Kibera slum which houses anywhere from 600 000 to 1 200 000 residents (*Economist*, 3/5/2007).

Slums frequently comprise a 'complex mix of agriculture, cottage industry and residential use . . . often [involve] waste dumping and extraction of construction materials', and in some cases 'lie outside the geographical area of responsibility of local authorities' (Tacoli, 2008). They are characterized by wretched living conditions – inadequate access to drinking water and pollution of existing supplies – sometimes by toxic industrial chemicals, inadequate or non-existent sewerage facilities and solid-waste-disposal arrangements, lack of access to electricity supplies, severe air pollution (with concentrations of carbon monoxide, lead or suspended particulate matter greatly exceeding WHO safety limits), and serious congestion and overcrowding. Given that security of tenure is a rarity, few of the inhabitants have any incentive to improve their properties. Also, slums very often suffer from neglect, sometimes total, by city authorities with regard to provision of healthcare, education and other services.

Most slums – around 90 per cent – are located in the developing world. South Asia has the largest share, followed by Eastern Asia, sub-Saharan Africa and Latin America. China and India together have 37 per cent of the world's slums. In many parts of the developing world, most urban dwellers live in slums. In sub-Saharan Africa, where the slum population almost doubled in the 15 years from 1990 to 2005 to reach nearly 200 million, urbanization has become virtually synonymous with slum growth. As can be seen from Table 14.6, 72 per cent of the region's urban population lives in slum conditions. The overall figure for developing countries is 43 per cent.

Not unexpectedly, slum areas have a high incidence of acute *poverty*, and in many of the poorest developing countries the ratio of urban poor to total urban population is rising rapidly. It is estimated by the World Bank (2008a) that in 2007 around 30 per cent of all the world's poor were living in urban areas, this figure being expected to climb to 40 per cent by 2020, and to 50 per cent by 2035.

These conditions can lead to rapid environmental deterioration, serious health problems, and a feeling of hopelessness – resulting in the emergence of major problems with crime and child delinquency.

Given the prevalence of slums in cities in the developing world it is not surprising that, despite their making up the large majority of the world's urban areas, **no** cities in developing

Region	Percentage of urban population living in slums	Growth rate of slum population (% per annum)
North Africa	28	−0.15
Sub-Saharan Africa	72	4.53
South Asia	34*	2.20
East Asia	36	2.28
East Asia excluding China	25	1.76
Latin America & Caribbean	32	1.28
West Asia	33	2.71
South-East Asia	28	1.34
Oceania	24	3.24
DEVELOPING COUNTRIES	43	na

TABLE 14.6 Slums in developing countries: growth rate of slum populations and percentage of urban population inhabiting slums in 2005 – by region
* South Central Asia. na Not available.
Source: UN Habitat (2003) and UNFPA (2008).

countries make it into the 'top 40' in the 'liveability' rankings – which are based on around 40 physical and social amenity factors – for major cities worldwide.[8]

Slums and development

So what is the relevance of all this to development, especially given that slums are no new thing? They have long been with us – a much-discussed problem in eighteenth-century England – and in essence have not changed much. '*The difference today is one of scale.* Slum dwellers of the new millennium are no longer a few thousand in a few cities of a rapidly industrializing continent. [Europe] They include one out of every three city dwellers, a billion people, a sixth of the world's population' (UNFPA, 2008). And their numbers are growing rapidly – projected to reach 2 billion by 2040. In many locations they are swamping local authorities' capacity to improve the basic infrastructure and to provide essential services (Cohen, 2006). As a result, orderly expansion of enterprise activity is threatened by physical constraints on the one hand, and by antisocial activity on the other. Nowhere are these problems more acute than in the '**megacities**' – a megacity being an urban area with 10 million or more inhabitants. In 2005 there were 20 megacities and this figure is expected to rise to 22 by 2015, with 17 of these in developing countries. By that time their combined population will be around 360 millions.

Slums, megacities and the 'doomsday' scenario

The preceding paragraphs paint a worrying picture of the magnitude of the slum problems currently facing many rapidly growing urban areas. Even more extreme situations are predicted by alarmist 'futurists' if private enterprise activity and government initiatives for the slums fail to deliver at least the minimum acceptable numbers of jobs. Todaro's pessimistic

[8] Compiled by the Economist Intelligence Unit.

estimates of urban unemployment levels might be multiplied several times as intensified 'push' factors (in particular climate change, the associated degradation of agricultural land, and armed conflicts) accelerate the inflow of rural–urban migrants – for whom there are not, and cannot be, enough jobs since the speed of urban expansion significantly exceeds any feasible rate of job creation.

The worst fears of the policy-makers regarding the outcome of such a situation are summed up in various 'doomsday scenarios', usually set in megacities. Typically, large areas of these cities are seen slipping into an abyss of unemployment, poverty and 'social exclusion' so deep that there is no way back. In many vast slums 'A point of no return is reached when a reserve army waiting to be incorporated into the labour process becomes stigmatized as a permanently redundant mass, an excessive burden that cannot be included now or in the future, in economy and society.' Slums are seen as becoming centres of 'resistance' to civilized life, bases from which 'desperate masses', 'excluded populations', the 'dispossessed', the 'criminal syndicates', the 'urban terrorists', wage permanent war on the rest of society (Breman, quoted in Davis, 2006).

A less apocalyptic view

In fact, many analysts foresee a less apocalyptic future for the great cities of the developing world. They expect the future expansion of the largest urban areas, in particular the megacities, to be a more modest affair than some have predicted. This is partly because of the changing demographic scene in the larger cities themselves and partly because of anticipated changes in the dynamics overall of urban development.

To look first at large-city demographics: rates of urban growth have been falling fairly steadily in most parts of the world since the 1950s as is clearly indicated by Figure 14.2. Of the megacities in particular, only six (out of twenty) have grown at over 3 per cent per annum since the 1970s, and of these only Dhaka and Lagos are now forecast to grow at over 3 per cent per annum in the years to 2017. A further six megacities are expected to grow by less than 1 per cent per annum. Moreover, 'although the number of very large urban agglomerations is expected to continue to rise, they still account for a relatively small fraction of the world's total population or even the world's total urban population' (Cohen, 2006, p. 72). While still worrying, these figures are less dramatic than many earlier projections suggested.

These more modest growth figures for the larger cities, as well as reflecting a significant slowing of natural increase in the urban areas, support the expectation of a natural decline in city growth rates as city size increases – caused by the emergence of countervailing pressures tending to prevent unlimited growth of cities.

That countervailing pressures of some sort are already at work in the largest cities is evidenced by the fact that in many of them – notably Buenos Aires, Kolkata, Mexico City, São Paulo and Seoul – out-migration now actually exceeds in-migration. Precisely why this is so is still a matter for conjecture, but it seems very likely that *increasing external diseconomies in the urban areas*, in the form of rising congestion costs, pollution costs, infrastructure costs, and construction costs (associated with the increasing cost of urban land), are causing expansion of economic activity in some of the largest urban areas to cease, even move into reverse, with resources flowing outwards to cheaper operating environments in the smaller towns, and even back into the countryside. This interpretation of what is happening is consistent with a further demographic characteristic of many developing countries, the expansion of the smaller towns and cities (that is those with less than 500 000 population). More than half of all urban dwellers in developing countries currently live in such settlements, and they are expected to account for a large slice of urban growth in the future.

These pressures tending to discourage population growth in the largest cities may well be reinforced in the future as advances in computing and telecommunications technologies, production technologies and transportation technologies, permit the spatial fragmentation of economic activity without loss of efficiency – though 'working from home', as practised in developed economies, is still a long way away for most workers in developing countries.

Potential benefits and costs in rural areas

When we are examining the overall social and economic impact of rural–urban migration and urbanization on developing-country economies, it is necessary to consider the impact of the outflow of population on output and productivity in the rural 'source' regions. What effect does the outflow of labour have on output and productivity in the rural areas? And what are the social costs and benefits resulting from the outflow of people?

In fact, the impact of rural–urban migration on rural areas is ambiguous. The outflow of population can have either beneficial or harmful effects on rural areas – depending on the specific circumstances of the case.

Benefits

Remittances

An important result of the flow of migrants to the towns is the reverse flow of financial remittances. These may be used to improve consumption levels and living standards of those remaining in the countryside, may be ploughed back into education and other productive investments, or may be used to provide a source of rural credit where none is currently available. In some cases they may be devoted to construction of residential property, or productive assets, to be used by the remitter on his eventual return from the urban area (Deshingkar, 2006).

The magnitude of remittance flows in some developing countries is very significant. In Asia urban-to-rural remittances have been found to add significantly to the resources at the disposal of rural households. Particularly striking is the situation in China where the Ministry of Agriculture estimates that in 2004 remittances were almost as large as earnings from agriculture (Deshingkar, 2006). A further study suggests that, for Chinese provinces with high rural–urban migrant flows, remittances add 30 to 40 per cent to rural incomes (Wang, 2004). 'In India, remittances account for about one-third of annual incomes of poor and landless households, while in Bangladesh the Coalition for the Urban Poor estimated that migrants in Dhaka send up to 60 per cent of their incomes to relatives at home' (Deshingkar, 2006). 'These figures are staggering, and, although they should be treated with some caution because of the difficulties in obtaining reliable and comparable information, they certainly suggest that migration and the consequent income diversification are not just important but crucial for a growing number of rural households' (Tacoli, 2008, p. 8).

Possible increase in wage rates

The movement of labour from countryside to town may serve to tighten the labour market in the source region. However, this depends very much on the specific circumstances of the case; a contrary scenario is set out later in this chapter.

Increased demand for cash crops

The growth of cash demand for agricultural output by the burgeoning urban population will reinforce commercialization of agriculture and increase the incomes of many of those remaining in agriculture.

Reduced consumption in countryside

Depending on the current status of the rural labour market, internal migration to the city may improve conditions in the countryside by removing surplus (i.e., zero-productivity) labour, so cutting rural consumption without reducing rural production. (Naturally, this outcome hinges on the precise conditions prevailing in agriculture at the time; a contrary scenario is easily constructed – as is indicated below.)

Increased investment . . .

Out-migration from the countryside may also, where property ownership structures permit, lead to the consolidation of small, rented farms into larger, privately owned blocks. While this is a problem from the point of view of the displaced population, it may nevertheless bring benefits for others. Specifically, it may favour the kind of long-term investment in productivity-improving innovations by the proprietors which the displaced tenant farmers could not afford or were not inclined to make if their tenure were not secure, so that they could not be certain of reaping the full benefit from such investment. (The logic underlying unwillingness to upgrade someone else's asset reappears in modern guise in the much-quoted observation by Larry Summers, former President of Harvard University, that 'In the history of the world, no one has ever washed a rented car'.)

Costs

. . . or falling incomes and declining economic activity?

However, depending on the precise conditions prevailing in the rural labour market, the favourable outcomes for employment and incomes predicted above in the rural areas may not eventuate. Migration *can* have seriously adverse consequences for those remaining at home. In a downbeat scenario, migration leads to the loss of the labour, the income and the expenditures of the migrants. If the skills of migrating workers cannot be replaced, local agriculture may decline; family and community structures may decay through lack of funds; and those left behind, usually women and children, may face a future of poverty, bereft of development prospects.

One formal model incorporating elements of this scenario makes use of the concepts of *cumulative causation* and *backwash*. **Gunnar Myrdal**, a noted sceptic regarding the ability of the market to self-correct, argued that, far from being ironed out by migration of labour, regional disparities in wage rates and levels of activity tend to persist and, indeed, to reinforce themselves. Myrdal's (1968) theory of 'cumulative causation' as applied to the rural–urban scenario suggests that denuding the countryside of labour will go along with an increasing concentration of capital and entrepreneurship in the urban areas, leading to accelerating decline in the rural areas, and the opposite in the urban areas. As a result, marginal productivities of resources will *diverge*, rather than converge. 'Backwash effects' will cause wage rates to fall in the rural areas and rise in the towns, as part of a cumulative process which market forces will not correct. Thus, once the process begins, there is no self-equilibrating mechanism which will automatically, and quickly, restore parity between the rural and the urban areas.

Income distribution economy-wide

Income distribution is likely to shift sharply in favour of urban areas and against rural areas in the early phases of the urbanization/industrialization process, as urban income growth outstrips rural income growth by a sizeable margin. While the urban population is a minority and rural labour is not 'scarce', this will probably mean a rise in overall inequality. Thus China's Gini coefficient rose from 0.25 at the beginning of the economic reforms (say, in 1978) to around 0.41 in 2006 (Dollar, 2007). (A rise in inequality is *one* of the possible distribution effects of 'modern-sector-enlargement growth' in Fields' analysis, as expounded in Chapter 10. If it is true that China has left the 'unlimited labour' phase since the late 1990s, it would seem likely from Fields' reasoning that its Gini coefficient will henceforth be moving downward.)

Summary conclusions and policy implications

- In this chapter we have documented the very rapid growth of urban populations in the developing world over the twentieth century, and have noted that this process is expected to continue well into the current century, with a further 3 billion people added by 2050.

- Rural populations, in contrast, seem likely to stagnate, or even decline, as the process of rural–urban migration continues to be responsible for a significant proportion of the growth of urban numbers.

- The migration process has been driven by both 'pull' factors attracting rural dwellers to the towns and cities (notably higher wage levels; the opportunity to diversify the income sources and asset structures of rural households; improved access to education, health and other public services; and superior social amenities), and 'push' factors driving them from the villages (notably unemployment, environmental degradation, civil conflict and, in some countries, government policies embodying 'urban bias' – at the expense of agriculture and rural enterprise in general).

- The possible economic and social effects of continuing, massive, urban growth are matters of great concern to the governments of many developing countries, presenting them with an apparent policy dilemma. On the one hand, there is ample evidence to support the view that urbanization and economic growth go hand-in-hand. On the other, further expansion of cities leaves open the possibility that major problems – such as mass unemployment, further deterioration of living conditions in already slum-ridden urban areas, growing criminality, and social disorder – will cripple the urban areas, extinguishing their potential as growth poles and, in the worst-case scenario, leading to a complete loss of control of urban development. This may come about if the deteriorating situation is not tackled by the city authorities as a matter of priority. What policy measures might be suggested?

- It seems clear that the appropriate policy response is one which eschews the two extreme approaches noted in this chapter. 'Urban bias' of the kind which neglects the rural sector and encourages villagers to move to town to take advantage of 'distorted incentives' and subsidies unrelated to genuine economic opportunities, can result in rapid urbanization *without* economic growth (as discussed in Appendix 14.2 on the Online Learning Centre). This is probably the worst of all possible worlds as it brings with it the problems of urban growth without the economic growth needed to finance their amelioration.

▶

- At the same time, policies based on a fear of the possible adverse consequences of urbanization so strong that resources are pushed into the countryside irrespective of how much, or how little, economic return this yields, are also counterproductive. Where pro-rural measures are market-led and encourage the expansion of viable enterprise activities in the countryside, they stand a good chance of inducing some rural dwellers to remain in the villages and of moderating rural–urban migration levels. On the other hand, where the measures are merely an indiscriminate defensive reaction to urbanization, they may waste resources and do little to curb migration. It seems likely that many of the schemes aimed at stemming migration currently in place in around 100 developing countries are of the latter kind.

- So, what policy initiatives may be both *efficient* in terms of resource allocation, and *equitable* in that they do not unfairly penalize one group – urban dwellers or rural dwellers – in order to favour the other? The following might be considered.

  1 As a first step, **abandon measures that seek to deter people from migrating** to urban areas by, in effect, bribing them to stay in the countryside with resource-wasting 'make-work' schemes, or by imposing physical bans or restrictions on their movement, or by making living conditions in town difficult for them (through, for instance, denying them access to welfare benefits available to non-migrants).

  2 **Improve**, as far as is practicable, **conditions in the slums** – especially with regard to factors directly affecting the health of residents. Improved access to clean water and to effective sewerage systems are urgent priorities from a humanitarian standpoint and have the beneficial effect of improving the health, and thus the productivity, of the labour force.[9] Longer-term economic pay-offs are also available on investment by local authorities for improving access to education and for promoting gender equality. Given that many urban dwellers, especially in-migrants, remit funds to relatives in the countryside, improving the economic lot of the former is likely to have a directly favourable impact on conditions in the countryside by increasing the capacity to remit.

  3 **Support informal-sector enterprise** in general, by such relatively inexpensive measures as: (i) enabling slum dwellers to acquire a secure, formal title to their properties – so giving them collateral against which they may borrow to start a business (De Soto, 2000); (ii) encouraging the development of micro-enterprise by deregulating its operations (by, for instance, dropping any requirement that micro-enterprises require to purchase a permit if they are to operate); and (iii) promoting the development of micro-credit schemes by removing unnecessary counterproductive restrictions on their activities (for example, bans on borrowing by such schemes from outside sources). These measures will, once again, have favourable, if indirect, implications for rural dwellers by enhancing the capacity of in-migrants to remit funds back to their relatives in the villages.

  4 **Encourage** economic activity, and improve conditions in **the smaller urban centres**. This can be justified in terms *both* of the decentralization of urban economic activity (recognizing the importance of the 'countervailing pressures' mentioned earlier) *and* of the legitimate claims of smaller urban centres relative to those of the larger urban centres.

▶

---

[9] The Karachi 'civil society' low-cost sewerage scheme outlined in Chapter 8 might be a model.

▶
Decentralization is being hampered by the lack of capacity of the administrations of smaller urban centres to play their part in encouraging local economic activity: their capabilities for planning and implementation can be exceedingly weak. Yet the worldwide process of decentralizing governmental powers is heaping greater responsibility on them. As the population of smaller cities increases, their thin managerial and planning capacities come under mounting stress. New ways will have to be found to equip them to plan ahead for expansion, to use their resources sustainably and to deliver essential services'.

(UNFPA, 2008, Introduction)

Equally, at the welfare level, administration of smaller urban centres is very weak: 'A study by the US National Academy of Sciences of over 90 countries found that residents of smaller cities tended to have higher incidence of poverty and poorer provision of piped water, electricity, waste disposal and schools than was the case in the medium-sized and large cities' (National Research Council, 2003). Clearly, '. . . there are good reasons for putting smaller cities more centrally on the development agenda' (Cohen, 2006, p. 73).

5 As a counterpart policy, **invest in rural areas where there is a good economic case for support**. This will take some pressure off the urban areas – but should not be done in a way which diverts resources from more productive efforts in towns. Possible targets for funding include: (i) *Improving rural infrastructure* in order to increase productivity in agriculture; and (ii) *Encouraging the adoption of good husbandry* practices in agriculture especially with regard to ensuring sustainability of land resources (investing in reversing degradation of land will provide a dual pay-off – by stemming enforced abandonment of farming, and by increasing rates of return in agriculture so improving living standards in the countryside and discouraging migration to urban areas); (iii) *Making the process of remitting funds* to the rural areas – which, at present, can cause problems for poor urban-dwellers – *easier, speedier, and more secure.*

The ultimate destiny of the great urban centres of the developing world is not yet decided. Policy measures assisting the urban poor to engage in productive economic activity and to improve their own living conditions can steer the cities towards a prosperous future as centres of economic growth. Continued reliance on negative measures, in particular fruitless attempts to deter people from migrating to urban areas, waste resources now – and steadily increase the probability that megacities will become unmanageable centres of strife and despair.

Questions for discussion

14.1 Many developing countries have pressed, in WTO negotiations, for massive cuts in the protection afforded domestic agriculture by both the US and the EU. If such protection were removed what impact would you expect this to have on the urbanization process in the developing world?

14.2   Given that agglomeration economies and economies of scale reduce production costs in urban locations, what countervailing pressures prevent all economic activity in a given developing country from concentrating in just one single city?

14.3   Assess the view that the potential costs of the emergence of slum-filled 'megacities' across the developing world are so enormous that rigorous control of further rural-to-urban migration should be introduced as a priority matter.

14.4   Urban growth and economic growth are usually found to be positively related. However, in sub-Saharan Africa 'urbanization without growth' is common. Why might this be happening – and what are the possible consequences?

14.5   Why might government policies aimed at creating jobs in urban areas have the paradoxical effect of actually *increasing* urban unemployment rates?

14.6   What desirable 'gender effects' have been claimed to result from rural–urban migration?

14.7   What role might 'social capital' play in the rural–urban migration process?

14.8   Why is the 'second wave' of urbanization now being experienced in the developing world moving at a much faster pace than did the 'first wave' of urbanization in Europe and North America?

Additional reading and web resources

Economist, 3/5/2007, Special Report on 'Cities'.

Chandler, T. (1987) *Four Thousand Years of Urban Growth: A Historical Census*, St. David's University Press, Lewiston.

Campbell, Tim and Richard Stren, *Cities Transformed: Demographic Change and its Implications in the Developing World*, World Bank video presentation based on Montgomerie, M.R., R. Stren, B. Cohen and H.E. Reed (eds) (2003) *Cities Transformed: Demographic Change and its Implications in the Developing World*, National Research Council, National Academics Press, Washington, DC, at http://info.worldbank.org/etools/bSPAN/PresentationView.asp?PID=777&EID=393

UNFPA, *State of World Population 2007: Unleashing the Potential of Urban Growth* – video presentation: http://www.unfpa.org/swp/2007/multimedia/index.html

Online
Learning Center

To help you grasp the key concepts of this chapter check out the extra resources posted on the Online Learning Centre at ***www.mcgraw-hill.co.uk/textbooks/huq***

Among other resources, there are two appendices available:

- Appendix 14.1   Urbanization tables
- Appendix 14.2   Urbanization without growth in Africa

CHAPTER 15

Gender and Development

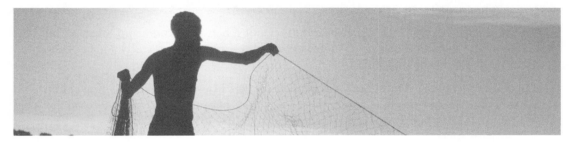

'Societies that discriminate by gender tend to experience less rapid economic growth and poverty reduction than societies that treat males and females more equally.'

'Studies . . . [of] more than 100 developing countries . . . find that measures of gender equality have significant, positive effects on growth and thus on poverty reduction'.

(World Bank)

Ignored until recently, gender issues are now seen to be directly relevant to many of the most important variables in the development equation discussed in this book: education, health, productivity of labour, population growth rates, mobilization of capital, enterprise, governance and, ultimately, economic growth.

Introduction

Discussion of gender issues is a relatively recent addition to the development debate. The publication that started the ball rolling was Ester Boserup's *Women's Role in Economic Development* published in 1970 – though it was nearly two decades later before the subject came to be accepted as 'mainstream', and even now textbook treatment tends to be sketchy and fragmented.

The emergence of gender as a variable worthy of serious consideration in the analysis of development processes can be attributed to the coincidence of two separate, though not unrelated, phenomena. The first was the strengthening of feminist sentiment, and in particular of the feminist focus on the widespread discrimination against women in developing countries (including disregard of women's human rights). This line of analysis was facilitated by, though it did not originate with, the rapid improvement in coverage, reliability and accessibility of data on developing countries – in particular, data broken down by gender. This improvement, which itself reflected the increasing interest in both official and academic circles in development, made possible the penetration of academic analysis into gender-related issues not hitherto identified as important. This led to a growing understanding of the importance of gender in many aspects of the development process. The result of these mutually reinforcing pressures has been widespread official recognition – by the World Bank, the United Nations and many other international agencies, as well as national governments – of the strength of the case for urgent action to promote 'women's participation in development'.[1]

BOX 15.1 TOOLKIT ON GENDER AND DEVELOPMENT

Gender gap. A systematic difference in the values, between women and men, of an important economic variable (such as the average wage rate), usually such as to imply that women are disadvantaged.

The 'missing women'. The shortfall of actual numbers of women in developing countries below demographers' original predictions. This arises because of failure to foresee the very high incidence of premature death of women – in child-birth or because of malnourishment.

Time poverty. Having inadequate time to carry out all the tasks one wishes, or is expected, to undertake.

Voice. Opportunity to express an opinion and to influence others.

Underclass. A group of individuals of particularly low social standing – usually carrying out low-prestige jobs or unemployed, and lacking the influence required to improve their circumstances.

BOX 15.2 ESTER BOSERUP

Ester Boserup, a Danish economist, wrote on agricultural and economic development. Her best-known work is a book on *The Conditions of Agricultural Growth: the Economics of Agrarian Change*, in which she argued that Malthus' fears that population was very likely to outrun food supplies (see Chapter 4 on this) were baseless since population pressure would stimulate favourable changes in agricultural technologies and productivity. Boserup's ground-breaking work, *Women's Role in Economic Development*, stimulated a major debate about the sources and impact of development. Key points here were that: women's crucial contributions to the development process were often overlooked since they were largely unpaid and outside the market; the development process itself – being ostensibly associated with male activities (including almost exclusively male employment in development projects and male involvement with modern technologies) – channelled benefits towards men and led women to be associated with the traditional and backward, and so to lose status.

In the next section summary data are presented on the nature and dimensions of the most important 'gender gaps' – the differences between women and men in their economic status, quality of life, and social standing. This is followed by a brief discussion of the reasons for

---

[1] A summary of current policy initiatives of these, and other, agencies is set out later in this chapter. No attempt is made here to pursue the arcane intricacies of the largely academic debates on 'Women in development versus gender in development', and on 'Efficiency versus empowerment'.

the existence of these gaps. A résumé is then presented of current thinking on the role of gender gaps as a factor influencing the rate of economic growth. It will be seen that the relevance claimed for gender factors is remarkably pervasive and profound, spanning areas as diverse as education, health, labour productivity, population growth, mobilization of investible funds, enterprise, and governance – with consequential broadly based effects on the rate of economic growth. The policy agenda flowing from analysis of the role of gender factors in the development process are summarized in the final section of the chapter.

The nature and dimensions of gender gaps in developing countries

Marked differences between the economic situation, quality of life, and socio-cultural standing of women and those of men, are common in developing countries. In this section key 'gender gaps' are identified and the extent of these differences illustrated.

Economic gaps

In most developing countries *poverty* is being 'feminized': that is, an increasing proportion of those deemed 'poor' is made up of women, and the gap between average male incomes and average female incomes is widening – so much so that some observers see women as 'the new underclass'.

	1990	1998	2005
Africa*	87.7	86.0	82.4
America & Caribbean**	80.2	85.7	87.3
Asia***	74.4	78.8	80.0

TABLE 15.1 Female wage rates as a percentage of male wage rates in developing countries
* Average (unweighted) of ratios for 6 countries.
** Average (unweighted) of ratios for 11 countries.
*** Average (unweighted) of ratios for 20 countries.
Source: ILO (2007).

In general, women work for lower wage rates than men and their employment opportunities are restricted to a narrower range of (usually less attractive) jobs than those open to men. Data on remuneration rates for males and females in a sample of 37 countries are set out in Table 15.1. Given the serious problems attached to constructing internationally comparable wage-rate statistics, the figures in the table should be regarded as indicative rather than precise values. Nevertheless, it is worth noting that, in the large majority (86 per cent) of the developing countries covered by the table, female remuneration rates were below male rates in all three years covered, and that there was no clear evidence of any general improvement in female rates relative to male rates over the 15-year span.

In addition to this, women are much more likely than men to work for no remuneration at all – as 'unpaid family workers'. Data here are patchy, but almost all the figures made available by the World Bank (2007) tend to confirm this. Striking examples among the larger developing countries include *Vietnam* where 50.3 per cent of all female employment is of this kind as against only 21.9 per cent for males, *Pakistan* (46.9 against 16.4 per cent), *Turkey* (49.0 and 8.2 per cent), *Egypt* (19.5 and 8.4 per cent), *Uganda* (40.5 and 10.3 per cent), *Sri Lanka* (20.9 and 4.2 per cent), *Morocco* (52.5 and 21.6 per cent), *Thailand* (35.2 and 16.0 per cent), and – the most unbalanced of all – *Bangladesh*, where a massive 73.2 per cent of all female employment goes unpaid compared with 10.1 per cent for males. Much of this work is in subsistence agriculture, in which many of the lighter tasks, such as weeding, are performed by women – the 'invisible farmers'.[2] Men do perform unpaid work

---

[2] So called by Caroline Sachs (1983).

in the household and in agriculture, but this tends to comprise a much smaller proportion of their 'economic activity'.

For those women who do wish to work for pay, the problem of unemployment looms larger than is the case for men. Again, the data are incomplete, but of the 55 developing countries for which recent data are available no fewer than 41 had higher unemployment rates for female workers than for males (World Bank, *WDR 2007*, p. 65). The figures in Table 15.2 below, although incomplete, tell the same story.

	WORLD			East Asia and Pacific			Europe and Central Asia+			Latin America and Caribbean		
	1980	1990	2004	1980	1990	2004	1980	1990	2004	1980	1990	2004
1. Population												
Female %	49.7	49.7	49.7		48.9	49.1	52.3	51.9	52.1	50.1	50.3	50.6
2. Life-exp at birth (years)												
Male	61	63	65		66	68	63	65	64	62	65	69
Female	65	67	69		60	72	72	73	73	68	71	75
3. Adult literacy (%, age > 15 Years))												
Male					87.2	94.6		97.9	99.2		86.4	91.0
Female					70.1	86.7		94.3	98.7		83.5	89.5
4. Labour force (total)												
Female %	39	40	40	43	44	44		46	45	29	34	40
5. Unemployment												
% Total labour force			5.7*	4.7	2.8	4.4		10.6*	10.6		6.2	9.5
% Female labour force								10.6*	10.7		7.1	11.8
6. Net primary school enrolment rate												
Male		89			98			91				95*
Female		84			93			89				93*
7. Primary school completion (% age group)												
Male					98	99		92	95		85	96
Female					96	97		93	94		89	97
8. Youth literacy rate (% people aged 15–24 yrs.)												
Male					96.9	98.2		99.2	99.3		92.7	96.3
Female					92.8	97.5		97.4	98.4		92.8	97.0
9. Total fertility rate (births per woman)	3.7	3.1	2.6		2.1	2.0		1.6	1.6	4.2	3.2	2.5
10. Maternal mortality (per 100,000)			410*		117			58			194	
11. Parliamentary seats (% women)		11	15		19*	18		8*	12		8	19

TABLE 15.2　Key gender statistics – world and major regions – 1980, 1990 and 2004
+ Excludes high-income countries.
* Year 2000.
Source: World Bank (2006) Table A7 (p. 281).

	Middle East & North Africa			South Asia			Sub-Saharan Africa		
	1980	1990	2004	1980	1990	2004	1980	1990	2004
1. Population									
Female %	49.5	49.4	49.5	48.3	48.4	48.7	50.3	50.3	50.1
2. Life-exp at birth (years)									
Male	57	63	68	54	58	63	47	48	46
Female		66	71	54	59	64	50	51	47
3. Adult literacy (% age > 15 Years)									
Male		64.7			59.5	71.9		61.0	
Female		38.8			33.9	46.4		40.7	
4. Labour force (total)									
Female %	20	23	27	33	31	29	43	43	42
5. Unemployment									
% Total labour force		15.2*	13.6		4.5				
% Female labour force		20.1*			5.0				
6. Net primary school enrolment rate									
Male		88	92	91*	90			51	68
Female		81	87		75	85		44	60
7. Primary school completion (% age group)									
Male		83	89		87	85		55	66
Female		71	86		65	78		47	56
8. Youth literacy rate (% people aged 15–24 yrs.)									
Male		80.0			70.2	82.5		76.2	
Female		59.4			49.9	65.3		60.9	
9. Total fertility rate (births per woman)	6.2	4.8	3.0	5.2	4.1	3.1	6.7	6.2	5.3
10. Maternal mortality (per 100,000)		183			564			921	
11. Parliamentary seats (% women)		4	6		6	9			13

TABLE 15.2 (*continued*)

Quality-of-life gaps

The quality of life of many women in developing countries is markedly inferior to that enjoyed by their male counterparts. This is both a cause and a consequence of the relatively weak economic situation of women. Here we focus on two key areas – health and education.

Nutrition and health: the 'missing women'

Women have a significant inbuilt biological advantage over men in their underlying greater longevity. However, demographic studies indicate that, for women in developing countries, this natural advantage is often seriously eroded by malnourishment (males typically having first claim on a family's dietary resources) and by a high incidence of a variety of life-shortening maladies – especially those associated with pregnancy and child-bearing (again, male family members are usually given priority where expenditures on medical treatment are concerned).

Although life-expectancy has been rising for both sexes in recent years in most, though not all, countries, a significant discrepancy exists between experience in high-income countries, where the gender gap in life expectancy is 6–8 years, and in the developing world where the difference averages only 2–3 years. A.K. Sen (1992) has noted that, in many developing countries especially in South Asia, men actually outnumber women, and he has estimated that, in 1990, more than 100 million women were 'missing' because of avoidable 'excess female mortality'.

Education

A major 'gap' is also evident in education. As the figures in Table 15.2 show, primary-school enrolment ratios in developing countries are generally higher for males than for females, and female literacy rates are correspondingly lower than male rates – notably in South Asia (46.4 against 71.9 per cent in 2004) and sub-Saharan Africa (40.7 against 61 per cent in 1990). In low-income countries 30 per cent of males are illiterate, compared with almost 50 per cent of females.

Socio-cultural-status gaps

For the majority of married women in developing-country families, the importance of their role in family life contrasts sharply with the *low esteem* they enjoy *in the family* and their *lack of decision-making authority* in that context. Women bear most of the responsibility for home-making and for managing the health and education of the children. Yet typically their often crucial contributions to family welfare are not reflected in their status within the family. Rather, the reverse is frequently true, with little importance being attached by the male head of the family to these contributions, and inadequate resources provided from the family budget to finance them.

In the broader social context women are again in a position of inferiority to males in many respects. Their *social mobility* is usually severely limited – in part because of the economic and educational handicaps mentioned above. This is often reinforced by a typically disadvantaged *legal status* so that, for instance, legislation on land rights may rule out ownership of land by women, while mercantile law may dictate that commercial documents and contracts cannot be validated by women – a husband's signature being required to regularize them. In terms of *political power*, women are, in most countries, marginal players. Female representation in parliaments, and in the upper civil service echelons, is almost invariably small. As Table 15.2 indicates, among regions the highest value for the proportion of parliamentary seats held by women in 2004 was 18 per cent for East Asia and the Pacific, and the lowest a negligible 6 per cent in Middle Eastern and North African countries. Only in NGOs, a non-traditional element of civil society, are women generally believed to make a significant contribution to leadership, though data to back up this perception are hard to find.

The causes of gender gaps

The existence, and persistence, of the gender gaps referred to above stem from a complex of interrelated factors. A fundamental cause is the greater value, and higher expectations, placed by many households on sons than on daughters. Promoting the success of male children typically means channelling a disproportionately large share of the family budget into providing *education, nutrition* and *health/medical-care* for boys – to the detriment of the educational attainment and health status of girls.

Exclusion from training and poorer health status, in turn, restrict the range of formal-sector employment opportunities, including government-sector jobs, open to girls, and greatly reduce their 'economic value' to their families. This encourages their diversion into low-grade (sometimes 'sweat-shop') formal employment, or into unpaid and (being outside the market) typically undervalued activities such as cooking, cleaning, collecting firewood and water, agricultural work – and child-rearing. Thus the expectation that the economic returns from investment in male children exceed those from investment in daughters becomes a self-justifying belief, a form of vicious circle.

Even if women attempt to break free from these constraints by seeking to move into independent private-sector activities, accessing credit for investment is likely to prove very difficult. Banks often share the view that rates of return on female enterprise are unlikely to be high. And, of course, lack of legal independence is very often a serious barrier to commercial success.

All of this helps explain the greater incidence of poverty – lack of command over resources – amongst women than amongst men in developing countries.

A further consequence of the diversion of most women away from formal-sector careers – in addition to their relegation to non-formal and domestic employment – is an increased emphasis on child-bearing. As the data in Table 15.2 indicate, in several regions – in particular, sub-Saharan Africa and South Asia – fertility rates, though falling, are still high. The latest World Bank data on age-specific fertility rates for women aged 15–24 years indicate that, even within this youngest decade of their fertile period, for the 40 developing countries for which figures were available, 21 had average rates in excess of 3.0 per women, six had rates in excess of 4.0, and one country, Uganda, had a rate of over 5.0 (World Bank, *WDR* 2007). The combination of early child-bearing and high fertility reinforces the adverse effects on health of malnourishment in childhood and subsequent relative lack of access to healthcare. This further reduces the economic potential of women and significantly increases, during childhood and child-bearing years, female morbidity and mortality rates (which include the high maternal mortality rates documented in Table 15.2) to levels often above male rates, an important cause of Sen's 'missing women' phenomenon mentioned earlier.

Gender gaps and development

A strong case can be made for the view that, over and above the obvious ethical dimension, discrimination against women of the kinds discussed above adversely affects the rate of economic growth in developing countries, and that removing, or reducing the extent of, such discrimination is likely to bring major gains for growth and development. (This is, in fact, a particularly important application of the general argument that discrimination between people in the work they are allowed to do, other than on the criterion of their relative capacity to perform it, is always likely to be economically and socially wasteful). Key specific issues in the gender context run in terms of human-capital formation, and market and institutional discriminatory practices.

Human capital formation and growth: women's education and health

Returns to investment in education and health in developing countries are typically high. Expanding women's education and improving their health status adds *directly* to the stock of *'human capital'*. This leads (as was noted in Chapter 4) to a rise in the growth rate during the phase when additional investment funds are being pumped into these areas and the capital stock is being augmented, which results in a permanent increase in per capita incomes. Additionally, to the extent that enhanced education of women better prepares them for adopting, adapting, and using new technologies, a permanent 'endogenous' increase in the growth rate may be achieved. Given the extent of the current disparities between the educational and health status of men and women, there is plenty of room for 'catch-up' in this context.

Over and above the straightforward favourable impact of human-capital formation referred to in the preceding paragraph, a number of important *indirect* benefits are likely to accrue. Thus:

- Compared with uneducated women, educated women place greater emphasis on, and are more knowledgeable about, the desirability of educating their own children – so extending the expansion of human capital into the next generation;
- Similarly, educated women are likely to be better informed about the importance of good nutrition, hygiene and healthcare for the well-being of their children. This, again, contributes to future human-capital formation and enhances the productivity of the next cohort of workers (Alderman and King 1998);
- An important aspect of development policy in most developing countries is cutting the population growth rate in order to reduce pressure on resources and the environment and to create space for per capita income growth. (The discussion of Malthus and population growth in Chapter 4 is relevant here.) There is a substantial body of evidence indicating that increased investment in women's education is an effective means of reducing population growth rates (see Figure 13.2 in Chapter 13). This works through several mechanisms:

  1 Education and employment of women have the effect of delaying marriage and the start of child-bearing, thus limiting fertility and the size of families. This results in healthier mothers and children, as well as releasing women for further education and employment after child-bearing. Both of these contribute to faster economic growth.
  2 A related point: education, by enhancing women's employment opportunities, increases the opportunity cost of having children since child-bearing and child-rearing usually involve prolonged, or permanent, absence from work. This provides a further incentive to curtail family size.
  3 Fewer children means enhanced availability of family resources per child for education and healthcare, so creating the potential for further capital formation and more rapid average-income growth in the future.
  4 Large families require a great deal of attention. Not only does this debar many mothers, often from a very early age, from education and formal employment, but it may well involve older children in helping to look after the family – so truncating their schooling, with obvious negative effects on human-capital formation.
  5 Educated women tend to be more aware of the benefits of contraception.

- Education and employment enhance women's economic status, which is often reflected in improved status within the family unit. This change not only lets women have their own funds to disburse, but may improve their 'voice', or influence, within the family, in particular with regard to how the family budget is spent – and women are known to be much more likely than men to channel funds towards children's education and healthcare (Hoddinot and Haddad, 1995). 'Increasing household incomes may not translate fully into improved health, education levels and lower fertility – if the income is hijacked by men' (Thomas, 1991). A corollary of this is that the effectiveness of expanded public provision of education and health infrastructure in promoting growth will be increased where women have a say in how household funds are deployed and are able to direct them into using such facilities. (Students of resource-allocation theory will note that the traditional approach, which regarded the household as the basic, homogeneous decision-making unit on family spending, did not take such intra-family distinctions into account.)

All of these mechanisms lead to more rapid growth by, either directly or indirectly, contributing to increasing the rate of human-capital formation and improving the quality of human capital. In many cases they are mutually reinforcing, making possible a break-out from the vicious circle of low per capita incomes, caused by low growth, itself the result of the poor education and health status – which are all that can be afforded because of low per capita incomes and large family size.

Gender relations: access to resources, institutional factors – and growth

Gender relations and gender-based specialization have an important bearing on the pace of economic growth and development through mechanisms other than the education/health/ human-capital nexus. Important among these mechanisms are:

- *Legal and customary restrictions on women's economic rights inhibit enterprise activity.* As noted earlier, in many developing countries women may not own land and are not free to enter into certain kinds of commercial and financial contracts. In agriculture, lack of ownership discourages women from investing in farm improvement. More generally, such restrictions impair women's capacity to access financial assets and to provide collateral against which to raise investment funds. Removing them seems likely to spur enterprise activity. (The introduction of microcredit schemes, discussed in Chapter 19, was, in part, a means of addressing this growth-restricting problem);

- *The customary division of labour in rural areas lacking adequate infrastructure creates 'time poverty'.* Many of the domestic tasks traditionally allocated to women in rural areas become particularly burdensome and time-consuming where infrastructure is lacking, often absorbing more hours than the typical male working day. For instance, fetching water (where there is no public water supply), transporting firewood and produce (where the local road system is not suitable for vehicles), and performing repetitive tasks manually rather than mechanically (where there is no public electricity supply), can absorb a great deal of time and energy, leaving very little of either for education or income-generating activities. Provision of appropriate infrastructure can relax this constraint;

- *Exclusion of women from formal-sector jobs limits earning power.* Many women migrants to towns have difficulty in finding formal-sector employment. This is often because of established patterns of job reservation for males (which may be excused on grounds of protecting women from difficult or strenuous work), or prejudice against employing women, or lack of educational qualifications. This kind of restriction is *prima facie* a barrier to efficient allocation of labour resources, and hence reduces total output. Many women, faced with this situation, are pushed into the low-paid informal sector and, despite often being heads of households, may be unable to afford education and healthcare for their children. The growth benefits to be had from deregulation of the labour market in this context are apparent.

Governance and law

Good governance and the suppression of corruption are important contributors to economic growth. There is some evidence – admittedly as yet by no means conclusive – to suggest that women may be less prone than men to adopt corrupt practices when in power (World Bank, *WDR*, 2001). If this is so, then gender equality may bring with it improved governance and hence faster growth.

Policy on gender and development

International support for gender-based development policies

In recent years several important commitments have been made by major international institutions, and in a number of world forums, to improving the lot of women in developing countries. The growing recognition that such measures are likely to have favourable effects on development has helped bring on-side players in the international arena that might not have been swayed by egalitarian arguments alone, and has added considerable impetus to the introduction of gender-based policies.

Particularly significant have been:

- The designation by the UN of 1976–85 as the *UN International Women's Decade*. This focused official attention on women, and resulted in the establishment of national women's organizations and ministries in many countries. It also brought about the widespread adoption of Women in Development (WID) policies in governments, donor agencies and NGOs;

- The strong statement made by the United Nations International Conference on Population and Development (held in Cairo in 1994) to the effect that 'the empowerment and autonomy of women and the improvement of their political, social, economic and health status is a highly important end in itself. In addition, it is essential for the achievement of sustainable development';

- The focus of the Fourth World Conference on Women: Action for Equality, Development and Peace (reflected in the *Beijing Declaration and Platform for Action*) was the advancement and empowerment of women in relation to women's human rights, women and poverty, and women and decision-making – to be achieved by 'gender mainstreaming' of many policies and programmes;

- The commitment embodied in the *Copenhagen Declaration* (made at the UN-sponsored World Summit for Social Development in 1995) to 'achieving equality and equity between women and men, and to recognizing and enhancing the participation and leadership roles of women in political, civil, economic, social and cultural life and in development';

- The World Bank's enthusiastic support for such policies, notably in its Policy Research Report entitled *'Engendering Development'* (Mason and King, 2001) and in several recent annual *'World Development Reports'*;

- The inclusion in the UN's Millennium Development Goals (MDGs) of the need to 'promote gender equality and empower women';

■ The four-year 'Gender Action Plan', beginning in 2007 and promoted by the World Bank in collaboration with national donors (notably Norway and Germany), designed to 'advance women's economic empowerment in order to promote shared growth [and] . . . gender equality'. The focus of this 'smart-economics' plan is women's empowerment in the economic sectors, most importantly infrastructure (energy, transport, water and sanitation); agriculture; private-sector development and finance.

Specific policies for economic growth through gender-equalization

Our discussion suggests that economic growth and the process of development may be significantly accelerated by the adoption of policy measures which promote more equal rights for women and seek to correct present prejudices. At the most general level, *empowerment of women* – that is, improving the social and political status of women, and giving them more control over their own life choices, especially with regard to education, employment and child-bearing – is seen as a social and ethical necessity, as well as being a particularly effective growth strategy. Empowerment may be promoted in a number of ways many of which are gender-specific, though, as the World Bank has pointed out, some important options may have a 'gender-neutral' *form* while yet favouring women in practice (World Bank, *WDR*, 2007). Specific policy options follow naturally from the discussion above and may be summarized as follows:

■ *Improve girls' education.* Improving girls' primary and secondary education is seen as the most effective way of promoting empowerment. Much has already been done to increase primary-school enrolments and attention is now shifting to secondary education. The next four requirements listed constitute elements of a strategy for improving girls' education.

■ *Build more schools closer to where people live.* The ostensibly gender-neutral policy of building more schools in rural areas turns out, in practice, to help in equalizing opportunities for schooling since girls' enrolment is more affected than boys' by the need to make lengthy trips to school (primarily because of perceived security problems) and since, in any case, female enrolment is currently at a lower level than male enrolment. These favourable effects can be reinforced if cash subsidies are made available to poor families to send, and keep, girls at school.

■ Reinforce the beneficial effects of increased rural school building by *cutting school fees* and increasing the number of *scholarships* for *girls*.

■ *Train more women teachers* and encourage girls to *study maths and science.*

■ *Make selective investments in infrastructure.* Where 'time poverty' is a problem for women – adversely affecting, amongst other things, their ability to take advantage of educational opportunities – appropriate investments in infrastructure can have significant effects. Thus, building roads in rural areas can release girls from hours spent in walking to collect firewood or water and to attend market. Improving public transport has a similar effect. Providing electricity and water supplies can also reduce the time burden on women of routine tasks.

■ *Guarantee reproductive health and rights.* Improving education on contraception and reproductive health in general, and providing improved access to obstetric care in particular, can greatly improve women's health as well as encouraging reduced family size. The improvements in girls' education proposed above can also assist in reducing family size, through delaying marriage by postponing the termination of education (at which point many girls get married) and, in some cases, by further delaying marriage by improving employability of female school-leavers. In addition, delaying marriage reduces the health risks, the diminished decision-making power in the family, and the vulnerability to domestic violence – which are the lot of many women who have large numbers of children.

■ *Improve employment prospects.* Improving women's employment prospects and earnings can have an important favourable impact on family spending on nutrition, health and education – as well as raising women's status in the household. Removing pro-male biases in employment legislation (including occupational segregation), encouraging equal pay, improving work place health and safety regulations (women often being particularly vulnerable to injury in the work-place) and providing government subsidies for child-care services and skills training can all play an important part here. Rather less obvious is the possibility of adopting trade policies aimed at increasing production (and exporting), and hence creating more jobs, in female-intensive occupations (for example, garment manufacturing). It will sometimes conveniently be the case that shifting to *non-discriminatory* trade policies has this effect. All these policy options have been found to narrow male–female wage gaps and increase employment levels of women with favourable effects on their status within their households.

■ *Facilitate women's entrepreneurial activity.* Permitting women to own and inherit assets, and removing legal barriers to their autonomy in enterprise activity, can have favourable effects on both women themselves and the national economy. Encouraging microfinance schemes can help in this direction.[3]

■ *Encourage women to enter government.* Increasing the numbers of women in parliament and in the upper echelons of the civil service is a very direct way to empower women and may also improve the quality of governance.

Summary conclusions

■ The central message of this chapter is that the widespread relegation of women in developing countries to the status of second-class citizens in the economic, social and political spheres has been costly – whether viewed ethically for the intrinsic value of equal treatment or instrumentally for its impact on economic growth.

■ Neglecting women's education and health, and placing barriers in the way of women's enterprise, have condemned them to unnecessarily severe poverty and have depressed their quality of life, as well as adversely affecting the efficiency of resource allocation and cutting growth rates in the developing world.

■ Put more positively, the empowerment of women along the lines outlined above offers the possibility of accelerating rates of economic growth both indirectly, by building-in long-term improvement in the stock of human capital, and directly, by permitting women to play a much more active role in the market.

---

[3] It is worth noting that the Grameen Bank, the original microcredit institution and one of the largest, incorporates in the 'Sixteen Decisions' which all members (male and female) must take, the restriction of family size – and this appears to have a negative impact on fertility.

Redrafting the policy agenda in developing countries to allow for much greater investment in women, and for the transformation of their status, creates a situation in which the 'cost' of correcting a serious social injustice is actually increased economic growth: a 'win-win' outcome.

Questions for discussion

15.1 What are the main 'gender gaps' between men and women in developing countries – with particular reference to their economic situation, quality of life, and socio-cultural standing?

15.2 Would you expect these 'gaps' to be wider – or narrower – in developed countries than in developing countries? Why?

15.3 What difference, if any, does the existence of significant 'gender gaps' in a developing country make to the prospects for economic growth?

15.4 What is meant by the statement that 'poverty is being feminized'? What evidence can you adduce in support of this contention?

15.5 What gender-related policy measures would you recommend for developing countries? Why?

15.6 What arguments might be advanced for, and against, the proposition that economic governance in developing countries would be improved if taken out of the hands of men and handed over to women?

15.7 It is usually assumed that the central aim of private-sector entrepreneurs in the developing world is to increase the profitability of their businesses. Why, then, would they employ relatively poorly qualified men rather than relatively well-qualified women – as women's rights campaigners claim they do?

Additional reading and web resources

The Oxfam journal *Gender & Development*, published three times per year, provides a useful up-to-the-minute overview of the topic together with articles, interviews and book reviews from researchers, academics, policy-makers, and practitioners. Each issue lists recent publications, electronic resources, and organizations in the field.

Inglehart, R. and P. Norris (2003) *Rising Tide: Gender Equality and Cultural Change Around the World*, Cambridge University Press, Cambridge, Mass.

Haddad, W.D. (1990) 'Education and development: evidence for new priorities', *World Bank Discussion Paper No. 95*, Washington DC, pp. 12–15.

Forsythe, N., R. Korzeniewicz, and V. Durrant (2000) 'Gender inequalities and economic growth', *Economic Development and Cultural Change*, **48** (2).

The main World Bank websites on Gender and Development are at: http://web.worldbank.org/WBSITE/EXTERNAL/TOPICS/EXTGENDER/0,,menuPK:336874~pagePK:149018~piPK:149093~theSitePK:336868,00.html (which focuses on the 'Smart Economics' gender equality strategy) and the more general: http://web.worldbank.org/WBSITE/EXTERNAL/TOPICS/EXTGENDER/0,,contentMDK:20260262~menuPK:489120~pagePK:148956~piPK:216618~theSitePK:336868,00.html

A short, but informative video on the World Bank's *Smart Economics* action programme is available at: http://go.worldbank.org/KB7CH9X3WO

World Bank papers on which *Engendering Development* was based can be found at: http://web.worldbank.org/WBSITE/EXTERNAL/TOPICS/EXTGENDER/0,,contentMDK:201917 32~pagePK:210058~piPK:210062~theSitePK:336868,00.html

A range of documents relating to Asian developing countries and generated by the Asian Development Bank can be found at: http://www.adb.org/Gender/default.asp

Work by the United Nations is discussed at: http://www.undp.org/women/

Data on gender and development are available on the World bank site at: http://web.worldbank.org/WBSITE/EXTERNAL/TOPICS/EXTGENDER/0,,contentMDK:202436 43~menuPK:489223~pagePK:148956~piPK:216618~theSitePK:336868,00.html

CHAPTER 16

Agricultural Development, Food Supply and Rural Transformation

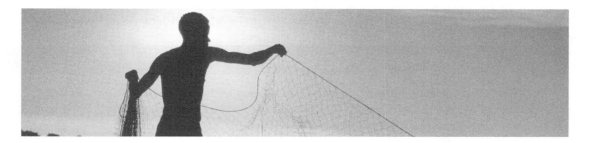

Though the share of GDP in agriculture has declined rapidly in much of the world, the sector (which is taken to include hunting, forestry and fishing) still dominates employment in a number of the poorest countries. The sector can and does contribute significantly towards the overall growth of a developing country's economy, and its expansion has a special potency for reducing poverty. The big 2007–08 increases in food prices have raised fears about possible long-run aggravation of the problems of food security. Hence the urgency of the quest for technological and other ways of increasing foodcrop productivity.

Introduction

As late as 1980 agriculture[1] could still be said to dominate the economies of the bulk of low-income and low-middle-income countries in the sense of engaging more than half of the *workforce*. One has to go back some decades further to a time when, even in low-income countries, it generally provided the preponderant share of the value of *output*; and its share on either test is still falling fast. This fading dominance is what remains of the life of hunting and gathering, husbandry and cultivation – of animals and plants – that had of necessity characterized most of the world's working population everywhere from time immemorial until very recent centuries. It is the modern importance in most of the world of 'industry' and services – not that of agriculture in many of the poorest developing countries – that is historically exceptional.

In providing a picture of the agricultural sector in developing countries, we begin by discussing changes in the relative importance of agriculture and in its productivity and

---

[1] 'Agriculture' is here taken to include forestry, hunting, and fishing, besides cultivation involving food and cash-crops, and animal husbandry.

salient features that it often displays: what by modern standards count as **low productivity** and **disguised unemployment**. Then we consider the **importance** of agriculture for economic growth, and the special potency of increases of agricultural product for poverty reduction. Accordingly, we discuss **technological advances**, referring in particular to the *'Green Revolution'*, which helped to transform agriculture in large parts of the developing world during the second half of the twentieth century, and to the newly emerging *GM crops* which appear to have the potential for revolutionizing agriculture anew. We refer also to the high social returns to agricultural R&D and its comparative neglect in developing countries. We then propose explanations for the big worldwide rises of 2007–08 in food prices and take up the issue of maintaining the growth of **food supplies** in order to restore and enhance food security. Finally, we identify some of the major **issues (urban bias, reforms of land distribution and tenure**, and **rural credit)** that arise in policy toward the agricultural sector.

BOX 16.1 TOOLKIT ON AGRICULTURAL DEVELOPMENT

Agricultural mechanization. The use of machinery and equipment for carrying out agricultural activities which in the past used to be conducted by men and women, or animals such as oxen and horses. Tractors have been the major form of equipment that has replaced the plough.

Agricultural productivity. Measured as the average agricultural value added per worker, it is often used to analyse the growth in agricultural output.

Agricultural sector. The part of the economy which is engaged in the cultivation of food and cash crops, besides other activities based on animals and plants including grazing, forestry, fishing and hunting.

Disguised unemployment. A situation in which a greater number of people are working than are required. Suppose only two labourers are required to cultivate a plot of land but five brothers are actually carrying out the work; we then have an example of disguised unemployment of three people.

Double cropping. The practice of producing two consecutive crops on the same plot of land in a year. That is, a second crop is grown after the harvesting of the first one.

Food security. A situation which guarantees the availability of food to a consuming unit, thus ensuring that a household will not suffer from starvation. About two billion people in the world lack food security.

GM crops. At the dawn of the twenty-first century the world is witnessing a major breakthrough in agricultural yield based on genetically-modified ('GM') crops: crops whose genetic make-up has been altered through a process called recombinant DNA or gene-slicing. The transformation is also referred to as the **gene revolution**.

Green revolution. A major technological breakthrough in agriculture which took place between the late-1960s and the mid-1970s, revolutionizing yields mainly of wheat, rice and corn (Maize) in many countries of Asia and Latin America. Water, fertilizer and high-yielding varieties of seeds have been the three major ingredients of this revolution.

Land reforms. Deliberate attempts to reorganize the distribution and terms of land occupancy, aimed either at increasing agricultural output or at improving the distribution of income from agriculture, or both. The reorganization can involve re-grouping of land-holdings, transfer of land ownership, confiscation and redistribution or nationalization of estates, and alteration of rental terms.

Lewis two-sector model. A two-sector model of economic growth advanced by Arthur Lewis (1954), in which the traditional agricultural sector provides its surplus labour to the modern industrial sector and, in the process, helps in capital accumulation and sustained development.

Low productivity in agriculture. Along with disguised unemployment, low productivity is a common feature of Third World agriculture. While land and labour productivities in agriculture have been increased greatly over traditional levels in developed countries as a result of the extensive application of technological improvements, the corresponding figures in developing countries have generally increased much less.

Marketable surplus. The quantity or value of output generated by the agricultural sector, over and above what is needed to satisfy its subsistence needs.

Primary products. Natural-resource-based commodities are called primary products and these include foodstuffs, agricultural raw materials, fishing and forestry products, and mining and quarrying outputs.

Rural credit. Loans made available to farmers. Given the small-scale nature of farming, in developing countries the traditional financial institutions find it difficult to provide credit to the farmers, hence the constraint faced by the small farmers in obtaining credit from 'formal' financial sources.

Share-cropping. A farming practice commonly found in the Indian sub-continent and elsewhere under which a farmer will cultivate a plot of land not owned by him, on an agreement to give an agreed share of the crop to the owner of the land.

Subsistence economy. This is an economy in which a production unit, often a household, produces mainly for its personal consumption of food, clothing and shelter, i.e., just to meet the basic necessities of life, and mainly to acquire these by direct production rather than through exchange. There is no attempt to accumulate wealth and most goods.

Subsistence farming. A type of farming in which crops or livestock are raised for the personal consumption of the farmer and his family and there is hardly any surplus.

Surplus labour. The availability of excess labour over and above the quantity demanded at the prevailing wage rate. In Arthur Lewis's two-sector model of the economy (1954), labour surplus at the going market wage rate is a driving force for capital accumulation.

Tenant farmer. One who will farm a plot of land without owning it, on an agreement to surrender a part of the output or of its proceeds to the owner of the land.

Urban-biased development. The notion that in developing countries government development policies often favour urban areas, and in the process rural areas are disadvantaged in access to basic services.

Village money lender. One who lends money to peasant farmers in order to meet their various needs including those for agricultural inputs and emergency living expenses.

Output and productivity changes

The developing world has been characterized in the not-so-distant past as the agricultural world, in contrast with the industrial world. This has become ever less appropriate, especially if we judge by the proportions of GDP from the various sectors. Early in the present century only a handful of countries still registered more than half of their GDP as originating in agriculture; but, as Table 16.1 shows, as late as 1995 well over half the *workforce* in *low-income* countries overall were engaged in agriculture.

If we go back far enough, the share of agriculture in the GDP of developing countries was also high. For 1965, as the table shows, the overall share for the low-income countries recorded was 42 per cent, though the share of the workforce was much higher, at 78 per cent. So at that time, it seems, three out of four working people in that large slice of the world's population were engaged in agriculture. Many of these were regarded as under-employed, and the term *disguised unemployment* (see Box 16.1) came to be used.

Diminishing GDP share in agriculture with increases in per capita income appears to be a general rule, as may be seen from Figure 16.1.

It is clear that the relationship is highly significant, though the R-square value, indicating the closeness of fit, at least to the *linear* relationship, is rather low. With the transformation of an economy then, as GDP per capita increases, the relative share of agriculture in the output of the economy declines. There is an almost L-shaped pattern shown in the scatter diagram. As GDP per capita reaches and surpasses a level of around $5000 (about a fifth of the way into the upper-middle-income range), the share of agriculture in GDP falls to about 5 per cent or below and we approach the horizontal part of the L. The clearly negative, though non-linear, relationship seems to be due, at least in part, to the relatively income-inelastic demand for food.

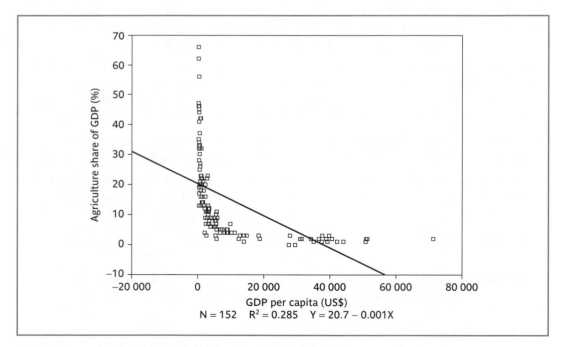

FIGURE 16.1 Per capita income and share of agriculture in GDP, 2006
The slope of the linear regression line is –0.001; the standard error of the slope is 0.00014; the t-statistic is –7.285; and the p-value is 0.000.

We shall see in Chapter 17 that any positive relationship that may have existed between income per head and the share of *manufacturing*, or of *'industry'*, in GDP is now negligible. The negative relationship with agriculture, however – even though now a rather weak one – persists.

As may be seen from Table 16.1, the relative share of agriculture in GDP in the three groups of countries (low-income, lower-middle-income and upper-middle-income) were respectively 42, 31 and 17 per cent of GDP in 1965, and 29, 18 and 7 per cent of GDP in 1995. Thus, over this period of 30 years, the low-income countries' share of agriculture in GDP fell by about 30 per cent, that of the lower-middles by about 40 per cent, and that of the upper-middles by nearly 60 per cent.

| | Agriculture's share in GDP and labour force | | | | | | | |
| | Share in GDP[a] | | | | Share in labour force[c] | | | |
	1965	1980	1995	2006	1965	1980	1995	2003–05[c]
Country Groups								
Low income	42	36	29	26	78	70 (73)	69	..
Lower middle income	31	22	18	12	66	56 (41)	36	..
Upper middle income	17	10 (8)	7	6	45	29 (31)	21	17.1
Selected Countries								
Bangladesh	53	50	26	20	84	74	64	51.7
Brazil	19	11	6	5	48	37	23	20.9
China	39	30	20	12	..	76	74	..
Egypt	29	18	17	14	55	61	43	29.9
Ghana	41	58	39	37	61	61	60	..
India	47	38	26	18	73	70	64	..
Indonesia	59	24	17	13	71	59	57	44.5
Kenya	35	33	31	27	86	83	80	..
Mexico	14	8	6	4	50	37	28	15.9
Nigeria	53	27	32	23	72	55	43	..
Pakistan	40	30	26	19	60	62	56	42.7
Philippines	26	25	22	14	58	52	45	37.2
South Africa	10	7	4	3	32	17	14	10.3
Tanzania[b]	46	46	47	45	92	86	84	..
Thailand	35	23	10	10	82	71	64	43.3
Uganda	52	72	49	32	91	89	93	69.1
Vietnam	..	..	27	20	79	73	72	58.8

TABLE 16.1 Agriculture's share in GDP and labour force in selected developing countries

Notes: [a] – components are at producer prices; [b] – covers mainland of Tanzania only; [c] – employment in agriculture as a percentage of total labour force. For 1980, labour force figures in brackets are from *WDR* 1997 while those without brackets are from *WDR* 1982. For 1965 the figure for the share of GDP in upper-middle-income countries as shown in brackets is from *WDR* 1995, p. 237.

Sources: World Bank, *World Development Indicators* 2008, Tables 3.2 and 4.2, (for data 1995 and 2006); *WDR* 1986 (for data 1965, GDP share pp. 184–5, labour share pp. 238–9); *WDR* 1997 (for data 1980 pp. 236–7); *WDR* 2008 (for data 2002–04 pp. 320–1); *WDR* 1982, 1995.

There was also a fall in the share of *employment* in agriculture. As the table shows, the
shares for the three groups of countries fell from 78, 66 and 45 per cent respectively in 1965
to 69, 36 and 21 in 1995 (and the upper-middles further to 17.1 per cent in 2003–05).
For the low-income countries this is a much less sharp fall than that in shares of GDP. The
fact that, in the low-income group, the decline in agriculture's share in total employment
over 1965–95 (by 12 per cent) has been slower than the decline in its share in GDP (by
31 per cent) implies that, for those countries, labour-productivity growth in agriculture has
been slower than in the rest of the economy.

Low productivity

Agricultural productivity, measured as the average agricultural value added per worker, is
found, as we might expect, to be significantly lower in low-income countries than that in
lower-middle-income and upper-middle-income countries (Table 16.2). The table also

	2000 US$		
	Agriculture Value-Added per Worker (2000 US$)		Per cent change for the period (1990–92 to 2001–03)
	1990–92	2001–03	
Country Groups			
Low-income countries	*315*	*363*	*15.2*
Lower-middle-income	*530*	*708*	*33.6*
Upper middle-income	*2139*	*2723*	*27.3*
Selected Countries			
Bangladesh	246	308	25.2
Brazil	1507	2790	85.1
China	254	368	44.9
Egypt	1686	1486	−11.9
Ghana	302	331	9.6
India	332	381	14.8
Indonesia	483	556	15.1
Kenya	335	327	−2.4
Mexico	2247	2704	20.3
Nigeria	170	172	1.2
Pakistan	586	691	17.9
Philippines	905	1017	12.4
South Africa	1796	2391	33.1
Tanzania	245	283	15.5
Thailand	501	586	17.0
Uganda	187	230	13.0
Vietnam	215	290	34.9

TABLE 16.2 Productivity growth in agriculture, 1990–92 to 2001–03
Source: World Bank, *WDR* 2008, pp. 340–41; percentage change is calculated.

shows that the low-income countries demonstrated lower proportional *growth* of labour productivity. During the period 1990–92 to 2001–03 their rise in productivity was only 15.2 per cent, while the corresponding figures were 33.6 per cent in the lower-middles and 27.3 per cent in the upper-middles (per annum, 1.3, 2.7 and 2.2 per cent respectively).

Given the significantly lower value-added per worker in low-income countries as shown in the table, there is, obviously, much room for improvement. Such optimism was backed up by research findings, for example those of Hayami and Ruttan (1970), who found that productivity differences can arise not only from natural-resource endowments but also from technology (as embodied in fixed or working capital) and human capital (broadly conceived to include the education, skill, knowledge and general capacity embodied in a country's population). Moreover, these three factors, between them capable of explaining 95 per cent of the differences in labour productivity at the time in the agriculture of the group of countries selected by Hayami and Ruttan, were found to be of roughly equal importance.

Disguised unemployment

Agriculture in the developing world is also characterized by the prevalence of disguised unemployment, a feature that has long attracted the attention of economists. The basic assumption in **Lewis's (1954) model**, which projects the use of agricultural surplus labour to expand the non-agricultural sector, is the existence of disguised unemployment in the rural economy.

Figure 16.3 in Appendix 16.1 (available on the Online Learning Centre for those who are interested) represents diagrammatically what is meant by disguised unemployment in a labour-surplus economy and follows the analysis of **Sen** (1975) and **Nurkse** (1953).

MP_L = marginal product of labour
MP_T = marginal product of labour time
SW = subsistence wage
TP = total product

If there is disguised unemployment, i.e., $MP_L = 0$, other things remaining constant, it is by definition possible to withdraw some workers permanently from the land without causing any fall in aggregate agricultural output. Furthermore, in a situation in which $MP_L > 0$, but $MP_L < SW$ and $SW = AP_L$, it follows from the definitions of the terms that reducing the input of labour at the margin will *raise its average product, that is the output per worker;* and moreover, if the working environment is flexible (i.e., there are variable daily hours subject to a maximum total), it should also be possible to take out some of the labour force from the agricultural sector *without causing any decline in its output.*

Whether surplus labour exists (that is whether labour's marginal product is zero) has, however, been disputed. Empirically one needs to demonstrate that the withdrawal of some of the labour force does not necessarily lead to a fall in total output. A study done by **Schultz** (1964) drew on evidence that in 1918–19 the worldwide influenza epidemic had caused the deaths of 8 per cent of the agricultural labour force in India. He found that output during the period declined and concluded that in India there was no agricultural surplus labour. However, there has been an extensive debate over this topic, and perhaps Schultz's interpretation fails to tell the whole story. The finding of a comprehensive study conducted on India by **Mathur** (1964, p. 168) at least qualifies it: 'On some farms the marginal product of family labour may be zero while on others it may be positive and in some cases even quite high.' It is also a matter of common experience that, in an agricultural sector dominated by household enterprises (such as is normally supposed to lie behind disguised farm unemployment), there are times in the year when the workforce may be fully employed and others when it is not. Large-scale reduction in the workforce through death, as in 1918–19, may then reduce total output, even though there are times in the year when the labour on hand is surplus to requirements. This is perhaps at least part of the reason why the withdrawal of much worker-time from agriculture in Mao Zedong's 'Great Leap Forward' of 1958–61 in China was so disastrous, even though it may well have been true that there was surplus farm labour at certain times of the year.

Agriculture's role in economic growth

Among the classical economists, **David Ricardo** was especially keen on emphasizing the importance of agriculture, given his concern with the limited supply of land and the resultant diminishing returns. Thus Ricardo believed that progress in agriculture contributed to increasing productivity in the economy of a country. As he observed,

> . . . the fall in the relative price of raw produce, in consequence of the improvement in agriculture, or rather in consequence of less labour being bestowed on its production, would naturally lead to increased accumulation; for the profits of stock would be greatly augmented. This accumulation would lead to an increased demand for labour, to higher wages, to an increased population, to a further demand for raw produce, and to an increased cultivation.
>
> *(Ricardo, 1817, pp. 103–4)*

Ricardo was, however, primarily concerned with the implications of the *decline* in profits and capital accumulation. He was convinced that, as there was a limit to the growth of output in agriculture, this would set an upper limit to capital formation in the non-agricultural sectors and hence to the growth that could be achieved in the economy.

In general, increasing agricultural productivity is considered as contributing to the economic development of a country in four main ways.

1 Agriculture is the source of foodstuffs and is a supplier of raw materials to the other sectors, and its expansion supplies the needs of an expanding economy.

2 By increasing savings and tax revenue, a growing agricultural output supports investment in the other expanding economic sectors.

3 An increasing 'marketable surplus' sold for cash by the agricultural sector helps to raise the demand for products of the other growing sectors of the economy. Marketable surplus for any period is the difference between total agricultural output and subsistence needs of food on the part of the producers.

4 Increased agricultural output helps to relax the foreign-exchange constraint of an economy as it enables the economy to earn foreign exchange: directly from exports of agricultural products or indirectly by saving foreign exchange through import-substitution.

Most of these points now seem so obvious that it would probably not have been considered necessary to state them at all if there had not been the fixation that some early discussions of development economics shared with some of the Marxists of the early twentieth century to the effect that industry was all-important and that agriculture was intrinsically backward and almost an unfortunate survival.

The above points are repeated by **Johnston and Mellor** (1961) who, in a classic article, succinctly analysed the contribution of agriculture to economic development under five categories:

1 Increase in food supply for domestic consumption
2 Release of labour for employment in the industrial sector
3 Higher domestic market for manufacturing output
4 Higher domestic savings
5 Foreign-exchange earnings from agricultural exports.

Simon Kuznets (1965) can also be credited with providing a summary view of the importance of agriculture, listing its contribution under three major categories: the product contribution, the market contribution and the factor contribution.

The product contribution

As viewed by Kuznets:

> An increase in the net output of agriculture represents a rise in the product of the country, since the latter is the sum of the increases in the net product of the several sectors.
> This type, which we may call the product contribution, can be briefly examined – as a contribution first to the growth of *total* net or gross product, and second to the growth of product per capita.
>
> *(Kuznets, 1965, p. 239)*

In particular, domestic agriculture will largely determine the growth potential of the non-agricultural sector. This is mainly because of the latter's dependence on the former not only for the supply of food but also in some countries for the raw materials it needs for its various sub-sectors, including for example textile manufacturing.

The ability of the agricultural sector to generate the **marketable surplus**, namely the difference between total agricultural output and the subsistence needs of the sector, may be crucial, especially at the early stage of development when the economy might not have the foreign exchange to import much food.

The marketable surplus can be either voluntary or involuntary. After an increase in labour productivity, the agricultural sector will find it possible to generate marketable surplus. However, a society may decide to adopt forcible procurement, as happened in Japan during the Meiji period (1868–1912), and in the Soviet Union in the 1920s after the Bolshevik Revolution.

In classical thought about the development process, marketable surplus formed an important concept. In the absence of such surplus, food prices would tend to rise, which would cause an increase in the wage bill and a fall in profit, thus slowing down industrial capital accumulation.

The market contribution

By the market contribution of agriculture we mean the demand for industrial goods that arises from agriculture and agricultural producers, a major source of autonomous demand. As a developing country starts its industrialization process, the market for the new goods being produced from the emerging manufacturing sector is likely to be provided by the domestic agricultural sector. Indeed, agriculture has been found to be an important ally of growth in all the major countries that went through the development process.

Agriculture's market contribution to economic growth was viewed by Kuznets (1965, pp. 244–5) in two main ways:

1 the purchase of some production items from other sectors, domestic or foreign
2 the sale of some of its own products, not only for buying the kinds of items listed above under **1**, but also to buy various consumer goods from other sectors, domestic or foreign.

Thus, the agricultural sector makes a contribution towards the emergence and growth of other sectors and also towards the development of international flows, in the same way as these other sectors and the international flows help agricultural output to grow and raise the consumption of those employed in the sector.

The factor contribution

Agriculture makes a 'factor contribution' through its supply of (i) labour and (ii) capital, the two main inputs for any growth to take place.

The ability of the agricultural sector to provide labour to other sectors of the economy, especially manufacturing, gives it a unique position in economic development. Indeed, the role of agriculture in providing labour for the emerging industrial sector of a developing economy formed the cornerstone of Arthur Lewis's growth model based on labour surplus. The availability of such labour (at slightly above a subsistence wage), he said, would enable the industrial sector to accumulate surplus and continue to reinvest it, thus helping to maintain the growth process.

The role of agriculture as a source of saving and capital-accumulation also hardly needs to be stressed. In developing countries, agriculture has traditionally been a very important source of financing investment for development. The several means by which this can be done are listed in Chapter 17.

Lewis, among others, emphasized the importance of agriculture for the economic development of underdeveloped countries, especially as he believed that the emerging industrial sector had to be supported with cheap food, and that this could be made possible through rapid transformation in agriculture.

The foreign-exchange contribution

One can credit a fourth contribution to the agricultural sector beside Kuznets's three: that of foreign exchange. The importance of this contribution is particularly crucial in the 'early' stages of development when a developing country is likely to depend heavily on exports of primary products. By making it possible to import the needed foreign goods, agriculture may remove a serious constraint on economic growth, in the same way as domestic savings are generally necessary for development to take place.

In their classic articles published in the early- and mid-1960s, **Chenery** and his associates[2] illustrated, in the form of dual-gap analysis, the crucial importance of foreign exchange in the development process. For a developing country, it seemed, the export–import gap is as

---

[2] See, for example, Chenery and Bruno (1962), Chenery and MacEwan (1966) and Chenery and Strout (1966).

significant as the savings-investment gap. Hence the once familiar concept of the 'two gaps' that can be faced by a developing country, which is explained in Chapter 5.

Special roles as emphasized by the World Bank, 2008

In the **2008** *World Development Report (WDR)*, the President of the World Bank considers agriculture as 'a vital development tool for achieving the Millennium Development Goal that calls for halving by 2015 the share of people suffering from extreme poverty and hunger' (World Bank, *WDR* 2008, p. xiii). That issue of the *WDR* focuses on the role of agriculture in development. It distinguishes three specific roles of agriculture: as an economic activity, a livelihood, and a provider of environmental services (ibid., pp. 2–3). It makes two points of interest, beyond those made above and below, relating to:

1 the numbers depending on agriculture directly for their livelihoods (about 2.5 billion), or as backstops when other sources of support fail, as when migrants to urban areas find themselves unemployed

2 the environmental costs and benefits that it generates, both considerable and of great policy importance.

The agricultural sector has been shown to have a large potential role in development (World Bank, *WDR* 2008, pp. 6–8) for at least two reasons:

1 *'[A]griculture has special powers in reducing poverty'* (ibid., p. 6). Agricultural growth is found to be significantly effective in reducing poverty all over the developing world. In China, in fact, agricultural growth has been estimated to be 3.5 times as effective in reducing poverty as growth in the non-agricultural sector. Agricultural growth has also been found to be highly effective in reducing poverty in Latin America and India and, more recently, in Ghana (ibid.).

2 Essentially an elaboration of one of Kuznets' 'market contribution' points mentioned above – *'agriculture can be the lead sector for overall growth in the agriculture-based countries'* (ibid.). There are countries in which staple foods are bulky or perishable, and in these cases staple food will be little traded internationally. So the productivity of the country's own agriculture will largely determine the price of its food, and this in turn will determine the cost of wage employment. Thus, in such agriculture-based economies, the competitiveness internationally of the tradable sectors will largely depend on agricultural productivity. As observed by the *WDR* 2008 (p. 7):

> Agricultural growth was the precursor to the industrial revolutions that spread across the temperate world from England in the mid-18th century to Japan in the late-19th century. More recently, rapid agricultural growth in China, India, and Vietnam was the precursor to the rise of industry.

Agricultural growth and poverty reduction[3]

There is now a consensus that agricultural growth is an important vehicle for reducing poverty so that, in many circumstances, the agricultural sector is an important arena for connecting the raising of output with the reduction of poverty.

---

[3] See, e.g., Mellor (2008) for a succinct discussion on a number of relevant issues.

Indeed, as already mentioned, agriculture is considered to have special potential for reducing poverty. Some recent World Bank cross-country estimates, mentioned above, show that 'GDP growth originating in agriculture is at least twice as effective in reducing poverty as GDP growth originating outside agriculture' (World Bank, *WDR*, 2008, p. 6).

Ravallion and Datt (1996) have carried out an extensive cross-section analysis and found that agricultural growth is the main driver of poverty reduction in low- and middle-income countries, although there is a significant lag in the timing of the impact. The lag might tempt people to dismiss the effect on poverty, but, according to Ravallion and Datt, the lag is mainly due to the indirect character of the impact. The poverty-reducing effect of agricultural growth is attributed to the reduction in food prices, the increase in farm employment, and the increase in rural non-farm employment.

However, agricultural growth may not always help in reducing poverty. In many Latin American countries, for example, where land distribution is highly skewed, the high-income groups, who are large landowners and, because of their monopsony power over their labour, tend to reap most of the gains from any technical improvement or market windfall, may not typically spend their marginal income on labour-intensive products originating in their domestic rural non-farm sectors, but rather on import-intensive products.

Lower food prices

As much as 80 per cent of the income of the very poor is spent on food, so that the price of food is a key determinant of their real income. The rapid increase in the production of food grains, following the Green Revolution, enabled the Asian countries in particular to maintain low food prices. As the food prices remained low in relation to those of other goods, real wage costs also remained depressed relative to industrial prices, which helped to increase employment. However, the case of sub-Saharan Africa is different. For many of its foodcrops there was no Green Revolution. So the region has continued to suffer from a shortfall in food supply as population has grown. In the case of Africa, estimates made by FAO and IFRI show that there is likely to be a continued shortfall of the supply of food, and the suffering of the poor there will persist (Eicher and Staaz, 1998).

Increase in farm employment

Given the relatively large size of the share of agriculture in the GDP of a number of developing countries (Table 16.1), any rapid growth of the sector is likely to have both direct and indirect positive impacts on employment. However, modern agricultural technologies are variously intended to increase labour- and land-productivity, so that their employment effect is not necessarily as labour-intensive as traditional agricultural technologies. So, for each 'ten per cent increase in agricultural output, employment increases [directly] by between less than three per cent and at most six per cent. Thus, the big impact of agricultural growth on employment comes indirectly through the non-farm sector' (Mellor, 2008, p. 102).

Farm-income-driven growth in rural non-farm employment

An increase in the incomes of an area's agricultural households can help greatly in increasing the non-farm employment in the area. Following increases of income for the farmers, the demand for many locally produced goods including housing materials and furniture will increase, thus causing an increase of rural employment and an eventual increase in the real wages of the non-farm sector in rural areas. One can also consider the multiplier effects of these expenditures following increases in income of the agricultural sector. Thus, it is not difficult to visualize the positive impact of increases in agricultural income on poverty reduction. However, such impacts will be missing if the incremental income is spent on imported goods and services as is often the case with rich and absentee land-owners. This of course has a bearing on the case for 'distributist' land reform – that is, reforms that redistribute large units of land property or tenure into smaller parcels.

Technological changes in agriculture

Over the past 50 years or so the world has witnessed major technological breakthroughs in agriculture. The first, known as the 'Green Revolution', which started to influence practice in a big way from the 1960s, has already transformed agriculture in many countries of the world; while the second, the emergence of Genetically Modified (GM) Crops through genetic engineering, has yet to take firm root, although it has already been extensively applied in certain countries and has attracted serious attention even more widely because of the vast potential it holds for output growth and cost reduction, and also because of some alleged environmental hazards that it incurs.

The Green Revolution

Between the late-1960s and the mid-1970s there was a dramatic increase in the production of cereals per hectare in a number of developing countries such as the Philippines, Mexico, India, Bangladesh and Pakistan, and the phenomenon soon came to be described as the 'Green Revolution' (see, e.g., Dobbs, 2006). There were three key inputs:

1 high-yielding varieties of seeds especially wheat (*Triticum aestivum*) and rice (*Oryza sativa L.*)
2 inorganic fertilizer (and also pesticides)
3 water (mainly by irrigation from groundwater).

The impact on agriculture was particularly strong in a number of Latin American and Asian countries including Mexico (certain parts), the Philippines, the Indian sub-continent, and Thailand.

This biological change was soon accompanied by mechanical change, which started with the use of tractors. In places, for example in the Indian Punjab, extensive farm mechanization has now involved 'the use of various types of machines and other agricultural implements during the production, transportation and processing of agricultural products' (Official Website of the Indian Punjab).

The biological aspect of the technical change resulted in a more intensive use of the land extending to double- or even triple-cropping. So more labour was needed, while the mechanical aspect of the change resulted in an increase in the capital–labour ratio as the resultant technical change was capital-augmenting. Thus, one could argue that while the high-yielding seed, fertilizer and water between them increased the productivity per unit of both land and labour, the increased use of machinery helped to raise mainly the productivity of labour. Thus, in labour-surplus countries, the adoption of machinery went against the conventional wisdom of encouraging labour-intensity.

	Average annual growth in percentages	
	1961–1980	**1981–2000**
Output Obtained	**3.20** *(3.08 Latin America)* *(3.65 Asia)* *(2.53 Middle East & North Africa)* *(1.70 sub-Saharan Africa)*	**2.19** *(1.63 Latin America)* *(2.11 Asia)* *(2.12 Middle East & North Africa)* *(3.19 sub-Saharan Africa)*
Area Cultivated	**0.68** *(1.47 Latin America)* *(0.51 Asia)* *(0.95 Middle East & North Africa)* *(0.52 sub-Saharan Africa)*	**0.386** *(−0.51 Latin America)* *(0.02 Asia)* *(0.61 Middle East & North Africa)* *(2.82 sub-Saharan Africa)*
Crop Yield (per unit area)	**2.50** *(1.59 Latin America)* *(3.12 Asia)* *(1.56 Middle East & North Africa)* *(1.17 sub-Saharan Africa)*	**1.81** *(2.15 Latin America)* *(2.09 Asia)* *(1.51 Middle East & North Africa)* *(0.36 sub-Saharan Africa)*

TABLE 16.3 Green Revolution: Growth in output, area cultivated and yield per hectare in developing countries, 1961–80, 1981–2000

Estimates show that between 1990 and 2007 crop yields increased at an average annual rate of 1.1 per cent.

Sources: Evenson (2008) and *Financial Times*, 2/6/2008, p. 9.

The 1960s and 1970s are considered to be the period when spectacular gains were registered in output and yield. As may be seen from Table 16.3, for the developing world as a whole from 1961 to 1980 (which is considered the *early* Green Revolution period), output increased at an annual average rate of 3.2 per cent; the corresponding growth rates in area cultivated and crop yield were 0.68 per cent and 2.50 per cent, respectively. In the late period of the Green Revolution (1981 to 2000), however, the rates of increase of the early period could not be maintained; the respective rates of increase in output, area and yield were 2.19 per cent, 0.39 per cent and 1.81 per cent. It was only sub-Saharan Africa that improved performance over the late period in both output and area, but in yield per hectare there was a fall in the pace of improvement even here, down from a growth rate of 1.7 per cent in the early period to one of 0.47 per cent in the late period.

The Gene Revolution

The world appears to be at the threshold of a new technological revolution in agriculture, which has been called the 'gene revolution', with genetically modified (GM) crops. As the *FDA Consumer Magazine* (Bren, 2003) has put it:

> Genetically engineered foods are produced from crops whose genetic makeup has been altered through a process called recombinant DNA, or gene splicing, to give the plant a desirable trait. Genetically engineered foods are also known as biotech, bioengineered, and genetically modified, although 'genetically modified' can also refer to foods from plants altered through other breeding methods.

The crops are genetically engineered. For example, by altering one or two genes in a plant the scientists can introduce a new characteristic while the basic features remain unaltered.

The first group of GM crops appeared in the mid-1990s following keen interest shown by a number of well-established chemical companies. The big companies that have entered this area include Monsanto and DuPont in the US, Bayer and BASF in Europe and Sava in Mexico. Seeds have already been produced for various GM crops including soyabeans, cotton and maize.

As farmers may be able to reduce production costs by planting GM crops, Third World countries facing food shortages are generally enthusiastic. However, estimates of the reductions in production costs vary from region to region. While the US and the developing countries are expected to achieve significant reductions in cost, the gains received by farmers in Western Europe are not likely to be great. Moreover, the fall in production costs is thought to be static, so that for dynamic gains it will be necessary to engage in developing new generations of varieties (Evenson, 2008, p. 99).

The GM crop revolution, however, has been facing strong opposition, especially in Western Europe. A number of NGOs including Greenpeace have been particularly vocal in their protests. There is a public perception that the GM crops can turn into 'monster' varieties. There is also a fear that a few large companies will control the technology of GM food and will be able to earn monopoly profits, so that farmers in developing countries will hardly benefit. Concern has also been expressed that a GM crop may adversely affect non-GM plants in neighbouring areas.

However, opposition to GM crops appears to be virtually non-existent among biological scientists. They point out that genetic modification of plants has been going on for hundreds of years. An example quoted is tangelos, a hybrid of grapefruit and tangerine, an outcome of genetic modification through plant breeding carried out by farmers using traditional methods. Other examples, among a huge number that might be cited, are hybrid corn and the many varieties of apples. With the hope of continuing the development of GM crops, the British Association for the Advancement of Science has even called for keeping secret the sites where GM trials are conducted.

At times there is vocal opposition in some developing countries, as for example in Zambia when it refused to accept GM grain as emergency aid in 2002 because of a fear of 'contaminating' local agriculture with GM strains and so blocking access to the EU market, but that objection was entirely the result of *EU policy*, which, arguably, was based on insubstantial fears and which said nothing about intrinsic disadvantages of GM crops. South Africa is reported at the time of writing (2008) to be growing GM maize, cotton and soyabeans.[4] A number of other developing countries have also already approved or are about to approve the widespread use of selected GM strains: in cotton (India) and maize (Egypt).[5] In fact, estimates show that 100 million hectares, which is about 8 per cent of the farming land in the world, is already under GM crops.[6]

R&D in agriculture: high social returns and comparative neglect

R&D investment in agriculture has been found to produce a high rate of return. The estimates made by Griliches (1958) showed that returns to investment in agricultural research could be very high. For example, research on hybrid corn was estimated to have an internal rate of

---

[4] *Financial Times*, 23/6/2008, p. 6.

[5] *Financial Times*, 3/6/2008, p. 13, 'Seeds of change': *FT* Series Part 2.

[6] *Financial Times*, 2/6/2008, p. 13, 'The end of abundance': *FT* Series Part 1.

Countries	Public R&D spending on agriculture (% agriculture value-added)
Developing Countries	
Bangladesh	0.44
China	0.43
Ghana	0.47
India	0.34
Indonesia	0.21
Nigeria	0.38
Pakistan	0.24
Tanzania	0.40
South Korea	1.73
Sri-Lanka	0.64
Philippines	0.41
Developed Countries	
Australia	3.38
Denmark	3.14
Japan	3.62
United States	2.65

TABLE 16.4 Public Expenditure on R&D in Agriculture, 2000
Source: World Bank, *World Development Report*, 2008, pp. 322–3.
Note: Public R&D spending in agriculture includes spending by government, non-profit-making bodies and universities, whether financed from fiscal sources or from the private-sector and international grants and loans.

return (IRR) of 43 per cent. Some recent estimates of IRR are available from a study by Evenson (2001). He found very high returns to investment in the research carried out by the international agricultural research centres. However, returns to investment in the programmes of *national* agricultural research centres are lower, particularly in sub-Saharan Africa. Estimates by the World Bank also point to high rates of return for R&D investment in agriculture:

> Decomposition of productivity gains consistently point to investment in research and development (R&D) as major sources of growth. Hybrid rice alone is estimated to have contributed half of the rice yield gains in China from 1975 to 1990. Improved varieties contributed 53 per cent of total-factor-productivity gains in the agriculture of the Pakistan Punjab from 1971 to 1994.
> *(World Bank,* WDR *2008, p. 52)*

However, in low-income countries, where private direct investment for agricultural research is almost non-existent, public expenditure on agricultural R&D has also been very low, as may be seen from Table 16.4. South Korea (only just below the Bank's high-income category in 2002) was a rare exception. Indeed, there has been stagnation in agricultural research investment in sub-Saharan Africa (Box 16.2).

BOX 16.2 STAGNATION IN AGRICULTURAL RESEARCH INVESTMENT IN SUB-SAHARAN AFRICA

'In contrast with other regions, such as Latin America and Asia, per-capita food availability in sub-Saharan Africa (hereafter, Africa) has decreased over time, and the region suffers from widespread food insecurity. As a result, the number of poor and undernourished people in Africa has increased substantially in recent decades. At the turn of the millennium, at least one in four Africans was undernourished.

'Africa continues to be highly dependent on the agricultural sector for its livelihood, employing more than 80 per cent of the labour force in many countries. Small-scale farmers predominate in a climate of increasing population pressure, food insecurity, very low (and declining) levels of agricultural productivity, and rapid natural-resource degradation. Lessening African poverty requires an increase in agricultural productivity.

▶ 'Agricultural research and development (R&D) investments are a crucial determinant of agricultural productivity through the introduction of improved crops and cropping practices, labour-saving technologies, improved quality of food storage, processing, and marketing. In addition to newly developed technologies, existing technologies need to be better disseminated throughout Africa.

'Considerable empirical evidence indicates high rates of return from agricultural R&D investments, making agricultural research a cost-effective way for governments to accelerate agricultural development.

'In recent years, reports from a number of influential initiatives . . . have pointed out the critical role of Science and Technology (S&T) for African economic and social development. NEPAD's Framework for African Agricultural Productivity (FAAP) emphasized the critical role of technical change and recommends a doubling of the current level of public agricultural R&D funding by 2015.'

But despite all this, overall growth in agricultural research investments in Africa has effectively stagnated over the past two decades increasing only 'at an average rate of about 1 per cent per year. This continent-wide trend masks significant variation among countries. During 1991–2000, about half the countries in [a] 27-country sample experienced a contraction in total agricultural research and development (R&D) spending. Declines often occurred during periods of political unrest or following the completion of large donor-funded projects. The majority of African agricultural research is still conducted by the public sector.'

Source: IFPRI, *Agricultural R&D in Sub-Saharan Africa: An Era of Stagnation*, Washington, DC, August 2006. (Report prepared by Nienke M. Beintema and Gert-Jan Stads.) For supporting material, see Alston and Veneer (2000), Benson (2004), Eicher (2004), Evenson (2001), Evenson and Gollin (eds) (2003), Thirtle, Lin and Piess (2003).

A challenge to food security?

The price panic of 2007–08

After three decades of relatively stable prices, in 2007–08 developing-country markets experienced unprecedented shifts in the prices of staple foodstuffs. Very sharp rises were experienced in the prices of many products – notably rice, wheat and corn, soya beans, meat, coffee and milk – and the world faced its worst food crisis in a generation. Shortages of food were sufficiently acute to trigger food riots in several countries as diverse as Guinea, Mauritania, Mexico, Morocco, Senegal, Uzbekistan and Yemen, and to lead a number of the countries most affected (notably China, India and Vietnam) to impose emergency measures such as price controls, cuts in retail taxes on basic foodstuffs, tariffs on exported grain, bans on exporting rice, and reductions in import tariffs on food.

As well as inducing immediate social turmoil, these events revived concerns about the possible reappearance of long-run problems with food security, and even of the rebirth of 'Malthus' Devil' (see Chapter 4). So – was this just a passing blip in prices, or a warning of something more long-lasting appearing on the horizon? Are there serious threats to the sustainability of food supplies? And what changes, if any, in developing country food security policies are indicated?

The causes of the 2007–08 price rises

The main apparent causes of the sharp 'spike' in food prices in 2007–08 come in several categories.

Immediate short-run causes

The sharp increases in food prices in 2007–08 can be blamed on *the running-down of stocks of foodstuffs* partly because of bad weather (and associated poor harvests) in the recent past, and partly as a reaction to the rising carrying-cost of stocks as prices have pushed upwards. In a 'thin' market (typically, in developing countries, sales of subsistence foods – domestic and international – comprise a relatively small part of total consumption) any change in the balance of supply and demand is likely to have an exaggerated impact on prices.

Longer-term demand-side factors

Several longer-term *demand-side* factors are tending to push up the prices of foodstuffs in developing countries:

- *Continued population growth* (at around 70 million additional people every year) is putting steady upward pressure on the total demand for food.

- *Rising incomes resulting from rapid economic growth in Asia* – in China and India in particular – have led to demand for an improved diet, in the forms of increased total consumption and a shift towards protein-rich and higher-quality materials. The overall demand for food is increasing and there has been a significant expansion in the market for meat. Since grain is an important input into meat production (1 kg of meat requires an input of around 7 kg of grain) this shift has put pressure on both meat prices and grain prices.

Longer-term supply-side factors

- *Sharply rising prices of oil and natural gas* push food prices up *directly* by increasing agricultural production costs in two ways. First, they increase the cost of operating farm machinery and transporting inputs and outputs. Second, they increase the cost of natural-gas-based fertilizers (around 30 per cent of total supply), and this in turn puts upward pressure on demand for, and prices of, other fertilizers – notably phosphatic fertilizers. Prices of many oil-based pesticides and herbicides are also directly affected by the price of oil.

- Rising oil prices push up food prices *indirectly* by further increasing the attractiveness of *diverting grain supplies from food production to biofuel production*. Thus, US ethanol production from grain is expected to tie up around 30 per cent of the total corn crop by 2010. This will inevitably put further upward pressure on food prices by reducing supplies of corn flour on international commodity markets, and by reducing the proportion of farmland available for food production.

This is a wholly new situation. True, biofuels predate the current concern over their impact on food prices by over a century. Thus the engine patented in 1898 by the eponymous Rudolph Diesel was originally designed to run on ground-nut oil. Two decades later, Henry Ford's Model T was to have used ethanol produced from maize or hemp. Neither of these 'green' innovations, however, survived the advent of cheap mineral oil (Booker and North, 2008). So, traditionally, the linking of the price of oil to agriculture has been via on-farm costs of energy use, transportation costs, and the prices of fertilizers. Under this regime, changes in the price of energy affect the price of food through its cost of production and delivery to market. Any impact on the *level of food supplies* is a derived effect reflecting the response of demand to increases in food prices. Now, with the advent of biofuels as a major 'agricultural' product, food and energy are, for the first time, *direct substitutes* in production since corn (and several other crops) can be turned into *either* fuel or foodstuffs. As a result, prices of food based on these crops will be closely tied to energy prices. A rise in the price of energy will divert land away from food production and towards biofuel production – so raising food prices by *both* pushing up the energy costs of agricultural production *and* reducing the acreage available for food products.

Very long-term supply-side factors

- Following the rapid increases of farm productivity in developing countries associated with the 'green revolution' – when crop yields increased by around 2 per cent per annum over the period 1970 to 1990 – the years 1990 to 2007 saw a *slow-down in improvements in farm productivity* to around 1 per cent per annum – lower than the rate of growth of population in developing countries – with further declines in prospect. Unless productivity can be increased faster than population growth, the possibility is created of the reappearance of a 'Malthusian' race between population growth and food supplies. As we have seen, the factors which headed off the problem in the eighteenth century were access to the hitherto unexploited land areas of the New World and improved agricultural technology. As is explained below, the former option of significantly expanding the land area under cultivation is no longer available to us.

- While there is some doubt as to the actual influence, if any, of *climate change* (on global warming, see Chapter 11) on the food price 'spike' of 2007–08, it seems inevitable that climate-induced trends in developing countries towards increased desertification and soil degradation, changing patterns of rainfall (bringing with them an elevated incidence of water shortages or drought, and more frequent flooding), and increased problems with plant diseases and insect infestation, will affect agricultural production adversely in the future – unless effective counter-measures are taken. Given the current problems with loss of formerly cultivated land, and the widespread practice of exploiting increasingly unsuitable locations, there seems to be little likelihood that the opening of new areas to cultivation can make for significant increases in food supplies.

Sustainability of food supplies

We have not, thus far, defined 'sustainability' in relation to food supplies in developing countries. A simple, intuitive definition can be modelled on that used in Chapter 11 in relation to overall economic growth, thus: **A 'sustainable' food-supply situation is one in which the supply available to the present generation meets its needs on a reliable basis and is 'sufficient, nutritionally adequate and safe . . . at the household, regional and global levels'** (FAO, 2006), **without compromising the ability of future generations to meet their own food needs**. Achieving this clearly requires much more than an instant solution to immediate food shortages, and is likely to involve policy measures that go beyond the agriculture sector itself.

Policies for securing sustainable food supplies

Policy options for establishing sustainable food supplies for the developing world fall, by and large, into two categories – those favouring a 'technical fix', often in conjunction with 'big agriculture', and those favouring evolutionary improvement of currently used systems (albeit with increased regard for environmentally sensitive aspects of agriculture, and for government responsibilities towards agriculture).

'The "big agriculture" approach sees the future lying with increases in production brought about by the application of relatively sophisticated technologies.' These would take two main forms – the use of genetically modified crops, and cultivation carried out, not by small-scale, peasant farmers, whose approach 'is not well suited to innovation and investment', but by replicas of 'the Brazilian model of large, technologically sophisticated agro-companies that supply the world market'. The scope for the latter is seen as considerable as 'there are still many areas of the world – including large swathes of Africa – that have good land that could be used far more productively if it were properly managed by large companies. To contain the rise in food prices we need more globalisation not less' (Collier *et al.*, 2008).

The 'evolutionary' approach to achieving sustainability of developing-country food supplies favours a twin-track combination of policies aimed at both rehabilitating failing sectors of agriculture and placing the entire industry on a path to sustained, long-run productivity improvement. Initially high-priority measures would be brought forward to provide, in the short/medium-term, a rescue-and-rehabilitation package aimed at low-productivity farmers and distressed rural communities. These initiatives would be backed up by a long-term programme of environmentally sensitive, productivity-improving measures.

The first part of the latter strategy involves a recognition of the fact that a vicious circle affects a sizeable segment of developing-country agriculture. Rural poverty leads to hunger. Hunger has a negative effect on the productivity of agricultural labour, encouraging bad husbandry, depletion of soils and decreasing yields – which reduce output and reinforce poverty. The key to a break-out from this cycle is the introduction of a pro-poor programme ('social security safety nets, cash transfers, health interventions, and food and nutrition programmes') which have the immediate effect of reducing the incidence of hunger, so permitting increased productivity, growth of agricultural output and further hunger reduction (FAO, 2006, p. 28).

In the longer term, increasing productivity will require improved infrastructure, agricultural research, education and extension – and assistance for farmers in identifying and funding the acquisition of agricultural technologies designed to raise productivity. However, in the (controversial) view of the Intergovernmental Panel on Climate Change [IPCC], 'Genetically modified (GM) crops . . . will not play a substantial role in addressing the challenges of climate change, loss of biodiversity, hunger and poverty.' The emphasis should be firmly on achieving sustainability through small-scale farming using environmentally friendly 'agro-ecological methods . . . with indigenous and local knowledge playing as important a role as formal science' (IPCC, 2008).[7]

---

[7] The IPCC (Intergovernmental Panel for Climate Change) report published in 2008, entitled *The International Assessment of Agricultural Science and Technology for Development* (IAASTD), was prepared through 'a unique collaboration initiated by the World Bank in partnership with a multi-stakeholder group of organizations, including the United Nations Food and Agriculture Organization, United Nations Development Programme, United Nations Environmental Programme, the World Health Organization and representatives of governments, civil society, private sector and scientific institutions from around the world'.

These 'evolutionary' proposals by devotees of the 'small is beautiful' approach to agricultural revival will, of course, require substantially increased public investment in agriculture – both from developing countries' own resources and through increased allocations from development-assistance budgets, which have tended to move away from agriculture in recent years. They will also have to be complemented by more 'traditional' policies such as investing in improved facilities for storing and transporting agricultural output; providing a solid context for agriculture by recognizing the importance of peace, stability and good governance; and ensuring that domestic policy in this area is not negated by unfavourable trade deals.

Treating these two 'approaches' as mutually exclusive alternative strategies seems a false dichotomy, under which GM crops risk being condemned by association. There is no reason whatever why the use of GM technology should imply large corporate farms. If the new seeds perform as intended, small farmers seem likely to adopt them as avidly as they did those of the Green Revolution. It is also arguable that, in implying that GM crops are to be judged on whether they provide solutions to climate change and loss of biodiversity, the IPCC is ensuring that they fail by requiring too much of them.

Agricultural development: challenges, policies, structures

Urban-biased policy

A common complaint in developing countries is that the government policies are biased towards urban areas. Such biases are reflected not only in the supply of utilities and infrastructural facilities such as electricity and road communications but also in the provision of basic services including education, health and housing. In the process, rural areas are neglected. The urban-biased nature of policy probably makes some contribution to the fact that real income is lower, and the proportional poverty headcount higher, in rural than in urban areas. (See Table 16.5, where it seems all the surveys, bar the more recent one for Sri Lanka, show a higher proportional poverty headcount for rural than for urban areas.[8]) This bias in policy has presumably contributed, among other things, to the influx of rural people to urban areas which is discussed in Chapter 14.

Michael Lipton (1968), who identified 'urban bias' in Indian planning, is one of the early writers to raise concern about it. As he subsequently argued (Lipton, 1977), in both developing and developed countries relatively little attention is received by the agricultural sector because of the existence and operation of complex social forces and processes. The people living in urban centres include most of the vocal minority, and among them will be those who determine the distribution of government development expenditures. The deficiencies of urban road and other physical facilities are also likely to receive preferential government attention because of higher media coverage, while the rural infrastructure is less publicized. Moreover, secondary industry is often located in urban areas; and that is another reason why housing, health, education and various utilities there usually have priority, and corresponding services for agriculture and its workers are neglected by comparison.

---

[8] And the Sri Lanka rural figure for 2002 must be dubious. It is so far below the corresponding figure from the 1995–96 survey, and also unconvincingly far below the national headcount figure, implying that the rural weight in the latter is very low.

Developing Countries	Population below national poverty line: percentage							
	Survey Year	Rural	Urban	National	Survey Year	Rural	Urban	National
Bangladesh	1995–96	55.2	29.4	51	2000	53	36.6	49.8
Brazil	1998	51.4	14.7	22	2002–03	41	17.5	21.5
China	1998	4.6	..	4.6	2004	..	..	2.8
Egypt	1995–96	23.3	22.5	22.9	1999–00	..	..	16.7
Ethiopia	1995–96	47	33.3	45.5	1999–00	45	37	44.2
Ghana	1998–99	49.6	19.4	39.5	2005–06	39.2	10.8	28.5
India	1993–94	37.3	32.4	36	1999–00	30.2	24.7	28.6
Indonesia	1996	..	..	17.5	2004	..	..	16.7
Kenya	1994	47	29	40	1997	53	49	52
Mexico	2002	34.8	11.4	20.3	2004	27.9	11.3	17.6
Nigeria	1985	49.5	31.7	43	1992–93	36.4	30.4	34.1
Pakistan	1993	33.4	17.2	28.6	1998–99	35.9	24.2	32
Philippines	1994	45.4	18.6	32.1	1997	36.9	11.9	25.1
Sri Lanka	1995–96	27	15	25	2002	7.9	24.7	22.7
Tanzania	1991	40.8	31.2	38.6	2000–01	38.7	29.5	35.7
Thailand	1994	..	..	9.8	1998	..	..	13.6
Uganda	1999–00	37.4	9.6	33.8	2002–03	41.7	12.2	37.7
Vietnam	1998	45.5	9.2	37.4	2002	35.6	6.6	28.9

TABLE 16.5 Urban and rural poverty in selected developing countries

Notes: Rural population below the poverty line is the percentage of rural population living below the national rural poverty line; urban population below the poverty line is the percentage of urban population living below the national urban poverty line; and national population below poverty line is the percentage of the country's population living below the national poverty line.

Source: World Bank, *World Development Indicators* 2008, pp. 64–6.

Manipulation of the terms of trade

In order to encourage industrial investment, a strategy that was used in a number of developing countries after 1950 was to turn the terms of trade against agriculture in favour of manufacturing. Pakistan was a typical case of the strategy, in which industry was intended to benefit at the expense of agriculture. According to the *Third Five Year Plan of Pakistan (1965–70)* (Government of Pakistan, 1965, p. 7):

> There was a considerable transfer of income from the agricultural sector to the industrial sector during the 1950s as the terms of trade were deliberately turned against agriculture through such policies as licensing of scarce foreign exchange earned primarily by agriculture to the industrial sector, compulsory procurement of food grains at low prices to subsidize the cost of living of the urban, industrial workers, generous tax concessions to industry and lack of similar incentives for commercial agricultural investment.

The strategy of favouring industry against agriculture was considered to be justified mainly on the grounds that the large-scale manufacturing sector had a higher marginal rate of savings than the agricultural sector; hence the conscious move to discriminate against agriculture. Thus, although the industrial capitalists were undertaking investments, it was the farmers, rich and poor, who were paying in large part for capital formation in the early days of Pakistan's planned economic development. There was thus a deliberate policy of taking away the surplus from the rural areas, though they were significantly poorer than the urban areas, and the strategy formed the basis of much of Pakistan's capital formation in the 1950s and 1960s. The policy had its model in Soviet industrialization, when the Bolshevik government that had come to power through the Russian revolution adopted from 1928 a deliberate strategy of industrialization, in which one measure was to appropriate any surplus generated by work on the land.

The policy of favouring the industrial sector has been seriously criticized. There is no guarantee that the industrialists will invest their surplus domestically in productive assets. In fact, they may transfer it, legally or illegally, outside the country. They may also decide to spend the profit they earn on luxury consumption such as of high-value housing. There is ample evidence that both of these things took place in Pakistan. In fact, in the face of serious opposition the government of Pakistan had to alter its strategy: 'some of the policies were changed after 1959 and incentives were given to agriculture'. However, large-scale industry has continued to enjoy the privilege of being treated as the leading sector of the economy.

Land ownership and tenure: structure and reform

There is a widespread desire for land reform, meaning a transformation of the terms on which land is held and by whom, and of the size-distribution both of *landholdings* and of units *of property-ownership* in land. The motives may be social justice or else productive efficiency and growth, or a combination of both, and these two may or may not pull in the same directions. So land reform has come in many shapes, some of them more or less opposite to others. Overlying these two main motives, ideology – collectivist or individualist – may play a role in determining the form, as may political motives: the desire to maintain power on the part of the government of the day.

As one possible classification, we can distinguish four main types – distributist, collectivizing, nationalizing and privatizing – while recognizing that the boundaries between them are not exactly clear in practice.

Distributist

This covers those with the general intention of distributing land-holding, and for preference ownership, as widely as possible among the cultivators, in units of more-or-less equal value, each to be controlled by a single cultivating household, and setting an upper limit to the size of the land that any individual can own. Japan's reform of 1946, under the aegis of the Allied Control Council representing the occupying powers, and Taiwan's of a few years later that largely followed it – again under the influence of an occupying force, the Nationalist government from the mainland – are notable modern examples. Both of them are generally rated successful economically and politically. Each of them reformed a previous system of private ownership, and in both cases by world standards the typical areas of land owned by one owner, and also the areas of land cultivated as single enterprises, had been small (Dore, 1959; Fei *et al.*, 1979, pp. 38–50). A case of a distributist reform, this time from a previous collective-cum-state system, was that of Albania in the early 1990s. This aimed to reverse the collectivization completed about 25 years earlier and also to provide a holding for every cultivating family. Though the resulting holdings were mostly extremely small, output promptly surged, with big changes in its product composition. With other Albanian reforms of the time it can be regarded as politically successful in giving a large proportion of the country's families at least a small piece of productive property (Clunies-Ross and Sudar (eds), 1998, pp. 84–5). Another *de facto* distributist reform from a collectivized system was China's introduction of its 'household-responsibility' system in the early 1980s. Though the collective legal form was retained, each 'team' unit of land, formerly cultivated collectively by 30 or so families, was normally divided into household units with each household given many of the capacities of an owner. With rises about the same time of crop prices paid by the state and increasing freedom of private trading, the response was again a sharp rise in output.

Collectivist and nationalized (state-owned and state-managed)

These two forms have often gone side by side, as in the Soviet Union after 1928 and in China and Albania from the 1950s, in all three cases after an earlier distributist reform. Other Communist countries in Eastern Europe and elsewhere took somewhat the same path, generally with some degree of imitation of the Soviet model. Most of the land in each case was collectivized in legal form; but, whether nominally nationalized or collectivized, the producing entities were under a fairly high degree of state control, and the now almost universal verdict on their performance in production is that it was poor.

Privatizing

These reforms can be distinguished from distributist ones in purpose, though one can readily shade into the other in practice. A privatizing reform may have no distributional objective. In its straight form, it would allow land – once it has been made over to private hands – to be traded freely, regardless of the effect on its *distribution* across owners and across operating units. On standard free-market arguments, this would be the most efficient solution, with the important qualification made by Doreen Warriner (1955/1964) that size may give the landowner monopoly/monopsony power in dealing with tenants, and the land-holder, whether owner or tenant, in dealing with employees. Doubtless owners, both rich and poor, would resent legal limitations on their rights to sell their land or to raise money on its security, and it is easy to see that quite often any such limitation could seem harmful to both potential buyer and potential seller, with no obvious gainer in a particular case. Even short of such a prohibition, however, there may still be ways in which a government could support the maintenance of widely distributed landholding – for example, through credit institutions geared to helping smallholders who might otherwise be forced off their land – so that it is a relevant question whether maintaining widely distributed, and therefore small, landholdings should be an unvarying object of policy enforced by law.

That is one question raised by the land-reform issue and not easily answered. Compassion – possibly also a sense of justice – would favour keeping smallholder families on their land – as tenants if not as owners – *if that is what they choose.* However, it can also be argued that, if they want the opportunity to raise money on the security of their land, this option should be open to them, and in practice that would mean that smallholders could in certain circumstances lose their land. So which solution would make the best trade-off between equity on the one hand and the efficiency that could be conducive to agricultural growth on the other might be difficult to decide, whatever the ethical standpoint.

What does now seem abundantly clear is that state farms and large collectives are generally very inefficient forms. It seems that there are special characteristics of most farming, especially mixed farming – such as the variety of tasks and the need for continual adaptation and improvization – that make control by a remote and impersonal boss, whether bureaucrat or collective board, and the administrative overheads of anything larger than a 'small enterprise' in the formal sector, dysfunctional. There may be exceptions for capitalist, highly mechanized farming of a single crop over a large area, such as some have proposed for some less-exploited and less-populated parts of Africa, but the extreme labour-saving character of the technology and environmental concerns may make these propositions dubious.

Yet we return to the relationship between farm size and land productivity. Where it is the case that land is scarce and labour is surplus, it is land productivity rather than labour-productivity that needs to be maximized.

There was once a notion that small farms would be efficient because they would be able to use cheap family labour, and members of the landholding family could be presumed to be highly motivated. Against this it is argued that small farms can not so readily use certain modern inputs such as tractors and irrigation. That in itself does not settle the question because we should first need to know whether relative factor scarcities (and hence factor prices) justify the use of tractors at *any* relevant scale. If they do, then there *will* quite probably be some economies of scale: it will pay to have a scale that will use the equipment (as nearly as possible) fully. However, with only one piece of expensive equipment (say the tractor), costs will not necessarily continue falling as size goes on rising beyond the one-tractor scale. However, if there is another type of expensive gear such as a pump, which it also pays to use as fully as possible, or even more so if there are several different types of equipment that are relevant, the chances of approaching a point at which both or all are fully engaged generally increase as the scale of the operation rises. These gains from increased scale have to be set against extra costs (diseconomies of scale), arising most probably for organizational and incentive reasons.

Relevant to the desirability of reforms is analysis of the *share-cropping* system which is a common feature in many Asian countries. When landowners lease out their land they often take their rent in the form of a share of the crop, say 50 per cent or 40 per cent. (They may also share the cost of some inputs, such as fertilizer or hybrid seeds, but, in order to simplify the analysis initially, we ignore that possibility. It can be brought in later, when its significance depends on the terms in which those expenses are shared.) **Alfred Marshall** (1890/1920) provided a meticulous analysis of share-cropping. Figure 16.2 helps to explain this.[9] Here HC shows the marginal product of the input (say, labour) provided by the tenant and GC the share of marginal product of the input that accrues to the tenant. If OW is the (opportunity) cost of the input, OA is the amount of input that the tenant will employ. OHFA is the output. But if the landowner was cultivating the land, she would use OB amount of input and would produce OHEB amount of output. So, under the sharecropping method less input is used than under owner-cultivation, which will mean that there is lower output.

To put it simply, the owner-cultivator (or the tenant paying a fixed cash rent) gets the full value of the extra output resulting from every extra unit of input that she contributes. She will continue increasing production up to the point at which the extra value of output produced is just equal to the extra cost of the input required. The share-cropper gets only say half the value of the extra output. He will stop increasing production at the point at which the value of the extra output is equal to *twice* the cost of the extra input required to produce it. If marginal gross revenue diminishes as output increases, then the sharecropper will settle at an output *lower* than the one at which the owner or fixed-cash-rent tenant would settle. And the latter level of output is the more socially efficient. It is the one at which the social marginal gross revenue equals the (social) marginal cost.

---

[9] This figure and explanation have been taken from Taslim, M.A. (1995), 'Agricultural land tenancy in Bangladesh: a review', from the book *Bangladesh Economy: Evaluation and Research Agenda*, edited by Selim Rashid (1995).

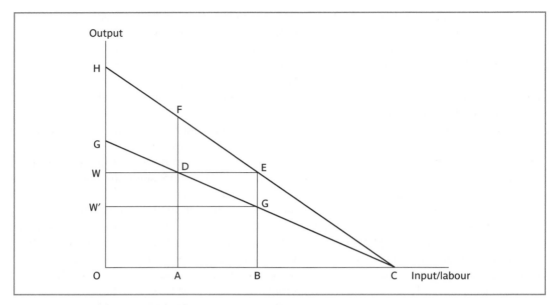

FIGURE 16.2 Output from share-cropping versus ownership-based cultivation

In an analysis of share-cropping, Zaman (1973) showed that the system was working inefficiently in Bangladesh. As tenants use less variable inputs such as water and fertilizer than they would if they were cultivating owners or tenants simply paying fixed cash rents, there is lower output under this than under the alternative arrangements, which is disadvantageous to both parties. Later on, the subject was studied by, among others, Hossain (1977) who also found the disincentive effect of share-cropping and concluded that 'the evidence lends support to the Marshallian proposition that sharecropping is an "inefficient" form of tenurial arrangement' (p. 332).

The advantage of share-cropping as against fixed rents for the tenant is that the risk is shared and sometimes that, beside the land, some of the capital is provided by the landlord in the form of a share in supplies. Presumably the advantage to the landlord is that he can charge a rent with a higher expected value than if it were fixed in cash. However, if the arrangement is socially inefficient, the implication is that both parties might gain if it were possible to reduce the tenant's risk and the cost of his capital in some other way, possibly with the help of crop insurance.

More generally on reform, there is a widespread belief in the need to distribute property and landholdings among the rural population (and not only current landholders) more equally, and a number of governments have professed such an objective. But redistributing, other than in a highly authoritarian state, is politically very difficult and risky.

Rural credit

A major constraint generally faced by the farmers in developing countries is the non-availability of credit from the traditional financial institutions. The problem arises, as John Brewster (1950) noted in a classic paper, because of the fact that agriculture is organized not only in small-scale units but also in a way that is spatially dispersed, so that the banks find it extremely difficult to monitor directly these large numbers of small farmers; hence the unwillingness on their part to lend any funds. This can be regarded as an 'agency' problem arising because of 'asymmetric knowledge' (this time it is the lender who is relatively ignorant).

We thus face a situation in which the small farmers have to depend on 'informal' sources, which include friends and relatives on the one hand and village money-lenders on the other. The money-lenders have remained a major source of finance (in cash and kind) to small-scale farmers. As can be seen from Box 16.3, a recent study in India has found that 'the share of the informal sector, notably traditional moneylenders and traders, in farmers' outstanding debts remains as high as 43.3 per cent at the all-India level'. Interest rates paid to money-lenders and commission agents are in the range of 18 per cent to 36 per cent. For production loans the question might at least be raised whether the extension of microfinance on the 'Bangladesh model' might offer useful possibilities, preferably backed by crop insurance to support the capacity of the borrowers to repay.

BOX 16.3 RURAL CREDIT: LOCAL LENDERS STILL RULE THE ROOST

'Despite a perceptible increase in the flow of rural credit from institutional sources, the share of the informal sector, notably traditional money-lenders and traders, in farmers' outstanding debts remains as high as 43.3 per cent at the all-India level.

'This share is higher than the national average in several agriculturally progressive states, including Punjab, Andhra Pradesh, Tamil Nadu and Rajasthan.

'The interest paid by farmers to money-lenders and commission agents is generally between 18 and 36 per cent, as revealed in a study on agriculture indebtedness in India, conducted by two agriculture economists of Punjab (R.S. Sidhu of the Ludhiana-based Punjab Agricultural University and Sucha Singh Gill of the Patiala-based Punjab University).

'The study has used the data of the 59th round of a survey conducted by the National Sample Survey Organization released in 2005.

'The study has concluded that deceleration in agriculture in the 1990s is one of the most important factors responsible for increasing indebtedness of farmers in the agriculturally advanced states.

'Manipur tops the list of states having a high share of moneylenders in rural credit. This works out as much as 81.9 per cent there.

'Money lenders' share in some other states is like this: 52.1 per cent in Punjab, 48.86 per cent in Andhra Pradesh, 63.8 per cent in Rajasthan, 42.6 per cent in Tamil Nadu, 58.3 per cent in Bihar, and 42 per cent in West Bengal.

'Farmers borrowing from non-institutional sources generally use their crop as collateral and commit to sell the output to lenders. The loans are also used to acquire inputs like seeds, fertilisers, insecticides and even consumer goods from the lenders.

'The inter-linked transactions take place largely because the lenders are usually engaged in the marketing of farm inputs, consumer goods and agriculture output, along with money lending.

'This has negative implications for agricultural development and cripples farmers' capacity to return loans and come out of debt traps, as the study report points out.'

Source: http://www.rediff.com/money/2006/jan/16credit.htm (Rediff India Abroad – 'As It Happens'), 23 March 2008 (from: Surinder Sud in New Delhi, 16 January 2006). Accessed 28 January 2009.

Summary conclusions

- Agriculture, though it has been witnessing significant and progressive declines in its GDP share, is still a very important sector in most developing countries. In low-income countries in 2006, its share in GDP was admittedly only 26 per cent, and much less in those of middle income. But, in employment, the dominance of agriculture in *low-income* countries persists; the data as available for 1995 show that 69 per cent of the labour force in low-income countries was then engaged in agriculture, and the corresponding figures were 36 and 21 per cent respectively in lower-middle- and upper-middle-income countries.

- Though low productivity and disguised unemployment are commonly considered two key features of agriculture in developing countries, the facts have been debated. While the low labour productivity (in relation to high-income countries and technical possibilities) is not disputed, the existence of disguised unemployment has at times been contested, by among others Schultz (1964). However, Lewis's labour-surplus model does seem to have fitted with labour-market behaviour in a large class of developing countries.

- The important role that agriculture plays in development has attracted the attention of a number of economists. David Ricardo (1817) is one of the early economists to emphasize the importance of agriculture given the scarcity of land and the resultant diminishing returns. Johnston and Mellor (1961) and Simon Kuznets (1965) are some of the other contributors who have helped articulate the special role that agriculture plays in economic development, in particular through the supply of output especially food, through development of markets, through the supply of labour, and through the earning of foreign exchange. The *World Development Report* 2008 considers agriculture a 'vital development tool for achieving the Millennium Development Goal that calls for halving by 2015 the share of people suffering from extreme poverty and hunger'.

- The success that is possible from technological changes is now apparent to us, especially because of the spectacular achievement of the Green Revolution which helped to transform a large part of Third World agriculture, with high growth in output and crop yield. These were remarkable during the earlier part (1961–80) of this period, though less impressive in the later part (1981–2000). At the start of the new Millennium, the world appears to be at the threshold of a new 'Gene Revolution', based on genetically engineered ('GM') crops: crops whose genetic make-up has been altered through a process called recombinant DNA, or gene-slicing. However, the Gene Revolution is facing some strong opposition, mainly in Western Europe, based on apocalyptic fears that have no support from scientists, coupled with anti-corporate suspicion. The successes of technological changes in the past have demonstrated that R&D in agriculture can produce high rates of return. For example, the social internal rate of return (IRR) of research in hybrid corn was estimated at 43 per cent. However, in low-income countries, while private investment in agricultural research is almost non-existent, public investment in R&D is also very low, often below 0.5 per cent of GDP.

- After three decades of relatively stable prices, in 2007–08 developing-country and world markets experienced unprecedented shifts in the prices of staple foodstuffs. As well as inducing immediate social turmoil, these events revived concerns about the possible reappearance of long-run problems with food security, and even of the rebirth of 'Malthus'

Devil'. The main short-run cause of the sudden rise in food prices has been the running down of stocks of foodstuffs (partly because of bad weather and associated poor harvests in the recent past, and, reinforcing this, a reaction to the rising carrying-cost of stocks as prices rose). From the demand side plausible long-term causes include the continued population growth and rising incomes resulting from rapid economic growth in Asia. From the supply side, sharply rising prices of oil and natural gas pushed food prices up directly by increasing agricultural production costs, and rising oil prices pushed up food prices indirectly by further increasing the attractiveness of diverting grain supplies from food to biofuel production. Two main (competing) policy directions have been suggested as means of establishing sustainable food supplies for the developing world. The first can be categorized as the 'technical fix', favouring bio-engineered ('GM') crops and large-scale corporate farming. The second, the 'evolutionary' approach, seeks to achieve sustainability of developing-country food supplies by, first, breaking (possibly with outside help) the vicious circle in which hunger and poverty reinforce each other, and then promoting small-scale, environmentally friendly farming, relying to a significant extent on 'local knowledge' relating to sustainable cultivation techniques. But it seems misleading to treat these approaches as if each of the two packages was indivisible.

- There is now strong evidence to show that agricultural growth is highly effective in reducing poverty. This has been confirmed, among others, by the findings of a study by Ravallion and Datt (1996). Their extensive cross-section analysis showed that agricultural growth can be the main driver of poverty reduction in low- and middle-income countries, although there is a significant lag in the impact achieved. The lag is due to the indirect character of the impact, which is attributed to the reduction in food prices, the increase in farm employment, and also the increase in rural non-farm employment.

- However, agricultural development in the Third World is faced with various challenges. First, policy in the developing world is typically urban-biased. As government policies are biased towards urban areas, the rural areas are neglected, not only in the development of utilities and infrastructural facilities such as electricity and road communications but also in the provision of basic services including education, health and housing. In some countries there has been a deliberate policy of turning the terms of trade against agriculture, as a means of favouring urban, industrial development. Until recently, many developing countries in their eagerness to promote industrial development, used to keep the prices of exports (which were often mainly of agricultural goods) depressed, while the prices of home-grown manufactured goods were kept artificially high by protection. The policies that emerged from the protectionist measures harmed the agriculturalists for the immediate benefit *of those with interests in industry* mainly based in urban areas (though not necessarily to the advantage of long-term industrial growth). With the liberalization that has been more recently in fashion, the old policy of turning the terms of trade against agriculture is, fortunately, no longer pursued as commonly as it was in the past.

- Second, there are perennial concerns on both efficiency and equity grounds over the structure of land ownership and tenure. 'Reforms' have taken various strongly divergent forms – distributist, collectivist, nationalizing, privatizing – with by now considerable experience of the various advantages and drawbacks. In present-day land tenure, an

▶ important concern is the system of share-cropping commonly practised in the Indian sub-continent. This is an inefficient form of tenurial arrangement because of the disincentives generated that have the effect of reducing output below the social optimum, and it may be possible to find more efficient ways of reducing the risk to cultivators, possibly with the help of crop insurance. Redistribution of ownership and holdings in land, and reform of tenures, has been widely approved but seldom carried out in a thoroughgoing and radical way except under authoritarian government (as in East Asia in the years just after the end of the Second World War and the Communist triumph in China).

- Third, the rural sector is at a disadvantage in its access to finance. As agriculture in developing countries is often organized on a small scale and is spatially dispersed, there is reluctance on the part of the traditional financial institutions to lend money to farmers. Consequently, not only is investment limited but also there is heavy dependence on the informal sector, that is on such people as village moneylenders and traders. A recent all-India study found that the average dependence of the farmers on informal money-lending is as high as 43.3 per cent. The interest rates charged are also high, ranging from 18 to 36 per cent. For production loans, the extension of microfinance on the 'Bangladesh model' might offer some possibilities, preferably backed by crop insurance.

World output of foodcrops must go on rising if it is to keep pace with rising world population and income. Even if the 2007–08 food-price rises turn out to be largely short-term phenomena, output will still have plenty of catching-up to do if it is to meet present nutritional needs adequately. In addition, if those in most need of them are to receive the necessary entitlements, much of the catching-up will need to be done by or on behalf of the very poor in the rural sector. The new GM agricultural technology has come at an opportune time, but it needs to be adapted or interpreted, and perhaps accompanied by other reforms, so that those most in need of it can use it productively.

Questions for discussion

16.1   Given that the share of agriculture as a percentage of GDP has fallen in all regions of the world, explain why expanding output in the sector is still considered to have an important role for economic development in Third World countries.

16.2   What is meant by 'marketable surplus' in agriculture? Is its role in development rightly considered as that of a source of finance for the growth of other sectors?

16.3   What are the possible and the probable causes of the increases in food prices that have taken place in and after 2007–08.

16.4   Explain the special importance asserted of the contribution of growth in agricultural output toward poverty reduction.

16.5   Explain the objections on efficiency grounds to share-cropping as a form of land tenure. Why, given those objections, which seem to indicate disadvantages to both landlord and tenant, do you think the system persists?

16.6   Why have large-scale farm collectives and state farms been generally so unsuccessful in production?

Additional reading

FAO [Food and Agriculture Organization] (2006) *The State of Food Insecurity in the World*, FAO, Rome.

Hayami, Y. and Ruttan, V.W. (1971, 1985) *Agricultural Development*, Johns Hopkins University Press, Baltimore.

Mellor, J.W. (2008) 'Agriculture and economic development', *The New Palgrave Dictionary of Economics*, edited by S.N. Durlauf and L.E. Blume, Palgrave Macmillan, Basingstoke, pp. 100–105.

Timmer, C.P. (1988) 'The agricultural transformation', in H.B. Chenery and T.N. Srinivasan (eds) *Handbook of Development Economics*, North-Holland, Amsterdam, vol. I, pp. 275–6.

Timmer, C.P. (2006) 'Agriculture and economic growth', in D.A. Clark (ed.), *The Elgar Companion to Development Studies*, Edward Elgar, Cheltenham, pp. 5–10.

World Bank (various issues), *World Development Indicators*, Washington, DC.

World Bank (2008) *World Development Report 2008: Agriculture for Development*, World Bank, Washington, DC.

Online *Learning* Center

To help you grasp the key concepts of this chapter **check out the extra resources posted on the Online Learning Centre at *www.mcgraw-hill.co.uk/textbooks/huq***

Among other resources, the following appendix is available:

- Appendix 16.1   Diagrammatic representation of disguised unemployment

CHAPTER 17

Industrialization and Development

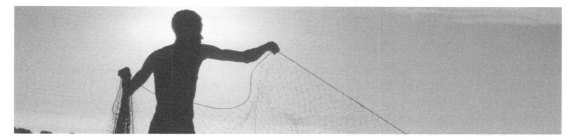

For a long time increasing affluence seemed to be intimately connected with growth in the importance of 'industry', and specifically of manufacturing, in the economy. However, in the late twentieth century the richest countries began to 'deindustrialize', while nearly all the big developing countries, a number of them still in the low-income class, became predominantly exporters of manufactures, and for some of them industry has become more important in their output than it is for some of the most affluent. Yet manufacturing seems likely to remain the main gateway through which a traditional economy must pass on its journey to secure affluence.

Introduction

This chapter faces the dual meaning attached to the term 'industrialization': on the one hand a change in an economy's **sectoral structure**, and on the other the attainment of, or the process of attaining, **secure affluence**. It seeks to explain how the two have been confused, and against this background to account for the paradoxical appearance of 'deindustrialization' in the richest countries.

We consider the sound reasons for supposing that the rapid growth of manufacturing (an 'industrial revolution') could be seen as virtually **a necessary *gateway*** to transformative economic growth for a largely traditional economy and may continue to be so; the apparent dilemma faced by mid-twentieth-century development economists in the need for 'balanced growth' if the fast-growing manufacturing that they desired was to find markets; and the solution – in the form of export-expansion – that began to emerge, not from theory but from events, in the late 1960s.

In this light we examine the choice, in **industrialization policy**, between the roles of state and market – with characteristic pitfalls when the state has overplayed its hand – and between closed-economy and open-economy strategies.

Finally we consider the Prebisch–Singer observations and hypotheses bearing on the **long-term trends in the terms of trade** between primary products and manufactures and between developing and developed countries, how far they have stood up to later investigation, and what relevance if any they may have to policy of and toward developing countries in the early twenty-first century, when manufacturing is coming to seem almost more characteristic of the poor 'periphery' than of the rich 'centre'.

BOX 17.1 TOOLKIT ON INDUSTRIALISATION

Balanced growth. A policy model forcefully advanced in the early 1950s by Ragnar Nurkse (1907–59), which argues for the simultaneous development of a large number of industries so that they can generate markets for one another. Earlier, in 1943, Paul Rosenstein-Rodan (1902–85) had advanced a similar argument for a '**Big Push**' theory.

Big push. The arguments for this policy are similar to those for the **balanced-growth policy**, but here it is specifically argued for investments to be undertaken in a big way – at a relatively high minimum scale – so that they enjoy not only external economies but also internal economies of scale. Paul Rosenstein-Rodan advanced in 1943 the theory of a need for a big push.

Capacity utilization. Output of a firm or a plant as measured against its installed (full) capacity. If the firm is producing only half of the output that could be produced with its full-capacity operation, the capacity-utilization rate is only 50 per cent.

Deindustrialization. A process of economic change now being experienced by some rich countries entailing a fall in the share of the manufacturing sector in national output and employment.

Export-pessimism. The assumption that the developing countries cannot depend on exports for significant economic growth either because they export primary goods which have inelastic demand or because they will be unable to break into established world markets for manufactures.

Export-promotion strategy. A strategy to promote exports of manufactured goods by removing obstacles to the expansion of export-based industries. (The policy has also been called an **outward-oriented industrialization strategy**.)

Income-elasticity of demand. This is measured by the proportionate change in the quantity demanded divided by the proportionate change in income of the purchasers. Responsiveness of the quantity of a good demanded to a change in the income of its buyers.

Import-substituting industrialization (ISI) strategy. A policy that actively supports local production of manufactured goods which were previously imported, as pursued by many developing countries in Latin America especially from the 1930s to the late 1980s and a number of Asian and African countries (at times vigorously) since the 1950s. The intellectual backing for the strategy has been provided by, among others, Raul Prebisch (1901–86) and Hans Singer (1910–2006). (The policy has also been called an **inward-oriented industrialization strategy**.)

Income terms of trade. A measure obtained when we divide the value index of a country's exports by the price index of its imports.

Inappropriate technologies. Technologies which produce goods at a high cost of production because the decision-makers fail to select the right type of machinery and equipment, or opt for the wrong scale of production, or select inappropriate products.

▶ **Industrialization policy.** Any deliberate attempt to promote the manufacturing sector, an objective that has been actively pursued by many developing countries since the 1950s.

Prebisch–Singer hypothesis. As put forward by Raul Prebisch and Hans Singer, this hypothesis (which was advanced independently by them in 1950) supposes that heavy dependence on the export of primary products, typical of developing countries in the mid-twentieth century and of a number still, is likely to lead to a deterioration in their terms of trade and to that extent a loss in income.

Price-elasticity of demand. Responsiveness of quantity of a good demanded to a change in its price: it is the proportionate change in quantity demanded divided by the proportionate change in price.

Terms of trade. The **net barter terms of trade** is the ratio of the index of export prices to that of import prices. A fall in export prices in relation to import prices is called a deterioration in the terms of trade. The secular deterioration of the terms of trade of primary-commodity exporters is a key feature in the **Prebisch–Singer hypothesis**.

Structural change and economic growth

One word, two meanings

The idea of **industrialization** has become thoroughly tangled with that of **development**. The subject can not be coherently discussed without awareness of the two separate meanings of the terms *industrialize* and *industrialization*. One sense of 'industrialization', the *structural* sense, refers to the shift in the pattern of a country's output and workforce toward manufacturing or toward secondary industry or toward 'industry' on a wider definition; and in this sense an 'industrialized' country is one in which the proportional importance of this sector (whichever exactly it is) has exceeded a certain point. So one writer (Sutcliffe, 1971, p. 18) ventured in the early 1970s to put arbitrary figures on the definition:

> a country 25 per cent of whose GDP arose in the industrial sector, of which at least 60 per cent was in manufacturing, and which had at least one-tenth of its population employed in industry would be counted as industrialized. Any country which did not satisfy these three criteria would not.

The other use of 'industrialized' is often simply a longer way of saying *developed* or *rich*, a country having an income per head above a certain level, maybe a high-income country under the World Bank's classification. However, as we said in discussion of the term in Chapter 1, some would *avoid* using it for certain classes of rich countries: broadly those whose affluence was highly and directly dependent on minerals or foreign military establishments or aid and might therefore readily contract drastically if the mineral resource ran out or ceased to be mined or the base or aid was removed.

Connection of economic growth with the structural move to 'industry'

Until well on in the twentieth century those countries that were 'industrialized' in the sense of rich, at least in the more restricted version of 'rich' in which the affluence was firmly based, would also be countries with relatively high proportions of output and workforce attributable to 'industry' (which includes mining and the operation of the 'utilities') and, within industry, to manufacturing; and conversely the ones that met those structural conditions would also be rich, with good prospects of so remaining. So industrialization in the first (structural) sense *seemed* to be *a necessary and sufficient condition* of industrialization in the restricted version of the second sense (secure affluence). To become reliably rich, a country had to swing heavily toward manufacturing. That was not so much argued as taken for granted by most mid-century development economists, such as Rosenstein-Rodan (1943), who was concerned not with *whether* expanding secondary industry was necessary for significant economic growth but *how* that expansion could be achieved. Marxists and non-Marxists alike made the same presumptions. Stalin's transformation of the Soviet economy, at its most intense in the years after 1928, was conceived as a massive expansion of industrial production, drawing workers and finance (in the sense of claims on output or value) from the agrarian sector. Major 'Western' writers such as Nurkse (1952), Rostow (1960) and Gerschenkron (1962) also saw development as being intimately linked with industrial production.

Reasons were given, as we shall see, why a switch to 'industry' was so important: what specific features manufacturing had that agriculture did not. But there was little doubt that it *was* important, so that 'industrialization' and 'development' came to be used almost interchangeably.

The paradox of deindustrialization in affluence

Then, in the later part of the century, events began to challenge the view that there was some special quality of 'industry' or of manufacturing that made its relative expansion a precondition for economic growth, and a certain relative importance of manufacturing within an economy a precondition (perhaps even a sufficient condition as well) for affluence. The rich countries generally – still growing richer – began to experience *deindustrialization*: 'industry' and manufacturing started *declining* in relative importance within output and employment.

Table 17.1 shows some of the changes in the sectoral origin of output. The **relative decline of agriculture** generally continued through the latter part of the century. It was **the service sector** that now expanded in a number of growing economies both rich and poor, though that sector in the late twentieth century, especially in the rich countries, covered a very different pattern of activities from those of the 'pre-industrial age' or indeed of the rich countries themselves a century earlier: there was far less domestic service, for example, and more of the service requirements of the knowledge economy.

As the table shows, even some of the countries that were or had quite recently been in the lower-income categories experienced some decline in the proportional importance of industry round the end of the century. In the case of South Korea this extended to a decline in the share of manufacturing itself, while the country's per capita GDP was still forging ahead; and even India showed a slight fall in the share of industry during a period of fast economic growth between 1998 and 2006, as the share of agriculture continued to drop and of services to expand – both of them quite sharply.

Moreover, India, Indonesia and Egypt in or around 2006 (a low-income and two low-middle-income countries) were all deriving *higher* proportions of output from industry than Australia, France, the UK or the US; and in or around 1998 Egypt and Indonesia were drawing higher proportions *from manufacturing specifically* than Australia, France,

Sector	Agriculture				Services			
	1965	1980	1998	2006	1965	1980	1998	2006
Egypt	29	18	17	15*	45	45	50	49*
India	44	38	25	18	34	39	45	55
Indonesia	56	24	15*	12	31	34	41*	46
South Korea	38	15	6	3	37	45	51	57
Pakistan	40	30	25	20	40	46	50	53
Australia	9	5	3*	3	51	58	71*	70
France	8	4	2*	2	54	62	72*	77
Italy	10	6	3*	2*	53	55	66*	71*
Japan	9	4	..	2*	48	54	..	68*
UK	3	2	2*	1	51	55	67*	73
US	3	3	2*	1	59	54	71*	77
	Industry				[within which Manufacturing]			
	1965	1980	1998	2006	1965	1980	1998	2006
Egypt	27	37	33	36*	....	12	26	17
India	22	24	30	28	16	16	19	16
Indonesia	13	42	43*	42	8	13	26*	28
South Korea	25	40	43	40	18	28	26	28
Pakistan	20	25	25	27	14	16	17	19
Australia	39	36	36*	27	26	19	14*	11
France	38	34	26*	21	27	24	19	..
Italy	37	39	31*	27*	35	28*	20*	..
Japan	43	42	..	30*	32	29	..	..
UK	46	43	31*	26	34	27	21*	..
US	38	33	27*	22	28	22	18*	..

TABLE 17.1 Proportions of value-added from the main sectors in GDP, various countries, 1965, 1980, 1998, 2006, percentages

Notes: An asterisk denotes a year other than the one specified but close to it. Because of rounding totals may not always add to 100.
Source: World Bank, World Development Reports 1990, 1999/2000, 2008. World Development Indicators 2008, pp. 202–4.

Germany, Italy, the UK or the US. Around 1998, on Sutcliffe's 1971 definition, Australia was no longer an industrialized country, and France and the US were running close and in fact would cease to qualify by 2006. On the other hand, in 2006 a number of low- and low-middle-income countries met at least one of Sutcliffe's tests, that of having 25 per cent or more of output from industry. These (not all covered in the table) included Bangladesh, Brazil, China, Colombia, Egypt, India, Indonesia, Pakistan, the Philippines, Thailand, and Vietnam (World Bank, WDR 2008, pp. 333, 340–1). It is almost as if being industrialized in the structural sense of the term is coming to seem more a feature of poorer countries than of the rich.

The very low (sometimes negative, effectively non-existent) relationship in the most recent years between income per head and the weight of industry or of manufacturing in

GDP is illustrated by the scatter diagrams and regression estimates in Figures 17.1 to 17.4. It seems from the scatter diagrams that what are now poor countries may have either high or low proportions of output from industry or from manufacturing, while more affluent countries generally have middling proportions, with some outliers (for industry as a whole as well as for manufacturing) very high or very low. In 1990, the positive relationship for industry as a whole, shown in Figure 17.1, is *almost* significant at the 5 per cent level, and that for manufacturing (Figure 17.2) is significant at the 10 per cent level, though the fit shown by R-square is very low in each case. In 2006 the relationship for industry has turned negative, and that for manufacturing is a long way from even 10 per cent significance. This fits with the way structural industrialization has seemed, from the other evidence we have given, to be moving. When we exclude the very small countries (the Guams and Greenlands) from the sample (in four similar regressions, results not shown here), only the relationship for manufacturing in 1990 is positive with as much as 10 per cent significance.

Why could growth in the weight of industry and manufacturing once have seemed so closely connected with the growth of income but now apparently cease to be so?

Probably only a small part of the answer is that there is some statistical artefact involved. If a group of workers providing IT services to a manufacturing concern change from being employees say to becoming a partnership that does the same work as before but now as an independent contractor, the workers and their product move in the statistics from 'manufacturing' to 'services'. Such outsourcing has become quite common.

Yet, even if such reclassification explained some part of the data that appeared to show *deindustrialization* in high-income countries, or there were other conditions explaining why the case of already affluent countries was different, there would remain the question why the

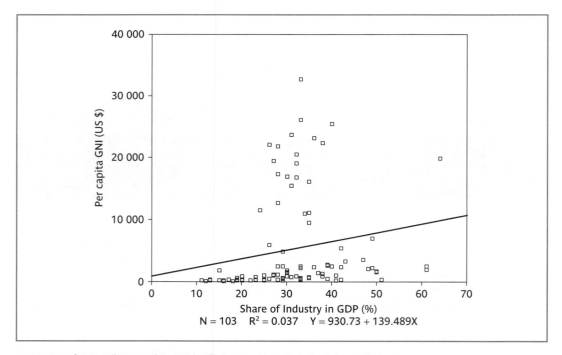

FIGURE 17.1 Scatter diagram of per capita GNI and share of industry in GDP, 1990
t statistic is 1.914, s.e. of slope is 72.89, slope is 139.489, p-value is 0.059.
Source: World Bank, *World Development Indicators* 2008.

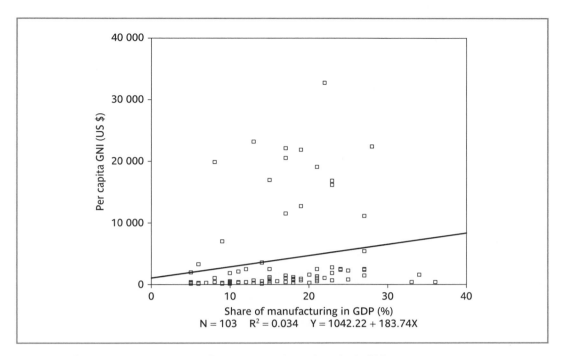

FIGURE 17.2 Scatter diagram of per capita GNI and share of manufacturing in GDP, 1990
t statistic is 1.739, s.e. of slope is 105.63, slope is 183.74, p-value is 0.086.
Source: World Bank, *World Development Indicators* 2008.

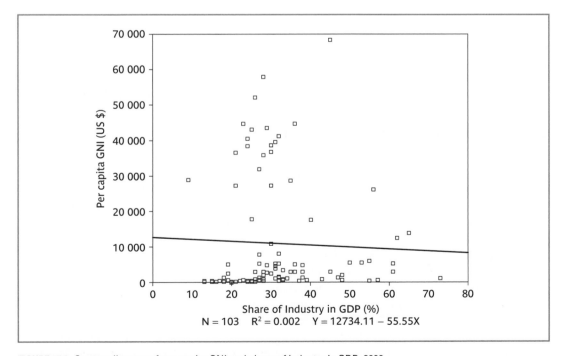

FIGURE 17.3 Scatter diagram of per capita GNI and share of industry in GDP, 2006
t statistic is –0.418, slope is –55.55, s.e. of slope is 132.77, p-value is 0.677.
Source: World Bank, *World Development Indicators* 2008.

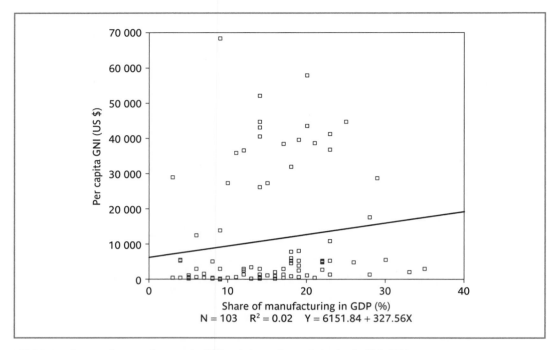

FIGURE 17.4 Scatter diagram of per capita GNI and share of manufacturing in GDP, 2006
t statistic is 1.35, slope is 327.56, s.e. of slope is 241.02, p-value is 0.177.
Source: World Bank, *World Development Indicators* 2008.

expansion of manufacturing had so long seemed, and indeed still seems, to be an essential part of the *path* to firmly based affluence for a low-income or low-middle-income country. The importance in secure economic growth of a shift of the workforce and output to manufacturing has scarcely been questioned. The questions of interest are **why it has been so important** and **by what means and at what initial cost it is worth pursuing.**

What is so special about manufacturing?

In answering this question we can simplify by considering only the shift of the workforce, as if labour was the only factor of production. But what is said about labour can be applied, *mutatis mutandis,* to other factors of production.

An obvious answer to the question is that manufacturing must be *more productive in net revenue per worker* at the margin (as valued in the relative prices of the time) than agriculture, from which much of the industrial workforce inevitably comes when manufacturing is growing fast from a low base. So, is manufacturing just intrinsically more productive per worker than agriculture? The answer to that question has to be no. Modern agriculture can be just as productive per worker as modern manufacturing. High-income countries can feed their people from the labour of a tiny fraction of the workforce that they used for the purpose before their industrial revolutions. Failing the capacity for big food imports, increased productivity per worker in agriculture is *a necessary accompaniment* of the rapid growth in non-agricultural activities that draws large numbers of workers into other activities. This may come about in part because the remaining workers are left with more land each from which to produce as a result of the industry-wards shift of the workforce, in part because the upward pressure on farm prices generated by the increasing numbers and income of workers in other sectors makes it possible and worthwhile to invest in equipment and other productive farm inputs, and in part because, historically, the range of known and accessible agrarian technology has expanded. The fact remains that more recently, in average labour product, agriculture has been able to enter the same league as secondary industry.

So it would seem that the explanation must be more dynamic. If a new sector can be found which is *initially* markedly more productive per worker at the margin than existing traditional activities – primary and secondary – (more productive in the sense of generating more earnings) *and* it can continue to expand while continuing to be more productive at the margin in what it earns, even while the *average* revenue-productivity of workers in the traditional sector is also rising, then, so long as these conditions last, the new sector can continue to draw workers from the old, and its own output can continue to grow. The new sector, as it increases its workforce and output, can drag the traditional sector up with it.

Mechanized manufacturing, even at first of a rather primitive kind, has apparently met these requirements for the new sector. In net value-added per worker it was decidedly more productive at the margin than traditional activities, and, if the value-added of the manufactures was reckoned in the prices of the traditional handicrafts that they displaced at the start of the industrial era, *much more productive*. This meant it would be capable of what must have seemed, at the start of the first industrial revolution (in Britain), quite explosive growth.

Certainly the 'first industrial economy' had advantages. It could offer goods – potentially right across the world – that used much less labour, and so could be sold much cheaper, than the handcraft products with which they competed. Subsequent entrants to mechanized manufacturing had to find new markets for it, or to extend it to new products, or to penalize foreign goods in their own domestic markets, or to produce even more cheaply. However, comparatively low-wage countries – Japan, India – were already producing textiles and clothing – those original staples of modern manufacturing – by mechanized methods on a large scale, and exporting them, well before the Second World War – and Japan was producing a much wider range than that. Low-wage countries were able to take over a large part of the British markets in cotton and jute textiles. Latecomers *could* enter the markets, especially if they came with low efficiency-wages.

Nevertheless, if the new sector (say manufacturing of consumer goods) is to expand continuously, it has to find an ever-growing market onto which to unload its products. The obvious solution might seem to lie in the fact that its domestic market would expand as its income all round expanded with the new lines of production. This, however, led, as explained under 'Balanced and unbalanced growth – and the big push' in Chapter 5, to an apparent problem for early development-economics thinkers, who were explicitly or implicitly supposing closed economies, or at least a market for exports that could increase only slowly. Manufacturing in a country might start with a relatively simple and limited range of goods. The domestic market for these goods would be correspondingly limited. Those whose incomes were increasing would want to buy a more varied range. If these were not produced locally, they would have to be bought from abroad. There would be additional demand for imports with no correspondingly increased source of earnings from exports. At the same time, the manufacturers would find that, with a limited range of products, their domestic market could not continue increasing in line with national income.

The apparent balanced-growth dilemma

This apparent dilemma led to the idea of the need for *balanced growth*, and for a *big push* – a sudden large addition to purchasing power and investment in order to make balanced growth possible – so that the manufacturers should have the capital and the markets that would promptly enable them to produce and sell enough of virtually everything to realize the potential economies of scale and to satisfy most of the demand that would be created. In the absence of the resources for a big push or before it had time to work itself out, manufacturers would need to be guided or directed or given incentives to produce a 'balanced' range of goods. While the range of goods that could be produced competitively was limited, taxes or restrictions would be needed on manufactured imports *both* to stop too much of the spending-power leaking abroad while there were no additional export earnings to pay for it *and* to encourage the domestic production of those goods for which there was currently a demand directed to imports.

So, manufacturing, though not always and everywhere necessarily more productive than other sectors, did have very suitable characteristics as a lead sector for a traditional economy to break through to higher productivity and income all round – as by the time of the Second World War it had done in Western Europe, within the lands of new European settlement in somewhat different circumstances, and to a point in Japan and the Soviet Union – *if only that problem of balancing demand with supply as the sector expanded could be solved.* We suggest that this insight was correct but that what for a number of years blocked understanding about how to make use of it was the *export-pessimism* fixation, a hangover from the experience of ex-colonies (including those in Latin America) in the inter-war years, and the apparent success of Stalinist planning. The big-push provided no solution – for one thing, because there was no chance it would happen, and, for another, because there was no hope for a moderately sized economy to approach self-sufficiency across the range of manufactures and still reap the potential economies of scale in each.

As we shall explain in this chapter and as has been mentioned in Chapter 5, Raul Prebisch and Hans Singer, very early in the story, threw up further 'dynamic' ideas about the suitability of manufactures as a growth sector, in this case in a context of international trade, but perhaps not all the implications that were eventually to reveal themselves were properly grasped at the time.

The export solution

The solution as it began to emerge from the late 1960s (though at first little recognized) was this. In fact, the world presented a huge potential market for simple, fairly standardized manufactures, such as much textiles and clothing. *Total market demand* for these goods was probably quite price-elastic (*unlike* that for tea or bauxite), but, because they were fairly standardized, they (*like* tea or bauxite this time) presented a highly price-elastic *demand to a comparatively small new entrant.* If a low-income, low-wage country could produce them cheaply enough and to an acceptable standard, it might have vast markets at its disposal. Also, despite persisting obstacles, there was considerable freeing of international trade in manufactures after 1945, with the formation of GATT, its non-discriminatory rules (for all their exceptions), and its successive rounds of negotiations. Conveniently too, as Prebisch and Singer had recognized, the world's demand for manufactures in general – and consequently for many classes of manufactures – increased faster than its real income.

To those that could get into manufacture at this global ground floor – initially the four East Asian 'Tigers', following the path trodden by Japan inter-war – their manufacturing sectors could expand very fast, drawing large numbers from agriculture as it did so and giving that sector the opportunity and the incentive to increase progressively its average labour productivity. It was not that manufacturing was *intrinsically* more productive than agriculture; rather that even low-technology modern mechanized manufacture was more productive per worker than *existing, traditional* agriculture, and that, once it had begun to produce for global markets, it became a new and wide open outlet for growth in self-supporting (unsubsidized) employment. As such it could not only generate extra income itself but also alter the context (the factor-proportions and possibilities of improvement) in which agriculture operated.

As the incomes and wage levels of these new entrants to the global markets for simple manufactures increased, and they added to their stocks of capital and human capital, their wage levels rose, and they tended to move up the scale into less unskilled-labour-intensive exports, leaving the field open for new relays of very-low-wage countries to enter, a development termed 'late industrialization' by Alice Amsden (1989) (see Box 17.2). This has happened in a big way with the Four Tigers and has begun to happen also with others, such as Thailand and Malaysia and China.

The apparently high proportions of output pertaining around the turn of the millennium to manufacturing in a number of still comparatively poor countries covering a large part of the world's population – even while the proportions in the rich countries decline – **do not mean that manufacturing has lost its potency as an accessible doorway to more or less rapid growth of output and income for the low-income and low-middle-income countries**. Quite the reverse. **It is rather that, in the countries that have reached affluence, marginal revenue products of the main factors of production across the various sectors will probably have become roughly equal, so that there is no longer any one sector in which investment can yield large, quick returns in national output and income through attracting resources from other sectors**. How the sectors then grow differentially in the most productive way will depend on factors such as changing final demand and technological advance, the latter of which in increasingly knowledge-based economies probably tips the scales toward services. In countries that have become affluent it is no longer important for manufacturing to increase differentially fast.

Incidentally, some of the important **service activities** too (such as computer programming and the manning of call centres) now have price-elastic export markets. For a low-income country such as India that happens to be able to enter these markets on a big scale, they may play the role in economic growth previously reserved to manufacturing.

That another sector, even one catering for the domestic market, might in certain conditions play a role similar to that of manufactured exports is perhaps illustrated by the experience of Colombia in the early 1970s, when, in response to indexation of deposit and mortgage interest rates designed to remove the distortion introduced by inflation into housing finance, there was a prolonged boom in **house building** that fed into a rapid rise in national income, one that might quite possibly have continued if the original reforms had remained in force (Sandilands, 1990, ch. 10). House building had the advantage for a foreign-exchange-constrained, labour-surplus economy that it was labour-intensive and domestic-materials-intensive, and, for the continuance of economic growth, that its demand in the circumstances was highly income-elastic, so that any resulting increase in income was fertile in its generation of further demand for its own output.

It has also been argued that an additional reason why a shift toward 'industry' contributes to growth is that it shows a higher propensity to save than agriculture. If this is so, at least when agriculture is still largely 'traditional', it may be because of the capitalist nature of enterprise and ownership in industry within market economies in contrast to the 'household' nature of organization in traditional farming.

From what has been said, the strategy of promoting industrialization *at the cost of* agriculture needs to be questioned. First of all, agriculture provides directly the livelihoods for a large part (in the poorest economies often still the majority) of the population, a part concentrated in the poorer segment. Agriculture can also, through the taxes it pays, be an important source of financing for the infrastructure element in industrial investment. (In the old command economies it was often heavily milked to finance industry, but this may have been carried to the point of being self-defeating.) In certain countries, agriculture will provide raw materials for industries. Incomes from agriculture will also offer an important market for the locally produced industrial goods; and, unless the country can afford to rely heavily on food imports, it will face difficulties if food production does not increase as output in other sectors, and income all round, increase. For industry to fulfil its role of opening the path to fast development, farm output must also grow.

BOX 17.2 SOME VIEWS OF LATE INDUSTRIALIZATION: ADVANTAGE OR HANDICAP?

Thorstein Veblen in 1915 had written on the 'advantages of backwardness', referring to what he regarded as Germany's advantage as a latecomer to industrialization over Britain. Alexander Gerschenkron (1962) updated and extended this theme to include Russia, France and Italy. Taking account of the insights of Gerschenkron, Alice Amsden (1989 and 2001) has tried to explore whether poor countries in the twentieth century could similarly take advantage of their relative backwardness. The gist of her answer seems to be no. Contrary to the view we have expressed in the text of the chapter, she regards the latest-comers as being under a handicap.

By contrast with the first industrial revolution that took place in the late eighteenth century in the UK, and the second industrial revolution that started some 100 years later in Germany and the US (both of which involved new products and processes), 'late industrialization' – that of countries that did not start the process until the twentieth century – has depended heavily on borrowed technology, and the story of their success is their ability to learn this technology fast.

The four East Asian Tigers – South Korea, Singapore, Taiwan and Hong Kong – are viewed as the shining examples of late industrialization. Amsden (1989) argues that industrialization was late in coming to these countries – and they remained backward for a long time – because they were too weak as states to mobilize forces for economic development, which would have involved fending off foreign aggression. She also believes that in modern history the state has always needed to intervene to spur economic activity. Moreover, she has no doubt that to catch up in the twentieth century has required still heavier doses of government support than in the century before because backwardness has been relatively greater. Thus, she believes that without a strong central authority (a necessary though not a sufficient condition), little industrialization can be expected in backward countries. She maintains that, even to maintain 'right' relative prices, it is necessary to have a strong state.

The late industrializers suffer from a serious disadvantage in that they are significantly lacking in knowledge-based assets. So 'successful late industrialization requires state support and initiative to create the possibility of overcoming the disadvantages of firms in latecomer economies.' (Weiss, 2002, p. 76). Indeed, these latecomers that are technology borrowers need to compete with the innovators of technology. The advantage of low wages

▶

that they enjoy is not enough, so that in Weiss's view they need various forms of government support including state subsidies, but, most important, they must use the opportunity provided by this support to raise the quality of their output and the efficiency of their production. They are challenging the superiority of the technology innovators, and their battleground is the shop floor, As observed by Hikino and Amsden (1994, pp. 291–2): 'It is on the shop floor where they must adapt borrowed technology to suit their targeted market size and other idiosyncratic conditions. It is also here where they subject borrowed technology to continuous incremental upgrading.'

Sources: Amsden (1989, 2001), Hikino and Amsden (1994), Weiss (2002).

Promoting industrialization

How can a developing country's government lead or help it to industrialize structurally, and to do so in such a way that the expansion of industry is indeed a path to economic growth?

Roles of government and market

Of over 200 countries that now exist in the world, there are only around 25 which can be called industrialized *in both senses of the word simultaneously*: rich (securely so) and at the same time, when compared with a traditional economy, structurally weighted significantly toward manufacturing. Britain was the first country to achieve what we would now regard as industrialization in the structural sense. It was followed by a number of West European countries and the USA and, progressively from the second half of the nineteenth century and into the twentieth, by Japan, the countries of North-west European overseas settlement, and in some degree a number of East and South European countries including Italy and Spain. Until the advent of the USSR after the First World War, structural industrialization had depended largely on private enterprise, though with various degrees and forms of government intervention. Further industrialization, in the USSR after 1928, and later in those East European countries that it dominated after 1945 and until 1989, was a matter almost entirely of state enterprise. One might perhaps have expected that the roads to industrialization open to the early industrializers would be different from those possible today because past industrialization achieved by other countries has altered the conditions of entry.

But, if so, how? Has the path for the newcomers of the late twentieth century and after been more or less difficult as a result?

In the 1950s and 1960s there was a considerable body of opinion holding that industrialization for agrarian countries was likely to involve much more state intervention than in the nineteenth-century (a 'socialist road'). This was based on speculation that the existence of already industrialized countries would make it difficult for newcomers to break in. Export-pessimism arising on this and other grounds led to the view that industrialization was unlikely to come about through the decisions of private firms to enter world markets for manufactured goods, and that consequently the demand for manufactures that would be needed to support the industrialization would have to be internally generated. This reasoning seemed to advance the need for government intervention in the pattern of industry, whether in a command economy such as that of the USSR or through 'democratic planning' such as was attempted in India and Pakistan.

The storming, in the latter part of the century, of world markets for manufactures (and some services) by products from developing countries in Asia, under predominantly private enterprise, has largely exploded the sweeping case for export-pessimism and with it the more comprehensive demands for state intervention. For reasons mentioned already, the huge globalized markets that were apparent by the second half of the twentieth century for some fairly standardized kinds of manufactures provided a convenient entry point for the manufactured exports of very-low-wage countries[1] and the first step on a ladder up which those countries could climb as their wage levels rose with increasing prosperity. The existence of already formed, highly competitive markets for large categories of manufactures seems to have been a help to these new entrants rather than a hindrance. But the degree and form of intervention conducive to industrialization as a path to rapid growth remains a lively question. Detailed discussion of the state-market balance, pursued to a point in Chapter 7, is what remains of the old 'capitalist-socialist' question.

The usual assumption now is that new enterprise in manufacturing should be left almost entirely to the private sector; that investment funds will be forthcoming if the business climate is favourable, the physical and social infrastructure is in place, and business opportunities are present and recognized; and that the state's role is rather to ensure that **institutions** determining the business climate *are* favourable, that the **infrastructure** *is* in place, and that **information** is provided so that business opportunities *are* recognized – and beyond that to compensate for, or correct, **externalities**. Institutions to promote technical progress, which is an important public good, include the provision of *technical education*, and fiscal incentives to encourage '*research and development*'. They can come under the general heading of infrastructure. (These matters are pursued further in Chapter 18.) It may still be debatable whether the state should in any circumstances provide *fiscal inducements or protection* for certain particular industries or products (as we discuss under industrialization strategies below), and whether there should be state *guidance* of greater or less intensity over the choice of industries, as was undoubtedly prevalent in the cases of Japan and South Korea, but, it is generally assumed, the actual entrepreneurship will not be the state's responsibility.

Infrastructure investment is a different matter. There state enterprise may often be essential, however much the government engages private contractors or other devices that use the skills and experience – or even the risk-taking – of private firms.

Pitfalls when the state was the entrepreneur

A number of pitfalls are thus avoided, pitfalls that could be anything up to disastrous when governments saw themselves as having the direct responsibility for industrial growth: of having to assemble the funds and actively invest them in manufacturing plant, not only in the necessary infrastructure. The following warnings refer to three types of pitfall that could easily be made when governments took the investment decisions themselves.

First, for the rate of industrial growth to be fast and consistent, it is necessary that the **choices of industries** for investment should be in accord with the nation's comparative advantage and have a potential for sustained development. It is only too easy for industrial projects planned by governments to choose industries on criteria other than profitability. Private investors may make mistakes but they will have a central concern for profitability.

---

[1] Strictly what is relevant is whether a country has low 'efficiency-wages', that is wages that are low even when the efficiency of the workers is taken into account.

ISIC	Sub-sector	1978	1980	1982
3211	Textiles	40.0	20.1	10.0
3212	Garments	38.1	29.9	20.2
381	Metals	28.2	28.4	42.5
3560	Plastics	10.6	19.1	20.0
3843	Vehicle Assembly	18.4	N.A.	15.0
313 & 314	Tobacco and beverages	50.0		N.A.
311	Food processing	40.8	30.0	N.A.
3231	Leather	31.3	20.9	18.0
3522	Pharmaceuticals	25.0	16.8	20.0
3525	Cosmetics	33.4	8.0	15.0
3519 & 3520	Paper and printing	31.0	28.4	25.0
3699	Non-metallic mineral manufacturing	47.0	29.7	15.0
35	Chemical	42.0	28.0	15.0
355	Rubber	21.6	16.4	27.0
3311	Wood processing	36.0	27.3	20.0
390	Miscellaneous	55.9	44.9	N.A.
3	All manufacturing industries	40.4	25.5	21.0

Table 17.2 Estimated rates of capacity utilization in Ghanaian manufacturing industries, 1978–82, in percentages
Note: Data for individual industries were obtained from Government of Ghana, Ministry of Industries; the estimate of capacity utilization for all manufacturing industries is a weighted arithmetic average, using weights proportional to value of gross output in 1975.
Source: Huq (1989), as obtained from Central Bureau of Statistics, Economic Survey, 1982, p. 69.

Governments on the other hand may be moved by politicians' personal preferences or by the capacity of schemes to attract public attention, quite apart from 'pork-barrel' reasons and clearly corrupt motives. If there are externalities, the government may need to ensure (by taxes or subsidies, for example) that they are taken into account by the private investors. But, with that qualification, the presumption is that the private investors will on the whole make more socially efficient investment decisions.

Second, lack of realistic evaluations on the viable **scale of production** can cause the establishment of larger-scale plants than are required or justified, given the markets, techniques, and input costs. In many developing countries, plants with larger scales of production have often been selected on the assumption that the large scale adopted will keep the unit cost of production low. In practice, what has happened is that many of these plants have remained highly underutilized, as may be seen from Table 17.2, which presents a picture of the low capacity-utilization that existed in Ghanaian industries around 1980 (Huq, 1989, pp. 142–5). The table includes the industries operated by the Ghana Industrial Holding Corporation (GIHOC), which was the main corporate instrument of the state investing heavily in industrial plant. As may be seen, capacity utilization in the various manufacturing sectors remained very low during the period 1978–82, ranging from 55.9 per cent (the highest recorded – in the 'miscellaneous' group – in 1978) to as low as 8 per cent (cosmetics in 1982). Moreover, there was a drastic fall in average capacity utilization in

GIHOC plants from 44.4 per cent in 1978 to 25.5 per cent in 1980, and further to 21 per cent in 1982. It is true that a number of factors, including serious price distortions that existed in Ghana at the time, were causing enormous obstacles to the industrial sector's operation, but it is also true that, even in more normal conditions, the level of utilization could remain significantly lower than anticipated. So, at the time of the decision-making it may be worthwhile to consider smaller-scale plants and to examine the viability of alternative scales at various levels of capacity utilization. One of the present authors remembers in 1970 visiting Tema, the ambitious industrial town in Ghana 20 miles or so from the capital, Accra. Though it had been built entirely since independence 12 years earlier, it was already a ghost town with vast empty structures that could be imagined as crumbling over the centuries and being eventually overgrown by vegetation.

Third, the choice for an investment of **inappropriate technologies** – those that fail to minimize costs of production – can cause the investment actually to *reduce* national output (as well as lowering employment) to lower levels than would have existed in the absence of the investment. In the 1970s and early 1980s the David Livingstone Institute at Strathclyde University conducted a number of industry studies in a wide variety of sectors including textiles, finished leather, bricks, beer, and sugar. An important finding was not only that there was a wide range of techniques for the investors to choose from, including variants that could be applied to particular stages of production, but also that there were techniques already being applied in developing countries that were particularly relevant at small to medium scales of production. It is not the case that there is one well-known technique for producing any good that, in each of the stages of production, is the most efficient under all conditions. Costs of various inputs and size of market have a large bearing on the choice. Industry planned by bureaucrats at the behest of politicians (or protection awarded by them on the basis of apparent 'need') may well overlook the possibilities of cost-minimization. Since Ghana built its white elephants, the fashion has changed. Governments have mostly given up the privilege of making these monumental mistakes. In 'directly productive activities', as distinct from power and communications and social-service infrastructure, it is now private firms, disciplined by the need to make ends meet, that take the decisions about where and in what to invest, and at what scale and with what techniques. Governments are responsible for setting the stages for these decisions – ideally, it can be argued, influencing them only through *institutions, infrastructure, and information* – unless there are identifiable externalities for which it needs to compensate. Tema stands as a warning against going beyond that short list.

Inward-oriented versus outward-oriented industrialization strategies

For reasons that may be apparent from what has been said, the 'capitalist-socialist' choice has often been associated with the choice between open-economy and closed-economy models. This latter choice is still a matter for debate, but mostly as a question of degree and form rather than pure principle.

Historically, Britain is cited as an example of the open-economy model, and the USSR as an example of the closed-economy model (Sutcliffe, 1971). Other Western countries and Japan did not, however, follow to the same extent the free-trade policy usually attributed to Britain, though the extent to which even Britain followed an open-economy model has been questioned. (e.g., Amsden, 1987, 1989). Indeed, at certain stages of their industrial development, many of these countries were as selective as the USSR in the import of goods.

Similarly, though the Soviet Union followed a policy of relative autarky, it depended on the industrialized countries for its supplies of many capital goods, in the absence of which the rate of its industrial growth would have been much slower. The 'model' is at most a broad pointer, and the detail is important.

Attempts at industrialization in many developing countries of Latin America, Asia and Africa, especially before 1980, followed an **import-substituting-industrialization (ISI) strategy**. Under this strategy, imports for which there is already demand are replaced by local production. The appeal of the strategy is two-fold. First, it is argued, the substitution of local products for imported goods saves foreign exchange and thus relaxes the balance-of-payments constraint. Second, it advances industrialization by guaranteeing markets for manufactures.

The application of the strategy necessitates protection of the local industry through duties on imported goods, import licensing, or even a ban on imports. The case for protection in those circumstances is based on a number of arguments (Meier, 1976, pp. 648–54), and below we mention two of these. (It is important to point out that Meier in the passage cited proceeds to challenge in detail all the arguments for ISI.)

The first argument is from history. The experience of the industrialized countries (other than the very earliest industrializers, notably Britain) has been held by some to show that industries originally developed through import-substitution account for a large proportion of industrial growth. Usually a developing country will start *assembling* the products by importing semi-finished components; the next process is the local production of some of the simpler components; and finally a stage may be reached when the product is fully locally made. This type of import-substitution-based production by stages can be found in many sectors, though it is common especially in engineering.

The second argument is from differences in income-elasticities of demand between the products of different sectors, with a belief (referred to further below in the discussion of the Prebisch–Singer thesis) that the elasticity is generally greater for manufactures than for primary products, and indeed greater than unity for manufactures in general, and that, before significant industrialization, a country will naturally be largely importing manufactures and exporting primary products. Suppose a country initially exports only primary products and imports all the manufactures that it uses. Any growth in average income will entail a more than proportional growth in purchases of manufactures and hence of imports; but the extent to which increases in importing will be possible will be limited by the country's export earnings, which, because they are based on primary products, may well grow irregularly and more slowly than the country's potential output per head and more slowly again than imports would need to grow in order for the country to realise that potential output. Hence, exclusive dependence on importing for manufactures will seriously limit the possibilities of income growth. Import-substitution will be needed to relax this constraint by economizing on the use of foreign exchange.

However, the import-substituting-industrialization strategy, which has at times appeared to work to a point – in the sense of enlarging the manufacturing sector – for countries such as China, India, Brazil and Mexico, has not been without serious criticisms.

First, to implement it, additional foreign exchange is necessary, at least in the early period, for importing machinery and equipment, raw materials, and components for the new industries. Thus the argument from foreign-exchange saving is not necessarily valid, at least at an early stage of development. Also, the ultimate import bill may turn out to be higher than it would have been without the import-substitution because the cost of protected local production can at times be so high that the protected industry generates *negative* net present value (NPV) even as assessed at low discount rates, as has long been well documented (Little *et al.*, 1970). For example, because of protected inefficiencies and wastefulness, the cost of the imported materials and components may be higher than the cost of importing the finished good would have been, so that the local process is subtracting, rather than adding, value. There may also be a situation where, even though local production costs are lower than the costs of corresponding imports, the protected industry, because of the monopoly power that one or a small cartel of firms in it can exert, still charges higher prices than those of the imports, so that the consumers are not able to enjoy the benefit of the lower-cost local production.

Second, an important weakness of the strategy is its built-in inefficiencies. It depends in a considerable degree on allocation of resources administered by the government, which, in many developing countries, has remained weak and often corrupt. Rent-seeking was often pursued on a massive scale, with monopolies created or protected by the government. There developed special rent-seeking groups which lobbied for control of production. The production so captured was likely to be markedly inefficient, but the monopoly power ensured sales, though at a higher cost of production and a lower output than there would have been in a competitive market (Krueger, 1987; Bardhan, 1997).

Third, by focusing attention on the overriding importance of the industrial sector, the ISI strategy created a clear bias against primary industry, thus leading to the neglect of the existing export production of many developing countries which was centred around primary produce. Thus, the new incentive structure under the ISI strategy often reduced the rate of growth of exports of the periphery, while the income-elasticity of demand for imports in many developing countries was not reduced. It was, therefore, inevitable that for many developing countries the external-payments constraint could be further tightened.

The alternative strategy, which has been extensively followed for a long time now by some countries such as Singapore, Taiwan, South Korea and Israel, is **industrialization by export-promotion/substitution**. In recent years, a number of other countries including China, India, Sri Lanka, Thailand, Indonesia, Malaysia, Egypt and Bangladesh have in one degree or another acted in accord with this strategy for achieving industrialization. There are two aspects of the strategy, or at least two ways of seeing it: first, export *substitution* that involves the replacement of traditional exports, which have often consisted of primary produce, by non-traditional exports such as processed primary products, semi-manufactures, or manufactures, but often by adding value to traditional exports or by moving into higher-value (sometimes niche-market) primary products; second, the *promotion* of manufactured exports by emphasizing the development of export-based industries some of which may be new to the country. As in the import-substituting-industrialization strategy, the easing of the external-payments constraint is an important consideration, but this time it is through the *earning* of foreign exchange rather than *conserving* it. The earning of one unit of foreign exchange through exports is, of course, equivalent to the saving of a unit of foreign exchange through import-substitution.

The export-substitution/promotion strategy, however, can also claim that the domestic resource cost of *saving* a unit of foreign exchange by import-substitution tends to be higher than the domestic resource cost of *earning* a unit of foreign exchange. Indeed, evidence available from empirical studies of input requirements of industrial imports and exports suggests that, if foreign exchange and capital are real constraints on development while labour is not, the value earned through exports, given the same use of scarce factors, is higher than the value of imports that could be saved through import-substitution (Sheahan, 1971).

Another important argument in favour of the export-promotion strategy is that the market for the industries encouraged or supported is worldwide and is not limited to the narrow scope of domestic demand. This can be of particular relevance for small and medium-sized countries with small domestic markets.

The superiority of export-promotion is all the more likely to be true if, as is usually the case, the import-substitution that is the alternative would need to be promoted by measures that raise domestic costs and remove the competitive forces that might otherwise impose a degree of efficiency. By contrast, the corresponding export expansion would have to make its way in highly competitive world markets.

It is obvious that foreign trade is the vehicle of growth in an export-led industrialization strategy, so that the country that practises it will be dependent on economic and other events in the outside world. Furthermore, if a number of developing countries want to export the same commodity, they may find that the market is limited. There may also be a serious reaction from the importing countries, where the domestic industry will be under pressure because of cheaper imports from developing countries. Such a reaction has been felt in the early 2000s, in the cases, to give some examples, of footwear in the European Union and textiles in the US.

However, it is notable that fast growth in the original four East Asian Tigers continued almost uninterrupted through the world recessions of the mid-1970s, early 1980s and early 1990s (Singapore's stumble around 1985 was an accident of its exchange-rate policy combined with the behaviour at that time of the dollar), when most of the rich countries and of Latin America, to say nothing of the low-income primary-exporters, were severely battered. Similarly China's growth since the 1980s has been little shaken (before 2008) by the vicissitudes of the late-1990s currency crises or the US setback at the turn of the millennium, or by chronic US protectionist agitation against its trade and exchange-rate policies.

The export-substitution strategy, particularly when it is directed towards the pursuit of labour-intensive processes and component manufacturing, has been criticized as the replacement of the nineteenth-century 'plantation society' with the twentieth-century creation of a 'branch plant society' (Helleiner, 1973). Vaitsos (1974) termed it a 'shallow development' insofar as the export-substitution strategy relies on foreign investment by vertically integrated multinational firms. However, such comments, over 30 years old at the time this book is written, seem, in the face of so much economic growth through these processes in the meantime, to belong in another world. Whatever the darker side of China's growth, its leaders are not likely to worry about similarities with the West Indies in 1850. Nor are those of the Four Tigers, now among the high-income countries.

Financing industrial growth: internal and external

For industries to develop, investment funds are needed. They can be financed in three main ways:

1 surplus generated within the industrial sector
2 surplus diverted from other sectors of the economy
3 funds obtained from abroad.

Much of the industrial investment in Britain in the eighteenth and nineteenth centuries was through the first source, i.e., surplus generated within the industrial sector. However, for a developing country hoping to invest in industries from a very small industrial base the amount available from the first source is likely to be small as the industrial sector itself is small. There is also no guarantee that a large surplus will necessarily bring big investment in industries. The industrialists may transfer the surplus, legally or illegally, outside the country. They may also spend the surplus for luxury consumption. Evidence available from Pakistan for the 1960s shows that the reinvestment ratio of the industrial sector was then significantly lower than expected (Haq, 1966).

A common source of financing for industrial investment in developing countries is by transferring funds from other sectors, particularly from agriculture. First, agricultural capitalists or landowners may use their funds voluntarily to finance investment in industries. Second, the surplus in the agrarian sector may be taxed away by the government and the funds transferred for industrial investment or for investment in infrastructure so as to encourage industrial investment. Third, policy measures may be adopted in such a way as to turn the terms of trade in favour of manufacturing and against agriculture. Fourth, government may decide to appropriate the surplus from peasants or landowners by taking over their property. A combination of the last three methods seems to have been followed for the Soviet Union for industrial financing in the 1930s, and many developing counties have applied the second and third measures, at times quite extensively.

A further source of financing for industrial investment is direct or indirect investment by foreign capitalists, foreign aid and loans, and investment by nationals living abroad. The industrial investment of a number of developing countries including Singapore and Hong Kong benefited greatly from foreign capitalists including MNCs. Foreign direct investment (see Chapter 23) features prominently in this age of globalization especially as the free flow of capital is now being widely practised and approved. Foreign aid and loans featured prominently in the industrial development of countries such as Israel and Taiwan, at least in their initial stage of development. In recent years non-resident nationals who have accumulated wealth and business experience living in some developed countries have been investing in the industrial sectors of a number of developing countries; China and India in particular have benefited from this source.

However, active policy concern about obtaining the funds for industrial investment, other than in public infrastructure – as if the state should be responsible for ensuring that they are forthcoming and that they are properly applied – no longer seems necessary in the way it used to be under the quasi-planned-economy regimes prevalent in developing countries before 1980. Whether the direct investment or commercial financing that is to be attracted is foreign or local, the same general policies on the part of the state seem to be appropriate. It is a matter of providing the appropriately favourable business conditions and publicizing them.

The Prebisch–Singer hypothesis

A highly influential argument for structural industrialization was advanced by Raul Prebisch of Argentina in a paper published in 1950 in his capacity as the Executive Secretary of the Economic Commission for Latin America (ECLA) (Prebisch, 1950). In the same year, Hans Singer also published a paper, putting independently a similar argument. So it is now commonly known as the Prebisch–Singer thesis or hypothesis. The hypothesis forms a part of a wider analysis of the relationship that exists between developed and developing countries. Behind the analysis was the assumption – much less true now than in 1950 – that developing countries export largely primary products.

The core of Prebisch's analysis is the differentiation of economic structure between the 'Centre' and the 'Periphery', roughly-speaking the developed and the developing worlds respectively. Prebisch advanced four 'stylized facts' of underdevelopment faced by Third World countries (Palma, 1987):

1 There is a growing gap in the level of income between the Centre and the Periphery.

2 There is persistent unemployment in the Periphery.

3 There is a persistent balance-of-payments problem in the Periphery (which imposes an important external constraint on the process of economic growth).

4 There is a tendency to secular deterioration of the terms of trade of the Periphery.

The last of these empirical generalizations – the tendency to deterioration of the terms of trade of the Periphery – has emerged as the best-known thesis of Prebisch and Singer. It was the observation on both their parts of the apparent fall of the terms of trade *of primary products* in the decades before the Second World War, and its interpretation as implying a long-term fall in the terms of trade *of developing countries,* that became famous. The theory was largely formulated in explanation of this observation and examination of the observation's implications.

According to Prebisch, if trade is left to an unregulated international market it will tend to work against the terms of trade of the Periphery because of strong forces that spring from the characteristics of both the Periphery's demand for imports and its supply of exports. In fact, to Prebisch, trade works as an exploitative force acting against the Periphery and this is a result of three main factors.

The first factor springs from the differences in the average income-elasticities of demand among different classes of exports, and this forms a core of the Prebisch hypothesis. As the income-elasticity of demand for primary produce is typically less than unity, while that for manufactured goods is much higher, specialization in primary produce by developing countries leads to wider income inequality.

The following illustration advanced by Thirlwall (2003) explains the effect. Let us assume that world income is growing by 3.0 per cent, while the elasticities of demand (E_d) for exports from developed and developing countries are different, as shown below.

E_d for exports from developing countries = 0.8; and

E_d for exports from developed countries = 1.3;

This will give us a growth rate of 2.4 per cent for exports from developing countries and one of 3.9 per cent for exports from developed countries.

If we assume that the exports of developing and developed countries are equal to imports from developed and developing countries respectively, there will be an initial disequilibrium in the balance of payments, since imports of developing countries will increase at the rate of 3.9 per cent, while their exports will increase at the rate of 2.4 per cent. To achieve equality of imports with exports for each of the two groups will require (by whatever precise mechanism of adjustment) falling real income in developing countries *in relation to that in developed countries.* For example, equilibrium in which each group's imports would be equal to its exports could be achieved if the growth rate of developing countries fell to 2.31 per cent and that of developed countries rose to 3.75 per cent. In that case both groups' exports (and by hypothesis also both groups' imports) would rise at 3 per cent but the income gap between them would rise continuously.

The second major factor refers to differences in the competitive structure in product and factor markets between developed and developing countries. Neoclassical economic theory suggests that, when competition exists, technological changes which result in increased productivity will lead to reduced product prices. Prebisch argues that this process operates at the Periphery where the product and labour markets are highly competitive, but not at the Centre where firms are able to dictate prices for their products because of the monopolistic forces that operate. Moreover, at the Centre, labour is unionized, so that it is able to bargain for higher real wages. Thus, the improvements in productivity that take place at the Centre are not likely to be passed to the consumers in the form of lower prices; rather this increased value will be distributed among the owners of capital in the form of higher profits and among the labourers in higher wages. It is, therefore, apparent that the differences in the competitive structure between the Centre and the Periphery, which help to keep prices of primary exports depressed relative to those of imported manufactured goods, will work against the interest of the Periphery. Hence the conclusion that trade will work as an 'exploitative' force, harming the Periphery while benefiting the Centre. (It should be said that the validity of the argument has been questioned, specifically its supposition that trade unions and oligopolistic firms in national markets will be able to alter not only the nominal prices they receive in domestic markets but also their real exchange terms in international trade; for example, that the world's clothing industry and its workers, with its immense number of independent firms – even supposing, for the sake of the argument, that it is confined to Centre countries (as of course it is not) – could and would act like a single cartel, conspiring to maintain all its prices in real terms whenever its costs fell.)

A third factor, which was subsequently raised by Prebisch (1984), writing two years before his death – mainly to strengthen his original hypothesis – refers to the differences in impact of the creation and diffusion of technological change. Technological change that takes place in the manufacturing sector, he argues, has a greater tendency than that taking place in other sectors to spread to the rest of the economy, so that positive externalities are higher there. The impact of any technological change that takes place in primary production is often confined to that sector.

Prebisch might appear superficially to contradict Ricardo's view of the implications of specialization according to comparative advantage, which implies that the developing countries (like others) will gain *from specialization*. Prebisch does indeed maintain that *productivity growth* in the primary sector will not benefit the primary-exporting countries. However, that is a completely different point. Belief in the gain from trade as a result of comparative advantage does not depend on any supposition that specialization in this sense *will lead to productivity growth* in the industry in which specialization occurs. So, the alleged fact that *productivity growth* in its product of specialization will not benefit the developing country does not for a moment imply that a primary-exporting country does not gain from specializing according to comparative advantage. If that were the case we might as well be advising all primary-exporting countries to become entirely self-supporting, regardless of their endowments. Coffee and petroleum exporter countries would produce only enough coffee and petroleum to meet their own domestic needs. This, to put it mildly, is completely counter-intuitive. What the Prebisch finding implies surely is just that primary-exporting countries *do not gain as much* from trade as they would like, and as they would have done under some other completely hypothetical circumstances. This may be regarded as *unfair* and as an additional case for aid, and it has been so used, but it surely does not imply that primary-exporters will gain by simply shutting up shop: having land under coffee turned over to producing rice for internal consumption, for example, and petroleum wells converted to domestic tourist attractions. (Prebisch does, however, contradict one element drawn from the Classical approach to the terms of trade: the belief that in the long term they will move in favour of primary production because of the fixed stock of land.)

However, on these various grounds, Prebisch argued that 'industrialization was an unavoidable prerequisite for development' (1984). He believed that for developing countries to achieve economic progress they would need 'to produce locally more of the highly income-elastic importables and to diversify exports towards more price-elastic, productivity-spreading commodities, i.e., a process of industrialization that should eventually lead towards exports of manufactured goods from the periphery'. This, presented here as if it was a distant dream, has, as we have seen, already happened in a big way! It was evident enough even at the time of this statement. In this sense by 1980 – if not indeed long before – Prebisch was beating on a wide-open door.

The Prebisch hypothesis: a critique

Prebisch provided a forceful case for government intervention to diversify the output of developing countries and, in particular, to pursue a strategy of industrialization. He was interpreted as supporting the foreign-trade pessimism that had been advanced earlier by, e.g., Rosenstein-Rodan (1943) and Nurkse (1952); and he thus strengthened the challenge against the Ricardian optimism centring around gains from foreign trade insofar as it applied to developing countries. With a number of arguments, emphasizing in particular the disparities between the income-elasticities of demand for imports between the Centre and the Periphery, Prebisch was considered to have provided a theoretical foundation for industrialization in developing countries.

However, the import-substituting-industrialisation strategy (ISI) that was probably boosted by the Prebisch–Singer hypothesis has attracted serious criticisms, some of which have been set out above.

There is a further criticism of Prebisch not concerned with the ISI strategy. By supposing that the Periphery produced primary commodities, while the Centre concentrated on manufactured goods, the Prebisch argument failed to recognize the fact that the Centre was a major producer of primary products. So, the potential impact on some developing countries of agricultural protection in the developed – latterly a major source of dispute in international trade negotiations – was ignored. Also, the fact that so much manufacturing has now moved to developing countries, depressing prices of manufactures in so doing, is at variance with the Prebisch image of international specialization, as well as throwing further doubt on the already shaky argument about the monopoly power at the Centre for keeping up the prices of manufactured goods.

As we have mentioned, the widespread use of the ISI strategy in the 1950s and 1960s in various countries of the developing world brought some apparent success in the sense of enlarging their manufacturing sectors. Whether this contributed much to real economic growth is another question. Some of the countries that appeared in that period to be doing well with some degree of ISI, such as South Korea, Taiwan and China, were arguably exceptions and sooner or later those three switched heavily into export-expansion. There were major failures in many countries of Asia, Africa and Latin America; in particular, sub-Saharan Africa turned out to be doing miserably badly. In cases such as Ghana and Nigeria, there were periods of clear economic decline.

Empirical evidence of the deterioration of the terms of trade (TT)

The question of whether there has been a long-run and continuing trend for the terms of trade to move against developing countries has been much debated. The question can be considered in two stages: first, whether the terms of trade have moved *against primary commodities*; and second, if so, whether the movement has been on balance *against developing countries*.

A concise survey of subsequent attempts since 1980 to test the hypothesis, in either of these two senses, is provided by Thirlwall (2006, pp. 552–5). (See also, from references in that survey, Bleaney and Greenaway, 1993; Cashin and McDermott, 2002; Grilli and Yang, 1988; Sapsford, 1985, 1988; Sarkar and Singer, 1991; and Spraos, 1980.) The survey's main thrust is to confirm the long-run decline of the terms of trade of primary commodities – one study, by Cashin and McDermott (2002), though regarding the variability of the series as more important than the trend, estimates a trend decline of 1.3 per cent a year, 83 per cent in all, between 1862 and 1999 – and to support the view that, at least until late in the twentieth century, this implied some (though less rapid) decline in the terms of trade of developing countries on average, with a contribution to this trend made by some decline even in the real export prices of developing countries' manufactures.

However, any decline in the real export prices of primary commodities has become less and less relevant to the position of developing countries in general against the developed. By the late 1990s most of the largest developing countries and a number of others were predominantly exporters of manufactures (to the extent of 50 per cent or more of the value of their merchandise exports). In or around 1997 (from a very incomplete listing) these included Bangladesh, Brazil, China, India, Malaysia, Mexico, Nepal, Pakistan, Philippines, Thailand, Tunisia, and Turkey (World Bank, *WDR* 2000, pp. 268–9), between them covering well over half of the world's population. The fact that even manufactured exports from these countries may be earning a bit less in real terms per unit over time need not cause much grief when total earnings from these manufactures are increasing fast. Insofar as demand for these countries' goods is price-elastic, reducing prices may have been a contributor to increasing receipts from sales. When a country is experiencing (as some are) a rapid increase in foreign-exchange earnings and in national income as a result of a continuous fast rise in its manufactured or service exports, it may not shed many tears over the fact that it would be earning even more if it could sell just as big a volume of exports but for rising rather than falling real prices.

Further evidence on the continuing validity of the empirical generalization made by Prebisch and Singer about terms on trade movements is given in Appendix 17.1 on the Online Learning Centre.

BOX 17.3 TARIFF REFORMS IN DEVELOPING COUNTRIES

Over the last few decades, there have been significant reforms in tariff rates in many developing countries, 'reforms' in this context implying reductions. Two studies help us to chart these developments, one by Jeffrey Sachs *et al.* (1995) and the other by David Dollar and Aart Kraay (2001).

In the context of an index specifically constructed, Sachs and Warner make a four-group country classification to show the levels of openness in various countries from the 1960s to the early 1990s, as shown in Table 17.3.

1992 is the end date of the Sachs–Warner study. On more recent developments, the Dollar–Kraay (2001) study shows the pattern and extent of post-1985 tariff reductions

▶

FULLY OPEN ECONOMIES	POLICY REVERSALS	LATE LIBERALIZERS	FULLY CLOSED ECONOMIES (1960–92)
Barbados 1967–92	Bolivia 1960–74, 1985–92	Argentina 1991–92	Algeria, Bangladesh,
Botswana 1979–92	Costa Rica 1960–61, 1985–92	Benin 1991–92	Burkina Faso,
Chile 1976–92	Ecuador 1960–82, 1991–92	Brazil 1991–92	Burundi, Cameroon,
Hong Kong 1960–92	El Salvador 1960–61, 1989–92	Colombia 1986–92	Central African Republic,
Indonesia 1971–92	Guatemala 1961, 1989–92	Gambia 1985–92	Chad, China, Congo,
Jordan 1965–92	Honduras 1960–61, 1991–92	Ghana 1985–92	Dominican Republic,
Malaysia 1963–92	Jamaica 1962–73, 1990–92	Guinea Bissau 1987–92	Egypt, Ethiopia, Gabon, Haiti, India,
Mauritius 1963–92	Kenya 1963–67	Guinea 1986–92	Ivory Coast,
Singapore 1965–92	Morocco 1960–64, 1991–92	Guyana 1988–92	North Korea,
S Korea 1961–92	Peru 1960–67, 1991–92	Mali 1988–92	Madagascar,
Taiwan 1963–92	Sri Lanka 1977–83, 1991–92	Mauritania 1992	Malawi,
Thailand 1960–92		Mexico 1986–92	Mozambique,
Yemen 1960–92		Nepal 1991–92	Myanmar, Niger,
		Nicaragua 1991–92	Nigeria, Pakistan,
		Paraguay 1989–92	Rwanda, Senegal,
		Philippines 1988–92	Sierra Leone,
		South Africa 1991–92	Somalia, Tanzania,
		Tunisia 1989–92	Togo, Trinidad,
		Turkey 1989–92	Zambia, Zimbabwe
		Uganda 1990–92	
		Uruguay 1990–92	
		Venezuela 1989–92	

TABLE 17.3 The Sachs-Warner openness index: country classification
Note: Years shown are periods during which the individual countries are classified as open economies.
Source: Weiss, J. (2002), as adapted from Sachs *et al.* (1995).

in a number of developing countries (listed as those with the largest falls in average rates of import tariff between the mid-1980s and the late 1990s). These may be seen from Table 17.4. Clearly reductions in that period of general liberalization were widespread and large.

It is manifest from this list that a number of major developing countries underwent large tariff reductions over the period of roughly a decade recorded here. As is apparent, the Dollar–Kraay list (Table 17.4) does not include the established open economies such as Singapore and Korea, nor does it include the late liberalizers such as Ghana and the Philippines. However, the list includes large economies such as Bangladesh, China, Egypt, India and Pakistan that were recorded by Sachs and Warner as fully closed during the 1960–1992 period.

COUNTRY	AVERAGE IMPORT TARIFF (%)	
	Mid-1980s	Late-1990s
Argentina	27.5	11.0
Bangladesh	92.7	26.0
Benin	42.8	12.7
Brazil	45.8	11.5
Burkina Faso	60.8	28.5
Cameroon	32.0	18.1
Central African Republic	32.0	18.8
China	38.8	20.9
Colombia	29.4	12.2
Dominica	31.9	15.0
Ecuador	34.3	11.7
Egypt	39.7	28.3
Ethiopia	29.6	16.3
India	99.4	38.3
Indonesia	27.9	13.2
Kenya	39.4	13.5
Nicaragua	22.1	10.7
Pakistan	69.2	41.7
Peru	45.0	13.3
Thailand	41.0	23.1
Uganda	25.0	13.0
Uruguay	33.7	9.6
Venezuela	31.1	12.7
Zambia	29.9	17.0

TABLE 17.4 Average import tariff rates in selected countries, mid-1980s and late-1990s
Source: Weiss, J. (2002), as taken from Dollar and Kraay (2001).

Summary conclusions

- Industrialization in the *structural* sense of a relative *shift of resources into 'industry'* (comprising manufacturing, mining, and utilities), and particularly into *manufacturing*, came to be so closely identified in people's minds with significant economic growth that the word 'industrialization' acquired a second meaning, which was simply *persistently fast economic growth* – or else the *attainment* of a high economic level – that does not depend on factors likely to be transient.

- However, *deindustrialization* – the reverse of structural industrialization – is now prevalent in the affluent economies, while their per capita incomes are still rising. As a result, the relative expansion of industry or manufacturing on the one hand and economic growth on the other have turned out from the late twentieth century to be *less closely connected* than they had seemed, so that it is important to distinguish between the two meanings.

- Yet, from the starting-point of a largely traditional economy, **the expansion of manufacturing still appears to play a key role** in starting and continuing such consistent and firmly based economic growth as may lead to modern affluence. At least all those countries now enjoying secure affluence *have had to pass through a period* of structural industrialization.

- This is not because manufacturing is *intrinsically more productive* per worker than agriculture, but rather that mechanized manufacture, starting as a new, additional source of income and employment at a point at which it is markedly more productive than existing traditional agriculture, can, *if it finds the markets for continuing, commercially viable expansion*, set in motion **a process through which both industry and agriculture move to progressively more productive uses of their workforces**.

- Early development economists, pessimistic about the possibilities for developing countries of breaking into world markets for manufactures, and bothered over how this continuous growth of industry could be matched in composition with *domestic markets* for its products – let alone make use in the process of the potential *economies of scale* – were driven to look for solutions in **balanced growth** that seemed to demand both a *big push* – a large injection of investment capital – and *government planning and control* of the industry that was to emerge.

- Linking domestic demand to the products of the newly established industries would inevitably involve import-substitution; and engineering this (without Soviet-style centralized direction of all investment decisions) would require *protection* of the new industries either by subsidies or by duties or quantitative restrictions on competing imports: the typical characteristics of an active policy of **import-substituting industrialization**. These distortions of markets reflected the excess costs of this approach to the expansion of manufacturing, which inevitably restricted the amount of growth in real income that could result. No examples of prolonged and consistent rapid economic growth proceeded from this inward-looking strategy *alone*, though there are still open questions whether some *initial* import-substitution, state-supported or not, is necessary in a country before it is likely to be able to export the types of goods concerned, and whether some government *guidance* on which sub-sectors to expand, with or without financial inducements, can be helpful.

- However, by the end of the 1960s a much more promising way of solving the problem of how to find appropriate markets for developing countries' growing industrial sectors had begun to emerge. This was **export-expansion**. So far from being closed to entrants from newly industrializing countries, the markets for manufactures in the late twentieth century – in spite of some import limitations imposed by both rich and poor countries – proved open enough. Quotas, such as those for textiles and clothing under the Multi-Fibre Arrangement, admittedly had a blocking and distorting effect, but overall 'the proof of the pudding was in the eating': fast growth through export of manufactures did occur and proceeded for the pioneering countries with little interruption. If a low-income, low-wage country could produce fairly standardized goods, of an acceptable quality, by highly labour-intensive methods, it could tap into huge markets, and then, as its incomes and wage levels rose, repeat the process with successively higher value-per-worker goods. This necessitated a move beyond low-technology manufacture. For such a move to be possible, there needed to be accompanying changes in other areas, particularly the technological capability of the workforce.

■ The continuous expansion of manufacturing, and the associated rise eventually in its labour-product and wage levels and in non-agricultural employment and income, would tend *to raise the labour-product in agriculture* along with it. The increasing output of manufactures would not of course have to depend *entirely* on exporting for its markets. As domestic income grew, so would the domestic markets for everything.

■ The countries, mostly in East and South-East, and eventually also South, Asia, that have followed this path, beginning at various times after 1960, were repeating more or less – with variants, in a different context, and much faster – the experiences of Britain and Japan in the previous two centuries.

■ **Deindustrialization** is most likely to occur when a country approaches affluence, and large, consistent gaps in marginal factor productivities among the main sectors have closed, so that further changes in sectoral balance are likely to reflect *changes in technology and in consumption choices*, public and private, as they occur, and possibly also *changes in the productive capacities of other countries*.

■ The case for industrialization does not imply that **agriculture** should be abandoned or neglected. In a number of developing countries agriculture is the main source of foreign exchange. In most, it provides a major source of employment and household livelihoods for a large part of the population, thus forming an important part of GDP; and, last but not unimportant, it generally plays the essential role of feeding all or most of the people.

■ In particular countries there may be possibilities other than manufactured exports for a labour-intensive, non-agricultural activity to grow explosively and pull the economy up with it. **Export of back-office and call-centre services** recently in India, and for a while **domestic housebuilding** in Colombia, played a similar role.

■ There is room for debate on how a government can best promote the establishment of manufacturing or some other industry that will lead to fast economic growth: whether it should provide guidance or even, in the early stages, protection. It is fairly generally assumed now that the actual entrepreneurship in manufacturing should be left to the private sector, but with the government ensuring the provision of suitable **institutions** (favourable to business activity), **infrastructure** (physical and social), and **information**; and beyond that **compensating for externalities**. But an important inclusion under either 'infrastructure' or 'externalities' is 'research and development' and technical training, either provided directly or encouraged through incentives. Any policy of assistance entailing the provision of state finance to particular parties or activities or incurring initial social cost in the form of market distortion should first be *evaluated quantitatively* to establish that it is likely to generate positive net present value over the lifetime of its effects.

■ There is, however, **no guarantee** that the government of any particular state will face an environment that enables fast growth through export of manufactures or analogous processes to take place, whatever the policy adopted.

- The case for structural industrialization was long held to be strengthened by the 1950 **observations of Prebisch and Singer** that appeared to show a long-term negative trend in the terms of trade of primary products in relation to manufactured goods in international exchange. At the time the observations were made in mid-century, the poorer countries were generally specializing internationally in primary products. Hence the 'falling terms of trade' was interpreted as an impediment to the economic progress of the developing countries. The preponderance of the many studies undertaken to test the reliability of the empirical generalization on various assumptions and over various periods have tended to support it. Perhaps the most persuasive of the explanations offered for this phenomenon was to do with differences in world income-elasticities of demand between the two classes of goods.

- Two lessons might be drawn from this: one misleading; the other, with qualifications, valid. The misleading one is that developing countries actually **suffer from their participation in international trade** so long as they export mainly primary products, and would do better to withdraw as far as possible into self-sufficiency and to forget about comparative advantage. The valid lesson that might have been drawn (though it was not at first made in precisely this form, and how far if at all it depends logically on the Prebisch–Singer observations about the terms of trade is debatable) is that developing countries currently depending for their exports on primary products may – if they have internationally low 'efficiency-wages' – **have considerable gains to make from becoming commercially viable exporters of manufactures**.

- Sixty years after Prebisch and Singer propounded their thesis, the relevance of any lessons that might have been learned from it for developing countries has changed. Now (2009) developing countries accounting for well over half of the world's population are predominantly exporters of manufactures. *Most of those that are not* are in this position *not* because their authorities have *no wish* for them to export manufactures, or because any outside authority (the Washington multilaterals, for example, to mention one popular Aunt Sally) has *forbidden it*. We infer from this that they are there for one of two reasons: either because their **policies** have – unintentionally – prevented it, or because their **endowments** of natural and human-made resources, including their geographical positions and culture and the extent of their enjoyment of international and domestic peace, have made it for the time being impossible.

Societies seeking transformative industrial growth through government entrepreneurship and import-substituting industrialization were mostly disappointed, but the alternative – of smoothing the path for export-expansion, with the state leading only through institutions, infrastructure (human and physical), and information, with or without some compensation for externalities – eventually came to light in various forms, with some striking successes.

Questions for discussion

17.1 Why does a structural move toward manufacturing appear at certain levels of income to be closely associated positively with economic growth while at higher levels the relationship seems to disappear or even possibly to be reversed?

17.2 Does Prebisch's Centre–Periphery illustration help to explain why structural industrialization is or should be viewed as an unavoidable prerequisite for economic development in developing countries?

17.3 Do the Prebisch–Singer observations about trends in the terms of trade between primary and secondary products have any relevant policy message for developing countries today?

17.4 What is the case against the usual form of a policy of import-substituting industrialization for a low-income country? Is there anything still to be said in favour of income-substituting industrialization in any circumstances?

17.5 Have changes in the world markets for manufactured goods since say 1900 made it more or less easy for new producer countries to gain export entry for their own manufactures?

17.6 What circumstances in a developing country, if any, are likely to make it impossible for its manufactures to gain significant entry to world markets, no matter what policies the country adopts?

Additional reading

Amsden, A. (1989) *Asia's Next New Giant: South Korea and Late Industrialization*, Oxford University Press, New York, ch. 1.

Cashin, P. and C.J. McDermott (2002) 'The long run behaviour of commodity prices: small trends and big variability', *IMF Staff Papers*, **49**, 2.

Palma, J.G. (1987) 'Prebisch, Raúl' in J. Eatwell, M. Milgate and P. Newman (eds) (1987), *The New Palgrave: a Dictionary of Economics*, Macmillan, London, vol. 2, pp. 175–91.

Prebisch, R. (1984) 'Five stages in my thinking on development' in G.M. Meier and D. Seers (eds) (1984), *Pioneers in Development*, Oxford University Press, New York, pp. 175–91.

Singer, H.W. (1987) 'The terms of trade and economic development', J. Eatwell, M. Milgate and P. Newman (eds) (1987), *The New Palgrave: a Dictionary of Economics*, Macmillan, London, vol. 4, pp. 626–8.

Spraos, J. (1980) 'The statistical debate on the net barter terms of trade between primary commodities and manufactures', *Economic Journal*, **90** (357).

Wade, R. (1990) *Governing the Market: Economic Theory and the Role of Government in East Asian Industrialization*, Princeton University Press, Princeton NJ, chs 1 and 4.

World Bank (1993) *The East Asian Miracle*, Oxford University Press/World Bank, New York, ch. 1.

Online *Learning* Center

To help you grasp the key concepts of this chapter check out the extra resources posted on the Online Learning Centre at ***www.mcgraw-hill.co.uk/textbooks/huq***

Among other resources, the following appendix is available:

- Appendix 17.1   More evidence on trends in the terms of trade

CHAPTER 18

Building Technological Capability

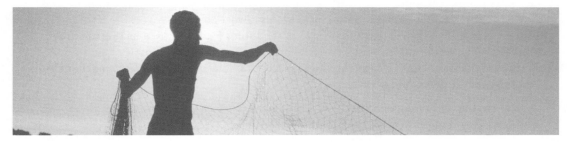

Policy-makers in developing countries have often failed to appreciate the importance of successful technology transfer. Hence the need to emphasize the building of technological capability. This entails both the personal possession of skills and experience (human capital) and the social possession of advances in know how (through R&D). Technology transfer takes place through a variety of routes, formal and informal, and the experiences of the East Asian 'dragons' provide important exemplars.

Introduction

Technological-capability building may be viewed as a process of learning, enabling a developing country to adopt successfully technologies imported from abroad. It refers to a country's ability to select, assimilate, use, maintain, adapt, design, and even create technology – capabilities required for the development of products and processes in response to a changing economic environment (see Huq, 1996).

The main focus in the chapter is on manufacturing, a sector to which the building of technological capability in developing countries is clearly relevant, but the implications of the analysis have a wider relevance.

The discussion starts with a comparison of the thinking of classical and neoclassical economics on technological development and choice and the relevance of both sets of insights for development economics. This leads on to evaluation of the radical case made for 'intermediate technology', an idea that was advanced in the 1960s and carried a strong appeal as a way of helping the poor, especially the rural poor.

Successive sections then deal with the economic evaluation of alternative technologies; the learning process involved in mastering technologies; the nature of technological capabilities; the justification for state financial support to the learning process; suitable forms of financial support; and the ways in which developing countries can pursue appropriate policies for supporting the development of technological capabilities within the rules and conventions of an open-world economy.

The various forms of technology transfer are listed in Box 18.2. There is also a box (18.3) illustrating briefly the acquisition of electronics technology by Korea, Taiwan, Singapore and Hong Kong, the four dragons of East Asia.

BOX 18.1 TOOLKIT ON TECHNOLOGICAL-CAPABILITY BUILDING

Appropriate technology. From an economic point of view, this refers to the technology which will make possible production at the lowest cost. However, the term has also been used in a loose sense to imply a type of technology (also known as **intermediate technology**) which is capital-saving and labour-using, and is designed for small-scale production, besides having some other essential characteristics suitable for sustainable development in developing countries.

Capital-saving technological progress. Innovations that enable more output to be produced from the same amount of capital as before.

Human-capital development. The acquisition by a person of knowledge, experience and skills, or of greater health and vigour, that enhances his or her potential contribution to production.

Intermediate technology. A technology which is neither of the large-scale sophisticated type nor of the traditional simple level, having some other important characteristics such as being capital-saving and labour-using. Ernst Schumacher (1911–1977) strongly advocated such technology and also worked earnestly to popularize it, with the belief that it would help the developing countries to achieve sustainable development with a strong 'grass-roots' foundation.

Labour-saving technological progress. Innovation that enables more output to be produced from the same amount of labour as before.

Least-cost technology. The least-cost technology for making a particular product is a combination of least-cost techniques selected for each and every one of the stages of production that go to make up the whole technology. In the selection process, the Present Values of Costs (PVCs) of the viable alternatives for each stage are systematically calculated.

Optimum input combination. This is the combination of inputs which, given the input prices, ensures production at the lowest total cost.

Production technique (technology). A method or a process for producing a required output, using a combination of inputs, say, labour and capital. It can be **labour-intensive** if it uses relatively more labour, or **capital-intensive** if it uses proportionately more capital.

Research & Development (R&D). The process of acquiring new knowledge about products and processes with the objective of improving them or even creating new products or processes. Along with **human capital development**, R&D is considered to be the core of technological-capability building.

Technological-capability building. This is the process of learning that enables a developing country to adopt successfully technologies imported from abroad. It enables a population to select, assimilate, use, maintain, adapt, design, and even create new technology.

▶

▶ **Technological progress.** New invention or innovation that makes possible the production of higher output with the same amount of labour and capital as before.

Technology transfer. A process through which a recipient in a developing country obtains, usually from a developed country, a production method involving hardware or software, or both. When the recipient manages to adapt the technology and, in the process, succeeds in mastering and even improving it, it is called **technology absorption**. And when the technology is being subsequently adopted by others with the help of the original recipient, it is called **technology diffusion**.

Classical and neoclassical perspectives[1]

The contributions from classical and neoclassical economists to theories of economic growth have already been discussed in Chapter 4. Here we are focusing on their thoughts and ideas relevant to factor use and advancement of technology.

In his classic treatise *An Inquiry into the Nature and Causes of the Wealth of Nations* (1776), **Adam Smith** (1723–1790) sought to account for the differences between countries in productive capability. In particular, he was enquiring why in the second half of the eighteenth century the people of Britain enjoyed a higher standard of living than people in other countries. He observed that a country's supply of 'the necessaries and conveniences of life' depended on two things: (a) the proportion of the people productively employed, and (b) more important, the productivity of those so employed. Superior productivity of labour (i.e., output per person), according to Smith, could be explained by the way the workers were organized in production, the skill they possessed, and the effectiveness of the tools and equipment with which they worked. The extent of the 'division of labour', that is the *degree of specialization*, was considered the key factor in Smith's analysis of productivity differences: the higher the degree of specialization, the greater the output per unit of labour. In speaking of specialization Smith had in mind *industrial* specialization, the division of labour amongst the separate trades and industries that operate within the economy. To illustrate, however, the implications of division of labour for productivity, he chose, as he put it, a rather trivial activity – pin-making – because in the case of this small-scale operation all the various specialized activities were conducted under the one roof, so that the operation and consequences of the principle of the division of labour were particularly evident to the observer.[2] Smith recognized that interlinked, specialized activities were in fact conducted simultaneously in different

---

[1] Roy Grieve provides very useful insights into the historical development of the relevant ideas; this section and the next draw heavily from his two articles (Grieve, 2003 and 2004). Indeed, the chapter has greatly benefited from his rigorous comments.

[2] The illustration of the pin factory was given by Adam Smith as follows: 'I have seen a small manufactory of this kind where ten men only were employed, and where some of them consequently performed two or three distinct operations. But though they were very poor, and therefore indifferently accommodated with the necessary machinery, they could, when they exerted themselves, make among them about twelve pounds of pins in a day. There are in a pound upwards of four thousand pins of a middling size. Those ten persons, therefore, could make among them upwards of forty-eight thousand pins in a day. Each person, therefore, making a tenth part of forty-eight thousand pins, might be considered as making four thousand eight hundred pins a day. But if they had all wrought separately and independently, and without any of them having been educated to this particular business, they certainly could not each of them have made twenty, perhaps not one pin in a day. . . . In every other art and manufacture, the effects of the division of labour are similar to what they are in this very trifling one' (Smith, 1776, bk. I, ch. 1).

locations, in different workshops, so that the fact of the division of labour by trades and industries, although an essential feature of the economy, was not so readily apparent as was division of labour on the pin-makers' shop floor (Smith, 1776, bk. I, ch. 1).

Taking a long view, Smith envisaged economic growth as a continuing process occurring over time with increasing division of labour, technological progress, and accumulation of capital over time. This would yield progressively rising productivity and real income per head.

Karl Marx (1818–1883) continued the classical economics tradition. Like Adam Smith, he was keen to understand the sources and the process of economic growth, although he was experiencing a significantly different industrial world from the one that had existed during Smith's time in the later part of the eighteenth century. Marx had witnessed the first half-century or so of the industrial revolution taking place during his lifetime, with machinery playing a much more prominent role than in Adam Smith's time. Still, just like Smith, he was keen to understand the factors that were responsible for contemporary levels of labour productivity and industrial capability.

As an economist, Marx was close to the classical tradition, analysing the role of machinery in the production process, the growth of mechanization and the factors that were helping in the application of science to production. He observed:

> The machine, which is the starting point of the industrial revolution, replaces the worker, who handles a single tool, by a mechanism operating with a number of similar tools set in motion by a single motive power. . . . As soon as tools had been converted from being manual implements of man into the parts of a mechanical apparatus, of a machine, the motive mechanism also acquired an independent form, entirely emancipated from the restraints of human strength. . . . (In time) large scale industry had to take over the machine itself . . . and produce machines by means of machines.

> But just as a man requires lungs to breathe with, so he requires something that is the work of human hands in order to consume the forces of nature productively. A water-wheel is necessary to exploit the force of water, and a steam-engine to exploit the elasticity of steam. . . . But the exploitation of these (natural) laws . . . necessitates costly and expensive apparatus. . . . it is clear at the first glance that large-scale industry raises the productivity of labour to an extraordinary degree by incorporating into the production process both the immense forces of nature and the results arrived at by natural science. . . .

(Marx, 1867, ch. 15)

So the great classical economists were keen to unravel the mystery of the growth of output and to understand how particular systems of production and the use of tools and machinery helped output per worker to increase. The essential message that emerged was clear: economic growth was the result of continuous improvements in the 'productive powers of labour' (progressively increasing productivity), obtained through technological progress.

In the latter part of the nineteenth century, with the advent of the 'marginalist' or 'neoclassical' school of economic theorists who envisaged economic questions as issues of choice resolved by rational, optimizing agents, attention was diverted from the dynamics of economic growth to static issues of utility maximization. The central concern of the new school was the formal conditions for optimal use of *given* resources in a static context, with an efficient equilibrium attained through substitution at the margin.

So the tools developed for analysing utility maximization in consumption are extended to model optimum input combination in production. The technique that maximizes output (given technology and resources) or minimizes costs (given factor prices) is represented as the optimal choice, as shown in Figure 18.1.

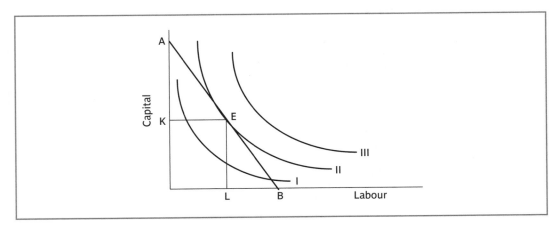

FIGURE 18.1 Optimum input combination

The cost line AB shows the different combinations of capital and labour available to the producer for a fixed outlay on inputs. Relative prices of labour and capital are represented by the slope of AB, while the curves I, II and III represent isoquants, signifying successively greater levels of output as one moves upward and to the right, each isoquant showing as we move along it different combinations of capital and labour (i.e., inputs) capable of producing the given level of output.

The optimal input combination is at point E on isoquant II, at the point of tangency between the given isocost line and the highest possible isoquant. From any other point on the isocost line, the producer will be able to obtain an increased quantity of output for the given expenditure by substituting one input for the other, so that the cost-minimizing/ output-maximizing factor combination is OL of labour and OK of capital. Thus, given the nature of the isoquant map, the optimum input combination depends on relative factor prices (shown by the slope of the isocost line, AB), which, in turn, depend on relative factor availabilities.

In determining the optimal choice of technique, the *relative factor prices* thus emerge as an important element of the model. In a developing country, with relatively abundant labour and scarce capital, shown by the relatively low slope of the isocost line GH in Figure 18.2, labour will be relatively cheap and capital relatively expensive. The investor will choose a labour-intensive method of production at point T, using more of the relatively cheap factor (labour), and less of the relatively dear factor (capital), than in an economy with less abundant labour in relation to capital. The figure also shows that in a developed country, with less labour in relation to capital, as shown by the steeper slope of the isocost line EF, a capital-intensive method of production will be chosen, as at point S. The growth of output in the developed country (DC), facing a higher capital-labour ratio, will follow the ray DC*, while growth in output in the developing country, facing a lower capital-labour ratio, will follow the ray LDC*.

The analytical tools advanced by the neoclassical school enable us to adopt a coherent approach to both production and consumption behaviour, *although the theoretical coherence has been criticized as illusory in practice.* Correspondingly, the model allows us to represent, in the case of production, how a producer may choose techniques in a way that *fails to make use of available resources* and thus fails to maximize output or minimize cost.

The neoclassical assumption of competitive markets is a useful analytical device but not necessarily a close representation of actual market behaviour. Market failure as a result of

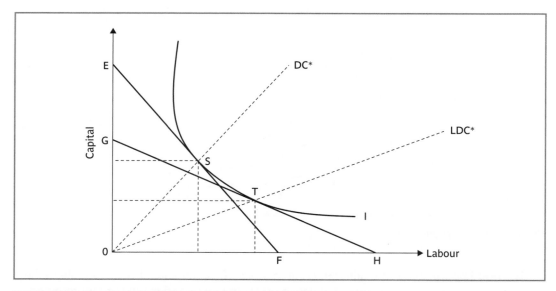

FIGURE 18.2 Optimum technical choice in developed and developing countries
Notes: DC = developed country; LDC = developing country.

departures from the ideal are recognized as common. For example, **the prices of factors often fail to reflect their true availability.** Thus, as has been observed in many situations, the actual choice of techniques in developing countries often hardly differs from that found in developed countries.[3] It is true that there are many other factors that have contributed to such technical choices, but the failure of factor prices to reflect factor availability has often featured prominently.

For the present purpose the major criticism of the neoclassical model of technical choice is its **static approach**. The effect of the passage of time is ignored, so that everything is analysed in a timeless context.

There is also in the model a built-in **presumption that at any scale of production there is an infinite range of techniques** – actually or potentially – with every possible combination of inputs represented. All that is required of the producer is to choose the input combination that will minimize costs for the output required. Because the relevant factor prices will reflect the relative abundance or scarcity of the factors, this combination will represent the most socially efficient use of resources. The model fails to consider the reality that different techniques are likely to emerge at different periods, in response to particular kinds of output and scales of production, so that, as argued by Grieve (2003, p. 27), the hypothetical techniques 'do not necessarily represent practicable alternatives for producing a particular volume of a specific product at a particular point in time'. Thus, the stylized neoclassical model stands in sharp contrast to the thinking of Smith and Marx, who were keen to understand technological improvements and the resultant productivity enhancement, based on actual innovations taking place over time.

---

[3] See, e.g., the David Livingstone Institute Series on Choice of Technique in Developing Countries, edited by Eric Rahim. The nine studies published under this series and the earlier two volumes from the David Livingstone Institute of Strathclyde University greatly help us to broaden our understanding on some relevant key empirical issues. See, e.g., D. Forsyth (1979), *The Choice of Manufacturing Technology in Sugar Production in Less Developed Countries*, HMSO, London; and E. Rahim (2003), 'Choice of Technique and Technology Policy in Developing Countries' in M. Huq (ed.) (2003a), *Building Technological Capability: Issues and Prospects*, UPL, Dhaka.

The neoclassical approach tended to treat technology choice as a mere matter of factor substitution, viewing technology as a sort of 'black box' which, in some mysterious way, was helping labour productivity and the process of production.[4] It may be recalled that the classical economists were keen to explore how specific systems of production, based on the use of particular tools and machines, helped labour productivity to increase. Thus, **classical thinking provided a vision of the *growth process*** with

> technology advancing and productivity increasing in a cumulative manner, an ongoing process driven by profit-seeking entrepreneurs' search for competitive advantage through undercutting and outplaying their rivals. Smith envisaged a dynamic sequence such that improved productivity in one sector of the economy, by lowering output costs, and raising real incomes of customers, thereby widened markets throughout the economy. These new market opportunities would then be exploited by other sectors via improvement of products and production methods, thus in turn lowering their costs, raising incomes, and further stimulating the cumulative process of growth.
>
> *(Grieve, 2004)*

Neoclassical orthodoxy of the late nineteenth and early twentieth centuries ignored too much of the classical heritage, in particular of the growth process resulting from continuous improvements of labour productivity. Classical growth economics had approached technology in the context of a dynamic model that had analysed the conditions of economic growth over time.

It may be added that development economics has had to be concerned *both* with the choice of techniques (the neoclassical preoccupation) *and* with the technical advance and accumulation of capital on which the classical writers laid such stress – outward movement of the technical frontier rather than simply finding the right position on its course – and it is the critical need to *realize* in developing countries this expansion of technical possibilities that leads to the importance of *building technological capability*.

Intermediate technology: a radical idea

Ernst Schumacher (1911–1977), a German economist who spent most of his life in Britain, is the founder of the 'radical' appropriate-technology movement which argued for the adoption of labour-intensive, small-scale methods of production. Because the techniques envisaged were neither standard 'modern' nor simple unimproved traditional, they were described as representing **intermediate technology**. In his ground-breaking book, *Small is Beautiful* (1973), which became a worldwide best-seller, Schumacher argued for avoiding the current practice of adopting modern large-scale, capital-intensive and labour-saving plants which, according to him, were not doing any good to the vast majority of people in developing countries, who were living in rural areas. Schumacher argued that, given the limited investible resources, developing countries would fail to create enough jobs by concentrating on the modern capital-intensive industries with high capital requirement per job. Such a

---

[4] Later writers (of the neoclassical persuasion) were less inclined to engage in close consideration of technological matters; Rosenberg (1982, p. vi) observes that '[these later writers] have long treated technological phenomena as events transpiring inside a black box . . . . the economics profession has adhered rather strictly to a self-imposed ordinance not to inquire too seriously into what transpires inside that box'. Similarly Rostow (1990, p. 454) observes: '. . . the formulation of marginal analysis round about 1870 . . . broke the rather easy, unembarrassed linkage of technological and economic analysis that had existed for over a century.'

focus, to Schumacher, would give rise to a situation of dualism, with a small, relatively high-income, modern sector as an island in the midst of a vast traditional economy with very low productivity; so Schumacher advocated the use of intermediate technologies:

> If we define the level of technology in terms of 'equipment cost per workplace', we can call the indigenous technology of a typical developing country – symbolically speaking – a £1-technology, while that of the developed countries could be called a £1,000-technology. The gap between these two technologies is so enormous that a transition from the one to the other is simply impossible. In fact, the current attempt of the developing countries to infiltrate the £1000-technology into their economies inevitably kills off the £1-technology at an alarming rate, destroying traditional workplaces much faster than modern workplaces can be created, and thus leaves the poor in a more desperate and helpless position than ever before. If effective help is to be brought to those who need it most, a technology is required which would range in some intermediate position between the £1-technology and the £1000-technology. Let us call it – again symbolically speaking – a £100-technology.

> Such an intermediate technology would be immensely more productive than the indigenous technology (which is often in a condition of decay), but would also be immensely cheaper than the sophisticated, highly capital-intensive technology of modern industry.
> *(Schumacher, 1973, pp. 148–9)*

In the report which Schumacher prepared for the Indian Planning Commission, he argued that 'a technology must be evolved which is cheap enough to be accessible to a larger sector of the community than the very rich and can be applied on a mass scale without altogether excessive demands on the savings and foreign exchange resources of the country' (Schumacher, 1981, p. 19). George McRobie, another principal exponent, argues, that

> to be appropriate the technology should be capable of local operation and maintenance, and local or at least indigenous manufacture; it should be owned and operated by its users, and result in a significant increase in their net (real or money) income; it should utilize to the maximum extent local and renewable raw materials and energy; and it should lend itself to widespread reproduction using indigenous resources and through the medium of local markets.
> *(McRobie, 1991, p. 169)*

Thus, according to this approach, for a technology to be 'appropriate' it must have **specific characteristics** (Stewart, 1985), such as (in comparison with typical commercial methods) being:

- More labour-using (high labour/output ratio, L/O)
- Less capital-using (low capital/labour ratio, K/L)
- Less skill-using
- Making more use of local material resources
- Being smaller scale
- Producing more appropriate products (e.g., a simpler product designed for lower-income groups, or more intensive in the use of local material resources).

The Intermediate Technology Development Group (ITDG), established in 1965 in London, has played a major part in popularizing this radical approach, often termed the 'Appropriate Technology' movement. Beside ITDG, known since 2005 as 'Practical Action', other organizations that have helped to develop and disseminate knowledge of this type of small-scale technology include Volunteers in Technical Assistance (VITA) in the US and the Brace Research Institute (Canada). They have been joined by others such as AT

International in the US, TOOL in Canada and the Appropriate Technology Development Association in India. International agencies such as UNICEF, the ILO, UNIFEM and IFAD have also helped various organizations to introduce intermediate technologies in developing countries. See Kaplinsky (1990), McRobie (1991) and Grieve (2003).

Such small-scale technologies are aimed at benefiting in particular the people in the lower-income groups. Given that high unemployment and low productivity have featured prominently in developing economies, it is not difficult to see the wide appeal of the notion of technologies whose equipment is easy to produce locally at much lower cost per unit than that of their 'modern' counterparts. ITDG catalogues and other publications have actively promoted the dissemination of these technologies, by providing designs and instructions for manufacturing machinery and equipment for use in agriculture and transport, construction, textile manufacturing, food processing, energy supply (biomass, biogas, micro-hydro, solar and wind), provision of safe water and healthcare.

During the 1960s and 1970s the approach became particularly appealing as, in the name of industrialization, many developing countries were importing, on a vast scale, the equipment for modern large-scale, capital-intensive technologies which were not operating fully and were also apparently failing to create adequate numbers of jobs. Indeed, many people started criticizing the use of modern capital-intensive technologies which were considered to be 'wrong' in terms of the scale of production, type of machinery and equipment, and even the goods produced (see, e.g., Stewart, 1977; Rahim, 2004).

The capital-saving and labour-using bias of this approach has strong similarities with some early criteria advanced by economists for evaluating investment in developing countries. An example is provided by Polak and Buchanan with their Minimum Capital/Output Ratio Investment Criterion (Sen, 1968).

The advocates of intermediate technology believed that it would 'help the poor to help themselves', by paving the way for a sustainable path of economic development with a strong 'grass-roots' foundation. According to Schumacher, the vast majority of people in developing counties, especially those living in rural areas, would find intermediate technologies much more accessible, in financing, operational and organizing skill, and marketing, than standard modern methods.

However, it should be mentioned that the approach suffers from a number of limitations. First, the limited availability of technologies of this type presents an obvious in-built constraint. Second, the capital-saving and labour-using bias, though appealing, can at times lead to the selection of techniques which are inferior financially or economically/socially or both, if efficient resource-allocation is the objective: that is, there may be alternative techniques which can give higher output than the technique chosen, given the financial input costs (or the economic/social input costs). There are some techniques indeed that are inferior *whatever* the relative prices of the inputs.[5] Third, the ITDG approach is more concerned with the increase of immediate employment and income and fails to take into account the objective of generating capital so as to maximize the present value of output and employment over a relevant future (Sen, 1968).

---

[5] For example, Huq and Islam (1992) found that, in the manufacture of fertilizer from natural gas, the labour-using, small-scale-technology variant, though it has significantly lower capital per unit of labour than the modern large-scale, capital-intensive variant, is an inferior technology in almost all areas of cost (it uses more of almost every input); in particular, the use of natural gas, the principal raw material, is found to be significantly higher per tonne of fertilizer produced. It should, however, be mentioned that both the above technology variants involve large investments costing millions of dollars and employing hundreds of people, so that even the capital-saving technology variant is not what may be called a small-scale technology in the ITDG context.

Technology evaluation based on economic efficiency

Morawetz (1974, p. 517) defined appropriate technology from an economic viewpoint as 'the set of techniques which makes optimum use of available resources in a given environment. For each process or project, it is the technology which maximizes social welfare if factors and products are shadow priced.' This test thus requires a profit-maximizing or cost-minimizing technology from the social point of view, and it is convenient to apply the conventional DCF (discounted-cash-flow) method to identify such a technology.

The NPV and IRR based on shadow prices.

The two versions of the DCF method, Net Present Value (NPV) and Internal Rate of Return (IRR), have been extensively used for evaluating investment projects, especially public-sector projects, in developing countries. In order to take care of the distortions in market prices, shadow prices are used. The incorporation of shadow prices for estimating NPVs for investment appraisal came to be widely used from the early 1970s, thanks to pioneering works produced under the auspices of the Organization for Economic Co-operation and Development [OECD] (Little and Mirrlees, 1968 and 1974) and the United Nations Industrial Development Organization [UNIDO] (Dasgupta, Marglin and Sen, 1972). These were designed to allow appraisers to take into account (in the shadow-prices that they used) all the main reasons why developing countries might judge market-price signals inadequate. Standard Conversion Factors (SCFs), often supplied by the World Bank, for correcting the distortions in market prices, have made life relatively easy for planners and project analysts. (These developments are expounded in Chapter 20.)

Identifying least-cost technology by social cost-efficiency analysis

If we suppose the same output yield from alternative technologies, an evaluation of the cost side can help us to obtain the 'least-cost technology' and also to rank various technologies on their relative costs.

During the 1970s this approach was extensively used for evaluating alternative technologies in a number of individual industry investigations conducted at the David Livingstone Institute (DLI), University of Strathclyde (the DLI studies).[6]

Put formally,

$$PVC = \sum_{n=1}^{t} \frac{(K_n + W_n + L_n + M_n + N_n) - V_n}{(1 + i)^n}$$

where,

PVC is present value of costs
K_n is fixed capital in year n
W_n is working capital in year n
L_n is labour cost in year n
M_n is material input costs in year n
N_n is non-material input costs in year n
V_n is residual value and recovery of working capital in year n
i is the discount rate.

---

[6] Nine of these studies were carried out during the second half of the 1970s, covering a diverse range of industries including leather manufacturing, machine tools, cotton textiles, brick manufacturing and corrugated board manufacturing. For an application of the methodology see, e.g., Huq and Aragaw (1981) and Khan and Rahim (1986).

By calculating PVCs for alternative techniques for each and every sub-process, and selecting least-cost techniques for each sub-process, we can identify the least-cost technology. *If all the cost variables are expressed in appropriate shadow-prices*, then the PVC will be in social/economic prices. We thus have a method which can help us to select a technology that can pass the economic-efficiency test of *society's* profit maximization.

This approach, comparing costs for the different methods of achieving a given outcome, is what is described in Chapter 20 as *cost-efficiency* (as distinct from *cost–benefit*) analysis, though the principle is exactly the same.

We can then qualify the choice by considering the likely degrees of capacity utilization with the techniques that otherwise come out as most eligible. This may rule out some for which the scale required would exceed the size of the probable market. We can also take into account risks and uncertainties, if any, by incorporating sensitivity analysis based on probability values.

However, the method is basically neoclassical in its approach in the sense of being static, and it ignores the questions of how in practice technologies, with the capacity to apply, modify or invent them, can best be introduced to the economies of the developing countries. The approach fails to consider many dynamic elements such as the costs and benefits of technology learning and the externalities generated.

In brief, the approach aims only to *select* the cost-minimizing technology (from the 'World Technology Shelf'). However, for a successful transfer of technology the following two other conditions also need to be satisfied (Centre on Transnational Corporations, United Nations, 1987).

1 The *assimilation and diffusion* of those technologies in the host economy

2 The development of *indigenous capacities for innovation.*

Mastering technology: a learning process

The literature which has been developing since the mid-1980s has been of great help in clarifying our understanding in this area. Contributors to the topic include Enos and Park (1988); Dahlman *et al.* (1987); Lall (1987 and 1992); (Huq *et al.*, 1992 and 1993); Hikino and Amsden (1994); Bell and Pavitt (1997); Huq (2003a and 2004); and Grieve (2003 and 2004).

An important feature of this new approach to technology evaluation is that it takes into account the development of technological capability. This is viewed as a process of learning which involves several components. A critical part of it is the **development of human capital**. This is the process that enables the labour force to select, instal, maintain, assimilate, design, manufacture and even create the technology. The workers do not need to be the inventors, but must have the ability to absorb borrowed technologies successfully. The mass educational development that took place in South Korea (and also in Singapore, Taiwan and Hong Kong) preceding their success in industrialization is often cited as a model of appropriate preparation.

Another important component is **Research & Development (R&D)**, considered to be the core of technological-capability building. It extends and elaborates the skills that are there to be mastered. The act of performing R&D is also an educative process for those engaged in it. So it may also be considered as an element in the human-capital investment, no less than straight operational experience. Freeman (1987) identifies a country's R&D with its national system of innovation and describes it as the decisive factor. The ease of absorbing new technologies in agriculture, thanks largely to the successful R&D carried out in Asian and South American countries, has contributed greatly to the success of the Green Revolution.

Country	Research and Development			Number of Scientists and Engineers in R&D (1987–1997)
(GNP per capita 1995, US$)	Year	As % of GDP	R&D per capita (US$)	(per million people)
Developed Countries				
UK (18 700)	1996	2.04 (1.4)	384	2448
Canada (19 380)	1997	1.66 (n.a.)	315	2719
France (24 990)	1997	2.25 (1.5)	545	2659
USA (26 980)	1996	2.64 (1.7)	655	3676
Germany (27 510)	1998	2.41 (1.5)	675	2831
Japan (39 640)	1996	2.80 (1.9)	1226	4909
Developing Countries				
Bangladesh (240)	1995	0.03 (n.a.)	0.1	52
India (340)	1994	0.73 (0.22)	2.4	149
Pakistan (460)	1997	0.90 (0.0)	4.4	72
China (620)	1995	0.61 (n.a)	3.8	454
Indonesia (980)	1994	0.07 (0.04)	1.0	182
Thailand (2740)	1996	0.13 (0.04)	4	103
South Africa (3160)	1993	0.70 (n.a.)	21	1031
Mexico (3320)	1995	0.24 (0.17)	11	93
Brazil (3640)	1996	0.81 (n.a.)	37	168
Malaysia (3890)	1996	0.24 (0.17)	11	93
South Korea (9700)	1994	2.60 (2.0)	271	2193
Taiwan (12 400)	1993	1.70 (0.8)	180	n.a.
Hong Kong (22 990)	1995	0.10 (n.a.)	23	98*
Singapore (26 730)	1995	1.13 (0.6)	300	2318

TABLE 18.1 Investment in R&D and the availability of scientists and engineers in R&D in selected developed and developing countries

Notes: Figures in brackets show: in col. (1) GNP per capita in US$ and in col. (3) R&D expenditures incurred by industry.

* Data for Hong Kong for the number of Scientists and Engineers refer to the period 1985–95.

Figures have been rounded off.

Sources: Given the difficulty of obtaining the relevant data, especially for developing countries, we have depended on various sources and in some cases there may be some slight discrepancies, e.g., the year of data relating to the percentage of R&D in the industrial sector may not exactly match with that of R&D expenditure as per cent of GDP. However, the discrepancies are not of such a magnitude as to provide any misleading information. The sources of data are UNESCO, *Statistical Yearbook* (various issues); World Bank, *World Development Report* (various issues); and ADB and OECD (1998), *The Future of Asia in the World Economy* (edited by Foy *et al.*).

There is a very high social rate of return from R&D in agriculture, typically exceeding 20 per cent and often higher than 40 per cent (Khan and Akbari, 1986). Unfortunately, however, in low-income developing countries R&D investment in the manufacturing sector is negligible.

As may be seen from Table 18.1, even the higher-income developing countries such as Malaysia, Mexico and Brazil are faring badly – at least very differently from the big high-income countries – when it comes to investment in R&D and also in the number of scientists and engineers engaged in R&D.

There is, however, a positive correlation of GNP per capita with R&D variables: the lower the per capita income the lower is the investment in R&D as a percentage of GDP.

A similar relationship is also observed between GNP per capita and the number of scientists and engineers in R&D, the correlation coefficient being stronger here (0.8740, n = 19) than in the former relationship (0.7142, n = 19); the causation, however, runs in both directions.

Among the attempts to evaluate how far the dynamic learning process of technological-capability building has proceeded, one can identify two major approaches, shown below.

Evaluation of economies on the basis of the level of technology adoption

This was advanced by Enos and Park (1988) while they were investigating a number of large-scale South Korean firms through individual case studies in the following industries: (a) Petro-chemicals, (b) Synthetic Fibres (c) Machinery, (d) Iron and Steel. The approach enables us to examine the incorporation of a foreign technology by looking into various phases of the transfer process, namely:

1 Planning and investigation
2 Negotiation with suppliers
3 Design of plant and equipment
4 Purchase of equipment, construction
5 Installation and initial operation
6 Production and maintenance ('minor' technical change)
7 Development of improved technique ('major' technical change).

These processes can be conveniently classified into three main stages:

- Stage 1: Selection/Purchase (**1** and **2**)
- Stage 2: Absorption (**1** to **6**)
- Stage 3: Diffusion (**7**).

The undeniably important Stage 1 in the process of technology transfer can be taken care of through the 'least-cost' identification outlined above, but Stages 2 and 3 definitely contain a number of dynamic elements that are not incorporated in the approaches already considered.

Absorption may be viewed as the initial process of technology adaptation[7] and involves the importer in mastering, learning, adapting and improving the technology. **Diffusion** refers to the final stage of technology transfer and is reached when the technology is subsequently adopted by others with the help of the original recipient. The technology-transfer deals in the British automobile industry between the British firm Rover and the Japanese firm Honda provide a very good example of the absorption of technology by Honda, which led subsequently to diffusion when Honda successfully sold improvements to others including Rover itself.

Evaluation on the basis of selected capabilities

This is another way of evaluating the transfer process, particularly some of the dynamic aspects, this time by viewing particular capabilities that are components in the general development of technological capability. Dahlman *et al.* (1987) originally suggested three

---

[7] See Huq *et al.* (1992 and 1993) for some in-depth evaluation of technology absorption in the context of fertilizer and machinery manufacturing in Bangladesh by viewing some relevant aspects such as designing, local manufacturing, assembling, installation and maintenance capabilities.

of these capabilities (production, investment and innovation), and subsequently Lall (1992) added a fourth (linkages).

1   *Production capability.* This is needed to operate productive facilities. It is reflected in productive efficiency and in the ability to adapt operations to changing market circumstances.

2   *Investment capability.* This is needed to establish new productive facilities and expand existing facilities. It is reflected in the project costs and in the ability to tailor project designs to suit the circumstances of the investment.

3   *Innovation capability.* This is needed to create new technology. It is reflected in the ability to improve technology or to develop new products or services that better meet specific needs.

4   *Linkages capability.* This is defined as the

> skills needed to transmit information, skills and technology to, and receive them from, component or raw-material suppliers, sub-contractors, consultants, service firms, and technology institutions. Such linkages affect not only the productive efficiency of the enterprise (allowing it to specialize more fully) but also the diffusion of technology through the economy and the deepening of the industrial structure, both essential to industrial development.
>
> *(Lall, 1987, p. 168)*

It is often difficult, however, to quantify the level of, say, absorption and diffusion, or to measure the various capabilities. Yet, in spite of the difficulties, the importance of the learning process can hardly be overemphasized. According to Hikino and Amsden (1994), developing countries wanting to compete effectively with advanced countries will have to 'sharpen their own managerial and organizational skills, shorten their learning period and . . . make incremental improvement'. They further highlight the fact that no technology is 'perfectly transferable' and adapted to the relevant market. The view that development requires more than just basic foreign technology investment was also supported by Nelson (1993), who found that countries also require *capabilities* in science and education if they are to be able to catch up.

Kaplinsky (1990, p. 25), a keen observer of technological change in developing countries, believes that 'development of technological capability is expensive; it takes time; and the greater the scientific content in production, the greater the cost, and the longer the wait'. The effective use of a new technology will depend on a number of factors including development of new skills, and improvement of managerial and administrative capability. Capability for selecting and installing new machinery and equipment, though important, is only an initial stage of technological-capability building. The recipient will also need to develop the required human skills for operating the plant and also for achieving product and process improvements so as to remain competitive in the market.

From the experience of the successful East Asian industrialization, it appears that the starting point is the introduction of technologies that are relatively accessible to developing countries, given existing resources and capabilities.[8] Gradually the recipient will be able to

---

[8] Pack (2000, p. 79) notes that Hong Kong, Korea, Singapore and Taiwan, having begun industrialization with import substitution, soon 'switched to export-orientation, the earliest exports consisting of labour-intensive manufactured products. In these products the relevant technology is largely embodied in imported equipment, and the requisite additional noncodified production knowledge is easily acquired from consultants or former employees of developed-country firms. A literate and numerate labour force is the important requisite at this stage of production, the need for highly-trained engineers and scientists being relatively limited.'

move up the ladder, taking up more advanced technologies. As found by Kim (1995, p. 94), Korea followed a 'dynamic strategy for industrialization', with progressive technological upgrading, starting with relatively labour-intensive light industries such as textiles, garments, footwear and simple electronics, and then gradually moving into more capital-intensive industries, such as steel and petrochemicals, and further on technologically complex sectors such as shipbuilding, car manufacturing and advanced electronics. Similarly, in Taiwan one finds a gradual shift from the acquiring of relatively simple technologies to the adoption of others, intensive in higher levels of skill and knowledge. At each stage a serious learning process is involved, so that there is a progressive development of technological capability.

The volume of high-technology exports can perhaps give an idea of the ability of a developing country not only to produce such goods but also to export them, thus ensuring technology-learning at some key stages. As may be seen from Table 18.2, in developing countries such as Malaysia, Korea, China and Brazil, high-technology exports have featured strongly, and in some cases have been even higher as a percentage of manufactured goods than those recorded by some developed countries. This gives a somewhat different picture of technological advance from that suggested for Malaysia and Brazil by the quantity of their

Country	GDP per capita in US$	Exports as % of GDP	Manufactured exp. % of merchandise exports	Manufactured exports: % of GDP	High technology exports as % of manufactured exports	High technology exports as % of GDP
Bangladesh	440	13.32	89	11.85	0	0.00
Pakistan	600	14.69	85	12.49	1	0.12
India	620	10.75	77	8.28	5	0.40
Sri Lanka	1 010	29.59	74	21.90	1	0.21
China	1 290	35.38	91	32.20	27	8.69
Egypt	1 310	10.22	31	3.17	1	0.01
Algeria	2 280	37.46	2	0.75	2	0.01
Tunisia	2 630	36.36	81	27.03	4	1.11
South Africa	3 630	27.78	58	16.11	5	0.63
Malaysia	4 650	108.02	77	83.18	58	47.97
Brazil	3 090	17.47	52	9.08	12	1.00
Korea Rep.	13 980	37.73	93	35.09	32	11.12
Israel	17 380	31.37	93	29.17	18	5.25
Italy	26 120	23.01	87	20.02	8	3.24
France	30 090	24.26	81	19.65	19	3.47
Germany	30 120	36.75	84	30.87	16	4.53
UK	33 940	17.14	78	13.37	26	3.27
US	41 400	6.74	80	5.39	31	1.74
Japan	37 180	11.99	93	11.15	24	2.73

TABLE 18.2 High-technology exports from selected developed and developing countries, 2004
Source: World Bank, *World Development Report* (various issues).

R&D investment and their numbers of scientists and engineers, as shown in Table 18.1. However, it is possible that the relevant abilities are still confined to the FDI sector; so we need more detailed information than is available in Table 18.2. (Pack's observation recorded in footnote 8 may point to a part-resolution of the apparent contradiction.)

BOX 18.2 FORMS OF TECHNOLOGY TRANSFER

Forms of technology transfer to developing countries can vary widely. There are **internalized** and **externalized** modes of the transfer process. In the former, the ownership and control of the technology transferred is with the supplier of technology, while in the externalized mode the ownership is with the recipient.

Formal and **informal** mechanisms both feature prominently in discussions of the transfer of technology to developing countries. The **formal mechanism** can include a number of sources, as shown below.

Foreign direct investment (FDI) has remained a key source of technology transfer to developing countries. Multinational corporations (MNCs) have been the major players here, building factories and operating them in developing countries. FDI flows to developing countries increased significantly in recent years, the nominal US$ value of gross inflows growing fourteen-fold from 1990 to 2007. Developing countries received nearly $150 billion FDI in 1996 and more than $500 billion in 2007. Their share of total FDI inflows, increased from 28 per cent in 1980 to 39 per cent in 2004; before falling to 27 per cent in 2007. However, the distribution of FDI flows among the developing countries has remained uneven. Thus, of the total FDI flows to the developing world in 2007, Asia attracted the highest share (64 per cent), followed by Latin America and the Caribbean (25 per cent), and Africa (nearly 11 per cent). (See the tables in Chapter 23.)

Joint Ventures involve domestic and foreign companies' reaching agreements to procure technologies, the latter usually supplying the technology and then operating it jointly with the former. Depending on the nature of the agreement, ownership of the technology will vary; but local ownership is generally an ultimate objective.

OEM (Original Equipment Manufacture) Agreements provide an inexpensive mechanism of technology transfer. It can be considered as a form of **licensing**; the recipient in the developing country obtaining authority from the supplier to manufacture the machines locally, without the need to become involved in the design. However, the original design may need modifications in the new local environment, so that the recipient will be at a disadvantage unless he/she can deal with the problem.

Purchase of technical assistance or a technical service agreement enables a recipient in a developing country to purchase the know-how from abroad, using foreign expertise. Thus there is no need to acquire the knowledge, which is a time-consuming and costly effort. However, this form of technology procurement, though easier and inexpensive, will keep the recipient dependent on foreign sources. **Management contracts**, **Sales/marketing contracts** and **Research contracts** are different versions of this type of technology transfer.

Turnkey Projects – where a foreign supplier of technology will establish the whole plant, will test its operation and will then hand it over to the recipient – can enable a developing

▶

▶ country to obtain technology quickly. As in FDI and licensing, the involvement of the recipient is negligible in the design of the plant and also in selecting the machinery and equipment and getting them installed.

Company Acquisitions. This form of transfer has been found by developing countries to be convenient, especially in situations in which developed countries want to close some old factories or companies that are no longer profitable for them to operate. The price paid is generally significantly lower than for new equipment.

The **informal mechanisms** comprise two main sources. First, by **getting the local technicians and engineers trained abroad**, and also taking advantage of the **return of nationals with training abroad**, a country can arrange to obtain foreign technologies. US-trained Korean and Taiwanese engineers were found to be very helpful in the development of the electronics industry in Korea and Taiwan (see Box 18.3).

Second, **imitation, copying and reverse engineering** have also been found to be important sources of technology transfer. Imitation and copying are particularly common in many instances. However, a transfer by this mode is largely dependent on the capability of the capital-goods sector of the recipient country. For example, in the 1970s and 1980s, a number of Indian firms producing machines for processing leather were found to be copying some of the models imported earlier or even using the blueprints.

Sources: Hobday (1994 and 1995).

Technology development in an age of globalization[9]

What is the best strategy for the development of technological capability? In this age of globalization, some might argue that the task of technological-capability building is best done without any government intervention.

This is too important a question to be settled by an appeal to ideology. In developing countries, as in any other country, such questions cannot reasonably be answered by deduction from a doctrine that government intervention is either a good or a bad thing – or a good or a bad thing specifically for developing countries. Much serious policy failure has resulted from that style of thinking.

Case for financial support

As far back as Adam Smith economists have accepted the case for government support to public education. In one form or another it is indisputably what we would now call a pure public good. *Certain elements* of general education at least produce benefits in which all (not only those individually being educated) can be expected to participate: no one can be excluded from these benefits on the ground of not being prepared to pay for them; and my enjoyment of them does not diminish yours. The question then is simply whether the accumulation of human capital represented by the nation's or community's acquisition of technological capability in the senses discussed in this chapter is one of those elements of

---

[9] This section draws heavily from M. Huq (2004).

public education, and if so whether, unless paid for in whole or in part by the state, it might not be provided.

Alternatively – as another way of looking at the same question – building technological capacity could be seen as conveying a **positive externality**. In other words, the total social gains from the learning that takes place under that heading are greater than the (private) gains for which the firms and others whose decisions generate the learning have to pay. So failing to subsidize the process risks under-investment on the part of the society in this element of human capital.

If any country accepts the imperative of development entailing significant and consistent economic growth, and expects that growth to involve manufacturing as a leading element, it seems likely to need technological capabilities *comparable in some way* to those acquired by the East Asian Tigers as they went through this process. But the details of what each requires will probably be peculiar to itself, depending on the particular industries that each will find it is developing.

Because the course of industrial development – which industries it involves – will depend largely on private decisions, the role of any state support must inevitably be to some extent that of going with the flow. Beyond formal trade and technician and professional training in engineering and related skills (of a *generalist* character in the sense that it is not tied to the needs of particular firms or particular lines of production), the case that may be made is for support, in the form of subsidies or tax concessions for example, of what R&D and specific training activities the firms themselves wish to undertake.

We have seen in the East Asian stories of successful industrial development that it may be more or less 'guided' in its choice of industries. South Korea provides an example at the guided end of the spectrum. At the same time we have seen (as in the extreme case of Ghana mentioned in Chapter 17) the risks of disastrous pitfalls when the state makes these decisions, especially if it also sets out to conduct the industrial investment itself. So we assume that the investment in relatively high-tech industries that is the subject of consideration will be essentially private-sector investment, with at most *influence* on the choice of industries on the part of the government. Whether under guidance or not, it will be the industries in which firms decide to invest about which the question must be raised whether their role as formal or informal instructors, and hence as investors in social capital, justifies state support.

On the other hand, can support of this kind be defended against possible international criticism on the ground that it is protectionist and in conflict with the (generally desirable) rules of international competition?

It is important here that a distinction is made between trade policy and technology policy, with the latter considered as a form of social investment. A completely liberal regime is more suited to the former than to the latter. Technology *trade* (in the sense of paying for imported material inputs and hiring imported intellectual property and know-how) is the type of activity that can fare adequately in a liberalized market. However, there are reasons for thinking that *technological-capability building* is a task that will experience difficulties in most developing countries if left entirely to market forces. This is because it is a matter very largely of **learning by doing**. Where experience of more or less high-tech activities is sparse in a particular host country, each new investment in these fields is a potential opportunity for learning on the part of the people and institutions of the host country to take place. If that learning occurs, it will generate a benefit to the host community over and above what the investment earns for the foreign or other investor. Similarly each act of R&D in such a context not only serves the commercial purposes of the investor but also extends the range of directly productive possibilities open to the host community while at the same time again potentially providing informal training in how such a development can be brought about: in how to 'do' R&D.

So, when it comes to technological-capability building through human-capital development and R&D initiatives, there are likely to be important '**positive externalities**': the market rates of return to the investors will exclude an important element in the social returns. Withdrawal of the state from any active role – in an all-out pursuit of liberalization – would entail ignoring those externalities and forgoing a possibility of actively supporting the home team's learning and hence its capacity for adaptation and innovation.

Furthermore, though domestic firms that are investors or potential investors may well have a medium-term interest in promoting the community's technological-learning process (over and above their immediate commercial interest in the outcome of their own individual investments), they will need to be *mobilized and co-ordinated* if they are to make jointly the necessary supportive outlays. One of the justifications for the existence of government is that is can solve such co-ordination problems.

So, evaluated from the viewpoint of *the country's own population*, such support can be justified on the ground that it is compensating for a positive externality, a potential gain to its people that would otherwise be ignored by the market, or (a closely related point) that it is paying for a pure public good.

Against *outside-world* opposition on the ground that such differential help to own-country industries departs from the liberal ideal, the answer is that it is justified on the same grounds as the financing of own-country technical education. A country that is low in an important element of human capital has an implicit right to invest in building it up.

Eligible forms of support

What possible forms of support should be considered?

Enough has probably been said in this book to warn against the approach that would set out to attract the high-tech industries that might be the source of the learning *at any cost*. Industries that private investors would not at least *contemplate* establishing in country A on commercial grounds are likely to be a millstone around the neck of any government that somehow induces the investors to introduce them. The first prerequisite is to adopt those general policies that will make foreign and indigenous investors feel secure and that will avoid burdening them with unnecessary costs. If that works in a country with very little manufacturing, it is likely to attract first relatively low-tech industries: bottling plants, clothing, textiles, certain forms of assembly, possibly as either 'market-seeking' or 'efficiency-seeking' investment from abroad (see Chapter 23). These should not be despised. You have to walk before you can run. The East Asian Tigers went through the same experience. If relatively low-tech industries flourish in the marketplace without extraordinary assistance and the essential infrastructure is in place and efficiency-wages are low enough, then more diversified investment may follow.

Part of the infrastructure required is **technical education**, 'generalist' in the sense that it is not tied to the needs of particular products and firms, but framed in quantity and content to be just sufficiently ahead of immediate manpower needs. Some of it at the higher 'professional' levels may be most efficiently carried out abroad, but overseas training has unfavourable as well as favourable aspects. Clearly maintaining formal trade, technician and professional training adequate to the direction and pace at which industry seems to be going is an important part of the support for the development of technological capability.

The other element of the capability-building is the informal part. Here it is highly desirable to frame the measures of support so that they do not involve favours to particular industries and firms. This is important not only to strengthen the defence against possible liberal objections, but also to keep the aid that is given efficient from the country's own viewpoint. So there might be **subsidies** or **tax concessions** on **R&D** and on industry-specific or firm-specific **technical-training programmes**. It would be necessary then to define R&D and technical training for the purposes of the measure, so that, as far as possible, it would provide a clear and unambiguous criterion, reducing the scope for executive discretion, which is always at risk of corruption and favouritism.

A third element, also directed at informal learning, would require knife-edge balancing on the part of government. This is ensuring that foreign investors in the relevant industries pass on the skills of their expatriate staff to local staff, through programmes, for example, of localization, understudying, mentoring. The risk is of course that the requirements will tie the firms up so that their activities are unduly impeded, or that firms that *might* invest fail to do so because they fear such impediments. To help resolve the conflict, there might be certain minimal requirements – on localization, say – laid down by law, and consultation with each firm on how it might set more ambitious targets for itself. There is always the possibility that negotiation might lead to solutions on localization that are win-wins, where the firm gets the credit for an ambitious programme *and* a reduction in its costs, while the country gets the additional human capital. There is a particular ground for subsidizing **localization programmes**, or at least the training associated with them. This is that they may involve a positive externality over and above the one to which we have referred. The externality lies in the fact that a firm that has invested in training one worker to a high level of skill may find her or him poached by another firm. The training firm's return, and maybe in advance its expected return, may then be, for that reason as well, below the full social return on the training investment.

Framework for technology policies

Technological-capability development in developing countries would thus call for the state to be prepared to play an active role, but without the illusion that a sufficiently active government can make *anything* desired possible. We have seen how **externalities** and **market imperfections** involved in technology development can 'justify' certain forms of intervention, both in the sense of making them rational as national policies and in that of defending them as consistent with international fair play; but it is also important to recognize the limits of those arguments, so as to form some rational idea of the *amount* of subsidy the externality could justify.

There are a number of developing countries that would seem at the moment far from being likely to host high-tech manufacturing industries, but it is probably worthwhile for these too (some of them with important mining activities and almost all of them with some involvement already in modern public utilities) to develop **explicit technology policies**.

A major task of technology policy in developing countries is to provide the institutional and organizational framework that would allow the various 'actors' in the development process to interact. The actors concerned include the state; the investors – foreign and local; the training institutions, universities and research establishments; and accreditation bodies. However, such a framework and the incentives for the actors to interact fruitfully are generally conspicuous by their absence in developing countries.

Given the institutional and organizational fragmentation and the widespread 'capacity deficits' characterizing the socio-economic formation of developing countries, unmitigated adherence to liberalization policies is unlikely to help the task of technology-capability building. As noted above, the interventionist role of the state, expressed *inter alia* in the form of technology policy with commitment and focus, is crucial for the development of technological-capability building. Globalization would in the meantime be expected to broaden the outlook of policy, thus orienting its focus towards the wider and long-term objective of sustainable economic development.

The main concern is how a developing country can acquire the ability to adopt imported technologies successfully. Human-capital development and R&D will undoubtedly remain important elements in the learning process. It is not an easy task, and a country's government will need to remain committed to a coherent supporting role if the objective is to be achieved.

What we now know is that certain countries that were not long ago in the middle-income, or even the low-income, range have moved into the high-income class; that acquiring technological capability seems to have been an important ingredient of their success; and that there is every sign that they have followed deliberate policies for reaching that goal.

BOX 18.3 TRANSFER OF TECHNOLOGY IN THE ELECTRONICS SECTOR: THE 'FOUR TIGERS' OF EAST ASIA

Hobday (1994) addresses the growth of the East Asian NICs (Korea, Taiwan, Singapore and Hong Kong) with particular reference to the electronics sector, chosen because it is the largest single export industry in three of the four countries (Hong Kong being the exception) and the fastest growing export industry in all the four NICs during the 1980s. The evidence shows that 'firms in the NICs exploited foreign investment, technology and marketing channels to their advantage, gradually learning the skills needed to compete internationally. Local firms successfully coupled export and technological developments, allowing export market needs to focus technology investments and provide a channel for foreign technology acquisition.' (Hobday, 1994, p. 335).

One particularly interesting result in Hobday's study is the finding that, of the four Dragons or Tigers (Korea, Taiwan, Singapore and Hong Kong), the two that operated a more restrictive policy towards Foreign Direct Investment (Taiwan and Korea) were the countries where it was local firms rather than transnational companies that provided the main stimulus for the development of the electronics industry. This raises a policy dilemma for developing countries, many of which operate 'open door' approaches to FDI.

During the 1980s the OEM (Original Equipment Manufacture) agreement was probably the most important mechanism through which technology in electronics was acquired in Korea, Taiwan and Hong Kong (and this contrasts with Singapore which depended heavily on FDI). As soon as local firms gained capabilities to operate independently, joint ventures tended to be superseded by OEM and licensing. Informal mechanisms of technology transfer, e.g. training of local technicians and engineers abroad and the return of nationals with training abroad (e.g. US-trained Korean and Taiwanese engineers), also featured in the development of the electronics industry. Other informal means such as imitation, copying and reverse engineering also contributed towards technology acquisition by the NIC firms engaged in the electronics industry.

Which is the best mode of technology transfer for building capability in a developing country? The answer to the question will, obviously, need to be carefully considered by the developing country concerned in the light of its specific circumstances. However, for building technological capability there is much to be said for the modes of transfer which will force the developing-country firm to engage itself directly in the search and direct purchase of machinery and equipment, and also the design of the plant, and its installation, operation and maintenance.

Source and Note: Hobday (1994). The mechanisms of transfer, identified through literature survey and field research and recorded here and in Box 18.2, apply to the NICs (Korea, Taiwan, Singapore and Hong Kong) covered in Hobday's study.

Summary conclusions

- **Technological-capability building is a learning process**, defined as the ability to select, assimilate, use, maintain, adapt, design, and even create technology – capabilities required for the development of products and processes in response to a changing economic environment.

- The main concern is how a developing country can acquire the required abilities, thus enabling it successfully to adopt and adapt imported technologies and use them as a springboard for further innovations.

- It is apparent that one needs to go beyond the neoclassical framework of static technical choice in order to take proper account of technological-capability building. Development economics, accepting the imperative of economic growth, inevitably returns to classical modes of thought, being concerned with the progress of technology and the accumulation of capital, now extended to human capital. The conventional approach of efficient technology choice based on factor prices, even if it is extended to social prices, fails to consider fully the essential learning process involved in the accumulation of human capital. So modern technology policy has to consider *both* efficient choice of techniques as seen from a static viewpoint *and* the progress of technology and accumulation of human capital as considered in a dynamic context.

- Intermediate technology (IT) represents an ideal of techniques of production that are more productive per worker than traditional methods but have lower capital–labour ratios, and lower technically optimum scales of production, than standard modern techniques. It was intended to provide a way into higher productivity that would be accessible to poor people and enable independent small household enterprises to keep their autonomy. Insofar as they had lower capital–labour ratios than standard modern techniques, it was thought that these devices might well be more economically efficient than those techniques for a low-wage, capital-poor country.

- However, there is limited range of IT devices; and there is no guarantee that there will be one device to suit every need, let alone one that will, at least for certain factor-price ratios, not be inferior to the latest modern technology.

- The learning process involved in the acquisition of technological capability involves both formal and informal modes of learning.

▶

- On various criteria most developing countries are very low on technological capability. But a few, notably Malaysia and China (together with South Korea, which until recently counted as a developing country), export high-tech products in higher proportions of value to their national incomes than some developed countries including Israel, France and Italy.

- Technological capability entails *both* the personal possession of skills and experience (human capital) *and* the social possession of advances in know-how (the product of R&D). But these can not be sharply divided. Participation in R&D is itself a learning experience.

- In the framing of a strategy for technology, the case for considering state financial support rests on the belief that the informal learning that takes place when there is a high-tech investment in a country with limited high-tech activity constitutes a positive externality, and can also be considered a form of education that is a pure public good. Private investors who corporately might benefit in the medium term from the capability-building (and who would be prepared to pay extra for it) might need some form of mobilization and co-ordination to bring this about. Either way, there is a case for state action, even if only in a consultative form.

- Eligible forms of state support for advanced technology include provision for formal 'generalist' technical education at trade, technician and professional levels, some of it possibly undertaken abroad; subsidies or tax-concessions for closely-defined R&D and industry-specific or firm-specific technical-training; and rules, negotiated agreements, or financial incentives (or any two or all three) for measures to support the transfer of experience and know-how (as by localization targets, under-studying, and mentoring). There are potential risks of over-regulation with the third of these devices.

- The framework of policy should be one in which every developing country has at least a rudimentary technology policy, even if it now has very little manufacturing industry. The technologies used in mining and utilities also have educational possibilities. Formal technical training should keep a small step ahead of manpower demand. Other forms of assistance should as far as possible be framed to be impartial among industries and to minimize reliance on executive discretion, and their conditions should be fully public so as to strengthen their incentive effects. This will mean that the support will in practice largely follow investors' choice of industries but at the same time give encouragement at the margin to those with technological-learning possibilities. It will be important for the authorities to resist the temptation of offering big inducements to particular industries and firms that show no inclination to invest in the country unassisted. For attracting investment that is worthwhile, it is probably best to stick to general policies offering business of all sorts *non-discrimination (except on grounds of some definable externality), macroeconomic stability, security*, and *predictability*.

Every developing country, even one with very little manufacturing industry, needs a technology policy, however rudimentary. Modern technology will be involved in mining and utilities, as well as in manufacturing. Transfers of whatever know-how is available will need to take place. This will require the provision of formal technical education (a public good); suitable forms of partnership between government and foreign firms; encouragement of R&D and of industry-specific and firm-specific training (which will have positive externalities); and recognized conventions, or an individual understanding with each important inward investor, on localization.

Questions for discussion

18.1 Why might neoclassical analysis be considered an inadequate guide on its own for technology transfer to developing countries?

18.2 Why does the concept of 'technological-capability building' ask us to incorporate dynamic elements such as 'absorption' and 'diffusion' of technology?

18.3 Why is 'technological-capability building' viewed as a process of learning? Discuss the main elements and the policy implications of such technological-capability building.

18.4 What are some possible pitfalls (a) in policies to subsidize certain high-tech firms; and (b) in laying down rules about the transfer of technology to local people?

18.5 Is it sensible to set particular value on high-tech investment? If so, why?

18.6 Should the government of a developing country 'pick winners' to support among possible industries that might be brought in by foreign investors? Why, or why not?

Additional reading

Dahlman, C.J., B. Ross-Larson and L.E. Westphal (1987) 'Managing technological development: lessons from the newly industrializing countries', *World Development*, **15** (6).

Enos, J.L. and W.H. Park (1988) *The Adoption and Diffusion of Imported Technology: the Case of Korea*, Croom Helm, London.

Hobday, M. (1993) 'Technological learning in Singapore: a test case of leapfrogging', *Journal of Development Studies*, **30** (1).

Huq, M. (2003) *Building Technological Capability: Issues and Prospects*, University Press, Olaka.

Lall, S. (1992) 'Technological capabilities and industrialization', *World Development*, **20** (2), pp. 165–86.

Schumacher, E.F. (1973/1993) *Small is Beautiful: a Study of Economics as if People Mattered*, Vintage Books, London.

PART 5
Finance

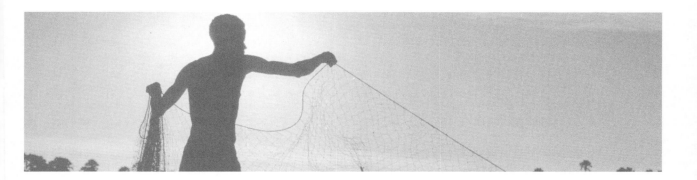

CHAPTER 19

Domestic Finance

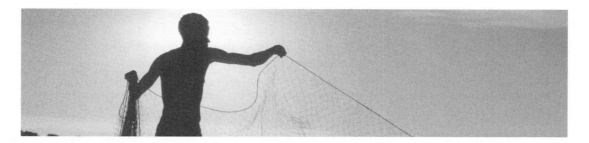

Much of the action that might be taken to promote economic growth or to improve the lot of the poor requires spending on someone's part – governments, investors, or charitable and public-interest bodies – who may be based at home or abroad. Analysing how the finance required can be provided opens possibilities of mobilizing more funds more fairly and using them better.

Introduction

The question in this chapter is **how purchasing-power can be mobilized *from within a country* to promote economic growth and current welfare.** The funds may be assembled and put to use either by government (public finance) or by individuals, associations, and corporations (private finance).

Answering the question concerns both how the funds are to be **raised** and how they are to be **spent**. This chapter is primarily about how funds can be raised, but, when it comes to private finance, the two questions can not be completely separated. So we shall discuss first how finance may *effectively – and efficiently and fairly – be mobilized for the public sector,* with attention to the special circumstances of developing countries; and second how arrangements can encourage funds to be *efficiently and fairly channelled to, and used by, private investors.* Other chapters deal with the much more complex questions of what classes of activities the state should undertake (Chapter 7), and deciding from among those activities how financial resources coming under the control or influence of the state may most advantageously be spent (Chapter 20).

Under **public domestic finance**, we consider a government's potential **sources of revenue** (taxes, charges, and enterprise profits), with attention to the advantages and drawbacks of various classes of *tax*; the debate over how far there should be *charges for government services*; and how net *revenue from state-owned enterprises* may be increased.

The mobilization and direction of **private domestic finance** we consider mainly as a question of **motivation** of investment and **intermediation** of funds between savers and investors. Governments' role in motivation of investment we shall treat as involving (a) the enhancement of *security* for potential investors, through legal institutions and possibly also measures of 'social security', while (b) minimizing unnecessary impositions and regulation. Under intermediation, we consider the case for and against *financial liberalization* as a default principle, and devices such as *microfinance* for enabling investments to be made by, and in the interests of, very poor people.

Finally we consider several elements of potential **international tax co-operation** that could very probably bring large amounts of additional revenue – much of it from what are really their own domestic sources – to developing countries, while at the same time, with any given set of tax rates, generally expanding, or at least not reducing, the tax revenue available to the developed countries and making its incidence fairer and more efficient.

In Appendices, we consider the objective of **neutrality** in taxation; and some taxes that appear close to satisfying it; some broadly neutral and equitable devices suitable for raising **local-government revenue**; and an approach to neutral taxation of **natural-resource projects**. These are available on the Online Learning Centre.

BOX 19.1 TOOLKIT OF TERMS

Public goods. These are goods, such as law and order, that possess one or both of the characteristics: non-excludability and non-rivalry. Non-excludability means that those who will not contribute to paying for them cannot be excluded from using them and this makes it impossible to pay for providing them by charging for their use. Non-rivalry means that one person's enjoyment of the goods does not reduce anyone else's capacity for enjoying them and means that, even if it was possible to exclude non-payers from using them, it would be socially wasteful to do so. 'Pure' public goods possess both characteristics. See Chapter 7 for further explanation.

Merit goods. These are goods, which, though they do not possess the properties of public goods, the state sees it as desirable that all should be free to enjoy. It therefore provides them free of charge. See also Chapter 7.

Neutrality. This term, applied to a tax or other policy measure, means that it does not alter behaviour except as is necessarily entailed by the purpose of the tax or measure. So, a neutral tax reduces the spending of those legally obliged to pay it but does not alter their behaviour except as would follow directly from their having less to spend. See Appendix 19.1, available on the Online Learning Centre.

Financial repression refers to the setting of upward limits to interest rates below rates that would otherwise apply in the market.

Financial intermediation refers to the role of financial institutions in channelling funds from savers to investors or converting assets from one form into another, as from mortgages into securities.

Direct taxes are taxes assessed on persons, usually on their incomes or wealth or some particular form of property.

Indirect taxes are taxes assessed on transactions, such as purchases and sales.

Domestic finance for development

'Development' we have been taking in this book to cover not only economic growth but also advances in current welfare, and, because each dollar's-worth of benefits means more to the poor than to the rich, especially in the welfare of the poorest. 'Finance' here is taken to cover the means of procuring goods and services; hence 'domestic finance for development' concerns the question how buying-power can be mobilized from within the country and directed to promoting economic growth and welfare. To be truly domestic in origin, the funds must represent saving on the part of the population, as a result either of private decisions (individual or corporate) or of government transactions.

Finance may of course also come from foreign savings. We consider these sources in Chapters 21 to 24.

Relevance of the rate of domestic savings

Fast-growing economies must necessarily be high investors. The 'vicious-circle-of poverty' model, popular in early attempts to explain obstacles to economic growth, implied that low-income populations would spontaneously save especially *low* proportions of their incomes; that for this reason their net investment would be low or zero; and hence that growth might be impossible for them unless measures were taken to increase their savings rates. By implication it was the propensity to save that would determine the rate of investment and hence be the main mover in economic growth, rather than any independent propensity to invest. (We have seen in Chapter 4 the subsequent doubt over this relationship that followed the neoclassical critique, with the emphasis instead thrown onto technical progress, originally treated as exogenous.) Early discussions of growth in poor countries tended to direct attention to the need to increase the national savings rate. This might be achieved by the state through various means, of which the most obvious would be increasing government revenue in relation to government spending on 'consumption'. The state might then either invest the extra revenue itself or channel it to private investors. Another thought was that bank interest-rates on deposits might be raised to increase savings. On this latter point (see the discussion of 'financial repression' below), however, a common view now, with some basis in evidence, is that any positive responsiveness of *personal savings* to bank interest-rates is probably low, while raising deposit rates will probably entail raising lending rates as well, which will be discouraging to investment.

However, seeing the question primarily as one of increasing the propensity to save, rather than of increasing the readiness to invest, and the propensity to save as depending on relative poverty, has come to seem misleading, for several reasons, beside those that follow from the neoclassical critique of the relationship between saving and growth.

First is the lack of a positive relationship across groups of countries between average incomes and savings rates. It is apparent from the figures in Table 19.1 that, across income groups of countries, it is by no means true that the poorer the country is the lower is its savings rate. Among the four groups, the high-income countries have the *lowest* rate in 2005, and the low-income group the *second-highest* in both 1987 and 2005. Relatively low national savings rates, it would seem, are not the inevitable or even typical *effect* of relative poverty.

Second, a country's domestic investment (investment within the country) is not rigidly limited by its domestic savings. There are big international capital movements. The savings generated in one country may be financing investment in another. Some capital movement is from the rich to the poor: Table 19.1 shows low- and low-middle-income countries in 1965, and low-income countries in 1987 and 2005, with somewhat higher rates for domestic investment than for domestic saving, which implies that there was net movement of funds from outside those countries. However, funds are not always moving from the richer to the poorer. Both classes of middle-income countries are net providers of funds in 2005; and one of the most striking processes of the early-twenty-first-century world is the

	Domestic savings			Gross domestic investment		
	1965	1987	2005	1965	1987	2005
World	20	22	21	20	21	21
Low-income countries	19	26	24	20	28	27
Low-middle-income countries	18	21	31	20	21	29
Upper-middle-income countries	24	27	23	23	25	22
High-income countries	21	21	20	20	21	20
Among low- and middle-income countries						
East Asia*	23	35	38	23	30	34
Europe, M East & N Africa	20	n.a		22	n.a.	
Europe & C Asia			23			23
M East & N Africa			27			26
South Asia	15	19	26	18	22	28
Latin America & Caribbean	21	20	23	20	18	20
Sub-Saharan Africa	14	13	20	14	16	20

TABLE 19.1 Savings and investment rates out of GDP, country-group averages, various years, percentages
Notes: * East Asia and Pacific in 2005.
Some of the figures do not relate precisely, over all the groups averaged, to the years given.
Source: World Bank, *World Development Report 1989*, pp. 180–1; *2007*, pp. 294–5.

consistent net movement of funds out of East Asian countries – some, such as China, of relatively low income – which tend to run big external surpluses on current account, and into the United States, which runs a huge deficit.

Third, reputable people and corporations with a clear desire to invest in a particular country and expectation of a sufficiently high rate of return, can often, so long as they are not blocked by local regulation and bureaucratic obstruction, obtain funds for their investments – if necessary from abroad – even when domestic 'money' is 'tight' in the target country, and can and do invest. Insofar as the net value of what they produce ends up as additional income for entities, public or private, within the country, their investment will also be likely to *generate* domestic savings.

However, *fast-growing* countries do still tend, as we would expect, to have high savings rates. For example, in the World Bank figures for 1987 (source as for Table 19.1), the only economies listed with savings rates of 30 per cent or more were Japan, Hong Kong, Singapore, Yugoslavia, Gabon, South Korea, Malaysia, and China. With the exceptions of Yugoslavia and Gabon, these were all countries that had grown notably fast over 1980–87 (even Japan in comparison with the high-income countries outside this list). Table 19.1 also shows savings rates for East Asia (1987) and East Asia and Pacific (2005) as *much* higher than for the other regional groups of low- and middle-income countries. It does seem that *high savings rates and fast growth go together*, though it is not obvious from this how much is cause and how much effect.

Quite probably, treating the promotion of economic growth as a matter of increasing national savings rates is putting the cart before the horse. Rather there are certain things that need to be *done* (or *avoided*) by governments to enhance the *demand* for investment.

Unnecessary obstructions to productive private investment need to be removed. Vital items of *physical infrastructure* have to be created, through private or public investment. There will be *public goods*, such as the protection of life and property – shading off into *merit goods* such as education and health services – that are crucial not only for current welfare but also for encouraging investment.

Much of this involves government spending. So promoting economic growth still leads to the question (among others) how **public** funds can and should best be raised.

Over the **private** segment we have to ask first how to foster the *motives* for investment, including self-financed investment; and second how to ensure that *intermediation* is working efficiently and fairly: so that funds that some people would be willing to save will be made available to others, including the very poorest, who would be willing and able to invest them productively.

Public domestic finance

Governments collect *revenue* so as to divert spending power away from private purposes in order to make room for the claims of the public sector on the economy's productive capacity – without increasing state debt or relying on inflation.

Government revenue and the alternatives

Current spending-power *can* certainly also be diverted to the public sector by **borrowing from the domestic market**. In some developing countries, there are very limited possibilities here, with virtually no domestic capital market, so that most of their government borrowing has to be from abroad. Where domestic borrowing *is* possible, there are two disadvantages that have to be considered. One is the immediate *'crowding-out'* effect: limiting the availability of private funds for investment and raising their price, though this may not be of great importance where there is fairly free movement of funds internationally. The second is of course the *future burden* of payments to service the loans, which will require higher tax rates, or less capacity for public spending, in the future than would otherwise obtain *unless the borrowed funds make possible a sufficiently increased tax-base as a result of raising national income*.

This relationship leads to the idea ('the golden rule') that borrowed funds should finance 'investment' rather than 'consumption', in other words the rule that public borrowing should not exceed spending on public investment, at least over the medium-term ('the cycle', however precisely that term is understood). However, identifying recurrent government expenditure with *consumption* and capital expenditure with investment for this purpose is arbitrary. Recurrent expenditures on health or education or transport – for example on the supply of life-prolonging medicines for AIDS, or payment of elementary teachers, or critical road maintenance – may make an important contribution to future income, though sometimes only after a considerable gestation period. On the other hand, capital projects without the corresponding recurrent-spending provision (school buildings without teachers, roads without maintenance) may be completely unproductive. More generally, the fact that borrowed funds are limited to the financing of 'investment' (in whatever sense) does not guarantee that available funds will be generated in future for the servicing and repayment of the loans. A rule such as this may offer a crude check on over-borrowing, but sensible budgeting requires more sophisticated methods, with projection of future cash-flows.

Foreign borrowing *also* of course brings a future burden of debt, with the added complication that servicing of the loans has usually to be made in foreign currency. This is discussed in Chapter 22.

Up to a point spending power can also be diverted to the state by **money-creation** (the so-called *'inflation-tax'*) – but only temporarily unless other sources of money-creation are dropping or there is continuing unexpected (and therefore *increasing*) inflation. Although, as outlined in Chapter 12, there is some evidence that, at modest rates of inflation, perhaps up to 8 per cent a year, inflation and growth may be positively related – possibly because at least mild inflation is often a by-product of the structural change that growth entails – *ever-increasing* rates of inflation bring highly undesirable effects.

Government **revenue** (as distinct from borrowing and money creation) can come from three main domestic sources: **taxes**, **service charges** (sums paid in exchange for the receipt of some good or service), and **profits from government-owned enterprises**. Taxes are generally by far the most important, at least for *national*-government activity, in both rich and poor countries.

Taxes

Types of tax available

Taxes may be **direct** (assessed on *persons*, individual or corporate) or **indirect** (assessed on *transactions*, as in importing, exporting, production, or sales).

The amount of a direct tax, except in the now increasingly rare case of what are called 'head taxes' or 'poll taxes', is normally based on some measure of income (including corporate profit) or wealth, or the amount or value of some particular asset held, such as buildings or land.

The amount of an indirect tax may be based on the *quantity* of some good involved in the transaction (a *specific* tax) or on the *value* of the good or service concerned (an *ad valorem* tax). Import taxes are often referred to as *tariffs*. *Excises* are specific taxes on the *output* of some clearly defined product, such as whisky or cigarettes or petrol, with *imports* of the product often added in. *Sales taxes* are *ad valorem* indirect taxes collected on sales of *a wide range* of goods and services, usually sales of goods for investment or final consumption rather than intermediate goods, though they may be collected either at the retail or at the wholesale point. *Turnover taxes* are *ad valorem* indirect taxes collected on *gross* output of a wide range of producing firms. *Value-added taxes* (VATs) are *ad valorem* indirect taxes assessed on *net* output at every stage of production and distribution. If their rate is uniform and their cover complete, they are in principle equivalent to uniform-rate sales taxes on all final goods and services assessed at the retail point.

Criteria of choice of taxes

So there is a variety of kinds of tax from which in principle a government can choose. Ideally the criteria of choice are the **economic efficiency** and **equity** of the various kinds of tax (though these are often discussed on the questionable assumption that whatever the law requires to be collected is in fact collected). (See, on economic efficiency, Appendix 19.1, available on the Online Learning Centre.)

In practice, governments have to pay a lot of attention to **political acceptability**. This counts in favour of taxes that are not noticed, or at least *changes* that are not noticed in the type or level of tax. (The maxim 'an old tax is a good tax' derives part of its force from the experience that a tax or a rate of tax is more likely to be acceptable if it is familiar; it is *change* that arouses opposition.) The criterion of political acceptability also counts *against* taxes that offend powerful interests, and, at the other end of the scale of wealth and power, *against* visible taxes on essential items of mass consumption, such as the onetime British Indian salt tax, against which Gandhi led his famous march.

The fourth big consideration is **how easily and reliably the tax can be administered** – and hence how *cheaply* for any given amount of revenue. (Incidentally a tax whose administration is *watertight* will also tend on that account to be more fair and more economically efficient. If it is true that *discrimination* (between different goods, for example) on the part of a tax on any ground – other than to compensate for an externality – is *prima facie* economically inefficient, then discrimination *specifically against honest citizens* will be inefficient as well as unfair.) Even an otherwise quite economically inefficient or unfair tax is likely to be made *worse* on both grounds if people who ought by law to be paying it are not. The more administratively complex a tax is, the more executive discretion there is likely to be in its administration, which makes it more prone to corruption as well as less watertight on other grounds.

This last factor – ease of effective administration – has a bearing on such typical differences in patterns of taxation as there are between rich and poor countries. Some forms of tax – particularly income taxes and VATs, for which the administration is complex – are generally harder and therefore more costly *pro rata* (in relation to other taxes) to administer effectively in poor countries than in rich. It is in large part for administrative reasons that the proportion of the population that income taxes cover is typically less in poorer countries. (VATs and income taxes also put particular administrative burdens *on those who have to pay them*.)

We could say that the 'principles of taxation' are the same across countries with different average-income levels; but differences among societies in patterns of ownership and business organization (such as the importance of the 'informal sector'), in the prevalence of formal education perhaps, and in institutions, especially those of government, dictate some difference in choices among tax instruments. The diversity among developing countries means of course that their responses to these elements will be far from uniform, but there are certain characteristic differences from affluent countries.

Developing-country tendencies in tax choice and reasons for them

Developing countries tend to have lower proportions of national income taken as tax or as total government revenue than rich countries. The scatter diagram in World Bank (*WDR* 2002, p. 110, not shown here) shows this clearly. Table 19.2, dealing with central-government revenue alone and based on eleven developed, and 31 large to medium-sized developing, countries, shows an average difference of five percentage points, between the developed and developing countries sampled, in the proportions of GDP taken as tax by the centre.

So there seems to be at least some tendency for the developing countries to raise lower proportions of national income as tax revenue. Insofar as this is true, it probably reflects either the comparative weakness of

	Percentage
Developing countries of 10 million or more population (31*)	19.2
Developed countries (11*)	24.4

TABLE 19.2 Percentages of GDP collected as central-government tax and social-security contributions, selected developed and developing countries, weighted averages, 2005
* Countries as in Table 19.3 overleaf.
Source: As for Table 19.3 overleaf.

government institutions or the importance of the informal sector. The informal sector is difficult to tax directly because there are so many operators with such comparatively little income and turnover, often with no checkable records. A further possible explanation is that it is 'ultimately' a matter of the public's choice in consumption: that, for reasons associated with relative poverty, 'private' goods – provided normally through the market, goods such as food and shelter – tend to be or to seem *more essential* than in richer countries *in relation to* the goods normally provided by governments.

Developing countries also tend to rely more relatively on indirect taxes as against direct, and very probably for much the same reasons as the first two just mentioned: relative bureaucratic effectiveness and the informal sector's prominence. Tariffs and excises particularly can generally be collected at a small number of points (at production or import) from a relatively small number of producers or traders, where the *tax base* (the volume or value on which the tax is based) will often be relatively easy to determine or check. Table 19.3 for 2005 bears out the smaller importance, within total central-government revenue, of direct taxes (income tax and social-security contributions taken together) as against indirect, in low- and middle-income countries. Comparison of this table with one for 1978–80 in Prest (1985, p. 21) shows very much the same picture then, with the difference that direct taxes (and within them social-security contributions) had risen somewhat in relative importance in the meantime within both developed and developing countries.

Tendencies among indirect taxes

Among indirect taxes, the poorest countries particularly have often relied mainly on duties levied on overseas trade or on production of primary export commodities. Table 19.3 gives evidence of some remaining tendencies in this direction. A further scatter diagram in World Bank (*WDR*, 2002, p. 110) shows a clear negative relationship between a country's average income and its reliance on external-trade taxes. Comparing Table 19.3 with the one given by Prest for 25 years earlier suggests that this dependence on foreign-trade taxes fell after 1980 in accord with the generally increased faith in markets among policy-makers – and more strikingly in developing countries, where those taxes had still been of some importance in 1980, and the tendency to drop them derived additional force from the advocacy of the World Bank and IMF.

Type of revenue	Non-oil developing countries* (averages)	Industrial countries (averages)
Taxes on income and profits	26.8	42.3
Social security contributions	20.2	40.2
Domestic taxes on goods and services	36.0	14.7
Taxes on international trade and transactions	10.1	0.7

TABLE 19.3 Percentages of central government revenue (excluding grants and non-tax revenue), 2005, weighted averages

The table is based on figures for 11 developed and 31 developing countries.

* Among developing countries those with less than 10 million population (and Algeria) were excluded, so that most of the countries with the most extreme dependence on oil are not represented, but Indonesia, Mexico, Iran and Russia are included. The sample of developing countries is much smaller than Prest's (1985, p. 21) for 1978–80.

Source: Derived from IMF, *Government Finance Statistics Yearbook 2005*, pp. 19–21.

The general preference for tariffs and excises among indirect taxes implies a reluctance to make much use of general sales taxes, which, at least if collected from retailers, would usually involve dealing with a very large number of small, informal-sector shopkeepers. The alternative of a value-added tax (VAT), if undertaken rigorously, would not only entail this last handicap but also require reliable record-keeping right through the chain of production. On the whole, the lower the number of individuals or businesses with whom the tax authorities need to have dealings, and the larger and more sophisticated on average they are, the lower the administrative cost of collecting any form of tax is likely to be in relation to the revenue realized. A general sales tax would on those grounds be better imposed at the wholesale than at the retail point – and evidence (Due, 1970, *passim*) suggests that, at least before pressure was applied by international organizations in favour of VAT, developing-country governments generally responded accordingly.

VAT illustrates the conflicts that often arise between the various criteria. Its first ostensible advantage is that it does not discriminate between different classes of goods. This would be true if the tax were really applied universally at a single rate (which it generally is not), and it is regarded 'in principle' as a mark of economic efficiency. VAT's second advantage is that it should provide an incentive for producers further on down the chain of production to insist that *their suppliers* pay the taxes due because they (the producers further down) can then claim back the amounts their suppliers have paid. The first potential disadvantage of a VAT in a developing country is that it requires extensive, accurate record-keeping and form-filling by all producers (including retailers), which is at best a burden and at worst may be beyond the habits and skills of many. This makes it also expensive to enforce for revenue departments, which are often under-resourced even before VAT is introduced and yet have been pressured to use it to replace simple, straightforward import taxes (cheap to collect but with a tendency to be economically inefficient because of their discrimination against foreign trade and reduction of competition). A further drawback of VAT is that exemptions or reduced rates for particular goods (which in any case tend to negate one of its alleged advantages) are more complex to introduce administratively than they would be with conventional sales taxes. Without exemptions VAT acts as a proportional, or even slightly regressive tax, which arguably burdens the poor excessively. That characteristic in turn is the obverse of a third alleged advantage – its comprehensiveness – which entails at least an element of fairness: that it draws some revenue from a number of classes of people who, legally or illegally, will not be paying income tax.

Tendencies among direct taxes

Foreign direct investments in a country will generally be embodied in relatively large enterprises and will be subject to public-reporting requirements, and therefore – given reasonably honest and competent revenue administration – they will be comparatively cheap (per unit revenue) and easy to tax directly. Since, in a number of developing countries, a high proportion of formal-sector business is foreign-owned, taxes imposed on multinational enterprises can well form a large part of corporate-profit tax collected there or indeed of direct-tax proceeds generally. This raises a dilemma for the government. Where the potential investors have a choice of location for their investments, making the tax regime too severe may lead them to take their investment elsewhere. Yet going all-out to attract investors through very low corporate tax rates or tax concessions to foreign investors risks surrendering unnecessarily a highly important potential source of revenue. We shall discuss below how this dilemma can be at least reduced, especially with natural-resource projects, and how co-ordinated international action might remove another element in it. (See, below,

'Role of international tax co-operation: the neglected agenda'; and Appendix 19.3, 'Neutral taxes for natural-resource projects' available on the Online Learning Centre.)

If tariffs, excises, and income taxes, including profit taxes on multinationals – and general sales taxes or VAT too if they are not anyway in the too-difficult box – are all directed to central government, or in federal systems divided between federal and state or provincial governments, we may wonder what fruitful tax instruments are left – reasonably efficient and fair, and not too difficult to administer – for local governments. Their sources of finance vary considerably from one country to another. A large part in some systems comes to them as general or specific grants from the centre. They may have exclusive rights to certain forms of tax, for example taxes on land or real estate. They may collect fees for various kinds of licence, in which case the temptation is to overburden business with charges and formalities and subject it to arbitrary decisions. Or they may be able to tax on some of the same bases as central authorities, so that there is potentially more than one layer of sales tax, for example. Generally subordinate authorities, including states or provinces, may not collect taxes on international transactions. In all this there is a risk of excessive taxation in total, or that subordinate authorities will be driven to clog up the working of the economy with excessive licence requirements if they do not have other, less potentially wasteful, revenue opportunities. For one possible set of constructive contributions to local taxation, see Appendix 19.2, 'Quest for fair, efficient, and manageable local taxes' available on the Online Learning Centre.

Service charges

Service charges can usefully be imposed for services or goods to which 'the exclusion principle' can be applied: that is, that the person who will not pay can be prevented from enjoying the service. They *cannot* usefully be employed for what are in the strict sense 'public goods' such as 'law and order' or clean waterways or the elimination from an area of some contagious disease. But charges *can* be imposed for schooling, or piped water, or individual vaccinations – and other cases of what may be classed as 'merit goods'. (The terms 'public good' and 'merit good' are explained in Box 19.1 above, and public goods at greater length in Box 7.1 of Chapter 7.)

For much of the 1980s and 1990s the World Bank favoured **the use of charges for services that governments had often provided free of charge**, such as water and schooling. Arguments that can be used in favour are: that charges, where they can be used, discourage waste and on that ground are *prima facie* more economically efficient than taxes as means of financing the same activities; that charges (on top of existing taxes) will allow the state to provide more of the essential services or to improve them; that the collection of charges rather than additional taxes will be cheaper and more reliable administratively; that, if people want services enough, they will pay for them; that, if the charges for a service – say, piped water in any area – are earmarked for providing the service in the area, the provision will reflect the importance the users place on it; and finally that having to pay for water is better than having no local water supply at all, as can easily happen – and particularly to people in the poorest areas – when the government makes the investment decisions while the budgeting process and the way the bureaucracy works are not such as to relate supply closely to local demand or need.

On the other side of the argument is the objection on equity grounds that some very poor families – who may previously have enjoyed water and schooling free of charge – will not be able to pay the charges for one or the other or both. A possible answer to this is that the very poor can be subsidized, either by cash payments based on say household size or by giving them vouchers for the services. The trouble is that such means-tested grants are rarely provided in developing countries – though admittedly, as mentioned in Chapter 10, such provision has become less rare in very recent years. Such safety-net measures to provide free services for the poorest people and not to others require a way of assessing, at least roughly, the incomes of huge numbers of people, and hence need the administrative structures for doing this effectively.

A further, political, objection to imposing charges where they have not previously existed, one which must weigh heavily with politicians, is that people, even the moderately rich, will object strongly to being made to pay for something they regard as essential and have previously enjoyed free of charge.

Much the same issues arise as over **subsidization of commodities of common use**, such as food staples – with the difficulties of rational policy greatest where subsidies have already become established. The case against *general* subsidization of food staples has been given in Chapter 10 in connection with famine relief. Subsidizing rice or maize universally is a highly inefficient instrument for reducing poverty.

Profits from state-owned enterprises

The trouble with these as a source of revenue is that profits from state-owned enterprises are often meagre, if not negative. There is a variety of possible reasons for this phenomenon, which is not confined to developing countries: political interference with management; popular criticism of enterprises that do show profits as if this is something disreputable in an institution set up for the common good; lack of the discipline of competition, especially where the enterprise is a monopoly, as many owned by government are; and the difficulty of imposing internal discipline where the workers and their, often powerful, trade unions are confident that the business will not be allowed to fail, however poor its commercial performance.

Various **remedies for this poor revenue performance** may be considered, most involving the removal of management of the enterprises as far as possible from 'politics', and placing them so that they are obliged to act more like firms in a competitive market. So, it might seem, management might be insulated from 'political' intervention by subjecting it to an independent board like that of a privately owned corporation, and the enterprise might be required to make its way in the marketplace like any other business. The difficulties that can arise here stem from the fact that it is often *not like* any other business. The members of an independent board, if they have no financial stake in the enterprise's success, may not be highly motivated to improve its commercial performance. Moreover, often the product will be some essential service not otherwise available, so that the government simply cannot allow the business to fail, even if continuing it entails financial losses.

The **privatization** solution – and how to overcome its drawbacks in the case of public utilities that are 'natural monopolies' – is discussed in Chapter 7.

Revenue-effort versus revenue-efficiency

It is rightly considered in some contexts a mark of achievement for a developing country to manage a high ratio of government revenue to national income: a high *revenue-effort*. More revenue in principle allows the state to do more of the many valuable things that a state can do, but taxes in themselves are a burden on the public, and are likely to be a disincentive in some degree to productive activity. A developing country with a relatively high level of total taxation for its income level, such as Brazil, is not necessarily noted for a correspondingly large expenditure on health, education and roads. At worst, like excessive regulation, taxes can impose deadweight costs on enterprises with no significant advantage.

The moral is not *only* that there is a trade-off and that a compromise has to be sought between the desirable uses of revenue and the costs and burdens of raising it. Rather, whatever the compromise adopted over the volume of revenue, it is important to scrutinize the economic inefficiencies arising from particular forms of tax by their nature against the amounts of revenue they raise, the administrative costs of raising it, and the possibilities of raising it by other means: with a view to keeping the *total economic burden* of whatever amount of tax is collected as low as possible. It is highly desirable to keep in mind the ideal of *neutrality* in taxation (see Appendix 19.1, available on the Online Learning Centre), by definition a condition in which there is *no excess burden* of the tax considered independently of its administrative costs.

Complete neutrality is in many circumstances an unachievable ideal, but treating neutrality as an important criterion of a satisfactory tax system (alongside equity, acceptability, and administrative practicality and cost) may help avoid some of the unintended side-effects.

As hinted above, some of the worst inefficiencies (combined with deplorable inequity) arise when tax administration is corrupt: when officials or politicians drain off revenue for their personal use or, because of bribes or personal connections, tax certain favoured members of the public less than the law requires. Minimizing corruption where it exists – discussed in Chapter 6 – is the first (and unfortunately often the most difficult) requirement of a productive and fair system of public finance.

Private domestic finance: motivating investment, and providing capital through intermediation

Public-policy questions here can be considered under the general headings of *motivating investment* and providing capital through *intermediation*.

Motivating investment involves legislation and its implementation geared to giving investors – large and small, formal and informal – security, and some elements of relevant knowledge (such as about the soundness of other firms, especially financial institutions, with which they may have dealings), *without* burdening them with *unnecessary* impositions and regulatory requirements. It may also be helped by forms of risk-reduction – insurance – provided, or under-written, or approved for general soundness, by the state.

Intermediation refers to the movement of funds through intermediary institutions from savers to investors. We shall discuss it under two overlapping sub-heads: regulation of financial institutions and markets; and facilitating production loans for the very poor.

Motivating investment

Law and legalization

Investors will want to know that their physical and financial assets will be secure; that they are likely to be able to collect from their creditors; that firms with which they deal are what they appear to be; that they will be eligible to borrow and to be offered adequate insurance if their business position and policy are sound; that they will be free from official extortion or demands for extra-legal payments as conditions for carrying on their business; and that the burden of regulations and of official formalities and financial demands will be kept to a minimum. This requires a basic framework of property law, together with *positive regulation* for the maintenance of transparency – about, for example, the financial status of firms of significant size – and for the recovery of debts; licensing requirements for banks and firms offering financial services; at the same time, sufficient legal protection for banks and insurance companies to encourage them to offer their services widely.

On the other hand it dictates that *unnecessary* regulation should be avoided, not only because of the direct burden it imposes on productive activity but also because of the opportunity it gives for illegal and corrupt impositions; and similarly that taxes, especially the more 'distorting' (less neutral) ones on particular transactions rather than on total income or expenditure, should be kept to the minimum. Brazil might be thought a fairly extreme example of bureaucratic burdens. A survey cited in 2007 (*Economist*, 14/4/2007, Special Report, p. 6) reports that opening a business there requires 17 procedures and takes on average 152 days. (Canada at the other extreme is reported to need only one procedure.) Apart from all else, each procedure in a case like this gives opportunities for demanding bribes; the investor will have plenty of reason to pay what is asked in order to speed the process along. (See also Box 19.2.)

BOX 19.2 KEEPING SMALL INFORMAL BUSINESS INSECURE – AND ILLEGAL – IN PERU

Hernando de Soto, writing in 1989, asserted that, in the city of Lima at that time, meeting all the requirements for legally acquiring a plot of building land took 83 months, one of the three main elements in the process alone involving 207 bureaucratic steps (each taking about one working week) in 48 different government offices, with a total cost over $2000, which represented more than four years' earnings for someone on the legal minimum wage. A trial attempt to obtain permission to open a small store showed that it would take 43 days and cost in cash fifteen times the monthly minimum wage. The setting up of a market by an association of traders would take at least 14.5 years from the time the idea was formulated. Getting permission to operate a bus route would take 26–27 months. The great bulk of all these activities in Lima at the time were undertaken by small operators – and, not surprisingly, illegally.

Source: Hernando de Soto (1989), *The Other Path: the Economic Answer to Terrorism*, Basic Books, New York, pp. 136–9; 142–3; 143–4; 146.

It is of particular concern for the state to support, and not obstruct, investment in the small-scale informal sector, such as the kinds of business mentioned in Box 19.2 and investments by people in their own housing. Third World cities commonly have huge numbers of their people living in considerable insecurity and squalor within informal settlements, where they must make a living somehow but have no legal title to their dwellings or to the land they occupy. The tenure insecurity increases their vulnerability to predatory gangs and corrupt police. Improving their houses, or operating businesses from them, will be precarious at best. Giving them ownership rights over the land they occupy and what is on it will be at least a highly relevant first step toward the security that will make investment worthwhile. The need for legalizing *de facto* house ownership is one major strand in De Soto's large theme. William Easterly (2006, p. 90) expounds it:

Property rights also determine whether markets work. Do I have title to the land, building and equipment making up my taco stand? Hernando de Soto noted in his great book *The Mystery of Capital* that the majority of land occupied by the poor urban majorities in the developing world does not have legal title – *nobody* owns it. Only if I felt secure that I would keep my taco stand would I invest in more sanitary food-processing equipment. I can borrow from a bank to purchase such equipment only if I have title to the property to put down as collateral. Only then will the bank feel secure that I will not abscond with the loan. Even then, the loans will be available only if the laws allow the bank to take my taqueria if I default on the loan. . . .

De Soto argues that suitable legal rights are essential if businesses are to have the confidence and credit to expand. Those that remain illegal not only suffer the positive burdens of illegality (such as the need to pay bribes to officials and to remain small and inconspicuous) but also lack the support of banking and insurance and of being able to sue for the recovery of debts. Yet the immense obstacles put in the way of becoming legal at the time he wrote simply excluded from the protection of the law those who were doing most of the house-building and most of the retail trade and providing most of the public transport. What was needed was law, but law shaped by the needs of the hundreds of thousands of small investors and taking cognisance of the informal rules that they were applying.

Buffers to support risk-taking

Relevant also to the motivation for taking the risks of innovation and investment – especially perhaps in rural industries where success depends so much on weather and events outside the producer's control – are the various forms of insurance (in the broadest sense) that will provide support if things go wrong: crop insurance; loan agreements with contingency clauses; guarantees of relief in emergencies, involving at best perhaps some regular and reliable social safety-net providing minimal subsistence. In other words there is a need to exploit the *potential* that devices ranging from forms of *business insurance*, some of it possibly provided commercially, to *social-safety-net systems for relieving extreme poverty*, may give enough reassurance for the risks of a venture to be accepted.

Intermediation

Conditions of lending and borrowing: the financial-repression debate

Developing-country governments have often in the past set limits to rates of interest on bank deposits and bank loans. This probably reflected popular views about 'usury' combined with the idea that lower rates of interest would be more encouraging to investment. The practice was challenged by Ronald McKinnon (1973) and Edward Shaw (1973), independently, though through publications in the same year. Keeping interest rates below those that would prevail in a free market was described as *financial repression*. (See Meier 1989, pp. 205–12, an extract from Ronald McKinnon.)

The crux of the argument against financial repression is based on simple market analysis: that less funds will flow into the banks if real interest-rates are lower and, consequently, they will be able to lend less. This argument against financial repression does not rely on supposing that the actual *rate of private saving* responds positively to interest-rates, on which there is conflicting evidence. It is rather that, for want of other financial instruments, small savers in developing countries have to rely for accumulating liquid reserves on the use of cash or bank deposits unless they are to tie up their assets in such 'non-financial' forms as jewellery or land. The presence of low, possibly negative, real interest-rates on bank deposits, even if does not inhibit their *saving*, will encourage them to *accumulate* their assets in non-financial forms, where they will not be readily available for productive investment by others.

On the demand side, because of interest-rates below the market equilibrium, not only will loans for investment be restricted in volume, forcing investors to rely more on self-finance, but also, because of excess demand for the loans, their allocation will be arbitrary – in the sense of depending on factors such as the value of the borrower's collateral, or personal favour (Fry, 1982) – rather than being determined by investors' expectations of returns, and this will be inefficient.

Any inflation will aggravate these tendencies, easily generating *negative* real rates of interest when the nominal rates are capped, so further encouraging savers to use traditional non-financial hedges against inflation rather than depositing in banks, and further increasing the unsatisfied demand for investible funds.

McKinnon and Shaw argue also that financial repression, by reducing bank lending, inhibits the development of the financial system, as proxied by M2 money supply, and they invoke evidence relating the rate of growth of M2 positively to that of the economy.

By the end of the 1980s or before, the McKinnon–Shaw analysis of financial repression had become conventional wisdom, and financial liberalization had come to be accepted in the general movement to liberalization over the 1980s. Allowing interest rates to be more market-determined went naturally with the winding-down of centrally directed credit-rationing. (See, for detail, World Bank, *World Development Report* 1989, esp. pp. 122–32.)

However, it is the case now that not only have the *a priori* arguments against financial repression been subject to question but that also the empirical evidence against seems at best ambiguous.

Furthermore, the arguments against financial repression, even if valid, do not necessarily imply support for all forms of financial liberalization. The currency crises of the late 1990s raised strong doubts about complete liberalization – regardless of circumstances – in international capital movements. Earlier, the World Bank (1989, p. 127), in a report generally strongly favourable to complete financial liberalization, nevertheless set out several conditions under which any of which the benefits of some forms of liberalization might be dubious: macroeconomic instability, a highly distorted price system, and the absence of 'adequate prudential regulation and banking supervision' to replace direct intervention. Whether heeding these qualifications would have been enough to prevent the 'East Asian crisis' of 1997 is, however, questionable.

The following are some doubts about the McKinnon–Shaw argument. (This passage owes much to Thirlwall, 2006, pp. 426–30.)

First, it supposes that funds for investment will be better allocated by banks than by informal-sector investors using their own or acquaintances' savings, though the latter may well be better placed to make judgements about their own investment projects than the banks will be about similar ventures presented to them for finance, and this may be especially important socially when, as de Soto's (1989) evidence suggests was the case in Lima, informal-sector investments are fulfilling the bulk of certain irreplaceable public-service functions.

Then it supposes that bank lending to investors will be less efficient the less funds the banks have to lend, whereas banks do not necessarily lend all the funds they have available, and with more to lend they may well be motivated still to perverse selection by the over-caution and favouritism mentioned by Fry (1982).

Relatedly, it supposes that banks' capacity to lend to the private sector will be rigidly determined by their levels of deposits. In fact, banks typically lend multiples of their deposits, and the limits are determined by conventions and official directives. Policy will determine too how far they are obliged or induced to lend to government.

Thirlwall (ibid.) also cites several empirical studies that at least cast doubt on whether raising real interest rates increases either saving or investment. A World Bank study, however, (1989, pp. 32–3) shows a marked difference in productivity of investment in favour of those developing countries that have *positive* real interest-rates over those *with real rates below minus 5 per cent*. Following the idea that there may be a trade-off between lending rates that are too high and deposit rates that are too low, an empirical study by Fry (1997; cited Thirlwall, 2006, p. 429) over 85 countries and 25 years pointed to a real interest-rate of zero as one that would maximize growth.

The case against financial repression is not as strong or unambiguous as has sometimes been supposed. What seems to be loosely agreed, however, is that *negative* real rates of interest need to be avoided.

Colombia's experience with housing finance (see Box 19.3) gives support to objections against negative real interest-rates and to the advantage of eliminating them.

BOX 19.3 HOUSING FINANCE IN COLOMBIA

Colombia switched in 1972 from negative to significantly positive real interest-rates over housing finance through the creation of intermediaries that indexed to inflation the rates on what they lent and borrowed. This provides one striking example of the gains that can be made in certain circumstances from removing financial repression. As discussed in Chapter 12, there are special characteristics of domestic-housing finance (notably the need for long-term loans), and these may account in part for the strength of the result in this case. The change set in motion a boom in house-building that not only boosted national income by satisfying a latent ('repressed') consumer demand for accommodation but also generated a big reduction in unemployment because of the labour-intensive and domestic-materials-intensive nature of the house-building industry.

Source: Information derived from R.J. Sandilands (1990), *The Life and Political Economy of Lauchlin Currie*, Duke University Press, Durham NC and London, ch. 10.

Lending to the very poor: microcredit

Generally lending to the poorest people has no appeal for commercial banks. Creditworthiness would be difficult to determine; costs per transaction would be unduly high; satisfactory collateral could not be expected. Lending by government 'development banks', supposedly targeting small commercial borrowers, has generally failed to reach the very poor, and these institutions have been notoriously bad at recovering service payments from their borrowers.

The microfinance or microcredit movement, as the terms are now understood, is generally dated as starting in 1976, with an experimental project undertaken by Dr **Muhammad Yunus**, in the vicinity of Chittagong University in Bangladesh – though it was at least foreshadowed by schemes in Africa dating back to 1968. The project developed into the Bangladesh Grameen Bank, a multi-million-dollar, not-for-profit enterprise. Microfinance involves lending for purposes of production to very small borrowers, often but not always the very poorest, often but not always women, with devices that generally ensure very low rates of default. The Grameen Bank is now one of three very large not-for-profit NGOs in

Bangladesh – with other lenders, including some that are commercial banks, elsewhere in Asia and in Africa and the Americas – all administering what is counted as microfinance.

By the end of 2001 there were estimated to be 54.9 million people across the world who could be classed as microcredit borrowers, of whom 26.8 million had been among the poorest people at the time of their first loans. At this time, by a rough estimate, there were about 10 million micro-borrowers in Bangladesh, with about 3 million having loans from each of the three big micro-lenders, the great bulk of these borrowers people who were poor by the very low national standards. Estimates from a few years earlier (Morduch, 1999, p. 1574) suggested nearly 3 million in Indonesia, though with less concentration on the poor. With 25 million or so poor households across the world borrowing, 100 to 150 million individuals might be affected. A 'summit' of the movement in 1997 aimed to reach 100 million poor borrowers across the world by 2005.

BOX 19.4 A FAMILY UNBOUND THROUGH MICROCREDIT

'. . . There are millions of women like Saraswathi Krishnan who lives in India. "When my children cried at night from hunger, I felt like dying", Saraswathi recalled. . . . Eventually, when the roof of their tiny hut was about to collapse, having no jewelry or other assets to pledge for a loan to repair it, Sarawathi sold her seven-year-old daughter into bonded labor to a local merchant for 2000 Indian rupees (about US$40).

'. . . Five years later, Saraswathi joined Working Women's Forum, a women's self-help and microcredit program based in Madras, India. With her first loan she paid off her debt to the merchant, freeing her daughter, who now attends school, and began a small vegetable-selling business.

'With a second loan she bought her sixteen-year-old son a loom. Previously he would bring home around $5 a month doing odd jobs for wealthy families. With the loom, he can weave two saris per month, earning him $25 per month.

'Now Sarawathi's vegetable business is thriving as well, thanks to her hard work and the training she has received from the program. . . . With the family's new sources of income, Saraswathi has a sense of pride and security she has never before experienced. "I will never mortgage my children again; they will be educated. Now I see to it that my husband is good and does not beat me any more."'

Source: S. Daley-Harris (ed.) (2002), *Pathways out of Poverty: Innovations in Microfinance for the Poorest Families*, Kumarian Press, Inc., Bloomfield, Connecticut, p. xi.

Lending practices vary across the institutions. The Grameen Bank has set the popular stereotype of a micro-lender, with its concentration on the very poorest (generally people with less than half an acre of land each); its strong bias toward women clients; the fact that it does not require collateral; its organization of borrowers in 'solidarity groups' of around five people each, who take responsibility for each other's obligations; its bait of further loans to clients who meet repayment schedules ('progressive lending'); and its very low rate of defaults. Morduch's (1999) summary of the position across the world at the end of the last century indicates that not all the institutions regarded as microcredit lenders have an exclusive direction to the poorest. Most, but not all, do have at least some bias toward women. Most do not require collateral, though some do. Solidarity groups have been widely copied but are only one of the methods adopted to promote discipline among borrowers. 'Progressive lending' is very nearly universal and, in almost all programmes, rates of default (at well below 10 per cent) are very low by the standards of small institutional lending in developing countries before the 1980s.

Are microcredit institutions self-supporting financially? Of the three big Bangladesh lenders, only the smallest, ASA, was judged by one outside analyst in the late 1990s even arguably to be completely self-supporting (Goodwin-Groen, 1998, p. 8), and some doubts have been expressed over the interpretation of this claim. Morduch's evidence from the late 1990s suggests that those that are clearly self-supporting tend to be those *not* concentrating heavily on the poor. At the same time, while Morduch appears to be using the most exacting definition of self-sufficiency, he argues (p. 1591), from the experience of BRAC, a third big Bangladeshi lender, that the Grameen Bank could have raised its lending rate from 20 per cent to 32 per cent (nominal) without significant loss of custom and, if it had done this, would have become genuinely self-supporting. At the time of writing the Grameen Bank claims to be self-supporting.

The importance of the capacity to cover fully all costs, including the cost of capital, is that it would make possible flows of funds from the commercial markets up to whatever the organizational capacity of the system was. Experience has generally supported the advantage or necessity of avoiding any direct government involvement in microfinance other than some straight provision of funds; and, if there is to be serious concentration on the poor, the involvement in the organization of a not-for-profit NGO – which may be a huge one such as Grameen or BRAC or ASA – is probably essential.

Statistical evidence of the boost to national income or to the incomes of the poor arising from microcredit has not been entirely satisfactory. However, apart from much moving anecdotal evidence of the gains to poor borrowers (for example, Yunus, 1984), the fact that tens of millions of people who are poor by the most exacting standards are ready to borrow for business purposes at quite high rates of interest, are able to meet their obligations, and are willing to come back for more, is evidence that could hardly be stronger of gains in human material welfare under conditions in which they are most needed.

Role of international tax co-operation: the neglected agenda

There has already been significant international tax co-operation: principally for avoiding 'double-taxation' on people and firms that earn in more than one country or reside in one country and earn income in another. It is regarded as inefficient, as well as unfair, if anyone is taxed twice on the same income simply because of choosing – or finding it most productive – to live or work in this way. In that case the person or firm would have an incentive, imposed for no good reason, to live or to earn other than where it was most pleasant or profitable. Often pairs of countries have reached bilateral double-taxation agreements, providing that someone domiciled in one country but having a source of income in another should be taxed on that income in one but not both. Where there is no double-taxation agreement, as has often been the case between developed and developing countries, the home country (the one where the person is domiciled or the company registered) normally adopts one of three methods for avoiding double taxation: exemption, deduction, or credit.

Exemption simply involves refraining from taxing again income (including company profits, of course) that has been already taxed abroad. *Deduction* means treating the tax paid abroad as a deductible expense to set *against income* for purposes of tax in the home country. *Credit* offsets tax paid abroad *against tax* that would otherwise be payable in the home country, so that the amount of tax that the person or corporation pays *altogether* on the income amounts to what would be due on it abroad or what would be due on it in the home country, *whichever is the higher.*

In spite of these co-operative arrangements, the rules and practices of the various national tax jurisdictions are constructed largely independently of each other. This is less and less satisfactory as economic activities and opportunities become more and more international. It gives opportunities for tax to be *evaded* (that is, escaped illegally) or *avoided* (legally, but often against the intentions of the taxing authorities), and for mutually destructive *tax-competition* between countries over the terms and rates of the taxes. As a result of the evasion, avoidance, and tax-competition, developing countries forgo large amounts of annual revenue – probably at least as much as they have normally received in Official Development Assistance – that beyond dispute would be rightfully theirs and which they might otherwise enjoy.

The measures needed to block these holes in the system would leave the developed countries too, taken as a body, in a better revenue position, very probably with greater absolute gains than those of the developing countries.

There are three main sources of leakage, giving scope in the main to *evasion*, ostensibly-legal *avoidance*, and *self-defeating tax-competition* respectively. These sources are *tax-exemption for portfolio income earned by foreigners* in the major financial centres; *tax treatment of the enterprise income of multinational firms* producing in several jurisdictions; and *tax concessions given by host countries to foreign direct investment*. Exacerbating or even arguably creating the first two problems is lack of communication or transparency: the bank secrecy allowed in certain jurisdictions, and failure of the authorities of different jurisdictions to share information.

Tax exemption on interest earned by foreigners

First is the scope for evasion arising from the fact that potential taxpayers can profitably hide from their own authorities their property-income earnings by transferring capital to other jurisdictions where its earnings will not be taxed. When capital and its owner are in different tax jurisdictions, it is far easier to tax if the tax is collected in the first instance at source, that is where the income is earned. If the authority in that jurisdiction fails to do this, and also fails to inform the authorities in the earner's home country, the earner can easily avoid being taxed altogether.

The jurisdictions that enable this to happen may be what we normally associate with the term *tax-havens*: tiny states – tropical islands or picturesque European principalities – where little business goes on apart from 'financial services'. However, they may also be rich-world financial centres, and not just those deliberately geared to banking secrecy such as Switzerland and Luxembourg. It has been said that the really important tax-havens are in sites such as London, New York, and Frankfurt. Rules operating there are an important part of the story. This is especially so because, since 1984, the other rich countries have followed the US in *ceasing to apply a withholding tax* to portfolio-investment income earned in their jurisdictions by non-citizens or non-residents (in the case of the US 'non-resident aliens'). The exemption had been introduced in the US in response to conditions particular to the time. Its clearly attributable immediate effect was a large 'capital flight' from Latin America to the US. In these new conditions, the attraction for many developing-country residents of holding their deposits in rich-country banks was for obvious reasons irresistible. If the interest earned was not declared for tax purposes in the recipient's own country, it would be simply tax-free, while the capital would also be (it was no doubt assumed) in a thoroughly safe place.

Meanwhile the home country would lose not only the tax legally due from its resident but also the presence of the financial capital on which the taxable income was earned. By following the lead of the US, the rich countries offered similar incentives for flight and opportunities for evasion to each others' residents as well as to those of developing countries. Avi-Yonah (2000, p. 1599) gives reason for believing that at the time he wrote the revenue loss to developing countries from this source might be at least of the order of $30 billion a year.

Since 1996 both the EU and the OECD have made moves toward preventing these losses of revenue (Avi-Yonah, 2000, pp. 1554–62; *Economist*, 24/2/2007, 'A special report on offshore finance; esp. pp. 15–16), but in neither case with the complete unanimity needed among members for radical measures. The EU's savings directive, which came into force in 2005, was very restricted in its scope so that it would do nothing for the tax-evasion problems of developing countries. The OECD's 'harmful-tax' project, started in 1996, was supported by most of its member countries, but not by Austria, Belgium, Luxembourg, or Switzerland. It was directed at full exchange by its members of tax-relevant information on the international movement of capital and service income. The OECD has also tried to persuade the smaller offshore tax havens to follow similar practices of transparency and exchange of information. Of 35 listed in 2000, all but five (three of them in Europe) had complied by early 2007 (*Economist*, 24/2/2007, ibid.). There have also been a few bilateral exchange-of-information agreements between individual tax-havens and particular major countries, chiefly the US (ibid.) It remains to be seen whether these exchanges of information will greatly restrict the opportunities for evasion of developing countries' taxes.

Avi-Yonah (2000, pp. 1667–70) proposes a much more direct approach: a high level of withholding tax (say 40 per cent) imposed by all co-operating countries on all interest, royalties, management fees, and dividends payable to non-residents, the tax remittable in full (unless there are bilateral tax agreements between the two countries concerned with which this would be inconsistent) to all those payers who can give evidence that the income on which it is based has been notified to the tax authorities in their respective countries of residence. It would be left to these authorities whether, once apprised of the information, they levied any tax and at what rate they chose to do so. The rate of the withholding tax would be designed to be at least as high as the highest for which the taxpayers would be liable in their home countries, so that the incentive to capital flight from the taxpayers' home countries would be removed.

Tax treatment of multinational firms producing in several jurisdictions

Here the trouble is not only – perhaps not mainly – evasion but rather avoidance that allows a firm to be taxed overall at a rate lower than it would pay if its total income were to be taxed in any one of the jurisdictions where its main operations take place.

There are two cases: where it *reports* its activities to the various tax jurisdictions in such a way as reduce its tax liability; and where it actually *sites* its operations to the same effect.

To take the case of 'tax-efficient' *reporting* first: the usual practice is that the firm is obliged to pay tax in each country's jurisdiction on that part of its income deemed to be earned in that country. But there can be no unambiguous way of determining how much of its income is generated in any one of the countries. Methods of calculating income are not necessarily the same from one jurisdiction to another; tax rates differ; and there are concessions particular to individual countries. So a firm may be able to gain by shifting parts of its income for tax purposes to the jurisdiction that will treat them most favourably. 'Transfer-pricing' (choosing prices favourable to tax-avoidance for charging its branches or subsidiaries in one country for inputs bought from its branches or subsidiaries in another) is one way of doing this, but there are other ways in which activities can be 'shifted' for reporting purposes.

Vito Tanzi (1995, pp. 101–3) cites four studies that use evidence – on foreign corporations in the US and US corporations abroad – which points strongly to the conclusion that shifting of declared income between jurisdictions is a significant source of loss of revenue. (For example, in each year from 1982 to 1990, taxable income reported by foreign-controlled US corporations bore between a half and a twentieth of the proportion – either to receipts or to assets – of the taxable income reported by other US corporations.)

That is one class of problem for the revenue services: 'tax-efficient accounting' – efficient of course for the tax payer, not for the society – by which income will be reported where it will be taxed most favourably.

A second is the actual *siting* of some of a firm's operations so that it, legally and openly, avoids tax, or pays very low rates, on them. This can come about because the site chosen charges low or no taxes on income generally, or because it gives preferences for certain purposes to foreign investors, or because the firm, though selling say in a particular jurisdiction, is not held to have a 'permanent establishment' there, which is usually a condition for being taxable. Beside low-tax and no-tax havens, there are preferential 'headquarters-tax-havens' and 'production-tax-havens' set up specifically to attract foreign investors. If the individual or company owning the firm can not only locate some relevant activity but also establish residence in one of these havens, or if its country of residence gives *exemption* (as distinct from *deduction* or *credit,* as explained above) from tax to a resident on activities taxed elsewhere (at however low a level), the firm can get the full benefit of the lenient tax-treatment on offer.

There are two broad approaches that the international community might adopt to counter these sources of revenue loss.

One, mainly directed at the first of the two problems, is suggested by Tanzi. This is to follow the example of what is called the *'Massachusetts formula'* that has been used by a number of states in the USA. The essence of this device would be that an individual's or corporation's *whole* income should be reported to *each* of the jurisdictions in which any of it is taxable and reported according to that jurisdiction's own rules. The claim on the tax due from the firm would then be divided among the jurisdictions according to some objective indicator of the relative importance of its activities in each – for example, the proportions of its workforce in each country. Then, for example, a country with 40 per cent of the workforce would collect 40 per cent of the tax that would have been due if the whole income reported had been taxable in that country under its own laws.

The second approach – addressed particularly to the second problem ('tax-efficient' location) – is probably not a full alternative but may be a supplement in many of the cases, as argued by Avi-Yonah (2000, pp. 1664–6, 1670–4). This is that *all the OECD guidelines that could remove or reduce the incentive to maintain preferential regimes should be followed* (on transfer-pricing, on the elimination of preferences designed to attract foreign investment, and on various other measures discussed below in the section on 'Tax concessions given to attract foreign direct investment').

Tax concessions given to attract foreign direct investment

In order to attract direct investment from abroad, it has been common for developing countries to adopt either low general income-tax rates or such concessions as low preferential rates or initial tax-holidays for foreign establishments. These concessions can undoubtedly have some effect in attracting investment, though there has long been evidence that other factors, such as the riskiness implied by official attitudes and policies, and other transaction costs of doing business in the country concerned, also weigh heavily (Aharoni, 1966). Furthermore, where the host country has a valuable natural resource in which extractive firms are interested, and the tax liability is designed to fall fairly closely on the economic rent of the resource exploitation (see Appendix 19.3, available on the Online Learning Centre), concessions made to attract them are likely to be unnecessary.

Moreover, where a number of developing countries are competing against each other with tax concessions, it is clear that the competition can easily become self-defeating: taken together they will attract few more foreign firms, and very probably earn less revenue, than if they could make a pact together to tax at some agreed 'normal' rate. It is of course a possibility that, if all developing countries taxed inward investment less heavily than developed countries, they would between them attract more investment than if all, rich and poor, taxed at the same rate. However, a foreign firm considering investing in a developing country is likely to be making the choice because of some advantage particular to the country (such as a natural resource or a large internal market), or for the sake of some advantage that a wide range of developing countries have over the developed, such as lower labour costs. It does seem likely that competing against each other with tax concessions leaves developing countries as a body with less revenue from the foreign investments that they have, without significantly expanding the volume of those investments.

Gurtner (2002), on admittedly contestable assumptions, estimates developing countries' loss of revenue from tax competition to be of the order of $35 billion a year.

The developing countries need to find ways of avoiding competition with each other, but how? It does seem that the *incentives* to apply low or discriminatory rates in order to attract foreign investment might be removed by an agreement on the part of the authorities in the home countries of the investors to follow some simple rules that will incidentally generally also favour their own revenue take. If these home countries (i) extended their tax systems, in a way very few now do, so that *all* the overseas earnings of people and companies domiciled within their jurisdictions (not just the part remitted to the home country) would be in principle taxable, and (ii) used the *credit* method in all cases as the means of allowing for tax already imposed in the host country; the effect would be that the host country could not increase its attractiveness to a foreign investor by lowering the rate of tax applying to the investor (so long as the host country's rate of tax *was not higher than that in the home country*).

Say the tax rate on profits in the home country was 30 per cent, and that in the host country was 20 per cent. Under the credit method, the investor would pay 20 per cent to the host and 10 per cent to the home country. Lowering the host-country rate that applied to the investor from 20 per cent to 10 per cent would not benefit the investor, who would still pay 30 per cent in all and would not find this particular host country any more attractive as a result of its reduced tax rate, but this time the host country would take only half as much as before. So, lowering the rate charged by the host country would not make it any more attractive but simply reduce its revenue. In fact the host country might as well charge the full 30 per cent. Any reduction below that rate would be simply transferring revenue unnecessarily to the investor's home country. So, if all potential 'home' countries followed these rules, all incentives to tax-competition on the part of host countries would be removed.

General: toward watertight systems

A watertight tax system is a global public-good. It can only be achieved by co-ordination among national tax authorities. Apart from a relatively small number of (mostly very small) countries that have made a large part of their income through concealing the incomes of others, all are likely to increase their revenue as a result. For developing countries as a group the gains from blocking the holes have been estimated as very probably exceeding the total received in financial aid. It is demoralizing and economically inefficient in the extreme to maintain systems that act discriminatorily *against law-abiding* businesses and households.

The main thrust of reform pressed by the OECD is toward transparency and full disclosure between one tax authority and another, and from banks to tax authorities. Tax-havens, large and small, would cease to menace the receipts of other states once all the information they had and all that they could oblige banks within their jurisdictions to provide was available to other interested revenue departments.

To facilitate among other things the use of the Massachusetts formula mentioned above, we might look forward to a time when every potential taxpayer in the world had a computer-readable identification number that embodied many of his or her characteristics relevant to tax-liability, with groups of digits in it representing each of the jurisdictions in which she or he had been earning. We might also hope for further movement toward common accounting standards and as far as possible toward a uniform way of computing taxable income, so that a common form might be used on which any taxpayer would submit an identical return to each relevant jurisdiction. Without these developments a common form would be difficult to devise.

However, it would emphatically not be necessary for all participating jurisdictions to apply the same rate of tax.

We might expect movement toward full sharing of tax information, and common standards, to get under way initially through co-operation among a small group of likeminded countries, which might be able to demonstrate the possibilities and the advantages of this form of co-operation. Once a workable system was in place, most developing countries would probably have considerable gains to make from joining.

A world tax organization

Agreements promoting world co-operation for closing tax loopholes and removing incentives for 'self-defeating tax competition' would constitute a global public good. Realizing them would depend on negotiation. We suggest that a world tax organization, somewhat along the lines of the World Trade Organization (WTO), should be set up, with an expert secretariat given a brief for promoting agreement between national tax authorities on action (supported by legislative change where necessary) to reduce revenue loss. There might be agreement reached among founding members of the organization on the general principles that were to govern a settlement and on such rules of conduct as might be accepted in the meantime. It might then work like the WTO through successive rounds of negotiation, each with a proximate set of targets. There might be some rules to which all members were obliged to adhere, and others accepted as aspirations and followed by a subset of members.

Summary conclusions

- Developing countries tend to raise a smaller proportion of national income as government revenue than richer countries, to raise a lower proportion of tax revenue from direct taxes, and to raise a higher proportion of their indirect taxes from foreign trade; but the differences are not sharp; and there has been a recent movement by developing countries away from taxes on foreign trade. These differences can be plausibly attributed in part to differences in industrial structure and institutions, and not solely to politics or lack of political will. Higher tax–GDP ratios are not necessarily better. It depends on how the revenue is used and the form of the taxes applied. But in many developing countries there are recognized high-priority needs for public spending that are not met.

- From the range of tax instruments available, criteria of choice include ideally *economic efficiency* and *equity* but also inevitably *political acceptability* and *ease of administration*, which will be reflected in the cost or completeness of collection.

- *Neutrality* is an important criterion in choice of instruments, but near-complete neutrality is generally deemed impossible to combine to the necessary degree with other desirable features in major national taxes. However, workable approaches to neutrality may advantageously be practised in some fruitful local taxes and in the taxing of natural-resource projects.

- *Watertight administration* of taxation and the avoidance of corruption is of the utmost importance. Corruption is likely to aggravate greatly any economic inefficiency and inequity; and it encourages cynicism, which is likely to undermine progressively the tax administration.

- A number of arguments can be put for using *service charges*, rather than general taxation, to pay for government-provided services that do not have the character of public goods. However, there are also arguments of equity against charging for some of the services over which charging would be possible, and there may be further obstacles of political unacceptability, especially when the services have previously been provided free of charge. Less acute conflict of considerations arises with *general* subsidization of the purchase of food staples, which is likely to be a costly and inefficient way of raising the entitlements of the poorest people to food.

- *Profits of state-owned enterprises* are a potential source of public revenue, but often their yield is negative. There are a number of possible ways, not all of them entailing privatization, and partly depending on the particular circumstances of the industries concerned, in which this may be remedied while the potential abuses of natural monopolies are avoided.

- State policy to promote the efficient direction of private funds into productive investment, with due attention to fairness, requires a specific mixture of action and inaction. The topic can be divided between, first, *motivating investment* and, second, *intermediation*.

- Motivating investment can entail imposing the regulation necessary to provide business with essential elements of security and information, but at the same time avoiding rules, bureaucratic procedures, and licensing requirements, that are not necessary for protecting the public or other enterprises. In the case of the huge numbers of people in most big cities that have no legal claims to their houses and land, a prime requirement for encouraging their informal-sector investment, including any communal investment, is to give them firm property titles. Informal-sector enterprise generally needs to be

▶
brought, on terms that it can manage, within the protection of the law. Forms of business insurance and of social insurance or social safety-nets may also have a role in encouraging innovation and investment, especially in small-scale agriculture.

■ On intermediation, there is a widely believed case, on grounds of *a priori* reasoning, that government intervention to set upper limits to banks' rates of interest for lending or borrowing ('financial repression') inhibits intermediation and reduces the funds available for investment and the efficiency with which they are allocated. However, there is also both *a priori* reasoning and empirical evidence tending to cast doubt on the unqualified case against financial repression, but at the same time fairly general agreement, backed to an extent by evidence, that *negative* real rates of bank interest are harmful.

■ The microcredit movement that started (in its present most widespread forms) in Bangladesh now covers across the world tens of millions of very small business borrowers, many of them women, a high proportion of them drawn from among those below extreme poverty lines, who display very low rates of default and generally a willingness to return for further loans.

■ International tax co-operation has the potential for greatly increasing the revenue of developing countries from activities within their jurisdictions and from the incomes of their own residents. In particular this requires an end to the exemptions given by most developed countries to portfolio earnings generated within their jurisdictions by non-citizens or non-residents; joint arrangements for taxing multinationals among the authorities of all the jurisdictions in which they operate; and measures to remove the incentives that individual developing countries have to compete with each other through tax concessions to attract foreign direct investment. More broadly it requires transparency and communication among governments on matters of common tax interest. In absolute terms, a number of these measures will also be of even greater revenue advantage to the developed countries than to the developing countries, though probably of more vital importance to the latter. This win-win character increases the likelihood that the measures may eventually prove politically attainable. There is a strong case for the creation of an international tax organization, with an expert secretariat and a brief to foster negotiations toward co-operative action for preventing revenue loss.

International tax co-operation has the potential for significantly increasing tax revenue virtually everywhere without increasing tax rates. (The exceptions are the small tax-havens that live off the illegality or dubious legality of those who resort to them.) Alternatively it may be used to allow tax rates to be reduced without reducing the revenue they generate. And, by making it harder to evade or avoid paying taxes, it could have the effect of allocating their burden more fairly.

Questions for discussion

19.1 What do you understand by 'neutrality' in taxation? With developing countries in mind, give examples where you think tax neutrality might be important, or the lack of neutrality an obstacle, to growth or welfare.

19.2 Referring to the criteria on which tax systems are judged, discuss critically the case for replacing import duties by a value-added tax (VAT), either in some particular developing country about which you have some knowledge or in developing countries in general.

19.3 What are the grounds for the judgement that corruption in the administration of taxation introduces both economic inefficiency and unfairness into the system or increases any inefficiency or unfairness that already exists?

19.4 What possible lines of attack are available for preventing small specialized tax-havens from furthering tax-evasion?

19.5 Explain why the exemption from income tax given by most major developed countries to interest income earned in their jurisdictions by non-residents is an important source of evasion of the taxes due to authorities elsewhere, and notably in developing countries.

19.6 Can further international tax co-operation among rich and poor countries be run as a positive-sum game for all the participating governments? Who, if any, are likely to be the losers?

19.7 What are the arguments for and against 'service-charges' as means of paying for schooling, health services, and water?

19.8 With reference to developing countries, say what forms of government regulation of business you think are essential. What measures might be taken to prevent business regulation from becoming unduly obstructive?

Additional reading

Avi-Yonah, R.S. (2004) 'Bridging the North/South divide: international redistribution and tax competition', *Michigan Journal of International Law*, **26**, 1, Fall, pp. 371–87.

De Soto, H. (1989) *The Other Path: the Economic Answer to Terrorism*, Basic Books, New York.

This is the work of an inveterate crusader and organizer, who has achieved substantial success in reform of the monstrously dysfunctional system of mixed regulation and neglect regarding business and housing that he describes and analyses in the city of Lima. You don't need to read it all to get the sense of the situation and the answers he prescribes.

Economist 24/2/2007, 'A special report on offshore finance'.

Meier, G.M. (1989) *Leading Issues in Economic Development*, 5th edn, 'Case against financial repression', pp. 205–12.

Morduch, J. (1999) 'The microfinance promise', *Journal of Economic Literature*, **XXXVII**, December, pp. 1569–1614.

 Online
Learning Center

To help you grasp the key concepts of this chapter check out the extra resources posted on the Online Learning Centre at *www.mcgraw-hill.co.uk/textbooks/huq*

Among other resources, there are three appendices available:

- Appendix 19.1 Quest for a neutral and equitable tax
- Appendix 19.2 Quest for fair, efficient and manageable local taxes
- Appendix 19.3 Neutral taxing of natural-resource projects

CHAPTER 20

Elaboration of Economic Project-Appraisal

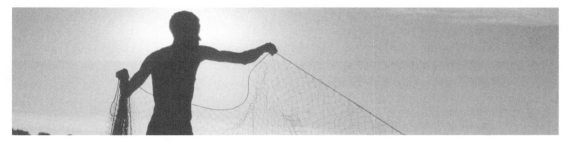

New twists to economic cost–benefit analysis were designed to allow appraisers to reflect
the special insights, hunches, observations and aspirations of development economics in
quantitative form. Among the circumstances for which allowance was made were the
informal sector of household enterprises and distortion by policy of the price system.
The special aspirations were for faster growth – presumed to follow from higher
investment – and greater equalization.

Introduction

Project-appraisal refers to **cost–benefit analysis** and **cost-efficiency analysis**. *Economic*
project-appraisal is used here to mean project-appraisal from the viewpoint of the society
at large rather than of any individual business or person.

Modifications introduced around 1970 to economic project-appraisal allowed some of
the insights of development economics to be systematically taken into account in decisions
over public spending. This chapter describes those modifications.

For a start, we outline the role and logic of conventional **economic** appraisal, its
relationship to **financial** appraisal, and why modifying it to take account of conditions in
developing countries was deemed necessary.

In outlining the elaborations introduced into cost–benefit analysis, we distinguish the two
levels of appraisal: *efficiency appraisal* and *social appraisal*; we present the main differences
between the approaches adopted by the two pioneering studies to the central problem of
widespread price distortions and the aspiration to faster growth; and we expound the
principles, in their developed form, of the appraisal method that became standard in the
lending and aid decisions of the World Bank and a number of other international and
national providers of project finance to developing countries.

This involves questions relating to the numéraire; the discount rate for time used to represent
the shadow-price of capital; the discount for consumption or premium for investment; the
weighting of consumption benefits according to the poverty of the people who receive them;
the shadow wage-rate; and general revaluation for appraisal purposes of inputs and outputs.

After that we discuss how economic project-appraisal can be most usefully incorporated into public decision-making.

Finally we say something about the changing historical context through which the methods, new around 1970, have travelled, and the extent to which their special characteristics are still relevant.

Appendices give the formal derivations of some of the formulations introduced in the body of the chapter, and also a highly simplified example of appraisal in practice to show the stages that might be followed. All four appendices are available on the Online Learning Centre.

BOX 20.1 TOOLKIT FOR ECONOMIC PROJECT-APPRAISAL

APRs. Accounting-price ratios, ratios of 'accounting' or 'shadow' prices used in economic appraisal to actual market prices.

ARI. Accounting rate of interest, the rate of interest used to discount for time in economic project-appraisal.

AWR. The **accounting wage-rate** or **shadow wage-rate**, usually for unskilled labour unless otherwise specified, is the (unskilled) wage-rate used in economic project-appraisal.

Border prices as against **market prices**. Border prices of goods or services imported or exported are the prices those goods and services would have 'at the border' without any duties or subsidies that might be applied to them by the home government. They would correspond to c.i.f. (cost, insurance and freight) prices for visible imports and f.o.b. (free on board) prices for visible exports. In the Little–Mirrlees version of project-appraisal, border prices are used as a way of correcting for policy-imposed distortions in the price system so as to have more realistic estimates of the relative costs and values to the society of various items than would be provided by market prices. Non-traded goods and services are revalued in the nearest equivalents to border prices.

CCF. Consumption conversion factor. In the Little–Mirrlees method the CCF is the factor that, on weighted average across all goods and services, would – as a short-cut approximation – need to be applied to market prices in order to convert them to border prices. It can be regarded as an average APR (see above) for the Little–Mirrlees method. The corresponding factor in the UNIDO method *to convert border prices to market prices* is the **SER (shadow exchange rate)**, ideally the reciprocal of the CCF.

Cost–benefit analysis (CBA) and **cost-efficiency analysis (CEA)**. The difference here is that CBA attempts to take account of *all* costs and benefits of a project so that it gives a net-present-value (NPV) of the project which in principle can be compared with the NPV of any other project whatever its character; while CEA constructs the problem simply to compare *different ways of achieving a particular given result*. So CEA needs to quantify in NPV form *only the net costs* of achieving the given result; and the NPV that it calculates is relevant only for comparisons of other ways of achieving the same outcome.

CRI. Consumption rate of interest, the rate (per cent per year) at which people – in their capacity as consumers – discount future consumption benefits for time.

▶ **DCF. Discounted cash flow,** the now-standard method of valuing investments or loans that takes account of both the inflows and the outflows of cash (or alternatively the economic benefits and costs) expected, and how far into the future each of them is expected to occur. It is equally applicable to financial and to economic appraisal (see below).

Economic appraisal and **financial appraisal.** Conducted by DCF methods (see above) these are identical in their arithmetical form, but financial appraisal takes account of positive and negative cash flows relevant to a particular business, while economic appraisal takes account of benefits and costs for the total society. (Economic appraisal in this sense is often called 'social appraisal', but 'social appraisal' is used here in a narrower sense; see below).

Efficiency appraisal and **social appraisal.** As the terms are used here, these are two *levels* of *economic appraisal.* Efficiency appraisal treats units of income generated by a project alike regardless of the purpose for which the income will be used or who receives it. Social appraisal allows the possibility of treating some units of income as more valuable than others: for example, income destined for investment more highly than income destined for consumption, or 'uncommitted social income' more highly than income available to the private sector, or income passing to poor consumers more highly than what goes to the rich.

LM and **LMST. Little-Mirrlees** and **Little–Mirrlees–Squire–van der Tak.** This is the most commonly used strand of methodology on economic project appraisal elaborated for developing countries.

MPI. Marginal product of investment. This term as used here corresponds to the internal rate of return (IRR), used within this context in an economic, rather than a financial, sense.

NPV. Net present value, or **discounted net present value,** the value of a project or loan reached by a DCF calculation.

Numéraire. The system of units in which some quality or outcome is assessed or valued.

OECD. Organization for Economic Co-operation and Development. See Box 12.1.

UNIDO. United Nations Industrial Development Organization. A UN Specialized Agency with headquarters in Vienna. It sponsored the study leading to the project-appraisal method devised by Partha Dasgupta, Stephen Marglin and Amartya Sen.

Jumping-off point: earlier cost–benefit analysis

Economic cost–benefit analysis is designed to help policy-making by balancing the overall value to society of one potential public project (or publicly protected or subsidized project) against that of others. (We use 'economic' rather than the more common 'social' in this context because of the narrower meaning given here to 'social', as explained below and in Box 20.1.) Purely *financial appraisal*, which estimates financial profitability, is clearly *inadequate* for the purpose on its own – even though it is still important as *a component* in the process of judging projects – since government projects are not usually designed solely or primarily for financial profit, and often their most important output is not marketed.

'What have we now established? First, a project is not just some grand design for a steelworks, a river valley, or a supersonic passenger plane which will be described (and normally recommended) in several tomes, and be considered (and normally approved) by a Cabinet Committee. It is any item of investment which can be separately evaluated. Thus, projects are considered and evaluated at all levels from a junior engineer to the Planning Commission or the World Bank. They are also analysed at all depths, from the back of the envelope to many volumes of erudite programming and scientific guesswork or prediction. Secondly, project *decisions* are taken at all levels: the process of design consists of rejecting and accepting alternatives, many of which are projects in our sense of the term.

'It is clearly desirable that all projects should be evaluated, so far as possible, by applying the same principles. Otherwise inconsistent decisions are certain to be made. Thus our junior engineer, or settlement planner, should be guided by the same rules and methods as are used in the final appraisal of the steelworks or the river valley scheme.

'The above kind of planning harmony should not be too difficult to achieve in the case of a corporation whose sole aim is to maximize its . . . present value . . . The planning engineer then knows that he should plan with this aim in view. He will have to predict market prices in so doing, these being the prices which the corporation faces. As against this, it quite often happens that executives get a hunch about some scheme, and become personally committed to promoting it or opposing it as the case may be. It is not then difficult for them to steer their predictions to support their case. The board is often in no position to check the predictions, and may well not understand how they were arrived at. The same applies in the case of a nationalized industry and its responsible ministry; and in the case of spending ministries and the planning department or finance ministry.

'In general, we shall see that harmony is much more difficult to achieve when one is trying to plan for maximum social advantage for a whole country. This book can be considered as an exploration of the means of achieving this very difficult aim.'

Source: I.M.D. Little and J.A. Mirrlees, *Project Appraisal and Planning for Developing Countries* (1974), Heinemann, London, pp. 5, 6.

Economic as against financial appraisal

Economic appraisal of projects follows the same *arithmetic* as financial appraisal. (We assume that financial appraisal will be conducted by discounted cash-flow, though other methods are still sometimes used.) In either case, a net benefit is estimated for each period of the project's prospective life, and these net benefits for the various periods, discounted for time, are added together to give an expected net present value (NPV) for the project. The difference is that in financial appraisal the positives and negatives in each period are cash inflows and outflows, while in economic appraisal they are benefits and costs to the society. In either case:

$$NPV = \sum_{t=0}^{n} [(B_t - C_t)/(1 + i)^t] \tag{20.1}$$

where   NPV is the net-present value of the project

$t = 0,1,2 \ldots$, n is the number of years from the original investment

n is the lifetime of the project in years

i per year is the discount-rate for time

B_t and C_t are the benefits and costs respectively in year t

B and C in financial appraisal are cash inflows and outflows, while in economic appraisal they are benefits and costs for society.

Discounting for time is used in both financial and economic appraisal because £100 received in year 1 can, through lending or investment, grow into say £105 in year 2, and is therefore more valuable than £100 received in year 2, and, for this and other reasons, people do actually value £100 (whether in cash or in non-cash benefits) received in year 1 more than £100 received in year 2.

The challenge for economic appraisal that does not have to be faced by financial appraisal is to put values on those of the project's benefits and costs that have no market price, and, where there *are* market prices, to take account of 'externalities' that will make the economic price of an input or output (its value or cost to the public at large) greater or less than is indicated by its market price. Prices invented or adapted in this way, differing from market prices in order to reflect values (benefits and costs) to society, are called *shadow prices* or *economic* (or *social*) *prices* or *social-accounting prices*, or (confusingly) *accounting prices*. ('Accounting prices' in this sense are definitely *not* the prices normally used by accountants.)

Cost–benefit analysis and cost-efficiency analysis

Economic appraisal of projects can take the form of either *cost–benefit analysis (CBA)* or *cost-efficiency analysis (CEA)*. *Cost-efficiency analysis* is used when a comparison can be made between several projects that have the same output and represent simply different ways of achieving the same objective: say, several ways of smelting and refining aluminium from the given output of a bauxite mine; or of eliminating malaria from an area; or of providing an airfield of a given capacity. The benefits and costs *other than that of the principal output* will be evaluated in the way outlined above to give in effect a *cost–benefit analysis yielding a NPV **of all the rest***, so that the net costs of the various ways of achieving the objective can be compared. This, in principle, removes the need to set a value on the main output, since that will be common to all the projects. In fact, however, the main outputs of the various projects that are considered together will not always be *identical*, so that some of the task of evaluating them may remain. Here we treat CEA as a variant of CBA and use the term CBA to apply to both.

Conventional CBA

Conventional economic appraisal, as normally applied in developed countries, has started from the price system as it is, departing from it only where there are considered to be externalities that dictate an economic price different from the price in the market or where an input or an output (commonly the main output of the project such as a bridge or a clinic) has no market price because it is not for sale.

This is difficult enough, but methods – approximate, imperfect, not necessarily consistent with each other in the verdicts to which they lead – have been devised for valuing the financially unpriced items. Sugden and Williams (1978/1983) is one text that gives an introduction to these methods, distinguishing between on the one hand those that rely on consumers' choices expressed by their behaviour, or their accounts of what their behaviour would be in hypothetical situations ('individuals' valuations'); and, on the other hand, appraisers' or planners' judgements ('decision-makers' valuations'). Either way, the methods involve elements of judgement, elements that *go beyond* the prediction of tangible outcomes, which economic appraisal, just like financial appraisal, also has to make. Hence the results of economic appraisal have elements of uncertainty and unreliability about them over and above those of financial appraisal, and are quite likely to be controversial.

It follows that economic CBA results do not necessarily provide knock-down arguments for preferring one project over another. They are best seen as an important *aid* to achieving, in the public interest, rationality and consistency in government spending policy.

Adapting economic appraisal for developing countries

Two groups of economists, working independently at about the same time, made the pioneering moves to render economic appraisal more relevant to the special needs of developing countries. They were Ian Little and James Mirrlees (LM), in a publication for the OECD (1968), and Partha Dasgupta, Stephen Marglin, and Amartya Sen (DMS), reporting for UNIDO (Dasgupta *et al.*, 1972). Their insights were similar, though the operational solutions they proposed were different, as we shall see, in two respects. It can be said that their work was designed to make development economics *operational*. They showed how the bearing of some of its insights in particular cases could be jointly *quantified* in order to help illuminate policy choices and to guide with a degree of consistency the decisions made.

The Little–Mirrlees (LM) proposal, which was the more radical, saw the light first. Whether mainly for this or for other reasons, it formed the foundation of the method that has come to be most widely used. LM moved from their original publication, brief and lucid, to a longer book (1974), which introduced new elements. The expanded ideas of this later version were condensed, with the idea of making them more readily applied, by Lyn Squire and Herman van der Tak (1975), in a short book commissioned by the World Bank. It is this version – 'Little-Mirrlees-Squire-Van der Tak' (LMST) – that has been used and promoted by the World Bank, the Inter-American Development Bank, and other international lenders and providers of project aid. A useful manual on the method, with a number of case studies, is Powers (ed.) (1981),[1] with a lucid introduction by the editor to the theory in its first 60 pages. There was also some further development of the UNIDO manual.

Why economic appraisal was deemed to need adaptation

There are four main reasons prompting the new project-appraisal methods, two of them leaning toward descriptive generalizations about the world, and two toward value judgments.

1 The *price system* was held to be so heavily '*distorted*' in many developing countries by government duties, subsidies, and restrictions, coupled typically with considerable over-valuation of the countries' currencies, that it formed a poor starting-point for the relative valuation of project inputs and outputs.

---

[1] This book, drawn on extensively here, was formerly (and is possibly still) distributed free of charge by the Inter-American Development Bank.

2   Structural features of many developing economies – such as the dualism between formal and informal sectors, and the predominance of household enterprises in traditional agriculture – combined with these policy distortions to have important implications for *labour markets*. There was often a high level of urban unemployment, and also (arguably) of urban underemployment and of surplus labour in agriculture, which raised complex questions about the effective opportunity-cost of unskilled labour and hence about the appropriate shadow wage-rate for appraisers to use.

3   The prevailing view that the *rate of economic growth needed to be increased* was held to imply that the existing rate of investment, and consequently of saving, was sub-optimal and that policy needed to boost savings rates.

4   *Income distribution* was held to be *too unequal*, and direct redistribution was considered difficult. This could be taken to imply that extra consumption for poorer people should have a higher priority in the assessment of projects than extra consumption for richer people.

Considered individually, these peculiarities could have pushed project choices in opposite directions. A presumed need to increase the savings rate could have favoured *capital-intensive* methods because they would shift income toward corporations and richer people, who would be expected to have higher saving-rates than the average. On the other hand, recognition that market wage-rates in the formal sector exceeded the marginal opportunity-cost of labour might have dictated greater *labour-intensity* than markets signalled, which would probably have shifted disposable income towards the poorer. By providing frameworks for quantifying these considerations, the OECD and UNIDO teams enabled them to be balanced against each other.

We proceed to outline key elements of the schemes. The exposition below of LMST draws heavily on Powers (1981), largely using his notation.

Efficiency accounting and social accounting: two levels of economic appraisal

This is a distinction absent in the original studies but introduced for essentially practical reasons by Squire and van der Tak and present in the later versions of LMST. One key innovation of both the original studies was provision for weighting income directed to consumption less highly than the same amount of income directed to investment, as a way of reflecting the judgement that the rate of economic growth was sub-optimal. The 1974 version of LM also allows for the possibility that income available without restriction to the state ('uncommitted social income') may be treated as more valuable than income available for private investment, and also that income for consumption may be rated more highly the poorer the class of people to whom it will go.

What later came to be called **efficiency accounting** ignores the possibility of making any of these distinctions. Efficiency accounting revalues the price system so as to reflect better the economic opportunity-cost of resources in production, but, having done this, treats the income arising from projects as homogeneous, regardless of who will use it or for what.

Social accounting (with the 'social' used here in a more restricted sense than it is often used in other contexts) does allow for the possibility of making distinctions between equal amounts of income according to their probable use and according to their distribution among classes of people.

Powers, writing in 1981 from experience in the Inter-American Development Bank, submitted that few developing-country administrations had at that time reached the point of consistently revaluing prices as required for satisfactory efficiency accounting, and argued that, until that hurdle had been surmounted, it was better that they should not attempt the additional complication of social accounting in this restricted sense.

Of the four issues that the extensions to CBA were designed to address, efficiency appraisal deals only with the first two ('distortions' of prices, including that of labour). Social appraisal covers *in addition* the third and fourth (concerns over future growth and over distribution).

Numéraire

This term refers to the unit of value – the standard of value – in terms of which costs and benefits are to be counted. If the same goods were to be valued differently according to whether they would be destined *for consumption or for investment,* then a decision would have to be made over which was to be treated as the standard of value. But a prior question – important even if only *efficiency* appraisal were to be attempted – was the choice of the foundation from which *the system of relative prices of goods and services* would be built up.

To both these questions the two teams gave different answers. On the second question, both envisaged a set of relative prices that might be substantially different from the set prevailing in the market. But there would need to be some objective starting-point: an actual set of relative prices – a set considered to approximate to relative *social* values or costs – in terms of which the rest of the price system could be usefully revalued.

In an *ideal* market system, with perfect competition and with all goods and bads priced, the ratio of two goods' marginal costs would be the same as the ratio of their marginal values. Then the actual price system would reflect adequately the relative costs and values at the margin of any pair of goods or factors, and any revaluation for economic appraisal would be unnecessary.

Because we do not have such an ideal market system, and revaluation for economic appraisal *is* necessary, we have to look for some set of actual prices that reflects (more or less) *either* relative marginal (economic) values *or* relative marginal (economic) costs, and then revalue the rest so that their costs or values bear the right proportions to those in the original set.

The LM method: investment income (or uncommitted social income) at border prices as the numéraire

LM base their system of relative valuation on *'border' prices in convertible foreign exchange,* with the standard unit of value a unit of *income destined for investment.* Their numéraire was described as *investment income at border-prices. Border prices* are relative import and export prices as they would be without any tax or subsidy on importing or exporting (c.i.f. for visible imports, f.o.b. for visible exports). On the assumption that the home country is 'small' in the economic sense – that is to say that its own trade makes a negligible difference to the world prices that it faces – relative border prices for tradables represent a system of relative values *outside the country's own influence* that does show objectively the rates of exchange of various goods and services in its dealings with the rest of the world: how much of A it can get for each unit of B.

If the border price at import of a particular model of truck equals the border price at export of 40 000 T-shirts or 10 tonnes of coffee beans, it can be said that the truck and the 10 tonnes of coffee and the 40 000 T-shirts are of equivalent value for the country, regardless of what taxes or subsidies the government may actually impose on them.

However, if the truck had to pay a 100 per cent import duty while shirts and coffee could be sold in the country without duty, its *market* price would be equal (just 'inside' the border) to that of 20 tonnes of coffee or 80 000 T-shirts. *That set of market prices* would greatly exaggerate the truck's *marginal opportunity-cost* for the country (the resources required – what sacrifice would need to be made – to import it), and consequently, if the 100 per cent duty were not assumed to be an unavoidable fixture, would also exaggerate the *marginal value* of producing it domestically instead of importing it. If in these circumstances a vehicle-building project for the country were to be appraised with the trucks produced valued at their *market* prices, then, other things being equal, the *economic value* of the output of the project (the number of T-shirts it could release to pay for imports of other things through reducing the need to import trucks) would be *exaggerated* by 100 per cent. *That* appraisal might declare the project economically profitable, while one at border prices might indicate (correctly) that it was wasteful.

Similarly, the border price of a litre of petroleum, whether imported or exported, might be the same as that of a T-shirt. If, however, the government subsidized the domestic use of petroleum by 50 per cent, and a project to produce T-shirts with petroleum as a fuel were to be appraised *at market prices*, the cost *to the country* of the petroleum used (what *the country* would have to pay to import the petroleum, or alternatively what it could have earned for exporting it), in relation to the value of the T-shirts produced at border prices, would be greatly *under-rated*, and again the project might wrongly be judged as economically profitable.

The border prices do not need to be *expressed* in foreign currency. Whether we call the unit – which might be the border price of a litre of petroleum – one pound, or 200 yen, or 2000 won – is immaterial. It is the *relative* values and costs that are of interest. Expressing them in the domestic currency is probably the most convenient way.

Where final or intermediate goods or services, or factor services such as certain forms of skilled labour, are directly imported or exported, there is no difficulty in assigning them border prices. And there will be some items which, while not actually imported or exported at the time, are of kinds that are *tradable*: there *are* prices at which they *could* be bought or sold internationally. If the reason that they are not traded internationally is simply the existence of price distortions arising from some act of policy, then these potential prices at which they could be imported if there were no distortions are the ones to use for the appraisal.

The difficulty arises with goods or factor services of a kind not likely to be tradable abroad in any circumstances (cooked meals, the services of garage mechanics), or at least not under current (even undistorted) price-cost conditions. An extreme example, and key to much else, is the unskilled wage-rate, considered in more detail below. One solution would be to fix on the most relevant estimate of the marginal product per worker-year of this kind of labour and express this as the amount of some good or basket of goods that has a border price. This might be a quantity of a staple foodgrain of which there are (or, if distortions were removed, would be) either imports or exports. It might be a *basket* of tradable crops in the proportions in which they are produced.

Once border-price equivalents have been given in this way to a few non-tradable inputs, then, with the help of known input–output relationships in the economy, rough border-price equivalents can in principle be allotted to the non-tradables, by sector if not by individual product.

A ratio could then be found for the total output of each sector between its value at border prices and its value at market prices. The average of these ratios, weighted by their importance in final goods, would give a *consumption-conversion-factor (CCF)* for the economy. The CCF would be the factor by which a value in market prices would have to be multiplied to give its rough working equivalent in border prices.

To specify that the numéraire is investment income (or that it is consumption income) is relevant if investment is to be rated more highly per unit than consumption. Income for consumption will in that case be valued at a discount, and that is the essence of the original LM approach. The later version of the LM numéraire, however, specified that the standard should be *uncommitted social income*, that is public-sector income freely available to the state for spending. This would allow for the possibility that income committed to private investment might be rated less highly than income that was available to the state and free to be used for any social purpose.

It may be said that the LM method proceeds primarily from the side of *relative costs*.

The UNIDO alternative for numéraire: consumption income at domestic market-prices

The UNIDO method could by contrast be said to start from *relative values* rather than *relative costs*. Its numéraire is *consumption at domestic market prices*. A rationale here is that, from society's viewpoint, the purpose of production is ultimately consumption, so that the amount of consumption should be the ultimate measure of value produced, and that the relative marginal social value of the various consumer goods is their relative marginal value *to consumers*, which, unless the goods are quantitatively rationed and sold at centrally fixed prices, will be reflected by the relative prices at which they sell, even if those prices have been distorted by taxes and subsidies. (A consumer will buy each of them up to the point at which their relative marginal values to herself are proportional to their relative prices, however those prices have been doctored.)

Of course this method does not simply use *all* market prices undoctored. To remove the effect of the 'distortions', however, applying as they typically do particularly to foreign trade, it translates the foreign-exchange border prices by a *shadow exchange rate (SER)* to their approximate equivalents in domestic-currency prices for consumer goods. This is analogous – in fact the direct converse – to the way in which the LM method converts domestic market prices by the consumption conversion factor (CCF) approximately to border prices. The SER for the economy is reached by a similar weighted-averaging process of sectoral ratios. (Both the shadow exchange rate and the consumption conversion factor – ideally each other's reciprocals – are short-cuts involving a degree of approximation.)

In the UNIDO system a preference for investment over consumption will be expressed by a premium for investment rather than a discount for consumption.

Does the difference in numéraires matter?

The difference between the two versions on this last point is purely a matter of expression. However, starting from domestic market prices of consumer goods rather than border prices of tradables could make a difference in particular cases. The fact that relative domestic market prices differ from relative border prices is after all one main reason for using shadow prices. That an argument can be made for either as a starting-point, and that neither is ideal, is comparable to an *index-number problem*. The choice between the two is analogous to that between weighting a consumer price index by the initial and by the final composition of consumption.

Balance of advantage between the two versions of the numéraire

Both teams doubtless started with the hope that the analysis itself would help to shift practices away from the distorting policies by making their implications more obvious. The stronger the expectation that this will happen, it might be argued, the stronger is the case for border prices as the standard, since it will mean that the standard remains fairly constant while relative market prices change. Reform involving reduction of distortions will after all not alter border prices, at least if the economy is 'small', but will bring domestic market prices into closer correspondence with them.

Accounting-price ratios

Accounting-price ratios (APRs) in LMST are ratios of accounting prices (shadow prices) to market prices of goods or factors. The CCF is a form of *aggregate* APR: a weighted average of APRs covering the range of final goods.

The accounting price of capital

The accounting price of capital is the discount rate used in the appraisal, in effect the economic cost set on time. Both LMST and UNIDO virtually say that in practice the discount rate will have to be determined by trial-and-error but, for the sake of understanding, and of consistency with other elements in the system, both consider the bearing on the question of the marginal productivity of investment and the public's rate of discounting the future.

LMST uses the terms 'accounting rate of interest' (ARI) and 'consumption rate of interest' (CRI), beside the concept of the marginal product of investment (MPI). The MPI is the marginal product of public investment in efficiency accounting prices: in effect an (economic) internal rate of return on the marginal project. The CRI is the rate at which people – in their capacity as consumers – discount future consumer benefits. The ARI is simply the discount rate, however derived, used in the appraisal. The UNIDO *Guidelines* calls the CRI the 'social rate of discount' and supposes that it will also be in principle the rate to be used in the appraisal (Dasgupta *et al.*, 1972, ch. 13); it would ideally be used as what LMST calls the ARI.

The logic of determining the CRI

People may discount future benefits for one or both of two reasons. One may be regarded as rational. This is that they expect to be richer in the future and therefore, because of *diminishing marginal utility of consumption* as consumption rises, rate future incremental units less highly than present ones. The other is described as *pure-time preference*. This is arguably irrational – due simply to shortsightedness – but it may have something to do with uncertainty about the future and the idea that a bird in the hand is worth two in the bush.

Because of the intrinsic difficulty of even *defining* operationally the rate at which people in the aggregate discount the future – let alone the practical difficulties of determining it on whatever definition – giving it a value, insofar as that is necessary, must come into the category of a 'decision-makers' valuation', involving a degree of value judgement. However, the appraiser may push the determination of the *first* of the two components further back by saying that it depends logically on two relationships: the expected rate of growth (g) of average consumption, and the elasticity of marginal utility to the level of average consumption (–n). Fixing the magnitude (n) of the elasticity will again be largely a matter of value judgement, but consistency will demand that it should be given the same value in this context as in the determination of *distribution weights* discussed below. The CRI (i) is then given by

$$i = ng + r \text{ where r is the rate of pure-time-preference} \qquad (20.2)$$

LMST recommends the pragmatic solution of determining the ARI (the discount rate for time to be used in the appraisals) by trial-and-error so as to give, as near as possible, positive NPVs to a set of public-sector projects whose aggregate capital costs equal the discretionary public resources available for investment in total – no more and no less. In other words, choose the discount rate so that it will give just enough *positive* NPV results to use all the resources available for investment. The ARI used might thus vary over time. (The UNIDO *Guidelines* proposes something probably similar in practice, with the estimated CRI – the 'social rate of discount' – used, but probably only as *one of several* rates that between them – with simultaneous variation of other key parameters – will point to the economic return on the project and enable it to be compared with that of others.)

Insofar as funds are freely available from abroad, it has been suggested that the real rate of interest charged internationally on these funds can be taken to set a lower limit to the ARI (Powers, 1981, p. 47).[2] However, there are snags in any attempt to treat as eligible *all* public projects that register positive efficiency or social NPVs when this international interest rate is used as the discount rate. This is because foreign loans have to be serviced in actual foreign exchange, whereas the benefits from public projects as appraised on efficiency or social grounds will naturally include as outputs elements that represent no cash inflow so that the projects' 'surplus' as assessed is not necessarily *negotiable for servicing loans.*

The discount for consumption (or premium for investment)

If q is the MPI, the efficiency equivalent of the internal rate of return on the marginal project, and both q and i (the CRI) are for simplicity assumed to represent rates constant for ever with no reinvestment of the additional income generated in future years, then switching one unit of income in year 0 from consumption to investment will give rise to an additional income stream of q per year, which will by assumption represent additional consumption, but the value of this stream to the consumers will be found by discounting it at the rate of i per year. So there will be a constant stream of consumer benefits, amounting to q, each year, which will have to be discounted by $(1 + i)$ in year 1, $(1 + i)^2$ in year 2, and so on. The present benefit arising from the surrender to investment of a unit of consumption in year 0

---

[2] Powers indicates that the *nominal* rate will be LIBOR (the London Inter-Bank Offering Rate) plus a premium determined by the credit standing of the borrowing government, and that this will have to be deflated by an expected inflation rate in foreign-currency import and export prices to give the *real* rate.

will be the sum of a continuous stream of q values, each multiplied in order by a term of an infinite geometric series, $1/(1 + i)$, $1/(1 + i)^2$, ..., $1/(1 + i)^n$, ..., that adds up to $1/i$. The discounted stream of additional consumer benefits will therefore have a present value (NPV) given by:

$$NPV = \sum_{t=1}^{\infty} [q/(1 + i)^t] = q \cdot \sum_{t=1}^{\infty} [1/(1 + i)^t] = q \cdot 1/i = q/i \qquad (20.3)$$

If $q/i > 1$, transferring a unit of income at the margin from consumption to investment will benefit the consumer, increasing her present value by $(q/i - 1)$ units. It will imply that investment has previously been suboptimal; in other words it will fit the frequent judgement made about developing countries that investment needs to be increased by increasing saving. (On this reasoning, savings and investment ought ideally to be increased until q has fallen to the point at which it equals i, the CRI.) If q is 5 per cent and i is 3 per cent, then transfer of a unit of consumption to investment raises consumers' NPV by $(1.05/1.03 - 1)$ of a unit, that is roughly 0.02 of a unit. So investment income per unit is worth at the margin approximately 1.02 as much as the same amount of consumption income. Hence q/i gives the appropriate proportional *premium* factor to be applied to *investment* in the UNIDO method, or alternatively i/q is the appropriate *discount* factor for *consumption* in LMST.

If v represents the valuation-weighting of uncommitted social income *at border prices* in relation to that of consumption income *at market prices*,

$$v = q/i(CCF) \qquad (20.4)$$

where CCF is the consumption-conversion factor that has to be used to multiply aggregates in market prices to convert them to border prices (here appearing in the denominator because the conversion is in the opposite direction).

If we were to abandon the assumption of no reinvestment of the additional income stream and to suppose that there *is* reinvestment, at a constant proportion each year, s, of the extra income generated by the original investment, then, so long as $q > i$ and $i > sq$, the premium factor to be applied to investment will be higher than q/i (or the discount factor applied to consumption lower than i/q).[3]

Distribution-weighting

Social (as distinct from efficiency) appraisal allows various bodies of income generated by a project to be evaluated differently, not only according to whether the income will be destined for public uses, private investment, or private consumption, but also according to *whose* private consumption will be augmented. This can be done by using different weighting factors, D_c, for the consumption of beneficiaries at different consumption or income levels. The consumption-weighting derived above from the CRI (i) and the MPI (q) can be taken to be the weighting for consumers at the *average* per capita consumption level $\bar{c}$, these being representative of the beneficiaries of the additional unit of investment. The distribution weights might be fixed arbitrarily, but more satisfactory – because it makes the implications of the decision more obvious – is to base them on a stated welfare function.

---

[3] This is demonstrated in Squire and Van der Tak (1975, p. 105).

Because the reasoning for basing the distribution weights on a coherent welfare function may seem excessively mathematical to some readers, we transfer the continuation of the argument to Appendix 20.2, which is available on the Online Learning Centre.

Accounting wage-rate

The shadow wage-rate or accounting wage-rate (AWR) is clearly a highly important parameter of any appraisal. We shall consider it first for purposes of efficiency appraisal.

In efficiency appraisal

We need to distinguish unskilled, domestic skilled, and expatriate labour. The relevant efficiency accounting wage in the LMST system will be the opportunity cost in border prices of a unit of the labour concerned.

It has been put forward as a reasonable supposition for most developing countries that domestic **skilled labour** of most kinds is 'scarce' and will tend to be fully employed. In that case it will be adequate to use the market wage converted to border prices as the accounting wage-rate for that class of labour under LMST.

For **expatriate labour**, on the assumption that it is brought in because not enough comparable domestic workers are available, one simple solution would be to take the pay expressed in foreign exchange as the cost in border prices. However, insofar as some of the pay will be spent within the country, buying directly or indirectly non-scarce factors such as unskilled labour whose price is above its opportunity cost, and at domestic prices that possibly overstate costs in border prices, downward adjustments to the cost may be considered necessary for the part of the pay so spent.

The difficult question, however, is the price to put on **unskilled labour**. The aim will be to use its marginal opportunity cost – that is, the marginal product of the labour (MPL) forgone in alternative uses (in domestic prices), and to multiply this by the CCF to convert it to border prices. The significance of the value reached is this: the *lower* the AWR set on unskilled labour, the greater the extent to which the appraisal will be geared to ***increasing unskilled employment***.

The practical challenge will be to set a realistic value on the marginal product. Is the relevant MPL the marginal product in traditional agriculture, or the marginal product in the urban informal sector? Insofar as an additional job in the urban formal sector draws one or more workers from the villages, should the cost of the additional urban infrastructure needed be added in? The Lewis model – devised at a time when, and in countries for which, the source of additional formal-sector workers was likely to be traditional household agriculture, in which the product of the marginal worker might be very low – would suggest an AWR well below the formal-sector wage. However, the Harris–Todaro model, apparently fitting evidence in East Africa in the 1960s and 1970s and, like the Lewis model, recognizing that the urban formal-sector wage was above the forgone marginal product *per worker*, nevertheless supposed that each extra worker employed at these wages would draw *more than one worker* on average from the rural scene, so that the opportunity cost might well approach the actual wage-rate.

However, field evidence from Delhi assembled and analysed by Biswajit Banerjee (1983) indicated that a large proportion of labour migrants to the city came either with work pre-arranged or with fairly confident prospects of work through relatives or acquaintances, in either the informal or the formal sector. This, in contrast to the Harris–Todaro probabilistic model of rural–urban migration, suggests that on average each extra urban job will *not* attract more than one labour migrant and may even attract less because it may also draw workers from the urban unemployed. (The research also indicates that informal-sector – waged or non-waged – work is not necessarily an inferior second-best for workers to jobs in the formal sector.) It seems that each country or region needs to determine the MPL to be used according to its own conditions at the time.

It would be ideal – but is only to a limited degree possible – to make an assessment, for each of the various types and locations of projects in a country, as to the sources from which their marginal labour is likely to be drawn. The efficiency wage-rate may be taken as the weighted average of marginal products of labour in several alternative activities, with appropriate accounting-price ratios attached to each according to the extent that its cash value represents international or domestic market prices.

Powers (*ibid.*, p. 34) gives the expression for the efficiency wage as

$$\sum a_i\, m_i\, APR_i$$

where a_i is the weighting factor for the importance of activity i as a labour source,
m_i is the marginal product forgone in activity i,
APR_i is the accounting-price-ratio for the price of the product of i.

He adds also a further term, sCCF, to take account of any disutility to the worker of the extra labour or change of employment entailed, s being the measure of the disutility in market prices.

In social appraisal

The social appraisal adds an additional term to take account of (a) the effect on consumption of the additional payment made to the workers employed in the project (or in projects of the kind in general) over what they would otherwise have earned, and (b) the social cost per unit attributed to that additional consumption because of its implicit diversion of resources from 'uncommitted social income'. The term is

$$C\,(CCF - D)$$

where   C is the additional consumption in market prices,
D is the distribution weighting for the consumption level of the benefiting consumers, higher the lower is that consumption level (see Appendix 20.2).

We can see that formula in this way: the whole of the additional consumption (in border prices), the (C.CCF) term, is first treated as a cost; then that cost is reduced by the (C.D) term, which expresses the positive value of the extra consumption. D as defined equals CCF at the critical consumption level, c* which can be taken as a minimum tolerable level, a poverty line.

So at that critical consumption level the expression in brackets, and hence the whole term, becomes *zero*, which fits with the fact that, for consumers at that critical level, extra consumption is treated as being of as high a priority as extra expenditure out of uncommitted social income.

If a term is included for the disutility of the additional labour, it will now be expressed as sD, rather than s(CCF). This is because any disutility of extra labour is taken to involve a greater social cost the poorer the worker.

The full expression for the social-accounting unskilled-wage-rate is then

$$AWR^u = \sum_i a_i\, m_i\, APR_i + \Delta c \,.\, (CCF - D) + sD \tag{20.5}$$

where Δc is the increase in consumption per worker.

The second and third terms in the shadow unskilled wage expression have no analogues for skilled labour, and the social wage for skilled labour is thus the same as the efficiency wage.

Totalling the accounting costs of inputs and values of outputs

The formula given above for the social-accounting price of unskilled labour can be taken as giving the general form for the social-accounting price of any factor input. It is the forgone output per unit at efficiency prices plus the net 'cost' of any extra consumption, distribution-weighted. We might add a further term if there seemed to be extra disutility involved for the providers of the factor input. For very large projects we might need to add terms reflecting costs on a macro scale, such as the cost of extra urban infrastructure if large numbers of people were likely to be drawn from countryside to cities.

The social-accounting value of any element of output is similarly its value at efficiency prices minus the 'cost' of the extra consumption, distribution-weighted

Adding up the figures

Where inputs and outputs have financial prices attached, they have to be revalued to express them in either efficiency- or social-accounting prices, whichever form of appraisal is involved.

For the costs, the aim would be to divide these financial costs among a limited number of categories, to each of which an appropriate APR could be applied in order to convert it to an economic-cost equivalent. So the financial costs could be divided among (1) actual imports and other tradables (whose border prices would be given an APR of 1.0); (2) various domestic factors of production (such as unskilled, skilled, and expatriate labour, use of land, and entrepreneurial services, each of which would have its own APR); and (3) 'non-costs' – taxes together with pure profit and interest elements in costs – (all of which would be given an APR of zero). Beside direct use of the factors and of tradables and payment of taxes, there would be intermediate inputs not directly tradable, which would have, if possible, to be reduced to their costs in the basic elements: tradables, domestic factors, and taxes.

To facilitate this operation, it would be highly desirable that the national planning body should have derived, by 'inverting' a national input–output matrix, the relevant proportions of these basic elements in the market values of the products of each industrial sector. (An input–output matrix shows in what proportions the value of the output of each each industry or industrial sector embodies (1) the costs of the products of each other industry or sector; (2) costs of the direct use of primary factors of production; (3) costs of imports; and (4) other 'costs' such as taxes and profits. An arithmetical procedure known as *inversion* enables the market value of the output of each sector to be divided proportionately according to its *direct and indirect* dependence on imports; on the various primary factors; and on the 'other' elements regarded for the present purpose as 'non-costs'.)

So, by dividing the intermediate-input costs for the project into sectors, the project appraisers should be able to allocate the costs in each sector *approximately* among a few basic elements. This would allow the total financial costs of the project to be divided among (*direct and indirect*) costs of tradables; of each of the handful of factors (possibly just unskilled, skilled, and expatriate labour); and of taxes, profits, and interest. Each total would then be multiplied by an appropriate conversion factor to convert it to border prices (by 1.0 for the tradables, 0.0 for the taxes and other 'non-costs', and perhaps the CCF for skilled wages, and so on). The numbers used for an efficiency appraisal would differ from those used for a social appraisal.

Alternatively the national planners might themselves use the input–output table to calculate APRs for each sector, so achieving the same effect but leaving one less step to be done by the appraisers in the particular case.[4]

Any increase in saleable output as a result of the project could have its financial value similarly allocated, and the components multiplied by the appropriate ratios, to convert it to the equivalent of border prices of tradables. The difficult part – and inevitably the main analytical preoccupation of traditional CBA – is valuing the non-marketable or non-marketed benefits. This is a huge question that we shall not attempt to broach here. (There is some discussion of the valuation of environmental benefits in Chapter 11.) However, two points need to be made about the use of the LMST method in these estimates. One is that valuations made in market-price equivalents would have to be converted by the CCF to border prices. The other is that, with some projects in developing countries, the distribution of benefits may be central to their purposes. An example is the appraisal of a low-income-housing project in Kenya (Hughes, in Little and Scott, 1976, pp. 43–87). An efficiency appraisal could miss the main point. The example also shows the complexity of assessing distribution in a case such as this and the ingenuity required for dealing with it.

BOX 20.3 SHOULD THE PROJECT ANALYSIS BE EXTENDED TO 'SOCIAL' AS WELL AS 'EFFICIENCY' APPRAISAL? (FROM POWERS' SUMMARY OF HIS 'OVERVIEW OF THE LMST SYSTEM')

'The focus of this chapter has been on how a national study should estimate the accounting prices for three broad economic categories: goods and services, labor, and capital. The national accounting prices (or parameters) are useful for general economic policy analysis, but their most immediate use is in project appraisal to value inputs consumed and outputs produced by public investment. It was argued that correct valuation of project benefits and costs in the public sector leads to improved resource allocation and contributes to higher economic growth.

'Concern about distributional equity for project beneficiaries may also be introduced into the accounting prices, although at an extra cost in terms of information, time, and manpower. Only the briefest outline was given on how the efficiency and distributional aspects are brought together to form social accounting prices. The emphasis placed on efficiency accounting prices is for practical rather than ideological reasons; few national planning offices in developing countries manage to estimate and use efficiency accounting prices correctly, yet it is important to master this phase before moving to the more elaborate social accounting prices. The two contexts of investment appraisal should not be viewed as wholly separate, however. Both efficiency and social accounting prices share a common theoretical framework, and much of the data and experience obtained in the efficiency context can be put to good use in the latter as well.'

Source: Terry A. Powers (ed.) (1981), *Estimating Accounting Prices for Project Appraisal*, Inter-American Development Bank, Washington, DC, p. 59.

---

[4] See, for the use of input–output tables in this way, Powers, 1981, pp. 61–121, where he also discusses abbreviated 'semi-input–output tables' specifically designed for deriving APRs nationally or for particular sectors. Examples are in later chapters of the same book and in Little and Scott, 1976, pp. 15–87 (chapters by Anne M. Forbes and Gordon Hughes).

Use of project-appraisal in policy

We make several points

- Though the aim in devising the methods and parameters of project-appraisal is to signal by a positive NPV that a project should be undertaken, and by a negative NPV that it should not, a government's new-project spending will not be *determined to anything like that extent* by project-appraisal. At most we can hope that a systematic appraisal will be of *some help toward greater rationality and fairness*. When it gives a *clear negative* answer, this may provide ammunition against a wasteful project of a pork-barrel kind or one that does disproportionate favours to some sector of the population: a project that may well have powerful interests behind it or be a pet scheme of some politician or influential person. A *clear positive*, on the other hand, will provide international project-lenders with a strong *prima facie* case for considering a project presented to them for funding.

- It is quite likely that the allocation of funds among major spending heads such as transport and health will be made independently of project appraisals. So comparison among projects on the basis of appraisal may often have to be *within these sectors rather than between them*. The choice might be between different patterns of trunk roads or routes for oil pipelines, or between different strategies for dealing with AIDS or malaria. It might be a choice between the modest and the spectacular: between new main highways and rural feeder roads or a programme of road maintenance; between a new major hospital and rural clinics or a major additional training programme for ancillary medical staff. The more spectacular venture is likely to appeal to the politicians, with the risk that more modest but more valuable projects are overlooked. The appraisal might come down clearly on one side. This will be especially valuable when it is the side that has less political appeal. Though the projects for appraisal would naturally arise from the sectoral departments, which would need to *inform* any appraisal, it would probably be best for the appraisal to be done by a body independent of the unit that has put the project forward.

- Because the parameters used in appraisal are inevitably controversial, it is useful if each result can come with a *sensitivity analysis*, allowing for variation not only of projections of observable outcomes (optimistic, middle, and pessimistic projections, say) but also of the key parameters such as the discount rate, the shadow price for unskilled labour, and any distribution-weighting system or discount for consumption. If all or almost all of the variants leave the verdict positive, or all or almost all leave it negative, the case, whether plus or minus, is very strong.

- Nevertheless, there need at any one time to be *standard parameters* laid down that will be used for the *central* estimates across all appraisals in the country. These would include discount rate and shadow unskilled-wage-rate, and, where they are available, accounting price ratios for the various industrial sectors. They may well be changed over time.

- Investment projects whose benefit depends on additional *future recurrent spending*, as on maintenance or staffing, need to have those recurrent costs, discounted of course for time, included in the appraisal.

- Sometimes the *financing method* needs to be *included* in the appraisal. This will be so when the project comes with a particular financial package attached, as will be the case with a project-tied international concessional loan. The loan's projected financial inflows and outflows in a case such as this should be added to the benefits and costs of the project for each period – at their full value if they are in foreign exchange and the appraisal is being conducted in border prices.

■ Yet also, as hinted above, the *straight financial implications* for future cash-flows of any international loan to the government need *also* to be considered in the light of other debt obligations – and independently of the project to be financed unless the two form an inseparable package with each a condition of the other. This is because projects, even if they are appraised as having clear net social benefits, will not necessarily generate negotiable foreign-exchange surpluses that can be used in the servicing of international loans.

■ More generally, it will be a consideration for public-financial management that projects that correctly show a positive economic NPV *will not necessarily yield a surplus for the government finances* over any period short enough to be of interest. Because there are almost always fiscal constraints, it will be tempting for finance ministers to choose projects that are expected to yield a financial return over those that are not – even if the latter show higher economic NPVs. There may well be difficult choices.

■ One of the aims of the new methods was to *make policy-generated distortions of the price system more obvious and so encourage their removal*. The outcome sought has to an extent been realized in the behaviour of governments in a number of countries, though it is not clear how critical the contribution of the new CBA has been.

Place of the methods in the changing policy context

The LM and UNIDO methods were devised at a time when it was still widely assumed that the choice of industries, and hence often of 'industrial projects', would be largely made by governments. Funding might be sought from the World Bank or the regional development banks or from overseas governments. Governments and foreign or multilateral funders needed to make judgements about the suitability of industrial projects. For privately owned industrial enterprises there were often very high rates of protection through tariffs or import quotas. So, two important policy questions were industrial-project selection and judgements on appropriate levels of protection. For both these purposes, economic/social methods of appraisal were needed. They provided a method for a rational critique of industrial and trade policy.

However – in part, perhaps, because of the promulgation of these methods, which helped to make some of the ideas of development economics operational – the policy context through the course of the 1970s and 1980s changed. High protection and direct industrial investment or industrial-project choice on the part of governments went increasingly out of fashion. The methods and their logic remained as a rampart against capricious project choice and undue trade restriction, but the actual choice of projects and industries has been increasingly left to private enterprises.

As a result the role of social project appraisal in developing countries has come closer to that typical in rich countries: deciding among potential infrastructural or environmental projects or social-welfare outlays. Policy-driven price distortions are generally less important than in the 1970s, though traditional agriculture and the urban informal sector are still prevalent enough, especially in the poorest countries, to justify special treatment of unskilled wages. And inequality retains its particular seriousness (in the absence of comprehensive social safety nets) in most low-income and low-middle-income countries, so as arguably to call for distribution weighting, which is probably not used much in appraisals conducted in rich countries.

Summary conclusions

- The methods used for economic, as distinct from purely financial, appraisal of public or publicly supported projects were extended around 1970 to take account of the particular conditions and aspirations of developing countries.

- The special features specifically addressed were the widespread 'distortion' by policy of market prices; labour-market conditions, involving apparently extensive unemployment and underemployment, arising from the structure of the economy; the aspiration for increasing the rate of economic growth; and the perceived need to use project-choice decisions to improve income distribution.

- It was found useful, when the methods came to be applied, to distinguish two levels of appraisal: efficiency appraisal, which dealt with only the first two of these four features; and social appraisal (in a special narrow sense of 'social'), which dealt with all four.

- The two teams of economists that pioneered the developments of the method worked on essentially the same theory and objectives but framed the procedures that they recommended somewhat differently. The differences between them are not likely to have had much impact on the answers generated. The procedures devised by Little and Mirrlees and developed by Squire and van der Tak came to be standard, in part through their adoption by the World Bank. The World Bank's emphasis on the need for economic appraisal of projects to be funded has made it inevitable that many developing countries should attempt it.

- Both of the two procedural systems aimed to embody a coherent theory and an explicit welfare function in their development of standard cost–benefit methods.

- Both probably embodied the hope that making the policy-based distortions more obvious would lead to their progressive elimination: a process which, for that or other reasons, has to an extent occurred.

- A reasonable hope has been that project-appraisal which specifically takes account of the conditions and aspirations of developing countries – reinforced by the influence of the international lenders – will help make public-investment decisions more rational: both *more efficient* and *fairer*.

- The types of project ('directly productive activities' – as distinct from infrastructure – undertaken by government agencies) for which the new twists to social appraisal were particularly designed have become much less prevalent in developing countries since the early 1970s – a change that the LMST and UNIDO manuals may have played some part in bringing about – but the existence of the systems embodied in those manuals provides some fortification against high protection and capricious project choice, and some of their features designed particularly for developing countries retain their relevance.

The results of a social project-appraisal are unlikely to be the sole determinant of project choice. But quantification of the factors considered to be economically/socially important in the decision allows them to be balanced against each other and tends to weaken the case for particular choices that are based on caprice or favouritism. Quantifying special considerations operating, or held to operate, in developing countries is a check on their overuse as arguments for the defence of sectional interests.

Questions for discussion

20.1 The wage for unskilled workers in a project under consideration is 2000 rupiah per week. But it is claimed that the marginal product of labour is only 750 rupiah per week. What is the meaning of 'marginal product' in this context?

20.2 How can social appraisal be made to reflect the value judgement that the rate of economic growth is too low?

20.3 A government agency undertaking economic project-appraisal formerly used existing market wage-rates to represent the social cost of using unskilled labour. It has now switched to using shadow unskilled wage-rates that are substantially lower than the market wage-rates while other prices used in the appraisal have remained very much the same as before. What is likely to be the effect of this switch on the allocation of resources?

20.4 A certain country's currency, the dong, has had an official exchange rate of four dongs to the US dollar. All projects financed by the country's development bank have been appraised in financial terms only. But a decree has gone out that henceforth appraisals will be done in shadow prices, with the shadow-price system generally based on market prices but using a shadow exchange-rate of 20 dongs to the dollar. What effect is this change likely to have on the choice of projects?

20.5 How does CEA differ from CBA?

20.6 What is meant by the 'economic opportunity-cost' of a factor of production such as land?

20.7 What would be the effect on resource allocation of simply increasing the discount rate used in project appraisal?

Additional reading

Meier, G.M. (1984, 1989) *Leading Issues in Economic Development, 4th and 5th editions,* Oxford University Press, New York and Oxford.

The 4th edition, pp. 637–706, and the 5th edition, pp. 467–510, each gives a series of extracts (the two sets of course overlapping) on project appraisal. Either is well worth at least browsing for items of interest.

Powers, T.A. (ed.) (1981) *Estimating Accounting Prices for Project Appraisal,* Inter-American Development Bank, Washington, DC.

The first 60 pages of text in this book contain a clear and concise exposition (largely drawn upon here) by Powers of the logic of the LMST method. The book is published by the Inter-American Development Bank, which used to distribute copies free of charge. If it no longer does so, there should still be copies on the second-hand market. The rest of the book deals with actual appraisals conducted in the Americas.

Sugden, R. and A. Williams (1978–83) *The Principles of Practical Cost-Benefit Analysis,* Oxford University Press, Oxford.

This is a standard introduction to 'conventional' CBA with the focus principally on developed countries.

Hanley, N. and C.L. Spash (1993) *Cost-Benefit Analysis and the Environment*, Edward Elgar, Aldershot, Hants.

Environmental costs and benefits broadly considered raise the *main* evaluation problems in affluent countries, where the *re-pricing* that is the central subject-matter of the UNIDO and LMST studies is less important. But environmental costs and benefits of course have also to be valued in developing countries.

Online
Learning Center

To help you grasp the key concepts of this chapter check out the extra resources posted on the Online Learning Centre at *www.mcgraw-hill.co.uk/textbooks/huq*

Among other resources, there are four appendices available:

- Appendix 20.1   The equivalence 'in principle' of LM and UNIDO methods for appraising a car-production project
- Appendix 20.2   Determining distribution weights from a coherent welfare function
- Appendix 20.3   Fixing a shadow-wage for unskilled labour
- Appendix 20.4   Processes involved in an LMST appraisal – a hypothetical example

CHAPTER 21

Foreign Aid

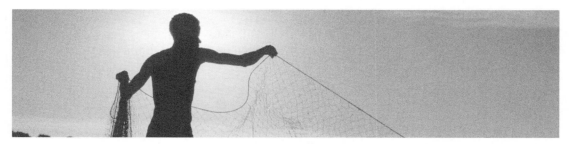

Foreign aid – public and private – to developing countries has had some remarkable achievements to its credit, notably in disease control and the development of greatly improved crop strains. It has *probably* increased rates of economic growth. But it has not moved mountains as has sometimes been hoped. Is it that there was too little; or the wrong kinds; or bad administration; were the hopes misplaced; or was the whole structure wrongly conceived?

Introduction

The chapter starts by considering how inter-governmental aid compares in **scale** with other forms of capital inflow to developing countries; how the relative weight of aid among inflows has **changed**; why aid, namely official grants and concessional loans, nevertheless has its own special **importance**; and how aid is **distributed** across both donor and recipient countries, both absolutely and in relation to the size of their economies.

We then give **definitions** of terms and explain the various **distinctions of kind** in the aid business and some reasons for preferring one kind rather than another. We classify the **motives** behind official aid. We consider **expectations and aspirations** for the effects of aid when its motive is essentially humanitarian, and what might be (as against what have been) the implications for aid of taking seriously the *Millennium Development Goals*.

We consider the concept of **aid-absorptive capacity** and whether it is useful, and, if it is, why deficient absorptive capacity arises.

Then we consider the empirical **evidence for the impact of aid on economic growth** and next expound and examine **the recent debate on aid** between two prominent advocates, Jeffrey Sachs and William Easterly – one of them now a strong critic of the present aid scene – giving attention also to a third with a highly distinctive approach, Paul Collier; and from them we formulate ideas of how aid might serve its purpose better, some of which are foreshadowed in the section next following.

So finally we consider **new directions in aid**, both emerging and possible: first, potentially acceptable *sources of additional development finance* to match what appear to be urgent needs that are otherwise likely to remain unsatisfied; and second, new and prospective *arrangements for fruitfully channelling* additional or existing funds that are available internationally for development.

BOX 21.1 TOOLKIT FOR FOREIGN AID

Aid-absorptive capacity. How far a government or other recipient of aid can effectively use it (or how much it can effectively use).

Bilateral and multilateral aid. **Bilateral** (two-sided) aid is aid given by one government to another. **Multilateral** (many-sided) aid is aid given by an international institution representing a number of governments.

Concessional loans. Loans made on more favourable terms than those available in commercial markets.

DAC. Development Assistance Committee of the OECD (see below). This includes almost all the high-income member countries of the OECD who give substantial amounts of aid ('ODA' and 'OA': see below). It is essentially a source of public information and mutual consultation about foreign aid, but its members agree on certain targets in their aid, and the DAC as an institution monitors the attainment of those targets.

FDI. Foreign direct investment, which is private commercial investment in one country by an individual, company or other entity resident in another – by either starting a producing business or buying one (or shares in one) already in existence – provided the intention of the investor is to play an active role in management of the business.

FPI, PFI. Foreign portfolio investment, which is the purchase by a resident in one country of financial assets (taken to include company shares) issued in another, provided the purchaser of the shares does not intend to play an active role in the business whose shares they are.

Fungibility. In the context, this term refers to the capacity of resources given or appropriated for one purpose to be effectively used for another, for example when foreign aid received to finance a health project releases funds that would otherwise have been spent on the project so that the receiving government can spend more on weapons.

Grant element of a concessional loan is the proportion that the **grant equivalent** of the loan (see below) bears to its face value.

Grant equivalent of a concessional loan is the value of a free grant that would have the same net present value (NPV) to the recipient as the loan.

Multilateral aid. See 'Bilateral and multilateral aid' above.

OA. Official Aid. For precise definition of the term is used by the DAC, see Appendix 21.2.

ODA. Official Development Assistance. As the terms are commonly used, this refers to **foreign aid**. For precise definition as the term is used by the DAC, see Appendix 21.2.

OECD. Organization for Economic Co-operation and Development. A Paris-based intergovernmental think-tank, source of information, and co-ordinator, formed by the governments of most of the high-income countries, and a few countries of upper-middle income.

Programme aid. See 'Project aid and programme aid' below.

Project aid and programme aid. **Project aid** is aid given exclusively to finance a particular project. **Programme aid** is aid whose use is less restricted, so that the recipient government has some discretion over the purposes for which it is spent. It may be either **sectoral aid** (which means that it may be spent at the discretion of the recipient but only within a specified sector such as education) or **general budget support** (which may be spent entirely at the discretion of the recipient).

Tied (source-tied) aid and untied aid. **Source-tied aid** (now normally called simply 'tied aid') must be spent on goods or services originating in the donor country. **Untied aid** is subject to no such restriction.

Aid in the context of capital inflows

Relative magnitudes of various flows

In the 1950s and 1960s official aid exceeded private capital flows to developing countries. This position has now long been reversed, at least *before* flows in the other direction (interest payments and profit remittances) are netted out, with the late 1960s the crossover period. Table 21.1 shows the magnitudes of official-aid flows and private commercial flows from those countries ('DAC countries') that are members of the Development Assistance Committee of the OECD (the Organization for Economic Co-operation and Development, a rich-country governments' think-tank). These DAC countries comprise nearly all of the *high-income* countries that give official aid, and between them give the overwhelming bulk of it. (Other donor countries *for which the DAC had evidence* – which *excluded* China and India – contributed about $5 billion a year around 2005, equal to about 5 per cent of the DAC total, with Saudi Arabia responsible for about a third of this. DAC statements in its 2006 Report suggest that the all-inclusive total could well have been substantially higher, probably $7 billion or more, and would be likely to grow faster than that from DAC countries.)

Clearly the private flows reported in Table 21.1 were well above official aid in both 2000 and 2005 and as far back as 1980. Both roughly doubled in nominal terms over the five-year period to 2005, but 2005 was regarded at the time as an exceptionally high year for aid because of extensive debt-forgiveness – and even so the proportional increase in the private flows over that period was slightly higher.

	Current prices						Constant 2000 prices					
	1960	1970	1980	1990	2000	2005	1960	1970	1980	1990	2000	2005
ODA (as % of donors'	4.67	6.81	26.78	54.08	53.75	106.78	31.11	32.17	44.51	57.61	53.75	84.43
GNP/GNI)	(0.52)	(0.34)	(0.37)	(0.35)	(0.22)	(0.33)						
Private	3.15	6.74	40.63	n.a.	80.78	178.64	20.99	31.84	67.53	..	80.78	141.25

TABLE 21.1 Official Development Assistance (ODA) and private capital flows from DAC members to developing countries, US$ billions in current and constant-2000 prices, 1960–2005
Note: Deflator as in Table 21.2 below, extended back beyond 1980 by a DAC deflator for GNI of DAC countries.
Source: OECD, *International Development Statistics Online*, at http://www.oecd.org/dac/stats, consulted May 2007; OECD, *Development Assistance Report*, various issues.

	1985	1990	1995	2000	2005
Current prices	61.8	95.7	227.4	228.1	443.4
Constant year-2000 prices	111.4	101.9	197.29	228.1	350.6

TABLE 21.2 Net resource flows to developing countries, 1985 to 2005, billion US dollars in current and constant-2000 prices
Notes: 1. Deflation is by an index compiled by the DAC for deflating dollar prices in international transfers from DAC donors
2. These figures do not deduct from the inflows interest paid abroad on long-term debt or profit remittances on inward foreign investment. They exclude short-term debt transactions, loans from the IMF, and technical-assistance grants. They also exclude migrant remittances and other private unrequited transfers.
Sources: World Bank, *Global Development Finance*, 2006, vol. ii, p. 2. OECD, Development Assistance Committee, *1998* and *2006 Reports* (for deflators).

	1985	1990	1995	2000	2005
Net inflow of long-term loans	59.1	44.8	33.5	7.2	20.7
FDI net	19.1	22.7	46.2	74.0	53.6
Portfolio equity flows	0.0	3.6	6.4	6.2	13.8
Grants	21.7	28.9	13.9	12.6	11.9

TABLE 21.3 Distribution of net resource flows into developing countries among forms of inflow, 1985 to 2005, % of the totals of Table 21.2
Note: See note 2 to Table 21.2 above.
Source: As in Table 21.2 above.

The DAC figures in Table 21.1 are not easy to reconcile in detail with those implied by Tables 21.2 and 21.3, where private flows (and total net resource flows) seem much higher, and aid (if we take it as 80–90 per cent comprising grants) much lower. Some, but not much, of the discrepancy is explained by the fact that Table 21.1 refers to flows from DAC members only. We can go some way to explaining the remaining discrepancy. In any case the broad private–official difference has the same sign throughout in Tables 21.2 and 21.3 as in Table 21.1.

However, the picture can be further elaborated by subtracting (2) interest paid out on long-term debt, and profit remittances on private investment, from (1) net inward 'resource flows', to give (3) *net inward 'transfers'*, as shown in Table 21.4. If these recurrent outward flows of interest and profit were to be deducted from the relevant parts of the data used in Table 21.3, which would overwhelmingly mean from the private-flow elements, official net inward transfers would exceed private at least as late as 1985.

Other features revealed by the tables are the large increase of direct investment in relation to loans from 1995, and the emergence of net portfolio equity investment: from nothing in 1985 to a substantial figure in more recent years.

The main element still missing for completing the picture is migrant remittances. There is great uncertainty about the magnitude of these flows, but we mention an estimate of $199 billion for 2006. Reasons are given in Chapter 24 why that is almost certainly a large

	1985	1990	1995	2000	2005
Net resource flows (1)	61.8	95.7	227.4	228.1	443.4
Outward interest & profit payments (2)	63.1	68.3	111.2	177.7	228.8
Net inward 'transfers'* (3) = (1) − (2)	−1.3	27.4	116.2	150.4	214.6

TABLE 21.4 Net transfers to developing countries, 1985 to 2005, US$ billion at current prices
Note: *The term 'transfers' as used here and by the DAC is both wider and narrower than in its standard use in balance-of-payments statistics, where it refers to all flows that are *'unrequited'* and no others. Unlike the 'transfers' presented here, it would *include* free grants from private sources and migrants' remittances (and also in principle technical-assistance grants, though they might be largely balanced by related outflows), but it would *exclude* movements representing investment and loans, or income therefrom.
Source: As in Table 21.2 above.

underestimate. As it stands, however, it would put remittances at nearly twice the DAC aid figures, even for 2005 and 2006, when aid was exceptionally high. See Table 24.6 in Chapter 24, which shows net ODA against net inward FDI and migrant remittances from 1995. According to that table remittances surpassed ODA from 1997. Other comparisons are given in Chapter 24, where the point is also made that remittances are *more reliable* than either official development aid or FDI.

The gist of the story is that aid has decreased in relative importance among financial inflows to developing countries fairly consistently since 1960, and especially in relation to direct investment, and almost certainly to migrant remittances.

Special function of 'aid'

Aid still has special functions, at least potentially. What will be treated here as 'aid' is Official Development Assistance (ODA) and Official Aid (OA) in DAC terminology (see definitions in Appendix 21.2). 'Official' indicates that it is given by governments directly or by international organizations ('multilaterals'). This means that it differs from the other flows we are considering – migrant remittances and all forms of commercial investment and lending – which are matters of private decision. So public policy enters directly into the aid-giving decisions. Any public aspirations to a less deprived, fairer, more equal world could admittedly be reflected also in changes in the *conditions*, the *rules*, under which commercial trade and investment and migrant transfers are carried on; and world public policy on these matters may arguably be *quite as important* as direct aid decisions; but, among the international financial flows, aid alone can ('in principle') be deliberately directed by public decisions to economic-growth and welfare objectives. In other words, governments and international bodies may use the aid lever directly for public-policy purposes, though in fact it is only to a very limited extent that they do so *by common arrangement*.

The idea of aid as filling several gaps

What was called **two-gap analysis**, explored in Chapter 5, implied that growth-generating investment was likely to require not only adequate proceeds of domestic saving but also foreign exchange, which might or might not be present in sufficient quantity for the savings to be converted into investment. Foreign aid in convertible currency, it was argued, would meet not only the 'savings gap' but also any foreign-exchange gap that might not otherwise be met by the equivalent savings. A further twist is that some crucial elements in economic growth – much physical and social infrastructure – require outlays by the state. Raising enough revenue to finance these outlays may face political obstacles. Almost all official aid passes not only *from* but *to* governments. By this reasoning that is an additional advantage, relieving a third limitation, the *fiscal constraint.*

Over time, two-gap analysis has come to feature less in thinking than it did in the earlier decades. This is in part because of greater trust in the possibilities of substitutability between resources through international trade. Emphasis on the fiscal constraint has also languished, possibly because there has come to be greater awareness of 'government failure' coupled with the belief that aid has often failed to deliver what has been expected of it by donors.

Distribution of aid by donor

Early in the post-war era the idea developed of an obligation among the rich countries to devote a proportion of their income to economic aid, something like a proportional tax. The aspiration originally set by the UN General Assembly was a uniform rate of 1 per cent of national income. France, with its large budget support to colonies and ex-colonies, was one of the few countries to reach that target in the 1960s. As the importance of private capital inflows grew, the target was relaxed by the General Assembly in 1970 to include these movements within the required 1 per cent, but still with a target, now of 0.7 per cent, for official aid. That 0.7 per cent has remained an aspiration, though, after France's performance dropped off from the late 1960s, only a few comparatively small countries – mainly the Netherlands, the Scandinavians, and Luxembourg – have fairly consistently met the target. In absolute amounts given, the US, with the world's third-highest population and one of its very highest incomes per head, has been the biggest individual donor in many, though not all, years; but, in spite of having started the aid fashion with its generous and extremely successful Marshall Plan, the US has dropped to a point at which, by the end of the century, it had long been at or near the bottom among the DAC countries in the proportion of its aid to national income.

Table 21.5 shows that the aid total rose considerably between 2000 and 2005: in real terms by about 58 per cent, and by about 32 per cent between 2004 and 2005 alone. The large debt-forgiveness of 2005 to poor countries, mainly consisting of big reliefs arranged through the Paris Club of rich creditor-governments with Iraq and Nigeria, amounted to $22.699 billion in current prices, which accounted for about half of that year's real increase in aid over 2000 (OECD, 2007, p. 132). Debt-forgiveness continued on a large scale in 2006.

The Sachs Report (UN, 2005) on strategy to achieve the Millennium Development Goals advocates increasing aid from high-income countries from around 0.25 per cent of donor national income in 2003 to around 0.44 per cent in 2006 (well ahead of what was actually to be attained in spite of the extra debt-forgiveness of that year) and 0.54 per cent by 2015. From ostensible future commitments made by DAC members in 2005, the DAC projected that ODA from the DAC would increase from $80 billion in 2004 to $130 billion (at 2004 prices) in 2010, and that aid to Africa would double over the same period. Staff of the Millennium Project, probably working from similar projections and in the same prices, calculated the difference between ODA needs and the lesser sums that had been projected by the donors at the time the report was compiled as $48 billion in 2006, $50 billion in 2010, and $74 billion in 2015.

	US$ billions at current prices			% of donors' GNI		
	2000	**2005**	**2006***	**2000**	**2005**	**2006***
DAC members total	53.749	106.777 (84.429)**	103.940	0.22	0.33	0.30
Australia	0.987	1.680		0.27	0.25	0.30
Austria	0.440	1.573		0.32	0.52	0.48
Belgium	0.820	1.963		0.36	0.53	0.50
Canada	1.744	3.756		0.25	0.34	0.30
Denmark	1.664	2.109		1.06	0.81	0.80
Finland	0.371	0.902		0.31	0.46	0.39
France	4.105	10.026		0.30	0.47	0.47
Germany	5.030	10.082		0.27	0.36	0.36
Greece	0.226	0.384		0.20	0.17	0.16
Ireland	0.234	0.719		0.29	0.42	0.53
Italy	1.376	5.091		0.13	0.29	0.20
Japan	13.508	13.147		0.28	0.28	0.25
Luxembourg	0.123	0.256		0.71	0.86	0.89
Netherlands	3.135	5.115		0.84	0.82	0.81
New Zealand	0.113	0.274		0.25	0.27	0.27
Norway	1.264	2.786		0.76	0.94	0.89
Portugal	0.271	0.377		0.26	0.21	0.21
Spain	1.195	3.018		0.22	0.37	0.32
Sweden	1.799	3.362		0.80	0.94	1.03
Switzerland	0.890	1.767		0.34	0.44	0.39
UK	4.501	10.767		0.32	0.47	0.52
USA	9.955	27.622		0.10	0.22	0.17

TABLE 21.5 Distribution of aid among DAC donors, 2000, 2005, and 2006: total ODA, net disbursements
Notes: * Provisional.   ** Figure in brackets is in year-2000 prices.
Source: OECD, Development Assistance Committee, International Development Statistics Online; http://www.oecd.org/dac/stats, consulted June–August 2007.

Distribution of aid across recipients

Aid from the DAC members has gone to about 180 countries, which comprise almost all those of low and middle income. Their receipts *per head* have been notoriously unequal, with smaller countries having a strong tendency to get a higher rate. The poorer countries, moreover, have not necessarily done better on that measure than those less poor. DAC figures for 2004–5 (OECD, 2007) admittedly show that low- and low-middle-income countries received 96 per cent of the bilateral (direct government-to-government) aid; but the division between low-income (47 per cent) and low-middle-income (49 per cent) shows them as getting roughly the same amounts *per head*, when a decided balance in favour of the former (which have about three times as many people absolutely as the lower-middles *living at less than a dollar a day*) might have been expected. Of six world regions, sub-Saharan Africa received the biggest absolute share of bilateral aid at 32.5 per cent.

Figures for 2004–5 (OECD, 2007, pp. 15–17) are not typical, both because of the debt-forgiveness of 2005, heavily biased to Iraq and Nigeria, and also because of the special position at the time of Iraq and Afghanistan as theatres of war. In that two-year period, Iraq was by far the largest absolute recipient with about *an eighth* of the world total, though it has only about 0.4 per cent of developing-country population. Afghanistan took about 2 per cent. With the exception of Sudan and, surprisingly, Ghana, the rest of the ten largest recipients were all countries with large populations, but not all of the poorest: China and Egypt were included, while Bangladesh and Pakistan, decidedly poorer, were not. The world distribution of aid receipts, decided largely by donor governments working independently of each other, does not follow any clear principle of fairness or relative need. The source indicates that the identity of the ten largest recipients changes from year to year.

The Sachs Report for the Millennium Project (UN, 2005) advocated a selective approach, with heavy concentration of aid on those recipient countries geared by the character of their governance to make good use of the resources provided.

Definitions and forms of aid

For definitions of terms and abbreviations not explained here, see Appendix 21.2.

Military and civil assistance

The DAC includes among the defining features of ODA (Official Development Assistance) and OA (Official Aid) that they have 'economic development and welfare' as their main objective. Whether as a statement of motivation this is in fact the case *with all that passes for aid* is a matter for investigation, but the definition is agreed *to exclude flows for military purposes*. Military aid was important particularly in the Cold War and Apartheid period and has continued to be so in some more troubled areas where great powers' objectives are affected, but it is not included within the totals in this chapter.

Grants and concessional loans in aid: grant equivalent and grant element in loans

Concessional loans are loans made on more favourable financial terms than are available in the commercial market. Where loans are sufficiently concessional, they are treated as part of aid.

The *net present value (NPV)* of a loan, as calculated from its capital inflows and the offsetting outflows required to service it – all discounted for time at some standard rate – is called the *grant equivalent* of the loan. This means the amount of outright grant to which its value in straight financial terms is equivalent. The discount rate used by the DAC for this purpose is 10 per cent. (Near the start of Chapter 20 is a brief account of how the NPV of a series of cash flows is calculated.)

The ratio of a loan's grant equivalent to its face-value is called its *grant element*, usually expressed as a percentage. It will be higher the longer the *maturity* of the loan, the lower the *interest rate*, and the longer the *grace period* before repayment has to begin.

Where a loan has *a grant element of 25 per cent or more*, it is treated by the DAC as part of aid from the lender to the borrower. In the DAC's valuation of ODA, concessional loans that meet the 25-per-cent test are included *at full face-value*. An alternative measure, *effective development aid (EDA)*, proposed in a World Bank publication of 1998, includes – perhaps more reasonably – *all* a country's official loans to developing countries, but each *valued only at its grant equivalent*. (A further way in which EDA differs from ODA is that EDA excludes technical-assistance grants and debt-forgiveness. The reasons for this are probably that technical assistance outlays typically consist largely of consultant fees paid to nationals of the donor country; while debt-forgiveness often entails additional net cash-flows to the recipient that are less than what is technically the grant-equivalent of the debt forgiven.)

The debt problems of developing countries in the 1980s – and more particularly those in the 1990s, which were commonly over loans from governments and multilaterals – have widely been taken as favouring the giving of aid in the form of grants rather than loans, and the recent trend has been in that direction. About half the donor countries over 2004–5 had grant-only aid programmes, with most remaining loans designed for infrastructure projects. Of the exceptions among donors, the most striking was Japan, with about 40–50 per cent of its aid in loan form. For the DAC in total over 2004–5, only 11 per cent of ODA consisted of loans, and these loans had a grant element on weighted average of about 70 per cent (OECD, 2007, p. 183).

Bilateral and multilateral aid

An element in the early aspirations for development aid was that it should be a world project administered impartially. This led to the hope that most of it might be 'multilateral' (many-sided), that is coming through international institutions, such as the World Bank and the UN Agencies. This is not what has happened. Most aid is 'bilateral': from one country's government to another's. Multilateral aid has never been more than a minor fraction of the total. Aid from multilaterals is included within the DAC's totals of ODA. The multilaterals (with respect to their grants and concessional loans) are largely, but not entirely, financed by DAC members.

If aid from the European Commission (EC), acting for the European Union, is included as multilateral, then multilateral concessional flows in 2005 are given as $26.7 billion, which is equal to 25 per cent of the total of DAC aid in 2005 (OECD, 2007, p. 175). DAC members' contributions to multilaterals was only a little lower than that total at $24.6 billion (ibid., p. 171).

Project and programme aid

Here the question is how far the use of the aid is determined by the donor government. *Programme aid* includes *general budget support*, which leaves the recipient government completely free over its use; and also *sectoral aid*, where the donor specifies the sector (such as education or transport) but leaves the recipient to decide on the use of the aid *within that category*. The term '*project aid*' is sometimes applied to all non-programme aid, but this would mean including humanitarian outlays made in emergencies. Better perhaps to use the term '*non-programme aid*'. There is a dilemma for donors over how restrictive they should be. Being over-prescriptive risks overriding responsibly determined recipient priorities and failing to use local knowledge and to respond to local perceptions of need. There is a particular risk of overlooking political factors, such as potential sources of conflict, that may have a large impact on how useful the aid can be. On the other hand, a hands-off policy, under which the aid could not be attached by agreement with the donor to any pre-agreed object and its use could not be monitored, might leave the donor without much assurance that the aid had been used well or even with integrity. However, for donor governments that wish to impose certain priorities (for example, to prevent their aid from being used for increasing armaments), there is the problem of what is called *fungibility* of earmarked funds: it can be hard to prevent aid earmarked for, say, health spending from being used to release resources *that would otherwise have been devoted to health* to be spent instead on, say, additional military aircraft, so that the effect of the aid is to increase military rather than health spending.

Latterly, the international community (encouraged by the UN in its Millennium Project) has been inclined to treat a certain number of developing countries, including several of the poorest in sub-Saharan Africa, as reliable in setting priorities and consistently translating them into spending commitments, and consequently to support those countries' own programmes and to direct funds differentially to them. Other recipients may be required to propose projects that can be evaluated in advance by the donor and specifically monitored as they proceed. The World Bank was designed to be a project-lender, but its Structural-Adjustment Loans, instituted in 1979, though tied to reforms, constitute programme aid, with the actual use of the funds fairly open.

The proportion of ODA in 2005 given as programme aid was 47 per cent, roughly half of this as general budget support and half as sectoral aid (OECD, 2007).

Source-tied and source-untied aid

Aid that is given by the donor *in kind*, or for which some or all of the purchases must be made from the donor country, is described as *source-tied* or simply *tied*. Most 'technical assistance' is tied aid in that the advisors (whose employment accounts for most of the cost of technical assistance) are almost always from the donor country.

Arguments used by donors in the past for source-tying are that their countries can afford more aid if it is given that way; or (for domestic consumption) that they can promote their own countries' products and tie the recipients into further purchases for maintenance and replacements. For the recipients, tying means that they can not obtain the goods or services to be financed by the aid from the cheapest supplier. This may substantially reduce the value of the aid, all the more so if it effectively binds them to future purchases from the same source. If the tied aid is given by way of a not-very-concessional loan, the deal may even be, in a straight financial sense, of negative value to the recipient country. In other words, the country might do better getting the inputs more cheaply and borrowing the cost in the market.

Source-tying by DAC countries is almost certainly less prevalent than it once was. Of the DAC aid *for which tying status had been reported*, the proportion *untied* in 2005 was given as 91.8 per cent (OECD, 2007, p. 184). However several important countries, covering nearly 25 per cent of the aid, had not reported on the subject, which leads to the suspicion that the true figure untied was in fact substantially lower. Aid from the UK and Ireland was 100 per cent untied, and that from Germany, France, and Sweden each well over 90 per cent. According to Easterly (2006, p. 192; citing OECD, 2001), the US, whose rate is not reported in the figures just quoted, *ties* about 75 per cent of its aid.

Motives of aid

U nless a country is a complete autocracy or oligarchy, what is meant by the motives of its aid has to include the motives not only of the politicians and officials who directly make the aid decisions but also the motives of all those who advocate it, lobby for it, or tacitly expect it. It would be very surprising if there were one single motive. The individual politicians and officials themselves, and public advocates of aid, may themselves each have a mixture of motives. As a rough guide to thinking about the matter while avoiding the worst over-simplifications, we could divide the motives four ways.

Humanitarian

There is a concern, however vague, to mitigate at least the worst extremes of poverty across the world; a sense of a shared responsibility for pursuit of that objective and a desire to have some part in it. Without some such concern among a significant proportion of donor populations, aid would surely be much lower than it is. The pro-aid campaigning groups are almost entirely humanitarian in their arguments. Even in the US, the rich country with the most vocal opposition to foreign aid, a survey of public attitudes showed a surprising level of support for it, coupled with a huge *overestimate* of the amount actually given, with a median choice of 5 per cent as the proportion it *should* bear to government spending (about eight times as high as the actual amount!) (Kull and Destler, 1999). The Landau Report (France, 2004b, p. 61) cites surveys as showing that 92, 79, 78, 74, and 74 per cent, of the public in respectively Germany, the US, the UK, France and Japan backed development aid in principle, and other surveys as finding that *increasing* aid was supported by 96 per cent in France, and 83, 81, 72, and 68 per cent, respectively in Germany, the US, the UK, and Japan. It would seem likely that the *public* support for aid in general, however ill-informed and removed from consideration of the opportunity costs some of it may be, is based largely on humanitarian grounds.

Political – general

Arguments are sometimes put for increasing aid on the grounds that a world with less poverty and faster economic growth is likely to be a more peaceful world. This may be at the backs of the minds of some decision-makers and campaigners, but the very long term over which any country's donations, unless highly concentrated in particular trouble-spots, can be expected – at best – to make a significant difference to the prevalence of unrest probably prevents this motive from carrying much weight. The rather small proportions of their resources that most donor countries now give indeed suggest that their politicians do not take this consideration very seriously. It may on the other hand have bulked quite large in the motivation of the very liberal US aid given to Western Europe (and offered to Eastern Europe) under the Marshall Plan in the late 1940s, when unrest and disaffection were expected to favour Soviet-aligned Communist parties.

Political – particular

Yet, undoubtedly much aid has been targeted on particular countries with the idea of supporting their regimes or recruiting their support. This has been recognized in Japan's apparent inducements to small countries, often without any whaling interests of their own, to become members of the International Whaling Commission, where they can support Japan's position. Taiwan's aid has often been linked, explicitly or implicitly, to recognition of its legitimacy. The fact that Israel and (after 1977) Egypt have for so much of the time been around the top of the lists of US aid recipients reflects strong attachment within the US to maintaining the position of Israel and seeking allies in the 'Middle East'. France has used military and civil aid to retain the attachment of independent states from its former African empire. In the Cold War both sides plainly used aid to keep specific developing-country governments onside or at least neutral.

Commercial

Commercial objectives are not always explicit, and they seem to play a larger part in the motivation of some countries' aid than in that of others. Japan has been regarded as more commercially motivated than most in the direction of its aid, favouring destinations likely to be important markets for its goods or sites of its direct investment. However, only 10.4 per cent of its aid was reported as wholly or partly tied in 2005 (OECD, 2007, p. 184). It is probable that any commercial objectives sought through Japan's aid are pursued largely through maintaining good relations rather than by using the aid for what is in effect marketing. China similarly in most recent years has apparently used aid to facilitate secure supplies of energy and minerals, as in Sudan and elsewhere in Africa, but its more important instrument for that purpose is probably political support (Sudan again). There is competition among arms-exporting countries over purchase terms on supply contracts for weapons, but any loan concessions given for these purposes are excluded by definition from ODA.

Expectations and aspirations of humanitarian aid

Insofar as humanitarian motives rule, aid may reasonably be hoped or expected to do one or both of two things: to **contribute funds** for promoting economic growth and poverty reduction; and to **influence policy** in directions favourable to these same two objectives or others of a humanitarian nature. Aid is only one of the ways in which rich countries may enhance the resources available to poorer countries for growth and poverty reduction. Their own *foreign-trade policies* too are highly relevant. Aid is also only one of the ways in which they can influence developing countries' own policies toward effective pursuit of these ends. Appropriate trade agreements, in which each side agrees to be more open, *can be* a win-win game, as can agreements on tax co-operation (see the last part of Chapter 19).

Millennium Development Goals

The eight Millennium Development Goals (MDGs), adopted by the UN General Assembly in the year 2000 for fulfilment by 2015, are set as world objectives. The Goals, with their 'Targets' and 'Indicators' are listed in Appendix 21.1 at the end of this chapter. Most of the Goals are fairly concrete and specific, all (except arguably the last) concerned with present material welfare rather than economic-growth rates, and each (except the last) having as sub-heads at least one quantified 'Target' out of 18 Targets more detailed than the Goals, and each with a varying number of Indicators, summing to 48 in all, mostly quantitative, to measure how far the Goals are being achieved. Several of the quantified targets are expressed as proportional changes in specific welfare variables between 1990 and 2015 (see the table in Appendix 21.1). This indicates how far the various regions of the world had already gone from the base year of 1990 toward achieving the MDGs by around the year 2000, when the Goals were adopted by the UN, and how the rate of improvement might or might not need to be increased if each Goal was to be reached by 2015.

Though the proportional changes are expressed as changes in world totals, they have generally been taken (for example, by the UN Millennium Project) as to be applied also to each country individually. Attention has been given to the information necessary for each country (the 48 'Indicators') and the organization needed in each, with a proposal that each should mobilize, for pursuit of the goals, *increased domestic resources 'by up to four per cent of GNP by 2015'*. They are also enjoined to calculate the need for ODA (UN, 2005, '10 key recommendations', p. 1).

Promulgation of the goals shifts the emphasis in 'development' and 'aid for development' decisively from increasing growth rates (however necessary that may be as a means) to concrete reduction in poverty and general deprivation, notably in health, education, nutrition, access to water and sanitation, and gender equality, as well as in the cutting of straight income-poverty (in its most extreme expression: life on less than a dollar a day). Many of the direct poverty-reducing measures may themselves serve to increase growth rates, but the effect will often be long delayed, and there may be other spending projects, as on transport, that could be expected to increase growth rates more immediately for a given volume of resources employed. So, for the developing-country governments, and civil-society bodies prodding them, and consequently also for foreign governments and NGOs providing assistance, there will be *trade-offs over time* among different ways of promoting the desired benefits for the poorest, as well as *trade-offs between income classes*. The choice is perhaps eased if the results found by Clemens, Radelet, and Bhavnani (2004), mentioned below, are supported by subsequent research.

Baulch (2006) explores the extent to which the MDGs have influenced the character of aid funds. He finds that World Bank and UK aid goes predominantly to low-income countries, and US and European Commission aid predominantly to middle-income countries. Specifically on the extent to which aid is concentrated on populations most deficient in four of the MDG indicators (one-dollar-a-day poverty, young-child malnutrition, under-5 mortality, and non-attendance at primary school), he finds that among the nine major donors the World Bank and the UK tend to concentrate on countries that are worst on these indicators, as to a less extent do the Netherlands and the UN, while the US and the European Commission concentrate on those already best, followed in this by Japan, Germany, and France. However, all donors, including the World Bank and the UK, contribute much less to the very populous and deprived countries than those countries' shares of global poverty, child malnutrition, and under-5 mortality suggest is needed (ibid., p. 944). Altogether this does not suggest any strong influence of the MDGs on the setting of priorities. If there had been, we should expect a consistent bias among donors towards those lowest on the Millennium targets, and contributions to countries in rough relationship to their shares in the world's extreme poverty.

Aid-absorptive capacity

A country's absorptive capacity for aid means **the maximum amount that it can effectively use**. The idea of absorptive capacity, if it is valid, can serve as a guide to allocation of aid among potential recipients. But is it valid? Can there be simply too much aid, or at least more than enough? Doubts may well arise over whether an absorption limit can usefully be estimated *on aggregate aid to a whole country* rather than to particular sectors and kinds of project. A country's administration may be able to deal with no more major road-building projects but plenty of additional health-service workers. However, if further spending of particular kinds or in particular sectors can not adequately be managed, even though the objects to which it might be allocated may undoubtedly be important needs, it seems fair perhaps to refer to limits of absorptive capacity *in those areas*.

There are four linked or overlapping possibilities for explaining limits where they exist: dysfunctional formal institutions; unsuitable informal institutions (habits and expectations); lack of expertise; or failures in integrity. The question then arises whether further aid or consultation in some form could be provided to generate changes that might **relax the limits** – through, say, advising on improvement of the formal administrative institutions; through formal and motivational training courses; and through use of the influence that comes with aid to discourage corruption and encourage performance. There may be possibilities of concentrating aid in the sectors that work best and by-passing faulty arms of local administration. Judgements of the capacity of recipients to deal with certain amounts and forms of aid may be inevitable, but, where additional resources are ostensibly seriously needed, attempts might be made jointly among the donor community to help *expand the capacity*. This might be one of the ways in which more co-operation among donors could add value.

The experience of one of the present authors, mainly in the Pacific Islands, however, confirms that absorptive capacity can indeed be a problem for the donors and points to some of the apparent anomalies and dilemmas in aid relationships, and the expedients adopted to resolve them. Many donors active in the Pacific try to standardize projects across countries in order to simplify project management. The European Commission sets 'themes', narrowly defined, to which the local representatives are meant to adhere (even when projects may not be entirely suitable). The Asian Development Bank works in much the same way. There is some sense in this in that it gives the representatives some applicable expertise, but it may mean that projects on offer are not tailored to the recipient's circumstances or expressed choices. There is also tacit agreement across most donors that each of them will have its own country or sector 'specialisms', one of the reforms proposed by Easterly as mentioned later in this chapter. Recipients then know to which donor they should go first over say health projects. This is in order to minimize competition or duplication between donors. Another phenomenon encountered in some African countries and in the Pacific is that an aid representative of a donor country will often end up acting as a covert ally of the host country and trying to outmanoeuvre the donor organization back home. (This may be one reason why three years is usually the maximum length of stay for a representative.)

A possible source of waste and friction is the widespread practice of allocating local donor offices specific amounts to spend, often obliging them to unload the funds on what they know to be non-viable projects. At least until the mid-1990s the World Bank was quite willing to go along what was often an obvious fiction that loans for a project could be serviced and repaid from the increased tax revenue resulting from the growth in GNI that would be brought about by the project. Where part of the justification for the project was in the form of non-financial benefits, the problem raised by this pretence could be especially serious. Much the same was true regarding running costs; donors were often fully aware that the recipient country had no capacity for (and sometimes no intention of) *maintaining or using* a proposed new asset, such as a highway or hospital, adequately – but gave the funds to construct it anyway. It seems that motivations on the ground, generated by the institutions for the giving and receiving of aid, may work against the aid's efficient allocation and effective use.

Empirical evidence on the bearing of aid on economic growth

Here there is a profusion of empirical studies, with apparently conflicting results, reaching back over at least four decades. Their results are usefully summarized by Mark McGillivray, Simon Feeny, Niels Hermes, and Robert Lensink (2006), who manage to organize them, and, without resolving the contradictions, draw from the studies one seemingly important conclusion. McGillivray *et al.* divide the studies into those up to the year 1996, and those after it. The watershed is the publication of the papers that fed into the World Bank report, *Assessing Aid* (World Bank, 1998).

The studies they summarize *before* the watershed are all concerned directly with whether aid does or does not appear to favour growth, or with closely related questions such as whether aid, or the presence of foreign-capital inflows generally, has a negative impact on domestic savings.

Of four studies *concerned with effects on domestic savings*, three find a negative impact, and one, no impact. (If there were indeed a negative impact on domestic savings, this would not be *conclusive* evidence that there could be no positive impact on growth. Total resources for investment might still be higher than if there had been no aid or inward capital flows. Some of the public-sector 'consumption' expenditures that might have increased as a result of the aid – as on education and health – could have had favourable long-term effects on growth. On the other hand, a finding of a *positive* impact or none on domestic savings would *enhance* the case for a positive impact on growth.) Of those seven studies from this period *concerned directly with effects on growth*, three find a positive impact, and four, no impact. So far, there is little conclusive one way or the other.

The change from 1997 is that the impact question was in most cases posed differently: *on what does any favourable effect of aid on growth depend?* This followed the approach of Burnside and Dollar (1997), on which, with related studies, *Assessing Aid* drew. These studies tested whether the positive impact of aid depended on a particular compound policy-variable; and they found that it did. The policy variable was designed to reflect the fiscal surplus, the inflation rate, and trade openness. In the estimation, explanatory variables included both (a) aid and (b) the product of aid and this policy index. Most subsequent studies on the question adopted a broadly comparable approach. McGillivray *et al.* list a further 17 whose answers can be readily compared, and review others. Of the 18, all have as explanatory variables *aid (per head)*, together with one or more of: a *squared* aid term (to test the hypothesis of diminishing returns to aid); a term that is *a product of aid and a policy variable* (not necessarily similar to that used by Burnside and Dollar); and a term that is *a product of aid and some other variable*. Three of the 18, all three involving as researchers either or both of David Dollar and Paul Collier, found that the effectiveness of aid depended on the policy environment. Nine concluded that it did not. Other variables on which aid-effectiveness was found to depend included political stability (two studies); institutional quality; democracy; climate (aid more effective the *worse* the climate); and whether or not the country was in the tropics (aid *less effective* in that case). (A study outwith the 18 found aid less effective the more *volatile* it was.) Seven found diminishing returns to aid; one, by contrast, that it was effective only *above* a certain threshold; and, beside this last, four of those that used the squared term to test for diminishing returns did not find evidence of any. However, of the 18, only one found that 'aid is not effective in stimulating growth'. The implication of all the others' findings was taken by McGillivray *et al.* – on the supposition that the possibility of reverse causation had been excluded – to be that aid *would* be effective in stimulating growth, at least in certain circumstances.

The lack of consensus about what those circumstances are leaves a big gap in our understanding of what is needed to make aid 'work'; but the studies strongly suggest that it is worthwhile persevering with aid, even if *only* for the sake of growth. The conclusion from seven of them that aid's effectiveness depends on policy or institutions *in some form* is after all plausible.

As McGillivray *et al.* conclude:

> One controversy has, it seems, been settled: one way or another, aid does appear to work. By that, it is meant that growth would be lower in the absence of aid. One can reasonably infer from this finding that poverty would be higher in the absence of aid.

Consideration of *the mechanism by which aid may become 'effective'* leads to the obvious possibility that different forms of aid will have different effects, that some forms will be more effective than others, and that the period over which the effect is measured will have a bearing on which forms register as effective and how much so. Clemens *et al.* (2004) follow up the hunch that the growth impact of aid will vary with the kind of aid and the period over which the effect is assessed. They divide aid into three types: (a) humanitarian and emergency aid, which they expect to be negatively correlated with growth since it comes when and where things are going wrong; (b) aid that is likely to affect growth only over a long period, such as for health and education; and (c) aid 'that plausibly could stimulate growth in four years'. In this last category, which they say comprises 53 per cent of all aid, they include support for investments in infrastructure; budget and balance-of-payments support; and aid for productive sectors such as industry and agriculture. They examine the impact of *this third class* within a period of four years after it is received; and they find a positive causal relationship between this aid and *growth within the four-year period after it is received*. The estimated impact of this form of aid on growth is two or three times as large as the effect estimated from studies that use *aggregate* growth for the explained variable. This perhaps suggests that quite potent effects on growth can occur simply from the release of spendable funds and its multiplier effects, with any foreign-exchange constraint relaxed by the fact that the aid comes in foreign-exchange form. (So perhaps, we may speculate, it is the fact of extra spending rather than the object of the spending that is mainly responsible for the extra growth within the four-year period.) The growth result does not depend 'crucially' on the recipient country's level of income or quality of institutions and policies. The result itself, however, was questioned by further testing of the same data (Rajan and Subramaniam, 2005).

The Olympian debate on aid: Easterly vs Sachs

Jefferey Sachs's *The End of Poverty: how we can make it happen in our lifetime* (2005) and William Easterly's *The White Man's Burden: why the West's efforts to aid the Rest have done so much ill and so little good* (2006) are rightly treated as two sides of a debate, though it is wrong to see the sides as for and against aid. Yet Easterly comes out strongly against the approach embodied in Sachs's book, in the Millennium Development Goals with whose implementation Sachs has been charged, and in the publications of the Millennium Project under his direction. Both books are extremely readable, passionate, and reasoned. Both authors write from extensive experience of developing countries.

First: **some elements in the rhetoric tending to exaggerate the disagreement**, and **some lines of agreement**, between them. When Easterly talks of 'aid', he is not referring only to financial aid but to the whole complex of ostensibly benevolent *intervention* by 'the West' in the rest of the world: policy advice, policy conditions for aid and co-operation, past colonization and imperialism, modern regime change. Set aside the fact that it may be loading the dice against to include nineteenth-century European policies in India or exploitation of Java and the Congo as 'aid'; the point here is that he is by no means against financial aid and there is nothing to indicate that he is keen to reduce it. He is rather concerned for its better use, as he sees it, with more realistic goals: 'I and other like-minded people keep trying, not to abandon aid to the poor but to make sure it reaches them' (2006, p. 5).

Sachs for his part is not arguing for aid *indiscriminately*, rather for its importance at a number of crucial points in recent history, when it was or was not provided, and for a number of crucial purposes now – purposes which between them require much more aid than is currently forthcoming, though amounts that are nonetheless easily manageable by the developed countries. Both are highly critical of some of the policies, past or current, of the World Bank and IMF and consequently of the governments of the large developed countries that ultimately control those institutions. Both believe in the value of markets and are certainly no enemies of globalization, but they recognize the critical need for enforced and internalized rules to control the abuses to which unrestrained private enterprise is prone, and institutions to compensate for the adverse fall-out from globalization. Both have a considerable measure of faith in the capacity of ordinary people to take advantage of opportunities for material betterment under certain conditions, though Sachs places greater hope in the possibility that benevolent and informed outsiders can and will help to create these conditions. The two agree that there is no single Big Idea, no key that will unlock the door to 'development'. Both are concerned principally to relieve human misery and powerlessness: to reduce poverty.

What Sachs attempts is evident from the audacious title of his book. 'We can end poverty by 2025 . . . and change the world forever', says its back cover. Like the UN Millennium Project, which he directs, it starts with the premise that certain objectives *must* be achieved, and proceeds to say in broad terms what actions could make this possible: how much extra finance, what international co-ordination, what deployment of expertise, what local co-operation. There are plenty of tried-and-tested technical devices – against the mass-killer and mass-debilitating diseases, for child nutrition, for family planning, for mini-power-generation, for getting investment finance to be used by the very poor – none of them vastly expensive in relation to their pay-offs, and well within the combined capacity of local effort and foreign donors to pay.

Much of the early part of the book draws on Sachs's previous experience as an adviser and seems intended to show that the *giving or withholding* of what seemed at the time to be large sums (in debt-forgiveness, stabilization backstops, and other forms) at critical points has made enormous differences: *giving for better, or withholding for worse*. The latter part counters arguments for despair; puts flesh onto the idea of breaking local vicious circles of poverty; gives ten examples of achievements on a world scale (seven of the ten concerned with health or reproduction); and takes us to various localities in the developing world to show how, with an open mind about the specific needs of particular times and places – the diagnostic approach – big improvements can be made on the ground.

The clear hope, explicit in the account of the Sauri project, mentioned below, is that this kind of experience can, with enough support, be replicated so as virtually to end extreme poverty and economic decline worldwide and to release every country for continuing material improvement. He does appear to see extreme poverty as involving people in a vicious circle which has to be, and can be, broken *with the help* of outside action, and he treats economic growth as a matter of stages through which now-very-poor countries can be expected to pass: Bangladesh at present, for example, with its big, though extremely low-paid industrial workforce, a step ahead of much of Africa.

Easterly counters with what is really a different view, not just of financial aid but of development and indeed of how the world works. Briefly, it's no good starting with the idea that some end *must* be met, regardless of experience of what is possible, and then letting the Planners work out how to do it. Reducing poverty is the work of 'Searchers', who tease out better ways of solving immediate problems, rather than of 'Planners'.

> I was among the many who have tried to find the answer to the question of what the end of poverty requires of foreign aid. I realized only belatedly that I was asking the question backward: I was captive to a planning mentality. Searchers ask the question the right way around: What can foreign aid do for poor people?'. . . . Aid agencies cannot end world poverty, but they can do many useful things to meet the desperate needs of the poor and give them new opportunities. For example, instead of trying to 'develop' Ethiopia, aid agencies could devise a program to give parents cash subsidies to keep their children in school. . . .
>
> *(Easterly, 2006, p. 11)*

Improvement involves varied and piecemeal processes – building on existing expectations, social relations, and habits of mind – that emerge over time to enable markets to work, and governments to work, for the general good. People from outside, unaware of the way existing systems, however imperfectly, operate, and trying to impose models from the West, may easily damage what there is without achieving what they intend. 'Planners' can not create markets; nor can they create democracy and the rule of law. So Planners cannot use quantities of cash to generate sustained, fast economic growth. What can be done with aid is help meet a variety of desperate human needs. Aid ought to be used to serve the world's poor, they are its customers; but aid administered, as it mainly is, by 'Planners' lacks feedback from, and accountability to, those customers. That is why, very little, so Easterly claims, seems to have been accomplished with the help of financial aid over 50 years, despite a series of past targets (as for universal access to water or primary schooling) similar to the Millennium Development Goals. Easterly is against the whole approach of fixing visionary (in his view utopian) targets and then working out centrally what they entail.

Quite apart from the fact that we don't know how to generate 'development' (by which he means economic growth), there is, Easterly argues, a serious obstacle in the way aid is currently organized even to meeting much more specific needs. This is typified in the way the implementation of the Millennium Project is envisaged, with the UN Secretary-General 'coordinating the actions of officials in six UN agencies, the UN country teams, the World Bank, the International Monetary Fund, and a couple of dozen rich-country aid agencies . . .' (2006, p. 6), for the adoption by myriad bodies across the world of 449 named kinds of intervention. This must lack the accountability – of specific people for specific results – that is necessary to ensure that anything happens. 'Collective responsibility for Millennium Development Goals or any other goals does not work' (2006, p. 205).

On the other hand,

Searchers could find ways to make a specific task – such as getting medicines to dying children – work if they could concentrate on that task instead of on Big Plans.

(2006, p. 7)

How can these two rational and informed writers with such largely shared values differ so radically? **Three underlying differences of basic approach** – closely linked – stand out: about *realistic public targets*, about *scale* in action for improvement, and about *the right location for initiative*.

First, Easterly does not accept that *speeding economic growth* is a reasonable policy objective, let alone one in which targets can realistically be set. Foreign aid can help meet some concrete, 'desperate needs' of great human importance. We simply don't know how it could be used to bring about rapid growth. We know a certain amount about what the requirements for sustained growth are. What we don't know is how 'Planners' can generate those requirements. (Certainly, we might agree, where fast and long-continued growth has occurred, as in much of East and South-East Asia, and more recently in India, this to all appearances has had little or nothing to do with any international plan or donation directed at bringing it about. Much has often been made of the fact that South Korea and Taiwan received substantial US aid in the 1950s and 1960s. This was used to disparage their achievement. But all that is long-past history. Their rapid growth is not. The Korean and Taiwanese industrial revolutions were no more deliberately concocted by outside benevolence than those of Japan and China.) By implication Easterly also seems to be rejecting the need for world co-ordination and scale even in certain specific welfare programmes – although he admits successes for aid in some of the major health achievements called in evidence by Sachs that depended heavily on international projects. His apparent aspiration that all aid should go through an 'open market' for the sponsoring of projects – submitted individually for help by their immediate beneficiaries – seems to rule out the co-ordinated application locally of a number of different inputs as in Sachs's example of the Sauri villages in Kenya (see Box 21.1), let alone the big world efforts against smallpox, polio, and malaria.

Sachs, by contrast, seems to believe that economic growth is a natural state. If it is not occurring, we should look for *obstacles* of various types that may be blocking it. No less than Easterly, he disavows a belief in any single expedient for bringing growth about. Instead, he proposes a clinical diagnostic approach: look and test for *which of the various possible factors may have gone wrong*. He also seems to believe, or hope, that using foreign help in dealing comprehensively and sustainably with the diverse material-welfare needs of individual poverty-stricken rural communities, each for a limited period, opens possibilities of aggregating up to produce comparable economic growth for the whole rural economy. This seems to follow from the implications he draws from experience with the Sauri area (2005, pp. 226 ff.). There need be no conflict: in a virtuous circle, economic growth, *bringing poverty reduction in its wake*, can and will also *follow from* appropriate forms of poverty reduction.

The **second** major difference, not unrelated, refers to the potential of aggregate planning, with aggregate targets, worked out in New York or Washington or national capitals, and more broadly with *the advantages of co-ordination and scale*. Easterly, as we have seen, opposes 'Planners' to 'Searchers'. The Searchers are people working on the ground and finding better ways of doing things. He cites a number of examples of successful Searchers. One, for example, is Mohammed Yunus, who found a way of making micro-lending viable (as outlined in our Chapter 19 under 'Lending to the very poor: microcredit'). No planner can make such new ideas, generated as they are from hands-on experience, happen by propounding a target.

Sachs, on the other hand, believes that many targets such as those in the MDGs *can* be achieved if enough resources are devoted to them, and that having a global plan, with the goals propounded and universally agreed, gives a handle for screwing out the resources. His examples of how world-scale projects, such as the elimination of smallpox, or the near-elimination of polio, or what at one time seemed a close approach to the elimination of malaria from much of its range, can take place with a technical lead from the World Health Organization (WHO, a UN agency), and with funding from multilaterals or private foundations, throw doubt on some of Easterly's assertions of impossibility. Co-ordinating projects on a national or regional or world scale is sometimes necessary. It may also be possible. Often there is no need to wait around for Searchers. The techniques are known. Granted that implementation may require respectful co-operation with local partners – state or non-state – to take account of local attitudes and circumstances, achievements – with smallpox, polio, river-blindness, family-planning, child mortality, green-revolution foodgrains – are nevertheless there to see.

A **third** arguable difference, though at most one of degree, is related to how far decisions over the spending of aid should be peripheral rather than central: both how far they should be taken or influenced by authorities outside the receiving country, and how far they should be determined by governments at all rather than by people closer to the action and to those affected by it. Easterly is impressed by how often the actors in 'the West', multilaterals and all, have got it wrong: through ignorance or ideology, they have given what was not wanted, or else they have pressed policy conditions that were dysfunctional on the recipient countries. He deplores also the way aid agencies have mostly refused to extend aid to recurrent expenses that follow from the capital projects they have financed, resulting in unmaintained roads, clinics without medicines, and schools without teachers. He highlights also the extent to which recipient governments become smothered in administration by aid relationships.

> The 'growth industry' in Tanzania is actually bureaucracy. Tanzania produced more than 2,400 reports a year for its aid donors, who sent the beleaguered recipient one thousand missions of donor officials per year.
>
> *(2006, p. 166)*

Most significantly he discusses how receiving governments have misused and diverted aid given, and how far aid from certain donors including the IMF has even been concentrated on highly corrupt and brutal governments (who of course often rule over the poorest countries, which surely helps to explain why). From these experiences he draws the conclusion that it is futile to use aid *as a way of reforming bad governments*.

To these apparent pieces of evidence about the ineffectiveness of aid, however, there are *prima facie* interpretations different from those Easterly gives. Could it be that there has not been *enough* aid to have a reasonable prospect of effectiveness? The huge sums that Easterly cites for total aid since the business began need to be divided by something over 50 for the years over which they have been spread, and then perhaps by say 3 billion to get the average annual amount per head of the people in the recipient countries. If the resulting amount per recipient head per year turned out to be say 30 dollars in present prices, perhaps we should not so readily have expected miracles from it and, as we saw in Chapter 2, there have in fact been big improvements in longevity, young-child mortality, nutrition. No one could or does claim that they are all due to aid or to anything governments have done, but to deny *any* contribution from external aid and international projects would surely be equally unreasonable.

Sachs for his part clearly believes that the rich world has resources of expertise which, properly mobilized and financed and with local support, can make huge differences on the ground. Witness the Sauri project again, where a programme of improvements worked out by Columbia University's Earth Institute seemed, at relatively low cost, to be radically transforming the material position of a community of 5000 poor people, whose poverty had previously been extreme and deepening (*Economist*, 9/6/2007, p. 60, see Box 21.1.) Sachs does not believe that all recipient governments are a dead loss at dealing with priorities and administering funds, and in fact proposes, in the UN Millennium Project documents (UN, 2005), that certain governments, including some in Africa, should have aid in 'programme' form, that is, to spend according to their own priorities. Though he may have some hope of *reforming governance* by selective aid allocation, that is presumably not the only or main reason for it. At the same time he would probably not entirely disagree with Easterly's proposal for winding down some forms of interference in recipient countries' policies,

Paul Collier, whose book, *The Bottom Billion* (2007), has been mentioned in Chapter 10, takes a different view of the role of aid from either Sachs or Easterly, mainly because he has a somewhat different position on the priorities in world development. He sees the urgent task as that of *setting on a growth path* those countries – most of sub-Saharan Africa, Central Asia, and a few others – whose incomes per head have been stagnant or falling. He sees each of them as caught in one or more of several 'traps'. The urgency of breaking those traps is that they easily generate vicious circles: poverty begets coups and armed conflict, which aggravate poverty, and between them they readily exacerbate the decline by worsening governance. Aid can have a role in helping to break open the traps, but when and where it is needed and in what form varies with the precise situation. Too much in the wrong form or at the wrong time may do harm rather than good. Collier relies heavily for his conclusions on empirical research in which political factors play a large role. No simple statement of his view of the roles of aid could do them justice.

BOX 21.2 TRANSFORMING SAURI: A GROUP OF VILLAGES IN WESTERN KENYA

Jeffrey Sachs (2005, pp. 234–5) outlines a list of inputs compiled by technical experts from Columbia University, as means for this miserably and increasingly poor rural community of 5000 people to emerge from its extreme poverty into continuous growth. These inputs – to be provided initially through outside finance at a cost roughly estimated in 2005 at $70 per person per year for about five years – would, it was hoped, reduce malaria transmission by about 90 per cent, cut mass deaths from AIDS, double or triple food yields per hectare, improve school attendance, reduce water-borne disease, and raise cash incomes (through crop sales, food processing, carpentry, clothes production, horticulture, aquaculture, and animal husbandry), in consequence drastically reducing chronic hunger and malnutrition.

An *Economist* correspondent with past Kenya experience made the following judgement in 2007:

> In the rural areas [of Kenya], the prospects are often grimmest, as the population swells and landholdings shrink. But a stirring and original experiment is being conducted by the UN, in

cahoots with Columbia University's Earth Institute and spearheaded by Jeffrey Sachs to stimulate a clutch of Millennium villages as models for emulation elsewhere. The early results of Kenya's prototype village, in Sauri in Western Kenya, where two-thirds of the people . . . live on less than $1 a day, are astonishing.

With an annual budget amounting to $50 a head administered by a UN team consisting mostly of bright young Kenyans, the Sauri villagers have apparently seen their rate of malaria go down from 43% to 11% (due to the provision of bed-nets), while school results have leapt (due partly to proper lunches). Maize production has soared five-fold (due mainly to fertilisers) and receipts from crop sales have steadied thanks to a cereals bank.

The big question is what happens after the projected five-year span of tutelage when the overseers go away – not to mention the extra help from an American philanthropist, George Soros, and sundry Norwegian and Japanese donors. That fragile and rotten thing, the Kenyan state, will have to help sustain those dramatic improvements, by providing decent teachers, doctors and farm advisers – just what Kenyans have most lacked. (*Economist*, 9/6/2007, p. 61)

Is there **a reasonable resolution between the Sachs and Easterly positions**? The most 'extreme' suggestions of the two sides each has its appeal. Sachs's vision that something comparable to the Sauri experiment might be repeated, with variations following diagnoses of local needs, right across the 22 million or so people of rural Kenya, provided only the initial funds can be obtained from outside the country, is irresistible before we come to nuts and bolts. It might take say $1.5 billion for each year of the initial five-year periods if all were taken simultaneously – perhaps a third as much a year if they were staggered over 15 years: large as an *addition* to Kenya's aid receipts, but not right off the scale. Social cohesion in each area might, as Sachs suggests, ensure enough accountability (of the recipients to each other and to the donors). Yet it is when we think of the mechanics of drawing up so many individual local plans with comparable expertise to that of the Earth Institute that courage wavers; and part of the apparent success in Sauri surely depends on by-passing the government. Yet – wherever the funds come from – if the government bureaucracy is to be by-passed, there must be an external body to dispense the funds and to co-ordinate with each group of villages, even if that body is a locally-based NGO or alliance of NGOs, one that must be able in that case to operate on a considerable scale. There may also be worries about the *fallacy of composition*: for example, fears that a radical increase in food or cash-crop production over such a wide field will lead to drastic falls in prices received. (Great to have lots more corn *if* the urban economy is poised for explosive growth, and great *if* the farmers can find new export products with buoyant world markets.) Scaling up further to cover the whole of sub-Saharan Africa – not mentioned by Sachs but hard not to consider if we are thinking of 'ending world poverty' by 2025 – multiplies all the doubts many times, even though *funding* at the Sauri rate might not be completely out of the question.

Easterly's more extreme suggestions are made tentatively; but one, clearly following from much of the argument, is to take aid as far as possible out of the hands of governments in recipient countries. This is the same direction as is suggested by Sachs's Sauri experiment. It would raise the same questions about the need for a parallel bureaucracy, except that Easterly's vision would not require everything to be done at once or in a co-ordinated fashion. He envisages also something like a market for aid, with the donor agencies, including NGOs, accepting bids (he sees them as competing for bids) from a variety of bodies on the spot. These would presumably be individual villages, town councils, clinics, schools, companies, cooperatives – proposing to provide water, sewerage, electrification, schools, teachers, equipment, medicines, health-workers, feeder roads, maybe even conditional cash grants to the poorest. He looks at ways, some already tried on a small scale, in which this might be done: an Internet exchange site, for example, or vouchers (pp. 376 ff.) A difficulty in all these decentralized schemes might be getting the necessary information, about the proposal and the proponents, to the donor agencies or clearing-sites. He proposes that the various agencies might specialize, presumably on either individual recipient countries or particular branches of welfare such as health or even particular diseases, which might both increase the total effective stock of useful expertise and make the individual agencies more readily answerable for results. (Yet the awkwardness of this persuasive suggestion for the rest of his thesis is that it ostensibly requires the co-ordination that he elsewhere seems to reject or to regard as impossible.) He suggests also that the various agencies might jointly fund a system of completely independent evaluation.

Two forms of vicious/virtuous circle: Sachs and Collier

Though Collier and Sachs are not ranged against each other in the way that Easterly opposes Sachs, their emphases are different, with Collier's models explicitly involving political variables. Both, as we've seen, invoke *vicious-circle* (or virtuous-circle) mechanisms. However, the circle that **Sachs** sees is that, properly chosen, *measures directly improving welfare will also release economic growth* and it is the choice, from among these measures, of those appropriate to the situation that is important. **Collier**, on the other hand, seems to suppose that it is growth on which attention should be concentrated; that welfare improvement will follow; and that (apart from the case in which a country is landlocked, about which not much can be done) *the key interaction is between growth and essentially political factors* such as how bad government is, how malign the effect of any resource bonanza is likely to be, and especially the risk of violent conflict.

So in Sachs's instances the key ingredient in the circle seems to be *funding*, with the precise use of the funding to be determined from one situation to another. Collier tries to find more general guidance *on the circumstances in which outside funds are likely to be helpful and what their uses should be.* He is also wary of the possibility that financial aid in the wrong amounts or wrong political junctures may have the often undesirable effects of a natural-resource bonanza (though his empirical estimate is that the effect of financial aid is likely on the whole to be better than that). In his view – if we may interpret – *bad government* and *violent conflict* should be seen as candidates for points at which the circle must be broken.

In the case of conflict there is a possible solution: international peacekeeping forces. In a recent co-authored paper, using numbers based on experience of recent conflicts and estimation of the effect of conflict on income and of income on the likelihood of further conflict, he and his colleagues compare the cost-effectiveness to be expected from peacekeeping as against typical financial assistance as a way of contributing to growth; and they find a peacekeeping force superior (Collier *et al.*, 2008; as reported in the *Economist*, 17/5/2008, p. 77). Where UN-type peacekeeping is an available option, that is an encouraging finding, because avoiding violent conflict is of course good in itself, and can be regarded as a highly desirable by-product of that way of pursuing economic growth.

It might be good if paying for genuinely multilateral peacekeeping could be treated as development aid.

This is not in conflict with Sachs's approach but it is more specific over the most useful way of breaking the circle for some of the poorest countries; and the emphasis on conflict seems only too relevant in much of sub-Saharan Africa.

BOX 21.3 TWO OF A NUMBER OF LARGE-SCALE SUCCESSES OF AID IN HEALTH

The following are two of the ten highly fruitful large-scale projects financed and undertaken through foreign aid of various kinds that are outlined by Jeffrey Sachs (2005, pp. 259–65).

'The Global Alliance for Vaccines and Immunization

'By the late 1990s, the campaign for childhood immunizations needed fortifying in two major ways. First, many new immunizations had been developed and adopted in the rich countries, but because of costs and lack of training and facilities, they had not been introduced into poor countries. Second, coverage rates achieved by the early 1990s had slipped, often the result of intensifying poverty and economic crisis in sub-Saharan Africa and other regions. Bill Gates stepped up to the effort, announcing an initial gift of $750 million from the Bill and Melinda Gates Foundation to reenergize the effort. The Global Alliance on Vaccines and Immunizations was launched in 2000 to guide the new effort. In the first years of its operation, the alliance made commitments of $1.1 billion to poor countries, and it had achieved a series of striking results. As of 2004, the alliance reported 41.6 million children vaccinated against hepatitis B; 5.6 million children vaccinated against Haemophilus influenzae type b (Hib); 3.2 million children vaccinated against yellow fever; and 9.6 million children vaccinated with other basic vaccines. . . . Its strategy has depended on the coupling of standardized technologies with systems of mass distribution . . . .

'The Campaign Against Malaria

'During the 1950s and 1960s, the World Health Organization launched a series of efforts directed at eradicating malaria. Sometimes judged to have been a failure, since malaria was certainly not eradicated, these efforts can be seen as a stunning success for certain parts of the world where the scourge of malaria was eliminated or brought dramatically and decisively under control. Well over half the world's populations living in endemic regions in the 1940s were largely freed of malaria transmission and mortality as a result of WHO's concentrated efforts . . . Africa, alas, was neither part of the program at the time, nor a beneficiary of its results until today. The standardized technologies that produced these regional, if not global, successes were two: the use of DDT and other pesticides to reduce the transmission of the disease and the use of chloroquine and other new antimalarial drugs to treat cases of it. (Newer technologies, especially antimalarial bed nets and artemisinin-combination therapies to treat the disease, combined with DDT where appropriate, can dramatically reduce the burden of the disease in Africa but will not eliminate the transmission entirely.)'

Source: Jeffrey Sachs, *The End of Poverty: how we can make it happen in our lifetime,* Penguin, London, 2005, pp. 261–2.

A resolution?

Reserving judgement on the more extreme hopes or suggestions on all sides, we may perhaps look for **developments along the following lines that might be accepted by all three protagonists**, though some of them would have implied 'ifs', and the question of policy 'conditionality' – in other words policy intervention – is evaded.

- *More funds* for aid, provided the way is cleared for them to be used for meeting welfare needs;
- Less subordination of aid to the priorities of particular *donor governments*;
- Less reliance in administering aid programmes on *recipient governments*;
- More *concrete, attainable, and testable objectives*;
- More *specific responsibilities* accepted by individual foreign governments, and other donors;
- Aid flows *more reliable*;
- Reduced *burden of aid-bureaucracy* on recipient governments;
- More effective ways of pursuing *co-ordination on the donor side*;
- A very high priority, in the use of potential aid funds, to UN-type *peacekeeping* – where that is relevant and possible – undertaken at a level likely to be effective.

It will be suggested below under 'New directions' how some of these pointers might be, or have already begun to be, followed.

New directions in aid: new sources and new channels

Objectives

From the general discussion and consideration of the arguments put by Sachs, Easterly, and Collier, we have tentatively defined in the paragraph above nine objectives as (largely) uncontroversial.

We shall discuss first ways of increasing funds available for development through international action; and then the ways, already present in embryo or possible, in which aid might be managed better from the donor side.

Additional development finance from international action

We confine the discussion in what follows to devices that might be used to increase funds available for public objectives, to be used by governments or multilaterals or by NGOs, with exclusively social goals. So we omit here ways of encouraging and supporting migrant remittances and private investment, important as they both are. We also omit for the present ways that may be found of increasing budgeted transfers from foreign governments, though it may turn out that most of the increased aid will have to come from that source. Instead, we look for ways that may be less fiscally costly or politically difficult for the governments of the rich world than simply increasing their own outlays on ODA, and that may help fill the gaps when the governments' willingness for increasing their own bilateral aid or their budgeted contributions to multilaterals has reached its limit.

Global tax co-operation

In the last section of Chapter 19, we discussed the ways in which tax co-operation could increase the revenue of developing countries. The tactical advantage of these methods is that they may well be, in fact often will be, of fiscal benefit rather than cost to the rich countries as well.

Private donations

An estimate in the early years of the century was that there was $8.37 trillion held in private fortunes of more than $30 million each. Tapping more of that wealth for world poverty-reduction presents a tantalizing challenge. Funding by private individuals and foundations of activities with an international-development purpose is not new, though it has been of increasing importance around the turn of the century. The crop research behind the 'green revolution' that bore abundant fruit from the late 1960s was funded by the Rockefeller and Ford Foundations. By 2003, the Bill and Melinda Gates Foundation had committed more than $2 billion to 'alliances in global health'; its most notable contribution has been in immunization of children, paying at one time three-quarters of the finance for the Vaccine Fund associated with the Global Alliance for Vaccination and Immunization. Rotary International at the same time had raised $450 million, together with the services of large numbers of volunteers, toward the final eradication of polio (Stansfield, 2002, pp. 94, 99). There are plenty of other examples in the health field. Attracting finance from such sources may depend largely on the capacity of health or education or food-research 'entrepreneurs' to present 'packages' of manifest human value to those who have the funds to dispense (see Micklewright and Wright, 2004).

Special Drawing Rights (SDRs)

We have outlined in chapter 12 the role of the IMF's SDRs and the rules applying to them. This was in the discussion of their use in stabilization through enabling developing countries to obtain almost costlessly additional international reserves. At the end of the section in that chapter on SDRs, we explained why further issues of SDRs might also permit the rich countries to transfer their receipts of SDRs to developing countries. While the recipients simply held the SDRs as reserves, it would be at no cost to either party on the (inevitable) assumption that the recipient countries would pay the interest due *to* the IMF on the SDRs from the countries that were their original recipients, while they (the secondary recipients) themselves would be receiving interest of the same amount *from* the IMF for so long as they continued to hold the SDRs. If, however, these secondary recipients wanted to *spend* these assets rather than using them to expand reserves, they would cease to receive the interest from the IMF and would in effect be financing that spending with loans that charged the (low) SDR interest-rate and had no maturity date. Where these countries already had debts contracted on less favourable terms, they would be able to buy these debts out through the SDRs and so reduce their servicing obligations. Thus, issue and transfer of SDRs could have a role in 'development finance', but not as the equivalent of free grants unless the recipients were simply to hold the assets as reserves.

Global lottery or 'premium bond'

A further possibility is that one of the international organizations might raise funds by running a lottery, or by issuing 'premium bonds' (bonds paying little or no real interest but giving the holder the possibility of a large prize) as the UK Treasury does. This is examined by Addison and Chowdhury (2004).

Global taxes

The term *global taxes* refers here to taxes collected by national governments under some form of international agreement and for some global purpose. No international organization yet in existence has taxing powers, or of course any tax-collecting mechanism. Making the tax global can only be by consensus of all the governments taking part. This has to be said because of the hysterical and misleading propaganda sometimes directed at any idea of a global tax.

The forms of global tax seriously discussed are all of them *indirect* taxes on particular transactions or activities. It could always be argued that an income tax levied on every country (or every high-income country) at rates progressive in relation to the countries' incomes per head would be administratively simpler and plainly more equitable than any of the indirect taxes considered. That would be relevant if such a direct tax had the slightest chance of being generally accepted. However, we have seen how patchy compliance has been among the rich countries with an analogous obligation to devote 0.7 per cent of income to foreign aid. The hope is that some form of indirect tax for the purpose of supplementing existing aid might prove more acceptable to those who have to draw up government budgets and to the public opinion that they have to consider. One appealing idea is that the tax might be acceptable because it is levied on a negative externality: some polluting or otherwise undesirable activity. So taxing would kill two birds with one stone; a 'double dividend'. One problem here is that the two functions may become to some extent competitive: the rate of tax suitable for one function may be less than ideal for the other. More serious is that, if the anti-pollutant tax would have been applied anyway, government and public may not see any strong reason why the revenue should not be used domestically like that from any other tax. We consider four such taxes with, at first glance, obvious appeal.

Tax on arms sales or arms traded internationally   This is mentioned because it is one tax instrument specifically supported by the Quadripartite Report from the Governments of France, Brazil, Chile, and Spain in 2004 (France, 2004a, pp. 36–41). The Report advocates a tax (effectively a VAT) on all arms sales, not only those internationally traded, though its discussion mainly calls attention to the tax's disadvantages and difficulties. (The Report also argues for a currency-transaction tax – discussed below – and for the development use of SDRs; and France at the time was advocating, and was itself about to join others in applying, a tax on air tickets.) One awkward feature of an arms-sales tax is that governments would largely be taxing themselves and their activities. (The legal arms trade, the only part of it that is taxable, will mainly have governments as the buyers, and often too as the sellers.) Governments all over the world, rich and poor, are buying arms and obviously try to get them as cheaply as possible. Other governments are selling them or exerting themselves to support the sales of resident arms producers. We might wonder how much zeal they will show in taxing themselves and their favoured producers. There will be great opportunities for fudging, especially when governments are producing arms for their own use. Moreover, whoever formally pays the tax, buyers or sellers, it is hard to say who will bear most of the burden. It is not improbable that the buyers will bear a large part, and this could easily mean that the poorer countries, which often spend heavily on arms in relation to their incomes, will be paying a higher proportion of their income on this tax than the rich.

A carbon tax   This is attractive not only because of its double-dividend character but also because a very small rate of tax applied uniformly across the world on carbon content (or its greenhouse-effect equivalent) would raise considerable revenue. (It was worked out recently that a tax equivalent to 5 US cents per US gallon of gasoline would raise about $130 billion a year if – as seems likely – the tax did not significantly deter consumption. High-income countries alone at the same rate would raise about $60 billion.)

As has just been implied, tax at that level would make very little difference to carbon use. A compromise reached to implement both arms of the 'double dividend' by taxing much more highly (which over a considerable range *would* very probably yield more revenue, not less) might also set a limit to the proportion of the revenue that would be used for global purposes and let the country collecting the tax keep the rest. If poor as well as rich countries submitted globally all (or equal proportions) of what they collected, and the tax rate was uniform, poorer countries would often be submitting higher proportions of their incomes than richer ones, because the poorer often have relatively high carbon-intensities in their output, but the worst of the injustice of this could be avoided by directing proceeds from the rich countries alone to global development.

However, as with arms sales, it might be difficult to keep all collecting governments steady in the resolve to submit the whole or a large part of the revenue internationally, or indeed difficult to get the agreement in the first place. At the same time, it may be worth persevering with this idea, especially as concern over global warming is increasing, so that the unthinkable may become thinkable. Taxing is an *efficient* way of pursuing the objective of reducing greenhouse emissions. Those unduly hurt by the tax may be compensated in other ways. Funds received internationally might be earmarked, wholly or partly, for emissions-reducing investments, or for measures to protect from, or to remedy, or at least palliate, the adverse effects of global warming (such as inundation in some areas, persistent drought in others).

Tax on air travel   This is mentioned because an air-ticket levy was floated in 2004 by the government of France as a possible universal tax for international development, and was approved by around 40 governments at the time. At least 19 governments have taken measures to apply it, including France, Norway, South Korea, the UK, and a number of developing countries. At the rates applied by France, the estimated annual revenue would be about 200 million euros, or $250 million dollars, and it was to be used to combat HIV/AIDS, malaria, and tuberculosis. There is a strong case on negative-externality grounds for taxing air travel, principally because of its very high carbon emissions and the fact that, by longstanding international agreement, aircraft fuel has not been taxed. Taxing tickets rather than fuel is a definite second-best but is administratively easy and watertight. Taxing aircraft fuel generally at rates comparable to the highest applied in Europe to fuel for road travel would presumably make a big contribution to filling the funding gaps of the Sachs report, but, to be effective on international flights in or out of any particular country, it would have to be applied fairly generally across the world.

A currency-transaction tax (CTT)   This device, proposed as a universal tax on currency exchanges in the wholesale market, came out of the shadows from the late 1990s, with the recognition that institutions were by then such that it could be effectively collected through financial clearing and settlement systems, and the further recognition that taxing foreign exchanges for *stabilization* purposes could be operated (by individual countries, temporarily, and *ad hoc*) quite independently of any universal and regular revenue use of a CTT (Schmidt, 1999, 2000, 2001). Systematic empirical estimation of the elasticity of activity in the markets with respect to rates of tax has suggested that a tax rate of 0.005 per cent – chosen conservatively, because of its relationship to the observed variation in the market 'spread', as highly unlikely to disturb the market fundamentally, could be expected to raise over $30 billion a year, provided the monetary authorities of the US, the Euro area, Japan, and Britain co-operated in collecting the tax (Schmidt, 2008). If they co-operated in the venture, collection could be very close to complete. There would, it seems, be no sense in imposing and collecting it any other way. The burden of the tax would be borne across the world, and we might hope that it would be completely out of the question for the four collecting authorities to regard themselves other than as performing this task (at very little cost to themselves because of the mode of collection) for the world at large. The tax – collected other than as an emergency currency-stabilization measure on transactions in one particular currency by that currency's own issuing authority – would rightly require substantial world approval; it would be raised for global purposes, or it should not be raised at all. This distinguishes it from the other tax devices mentioned here, all of which could be collected by individual jurisdictions and plausibly claimed to be their own.

New channels

Certain developments that have already occurred since the late 1990s begin to meet some of Easterly's criticisms by emphasizing specificity of attainable objectives and accountability of particular agents; real possibilities, rather than paper aspirations, of concerted action by donors; and reduction of the bureaucratic burden of aid on the recipient governments. Other devices that *might* do so are not remote from possibility, particularly if reasonably large funds from new sources – either of undeniable global provenance or earmarked by agreement for global purposes – can be tapped.

Promulgation of the **Millennium Development Goals** (see this chapter's Appendix 21.1) in 2000 fixes attention on variables *directly impinging on welfare and capable of being directly and measurably altered* by official action, rather than on the elusive target of higher economic growth.

Formation of **Global Funds** and associated alliances – such as the Global Fund to Fight AIDS, Tuberculosis and Malaria (GFATM), started in 2001, and the Vaccine Fund, associated with the Global Alliance for Vaccination and Immunisation (GAVI) – has *tempered the generalism of the aid business* by giving particular bodies specific and limited responsibilities, for which they can call on technical advice wherever it is to be found. These funds have been called 'multiactor global funds' (Heimans, 2008) in that they involve, as participants in funding or control or both, governments and international organizations on the one hand, and, on the other, the private sector (which can cover NGOs, charitable foundations, corporations or industry groups, educational and research institutions, wealthy individuals, and as donors the general public). Heimans (2008), while recognizing in these funds possibilities of new ideas and initiatives freed from traditional boundaries and bureaucracies, also faces the possibility that they may be more restricted owing to the number of entities that they represent, or at the other extreme that they may not be sufficiently accountable. **International networks on particular objectives** include but go beyond the Global Funds, which could be, like the GFATM, primarily governmental in inspiration. A variety of combinations of private and public participation in organization and funding and knowledge-support are possible. Stansfield, (2003, pp. 94–9) and Sachs (2005, p. 283) give a number of examples in the health field.

A further device, so far implemented only as a pilot, is the **International Finance Facility (IFF)**, a scheme proposed by Gordon Brown, then British finance minister, in 2003. The particular idea here was that aid expenditures could be brought forward through borrowing against future aid commitments. It was intended to involve all the rich donors, but in its original ambitious form received strong support only from France and Britain. An advantage might have been that, as the financial commitments were accepted jointly, there would have had to be co-ordination among the donor countries, though this aspect tended to be played down for presentational purposes. So far the outcome has been a pilot project ('IFF Im.') – one outcome of the 2005 G8 meeting – on a smaller scale than was originally envisaged, to support immunization of children under the GAVI, expected for a period of some years to increase the annual funds available, for that purpose and under those auspices, by $500 million over and above the $600 million a year previously spent. Six donor governments have agreed to participate (OECD, 2007, p. 20). The case for using this device for that particular purpose may depend on the belief that spending at a high enough level now will yield some once-for-all achievements in conquering certain diseases.

A further innovation of 2005–6 is an **Advanced Market Commitment** for new vaccines against certain tropical diseases that otherwise lack enough commercial prospects to attract the research and development needed from pharmaceutical companies. The idea, advocated for some years by Sachs, is that donors would guarantee a market once the appropriate vaccine was discovered. This is a form of aid that would only be paid out when the object was achieved (ibid.).

In order to concentrate donor action more usefully in each particular recipient country and to reduce the bureaucratic burden each of them has to bear, Sachs (2005, pp. 285–7) proposes **something like a 'one-stop shop'** in each recipient country, with a UN representative serving as the channel through which all the donor agencies, including the World Bank and IMF, deal with the recipient. This is a long way from what happens at present, but the possibility of something of the kind, whichever agency is to act as the main contact point, clearly increases as and if more of the aid comes through multilateral channels.

Tapping any large source of funds that is clearly international (such as, for reasons we have pointed out, a general currency-transaction tax) raises the question how such funds are to be administered for global welfare purposes. A suggestion of one way in which this might be done acceptably to all the major players is given by Clunies-Ross and Langmore (2008). The idea is that a new arm of the World Bank should be created for this purpose, with authorization to give aid in grant form and to give it not only through sovereign governments but also through subordinate governments, NGOs, multisectoral networks, and other multilaterals. Its brief might be set by the UN General Assembly under inter-agency advice; and there should be full transparency and independent scrutiny of the new entity's performance. Other equally satisfactory arrangements might well be possible, but it seems that a large new source of funds – of undeniably world provenance or otherwise committed to world disposal – would give the world an opportunity for creating a co-ordinating force with real influence among the donors in each receiving area and overall.

Over and above the humanitarian needs embodied in the Millennium Development Goals, the prospect, from as early perhaps as the second decade of the century, of extraordinary costs for the palliation of the potentially lethal effects of climate change – palliation through, for example, flood control, sea defences, desalination, long-distance transfer of water, and, in the (almost unthinkable) extreme, resettlement of very large numbers of people, possibly several or all of these – makes a large fund genuinely **at world disposal** an urgent necessity.

Summary conclusions

- The humanitarian **purpose** of promoting 'development' and hence of 'development aid' is to reduce world poverty, and to open to an increasing range of the world population an enhancement of freedom that depends in part on realizing ever more widely the material advantages of present world technology and organization.

- **Official development assistance** (grants and concessional loans from governments and multilaterals) is now quantitatively much less important than the sum of **other sources** of external capital-flow to developing countries – direct and portfolio investment, commercial loans, migrant remittances – but it is the part that can be deliberately directed by public policy to promote economic growth and poverty reduction.

- However, official aid is also not the only form of flow that is social, rather than commercial, in its motivation. There has been increasing importance of funds coming from **private fortunes or foundations**, and from or through **NGOs**.

- The **level** of official development assistance given by the high-income countries, except from a small number of (small) countries, has consistently fallen short of the aspirations to which those countries have committed themselves through international resolutions. Its **distribution** among recipient countries has not been at all closely related to their needs as indicated by populations or income levels or degrees of poverty. Even for much of the minor share that comes through the multilaterals, aid has not fitted in any obvious way into a **strategy** of world development. Also, the strategy or strategies broadly promoted by the World Bank and IMF in their own lending decisions have not been, in their entirety, universally approved.

- Whether aid has worked *to promote economic growth* has been questioned. There have been conflicting answers from econometric studies. Yet recently there have been a number of results from which together the conclusion has been drawn that, at least under some conditions, aid contributes to economic growth. But on the question of what those conditions are, how far they can be generated by policies, and if so by which policies, those studies offer no consensus.

- After consideration of the Sachs–Easterly 'debate' and the recent contributions of Collier, we suggested the need for substantially larger amounts of aid *provided it can be used successfully in the interest of the poor, and for eight directions of change mainly in the way aid is managed internationally*. It appeared that change in some of these directions was already occurring.

- As ways of *increasing the volume* of development finance, we mentioned the various forms of international tax cooperation discussed in Chapter 19 and five broad possible sources of additional external aid that would *not* involve donor governments in additional budgetary allocations to bilateral aid or contributions to international institutions (ODA in the usual sense), including as one option 'global taxes'. Among these one possibility at least, a currency-transaction tax, could raise funds of clearly global provenance in sufficient amount to give an international body allowed to administer it an effective co-ordinating role among aid donors.

▶
- Beyond the objectives of the Millennium Development Goals, the prospects of hugely costly expenses for palliating the human effects of climate change makes urgent the need for a large fund fully at global disposal.

- Under '*new directions*' for aid, we considered recent changes that have already moved very tentatively toward 'additional sources'; toward greater 'sectoral' specialization of aid through various forms of 'network' and greater co-ordination among donors, public and private; toward reducing reliance on recipient governments for administering aid receipts; and toward closer orientation to concrete welfare improvements. We also aimed to suggest how changes in those directions might be furthered by realization of a large new source of funds that were indisputably 'global', rather than national, in provenance.

It is hard to doubt the *potential* of foreign aid – in amounts well within the capacity of the donor countries to pay while scarcely noticing it – to generate big welfare improvements, even if not spectacular economic growth. Something – lack of a sense of urgency, itself possibly related to the other obstacles such as internal or international politics, or administrative weaknesses or lack of co-ordination among donors – seems to get in the way. There are promising options for substantially increasing the volume of aid, including, but not only, fulfilment by the donors of the targets that they have accepted – but ingenuity and flexibility, such as are already evident in some new initiatives, are also needed in order to overcome the widely recognized weaknesses in what actually happens.

Questions for discussion

21.1 Suppose that the necessary funds (say $12 billion a year for 15 years) could be obtained. How realistic would it be to make arrangements for replicating the Sauri-type improvements, adjusted to local conditions and needs, over 15 years across say 90 per cent of the rural population of sub-Saharan Africa?

21.2 Would you agree with the assertion that decisively improving living conditions for the poor in informal settlements around Third World cities is mainly a political task – for them and/or for their governments?

21.3 Should the giving of aid be *conditional* on the fulfilment by recipient governments of reforms of policy or of systems of accountability – sometimes at least, or else never? On what conditions, if any, of policy or practice, should donors insist?

21.4 Is there ever validity in the idea (as invoked, for example, by Jeffrey Sachs over the condition of areas such as Sauri) of using foreign aid to break a vicious circle of poverty?

21.5 What do you think of Paul Collier's view that a military peacekeeping force may be the most cost-effective way in which the outside world can contribute to the development of a conflict-prone country?

21.6 Is source-tying of aid ever justified?

Additional reading

Collier, P. (1997) *The Bottom Billion: why the poorest countries are failing and what can be done about it,* Oxford University Press, Oxford.

Easterly, W. (2006) *The White Man's Burden: why the West's efforts to aid the Rest have done so much ill and so little good,* Penguin Press, New York.

McGillivray, M., S. Feeny, N. Hermes and R. Lensink (2006) 'Controversies over the impact of development aid: it works; it doesn't; it can, but that depends . . .', *Journal of International Development,* **18**, pp. 1031–50.

Sachs, J.D. (2005) *The End of Poverty: how we can make it happen in our lifetime,* Penguin, London.

Stiglitz, J. (2006) *Making Globalization Work,* Allen Lane, London.

UN (2005) UN Millennium Project, *Investing in Development,* New York, January ['the Sachs Report']. Found at http://unmp.forumone.com/eng_html_07.html.

The recent works by Collier, Easterly and Sachs, taking three highly distinct positions, are worth reading in full and all read extremely well: Sachs, guardedly and conditionally optimistic; Easterly, anti-establishment and maybe stronger on pulling down than on building up; Collier, persistently using systematic empirical investigation to feel his way through the thickets blocking the path for the poorest countries out of stagnation or worse. McGillivray, Feeny, Hermes and Lensink give an up-to-date account as of 2006 of research on the aid-and-growth question. Stiglitz, in the less famous of his two recent popular books, takes the whole field of world policy toward the developing countries and looks for institutions, consistent with the positive contributions of globalization, that in a number of areas will make the system work better for the poor.

Appendix 21.1 The Millennium Development Goals[1]

Millennium Development Goals (MDGs)

Goals and Targets		Indicators
Goal 1: Eradicate extreme poverty and hunger		
Target 1:	Halve, between 1990 and 2015, the proportion of people whose income is less than one dollar a day	1. Proportion of population below $1 per day 2. Poverty gap ratio [incidence [*21] depth of poverty] 3. Share of poorest quintlle In national consumption
Target 2:	Halve, between 1990 and 2015, the proportion of people who suffer from hunger	4. Prevalence of underweight children (under-five years of age) 5. Proportion of population below minimum level of dietary energy consumption
Goal 2: Achieve universal primary education		
Target 3:	Ensure that, by 2015, children everywhere, boys and girls alike, will be able to complete a full course of primary schooling	6. Net enrolment ratio in primary education 7. Proportion of pupils starting grade 1 who reach grade 5 8. Literacy rate of 15-24 year olds
Goat 3: Promote gender equality and empower women		
Target 4:	Eliminate gender disparity In primary and secondary education preferably by 2005 and to all levels of education no later than 2015	9. Ratio of girls to boys in primary, secondary and tertiary education 10. Ratio of literate females to males of 15-24 year olds 11. Share of women In wage employment In the non-agricultural sector 12. Proportion of seats held by women in national parliament
Goal 4: Reduce child mortality		
Target 5:	Reduce by two-thirds, between 1990 and 2015, the under-five mortality rate	13. Under-five mortality rate 14. Infant mortality rate 15. Proportion of 1 year old children immunised against measles
Goal 5: Improve maternal health		
Target 6:	Reduce by three-quarters, between 1990 and 2015, the maternal mortality ratio	16. Maternal mortality ratio 17. Proportion of births attended by skilled health personnel
Goal 6: Combat HIV/AIDS, malaria and other diseases		
Target 7:	Have halted by 2015, and begun to reverse, the spread of HIV/AIDS	18. HIV prevalence among 15-24 year old pregnant women 19. Contraceptive prevalence rate 20. Number of children orphaned by HIV/AIDS
Target 8:	Have halted by 2015, and begun to reverse, the incidence of malaria and ether major diseases	21. Prevalence and death rates associated with malaria 22. Proportion of population in malaria risk areas using effective malaria prevention and treatment measures 23. Prevalence and death rates associated with tuberculosis 24. Proportion of TB cases detected and cured under DOTS (Directly Observed Treatment Short Course)
Goal 7: Ensure environmental sustainability*		
Target 9:	Integrate the principles of sustainable development into country policies and programmes and reverse the toss of environmental resources	25. Proportion of land area covered by forest 26. Land area protected to maintain biological diversity 27. GDP per unit of energy use (as proxy for energy efficiency) 28. Carbon dioxide emissions (per capita) [Plus two figures of global atmospheric pollution: ozone depletion and the accumulation of global warming gases]

[1] The first ten years of the 25-year period adopted for achieving the Goals.

Target 10:	Halve, by 2015, the proportion of people without sustainable access to safe drinking water	29. Proportion of population with sustainable access to an Improved water source
Target 11:	By 2020, to have achieved a significant improvement in the lives of at least 100 million slum dwellers	30. Proportion of people with access to Improved sanitation 31. Proportion of people with access to secure tenure [Urban/rural disaggregation of several of the above indicators may be relevant tor monitoring Improvement in the lives of slum dwellers]

Goal 8: Develop a Global Partnership for Development*

Target 12:	Develop further art open, rule-based, predictable, non-discriminatory trading and financial system Includes a commitment to good governance, development, and poverty reduction – both nationally and internationally	**Some of the indicators listed below will be monitored separately for the Least Developed Countries (LDCs), Africa, landlocked countries and small island developing states.** **Official Development Assistance** 32. Net ODA as percentage of DAC donors' GNI [targets of 0.7% in total and 0.15% for LDCs] 33. Proportion of ODA to basic social services (basic education, primary health care, nutrition, safe water and sanitation)
Target 13:	Address the Special Needs of the Least Developed Countries Includes: tariff and quota free access for LDC exports; enhanced programme of debt relief for HIPC and cancellation of official bilateral debt; and more generous ODA for countries committed to poverty reduction	34. Proportion of ODA that is untied 35. Proportion of ODA for environment in small island developing states 36. Proportion of ODA for transport sector in land-locked countries
Target 14:	Address the Special Needs of landlocked countries and small island developing states (through Barbados Programme and 22nd General Assembly provisions)	**Market Access** 37. Proportion of experts (by value and excluding arms) admitted free of duties and quotas 38. Average tariffs and quotas on agricultural products and textiles and clothing 39. Domestic and export agricultural subsidies in OECD countries 40. Proportion of ODA provided to help build trade capacity
Target 15:	Deal comprehensively with the debt problems of developing countries through national and international measures in order to make debt sustainable in the long term	_Debt Sustainability_ 41. Proportion of official bilateral HIPC debt cancelled 42. Debt service as a percentage of exports of goods and services 43. Proportion of ODA provided as debt relief 44. Number of countries reaching HIPC decision and completion points
Target 16:	In cooperation with developing countries, develop and implement strategies for decent and productive work for youth	45. Unemployment rate of 15-24 year olds
Target 17:	In cooperation with pharmaceutical companies, provide access to affordable, essential drugs in developing countries	46. Proportion of population with access to affordable essential drugs on a sustainable basis
Target 18:	In cooperation with the private sector, make available the benefits of new technologies, especially information and communications	47. Telephone lines per 1000 people 48. Personal computers per 1000 people

* _The selection of indicators for Goals 7 and 8 is subject to further refinement_
Source: Reproduced by permission from: S. Devarajan, M. J. Miller and E. V. Swanson 'Goals for Development: History, Prospects and Costs World Bank Policy Research Working Paper, WPS 2819, April 2002

Appendix 21.2 OECD Development Assistance Committee (DAC)'s aid and capital-flow terminology

ODA (Official Development Assistance) and OA (Official Aid). Both of these categories cover (a) grants and (b) loans of more than a year's term and with a 25 per cent or more grant-element, that come from official sources, and are given primarily for economic development and welfare. They include technical-co-operation grants but not flows for military purposes. The only difference between ODA and OA is in the list of recipients covered. OA has covered payments to 'transitional countries' and some 'advanced' developing countries; ODA, to the rest.

ODF (Official Development Finance) is wider than ODA in that it *also* includes *non-concessional* developmental loans from multilaterals, and also bilateral developmental loans with *less than* a 25 per cent grant element.

OOFs (Other Official Flows) cover flows, to countries on DAC lists of aid-recipients, that are ineligible as ODA or OA because they are not developmental or have too low a grant element. It is not clear whether they overlap with ODF.

Net flows. In the case of loans, net flows are the incoming amounts disbursed, net of outflows for amortization or repatriation of capital (but not outflows of interest) – all net of corresponding movements in the reverse direction. World Bank figures cited in the chapter clearly use the term to include also the corresponding flows for direct investment and portfolio equity investment, and also grants.

Net transfers. For loans, these are net flows *minus* net outward interest payments. (Again they can be extended to include the corresponding figures for investment, with profit remittances and dividends deducted in the same way as interest.)

Private flows. These cover flows on market terms out of private-sector resources: direct and portfolio investment and a variety of forms of loans; together with private grants (grants made by NGOs, and presumably also individual philanthropists, net of any government subsidies). It is not clear in the source whether they include net migrant remittances.

Debt-service ratio. A country's debt-service ratio on its stock of borrowings is taken by the DAC as:

(Interest payments and loan-amortization out)   *divided by*
(Exports of goods and services *plus* private inward transfers)

Source: OECD (2007), *Development Assistance: Efforts and Policies, 2006 Report*, OECD, Paris.

CHAPTER 22

Loans and Debt

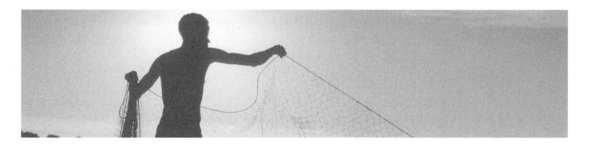

Borrowing abroad by developing-country governments may be reasonable and responsible. However, giving concessional loans as a form of aid in place of the equivalent grants is advantageous only in special circumstances and raises hazards for the recipient countries. Over-indebtedness on the part of governments may be from painful to disastrous for their own peoples, and in the 1980s the sovereign debts of twenty or so middle-income countries threatened the whole international financial system.

Introduction

We outline first the **case that may be made for lending** to, and borrowing by, developing-country governments (in relation to possible alternatives), and its possible flaws and pitfalls.

We then consider **the two crises** of sovereign-debt experience that started respectively in the 1980s and 1990s, referring to: (a) the *policy responses* of the international community, with the criticisms that might have been made of them; and (b) in the case of the 1980s crisis particularly, *what on the face of it might well have been done instead.*

Finally, we explore proposals for **improving** (i) the behaviour of potential borrowers, (ii) the responses of the international agencies when avoidable pain threatens the peoples of developing-country debtors, and (iii) the character of lending and borrowing instruments and institutions.

BOX 22.1 TOOLKIT ON LOANS AND DEBT TERMINOLOGY

Concessional loan. Loan whose terms (a combination of interest-rate, grace period, and maturity, and any other special phasing of payments in and out) are more favourable than the most favourable available to the borrower in the commercial market.

Debt-equity swaps. Arrangements by which debtor-governments that are having difficulties with servicing are relieved of their debts by giving their creditors equities (shares) – in principle of equivalent value – in enterprises that they own. While leaving the value of the debtor-government's assets on paper the same, this may relieve its problems over cash flow.

Debt servicing. Payments due by debtors in the form of interest and repayment of the capital sum borrowed.

Debt overhang. Excess cost to lenders and borrowers of the fact that a state or person is so heavily in debt that there is doubt about whether the existing debts or others subsequently incurred will be honoured. The excess cost arises from the uncertainty and from the reaction of lenders to it.

Debt-standstill. Temporary cessation (in effect delay) of a debtor's obligations to repay principal.

Grace period on a debt. Time after the making of the loan before repayment of principal begins.

Grant-equivalent of a loan. This is the amount of free grant that would have the same value as the NPV of the loan. It would thus depend on the discount rate applied in calculating the NPV. Strictly, if the lender and the borrower applied different discount rates, the same loan would have a grant-equivalent for the lender different from that for the borrower.

HIPCs. 'Heavily indebted poor countries', a term that began to be used in the 1990s for a set of 40 or so (mostly low-income) debtor countries.

Maturity of a loan. The time from first receipt of the loan by the borrower to the date at which it must be completely repaid.

Moratorium on a debt. Cancellation or suspension of payments due on the debt.

Net present value (NPV) of a loan. Exactly comparable to the (discounted) net present value of an investment project. (See for a formula the start of Chapter 20.) It is the sum of the net positive cash-flows on the loan to the borrower in each period of the loan's life, with the net value for each period discounted for time from the starting-point. A concessional loan will by definition have a positive NPV for the borrower or a negative NPV for the lender, or both. The *real* NPV of a project or a loan is the NPV adjusted to allow for inflation, either by expressing each item of cash-flow in (projected) constant (e.g., year-0) prices or by using a discount rate augmented to take account of (projected) inflation.

Rescheduling of a debt. Altering the amounts and timing of the servicing payments due on a debt (usually in order to ease the pressure on the debtor), generally extending the time within which the repayment must be completed, but usually without reducing the real net present value of the servicing payments in total.

Sovereign debt. Debt owed by governments.

State-dependent clauses in loan contracts. Clauses that provide that the obligations of parties will be altered (usually the debtors' obligations reduced or delayed) on the occurrence of certain defined events over which the parties themselves have no control.

The case for the value of loans to developing-country governments

Aid through concessional loans, as against grants

In favour of loans rather than grants as forms of aid, it has been argued that donors may be able to give a larger capital value of aid in the form of concessional loans than in grants. However, this implies that there can be a choice between a grant A and a loan B such that they are of equal cost to the lender/donor but that the loan is of greater value to the recipient. If every loan had a unique grant-equivalent, this could not be so, but a loan's grant-equivalent depends on the discount rate applied. If the lender/donor and the recipient use *different* discount rates, with the one applied by the recipient *higher*, the recipient may value B more highly than A, while the donor/lender regards them as of equal cost to itself. The recipient, in other words, might be in more of a hurry than the donor; or else it might have to borrow at higher interest rates in the commercial markets than would the donor. If that were the case, this argument for a loan rather than a grant might hold.

There are, however, extra disadvantages ('debt overhang', explained below) from simply being in debt. As we have mentioned in Chapter 21, experience has come to favour grants rather than loans as a form of aid to developing countries. Nevertheless, there may be cases in which the notorious difficulties of the 1980s and 1990s over sovereign debt need not arise. An example might be a loan for an infrastructure-type project (such as a toll-bridge) that will produce negotiable cash returns over an extended period sufficient to amortize the loan.

Loans to governments on commercial terms

Commercial loans – raised from banks or through issues of bonds – are of *financial* value to the borrowing government if the financial return on the project financed is greater than the effective rate of interest on the loan. Any additional *social* return – the bridge may not only pay for itself by tolls but in addition reduce cash or consumption costs to the public – enhances the value to the borrowing country's people. All the same, apart from any social appraisal that is made about the whole project including the loan, it is important for a government also to make a purely financial assessment from a fiscal (government-finance) viewpoint. A government has to cover itself financially. Hence the surplus used to service the foreign loan has to be negotiable and available in foreign currency. So, before a government borrows, the loan needs to be appraised financially and in the light of the government's other foreign-currency servicing commitments, whatever the non-fiscal benefits of the deal.

Addison (2008, p. 232) makes the point that, because of 'very high social returns from investing in primary education, basic health care, and safe water and sanitation – rates of return that exceed concessional, and even commercial, rates of interest – it makes sense to borrow both domestically and externally for poverty reduction and national development'. On a long enough perspective this must indeed be true; but, where the costs are financial in the fairly short term and the benefits are not, a borrowing government can not rely on these long-term verities alone but must also make timed projections of possible cash flows to ensure it can meet its servicing costs for the loans when they become due without imperilling its other objectives.

The hazards of borrowing for developing-country governments appear from the series of events of the 1980s and 1990s outlined below.

Inward portfolio-capital movements to private or public entities

There is a third form of international lending and borrowing. Foreign residents may deposit money in a country's banks, or buy its bonds or bills, or buy its equities without the intention of controlling the companies that issue them. This is 'portfolio investment'. It may happen of course quite independently of any decision by the country's government. This will tend to raise the currency's exchange value, which may or may not be welcome. If this inward capital movement has been extensive, the risk is that it may be rapidly reversed. This risk and ways of dealing with it have been discussed in Chapter 12.

Debt in these three forms has been involved in three series of events, each traumatic for a number of developing countries. Having considered the East Asian and other currency crises of 1997–9 briefly in Chapter 12, we shall concentrate here on the other two: the middle-income-countries' debt crisis of the 1980s; and the plight of, and attempted remedies for, the heavily indebted poor countries in the mid-1990s and after.

BOX 22.2 THE LOST DECADE: A VIEW FROM THE CENTRE

'. . . An international debt crisis erupted in 1982 as one developing country after another was forced to retrench from the excessive borrowing levels of the late 1970s. A combination of damaging external shocks – high world interest rates, adverse shifts in the terms of trade, and weak demand in industrial countries – and unsustainable economic policies at home destroyed the ability of many developing countries to service their external debts. Debtors then had to choose between defaulting on their debts or attempting to adjust policies by enough to reduce their external deficits to a financeable level. Most countries chose the latter approach . . . .

'The effects of the debt crisis were contained in the early 1980s through a "case-by-case" strategy in which external financial support was provided to countries willing to adjust their economic policies. That strategy succeeded in preventing a series of defaults on sovereign debts, but it did not lead to an early resumption of normal relations between debtors and creditors . . . . The debt strategy also succeeded in greatly reducing the payments deficits of many developing countries, but it did so more by forcing a reduction in imports than by fostering growth in exports.

'By 1985, a consensus was forming among officials in creditor countries that new approaches were needed for a more favorable and more sustainable solution to the crisis. The focus of the debt strategy during the next few years was to encourage indebted countries to undertake growth-oriented structural reforms, financed largely by longer-term loans from the World Bank and the regional development banks, and to encourage commercial banks to resume net lending to countries undertaking such reforms. That effort failed to generate either long-term growth or even much long-term financing, and by 1988 almost all of the countries hit by a debt crisis several years earlier were still struggling to escape from it. For much of the developing world, the 1980s were to be a "lost decade" for economic growth.

'The denouement of the debt strategy arrived when the realization took hold that a high-growth equilibrium could be obtained only through debt-reduction. The debt-relief approach had two prongs: one aimed at the low-income countries that owed most of their external debt to creditor governments, and the other aimed at the middle-income countries that were heavily indebted to commercial banks.'

Source: James M. Boughton, *The IMF and the Silent Revolution: Global Finance and Development in the 1980s*, IMF, Washington, DC, 2000, pp. 22, 23.

The debt crisis of the 1980s

Boost to sovereign borrowing from the 1970s oil-price rises

The oil-price rises engineered by the OPEC cartel at the end of 1973 imposed a substantial burden on all countries that were net importers of hydrocarbons. It also gave an initial boost to costs in money terms in many forms of production in most parts of the world, and hence to prices. This price rise was widely met by deflationary action. These effects contributed strongly to ending the world boom of the early 1970s and, with more or less delay, to depressing the prices of metals and other raw materials. At first there seemed to be a mitigating factor for many of the middle-income countries. The richest among the countries specializing in oil-exporting, such as those of the Gulf, accumulated big surpluses as a result of the oil-price rises. To make the surpluses earn, they 'recycled' them into the world's financial institutions, which became awash with funds for lending on. Governments of middle-income countries were not averse to borrowing funds that the institutions were desperate to lend. Through the late 1970s and early 1980s, this recycling was not discouraged by the Washington multilaterals. It was even argued by some that the developing world had gained on balance from OPEC's intervention in the system. At all events the world economy would have been far more depressed if the OPEC countries' accumulated receipts had simply lain idle. Some sages maintained that the oil-price rises merely reflected the increasing natural scarcity of energy resources with their progressing exploitation and that the price would continue on a rising trend indefinitely. Anyone who believed this could draw the conclusion that more and more oil-producer surpluses would become available for borrowing and that more and more borrowing would be necessary to maintain the activity of the world economy. The further sharp oil-price rises of 1979 and 1980 easily reinforced these beliefs.

Yet nemesis was to come very soon. The sustained period of high oil prices had drawn new fields and whole new domains into oil production, and, through the resulting recession, had depressed oil demand. After 1980 the oil price ceased to rise, and then after 1981 it fell, until by early 1986 it had dropped close to where it had been in real terms in mid-1973. The governments of some poorer oil exporters such as Nigeria and Algeria had spent recklessly as if the oil boom would never end, and in addition their governments had borrowed freely on the strength of their oil wealth. A number of non-oil-exporting, middle-income countries, mainly in Latin America and Eastern Europe, had also borrowed freely, relying on fresh loans to turn over earlier ones as they fell due. The lenders had to trust that the borrowing governments would be able to service their debts; the borrowing governments had to trust the lenders to come up with fresh loans. The spell was broken in late 1982. Mexico, which had been both an oil exporter and a large borrower, found difficulty in servicing its debts. The flow of new funds threatened to dry up as lenders were scared off further lending and feared for their existing holdings. Their unwillingness to lend could easily cause their fears to be fulfilled by making the debtor governments unable or unwilling to pay. The market value of the loans made to the heavily indebted governments plummeted.

So began the 1980s debt crisis, which haunted *both* the 20-odd developing countries involved as debtors to private lenders *and* international banks both large and small, until near the end of the decade. In retrospect it was clear there had been recklessness on both sides. The lending institutions, and with them the whole international system of intermediation of capital, were threatened with collapse, or so it was widely believed. The borrowing countries were torn between severe austerity and default.

One way or another, a tolerable outcome would have required a high degree of prompt co-operation: among the debtor governments; or among the major developed powers; or among the lenders (or perhaps also *between* lender and borrower groups) – and in any case with a large input of imagination and vision. In the absence of spontaneous moves of this character, the IMF staff made heroic efforts to avert the worst: by dealing with one debtor country after another, each time trying to get from its government a commitment to a degree of austerity and fiscal discipline, and from its creditors – around 800 of them in the extreme case of Brazil, 500 for Mexico (Boughton, 2001, pp. 309, 377) – agreement both to accept 'rescheduling' of the debt (lengthening the time over which it would have to be repaid, though generally without any reduction in the real time-discounted cost of servicing it) and also to continue lending. There was lubricating back-up from the Paris Club of rich-government lenders and from the IMF itself. There were, not surprisingly, great difficulties in reaching these agreements, and the process might have to be repeated several times for one country.

Release for a number of countries had to await the acceptance by the US in early 1989 (at the start of the term of the first President Bush) of what was effectively debt-reduction through **Brady bonds**, so named after the then US Treasury Secretary. (A detailed but highly readable account of these events is given in Boughton, 2001, chs 6–12.)

Mistakes: on whose part? And what might have been done to end the crisis?

Largely as a result of the debt crisis, most of Latin America and several other countries went through nearly a decade of low growth and instability, with reductions in government spending that inevitably fell hardest on the poor and depressed a number of welfare indicators. There was a slow recovery from the world recession of the early 1980s. Who or what was to blame?

One view is that, by borrowing heavily and spending the proceeds, Brazil, Mexico, Argentina, and the rest performed a service for the world economy. They helped to keep up effective demand for goods and services when there were strong tendencies to recession through accumulation of unspent surpluses. In the circumstances, boosting world demand was providing a global public-good, and they ought to have been rewarded by being bailed out by the rest of the world, which was in a sense in *their* debt. No country gained from plunging its poor into deeper misery because the lenders had panicked – just as no one would have gained if the debtor countries' default had ruined a number of the world's major banks. A more rational world might have made a bargain with the debtor countries to provide them with abundant cheap or costless credit while they slowly rectified their debtor positions. But in any case existing institutions did not make this possible: there is no world body capable then or now of creating and granting such credit. (Only thorough re-casting of the rules and mystique covering Special Drawing Rights – the form of international 'money' that the IMF *can* issue – could have made the global institutions suitable for this purpose.)

Granted that this was impossible and so recognized, it seems in retrospect that both lenders and borrowers had been extremely reckless; but they may have been beguiled by the myth of the ever-rising oil price and the misleading maxim that a government can never be bankrupted. As it was, the market value to the creditors of the loans to each borrowing government fell to various fractions of their face value (Bolivia's at one time to 11 per cent).

One debt-reducing solution mooted – that might have greatly mitigated the pain to the debtors while leaving the lenders in not much (if any) worse a position than the one they were in – was to reduce the face value of the loans (and hence the debtors' obligations) closer to their (collapsed) market value, while making agreements to ensure that the written-down loans would be honoured in full even at the expense of other servicing obligations of the debtor governments. The formation of an **intermediary** that would buy the loans at their market price and issue new ones of lower face-value was debated (as in Corden, 1988). This would reduce or remove what is called **debt overhang**: the extra cost of debt to the parties because of *uncertainty* over whether it would be honoured. The immediate cost of the overhang to the debtor governments in this case lay principally in the difficulty they had in obtaining further loans, on which they had largely relied to service the old ones; but the uncertainty and disruption inherent in the crisis also inevitably discouraged any form of investment, domestic or foreign. For the creditor banks the cost was a reduction in the value of their assets. It was a loss to each party without a corresponding gain to the other. Once the servicing obligations had been reduced to levels that were clearly manageable, the worst of the uncertainty would have disappeared. A deal to achieve this could presumably have been constructed so as to leave the creditors with claims of no less market value than before it was made. (In theoretical terms, if there had been an excess cost of debt overhang in this sense, the removal of the debt could be done in such a way as to constitute a **Pareto-improvement**: producing benefits to both sides, or else to one with no harm to the other.) However, the Reagan Administration in the US, in office until early 1989, was unwilling to countenance any open debt-forgiveness. So the IMF, determined to save the financial system from disaster, may have thought it had no alternative to finding grounds of agreement that would ostensibly allow the creditors eventually to be paid in full.

Before the Brady Plan of early 1989, only Bolivia in 1986–7, and to a modest degree Mexico in 1987–8, were offered anything in the nature of forgiveness of debt owed *to the private sector* (Boughton, 2001, pp. 484–91). (The Paris Club of rich-government lenders had a few months earlier begun measures containing some elements of debt-forgiveness for loans *from governments*, with the so-called Naples, and later Toronto, conditions.) But, with the issue of the Brady bonds, debt-reduction seems to have been critical in ending the crisis in some important cases (Boughton, 2001, pp. 499–531).

BOX 22.3 VIEW FROM THE PERIPHERY: ONE RELATIVELY RICH INDEBTED COUNTRY IN THE LATE 1980s

'Even Argentina, where malnutrition and other forms of acute social deprivation were traditionally minimal, shows the stamp of decline. Malnutrition is no longer a marginal phenomenon. Miguel Teubal reported in 1986:

> According to official sources, there are 685,000 children in Greater Buenos Aires alone who don't eat enough to stay alive – a minister said this – plus another 385,000 children in the province of Buenos Aires, or a third of the children under 14 in this province. One of the first acts of the new civilian government was to institute the National Food Program . . . to hand out supplementary food rations to families whose basic needs were not being met. In May 1985, 5.6 million people, or 18 per cent of the entire population, were receiving this assistance. We also have to count on foreign Non-governmental Organizations, the Churches and the school lunch program which was launched to try to avoid school drop-outs. In many cases, this lunch is the only food the children receive all day.

'A doctor [in a small city 340 miles from Buenos Aires] says that 5 per cent of the children are born with serious deficiencies because the mothers are malnourished. He attributes 35

▶ infant deaths per thousand to hunger. Official figures show 28 per cent of Buenos Aires inhabitants malnourished, but as many as 40 to 50 per cent suffer from hunger in the poorer provinces of the north. There is even one small province (with a largely Indian population) where fully 59 per cent of the children under 5 are considered *desnutridos*.

'Meanwhile, Argentina is exporting more food than ever before in its history in order to reimburse its $54 billion debt. But it must compete against heavily subsidized wheat exports from the US and the EEC, which also happen to be its largest creditors . . . .

'The Alfonsín government [the first democratic government after the fall of the military junta in 1983], in spite of electoral promises that "debt will not be paid with the sacrifices of the people", has fallen into line and behaved so far, as a model debtor.'

Source: Susan George, *A Fate Worse than Debt*, Penguin, London, 1988, pp. 136–7.

The solution might have come earlier if the debtor governments had combined to bargain as a block. They might have threatened collectively to default if a stipulated measure of debt reduction had not been given. That threat could surely have been made quite credible and its prospect was of a disaster for the lenders. By this means debt reduction might have been forced on the creditors much earlier, with the connivance of the multilaterals. Debt reduction had been persuasively advocated earlier by some members of IMF staff and other highly reputable economists, and had been supported by the governments of Japan and France (Boughton, 2001, pp. 480–1). As it was, the debtor governments were dealt with one by one. They made no serious attempt to use their combined bargaining power. They ignored the opportunity expressed in the maxim that, if you owe someone a trillion dollars and can't pay, *the other party* is in trouble. It is notable that Argentina, in a later episode of unmanageable debt, *unilaterally* began to default in late 2001, when it faced a desperate domestic situation, economically and politically. With other measures such as the floating of its exchange rate, it then began fairly quickly to recover, and eventually in 2005 it was able to induce its creditors to accept repayment of 35 per cent only of the value of their loans (Stiglitz, 2006, pp. 220–5; Easterly, 2006, pp. 232–4).

Low-income-country debt problem of the 1990s and the HIPC Initiatives

The two HIPC stages and their background

The difficulties of certain low-income countries over debt in the early 1990s moved the World Bank (through its soft-loan arm, the IDA) and the IMF jointly to launch a cautious and conditional programme of debt reduction. The institutions were joined by the African Development Fund (AfDF), and the initiative depended on the co-operation of the Paris Club of rich-country creditor governments, though participation by any government was voluntary. Commercial creditors were also encouraged to participate. The initiative came in response to an unusually effective world-scale campaign for debt-cancellation, 'Jubilee 2000'. Forty-one (later 40) low-income countries were identified as 'heavily-indebted low-income countries' (HIPCs, the 'P' standing for 'poor'). Their exceptional debt position among low-income and low-middle-income countries is shown in Table 22.1. The nature of their 'crisis' differed

Country category	1980–84	1985–89	1990–94	1995–2000
HIPCs	38	70	120	103
Other IDA countries*	21	33	38	33
Other lower-middle-income countries	22	30	27	26

TABLE 22.1 External debt as percentage of GDP, HIPCs and others, period averages
Note: * Countries of low enough income to be eligible for loans from the International Development Association.
Source: 'The HIPC Initiative: progress and prospects' in *Précis*, Winter 2003, no. 320, World Bank Operations Evaluation Department.

from the debt crisis of the 1980s, which had concerned middle-income countries, and debts overwhelmingly to private financial institutions. The countries arousing concern in the 1990s were in the low-income class, and their debts were overwhelmingly to *official* creditors, many of them for concessional loans, and quite a high proportion to the multilaterals. To qualify for relief under the initiative, a country had to be poor enough to be eligible for loans from the World Bank's International Development Association (IDA), and its debt had to bear a ratio to exports of no less than 220 per cent, or else to government revenue of no less than 280 per cent (the limits reduced to 150 per cent and 250 per cent respectively from 1999).

The HIPC Debt Initiative has provided debt reduction to certain governments on conditions. The conditions are, first, certain tests of fiscal responsibility designed to ensure that the position of reduced debt will be sustained, and second, evidence of commitment to use a part of fiscal resources for increasing growth and reducing poverty.

The obligation for spending to reduce poverty became more prominent – while eligibility for relief under the scheme was extended – under the Enhanced HIPC Debt Initiative (E-HIPC) approved by the Group of Seven major industrial countries (G7) in 1999. Each aspiring beneficiary was then required to provide a Poverty Reduction Strategy Paper. The idea was that the HIPC government would prepare its own proposals on both fiscal disciplines and poverty reduction, so that it would 'own' the policies. If its proposals were approved and it had showed a long enough period of performance, it could be regarded as having reached a 'decision point', when it would have its *servicing* obligations reduced.

After a further period of seriousness over what it had proposed, it would reach a 'completion point', which would be the cue for applying the full programme of debt reduction, *including principal*. The reduction in the principal of any loan would of course mean that the concession was irrevocable.

The idea was that those countries that had reached the completion point would have their debt ratios reduced to below the critical levels that had determined their classification as HIPCs: debt stock 150 per cent to exports or 250 per cent to government revenue. Those that had reached the completion point would be eligible to have their debts *to the three participating multilaterals* reduced under what was technically a separate scheme, the **Multilateral Debt Relief Initiative (MDRI)**.

Achievements of the HIPC Initiatives (HIPCI)

The upshot hoped for from debt reduction was two-fold: encouraging inward capital flows, both direct and portfolio, because further lending would be less risky and the general macroeconomic situation more stable; and making possible extra fiscal spending for promoting growth and reducing poverty (Addison, in Addison and Mavrotas 2008, pp. 225–8).

By late 2006, ten years after the start of the initiative, 29 of the 40 countries had reached the decision point, and of these 19 had reached the completion point, so qualifying for MDRI relief as well as irrevocable relief on *bilateral* loans. Debt relief was expected eventually to reduce the debt stocks of the 29 that had reached decision point by nearly 90 per cent on average. Debt relief committed by late 2006 amounted to $41.3 billion under the HIPC Initiative and $18.3 billion under the MDRI, both in end-2005 NPV (net-present-value) terms. It was estimated that (expressed in the same terms) full application of relief to all 40 countries would cost $63.2 billion under the HIPCI and $24.9 billion under the MDRI (IDA and IMF, 2006).

The *formulation* (at least) of a **poverty-reduction strategy** had become a recognized responsibility; and certain countries such as Uganda had taken deliberate measures to *demonstrate* the use made for social expenditures of the funds they had received by way of debt reduction.

Debt-service-to-export ratios of the 29 had been reduced from 14 per cent on average a year before the decision point to 6 per cent on average five years after. Poverty-reducing expenditures by the 29 had increased by almost 3 per cent of GDP between 1999 and 2005 (ibid.).

Criticisms and limitations of the HIPC scheme

Following are some of the criticisms that have been made, not necessarily all mutually consistent.

Delay in debt relief

Because of the conditions imposed, actually granting debt relief seemed to some unduly **delayed**. Over the first three years of the scheme, only six countries had reached decision point, of which four had reached completion point.

Imperfect additionality; tendency to deplete other aid

The assumption of the initiative was **additionality**: that is, that debt relief should be additional to other aid, rather than having the effect of reducing other aid, either to the HIPC countries or to others. But there was no mechanism to ensure that this happened. In fact, as of 2003, the judgement was made that 'HIPC countries are indeed receiving an increasing share of declining global aid resources relative to other poor countries . . . but they are not receiving additional funds compared to what they were getting before the creation of the Initiative (that is, before 1996)' (World Bank, 2003, p. 3). In other words, other poor countries were receiving less than before, and the HIPC 40 (debt-relief included) were receiving no more than before. In an important sense the other poor countries were paying for the debt relief given to the HIPCs. The bad incentive and other effects of this could not have been remedied unless more funds had been made available by the donors (ibid.).

Unfairness, moral hazard

Countries, even very poor ones such as Bangladesh, that had behaved prudently and been fiscally responsible did not benefit at all from the Initiative, and in fact, as the last paragraph shows, were likely *actually to have been harmed* by it.

Little emphasis on growth-related policies except spending on education and health

This assessment was made by Addison *et al.*, (2004, p. 15). They said that the growth performance of HIPCs had been 'lamentably low', which meant that tax receipts, and consequently government spending, including spending for the benefit of the poor, had been stagnant or even declined; while accelerated economic growth itself, given other supporting measures, *could have* contributed directly to poverty reduction *if it had occurred*.

Conditionality related to inputs rather than outputs

This judgement applies to growth-enhancing and poverty-reducing spending. It is always easier to measure what is spent than what the spending achieves, and the effect of that limitation means that the assessment of performance can not be satisfactory, and any incentive to generate results is probably weak.

Failure to take account of, and tackle, unexpected setbacks

This criticism, relevant to much policy related to foreign-debt problems, comes from a number of quarters (e.g. in relation to the HIPC, Nissanke and Ferrarini, 2004, p. 48, citing over the general principle Krugman, 1988). There ought to have been arrangements made in advance to deal with contingencies. Krugman shows why agreeing in advance in loan negotiations to **'state-contingent' relief** – relief related systematically to adverse events over which the debtor has no control – improves the trade-off for the parties: in other words, increases efficiency.

Need to override fiscal conditionality in certain cases in order to avoid internal conflict

Twelve of the HIPCs are affected by violent internal conflict. Addison *et al.*, (2004, p. 15, citing Addison, 2003, and Addison and Murshed, 2003) give reasons for considering political, as well as economic, criteria for giving debt relief: if, for example, extra spending in a dissident region might avert conflict.

BOX 22.4 DOUBTS ABOUT THE FISCAL PAY-OFF TO HIPC DEBT RELIEF

'For the HIPCs that have reached the decision-point, the data suggest a rise in poverty-reducing expenditure, as classified by the IMF and the World Bank . . . . This is welcome news, but all such numbers must be treated with caution; budgeted resources frequently do not reach intended beneficiaries . . . . and, in contrast to the conclusions of the Bank-Fund study just cited, Chauvin and Kraay (2005) find little evidence that debt relief has had a positive effect on the level and composition of public spending in HIPCs. And even well-spent money may not achieve the desired outcomes. Take health, for example. More funding for training health personnel will show up as a desirable rise in health expenditure, but whether health indicators improve proportionately to spending depends on the effectiveness of those personnel (that is, on the health-care system in which they operate) and, indeed, on whether they remain in their own country when trained. There are more Malawian doctors in my home city – Manchester – than in all of Malawi . . . .

'A great deal comes down to "governance". Donors continue to struggle with recipient corruption, strategies wavering between using aid to induce reform (for example, establishing anti-corruption commissions) to withholding aid to punish corrupt politicians. Overall, however, the effect of corruption on aid allocations appears to be weak; Svensson (2000) finds no evidence that donors allocate aid towards the less corrupt, for example. This is one reason why the HIPCs, with their legacy of past aid loans, are found

▶

disproportionately among the worst performers in the Transparency International Index of Corruption . . . , with one (Chad) at the very bottom.

'Large amounts of oil revenue are "missing" from the fiscal accounts of Nigeria and São Tomé and Príncipe, while Chad and the World Bank were recently in dispute over the revenue-allocating mechanism created as a condition of the Bank's financing Chad's oil pipeline project . . . . For the oil-producers, initiative such as the Extractive Industries Transparency Initiative (EITI), which was championed by the Africa Commission, need more action on the "supply-side" of corruption, including vigorous prosecution of those from the North who offer bribes in the South.'

Source: Tony Addison, 'Debt relief: the development and poverty impact', in Addison and Mavrotas 2008, pp. 226, 228.

Given that, taken as a whole, the aid given as debt-relief under the HIPC initiatives was not (at least up to 2003) *'additional'*, it could be argued that any overall benefit for poor countries must depend on (a) the importance of *removing 'debt overhang'* and (b) the effectiveness of the conditionality imposed for *enhancing fiscal responsibility and pro-poor spending.*

By contrast the debt relief of 2005 and 2006 following from the Gleneagles Agreement between the G8 countries seems to have been, on any reasonable judgement from the much increased quantities of aid over those years, 'additional' at least in some degree, though the addition was *highly biased* toward a few recipients. (It is notable, however, that debt forgiveness does not raise immediate net cash inflows by its own value in the first year as is the case with other forms of aid disbursed. Net inflows are raised over a period into the future, but in each year only by the reduced annual servicing charges. Where the loans remitted are highly concessional or are not being fully serviced, the present value of the debt forgiveness may be a long way short of its nominal amount.)

Reducing the incidence and duration of debt crises and difficulties

Role of the borrowing governments

There are certain rules of prudence that borrowing governments might adopt, such as *not* incurring new debts, foreign or domestic, *without viewing* their total servicing obligations year by year into the future and *without considering* how far any additional investments so financed will generate the *negotiable* resources for servicing the loans. Naturally countries with weak governance or political turmoil are unlikely to act by the best fiscal canons.

Role of lenders, private and official

It is to be hoped that both investment banks and institutions in the market for the bonds of developing-country governments will have learned the lessons of the 1980s and pay serious attention to the sustainability of the obligations of the governments to whom they lend.

For official providers of finance, there has been a mixed picture. Governments, as we have seen, have largely turned away from giving aid in the form of concessional loans; but the Washington multilaterals, bound by their constitutions, are still lenders rather than givers, even though some of the loans are on highly concessional terms. It seems a natural move for the World Bank before long to be empowered to give a considerable part of its funding in the form of grants, as some of its influential staff are believed to hope.

Regular means of escape from debt difficulties when they arise

There was discussion around the year 2000, stemming from prominent central-bank and IMF staff and others, of **regular procedures** for dealing with sovereign-debt difficulties (e.g., Haldane and Kruger, 2001; Krueger, 2002b), *with a closely defined and predictable role for the IMF*. There could be two broad possibilities: first, measures to deal with illiquidity, based on the assumption that, given time or further credit, debt obligations can be reduced by the debtors themselves to a manageable level; and second, measures to reduce the net present value of debt. Most of the official-level discussion dealt with mechanisms for relieving **illiquidity** and its effects, and signals for precipitating their use.

Relieving illiquidity

This covers **standstills** (when servicing is temporarily halted); **rescheduling** (when extra credit is arranged to lengthen the maturity of loans and hence to reduce the *annual* servicing obligations on existing loans); **debt-equity swaps** (which, in place of the claims entailed by the loans, give creditors equity, of comparable expected value, in potentially profitable projects at the disposal of the debtor-government); or, to facilitate these measures or in addition**, credit from the IMF**. All these devices can be designed to leave the parties with unchanged expected financial NPV, but with the advantage that debtor governments are given more time to mitigate the effects on their people of meeting their liabilities, and that any reduction of the uncertainty associated with 'debt overhang' may in itself leave all – debtors and creditors – simultaneously in a better position than before.

Increasing debtors' net worth: debt reduction

This heading covers actual **debt forgiveness**, as under the Brady Plan, or Argentina's eventual agreement with its creditors in 2005, or the HIPC Initiative. On paper the debtors gain in financial expected NPV at the expense of the creditors, but again with the important qualification that *reducing uncertainty* gives a potential bonus to both, so that, when this debt-overhang effect is taken into account, an arrangement may be reached under which both gain. Hence there are grounds for negotiation, enhanced by the fact that the debtor may threaten default.

Rules to facilitate agreement

In order to facilitate agreement on reliefs of either type – reducing illiquidity or reducing debt – provisions may be made by various countries – in their law applying to sovereign-loan agreements, or in the individual agreements – that **a defined majority of creditors** should be empowered to agree to the appropriate **relaxation** of the debtors' obligations.

Longer-term devices: inbuilt safety-valves in loan agreements

There are various possible safety-valve provisions that a government issuing bonds might write into their terms and which might be accepted as international good practice. Measures of this kind that reduce uncertainty for the debtor-governments do not necessarily increase it commensurately for the lenders. They may require some increase in the effective rate of interest, in order to satisfy the lenders, but this will not necessarily outweigh the value of the safety-valves to the borrowers. In other words, the devices may be framed to increase efficiency. Examples are **'state-dependent' remissions in servicing** as already mentioned, 'state-dependent' meaning that they depend on changes in 'the state of the world' rather than anything the debtor has done or not done. As an example, it might be agreed that interest or total-servicing obligations would be reduced or postponed if the terms of trade of the debtor country were to fall by more than a certain proportion. Such a provision could be argued to increase efficiency *not only because of the reduction in uncertainty* but also because it *weakens the case for* ad-hoc *concessions* to debtors and consequently *reduces 'moral hazard'*, which in this case might arise from the debtor's belief that it can *expect* concessions *ad hoc* when it gets into difficulties, so that it is tempted to behave with excessive profligacy.

Another safety-valve device that might be written in when loans are issued is **variable maturity** (meaning that within certain limits the maturity of the bond might be extended, either automatically or at the discretion of the debtor – at the cost, for example, of a formula-determined rise in interest rate).

Summary conclusions

- It is only under rather limited conditions that aid-type concessional loans have advantages to donor and recipient on balance over grants, and the recent tendency in bilateral aid has been to move away from loans.

- Debts incurred by governments, and private debts incurred through portfolio investment and other short-term capital movement, have been shown to embody **serious risks to developing countries** if they are not carefully limited and managed, and these hazards can spread **to the world at large**.

- For a number of years, the world **badly mismanaged the debt crisis of the 1980s**, arguably in part because of a lack of flexibility and imagination on the part of some of the rich-country governments, and in part because of the unreadiness of the main debtor governments to combine and bargain for a debt reduction of the kind that was finally adopted to general advantage.

- **Debt-reduction**, on certain conditions, was adopted as the aim in the **Heavily Indebted Poor Countries Initiative** of 1996, and after ten years it had been achieved permanently for about half the countries involved, with another quarter relieved more provisionally. Various criticisms were made of the Initiative, largely on grounds of slowness and inflexibility and of the fact that aid in the form of debt forgiveness was **not normally additional** to the aid that would have been given to poor countries otherwise, which meant that it worked to the detriment of the more fiscally responsible, indeed at their

▶

expense, with – beside the injustice – potentially bad incentive effects. The evidence of poverty reduction and especially growth as a result of the Initiative was also patchy at best.

■ There was consideration around the turn of the century of **more regular international arrangements** for dealing with sovereign-debt problems, but mostly as problems of illiquidity rather than insolvency. There have been suggestions for having routine provisions that in certain circumstances there may be measures to relieve the illiquidity of the debtors, such as rescheduling, standstills, and debt-equity swaps. Cases have also been made for embodying in the terms of bonds or other sovereign-debt contracts rules that allow the creditors by a form of *majority decision* to relax the debtors' obligations.

■ Strong arguments have also been put (on grounds, among others, of efficiency) for inserting *'state-dependent' clauses* in the terms of bonds or other sovereign loan contracts (possibly in exchange for somewhat higher expected interest rates) so as to relax servicing obligations routinely when defined adverse events outside the debtor's control occur. *Variable maturity* might also be applied to loans as a further safety-valve available to debtors under defined conditions.

The 1980s debt crisis, it now seems, might have been ended much earlier to the advantage of all sides, given more imagination, and more co-operation especially among the debtor-governments. The verdict on how the 1990s crisis was treated is less certain, but to an extent the rescue has had the unintended consequence that the gains for a number of the heavily indebted poor countries have been made at the expense of other poor countries. Moreover, for some of the beneficiaries' populations the gains in poverty reduction have been tenuous. There has been some sensible but possibly rather timid thought about how to react better to sovereign-debt difficulties in future.

Questions for discussion

22.1 In what circumstances might the forgiveness of foreign debts of developing-country governments be of value to both creditors and debtors? What is the meaning of *debt overhang*?

22.2 Why do you think the large and important Latin American debtor governments made no notable attempt to use their joint bargaining-power in the debt crisis of the 1980s so as to obtain much earlier the kind of debt-forgiveness finally granted with the Brady bonds from 1989? If they were afraid to do so, was this fear misguided?

22.3 Does debt forgiveness necessarily lead to 'moral hazard' *on the part of borrowing governments*? In other words, does it make them borrow more recklessly than they otherwise would? If so, does it matter?

22.4 Does effective 'bailing-out', under the IMF's auspices, of private creditors when they have possibly unrecoverable debts owed to them (an interpretation that may be put on a number of the settlements between private banks and debtor-governments in the 1980s) lead to moral hazard *among lenders*? If so, does it imply that the arrangements ought not to have been made?

22.5 How might 'state-dependent' clauses in loan contracts (clauses that relax the debtors' obligations on the occurrence of certain defined adverse events beyond their control) contribute to the *efficiency* of incentives to the borrowers?

Additional reading

Addison, T. and S.M. Murshed (2003) 'Debt relief and civil war', *Journal of Peace Research*, **40** (2), pp. 159–76.

Boughton, J. (2001) *Silent Revolution: the International Monetary Fund 1979–1989*, IMF, Washington, DC, chapter 6 (pp. 267–80). [The ground is covered in much more detail in chapters 7–12.]

Corden, W.M. (1988) 'An international debt facility', *IMF Staff Papers*, **35** (3), September, pp. 401–21.

Haldane, A. and M. Kruger (2001) 'The resolution of international financial crises: private finance and public funds', mimeo., Bank of England and Bank of Canada, November.

Krugman, P. (1988) 'Financing vs forgiving a debt overhang', *Journal of Development Economics*, **29**, pp. 253–68.

CHAPTER 23

Foreign Direct Investment

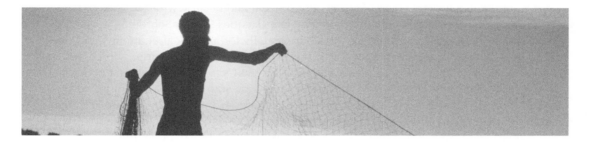

*'Attracting foreign direct investment is at the top of
the agenda for most countries.'*

(World Bank, 2007a)

*'Developing countries have been strongly advised by
international organizations and other external advisors to
rely primarily on foreign direct investment (FDI) as a source
of external finance. It is argued that FDI is superior to
other types of capital inflows in stimulating economic growth.'*

(Nunenkamp and Spatz, 2003)

Introduction

Foreign direct investment (FDI[1]) is traditionally thought of as funds transferred by a multinational corporation (MNC[2]) from a source country to a 'host' country in order to finance the setting-up and operating of a subsidiary or an affiliate there. 'Direct' investment differs crucially from portfolio investment in that the former involves the investor in actually *operating* a production facility in which it has a 'lasting interest'[3] whereas portfolio investment refers to the purchasing of shares, or other financial assets, and does *not* entail any management role for the investor. For this reason FDI is usually seen as being inherently more difficult to liquidate than a purely financial investment, hence implying a greater level

---

[1] Also sometimes referred to as private foreign investment (PFI). This abbreviation is not used in this sense here, but instead indicates Portfolio Foreign Investment.

[2] Also known as transnational corporations (TNCs) and multinational enterprises (MNEs).

[3] A 'lasting interest' is generally taken to mean a share of 10 per cent or more of the voting rights in an enterprise.

of commitment by the MNC to the host country. (However, as we shall see, the true picture is often more complex than this.)

FDI has, of course, existed for a very long time, early involvement taking the forms of overseas trading bases and plantations. However it was only in the 1960s that FDI became an important focus of interest for economists. Initially attention centred on the implications of the growing flow of American direct investment into Europe. Backed up by massive financial resources, superior technical know-how, and advanced management systems, the incoming US firms seemed likely to out-compete and destroy wide swathes of European industry, a view advanced very effectively by Jean-Jacques Servan-Schreiber (1968) in his influential *The American Challenge* (which, unusually for a political-economy tract, sold over 600 000 copies). Subsequently, as FDI flows to developing countries (which are seen as being at an even greater 'disadvantage' vis-à-vis MNCs than are developed countries) have expanded to the point where they are a significant source of finance for growth – the proportion of all capital formation in developing countries financed by inward FDI rose from 4.7 per cent in 1970 to 13.8 per cent in 2006 – discussion of the implications of this phenomenon has become a major preoccupation of development economists.

The structure of this chapter

The following section of this chapter sketches the evolution of FDI flows to the developing world in terms of their magnitude, distribution across countries, sources, industrial composition, and contribution to local capital formation.

In the third section we look at the motives of firms which seek to transform themselves into MNCs: why do they do it? This is an important issue since, clearly, policies designed to attract FDI must take the aims and preferences of potential investors into account. Then, in the subsequent section, we ask what experience tells us about the potential gains and losses for host countries associated with inward FDI, and how these are conditioned by characteristics of the host countries and of the MNCs themselves. Once all this information is available, appropriate policies for attracting appropriate kinds of FDI can be formulated.

BOX 23.1 AN FDI TOOLBOX

'**Roundtripping' investment.** A manoeuvre involving transferring domestic investment funds to a foreign country and then repatriating them, ostensibly as FDI. A firm intending to invest in a project at home may first transfer the investment funds to a subsidiary firm in a second country. The subsidiary returns the funds, apparently as 'FDI', to finance the project – at the same time benefiting from any inducements, such as tax holidays, offered by the home country to foreign investors. The funds have been 'roundtripped', and will appear as 'FDI' in the national accounts of the home country – so exaggerating the true value of inward investment.

Special Purpose Entity (SPE). A commercial entity, usually a firm, set up specifically to facilitate a particular financial, or legal, manipulation (as opposed to engaging in ongoing, orthodox trading). SPEs are often short-lived, being wound up once the transaction is completed. The 'subsidiary firm' referred to in the explanation of 'roundtripping' (above) would usually be an SPE.

▶

> **Proprietary knowledge.** Exclusive knowledge, usually owned by a firm – often as the result of R&D activity. Such knowledge may not be used without the permission of the owner, which may be granted for a fee. Legal protection of proprietary knowledge is particularly important where the cost of generating that knowledge is high but the cost of exploiting it is low.
>
> **'Fire sale'.** A situation in which the prices of assets, physical or financial, are seen as very low – probably significantly below the true long-run value of the assets. Fire sales may be caused by a sudden need to liquidate assets – perhaps as the result of a financial crisis, such as the Asian crisis of 1997–98.

The focus then shifts from the analysis of 'traditional' forms of FDI to consider important recent developments – in particular implications of the rapid rise in FDI *from developing countries*, the growth of cross-border mergers and acquisitions, and the effects of globalization, especially the pressures created by the WTO's 'level- playing-field' programme. The chapter ends with a brief summary of the key findings suggested by the earlier discussion.

Dimensions of FDI

Growth and magnitudes of FDI

A key reason for the widespread interest in FDI is its very rapid growth since the 1980s and its impressive absolute scale. Figure 23.1 (which is based on Table 23.9 in Appendix 23.1 on the Online Learning Centre) shows clearly the explosive expansion of gross and net inflows of FDI into developing countries between 1970 and 2005.

As indicated in Table 23.1, total (or *gross*) FDI receipts of developing countries grew from US$3.9 billions in 1970 to an estimated US$379.1 billions in 2006. This represents a 97-fold increase, somewhat larger than the 89-fold growth of flows to developed countries. Over the period to 2005 *net* inward flows of FDI into developing countries rose by a factor of 52. In none of the 37 years covered by the data did outflows come near to exceeding inflows.[4] As a result of these changes the share of gross worldwide FDI going to developing countries rose (albeit somewhat unsteadily) from 29.1 per cent in 1970 to a peak of 38.7 per cent in 2004, falling back to 29.0 per cent in 2006 (see Table 23.2). Over the same years, the geographical distribution of FDI flows to the developing world changed significantly. Figure 23.2 provides the absolute US$ values and Table 23.3 the percentage breakdown of the gross flows to developing countries only. With regard to the latter, three shifts stand out – the very sharp fall in Africa's share, the decline in the share of Latin America/Caribbean, and the massive increases in the shares of West Asia and East Asia. (The main recipients of FDI in the regional groupings used in these tables are footnoted below. A complete listing of the members of all countries in each group is given in Table 23.10 in Appendix 23.1 on the Online Learning Centre.)

---

[4] It should be noted that FDI data drawn from different sources do not always tally exactly. (See, for instance, Table 23.1, and Table 23.9 in Appendix 23.1 on the Online Learning Centre.) Discrepancies in published figures arise largely from the frequent need to use different sources in compiling different data sets and the lack of uniformity in data collection methods used by these sources. However, such discrepancies are not sufficiently large as to affect our discussion materially.

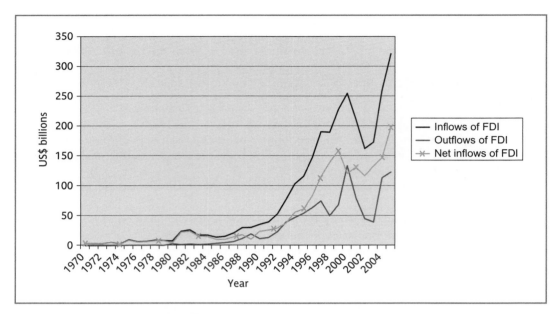

FIGURE 23.1 FDI and developing countries: inflows, outflows, and net inflows: 1970–2005
Source: Based on data drawn from UNCTAD (2007c)

HOST REGION	1970 (US$ billion)	1993–1998 (Annual Average) (US$ billion)	1999 (US$ billion)	2000 (US$ billion)	2001 (US$ billion)	2002 (US$ billion)	2003 (US$ billion)	2004 (US$ billion)	2005 (US$ billion)	2006 (US$ billion)
World Total	13.4	401.7	1092.1	1396.5	825.9	716.1	632.6	742.1	945.8	1305.9
Developed Countries	9.6	256.2	849.1	1133.7	599.3	441.2	358.5	418.9	590.3	857.5
Developing Countries	3.9	138.9	232.5	266.8	221.4	163.6	175.1	283.0	314.3	379.1
Africa	*1.3*	*7.1*	*11.9*	*9.6*	*19.9*	*13.0*	*18.5*	*18.0*	*29.6*	*35.5*
Latin Am. and Caribbean	*1.6*	*47.9*	*108.6*	*109.0*	*89.4*	*54.3*	*46.1*	*94.3*	*75.5*	*83.8*
West Asia	*0.1*	*3.5*	*1.9*	*3.5*	*7.2*	*6.0*	*12.3*	*20.8*	*41.6*	*59.9*
East Asia	*0.2*	*51.6*	*77.3*	*116.3*	*78.8*	*67.4*	*72.2*	*106.3*	*116.3*	*125.8*
South Asia	*0.1*	*2.9*	*3.1*	*4.7*	*6.4*	*7.0*	*5.7*	*7.6*	*9.9*	*22.3*
South-East Asia	*0.5*	*25.3*	*29.3*	*23.5*	*19.6*	*15.8*	*19.9*	*35.2*	*41.1*	*51.5*
Oceania	*0.1*	*0.4*	*0.4*	*0.3*	*0.1*	*0.1*	*0.4*	*0.7*	*0.4*	*0.3*

TABLE 23.1 Total FDI inflows by host region: 1970 and 1993–2006 (US$ billion; current prices)
Source: UNCTAD, *World Investment Report* (various editions), and *Handbook of Statistics* (various editions), Geneva.

RECEIVING REGION	1970 (%)	1993–1998 (annual average) (%)	1999 (%)	2000 (%)	2001 (%)	2002 (%)	2003 (%)	2004 (%)	2005 (%)	2006 (%)
Developed Countries	71.6	63.8	77.7	80.4	72.0	71.4	64.3	55.7	59.2	65.7
Developing Countries	28.1	34.6	21.3	18.9	26.6	26.5	31.4	38.7	36.5	29.0

Table 23.2 Percentage distribution of total FDI inflows between developed and developing countries: 1970 and 1993–2006*
* The balance of total inflows went to CIS countries.
Source: UNCTAD, *World Investment Report* (various editions), Geneva.

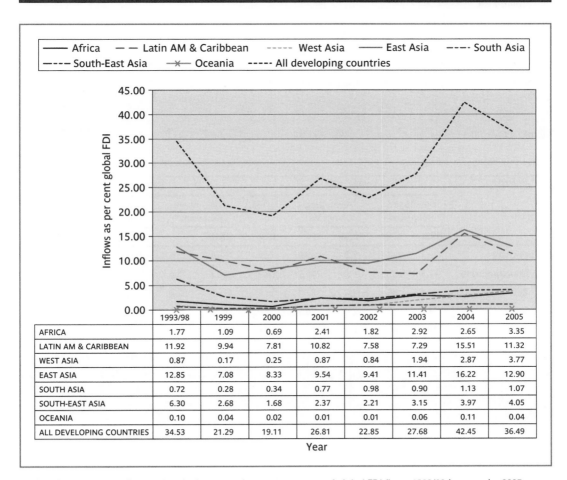

FIGURE 23.2 Inflows of FDI into developing countries as percentage of global FDI flows 1993/98 (average) – 2005
Source: Based on data drawn from UNCTAD, *World Investment Report* (various editions), Geneva.

Table 23.4 provides figures (annual averages) on the broad sectoral distribution – Primary Production, Manufacturing, Services, and Other – of FDI across developed and developing countries in 1989–91 and 2003–05. In both groups of countries the shares of investment going to Primary activities was less than 15 per cent in both periods. Investment in Manufacturing was dominant in developing countries in the earlier period, whereas the

RECEIVING REGION	1970 (%)	1993–1998 (Ann. Av.) (%)	1999 (%)	2000 (%)	2001 (%)	2002 (%)	2003 (%)	2004 (%)	2005 (%)	2006 (%)
Africa	33.3	5.11	5.12	3.60	8.99	7.95	10.57	6.25	9.18	9.36
Latin Am. and Caribbean	41.0	34.49	46.71	40.85	40.38	33.19	26.33	36.55	31.02	22.1
West Asia	2.6	2.52	0.82	1.31	3.25	3.67	7.02	6.76	10.32	15.8
East Asia	5.1	37.15	33.25	43.59	35.59	41.20	41.23	38.22	35.36	33.18
South Asia	2.6	2.09	1.33	1.76	2.89	4.28	3.26	2.65	2.93	5.88
South-East Asia	12.8	18.21	12.60	8.81	8.85	9.66	11.36	9.35	11.10	13.58
Oceania	2.6	0.29	0.17	0.11	0.05	0.06	0.23	0.25	0.12	0.08
TOTAL*	100	100	100	100	100	100	100	100	100	100

TABLE 23.3 Percentage distribution, by host region, of FDI flows to developing countries: 1970–2006
* errors due to rounding.
Source: Base on data from UNCTAD, *World Investment Report* (various editions), and UNCTAD, *Handbook of Statistics* (various editions), Geneva.

SECTOR	1989–1991*					2003–2005*				
	Developed Countries		Developing Countries		TOTAL	Developed Countries		Developing Countries		TOTAL
	US$b	%	US$b	%	US$b	US$b	%	US$b	%	US$b
Primary	9.1	6.1	3.3	9.5	12.4	69.1	13.5	16.8	7.9	85.9
Manufacturing	47.7	32.1	16.5	47.2	64.2	83.7	16.4	82.1	38.5	165.8
Services	83.6	56.3	11.3	32.4	94.9	315.9	62.0	106.1	50.0	422.0
Other	8.2	5.5	3.8	10.9	12.0	41.5	8.1	7.7	3.6	49.2
TOTAL	148.6	100.0	34.9	100.0	183.5	510.2	100.0	212.7	100.0	722.9

TABLE 23.4 Inward flows of FDI into developing countries by sector 1989–1991 and 2003–2005 (US$ billions at current prices; and %)
* Annual averages.
Source: UNCTAD (2007) *FDI On-line.*

Services sector was easily the largest target in developed countries. However, by 2003–05 investment in Services dominated in both groups of countries.

The substantial growth in FDI has not, however, been felt in all developing countries. The shares of total FDI going to individual countries are highly skewed. Some get large inflows, others next to nothing. Thus, in 2005 only 17 developing countries out of the 170 (including Commonwealth of Independent States [CIS] countries) for which data are available, absorbed 86 per cent of all FDI going to the developing world. The main recipients were China (23 per cent), Hong Kong (11 per cent), Singapore (6 per cent), Mexico (6 per cent) and Brazil (6 per cent). The others in this favoured group of 17 were South Africa, the British Virgin Islands, the Cayman Islands, Argentina, Chile, Colombia, South Korea, India,

Indonesia, Saudi Arabia, Turkey and UAE. Even within this small group, not all members saw the inflow of FDI turned into productive assets. In particular, in two cases – the British Virgin Islands and the Cayman Islands – the funds were channelled through financial institutions to be used subsequently to purchase productive assets in *other* countries.

Operating dimensions of leading MNCs

A glance at the operating dimensions of the larger MNCs confirms the enormous size of these firms. Many MNCs are very big indeed; according to the *Fortune Global 500*[5] listing, the top ten had, in 2006–7, total revenue of US$2435 billion, or more than the total GDP in 2006 of 125 developing countries taken together and somewhat greater than the GDP of Italy. The same ten employed 3.25 million people worldwide, while the top 100 MNCs employed around 8 million people in their overseas operations alone.

BOX 23.2 LARGE MNCS AND SMALL COUNTRIES

The table shows revenue and number of employees of each of the world's three largest MNCs (as ranked by revenue earned in 2007), and the GDP and population (in 2007) of three of the smallest developing countries (as ranked by GDP). Wal-Mart's revenue, at $378.8 billion, is 1894 times Palau's GDP, and the retail giant could employ Palau's entire population 103 times over.

Firm	Employees	Revenue ($b)	Country	GDP ($b)	Population
Wal-Mart	2 055 000	378.8	Dominica	0.3	73 000
Exxon-Mobil	170 100	372.8	St. Kitts & Nevis	0.5	49 000
Royal Dutch Shell	104 000	355.8	Palau	0.2	20 000

Source: World Bank (2008c), and *Global Fortune 500*, at www.money.cnn.com/magazines/fortune/global500/2007/

The industrial composition of the major MNCs is highly concentrated. In 2006–7, the top 50 firms (in terms of sales) were covered by only 6 industry categories: 19 were in banking or insurance; 12 were petroleum firms; 8 were motor-vehicle manufacturers; 7 made electronic, electrical and telecommunications equipment; and 4 were in retail or wholesale activities.

The source-country composition of the largest MNCs is also highly concentrated. The 50 largest firms in 2006–7 were based in only twelve countries – the US (nineteen firms), France (six), Japan (five), Germany (four), the UK and China (three each), Switzerland, Italy, the Netherlands, and Belgium (two each), and Mexico and South Korea (one apiece).

Growing dependence of developing countries on FDI for capital formation

Along with the rapid increase in FDI flows has come a growing dependence in many developing countries on FDI as a source of funds for fixed capital formation. Thus, in 1970 only around 10 per cent of all developing countries for which figures were available funded

---

[5] Quoted in www.money.cnn.com/magazines/fortune/global500/2007/

more than one-fifth of their fixed capital formation from this source. By 2006 this figure had risen to 45 per cent of developing countries. (Detailed figures are given in Table 23.9 in Appendix 23.1 on the Online Learning Centre.)

A word of warning regarding the interpretation of data on FDI 'inflows'

Having drawn attention to the vast dimensions of FDI flows, we must point out that the bare figures exaggerate the true magnitude of inflows of new capital into developing countries. In fact, some of these funds will have been 'roundtripped'; that is, they will have been remitted by a firm in country A to an affiliate, or to a firm set up specifically to handle the funds – a 'Special Purpose Entity', or SPE – in country B, then returned to A as 'FDI' in order to take advantage of the benefits offered by A to incoming firms. These benefits may take the form of, for instance, lower corporation tax rates than those paid by domestic firms or lower tariff rates on imported raw materials. Estimates of the extent of 'roundtripping' are still little more than guesses, but it is claimed that between 25 per cent and 45 per cent of all FDI flowing into China in recent years was actually Chinese funds, much of this sent to affiliates in Hong Kong, then channelled back to China. Clearly, such 'roundtripping' can lead to double-counting of FDI flows.

A second feature of FDI data is that not all of the funds involved are used to buy *new* capital assets. An increasing proportion of FDI is used to buy pre-existing assets through cross-border mergers and acquisitions (M&A). In the short run, at any rate, these flows simply finance a change of ownership of assets, though it is possible, of course, that the new owner may subsequently expand its stake in the overseas entity. A variation on this theme is the take-over of an existing firm by a foreign 'private-equity' firm. (These matters are discussed further in the following section.)

Last, a striking feature of FDI flows as they are currently measured is that a significant proportion of all flows to and from developing countries passes through a second form of SPE, 'offshore financial centres' (commonly known as 'tax-havens'). Over the years 2000 to 2005 around 10 per cent of all FDI inflows to developing countries actually went to tax-havens in the Caribbean, notably the Cayman Islands and the British Virgin Islands. Funds remitted by MNCs to tax-havens are often used to set up new firms – holding companies or other non-operating entities – designed to channel ('trans-ship') cash to other countries, developed or developing, for investment there. The aim of such manoeuvres is to provide MNCs with bases in countries in which no, or very little, corporation tax is levied, and where, very often, other advantages are available, such as limited disclosure requirements and limited regulation of corporate activities.

The true extent of these activities is currently being studied as a matter of urgency by the various agencies, such as UNCTAD, interested in producing accurate figures on the dimensions, sources, and direction of FDI.

Foreign direct investment: motives and impact

Introduction

If developing countries are to derive full advantage from inward flows of FDI it is important that their policy-makers are aware of the aims of the firms responsible for it, the potential impacts of FDI on host economies, and the domestic factors conditioning such effects. These matters are examined in detail below in order to highlight issues relevant to policy formulation in this important area.

Why do firms invest abroad? And what might deter them?

Why do firms invest abroad? Why do they take the trouble to set up subsidiaries in foreign countries when they could simply supply overseas markets by exporting, or could license foreign firms to use their patents or technology for a suitable fee?

A convincing answer to this question was first put forward by Stephen Hymer in his PhD dissertation (presented in 1960 but not published until 1976). Hymer concluded that FDI depends on the existence of *imperfect competition*. Investing abroad increases a firm's profits by extending exploitation of some *monopolistic advantage* possessed by the firm, for instance a unique technology, ownership of a patent not available to others, or the special skills (manual, technical or managerial) of its employees – in a way not possible from the home base. The additional advantage resulting from expansion into a new overseas location may take a variety of forms, for instance reduced transport costs, cheaper labour or raw materials, availability of tariff protection, or preferential tax treatment by the host-country government.

Building on this insight regarding the necessary conditions for FDI, Dunning (1977) differentiated between two alternative motives which may prompt MNCs to set up operations in specific locations. Some firms are attracted by the prospect of increasing profitability by setting up production units in developing countries in order *to sell their products into the local markets*. The gains from such '**market-seeking**', or 'horizontal', FDI will be greater the larger are the local markets, the greater their growth potential, and the higher the level of protection offered by tariffs on competing imports. Other, '**efficiency-seeking**' firms, *attracted by the availability of cheaper inputs and hence lower production costs in the host countries* than at home, shift one or more segments of their production process to the host country in order to cut costs of production. This is 'vertical' FDI. Here the cost and efficiency of local inputs such as labour, raw materials, and infrastructure relative to costs in the source country, will be key considerations in the investment-decision process.

Beyond this, a wide range of host-country policies and characteristics may play a part in determining the volume of FDI in any one period and how it is allocated across countries. The most common kinds of measure designed specifically to attract FDI are the **financial inducements** offered by prospective host governments. These include *special fiscal treatment* (for instance 'tax holidays' during which a reduced rate of corporation tax, or none, is paid; accelerated writing-off of depreciation costs against tax liabilities; or duty-free importing of capital equipment and raw materials); *grants or subsidies* (such as assistance with set-up costs, provision of infrastructure, and rent-free factories); or *protection against local and foreign, or just foreign, competition* (relevant in the case of 'market-seeking' investment).

However, while such benefits are unlikely to be refused by MNCs, experience suggests that they are rarely decisive in determining whether or not firms opt to invest overseas, particularly as they can be withdrawn at the stroke of a pen. Rather, they are likely to influence location decisions by firms *already committed* to foreign investment. Even then, there is ample evidence that a much more effective form of 'inducement' for most firms is the provision of **a congenial, stable, and dependable environment** in which to do business. This usually amounts to removing, or ameliorating, the many operating problems which often confront MNCs in developing countries. These include:

- *Bureaucratic problems:* Complex regulatory systems and procedures relating to, for instance, obtaining permission to invest and to open a business; employing foreign workers; and registering property;
- *Financial problems:* Currency conversion controls; restrictions on remission of profits, dividends and royalties to the source country; difficulty in obtaining credit locally;

- *Legal problems:* Inability to enforce contracts effectively; lack of protection for investors; difficulty in establishing and enforcing property rights (including rights in intellectual property);
- *Governance problems:* Corruption; poor macroeconomic management (leading to, for instance, weak local economic performance, failure to control inflation, volatility of exchange rates, and postponement of spending on infrastructure and utilities); inability to control crime; civil disturbances.

Many of these factors are incorporated in the *Ease of Doing Business Index* prepared each year by the World Bank. This brings together ten factors believed to be important in determining the extent to which a local regulatory environment is, or is not, conducive to the satisfactory running of a business, with special reference to: starting a business, obtaining business licences, employing labour, registering property, getting credit, protecting investors, paying taxes, trading across borders, closing a business, and the effectiveness of provisions for enforcing contracts. The 'ease' with which firms can conduct business was found to vary widely across the 175 countries covered by the Index for 2007. By and large developed countries occupied the top end of the ranking (16 out of the top 20). African countries occupied 25 of the bottom 30 places. Singapore had the distinction of being the easiest country in which to do business. The average ranking (1 being the most business-friendly and 175 the least) of each of the main country groupings in 2007 was:

Region	Developed	East Asia	Oceania	West Asia	Latin Am. & Caribbean	South-East Asia	South Asia	Africa
Average ranking	26	44	73	80	87	91	108	138

On the specific, and very important, issue of corruption, the *Corruption Perceptions Index*, compiled annually by Transparency International (explained with scores and rankings in Chapter 6) ranks 180 countries by their perceived levels of corruption in government, as estimated by expert assessments and opinion surveys. The Index suggests the existence of a strong tendency for a high incidence of corruption to be associated with low per capita income; 40 per cent of countries experiencing 'rampant corruption' are classified by the World Bank as low-income countries. 'Somalia and Myanmar share the lowest score . . . deeply troubled states such as Afghanistan, Iraq, Myanmar, Somalia and Sudan remain at the very bottom of the Index.'

All these considerations lead on very directly to identification of the policy measures aimed at encouraging FDI adumbrated later in this chapter.

The impact of FDI on host developing economies

> The effects of FDI can sometimes barely be perceived, while other times they can be absolutely transformative.
>
> *(World Bank)*

Introduction

Developing countries that seek to attract inward FDI do so because they expect the impact of that investment to be beneficial for the home economy. We now go on to look at what the *a priori* economic theory built up over several decades suggests the most important potential benefits, and costs, of such investment might be, and what the available evidence has to say on the realities of the situation. An important caveat before we begin: a major difficulty with this analysis is that the list of potential impacts is long; MNCs themselves come in a very wide range of shapes and sizes; and host countries are both numerous and varied in their levels of development, administrative capacity to deal with foreign firms, and political attitudes. It is not surprising that, despite several decades of analysis, there is still a very active debate on many aspects of the impact of inward FDI. Furthermore, as with many other financial instruments, the nature of FDI does not stand still but becomes more complex and diverse as time goes by – so continuously demanding fresh appraisals of its consequences for host economies.

In what follows the impact of FDI on host developing-country economies is examined with respect to:

- The effects of capital inflows *per se*
- The 'package' of know-how and skills which accompanies FDI
- Implications for the host-country balance of payments
- The contribution to local fiscal revenue
- Environmental effects
- Socio-economic effects
- Political effects.

In each case the hypothetical pros and cons are summarized, and a synopsis presented of research findings on the key issues.

Last, the central questions underlying all of this discussion – *what is the effect of FDI on growth in developing countries, and what conditions this effect?* – are considered in the light of available evidence.

The effects of capital inflows per se

At first glance it appears obvious that FDI will have beneficial effects on host developing countries. The flow of capital from the source to the host country will help to alleviate any shortages of domestic savings, adding to the local capital stock and thus, as the growth theories deployed in Chapter 4 argue, leading to a permanent increase in the growth rate, or to a transitional increase as the economy moves to a higher equilibrium level of per capita income. These favourable effects on GNP and GNP per capita will be doubly beneficial as they will very probably be accompanied by increased levels of employment. Furthermore, the new demand, by MNCs, for local products as inputs will stimulate productive activity by creating 'linkages' to local firms, and by encouraging competition – a process sometimes referred to as 'crowding-in'.

How far can we depend on these potential benefits? What if incoming firms borrow some, or all, of their capital requirements locally (which may not be difficult since their credit ratings are typically superior to those of most local borrowers)? Given the prevailing shortage of domestic capital, might this 'crowd-out' local commercial borrowers? If so, this could materially reduce the expected benefits from FDI, as there would now be no immediate favourable foreign-exchange or balance-of-payments impact in the absence of an inward capital flow. Again, what if incoming firms form 'enclaves' with little contact with the domestic sector? Or if local competitors are forced out of business by MNCs either because the latter are more efficient or because they receive preferential treatment from the host government in the forms, for instance, of 'tax holidays' or even exclusive access to resources? The resultant decline in demand for capital by the domestic sector could lead to a fall in domestic savings, so that incoming funds (if any) simply replace local savings, with no net increase in investment or the level of economic activity.

The empirical evidence on these issues is mixed. Research published by UNCTAD suggests that crowding-out of domestic investment by FDI is common in Latin America, but that crowding-in is the dominant effect in Asia and Africa (Agosin and Mayer, 2000). One important, and fairly obvious, reason for this is that the potential for crowding out varies from industry to industry, depending on the extent of local participation. This is certainly consistent with the finding that China's rapidly expanding FDI in extractive industries (oil and minerals) in Africa, where there is minimal local activity in these sectors, has had very little crowding-out effect (Gedu, 2006).

The 'package' of know-how and skills that accompanies FDI

FDI funds are often accompanied by a beneficial 'package' of technological know-how and skills (manual, technical, entrepreneurial and managerial) all of which are typically in short supply in developing countries. The components of this 'package' will themselves raise average productivity directly in the host country. Moreover, and potentially even more important, there will often be beneficial 'spillovers' to the host economy as know-how, skills and capacity for innovation are spread to local firms through a 'diffusion' process. The nature of this diffusion process will vary with the precise circumstances of the situation, but may arise through:

- 'Linkages' with local firms; that is, purchases of inputs from local firms, or sales of outputs to local firms. (In the former case, the MNC may provide suppliers with the technical and managerial know-how required to produce the inputs to the required standard and in a timely and efficient manner. In the latter, advice may be given to local firms on how the MNC's products may be best used to improve their own products or efficiency.)

- Training of local labour in manual and management skills. (This will create a pool of skilled labour which will augment the 'diffusion' process when and if these workers move back into the domestic sector.)

- Direct emulation by local firms of MNCs' methods, in some cases forced on the former by the need to compete effectively with the incoming firms.

With regard to the advantages of improved access to new technologies, a counter-case is often made to the effect that MNCs, which originate for the most part in high-wage countries, are likely to bring with them 'inappropriate', capital-intensive technologies suited to their home economies rather than the labour-intensive technologies needed to provide jobs in low-wage, high-unemployment countries. Were such MNCs to supplant ('crowd-out') local firms, total employment might actually *fall* as a result. (An example here might be the introduction by an incoming sugar-producing MNC of mechanical sugar-cane harvesters, each capable of replacing up to 500 of the cane-field labourers previously employed on the cane farms.)

A great deal of effort has gone into researching the issue of the appropriateness, or inappropriateness, of the technologies used by MNCs in developing countries. Many studies agree that MNCs do tend to be more capital-intensive than their local counterparts. And there are numerous (frequently recounted) horror stories of developed-country technology that failed to deliver the goods when transplanted to the tropics. (One of the most spectacular of all technology-based failures was the 'Ground Nut Scheme' in Tanzania – a British project designed to develop a ground-nut plantation covering 150 000 acres

(607 km²), which, in part because of the use of totally unsuitable equipment, was abandoned after four years, having yielded only 2000 tons of output. This was, however, a government-run, rather than a private-sector, project.)

At the same time, it is not plausible to suggest that MNCs would deliberately and systematically select technologies that reduced the profitability of their operations. It seems likely that investing in 'excessive' capital-intensity, if this happens, is actually a rational response to the fact that capital is cheaper (in relation to labour) to MNCs than to local firms, or to the availability to MNCs of technology (albeit not ideally suited to local cost conditions) at much lower cost than to local firms. One further important consideration is that there is often a close connection between the sophistication of technology and the quality of product so that labour-intensive technologies may be unable to produce the high-quality output often demanded in export markets. (A good example here is sugar – which can certainly be produced in very labour-intensive ways, but not to the high degree of refinement preferred in world markets.)

It is also the case that some MNCs prefer *not* to transfer complex or advanced technologies to developing-country subsidiaries because of difficulties experienced with protection of proprietary knowledge in these countries. Despite the efforts of the World Intellectual Property Organization (WIPO), theft of intellectual property is still a matter of concern for many firms, and the risks increase when such property is deployed far from home and in unfamiliar legal jurisdictions. (Some aspects of the transfer of technology and the development of facility in its use and adaptation have been discussed in Chapter 18.)

On diffusion of know-how and spillovers the evidence is more clear-cut. While local firms tend to have a higher propensity to develop backward linkages to local suppliers than do MNC affiliates, and there is considerable variation across industries, nevertheless in-country procurement by these affiliates can be significant. Thus, at the low end of the scale, in the garment industry backward linkages from MNCs to local firms are typically small – as low as 5 to 10 per cent of the total value added. But automobile-industry values of 19 to 25 per cent (in Thailand) and 30 per cent (in Mexico) have been reported. Also, in the production of electrical and electronic goods local purchases by MNCs in the range 25 per cent (Mexico) to 60 per cent (Malaysia) of value-added have been recorded.[6] Possible means of increasing this important benefit from FDI are considered in a subsequent section.

Implications for the host-country balance of payments

Two key issues arise with regard to the balance-of-payments impacts of FDI in developing countries. The first concerns the relative merits of financing investment through FDI and through portfolio foreign investment (PFI). The second concerns the expected impact of the operations of MNCs on current-account payments and receipts.

FDI versus PFI – the stability issue It is often suggested that, where there is a choice for funding investment between PFI and FDI, the latter is superior. This is because it is held to be less volatile as it brings with it no obligations to repay and involves more commitment to the host economy than does PFI. While the latter usually involves obligations to remit to the source country both interest and, ultimately, the original capital, FDI involves no such fixed obligations and may, in the event that the project is not profitable, involve nothing worse than the writing-off by the foreign owner of the investment.

Put another way, FDI is more 'reliable' than PFI in that the former is, to use Krugman's term, 'bolted down' and cannot be withdrawn as easily as the much more liquid portfolio

---

[6] For an analysis of the 'linkages' issue see UNCTAD (2001) or http://www.unctad.org/en/docs/wir2001_en.pdf

investments. Investment in a production facility creates an inherently less liquid asset since entry costs are typically much higher than is the case for the acquisition of a financial asset, and exit costs are also likely to be much higher. FDI investments are therefore more difficult to repatriate to the source country than is the value of portfolio instruments. From this perspective FDI appears to be a relatively *stable* form of long-term funding, bringing with it a much lower probability of creating financial and balance-of-payments problems than PFI funds, which are potentially 'hot money' that can be withdrawn at any point. This certainly proved to be the case during the financial crises in Mexico (1995), and East Asia (1997–98), when net inward flows of FDI remained fairly stable while those of private portfolio equity and debt, especially short-term flows, turned seriously negative. Some analysts go so far as to describe short-term capital inflows as 'bad cholesterol' which, to mix metaphors, is 'the first to run for the exits in times of trouble', and which may trigger boom-bust cycles, unlike less mobile 'good cholesterol' in the form of FDI (Hausman and Fernandez-Arias, 2000).

Again, it can be argued that MNC investors are less likely than PFI investors (or lenders) to be affected by fears of depreciation of host-country exchange rates. In particular, a depreciation of the local currency will have little impact on an established 'market-seeking' firm, since it will divert local demand towards, rather than away from internal suppliers. 'Efficiency-seeking' firms will be in a different position. On the one hand, insofar as their *raison d'être* is to supply affiliates with intermediate products, the loss of revenue in dollar terms will be cancelled out by a fall in the dollar cost of their products supplied to affiliates. That is, for intra-firm transactions the effect of the depreciation nets out. Only if the efficiency-seeking affiliate wishes to export to third parties does depreciation of the host currency become a potential problem and, even then, if demand elasticities are high, the ultimate effect may be beneficial to the firm.

However, this favourable view of FDI needs to be qualified. In practice, the mobility of FDI may be greatly increased should the parent firm wish to do so. Given their typically good credit rating in host countries, MNC affiliates may be able to borrow funds locally against the collateral of their fixed assets (backed up by the good name of the parent firm) and remit these funds to their parent, thus in effect liquidating their local investment and reversing any initial inflow of capital funds. Alternatively, local investors may be encouraged to buy the equity of MNC subsidiaries. One danger here is that the detailed knowledge possessed by MNCs regarding the viability of their subsidiaries could, in principle, be used to identify weaker units – with a view to selling them on to local investors at prices inflated by the mistaken (local) belief that MNCs are always 'blue chip' firms. Clearly, such 'adverse selection' would mean that FDI imposed a burden on host countries.

Furthermore, many MNCs remit funds regularly to the parent in the form of dividends, royalties, management fees or interest payments, so nullifying a second supposed advantage over PFI. (And such remittances may be substantial. One striking case in point is that of the tuna canning firm Solomon Taiyo, a subsidiary of the Japanese Taiyo Corporation, which has operated in the Solomon Islands since 1973 but has made overall losses in every year, and an operating profit in only one year. The explanation for the satisfaction of the parent firm with this performance is that large sums are remitted to it annually by Solomon Taiyo in the form of royalties, management fees and marketing fees, all non-taxable at source.)

Other sources of instability   FDI may introduce instability in the balance of payments, and instability in the level of economic activity, in two other ways. First, year-on-year variation in inflows can be large. The unstable nature of FDI flows from one year to the next is evidenced by the 41 per cent fall in gross inflows worldwide in 2001 as against 2000, and the 38 per cent rise in 2006 over 2005 – shown in Table 23.1. This may well lead to balance-of-payments instability in host countries, with consequential problems of maintaining macroeconomic stability. Such volatility is largely beyond the control of developing countries, stemming from a variety of causes such as fluctuations in foreign exchange rates (which affect costs of FDI to investing companies) and, more generally, operating and profitability conditions in source countries.

Second, independently of the debate over 'FDI versus PFI' as sources of instability, it is sometimes argued that aggregate levels of activity of MNC subsidiaries, as a group, are subject to greater variation than is the case with local firms simply because the foreign-owned firms have the option of leaving the country. This is usually expressed by saying that MNCs are 'footloose'. Here the evidence needs to be interpreted with care. A study of foreign investment in Indonesia, a country which has a very large foreign-owned sector and which is often held to have been particularly disadvantaged by departures and closures of foreign-owned firms, shows clearly that, over a 15-year period, while the rate of closures of similarly-sized foreign and local firms making similar products *with similar efficiency levels* was significantly *higher* for the former group, *overall* the foreign firms displayed a significantly *lower* closure rate because of their typically much greater efficiency (the result, in part, of their greater average size) and hence lower probability of becoming unprofitable. From the point of view of the instability issue, the latter finding would appear to be the more relevant (Bernard and Sjoholm, 2003).

Investment, exports and imports   Inward FDI may be expected to affect the balance of payments of host countries through its impact on both capital and current accounts. Insofar as there is an initial (and possibly subsequent) capital inflow, this will have a favourable impact, though it is to be expected that a large part of the invested funds will be used to pay for imports of plant and machinery, since only relatively simple capital goods (including buildings) are likely to be available locally. Moreover, it is possible that some of the capital spending may be in kind, in the form of equipment supplied by affiliates.

The precise nature of the role played by FDI in the export performance of developing countries is a matter of some debate, largely because of lack of detailed data on the trading performance of MNCs relative to non-MNCs, compounded by many MNC affiliates' practice of 'transfer pricing'. This means that they trade within their own firms at prices that do not reflect accurately the market value of the goods (as discussed in the following section).

What is known is that the trading performance of the subsidiary of an MNC will depend heavily on the reason for its presence in the host country. Thus the many affiliates that are 'efficiency-seekers', for which the intention is to export all, or almost all, production in fulfilment of their roles as integral parts of a vertical international production structure, will arrive with a ready-made export market for their output. They will either supply the parent firm or affiliates with raw materials or intermediate products, or will supply overseas customers already lined up by the parent firm (or, at the very least, they will get help from the parent in finding customers), and this will clearly be a plus for the host-country current account. Given the problems frequently encountered in developing countries in meeting debt-servicing obligations and avoiding destabilizing import surpluses, this would be a welcome consequence of FDI (though there may well be a partial offset in the form of payments for imports of intermediate goods).

This contrasts sharply with the situation faced by many host-country firms which, lacking market clout, know-how, and reputation, often experience great difficulty in penetrating export markets.

It is also worth noting that, by diversifying a host country's export range, 'efficiency-seeking' FDI may help to stabilize export earnings in the face of fluctuations in demand for individual products.

However, where FDI is designed to target local consumers ('market-seeking FDI'), the expectation is that the export performance (if, in fact, there are any exports) will be considerably weaker on average than is the case with efficiency-seekers. Market-seeking FDI may, however, replace imports so that its net impact on the current account is ambiguous. The only conclusion that is fairly certain is that it is unlikely to have as favourable an impact as efficiency-seeking FDI.

This having been said, it is necessary to recall the strikingly buoyant export performance of several Asian countries that have received substantial inflows of FDI. It is also relevant to note that somewhere in the region of one-third of world trade consists of intra-MNC trade (that is trade between the various affiliates comprising individual MNCs), and that MNCs account for around two-thirds of all world trade.

Tax take: the contribution to local fiscal revenue

The operations of MNCs themselves, and the increased levels of economic activity that they promote, should result in increased tax revenue for the host government. This benefit will, however, be reduced, or limited, to the extent that the host has offered inducements to incoming firms in the form of tax holidays, free or subsidized premises, or exemption from import tariffs, value-added tax, or other fiscal impositions. And some inducement schemes can be very generous. For example, according to the terms of an investment-promotion scheme in Belize (see Box 23.3), the inducements offered would appear to rule out virtually all possible fiscal benefits for the Belize Treasury resulting from the presence of incoming firms – beyond the personal taxes paid by its expatriate employees![7]

BOX 23.3 MANUFACTURING SITE: EXPORT PROCESSING ZONE (EPZ) IN BELIZE

One company in Belize offers assistance in setting up any kind of operation in tax-havens or incorporation of companies in just 24 hours. It explains that Belize's EPZ programme is intended to attract both local and foreign investment to boost production for export with a focus on manufactured goods and non-traditional agricultural products.

The benefits available to companies operating in an EPZ in Belize according to this company include:

- Full import and export duty exemptions
- Exemptions from capital gains tax, property and land taxes, excise, sales and consumption taxes, taxes on trade turnover, on foreign exchange and transfer tax
- Tax holiday of 20 years with an option to extend and deduct losses from profits following the tax-holiday period
- Dividend tax exemption in perpetuity
- Opportunity to open foreign-currency bank accounts in Belize and abroad
- Opportunity to sell, lease or transfer items, goods and services within an EPZ

---

[7] See www.diloffshore.com/

> - Customs inspection at the Zone for expediency
> - Work permits at no cost for all professional and technical staff
> - Exemption from the Supplies Control Act and its regulations
> - No import restrictions on raw materials
> - No import or export licensing requirement
> - No trade licences.
>
> *Source:* Dominion International Limited.

Moreover, many MNCs have the ability to move profits from one country to another by using 'transfer-pricing' on intra-company sales and purchases. Depending on the direction MNCs wish to shift their profits, this process involves the covert exporting of funds by selling exports to an affiliate at an artificially low price (or buying imports from an affiliate at an artificially high price), or importing funds by doing the opposite (that is, under-paying for intra-firm imports or over-invoicing for intra-firm exports). Such a manoeuvre has the effect of shifting taxable profits from one affiliate to another and, if the latter is in a low-tax jurisdiction, of reducing, perhaps very substantially, the amount of tax payable by the company.

Examples of falsely priced export items have included such outlandish 'bargain' items as bulldozers priced at US$527.94 each and forklift trucks priced at US$384.14, while over-priced imports include electric torches at US$5000 each and toothbrushes at US$5655 each. The study featuring these clearly false prices concluded that transfer-pricing by MNCs cost the US Treasury around US$53.1 billion in 2001 alone (Pak and Zdanowicz, 2002). A second study, commissioned by the US Internal Revenue Service, estimates that, for 686 MNCs found to have been shifting income out of the USA by transfer-pricing, the declared average rate of return on overseas assets was 11.3 per cent against only 2.4 per cent on US assets, implying a shifting overseas of US$62 billion of pre-tax income (Christian and Schultz, 2005). Other estimates put the total losses to the US Treasury as high as US$200 billion per year. Clearly, developing countries are likely to be at least as vulnerable as the US to such manoeuvres.

Environmental impacts

The debate over the environmental impact of FDI in developing countries has focused on three possibilities. The first is the capacity multinationality gives to a firm to *shift any environmental problems* associated with its processes from countries which are intolerant of such problems to countries – particularly developing countries – which tend to be more lenient in this respect because of their greater need for industrial development and their weaker regulatory capacity. Hence the claim that MNCs are engaged in a 'race to the bottom', that is, a race to move polluting industries, such as paper-making and production of certain chemicals, to countries where environmental legislation is least restrictive or effective and where, for this reason, they will do most damage. The more rapid the expansion of FDI in the developing world, the worse the problem will be.

A second observation is that, independently of the consideration discussed above, a considerable slice of FDI in developing countries happens to be in industries which are inherently pollution-intensive, in particular, mining and petroleum extraction. Once again, the local capacity to deal with the problem is very likely to be deficient.

Third, a contrary view sees MNCs' operations in developing countries as likely to be *less* polluting than the activities of local firms. The perception here is that local firms are unlikely to have the technical know-how, or the funds, required to deal with the environmental problems they create, whereas branches of MNCs do have these capacities and, at the same time, have the added incentive of wishing to be seen as 'good citizens'.

As with most of the issues covered in a critique of MNCs' operations in developing countries, this one cannot be settled on the basis of *a priori* argument alone. Whether or not MNCs are 'cleaner' than local firms (and, if so, where? in which industries? and to what extent?) are empirical matters requiring recourse to the facts of individual cases. As yet, conclusive evidence is not available.

Socio-economic effects

Except for extreme cases where incoming MNCs simply replace local competitors and buy nothing from local firms, it seems likely that their advent will lead to an increase in *employment* in the host economy, and there is considerable evidence to the effect that this is usually the case. Further, *wage-rates* paid by MNCs tend to be higher for any given skill level than those paid by local firms (an obvious benefit to those receiving these higher rates, but possibly leading to the draining of better-quality labour away from local firms to the MNCs, which are in a position to 'cherry-pick' the best candidates for employment, and to the creation of a new, narrowly based labour 'elite'). An additional benefit to local employees of the multinational nature of their employer is the possibility of work overseas in other affiliates of the parent firm and *broader career-development prospects* generally.

Reflecting the practices prevalent in their home economies, *working conditions* in MNC branches operating in developing countries are generally found to be superior to those in competing local firms, and MNCs are much less likely than local firms to be involved in *undesirable employment practices* such as the use of child labour.

Insofar as MNCs tend to locate in cities (and, with the obvious exception of firms in extractive or plantation industries, whose locations are dictated by resource availability, there *is* a tendency for MNCs to cluster in the largest towns in developing countries), this may tend to *reinforce pressures created by urbanization* (discussed in detail in Chapter 14) and *increase the disparity between rural and urban incomes*.

It has also been suggested that the nature of the goods produced by some MNCs may encourage 'undesirable', or *'inappropriate', patterns of consumption* with non-traditional sophisticated consumer goods and 'consumerism' replacing the earlier culture which emphasized healthier food and home-grown products.

Political effects

Host governments, and in some cases segments of local populations in developing countries, are often uneasy about the presence of foreign firms on their territory. The main concerns, some valid, some largely imagined, relate to possible infringements of sovereignty, and encouragement by MNCs of malpractice by local officials and legislators. They may be summarized as follows:

- *MNCs may possess considerable bargaining power.* Governments may find foreign-owned firms to be more difficult to influence than domestic firms. Size and sophistication often bring with them enhanced bargaining power vis-à-vis domestic legislators (and firms) due to a combination of superior legal, managerial and economic capacity. This is especially so where smaller countries are concerned, given that much FDI comes from

MNCs which are 'larger' (in terms of total output) than many of these countries. Moreover, most MNCs possess the ultimate capacity to escape the attentions and legislation of host governments altogether by simply leaving the country.

- *MNCs 'above the law'.* Some MNCs can put themselves, in effect, above the law by using their ability to render the detail of their operations non-transparent through transfer-pricing, working through tax-havens and other devices that make it impossible for relatively poorly resourced local Revenue departments to unravel exactly what is going on. Furthermore, use of their considerable political or financial influence to bend or by-pass local laws and to encourage corruption amongst legislators is not unknown.

- *Extraterritoriality.* Governments of MNCs' *home* countries may attempt to impose their domestic legislation on the overseas subsidiaries (with regard to accounting practices, remittance practices, or labour-relations codes on working conditions, health and safety, child labour, and so on) a practice often seen as intrusive and unacceptable by host-country legislators.

- *Anti-capitalist sentiment.* In the early post-colonial, 'pre-globalization' era – say from the 1960s to the 1980s – the prevalent political bias in many developing countries was left-of-centre. Although FDI can be, and is, undertaken by state-owned enterprises, it is overwhelmingly a 'free-market' phenomenon. Given that MNCs are often viewed as standard bearers of capitalism *par excellence*, it is not surprising that, in the past, they were regularly treated with caution, even hostility, by developing-country governments. Such sentiments are much diminished in the new millennium, but have not entirely disappeared.

FDI and growth in developing countries

We have thus far considered a number of possible effects of FDI on host economies. We conclude this section by examining what is often considered, by both host countries and economists, to be the overarching issue: what is the impact of inward FDI on *growth rates* in host developing economies?

The short answer to this question is that experience is mixed. A large numbers of studies of a wide range of host countries have generated contradictory findings. In cases where FDI *is* accompanied by increased growth, establishing the direction of causation has often proved difficult. (Does FDI cause growth, or does growth attract FDI – or both?) Nevertheless, despite the ambiguity of its overall outcome, this research has led many analysts to a useful conclusion with important policy implications, aptly summarized as follows:

> Positive growth effects of FDI are anything but guaranteed. Rather, host country and industry characteristics as well as the interplay between both sets of characteristics have an important say on the growth impact of FDI in developing countries.
>
> *(Nunenkamp and Spatz, 2003)*

So what are these 'characteristics' that condition the impact of inward FDI on growth rates, and how do they affect the outcome? The results of a large number of studies may be boiled down into the following summary listing of influences.

Host-country characteristics

- *The quality of local labour.* A well-developed education system in the host country, providing an adequate supply of skilled labour enhances the positive impact of FDI by both improving the productivity of the MNC and increasing the 'absorptive capacity' of the local sector for positive spillovers into that sector;

■ *High levels of corruption, lack of protection of property rights, a generally weak system of law enforcement, and high levels of discretionary behaviour* by government officials all discourage inward FDI, reduce the efficiency and favourable impact of those MNCs that do invest, and make them less likely to deploy commercially valuable know-how in the host country because of the difficulty of protecting ownership of such know-how.

BOX 23.4 THE KEY TO AVOIDING CORRUPTION IN CHINA?

A consultancy firm currently operating in China says 'the law against commercial corruption there is rarely enforced and, when it is, prosecutions usually have additional motives'. It advises foreign firms to

start their operations from scratch and impose their ethical standards from day one. They also need to avoid hiring 'tribes' – groups of workers from the same region, or who speak the same dialect. Such groups are known to move systematically between businesses, especially foreign ones. Training is important too, as are regular audits. But even though there is a growing push for a clampdown, the resistance to change is strong. *Fu ze ren bu zai*, 'the man with the key is not here', is a common way of asking for a bribe. Alas, the man with the key to solving China's corruption problem is nowhere to be found either.

Source: Based, with quotations, on an article in *Economist*, 4/8/2007, p. 55.

FDI characteristics

■ *The volatility of FDI inflows.* The more variable the size of inflows from year to year the less favourable the impact;

■ *'Efficiency-seeking' FDI*, which is motivated by the desire to use cheap local inputs in order to reduce the MNC's production costs, is more likely to bring with it technology that is appropriate to the host's level of development, and this in turn increases the potential for beneficial spillovers into the local economy. *Market-seeking FDI*, which is aimed at supplying local consumers in host countries rather than reducing the production costs of the particular processes transferred to the host country, may not have this favourable characteristic. Moreover, since market-seeking FDI does not generate export earnings whereas efficiency-seeking FDI does, the latter is likely to have a more beneficial long-run impact on the host's balance of payments;

■ *Resource-seeking MNCs* (for example mining companies) will often be found in enclaves with few backward or forward linkages to the local economy. However, where resource-seeking MNCs find it necessary to develop, at their own expense, local infrastructure in remote areas in order to service their labour force (residential, medical and educational facilities) or to facilitate production and transportation (utilities and roads), this will represent a benefit to the host economy.

■ Where *incoming firms' investment is heavily 'leveraged'* (in the sense that the MNC has borrowed a significant part of its capital locally) the growth-promoting gains from that investment will not be as large as in cases where all funds are imported, since the borrowed funds are no longer available for investment by local firms.

- *FDI is found to have a greater impact than PFI* on overall levels of investment (and hence, very probably, on growth) in the host country. A broadly based study of recipients of both forms of investment found that, whereas a $1 inflow of FDI typically induced a rise of a further $1 in domestic investment, an inflow of PFI had no detectable impact on local investment (Bosworth and Collins, 1999).

Interactive factors

- *Openness to trade* on the part of the host country. The increasingly complex global integration strategies pursued by many 'efficiency-seeking' MNCs, such that their production processes are split up over several countries, are facilitated by freedom from barriers to trade in intermediate goods between countries. Thus FDI will have a greater favourable impact the more 'open' the host economy.

- *The greater the gap between the technology transferred* by the MNC and the technology 'typical' of the host country, the smaller the favourable impact on the host because of the increased difficulty of transferring technology to local competitors, suppliers and customers.

- The *competitive power of the MNC* in local markets. Where incoming firms destroy local competition the growth effects of FDI are reduced. Where they stimulate local competition, growth effects are increased. The former is more likely with market-seeking FDI than with efficiency-seeking FDI, since market-seeking firms are likely to be in direct competition with local firms whereas efficiency-seekers rarely will be.

FDI from developing countries[8]

Developing countries are emerging as a significant source of FDI. According to UNCTAD, in 2006, of around 77 000 MNCs worldwide (with over 770 000 foreign affiliates) some 19 000 originated in developing countries. The bulk of the parent companies based in the developing world were located in East Asia (Korea had 7500 and China 3500) with a further 2000 each in Latin America and the Caribbean, and in West Asia. Africa had around 750 and South Asia and South-East Asia had fewer than 1000 between them. Developing countries in Oceania had only 15.

The flow of investment from these countries is accelerating rapidly. In 2002 the figure was $16 billion; by 2006 this had climbed to over $40 billion (with around one-third going to other developing countries). The outward FDI stock belonging to developing nations increased from $72 billion in 1980 to $149 billion in 1990, and to over $1 trillion in 2005, and the number of developing countries with outward FDI stocks exceeding US$5 billion rose from only six in 1990 to 25 in 2005. In the latter year developing countries accounted for some 17 per cent of world outflows of FDI. The major growth area in the recent past has been outflows from China, India, Brazil and West Asia, fuelled by petrodollars, higher prices and, in China's case in particular, increased demand for commodities and rapid domestic economic growth. A number of MNCs based in developing countries have become major international companies, and FDI from these is now a significant part of investment inflows into other developing countries.

Since large FDI flows between developing countries are a relatively recent phenomenon, a definitive critique of their effects is not yet available. But the impact seems likely to be

---

[8] The main source of material for this section is UNCTAD (2007b).

similar to that of FDI originating in developed countries. However, certain distinctive features may be expected to emerge with regard to the impact on both source and host countries (see below).

Implications for source developing countries

■ *Investing abroad will present some developing source countries with the opportunity for firms to enter new markets* thus diversifying their customer base, perhaps to the point at which they become global players (as some Asian firms have already done).

■ *Becoming MNCs may push firms into providing enhanced transparency over their domestic corporate activities* because tougher overseas requirements in this area spill over into the domestic context.

■ *Investing abroad, especially in developing countries, will provide opportunities for 'strategic-asset-seeking' firms* (especially through the mergers and acquisitions (M&A) form of FDI) *to acquire assets* such as special skills, know-how, technology, R&D facilities, brand names, and distribution networks. This will facilitate 'leap-frogging' and moving up the 'value chain' for such developing-country firms;

■ *Enhanced linkages and spillovers* from the investing firms will be available to non-MNCs in source developing countries.

■ *Increased pressure may develop to restructure domestic industries* because of moves by local MNCs (as part of a strategy permitted by their international status) to alter the composition of their domestic output, employment and exports, and to redeploy resources released from low-value-added activities.

■ The capacity to invest abroad may be used by some firms to create channels for *capital flight*.

■ A programme of foreign investment originating in a developing country *may reduce domestic investment*. However, such evidence as is available suggests that, while FDI has the *initial* effect of reducing gross domestic capital formation, this will be followed by a revival to a level at least as high as the initial one. This was experienced by Singapore, where the revival of domestic investment commenced around two years after the initial outflow of funds (Wu *et al.*, 2003). Of course, if MNCs have a preference for taking up new investment opportunities overseas to the exclusion of new investment at home, a clear conflict between the interests of the firm and the source country is created.

■ *Jobs may be lost*, at least during a transition period, if outward investment results in major restructuring of the parent firms. Permanent 'hollowing out' of parts of the economy, due to the exporting of manufacturing capability to overseas subsidiaries, may lead to the permanent loss of demand for certain skills, especially in the more advanced developing countries.

■ *Fiscal revenue may be lost* if the FDI leaves the developing countries simply in order to reduce corporation-tax bills. For instance, UNCTAD has estimated that around two-thirds of Brazil's US$53 billion stock of outward FDI has been carried out for this reason, being focused on the Cayman Islands and the British Virgin Islands – both tax-havens. While this practice may have advantages for the firms concerned, it is obviously costly from the point of view of the source nation as a whole.

Implications for host developing countries

It is also possible to point to some distinctive effects on host countries of the flow of FDI from developing countries to other developing countries:

- It has been suggested that FDI from developing countries will, because of the similar 'industrial distribution of developing country FDI and the technological attributes of *developing country MNCs*', be able '*to interact more effectively with domestic firms in host developing economies* than [would] affiliates . . . from developed countries' (UNCTAD, 2006, p. 196). One specific manifestation of such benefits might be a tendency for technologies transferred from a developing country to be 'more appropriate' than if the source country were much wealthier than the host country (Aykut and Ratha, 2004).

  However, similarity of industrial structures can cut both ways. Whereas 'market-seeking' FDI from developed countries will, in some cases, introduce new products, so that there is no direct competition with local firms, this is much less likely with FDI from developing countries, with the result that *local firms, no longer protected by import tariffs and non-tariff barriers, can expect to be exposed to much more serious, possibly fatal, competition* from such incoming investment.

- Again, it is by no means clear that MNCs from developing countries are always paragons of environmental virtue when operating in other developing countries. It is not unknown for such firms to be criticized for insensitive exploitation – and over-exploitation – of natural resources. *Developing-country MNCs are less subject to pressure from 'green' organizations back home than are developed-country firms*, which often operate in the full glare of the environmental spotlight.

BOX 23.5 WHAT IS AN ARGENTINIAN COMPANY?

The large firm Bunge and Born (now Bunge) is often held to be one of Argentina's first home-grown MNCs. But is Bunge Argentinian? A brief history of the firm provided by the OECD indicates how modern patterns of corporate evolution can make identification of 'nationality' very difficult. 'The company was founded in Holland in 1818, soon after which it moved to Belgium and then Argentina. It was in Argentina that it really expanded, becoming one of the world's leading marketers of agricultural commodities. In the 1970s the company moved again because of political instability, this time to Brazil. By the following decade, Bunge and Born had diversified into numerous activities up and down the food production chain throughout the American continent. In 1999, after undergoing a deep restructuring and refocusing on its core business (agriculture), the company changed "nationality" yet again and set up its headquarters in New York . . . where [as] Bunge [it] began to trade its shares on the stock exchange in 2001.'

Bunge continues to be involved in FDI. But is it an Argentinian – or an American – MNC?

Source: Hans Christiansen (2007), *Trends and Recent Developments in Foreign Direct Investment*, OECD, Paris.

Cross-border mergers and acquisitions:

Cross-border mergers and acquisitions (M&A) are an increasingly significant component of FDI. As the figures in Table 23.5 show, the total value of such transactions worldwide, standing at $150.6 billion in 1990, more than doubled between 1990 and 2004, with particularly rapid acceleration post-1999, and grew by a massive 88 per cent between 2004 and 2006. Over that period M&A accounted for a large part of the total increase in global FDI. The developing-country component expanded by a factor of five over 1990–2004 and, in 2004, was equivalent to 35.1 per cent of outward FDI coming from developing countries.

Year	1990	2004	2006
World	**150.6**	**380.6**	**716**
By Developed Countries	*143.1*	*339.8*	
By Developing Countries**	*7.2*	*39.8*	
Africa	*0.1*	*2.7*	
Latin Am. & Caribbean	*1.6*	*16.5*	
West Asia	*2.1*	*1.3*	
South Asia	*	*0.9*	
East Asia	*2.7*	*5.2*	
South-East Asia	*0.6*	*13.2*	
Oceania	*	*	

TABLE 23.5 Cross-border mergers and acquisitions – purchases of assets 1990, 2004 and 2006 (US$ billions)
* negligible.
** Full particulars of membership of developing-country groupings are given in Table 23.10.
Source: UNCTAD (2007b) and *FDI On-line*.

Insofar as no new physical assets are created by cross-border M&A deals, whereas 'real' MNCs invest in new 'green-field' factories, their inclusion in FDI data exaggerates the immediate significance of inward foreign investment for levels of economic activity. It is believed, however, that a significant proportion of such deals are carried out with a view to building on the industrial base acquired through the share purchase, so their long-run impact on output should be positive.

Less certain is the long-run impact on the M&A scene of large-scale participation by US-based and UK-based collective-investment funds – mainly private-equity and hedge funds. UNCTAD has guesstimated that, in 2005, private-equity firms acquired around US$13.5 billion in developing-country assets, making them serious players on the development-finance scene. (In comparison, the World Bank, in the same year, disbursed a total of US$22.3 billion in loans). Private-equity firms, usually focusing on existing firms which are underperforming, generally hold their shares for 5–6 years, which is longer than typical portfolio investors but not long enough to be seen as typical 'direct' investors.

The implications of this new initiative are hard to predict. On the one hand, there is concern that the intervention of private-equity firms in developing-country economies may simply result in asset-stripping or the radical reorientation (probably downsizing) of firms in ways not necessarily compatible with development priorities. On the other, the private-equity firms themselves emphasize their overriding interest in putting ailing firms back on a sound commercial footing (so averting possible closure). They suggest, too, that where host-country governments are currently resisting deregulating industry and liberalizing their economies, the prospect of the rapid withdrawal of private-equity capital may act as a 'useful corrective'.

BOX 23.6 PRIVATE EQUITY INVESTORS: ASSET STRIPPERS – OR DEVELOPMENT TYCOONS?

Private equity investors 'are certainly unabashed about their motives. It's profits, pure and simple . . . For 60 years and more development economists have lurched from one fad to another in their attempts to allocate billions upon billions of dollars of development aid. The result has been little noticeable development . . . a steady supply of "bridges to nowhere". In contrast . . . private equity firms have the expertise, not to mention the incentives, to identify genuine opportunities for productive investment . . . Nor do they make their profits in isolation – they do so largely by increasing the productivity of the firms in which they invest, which has the knock-on effect of improving life for the workers.'

Source: Based on Joseph Sternberg, 'Crowding out the UN', *New York Sun*, 1/10/2006.

There is also concern that a significant proportion of M&A inflows of FDI may be the result of 'fire sales'. These are deals in which failing local firms subjected to severe liquidity constraints during a financial crisis (usually exacerbated by portfolio and debt outflows) are sold off cheaply to foreign investors. Striking examples of such disadvantageous deals were evident during the Asian financial crisis in the late 1990s. With both the Korean currency and the Korean stock market in free fall and capital flight rampant, the price for which many local firms could be bought by foreign buyers fell dramatically. Thus, Korean Airlines, which operated over 100 aircraft, was valued by the market at only US$240 million (net), equivalent to the cost of just two jumbo jets. Given the unfavourable terms on which such 'fire-sale' transactions are carried out, such FDI inflows are likely to be harmful to the host country.

Finally, it is appropriate to mention in the present context the emergence in 2007 of *sovereign-wealth funds (SWFs)*. These are funds set up by governments, many of them in developing countries, which judge that the value of their foreign-exchange reserves, accumulated as a result of their success in expanding exports, far exceeds the level required to maintain their present exchange rates. Most of these 'surplus' funds have traditionally been invested in very liquid, low-risk, securities such as US government bonds. This practice has, however, created two problems. First, low-risk assets usually earn a low rate of return. Second, excessive concentration of reserves in assets denominated in one, or a small number of, currencies creates a situation in which a sizable sell-off of these assets could seriously depress the currency in which they are denominated, usually the US$, so significantly reducing the proceeds from the sales. Consequently, a number of countries, notably China, India and Singapore, are channelling reserves into SWFs. The bulk of initial operations were of a PFI kind but it is likely that many SWFs will follow the lead of Singapore's state investment company, Temasek – which has purchased a Thai telecommunications group as well as stakes in two banks in China – and move beyond purchasing minority shareholdings to acquiring existing firms.

The funds available to some SWFs, especially those in China and India, are sufficiently large to enable them to acquire large stakes in foreign companies. Where these are seen as having strategic importance in economic or political terms, such as the proposed Indian multi-billion fund for investment in overseas energy operations, this could trigger serious concern in target countries about this new form of FDI.

WTO ambitions with regard to FDI

The World Trade Organization [WTO] seeks to extend the deregulation of foreign direct investment well beyond the present position. Its ultimate aim is to bring about a situation in any given country in which foreign and local firms are treated virtually identically. With a few exceptions (for instance, key national defence industries) host governments would be obliged to accord 'national treatment' to incoming firms across not just manufacturing industries, but also in the much more contentious area of core service industries such as banking, insurance, health, education, transport, telecommunications and retailing. A move of this kind would appear to promise greatly reduced risk for MNCs and hence lead to a significant, sustained increase in FDI. However, many developing countries oppose this massive extension of the range of industries open to outside firms, not least because, in many cases, local firms are just becoming established in these industries, are not yet equipped to take on the international giants, and would probably fare badly if exposed prematurely to competition from incoming MNCs. Additionally, in some countries the government has a sizable stake in what can be highly profitable service activities and does not wish to relinquish this source of revenue. And, of course, the loss of local control over an important sector of the local economy, and the associated curtailing of sovereignty, is unpopular with many politicians and private citizens.

Outsourcing by 'offshoring'

Starting in the early 1990s, MNCs began to 'outsource' service functions to 'offshore' (overseas) locations in developing countries. Rapid technical improvements and cost reductions in global telecommunications services have made it possible to carry out a widening range of tasks at arm's length. In particular, the outputs of paper-based, back-office activities (ticketing, bill preparation, and so on) are often capable of being digitalized and communicated electronically where the appropriate computing skills are available, India being the location of choice thus far. Furthermore, numerous MNCs have located software development in India either in subsidiaries set up for the purpose or, increasingly, in joint ventures with locally owned firms.

At a somewhat more prosaic level, straightforward telephone enquiries to businesses located in developed countries can be cheaply re-routed to call-centres overseas. Demand for such services is predominantly English-speaking, from the UK and the US. This again favours operators located in India which has a large population of English speakers. (Around 80 per cent of the two million students graduating every year from colleges in India speak English.)

As well as reducing costs (Indian wage rates being as low as 10 per cent of call-centre rates in the UK) offshoring often adds a new dimension to MNC activities by creating networks of firms which are open for business, round the globe, 24 hours a day.

These moves are presumably good for MNC profits and work both to increase employment and (possibly) wage rates in India. Some commentators have maintained that *both* source *and* host countries are likely to gain from the process. A study carried out by the McKinsey Global Institute sees offshoring as creating only 'winners'. When to the savings accruing to the MNC are added additional profits earned in the overseas operation (and remitted to the US), entrained exports from the US to subsidiaries in India, and output of redeployed workers in the US, it seems that 'Everyone's a winner'. The calculation set out in Table 23.6 suggests that every $1 spent on offshoring by US firms in 2002 resulted in benefits to the US of $0.71–$1.14, and benefits to India of $0.33.

US		INDIA	
Savings accruing to US investors/customers	$0.58	Labour	$0.10
Imports of US goods and services by providers in India	$0.05	Profits retained in India	$0.10
Transfer of profits by US-based providers in India to US	$0.04	Suppliers	$0.09
Net direct benefit retained in US [sub-total]	*$0.67*	Central Government taxes	$0.03
Value from US labour re-employed	$0.04–$0.47	State Government taxes	$0.01
Potential net benefit to US	**$0.71–$1.14**	**Net Benefit to India**	**$0.33**

TABLE 23.6 'Everyone's a winner': benefit per $1 of US spending offshore in India in 2002
Source: 'Offshoring: is it a win-win game?', McKinsey Global Institute, San Francisco, 2003.

This optimistic finding has been reinforced by the conclusions of a study by Klein (2004) which sees offshoring of IT software and services activities by US MNCs as likely to generate cost savings, additional profits and improved productivity in US-based operations, with resultant favourable impacts on real GDP, real wages and employment in the US.

However, these findings do not go unchallenged. There is considerable dispute as to the long-term impact on source countries of international migration of jobs resulting from relocations through offshoring (together with relocations carried out for other reasons). Indeed, relocation of jobs to developing countries is held to be an important cause of the 'hollowing out' of industry in developed countries and of the 'jobless recoveries' from recessions there. One particularly striking forecast (Blinder, 2007) sees between 35 and 40 million American jobs as vulnerable to displacement by workers in India who provide the same service or product electronically. 'I believe this phenomenon is going to be the most important issue at the intersection of economics and politics for the next generation.'

Policies on FDI

Policy options for host countries

Despite the risks attached to encouraging inward flows of FDI, a large majority of developing-country administrations feel that this is the path to follow. What policy measures seem most likely to enable them to achieve the end of increasing inward direct foreign investment? And what factors make potential investors prefer one developing country to another?

Our earlier discussion suggests that the central thrust of policy should be the creation of a *supportive business environment*. This involves removing obstructive and unnecessary regulation of FDI (and of business in general); reinforcing the domestic economy (in order to bolster its capacity to provide inputs for the foreign-owned sector and provide a more dynamic market for the output of market-seeking FDI); and improving the quality of governance. Specific initiatives in these three directions might include:

- Improving the skill levels of the labour force; facilitating provision of better, and better access to, primary, secondary, and tertiary education;
- Upgrading physical infrastructure: providing reliable, well-developed, transport systems, public utilities, and telecommunications;
- Opening up, to some degree, certain 'closed' or highly regulated fields, in particular service activities such as banking, insurance, telecommunications, retailing and healthcare;
- Removing the more restrictive controls on the free movement, in and out, of capital;
- Continuing the process of liberalizing trading regimes. In most developing countries import tariffs are now fairly low, but non-tariff barriers often remain a major restraint on trade in many countries;
- Combating local corruption;
- Upgrading 'soft infrastructure' – laws, institutions and financial markets;
- Reinforcing and broadening legal support for business activity especially in the commercial sphere;

- Removing, as far as practicable and prudent, legal, administrative and regulatory barriers to enterprise activity, and actively fostering competition in the marketplace;
- Providing long-term stability and predictability in legislation affecting foreign investors and reducing the complexity of such legislation;
- Assuring protection of property rights, including intellectual property;
- Assuring enforcement of contract (India is criticized in this respect; the law's delay there has resulted in a backlog of some 26 million cases);
- Providing long-term macroeconomic stability (as the 'condition of the host economy' is likely to be an important factor for potential investors).

Consideration might also be given to providing tariff and non-tariff *incentives*, including direct assistance to incoming firms by exempting them from corporation taxation and providing tax-free industrial zones. However, most of the evidence on such special deals suggests that MNCs are frequently concerned that they may prove to be transient, and prefer that similar trade and tax treatment be accorded to all investors, foreign and domestic.

A relatively novel means of increasing inward FDI is by encouraging nationals (or their descendants) who have moved abroad to invest in the 'old country'. For larger countries that have experienced significant emigration, this may be a potentially important source of funds. Thus the boom in investment in China was kick-started by investment by ethnic Chinese living in South-East Asia. Indeed, between 1985 and 1996, around two-thirds of inward investment into China, much of it FDI, came from this source. Keeping in touch with such potential sources of finance, through Chambers of Commerce, overseas commercial missions, and the like, can yield long-term benefits.

Again, some developing countries may be able to attract inward FDI by capitalizing on cultural and language affinities stemming from former colonial links. Thus, African countries may have an advantage in this respect for interesting firms from the UK and France in investing, and Latin American countries may have a similar advantage in dealing with Spanish MNCs.

Last, there is scope for encouraging further expansion of *bilateral investment treaties* (BITs). Such treaties establish, on a reciprocal basis, the terms and conditions under which MNCs will operate in pairs of countries. Typically, they include guarantees of 'fair and equitable treatment', protection from expropriation, and unrestricted international transfer of funds – backed up by a dispute-resolution mechanism (which usually provides for international arbitration under the aegis of the International Center for the Resolution of Investment Disputes).

Policy actions on FDI by host developing countries

Regulating incoming direct foreign investment

Since the early 1990s many developing countries have made major unilateral efforts to attract FDI by altering their regulatory systems. UNCTAD publishes an annual summary of changes in regulatory policies, dividing them into 'favourable' and 'unfavourable' measures. As Table 23.7 shows, the tide of regulation, as measured by the *absolute* number of measures annually, has been flowing strongly in the 'favourable' direction (though the picture is clouded somewhat by a steady increase in the *proportion* of new measures unfavourable to FDI). The most popular forms of 'favourable' measures in the years 1992 to

YEAR	Countries Changing FDI Rules (number)	Rule Changes (number)	Changes Favourable to FDI (number)	Changes Unfavourable to FDI (number)
1992	43	77	77	0
1993	57	100	99	1
1994	49	110	108	2
1995	64	112	106	6
1996	65	114	98	16
1997	76	150	134	16
1998	60	145	136	9
1999	63	139	130	9
2000	69	150	147	3
2001	71	207	193	14
2002	70	246	234	12
2003	82	242	218	24
2004	102	270	234	36
2005	93	205	164	41

TABLE 23.7 Changes in rules on FDI, 1992–2005
Source: UNCTAD (2006) Table I.11.

2005 were reductions in corporate tax rates, liberalization of FDI access to sectors hitherto reserved for local firms (notably in service activities) and simplification of FDI-approval procedures. The growing numbers of changes unfavourable to FDI were largely concentrated in natural-resource sectors, often involving preferential treatment of domestic firms and restrictions on extraction volumes available to MNCs.

Entering into investment and taxation treaties

Developing countries have also sought to increase their attractiveness to MNCs by entering into BITs with other countries. In addition, the number of double-taxation treaties (DTTs), which co-ordinate tax treatment of MNCs across source and host countries, has also been expanding rapidly. By the end of 2005 no fewer than 2495 BITs and 2785 DTTs were in place worldwide, developing countries being involved in around 75 per cent of the former and 58 per cent of the latter; BITs between developing countries numbered 644 and DTTs between developing countries 399. Table 23.8 summarizes the regional structure of participation in such agreements.

The proliferation of these international agreements is, in principle, an important contribution to improving the investment climate and encouraging the expansion of FDI. However, the growing complexity of the web of treaties creates problems for policy-makers seeking to draft, analyse and implement a transparent set of rules which is internally and internationally consistent and which can be overseen by the often under-resourced legal and negotiating staff available in many developing countries. The potential for building in 'incoherence' is considerable, as is made clear in Box 23.7.

Region	Bilateral Investment Treaties		Double Taxation Treaties	
	Countries (number)	Total Treaties	Countries (number)	Total Treaties
Asia and Oceania***	31	1003	36	968
Latin America and Caribbean***	13	464	9	322
Africa***	21	660	17	436
South-East Europe and CIS***	15	671	27	576
Developed Countries	45	1511	38	2111
Developing Countries	60	1878	53	1604
Least Developed Countries	16	399	5	184
Between Developing Countries	20	644	25	399

TABLE 23.8 Regional structure of BITs* and DITs** at end 2005
* Bilateral Investment Treaties. ** Double Taxation Treaties. *** Developing countries only.
Source: UNCTAD (2006) Table I.12.

BOX 23.7 INCOHERENCE AND INTERNATIONAL INVESTMENT AGREEMENTS

The expansion of the network of international investment agreements (IIAs) has given rise to various forms of *potential incoherence* between different agreements. For example:

- While most BITs leave it to the discretion of the host country to decide whether, and how, foreign investment should be admitted, free-trade-area rules often include establishment rights for foreign investors – so cutting across, and possibly conflicting with, the terms of IIAs.

- Different modes of investment liberalization in IIAs may affect coherence. For instance, regional economic integration agreements (such as the North American Free Trade Agreement (NAFTA)) may establish *up-front* liberalization, whereas the multilateral General Agreement on Trade in Services (GATS) provides for *gradual* market access. As a result, the degree of liberalization may be unclear for an economic activity covered by both agreements in the same host country.

- The Energy Charter Treaty includes an exception clause concerning the protection of the essential security interests of contracting parties. Many BITs do not contain similar provisions.

There may also be cases of *unintended incoherence* between treaties. For instance, the Most Favoured Nation (MFN) clause may, against the intention of a contracting party, incorporate into the IIA containing this clause certain procedural or substantive rights from other IIAs. Another example is the so-called 'umbrella' clause, which extends the protection of the IIA to 'any other obligation' of the contracting parties in respect of an investment. As a result, a breach by a host country of such other obligations (e.g. one

▶ deriving from a contract with a foreign investor) may be a violation of the IIA, and the latter's dispute settlement mechanism applies – an outcome that may not be desired by a contracting party to the IIA. The risk of incoherence is especially high for developing countries that lack expertise and bargaining power.

Source: Adapted from UNCTAD (2006), Box 1.7.

Policy options for source countries

The impact of these policies on flows of inward FDI will be reinforced if conditions in *source* countries favour increased outflows of direct investment. In particular, source-country firms are likely to invest more in overseas production when macroeconomic growth rates in the source country are high, interest rates low, and corporate profitability high. It is, however, unlikely that source-country economic policies will be designed specifically to favour these outcomes *in order to bring about* an increase in outflows of FDI – since this is rarely a priority in itself.

Summary conclusions

- Foreign direct investment makes an important contribution to capital formation in many developing countries. Flows of FDI to the developing world in nominal terms (current prices) grew by a factor of nearly one hundred between 1970 and 2006, pushing up the overall share of investment financed in this way from 4.7 per cent to 13.8 per cent.

- Given that most developing countries now seek to attract FDI, an understanding of the motives driving foreign investment is important for policy formulation.

- Possession of some monopoly advantage which can be exploited by becoming involved in foreign investment is usually seen as a necessary condition for a firm's going multinational.

- However, it is by no means a sufficient condition. Firms may well be deterred from investing if the business environment in a potential host country is rendered uncongenial to enterprise activity by, for instance, excessive bureaucratic interference, over-regulation (especially of financial flows), inadequate legal support for investors, or weak or corrupt government. These problems remain an important impediment to FDI in many countries, especially low-income countries.

- FDI has the potential to confer major benefits on host economies. It can constitute an important source of funds for countries with inadequate domestic savings. It may bring with it a 'package' of technical know-how, skills and commercial dynamism which can directly increase overall productivity, output, employment and incomes (with consequential increases in fiscal revenues) and which can trigger improvements in the efficiency of the domestic sector by 'diffusion' of know-how and skills through training of indigenous labour, through the growth of commercial linkages and 'spillovers', and

▶

through the creation of a more vigorous commercial business climate. It may also have a favourable impact on the balance of payments via the capital inflows required to finance the setting up and expansion of production facilities and, in the case of 'efficiency-seeking' firms, through expanded exports.

- However, these benefits may fail to materialize if incoming firms finance their activities through local borrowing and crowd out indigenous firms, drive local competitors out of business, introduce capital-intensive technologies which destroy jobs rather than creating them, or avoid contributing to local tax revenues by indulging in transfer-pricing or by taking advantage of major fiscal concessions. Problems may also arise if MNCs are 'footloose' rather than committed to remaining in the host economy, or are insensitive to local attitudes to environmental, social or political matters.

- The overall balance of these pros and cons may be positive or negative, depending on the circumstances of individual firms and countries. The evidence on the overall impact of FDI on growth rates is mixed.

- What is clear, however, is that for most developing countries FDI offers significant attractions provided that appropriate and effective policies can be put in place which create a business environment congenial to incoming firms and provide adequate protection against the costs that can be inflicted on vulnerable host economies by the multinational giants.

- The foregoing paragraphs reflect preoccupations which go back to the early days of the debate on FDI. The new millennium has seen important new considerations emerge which seem certain to add to the complexity of the debate on the balance of costs and benefits associated with FDI, and on policies towards it. Prominent amongst these are the following:

1 *The rapid growth of MNCs originating in developing countries.* (Will they behave in the same way, and have the same impact on host developing countries, as 'traditional' MNCs? Or will wholly new effects emerge?)

2 *The burgeoning of cross-border mergers and acquisitions by private-equity and hedge funds and, probably, by sovereign-wealth funds.* (Will these improve efficiency, or lead to asset stripping, or, in the case of SWFs, to increased concerns over infringement of sovereignty in host economies?)

3 *The deregulation of FDI being pushed by the WTO and its supporters.* (Will full 'national treatment' of FDI in developing countries come to pass and, if so, what are the likely economic, social and political implications for developing countries?)

4 *The dramatic acceleration in the 'offshoring' of developed-country jobs to developing countries by MNCs.* (Will this continue and, if so, with what consequences for host and source economies, and for developed-country policies on 'openness' in the international economy?)

A major concern over MNCs for their *source countries* is that their impact on host economies often extends far beyond purely commercial interactions; their presence can have important *political* effects. The *Economist* (6/02/04) quotes a leading commentator on international business as saying 'I love American brands, but they are losing friends around the world and it is vital to the interests of America to change this'; his survey of attitudes towards American MNCs in 17 countries 'told a by-now familiar story – America, and American business, was viewed as arrogant and indifferent toward others' cultures; exploitative, in that it extracted more than it provided; corrupting, in how it valued materialism above all else; and willing to sacrifice almost anything in an effort to generate profits'.

Questions for discussion

23.1 The World Trade Organization wishes to introduce rules banning host governments from discriminating in favour of local firms, and against incoming MNCs, in trade-related matters. What are the potential costs and benefits for developing countries of such a move?

23.2 What differences, if any, would you expect to find in the impact on host developing countries of FDI by, respectively, multinational corporations, sovereign wealth funds, and private equity firms?

23.3 What are the advantages, and the disadvantages, associated with financing industrialization in developing countries through, respectively, foreign direct investment (FDI) and portfolio foreign investment (PFI)?

23.4 What are the key differences between 'market-seeking' and 'efficiency-seeking' MNCs? In what ways are their respective impacts on host developing countries likely to differ?

23.5 Is inward FDI likely to increase growth rates in developing countries?

23.6 What policies might be recommended to a developing country seeking to attract FDI?

23.7 What are the main costs and benefits likely to arise from the 'offshoring' of jobs by MNCs?

Additional reading and web resources

Key reference works in this field are: UNCTAD, *World Investment Report* (annual) available at http://www.unctad.org/Templates/Page.asp?intItemID=1485&lang=1;UNCTAD (2007b); *Handbook of Statistics, 2006–7*, Geneva (at *UNCTAD Handbook of Statistics On-line*); UNCTAD, *Foreign Direct Investment Database*, Geneva (Annual);
UNCTAD, *Transnational Corporations* (Journal published by UNCTAD, Geneva, 3/annum); World Bank (2007c), *Global Development Finance: The Globalization of Corporate Finance in Developing Countries*, Washington, DC and http://www.worldbank.org/prospects; OECD (2000a).

Daniel Litvin (2004) *Empires of Profit: Commerce, Conquest and Corporate Responsibility*, South Western Educational Publishing.

A readable account of social and political reactions to incoming MNCs, and the complex problems faced by MNCs in framing responses to these reactions.

Christiensen, H. and Goldstein, A. (2007) *Trends and Recent Developments in Foreign Direct Investment*, OECD, Paris.

To help you grasp the key concepts of this chapter check out the extra resources posted on the Online Learning Centre at ***www.mcgraw-hill.co.uk/textbooks/huq***

Among other resources, the following appendix is available:

■ Appendix 23.1   Tables on foreign direct investment

CHAPTER 24

International Migration and Remittances

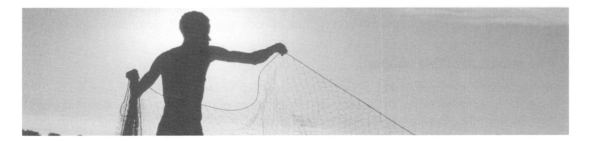

'Nearly 200 million people live outside their country of birth. Future pressure for international migration will be great . . . The major issues are how to adapt to large-scale international migration and improve its development impact'.

(World Bank)

Remittance flows to developing countries are now twice as large as total official development assistance. For some countries they are the main source of foreign exchange.

Introduction

Until recently, *internal* migration was the main focus of interest of economists studying migration and, surprising as it may now seem, 'International migration . . . was simply not a major policy issue' (Skeldon, 2003). However, in recent years, international migration has attracted increasing attention. This is, in part, because of the significant shift in the direction of such migration. Whereas in earlier times international migration was largely from, and to, relatively developed areas – for instance, Europeans migrating to the Americas – current flows are now very largely from developing countries to developed countries. Tightening immigration laws in the former 'settler' countries have been partly responsible for this change (by reducing emigration from other developed countries), as have falling fertility rates in Europe and associated declines in the growth rate of local labour forces (by increasing demand for immigrant labour from developing countries).

An important outcome of this change in migration patterns, from a development perspective, is the rapidly increasing magnitude of financial flows from migrants back to their countries of origin. These have become a major source of funding for both consumption and investment in these countries. The potential of migrants' remittances as a source of development finance is indicated by the facts that, by 2005, international migrants made up around 9 per cent of the population of developed countries and 3 per cent of the world's population – sufficient numbers, if assembled in one country, to make it the fifth most populous in the world (IOM, 2007). By that year, the level of annual remittances by workers to developing countries far exceeded that of development assistance ('aid'), and was equivalent to nearly 80 per cent of the level of inward direct investment (FDI) into the developing world.

The earlier 'under-researching' of international migration is in part attributable, according to the World Bank, to 'political sensitivities and lack of reliable statistics'. The Bank itself is in large measure responsible for the vastly improved flows of data and research findings on the phenomenon in recent years – a response to its belief that international migration has enormous implications for growth and welfare in both 'source' and 'destination' countries.

The structure of this chapter

In this chapter we first examine in detail the *magnitude* of international migration flows from developing countries, the sources and destinations of migrants, and the size of migrant 'stocks' in host countries. We then investigate possible *motives* for international migration; beginning with 'traditional' 'push' and 'pull' explanations, we move on to consider the possible role of family-income-diversification strategies, and conclude by outlining a 'stages' theory of migration rooted in the dynamics of the development process itself. Last, the *impact* of international migration – benefits and costs – on the source and host countries, and on the migrants themselves, is assessed, some possible orders of magnitude being derived from the results of a general equilibrium analytical exercise.

BOX 24.1 A MIGRATION AND REMITTANCE TOOLKIT

Mode 4. The international migration of labour ('natural persons') in order to work abroad is seen by the WTO, under the General Agreement on Trade in Services (the GATS) as one of four ways ('modes') in which services may be exported. The other modes are *cross-border supply* (where the supplier remains at home and exports the service, usually by mail or electronically – e.g. international banking services), *consumption abroad* (where the consumer moves to the supplying country – e.g. tourism), and *commercial presence* (where a supplier in one country sets up a sales outlet abroad – e.g. a hotel chain).

Brain gain. This term is often used to refer to a situation in which migrants from developing countries return to work in their country of origin with augmented human capital – having acquired valuable skills, qualifications or work experience while working abroad. It is also used to refer to the flow of technological and managerial know-how directed back to the country of origin by migrants, and even to the phenomenon whereby some developing-country residents, stimulated by the possibility of emigrating, undertake studies – and then decide to remain at home. Confusingly, the term is increasingly applied to any net improvement in the skill profile of labour forces – including those in developed countries – resulting from immigration.

Demographic transition. A common demographic experience as countries develop is that, beginning with a steady state characterized by high death and birth rates, death rates decline while birth rates remain high (so population rises rapidly). Then birth rates, too, decline, so that population growth rates fall. Eventually, as birth rates level off and death rates remain low, a new equilibrium is reached with much lower birth and death rates than in the initial situation; the country has passed through the 'demographic transition' (see Chapter 13 for a detailed analysis).

The dimensions of international migration since 1950[1]

The figures in Table 24.1 show how radically both the magnitude and the geographical pattern of international migration have changed since 1950. During the 1950s gross flows averaged around 800 000 per annum, with movements into and out of developing countries as a group roughly in balance – the same, therefore, being the case for developed countries. Within the developing group, Africa, Latin America and the Caribbean were net sources of migrants, while Asia was a net recipient. Within the more developed regions the important flows were those from Europe to North America (the USA and Canada), and to Oceania (Australia and New Zealand). By the 1990s all three of the more developed regions had become large-scale net recipients of immigrants (running now at around 2.5 million per annum), while less developed regions were now significant suppliers of these migrants, numbers having increased fairly steadily over the intervening decades, though migration from the 'least developed' countries collapsed after 1990, being replaced by sharply increased numbers from the better-off members of the developing-country group. (Note that these data on international migration are net figures, and the true number of *movements* will be much larger.)

The projections in the table suggest, with the exception of a significant increase in emigration from least developed countries, a continuation of these trends into the 2020s. (However, the room for error in making migration projections should not be underestimated. In a celebrated example of serious miscalculation, prior to the accession to the EU of several Eastern European countries in 2004, the UK Government predicted that they would provide no more than 15 000 in-migrants per annum for the UK. In fact, by 2008 estimates of immigration *from Poland alone* ranged from 600 000 to 1 million people.)

	Net number of migrations (thousands)							
	1950–1960	1960–1970	1970–1980	1980–1990	1990–2000	2000–2010*	2010–2020*	2020–2030*
More developed regions	–3	556	1088	1530	2493	2902	2268	2269
Less developed regions	3	–556	–1088	–1530	–2493	–2902	–2268	–2269
Least developed countries	–104	–148	–447	–788	–37	–29	–277	–373
Other less developed countries	108	–409	–641	–742	–2456	–2873	–1991	–1896
Africa	–125	–242	–289	–267	–310	–416	–377	–395
Asia	194	–22	–377	–451	–1340	–1311	–1210	–1221
Europe	–489	–31	288	441	1051	1271	799	805
Latin America and the Caribbean	–68	–293	–415	–781	–775	–1108	–616	–590
Northern America	403	479	748	972	1277	1453	1305	1305
Oceania	85	109	44	86	96	111	99	99

TABLE 24.1 Average annual net number of international migration movements to or from each region and major area, 1950–2030
* projection
Source: Adapted from United Nations Population Fund (UNFPA, 2007b) – 'medium variant' of estimates.

[1] Key sources of data used in this section are: International Organization for Migration (2007) and UN (2006).

PERIOD	1960–1965	1965–1970	1970–1975	1975–1980	1980–1985	1985–1990	1990–1995	1995–2000	2000–2005
PER CENT INCREASE (%)	3.8	3.6	6.8	14.4	11.8	39.5	6.6	7.0	7.9

TABLE 24.2 Five-year growth rates of numbers ('stocks') of international migrants: 1960–2005
Source: Adapted from United Nations Population Fund (UNFPA, 2007b) – 'medium variant' of estimates.

The corresponding five-year *growth rates* of the worldwide *stock* of migrants are shown in Table 24.2. Clearly the pace of immigration has risen over the period as a whole, though not uniformly, with a rapid acceleration from 1960–65 to 1985–90 (especially over the last of these five-year periods, when growth of 39.5 per cent was recorded, though this figure includes a substantial number of persons classified as migrants simply because of changes in national boundaries, especially in the former USSR), followed by almost as dramatic a decline thereafter. This decline is in part due to the boundary changes, in part to a sharp increase in temporary/short-term migration at the expense of permanent/long-term migration, so that gross flows increased faster than net flows.

Figure 24.1 tracks the *absolute size* of the global 'stock' of international migrants post-1960, showing a near three-fold rise from 75.5 millions in 1960 to 190.6 millions in 2005.[2] (In addition to these numbers, there are an estimated 30 to 40 million unauthorized migrants worldwide, comprising 15–20 per cent of the world's immigrant stock.)

Figure 24.2 gives a breakdown of the global stock of international migrants, in terms of their shares of the populations of the more developed and the less developed regions, from 1960 to 2005.

The official stock figures correspond, as Figure 24.2 illustrates, to an increase from 2.5 per cent of the world's population in 1960 to 3.0 per cent in 2005, though the increase

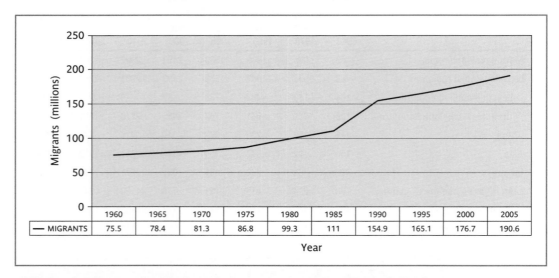

	1960	1965	1970	1975	1980	1985	1990	1995	2000	2005
— MIGRANTS	75.5	78.4	81.3	86.8	99.3	111	154.9	165.1	176.7	190.6

FIGURE 24.1 Cumulative total number ('stock') of international migrants: 1960–2005 (millions)

---

[2] The data on which Figures 24.1 to 24.4 are based are from International Organization for Migration (IOM, 2007) and United Nations Population Fund (UNFPA, 2007b).

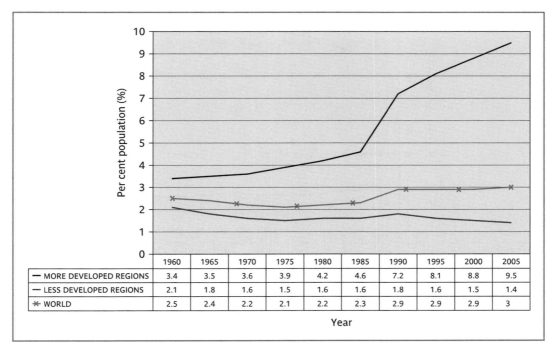

	1960	1965	1970	1975	1980	1985	1990	1995	2000	2005
— MORE DEVELOPED REGIONS	3.4	3.5	3.6	3.9	4.2	4.6	7.2	8.1	8.8	9.5
— LESS DEVELOPED REGIONS	2.1	1.8	1.6	1.5	1.6	1.6	1.8	1.6	1.5	1.4
✳ WORLD	2.5	2.4	2.2	2.1	2.2	2.3	2.9	2.9	2.9	3

FIGURE 24.2 International migrants as per cent population of world, of more developed, and of less developed countries: 1960–2005

has been asymmetric, with immigrants increasing their share of the population in more-developed regions from 3.4 per cent to 9.5 per cent, while declining in relative importance in less-developed regions from 2.1 per cent to only 1.4 per cent of the total population.

Figure 24.3 shows the breakdown of the same stock of migrants by host *continent*, again as percentages of host population. Declines are seen in Africa, Asia, and Latin America and the Caribbean, and increases in Europe and North America (in both of which the immigrant share more than doubled between 1960 and 2005), and in Oceania (primarily Australia) which had the highest overall figure in 2005 at 15.2 per cent. It is estimated that, in addition to these official numbers, there were, in 2005, over 7 million undocumented migrants in Europe and over 10 million in the US.

The *sources*, by continent, of the migrant stock over the years 1960–2005 are shown in Figure 24.4. Here the ranking has changed in one significant respect over the period, in that Europe has overtaken Asia as the main source of international migrants, largely because of movements between member states of the EU and of the former USSR. The North American share of the source of migrants has also increased sharply, in this case mainly because of movements into the US from Mexico.

Looking more closely at the most recent years for which data are available (2000 to 2005), we see from the figures in Table 24.3 that ten countries accounted for almost 77 per cent of all emigrants, and 10 countries absorbed nearly 80 per cent of all immigrants (with over one-third going to the US, though the EU as a whole absorbed a slightly higher proportion – 37.0 per cent). Clearly, given that the data cover 133 countries, the patterns of both emigration and immigration across countries are highly skewed.

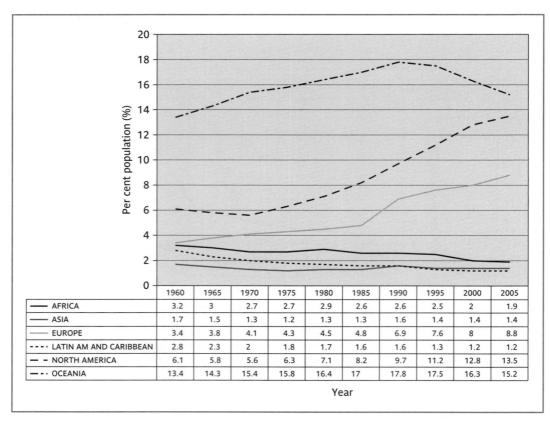

	1960	1965	1970	1975	1980	1985	1990	1995	2000	2005
AFRICA	3.2	3	2.7	2.7	2.9	2.6	2.6	2.5	2	1.9
ASIA	1.7	1.5	1.3	1.2	1.3	1.3	1.6	1.4	1.4	1.4
EUROPE	3.4	3.8	4.1	4.3	4.5	4.8	6.9	7.6	8	8.8
LATIN AM AND CARIBBEAN	2.8	2.3	2	1.8	1.7	1.6	1.6	1.3	1.2	1.2
NORTH AMERICA	6.1	5.8	5.6	6.3	7.1	8.2	9.7	11.2	12.8	13.5
OCEANIA	13.4	14.3	15.4	15.8	16.4	17	17.8	17.5	16.3	15.2

FIGURE 24.3 International migrants as percentage of population of host countries: 1960–2005

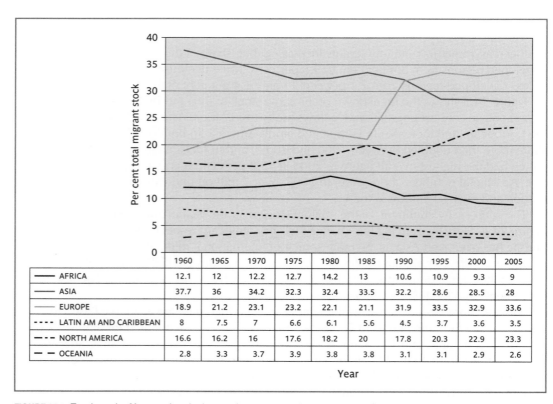

	1960	1965	1970	1975	1980	1985	1990	1995	2000	2005
AFRICA	12.1	12	12.2	12.7	14.2	13	10.6	10.9	9.3	9
ASIA	37.7	36	34.2	32.3	32.4	33.5	32.2	28.6	28.5	28
EUROPE	18.9	21.2	23.1	23.2	22.1	21.1	31.9	33.5	32.9	33.6
LATIN AM AND CARIBBEAN	8	7.5	7	6.6	6.1	5.6	4.5	3.7	3.6	3.5
NORTH AMERICA	16.6	16.2	16	17.6	18.2	20	17.8	20.3	22.9	23.3
OCEANIA	2.8	3.3	3.7	3.9	3.8	3.8	3.1	3.1	2.9	2.6

FIGURE 24.4 Total stock of international migrants by source regions: 1960–2005 (percentage of stock)

Major Sources of Migrants		Major Recipients of Migrants	
Country	**Per Cent Total**	**Country**	**Per Cent Total**
Mexico	12.5	US	36.3
China	12.2	Spain	12.7
Pakistan	11.3	Germany	6.9
India	8.8	Canada	6.6
Iran	8.6	UK	4.3
Indonesia	6.3	Italy	3.8
Philippines	5.6	Sierra Leone	2.7
Ukraine	4.4	Russian Federation	2.5
Kazakhstan	3.8	France	1.9
Sudan	3.2	Hong Kong (China)	1.9
TOTAL	**76.7**	**TOTAL**	**79.6**

TABLE 24.3 The ten countries supplying or receiving most migrants: 2000–2005

Note: These figures exclude data for the very smallest countries. In the year 2000, in seven countries immigrants made up more than 60 per cent of the population: Andorra, Guam, Holy See, Macao, Monaco, Qatar and the UAE.

Sources: International Organization for Migration (IOM, 2005) and United Nations Population Fund (UNFPA, 2007b).

It is also worth noting that, although the figures in Table 24.3 do reflect the general trend for migration to be from developing countries to developed countries, there are some exceptions. Also, there is a small group of countries attracting appreciable numbers of migrants, some of which (notably Thailand and Malaysia) are still in the middle-income class and others (such as Israel, Kuwait, Qatar, Saudi Arabia, Singapore, and the UAE) would have counted as 'developing countries' until two to four decades ago.

Last, in view of the publicity given to refugees in recent years, it is of interest to compare their numbers with those of other international migrants. The figures in Table 24.4 show that in 1960 the population of international refugees corresponded to 2.9 per cent of the total population of migrants. This figure climbed to a peak of 11.9 per cent in 1985/90 and had fallen back to 7.1 per cent by 2005. Countries receiving large numbers of refugees include Jordan and Syria (from Iraq) and several African countries, including Sierra Leone (mainly from neighbouring countries). Refugee flows also explain the fact that Pakistan and Iran have been major sources of migrants, many of these being Afghani refugees returning home.

YEAR	**1960**	**1965**	**1970**	**1975**	**1980**	**1985**	**1990**	**1995**	**2000**	**2005**
REFUGEES	2.2	3.9	3.9	4.2	9.1	13.2	18.5	18.5	15.7	13.5
REFUGEES % MIGRANTS	2.9	5.0	4.8	4.8	9.2	11.9	11.9	11.2	8.9	7.1

TABLE 24.4 Number ('stock') of international refugees: 1960–2005 (millions)

Source: Based on data from UN (2006), http://esa.un.org/migration.

What factors determine the rate and pattern of international migration?

Introduction

An understanding of the factors influencing the rate and pattern of international migration is important for purposes of formulating policies aimed at improving its benefits and reducing its costs. As with internal migration, traditional analysis of these factors ran in terms of 'push-pull' influences and focused heavily on financial considerations. In recent years there has been a considerable deepening of the understanding of the complexity of the motivation (often non-economic) driving international migration, though in practice much of the 'new migration theory' can still be set in a push-pull framework as is done in (b) below. Moving beyond this, in (c) we look at what amounts to a 'stages' model of international migration, the (somewhat inelegantly named) 'hump theory'.

Key influences on international migration

A wide range of fundamentally financial *'push'* and *'pull'* influences are believed to affect international migration rates and patterns. It seems likely that significant numbers of residents of developing countries are attracted by such obvious advantages (or perceived advantages) of life in developed countries as improved economic opportunities – higher wages, more congenial work, and better promotion prospects than in the country of origin; the availability of superior education and medical facilities, often provided by the state; the possibility, for those with appropriate tastes, of access to what they see as a more varied and rewarding social life than that offered by the home country (especially in the rural areas); and, for some, the availability of a welfare 'safety net' in the form of financial, and other, support provisions for those falling out of work, taken ill, or otherwise socially disadvantaged.

In other cases people may be 'pushed' out of their own countries by a dearth of jobs, by the desire to escape (as refugees or asylum seekers) from areas affected by civil strife, military conflicts, or religious and ethnic discrimination, or by natural disasters.

At the same time, various 'facilitating' factors may affect the feasibility or desirability of migrating:

- *Immigration policies* of the receiving countries are, of course, crucial. Some countries actively encourage specific kinds of labour to enter, while discouraging others. Some countries impose annual quotas on entry. Still others adopt an 'open door' approach.

- *Shortages of labour* in destination countries are likely to make employers there more willing to accept migrants. And shortages are found at all levels – from professional, through skilled manual, down to the more menial manual labour now falling out of favour with local workers, who often have access to generous welfare provisions. The extent to which particular grades of labour are attracted to given countries tends to be influenced, other things being equal, by the *relative* differentials between home and overseas pay levels. Thus, in the case of Mexico, although professionals can increase their earnings by migrating to the US, migration flows are dominated to a disproportionate extent by unskilled migrants since relative wage differentials in the two countries for the unskilled are much greater than for the highly skilled.

- *Cultural affinity*, in particular in the form of familiarity with the language of the target country, and some knowledge of the broad social background there, may also act as an incentive for migrants to locate in a particular country as well as making them more attractive to that country. Most international migrants do not select a destination country at random, nor do they necessarily choose to locate where monetary rewards are greatest, nor in the nearest developed country. Many choose to locate in a country of which their home was once a colony, this preference being facilitated by the well-established formal diplomatic/consular institutions remaining there and by other continuing links such as student-exchange programmes, tourism, trade, and the presence of multinational corporations. Again, active *labour recruitment* overseas has often focused, during periods of labour shortage, on former colonies – for example recruitment by the UK from the Caribbean and by France from North Africa.

- *Source-government support.* In some developing countries governments are well aware of the potential benefits accruing (mainly in the form of remittances) from nationals seeking employment abroad, and provide active support programmes for emigration.

- *Social networks* – sometimes termed *'friends and family'* groups – are believed to be important in several ways. Their presence in the target country will not only make the transition easier (by helping with housing, overcoming legal barriers to entry and employment, and easing cultural assimilation), and therefore more likely to happen, but may even be the critical factor which makes migration possible, especially where 'reuniting families' is an element in the target country's immigration policy. *Household* influences (as opposed to individual initiatives) may also operate through a mechanism similar to that believed to underlie much rural-urban migration, such that migrants move abroad in order to *address problems arising at home*.

  Thus families

  self-insure by sending one or more members overseas for work. By allocating members to different labor markets in multiple geographic regions – domestic and foreign – a household can diversify its labor portfolio and reduce risks to income, as long as conditions in the different labor markets are weakly or negatively correlated . . . By sending a family member temporarily abroad for work, a household can accumulate savings and overcome failures in capital and consumer credit markets by self-financing production or consumption. . . . Whereas the rational actors posited by neoclassical economics take advantage of a temporary geographic disequilibrium in labor markets to move abroad *permanently* to achieve higher lifetime earnings, the rational actors assumed by the new economics of labor migration seek to cope with failures in insurance, futures, capital, and credit markets *at home* by moving abroad *temporarily* to repatriate earnings in the form of regular remittances or lump-sum transfers. (Ozden and Schiff, 2006)

- *Geographical proximity* to the target country is also likely to influence some migrants because of the easier, and cheaper, access this implies. Again, the presence of branches of *multinational corporations* in a developing country may create opportunities for local employees to migrate in order to work in affiliates elsewhere. Last, for some, migration is facilitated by labour brokers or, for the less fortunate, by *labour smugglers or traffickers.*

- Beyond all this, there is also a strong element of *cumulative causation* in the migration system, with earlier migrants to a particular location smoothing the entry path for subsequent migrants to that location.

A 'stages' theory of international migration: the 'Migration Hump'

It is widely agreed that, in Massey's words,

> While the simple neoclassical reliance on wage differentials to explain international migration is naïve – in practical terms, however, large-scale international movement is rarely observed in the absence of a wage gap; but the existence of a wage differential still does not guarantee international movement, nor does its absence preclude it.
>
> *(Massey, 2003)*

Ozden and Schiff (2006) confirm that

> The principal cause of south-north migration is, in most cases, the difference in (the present value of) expected real wages, adjusted for migration costs. These costs increase with the distance between source and destination countries, and decline with social networks in the destination country. . . . Migration flows and remittances would be expected to rise with the difference in expected real wages and decline with migration costs.

However, although differences between wage levels in source and receiving countries are crucial, the relationship is complex, the propensity to emigrate varying in a non-linear fashion with the wage-gap as development proceeds in the source country. As per capita income rises in a given developing country, so does emigration, until a critical income level is reached, after which emigration declines. This process is illustrated in Figure 24.5.

At very low levels of per capita income – in Phase A, to the left of the point X on the horizontal axis – few people can afford to migrate internationally (though they may migrate internally). As per capita incomes rise above X, the economy enters Phase B where increasing numbers can afford to move abroad, and at the same time are encouraged to do so by the fact that local employment opportunities are still fairly limited and poorly paid. However, once the 'critical level', Y, is passed (i.e. in Phase C) local wage-rates and job opportunities have improved sufficiently to make emigration progressively less attractive relative to the option of remaining at home, and international migration declines. Thus,

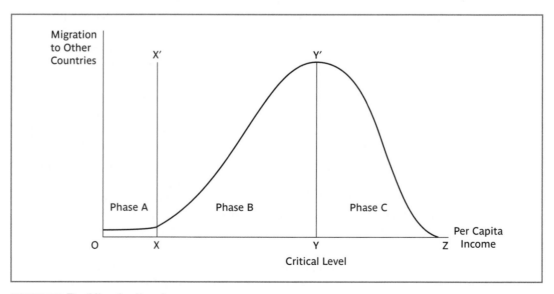

FIGURE 24.5 The 'Migration Hump'

international migration comes to be seen as a *consequence of development* not the result of acute poverty or marginalization.

Many countries have already passed through this process – in the 1960s and 1970s now-developed countries such as Spain, Portugal, Greece, Ireland and Italy and, more recently, countries such as, Korea, Taiwan and Malaysia – but it seems safe to assume that much of sub-Saharan Africa is still in Phase A.

> By far the world's poorest continent, Africa has generated remarkably few migrants to the major labor-scarce countries despite the massive gains that it would bring to the migrants. True, migration pressure, as reflected by illegal flows between North Africa and southern Europe, has often hit the headlines. Also, the share of Africans in legal immigration to the US has increased. Yet, real incomes in Africa are but a tiny fraction of those in Europe and North America so the incentive to emigrate should be huge. Indeed, the gaps are many times larger than those that gave rise to the mass emigrations from Europe a century ago.
>
> *(Hatton and Williamson, 2002)*

The profile of the 'hump', in particular the location of the increasing and decreasing phases of international migration, is believed to be intimately linked to the 'demographic transition' in the source country (see Chapter 13). Poor countries, in the demographic 'pre-transition' state, typically display low levels of international migration, for reasons explained above. As mortality declines and population begins to grow rapidly – in 'the early transitional society' – pressure to migrate internationally intensifies, affecting, in particular, the population of working age, especially the younger cohorts. With per capita incomes also rising, Phase B on Figure 24.5 is reached. In the 'late-transition' stage of demographic evolution, with fertility falling rapidly and a significant decrease in population growth rates, Phase C of the migration cycle is entered, and migration begins to decline. At length, as fertility and mortality are stabilized at low levels in the 'advanced society', net migration reverses direction, and the country becomes a net recipient of migrants (Zelinsky 1971).

The results of econometric investigations suggest that, at the 'critical level' of per capita income in the source country, the destination country's per capita income may typically be of the order of something over four times the level of the source country's per capita income. Thus Bohning (1994) estimates the multiple as lying on the range 3:1 to 4.5:1, while Martin and Taylor (1996) suggest a range of 4:1 to 5:1.

BOX 24.2 PROMOTING DEVELOPMENT MAY PROMOTE INTERNATIONAL MIGRATION

The 'hump' theory of the evolution of international migration suggests, somewhat paradoxically, that one outcome of success in promoting development in the poorest countries may be a much *increased* outflow of migrants from these countries – as rising incomes, combined with continuing poor employment opportunities at home, create the conditions known to favour emigration.

A summary view of key conclusions on the determinants of the rate and pattern of international migration

Research on international migration has indicated that, of the various possible influences on international migration discussed above, the most powerful influences on rates and patterns appear to be:

- *The existence of per capita income gaps between rich, high-wage countries and poor, low-wage countries:* as per capita income in the poorer country increases, international migration at first increases from a low level along the 'migration hump', reaches a maximum, then declines to zero, ultimately becoming negative;

- *Poverty constraints:* extremely poor countries (the 'least developed' countries), which might be expected to benefit most from international migration of workers, are *not*, in fact, major sources of migrants, the cost of migration and general lack of skills being serious inhibiting factors;

- *Demographic factors* (in the form of the 'demographic transition') play an important part in determining when international emigration begins in earnest, and also *who* migrates, young adults being the majority group;

- *The size of the foreign-born migrant stock* from the sending counties currently residing in the receiving countries has a major bearing on the magnitude and direction of future inflows of migrants.

The impact of international migration

Introduction

In this section we first itemize and discuss briefly the various costs and benefits expected to accrue to source and receiving countries, and to migrants, as a result of international migration of labour, with particular reference to the flows of funds from migrants to their countries of origin. Then, in order to provide some broad notion of the overall orders of magnitude of the expected macroeconomic impacts on both sets of countries, we present in abbreviated form the results of a major simulation exercise of the labour-migration process. Finally, we summarize the overall global effects of international worker migration.

The impact of international migration on the source country: benefits

The benefits from international migration accruing to a source country and its nationals are numerous and diverse. The immediate, and most obvious, benefits from international migration accrue to the *migrants themselves, who enjoy expanded income levels* in the destination countries. However, their incomes and activities give rise to a wide range of benefits which accrue to the source country. Important among these are remittances, inward foreign investment, and international trade.

Remittances: magnitudes and direction of flows

Remittances of funds by overseas migrant workers to their home countries have become a major element in externally sourced finance for many developing countries in recent years, and probably rank as the main single benefit resulting from international migration. In 1970 the officially recorded global total was relatively insignificant at US$3 billion, but by 2006 this had climbed to an estimated US$199 billion and, by 2008, to somewhere in the range $240 to $300 billion. As Figure 24.5 shows, in 2006 this flow of funds was equivalent to almost twice the value of net official development assistance ('aid') in the same year, and two-thirds of the value of net inward foreign direct investment (FDI) by multinational corporations. Moreover, it is believed that the published statistics seriously underestimate the true total as many workers make transfers in kind, or remit money through 'informal'

TOP 10 RECIPIENTS	US$(billion)	TOP 10 SHARE OF GDP	SHARE OF GDP (%)
INDIA	21.7	TONGA	31.1
CHINA	21.3	MOLDOVA	27.1
MEXICO	18.1	LESOTHO	25.8
FRANCE	12.7	HAITI	24.8
PHILIPPINES	11.8	BOSNIA HERZEGOVINA	22.5
SPAIN	6.9	JORDAN	20.4
BELGIUM	6.8	JAMAICA	17.4
GERMANY	6.5	SERBIA & MONTENEGRO	17.2
UK	6.4	EL SALVADOR	16.2
MOROCCO	4.2	HONDURAS	15.5
		All Upper Middle Income LDCs	0.7
		All Developing Countries*	1.3

TABLE 24.5 Remittances to selected countries in 2004
Sources: World Bank (2006a). * Ratha, D. (2003).

channels – by post, or on their persons when they return home – and hence by-pass official recording systems. Remittance flows are known to be the largest single source of foreign exchange for some countries. They are also a more reliable, and less variable, source of funds from year to year than FDI and development aid.

Uses and impact of remittances

As the figures in Table 24.5 show, in 2004 remittances were a substantial component of income for many countries. Though this was not the case for the largest recipients, India and China (for which remittances amounted to around 2.7 per cent and 1 per cent of GDP, respectively), for some small countries, remittances were vital to maintaining living standards. Six countries received estimated amounts equal to over 20 per cent of GDP (probably comprising about 20 per cent of gross national disposable income) in this form.

A brief summary of the various contributions made by workers' remittances to welfare and development in the source country would include:

■ In many source countries remittances play an important role in directly *relieving poverty* or *keeping recipients out of poverty*. Though it is true that remittances, in the main, benefit relatively non-poor households rather than the very poorest – since members of the latter are less likely to migrate overseas – the contribution to welfare can be substantial. For example, it has been estimated that, if remittances to Lesotho (a poor, land-locked country surrounded by South Africa) were to cease completely, between 11 and 14 per cent of families currently above the poverty line would fall below it. Similarly, in Morocco it is believed that about 1 170 000 Moroccans would fall back to absolute poverty without their receipts of incoming remittances. In Guatemala, internal and international remittances taken together typically make up between 50 and 60 per cent of the incomes of the poorest people – while in India in 2005–6 international remittances exceeded government spending on health and education combined.

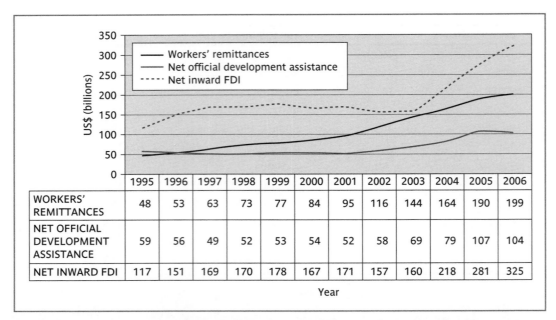

FIGURE 24.6 Flows of workers' remittances, official development assistance and FDI to developing countries: 1995–2006
Source: World Bank, *Global Development Finance* (various), Washington, DC.

	1995	1996	1997	1998	1999	2000	2001	2002	2003	2004	2005	2006
WORKERS' REMITTANCES	48	53	63	73	77	84	95	116	144	164	190	199
NET OFFICIAL DEVELOPMENT ASSISTANCE	59	56	49	52	53	54	52	58	69	79	107	104
NET INWARD FDI	117	151	169	170	178	167	171	157	160	218	281	325

- Remittances contribute substantially to *income growth* in the source country by enabling migrants and their families back home to *invest* in agriculture and other private enterprise. The once prevalent view that remittances were simply used to finance expanded consumption in the source country has proved to be mistaken. Recipient households consistently tend to display a higher propensity to invest in small businesses, including microenterprises, than do non-migrant households, and remittance levels are positively associated with levels of family economic activity and wealth (Martin and Taylor 1996). In any case, increased household spending on 'consumption' in the forms of healthcare, schooling and housing can have important favourable effects on human capital and productivity. Positive multiplier effects will also help to spread the benefits to non-migrant households.

- Remittances can help to *improve income distribution* in the receiving country, and appear to be a more efficient means of so doing than official development programmes, whether locally funded or aid-financed.

- Regular inflows of remittances can improve a country's *balance-of-payments* situation and also, by favourably affecting its *international creditworthiness* for external borrowing, enable borrowing to be carried on at better terms.

- Remittances are a 'bottom-up' way of delivering resources to those who actually need and use them, and *by-pass costly bureaucratic and administrative procedures associated with most development assistance.*

- The *skills and knowledge* that returning migrants have acquired through work experience and/or education abroad can be of considerable value in driving industrialization forward in the source country.

- *Technology transfer* may take place via migrants, either while they are abroad or on their return.

- More generally, counter-flows of *knowledge, new attitudes, and cultural influence* may result from international migration (Newland and Patrick 2004).

- *Market development* for source-country exports may be undertaken by migrants while abroad. (This may include outsourcing of production for receiving-country firms).

- Migrants may promote *tourism* in their home country while overseas – and may return home from time to time as 'tourists'.

- Last, where unemployment is a serious problem in a developing country, international migration is a useful *'safety valve'* reducing pressures on the local labour market.

The impact of international migration on the source country: costs

International migration may involve costs for the source country:

- *The loss of the output* produced by previously employed labour (unless similarly qualified unemployed persons are available to replace them);

- *The brain drain* – that is, the loss of skilled migrants' production and human capital, together with the loss of the positive externalities they generate for the source-country society (increased productivity of colleagues, provision of key services in health and education – which themselves have positive externalities – and fiscal externalities arising from the fact that they are net contributors to the public finances), together with the writing-off of past expenditures on training these individuals. It is clear that the impact of the brain drain on some small economies has been very damaging (thus Haiti and Jamaica lose around 80 per cent of their graduates to migration). However, it is argued that in many countries it is not an issue, especially where there is already serious 'graduate unemployment', where the majority of migrants are unskilled (as is often the case), where remittances are used to finance further training, and where returning migrants who have gained work experience or training abroad provide a 'brain gain'.

Benefits and costs to migrants

- The key benefits to migrants are the *increased incomes* earned in the receiving country, *access to higher-quality education and health facilities* than those available at home, and (in some cases) the provision of welfare benefits.

- Costs come in the form of the *disruption of family and social life* due to separation from relatives, friends and culture, the need (in many cases) to engage in heavy or unpleasant tasks and, in some countries, hostility on the part of certain elements in the host society, together with inadequate effective legal protection.

The impact of international migration on recipient countries

Benefits to recipient countries

By augmenting the labour force in the recipient country and, very probably, inducing additional investment there, international migration adds to the factor base and may thus push the level of GDP above the long-run trend level. For example, the favourable impact on the annual rate of growth in Greece has been estimated to lie in the range 1.5–2.0 percentage points (*Economist*, 5/1/2008, 'Special Report on migration', p. 6). At the same time, in-migration can help to hold wage levels steady, so helping to blunt inflationary pressures – which represents a gain to local consumers – and creating the possibility that associated gains may accrue to the owners of complementary factors of production (*capital and land*). (From the simple self-interested view of the pre-existing population, the question is of course whether the addition of the migrants raises income *per head* and how any additional income is distributed. This is a complex question. The simulation of Walmsley *et al.* (2005) reported below involves an attempt to answer it.)

BOX 24.3 CHANGING PATTERNS OF INTERNATIONAL MIGRATION

'Cobh, a bustling tourist town in southern Ireland . . . used to be famous for exporting people. Some 2.5 million Irishmen and women embarked for America from its quayside, and its great and gloomy neo-gothic cathedral was paid for by remittances. Now, like the rest of Ireland, Cobh heaves with foreign workers. There are Poles on building sites, Latvians who own a shop selling dumplings, *sauerkraut* and other continental delicacies, a South African in the tourist office and another driving a taxi, Chinese in restaurants, a Bangladeshi managing a fishing business, and so on. [When] a hotel owner . . . recently advertised for a receptionist, none of the 200 applicants was Irish.' (*Economist*, 5/1/2008, 'Special Report on migration', p. 5)

It has been argued that *the required gains are likely to occur and are likely to be long-term*.

The current demographic trends in developed countries point toward significant potential economic gains from migration. The labor forces in many developed countries are expected to peak around 2010 and decline by around 5 percent in the following two decades, accompanied by a rapid increase in dependency ratios. Conversely, the labor forces in many developing countries are expanding rapidly, resulting in declines in dependency ratios. This imbalance is likely to create strong demand for workers in developed countries' labor markets, especially for the many services that can only be supplied locally – or which local workers are unwilling to take up, for instance cleaning and nursing.

(Harris, 2002)

Costs to recipient countries

While countries hosting migrant workers may expect to gain from their presence, there may also be costs, or concerns, of various kinds, to be considered.

In the *labour market*, where in-migrants compete with local labour for jobs, some locals will lose out especially if migrants are willing to work for lower wages, possibly on an 'informal' basis in what is, otherwise, a regulated market (e.g., unionized, or subject to statutory minimum wage rates, or to restrictions on hours of work, and health and safety rules).

With regard to *public services*, in-migration can put pressure on the housing stock, on education and on health facilities – creating shortages and adversely affecting the quality of delivery, which will affect both the migrants and local people.

Last, the perceived *threat to the local cultural identity* posed by 'alien' communities (especially where migrants comprise a sizeable proportion of the population and are not readily assimilating) appears to be a common problem.

Magnitudes of macroeconomic and sectoral impacts

Insights into the potential overall broad orders of magnitude of the macroeconomic and sectoral impacts of international labour migration from developing to developed countries may be gleaned from an examination of the results of a simulation study carried out using a computable general-equilibrium model (Walmsley *et al.*, 2005). The global CGE model was developed by Walmsley *et al.* to examine the impact of a putative substantial increase in the level of temporary international migration of skilled and unskilled labour from developing countries to developed countries. The study, in which the increase in immigration was set at a number of workers equivalent to 3 per cent of the total labour force of the developed economies, was intended to throw light on the likely impact of a move to a more immigration-liberal regime in what is known as 'Mode 4' – the international movement of 'natural persons' for temporary employment – but provides a range of results of broader interest. While the specific results quoted below depend heavily on the assumptions made regarding the structure and responsiveness of the host economy, and hence should not be taken to represent any host economy in particular, they do provide a useful indication of the general direction in which inflows of migrant labour tend to push important macroeconomic variables, as well as giving some indication of the rough orders of magnitude of the resultant macroeconomic changes.

The key results for the *receiving* countries were as follows:

- Real GDP increases because of the increase in the employed labour force.
- Wage-rates fall – again because of the increase in the labour supply.
- The increase in output results in a decline in the terms of trade (that is, the ratio of export prices to import prices) and thus depresses the real exchange-rate (i.e., the nominal exchange rate adjusted for changes in relative prices at home and abroad).
- Exports rise (by 2.5 per cent) as a result of the fall in the real exchange-rate (though this result does not allow for the likelihood that the new immigrants and the local residents may well have different consumption patterns).
- Imports increase by (0.12 per cent) as incomes, and the number of consumers, rise (a result likely to be affected by the assumption of identical consumption patterns).
- The trade balance improves as exports increase more rapidly than imports.
- The current account, however, deteriorates because of the expected increase in remittances to the source countries of the migrant labour.
- The increase in the labour supply, together with the increased level of economic activity, raise the return on capital causing investment to rise, so increasing the size of the capital stock.
- The overall gain for permanent residents of the developed receiving countries is put at $US382 per capita per annum, of which the bulk ($US227 per capita) stems directly from increased inflow of unskilled labour.
- The incoming skilled and unskilled migrant workers each gain – by $US8000 per annum and $US6500 per annum, respectively.
- Migrants already working in the developed economies lose as wages fall because of the rise in the supply of labour.

The impact on the output of each *sector* of the receiving nations was found to depend on the extent to which that sector uses skilled, and unskilled, labour. Thus, agriculture and light manufacturing gain more in output from unskilled migrant labour than from skilled labour, and the reverse is true for other manufacturing and service industries.

Outcomes for the *source* developing countries were, in the main, the reverse of those for the receiving developed countries:

- The decline in the labour supply results in a rise in wage-rates and prices.
- This corresponds to a rise in the real exchange-rate.
- As a result exports fall and imports increase.
- So the balance of trade deteriorates.
- The trade balance change is more than offset by the increase in inward remittances.
- Returns to capital fall because of a rise in the capital-intensity of production.
- On average, the residents of the source countries gain $US4.60 per capita per annum as a result of the migration of unskilled labour, and $US1.35 per capita per annum as a result of the emigration of skilled migrants. (In most countries, the outcome is favourable.)
- Workers in the source countries gain as wages there rise because of the fall in the supply of labour.

In sum, this simulation exercise found that significant gains can arise as a result of liberalizing the movement of labour (especially unskilled labour) from developing to developed countries. This resulted in a significant rise in world GDP.

Impact on the global economy

The general conclusion to be drawn from the discussion in this chapter is that there are considerable gains to be had from international migration for both source and recipient countries. However, with regard to such migration, we have thus far considered only those bilateral costs and benefits affecting the participating economies. Moving beyond this to consider possible multilateral impacts of liberalizing migration regulations, we infer that it seems likely that reformulating immigration policies in such a way that workers are permitted to move to where they are most productive would bring significant gains in output and income. Migrants themselves would benefit, as would the source and recipient countries, and the global economy as a whole – to yield what has been termed by the World Bank (2006a) a 'win-win-win' situation.

Confirming this, the study referred-to above (Walmsley *et al.*, 2005), concludes that the contribution of an increase in the number of migrants equal to 3 per cent of the labour force of the OECD countries would result in a '*global welfare gain* surpassing those obtained from the removal of all trade barriers, with significant gains for all parties involved'.

Further multilateral benefits might be expected in the field of international trade. In this context the information some migrant workers possess on conditions at home – on potential market opportunities, consumer preferences, business codes, and local legal regimes – could materially reduce transaction costs and facilitate more efficient international trade and contract enforcement across national boundaries.

Last, significant volumes of funds are being invested directly in their home countries by international migrants. Foreign-direct-investment activities typically face even more complex information problems than international-trade transactions. Direct investment generally requires long-term interactions with diverse factors ranging from suppliers and workers to government markets and the legal and regulatory regimes in the host country. Contractual and informational problems can be quite severe, which is why variables related to governance and legal regimes are found to be among the most important determinants of FDI flows into a country. 'The investor needs to have detailed knowledge of the consumer, and of the labour and other inputs' (Javorcik, 2006). For all these reasons it seems likely that a positive relationship will exist between out-migration of labour and both the 'quality' and the quantity of foreign direct investment moving in the opposite direction.

BOX 24.4 A POSTSCRIPT ON THE FUTURE OF INTERNATIONAL MIGRATION

'. . . [A] word about South-South migration. How long will it be before successful development will shift the target of the emigrating poor from OECD labour markets to those which have recently arrived or shortly will have arrived on the industrial scene? After all, there may be more skills to learn in a newly industrial country's manufacturing job, which is also closer to the poor sending region, than in a post-industrial country's domestic service job, which is also farther away. These opportunities will most assuredly change the direction of South-North flows in a more South-South direction . . . creating new problems for the newly industrial country. The future rise of South-South migration will, no doubt, take those analysts who ignore history by surprise. It will not take economic historians by surprise. After all . . . South-South migration is not new. It is just ignored by economists.'

(Hatton and Williamson, 2002, p. 25)

Summary conclusions

- This chapter has examined international migration – particular attention being paid to the flows of funds generated by *migrants' remittances*. As in the analysis of internal migration, traditional 'push-pull' factors are important influences on the migration process, but these must now be integrated into a more complex 'stages' theory of migration than is generally used in examining domestic migration.

- We have noted that the flow of remittances from migrants to the home base has emerged as a key development variable, easily outstripping official aid in importance and, for some countries, dwarfing FDI as a source of funds. The multiple role of remitted funds for consumption and for both directly productive and social investment is already important and promises to become even more so.

- Indeed, the development potential inherent in worker migration (for both source and recipient countries) is now seen to be massive – greater, according to the outcome of one recent modelling study, than that of trade liberalization. It is apparent that evolving internationally acceptable policies for facilitating the flows of workers towards the developed countries (possibly under the aegis of the WTO), encouraging the reverse flow of remittances, and ensuring their effective use, are three of the key policy issues of the coming decade.

In the pressure on their people to migrate, conditions in much of Africa today resemble those in Europe at the time of the mass emigrations of the late nineteenth century; wage-rates are much lower than those in potential host regions and population is growing rapidly. And these pressures are reinforced by a further problem – the serious depletion of the resource base in many African countries. How will the wealthy countries respond to demands in, say, twenty years' time, for access by migrants in numbers far exceeding the levels that left Europe in the 'first wave' of global migration?

Questions for discussion

24.1   Why, and in what ways, might migration of labour from developing to developed countries affect international trade and investment flows between these groups of countries?

24.2   In relation to international migration, attention tends to focus on flows from developing countries to developed countries. But migrants also move between developing countries, and from developed countries to developing countries. What explanations can you offer for these latter flows – and what effects would you expect them to have on host and source nations?

24.3   Why do people migrate? How have the motives for migration, and its effects, changed over the last century?

24.4   What is the connection between poverty and the propensity to migrate?

24.5   What are the main costs and benefits for recipient countries of the migration of labour from developing to developed countries?

24.6   What are the main costs and benefits for source countries of the migration of labour from developing to developed countries?

Additional reading and web resources

Borjas, G.J. (1994) 'The economics of immigration', *Journal of Economic Literature*, **32** (4).

Castles, S. and M.J. Miller (1998) *The Age of Migration: International Population Movements in the Modern World*, London, Macmillan.

Cohen, R. (ed.) (1995) *The Cambridge Survey of World Migration*, Cambridge University Press, Cambridge.

Economist, 5/1/2008, 'A Special Report on migration' after p. 42.

Harris, J.R. and Michael P. Todaro (1970) 'Migration, unemployment and development: a two-sector analysis', *American Economic Review*, **60**.

Ozden, C. and M. Schiff (eds) (2006) *International Migration, Remittances and the Brain Drain*, Palgrave Macmillan and World Bank, Basingstoke.

Parsons, C., Skeldon, R., Walmsley, T. and Winters, L.A. (2005) 'Quantifying the International Bilateral Movements of Migrants', Migration DRC Working Paper T13, http://www.migrationdrc.org/publications/working_papers/WP-T13.pdf

University of Sussex database on the Development Research Centre website data. For more on this see the DRC website at http://www.migrationdrc.org/publications/working_papers.html

Migration Policy Institute Database: http://www.migrationinformation.org

International Labour Organization, International Labour Migration Database: http://www.ilo.org/public/english/protection/migrant/ilmdb/ilmdb.htm

PART 6
Conclusion

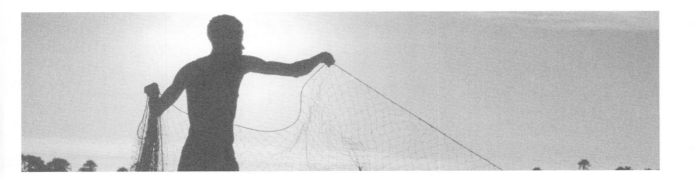

CHAPTER 25

Guidelines, Judgements and Possibilities

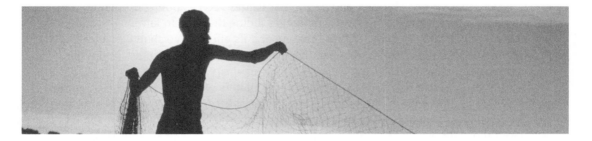

There are differences of emphasis and degree between economic thinking applied to the poorer developing countries and that applied to the rich world – because of the different relative importance of phenomena such as the informal sector and social inequality, and of the pressing aspiration for economic growth. However, certain habits of thought, such as separating efficiency from equity considerations and a disposition to look for ways of 'improving trade-offs', are no less essential to one than to the other. And thought about policy in both requires a readiness to look for solutions in the state, the market, and civil society – all three, with the possibility of drawing on two of them or on all three together.

Introduction

This final chapter will bring together our attempts at summary responses to **three questions** on which readers of the book may have been looking for answers.

First, is there a **different economics** needed for understanding developing countries and framing policies in and for them from the models and habits of mind that have constituted economics as commonly taught and understood in the rich countries of 1950 or the rich countries of today? We shall suggest there are certain differences but certain very important constants.

Then, second, readers may reasonably hope to come away with some idea of the **conditions for economic growth**: where and why it has happened significantly or even spectacularly in recent years; and how communities – or the world – can generate and speed it.

Third, they may want some idea of what can be done, through economic growth or by other means, to '**make poverty history**'. This after all is the object of the exercise for most of us: at least *to remove or radically to reduce the extreme deprivations* that exist of nutrition, healthcare, access to knowledge, and physical and economic security, and in general of freedom, dignity and capacities for creative action. In such conditions of poverty – on the narrowest and most sparing definition of poverty used internationally (in its latest version) – nearly a billion and a half of the world's people live, and these are deprivations that seem to many *unnecessary* in the technical sense that potential global *resources* – if we take into account that so much hangs on technical knowledge and the capacity to disseminate and extend it – are *far more than adequate* to remove them, and to do so sustainably, if only the understanding and political will and institutions are there. We shall summarize three arms of an approach to reducing poverty, and what contribution might be made by aid from abroad and by modifications of international institutions.

We shall end with reference to the **interaction** of movement for economic growth and poverty reduction with each other and with other **values** such as political freedom and human rights, and with the other main **challenges** facing the human family, most urgently keeping the peace and checking climate change and its effects. We shall consider the potential conflicts and synergies between these aspirations and challenges, and what they demand of economic thinking.

The answers involve expressions of opinion on matters of controversy. The questions about growth and poverty in particular can not be answered with any sense of completeness or finality. Values inevitably enter into the answers, and our knowledge about some of the behavioural questions is partial and tentative. But there are relevant statements that can be made, with varying degrees of confidence, and reasonable suggestions, and we try to give some of them.

Paradigms for policy in development economics

First what attitudes and habits of mind do we need to bring to the study of economic policy for development? Does poor-country economics require us to identify different paradigms from those applicable to rich countries – or to those that were already rich in the mid-twentieth century?

The differences

Our answer to that last question is a mixture of *yes* and *no*. First, there are some characteristic differences, at least in degree, between the resources and institutions of the two categories of society that have a bearing on the way their economies behave and the common aspirations of policy for them. Some of these might be thought of as *strictly economic* and some rather as *politico-economic*.

In the first category are such features as the greater importance of *the informal sector* in poorer countries and greater *flexibility in the price of labour* (which two elements are bound together), and at the same time, paradoxical as it may seem, the extent of *labour surplus* in the form of underemployment and unemployment that the Lewis and Harris–Todaro models have attempted to represent and explain.

In the second category are the greater *weakness of government institutions* and, paradoxically again, the greater *penchant for government regulation* of business activity, but also, extremely important, the greater *inequality* among classes of people in social power (not necessarily represented adequately by measurable income-inequality).

In most of these features, there is considerable variation *among* developing countries (more than among the affluent), and all the differences are in any case matters of degree. As far as we know, the underlying human material – divorced from cultural, historical and institutional elements and from the particular positions in which individuals have found themselves – is much the same; and study of the economics of developing countries has had light to shed on the affluent. Nevertheless, it is still important for those coming to developing countries with the assumptions normal among the developed to take certain phenomena – the informal sector, and corruption, and inequality of power and respect among people – much more seriously than policy discourse in rich societies commonly does.

There is another element of inequality that is important to policy for developing countries: inequality *between* rich and poor countries in international transactions. Reasoning about international institutions, such as trade and intellectual-property rules, needs to take account of the unequal position of developing countries; though the developing countries themselves may take action to counteract this inequality by co-ordinating strategy among themselves in international negotiations (Braithwaite, 2004; Clunies-Ross and Langmore, 2008).

So, development economics brings us starkly face to face with **inequality** and its implications for both equity (justice) and efficiency. A frequent value axiom of development-policy discourse is that inequality needs to be reduced. Economists in the Western tradition are at risk of underplaying inequality or ignoring it. The great neoclassical economist Alfred Marshall kept a picture of a starving man on his desk to remind him of the reason for his work, which suggests that he saw the risk. The study of developing countries in a world context does of course face us with inequality much more acutely than study confined to the affluent world.

A further feature that may be classed as political is the sense of an **imperative for economic growth** – implying that the growth rate is less than optimal – a view of the world that is typically taken for granted as part of the framework for policy in developing countries: the idea that the role of 'developing economies' is *to grow*.

We may say, to summarize, that the four important groups of considerations that typically differentiate policy conditions in developing from those in rich countries are *peculiarities of labour markets*, *relative weakness of government institutions coupled with a greater propensity to regulate*, the *imperative of greater equality*, and the *imperative of growth*. The opportunity to take account of these four elements was built into the elaborations of cost–benefit analysis introduced from 1968 to fit the conditions of developing countries (Chapter 20).

However, transcending differences in institutions and the distribution of social power, there are certain habits of mind characteristic of economists that are vital to constructive policy formation everywhere.

Universal economic habits of mind

Making choices among ends: improving the trade-off

As with all economic policy there are choices to be made by developing countries between pairs of 'goods' that may be rivals, such as growth and equity; growth and sustainability; equalizing redistribution of assets and security of property; personal security and social efficiency.

Between the members of each of these pairs, there is a 'trade-off': which is to say that, though having more of one *may* entail having less of the other, that does not mean that the members of each pair are *in all circumstances* rivals, or that the rivalry that exists between them under any one set of arrangements cannot be reduced. Growth and increasing equality, for example, may to a point be made mutually consistent, as became proverbial in the development policy of Taiwan in the 1960s and 1970s.

The job of economic policy-makers is to look for ways of 'improving the trade-off': finding a *more efficient* compromise between the two partly-competing objectives, delivering more of one good without having to make do with less of the other. Maybe the most important lesson from economic theory is that many such possibilities exist. Contrary to what it was once the fashion for economists to say, there *are* free lunches to be found. That was perhaps the crowning insight of Adam Smith: that under certain conditions people's pursuit of their own individual interests serves the common interest and indeed each other's interests. In fact, all trade in which a pair of people engage between themselves willingly and in full knowledge of the facts must be presumed to be to the benefit of both. In addition – just as there are 'deals' to be made between pairs of *people* that benefit *both* members of the pair – there are also deals to be made between pairs of social goods that potentially advance *both*. There are institutional changes, as well as interpersonal transactions, with a positive welfare sum.

Keynesian economics, in the aftermath of the Great Depression of the 1930s, also revealed a free lunch, so much so that its enthusiasts talked of the widow's cruse, referring to the story of Elijah and the widow of Zarephath whose flask produced an inexhaustible supply of oil. This free lunch had limits as Keynes was aware, and changed circumstances 35 to 40 years later made them tighter, but there are signs of its rediscovery in full force in 2009. It was an aspect of a wider truth: measures to *stabilize* real expenditure and income (prices too) can have a win-win character, and this applies *mutatis mutandis* just as much to poor countries as to the rich.

We called attention to another free lunch – or at least a win all round save for the enemies of fairness and legality – in the possibilities of greater international co-operation on taxation.

The importance of seeking these ways in which the trade-off between competing social objectives can be improved can hardly be exaggerated. It is simply the quest for positive-sum deals between people writ large. For example, in checking climate change, there are serious obstacles, political and technical, to doing what urgently needs to be done. There is inevitably a trade-off between current economic growth as it is usually measured and the element of sustainability that consists in limiting climate change in the future. Addressing the environmental objectives *in the most efficient way* – that is with the least cost in income and growth – may be the only acceptable way of doing it at all, and hence a matter of life and death. Here standard simple economic analysis needs to be kept in full play to find the efficient solutions.

Conflict also of great economic and political importance occurs between the urge for globalization as a means toward economic growth and the contrary urge for personal economic security, which for many individuals globalization (like technical change) tends to disturb. Those that fear disturbance from globalization are likely to oppose it in general or in particular. It is important for the authorities to combine the advantages of globalization with as much stability as possible for those that may fear being adversely affected by it – through such means as compensation packages for those displaced, through the various micro and macro ways of helping to stabilize the level of economic activity and hence in general to stabilize individuals' incomes (Chapter 12), and through social safety-nets as a last resort.

One of the key insights of economists is that in policy choices *allocative efficiency* can be separated from *distributional fairness*. A decision over whether to say yes or no to a particular proposal might seem to pose a dilemma in which more efficiency means less justice and vice versa. But in that case the range of possibilities should as far as possible be broadened – by breaking up what appear to be policy 'packages' – in the hope of finding a way of improving the trade-off.

So: recognize that there are choices to be made between ends. Achieving a desirable goal will not necessarily be costless. But there may be ways of reducing the costs, reducing the rivalry. Recognizing this and exploring how it may be done is the economist's first big contribution to policy.

Choosing the means: market, state, and civil society

A second major contribution is to recognize the need for keeping a completely open mind toward the three main means through which economic and social goals can be pursued: market, state, and civil society. This lesson of the first half-century of development economics is one that might have been learned – with only a little imagination – from Adam Smith and Ricardo. Trying to run society on any one of the three engines alone will bring its disasters, as it has already done.

The nightmare of the Soviet economic system, with the attempted suppression of all market activity and of any autonomous contribution from civil society, brought with it inhuman tyranny and kept the world's second military power and those it could dominate politically in a state of intellectual repression and relative material poverty. Another exemplar that heavily influenced early thought on development in the Third World was Indian 'democratic-planning'. This, though it avoided Soviet-style tyranny in India itself, nevertheless gave free rein to a bureaucratic impulse to control everything, which had the effect of suppressing much economic activity rather than promoting it and of increasingly fostering arbitrary privileges.

Nonetheless, the failure of one extreme experiment should not lead policy-makers to the opposite pole. The temptation for those that liked neat solutions was to opt instead for 'market-fundamentalism', subjecting to a market mechanism every transaction for which that would be possible. This risked ignoring the inefficiency and unfairness that might arise from asymmetrical knowledge and power and from multiple-equilibria in asset markets, and ignoring also the negative externalities following from instability in income. The 2007–09 world economic crisis arguably shows the risk of relying too exclusively on the market in the public management of the financial sector.

Utopian communities are so rare that there is as little risk now as in Adam Smith's day that we shall look to the benevolence of the butcher or baker for our dinner. We shall not go overboard in that way for civil society. The mistake today would rather be to neglect civil society's role – and that of the active humanity that underlies it – in, at the very least, supporting the observance of the rules of behaviour on which the market and the state at their best depend for their efficiency and fairness. As we have seen (Chapter 8), active humanity, acting through institutions of civil society, can transform very much for the better the provision of physical infrastructure, or the management of a common resource, or the working of a manufacturing enterprise, or the meeting of a depressed and deprived community's social needs.

We have this range of instruments then at our disposal. Some are suited for some purposes and some for others. As we have suggested in Chapter 7, the question of where the lines are best drawn in a particular country and time may depend on the character of the institutions and the administrative capacity present there and then rather than going by a single set of rules. And it is not a simple matter of *either–or*. State and market can be invoked together. For example, while still relying on a market mechanism for allocation, the state may properly influence the prices in the case of an externality, either by levy or subsidy or by acting itself as a market participant. But there are some standard guidelines on the cases for state intervention that help to clarify thought.

Furthermore, *active humanity*, the motivating force of civil society – involving trust and trustworthiness, responsibility, and creativity – is always likely to enhance the effectiveness and productivity of *appropriate* state and market measures. (Where the rules are clearly fair and efficient, a sense of responsibility will encourage compliance with them.) Also, because the exercise of trust/trustworthiness and responsibility – at least where they are reciprocated – and of creation, are in general pleasurable, what is achieved through them socially is quite likely to be costless or even to have its value enhanced by the means of supplying it.

It is difficult not to see in most of the successor states of the Soviet Union the gaping hole in social arrangements – even after attempts had been made to revive markets – where civil society had been systematically repressed for 70 years.

It is vital to look at market, state and civil society critically and pragmatically, not idolizing any of them by erecting it into an exclusive ideology.

Economic growth

In 2005, for the first time since the dawning of the industrial age, emerging economies accounted for more than half of global GDP at PPP.

(Economist, *20/9/2008, p. 6*)

Why economic growth happens – or fails to happen

This is still in part **a mystery**. We can say that, from the meanings of the terms, it must be due to some combination of increased factor inputs and improved techniques, and even go to the trouble of dividing the contributions accordingly. This, however, tells us nothing much of interest from the economist's viewpoint: nothing as a matter of social causation on *why* the investments or improvements happen. If a theatre is being built, the interesting answer to the question *why* is *not* that so much concrete and glass and tiles and textiles and the rest have been brought together. The relevant *why* has to be why one or a number of people have decided to risk building the theatre, and why others have been prepared to risk providing the finance and the insurance.

It is the amassing together of such decisions and others in one locality that constitutes economic growth in that place. The actions taken may be small improvements that are virtually costless (though still possibly of substantial value). Or they may involve large and expensive ventures. The investors and financiers may be poor individuals working within the informal sector, or they may be large corporations, but if the investors and financiers and insurers decide, in view of the conditions, that the investment can take place, then it will. The puzzle we should have to solve in order to explain growth is what causes more than a critical number and weight of such decisions to be taken in one area or at one time rather than another, and what causes investors in some places to become progressively more productive themselves or to displace others who are less productive. Beside the objective market opportunities in, or accessible through, the areas concerned, it is probably a matter of learning opportunities, competitive pressures, how far the business environment is objectively and subjectively favourable, and the attitudes of mind of the potential investors and financiers. We are faced with the task of fitting this (partly *a priori*) reasoning with experience about the publicly known circumstances in which relatively fast growth is recorded.

Where is it happening?

The world has found no general formula for generating consistent fast economic growth in income per head for the low- and middle-income countries: say at an average of 5 per cent or more a year, enough to double average income within 15 years. Yet, growth averaging as fast as that has been occurring, for low-income and low-middle-income countries covering now a large part of the world's people. In some cases this has gone on for only a few years so far, though with prospects of continuing, but in others it has already proceeded over decades.

If we separate this continuous, fast economic growth, beginning at various times in the half-century from 1950, from the irregular and fluctuating growth based on mineral and hydrocarbon exports, we find it concentrated until the time of writing in one area of the world: East Asia, and less consistently South-East Asia, and more recently also South Asia, regions that between them happen to contain well over half the world's people. There have lately been rates of transformation there comparable to those of which some of the early Asian and African independence leaders only dreamed.

The 2008 Commission on Growth and Development chaired by Michael Spence (combining in its membership a galaxy of scholarship and policy experience) identifies 13 countries that had experienced growth in total (not *per capita*) GDP of 7 per cent a year over a period of at least 25 years since 1950, and two others (India and Vietnam) in which they expected similar feats to be recorded. Of these 15, all but four were in East, South-East or South Asia. One of the remaining four was Brazil, whose spurt of exceptional growth had ended by the 1970s. The other three were very small states (with less than 4 million people each): Oman, Botswana and Malta (Spence *et al.* 2008, pp. 19–20).

It now seems that, round about the year 2000 and after, another group may have been in process of joining them: the ex-Communist 'transition' countries of East and Central Europe, reviving spectacularly after a disastrous time for most through much of the 1990s. Their spurt in the early 2000s applied not only to Russia and Azerbaijan, which were boosted by the oil boom, but also to Albania, Armenia, Belarus, Bosnia, Bulgaria, Estonia, Georgia, Latvia, Lithuania, Moldova, Romania, Serbia, the Slovak Republic and Ukraine, all with annual growth rates *per head* over the six years from 2000 to 2006 of 5 per cent or more, and eleven of them, including Ukraine, of 7 per cent or more. At the time of writing it may be too early to judge this as an economic miracle rather than a rebound from the miserable (for them) 1990s. Those involved are middle-income countries, a number of them upper-middle. For that reason their transformation is likely to be less spectacular, and what they have been achieving less revolutionary, than for those that started really poor. But they are worth watching, even if they seem for a while to succumb to the general collapse of growth from 2008.

Beyond geographical concentration, a common feature of the East and South-East and South Asian countries' consistent-fast-growth experience is that it depended heavily on manufactured or, to a lesser extent, service exports (notably of services rendered tradable by the communication revolution), and that in most cases it seemed to begin after a deliberate change of policy in the direction of openness to the world: measures to encourage overseas trade or foreign direct investment or both. The change was most striking in China and Vietnam, with their controlled economies, previously concerned for self-sufficiency, where the shift to openness (after 1978 and after 1986 respectively) was combined with a much greater reliance domestically on market mechanisms. South Korea's authorities, who (like the Japanese from *their* own early modernization starting about ninety years before) were unenthusiastic at first about foreign direct investment, nevertheless adapted their trade policy so that the measures they had adopted for import-substitution should not discourage exports. Taiwan abandoned its import-substitution policy around 1960 and moved close to the same league in openness as Hong Kong and Singapore. India liberalized both its external and its domestic-market policy in stages, though incompletely, principally from a 1991 beginning.

These countries, growing faster proportionally than those in the rich world, either at the time or (except for Japan) earlier or ever, have been fulfilling some theorists' predictions of *convergence* between rich and poor. If they go on at this rate, they will 'catch up'. Singapore and Hong Kong have already done so, and are now among the world's richest. Taiwan and South Korea already count in the high-income class.

At the other extreme are those countries that comprise what Paul Collier (2007) calls *the bottom billion*: those that for much of the time (except in primary-commodity booms or after new resource discoveries or in recovery after wars) have stagnated or fallen in income per head. These comprise in his classification most of sub-Saharan Africa, Central Asia, and a few others, such as Myanmar/Burma, Laos, Haiti and Bolivia. For them, the gap with the rich has generally widened. The proportional gap between sub-Saharan Africa and the rich world *increased* over the half-century, especially after 1980.

In between are most of the rest, not so obviously successful or problematic, including most of Latin America, Western Asia and North Africa. Brazil experienced a prolonged burst of fast development after 1950, but – like much of the rest of Latin America – also periods of chronic instability, notably over the last quarter of the century. Some other countries, such as Egypt, have shown similarities with East Asia but with more modest growth.

So, sixty or so years after development economics first roused wide and consistent interest, the income gap between the extremes is on the face of it as great as ever or greater, but we seem to be heading for a world in which the distribution of rich and poor is very different from that in 1950. The rich nations of that time are still rich, but others have joined them, and a further huge cohort of people shows prospects of doing so over the next fifty years or sooner, world order and the physical environment permitting.

What makes it happen?

What has been the compass that has got the Asian fast-developers to where they are? We don't know the whole story but we have some clues.

It is certainly *not* the development economics of the 1950s and 1960s with its export-pessimism and distrust of economic relationships with rich countries. In fact, opening to trade and (often also) to inward investment typically appears to have played a key, or at least a triggering, role in their outbursts of growth. At the same time, they have not conformed unreservedly to the economically liberal 'Washington consensus', or less politely 'market-fundamentalism' – promoted by the multilaterals and (more or less) by the US in the 1980s – which aimed in general to minimize government intervention. China, though allowing and eventually encouraging private enterprise after 1978, nevertheless retained much of the substance of the big state-owned enterprises from its centralized-economy period and much arbitrary power of local officials over moderate-sized private enterprises. South Korea, like Japan from the late nineteenth century, supported private enterprise but in a 'guided' form, with favoured companies given the privileges and responsibilities of fulfilling the state's development plans. China, against IMF doctrine at the time, continued through the 1990s to control its international capital movements, and – not coincidentally – escaped the contagion of the currency crises to which Thailand, Indonesia, Malaysia and South Korea, followed by Russia and Brazil, succumbed in and after 1997. (Malaysia imposed controls after the event.) China also opened at first very hesitantly to FDI in the 1980s, imposing various limiting conditions that were successively relaxed.

It would appear that not only have the fast-growers not followed a stereotyped doctrine. Their policies toward the outside world have also varied among themselves. Yet there does seem to have been this common element: that they had all oriented themselves to exporting, in some cases as a radical reversal of previous policies, before their individual phases of fast growth began.

It would be encouraging to many of us – with prejudices from either end of the state-versus-market spectrum – to believe that relatively uncorrupt government and the rule of law distinguished these 'successful' developing countries from others less successful in their growth records. But it is not clearly or consistently so (see Table 6.1). Singapore certainly rated exceptionally highly in 2007 for its lack of perceived corruption on TI's scale, and Hong Kong also scored very well (both even a bit more so than Japan, the US or Germany in 2007). Taiwan, Malaysia and South Korea rated quite well, and it may not be entirely fortuitous that Botswana came out as the least corrupt society in Africa as well as the fastest-growing. China and India, by contrast, ranked only 72nd-equal in the total of 180 countries, Vietnam 118th-equal, and Indonesia 143rd-equal. China is notoriously far from being an arena in which the rule of law prevails, but it has been suggested (Chapter 6) that the system of patronage from officials possibly provides enough security and predictability for investors who know the ropes: that the corruption that is simply illegal, but controlled by conventions and understandings, may be better for business and growth than the corruption that is unmoderated and unpredictable.

Is there any likely characteristic relevant to growth in the fact that all those countries that were the fastest growers over the last 20 years of the last century are close to each other geographically? If India had not strikingly joined the company later, it would be tempting to suppose, as we suggested in Chapter 2, that the clue might be some favourable element in Chinese culture. Korea and Japan and Vietnam had all been greatly influenced culturally by China. In a cultural sense, Singapore is virtually a Chinese city, and Taiwan is a Chinese island, and it seems to be very largely true that many of the major entrepreneurs of Thailand, Malaysia, and Indonesia belong to families of Chinese origin, in some countries more, in some less, assimilated into the host populations. But India's position among the fast-growers does not so easily fit that hypothesis.

Yet there may be similarities of resources in the broadest terms – including in a rather looser sense culture – that are plausibly relevant to the capacity to get onto the world's industrial ladder and that characterize China and its diaspora, India, Japan, Vietnam, and Korea and parts at least of South-East Asia: a high ratio of people to usable agricultural land, which may have instilled habits of planning and economizing and left these economies, in their largely traditional state, with a low 'efficiency wage'; and at the same time ancient, literate civilizations, with highly educated elites and long-standing specialization among skills and functions.

If growth depends to a large extent on private investment, and private investment depends on the readiness of people to take risks in a way that is simultaneously imaginative, well-informed and rational, it would not be surprising if the prevailing culture – habits and attitudes – played an important part in its prevalence.

It is possible that these endowments – shared to some extent with the original industrializers of Western Europe – coupled with a reasonable degree and duration of civil order (after 1870 for Japan, after various dates in the second half of the twentieth century for the rest) and financial stability, provided the preconditions. Then opening to the world and to a measure of market mechanisms domestically was plausibly the other main element needed.

Japan and the 'Four Tigers', at the start of their periods of fast growth, seem also to have been distinctly more advanced in general education than countries at comparable income levels, and China in the 1970s more so than most other low-income countries. Tentatively we suggest that a certain accumulated investment in human capital may have been another requirement.

It may then be that consistent growth at the high rates recently experienced in much of Asia depends on:

1 a world **open** to absorbing large additions to supplies of manufactured imports (and later also service imports);

2 an appropriate endowment of '**resources**', including widely spread **experience** and **habits of mind** in the country concerned, that are suited to entrepreneurship, coupled *initially* with low 'efficiency-wages' (real wages with their costs discounted for the efficiency with which work is carried on);

3 a modicum of **civil order**, **respect for property**, and financial and macroeconomic **stability**;

4 significant cumulative investment, public or private or both, in **health**, **education and training**;

5 **policies** that *avoid blocking or discouraging* enterprise, or business relations with the outside world, or (unless for good reason) the internal operation of markets.

Given that the world today satisfies condition **1**, there would then be four further conditions to be fulfilled: one broadly a matter of culture and possibly outside the capacity of any government to generate if it is not already present; one the framework of predictability, which any government needs to value for its own sake; one some elements of past and present human development, itself perhaps owing something to prevailing habits and attitudes of the public; and the last simply a matter of policy.

Though they express it differently, there is considerable overlap between this list and the common features that the members of the Spence Commission find among their 15 fast-developers (Spence, *et al.*, 2008, pp. 21–8). They recognize the relevance of the world's post-1950 trading environment, and they state essential elements that broadly cover (though they go beyond) conditions **3**, **4** and **5** above. But they do not venture into questions of culture and habits of mind, allowing their list to be one simply of what may be *necessary* conditions.

The five conditions that they judge to be satisfied by all their fast-growing economies are the following (p. 21):

1 They fully exploited the world economy

2 They maintained macroeconomic stability

3 They mustered high rates of saving and investment

4 They let markets allocate resources

5 They had committed, credible, and capable governments.

Under the third point the Commission observed that the successful economies in their periods of rapid growth all devoted 25 per cent or more of GDP to investment, most of it provided domestically. Of this 5 to 7 per cent of GDP was on physical infrastructure, and an additional 7 to 8 per cent of GDP (technically not all of it counted as investment) was spending on human capital (health, education and training). (The physical infrastructure requirement is one that should probably be added to our list.)

How far the successful economies fulfilled some of these conditions (notably the fifth) must inevitably be to some extent a matter of judgement.

The Commission members' view of the relevance of openness to the world economy was that it meant that the successful economies *both* imported ideas from the outside world through trade and incoming investment *and* earned foreign exchange by providing goods to the outside world, which subjected them to competition. There was a large emphasis in their analysis of the impact of outside-world contact on both *learning* and *competition*. Growth would inevitably slow down once the developing economy had absorbed most of the current lessons and there was no longer a big gap between the relevant know-how inside and that outside. So countries at the rich end of the spectrum will grow comparatively slowly: they have less to learn from the outside world. On similar reasoning we could suggest that another marker of the point at which possibilities of further *very fast* growth might stop could be that the developing economy was selling a range of goods to the outside world similar in technological sophistication, or in relative factor-proportions in production, to those that it was buying from that world: that it was moving into the arena of *intra-industry trade* (trade within, rather than between, industries), which has tended to characterize trade in manufactures between rich economies.

If the general character of our own statement of the conditions of fast growth is broadly sound, policy will be relevant, but also what a country brings in the way of endowments, physical and human, current and historical, but with the *natural* physical resources possibly the least important component. A country *cannot expect* to generate very rapid growth *unless* the most elusive element, the cultural conditions – the habits and attitudes – are present. However, if they *are* present, its government can still *block* growth by adopting **policies that discourage enterprise or business relations with the outside world**, limiting external transactions, tying up commercial and productive activity in regulations, treating the investors on whom growth depends as *prima facie* criminals; and it does seem that these were policies widely adopted by developing countries in the third quarter of the last century.

It is also obvious that opportunities for development in all good senses are obliterated if there is **armed conflict** affecting much of the country. Paul Collier (2007) has drawn attention to the vicious circles that easily develop between warfare and economic stagnation or decline. In Africa, where the phenomenon has been so common, this leads to a *prima facie* need for outside action *either* to put a stop to fighting *or* to rescue an economy directly from otherwise irremediable misery (in the last resort, he proposes, through straight welfare expenditures). Where a government that is recognized as legitimate, or both sides in a conflict, will accept UN troops as peacekeepers, this avoids some of the difficulties of foreign military intervention. But, for this solution to be effective, the UN has often needed more resources than it has available for the purpose.

Even if the cultural conditions for very rapid growth are absent or present only in attenuated form, it is rational to fulfil as far as possible the other conditions – those that depend on policy, 3, 4 and 5, or the five stated by the Spence Commission – so as to make the best of what growth possibilities there are in the existing cultural and other underlying circumstances. Promoting growth should be seen not as all-or-nothing but as something incremental, something to which not only some big public decisions but also a huge number of small decisions, private and public, may contribute.

It seems very likely that much additional growth across the world can be achieved by policy moves in the directions indicated by **3**, **4** and **5**: a stable business and macroeconomic environment, systematically enhanced human capital, economic openness, and deregulation wherever regulation is unnecessary for the public good and contrary to the interests of the poor. This in turn will increase the prospects of the *spontaneous* element in poverty reduction, and at the same time make all the aspects of it *that depend more directly on policy and public resources* easier to achieve.

As well as maintaining incentives for the private sector to provide resources and to allocate them efficiently, governments will need to husband their own resources, using budgetary disciplines that keep spending decisions as immune as possible from the whims of individual politicians or pressure from vested interests. For the bigger decisions it would be appropriate to use both financial and economic cost–benefit analysis, not necessarily as a binding decider but as at least a defence against the worst mistakes. In short the rules of good economic housekeeping apply here no less than in the rich world and can be expected to favour economic growth and attainment.

Where we might expect fast economic growth in the near future

If the resource pattern in the broad sense in which we have used the term 'resource', including certain cultural characteristics, provides the background precondition, we may reasonably hope that Bangladesh and Pakistan, which share so much historically with India – and maybe also Egypt – will find a way of treading a similar path if the economic policies are right and civil order is maintained. Also Brazil, though very different in physical resources from the East and South Asians, was one of the world's fast-developers for a period before 1980, until it was knocked off course, in part at least by its financial instability and debt; and it has already used its rare range of endowments for a big expansion of agricultural exports together with manufactures. These four big countries cover between them over half a billion people. Bangladesh, its citizens pressed to the limit to survive on their tiny patch of earth, must undergo a big transfer of people out of agriculture. This is happening but not fast enough. Possibly enough political stability there might let the process rip.

BOX 25.1 MIRACLES?

'*Economic miracles do happen, but as yet we do not know how to make them.*'

Source: Gerald M. Meier and James E. Rauch, *Leading Issues in Economic Development*, 8th edition, Oxford University Press, New York, 2005, p. 41.

Making poverty history?

The hope of making poverty history – or, to be much less ambitious, eliminating say in the first quarter of the present century most of the one-dollar-a-day poverty that serves as a marker for the multiple deprivations and insecurities that typically go with it – cannot, it seems, *rely on* fast (East-Asian-rate) economic growth, very helpful though that growth can be if it occurs. This is *both* because we have no sure way of inducing such fast economic growth *and* because fast growth does not *guarantee* quick or universal poverty reduction.

The three big reservoirs of extreme poverty have been until recently South Asia, sub-Saharan Africa, and China. However, in China's case unskilled wages had been rising over the ten years from around 1998 to the time this book was sent for publication. This suggests that China has passed the turning-point at which it has moved out of the Lewis 'unlimited-labour' world. Beyond that point workers on the lowest labour-incomes, rural and urban, are likely to get the advantage of continuing growth, as unskilled labour becomes increasingly 'scarce'. Growth *then* becomes the proverbial rising tide that lifts many (though not in itself all) boats. India, where the export boom in services depends on more skilled labour, has not yet shown signs of reaching the same point. The latest estimate in the World Bank's *WDR* (2008b) of the proportion of extremely poor people in China (2004) was 9.9 per cent, and in India (2004–5) 34.3 per cent (World Bank, 2008, p. 336).[1] There is still a huge burden of extreme poverty in India, which may not respond much *immediately* to further economic growth (if the supposition that it is still in the 'Lewis world' is correct), but a continuation of growth at recent rates should surely absorb the surplus labour before long.

Much can be done against such extreme poverty even where there is only modest economic growth. Striking examples are Sri Lanka in the fairly recent past and Kerala up to the time of writing. There have also been cases in which lowish-income countries have been able to ride times of serious crop failure with no loss of life and even sometimes improved child nutrition. But passively accepting stagnation at a low level in output is hazardous, for reasons implied by Collier (2007). A vicious circle, in which on one side *income that is low and stagnant or falling*, and on the other *armed conflict*, feed into each other, can so easily develop. The lesson from Collier would seem to be that neither those within the country nor the outside world should be content with stagnant or falling income. The vicious circle should be broken at whatever point that is possible. Though there is no positive formula for generating really fast growth, there are, as we have implied, plenty of impediments to growth common enough in developing countries that can be targeted for removal: kleptocracy and all varieties of macro-corruption (which deplete the resources for physical- and human-capital investment), over-regulation, insecurity of property, restriction of foreign trade and investment.

Three lines of attack on poverty

There are three arms of an attack on poverty, each of which can to a point stand on its own but should if at all possible be combined with the others.

One is an equalizing growth policy – a rational growth policy geared to equalization, the Taiwan solution – giving growth an equalizing cast by, for example, opening to world competition in manufactures (which for suitable candidates serves both growth and equalization purposes), decentralizing industry where this can be done without manifest excess cost, giving a labour-using slant to public procurement.

A second – the Sri Lanka and Kerala, possibly also Cape Verde, approach – is concentrating on providing public and merit goods, principally in the form of extending and improving health services, nutrition of vulnerable groups, education and training. This will probably contribute to growth *potential*, but the other measures needed for realizing that potential may be neglected.

A third – we can now perhaps call it the Indian and South American line – is offering social safety-nets for those without minimally adequate means of support. This is intrinsically difficult in poor countries, with its conundrums not yet fully cracked but under assault.

---

[1] As mentioned in Chapter 10, China's total PPP GNI for 2006 was revised downward by 40 per cent and India's by 35 per cent as a result of the building-in of the implications of the 2005 price survey, which gave a picture of much higher prices, and in consequence lower real income, in China and India than had been supposed (World Bank, *WDI* 2008, pp. 1–5; *WDR* 2008; A. Seidel, *Financial Times*, 14/11/2007, p. 15; *Economist*, 24/5/2008, p. 110). This would raise the extreme-poverty headcounts for both: China's, it seems, on a slightly less rigorous test than before, to about 16 per cent. But this would not have falsified the view that there had been a big *fall* in extreme poverty in China since 1990.

The best solution would be to combine the three elements. Conceptually and politically the second is likely to be easiest. But without the other two it has obvious shortcomings.

To maximize the improvement in human security, there needs also to be a serious national policy of economic stabilization (Chapter 12).

Equalizing growth policies

A rational growth policy, in view of what has been said above about the conditions favourable to economic growth, would appear to be one in which a government has a steady framework of property rights, rule of law and economic stabilization; invests or promotes investment in the physical and human infrastructure of production, particularly in education and training; keeps open to foreign trade and generally also to investment from abroad; and avoids regulation of business activity and consumption except where there is a strong social case for it. Even though the land redistribution and rural industrialization of the Taiwan experience might be out of the question (for political and natural-endowment reasons respectively), this pro-growth programme in itself, pursued impartially, would have some of the equalizing slants (labour-intensity, intensive human-resource development) mentioned as part of the Taiwan recipe.

Beyond that there are at least three fairly persuasive prescriptions for contributing to growth – all of them mentioned at points in this book – by particular devices whose impact is directly beneficial to some of those who are very poor.

These three comprise first, as argued comprehensively by Hernando de Soto, *legalizing the informal sector* as far as possible, giving *firm titles* for housing in informal settlements and minimizing the bureaucratic obstacles to legal registration of even the smallest businesses (Chapters 14 and 19). A second is for *microfinance*: large numbers of very small business loans to many of the poorest people, administered in ways that go close to guaranteeing their servicing and repayment (Chapter 19). A third is for the promotion of *intermediate technology*: productive equipment and methods that involve techniques, inputs of capital and scales of production such that they are accessible (preferably without subsidy) to operators with very little access to capital or high-tech skills (Chapter 18, where reservations to the case are also entered). These methods are not guaranteed to give big returns in economic growth, but, at least if they can be pursued with very little net subsidy, the strong presumption is that they will be favourable, and all are calculated not only to make poor people tangibly richer but also to give them more sense of freedom and control.

Supplying public and merit goods

National-government, civil-society, and world activity can be combined – with enough vision and will – to attack the many aspects of world poverty not measured directly by deficiency of personal cash income: disease, ignorance, environmental squalor, lack of access to capital, gender discrimination, lack of social power, and all aspects of insecurity (insecure tenure, lack of insurance against disasters, food insecurity, crop-earnings insecurity, general macroeconomic fluctuations). Some but not all these objectives could be pursued with enough cash, and some of the cash could come from outside.

Positively, to take some further examples, research could be pursued to obtain improved crops for developing-country conditions, as happened spectacularly in the 'green revolution' of the 1960s and could probably happen again now with further miracles possible through GM crops (Chapter 16); and there can be considerable enhancement of both research and action programmes for the elimination of the main remaining infectious diseases. At great but probably diminishing expense, ARV drugs could before long be provided universally for susceptible patients with AIDS, the big orphan-maker; and, given suitable resources (for spraying and impregnated bednets, with pharmaceuticals filling the gaps), malaria, the child-killer, could be seriously curbed.

These last are fields in which global action – by international agencies such as the World Health Organization, and by private foundations – has been particularly fruitful. Of the ten examples of highly successful 'aid' ventures of regional or global scale listed by Jeffrey Sachs (2005, pp. 259–65), seven (if we include family-planning) are health projects, and one is the private-foundation research that produced the green revolution. With suitable public-sector incentives (where market incentives are lacking because of the poverty of the beneficiaries), commercial pharmaceutical and biotechnology firms may be induced to do the relevant research and development – though most easily if the incentives are international.

Stabilizing measures and disciplines

Reducing the insecurity that is an important element in poverty requires, for a start, *stabilizing* action at a number of levels – world and national and local, official and commercial (Chapter 12) – many with no net financial cost.

Safety-nets and free services to support those most deprived; social insurance for the next layer up

Then, for human security there are further gaps to be filled by free schooling and health services, at least for the poorest, and by social safety-nets, and, for those not quite so poor, by part-contributory social insurance.

Income-safety-nets (as discussed in Chapter 10) need not be ruled out in developing countries, and have been coming increasingly into existence recently as one valid approach for reducing extreme poverty and insecurity.

It seems that some variant of either the South American conditional family allowance or the Indian cash-for-work scheme could be viable and affordable at a useful level if honestly and consistently administered, or they might be combined, though it might be difficult to eliminate anomalies and apparent unfairness from either. Some help from local civil society might be very desirable in administration.

International support for poverty reduction

This involves the closely related questions of expanding and improving aid, and modifying and enhancing the array of international organizations.

International economic organizations exist partly to provide **global public-goods** of potential material benefit to all countries, and partly to express the impulses of international **solidarity** in supporting the poverty-reducing and growth efforts of the developing countries. These two functions can not be entirely separated.

The background in 2008–9 is that much of the developing world is falling behind on the schedule for fulfilling the Millennium Development Goals by 2015, and that, for decades since aid targets for the rich countries have been propounded, most have failed to fulfil them; and there have been similar failures over targets for aid to Africa agreed by the G7 in 2005 at Gleneagles.

On **aid** we have asserted that more is needed; that far more could be provided at relatively little cost to the donor countries; and would be provided if they fulfilled their paper commitments, notably the one to give 0.7 per cent of income in aid. But reforms are needed to make the aid that is given more effective and to answer criticisms, some of which are undoubtedly valid.

In particular, bilateral aid from the various donors needs to be **co-ordinated** overall and in each recipient country, with one of the multilaterals recognized as co-ordinator. Beside making the aid itself more useful and effective, this could bring other benefits such as reducing the burden of aid bureaucracy on the recipient governments. We suggested that the **World Bank, with a much extended brief** (including a general capacity to make grants as well as loans possibly through a new arm, and scope to make grants or loans through agencies other than national governments), as well as under wider outside scrutiny, might be that co-ordinator, and that in that case it would be highly desirable for its influence among the donors to be increased through its acquisition of an own-source of funds separate from the contributions voted by member countries individually. There are funds of significant size that could plausibly be treated as of global provenance which might fill this role if that was generally agreed (see Chapter 21).

Some of the most successful projects involving aid, including a number of the ten cited by Sachs (2005, pp. 259–65), have been large co-ordinated efforts, principally in health and agricultural technology, outside national aid programmes and depending on multilaterals or private-foundation funding. Recently 'multiactor global funds', particularly on vaccination and infectious diseases, have become an important part of the scene (see Chapter 21).

We also suggested in the course of the book the possibility of **a more active world-stabilization role for the IMF** through extension of its power to issue and withdraw Special Drawing Rights (SDRs) for world counter-cyclical purposes, giving it more of the power and responsibility typical of a national central bank (Chapter 12). And we mooted (Chapter 19) the creation of an **international tax organization** to promote the tax co-operation that seems to have so much potential, especially but not only in the interest of developing countries. In addition (Chapter 12) we raised the possibility of an **earnings-insurance scheme** for the primary-exporting countries through their governments, following the principles of commercial insurance more closely in several respects than the existing IMF and EU systems, possibly to run alongside the World Bank's project for stabilizing *individual* primary-producers' incomes by giving them access for the purpose to the derivatives markets.

Economic growth and other values

We resolved in the first chapter of this book, following Amartya Sen, to treat 'development' – the desired outcome – as going well beyond economic growth to represent a comprehensive enlargement of human freedom. Economic growth, peace and civil order, and certain vital elements of environmental sustainability, are needed instrumentally for reducing material deprivation. Enlarged freedom also requires electoral democracy, freedom of political expression, the maintenance of individual human rights, and for those purposes and others the rule of law.

In an Olympian, humorous, and wonderfully balanced appraisal of the different patterns of achievements and failures of India and China, Sen argued in the mid-1990s against two positions taken officially at that time by India's and China's governments respectively.

At an international conference in 1994 'the official Indian position involved an attack on "the concepts of sustainable human development and of human security". . . Priority would have to be given, in this view, to focusing on economic variables, rather than on the constituents of so-called human development, including such "social" features as health services and educational opportunities' (Sen, 1995, p. 2). Sen calls this position POSH: 'postponability of social- and human-development'. In fact, by contrast with China at the time, where some of the pre-reform social legacy remained, health and education in India had been seriously neglected – except, as Sen mentions, in Kerala (p. 14). Sen argues, on a number of grounds, that the extraordinarily high prevalence in India of illiteracy and morbidity was not only bad in itself but a severe handicap, in spite of the economic reforms of the 1990s, to economic growth.

China's government, on the other hand, in practice as well as in its statements, takes a position that Sen calls PUSH: 'political unreadiness for human rights' – as a number of other governments have done (p. 3). The idea is that free elections and free expression and the capacity to assert human rights hinder economic growth, and that poor people do not value them highly in any case. Sen contests each part of that assertion. The evidence on the first element of it is at best ambiguous, while on the second he cites as one piece of evidence apparently against, the decisive rejection of India's Congress government in the election that was held effectively as something close to a plebiscite on its 'state of emergency' of the mid-1970s. Then 'the suppression of political and civil rights was firmly rejected, and the electorate of one of the poorest countries in the world showed itself to be no less keen on protesting against the denial of basic liberties and rights than it is in complaining about economic poverty' (p. 22).

Against the view that political rights are only a hindrance to material prosperity, Sen quotes a remarkable 1962 speech by Mao Zedong, in which Mao quite objectively blames the disaster of his 'Great Leap Forward' of 1959–61, in which 23 to 30 million people are reckoned to have died of famine, on the lack of democracy: 'Without democracy you have no understanding of what is happening down below; . . . top-level organs of leadership will depend on one-sided and incorrect material to decide issues . . .' (Mao Zedong, 1974, cited in Sen, op.cit., p. 28). And Sen argues that, in referring only to the 'informational' value of democracy and free expression, Mao understates the case for it. It also has an 'incentive' role for governments and a 'constructive' role in promoting public discussion through which people's needs can be formulated. This is in addition to what he regards as the 'intrinsic importance' of democracy (pp. 28–9).

With its admittedly faulty electoral democracy, and its free press, India has avoided major famines ever since its independence.

Sen takes the view that both political freedoms and human-social-development are of fundamental intrinsic value, and *in addition* both can contribute decisively to economic growth and material prosperity. There need be no conflict. All three can be pursued simultaneously. It is a matter of exploiting the potential synergies.

At a number of points in this book, we have come across cases in which the remedy for one ill is good instrumentally on other grounds or good in itself. Equality of rights and opportunities for women (Chapter 15) could be expected, almost unreservedly, through various mechanisms, to have a positive impact on economic growth. The most effective way of checking population growth seemed (Chapter 13) to be increasing women's education and reducing young-child mortality. Economic growth and poverty reduction would tend to reduce internal conflict. Checking internal conflict in turn would facilitate economic growth and poverty reduction (Chapter 10).

Some might argue that international migration, at least where it did not generate suspicions and hostility, could also qualify as a win-win (Chapter 24).

Increasing the revenue of developing countries appeared to be consistent with increasing the effectiveness, and therefore also fairness, of tax administration in rich countries, through international tax co-operation, without a need for either side to raise its tax rates. And there are other straightforward global public-goods of interest to rich and poor alike, notably peacekeeping – virtually anywhere and everywhere – and completing the elimination of a number of infectious diseases that can revive in regions from which they have almost disappeared. Further, economic stabilization is a win-win game, with the stability of any one country or occupational or industry group favourably affecting that of others. And removing unnecessary regulations is fiscally costless, but it may give a considerable boost to enterprises from the smallest to the largest, attract potential investors, increase real economic activity, and reduce the (real) price of services.

In a number of these matters there are still choices to be made by policy over priorities and timing on the use of limited resources, but intelligent exploitation of the synergies, helped where appropriate by international co-operation, can change 'either . . . or' into 'both . . . and'.

However, all favourable economic prospects – development, poverty reduction – depend on the world's political capacity to head off two apocalyptic threats: first, nuclear war or nuclear terrorism; and second, uncontrolled climate change. Without (1) determined moves toward a non-proliferation regime accepted by all significant states and a global system of securing supplies of fissile material[2] – or without (2) a tight world emission-reduction agreement, coupled with radical (and costly) interim ('palliative') measures to stop the habitat of tens of millions of people from becoming uninhabitable – all bets on world development and poverty are off.

The nuclear-proliferation and new-cold-war threat is worrying but the clock is not yet exactly ticking.

There is, however, one spectre at the feast that requires active and prompt exorcism and makes some conflict of purposes impossible to avoid. This is the risk – coming close to a certainty if nothing is done with global co-operation to stop it – to the environment, above all of climate change: a threat that large, densely inhabited parts of the earth will before very long become simply uninhabitable. Combating it will require sacrifices of consumption and of what we have come to think of as economic growth – arguably in part through false accounting (see Chapter 11). Because global co-ordinated action is needed, requiring at least some sacrifices, the political obstacles to averting disaster are enormous.

There are two ways in which economic reasoning can help. First, it can use its utmost ingenuity in devising **ways of sharing the sacrifices** that all parties – China, the US, Malawi, Mexico – can be brought to consider as fair. Second, it can make sure that the **incentives** put in place by any agreed system of control – rising environmental taxes, declining tradable quotas; those directly agreed internationally, those applied nationally – have the incentive effects intended, including (most important) adequate incentives for **further technological developments** (such as are happening all the time where the incentives are strong enough), which will almost certainly have to be a part of the mix if it is to do the job. Every scrap of ingenuity is needed here to improve the trade-off.

Beside reaching agreement on means for slowing and eventually halting the processes of anthropogenic climate change, there is a further large challenge unavoidable **because of the change already built in** before stability in atmospheric greenhouse-gas concentrations can be reached. This makes it only too likely that some inhabited areas will be almost continuously flooded, and others will run out of water. In fact, there are ominous signs that

---

[2] In early 2007 a 'utopian' proposal along these lines was made by twenty of the Americans outside the then Administration who were most influential and authoritative on foreign and strategic policy, including Henry Kissinger, George Schultz, William Perry and Sam Nunn (Epstein, 2007, p. 30).

these processes have already begun. To avoid the need for tens of millions of people either to die where they stand or to move and resettle (a political nightmare), a co-ordinated effort involving very large outlays on infrastructure is likely to be necessary.[3]

Devising a system of paying for this, as well as making the long-term changes needed in emissions, in a way that will appear fair to all parties will again involve the utmost ingenuity and flexibility and (to be realistic) extensive abandonment of the attitudes with which governments normally go into international negotiations.

So, the message with which the book ends is in many ways hopeful. There are abundant synergies to be exploited in the development business. All hangs of course on the substantial maintenance of world peace and the progressive neutering of nuclear weapons. Given that boon, there is much on the side of the world's people. Economic ingenuity has plenty of win-win possibilities and potential virtuous circles to exploit.

However, climate change poses the mother of all challenges. There are real conflicts of what is needed with many of the ingrained impulses and habits of mind to which governments and their publics are accustomed.

Together with the generosity of spirit that will be necessary, there has probably never been a greater need for cool economic thinking to improve the trade-offs in ways that are manifestly fair: to ransack the possibilities of efficiency and equity.

Summary conclusions

We sum up first with nine **generalizations relating to policy on growth and poverty**.

1 Although we have no formula for generating really fast growth on East Asian lines, which may depend in part on cultural habits and attitudes, there are in many countries potential policy measures by which the rate of growth can be increased, by suppressing or reversing: over-regulation; insecurity of property; restriction of foreign trade and investment; lack of appropriate investment in human capital, especially general education and technical training and public and clinical health services; inadequate investment in energy, communication and transport infrastructure; and kleptocracy and all varieties of macro-corruption that deplete resources for these useful purposes.

2 Even in low-income countries and in the absence of growth at significant rates there are usually a number of measures that a determined national government can take for significantly ameliorating poverty: through building equalizing and labour-using bias into its public-spending and private-investment and trade policies; through advancing the provision of public and merit goods bearing on health, education and nutrition; through macro-stabilization; through extending the protection, rather than the obstruction, of the law to the informal sector; through fostering (at arm's length) microfinance; and through social safety-nets. But without growth social development must still be limited and precarious.

---

[3] A recent *Economist* report (13/9/2008, pp. 74–5) gives a number of estimates by various bodies of the annual cost of preventing disasters on this account, of which the greatest is $86 billion a year by 2015. This seems at first sight large – of the same order as total annual ODA from the rich OECD countries – but it is encouragingly small in relation to annual world gross income, now of the order of $50 000 billion on exchange-rate equivalents (more in PPP).

3   Resources for these growth and poverty-reducing purposes could be increased by success in the suppression of macro-corruption; and their favourable effect on the poor could be enhanced by reduction of micro-corruption.

4   Poor countries' public revenue, and hence resources for public investment, human development and welfare policies, could be significantly increased by international tax co-operation of common benefit.

5   There is great unused potential for supporting poverty reduction that could be realized if rich OECD donors fulfilled their paper commitments on the scale of their bilateral aid and also adopted rational methods of aid co-ordination among themselves in consultation with the multilateral donors and with each of the recipients.

6   A bigger investment in UN – and other accepted multinational – peacekeeping could, beside its direct benefits, be a cost-effective way of achieving higher growth and more effective poverty reduction in a number of the poorest countries.

7   For supporting development there are a number of potential international sources of funding outside the usual bilateral channels.

8   Strategic co-operation among developing countries in international forums has the potential for significantly increasing their influence.

9   Some modifications of the briefs and the scales of funding of certain global institutions, in particular UN peacekeeping and the World Bank and IMF, and the addition of an organization to promote tax co-operation, could be used to enhance considerably the effectiveness of global responsibility for welfare. (See Appendix 25.1, available on the Online Learning Centre.)

In the development quest, there are abundant synergies between desirable objectives, and there are a number of potential virtuous circles. In particular, economic growth; the advancement of human security and social development; political freedom and human rights; and the avoidance of armed conflict: all can be pursued together in ways that are mutually supporting. However, the urgent need to check and eventually halt anthropogenic climate change, and to mitigate the potential disasters already built into the system by past changes, creates real conflict of purpose and requires not only unwonted generosity of spirit from governments and opinion-leaders in international negotiations but also the utmost economic ingenuity in identifying devices that are both rigorously efficient and recognized by all the major actors as fair.

Online Learning Center

To help you grasp the key concepts of this chapter check out the extra resources posted on the Online Learning Centre at *www.mcgraw-hill.co.uk/textbooks/huq*

Among other resources, the following appendix is available:

- Appendix 25.1   Modifying the working of global institutions

References

Abramovitz, M. (1956) 'Resource and output trends in the United States since 1870', *American Economic Review*, **46** (2) May, pp. 5–23.

ACP-EU *Courier* Special Issue (2000) *Cotonou Agreement*, Directorate General for Development, European Commission, Brussels, September.

Addison, T. (2008) 'Debt relief: the development and poverty impact', in Addison and Mavrotas (2008) *Development Finance in the Global Economy: the Road Ahead*, Basingstoke: Palgrave Macmillan, pp. 216–35.

Addison, T. (ed.) (2003) *From Conflict to Recovery in Africa*, Oxford and Helsinki: Oxford University Press for UNU-WIDER.

Addison, T. and A.R. Chowdhury (2004) 'A global lottery and a global premium bond', in Atkinson (2004) *New Sources of Development Finance*, Oxford: Oxford University Press, pp. 156–76.

Addison, T., H. Hansen and F. Tarp (eds) (2004) *Debt Relief for Poor Countries*, Basingstoke: Palgrave Macmillan.

Addison, T. and G. Mavrotas (eds) (2008) *Development Finance in the Global Economy: the Road Ahead*, Basingstoke: Palgrave Macmillan.

Addison, T. and S.M. Murshed (2003) 'Debt relief and civil war', *Journal of Peace Research*, **40** (2), pp. 159–76.

Ades, A. and E. Glaeser (1999) 'Evidence on growth, increasing returns, and the extent of the market', *Quarterly Journal of Economics*, **114** (3).

Agosin, M.R. and R. Mayer (2000) *Foreign Investment In Developing Countries: Does It Crowd In Domestic Investment?* UNCTAD Discussion Paper No.146, Geneva: United Nations Conference on Trade and Development.

Aharoni, Y. (1966) *The Foreign Investment Decision Process*, Cambridge, Mass: Harvard University.

Ahluwalia, M.S. (1974) 'Income inequality: some dimensions of the problem' in Chenery, H.B. *et al.*, *Redistribution with Growth*, Oxford: Oxford University Press, pp. 3–26.

Aisbett, E. (2005) *Why are the Critics so Convinced that Globalization is Bad for the Poor?* NBER Working Paper No. 11066, New York.

Alacevich, M. (2008) *The World Bank's Early Reflections on Development: A Development Institution or a Bank?*, Policy Research Working Paper No. 4670, Washington, DC: World Bank.

Alderman, H. and E.M. King (1998) 'Gender differences in parental investment in education', *Structural Change and Economic Dynamics*, **9**.

Alston, J.M. and R.J. Veneer (2000) 'Investments in African agricultural research', *World Development*, **25** (3), pp. 409–23.

Amsden, A. (1987) 'Imperialism', in Eatwell, J., M. Milgate and P. Newman (eds) *The New Palgrave: A Dictionary of Economics*, vol. 2, London: Macmillan, pp. 728–33.

Amsden, A. (1989) *Asia's Next New Giant: South Korea and Late Industrialization*, Oxford and New York: University Press, ch. 1.

Amsden, A. (2001) *The Rise of 'The Rest': Challenges to the West From Late-Industrializing Economies*, New York: Oxford University Press.

Anand, S. and S.M.R. Kanbur (1995) 'Public policy and basic needs provision: intervention and achievement in Sri Lanka', in Drèze, J., A. Guio and M. Murthi (eds) (1995) *Demographic Outcomes, Economic Output and Women's Agency*, STICERD Discussion Paper, London: London School of Economics, pp. 298–331.

Andres, L., D. Cuberes, M. Diouf and T. Serebrisky (2007) *Diffusion of the Internet*, Policy Research Working Paper No. 4420, Washington, DC: World Bank.

Arrow, K.J. (1962) 'The economic implications of learning by doing', *Review of Economic Studies*, **29**, pp. 155–73.

Asian Development Bank (ADB) and Organisation for Economic Cooperation and Development (OECD) (1998) *The Future of Asia in the World Economy*, edited by C. Foy, F. Harrington and D. O'Connors, Paris: OECD.

Atkinson, A.B. (1970) 'On the measurement of inequality', *Journal of Economic Theory*, **2**, pp. 244–63.

Atkinson, A.B. (ed.) (2004) *New Sources of Development Finance*, Oxford: Oxford University Press.

Atkinson, D. (1994a) *Radical Urban Solutions: Urban Renaissance for City Schools and Communities*, London: Cassell.

Atkinson, D. (1994b) *The Common Sense of Community*, London: Demos.

Avi-Yonah, R.S. (2000) 'Globalization, tax competition, and the fiscal crisis of the welfare state', *Harvard Law Review*, **113**, pp. 1575–676.

Avi-Yonah, R.S. (2004) 'Bridging the North/South divide: international redistribution and tax competition', *Michigan Journal of International Law*, **26** (1), Fall, pp. 371–87.

Aykut, D. and D. Ratha (2004) 'South-South FDI flows: how big are they?', *Transnational Corporations*, **13** (1).

Azhar, A., M.M. Huq, M.A. Khan, C. Lewis, A. Shibli, A. Siddiqui and S.H. Zaidi (eds) (2003) *Technology and Development in the New Millennium*, Karachi: Karachi University Press.

Baer, W. (1987) 'The resurgence of inflation in Brazil', *World Development*, **15** (8), August, pp. 439–76.

Bagchi, A.K. (1987) 'Industrialization' in Eatwell, J., M. Milgate and P. Newman (eds) (1987) *The New Palgrave Dictionary of Economics*, vol. 2, London: Macmillan, pp. 799–802.

Bairoch, P. (1989) *Cities and Economic Development: From the Dawn of History to the Present*, Chicago: University of Chicago Press.

Banerjee, B. (1983) 'The role of the informal sector in the migration process: a test of probabilistic migration models and labour market segmentation for India', *Oxford Economic Papers*, **35**, pp. 411, 414–20; extracted in Meier, G.M. and J.E. Rauch (eds) (2005) *Leading Issues in Economic Development* (8th edn), New York and Oxford: Oxford University Press, pp. 376–80.

Barco de Botero, C. and M. Smolka (2000) 'Challenges in implementing Colombia's Participacion en Plusvalias', *Land Lines*, **4**, March, pp. 4–7.

Bardhan, P. (1997) 'Corruption and development: a review of issues', *Journal of Economic Literature*, **35**, pp. 1300–46.

Barnett, H. and C. Morse (1963) *Scarcity and Growth: The Economics of Natural Resource Availability*, Resources for the Future, Baltimore: Johns Hopkins University Press.

Bauer, P.T. (1961) *Indian Economic Policy and Development*, Liverpool: George Allen & Unwin.

Bauer, P.T. (1971–6) *Dissent on Development*, London: Weidenfeld and Nicolson.

Bauer, P.T. (1981) *Equality, the Third World and Economic Delusion*, London: Weidenfeld and Nicolson.

Baulch, B. (2006) 'Aid distribution and the Millennium development Goals', *World Development*, **34** (6), pp. 933–50.

Bekaert, G., R. Campbell and C. Lundblad (2001) 'Emerging equity markets and economic development', *Journal of Development Economics*, **66** (2), December.

Bekaert, G., R. Campbell and C. Lundblad (2005) 'Does financial liberalization spur growth?', *Journal of Financial Economics*, **77** (1), July.

Bell, M. and K. Pavitt (1992) 'Accumulating technological capability in developing countries', in *Proceedings of the World Bank Annual Conference on Development Economics*, Washington, DC: World Bank, pp. 257–81.

Benjamin, B. (1968) *Demographic Analysis*, London: George Allen and Unwin.

Benson, T. (2004) *Africa's Food and Nutrition Security Situation: Where Are We and How Did We Get Here?*, 2020 Discussion Paper 37, Washington, DC: International Food Policy Research Institute (IFPRI).

Bernanke, B. and K. Rogoff (eds) (2000) *Macroeconomics Annual 2000*, Boston: NBER, MIT Press.

Bernard, A.B. and F. Sjoholm (2003) *Foreign Owners and Plant Survival*, NBER Working Papers 10039, New York: National Bureau of Economic Research.

Berry, R.A. and W.R. Cline (1979) *Agrarian Structure and Productivity in Developing Countries*, Baltimore: Johns Hopkins University Press.

Bhagwati, J. and S. Chakravarty (1969) 'Contributions to Indian economic analysis: a survey', *American Economic Review*, Supplement, September.

Bhalla, A.S. (ed.) (1975) *Technology and Employment in Industry*, Geneva: International Labour Office.

Biau, D. (2007) *Three Things We Should Know About Slums*, Statement made at the Twenty-first Session of the Governing Council of UN-HABITAT, Nairobi.

Biggelaar, C.D., R. Lal, K. Wiebe and V. Breneman (2004) 'The global impact of soil erosion on productivity I: absolute and relative erosion-induced yield losses', *Advances in Agronomy*, **81**, pp. 1–48.

Bilsborrow, R.E. (ed.) (1996) *Migration, Urbanization and Development: New Directions and Issues*, Norwell, Mass: Kluwer Academic Publishers – published in earlier draft form as (1996) *Symposium on Internal Migration and Urbanisation in Developing Countries: Implications, for Habitat II*, New York: UNFPA.

Binswanger, H., K. Deininger and G. Feder (1995) 'Power distortions, revolt and reform in agricultural land relations', in Behrman, J. and T. Srinivasan (eds) (1995) *Handbook of Development Economics*, vol. 3, New York: Elsevier.

Bird, G. and R. Ramkishen (2001) 'International currency taxation and currency stabilization in developing countries', *Journal of Development Studies*, **37** (3), pp. 21–38: cited in Chang, H.-J. and I. Grabel (2004), *Reclaiming Development: an Alternative Economic Policy Manual*, London and New York: Zed Books, p. 165.

Blattman, C., J. Hwang, and J.G. Williamson (2003) *The Terms of Trade and Economic Growth in the Periphery 1870–1983*, Working Paper 9940, National Bureau of Economic Research, Cambridge, Mass.

Bleaney, M. and D. Greenaway (1993) 'Long run trends in the relative prices of primary commodities and in the terms of trade of less developed countries', *Oxford Economic Papers*, **45**, pp. 349–63.

Blejer, M.L. and A. Cheasty (1988) 'High inflation, heterodox stabilization and fiscal policy', *World Development*, **16** (8), August, pp. 867–82.

Blejer, M.L. and N. Liviatan (1987) 'Fighting hyper-inflation: stabilization strategies in Argentina and Israel, 1985–6', *IMF Staff Papers*, **34** (3), September, pp. 409–30.

Blinder, A.S. (2007) Address to Conference on *Strategies for Improving Mobility of Workers*, Federal Reserve Bank of Chicago and Upjohn Institute for Employment Research, Chicago.

Böhning, W.R. (1994) 'Helping migrants to stay at home', *Annals of the American Academy of Political and Social Science*, **534**, pp. 165–77.

Booker, C. and R. North (2008) 'The great biofuel con', The *Sunday Telegraph*, London, July 13.

Borensztein, E. (1998) 'How does foreign direct investment affect economic growth?, *Journal of International Economics*, **45**.

Borjas, G.J. (1994) 'The economics of immigration', *Journal of Economic Literature*, **32** (4).

Boserup, E. (1965) *The Conditions of Agricultural Growth: The Economics of Agrarian Change under Population Pressure*, Chicago: Aldine.

Boserup, E. (1970) *Women's Role in Economic Development*, New York: St. Martin's Press.

Bosworth, B. and S. Collins (1999) *Capital Flows to Developing Economies: Implications for Saving and Investment*, Brookings Papers on Economic Activity, No. 1, Washington, DC: The Brookings Institution.

Boughton, J.M. (2000) *The IMF and the Silent Revolution: Global Finance and Development in the 1980s*, Washington, DC: IMF.

Boughton, J.M. (2001) *Silent Revolution: the International Monetary Fund 1979–1989*, Washington, DC: IMF, chapter 6, pp. 267–80.

Boulding, K. (1966) 'The Economics of the Coming Spaceship Earth', in Jarrett, H. (ed.) *Environmental Quality in a Growing Economy*, Baltimore: Johns Hopkins Press.

Bourguignon, F., D. Coyle, R. Fernàndez, F. Giavazzi, D. Marin, K. O'Rourke, R. Portes, P. Seabright, A. Venables, T. Verdier and L.A. Winters (2002) *Making Sense of Globalization: A Guide to the Economic Issues*, London: Centre for Policy Research.

BP (2008) *Statistical Review of World Energy, June 2008*, London: British Petroleum.

Brandt, W. (Chair – Independent Commission on International Development Issues) (1980) *North-South: a Programme for Survival* (the first 'Brandt Commission Report'), London: Pan.

Bren, L. (2003) 'The genetic engineering: the future of foods', *FDA Consumer Magazine*, November–December, http://www.fda.gov/educ/features/2003/603_food.html.

Bresser Pereira, L. (1987) 'Inertial inflation and the Cruzado Plan', *World Development*, **15** (8), August, pp. 1035–44.

Brewster, J. (1950) 'The machine process in agriculture and industry', *Journal of Farm Economics*, **32**, pp. 69–81.

Bringezu, S., H. Schütz, S. Steger and J. Baudisch (2004) 'International comparison of resource use and its relation to economic growth', *Ecological Economics*, **51** (1–2).

Brockerhoff, M. (1995) 'Fertility and family planning in African cities', *Journal of Biosocial Science*, **27**.

Brockerhoff, M. (1999) 'Urban growth in developing countries: a review of projections and predictions', *Population and Development Review*, **25** (4).

Brundtland Commission (1987) – see World Commission on Environment and Development (1987).

Brunetti, A. (1997) *Politics and Economic Growth*, OECD Development Studies, Paris: OECD; cited in Cartier-Bresson, J. (2000) 'The causes and consequences of corruption: economic analyses and lessons learnt', in OECD (2000b) *No Longer Business as Usual: Fighting Bribery and Corruption*, Paris: OECD.

Brunetti, A. and B. Weder (2003) 'A free press is bad news for corruption', *Journal of Public Economics*, **87**, pp. 1801–24.

Bruno, M. (1985) 'The reforms and macroeconomic adjustments: introduction', *World Development*, **13** (8), August, pp. 867–9.

Bryden, H.L., H.R. Longworth and S.A. Cunningham (2005) 'Slowing of the Atlantic meridional overturning circulation at 25° N', *Nature*, **438**, pp. 655–7, 1 December.

Burleigh, M. (2000) *The Third Reich: A New History*, London: Pan Books.

Burnside, C. and D. Dollar (1997) *Aid, Policies and Growth*, World Bank Policy Research Working Paper No. 1777, Washington, DC: World Bank.

Cable, V. (1999) *Globalization and Global Government*, Chatham House Papers, Royal Institute of International August, London.

Caiden, G. (1988) 'Toward a general theory of official corruption', *Asian Journal of Public Administration*, **10**.

Campbell, T. and R. Stren (2003) *Cities Transformed: Demographic Change and its Implications in the Developing World*, World Bank video presentation based on Montgomerie, M.R., R. Stren, B. Cohen and H.E. Reed (eds) (2003) *Cities Transformed: Demographic Change and its Implications in the Developing World*, National Research Council, Washington, DC: National Academies Press.

Cartier-Bresson, J. (2000) 'The causes and consequence of corruption: economic analyses and lessons learnt', in OECD (2000b) *No Longer Business as Usual: Fighting Bribery and Corruption*, Paris: OECD, pp. 11–27.

Cashin, P. and C.J. McDermott (2002) 'The long run behaviour of commodity prices: small trends and big variability', *IMF Staff Papers*, **49** (2).

Castles, S. and M.J. Miller (1998) *The Age of Migration: International Population Movements in the Modern World*, London: Macmillan.

Centre on Transnational Corporations (United Nations) (1987) *Transnational Corporations and Technology Transfer: Effects and Policy Issues*, New York: United Nations.

Chandler, T. (1987) *Four Thousand Years of Urban Growth: A Historical Census*, Lewiston: St. David's University Press.

Chang, H. (1993) 'The political economy of industrial policy in Korea', *Cambridge Journal of Economics*, vol. 17.

Chang, H. and I. Grabel (2004) *Reclaiming Development: an Alternative Economic Policy Manual*, London and New York: Zed Books.

Chang, J. (1992–3) *Wild Swans*, London: Flamingo (HarperCollins).

Chauvin, N. and A. Kraay (2005) 'What has 100 billion dollars of debt relief done for low income countries?', Unpublished paper, Washington, DC: World Bank; cited in Addison, T. and E. Mavrotas (eds) (2008) *Development Finance in the Global Economy: the Road Ahead*, Basingstoke: Palgrave Macmillan.

Chen, B. and G.Q. Chen (2007) 'Modified ecological footprint accounting and analysis based on embodied energy – a case study of the Chinese society 1981–2001', *Ecological Economics*, **61**.

Chen, N., P. Valente and H. Zlotnik (1998) 'What do we know about recent trends in migration?', in Bilsborrow, R.E. (ed.) (1996) *Migration, Urbanization and Development: New Directions and Issues*, Norwell, Mass: Kluwer Academic Publishers.

Chenery, H.B., M.S. Ahluwalia, C.L.G. Bell, J.H. Duloy and R. Jolly (1974) *Redistribution with Growth*, Oxford and New York: Oxford University Press.

Chenery, H.B. and M. Bruno (1962) 'Development alternatives in an open economy: the case of Israel', *Economic Journal*, **72**, pp. 79–103.

Chenery, H.B. and A. MacEwan (1966) 'Optimal patterns of growth and aid: the case of Pakistan', *Pakistan Development Review*, **6** (2), Summer, pp. 209–42.

Chenery, H.B. and A.M. Strout (1966) 'Foreign assistance and economic development', *American Economic Review*, **56**, pp. 679–733.

Chenery, H.B. and M. Syrquin (1975) *Patterns of Development, 1950–1970*, London: Oxford University Press.

Chenery, H.B. and L.J. Taylor (1968) 'Development patterns: among countries and over time', *Review of Economics and Statistics*, **50**, November, pp. 391–416.

Christian, C.W. and T.D. Schultz (2005) 'ROA-Based Estimates of Income Shifting by US Multinational Corporations', in *Recent Research in Tax Administration and Compliance*, Proceedings of the 2005 IRS Research Conference, Washington, DC: Inland Revenue Service. Also available at: http://www.docstoc.com/docs/698958/ROA-Based-Estimates-of-Income-Shifting-by-U-S-Multinational-Corporations---2005.

Christiansen, H. (2007) *Trends and Recent Developments in Foreign Direct Investment*, Paris: OECD.

Christiansen, H. and A. Goldstein (2007) *Trends and Recent Developments in Foreign Direct Investment*, Paris: OECD.

Chu, K.-y. and S. Gupta (eds) (1998) *Social Safety Nets: Issues and Recent Experiences*, Washington, DC: IMF.

Clark, C. (1939) *The Conditions of Economic Progress*, London: Macmillan.

Clark, C. (1969) 'The "population explosion" myth', *Bulletin of the Institute of Development Studies*, Sussex, May.

Clark, C. (1970) 'The economics of population growth and control: a communication', *Review of Social Science*, **28** (1), March, pp. 449–66.

Clark, D.A. (ed.) (2006a) *The Elgar Companion to Development Studies*, Cheltenham: Edward Elgar.

Clark, D.A. (2006b) 'Capability approach', in Clark, D.A. (2006a). *The Elgar Companion to Development Studies*, Cheltenham: Edward Elgar, pp. 32–42.

Clark, P.B. and J.J. Polak (2003) 'International liquidity and the role of the SDR in the international monetary system', *IMF Staff Paper*, **51** (1), pp. 49–71.

Clemens, M.S., S. Radelet and R. Bhavnani (2004, November) *Counting Chickens When They Hatch: The Short-Term Effect of Aid on Growth*, Working Paper 44, Washington, DC: Center for Global Development.

Clunies-Ross, A.I. (1991) *Economic Stabilization for Developing Countries*, Aldershot: Edward Elgar.

Clunies-Ross, A.I. (2001) *An Insurance Scheme for Stabilizing Incomes of Countries Exporting Primary Commodities*, Strathclyde Papers in Economics 2001/3, Department of Economics, Glasgow: University of Strathclyde.

Clunies-Ross, A.I. and J.V. Langmore (2008) 'Political economy of additional development finance' in Addison and Mavrotas (2008) *Development Finance in the Global Economy: the Road Ahead*, Basingstoke: Palgrave Macmillan, pp. 70–123. Also available at: http://www.wider.unu.edu/publications/dps/dps2006/dp2006-09.pdf.

Clunies-Ross, A.I. and P. Sudar (eds) (1998) *Albania's Economy in Transition and Turmoil, 1990–97*, Aldershot: Ashgate.

Coale, A.J. (1991) 'Excess female mortality and the balance of the sexes: an estimate of the number of "missing females"', *Population and Development Review*, **17**.

Coale, A.J. and E.M. Hoover (1958) *Population Growth and Economic Development in Low-Income Countries: A Case Study of India's Prospects*, Princeton, NJ: Princeton University Press.

Coase, R. (1960) 'The problem of social cost', *Journal of Law and Economics*, **3**.

Cohen, B. (2006) 'Urbanisation in developing countries: current trends, future projections, and key Challenges for sustainability', *Technology in Society*, **28** (1–2).

Cohen, D. (2007) 'Earth's natural wealth: an audit', *New Scientist*, May, 2007 and Reed Business Information Ltd. Also available at: www.science.org.au/nova/newscientist/027ns_005.htm and links from that address.

Cohen, R. (ed.) (1995) *The Cambridge Survey of World Migration*, Cambridge: Cambridge University Press.

Collier, P. (2007) *The Bottom Billion: Why the Poorest Countries are Failing and What Can be Done About It*, Oxford: Oxford University Press.

Collier, P., L. Chauvet and H. Hegre (2008) *The Security Challenge in Conflict-Prone Countries*, Copenhagen: Copenhagen Consensus, reported in: *Economist*, 17/5/2008, p. 77.

Collier, P. and D. Dollar (2002) *Globalization, Growth, and Poverty*, Washington, DC: World Bank.

Commission on Growth and Development (2008) *The Growth Report: Strategies for Sustained Growth and Inclusive Development*, Washington, DC: World Bank, 'Overview'.

Cook, C. (2001) 'Globalization and its critics', *Economist*, 29/9/2001.

Corbo, V. (1985) 'Reforms and macroeconomic adjustments in Chile during 1974–84', *World Development*, **13** (8), August, pp. 893–916.

Corden, W.M. (1988) 'An international debt facility', *IMF Staff Papers*, **35** (3), September, pp. 401–21.

Council on Environmental Quality (1981) *Global 2000: Report to the President* (Report to President James Carter, directed by Gerald O. Barney), Washington, DC.

Cypher, J.M. and J.L. Dietz (2004) *The Process of Economic Development* (2nd edn), London: Routledge.

Dahlman, C.J., B. Ross-Larson and L.E. Westphal (1987) 'Managing technological development: lessons from the newly industrializing countries', *World Development*, **15** (6).

Dahlman, C.J. and L.E. Westphal (1981) 'The meaning of technological mastery in relation to transfer of technology', *Annals of the American Political and Social Science*, **58**, London and New Delhi: Sage, pp. 12–26.

Daley-Harris, S. (ed.) (2002) *Pathways out of Poverty: Innovations in Microfinance for the Poorest Families*, Bloomfield, CT: Kumarian Press.

Dasgupta, P., S. Marglin and A.K. Sen (1972) *Guidelines for Project Evaluation*, New York: UNIDO.

David, P.A. and G. Wright (1999) *Early Twentieth Century Productivity Growth Dynamics: An Inquiry into the Economic History of 'Our Ignorance'*, Discussion Papers in Economic and Social History, No. 33, Oxford: University of Oxford.

Davis, M. (2006) *Planet of Slums*, London: Verso.

De Haan, A. (1999) 'Migration: a critical review of the migration literature', *Journal of Development Studies*, **36** (2), pp. 1–47.

De Haas, H. (2005) *Morocco's Migration Transition: Trends, Determinants and Future Scenarios*, Global Migration Perspectives No. 28, Geneva: Global Commission on International Migration.

De Mello, L. (1997) 'Foreign direct investment in developing countries and growth: a selective survey', *Journal of Development Studies*, **34** (1).

De Soto, H. (1989) *The Other Path: the Economic Answer to Terrorism*, New York: Basic Books.

De Soto, H. (2000) *The Mystery of Capital: Why Capitalism Triumphs in the West and Fails Everywhere Else*, New York: Basic Books.

Dennison, E.F. (1967) *Why Growth Rates Differ: Postwar Experience in Nine Western Countries*, Washington, DC: The Brookings Institution.

Dennison, E.F. (1974) *Accounting for United States Economic Growth 1929–1969*, Washington, DC: The Brookings Institution.

Deshingkar, P. (2006) *Internal Migration, Poverty and Development in Asia*, London: ODI.

Devarajan, S., M.J. Miller and E.V. Swanson (2002) 'Goals for Development: History, Prospects and Costs', World Bank Policy Research Working Paper, wps 2819, April, Washington, DC: World Book.

Devarajan, S., W. Swaroop and H. Zou (1996) 'What do governments buy? The composition of public spending and economic performance', *Journal of Monetary Economics*, **27**, pp. 313–44.

Diamond, J. (1998) *Guns, Germs and Steel: a Short History of Everybody for the Last 13,000 Years*, London: Vintage.

Diamond, J. (2006) *Collapse: How Societies Choose to Fail or Survive*, London: Penguin.

Dobbs, T.L. (2006) *Challenges Facing a Second Green Revolution: Expanding the Reach of Organic Agriculture* (internet source). http://www.plantmanagementnetwork.org/pub/cm/symposium/organics/Dobbs/

Dobson, W. and G.C. Hufbauer (2001) *World Capital Markets: Challenge to the G10*, Washington, DC: Institute for International Economics.

Dollar, D. (1992) 'Outward-oriented developing economies really do grow more rapidly: evidence from 95 LDCs, 1976–1985', *Economic Development and Cultural Change*, **40** (3), pp. 523–44.

Dollar, D. (2007) 'Asian Century or Multi-Polar Century?', World Bank Policy Research Working Paper No. 4174, March, Washington, DC: World Bank.

Dollar, D. and A. Kraay (2001) 'Trade, growth, and poverty', World Bank Policy Research Working Paper No. 2615, June, Washington, DC: World Bank.

Dollar, D. and A. Kraay (2004) 'Trade, growth, and poverty', *Economic Journal*, **114** (293), pp. 22–49.

Domar, E.D. (1946) 'Capital expansion, rate of growth, and employment', *Econometrica*, **14**, pp. 137–47.

Dore, R. (1959) *Land Reform in Japan*, London: Royal Institute of International Affairs and Oxford University Press.

Dornbusch, R. (1982) 'Stabilization policies in developing countries: what have we learned?', *World Development*, **10** (9), September, pp. 701–8.

Dreher, A. (2006) Does Globalization Affect Growth? Evidence from a new Index of Globalization, *Applied Economics*, **38** (10).

Dreher, A., N. Gaston and P. Martens (2008) *Measuring Globalization – Gauging its Consequences*, New York: Springer.

Drèze, J. (1995) 'Famine prevention in Africa: some experiences and lessons', in J. Drèze, A. Sen and A. Hussein (eds) *The Political Economy of Hunger, Selected Essays*, Oxford: Clarendon Press, pp. 554–604.

Drèze, J. and A.K. Sen (1989) *Hunger and Public Action*, Oxford: Oxford University Press.

Drèze, J. and A.K. Sen (1995) 'Introduction' to J. Drèze, A.K. Sen and A. Hussein (eds) *The Political Economy of Hunger, Selected Essays*, Oxford: Oxford University Press.

Drèze, J., A. Guio and M. Murthi (1995) *Demographic Outcomes, Economic Development and Women's Agency*, STICERD Discussion Paper, London: London School of Economics, also in *Population and Development Review*, **21** (2), pp. 281–305.

Drèze, J., A.K. Sen and A. Hussein (eds) (1995) *The Political Economy of Hunger, Selected Essays*, Oxford: Clarendon Press.

Due, J.H. (1971) *Indirect Taxation in Developing Countries*, Baltimore: Johns Hopkins Press.

Dunning, J.H. (1977) 'Trade, location of economic activity and the multinational enterprise: a search for an eclectic approach', in Ohlin, B., P.O. Hesselborn and P.M. Wijkman (eds) *The International Allocation of Economic Activity*, London: Macmillan, pp. 395–418.

Durlauf, S.N. and L.E. Blume (eds) (2008) 'Methodology of economics', *The New Palgrave Dictionary of Economics*, Basingstoke: Palgrave Macmillan, pp. 95–100.

Dyson, F. (2008) 'The question of global warming', *New York Review of Books*, LV, 10, 12/6/2008, pp. 43–5.

Easterlin, R.A. (2001) 'Income and happiness: toward an integrated theory', *Economic Journal*, **111**, July, pp. 465–84.

Easterly, W. (1997) *The Ghost of the Financing Gap: How the Harrod-Domar Growth Model Still Haunts Development Economics*, Washington, DC: World Bank.

Easterly, W. (2001) *The Elusive Quest for Growth*, Cambridge, Mass: MIT Press, pp. 153–5.

Easterly, W. (2006) *The White Man's Burden: Why the West's Efforts to Aid the Rest Have Done so Much Harm and so Little Good*, New York: Penguin Press.

Eatwell, J., M. Milgate and P. Newman (eds) (1987) *The New Palgrave Dictionary of Economics*, vol. 2, London: Macmillan, pp. 799–802.

Eckstein, A. (1977) *China's Economic Revolution*, Cambridge: Cambridge University Press.

Economist, 12/2/2005, p. 56.

Economist, 28/1/2006, p. 14.

Economist, 22/2/2007.

Economist, 24/2/2007, 'Special Report on offshore finance'.

Economist, 14/4/2007, 'A Special Report on Brazil', p. 6.

Economist, 3/5/2007, 'Special Report on cities'.

Economist, 9/6/2007, 'Going up or down', pp. 59–61.

Economist, 20/9/2007, 'Globalisation and emerging markets'.

Economist, 5/1/2008, 'Special Report on migration' – after p. 42.

Economist, 5/1/2008, 'The good, the bad and the president', p. 46;

Economist, 20/3/2008, 'Briefing: economics and the rule of law', pp. 95–7.

Economist, 19/4/2008, p. 81; 26/4/2008, pp. 71–2.

Economist, 17/5/2008, 'A dismal calculus', p. 77.

Economist, 13/9/2008, 'Climate change and the poor. Adapt or die', pp. 74–5.

Economist, 20/9/2008, 'A Special Report on Globalisation: A Bigger World', p. 6.

Economist, 24/5/2008, 'Briefing: inflation in emerging economies', pp. 101–3.

Ehrlich, P.R. (1968) *The Population Bomb*, New York: Ballantine Books.

Eicher, C.K. (2004) *Rebuilding Africa's Scientific Capacity in Food and Agriculture*, Background Paper No. 4, Commissioned by the Inter-Academy Council (AAC), Royal Netherlands Academy of Arts and Sciences, Amsterdam.

Eicher, C.K. and Staaz, J. (1998) *International Agricultural Development* (3rd edn), Baltimore: Johns Hopkins University Press.

Elliott, K. (1997) *Corruption and the Global Economy*, Washington, DC: Institute for International Economics.

Ellis, F. (2006) 'Vulnerability and coping', in Clark, D.A. (ed.) (2006), *The Elgar Companion to Development Studies*, Cheltenham: Edward Elgar, pp. 671–5.

Emmanuel, A. (1972) *Unequal Exchange: a Study of the Imperialism of Trade*, New York: Monthly Review Press.

Enke, S. (1971) 'Economic consequences of rapid population growth', *Economic Journal*, **81** (324), pp. 800–11.

Enos, J.L. and W.H. Park (1988) *The Adoption and Diffusion of Imported Technology: the Case of Korea*, London: Croom Helm.

Epstein, G., I. Grabel and K.S. Jomo (2003) 'Capital management techniques in developing countries', in Buira, A. (ed.) *Challenges to the World Bank and IMF*, London: Wimbledon Publishing Company, pp. 141–74.

Epstein, H. (2008) 'The strange history of birth control', *New York Review of Books*, **LV** (13), 14/8/2008, pp. 57–9.

European Bank for Reconstruction and Development, *Transition Report, 1996*, and *Transition Report, 1997*, London: EBRD.

Evenson, R.E. (2001) 'Economic impacts of agricultural research', in Gardner, B.L., and G.C. Rausser (eds) (2002) *Handbook of Agricultural Economics*, Amsterdam: Elsevier.

Evenson, R.E. (2008) 'Agricultural Research', in Duflauf, S.N. and L.E. Blume (eds) (2008) *New Palgrave Dictionary of Economics*, Basingstoke: Palgrave Macmillan.

Evenson, R.E. and D. Gollin (eds) (2003) *Effect on Productivity: The Impact of International Agricultural Research*, Wallingford, UK: CAB International.

Fei, J.C.H. and G. Ranis (1964) *Development of the Labour Surplus Economy: Theory and Policy*, Homewood: Irwin.

Fei, J.C.H., G. Ranis and S.W.Y. Kuo (1979) *Growth with Equity: the Taiwan Case*, Oxford: Oxford University Press.

Fernandez, R.B. (1985) 'The expectations management approach to stabilization in Argentina during 1976–82', *World Development*, **13** (8), August, pp. 871–92.

Fields, G.S. (1980) *Poverty, Inequality, and Development*, Cambridge: Cambridge University Press.

Financial Times (2 and 3 June, 2008) 'Part 1: The end of abundance' (2 June), and 'Part 2: Seeds of change' (3 June).

Financial Times (23 June 2008) 'Nestlé calls for Softer Line on GM', p. 6.

Fischer, S. (2003) *Globalization and its Challenges*, Ely Lecture, Washington: American Economic Association.

Flannery, T. (2005) *The Weather Makers*, London: Allen Lane.

Food and Agricultural Organization (FAO) (2006) *The State of Food Insecurity in the World 2006*, Rome: FAO.

Forsyth, D.J.C. (1979) *The Choice of Manufacturing Technology in Sugar Production in Less Developed Countries*, London: HMSO.

Forsythe, N., R. Korzeniewicz and V. Durrant (2000) 'Gender inequalities and economic growth', *Economic Development and Cultural Change*, **48** (2).

France (2004a) Government of France, with the Governments of Brazil, Chile, and Spain, *Action Against Hunger and Poverty*, Report of the Technical Group on Innovative Financing Mechanisms (the 'Quadripartite Report'), Paris, September.

France (2004b) Government of France, Rapport à Monsieur Jacques Chirac, Président de la République, Groupe du Travail sur les Nouvelles Contributions Financières Internationales, English version (the 'Landau Report'), Paris, December.

Frank, A.G. (1967) *Capitalism and Underdevelopment in Latin America*, New York: Monthly Review Press.

Frank, A.G. (1972) 'The development of underdevelopment', in Cockcroft, J.D., A.G. Frank and D.L. Johnson (eds) (1972) *Dependence and Underdevelopment*, Garden City, New York: Anchor Books, Doubleday.

Frank, A.G. and B.K. Gill (1996) *The World System: Five Hundred Years or Five Thousand?* London and New York: Routledge.

Frankel, J. and D. Romer (1999) 'Does trade cause growth?', *American Economic Review*, **89** (3), June.

Freeman, C. (1987) *Technology Policy and Economic Performance: Lessons from Japan*, London: Pinter.

Frey, B.S. and A. Stutzer (2002) *Happiness and Economics: How the Economy and Institutions Affect Human Well-being*, Princeton and Oxford: Princeton University Press.

Friedman, B.M. (2007) 'FDR and the depression: the big debate', *New York Review of Books*, **LIV** (17), 11/8/2007, pp. 26–9.

Fry, M.J. (1982) 'Models of financially repressed developing economies', *World Development*, **10** (9), September; cited in Meier, G.M. (1989) *Leading Issues in Economic Development* (5th edn), New York: Oxford University Press, pp. 210–11.

Fry, M.J. (1997) 'In favour of financial liberalisation', *Economic Journal*, **107** (442); cited in Thirlwall, A.P. (2006) *Growth and Development with Special Reference to Developing Countries* (8th edn), Basingstoke: Palgrave Macmillan, p. 429.

Galbraith, J.K. (1979) *The Nature of Mass Poverty*, Cambridge, Mass: Harvard University Press.

Garip, F. (2006) *How Does Migration History Change the Context of Migration? Analysis of 22 Communities in Nang Rong, Thailand*, Working Paper, Department of Sociology, Harvard University.

Garnaut, R. (2007) *Will Climate Change Bring an End to the Platinum Age?* Canberra: ANU.

Garnaut, R. (2008) *The Garnaut Climate Change Review*, Cambridge: Cambridge University Press.

Garnaut, R.G. and A.I. Clunies-Ross (1975) 'Uncertainty, risk aversion, and the taxing of natural-resource projects', *Economic Journal*, **85** (338), June, pp. 272–87.

Garnaut, R.G. and A.I. Clunies-Ross (1983) *Taxation of Mineral Rent*, Oxford: Oxford University Press.

Gedu, A. (2006) *Asian Drivers (China and India) and African Manufacturing: Issues and Challenges*, Paper Prepared for the African Economic Research Consortium.

Gemmell, N. (ed.) (1990) *Surveys in Development Economics*, Oxford: Basil Blackwell.

General Agreement on Tariffs and Trade (GATT) (1994) *The Legal Texts: The Results of the Uruguay Round of Multilateral Trade Negotiations*, Geneva: GATT Secretariat.

George, H. (1879/2007) *Progress and Poverty*, latest edition, New York: Robert Schalkenbach Foundation.

George, S. (1988) *A Fate Worse then Debt*, London: Penguin.

Gerschenkron, A. (1962) *Economic Backwardness in Historical Perspective: a Book of Essays*, Cambridge, Mass: Harvard University Press.

Getaneh, M. (2002) *Agricultural Development Models Reviewed*, Paper presented at First International Conference on Ethiopia (Organized by the Ethiopian Economic Association), October.

Ghatak, S. (2003) *Introduction to Development Economics* (4th edn), London: Routledge.

Ghatak, S. and K. Ingerscent (1984) *Agriculture and Economic Development*, Baltimore: Johns Hopkins University Press.

Ghemawat, P. (2007) 'Why the world isn't flat', *Foreign Policy*, March/April.

Gilbert, C.L. (1996) 'International commodity agreements: an obituary notice', *World Development*, **24**, pp. 1–19.

Gillis, M., D.H. Perkins, M. Roemer and D.R. Snodgrass (1996) *Economics of Development* (5th edn) New York: Norton.

Goldin, I. and K. Reinert (2007) *Globalization for Development*, Basingstoke: Palgrave Macmillan.

Goldsmith, E.R.D. and R. Allen (1972) *Blueprint for Survival*, London: Penguin Books.

Goode, R. (1984) *Government Finance in Developing Countries*, Washington, DC: Brookings Institution.

Goodwin-Groen, R. (1998) *The Role of Commercial Banks in Microfinance: Asia-Pacific Region*, Brisbane: Foundation for Development Cooperation.

Gordon, R.B., M. Bertram and T.E. Graedel (2006) 'Metal stocks and sustainability', *Proceedings of the National Academy of Sciences (PNAS)*, **103** (5), pp. 1200–14.

Gore, A. (2006) *An Inconvenient Truth: The Planetary Emergency of Global Warming and What We Can Do About It*, New York: Rodale Books.

Goss, C. (1986) *Petroleum and Mining Taxation: Handbook on a Method for Equitable Sharing of Profit and Risk*, Energy papers No. 19, London: Royal Institute of International Affairs.

Government of Ghana (1982) *Economic Survey*, Accra: Central Bureau of Statistics.

Government of Pakistan (1965) *The Third Five-Year Plan 1965–70*, June: Karachi, Planning Commission.

Greenspan, A. (2007) *The Age of Turbulence*, New York: Penguin Press.

Grieg-Gran, M. and A. Dufey (2005) *Economics-Based Approaches*, London: International Institute for Environment and Development.

Grieve, R. (2003) 'Perspectives on technology and development' in Huq, M.M. (ed.) *Building Technological Capability: Issues and Prospects – Nepal, Bangladesh and India*, Dhaka: Dhaka University Press.

Grieve, R. (2004) 'Appropriate technology in a globalizing world', *International Journal of Technology Management and Sustainable Development*, **3** (3), pp. 173–87.

Griffin, K. (1965) 'Financing development plans in Pakistan', *Pakistan Development Review*, **V**, 4.

Griliches, Z. (1958) 'Research costs and social returns: hybrid corn and related innovations', *Journal of Political Economy*, pp. 419–31.

Griliches, Z. and D. Jorgenson (1972) 'The measurement of productivity', *Survey of Current Business*, **52**, May.

Grilli, E.R. and M.C. Yang (1988) 'Primary product prices, manufactured goods prices, and terms of trade of developing countries: what the long run evidence shows', *World Bank Economic Review*, January.

Gunder Frank, A.G. (1972) 'The development of underdevelopment', in J.D. Cockcraft, A.E. Frank and D. Johnson (eds), *Dependence and Underdevelopment*, Garden City, NY: Archor Books, p. 3.

Gurtner, B. (2002) 'International tax competition and tax evasion in the developing countries', Speaking notes for the Friedrich Ebert Foundation Conference on Money Laundering and Tax Havens – the Hidden Billions for Development, New York, 8–9 July 2002, New York: Friedrich Ebert Stiftung.

Gwartney, J. and R. Lawson, with S. Russell, S. Sobel and P.T. Leeson (2007) *Economic Freedom of the World: 2007 Annual Report*, Vancouver, British Colombia: The Fraser Institute. (Data may be retrieved from www.freetheworld.com.)

Haddad, W.D. (1990) 'Education and Development: Evidence for New Priorities', World Bank Discussion Paper No. 95, Washington, DC: World Bank, pp. 12–15.

Hagen, E.E. (1962) *On the Theory of Social Change: How Economic Growth Begins*, IL: Homewood, Dorsey.

Hails, C. (2006) *Living Planet Report 2006*, Gland, Switzerland: World Wildlife Fund (WWF).

Haldane, A. and M. Kruger (2001) *The Resolution of International Financial Crises: Private Finance and Public Funds*, mimeo, Bank of England and Bank of Canada, November.

Hamilton, K. (2000) *Genuine Saving as a Sustainability Indicator*, Environment Department Papers No. 77, Washington, DC: World Bank.

Hanley, N., I. Moffatt, R. Faichney and M. Wilson (1999) 'Measuring sustainability: A time series of alternative indicators for Scotland', *Ecological Economics*, **28** (1), January.

Hanley, N. and C.L. Spash (1993) *Cost–Benefit Analysis and the Environment*, Aldershot, Hants: Edward Elgar.

Haq, M.Ut (1966) *The Strategy of Economic Planning: A Case-Study of Pakistan*, Oxford: Oxford University Press.

Harmsen, K. (2006) *Comments* to Conference on Desertification, Algiers, 17–19 December, 2006.

Harris, J.R. and M.P. Todaro (1970) 'Migration, unemployment and development: a two-sector analysis,' *American Economic Review*, **60**, pp. 126–42.

Harris, N. (2002) *Thinking the Unthinkable: the Immigration Myth Exposed*, London: Tauris.

Harrod, R.F. (1939) 'An essay in dynamic theory', *Economic Journal*, **49**, pp. 14–33. (Further developed in Harrod, R.F. (1948) *Towards a Dynamic Economics*, London: Macmillan.)

Hatton, T.J. and J.G. Williamson (2002) *What Fundamentals Drive Migration?*, NBER Working Paper No. 9159, Cambridge, Mass., p. 17, Sept.

Hausman, R. and E. Fernandez-Arias (2000) *Foreign Direct Investment: Good Cholesterol?* Inter-American Development Bank Working Paper No. 417, Washington, DC.

Hayami, Y. and V.W. Ruttan (1970) 'Agricultural productivity differences among countries', *American Economic Review*, **60** (5), pp. 895–911, December.

Hayami, Y. and V.W. Ruttan (1985) *Agricultural Development*, Baltimore: Johns Hopkins Press.

Heal, G., Dasgupta, P., Walker, B., Ehrlich, P., Levin, S., Daily, G., Maler, K.G., Arrow, K., Kautsky, N., Lubchenco, J., Schneider, S., and Starrett, D. (2002) *Genetic Diversity and Interdependent Crop Choices in Agriculture*. Beijer Discussion Paper 170. The Beijer Institute, The Royal Swedish Academy of Sciences, Stockholm.

Heal, G., P. Dasgupta, B. Walker, P. Ehrlich, S. Levin, G. Daily, K.G. Maler, K. Arrow and J.E. Hecht (2007) 'National environmental accounting: a practical introduction', *International Review of Environmental and Resource Economics*, **1**.

Hecht, J.E. (2005) *National Environmental Accounting: Bridging the Gap Between Ecology and Economy*, Baltimore: Johns Hopkins Press.

Heilbroner, R. (1974) *An Inquiry into the Human Prospect*, New York: W.W. Norton.

Heimans, J.J. (2008) 'Multi-actor global funds: new tools to address urgent global problems' in Addison and Mavrotas (eds) (2008) *Development Finance in the Global Economy: the Road Ahead*, Basingstoke: Palgrave Macmillan, pp. 151–69.

Helleiner, G.K. (1973) 'Manufacturing for export, multinational firms and economic development', *World Development*, July; cited in Meier, G.M. (1976) *Leading Issues in Economic Development* (3rd edn), New York: Oxford University Press.

Helleiner, G.K. (ed.) (1994) *Trade Policy, Industrialisation and Development*, Oxford: Clarendon Press.

Herrmann, R. (1983) *The Compensatory Financing Facility of the IMF: Analysis of Effects and Comparisons with Alternative Systems, Kieler Wissenschaftsverlag Vauk, Kiel*; cited in Hewitt, A.P. (1987) 'Stabex and commodity export compensation schemes: prospects for globalization', *World Development*, **15** (5), May.

Hervitz, H.M. (1985) 'The effects of migration on fertility: the case of Brazil', *International Migration Review*, **19** (2), pp. 293–318.

Hess, P. and C. Ross (1997) *Economic Development: Theories, Evidence and Policies*, Orlando: Dryden Press.

Hewitt, A.P. (1987) 'Stabex and commodity export compensation schemes: prospects for globalization', *World Development*, **15** (5), May, pp. 617–31.

Hicks, J. (1969) *A Theory of Economic History*, London: Oxford University Press.

Hikino, T. and A.H. Amsden (1994) 'Staying behind, stumbling back, sneaking up, soaring ahead: late industrialisation in historical perspective', in Baumol, W., R. Nelson and E. Wolff (eds) *Convergence of Productivity*, Oxford: Oxford University Press, pp. 286–315.

Hirsch, F. (1977) *The Social Limits to Growth*, London: Routledge and Keegan Paul.

Hirschman, A.O. (1958) *Strategy of Economic Development*, New Haven, Conn: Yale University Press.

Hobday, M. (1991) *Strategic Analysis in Science and Technology – Country Report on the Republic of Korea*, Brussels: Science Research Development (Commission of the European Union).

Hobday, M. (1993) 'Technological learning in Singapore: a test case of leapfrogging', *Journal of Development Studies*, **30** (1), October.

Hobday, M. (1994) 'Export-led technology development in the Four Dragons: the case of electronics'. *Development and Change*, **25** (2), pp. 333–61.

Hobday, M. (1995) 'East Asian latecomer firms: learning the technology of electronics', *World Development*, **23** (7), pp. 1173–93.

Hoddinott, J. and L. Haddad (1995) 'Does female income-share influence household expenditures?', *Oxford Bulletin of Economics and Statistics*, **57** (1).

Hossain, M. (1977) 'Farm size, tenancy and land productivity', *Bangladesh Development Studies*, **2** (4), pp. 285–378.

Hsieh, C. (2000) 'Comment' in Bernanke, B. and K. Rogoff (eds) (2000) *Macroeconomics Annual 2000*, Boston: NBER, MIT Press.

Huguet, J.W. (2002) *International migration and development: opportunities and challenges for poverty reduction*, Paper presented at the Fifth Asian and Pacific Population Conference, Bangkok, 11–17 December, 2002, UN ESCAP, Bangkok.

Huq, M.M. (1989) *The Economy of Ghana: the First 25 Years Since Independence*, London: Macmillan.

Huq, M.M. (1996) 'The role of the state in technology promotion in developing countries: an agenda for the Maghreb', in Zawdie, G. and A. Djeflat (eds) *Technology and Transition: the Maghreb at the Crossroads*, London: Frank Cass.

Huq, M.M. (2000) 'Technology policy for industrialization in a developing country: the case of Bangladesh', in Huq, M.M. and J. Love (eds) (2000) *Strategies for Industrialization: The Case of Bangladesh*, Dhaka: Dhaka University Press.

Huq, M.M. (ed.) (2003a) *Building Technological Capability: Issues and Prospects – Nepal, Bangladesh and India*, Dhaka: Dhaka University Press.

Huq, M.M. (2003b) 'Should developing countries adopt a technology policy?', in Azhar, A., M.M. Huq, M.A. Khan, C. Lewis, A. Shibli, A. Siddiqui, and S.H. Zaidi (eds) (2003) *Technology and Development in the New Millennium*, Karachi: Karachi University Press.

Huq, M.M. (2004) 'Building technological capability in the context of globalization: opportunities and challenges facing developing countries', *International Journal of Technology Management and Sustainable Development*, **3** (3), pp. 155–71.

Huq, M.M. and H. Aragaw (1981) *Choice of Technique in Leather Manufacture*, Edinburgh: Scottish Academic Press.

Huq, M.M. and K.M.N. Islam (1992) *Choice of Technology: Fertilizer Manufacture in Bangladesh*, Dhaka: Dhaka University Press.

Huq, M.M. and K.M.N. Islam (2003) 'Failure to absorb technology: a case study of fertiliser manufacturing in Bangladesh', in Huq, M.M. (ed.) (2003a) *Building Technological Capability: Issues and Prospects – Nepal, Bangladesh and India*, Dhaka: Dhaka University Press.

Huq, M.M., K.M.N. Islam and N. Islam (1993) *Machinery Manufacturing in Bangladesh: an Industry Study with Particular Reference to Technological Capability*, Dhaka: Dhaka University Press.

Huq, M.M. and J. Love (2000) 'Bangladesh industrialization since independence', in M.M. Huq and J. Love (eds) (2000) *Strategies for Industrialization:The Case of Bangladesh*, Dhaka: Dhaka University Press, pp. 1–23.

Huq, M.M. and J. Love (eds) (2000) *Strategies for Industrialization: The Case of Bangladesh*, Dhaka: Dhaka University Press.

Huq, M.M. and R. Prendergast (1983) *Machine Tool Production in Developing Countries*, Edinburgh: Scottish Academic Press.

Hymer, S.H. (1976) *The International Operations of National Firms: A Study of Direct Foreign Investment*, PhD Dissertation, (Published posthumously), Cambridge, Mass: MIT Press.

IFPRI (2006) *Agricultural R&D in Sub-Saharan Africa: An Era of Stagnation*, Washington, DC: IFPRI.

Ingham, B. (1995) *Economics and Development*, London: McGraw-Hill.

Inglehart, R. and P. Norris (2003) *Rising Tide: Gender Equality and Cultural Change Around the World*, Cambridge, Mass: Cambridge University Press.

Intergovernmental Panel for Climate Change (IPCC) (2001) *Climate Change 2001: Impacts, Adaptation and Vulnerability*, Intergovernmental Panel on Climate Change, Cambridge: Cambridge University Press.

Intergovernmental Panel for Climate Change (IPCC) (2008) *The International Assessment of Agricultural Science and Technology for Development (IAASTD)*, Washington, DC: World Bank.

Internal Displacement Monitoring Centre (2007) *Internal Displacement: Global Overview of Trends and Developments in 2006*, Geneva: Internal Displacement Monitoring Centre, April.

International Development Association (IDA) and International Monetary Fund (IMF) (2006) *Heavily Indebted Poor Countries (HIPC) Initiative and Multilateral Debt Relief Initiative (MDRI) – Status of Implementation, August 21, 2006*, Washington, DC: IDA and IMF. Found at: http://go.worldbank.org/85B908KVE0, accessed on 30/8/2007.

International Labour Office (ILO) (2007) *Yearbook of Labour Statistics*, Geneva: ILO.

International Monetary Fund (IMF), *World Economic Outlook*, various issues, Washington, DC: IMF.

International Monetary Fund (IMF) (1945) *Articles of Agreement*, Washington, DC: IMF.

International Monetary Fund (IMF) (1997) *World Economic Outlook*, Washington, DC: IMF.

International Monetary Fund (IMF) (2005) *Government Finance Statistics Yearbook 2005*, Washington, DC: IMF.

International Monetary Fund (IMF) (2007) *Annual Report on Exchange Arrangements and Exchange Restrictions*, Washington, DC: IMF.

International Organization for Migration (IOM) (2005) *World Migration 2005: Costs and Benefits of International Migration*, Geneva: IOM.

International Organization for Migration (IOM) (2007) *Global Estimates and Trends, 2007*, Geneva: IOM.

International Union for Conservation of Nature (IUCN) (1980) *World Conservation Strategy*, Gland, Switzerland: IUCN.

International Union for Conservation of Nature (IUCN) (2008) *2007 IUCN Red List of Threatened Species*, Gland, Switzerland: IUCN.

Iregui, A.M. (1999) *Efficiency Gains from the Elimination of Global Restrictions on Labour Mobility*, Bogota: Banco de la Republica.

Jacobs, J. (1984) *Cities and the Wealth of Nations*, Harmondsworth, Middlesex: Penguin.

Javorcik, B.S. (2006) *Migrant Networks and Foreign Direct Investment*, World Bank Policy Research Paper No. 4046, Washington, DC: World Bank.

Jayne, T.S., T. Yamano, M.T. Weber, D. Tschirley, R. Benfica, A. Chapoto and B. Zulu (2003) 'Smallholder income and land distribution in Africa: implications for poverty reduction strategies,' *Food Policy*, Elsevier, **28** (3), pp. 253–75, June. [Source taken from the Internet.]

Jiang, F. (2007) 'Lone migrants: China's growing underclass', *Harvard International Review*, **29** (3), Fall.

Johnson, I. (2003) *Statement* by the Vice-President of the World Bank's Environmentally and Socially Sustainable Development Network at the launching of *World Development Report 2003*, Washington, DC: World Bank.

Johnson, R.A. and S. Sharma (2004) 'About corruption', in R.A. Johnson (ed.) *The Struggle Against Corruption: A Comparative Study*, New York: Palgrave, cited in Senior, I. (2006) *Corruption – The World's Big C: Cases, Causes, Consequences, Cures*, London: Institute of Economic Affairs in association with Profile Books.

Johnston, B.F. and J.W. Mellor (1961) 'The role of agriculture in economic development', *American Economic Review*, **51** (4), September, pp. 566–93.

Jones, C.I. (2001) *Introduction to Economic Growth*, New York: Norton.

Jorge, J., S. Delfin and J. Page (2008) *Is Africa's Economy at a Turning Point?* Policy Research Working Paper No. 4519, World Bank, Africa Region.

Jorgenson, D. (1990) 'Productivity and economic growth', in Berndt, E.R. and J.E. Triplett (eds) (1990) *Fifty Years of Economic Measurement*, Chicago: University of Chicago Press.

Kaldor, N. (1961) 'Capital accumulation and economic growth', in Lutz, F.A. and D. Hague (eds) (1961) *The Theory of Capital*, International Economic Association, London: Macmillan, p. 178.

Kaldor, N. and J. Mirrlees (1962) 'A new model of economic growth', *Review of Economic Studies*, **29**, pp. 174–92.

Kaminsky, G.L. (2005) *International Capital Flows, Financial Stability and Growth*, DESA Working Paper No. 10, December.

Kanbur, S.M.R. (1991) 'Malnutrition and poverty in Latin America', in Drèze, J.K. and A.K. Sen (eds) (1991)*The Political Economy of Hunger*, vol. 3, Oxford: Clarendon Press, pp. 119–54.

Kaplinsky, R. (1990) *The Economies of Small: Appropriate Technology in a Changing World*, London and Washington: Intermediate Technology Publications and Intermediate Technology International.

Katz, J.M. (1987) *Technology Generation in Latin American Manufacturing Industries*, Dhaka: Macmillan.

Kaufmann, D. (1997) 'Corruption: some myths and facts', *Foreign Policy*, No. 107; cited in Cartier-Bresson, J. (2000) 'The causes and consequence of corruption: economic analyses and lessons learnt', in OECD (2000b) *No Longer Business as Usual: Fighting Bribery and Corruption*, Paris: OECD.

Kaufmann, D., A. Kraay and M. Mastruzzi (2007) 'Measuring corruption: myths and realities', in TI (Transparecy International) (2007) *Global Corruption Report* 2007, Cambridge: Cambridge University Press, pp. 318–23.

Kaufmann, D. and S.-J. Wei (1998) *Does 'Grease Money' Speed Up the Wheels of Commerce?*, NBER Working Paper No. 7093, April; cited in Cartier-Bresson, J. (2000) 'The causes and consequence of corruption: economic analyses and lessons learnt', in OECD (2000b) *No Longer Business as Usual: Fighting Bribery and Corruption*, Paris: OECD.

Kautsky, K., N. Lubchenco, J. Schneider and D. Starrett (2002) *Genetic Diversity and Interdependent Crop Choices in Agriculture*, Beijer Discussion Paper 170, The Beijer Institute, Stockholm: The Royal Swedish Academy of Sciences.

Kelly, K. (1999) *New Rules for the New Economy*, New York: Penguin.

Kennish, M. (2002) 'Environmental threats and the environmental future of estuaries', *Environmental Conservation*, **29**, pp. 78–107.

Keynes, J.M. (1920) *The Economic Consequences of the Peace*, New York: Harcourt, Brace and Howe.

Keynes, J.M. (1933/1972) 'Robert Malthus: the first of the Cambridge economists' in *Essays in Biography*, London: Macmillan.

Keynes, J.M. (1936) *The General Theory of Employment Interest and Money*, London: Macmillan.

Khan, A.R. and M. Hossain (1989) *The Strategy of Development in Bangladesh*, London: Macmillan (in association with OECD Development Centre).

Khan, H.M. and A.H. Akbari (1986) 'Impact of agricultural research and extension on crop productivity in Pakistan', *World Development*, **14** (6).

Khan, R. and E. Rahim (1986) *Corrugated Board and Box Production*, Edinburgh: Scottish Academic Press.

Kim, K. and D.M. Leipziger (1993) *The Lessons of East Asia: Korea – a Case of Government-Led Development*, Washington, DC: World Bank.

Kim, K.S. (1995) 'The Korean Miracle (1962–80) revisited: myths and realities in strategies and development', in H. Stein (ed.) *Asian Industrialization and Africa*, London: Macmillan, pp. 87–144.

Kim, L. (1980) 'Stages of development of industrial technology in a developing country: a model', *Research Policy*, **9**, pp. 254–77.

Kim, L. (1990) 'Korea: the acquisition of technology', in Soesastro, H. and M. Pangestu (eds) *Technological Change in the Asia Pacific Economy*, Sydney: Allen & Unwin.

Kim, L. and C.J. Dahlman (1992) 'Technology policy for industrialisation: an integrative framework and Korea's experience', *Research Policy*, **21**, pp. 437–52.

Kim, L. and R.R. Nelson (2000) *Technology, Learning, & Innovation: Experiences of Newly Industrializing Economies*, Cambridge: Cambridge University Press.

Kirkpatrick, C. and F. Nixson (1987) 'Inflation and stabilization policy in LDCs', in N. Gemmell (ed.) (1990) *Surveys in Development Economics*, Oxford: Basil Blackwell.

Klein, L. (2004) *The Comprehensive Impact of Offshore IT and Services Outsourcing on the US Economy and IT Industry*, Lexington, Mass.: Global Insight (USA) Inc.

Kose, M.A., E. Prasad, K. Rogoff and S.-J. Wei (2006) *Financial Globalization: A Reappraisal*, IMF Working Paper No. 06/189, Washington, DC: IMF.

Kreis, E.S. (1989) 'The inflationary process in Israel, fiscal policy, and the economic stabilization plan of July 1985', in Blejer, M.L. and K. Chu (eds) (1989) *Fiscal Policy, Stabilization and Growth in Developing Countries*, Washington, DC: IMF, pp. 309–45.

Krueger, A.O. (1974) 'The political economy of rent seeking society', *American Economic Review*, **64**.

Krueger, A.O. (1987) 'Rent seeking', in Eatwell, J., M. Milgate and P. Newman (eds) (1987) *The New Palgrave Dictionary of Economics*, London: Macmillan, vol. 4, pp. 147–9.

Krueger, A.O. (1998) 'Why trade liberalization is good for growth', *Economic Journal*, **108**, September.

Krueger, A.O. (2000) *Trading Phobias: Governments, NGOs and the Multilateral System*, John Bonython Lecture – available at www.cis.org.au/JBL/JBL00.htm

Krueger, A.O. (2002a) *Supporting Globalization*, Remarks at the 2002 Eisenhower National Security Conference.

Krueger, A.O. (2002b) *A New Approach to Sovereign Debt Restructuring*, Washington, DC: IMF.

Krugman, P. (1988) 'Financing vs forgiving a debt overhang', *Journal of Development Economics*, **29**, pp. 253–68.

Krugman, P. (1995) *Development, Geography and Economic Theory*, Cambridge, Mass: MIT Press.

Krugman, P. (1996) *The Fall and Rise of Development Economics* – available at http://www.wws.princeton.edu/pkrugman/dishpan.html.

Krugman, P. (1999) *The Return of Depression Economics*, London: Allen Lane, The Penguin Press.

Krugman, P. (2007) 'Who was Milton Friedman?', *New York Review of Books*, **LIV** (2), 15/2/2007, pp. 27–30.

Kull, S. and I.M. Destler (1999) *Misreading the Public: the Myth of a New Isolationism*, Washington, DC: Brookings Institution Press.

Kumar, M.S. (1989) 'The stabilizing role of the Compensatory Financing Facility: empirical evidence and policy implications', *IMF Staff Papers*, **36** (4), December, pp. 771–809.

Kuznets, S. (1955) 'Economic growth and income inequality', *American Economic Review*, **45**, March, pp. 1–28.

Kuznets, S. (1956–67) 'Quantitative aspects of the economic growth of nations', *Economic Development and Cultural Change* (10 entries).

Kuznets, S. (1963) 'Quantitative aspects of economic growth of nations: III, Distribution of income by size', *Economic Development and Cultural Change*, **11**, January, pp. 1–80.

Kuznets, S. (1965) *Economic Growth and Structure: Selected Essays*, New York: Norton.

Kuznets, S. (1966) *Modern Economic Growth: Rate, Structure and Spread*, New Haven, Conn. and London: Yale University Press.

Lall, S. (1987) *Learning to Industrialize*, London: Macmillan.

Lall, S. (1990) *Building Industrial Competitiveness in Developing Countries*, Paris: OECD Development Centre.

Lall, S. (1991) 'Explaining industrial success in the developing world' in Balasubramanyam, V.N. and S. Lall (1991) *Current Issues in Development Economics*, London: Macmillan.

Lall, S. (1992) 'Technological capabilities and industrialization', *World Development*, **20** (2), pp. 165–86.

Lall, S. (1996) *Learning from the Asian Tigers: Studies in Technology and Industrial Policy*, London: Macmillan.

Lall, S.V., S. Harris and Z. Shalizi (2006) *Rural-Urban Migration in Developing Countries: A Survey of Theoretical Predictions and Empirical Findings*, World Bank Policy Research Working Paper No. 3915, Washington, DC: World Bank, May.

Landes, D.S. (1998) *The Wealth and Poverty of Nations: Why Some are so Rich and Some are so Poor*, London: Little, Brown and Company.

Langlands, G. (1991) Undergraduate Dissertation, (unpublished), Department of Economics, University of Strathclyde, Glasgow.

Layard, R. (2005) *Happiness: Lessons from a New Science*, London: Allen Lane.

Leibenstein, H. (1957) *Economic Backwardness and Economic Growth*, New York: Wiley.

Lensink, K. and O. Morrissey (2001) *Foreign Direct Investment: Flows, Volatility and Growth*, Development Economics Study Group Conference, Nottingham: University of Nottingham.

Lewis, W.A. (1954) 'Economic development with unlimited supplies of labour', *Manchester School*, May.

Lewis, W.A. (1955) *The Theory of Economc Growth*, London: George Allen & Unwin.

Lim, E. (2001) *Determinants of, and the Relation Between, Foreign Direct Investment and Growth: A Survey*, Working Paper No. WP/01/175, Washington, DC: IMF.

Lindbeck, A. (ed.) (1992) *Nobel Lectures: Economics 1969–1980*, Singapore: World Scientific Publishing Co.

Lindert, P.H. and J.G. Williamson (2001) *Does Globalization Make the World More Unequal?* NBER Working Paper No. 8228, Cambridge, MA: National Bureau of Economic Research.

Lipton, M. (1968) 'The theory of the optimising peasant', *Journal of Development Studies*, **3**, pp. 327–51.

Lipton, M. (1977) *Why Poor People Stay Poor: Urban Bias in World Development*, London: Maurice Temple.

Little, I.M.D. and J.A. Mirrlees (1968) *Manual of Industrial Project Analysis for Developing Countries, (Volume II): Social Cost–Benefit Analysis*, Paris: OECD Development Centre.

Little, I.M.D. and J.A. Mirrlees (1974) *Project Appraisal and Planning for Developing Countries*, London: Heinemann Educational Books. This is a successor volume of their original study: (1968) *Manual of Industrial Project Analysis for Developing Countries (Volume II): Social Cost–Benefit Analysis*, Paris: OECD Development Centre.

Little, I.M.D. and M.F.G. Scott (eds) (1976) *Using Shadow Prices*, London: Heinemann Educational Books.

Little, I.M.D., T. Scitovsky and M.F.G. Scott (1970) *Industry and Trade in Some Developing Countries: A Comparative Study*, Oxford: Oxford University Press for OECD.

Litvin, D. (2004) *Empires of Profit: Commerce, Conquest and Corporate Responsibility*, Cincinnati, Ohio: South Western Educational Publishing.

Loh, J. (ed.) (2008) *2010 and Beyond: Rising to the Biodiversity Challenge*, Switzerland: WWF.

Lomborg, B. (2007) *Cool It!: The Skeptikal Environmentalist's Guide to Global Warming*, London: Cyan and Marshall Cavendish.

Loungani, P. and A. Razin (2001) 'How beneficial is foreign direct investment for developing countries?', *Finance and Development*, **38** (2).

Lucas, R.E. (1988) 'On the mechanics of economic development', *Journal of Monetary Economics*, **22**.

Lundvall, B.A. (1988) 'Innovation as an interactive process from user-producer interaction to the national system of innovation', in Dosi, G., C. Freeman, G. Silverberg and L. Soete (eds) *Technical Change and Economic Growth*, London: Pinter.

Lundvall, B.A. (1992) *National Innovation Systems: Towards a Theory of Innovation and Interactive Learning*, London: Pinter.

Mabro, R. (1967) 'Industrial growth, agricultural underemployment and the Lewis model', *Journal of Development Studies*, **3** (4), pp. 322–51.

Maddison, A. (2002) *The World Economy: a Millennial Perspective*, Paris: OECD, Ch. 3, pp. 125–67.

Maddison, A. (2006) *The World Economy*, Paris: OECD.

Maizels, A. (1995) 'New evidence on the North-South terms of trade', *South Letter*, **4**, December, pp. 16–19.

Mak, I. (2007) 'Bribe Payers Index (BPI) 2006', in TI, *Global Corruption Report 2007*, Cambridge: Cambridge University Press.

Mallampally, P. and K.P. Sauvant (1999) 'Foreign Direct Investment in Developing Countries', *Finance and Development*, **36** (1).

Malthus, T.R. (1798) *An Essay on the Principle of Population*, London: J. Johnson.

Malthus, T.R. (1830/1960) *A summary view of the principle of population*, in *On Population: Three Essays*, New York: American Library of World Literature.

Mansfield, C.Y. (1980) 'A norm for a stabilising budget policy in less developed export economies', *Journal of Development Studies*, **16** (4), July, pp. 401–11.

Mao Zedong (1974) *Mao Tse-Tung Unrehearsed, Talks and Lectures*, 1956–71. London: Penguin Books.

Marshall, A. (1890/1920) *Principles of Economics*, London: Macmillan, (8th edn) 1920.

Martin, A. (1972) *Minding Their Own Business*, London: Hutchinson.

Martin, P.L. and J.E. Taylor (1996) 'The anatomy of a migration hump', in Taylor, J.E. (ed.) *Development Strategy, Employment, and Migration: Insights from Models*, Paris: OECD.

Marx, K. (1967) *Capital: a Critique of Political Economy*, New York: International Publishers.

Marx, K. (1867)/(1990) *Capital*, Volume I, London: Penguin Books/New Left Review.

Mason, A.D. and King, E.M. (2001) (for World Bank), *Engendering Development Through Gender Equality in Rights, Resources and Voice*, Policy Research Report No. 21776, Washington, DC: World Bank.

Massey, D.S. (2003) *Patterns and Processes of International Migration in the 21st Century*, Johannesburg, South Africa: University of Pennsylvania, Conference on African Migration in Comparative Perspective.

Mathur, A. (1964) 'The anatomy of disguised unemployment', *Oxford Economic Papers*, **16** (2), pp. 161–93.

Matthews, K. (ed.) (1998) *The Economics of Politics and Money: The Selected Essays of Alan Walters*, Cheltenham: Edward Elgar.

Mauro, P. (1995) 'Corruption and growth', *Quarterly Journal of Economics*, **3** (442), pp. 681–712; cited in Cartier-Bresson, J. (2000) 'The causes and consequence of corruption: economic analyses and lessons learnt', in OECD (2000b) *No Longer Business as Usual: Fighting Bribery and Corruption*, Paris: OECD.

Mauro, P. (1997) 'The effects of corruption on growth, investment and government expenditure', in Elliott, K. (1997) *Corruption and the Global Economy*, Washington, DC: Institute for International Economics; cited in Cartier-Bresson, J. (2000) 'The causes and consequence of corruption: economic analyses and lessons learnt', in OECD (2000b) *No Longer Business as Usual: Fighting Bribery and Corruption*, Paris: OECD.

Mauro, P. (1998) 'Corruption and the composition of government expenditure', *Journal of Public Economics*, **69**, pp. 263–79.

Mazumdar, D. (1987) 'Rural-urban migration in developing countries', *Handbook of Regional and Urban Economics*, (2), New York: Elsevier.

McClelland, D. (1953) *The Achievement Motive*, New York: Appleton-Century-Crofts.

McGillivray, M., S. Feeny, N. Hermes and R. Lensink (2006) 'Controversies over the impact of development aid: it works; it doesn't; it can, but that depends . . .', *Journal of International Development*, **18**, pp. 1031–50.

McKinnon, R.I. (1964) 'Foreign exchange constraints in economic development', *Economic Journal*, **74**, pp. 388–409.

McKinnon, R.I. (1973) *Money and Capital in Economic Development*, Washington, DC: The Brookings Institution.

McKinnon, R.I. and D. Matheson (1981) *How to Manage a Repressed Economy*, Princeton Essays in International Finance, no. 145, Princeton, NJ: Princeton University; extracted in Meier, G. (ed.) (1989) *Leading Issues in Economic Development* (5th edn), New York and Oxford: Oxford University Press, pp. 205–10.

McLeod, R.H. and R. Garnaut (eds) (1998) *East Asia in Crisis: From Being a Miracle to Needing One?*, London and New York: Routledge.

McRobie, G. (1991) 'Technology transfer from North to South', in Huq, M.M., P. Bhatt, C. Lewis and A. Shibli (eds), *Science, Technology and Development: North-South Co-operation*, London: Frank Cass, pp. 163–75.

Mead, W.J. (1977) 'Cash bonus bidding for mineral resources', in Crommelin, M. and A.R. Thompson (eds), *Mineral Leasing as an Instrument of Public Policy*, Vancouver: University of British Columbia Press, pp. 46–57.

Meade, J.E. (1968) *The Growing Economy: Principles of Political Economy*, London: Allen and Unwin.

Meadows, D.H., D.L. Meadows, J. Randers and W.W. Behrens (1972) *The Limits to Growth: a Report for the Club of Rome's Project on the Predicament of Mankind*, New York: Earth Island, Universe Books.

Mehra, S. (1966) 'Surplus labour in Indian agriculture', *Indian Economic Review*, **1** (1). Reprinted in Chaudhuri, P. (ed.) (1972) *Readings in Indian Agricultural Development*, London: Allen & Unwin.

Meier, G.M. (ed.) (1976) *Leading Issues in Economic Development* (3rd edn) New York: Oxford University Press.

Meier, G.M. (ed.) (1984) *Leading Issues in Economic Development* (4th edn) New York and Oxford: Oxford University Press.

Meier, G.M. (ed.) (1989) *Leading Issues in Economic Development* (5th edn) (includes 'Case against financial repression', pp. 205–12), New York and Oxford: Oxford University Press.

Meier, G.M. (2004) *Biography of a Subject: an Evolution of Development Economics*, New York: Oxford University Press.

Meier G.M. and J.E. Rauch (eds) (2000) *Leading Issues in Economic Development* (7th edn) New York and Oxford: Oxford University Press.

Meier, G.M. and J.E. Rauch (eds) (2005) *Leading Issues in Economic Development* (8th edn) New York and Oxford: Oxford University Press.

Meier, G.M. and D. Seers (eds) (1984) *Pioneers in Development*, Oxford: Oxford University Press.

Mellor, J.W. (2008) 'Agriculture and economic development', in Durlauf, S.N. and L.E. Blume (eds) *The New Palgrave Dictionary of Economics*, Basingstoke: Palgrave Macmillan, pp. 100–5.

Menzel, A. (and 30 co-authors) (2006) 'European phenological response to climate change matches the warming pattern, *Global Change Biology*, **12** (10), pp. 1969–76.

Micklewright, J. and A. Wright (2004) 'Private donations for international development', in Atkinson A.B. (ed.) (2004) *New Sources of Development Finance*, Oxford: Oxford University Press, pp. 132–55.

Millennium Ecosystem Assessment (2005) *Ecosystems and Human Well-being: Biodiversity Synthesis*, Washington, DC: World Resources Institute.

Miller, W. (2006) 'Corruption and corruptiblity', *World Development*, **34**, pp. 371–80.

Ministry of Mines and Mineral Development (1978) *Zambia Mining Yearbook 1978*, Lusaka: Government of Zambia.

Mishra, A. (2006) 'Persistence of corruption: some theoretical perspectives', *World Development*, **34**, 2, pp. 349–58.

Montgomerie, M.R., R. Stren, B. Cohen and H.E. Reed (eds) (2003) *Cities Transformed: Demographic Change and its Implications in the Developing World*, National Research Council, Washington, DC: National Academies Press.

Morawetz, D. (1974) 'Employment implications of industrialisation in developing countries', *Economic Journal*, **84** (491).

Morduch, J. (1999) 'The microfinance promise', *Journal of Economic Literature*, **XXXVII**, December, pp. 1569–614.

Mosley, P. (1989) 'Crop and livestock insurance schemes in less developed countries', *Savings and Development*, **13** (1), pp. 6–19.

Murphy, K., A. Shleifer and R.W. Vishny (1989) 'Industrialization and the big push', *Journal of Political Economy*, **97**, pp. 1003–1026.

Myint, H. (1964) *The Economics of the Developing Countries*, London: Hutchinson.

Myrdal, G. (1957) *Economic Theory and Underdeveloped Regions*, London: Duckworth.

Myrdal, G. (1968) *Asian Drama: An Inquiry into the Poverty of Nations* (3 vols), A Twentieth Century Fund Study, New York, Pantheon and Harmondsworth, Middlesex: Penguin.

National Research Council (2003) *Cities Transformed: Demographic Change and its Implications in the Developing World*, Washington, DC: National Academies Press.

Nelson, R.R. (1956) 'A theory of the low-level equilibrium trap in underdeveloped economies', *American Economic Review*, **46** (5), December, pp. 894–908.

Nelson, R.R. (1993) *National Innovation Systems: A Comparative Analysis*, New York and Oxford: Oxford University Press.

Newland, K. with E. Patrick (2004) *Beyond Remittances: The Role of Diaspora in Poverty Reduction in their Countries of Origin: A Scoping Study*, Washington, DC: Migration Policy Institute for the Department of International Development – available at http://www.migrationpolicy.org/

Nissanke, M. and B. Ferrarini (2004) 'Debt dynamics and contingency financing: theoretical reappraisal of the HIPC initiative', in Addison, T., H. Hansen and F. Tarp (eds) (2004) *Debt Relief for Poor Countries*, Basingstoke: Palgrave Macmillan, pp. 24–58.

Nordhaus, W. (2008) *A Question of Balance: Weighing the Options on Global Warming Policies*, Newhaven: Yale University Press.

Nunenkamp, P. and Julius Spatz (2003) *Foreign Direct Investment and Economic Growth in Developing Countries: How Relevant Are Host-country and Industry Characteristics?*, Kiel Working Paper No. 1176, Kiel Institute for World Economics.

Nurkse, R. (1952) *Problems of Capital Formation in Underdeveloped Countries*, Oxford: Basil Blackwell.

Nye, H.L.M. and S.G. Reddy (2002) *Trade, Growth and Poverty: A Critique*, available at www.networkideas.org/feathm/jun2002/Trade_Growth_Poverty.pdf

ODI (2006) *Internal Migration, Poverty and Development in Asia*, Briefing Paper, London: Overseas Development Institute.

Ohlin, B. (1933) *Interregional and International Trade*, Cambridge, Mass: Harvard University Press.

Olesen, H. (2002) 'Migration, return and development: an institutional perspective', *International Migration*, **40** (5).

Organisation for Economic Cooperation and Development (OECD) (1998) *Open Markets Matter: The Benefits of Trade and Investment Liberalisation*, Paris: OECD.

Organisation for Economic Cooperation and Development (OECD) (2000a) *No Longer Business as Usual: Fighting Bribery and Corruption*, Paris: OECD.

Organisation for Economic Cooperation and Development (OECD) (2000b) *The OECD Guidelines for Multinational Enterprises. Draft Text and Commentary*, Paris: OECD.

Organisation for Economic Cooperation and Development (OECD) (2001) 'Untying aid to the least-developed countries', *Policy Brief*, July, Paris: OECD.

Organisation for Economic Cooperation and Development (OECD) (2007) *Development Assistance: Efforts and Policies, 2006 Report*, Paris: OECD.

Osei, B. (1996) The Terms of Trade of Sub-Saharan African Primary Commodity and Manufactured Exports, Unpublished PhD thesis, University of Strathclyde, Glasgow.

Ostrom, E. (1990) *Managing the Commons*, Cambridge: Cambridge University Press.

Ozden, C. and M. Schiff (eds) (2006) *International Migration, Remittances and the Brain Drain*, Basingstoke: Palgrave Macmillan and World Bank.

Pack, H. (1975) 'The choice of technique and employment in the textile industry' in Bhalla, A.S. (ed.) (1975) *Technology and Employment in Industry*, Geneva: International Labour Office, pp, 153–73.

Pack, H. (1992) 'Learning and productivity change in developing countries', in Helleiner, G.K. (ed.) (1992) *Trade Policy, Industrialization and Development: New Perspectives*, Oxford: Clarendon Press.

Pack, H. (2000) 'Research and development in the industrial development process', in Kim, L. and R.R. Nelson (2000) *Technology, Learning & Innovation: Experiences of Newly Industrializing Economies*, Cambridge: Cambridge University Press, ch. 3.

Pack, H. and L.E. Westphal (1986) 'Industrial strategy and technological change: theory versus reality', *Journal of Development Economics*, **22** (1), pp. 87–128.

Pak, S.J. and J.S. Zdanowicz (2002) *U.S. Trade with the World: an Estimate of 2001 lost U.S. Federal Income Tax Revenues Due to Over-invoiced Imports and Under-invoiced Exports*, Florida International University.

Palma, J.G. (1987) 'Prebisch, Raúl' in Eatwell, J., M. Milgate and P. Newman (eds) (1987) *The New Palgrave Dictionary of Economics*, vol. 2, London: Macmillan, pp. 175–91.

Pankaj Ghemawat, P. (2007) 'Why the World Isn't Flat', *Foreign Policy*, March/April.

Parr, J.F. and L.A. Sullivan (2005) 'Soil carbon sequestration in phytoliths', *Soil Biology and Biochemistry*, **37**, pp. 117–24.

Pearce, D. and G. Atkinson (undated) *Are National Economies Sustainable?: Measuring Sustainable Development*, Centre for Social and Economic Research on the Global Environment (*CSERGE*), Working Paper GEC 92–11.

Pearce, D.W., A. Markandya and E.B. Barbier (1989) *Blueprint for a Green Economy*, London: Earthscan Publications.

Pearce, D.W. and R.K. Turner (1990) *Economics of Natural Resources and the Environment*, Hemel Hempstead: Harvester Wheatsheaf.

Pereira, L.B. (1987) 'Inertial inflation and the Cruzado Plan', *World Development*, **15** (8), August, pp. 1035–44.

Perkins, D.H. and M. Syrquin (1989) 'Large countries: the influence of size', in Chenery, H.B. and T.N. Srinivasan (eds) (1989) *Handbook of Development Economics*, vol. 2, Amsterdam: North Holland, pp. 1725–6.

Perry, G.E., O.S. Arias, J.H. Lopez, W.F. Maloney and L. Servan (2006) *Poverty Reduction and Growth: Virtuous and Vicious Circles*, Washington, DC: World Bank.

Peters, T.J. and R.H. Waterman (1982) *In Search of Excellence: Lessons from America's Best-Run Companies*, London: Harper and Row.

Pfeiffer, D.A. (2006) *Eating Fossil Fuels*, Gabriola Island, British Columbia: New Society.

Politkovskaya, A. (2004) *Putin's Russia*, London: Harvill Press.

Pope, J. (2000) *Confronting Corruption: The Elements of a National Integrity System*, TI Source Book 2000, Berlin: Transparency International.

Potts, D. (2005) 'Counter-urbanisation on the Zambian Copperbelt? Interpretations and implications', *Urban Studies*, **42** (4).

Potts, D. (2006) 'Urban growth and urban economies in eastern and southern Africa: trends and prospects', in Bryceson, D. and D. Potts (eds) (2006) *African Urban Economies: Viability, Vitality or Vitiation?*, Basingstoke: Palgrave Macmillan.

Powers, T.A. (ed.) (1981) *Estimating Accounting Prices for Project Appraisal*, Washington, DC: Inter-American Development Bank.

Prasad, E., K. Rogoff, S. Wei and M.A. Kose (2003) *Effects of Financial Globalization on Developing Countries: Some Empirical Evidence*, Washington, DC: IMF.

Prebisch, R. (1950) *The Economic Development of Latin America and its Principal Problems*, Economic Commission for Latin America (ECLA), New York: UN Department of Economic Affairs.

Prebisch, R. (1984) 'Five stages in my thinking on development' in Meier, G.M. and D. Seers (eds) (1984) *Pioneers in Development*, New York: Oxford University Press, pp. 175–91.

Prest, A.R. (1985) *Public Finance in Developing Countries* (3rd edn), London: Weidenfeld and Nicolson.

Psacharopoulos, G. (1994) 'Returns to investment in education: a global update', *World Development*, **22** (9), September, pp. 1325–43.

Rahim, E. (2003) 'Choice of technique and technology policy in developing countries', in Huq, M.M. (ed.) (2003a) *Building Technological Capability: Issues and Prospects*, Dhaka: Dhaka University Press.

Rajan, R.G. and A. Subramaniam (2005) *Aid and Growth: What Does the Cross-Country Evidence Really Show?*, IMF mimeograph, April, Washington, DC.

Ranis, G. and J.D. Fei (1961) 'A theory of economic development', *American Economic Review*, **51** (4), pp. 533–51.

Ratha, D. (2003) 'Worker remittances: an important and stable source of external development finance', *Global Development Finance 2003*, Washington, DC: World Bank.

Ravallion, M. and G. Datt (1996) 'How important to India's poor is the sectoral composition of economic growth?', *World Bank Economic Review*, **10** (1), pp. 1–25, Washington, DC: World Bank.

Ravallion, M., S. Chen and P. Sangraula (2008) *Dollar a Day Revisited* and *China is Poorer Than We Thought, But No Less Successful in the Fight Against Poverty*, World Bank Working Papers 4620 and 4621, May; as reported in *Economist*, 25/5/2008, p. 110.

Rawls, J. (1971) *A Theory of Justice*, Oxford: Oxford University Press.

Rawski, T.G. (1979) *Economic Growth and Employment in China*, London: Oxford University Press.

Reisen, H. and M. Soto (2001) 'Which types of capital inflows foster developing-country growth?', *International Finance*, **4** (1), Spring.

Repetto, R., W. McGrath, M. Wells, C. Beer and F. Rossini (1989) *Wasting Assets: Natural Resources in the National Income Accounts*, Washington, DC: World Resources Institute.

Ricardo, D. (1817/1971) *On the Principles of Political Economy and Taxation*, London: John Murray, and Harmondsworth: Penguin Books.

Rock, M.T. and H. Bonnett (2004) 'The comparative politics of corruption: accounting for the East Asian paradox in empirical studies of corruption, growth and investment', *World Development*, **32** (6), pp. 999–1017.

Rodriguez, F. and D. Rodrik (2000) 'Trade policy and economic growth: a skeptic's guide to the cross-national evidence,' in Bernanke, B. and Rogoff, K. (eds) (2000), *Macroeconomics Annual 2000*, Boston: NBER, MIT Press.

Romer, P.M. (1986) 'Increasing returns and long-run growth', *Journal of Political Economy*, **94** (5).

Romer, P.M. (1994) 'The origins of endogenous growth', *The Journal of Economic Perspectives*, **8** (1), pp. 3–22.

Rosenberg, N. (1982) *Inside the Black Box: Technology and Economics*, New York: Cambridge University Press.

Rosenstein-Rodan, P.N. (1943) 'Problems of industrialisation of Eastern and Southeastern Europe', *Economic Journal*, **53**, June–September.

Rosenzweig, M.R. and H.P. Binswanger (1993) 'Wealth, weather risk and the composition and profitability of agricultural investments', *Economic Journal*, **103**, pp. 56–78.

Rostow, W.W. (1960) *The Stages of Economic Growth: A Non-Communist Manifesto*, Cambridge, Mass: Cambridge University Press.

Rostow, W.W. (1990) *Theorists of Economic Growth from David Hume to the Present*, New York and Oxford: Oxford University Press.

Sacerdoti, G. (2000) 'To bribe or not to bribe?' in OECD (2000a) *No Longer Business As Usual*, Paris: OECD.

Sachs, C. (1983) *The Invisible Farmers: Women in Agriculture*, Totowa, NJ: Rowman and Littlefield.

Sachs, J.D. (2005) *The End of Poverty: How We Can Make it Happen in Our Lifetime*, London: Penguin Books.

Sachs, J.D., G. Lange, G. Heal and A. Small (2005) *Global Initiative for Environmental Accounting*, New York: Population Division, UN Department of Economic and Social Affairs.

Sachs, J.D., A.M. Warner, A. Aslund and S. Fischer (1995) *Economic reform and the process of global integration*, Brookings Papers on Economic Activity, vol. 1995, (1), 25th Anniversary Issue, pp. 1–118.

Samuelson, P.A. (1954) 'The pure theory of public expenditure', *Review of Economics and Statistics*, **36**, November, pp. 387–9.

Samuelson, P.A. (1958) 'Aspects of public expenditure theories', *Review of Economics and Statistics*, **40**, November, pp. 332–8.

Sandilands, R.J. (1990) *The Life and Political Economy of Lauchlin Currie*, Durham, NC and London: Duke University Press.

Sapsford, D. (1985) 'The statistical debate on the net barter terms of trade between primary commodities and manufactures', *Economic Journal*, **95** (379), pp. 781–88, September.

Sapsford, D. (1988) 'The debate over trends in the terms of trade', in D. Greenaway (ed.) *Economic Development and International Trade*, London: Macmillan.

Sapsford, D., A. Sarkar and H.W. Singer (1992) 'The Prebisch-Singer terms of trade controversy revisited', *Journal of International Development*, **4** (3), May.

Sarkar, P. (1986) 'The Singer-Prebisch hypothesis: a statistical evaluation', *Cambridge Journal of Economics*, **10**, pp. 355–71, December.

Sarkar, P. and H.W. Singer (1991) 'Manufactured exports of developing countries and their terms of trade since 1965', *World Development*, **19** (4), April.

Satterthwaite, D. (2006) *Outside the Large Cities: The Demographic Importance of Small Urban Centres and Large Villages in Africa, Asia and Latin America*, Human Settlements Discussion Paper No. Urban 03, London: International Institute for Environment and Development.

Schiff, M. and A. Valdes (1998) *Agriculture and the Macroeconomy*, IBRD Policy Research Working Paper No. 1967, World Bank, Development Research Group, Washington, DC: World Bank.

Schmidt, R. (2000) 'A feasible foreign exchange transactions tax', in Bello, W., N. Ballard, and K. Malhotra (eds) *Global Finance: New Thinking on Regulating Speculative Capital Markets*, London and New York: Zed Books, pp. 215–38.

Schmidt, R. (2001) 'Efficient capital controls', *Journal of Economic Studies*, **28** (3), pp. 199–212.

Schmidt, R. (2008) *The Currency Transaction Tax: Rate and Revenue Estimates*, Tokyo: United Nations University Press.

Schultz, T.W. (1964) *Transforming Traditional Agriculture*, New Haven, CT: Yale University Press.

Schultz, T.W. (1981) *Investing in People: The Economics of Population Quality*, San Francisco: University of California Press.

Schultz, T.W. (1988) 'Education investment and returns', in Chenery, H.B. and T.N. Srinivasan (eds) *Handbook in Development Economics*, vol. 1, Amsterdam: North-Holland.

Schumacher, E.F. (1973/1993) *Small is Beautiful: a Study of Economics as if People Mattered*, London: Blond and Briggs/Vintage Books.

Schumacher, E.F. (1981) 'On technology for developing society', in McRobie, G. (ed.) (1981) *Small is Possible*, London: Jonathan Cape.

Seers, D. (1969) 'The meaning of development', *International Development Review*, **11** (4), December.

Seidel, A. (2007) 'The limits of a smaller, poorer China', *Financial Times*, 14/11/2007.

Semler, R. (1993) *Maverick!*, London: Century.

Sen, A.K. (1968) *Choice of Techniques* (3rd edn), Oxford: Clarendon Press.

Sen, A.K. (ed.) (1970) *Growth Economics*, London: Penguin Books.

Sen, A.K. (1975) *Employment, Technology and Development*, Oxford: Clarendon Press.

Sen, A.K. (1981) *Poverty and Famines: An Essay on Entitlement and Deprivation*, Oxford: Clarendon Press.

Sen, A.K. (1992) 'More than 100 million women are missing', *New York Review of Books*, December.

Sen, A.K. (1995) *Economic Development and Social Change: India and China in Comparative Perspectives*, STICERD No. 67, London: London School of Economics, December.

Sen, A.K. (1997) *Development Thinking at the Beginning of the 21st Century*, STICERD No. 2, London: London School of Economics, March.

Sen, A.K. (1998) 'Economic policy and equity: an overview', in Tanzi, V., K. Chu and S. Gupta (eds) *Economic Policy and Equity*, Washington, DC: IMF.

Sen, A.K. (1999) *Development as Freedom*, Oxford: Oxford University Press.

Senior, I. (2006) *Corruption – The World's Big C: Cases, Causes, Consequences, Cures*, London: Institute of Economic Affairs in association with Profile Books.

Servan-Schreiber, J.-J. (1968) *The American Challenge*, London: Harrish Hamilton.

Shapiro, C. and H. Varian (2000) *Information Rules: A Strategic Guide to the Network Economy*, Cambridge, Mass: Harvard Business School Press.

Shapiro, H. and L. Taylor (1990) 'The state and industrialization strategy', *World Development*, **18** (6), pp. 861–78.

Shaw, D.J. (2002) *Sir Hans Singer: the Life and Work of a Development Economist*, Basingstoke: Palgrave Macmillan.

Shaw, E.S. (1973) *Financial Deepening in Economic Development*, New York: Oxford University Press.

Sheahan, J. (1971) *Trade and Employment: Industrial Exports Compared to Import Substitution in Mexico*, Williams College Research Center for Development Economics, Research Memorandum 43; cited in Meier, G.M. (1976) *Leading Issues in Economic Development* (3rd edn), New York: Oxford University Press, p. 672.

Sidgwick, H. (1874, 1907) *Methods of Ethics* (7th edn), London: Macmillan.

Simon, J. (1981) *The Ultimate Resource*, Princeton, NJ: Princeton University Press.

Simon, J. and H. Kahn (1984) *The Resourceful Earth: A Response to Global 2000*, Oxford: Blackwell.

Singer, H.W. (1950) 'The distribution of gains between investing and borrowing countries', *American Economic Review*, **40** (2), May.

Singer, H.W. (1972) *Employment, Incomes and Equality*, Geneva: ILO.

Singer, H.W. (1987) 'The terms of trade and economic development', in Eatwell, J., M. Milgate and P. Newman (eds) *The New Palgrave: a Dictionary of Economics*, London: Macmillan, vol. 4, pp. 626–8.

Skeldon, R. (1997) 'Rural-to-urban migration and its implications for poverty alleviation', *Asia-Pacific Population Journal*, **12** (1).

Skeldon, R. (2003) *Interlinkages Between Internal and International Migration and Development in the Asian Region*, Bangkok: ESCAP.

Smith, A. (1776/1982) *An Inquiry into the Nature and Causes of the Wealth of Nations*, London: Strahan and Cadell.

Sobhan, R. (1993) *Agrarian Reform and Social Transformation: Preconditions for Development*, Dhaka, Bangladesh: UPL.

Solow, R.M. (1956) 'A contribution to the theory of economic growth', *Quarterly Journal of Economics*, **70**, pp. 65–94 – reprinted in Sen, A.K. (ed.) (1970) *Growth Economics*, Harmondsworth: Penguin Press.

Solow, R.M. (1957) 'Technical change and the aggregate production function', *Review of Economics and Statistics*, August, **39**, pp. 312–20.

Solow, R.M. (1970) 'A contribution to the theory of growth', in A.K. Sen (ed.), *Growth Economics*, Harmondsworth: Penguin Press.

Solow, R.M. (1987) Nobel Prize Lecture, in Odelberg, W. (ed.) (1987) *The Nobel Prizes 1987*, Stockholm: Nobel Foundation.

Spahn, P.-B. (1996) 'The Tobin tax and exchange rate stability', *Finance and Development*, **33**, June, pp. 24–7.

Spahn, P.-B. (2002) *On the Feasibility of a Tax on Foreign Exchange Transactions*, Report to the [German] Ministry for Economic Cooperation and Development, Bonn – available at: www.wiwi.uni-frankfurt.de/professoren/spahn/tobintax

Spence, M. *et al.* (2008) Commission on Growth and Development, *Report*, Conference edn, Washington, DC: World Bank.

Spraos, J. (1980) 'The statistical debate on the net barter terms of trade between primary commodities and manufactures', *Economic Journal*, **90** (357), 107–28, March.

Spraos, J. (1983) *Inequalising trade? A Study of Traditional North/South Specialisation in the Context of Terms of Trade Concepts*, Oxford: Clarendon Press.

Squire, L. and H.G. van der Tak (1975) *Economic Analysis of Projects*, Washington, DC: World Bank.

Srinivasan, T.N. (1998) 'Development and theories of endogenous growth' in Coricelli, F., M. di Matteo and F. Hahn (1998) *New Theories in Growth and Development*, Basingstoke: Macmillan, p. 114.

Stansfield, S. (2002) 'Philanthropy and alliances for global health', in Kaul, I., K. Le Goulven and M. Schnupf (eds) *Global Public Goods Financing: New Tools for New Challenges*, New York: United Nations Development Program, Office of Development Studies.

Stern, N.H. (2007) *The Economics of Climate Change: The Stern Review*, Cambridge: Cambridge University Press.

Sternberg, J. (2006) 'Crowding out the UN', *New York Sun*, 1/10/2006.

Stevens, R.D. and C.L. Jabara (1988) *Agricultural Development Principles: Economic Theory and Empirical Evidence*, Baltimore and London: Johns Hopkins University Press.

Stewart, F. (1977) *Technology and Underdevelopment*, London: Macmillan.

Stewart, F. (1985) 'Macro policies for appropriate technology: an introductory classification', in James, J. and S. Watanabe (eds) (1985) *Technology, Institutions and Government Policies*, London: Macmillan, pp. 19–48.

Stewart, F. (2006) 'Basic needs approach', in Clark, D.A. (2006a) *The Elgar Companion to Development Studies*, Cheltenham: Edward Elgar, pp. 12–18.

Stiglitz, J.E. (1974) 'Incentives and risk-sharing in sharecropping', *Review of Economic Studies*, **41**, pp. 219–55.

Stiglitz, J. (2002) *Globalization and its Discontents*, London: Penguin.

Stiglitz, J. (2006) *Making Globalization Work*, London: Allen Lane.

Sugden, R. and A. Williams (1978–83) *The Principles of Practical Cost–Benefit Analysis*, Oxford: Oxford University Press.

Sullivan, L.A. (2008) 'Letter to the editors', *New York Review of Books*, **LV**, 14, 25/9/2008, p. 95.

Sutcliffe, R.B. (1971) *Industry and Underdevelopment*, London: Addison-Wesley.

Svensson, J. (2000) 'Foreign aid and rent seeking', *Journal of International Economics*, **51**, pp. 437–61.

Tacoli, C. (2008) *Links Between Rural And Urban Development In Africa And Asia*, United Nations Expert Group Meeting on Population Distribution, Urbanization, Internal

Migration And Development, Population Division, Department of Economic and Social Affairs, New York: UN Secretariat.

Tannerfeldt, G. and P. Ljung (2006) *More Urban, Less Poor: an Introduction to Urban Development and Management*, London: Swedish International Development Cooperation Agency and Earthscan.

Tanzi, V. (1982) 'Fiscal disequilibrium in developing countries', *World Development*, **10** (12), December, pp. 1069–82.

Tanzi, V. (1995) *Taxation in an Integrating World*, Washington, DC: The Brookings Institution.

Tanzi, V. (1998) 'Corruption Around the World – Causes, Consequences, Scope, and Cures', IMF Working Papers 98/63, Washington, DC: International Monetary Fund.

Tanzi, V. and H. Davoodi (1997) 'Corruption, public investment and growth', IMF Working Paper 97/139, Washington, DC: IMF.

Tanzi, V., K.-Y. Chu and S. Gupta (eds) (1999) *Economic Policy and Equity*, Washington, DC: IMF.

Taslim, M.A. (1995) 'Agricultural land tenancy in Bangladesh: a review', in Rashid, S. (ed.) (1995) *Bangladesh Economy: Evaluation and Research Agenda*, Dhaka: Dhaka University Press.

Temple, J. (1999) 'The new growth evidence', *Journal of Economic Literature*, **37** (1), March, pp. 112–156.

Thirlwall, A. (2003) *Growth and Development with Special Reference to Developing Countries* (7th edn), Basingstoke: Palgrave Macmillan.

Thirlwall, A. (2006) *Growth and Development with Special Reference to Developing Countries* (8th edn), Basingstoke: Palgrave Macmillan.

Thirtle, C., L. Lin and J. Piess (2003) 'The impact of research-led agricultural productivity growth on poverty reduction in Africa, Asia and Latin America', *World Development*, **31** (12), pp. 1959–75.

Thomas, D. (1991) 'Gender differences in household resource allocation', *World Bank Living Standards Measurement Study Paper No. 79*, Washington, DC: World Bank.

Thompson, W. (1929) 'Population', *American Sociological Review*, **34** (6), pp. 959–75.

Timmer, C.P. (1988) 'The agricultural transformation' in Chenery, H.B. and T.N. Trinivasan (eds) *Handbook of Development Economics*, vol. 1, Amsterdam: North-Holland, pp. 275–6.

Timmer, C.P. (2006) 'Agriculture and economic growth', in Clark, D.A. (ed.) *The Elgar Companion to Development Studies*, Cheltenham: Edward Elgar, pp. 5–10.

Todaro, M.P. (1971) 'Income expectations, rural-urban migration and employment in Africa', *International Labour Review*, **104**, pp. 381–413, November.

Todaro, M.P. and S.C. Smith (2006) *Economic Development* (9th edn), Harlow, Middlesex: Pearson/Addison-Wesley.

Toye, J. (2006) 'Hans Singer and international development', *Journal of International Development*, **8**, pp. 915–23.

Transparency International (TI) (2007) *Global Corruption Report 2007*, Cambridge: Cambridge University Press.

Transparency International (TI) (2008) http://www.transparency.org/layout/set/print/, various links, accessed on 11/1/2008.

Ul Haque, N. and R. Sahay (1996) 'Do government wage cuts close budget deficits? Costs of corruption', *IMF Staff Papers*, **43** (4), December, pp. 754–78.

United Nations (1980) *Patterns of Urban and Rural Population Growth*, Population Studies Series No. 68, New York: United Nations Development of International Economic and Social Affairs.

United Nations (1987) *Transnational Corporations and Technology Transfer: Effects and Policy Issues*, UN Center on Transnational Corporations, New York: United Nations.

United Nations (2003) *Handbook of National Accounting: Integrated Environmental and Economic Accounting 2003*, New York: United Nations.

United Nations (2005) UN Millennium Project, *Investing in Development*, New York, January (the 'Sachs Report'). Found at http://unmp.forumone.com/eng_html_07.html, accessed on 18/02/05.

United Nations (2006) *Trends in Total Migration Stocks: The 2005 Revision*, New York: Population Division, Department of Economic and Social Affairs, UN Secretariat.

United Nations (2006a) *World Population Prospects: The 2006 Revision Population Database*, New York: Population Division, Department of Economic and Social Affairs, UN Secretariat.

United Nations (2007) *World Population Prospects: The 2006 Revision (Highlights)*, New York: Population Division, Department of Economic and Social Affairs, UN Secretariat.

United Nations Conference on Trade and Development (UNCTAD) (2001) *World Investment Report 2001*, Geneva: UNCTAD – available at http://www.unctad.org/Templates/Page.asp?intItemID=1485&lang=1.

United Nations Conference on Trade and Development (UNCTAD) (2006) *World Investment Report 2006*, Geneva: UNCTAD – available at http://www.unctad.org/Templates/Page.asp?intItemID=1485&lang=1

United Nations Conference on Trade and Development (UNCTAD) (2007a) *Trade and Development Report, 2007*, Geneva: UNCTAD.

United Nations Conference on Trade and Development (UNCTAD) (2007b) *Handbook of Statistics, 2006–2007*, Geneva: UNCTAD – available at www.UNCTAD Handbook of Statistics

United Nations Conference on Trade and Development (UNCTAD) (2007c) *Foreign Direct Investment Database*, (annual), Geneva: UNCTAD.

United Nations Conference on Trade and Development (UNCTAD) (2008a) *Development and Globalization: Facts and Figures*, Geneva: UNCTAD.

United Nations Conference on Trade and Development (UNCTAD) (2008b) *Globalization for Development: The International Trade Perspective*, Geneva: UNCTAD.

United Nations Conference on Trade and Development (UNCTAD) *Foreign Direct Investment Database*, Geneva: UNCTAD (Annual).

United Nations Conference on Trade and Development (UNCTAD) *Transnational Corporations* (Journal published by UNCTAD, Geneva; 3 per annum).

United Nations Conference on Trade and Development (UNCTAD) (2008c) *World Investment Report, 2008*, Geneva: UNCTAD – available at: http://www.unctad.org/Templates/webflyer.asp?docid=10502&intItemID=2068&lang=1&mode=toc.

United Nations Department of Economic and Social Affairs (ECOSOC) (2008) *Trends In Sustainable Development: Agriculture, Rural Development, Land, Desertification And Drought*, New York: UNECOSOC, Division for Sustainable Development.

United Nations Development Programme (UNDP) (2005) *Human Development Report 2005*, New York: Oxford University Press.

United Nations Educational, Scientific and Cultural Organization (UNESCO) *Statistical Yearbook* (various issues) Paris: UNESCO.

United Nations Environmental Programme (UNEP) (2007) *Global Environment Outlook: GEO4 – Environment for Development*, Nairobi: UNEP.

UN-HABITAT (2003) *The Challenge of Slums: Global Report on Human Settlements*, New York: UN-HABITAT, United Nations.

UN-HABITAT (2006) *State of the World's Cities 2006/7*, New York: UN-HABITAT, United Nations.

United Nations Population Fund (UNFPA) (1996) *State of World Population Report 1996: Changing Places: Population, Development and the Urban Future*, New York: UNFPA, Population Division, Department of Economic and Social Affairs, United Nations.

United Nations Population Fund (UNFPA) (2006a) *Trends in Total Migration Stocks: The 2005 Revision*, New York: UNFPA, Population Division, Department of Economic and Social Affairs, United Nations.

United Nations Population Fund (UNFPA) (2006b) *World Urbanization Prospects: The 2005 Revision*, New York: UNFPA, Population Division, Department of Economic and Social Affairs, United Nations.

United Nations Population Fund (UNFPA) (2007a) *State of World Population 2007: Unleashing the Potential of Urban Growth*, New York: UNFPA, Population Division, Department of Economic and Social Affairs, United Nations.

United Nations Population Fund (UNFPA) (2007b) *World Population Prospects: The 2006 Revision (Highlights)*, New York: UNFPA, Population Division, Department of Economic and Social Affairs, United Nations.

United Nations Population Fund (UNFPA) (2007c) video presentation: http://www.unfpa.org/swp/2007/multimedia/index.html

United Nations Population Fund (UNFPA) (2008) *World Urbanization Prospects: The 2007 Revision*, New York: UNFPA, Population Division, Department of Economic and Social Affairs, United Nations – available at www.esa.un.org/unup

Uphoff, N. (1996) *Learning from Gal Oya: Possibilities for Participatory Development and Post-Newtonian Social Science*, New York: IT Publications.

US Geological Survey, *Minerals Yearbook* (various years), Reston, VA: US Geological Survey.

Vaitsos, C.V. (1974) 'Employment effects of foreign direct investment', in Edwards, E.O. (ed.) (1974) *Employment in Developing Nations*, New York, pp. 39–41; cited in Meier, G.M. (1976) *Leading Issues in Economic Development* (3rd edn), New York: Oxford University Press, p. 676.

Van Den Berg, H. (2001) *Economic Growth and Development*, New York: McGraw-Hill.

Van Vuuren, D.P. and L.F. Bouwman (2005) 'Exploring past and future changes in the ecological footprint for world regions', *Ecological Economics*, **52** (1).

Veblen, T. (1915) *Imperial Germany and the Industrial Revolution*, New York and London: Macmillan.

Vu, M.T. (1984) *World Population Projections 1984: Short- and Long-term Estimates by Age and Sex with Related Demographic Statistics*, Washington, DC: The World Bank.

Wackernagel, M., N.B. Schulz, D. Deumling, A.C. Linares, M. Jenkins, V. Kapos, C. Monfreda, J. Loh, N. Myers, R. Norgaard and J. Randers (2002) 'Tracking the ecological overshoot of the human economy', *Proceedings of the National Academy of Sciences of the USA*, **99** (14).

Wade, R. (1990) *Governing the Market: Economic Theory and the Role of Government in East Asian Industrialization*, Princeton, NJ: Princeton University Press, chs. 1 and 4.

Waibel, M. (2008) *Migration to Greater Ho Chi Minh City in the Course of Doi Moi Policy: Spatial Dimensions, Consequences and Policy Changes with Special Reference to Housing*, Hamburg: University of Hamburg.

Walmsley, T., A. Winters, S. Amer and C. Parsons (2005) *Measuring the Impact of the Movement of Labour Using a Model of Bilateral Migration Flows*, 8th Annual Conference on Global Economic Analysis, Lübeck, Germany.

Wang, F.-L. (2004) 'Reformed migration control and new targeted people: China's *Hukou* system in the 2000s', *China Quarterly*, **177**, pp. 115–32.

Warriner, D. (1955/1964) 'Land reform and economic development', lecture delivered in 1955, reprinted in Eicher, C. and L. Witt (eds) (1964) *Agriculture in Economic Development*, New York: McGraw-Hill. Extracted in Meier, G.M. (ed.) (1984), *Leading Issues in Economic Development* (4th edn), New York and Oxford: Oxford University Press, pp. 468–71.

Weber, M. (1904) *The Protestant Ethic and the Spirit of Capitalism (Die Protestantische Ethik und der 'Geist' des Kapitalismus)* translated by Parsons, T. and A. Giddens (1930) London and Boston: Unwin Hyman.

Weber, S., N. Barma, M. Kroenig and E. Ratner (2007) 'How globalization went bad', *Foreign Affairs*, January/February.

Wei, S.-J. (1997a) 'How taxing is corruption on international investors?', NBER Working Paper No. 6030, National Bureau of Economic Research, Cambridge, MA; cited in Tanzi, 1998.

Wei, S.J. (1997b) *Why is Corruption So Much More Taxing Than Tax?* NBER Working Paper No. 6030, Cambridge Mass: National Bureau of Economic Research – cited in Tanzi, V. (1998) *Corruption Around the World – Causes, Consequences, Scope, and Cures*, IMF Working Papers 98/63, Washington, DC: International Monetary Fund.

Wei, S.-J. (2006) *Connecting Two Views on Financial Globalization: Can We Make Further Progress?* NBER Working Paper No. 13148, Cambridge, MA: National Bureau of Economic Research.

Weil, D.N. (2008) *Economic Growth* (2nd edn) Boston: Addison-Wesley.

Weiss, J. (2002) *Industrialisation and Globalisation: Theory and Evidence from Developing Countries*, London: Routledge.

White, M.J. and D.P. Lindstrom (2005) 'Internal Migration', in Poston, D. and M. Micklin (eds) *Handbook of Population*, Handbooks of Sociology and Social Research Series, New York: Springer.

White, M.J., L. Moreno and S. Guo (1995) 'The interrelation of fertility and geographic mobility in Peru: a hazards model analysis', *International Migration Review*, **29**, pp. 492–514.

Wilson, E.O. (2002) *The Future of Life*, New York: Alfred A. Knopf.

Winters, L.A. (2004) 'Trade liberalization and economic performance: an overview', *Economic Journal*, **114**, February.

Winters, L.A., T.L. Walmsley, Z.K. Wang and R. Gronberg (2002) 'Negotiating the Liberalization of the Temporary Movement of Natural Persons', Discussion Paper in Economics No. 87, Brighton: University of Sussex.

Wolf, M. (2005) *Why Globalization Works*, New Haven: Yale Nota Bene.

Woodhall, P. (2006) 'The new titans', *Economist*, 14/9/2006.

World Bank (1982) *World Development Report 1982*, New York: Oxford University Press.

World Bank (1984) *World Development Report 1984*, New York: Oxford University Press for the World Bank.

World Bank (1989) *World Development Report 1989: Financial Systems and Development*, New York: Oxford University Press for the World Bank.

World Bank (1990) *World Development Report 1990: Poverty*, New York: Oxford University Press for the World Bank.

World Bank (1992) *World Development Report 1992: Development and the Environment*, New York: Oxford University Press for the World Bank.

World Bank (1993a) *The East Asian Miracle*, New York: Oxford University Press for the World Bank, ch. 1.

World Bank (1993b) *World Development Report 1993: Investing in Health*, New York: Oxford University Press for the World Bank.

World Bank (1997) *World Development Report 1997: The State in a Changing World*, New York: Oxford University Press for the World Bank.

World Bank (1998) *Assessing Aid: What Works, What Doesn't, and Why*, Washington, DC: World Bank.

World Bank, International Task Force on Commodity Risk Management in Developing Countries (1999) *Dealing with Commodity Price Volatility in Developing Countries: A Proposal for a Market-based Approach*, Washington, DC: World Bank.

World Bank (2000) *World Development Report 1999/2000: Entering the 21st Century*, New York: Oxford University Press for the World Bank.

World Bank (2001a) *World Development Report 2000/2001: Attacking Poverty*, New York: Oxford University Press for the World Bank.

World Bank (2001b) *World Development Report 2002: Building Institutions for Markets*, New York: Oxford University Press for the World Bank.

World Bank, International Task Force on Commodity Risk Management in Developing Countries (2001c) *Delivering Price Insurance: Lessons from the Case Studies*, Washington, DC: World Bank. See also website: www.itf-commrisk.org

World Bank (2002) *World Development Indicators*, Washington, DC: World Bank.

World Bank (2003) World Bank Operations Evaluation Department, *Précis*, 'The HIPC Initiative: progress and prospects', No. 230, Washington, DC: World Bank, Winter.

World Bank (2006a) *Global Economic Prospects 2006: Economic Implications of Remittances and Migration*, Washington, DC: World Bank.

World Bank (2006b) *World Development Report 2007: Development and the Next Generation*, Washington, DC: World Bank, Table A7, p. 281.

World Bank (2007a) *Global Development Finance: The Globalization of Corporate Finance in Developing Countries*, Washington, DC: World Bank – available at http://www.worldbank.org/prospects

World Bank (2007b) *World Development Report, 2008: Agriculture for Development*, Washington, DC: World Bank.

World Bank (2007c) Worldwide Governance Indicators, http://info.worldbank.org/governance/wgi2007/.

World Bank (2008a) *World Development Indicators 2008*, Development Data Group, Washington, DC: World Bank.

World Bank (2008b) *World Development Report 2008: Agriculture for Development*, Washington, DC: Oxford University Press for World Bank.

World Bank (2008c) *World Bank Indicators Database* (revised September, 2008), Washington, DC: World Bank.

World Bank (various issues) *World Development Indicators*, Washington, DC: World Bank.

World Bank (various years) *Global Development Finance*, Washington, DC: World Bank.

World Commission on Environment and Development (the 'Bruntland Commission') (1987) *Our Common Future*, Oxford: Oxford University Press.

World Commission on the Social Dimensions of Globalization (2004) *A Fair Globalization: Creating Opportunities for All*, Geneva: ILO.

World Economic Forum (2007) *The Global Competitiveness Report 2007–2008*, Basingstoke: Palgrave Macmillan.

World Energy Council (2007) *Survey of Energy Resources 2007*, London: World Energy Council.

World Trade Organization (WTO) (2007) *International Trade Statistics 2007*, Geneva: WTO, November.

World Trade Organization (WTO) (2008) *The Doha Agenda* – available at www.wto.org/english/thewto_e/whatis_e/tif_e/doha1_e.htm

World Wildlife Fund (WWF) (2006) *Living Planet Report*, Gland, Switzerland: WWF.

Wu, F., T.M. Heng and T. Ho (2003) 'Outward FDI and its impact in the home economy: the case of Singapore', *Journal of Asian Business*, **19** (3).

Yunus, M. (ed.) (1984) *Jorimon of Beltoil Village and Others: in Search of a Future*, English edition translated by S.M. Islam and A. Rahman, Dhaka: Grameen Bank.

Zaman, M.R. (1973) 'Sharecropping and economic efficiency in Bangladesh', *Bangladesh Development Review*, **1** (2), pp. 149–72.

Zambia Mining Yearbook (1978), Lusaka: Government of Zambia.

Zawdie, G. and A. Djeflat (eds) (1996) *Technology and Transition: The Maghreb at the Crossroads*, London: Frank Cass.

Zelinsky, Z. (1971) 'The hypothesis of the mobility transition', *Geographical Review*, **61** (2).

Index

Note: locators in **bold** indicate definitions/descriptions